Everyday
GERMAN
Dictionary

Everyday

GERMAN

Dictionary

English-German
German-English

Mc Graw Hill

New York Chicago San Francisco Lisbon London Madrid Mexico City
Milan New Delhi San Juan Seoul Singapore Sydney Toronto

433.21
Eve

Copyright © HarperCollins Publishers Ltd. 2009. All rights reserved. Printed in the
United States of America. Except as permitted under the United States Copyright
Act of 1976, no part of this publication may be reproduced or distributed in any
form or by any means, or stored in a database or retrieval system, without the
prior written permission of the publisher.

1 2 3 4 5 6 7 8 9 10 11 12 13 14 15   QFR/QFR   1 9 8 7 6 5 4 3 2 1

ISBN   978-0-07-176880-1
MHID   0-07-176880-7

Library of Congress Cataloging-in-Publication Data

Everyday German dictionary.
        p.   cm.
     ISBN 0-07-176880-7 (alk. paper)
     1. German language—Dictionaries—English.   I. HarperCollins (Firm).

PF3640.E93   2011
433'.21—dc22   2011015834

McGraw-Hill books are available at special quantity discounts to use as premiums
and sales promotions or for use in corporate training programs. To contact a
representative, please e-mail us at bulksales@mcgraw-hill.com.

This book is printed on acid-free paper.

INHALT

Einleitung	vi
Abkürzungen	vii
Lautschrift	x
Regelmäßige deutsche Substantivendungen	xii
Unregelmäßige englische Verben	xiii
Unregelmäßige deutsche Verben	xvi
DEUTSCH-ENGLISCH	1
ENGLISCH-DEUTSCH	201

CONTENTS

Introduction	vi
Abbreviations	vii
Phonetic symbols	x
Regular German noun endings	xii
Irregular English verbs	xiii
Irregular German verbs	xvi
GERMAN-ENGLISH	1
ENGLISH-GERMAN	201

WARENZEICHEN

Warenzeichen, die unseres Wissens eingetragene Warenzeichen darstellen, sind als solche gekennzeichnet. Es ist jedoch zu beachten, dass weder das Vorhandensein noch das Fehlen derartiger Kennzeichnungen die Rechtslage hinsichtlich eingetragener Warenzeichen berührt.

NOTE ON TRADEMARKS

Words which we have reason to believe constitute trademarks have been designated as such. However, neither the presence nor the absence of such designation should be regarded as affecting the legal status of any trademark.

Abkürzungen

Abbreviations

auch	*a.*	also
Abkürzung	*abk, abbr*	abbreviation
Akronym	*acr*	acronym
Adjektiv	*adj*	adjective
Adverb	*adv*	adverb
Landwirtschaft	*Agr*	agriculture
Akkusativ	*akk*	accusative
Akronym	*akr*	acronym
Anatomie	*Anat*	anatomy
Artikel	*art*	article
Bildende Künste	*Art*	fine arts
Astronomie, Astrologie	*Astr*	astronomy, astrology
Auto, Verkehr	*Auto*	automobiles, traffic
Luftfahrt	*Aviat*	aviation
Biologie	*Bio*	biology
Botanik	*Bot*	botany
britisch	*BRIT*	British
schweizerisch	*CH*	Swiss
Chemie	*Chem*	chemistry
Film	*Cine*	cinema
Wirtschaft	*Comm*	commerce
Konjunktion	*conj*	conjunction
Dativ	*dat*	dative
Eisenbahn	*Eisenb*	railways
Elektrizität	*Elek, Elec*	electricity
besonders	*esp*	especially
und so weiter	*etc*	et cetera
etwas	*etw*	
Femininum	*f*	feminine
umgangssprachlich	*fam*	familiar, informal
übertragen	*fig*	figurative
Finanzen, Börse	*Fin*	finance
Fotografie	*Foto*	photography
Gastronomie	*Gastr*	cooking, gastronomy
Genitiv	*gen*	genitive
Geographie, Geologie	*Geo*	geography, geology
Geschichte	*Hist*	history
Imperativ	*imper*	imperative
Imperfekt	*imperf*	past tense
Informatik und Computer	*Inform*	computing
Interjektion, Ausruf	*interj*	interjection
unveränderlich	*inv*	invariable
unregelmäßig	*irr*	irregular
jemand	*jd*	
jemandem	*jdm*	
jemanden	*jdn*	

jemandes	*jds*	
Rechtsprechung	*Jur*	law
Konjunktion	*konj*	conjunction
Bildende Künste	*Kunst*	fine arts
Sprachwissenschaft, Grammatik	*Ling*	linguistics, grammar
Maskulinum	*m*	masculine
Mathematik	*Math*	mathematics
Medizin	*Med*	medicine
Meteorologie	*Meteo*	meteorology
Maskulinum und Femininum	*mf*	masculine and feminine
Militär	*Mil*	military
Musik	*Mus*	music
Substantiv	*n*	noun
Seefahrt	*Naut*	nautical, naval
Neutrum	*nt*	neuter
Zahlwort	*num*	numeral
oder	*o*	or
pejorativ, abwertend	*pej*	pejorative
Physik	*Phys*	physics
Plural	*pl*	plural
Politik	*Pol*	politics
Partizip Perfekt	*pp*	past participle
Präfix	*pref*	prefix
Präposition	*prep*	preposition
Pronomen	*pron*	pronoun
1. Vergangenheit	*pt*	past tense
Warenzeichen	®	registered trademark
Radio	*Radio*	radio
Eisenbahn	*Rail*	railways
Religion	*Rel*	religion
siehe	*s.*	see
	sb	someone, somebody
schottisch	*SCOT*	Scottish
Singular	*sing*	singular
Skisport	*Ski*	skiing
Sport	*Sport*	sports
	sth	something
Technik	*Tech*	technology
Nachrichtentechnik	*Tel*	telecommunications
Theater	*Theat*	theatre
Fernsehen	*TV*	television
Typographie, Buchdruck	*Typo*	printing
unpersönlich	*unpers*	impersonal
(nord)amerikanisch	*US*	(North) American
Verb	*vb*	verb
Hilfsverb	*vb aux*	auxiliary verb
intransitives Verb	*vi*	intransitive verb
reflexives Verb	*vr*	reflexive verb

transitives Verb	*vt*	transitive verb
vulgär	*vulg*	vulgar
Zoologie	*Zool*	zoology
zwischen zwei Sprechern	-	change of speaker
ungefähre Entsprechung	≈	cultural equivalent
abtrennbares Präfix	|	separable prefix

LAUTSCHRIFT   PHONETIC SYMBOLS

[:] Längezeichen, length mark
['] Betonung, stress mark
[*] Bindungs-R, 'r' pronounced before a vowel

alle Vokallaute sind nur ungefähre Entsprechungen
all vowel sounds are approximate only

VOKALE UND DIPHTHONGE

plant, arm, father	[ɑ:]	Bahn
fiancé	[ɑ̃:]	Ensemble
life	[aɪ]	weit
house	[au]	Haut
man, sad	[æ]	
but, son	[ʌ]	Butler
get, bed	[e]	Metall
name, lame	[eɪ]	
ago, better	[ə]	bitte
bird, her	[ɜ:]	
there, care	[ɛə]	mehr
it, wish	[ɪ]	Bischof
bee, me, beat, belief	[i:]	viel
here	[ɪə]	Bier
no, low	[əʊ]	
not, long	[ɒ]	Post
law, all	[ɔ:]	Mond
boy, oil	[ɔɪ]	Heu
push, look	[ʊ]	Pult
you, do	[u:]	Hut
poor, sure	[ʊə]	

KONSONANTEN

been, blind	[b]	Ball
do, had	[d]	dann
jam, object	[dʒ]	
father, wolf	[f]	Fass
go, beg	[g]	Gast
house	[h]	Herr
youth, Indian	[j]	ja
keep, milk	[k]	kalt
lamp, oil, ill	[l]	Last
man, am	[m]	Mast
no, manner	[n]	Nuss
long, sing	[ŋ]	lang

El Niño	[ɲ]	El Niño
paper, happy	[p]	Pakt
red, dry	[r]	rot
stand, sand, yes	[s]	Rasse
ship, station	[ʃ]	Schal
tell, fat	[t]	Tal
thank, death	[θ]	
this, father	[ð]	
church, catch	[tʃ]	Rutsch
voice, live	[v]	was
water, we, which	[w]	
loch	[x]	Bach
zeal, these, gaze	[z]	Hase
pleasure	[ʒ]	Genie

Regular German noun endings

nominative		genitive	plural	nominative		genitive	plural
-ade	f	-ade	-aden	-ist	m	-isten	-isten
-ant	m	-anten	-anten	-ium	nt	-iums	-ien
-anz	f	-anz	-anzen	-ius	m	-ius	-iusse
-ar	m	-ars	-are	-ive	f	-ive	-iven
-är	m	-ärs	-äre	-keit	f	-keit	-keiten
-at	nt	-at(e)s	-ate	-lein	nt	-leins	-lein
-atte	f	-atte	-atten	-ling	m	-lings	-linge
-chen	nt	-chens	-chen	-ment	nt	-ments	-mente
-ei	f	-ei	-eien	-mus	m	-mus	-men
-elle	f	-elle	-ellen	-nis	f	-nis	-nisse
-ent	m	-enten	-enten	-nis	nt	-nisses	-nisse
-enz	f	-enz	-enzen	-nom	m	-nomen	-nomen
-ette	f	-ette	-etten	-rich	m	-richs	-riche
-eur	m	-eurs	-eure	-schaft	f	-schaft	-schaften
-euse	f	-euse	-eusen	-sel	nt	-sels	-sel
-heit	f	-heit	-heiten	-tät	f	-tät	-täten
-ie	f	-ie	-ien	-tiv	nt, m	-tivs	-tive
-ik	f	-ik	-iken	-tor	m	-tors	-toren
-in	f	-in	-innen	-tum	m, nt	-tums	-tümer
-ine	f	-ine	-inen	-ung	f	-ung	-ungen
-ion	f	-ion	-ionen	-ur	f	-ur	-uren

Substantive, die mit einem geklammerten 'r' oder 's' enden (z.B. **Angestellte(r)** *mf*, **Beamte(r)** *m*, **Gute(s)** *nt*) werden wie Adjektive dekliniert:

Nouns listed with an 'r' or an 's' in brackets (eg **Angestellte(r)** *mf*, **Beamte(r)** *m*, **Gute(s)** *nt*) take the same endings as adjectives:

der Angestellte *m*   **die Angestellte** *f*   **die Angestellten** *pl*
ein Angestellter *m*   **eine Angestellte** *f*   **Angestellte** *pl*
der Beamte *m*   **die Beamten** *pl*
ein Beamter *m*   **Beamte** *pl*
das Gute *nt*
ein Gutes *nt*

UNREGELMÄßIGE ENGLISCHE VERBEN

present	past tense	past participle	present	past tense	past participle
arise (**arising**)	arose	arisen	**drink**	drank	drunk
awake (**awaking**)	awoke	awaked	**drive** (**driving**)	drove	driven
be (**am, is, are; being**)	was, were	been	**eat**	ate	eaten
			fall	fell	fallen
bear	bore	born(e)	**feed**	fed	fed
beat	beat	beaten	**feel**	felt	felt
become (**becoming**)	became	become	**fight**	fought	fought
			find	found	found
begin (**beginning**)	began	begun	**flee**	fled	fled
bend	bent	bent	**fling**	flung	flung
bet (**betting**)	bet	bet	**fly** (**flies**)	flew	flown
bid (**bidding**)	bid	bid	**forbid** (**forbidding**)	forbade	forbidden
bind	bound	bound	**foresee**	foresaw	foreseen
bite (**biting**)	bit	bitten	**forget** (**forgetting**)	forgot	forgotten
bleed	bled	bled	**forgive** (**forgiving**)	forgave	forgiven
blow	blew	blown			
break	broke	broken	**freeze** (**freezing**)	froze	frozen
breed	bred	bred			
bring	brought	brought	**get** (**getting**)	got	got, (US) gotten
build	built	built			
burn	burnt (o burned)	burnt (o burned)	**give** (**giving**)	gave	given
burst	burst	burst	**go** (**goes**)	went	gone
buy	bought	bought	**grind**	ground	ground
can	could	(been able)	**grow**	grew	grown
cast	cast	cast	**hang**	hung (o hanged)	hung (o hanged)
catch	caught	caught			
choose (**choosing**)	chose	chosen	**have** (**has; having**)	had	had
cling	clung	clung	**hear**	heard	heard
come (**coming**)	came	come	**hide** (**hiding**)	hid	hidden
cost	cost	cost	**hit** (**hitting**)	hit	hit
creep	crept	crept	**hold**	held	held
cut (**cutting**)	cut	cut	**hurt**	hurt	hurt
deal	dealt	dealt	**keep**	kept	kept
dig (**digging**)	dug	dug	**kneel**	knelt (o kneeled)	knelt (o kneeled)
do (**does**)	did	done			
draw	drew	drawn	**know**	knew	known
dream	dreamed (o dreamt)	dreamed (o dreamt)	**lay**	laid	laid
			lead	led	led

present	past tense	past participle	present	past tense	past participle
lean	leant (o leaned)	leant (o leaned)	shoot	shot	shot
			show	showed	shown
leap	leapt (o leaped)	leapt (o leaped)	shrink	shrank	shrunk
			shut (shutting)	shut	shut
learn	learnt (o learned)	learnt (o learned)	sing	sang	sung
leave (leaving)	left	left	sink	sank	sunk
			sit (sitting)	sat	sat
lend	lent	lent	sleep	slept	slept
let (letting)	let	let	slide (sliding)	slid	slid
lie (lying)	lay	lain			
light	lit (o lighted)	lit (o lighted)	sling	slung	slung
			slit (slitting)	slit	slit
lose (losing)	lost	lost	smell	smelt (o smelled)	smelt (o smelled)
make (making)	made	made			
			sow	sowed	sown (o sowed)
may	might	–			
mean	meant	meant	speak	spoke	spoken
meet	met	met	speed	sped (o speeded)	sped (o speeded)
mow	mowed	mown (o mowed)			
			spell	spelt (o spelled)	spelt (o spelled)
must	(had to)	(had to)			
pay	paid	paid	spend	spent	spent
put (putting)	put	put	spin (spinning)	spun	spun
quit (quitting)	quit (o quitted)	quit (o quitted)	spit (spitting)	spat	spat
read	read	read	split (splitting)	split	split
rid (ridding)	rid	rid	spoil	spoiled (o spoilt)	spoiled (o spoilt)
ride (riding)	rode	ridden			
ring	rang	rung	spread	spread	spread
rise (rising)	rose	risen	spring	sprang	sprung
run (running)	ran	run	stand	stood	stood
saw	sawed	sawn	steal	stole	stolen
say	said	said	stick	stuck	stuck
see	saw	seen	sting	stung	stung
seek	sought	sought	stink	stank	stunk
sell	sold	sold	strike (striking)	struck	struck
send	sent	sent			
set (setting)	set	set	strive (striving)	strove	striven
shake (shaking)	shook	shaken			
			swear	swore	sworn
shall	should	–	sweep	swept	swept
shine (shining)	shone	shone	swell	swelled	swollen (o swelled)

present	past tense	past participle	present	past tense	past participle
swim (**swimming**)	swam	swum	**wake** (**waking**)	woke (*o* waked)	woken (*o* waked)
swing	swung	swung	**wear**	wore	worn
take (**taking**)	took	taken	**weave** (**weaving**)	wove (*o* weaved)	woven (*o* weaved)
teach	taught	taught	**weep**	wept	wept
tear	tore	torn	**win**	won	won
tell	told	told	(**winning**)		
think	thought	thought	**wind**	wound	wound
throw	threw	thrown	**write**	wrote	written
thrust	thrust	thrust	(**writing**)		
tread	trod	trodden			

German Irregular Verbs

Infinitiv	Präsens 2., 3. Singular	Imperfekt	Partizip Perfekt
backen	bäckst, bäckt	backte o buk	gebacken
befehlen	befiehlst, befiehlt	befahl	befohlen
beginnen	beginnst, beginnt	begann	begonnen
beißen	beißt, beißt	biss	gebissen
bergen	birgst, birgt	barg	geborgen
betrügen	betrügst, betrügt	betrog	betrogen
biegen	biegst, biegt	bog	gebogen
bieten	bietest, bietet	bot	geboten
binden	bindest, bindet	band	gebunden
bitten	bittest, bittet	bat	gebeten
blasen	bläst, bläst	blies	geblasen
bleiben	bleibst, bleibt	blieb	geblieben
braten	brätst, brät	briet	gebraten
brechen	brichst, bricht	brach	gebrochen
brennen	brennst, brennt	brannte	gebrannt
bringen	bringst, bringt	brachte	gebracht
denken	denkst, denkt	dachte	gedacht
dringen	dringst, dringt	drang	gedrungen
dürfen	darfst, darf	durfte	gedurft
empfangen	empfängst, empfängt	empfing	empfangen
empfehlen	empfiehlst, empfiehlt	empfahl	empfohlen
empfinden	empfindest, empfindet	empfand	empfunden
erschrecken	erschrickst, erschrickt	erschrak	erschrocken
essen	isst, isst	aß	gegessen
fahren	fährst, fährt	fuhr	gefahren
fallen	fällst, fällt	fiel	gefallen
fangen	fängst, fängt	fing	gefangen
finden	findest, findet	fand	gefunden
flechten	flichtst, flicht	flocht	geflochten
fliegen	fliegst, fliegt	flog	geflogen
fließen	fließt, fließt	floss	geflossen
fressen	frisst, frisst	fraß	gefressen
frieren	frierst, friert	fror	gefroren
geben	gibst, gibt	gab	gegeben
gehen	gehst, geht	ging	gegangen
gelingen	–, gelingt	gelang	gelungen
gelten	giltst, gilt	galt	gegolten
genießen	genießt, genießt	genoss	genossen
geraten	gerätst, gerät	geriet	geraten
geschehen	–, geschieht	geschah	geschehen
gewinnen	gewinnst, gewinnt	gewann	gewonnen
gießen	gießt, gießt	goss	gegossen
gleichen	gleichst, gleicht	glich	geglichen
gleiten	gleitest, gleitet	glitt	geglitten

Infinitiv	Präsens 2., 3. Singular	Imperfekt	Partizip Perfekt
graben	gräbst, gräbt	grub	gegraben
greifen	greifst, greift	griff	gegriffen
haben	hast, hat	hatte	gehabt
halten	hältst, hält	hielt	gehalten
hängen	hängst, hängt	hing	gehangen
hauen	haust, haut	haute	gehauen
heben	hebst, hebt	hob	gehoben
heißen	heißt, heißt	hieß	geheißen
helfen	hilfst, hilft	half	geholfen
kennen	kennst, kennt	kannte	gekannt
klingen	klingst, klingt	klang	geklungen
kneifen	kneifst, kneift	kniff	gekniffen
kommen	kommst, kommt	kam	gekommen
können	kannst, kann	konnte	gekonnt
kriechen	kriechst, kriecht	kroch	gekrochen
laden	lädst, lädt	lud	geladen
lassen	lässt, lässt	ließ	gelassen
laufen	läufst, läuft	lief	gelaufen
leiden	leidest, leidet	litt	gelitten
leihen	leihst, leiht	lieh	geliehen
lesen	liest, liest	las	gelesen
liegen	liegst, liegt	lag	gelegen
lügen	lügst, lügt	log	gelogen
mahlen	mahlst, mahlt	mahlte	gemahlen
meiden	meidest, meidet	mied	gemieden
messen	misst, misst	maß	gemessen
misslingen	–, misslingt	misslang	misslungen
mögen	magst, mag	mochte	gemocht
müssen	musst, muss	musste	gemusst
nehmen	nimmst, nimmt	nahm	genommen
nennen	nennst, nennt	nannte	genannt
pfeifen	pfeifst, pfeift	pfiff	gepfiffen
quellen	quillst, quillt	quoll	gequollen
raten	rätst, rät	riet	geraten
reiben	reibst, reibt	rieb	gerieben
reißen	reißt, reißt	riss	gerissen
reiten	reitest, reitet	ritt	geritten
rennen	rennst, rennt	rannte	gerannt
riechen	riechst, riecht	roch	gerochen
ringen	ringst, ringt	rang	gerungen
rufen	rufst, ruft	rief	gerufen
salzen	salzt, salzt	salzte	gesalzen
saufen	säufst, säuft	soff	gesoffen
saugen	saugst, saugt	sog o saugte	gesogen o gesaugt
schaffen	schaffst, schafft	schuf	geschaffen
scheiden	scheidest, scheidet	schied	geschieden

Infinitiv	Präsens 2., 3. Singular	Imperfekt	Partizip Perfekt
scheinen	scheinst, scheint	schien	geschienen
scheißen	scheißt, scheißt	schiss	geschissen
schieben	schiebst, schiebt	schob	geschoben
schießen	schießt, schießt	schoss	geschossen
schlafen	schläfst, schläft	schlief	geschlafen
schlagen	schlägst, schlägt	schlug	geschlagen
schleichen	schleichst, schleicht	schlich	geschlichen
schleifen	schleifst, schleift	schliff	geschliffen
schließen	schließt, schließt	schloss	geschlossen
schmeißen	schmeißt, schmeißt	schmiss	geschmissen
schmelzen	schmilzt, schmilzt	schmolz	geschmolzen
schneiden	schneidest, schneidet	schnitt	geschnitten
schreiben	schreibst, schreibt	schrieb	geschrieben
schreien	schreist, schreit	schrie	geschrie(e)n
schweigen	schweigst, schweigt	schwieg	geschwiegen
schwellen	schwillst, schwillt	schwoll	geschwollen
schwimmen	schwimmst, schwimmt	schwamm	geschwommen
schwören	schwörst, schwört	schwor	geschworen
sehen	siehst, sieht	sah	gesehen
sein	bist, ist	war	gewesen
senden	sendest, sendet	sandte	gesandt
singen	singst, singt	sang	gesungen
sinken	sinkst, sinkt	sank	gesunken
sitzen	sitzt, sitzt	saß	gesessen
sollen	sollst, soll	sollte	gesollt
spinnen	spinnst, spinnt	spann	gesponnen
sprechen	sprichst, spricht	sprach	gesprochen
springen	springst, springt	sprang	gesprungen
stechen	stichst, sticht	stach	gestochen
stehen	stehst, steht	stand	gestanden
stehlen	stiehlst, stiehlt	stahl	gestohlen
steigen	steigst, steigt	stieg	gestiegen
sterben	stirbst, stirbt	starb	gestorben
stinken	stinkst, stinkt	stank	gestunken
stoßen	stößt, stößt	stieß	gestoßen
streichen	streichst, streicht	strich	gestrichen
streiten	streitest, streitet	stritt	gestritten
tragen	trägst, trägt	trug	getragen
treffen	triffst, trifft	traf	getroffen
treiben	treibst, treibt	trieb	getrieben
treten	trittst, tritt	trat	getreten
trinken	trinkst, trinkt	trank	getrunken
tun	tust, tut	tat	getan
verderben	verdirbst, verdirbt	verdarb	verdorben
vergessen	vergisst, vergisst	vergaß	vergessen
verlieren	verlierst, verliert	verlor	verloren

Infinitiv	Präsens 2., 3. Singular	Imperfekt	Partizip Perfekt
verschwinden	verschwindest, verschwindet	verschwand	verschwunden
verzeihen	verzeihst, verzeiht	verzieh	verziehen
wachsen	wächst, wächst	wuchs	gewachsen
waschen	wäschst, wäscht	wusch	gewaschen
weisen	weist, weist	wies	gewiesen
wenden	wendest, wendet	wandte	gewandt
werben	wirbst, wirbt	warb	geworben
werden	wirst, wird	wurde	geworden
werfen	wirfst, wirft	warf	geworfen
wiegen	wiegst, wiegt	wog	gewogen
wissen	weißt, weiß	wusste	gewusst
wollen	willst, will	wollte	gewollt
ziehen	ziehst, zieht	zog	gezogen
zwingen	zwingst, zwingt	zwang	gezwungen

a

à *prep* +*akk* at ... each; **4 Tickets ~ 8 Euro** 4 tickets at 8 euros each
A *abk* = **Autobahn** ≈ M (*Brit*), ≈ I (*US*)
Aal (-(e)s, -e) *m* eel

○ **SCHLÜSSELWORT**

ab *präp* +*dat* from; **Kinder ab 12 Jahren** children from the age of 12; **ab morgen** from tomorrow; **ab sofort** as of now ▷ *adv* **1** off; **links ab** to the left; **der Knopf ist ab** the button has come off; **ab nach Hause!** off you go home

2 (*zeitlich*): **von da ab** from then on; **von heute ab** from today, as of today

3 (*auf Fahrplänen*): **München ab 12.20** leaving Munich 12.20

4: **ab und zu** *od* **an** now and then *od* again

ab|bauen *vt* (*Zelt*) to take down; (*verringern*) to reduce
ab|beißen *irr vt* to bite off
ab|bestellen *vt* to cancel
ab|biegen *irr vi* to turn off; (*Straße*) to bend; **nach links/rechts ~** to turn left/right; **Abbiegespur** *f* filter lane

Abbildung *f* illustration
ab|blasen *irr vt* (*fig*) to call off
ab|blenden *vt, vi* (*Auto*) (**die Scheinwerfer**) **~** to dip (*Brit*) (*o* to dim (*US*)) one's headlights; **Abblendlicht** *nt* dipped (*Brit*) (*o* dimmed (*US*)) headlights *pl*
ab|brechen *irr vt* to break off; (*Gebäude*) to pull down; (*aufhören*) to stop; (*Computerprogramm*) to abort
ab|bremsen *vi* to brake, to slow down
ab|bringen *irr vt* **jdn von einer Idee ~** to talk sb out of an idea; **jdn vom Thema ~** to get sb away from the subject; **davon lasse ich mich nicht ~** nothing will make me change my mind about it
ab|buchen *vt* to debit (*von* to)
ab|danken *vi* to resign
ab|drehen *vt* (*Gas, Wasser*) to turn off; (*Licht*) to switch off ▷ *vi* (*Schiff, Flugzeug*) to change course
Abend (-s, -e) *m* evening; **am ~** in the evening; **zu ~ essen** to have dinner; **heute/morgen/gestern ~** this/tomorrow/yesterday evening; **guten ~!** good evening; **Abendbrot** *nt* supper; **Abendessen** *nt* dinner; **Abendgarderobe** *f* evening dress (*o* gown); **Abendkasse** *f* box office; **Abendkleid** *nt* evening dress (*o* gown); **Abendkurs** *m* evening class; **Abendmahl** *nt* **das ~** (Holy) Communion; **abends** *adv* in the evening; **montags ~** on Monday evenings
Abenteuer (-s, -) *nt* adventure; **Abenteuerurlaub** *m* adventure holiday
aber *conj* but; (*jedoch*) however; **oder ~** alternatively; **~ ja!** (but) of course; **das ist ~ nett von Ihnen** that's really nice of you
abergläubisch *adj* superstitious
ab|fahren *irr vi* to leave (*o* to depart) (*nach* for); (*Ski*) to ski down; **Abfahrt** *f* departure; (*von Autobahn*) exit; (*Ski*) descent; (*Piste*) run; **Abfahrtslauf** *m* (*Ski*) downhill; **Abfahrtszeit** *f* departure time
Abfall *m* waste; (*Müll*) rubbish (*Brit*), garbage (*US*); **Abfalleimer** *m* rubbish bin (*Brit*), garbage can (*US*)
abfällig *adj* disparaging; **~ von jdm sprechen** to make disparaging remarks about sb
ab|färben *vi* (*Wäsche*) to run; (*fig*) to rub off

ab|fertigen vt (*Pakete*) to prepare for dispatch; (*an der Grenze*) to clear; **Abfertigungsschalter** m (*am Flughafen*) check-in desk

ab|finden irr vt to pay off ▷ vr **sich mit etw ~** to come to terms with sth; **Abfindung** f (*Entschädigung*) compensation; (*von Angestellten*) redundancy payment

ab|fliegen irr vi (*Flugzeug*) to take off; (*Passagier a.*) to fly off; **Abflug** m departure; (*Start*) takeoff; **Abflughalle** f departure lounge; **Abflugzeit** f departure time

Abfluss m drain; (*am Waschbecken*) plughole (*Brit*); **Abflussrohr** nt waste pipe; (*außen*) drainpipe

ab|fragen vt to test; (*Inform*) to call up

ab|führen vi (*Med*) to have a laxative effect ▷ vt (*Steuern, Gebühren*) to pay; **jdn ~ lassen** to take sb into custody; **Abführmittel** nt laxative

Abgabe f handing in; (*von Ball*) pass; (*Steuer*) tax; (*einer Erklärung*) making; **abgabenfrei** adj tax-free; **abgabenpflichtig** adj liable to tax

Abgase pl (*Auto*) exhaust fumes pl; **Abgas(sonder)untersuchung** f exhaust emission test

ab|geben irr vt (*Gepäck, Schlüssel*) to leave (*bei* with); (*Schularbeit etc*) to hand in; (*Wärme*) to give off; (*Erklärung, Urteil*) to make ▷ vr **sich mit jdm ~** to associate with sb; **sich mit etw ~** to bother with sth

abgebildet adj **wie oben ~** as shown above

ab|gehen irr vi (*Post*) to go; (*Knopf etc*) to come off; (*abgezogen werden*) to be taken off; (*Straße*) to branch off; **von der Schule ~** to leave school; **sie geht mir ab** I really miss her; **was geht denn hier ab?** (*fam*) what's going on here?

abgehetzt adj exhausted, shattered

abgelaufen adj (*Pass*) expired; (*Zeit, Frist*) up; **die Milch ist ~** the milk is past its sell-by date

abgelegen adj remote

abgemacht interj OK, it's a deal, that's settled, then

abgeneigt adj **einer Sache** (*dat*) **~ sein** to be averse to sth; **ich wäre nicht ~, das zu tun** I wouldn't mind doing that

Abgeordnete(r) mf Member of Parliament

abgepackt adj prepacked

abgerissen adj **der Knopf ist ~** the button has come off

abgesehen adj **es auf jdn/etw ~ haben** to be after sb/sth; **~ von** apart from

abgespannt adj (*Person*) exhausted, worn out

abgestanden adj stale; (*Bier*) flat

abgestorben adj (*Pflanze*) dead; (*Finger*) numb

abgestumpft adj (*Person*) insensitive

abgetragen adj (*Kleidung*) worn

ab|gewöhnen vt **jdm etw ~** to cure sb of sth; **sich etw ~** to give sth up

ab|haken vt to tick off; **das** (**Thema**) **ist schon abgehakt** that's been dealt with

ab|halten irr vt (*Versammlung*) to hold; **jdn von etw ~** (*fernhalten*) to keep sb away from sth; (*hindern*) to keep sb from sth

abhanden adj **~ kommen** to get lost

Abhang m slope

ab|hängen vt (*Bild*) to take down; (*Anhänger*) to uncouple; (*Verfolger*) to shake off ▷ irr vi **von jdm/etw ~** to depend on sb/sth; **das hängt davon ab, ob ...** it depends (on) whether ...; **abhängig** adj dependent (*von* on)

ab|hauen irr vt (*abschlagen*) to cut off ▷ vi (*fam: verschwinden*) to clear off; **hau ab!** get lost!, beat it!

ab|heben irr vt (*Geld*) to withdraw; (*Telefonhörer, Spielkarte*) to pick up ▷ vi (*Flugzeug*) to take off; (*Rakete*) to lift off; (*Karten*) to cut

ab|holen vt to collect; (*am Bahnhof etc*) to meet; (*mit dem Auto*) to pick up; **Abholmarkt** m cash and carry

ab|horchen vt (*Med*) to listen to

ab|hören vt (*Vokabeln*) to test; (*Telefongespräch*) to tap; (*Tonband etc*) to listen to

Abitur (*-s, -e*) nt German school-leaving examination, ≈ A-levels (*Brit*), ≈ High School Diploma (*US*)

⬤ **Abitur**
⬤
⬤ The **Abitur** is the German
⬤ school-leaving examination which is
⬤ taken at the age of 18 or 19 by pupils
⬤ at a **Gymnasium**. It is taken in four
⬤ subjects and is necessary for entry to
⬤ university.

ab|kaufen *vt* **jdm etw ~** to buy sth from sb; **das kauf ich dir nicht ab!** (*fam: glauben*) I don't believe you

ab|klingen *irr vi* (*Schmerz*) to ease; (*Wirkung*) to wear off

ab|kommen *irr vi* to get away; **von der Straße ~** to leave the road; **von einem Plan ~** to give up a plan; **vom Thema ~** to stray from the point

Abkommen (*-s, -*) *nt* agreement

ab|koppeln *vt* (*Anhänger*) to unhitch

ab|kratzen *vt* to scrape off ▷ *vi* (*fam: sterben*) to kick the bucket, to croak

ab|kühlen *vi, vt* to cool down ▷ *vr* **sich ~** to cool down

ab|kürzen *vt* (*Wort*) to abbreviate; **den Weg ~** to take a short cut; **Abkürzung** *f* (*Wort*) abbreviation; (*Weg*) short cut

ab|laden *irr vt* to unload

Ablage *f* (*für Akten*) tray; (*Aktenordnung*) filing system

Ablauf *m* (*Abfluss*) drain; (*von Ereignissen*) course; (*einer Frist, Zeit*) expiry; **ab|laufen** *irr vi* (*abfließen*) to drain away; (*Ereignisse*) to happen; (*Frist, Zeit, Pass*) to expire

ab|legen *vt* to put down; (*Kleider*) to take off; (*Gewohnheit*) to get out of; (*Prüfung*) to take, to sit; (*Akten*) to file away ▷ *vi* (*Schiff*) to cast off

ab|lehnen *vt* to reject; (*Einladung*) to decline; (*missbilligen*) to disapprove of; (*Bewerber*) to turn down ▷ *vi* to decline

ab|lenken *vt* to distract; **jdn von der Arbeit ~** to distract sb from their work; **vom Thema ~** to change the subject; **Ablenkung** *f* distraction

ab|lesen *vt* (*Text, Rede*) to read; **das Gas/den Strom ~** to read the gas/electricity meter

ab|liefern *vt* to deliver

ab|machen *vt* (*entfernen*) to take off; (*vereinbaren*) to agree; **Abmachung** *f* agreement

ab|melden *vt* (*Zeitung*) to cancel; (*Auto*) to take off the road ▷ *vr* **sich ~** to give notice of one's departure; (*im Hotel*) to check out; (*vom Verein*) to cancel one's membership

ab|messen *irr vt* to measure

ab|nehmen *irr vt* to take off, to remove; (*Hörer*) to pick up; (*Führerschein*) to take away; (*Geld*) to get (*jdm* out of sb); (*kaufen, umg: glauben*) to buy (*jdm* from sb) ▷ *vi* to

decrease; (*schlanker werden*) to lose weight; (*Tel*) to pick up the phone; **fünf Kilo ~** to lose five kilos

Abneigung *f* dislike (*gegen* of); (*stärker*) aversion (*gegen* to)

ab|nutzen *vt* to wear out ▷ *vr* **sich ~** to wear out

Abonnement (*-s, -s*) *nt* subscription; **Abonnent(in)** *m(f)* subscriber; **abonnieren** *vt* to subscribe to

ab|raten *irr vi* **jdm von etw ~** to advise sb against sth

ab|räumen *vt* **den Tisch ~** to clear the table; **das Geschirr ~** to clear away the dishes; (*Preis etc*) to walk off with

Abrechnung *f* settlement; (*Rechnung*) bill

ab|regen *vr* **sich ~** (*fam*) to calm (*o* to cool) down; **reg dich ab!** take it easy

Abreise *f* departure; **ab|reisen** *vi* to leave (*nach* for)

ab|reißen *irr vt* (*Haus*) to pull down; (*Blatt*) to tear off; **den Kontakt nicht ~ lassen** to stay in touch ▷ *vi* (*Knopf etc*) to come off

ab|runden *vt* **eine Zahl nach oben/unten ~** to round a number up/down

abrupt *adj* abrupt

ABS *nt abk* = **Antiblockiersystem** (*Auto*) ABS

Abs. *abk* = **Absender** from

ab|sagen *vt* to cancel, to call off; (*Einladung*) to turn down ▷ *vi* (*ablehnen*) to decline; **ich muss leider ~** I'm afraid I can't come

Absatz *m* (*Comm*) sales *pl*; (*neuer Abschnitt*) paragraph; (*Schuh*) heel

ab|schaffen *vt* to abolish, to do away with

ab|schalten *vt, vi* (*a. fig*) to switch off

ab|schätzen *vt* to estimate; (*Lage*) to assess; **jdn ~** to size sb up

abscheulich *adj* disgusting

ab|schicken *vt* to send off

ab|schieben *irr vt* (*ausweisen*) to deport

Abschied (*-(e)s, -e*) *m* parting; **~ nehmen** to say good-bye (*von jdm* to sb); **Abschiedsfeier** *f* farewell party

Abschlagszahlung *f* interim payment

Abschleppdienst *m* (*Auto*) breakdown service; **ab|schleppen** *vt* to tow; **Abschleppseil** *nt* towrope;

Abschleppwagen m breakdown truck (Brit), tow truck (US)

ab|schließen irr vt (Tür) to lock; (beenden) to finish; (Vertrag, Handel) to conclude; **Abschluss** m (Beendigung) close, conclusion; (von Vertrag, Handel) conclusion

ab|schmecken vt (kosten) to taste; (würzen) to season

ab|schminken vr **sich ~** to take one's make-up off ▷ vt (fam) **sich** (dat) **etw ~** to get sth out of one's mind

ab|schnallen vr **sich ~** to undo one's seatbelt

ab|schneiden irr vt to cut off ▷ vi **gut/schlecht ~** to do well/badly

Abschnitt m (von Buch, Text) section; (Kontrollabschnitt) stub

ab|schrauben vt to unscrew

ab|schrecken vt to deter, to put off

ab|schreiben irr vt to copy (bei, von from, off); (verloren geben) to write off; (Comm: absetzen) to deduct

abschüssig adj steep

ab|schwächen vt to lessen; (Behauptung, Kritik) to tone down

ab|schwellen irr vi (Entzündung) to go down; (Lärm) to die down

absehbar adj foreseeable; **in ~er Zeit** in the foreseeable future; **ab|sehen** irr vt (Ende, Folgen) to foresee ▷ vi **von etw ~** to refrain from sth

abseits adv out of the way; (Sport) offside ▷ prep +gen away from; **Abseits** nt (Sport) offside; **Abseitsfalle** f (Sport) offside trap

ab|senden irr vt to send off; (Post) to post; **Absender(in)** (-s, -) m(f) sender

ab|setzen vt (Glas, Brille etc) to put down; (aussteigen lassen) to drop (off); (Comm) to sell; (Fin) to deduct; (streichen) to drop ▷ vr **sich ~** (sich entfernen) to clear off; (sich ablagern) to be deposited

Absicht f intention; **mit ~** on purpose; **absichtlich** adj intentional, deliberate

absolut adj absolute

ab|specken vi (fam) to lose weight

ab|speichern vt (Inform) to save

ab|sperren vt to block (o to close) off; (Tür) to lock; **Absperrung** f (Vorgang) blocking (o closing) off; (Sperre) barricade

ab|spielen vt (CD etc) to play ▷ vr **sich ~** to happen

ab|springen irr vi to jump down/off; (von etw Geplantem) to drop out (von of)

ab|spülen vt to rinse; (Geschirr) to wash (up)

Abstand m distance; (zeitlich) interval; **~ halten** to keep one's distance

ab|stauben vt, vi to dust; (fam: stehlen) to pinch

Abstecher (-s, -) m detour

ab|steigen irr vi (vom Rad etc) to get off, to dismount; (in Gasthof) to stay (in +dat at)

ab|stellen vt (niederstellen) to put down; (Auto) to park; (ausschalten) to turn (o to switch) off; (Missstand, Unsitte) to stop; **Abstellraum** m store room

Abstieg (-(e)s, -e) m (vom Berg) descent; (Sport) relegation

ab|stimmen vi to vote ▷ vt (Termine, Ziele) to fit in (auf +akk with); **Dinge aufeinander ~** to coordinate things ▷ vr **sich ~** to come to an agreement (o arrangement)

abstoßend adj repulsive

abstrakt adj abstract

ab|streiten irr vt to deny

Abstrich m (Med) smear; **~e machen** to cut back (an +dat on); (weniger erwarten) to lower one's sights

Absturz m fall; (Aviat, Inform) crash; **ab|stürzen** vi to fall; (Aviat, Inform) to crash

absurd adj absurd

Abszess (-es, -e) m abscess

ab|tauen vt, vi to thaw; (Kühlschrank) to defrost

Abtei (-, -en) f abbey

Abteil (-(e)s, -e) nt compartment

Abteilung f (in Firma, Kaufhaus) department; (in Krankenhaus) section

ab|treiben irr vt (Kind) to abort ▷ vi to be driven off course; (Med: Abtreibung vornehmen) to carry out an abortion; (Abtreibung vornehmen lassen) to have an abortion; **Abtreibung** f abortion

ab|trocknen vt to dry

ab|warten vt to wait for; **das bleibt abzuwarten** that remains to be seen ▷ vi to wait

abwärts adv down

Abwasch (-(e)s) m washing-up; **ab|waschen** irr vt (Schmutz) to wash off; (Geschirr) to wash (up)

Abwasser *(-s, Abwässer) nt* sewage
ab|wechseln *vr* **sich ~** to alternate; **sich mit jdm ~** to take turns with sb;
abwechselnd *adv* alternately;
Abwechslung *f* change; **zur ~** for a change
ab|weisen *irr vt* to turn away; *(Antrag)* to turn down; **abweisend** *adj* unfriendly
abwesend *adj* absent; **Abwesenheit** *f* absence
ab|wiegen *irr vt* to weigh (out)
ab|wischen *vt (Gesicht, Tisch etc)* to wipe; *(Schmutz)* to wipe off
ab|zählen *vt* to count; *(Geld)* to count out
Abzeichen *nt* badge
ab|zeichnen *vt* to draw, to copy; *(Dokument)* to initial ▷ *vr* **sich ~** to stand out; *(fig: bevorstehen)* to loom
ab|ziehen *irr vt* to take off; *(Bett)* to strip; *(Schlüssel)* to take out; *(subtrahieren)* to take away, to subtract ▷ *vi* to go away
Abzug *m (Foto)* print; *(Öffnung)* vent; *(Truppen)* withdrawal; *(Betrag)* deduction; **nach ~ der Kosten** charges deducted; **abzüglich** *prep +gen* minus; **~ 20% Rabatt** less 20% discount
ab|zweigen *vi* to branch off ▷ *vt* to set aside; **Abzweigung** *f* junction
Accessoires *pl* accessories *pl*
ach *interj* oh; **~ so!** oh, I see; **~ was!** *(Überraschung)* really?; *(Ärger)* don't talk nonsense
Achse *(-, -n) f* axis; *(Auto)* axle
Achsel *(-, -n) f* shoulder; *(Achselhöhle)* armpit
acht *num* eight; **heute in ~ Tagen** in a week('s time), a week from today
Acht *(-) f* **sich in ~ nehmen** to be careful *(vor +dat* of), to watch out *(vor +dat* for); **~ geben** to take care *(auf +akk* of); **etw außer ~ lassen** to disregard sth
achte(r, s) *adj* eighth; *siehe auch* **dritte**; **Achtel** *(-s, -) nt (Bruchteil)* eighth; *(Wein etc)* eighth of a litre; *(Glas Wein)* ≈ small glass
achten *vt* to respect ▷ *vi* to pay attention *(auf +akk* to)
Achterbahn *f* big dipper, roller coaster
achthundert *num* eight hundred; **achtmal** *adv* eight times
Achtung *f* attention; *(Ehrfurcht)* respect ▷ *interj* look out

achtzehn *num* eighteen; **achtzehnte(r, s)** *adj* eighteenth; *siehe auch* **dritte**; **achtzig** *num* eighty; **in den ~er Jahren** in the eighties; **achtzigste(r, s)** *adj* eightieth
Acker *(-s, Äcker) m* field
Action *(-, -s) f (fam)* action; **Actionfilm** *m* action film
Adapter *(-s, -) m* adapter
addieren *vt* to add (up)
Adel *(-s) m* nobility; **adelig** *adj* noble
Ader *(-, -n) f* vein
Adjektiv *nt* adjective
Adler *(-s, -) m* eagle
adoptieren *vt* to adopt; **Adoption** *f* adoption; **Adoptiveltern** *pl* adoptive parents *pl*; **Adoptivkind** *nt* adopted child
Adrenalin *(-s) nt* adrenalin
Adressbuch *nt* directory; *(persönliches)* address book; **Adresse** *(-, -n) f* address; **adressieren** *vt* to address *(an +akk* to)
Advent *(-s, -) m* Advent; **Adventskranz** *m* Advent wreath
Adverb *nt* adverb
Aerobic *(-s) nt* aerobics *sing*
Affäre *(-, -n) f* affair
Affe *(-n, -n) m* monkey
Afghanistan *(-s) nt* Afghanistan
Afrika *(-s) nt* Africa; **Afrikaner(in)** *(-s, -) m(f)* African; **afrikanisch** *adj* African
After *(-s, -) m* anus
Aftershave *(-(s), -s) nt* aftershave
AG *(-, -s) f abk* = **Aktiengesellschaft** plc *(Brit)*, corp. *(US)*
Agent(in) *m(f)* agent; **Agentur** *f* agency
aggressiv *adj* aggressive
Ägypten *(-s) nt* Egypt
ah *interj* ah, ooh
äh *interj (Sprechpause)* er, um; *(angeekelt)* ugh
aha *interj* I see, aha
ähneln *vi +dat* to be like, to resemble ▷ *vr* **sich ~** to be alike *(o* similar)
ahnen *vt* to suspect; **du ahnst es nicht!** would you believe it?
ähnlich *adj* similar *(dat* to); **jdm ~ sehen** to look like sb; **Ähnlichkeit** *f* similarity
Ahnung *f* idea; *(Vermutung)* suspicion; **keine ~!** no idea; **ahnungslos** *adj* unsuspecting
Ahorn *(-s, -e) m* maple
Aids *(-) nt* Aids; **aidskrank** *adj* suffering

from Aids; **aidspositiv** *adj* tested positive for Aids; **Aidstest** *m* Aids test

Airbag (*-s, -s*) *m* (*Auto*) airbag; **Airbus** *m* airbus

Akademie (*-, -n*) *f* academy; **Akademiker(in)** (*-s, -*) *m(f)* (university) graduate

akklimatisieren *vr* **sich ~** to acclimatize oneself

Akkordeon (*-s, -s*) *nt* accordion

Akku (*-s, -s*) *m* (storage) battery

Akkusativ *m* accusative (case)

Akne (*-, -*) *f* acne

Akrobat(in) (*-s, -en*) *m(f)* acrobat

Akt (*-(e)s, -e*) *m* act; (*Kunst*) nude

Akte (*-, -n*) *f* file; **etw zu den ~n legen** (*a. fig*) to file sth away; **Aktenkoffer** *m* briefcase

Aktie (*-, -n*) *f* share; **Aktiengesellschaft** *f* public limited company (*Brit*), corporation (*US*)

Aktion *f* (*Kampagne*) campaign; (*Einsatz*) operation

Aktionär(in) (*-s, -e*) *m(f)* shareholder

aktiv *adj* active

aktualisieren *vt* to update; **aktuell** *adj* (*Thema*) topical; (*modern*) up-to-date; (*Problem*) current; **nicht mehr ~** no longer relevant

Akupunktur *f* acupuncture

akustisch *adj* acoustic; **Akustik** *f* acoustics *sing*

akut *adj* acute

AKW (*-s, -s*) *nt* *abk* = **Atomkraftwerk** nuclear power station

Akzent (*-(e)s, -e*) *m* accent; (*Betonung*) stress; **mit starkem schottischen ~** with a strong Scottish accent

akzeptieren *vt* to accept

Alarm (*-(e)s, -e*) *m* alarm; **Alarmanlage** *f* alarm system; **alarmieren** *vt* to alarm; **die Polizei ~** to call the police

Albanien (*-s*) *nt* Albania

Albatros (*-ses, -se*) *m* albatross

albern *adj* silly

Albtraum *m* nightmare

Album (*-s, Alben*) *nt* album

Algen *pl* algae *pl*; (*Meeresalgen*) seaweed *sing*

Algerien (*-s*) *nt* Algeria

Alibi (*-s, -s*) *nt* alibi

Alimente *pl* maintenance *sing*

Alkohol (*-s, -e*) *m* alcohol; **alkoholfrei** *adj* non-alcoholic; **~es Getränk** soft drink; **Alkoholiker(in)** (*-s, -*) *m(f)* alcoholic; **alkoholisch** *adj* alcoholic

All (*-s*) *nt* universe

SCHLÜSSELWORT

alle(r, s) *adj* **1** (*sämtliche*) all; **wir alle** all of us; **alle Kinder waren da** all the children were there; **alle Kinder mögen ...** all children like ...; **alle beide** both of us/them; **sie kamen alle** they all came; **alles Gute** all the best; **alles in allem** all in all

2 (*mit Zeit- oder Maßangaben*) every; **alle vier Jahre** every four years; **alle fünf Meter** every five metres

▷ *pron* everything; **alles was er sagt** everything he says, all that he says

▷ *adv* (*zu Ende, aufgebraucht*) finished; **die Milch ist alle** the milk's all gone, there's no milk left; **etw alle machen** to finish sth up

Allee (*-, -n*) *f* avenue

allein *adj, adv* alone; (*ohne Hilfe*) on one's own, by oneself; **nicht ~** (*nicht nur*) not only; **~ erziehende Mutter** single mother; **~ stehend** single, unmarried; **Alleinerziehende(r)** *mf* single mother/father/parent

allerbeste(r, s) *adj* very best

allerdings *adv* (*zwar*) admittedly; (*gewiss*) certainly, sure (*US*)

allererste(r, s) *adj* very first; **zu allererst** first of all

Allergie *f* allergy; **Allergiker(in)** (*-s, -*) *m(f)* allergy sufferer; **allergisch** *adj* allergic (*gegen* to)

allerhand *adj* *inv* (*fam*) all sorts of; **das ist doch ~!** (*Vorwurf*) that's the limit; **~!** (*lobend*) that's pretty good

Allerheiligen (*-*) *nt* All Saints' Day

allerhöchste(r, s) *adj* very highest; **allerhöchstens** *adv* at the very most; **allerlei** *adj* *inv* all sorts of; **allerletzte(r, s)** *adj* very last; **allerwenigste(r, s)** *adj* very least

alles *pron* everything; **~ in allem** all in all; *siehe auch* **alle**

Alleskleber (*-s, -*) *m* all-purpose glue

allgemein *adj* general; **im Allgemeinen** in general
Alligator (-s, -en) *m* alligator
alljährlich *adj* annual
allmählich *adj* gradual ▷ *adv* gradually
Allradantrieb *m* all-wheel drive
Alltag *m* everyday life; **alltäglich** *adj* everyday; (*gewöhnlich*) ordinary; (*tagtäglich*) daily
allzu *adv* all too
Allzweckreiniger (-s, -) *m* multi-purpose cleaner
Alpen *pl* **die ~** the Alps *pl*
Alphabet (-(e)s, -e) *nt* alphabet; **alphabetisch** *adj* alphabetical
Alptraum *m* *siehe* **Albtraum**

○ SCHLÜSSELWORT

als *konj* **1** (*zeitlich*) when; (*gleichzeitig*) as; **damals, als ...** (in the days) when ...; **gerade, als ...** just as ...
2 (*in der Eigenschaft*) than; **als Antwort** as an answer; **als Kind** as a child
3 (*bei Vergleichen*) than; **ich kam später als er** I came later than he (did) *od* later than him; **lieber ... als ...** rather ... than ...; **nichts als Ärger** nothing but trouble
4: **als ob/wenn** as if

also *conj* (*folglich*) so, therefore ▷ *adv, interj* so; **~ gut** (*o* **schön**)**!** okay then
alt *adj* old; **wie ~ sind Sie?** how old are you?; **28 Jahre ~** 28 years old; **vier Jahre älter** four years older
Altar (-(e)s, Altäre) *m* altar
Alter (-s, -) *nt* age; (*hohes*) old age; **im ~ von** at the age of; **er ist in meinem ~** he's my age
alternativ *adj* alternative; (*umweltbewusst*) ecologically minded; (*Landwirtschaft*) organic; **Alternative** *f* alternative
Altersheim *nt* old people's home
Altglas *nt* used glass; **Altglascontainer** *m* bottle bank; **altmodisch** *adj* old-fashioned; **Altöl** *nt* used (*o* waste) oil; **Altpapier** *nt* waste paper; **Altstadt** *f* old town
Alt-Taste *f* Alt key
Alufolie *f* tin (*o* kitchen) foil
Aluminium (-s) *nt* aluminium (*Brit*), aluminum (*US*)

Alzheimerkrankheit *f* Alzheimer's (disease)
am *kontr von* **an dem**; **~ 2. Januar** on January 2(nd); **~ Morgen** in the morning; **~ Strand** on the beach; **~ Bahnhof** at the station; **was gefällt Ihnen ~ besten?** what do you like best?; **~ besten bleiben wir hier** it would be best if we stayed here
Amateur(in) *m(f)* amateur
ambulant *adj* outpatient; **kann ich ~ behandelt werden?** can I have it done as an outpatient?; **Ambulanz** *f* (*Krankenwagen*) ambulance; (*in der Klinik*) outpatients' department
Ameise (-, -n) *f* ant
amen *interj* amen
Amerika (-s) *nt* America; **Amerikaner(in)** (-s, -) *m(f)* American; **amerikanisch** *adj* American
Ampel (-, -n) *f* traffic lights *pl*
Amphitheater *nt* amphitheatre
Amsel (-, -n) *f* blackbird
Amt (-(e)s, Ämter) *nt* (*Dienststelle*) office, department; (*Posten*) post; **amtlich** *adj* official; **Amtszeichen** *nt* (*Tel*) dialling tone (*Brit*), dial tone (*US*)
amüsant *adj* amusing; **amüsieren** *vt* to amuse ▷ *vr* **sich ~** to enjoy oneself, to have a good time

○ SCHLÜSSELWORT

an *präp* +dat **1** (*räumlich: wo?*) at; (*auf, bei*) on; (*nahe bei*) near; **an diesem Ort** at this place; **an der Wand** on the wall; **zu nahe an etw** too near to sth; **unten am Fluss** down by the river; **Köln liegt am Rhein** Cologne is on the Rhine
2 (*zeitlich: wann?*) on; **an diesem Tag** on this day; **an Ostern** at Easter
3: **arm an Fett** low in fat; **an etw sterben** to die of sth; **an (und für) sich** actually
▷ *präp* +akk **1** (*räumlich: wohin?*) to; **er ging ans Fenster** he went (over) to the window; **etw an die Wand hängen/schreiben** to hang/write sth on the wall
2 (*zeitlich: woran?*) **an etw denken** to think of sth
3 (*gerichtet an*) to; **ein Gruß/eine Frage an dich** greetings/a question to you

▷ *adv* **1** (*ungefähr*) about; **an die hundert** about a hundred
2 (*auf Fahrplänen*): **Frankfurt an 18.30** arriving Frankfurt 18.30
3 (*ab*): **von dort/heute an** from there/today onwards
4 (*angeschaltet, angezogen*) on; **das Licht ist an** the light is on; **ohne etwas an** with nothing on; *siehe auch* **am**

anal *adj* anal
analog *adj* analogous; (*Inform*) analog
Analyse (-, -*n*) *f* analysis; **analysieren** *vt* to analyse
Ananas (-, - *o* -*se*) *f* pineapple
an|baggern *vt* (*fam*) to chat up (*Brit*), to come on to (*US*)
Anbau *m* (*Agr*) cultivation; (*Gebäude*) extension; **an|bauen** *vt* (*Agr*) to cultivate; (*Gebäudeteil*) to build on
an|behalten *irr vt* to keep on
anbei *adv* enclosed; ~ **sende ich ...** please find enclosed ...
an|beten *vt* to worship
an|bieten *irr vt* to offer ▷ *vr* **sich** ~ to volunteer
an|binden *irr vt* to tie up
Anblick *m* sight
an|braten *irr vt* to brown
an|brechen *irr vt* to start; (*Vorräte, Ersparnisse*) to break into; (*Flasche, Packung*) to open ▷ *vi* to start; (*Tag*) to break; (*Nacht*) to fall
an|brennen *irr vt, vi* to burn; **das Fleisch schmeckt angebrannt** the meat tastes burnt
an|bringen *irr vt* (*herbeibringen*) to bring; (*befestigen*) to fix, to attach
Andacht (-, -*en*) *f* devotion; (*Gottesdienst*) prayers *pl*
an|dauern *vi* to continue, to go on; **andauernd** *adj* continual
Andenken (-*s*, -) *nt* memory; (*Gegenstand*) souvenir
andere(r, s) *adj* (*weitere*) other; (*verschieden*) different; (*folgend*) next; **am ~n Tag** the next day; **von etw/jmd else; unter ~ sprechen** to talk about sth/sb else; **unter ~m** among other things; **andererseits** *adv* on the other hand
ändern *vt* to alter, to change ▷ *vr* **sich ~** to change
andernfalls *adv* otherwise

anders *adv* differently (*als* from); **jemand/irgendwo ~** someone/somewhere else; **sie ist ~ als ihre Schwester** she's not like her sister; **es geht nicht ~** there's no other way; **anders(he)rum** *adv* the other way round; **anderswo** *adv* somewhere else
anderthalb *num* one and a half
Änderung *f* change, alteration
an|deuten *vt* to indicate; (*Wink geben*) to hint at
Andorra (-*s*) *nt* Andorra
Andrang *m* **es herrschte großer ~** there was a huge crowd
an|drohen *vt* **jdm etw ~** to threaten sb with sth
aneinander *adv* at/on/to one another (*o* each other); ~ **denken** think of each other; ~ **geraten** to clash; **sich ~ gewöhnen** to get used to each other; ~ **legen** to put together
Anemone (-, -*n*) *f* anemone
an|erkennen *irr vt* (*Staat, Zeugnis etc*) to recognize; (*würdigen*) to appreciate; **Anerkennung** *f* recognition; (*Würdigung*) appreciation
an|fahren *irr vt* (*fahren gegen*) to run into; (*Ort, Hafen*) to stop (*o* call) at; (*liefern*) to deliver; **jdn ~** (*fig: schimpfen*) to jump on sb ▷ *vi* to start; (*losfahren*) to drive off
Anfall *m* (*Med*) attack; **anfällig** *adj* delicate; (*Maschine*) temperamental; ~ **für** prone to
Anfang (-(*e*)*s*, *Anfänge*) *m* beginning, start; **zu/am ~** to start with; ~ **Mai** at the beginning of May; **sie ist ~ 20** she's in her early twenties; **an|fangen** *irr vt, vi* to begin, to start; **damit kann ich nichts ~** that's no use to me; **Anfänger(in)** (-*s*, -) *m(f)* beginner; **anfangs** *adv* at first; **Anfangsbuchstabe** *m* first (*o* initial) letter
an|fassen *vt* (*berühren*) to touch ▷ *vi* **kannst du mal mit ~?** can you give me a hand? ▷ *vr* **sich weich ~** to feel soft
Anflug *m* (*Aviat*) approach; (*Hauch*) trace
an|fordern *vt* to demand; **Anforderung** *f* request (*von* for); (*Anspruch*) demand
Anfrage *f* inquiry
an|freunden *vr* **sich mit jdm ~** to make (*o* to become) friends with sb
an|fühlen *vr* **sich ~** to feel; **es fühlt sich gut an** it feels good

Anführungszeichen *pl* quotation marks *pl*

Angabe *f* (*Tech*) specification; (*fam: Prahlerei*) showing off; (*Tennis*) serve; **~n** *pl* (*Auskunft*) particulars *pl*; **die ~n waren falsch** (*Info*) the information was wrong; **an|geben** *irr vt* (*Name, Grund*) to give; (*zeigen*) to indicate; (*bestimmen*) to set ▷ *vi* (*fam: prahlen*) to boast; (*Sport*) to serve; **Angeber(in)** (*-s, -*) *m(f)* (*fam*) show-off; **angeblich** *adj* alleged

angeboren *adj* inborn

Angebot *nt* offer; (*Comm*) supply (*an +dat* of); **~ und Nachfrage** supply and demand

angebracht *adj* appropriate

angebunden *adj* **kurz ~** curt

angeheitert *adj* tipsy

an|gehen *irr vt* to concern; **das geht dich nichts an** that's none of your business; **ein Problem ~** to tackle a problem; **was ihn angeht** as far as he's concerned, as for him ▷ *vi* (*Feuer*) to catch; (*fam: beginnen*) to begin; **angehend** *adj* prospective

Angehörige(r) *mf* relative

Angeklagte(r) *mf* accused, defendant

Angel (*-, -n*) *f* fishing rod; (*an der Tür*) hinge

Angelegenheit *f* affair, matter

Angelhaken *m* fish hook; **angeln** *vt* to catch ▷ *vi* to fish; **Angeln** (*-s*) *nt* angling, fishing; **Angelrute** (*-, -n*) *f* fishing rod

angemessen *adj* appropriate, suitable

angenehm *adj* pleasant; **~!** (*bei Vorstellung*) pleased to meet you; **das ist mir gar nicht ~** I don't like the idea of that

angenommen *adj* assumed ▷ *conj* **~, es regnet, was machen wir dann?** suppose it rains, what do we do then?

angesehen *adj* respected

angesichts *prep +gen* in view of, considering

Angestellte(r) *mf* employee

angetan *adj* **von jdm/etw ~ sein** to be impressed by (*o* taken with) sb/sth

angewiesen *adj* **auf jdn/etw ~ sein** to be dependent on sb/sth

an|gewöhnen *vt* **sich etw ~** to get used to doing sth; **Angewohnheit** *f* habit

Angina (*-, Anginen*) *f* tonsillitis; **Angina Pectoris** (*-*) *f* angina

Angler(in) (*-s, -*) *m(f)* angler

Angora (*-s*) *nt* angora

an|greifen *irr vt* to attack; (*anfassen*) to touch; (*beschädigen*) to damage; **Angriff** *m* attack; **etw in ~ nehmen** to get started on sth

Angst (*-, Ängste*) *f* fear; **~ haben** to be afraid (*o* scared) (*vor +dat* of); **jdm ~ machen** to scare sb; **ängstigen** *vt* to frighten ▷ *vr* **sich ~** to worry (*um, wegen +dat* about); **ängstlich** *adj* nervous; (*besorgt*) worried

an|haben *irr vt* (*Kleidung*) to have on, to wear; (*Licht*) to have on

an|halten *irr vi* to stop; (*andauern*) to continue; **anhaltend** *adj* continuous; **Anhalter(in)** (*-s, -*) *m(f)* hitch-hiker; **per ~ fahren** to hitch-hike

anhand *prep +gen* with; **~ von** by means of

an|hängen *vt* to hang up; (*Eisenb: Wagen*) to couple; (*Zusatz*) to add (on); **jdm etw ~** (*fam: unterschieben*) to pin sth on sb; **Anhänger** (*-s, -*) *m* (*Auto*) trailer; (*am Koffer*) tag; (*Schmuck*) pendant; **Anhänger(in)** (*-s, -*) *m(f)* supporter; **Anhängerkupplung** *f* towbar; **anhänglich** *adj* affectionate; (*pej*) clinging

Anhieb *m* **auf ~** straight away; **das kann ich nicht auf ~ sagen** I can't say offhand

an|himmeln *vt* to worship, to idolize

an|hören *vt* to listen to ▷ *vr* **sich ~** to sound; **das hört sich gut an** that sounds good

Animateur(in) *m(f)* host/hostess

Anis (*-es, -e*) *m* aniseed

Anker (*-s, -*) *m* anchor; **ankern** *vt, vi* to anchor; **Ankerplatz** *m* anchorage

Ankleidekabine *f* changing cubicle

an|klicken *vt* (*Inform*) to click on

an|klopfen *vi* to knock (*an +akk* on)

an|kommen *irr vi* to arrive; **bei jdm gut ~** to go down well with sb; **es kommt darauf an** it depends (*ob* on whether); **darauf kommt es nicht an** that doesn't matter

an|kotzen *vt* (*vulg*) **es kotzt mich an** it makes me sick

an|kreuzen *vt* to mark with a cross

an|kündigen *vt* to announce

Ankunft (*-, Ankünfte*) *f* arrival; **Ankunftszeit** *f* arrival time

Anlage *f* (*Veranlagung*) disposition; (*Begabung*) talent; (*Park*) gardens *pl*, grounds *pl*; (*zu Brief etc*) enclosure; (*Stereoanlage*) stereo (system); (*Tech*) plant; (*Fin*) investment

Anlass (-es, Anlässe) m cause (zu for); (Ereignis) occasion; **aus diesem ~** for this reason; **an|lassen** irr vt (Motor) to start; (Licht, Kleidung) to leave on; **Anlasser** (-s, -) m (Auto) starter; **anlässlich** prep +gen on the occasion of

Anlauf m run-up; **an|laufen** irr vi to begin; (Film) to open; (Fenster) to mist up; (Metall) to tarnish

an|legen vt to put (an +akk against/on); (Schmuck) to put on; (Garten) to lay out; (Geld) to invest; (Gewehr) to aim (auf +akk at); **es auf etw** (akk) **~** to be out for sth ▷ vi (Schiff) to berth, to dock ▷ vr **sich mit jdm ~** (fam) to pick a quarrel with sb; **Anlegestelle** f moorings pl

an|lehnen vt to lean (an +akk against); (Tür) to leave ajar ▷ vr **sich ~** to lean (an +akk against)

an|leiern vt **etw ~** (fam) to get sth going

Anleitung f instructions pl

Anliegen (-s, -) nt matter; (Wunsch) request

Anlieger(in) (-s, -) m(f) resident; **~ frei** residents only

an|lügen irr vt to lie to

an|machen vt (befestigen) to attach; (einschalten) to switch on; (Salat) to dress; (fam: aufreizen) to turn on; (fam: ansprechen) to chat up (Brit), to come on to (US); (fam: beschimpfen) to have a go at

Anmeldeformular nt application form; (bei Amt) registration form; **an|melden** vt (Besuch etc) to announce ▷ vr **sich ~** (beim Arzt etc) to make an appointment; (bei Amt, für Kurs etc) to register; **Anmeldeschluss** m deadline for applications, registration deadline; **Anmeldung** f registration; (Antrag) application

an|nähen vt **einen Knopf (an den Mantel) ~** to sew a button on (one's coat)

annähernd adv roughly; **nicht ~** nowhere near

Annahme (-, -n) f acceptance; (Vermutung) assumption; **annehmbar** adj acceptable; **an|nehmen** irr vt to accept; (Namen) to take; (Kind) to adopt; (vermuten) to suppose, to assume

Annonce (-, -n) f advertisement

an|öden vt (fam) to bore stiff (o silly)

annullieren vt to cancel

anonym adj anonymous

Anorak (-s, -s) m anorak

an|packen vt (Problem, Aufgabe) to tackle; **mit ~** to lend a hand

an|passen vt (fig) to adapt (dat to) ▷ vr **sich ~** to adapt (an +akk to)

an|pfeifen irr vt (Fußballspiel) **das Spiel ~** to start the game; **Anpfiff** m (Sport) (starting) whistle; (Beginn) kick-off; (fam: Tadel) roasting

an|probieren vt to try on

Anrede f form of address; **an|reden** vt to address

an|regen vt to stimulate; **Anregung** f stimulation; (Vorschlag) suggestion

Anreise f journey; **der Tag der ~** the day of arrival; **an|reisen** vi to arrive

Anreiz m incentive

an|richten vt (Speisen) to prepare; (Schaden) to cause

Anruf m call; **Anrufbeantworter** (-s, -) m answering machine, answerphone; **an|rufen** irr vt (Tel) to call, to phone, to ring (Brit)

ans kontr von **an das**

Ansage f announcement; (auf Anrufbeantworter) recorded message; **an|sagen** vt to announce; **angesagt sein** to be recommended; (modisch sein) to be the in thing; **Spannung ist angesagt** we are in for some excitement ▷ vr **er sagte sich an** he said he would come

an|schaffen vt to buy

an|schauen vt to look at

Anschein m appearance; **dem** (o allem) **~ nach …** it looks as if …; **den ~ erwecken, hart zu arbeiten** to give the impression of working hard; **anscheinend** adj apparent ▷ adv apparently

an|schieben irr vt **könnten Sie mich mal ~?** (Auto) could you give me a push?

Anschlag m notice; (Attentat) attack; **an|schlagen** irr vt (Plakat) to put up; (beschädigen) to chip ▷ vi (wirken) to take effect; **mit etw an etw** (akk) **~** to bang sth against sth

an|schließen irr vt (Elek, Tech) to connect (an +akk to); (mit Stecker) to plug in ▷ vi, vr **(sich) an etw** (akk) **~** (Gebäude etc) to adjoin sth; (zeitlich) to follow sth ▷ vr **sich ~** to join (jdm/einer Gruppe sb/a group); **anschließend** adj adjacent; (zeitlich) subsequent ▷ adv afterwards; **~ an** (+akk) following; **Anschluss** m (Elek, Eisenb) connection; (*von Wasser, Gas etc*) supply; **im ~ an** (+*akk*) following; **kein ~ unter dieser Nummer** (*Tel*) the number you have dialled has not been recognized; **Anschlussflug** *m* connecting flight

an|schnallen *vt* (*Skier*) to put on ▷ *vr* **sich ~** to fasten one's seat belt

Anschrift *f* address

an|schwellen *irr vi* to swell (up)

an|sehen *irr vt* to look at; (*bei etw zuschauen*) to watch; **jdn/etw als etw ~** to look on sb/sth as sth; **das sieht man ihm an** he looks it

an sein *irr vi siehe* **an**

an|setzen *vt* (*Termin*) to fix; (*zubereiten*) to prepare ▷ *vi* (*anfangen*) to start, to begin; **zu etw ~** to prepare to do sth

Ansicht *f* (*Meinung*) view, opinion; (*Anblick*) sight; **meiner ~ nach** in my opinion; **zur ~** on approval; **Ansichtskarte** *f* postcard

ansonsten *adv* otherwise

Anspiel *nt* (*Sport*) start of play; **anspielen** *vi* **auf etw** (*akk*) to allude to sth; **Anspielung** *f* allusion (*auf +akk* to)

an|sprechen *irr vt* to speak to; (*gefallen*) to appeal to ▷ *vi* **auf etw** (*akk*) **~** (*Patient*) to respond to sth; **ansprechend** *adj* attractive; **Ansprechpartner(in)** *m(f)* contact

an|springen *irr vi* (*Auto*) to start

Anspruch *m* claim; (*Recht*) right (*auf +akk* to); **etw in ~ nehmen** to take advantage of sth; **~ auf etw haben** to be entitled to sth; **anspruchslos** *adj* undemanding; (*bescheiden*) modest; **anspruchsvoll** *adj* demanding

Anstalt (-, -*en*) *f* institution

Anstand *m* decency; **anständig** *adj* decent; (*fig, fam*) proper; (*groß*) considerable

an|starren *vt* to stare at

anstatt *prep* +*gen* instead of

an|stecken *vt* to pin on; (*Med*) to infect; **jdn mit einer Erkältung ~** to pass one's cold on to sb ▷ *vr* **ich habe mich bei ihm angesteckt** I caught it from him ▷ *vi* (*fig*) to be infectious; **ansteckend** *adj* infectious; **Ansteckungsgefahr** *f* danger of infection

an|stehen *irr vi* (*in Warteschlange*) to queue (*Brit*), to stand in line (*US*); (*erledigt werden müssen*) to be on the agenda

anstelle *prep* +*gen* instead of

an|stellen *vt* (*einschalten*) to turn on; (*Arbeit geben*) to employ; (*machen*) to do; **was hast du wieder angestellt?** what have you been up to now? ▷ *vr* **sich ~** to queue (*Brit*), to stand in line (*US*); (*fam*) **stell dich nicht so an!** stop making such a fuss

Anstoß *m* impetus; (*Sport*) kick-off; **an|stoßen** *irr vt* to push; (*mit Fuß*) to kick ▷ *vi* to knock, to bump; (*mit Gläsern*) to drink (a toast) (*auf +akk* to); **anstößig** *adj* offensive; (*Kleidung etc*) indecent

an|strengen *vt* to strain ▷ *vr* **sich ~** to make an effort; **anstrengend** *adj* tiring

Antarktis *f* Antarctic

Anteil *m* share (*an +dat* in); **~ nehmen an** (+*dat*) (*mitleidig*) to sympathize with; (*sich interessieren*) to take an interest in

Antenne (-, -*n*) *f* aerial

Antibabypille *f* **die ~** the pill; **Antibiotikum** (-*s*, *Antibiotika*) *nt* (*Med*) antibiotic

antik *adj* antique

Antilope (-, -*n*) *f* antelope

Antiquariat *nt* (*für Bücher*) second-hand bookshop

Antiquitäten *pl* antiques *pl*; **Antiquitätenhändler(in)** *m(f)* antique dealer

an|törnen *vt* (*fam*) to turn on

Antrag (-(*e*)*s*, *Anträge*) *m* proposal; (*Pol*) motion; (*Formular*) application form; **einen ~ stellen auf** (+*akk*) to make an application for

an|treffen *irr vt* to find

an|treiben *irr vt* (*Tech*) to drive; (*anschwemmen*) to wash up; **jdn zur Arbeit ~** to make sb work

an|treten *irr vt* **eine Reise ~** to set off on a journey

Antrieb *m* (*Tech*) drive; (*Motivation*) impetus

an|tun *irr vt* **jdm etwas ~** to do sth to sb; **sich** (*dat*) **etwas ~** (*Selbstmord begehen*) to kill oneself

Antwort (-, -*en*) *f* answer, reply; **um ~ wird gebeten** RSVP (*répondez s'il vous plaît*); **antworten** *vi* to answer, to reply; **jdm ~** to answer sb; **auf etw** (*akk*) **~** to answer sth

an|vertrauen *vt* **jdm etw ~** to entrust sb with sth

Anwalt (-s, Anwälte) m, **Anwältin** f lawyer

an|weisen irr vt (anleiten) to instruct; (zuteilen) to allocate (jdm etw sth to sb); **Anweisung** f instruction; (von Geld) money order

an|wenden irr vt to use; (Gesetz, Regel) to apply; **Anwender(in)** (-s, -) m(f) user; **Anwendung** f use; (Inform) application

anwesend adj present; **Anwesenheit** f presence

an|widern vt to disgust

Anwohner(in) (-s, -) m(f) resident

Anzahl f number (an +dat of); **an|zahlen** vt to pay a deposit on; **100 Euro ~** to pay 100 euros as a deposit; **Anzahlung** f deposit

Anzeichen nt sign; (Med) symptom

Anzeige (-, -n) f (Werbung) advertisement; (elektronisch) display; (bei Polizei) report; **an|zeigen** vt (Temperatur, Zeit) to indicate, to show; (elektronisch) to display; (bekannt geben) to announce; **jdn/einen Autodiebstahl bei der Polizei ~** to report sb/a stolen car to the police

an|ziehen irr vt to attract; (Kleidung) to put on; (Schraube, Seil) to tighten ▷ vr **sich ~** to get dressed; **anziehend** adj attractive

Anzug m suit

anzüglich adj suggestive

an|zünden vt to light; (Haus etc) to set fire to

an|zweifeln vt to doubt

Aperitif (-s, -s (o -e)) m aperitif

Apfel (-s, Äpfel) m apple; **Apfelbaum** m apple tree; **Apfelkuchen** m apple cake; **Apfelmus** nt apple purée; **Apfelsaft** m apple juice; **Apfelsine** f orange; **Apfelwein** m cider

Apostroph (-s, -e) m apostrophe

Apotheke (-, -n) f chemist's (shop) (Brit), pharmacy (US); **apothekenpflichtig** adj only available at the chemist's (o pharmacy); **Apotheker(in)** (-s, -) m(f) chemist (Brit), pharmacist (US)

Apparat (-(e)s, -e) m (piece of) apparatus; (Tel) telephone; (Radio, Tv) set; **am ~!** (Tel) speaking; **am ~ bleiben** (Tel) to hold the line

Appartement (-s, -s) nt studio flat (Brit) (o apartment (US))

Appetit (-(e)s, -e) m appetite; **guten ~!** bon appétit; **appetitlich** adj appetizing

Applaus (-es, -e) m applause

Aprikose (-, -n) f apricot

April (-(s), -e) m April; siehe auch **Juni ~, ~!** April fool!; **Aprilscherz** (-es, -e) m April fool's joke

apropos adv by the way; **~ Urlaub ...** while we're on the subject of holidays ...

Aquaplaning (-(s)) nt aquaplaning

Aquarell (-s, -e) nt watercolour

Aquarium nt aquarium

Äquator m equator

Araber(in) (-s, -) m(f) Arab; **arabisch** adj Arab; (Ziffer, Sprache) Arabic; (Meer, Wüste) Arabian

Arbeit (-, -en) f work; (Stelle) job; (Erzeugnis) piece of work; **arbeiten** vi to work; **Arbeiter(in)** (-s, -) m(f) worker; (ungelernt) labourer; **Arbeitgeber(in)** (-s, -) m(f) employer; **Arbeitnehmer(in)** (-s, -) m(f) employee; **Arbeitsamt** nt job centre (Brit), employment office (US); **Arbeitserlaubnis** f work permit; **arbeitslos** adj unemployed; **Arbeitslose(r)** mf unemployed person; **die ~n** pl the unemployed pl; **Arbeitslosengeld** nt (income-related) unemployment benefit, job-seeker's allowance (Brit); **Arbeitslosenhilfe** f (non-income related) unemployment benefit; **Arbeitslosigkeit** f unemployment; **Arbeitsplatz** m job; (Ort) workplace; **Arbeitsspeicher** m (Inform) main memory; **Arbeitszeit** f working hours pl; **gleitende ~** flexible working hours pl, flexitime; **Arbeitszimmer** nt study

Archäologe (-n, -n) m, **Archäologin** f archaeologist

Architekt(in) (-en, -en) m(f) architect; **Architektur** f architecture

Archiv (-s, -e) nt archives pl

arg adj bad; (schrecklich) awful ▷ adv (sehr) terribly

Argentinien (-s) nt Argentina

Ärger (-s) m annoyance; (stärker) anger; (Unannehmlichkeiten) trouble; **ärgerlich** adj (zornig) angry; (lästig) annoying; **ärgern** vt to annoy ▷ vr **sich ~** to get annoyed

Argument (-s, -e) nt argument

Arktis (-) f Arctic

arm *adj* poor

Arm (-(e)s, -e) *m* arm; (*Fluss*) branch

Armaturenbrett *nt* instrument panel; (*Auto*) dashboard

Armband *nt* bracelet; **Armbanduhr** *f* (wrist)watch

Armee (-, -n) *f* army

Ärmel (-s, -) *m* sleeve; **Ärmelkanal** *m* (English) Channel

Armut (-) *f* poverty

Aroma (-s, Aromen) *nt* aroma; **Aromatherapie** *f* aromatherapy

arrogant *adj* arrogant

Art (-, -en) *f* (*Weise*) way; (*Sorte*) kind, sort; (*bei Tieren*) species; **nach ~ des Hauses** à la maison; **auf diese ~ (und Weise)** in this way; **das ist nicht seine ~** that's not like him

Arterie (-, -n) *f* artery

artig *adj* good, well-behaved

Artikel (-s, -) *m* (*Ware*) article, item; (*Zeitung*) article

Artischocke (-, -n) *f* artichoke

Artist(in) (-en, -en) *m(f)* (circus) performer

Arznei *f* medicine; **Arzt** (-es, Ärzte) *m* doctor; **Arzthelfer(in)** *m(f)* doctor's assistant; **Ärztin** *f* (female) doctor; **ärztlich** *adj* medical; **sich ~ behandeln lassen** to undergo medical treatment

Asche (-, -n) *f* ashes *pl*; (*von Zigarette*) ash; **Aschenbecher** *m* ashtray; **Aschermittwoch** *m* Ash Wednesday

Asiat(in) (-en, -en) *m(f)* Asian; **asiatisch** *adj* Asian; **Asien** (-s) *nt* Asia

Aspekt (-(e)s, -e) *m* aspect

Asphalt (-(e)s, -e) *m* asphalt

Aspirin® (-s, -e) *nt* aspirin

aß *imperf von* **essen**

Ass (-es, -e) *nt* (*Karten, Tennis*) ace

Assistent(in) *m(f)* assistant

Ast (-(e)s, Äste) *m* branch

Asthma (-s) *nt* asthma

Astrologie *f* astrology; **Astronaut(in)** (-en, -en) *m(f)* astronaut; **Astronomie** *f* astronomy

ASU (-, -s) *f abk =* **Abgassonderuntersuchung** exhaust emission test

Asyl (-s, -e) *nt* asylum; (*Heim*) home; (*für Obdachlose*) shelter; **Asylant(in)** *m(f)*, **Asylbewerber(in)** *m(f)* asylum seeker

Atelier (-s, -s) *nt* studio

Atem (-s) *m* breath; **atemberaubend** *adj* breathtaking; **Atembeschwerden** *pl* breathing difficulties *pl*; **atemlos** *adj* breathless; **Atempause** *f* breather

Athen *nt* Athens

Äthiopien (-s) *nt* Ethiopia

Athlet(in) (-en, -en) *m(f)* athlete

Atlantik (-s) *m* Atlantic (Ocean)

Atlas (- o Atlasses, Atlanten) *m* atlas

atmen *vt, vi* to breathe; **Atmung** *f* breathing

Atom (-s, -e) *nt* atom; **Atombombe** *f* atom bomb; **Atomkraftwerk** *nt* nuclear power station; **Atommüll** *m* nuclear waste; **Atomwaffen** *pl* nuclear weapons *pl*

Attentat (-(e)s, -e) *nt* assassination (auf +akk of); (*Versuch*) assassination attempt

Attest (-(e)s, -e) *nt* certificate

attraktiv *adj* attractive

Attrappe (-, -n) *f* dummy

ätzend *adj* (*fam*) revolting; (*schlecht*) lousy

au *interj* ouch; **~ ja!** yeah

Aubergine (-, -n) *f* aubergine, eggplant (US)

🔵 **SCHLÜSSELWORT**

auch *adv* **1** (*ebenfalls*) also, too, as well; **das ist auch schön** that's nice too *od* as well; **er kommt — ich auch** he's coming — so am I me too; **auch nicht** not ... either; **ich auch nicht** nor I, me neither; **oder auch** or; **auch das noch!** not that as well!

2 (*selbst, sogar*) even; **auch wenn das Wetter schlecht ist** even if the weather is bad; **ohne auch nur zu fragen** without even asking

3 (*wirklich*) really; **du siehst müde aus — bin ich auch** you look tired — (so) I am; **so sieht es auch aus** it looks like it too

4 (*auch immer*); **wer auch** whoever; **was auch** whatever; **wie dem auch sei** be that as it may; **wie sehr er sich auch bemühte** however much he tried

audiovisuell *adj* audiovisual

🔘 SCHLÜSSELWORT

auf *präp* +dat (*wo?*) on; **auf dem Tisch** on the table; **auf der Reise** on the way; **auf der Post/dem Fest** at the post office/party; **auf der Straße** on the road; **auf dem Land/der ganzen Welt** in the country/the whole world

▷ *präp* +akk **1** (*wohin?*) on(to); **auf den Tisch** on(to) the table; **auf die Post gehen** go to the post office; **auf das Land** into the country; **etw auf einen Zettel schreiben** to write sth on a piece of paper

2: **auf Deutsch** in German; **auf Lebenszeit** for my/his lifetime; **bis auf ihn** except for him; **auf einmal** at once; **auf seinen Vorschlag (hin)** at his suggestion

▷ *adv* **1** (*offen*) open; **auf sein** (*umg*) (*Tür, Geschäft*) to be open; **das Fenster ist auf** the window is open

2 (*hinauf*) up; **auf und ab** up and down; **auf und davon** up and away; **auf!** (*los!*) come on!

3 (*aufgestanden*) up; **auf sein** to be up; **ist er schon auf?** is he up yet?

▷ *konj*: **auf dass** (so) that

auf|atmen *vi* to breathe a sigh of relief

auf|bauen *vt* (*errichten*) to put up; (*schaffen*) to build up; (*gestalten*) to construct; (*gründen*) to found, to base (*auf* +akk on); **sich eine Existenz ~** to make a life for oneself

auf|bewahren *vt* to keep, to store

auf|bleiben *irr vi* (*Tür, Laden etc*) to stay open; (*Mensch*) to stay up

auf|blenden *vi, vt* (**die Scheinwerfer**) **~** to put one's headlights on full beam

auf|brechen *irr vt* to break open ▷ *vi* to burst open; (*gehen*) to leave; (*abreisen*) to set off; **Aufbruch** *m* departure

auf|drängen *vt* **jdm etw ~** to force sth on sb ▷ *vr* **sich ~** to intrude (*jdm* on sb); **aufdringlich** *adj* pushy

aufeinander *adv* (*übereinander*) on top of each other; **~ achten** to look after each other; **~ schießen** to shoot at each other; **~ vertrauen** to trust each other; **~ folgen**

to follow one another; **~ prallen** to crash into one another

Aufenthalt *m* stay; (*Zug*) stop; **Aufenthaltsgenehmigung** *f* residence permit; **Aufenthaltsraum** *m* lounge

auf|essen *irr vt* to eat up

auf|fahren *irr vi* (*Auto*) to run (*o* to crash) (*auf* +akk into); (*herankommen*) to drive up; **Auffahrt** *f* (*am Haus*) drive; (*Autobahn*) slip road (*Brit*), ramp (*US*); **Auffahrunfall** *m* rear-end collision; (*mehrere Fahrzeuge*) pile-up

auf|fallen *irr vi* to stand out; **jdm ~** to strike sb; **das fällt gar nicht auf** nobody will notice; **auffallend** *adj* striking; **auffällig** *adj* conspicuous; (*Kleidung, Farbe*) striking

auf|fangen *irr vt* (*Ball*) to catch; (*Stoß*) to cushion

auf|fassen *vt* to understand; **Auffassung** *f* view; (*Meinung*) opinion; (*Auslegung*) concept; (*Auffassungsgabe*) grasp

auf|fordern *vt* (*befehlen*) to call upon; (*bitten*) to ask

auf|frischen *vt* (*Kenntnisse*) to brush up

auf|führen *vt* (*Theat*) to perform; (*in einem Verzeichnis*) to list; (*Beispiel*) to give ▷ *vr* **sich ~** (*sich benehmen*) to behave; **Aufführung** *f* (*Theat*) performance

Aufgabe *f* job, task; (*Schule*) exercise; (*Hausaufgabe*) homework

Aufgang *m* (*Treppe*) staircase

auf|geben *irr vt* (*verzichten auf*) to give up; (*Paket*) to post; (*Gepäck*) to check in; (*Bestellung*) to place; (*Inserat*) to insert; (*Rätsel, Problem*) to set ▷ *vi* to give up

auf|gehen *irr vi* (*Sonne, Teig*) to rise; (*sich öffnen*) to open; (*klar werden*) to dawn (*jdm* on sb)

aufgelegt *adj* **gut/schlecht ~** in a good/bad mood

aufgeregt *adj* excited

aufgeschlossen *adj* open(minded)

aufgeschmissen *adj* (*fam*) in a fix

aufgrund, auf Grund *prep* +gen on the basis of; (*wegen*) because of

auf|haben *irr vt* (*Hut etc*) to have on; **viel ~** (*Schule*) to have a lot of homework to do ▷ *vi* (*Geschäft*) to be open

auf|halten *irr vt* (*jdn*) to detain; (*Entwicklung*) to stop; (*Tür, Hand*) to hold open; (*Augen*) to keep open ▷ *vr* **sich ~** (*wohnen*) to live; (*vorübergehend*) to stay

auf|hängen *irr vt* to hang up
auf|heben *irr vt* (*vom Boden etc*) to pick up; (*aufbewahren*) to keep
auf|holen *vt* (*Zeit*) to make up ▷ *vi* to catch up
auf|hören *vi* to stop; **~, etw zu tun** to stop doing sth
auf|klären *vt* (*Geheimnis etc*) to clear up; **jdn ~** to enlighten sb; (*sexuell*) to tell sb the facts of life
Aufkleber (*-s, -*) *m* sticker
auf|kommen *irr vi* (*Wind*) to come up; (*Zweifel, Gefühl*) to arise; (*Mode etc*) to appear on the scene; **für den Schaden ~** to pay for the damage
auf|laden *irr vt* to load; (*Handy etc*) to charge; **Aufladegerät** *nt* charger
Auflage *f* edition; (*von Zeitung*) circulation; (*Bedingung*) condition
auf|lassen *vt* (*Hut, Brille*) to keep on; (*Tür*) to leave open
Auflauf *m* (*Menschen*) crowd; (*Speise*) bake
auf|legen *vt* (*CD, Schminke etc*) to put on; (*Hörer*) to put down ▷ *vi* (*Tel*) to hang up
auf|leuchten *vi* to light up
auf|lösen *vt* (*in Flüssigkeit*) to dissolve ▷ *vr* **sich ~** (*in Flüssigkeit*) to dissolve; **der Stau hat sich aufgelöst** traffic is back to normal; **Auflösung** *f* (*von Rätsel*) solution; (*von Bildschirm*) resolution
auf|machen *vt* to open; (*Kleidung*) to undo ▷ *vr* **sich ~** to set out (*nach* for)
aufmerksam *adj* attentive; **jdn auf etw** (*akk*) **~ machen** to draw sb's attention to sth; **Aufmerksamkeit** *f* attention; (*Konzentration*) attentiveness; (*Geschenk*) small token
auf|muntern *vt* (*ermutigen*) to encourage; (*aufheitern*) to cheer up
Aufnahme (*-, -n*) *f* (*Foto*) photo(graph); (*einzelne*) shot; (*in Verein, Krankenhaus etc*) admission; (*Beginn*) beginning; (*auf Tonband etc*) recording; **Aufnahmeprüfung** *f* entrance exam; **auf|nehmen** *irr vt* (*in Krankenhaus, Verein etc*) to admit; (*Musik*) to record; (*beginnen*) to take up; (*in Liste*) to include; (*begreifen*) to take in; **mit jdm Kontakt ~** to get in touch with sb
auf|passen *vi* (*aufmerksam sein*) to pay attention; (*vorsichtig sein*) to take care; **auf jdn/etw ~** to keep an eye on sb/sth

Aufprall (*-s, -e*) *m* impact; **auf|prallen** *vi* **auf etw** (*akk*) **~** to hit sth, to crash into sth
Aufpreis *m* extra charge
auf|pumpen *vt* to pump up
Aufputschmittel *nt* stimulant
auf|räumen *vt, vi* (*Dinge*) to clear away; (*Zimmer*) to tidy up
aufrecht *adj* upright
auf|regen *vt* to excite; (*ärgern*) to annoy ▷ *vr* **sich ~** to get worked up; **aufregend** *adj* exciting; **Aufregung** *f* excitement
auf|reißen *irr vt* (*Tüte*) to tear open; (*Tür*) to fling open; (*fam: Person*) to pick up
Aufruf *m* (*Aviat, Inform*) call; (*öffentlicher*) appeal; **auf|rufen** *irr vt* (*auffordern*) to call upon (*zu* for); (*Namen*) to call out; (*Aviat*) to call; (*Inform*) to call up
auf|runden *vt* (*Summe*) to round up
aufs *kontr von* **auf das**
Aufsatz *m* essay
auf|schieben *irr vt* (*verschieben*) to postpone; (*verzögern*) to put off; (*Tür*) to slide open
Aufschlag *m* (*auf Preis*) extra charge; (*Tennis*) service; **auf|schlagen** *irr vt* (*öffnen*) to open; (*verletzen*) to cut open; (*Zelt*) to pitch, to put up; (*Lager*) to set up ▷ *vi* (*Tennis*) to serve; **auf etw** (*+akk*) **~** (*aufprallen*) to hit sth
auf|schließen *irr vt* to unlock, to open up ▷ *vi* (*aufrücken*) to close up
auf|schneiden *irr vt* to cut open; (*in Scheiben*) to slice ▷ *vi* (*angeben*) to boast, to show off
Aufschnitt *m* (slices *pl* of) cold meat; (*bei Käse*) (assorted) sliced cheeses *pl*
auf|schreiben *irr vt* to write down
Aufschrift *f* inscription; (*Etikett*) label
Aufschub *m* (*Verzögerung*) delay; (*Vertagung*) postponement
Aufsehen (*-s*) *nt* stir; **großes ~ erregen** to cause a sensation; **Aufseher(in)** (*-s, -*) *m(f)* guard; (*im Betrieb*) supervisor; (*im Museum*) attendant; (*im Park*) keeper
auf sein *irr vi siehe* **auf**
auf|setzen *vt* to put on; (*Dokument*) to draw up ▷ *vi* (*Flugzeug*) to touch down
Aufsicht *f* supervision; (*bei Prüfung*) invigilation; **die ~ haben** to be in charge
auf|spannen *vt* (*Schirm*) to put up
auf|sperren *vt* (*Mund*) to open wide; (*aufschließen*) to unlock
auf|springen *irr vi* to jump (*auf +akk*

onto); (*hochspringen*) to jump up; (*sich öffnen*) to spring open

auf|stehen *irr vi* to get up; (*Tür*) to be open

auf|stellen *vt* (*aufrecht stellen*) to put up; (*aufreihen*) to line up; (*nominieren*) to put up; (*Liste, Programm*) to draw up; (*Rekord*) to set up

Aufstieg (-(*e*)*s*, *-e*) *m* (*auf Berg*) ascent; (*Fortschritt*) rise; (*beruflich, im Sport*) promotion

Aufstrich *m* spread

auf|tanken *vt, vi* (*Auto*) to tank up; (*Flugzeug*) to refuel

auf|tauchen *vi* to turn up; (*aus Wasser etc*) to surface; (*Frage, Problem*) to come up

auf|tauen *vt* (*Speisen*) to defrost ▷ *vi* to thaw; (*fig: Person*) to unbend

Auftrag (-(*e*)*s*, *Aufträge*) *m* (*Comm*) order; (*Arbeit*) job; (*Anweisung*) instructions *pl*; (*Aufgabe*) task; **im ~ von** on behalf of; **auf|tragen** *irr vt* (*Salbe etc*) to apply; (*Essen*) to serve

auf|treten *irr vi* to appear; (*Problem*) to come up; (*sich verhalten*) to behave; **Auftritt** *m* (*des Schauspielers*) entrance; (*fig: Szene*) scene

auf|wachen *vi* to wake up

auf|wachsen *irr vi* to grow up

Aufwand (-(*e*)*s*) *m* expenditure; (*Kosten a.*) expense; (*Anstrengung*) effort; **aufwändig** *adj* costly; **das ist zu ~** that's too much trouble

auf|wärmen *vt* to warm up ▷ *vr* **sich ~** to warm up

aufwärts *adv* upwards; **mit etw geht es ~** things are looking up for sth

auf|wecken *vt* to wake up

aufwendig *adj siehe* **aufwändig**

auf|wischen *vt* to wipe up; (*Fußboden*) to wipe

auf|zählen *vt* to list; **Aufzählungszeichen** *nt* bullet

auf|zeichnen *vt* to sketch; (*schriftlich*) to jot down; (*auf Band etc*) to record; **Aufzeichnung** *f* (*schriftlich*) note; (*Tonband etc*) recording; (*Film*) record

auf|ziehen *irr vt* (*öffnen*) to pull open; (*Uhr*) to wind (up); (*fam: necken*) to tease; (*Kinder*) to bring up; (*Tiere*) to rear ▷ *vi* (*Gewitter*) to come up

Aufzug *m* (*Fahrstuhl*) lift (*Brit*), elevator (*US*); (*Kleidung*) get-up; (*Theat*) act

Auge (-*s*, *-n*) *nt* eye; **jdm etw aufs ~ drücken** (*fam*) to force sth on sb; **ins ~ gehen** (*fam*) to go wrong; **unter vier ~n** in private; **etw im ~ behalten** to keep sth in mind; **Augenarzt** *m*, **Augenärztin** *f* eye specialist, eye doctor (*US*); **Augenblick** *m* moment; **im ~** at the moment; **Augenbraue** (-, *-n*) *f* eyebrow; **Augenbrauenstift** *m* eyebrow pencil; **Augenfarbe** *f* eye colour; **seine ~** the colour of his eyes; **Augenlid** *nt* eyelid; **Augenoptiker(in)** (-*s*, -) *m(f)* optician; **Augentropfen** *pl* eyedrops *pl*; **Augenzeuge** *m*, **Augenzeugin** *f* eyewitness

August (-(*e*)*s o* -, *-e*) *m* August; *siehe auch* **Juni**

Auktion *f* auction

⊙ **SCHLÜSSELWORT**

aus *präp* +dat **1** (*räumlich*) out of (*von ... her*) from; **er ist aus Berlin** he's from Berlin; **aus dem Fenster** out of the window

2 (*gemacht/hergestellt aus*) made of; **ein Herz aus Stein** a heart of stone

3 (*auf Ursache deutend*) out of; **aus Mitleid** out of sympathy; **aus Erfahrung** from experience; **aus Spaß** for fun

4: **aus ihr wird nie etwas** she'll never get anywhere

▷ *adv* **1** (*zu Ende*) finished, over; **aus sein** to be over; **aus und vorbei** over and done with

2 (*ausgeschaltet, ausgezogen*) out (*Aufschrift an Geräten*) off; **aus sein** (*nicht brennen*) to be out; (*abgeschaltet sein: Radio, Herd*) to be off; **Licht aus!** lights out!

3 (*nicht zu Hause*): **aus sein** to be out

4 (*in Verbindung mit von*): **von Rom aus** from Rome; **vom Fenster aus** out of the window; **von sich aus** (*selbstständig*) of one's own accord; **von ihm aus** as far as he's concerned

aus|atmen *vi* to breathe out

aus|bauen *vt* (*Haus, Straße*) to extend; (*Motor etc*) to remove

aus|bessern *vt* to repair; (*Kleidung*) to mend

aus|bilden *vt* to educate; (*Lehrling etc*) to train; (*Fähigkeiten*) to develop; **Ausbildung**

f education; (*von Lehrling etc*) training; (*von Fähigkeiten*) development

Ausblick *m* view; (*fig*) outlook

aus|brechen *irr vi* to break out; **in Tränen ~** to burst into tears; **in Gelächter ~** to burst out laughing

aus|breiten *vt* to spread (out); (*Arme*) to stretch out ▷ *vr* **sich ~** to spread

Ausbruch *m* (*Krieg, Seuche etc*) outbreak; (*Vulkan*) eruption; (*Gefühle*) outburst; (*von Gefangenen*) escape

aus|buhen *vt* to boo

Ausdauer *f* perseverance; (*Sport*) stamina

aus|dehnen *vt* to stretch; (*fig: Macht*) to extend

aus|denken *irr vt* **sich** (*dat*) **etw ~** to come up with sth

Ausdruck *m* (*Ausdrücke*) expression ▷ *m* (*Ausdrucke*) (*Computerausdruck*) print-out; **aus|drucken** *vt* (*Inform*) to print (out)

aus|drücken *vt* (*formulieren*) to express; (*Zigarette*) to put out; (*Zitrone etc*) to squeeze ▷ *vr* **sich ~** to express oneself; **ausdrücklich** *adj* express ▷ *adv* expressly

auseinander *adv* (*getrennt*) apart; **~ gehen** (*Menschen*) to separate; (*Meinungen*) to differ; (*Gegenstand*) to fall apart; **~ halten** to tell apart; **~ schreiben** to write as separate words; **~ setzen** (*erklären*) to explain; **sich ~ setzen** (*sich beschäftigen*) to look (*mit* at); (*sich streiten*) to argue (*mit* with); **Auseinandersetzung** *f* (*Streit*) argument; (*Diskussion*) debate

Ausfahrt *f* (*des Zuges etc*) departure; (*Autobahn, Garage etc*) exit

aus|fallen *irr vi* (*Haare*) to fall out; (*nicht stattfinden*) to be cancelled; (*nicht funktionieren*) to break down; (*Strom*) to be cut off; (*Resultat haben*) to turn out; **groß/klein ~** (*Kleidung, Schuhe*) to be too big/too small

ausfindig machen *vt* to discover

aus|flippen *vi* (*fam*) to freak out

Ausflug *m* excursion, outing; **Ausflugsziel** *nt* destination

Ausfluss *m* (*Med*) discharge

aus|fragen *vt* to question

Ausfuhr (-, -en) *f* export

aus|führen *vt* (*verwirklichen*) to carry

out; (*Person*) to take out; (*Comm*) to export; (*darlegen*) to explain

ausführlich *adj* detailed ▷ *adv* in detail

aus|füllen *vt* to fill up; (*Fragebogen etc*) to fill in (*o* out)

Ausgabe *f* (*Geld*) expenditure; (*Inform*) output; (*Buch*) edition; (*Nummer*) issue

Ausgang *m* way out, exit; (*Flugsteig*) gate; (*Ende*) end; (*Ergebnis*) result; **„kein ~"** 'no exit'

aus|geben *irr vt* (*Geld*) to spend; (*austeilen*) to distribute; **jdm etw ~** (*spendieren*) to buy sb sth ▷ *vr* **sich für etw/jdn ~** to pass oneself off as sth/sb

ausgebucht *adj* fully booked

ausgefallen *adj* (*ungewöhnlich*) unusual

aus|gehen *irr vi* (*abends etc*) to go out; (*Benzin, Kaffee etc*) to run out; (*Haare*) to fall out; (*Feuer, Licht etc*) to go out; (*Resultat haben*) to turn out; **davon ~, dass** to assume that; **ihm ging das Geld aus** he ran out of money

ausgelassen *adj* exuberant

ausgeleiert *adj* worn out

ausgenommen *conj, prep +gen o dat* except

ausgerechnet *adv* **~ du** you of all people; **~ heute** today of all days

ausgeschildert *adj* signposted

ausgeschlafen *adj* **bist du ~?** have you had enough sleep?

ausgeschlossen *adj* (*unmöglich*) impossible, out of the question

ausgesprochen *adj* (*absolut*) out-and-out; (*unverkennbar*) marked ▷ *adv* extremely; **~ gut** really good

ausgezeichnet *adj* excellent

ausgiebig *adj* (*Gebrauch*) thorough; (*Essen*) substantial

aus|gießen *irr vt* (*Getränk*) to pour out; (*Gefäß*) to empty

aus|gleichen *irr vt* to even out ▷ *vi* (*Sport*) to equalize

Ausguss *m* (*Spüle*) sink; (*Abfluss*) outlet

aus|halten *irr vt* to bear, to stand; **nicht auszuhalten sein** to be unbearable ▷ *vi* to hold out

aus|händigen *vt* **jdm etw ~** to hand sth over to sb

Aushang *m* notice

Aushilfe *f* temporary help; (*im Büro*) temp

aus|kennen *irr vr* **sich ~** to know a lot

(*bei, mit* about); (*an einem Ort*) to know one's way around

aus|kommen *irr vi* **gut/schlecht mit jdm ~** to get on well/badly with sb; **mit etw ~** to get by with sth

Auskunft (-, *Auskünfte*) *f* information; (*nähere*) details *pl*; (*Schalter*) information desk; (*Tel*) (directory) enquiries *sing* (*kein Artikel, Brit*), information (*US*)

aus|lachen *vt* to laugh at

aus|laden *irr vt* (*Gepäck etc*) to unload; **jdn ~** (*Gast*) to tell sb not to come

Auslage *f* window display; **~n** *pl* (*Kosten*) expenses

Ausland *nt* foreign countries *pl*; **im/ins ~** abroad; **Ausländer(in)** (-s, -) *m(f)* foreigner; **ausländerfeindlich** *adj* hostile to foreigners, xenophobic; **ausländisch** *adj* foreign; **Auslandsgespräch** *nt* international call; **Auslandskrankenschein** *m* health insurance certificate for foreign countries, ≈ E111 (*Brit*); **Auslandsschutzbrief** *m* international (*motor*) insurance cover (*documents pl*)

aus|lassen *irr vt* to leave out; (*Wort etc a.*) to omit; (*überspringen*) to skip; (*Wut, Ärger*) to vent (*an +dat* on) ▷ *vr* **sich über etw** (*akk*) **~** to speak one's mind about sth

aus|laufen *irr vi* (*Flüssigkeit*) to run out; (*Tank etc*) to leak; (*Schiff*) to leave port; (*Vertrag*) to expire

aus|legen *vt* (*Waren*) to display; (*Geld*) to lend; (*Text etc*) to interpret; (*technisch ausstatten*) to design (*für, auf +akk* for)

aus|leihen *irr vt* (*verleihen*) to lend; **sich** (*dat*) **etw ~** to borrow sth

aus|loggen *vi* (*Inform*) to log out (*o* off)

aus|lösen *vt* (*Explosion, Alarm*) to set off; (*hervorrufen*) to cause; **Auslöser** (-s, -) *m* (*Foto*) shutter release

aus|machen *vt* (*Licht, Radio*) to turn off; (*Feuer*) to put out; (*Termin, Preis*) to fix; (*vereinbaren*) to agree; (*Anteil darstellen, betragen*) to represent; (*bedeuten*) to matter; **macht es Ihnen etwas aus, wenn ...?** would you mind if ...?; **das macht mir nichts aus** I don't mind

Ausmaß *nt* extent

Ausnahme (-, -*n*) *f* exception; **ausnahmsweise** *adv* as an exception, just this once

aus|nutzen *vt* (*Zeit, Gelegenheit, Einfluss*)

to use; (*jdn, Gutmütigkeit*) to take advantage of

aus|packen *vt* to unpack

aus|probieren *vt* to try (out)

Auspuff (-*(e)s, -e*) *m* (*Tech*) exhaust; **Auspuffrohr** *nt* exhaust (pipe); **Auspufftopf** *m* (*Auto*) silencer (*Brit*), muffler (*US*)

aus|rauben *vt* to rob

aus|räumen *vt* (*Dinge*) to clear away; (*Schrank, Zimmer*) to empty; (*Bedenken*) to put aside

aus|rechnen *vt* to calculate, to work out

Ausrede *f* excuse

aus|reden *vi* to finish speaking ▷ *vt* **jdm etw ~** to talk sb out of sth

ausreichend *adj* sufficient, satisfactory; (*Schulnote*) ≈ D

Ausreise *f* departure; **bei der ~** on leaving the country; **Ausreiseerlaubnis** *f* exit visa; **aus|reisen** *vi* to leave the country

aus|reißen *irr vt* to tear out ▷ *vi* to come off; (*fam: davonlaufen*) to run away

aus|renken *vt* **sich** (*dat*) **den Arm ~** to dislocate one's arm

aus|richten *vt* (*Botschaft*) to deliver; (*Gruß*) to pass on; (*erreichen*) **ich konnte bei ihr nichts ~** I couldn't get anywhere with her; **jdm etw ~** to tell sb sth

aus|rufen *irr vt* (*über Lautsprecher*) to announce; **jdn ~ lassen** to page sb; **Ausrufezeichen** *nt* exclamation mark

aus|ruhen *vi* to rest ▷ *vr* **sich ~** to rest

Ausrüstung *f* equipment

aus|rutschen *vi* to slip

aus|schalten *vt* to switch off; (*fig*) to eliminate

Ausschau *f* **~ halten** to look out (*nach* for)

aus|scheiden *irr vt* (*Med*) to give off, to secrete ▷ *vi* to leave (*aus etw* sth); (*Sport*) to be eliminated

aus|schlafen *irr vi* to have a lie-in ▷ *vr* **sich ~** to have a lie-in ▷ *vt* to sleep off

Ausschlag *m* (*Med*) rash; **den ~ geben** (*fig*) to tip the balance; **aus|schlagen** *irr vt* (*Zahn*) to knock out; (*Einladung*) to turn down ▷ *vi* (*Pferd*) to kick out; **ausschlaggebend** *adj* decisive

aus|schließen *irr vt* to lock out; (*fig*) to exclude; **ausschließlich** *adv* exclusively ▷ *prep +gen* excluding

Ausschnitt m (Teil) section; (von Kleid) neckline; (aus Zeitung) cutting

Ausschreitungen pl riots pl

aus|schütten vt (Flüssigkeit) to pour out; (Gefäß) to empty

aus|sehen irr vi to look; **krank ~** to look ill; **gut ~** (Person) to be good-looking; (Sache) to be looking good; **es sieht nach Regen aus** it looks like rain; **es sieht schlecht aus** things look bad

aus sein irr vi siehe **aus**

außen adv outside; **nach ~** outwards; **von ~** from (the) outside; **Außenbordmotor** m outboard motor; **Außenminister(in)** m(f) foreign minister, Foreign Secretary (Brit); **Außenseite** f outside; **Außenseiter(in)** m(f) outsider; **Außenspiegel** m wing mirror (Brit), side mirror (US)

außer prep +dat (abgesehen von) except (for); **nichts ~** nothing but; **~ Betrieb** out of order; **~ sich sein** to be beside oneself (vor with); **~ Atem** out of breath ▷ conj (ausgenommen) except; **~ wenn** unless; **~ dass** except; **außerdem** conj besides

äußere(r, s) adj outer, external

außergewöhnlich adj unusual ▷ adv exceptionally; **~ kalt** exceptionally cold; **außerhalb** prep +gen outside

äußerlich adj external

äußern vt to express; (zeigen) to show ▷ vr **sich ~** to give one's opinion; (sich zeigen) to show itself

außerordentlich adj extraordinary; **außerplanmäßig** adj unscheduled

äußerst adv extremely; **äußerste(r, s)** adj utmost; (räumlich) farthest; (Termin) last possible

Äußerung f remark

aus|setzen vt (Kind, Tier) to abandon; (Belohnung) to offer; **ich habe nichts daran auszusetzen** I have no objection to it ▷ vi (aufhören) to stop; (Pause machen) to drop out; (beim Spiel) to miss a turn

Aussicht f (Blick) view; (Chance) prospect; **aussichtslos** adj hopeless; **Aussichtsplattform** f observation platform; **Aussichtsturm** m observation tower

Aussiedler(in) (-s, -) m(f) émigré (person of German descent from Eastern Europe)

aus|spannen vi (erholen) to relax ▷ vt **er hat ihm die Freundin ausgespannt** (fam) he's nicked his girlfriend

aus|sperren vt to lock out ▷ vr **sich ~** to lock oneself out

Aussprache f (von Wörtern) pronunciation; (Gespräch) (frank) discussion; **aus|sprechen** irr vt to pronounce; (äußern) to express ▷ vr **sich ~** to talk (über +akk about) ▷ vi (zu Ende sprechen) to finish speaking

aus|spülen vt to rinse (out)

Ausstattung f (Ausrüstung) equipment; (Einrichtung) furnishings pl; (von Auto) fittings pl

aus|stehen irr vt to endure; **ich kann ihn nicht ~** I can't stand him ▷ vi (noch nicht da sein) to be outstanding

aus|steigen irr vi to get out (aus of); **aus dem Bus/Zug ~** to get off the bus/train; **Austeiger(in)** m(f) dropout

aus|stellen vt to display; (auf Messe, in Museum etc) to exhibit; (fam: ausschalten) to switch off; (Scheck etc) to make out; (Pass etc) to issue; **Ausstellung** f exhibition

aus|sterben irr vi to die out

aus|strahlen vt to radiate; (Programm) to broadcast; **Ausstrahlung** f (Radio, Tv) broadcast; (fig: von Person) charisma

aus|strecken vr **sich ~** to stretch out ▷ vt (Hand) to reach out (nach for)

aus|suchen vt to choose

Austausch m exchange; **aus|tauschen** vt to exchange (gegen for)

aus|teilen vt to distribute; (aushändigen) to hand out

Auster (-, -n) f oyster; **Austernpilz** m oyster mushroom

aus|tragen irr vt (Post) to deliver; (Wettkampf) to hold

Australien (-s) nt Australia; **Australier(in)** (-s, -) m(f) Australian; **australisch** adj Australian

aus|trinken irr vt (Glas) to drain; (Getränk) to drink up ▷ vi to finish one's drink

aus|trocknen vi to dry out; (Fluss) to dry up

aus|üben vt (Beruf, Sport) to practise; (Einfluss) to exert

Ausverkauf m sale; **ausverkauft** adj (Karten, Artikel) sold out

Auswahl f selection, choice (an +dat of); **aus|wählen** vt to select, to choose

aus|wandern vi to emigrate

auswärtig adj (nicht am/vom Ort) not

local; (*ausländisch*) foreign; **auswärts** *adv* (*außerhalb der Stadt*) out of town; (*Sport*) **~ spielen** to play away; **Auswärtsspiel** *nt* away match

aus|wechseln *vt* to replace; (*Sport*) to substitute

Ausweg *m* way out

aus|weichen *irr vi* to get out of the way; **jdm/einer Sache ~** to move aside for sb/sth; (*fig*) to avoid sb/sth

Ausweis (*-es, -e*) *m* (*Personalausweis*) identity card, ID; (*für Bibliothek etc*) card; **aus|weisen** *irr vt* to expel ▷ *vr* **sich ~** to prove one's identity; **Ausweiskontrolle** *f* ID check; **Ausweispapiere** *pl* identification documents *pl*

auswendig *adv* by heart

aus|wuchten *vt* (*Auto: Räder*) to balance

aus|zahlen *vt* (*Summe*) to pay (out); (*Person*) to pay off ▷ *vr* **sich ~** to be worth it

aus|zeichnen *vt* (*ehren*) to honour; (*Comm*) to price ▷ *vr* **sich ~** to distinguish oneself

aus|ziehen *irr vt* (*Kleidung*) to take off ▷ *vr* **sich ~** to undress ▷ *vi* (*aus Wohnung*) to move out

Auszubildende(r) *mf* trainee

Auto (*-s, -s*) *nt* car; **~ fahren** to drive; **Autoatlas** *m* road atlas; **Autobahn** *f* motorway (*Brit*), freeway (*US*); **Autobahnauffahrt** *f* motorway access road (*Brit*), on-ramp (*US*); **Autobahnausfahrt** *f* motorway exit (*Brit*), off-ramp (*US*); **Autobahngebühr** *f* toll; **Autobahnkreuz** *nt* motorway interchange; **Autobahnring** *m* motorway ring (*Brit*), beltway (*US*); **Autobombe** *f* car bomb; **Autofähre** *f* car ferry; **Autofahrer(in)** *m(f)* driver, motorist; **Autofahrt** *f* drive

Autogramm (*-s, -e*) *nt* autograph

Automarke *f* make of car

Automat (*-en, -en*) *m* vending machine

Automatik (*-, -en*) *f* (*Auto*) automatic transmission; **Automatikschaltung** *f* automatic gear change (*Brit*) (*o* shift (*US*)); **Automatikwagen** *m* automatic

automatisch *adj* automatic ▷ *adv* automatically

Automechaniker(in) *m(f)* car mechanic; **Autonummer** *f* registration (*Brit*) (*o* license (*US*)) number; **Autoradio**

nt car radio; **Autoreifen** *m* car tyre; **Autoreisezug** *m* Motorail train® (*Brit*), auto train (*US*); **Autorennen** *nt* motor racing; (*einzelnes Rennen*) motor race; **Autoschlüssel** *m* car key; **Autotelefon** *nt* car phone; **Autounfall** *m* car accident; **Autoverleih** *m*, **Autovermietung** *f* car hire (*Brit*) (*o* rental (*US*)); (*Firma*) car hire (*Brit*) (*o* rental (*US*)) company; **Autowaschanlage** *f* car wash; **Autowerkstatt** *f* car repair shop, garage; **Autozubehör** *nt* car accessories *pl*

Avocado (*-, -s*) *f* avocado

Axt (*-, Äxte*) *f* axe

Azubi (*-s, -s*) *m* (*-, -s*) *f* akr = **Auszubildende** trainee

b

swimming trunks *pl*; **Badekappe** *f* swimming cap; **Bademantel** *m* bathrobe; **Bademeister(in)** *m(f)* pool attendant; **Bademütze** *f* swimming cap

baden *vi* to have a bath; (*schwimmen*) to swim, to bathe (*Brit*) ▷ *vt* to bath (*Brit*), to bathe (*US*)

Baden-Württemberg (*-s*) *nt* Baden-Württemberg

Badeort *m* spa; **Badesachen** *pl* swimming things *pl*; **Badetuch** *nt* bath towel; **Badewanne** *f* bath (tub); **Badezimmer** *nt* bathroom

Badminton *nt* badminton

baff *adj* **~ sein** (*fam*) to be flabbergasted (*o* gobsmacked)

Bagger (*-s, -*) *m* excavator; **Baggersee** *m* *artificial lake in quarry etc, used for bathing*

Bahamas *pl* **die ~** the Bahamas *pl*

Bahn (*-, -en*) *f* (*Eisenbahn*) railway (*Brit*), railroad (*US*); (*Rennbahn*) track; (*für Läufer*) lane; (*Astr*) orbit; **bahnbrechend** *adj* groundbreaking; **BahnCard®** (*-, -s*) *f* rail card (*allowing 50% or 25% reduction on tickets*); **Bahnfahrt** *f* railway (*Brit*) (*o* railroad (*US*)) journey; **Bahnhof** *m* station; **am** (*o* **auf dem**) **~** at the station; **Bahnlinie** *f* railway (*Brit*) (*o* railroad (*US*)) line; **Bahnpolizei** *f* railway (*Brit*) (*o* railroad (*US*)) police; **Bahnsteig** (*-(e)s, -e*) *m* platform; **Bahnstrecke** *f* railway (*Brit*) (*o* railroad (*US*)) line; **Bahnübergang** *m* level crossing (*Brit*), grade crossing (*US*)

Bakterien *pl* bacteria *pl*, germs *pl*

bald *adv* (*zeitlich*) soon; (*beinahe*) almost; **bis ~!** see you soon (*o* later); **baldig** *adj* quick, speedy

Balkan (*-s*) *m* **der ~** the Balkans *pl*

Balken (*-s, -*) *m* beam

Balkon (*-s, -s o -e*) *m* balcony

Ball (*-(e)s, Bälle*) *m* ball; (*Tanz*) dance, ball

Ballett (*-s,*) *nt* ballet

Ballon (*-s, -s*) *m* balloon

Ballspiel *nt* ball game

Ballungsgebiet *nt* conurbation

Baltikum (*-s*) *nt* **das ~** the Baltic States *pl*

Bambus (*-ses, -se*) *m* bamboo; **Bambussprossen** *pl* bamboo shoots *pl*

banal *adj* banal; (*Frage, Bemerkung*) trite

Banane (*-, -n*) *f* banana

band *imperf von* **binden**

Band (*-(e)s, Bände*) *m* (*Buch*) volume ▷ (*-(e)s, Bänder*) *nt* (*aus Stoff*) ribbon, tape;

B *abk* = **Bundesstraße**

Baby (*-s, -s*) *nt* baby; **Babybett** *nt* cot (*Brit*), crib (*US*); **Babyfläschchen** *nt* baby's bottle; **Babynahrung** *f* baby food; **Babysitter(in)** *m(f)* babysitter; **Babysitz** *m* child seat; **Babywickelraum** *m* baby-changing room

Bach (*-(e)s, Bäche*) *m* stream

Backblech *nt* baking tray (*Brit*), cookie sheet (*US*)

Backbord *nt* port (side)

Backe (*-, -n*) *f* cheek

backen (*backte, gebacken*) *vt, vi* to bake

Backenzahn *m* molar

Bäcker(in) (*-s, -*) *m(f)* baker; **Bäckerei** *f* bakery; (*Laden*) baker's (shop)

Backofen *m* oven; **Backpulver** *nt* baking powder

Backspace-Taste *f* (*Inform*) backspace key

Backstein *m* brick

Backwaren *pl* bread, cakes and pastries *pl*

Bad (*-(e)s, Bäder*) *nt* bath; (*Schwimmen*) swim; (*Ort*) spa; **ein ~ nehmen** to have (*o* take) a bath; **Badeanzug** *m* swimsuit, swimming costume (*Brit*); **Badehose** *f*

(Fließband) production line; *(Tonband)* tape; *(Anat)* ligament; **etw auf ~ aufnehmen** to tape sth ▷ (-, -s) *f (Musikgruppe)* band
Bandage *(-, -n) f* bandage; **bandagieren** *vt* to bandage
Bande *(-, -n) f (Gruppe)* gang
Bänderriss *m (Med)* torn ligament
Bandscheibe *f (Anat)* disc; **Bandwurm** *m* tapeworm
Bank *(-, Bänke) f (Sitzbank)* bench ▷ (-, -en) *f (Fin)* bank
Bankautomat *m* cash dispenser; **Bankkarte** *f* bank card; **Bankkonto** *nt* bank account; **Bankleitzahl** *f* bank sort code; **Banknote** *f* banknote; **Bankverbindung** *f (Kontonummer etc)* banking *(o* account) details *pl*
bar *adj* **~es Geld** cash; **etw (in) ~ bezahlen** to pay sth (in) cash
Bar *(-, -s) f* bar
Bär *(-en, -en) m* bear
barfuß *adj* barefoot
barg *imperf von* **bergen**
Bargeld *nt* cash; **bargeldlos** *adj* non-cash
Barkeeper *(-s, -) m*, **Barmann** *m* barman, bartender *(US)*
barock *adj* baroque
Barometer *(-s, -) m* barometer
barsch *adj* brusque
Barsch *(-(e)s, -e) m* perch
Barscheck *m* open *(o* uncrossed) cheque
Bart *(-(e)s, Bärte) m* beard; **bärtig** *adj* bearded
Barzahlung *f* cash payment
Basar *(-s, -e) m* bazaar
Baseballmütze *f* baseball cap
Basel *(-s) nt* Basle
Basilikum *(-s) nt* basil
Basis *(-, Basen) f* basis
Baskenland *nt* Basque region
Basketball *m* basketball
Bass *(-es, Bässe) m* bass
basta *interj* **und damit ~!** and that's that
basteln *vt* to make ▷ *vi* to make things, to do handicrafts
bat *imperf von* **bitten**
Batterie *f* battery; **batteriebetrieben** *adj* battery-powered
Bau *(-(e)s) m (Bauen)* building, construction; *(Aufbau)* structure; *(Baustelle)* building site ▷ *m (Baue) (Tier)* burrow ▷ *m (Bauten) (Gebäude)* building;

Bauarbeiten *pl* construction work *sing*; *(Straßenbau)* roadworks *pl (Brit)*, roadwork *(US)*; **Bauarbeiter(in)** *m(f)* construction worker
Bauch *(-(e)s, Bäuche) m* stomach; **Bauchnabel** *m* navel; **Bauchredner(in)** *m(f)* ventriloquist; **Bauchschmerzen** *pl* stomach-ache *sing*; **Bauchspeicheldrüse** *f* pancreas; **Bauchtanz** *m* belly dance; *(das Tanzen)* belly dancing; **Bauchweh** *(-s) nt* stomach-ache
Baudenkmal *nt* monument
bauen *vt, vi* to build; *(Tech)* to construct
Bauer *(-n o -s, -n) m* farmer; *(Schach)* pawn; **Bäuerin** *f* farmer; *(Frau des Bauern)* farmer's wife; **Bauernhof** *m* farm
baufällig *adj* dilapidated; **Baujahr** *adj* year of construction; **der Wagen ist ~ 2002** the car is a 2002 model, the car was made in 2002
Baum *(-(e)s, Bäume) m* tree
Baumarkt *m* DIY centre
Baumwolle *f* cotton
Bauplatz *m* building site; **Baustein** *m (für Haus)* stone; *(Spielzeug)* brick; *(fig)* element; **elektronischer ~** chip; **Baustelle** *f* building site; *(bei Straßenbau)* roadworks *pl (Brit)*, roadwork *(US)*; **Bauteil** *nt* prefabricated part; **Bauunternehmer(in)** *m(f)* building contractor; **Bauwerk** *nt* building
Bayern *(-s) nt* Bavaria
beabsichtigen *vt* to intend
beachten *vt (Aufmerksamkeit schenken)* to pay attention to; *(Vorschrift etc)* to observe; **nicht ~** to ignore; **beachtlich** *adj* considerable
Beachvolleyball *nt* beach volleyball
Beamte(r) *(-n, -n) m*, **Beamtin** *f* official; *(Staatsbeamter)* civil servant
beanspruchen *vt* to claim; *(Zeit, Platz)* to take up; **jdn ~** to keep sb busy
beanstanden *vt* to complain about
beantragen *vt* to apply for
beantworten *vt* to answer
bearbeiten *vt* to work; *(Material, Daten)* to process; *(Chem)* to treat; *(Fall etc)* to deal with; *(Buch etc)* to revise; *(fam: beeinflussen wollen)* to work on; **Bearbeitungsgebühr** *f* handling *(o* service) charge
beatmen *vt* **jdn ~** to give sb artificial respiration

beaufsichtigen vt to supervise; (bei Prüfung) to invigilate

beauftragen vt to instruct; **jdn mit etw ~** to give sb the job of doing sth

Becher (-s, -) m mug; (ohne Henkel) tumbler; (für Jogurt) pot; (aus Pappe) tub

Becken (-s, -) nt basin; (Spüle) sink; (zum Schwimmen) pool; (Mus) cymbal; (Anat) pelvis

bedanken vr **sich ~** to say thank you; **sich bei jdm für etw ~** to thank sb for sth

Bedarf (-(e)s) m need (an +dat for); (Comm) demand (an +dat for); **je nach ~** according to demand; **bei ~** if necessary; **Bedarfshaltestelle** f request stop, flag stop (US)

bedauerlich adj regrettable; **bedauern** vt to regret; (bemitleiden) to feel sorry for; **bedauernswert** adj (Zustände) regrettable; (Mensch) unfortunate

bedeckt adj covered; (Himmel) overcast

bedenken irr vt to consider; **Bedenken** (-s, -) nt (Überlegen) consideration; (Zweifel) doubt; (Skrupel) scruples pl; **bedenklich** adj dubious; (Zustand) serious

bedeuten vt to mean; **jdm nichts/viel ~** to mean nothing/a lot to sb; **bedeutend** adj important; (beträchtlich) considerable; **Bedeutung** f meaning; (Wichtigkeit) importance

bedienen vt to serve; (Maschine) to operate ▷ vr **sich ~** (beim Essen) to help oneself; **Bedienung** f service; (Kellner/Kellnerin) waiter/waitress; (Verkäufer(in)) shop assistant; (Zuschlag) service (charge); **Bedienungsanleitung** f operating instructions pl; **Bedienungshandbuch** nt instruction manual; **Bedingung** f condition; **unter der ~, dass** on condition that; **unter diesen ~en** under these circumstances

bedrohen vt to threaten

Bedürfnis nt need

beeilen vr **sich ~** to hurry

beeindrucken vt to impress

beeinflussen vt to influence

beeinträchtigen vt to affect

beenden vt to end; (fertigstellen) to finish

beerdigen vt to bury; **Beerdigung** f burial; (Feier) funeral

Beere (-, -n) f berry; (Traubenbeere) grape

Beet (-(e)s, -e) nt bed

befahl imperf von **befehlen**

befahrbar adj passable; (Naut) navigable; **befahren** irr vt (Straße) to use; (Pass) to drive over; (Fluss etc) to navigate ▷ adj **stark/wenig ~** busy/quiet

Befehl (-(e)s, -e) m order; (Inform) command; **befehlen** (befahl, befohlen) vt to order; **jdm ~, etw zu tun** to order sb to do sth ▷ vi to give orders

befestigen vt to fix; (mit Schnur, Seil) to attach; (mit Klebestoff) to stick

befeuchten vt to moisten

befinden irr vr **sich ~** to be

befohlen pp von **befehlen**

befolgen vt (Rat etc) to follow

befördern vt (transportieren) to transport; (beruflich) to promote; **Beförderung** f transport; (beruflich) promotion; **Beförderungsbedingungen** pl conditions pl of carriage

Befragung f questioning; (Umfrage) opinion poll

befreundet adj friendly; **~ sein** to be friends (mit jdm with sb)

befriedigen vt to satisfy; **befriedigend** adj satisfactory; (Schulnote) ≈ C; **Befriedigung** f satisfaction

befristet adj limited (auf +akk to)

befruchten vt to fertilize; (fig) to stimulate

Befund (-(e)s, -e) m findings pl; (Med) diagnosis

befürchten vt to fear

befürworten vt to support

begabt adj gifted, talented; **Begabung** f talent, gift

begann imperf von **beginnen**

begegnen vi to meet (jdm sb), to meet with (einer Sache dat sth)

begehen irr vt (Straftat) to commit; (Jubiläum etc) to celebrate

begehrt adj sought-after; (Junggeselle) eligible

begeistern vt to fill with enthusiasm; (inspirieren) to inspire ▷ vr **sich für etw ~** to be/get enthusiastic about sth; **begeistert** adj enthusiastic

Beginn (-(e)s) m beginning; **zu ~** at the beginning; **beginnen** (begann, begonnen) vt, vi to start, to begin

beglaubigen vt to certify; **Beglaubigung** f certification

begleiten vt to accompany;

Begleiter(in) *m(f)* companion;
Begleitung *f* company; (*Mus*)
accompaniment
beglückwünschen *vt* to congratulate
(*zu* on)
begonnen *pp von* **beginnen**
begraben *irr vt* to bury; **Begräbnis** *nt*
burial; (*Feier*) funeral
begreifen *irr vt* to understand
Begrenzung *f* boundary; (*fig*) restriction
Begriff (*-(e)s, -e*) *m* concept; (*Vorstellung*)
idea; **im ~ sein, etw zu tun** to be on the
point of doing sth; **schwer von ~ sein** to
be slow on the uptake
begründen *vt* (*rechtfertigen*) to justify;
Begründung *f* explanation;
(*Rechtfertigung*) justification
begrüßen *vt* to greet; (*willkommen heißen*)
to welcome; **Begrüßung** *f* greeting;
(*Empfang*) welcome
behaart *adj* hairy
behalten *irr vt* to keep; (*im Gedächtnis*) to
remember; **etw für sich ~** to keep sth to
oneself
Behälter (*-s, -*) *m* container
behandeln *vt* to treat; **Behandlung** *f*
treatment
behaupten *vt* to claim, to maintain ▷ *vr*
sich ~ to assert oneself; **Behauptung** *f*
claim
beheizen *vt* to heat
behelfen *irr vr* **sich mit/ohne etw ~** to
make do with/without sth
beherbergen *vt* to accommodate
beherrschen *vt* (*Situation, Gefühle*) to
control; (*Instrument*) to master ▷ *vr* **sich**
~ to control oneself; **Beherrschung** *f*
control (*über +akk* of); **die ~ verlieren** to
lose one's self-control
behilflich *adj* helpful; **jdm ~ sein** to help
sb (*bei* with)
behindern *vt* to hinder; (*Verkehr, Sicht*) to
obstruct; **Behinderte(r)** *mf* disabled
person; **behindertengerecht** *adj* suitable
for disabled people
Behörde (*-, -n*) *f* authority; **die ~n** *pl* the
authorities *pl*

○ SCHLÜSSELWORT

bei *präp* +dat **1** (*nahe bei*) near; (*zum*
Aufenthalt) at, with; (*unter, zwischen*)
among; **bei München** near Munich; **bei**

uns at our place; **beim Friseur** at the
hairdresser's; **bei seinen Eltern wohnen**
to live with one's parents; **bei einer Firma**
arbeiten to work for a firm; **etw bei sich**
haben to have sth on one; **jdn bei sich**
haben to have sb with one; **bei Goethe** in
Goethe; **beim Militär** in the army
2 (*zeitlich*) at, on; (*während*) during
(*Zustand, Umstand*) in; **bei Nacht** at night;
bei Nebel in fog; **bei Regen** if it rains; **bei**
solcher Hitze in such heat; **bei meiner**
Ankuft on my arrival; **bei der Arbeit**
when I'm *etc* working; **beim Fahren** while
driving

bei|behalten *irr vt* to keep
Beiboot *nt* dinghy
bei|bringen *irr vt* **jdm etw ~** (*mitteilen*) to
break sth to sb; (*lehren*) to teach sb sth
beide(s) *pron* both; **meine ~n Brüder** my
two brothers, both my brothers; **wir**
~ both (*o* the two) of us; **keiner von ~n**
neither of them; **alle ~** both (of them); **~s**
ist sehr schön both are very nice; **30**
~ (*beim Tennis*) 30 all
beieinander *adv* together
Beifahrer(in) *m(f)* passenger;
Beifahrerairbag *m* passenger airbag;
Beifahrersitz *m* passenger seat
Beifall (*-(e)s*) *m* applause
beige *adj inv* beige
Beigeschmack *m* aftertaste
Beil (*-(e)s, -e*) *nt* axe
Beilage *f* (*Gastr*) side dish; (*Gemüse*)
vegetables *pl*; (*zu Buch etc*) supplement
beiläufig *adj* casual ▷ *adv* casually
Beileid *nt* condolences *pl*; (*mein*)
herzliches ~ please accept my sincere
condolences
beiliegend *adj* enclosed
beim *kontr von* **bei dem**
Bein (*-(e)s, -e*) *nt* leg
beinah(e) *adv* almost, nearly
beinhalten *vt* to contain
Beipackzettel *m* instruction leaflet
beisammen *adv* together;
Beisammensein (*-s*) *nt* get-together
Beischlaf *m* sexual intercourse
beiseite *adv* aside; **etw ~ legen** (*sparen*) to
put sth by
Beispiel (*-(e)s, -e*) *nt* example; **sich** (*dat*)
an jdm/etw ein ~ nehmen to take sb/sth
as an example; **zum ~** for example

beißen (*biss, gebissen*) *vt* to bite ▷ *vi* to bite; (*stechen: Rauch, Säure*) to sting ▷ *vr* **sich ~** (*Farben*) to clash

Beitrag (*-(e)s, Beiträge*) *m* contribution; (*für Mitgliedschaft*) subscription; (*Versicherung*) premium; **bei|tragen** *irr vt, vi* to contribute (*zu* to)

bekannt *adj* well-known; (*nicht fremd*) familiar; **mit jdm ~ sein** to know sb; **~ geben** to announce; **jdn mit jdm ~ machen** to introduce sb to sb; **Bekannte(r)** *mf* friend; (*entfernter*) acquaintance; **bekanntlich** *adv* as everyone knows; **Bekanntschaft** *f* acquaintance

bekiffen *vr* **sich ~** (*fam*) to get stoned

beklagen *vr* **sich ~** to complain

Bekleidung *f* clothing

bekommen *irr vt* to get; (*erhalten*) to receive; (*Kind*) to have; (*Zug, Grippe*) to catch, to get; **wie viel ~ Sie dafür?** how much is that? ▷ *vi* **jdm ~** (*Essen*) to agree with sb; **wir ~ schon** (*bedient werden*) we're being served

beladen *irr vt* to load

Belag (*-(e)s, Beläge*) *m* coating; (*auf Zähnen*) plaque; (*auf Zunge*) fur

belasten *vt* to load; (*Körper*) to strain; (*Umwelt*) to pollute; (*fig: mit Sorgen etc*) to burden; (*Comm: Konto*) to debit; (*Jur*) to incriminate

belästigen *vt* to bother; (*stärker*) to pester; (*sexuell*) to harass; **Belästigung** *f* annoyance; **sexuelle ~** sexual harassment

belebt *adj* (*Straße etc*) busy

Beleg (*-(e)s, -e*) *m* (*Comm*) receipt; (*Beweis*) proof; **belegen** *vt* (*Brot*) to spread; (*Platz*) to reserve; (*Kurs, Vorlesung*) to register for; (*beweisen*) to prove

belegt *adj* (*Tel*) engaged (*Brit*), busy (*US*); (*Hotel*) full; (*Zunge*) coated; **~es Brötchen** sandwich; **der Platz ist ~** this seat is taken; **Belegzeichen** *nt* (*Tel*) engaged tone (*Brit*), busy tone (*US*)

beleidigen *vt* to insult; (*kränken*) to offend; **Beleidigung** *f* insult; (*Jur*) slander; (*schriftliche*) libel

beleuchten *vt* to light; (*bestrahlen*) to illuminate; (*fig*) to examine; **Beleuchtung** *f* lighting; (*Bestrahlung*) illumination

Belgien (*-s*) *nt* Belgium; **Belgier(in)** (*-s, -*) *m(f)* Belgian; **belgisch** *adj* Belgian

belichten *vt* to expose; **Belichtung** *f* exposure; **Belichtungsmesser** (*-s, -*) *m* light meter

Belieben *nt* (**ganz**) **nach ~** (just) as you wish

beliebig *adj* **jedes ~e Muster** any pattern; **jeder ~e** anyone ▷ *adv* **~ lange** as long as you like; **~ viel** as many (*o* much) as you like

beliebt *adj* popular; **sich bei jdm ~ machen** to make oneself popular with sb

beliefern *vt* to supply

bellen *vi* to bark

Belohnung *f* reward

Belüftung *f* ventilation

belügen *irr vt* to lie to

bemerkbar *adj* noticeable; **sich ~ machen** (*Mensch*) to attract attention; (*Zustand*) to become noticeable; **bemerken** *vt* (*wahrnehmen*) to notice; (*sagen*) to remark; **bemerkenswert** *adj* remarkable; **Bemerkung** *f* remark

bemitleiden *vt* to pity

bemühen *vr* **sich ~** to try (hard), to make an effort; **Bemühung** *f* effort

bemuttern *vt* to mother

benachbart *adj* neighbouring

benachrichtigen *vt* to inform; **Benachrichtigung** *f* notification

benachteiligen *vt* to (put at a) disadvantage; (*wegen Rasse etc*) to discriminate against

benehmen *irr vr* **sich ~** to behave; **Benehmen** (*-s*) *nt* behaviour

beneiden *vt* to envy; **jdn um etw ~** to envy sb sth

Beneluxländer *pl* Benelux countries *pl*

benommen *adj* dazed

benötigen *vt* to need

benutzen *vt* to use; **Benutzer(in)** (*-s, -*) *m(f)* user; **benutzerfreundlich** *adj* user-friendly; **Benutzerhandbuch** *nt* user's guide; **Benutzerkennung** *f* user ID; **Benutzeroberfläche** *f* (*Inform*) user/system interface

Benzin (*-s, -e*) *nt* (*Auto*) petrol (*Brit*), gas (*US*); **Benzingutschein** *m* petrol (*Brit*) (*o* gas (*US*)) coupon; **Benzinkanister** *m* petrol (*Brit*) (*o* gas (*US*)) can; **Benzinpumpe** *f* petrol (*Brit*) (*o* gas (*US*)) pump; **Benzintank** *m* petrol (*Brit*) (*o* gas (*US*)) tank; **Benzinuhr** *f* fuel gauge

beobachten *vt* to observe;
  Beobachtung *f* observation
bequem *adj* comfortable; (*Ausrede*)
  convenient; (*faul*) lazy; **machen Sie es**
  sich ~ make yourself at home;
  Bequemlichkeit *f* comfort; (*Faulheit*)
  laziness
beraten *irr vt* to advise; (*besprechen*) to
  discuss ▷ *vr* **sich ~** to consult; **Beratung** *f*
  advice; (*bei Arzt etc*) consultation
berauben *vt* to rob
berechnen *vt* to calculate; (*Comm*) to
  charge; **berechnend** *adj* (*Mensch*)
  calculating
berechtigen *vt* to entitle (*zu* to); (*fig*) to
  justify; **berechtigt** *adj* justified; **zu etw**
  ~ sein to be entitled to sth
bereden *vt* (*besprechen*) to discuss
Bereich (*-(e)s, -e*) *m* area; (*Ressort, Gebiet*)
  field
bereisen *vt* to travel through
bereit *adj* ready; **zu etw ~ sein** to be
  ready for sth; **sich ~ erklären, etw zu tun**
  to agree to do sth
bereiten *vt* to prepare; (*Kummer*) to
  cause; (*Freude*) to give
bereit|legen *vt* to lay out
bereit|machen *vr* **sich ~** to get ready
bereits *adv* already
Bereitschaft *f* readiness; **~ haben** (*Arzt*)
  to be on call
bereit|stehen *vi* to be ready
bereuen *vt* to regret
Berg (*-(e)s, -e*) *m* mountain; (*kleiner*) hill; **in**
  die ~e fahren to go to the mountains;
  bergab *adv* downhill; **bergauf** *adv* uphill;
  Bergbahn *f* mountain railway (*Brit*) (*o*
  railroad (*US*))
bergen (*barg, geborgen*) *vt* (*retten*) to
  rescue; (*enthalten*) to contain
Bergführer(in) *m(f)* mountain guide;
  Berghütte *f* mountain hut; **bergig** *adj*
  mountainous; **Bergkette** *f* mountain
  range; **Bergschuh** *m* climbing boot;
  Bergsteigen (*-s*) *nt* mountaineering;
  Bergsteiger(in) (*-s, -*) *m(f)* mountaineer;
  Bergtour *f* mountain hike
Bergung *f* (*Rettung*) rescue; (*von Toten,
  Fahrzeugen*) recovery
Bergwacht (*-, -en*) *f* mountain rescue
  service; **Bergwerk** *nt* mine
Bericht (*-(e)s, -e*) *m* report; **berichten** *vt,
  vi* to report

berichtigen *vt* to correct
Bermudadreieck *nt* Bermuda triangle;
  Bermudainseln *pl* Bermuda *sing*;
  Bermudashorts *pl* Bermuda shorts *pl*
Bernstein *m* amber
berüchtigt *adj* notorious, infamous
berücksichtigen *vt* to take into
  account; (*Antrag, Bewerber*) to consider
Beruf (*-(e)s, -e*) *m* occupation;
  (*akademischer*) profession; (*Gewerbe*)
  trade; **was sind Sie von ~?** what do you
  do (for a living)?; **beruflich** *adj*
  professional
Berufsausbildung *f* vocational training;
  Berufsschule *f* vocational college;
  berufstätig *adj* employed;
  Berufsverkehr *m* commuter traffic
beruhigen *vt* to calm ▷ *vr* **sich ~** (*Mensch,
  Situation*) to calm down; **beruhigend** *adj*
  reassuring; **Beruhigungsmittel** *nt*
  sedative
berühmt *adj* famous
berühren *vt* to touch; (*gefühlsmäßig
  bewegen*) to move; (*betreffen*) to affect;
  (*flüchtig erwähnen*) to mention, to touch on
  ▷ *vr* **sich ~** to touch
besaufen *irr vr* **sich ~** (*fam*) to get
  plastered
beschädigen *vt* to damage
beschäftigen *vt* to occupy; (*beruflich*) to
  employ ▷ *vr* **sich mit etw ~** to occupy
  oneself with sth; (*sich befassen*) to deal
  with sth; **beschäftigt** *adj* busy, occupied;
  Beschäftigung *f* (*Beruf*) employment;
  (*Tätigkeit*) occupation; (*geistige*)
  preoccupation (*mit* with)
Bescheid (*-(e)s, -e*) *m* information;
  ~ wissen to be informed (*o* know) (*über*
  +akk about); **ich weiß ~** I know; **jdm**
  ~ geben (*o* **sagen**) to let sb know
bescheiden *adj* modest
bescheinigen *vt* to certify; (*bestätigen*) to
  acknowledge; **Bescheinigung** *f*
  certificate; (*Quittung*) receipt
bescheißen *irr vt* (*vulg*) to cheat (*um* out
  of)
beschimpfen *vt* (*mit Kraftausdrücken*) to
  swear at
Beschiss (*-es*) *m* **das ist ~** (*vulg*) that's
  a rip-off; **beschissen** *adj* (*vulg*)
  shitty
beschlagnahmen *vt* to confiscate
Beschleunigung *f* acceleration;

Beschleunigungsspur f acceleration lane

beschließen irr vt to decide on; (beenden) to end; **Beschluss** m decision

beschränken vt to limit, to restrict (auf +akk to) ▷ vr **sich ~** to restrict oneself (auf +akk to); **Beschränkung** f limitation, restriction

beschreiben irr vt to describe; (Papier) to write on; **Beschreibung** f description

beschuldigen vt to accuse (gen of); **Beschuldigung** f accusation

beschummeln vt, vi (fam) to cheat (um out of)

beschützen vt to protect (vor +dat from)

Beschwerde (-, -n) f complaint; **~n** pl (Leiden) trouble sing; **beschweren** vt to weight down; (fig) to burden ▷ vr **sich ~** to complain

beschwipst adj tipsy

beseitigen vt to remove; (Problem) to get rid of; (Müll) to dispose of; **Beseitigung** f removal; (von Müll) disposal

Besen (-s, -) m broom

besetzen vt (Haus, Land) to occupy; (Platz) to take; (Posten) to fill; (Rolle) to cast; **besetzt** adj full; (Tel) engaged (Brit), busy (US); (Platz) taken; (WC) engaged; **Besetztzeichen** nt engaged tone (Brit), busy tone (US)

besichtigen vt (Museum) to visit; (Sehenswürdigkeit) to have a look at; (Stadt) to tour

besiegen vt to defeat

Besitz (-es) m possession; (Eigentum) property; **besitzen** irr vt to own; (Eigenschaft) to have; **Besitzer(in)** (-s, -) m(f) owner

besoffen adj (fam) plastered

besondere(r, s) adj special; (bestimmt) particular; (eigentümlich) peculiar; **nichts ~s** nothing special; **Besonderheit** f special feature; (besondere Eigenschaft) peculiarity; **besonders** adv especially, particularly; (getrennt) separately

besorgen vt (beschaffen) to get (jdm for sb); (kaufen a.) to purchase; (erledigen: Geschäfte) to deal with

besprechen irr vt to discuss; **Besprechung** f discussion; (Konferenz) meeting

besser adj better; **es geht ihm ~** he feels better; **~ gesagt** or rather; **~ werden** to improve; **bessern** vt to improve ▷ vr **sich ~** to improve; (Mensch) to mend one's ways; **Besserung** f improvement; **gute ~!** get well soon

beständig adj constant; (Wetter) settled

Bestandteil m component

bestätigen vt to confirm; (Empfang, Brief) to acknowledge; **Bestätigung** f confirmation; (von Brief) acknowledgement

beste(r, s) adj best; **das ~ wäre, wir ...** it would be best if we ... ▷ adv **sie singt am ~n** she sings best; **so ist es am ~n** it's best that way; **am ~n gehst du gleich** you'd better go at once

bestechen irr vt to bribe; **Bestechung** f bribery

Besteck (-(e)s, -e) nt cutlery

bestehen irr vi to be, to exist; (andauern) to last; **~ auf** (+dat) to insist on; **~ aus** to consist of ▷ vt (Probe, Prüfung) to pass; (Kampf) to win

bestehlen irr vt to rob

bestellen irr vt to order; (reservieren) to book; (Grüße, Auftrag) to pass on (jdm to sb); (kommen lassen) to send for; **Bestellnummer** f order number; **Bestellung** f (Comm) order; (das Bestellen) ordering

bestens adv very well

bestimmen vt to determine; (Regeln) to lay down; (Tag, Ort) to fix; (ernennen) to appoint; (vorsehen) to mean (für for); **bestimmt** adj definite; (gewiss) certain; (entschlossen) firm ▷ adv definitely; (wissen) for sure; **Bestimmung** f (Verordnung) regulation; (Zweck) purpose

Best.-Nr. abk = **Bestellnummer** order number

bestrafen vt to punish

bestrahlen vt to illuminate; (Med) to treat with radiotherapy

bestreiten irr vt (leugnen) to deny

Bestseller (-s, -) m bestseller

bestürzt adj dismayed

Besuch (-(e)s, -e) m visit; (Mensch) visitor; **~ haben** to have visitors/a visitor; **besuchen** vt to visit; (Schule, Kino etc) to go to; **Besucher(in)** (-s, -) m(f) visitor; **Besuchszeit** f visiting hours pl

betäuben vt (Med) to anaesthetize; **Betäubungsmittel** nt anaesthetic

Bete (-, -n) f **Rote ~** beetroot

beteiligen *vr* **sich an etw** (*dat*) ~ to take part in sth, to participate in sth ▷ *vt* **jdn an etw** (*dat*) ~ to involve sb in sth; **Beteiligung** *f* participation; (*Anteil*) share; (*Besucherzahl*) attendance
beten *vi* to pray
Beton (-*s*, -*s*) *m* concrete
betonen *vt* to stress; (*hervorheben*) to emphasize; **Betonung** *f* stress; (*fig*) emphasis
Betr. *abk* = **Betreff** re
Betracht *m* **in** ~ **ziehen** to take into consideration; **in** ~ **kommen** to be a possibility; **nicht in** ~ **kommen** to be out of the question; **betrachten** *vt* to look at; ~ **als** to regard as; **beträchtlich** *adj* considerable
Betrag (-(*e*)*s*, *Beträge*) *m* amount, sum; **betragen** *irr vt* to amount (*o* come) to ▷ *vr* **sich** ~ to behave
betreffen *irr vt* to concern; (*Regelung etc*) to affect; **was mich betrifft** as for me; **betreffend** *adj* relevant, in question
betreten *irr vt* to enter; (*Bühne etc*) to step onto; „**Betreten verboten"** 'keep off/out'
betreuen *vt* to look after; (*Reisegruppe, Abteilung*) to be in charge of; **Betreuer(in)** (-*s*, -) *m(f)* (*Pfleger*) carer; (*von Kind*) child minder; (*von Reisegruppe*) groupleader
Betrieb (-(*e*)*s*, -*e*) *m* (*Firma*) firm; (*Anlage*) plant; (*Tätigkeit*) operation; (*Treiben*) bustle; **außer** ~ **sein** to be out of order; **in** ~ **sein** to be in operation; **betriebsbereit** *adj* operational; **Betriebsrat** *m* (*Gremium*) works council; **Betriebssystem** *nt* (*Inform*) operating system
betrinken *irr vr* **sich** ~ to get drunk
betroffen *adj* (*bestürzt*) shaken; **von etw** ~ **werden/sein** to be affected by sth
betrog *imperf von* **betrügen**; **betrogen** *pp von* **betrügen**
Betrug (-(*e*)*s*) *m* deception; (*Jur*) fraud; **betrügen** (*betrog, betrogen*) *vt* to deceive; (*Jur*) to defraud; (*Partner*) to cheat on; **Betrüger(in)** (-*s*, -) *m(f)* cheat
betrunken *adj* drunk
Bett (-(*e*)*s*, -*en*) *nt* bed; **ins** (*o* **zu**) ~ **gehen** to go to bed; **das** ~ **machen** to make the bed; **Bettbezug** *m* duvet cover; **Bettdecke** *f* blanket
betteln *vi* to beg
Bettlaken *nt* sheet
Bettler(in) (-*s*, -) *m(f)* beggar

Bettsofa *nt* sofa bed; **Betttuch** *nt* sheet; **Bettwäsche** *f* bed linen; **Bettzeug** *m* bedding
beugen *vt* to bend ▷ *vr* **sich** ~ to bend; (*sich fügen*) to submit (*dat* to)
Beule (-, -*n*) *f* (*Schwellung*) bump; (*Delle*) dent
beunruhigen *vt* to worry ▷ *vr* **sich** ~ to worry
beurteilen *vt* to judge
Beute (-) *f* (*von Dieb*) booty, loot; (*von Tier*) prey
Beutel (-*s*, -) *m* bag
Bevölkerung *f* population
bevollmächtigt *adj* authorized (*zu etw* to do sth)
bevor *conj* before; **bevor|stehen** *irr vi* (*Schwierigkeiten*) to lie ahead; (*Gefahr*) to be imminent; **jdm** ~ (*Überraschung etc*) to be in store for sb; **bevorstehend** *adj* forthcoming; **bevorzugen** *vt* to prefer
bewachen *vt* to guard; **bewacht** *adj* ~**er Parkplatz** supervised car park (*Brit*), guarded parking lot (*US*)
bewegen *vt* to move; **jdn dazu** ~, **etw zu tun** to get sb to do sth ▷ *vr* **sich** ~ to move; **es bewegt sich etwas** (*fig*) things are beginning to happen; **Bewegung** *f* movement; (*Phys*) motion; (*innere*) emotion; (*körperlich*) exercise; **Bewegungsmelder** (-*s*, -) *m* sensor (*which reacts to movement*)
Beweis (-*es*, -*e*) *m* proof; (*Zeugnis*) evidence; **beweisen** *irr vt* to prove; (*zeigen*) to show
bewerben *irr vr* **sich** ~ to apply (*um* for); **Bewerbung** *f* application; **Bewerbungsunterlagen** *pl* application documents *pl*
bewilligen *vt* to allow; (*Geld*) to grant
bewirken *vt* to cause, to bring about
bewohnen *vt* to live in; **Bewohner(in)** (-*s*, -) *m(f)* inhabitant; (*von Haus*) resident
bewölkt *adj* cloudy, overcast; **Bewölkung** *f* clouds *pl*
bewundern *vt* to admire; **bewundernswert** *adj* admirable
bewusst *adj* conscious; (*absichtlich*) deliberate; **sich** (*dat*) **einer Sache** (*gen*) ~ **sein** to be aware of sth ▷ *adv* consciously; (*absichtlich*) deliberately; **bewusstlos** *adj* unconscious; **Bewusstlosigkeit** *f* unconsciousness;

Bewusstsein (-s) *nt* consciousness; **bei ~** conscious

bezahlen *vt* to pay; (*Ware, Leistung*) to pay for; **kann ich bar/mit Kreditkarte ~?** can I pay cash/by credit card?; **sich bezahlt machen** to be worth it; **Bezahlung** *f* payment

bezeichnen *vt* (*kennzeichnen*) to mark; (*nennen*) to call; (*beschreiben*) to describe; **Bezeichnung** *f* (*Name*) name; (*Begriff*) term

beziehen *irr vt* (*Bett*) to change; (*Haus, Position*) to move into; (*erhalten*) to receive; (*Zeitung*) to take; **einen Standpunkt ~** (*fig*) to take up a position ▷ *vr* **sich ~** to refer (*auf +akk* to); **Beziehung** *f* (*Verbindung*) connection; (*Verhältnis*) relationship; **~en haben** (*vorteilhaft*) to have connections (*o contacts*); **in dieser ~** in this respect; **beziehungsweise** *adv* or; (*genauer gesagt*) or rather

Bezirk (-(*e*)s, -*e*) *m* district

Bezug (-(*e*)s, *Bezüge*) *m* (*Überzug*) cover; (*von Kopfkissen*) pillowcase; **in ~ auf** (+*akk*) with regard to; **bezüglich** *prep* +*gen* concerning

bezweifeln *vt* to doubt

BH (-s, -s) *m* bra

Bhf. *abk* = **Bahnhof** station

Biathlon (-s, -s) *nt* biathlon

Bibel (-, -*n*) *f* Bible

Biber (-s, -) *m* beaver

Bibliothek (-, -*en*) *f* library

biegen (*bog, gebogen*) *vt* to bend ▷ *vr* **sich ~** to bend ▷ *vi* to turn (*in +akk* into); **Biegung** *f* bend

Biene (-, -*n*) *f* bee

Bier (-(*e*)s, -*e*) *nt* beer; **helles ~** ≈ lager (*Brit*), beer (*US*); **dunkles ~** ≈ brown ale (*Brit*), dark beer (*US*); **zwei ~, bitte!** two beers, please; **Biergarten** *m* beer garden; **Bierzelt** *nt* beer tent

bieten (*bot, geboten*) *vt* to offer; (*bei Versteigerung*) bid; **sich** (*dat*) **etw ~ lassen** to put up with sth ▷ *vr* **sich ~** (*Gelegenheit*) to present itself (*dat* to)

Bikini (-s, -s) *m* bikini

Bild (-(*e*)s, -*er*) *nt* picture; (*gedankliches*) image; (*Foto*) photo

bilden *vt* to form; (*geistig*) to educate; (*ausmachen*) to constitute ▷ *vr* **sich ~** (*entstehen*) to form; (*lernen*) to educate oneself

Bilderbuch *nt* picture book

Bildhauer(in) (-s, -) *m(f)* sculptor

Bildschirm *m* screen; **Bildschirmschoner** (-s, -) *m* screen saver; **Bildschirmtext** *m* viewdata, videotext

Bildung *f* formation; (*Wissen, Benehmen*) education; **Bildungsurlaub** *m* educational holiday; (*von Firma*) study leave

Billard *nt* billiards *sing*

billig *adj* cheap; (*gerecht*) fair

Binde (-, -*n*) *f* bandage; (*Armbinde*) band; (*Damenbinde*) sanitary towel (*Brit*), sanitary napkin (*US*)

Bindehautentzündung *f* conjunctivitis

binden (*band, gebunden*) *vt* to tie; (*Buch*) to bind; (*Soße*) to thicken

Bindestrich *m* hyphen

Bindfaden *m* string

Bindung *f* bond, tie; (*Skibindung*) binding

Bio- *in zW* bio-; **Biokost** *f* health food

● **Bioladen**
●
● A **Bioladen** is a shop which specializes
● in selling environmentally friendly
● products such as phosphate-free
● washing powders, recycled paper
● and organically grown vegetables.

Biologie *f* biology; **biologisch** *adj* biological; (*Anbau*) organic

Birke (-, -*n*) *f* birch

Birne (-, -*n*) *f* (*Obst*) pear; (*Elek*) (light) bulb

 SCHLÜSSELWORT

bis *präp* +*akk, adv* **1** (*zeitlich*) till, until; (*bis spätestens*) by; **Sie haben bis Dienstag Zeit** you have until *od* till Tuesday; **bis Dienstag muss es fertig sein** it must be ready by Tuesday; **bis auf weiteres** until further notice; **bis in die Nacht** into the night; **bis bald/gleich** see you later/soon

2 (*räumlich*) (up) to; **ich fahre bis Köln** I'm going to *od* I'm going as far as Cologne; **bis an unser Grundstück** (right *od* up) to our plot; **bis hierher** this far

3 (*bei Zahlen*) up to; **bis zu** up to

4: **bis auf etw** *akk* (*außer*) except sth (*einschließlich*) including sth

▷ *konj* **1** (*mit Zahlen*) to; **10 bis 20** 10 to 20

2 (*zeitlich*) till, until; **bis es dunkel wird** till *od* until it gets dark; **von ... bis ...** from ... to ...

Bischof (*-s, Bischöfe*) *m* bishop
bisher *adv* up to now, so far
Biskuit (*-(e)s, -s o -e*) *nt* sponge
biss *imperf von* **beißen**
Biss (*-es, -e*) *m* bite
bisschen *adj* **ein ~** a bit of; **ein ~ Salz/Liebe** a bit of salt/love; **ich habe kein ~ Hunger** I'm not a bit hungry ▷ *adv* **ein ~** a bit; **kein ~** not at all
bissig *adj* (*Hund*) vicious; (*Bemerkung*) cutting
Bit (*-s, -s*) *nt* (*Inform*) bit
bitte *interj* please; (*wie*) **~?** (I beg your) pardon?; **~** (**schön**)**!** (*als Antwort auf Dank*) you're welcome, that's alright; **hier, ~** here you are; **Bitte** (*-, -n*) *f* request; **bitten** (*bat, gebeten*) *vt, vi* to ask (*um* for)
bitter *adj* bitter
Blähungen *pl* (*Med*) wind *sing*
blamieren *vr* **sich ~** to make a fool of oneself ▷ *vt* **jdn ~** to make sb look a fool
Blankoscheck *m* blank cheque
Blase (*-, -n*) *f* bubble; (*Med*) blister; (*Anat*) bladder
blasen (*blies, geblasen*) *vi* to blow; **jdm einen ~** (*vulg*) to give sb a blow job
Blasenentzündung *f* cystitis
blass *adj* pale
Blatt (*-(e)s, Blätter*) *nt* leaf; (*von Papier*) sheet; **blättern** *vi* (*Inform*) to scroll; **in etw** (*dat*) **~** to leaf through sth; **Blätterteig** *m* puff pastry; **Blattsalat** *m* green salad; **Blattspinat** *m* spinach
blau *adj* blue; (*fam: betrunken*) plastered; (*Gastr*) boiled; **~es Auge** black eye; **~er Fleck** bruise; **Blaubeere** *f* bilberry, blueberry; **Blaulicht** *nt* flashing blue light; **blau|machen** *vi* to skip work; (*in Schule*) to skip school; **Blauschimmelkäse** *m* blue cheese
Blazer (*-s, -*) *m* blazer
Blech (*-(e)s, -e*) *nt* sheet metal; (*Backblech*) baking tray (*Brit*), cookie sheet (*US*); **Blechschaden** *m* (*Auto*) damage to the bodywork
Blei (*-(e)s, -e*) *nt* lead
bleiben (*blieb, geblieben*) *vi* to stay; **lass**

das ~! stop it; **das bleibt unter uns** that's (just) between ourselves; **mir bleibt keine andere Wahl** I have no other choice
bleich *adj* pale; **bleichen** *vt* to bleach
bleifrei *adj* (*Benzin*) unleaded; **bleihaltig** *adj* (*Benzin*) leaded
Bleistift *m* pencil
Blende (*-, -n*) *f* (*Foto*) aperture
Blick (*-(e)s, -e*) *m* look; (*kurz*) glance; (*Aussicht*) view; **auf den ersten ~** at first sight; **einen ~ auf etw** (*akk*) **werfen** to have a look at sth; **blicken** *vi* to look; **sich ~ lassen** to show up
blieb *imperf von* **bleiben**
blies *imperf von* **blasen**
blind *adj* blind; (*Glas etc*) dull; **Blinddarm** *m* appendix; **Blinddarmentzündung** *f* appendicitis; **Blinde(r)** *mf* blind person/man/woman; **die ~n** *pl* the blind *pl*; **Blindenhund** *m* guide dog; **Blindenschrift** *f* braille
blinken *vi* (*Stern, Lichter*) to twinkle; (*aufleuchten*) to flash; (*Auto*) to indicate; **Blinker** (*-s, -*) *m* (*Auto*) indicator (*Brit*), turn signal (*US*)
blinzeln *vi* (*mit beiden Augen*) to blink; (*mit einem Auge*) to wink
Blitz (*-es, -e*) *m* (flash of) lightning; (*Foto*) flash; **blitzen** *vi* (*Foto*) to use a/the flash; **es blitzte und donnerte** there was thunder and lightning; **Blitzlicht** *nt* flash
Block (*-(e)s, Blöcke*) *m* (*a. fig*) block; (*von Papier*) pad; **Blockflöte** *f* recorder; **Blockhaus** *nt* log cabin; **blockieren** *vt* to block ▷ *vi* to jam; (*Räder*) to lock; **Blockschrift** *f* block letters *pl*
blöd *adj* stupid; **blödeln** *vi* (*fam*) to fool around
blond *adj* blond; (*Frau*) blonde

⬤ **SCHLÜSSELWORT**

bloß *adj* **1** (*unbedeckt*) bare (*nackt*) naked; **mit der bloßen Hand** with one's bare hand; **mit bloßem Auge** with the naked eye

2 (*alleinig, nur*) mere; **der bloße Gedanke** the very thought; **bloßer Neid** sheer envy

▷ *adv* only, merely; **lass das bloß!** just don't do that!; **wie ist das bloß passiert?** how on earth did that happen?

blühen vi to bloom; (fig) to flourish
Blume (-, -n) f flower; (von Wein) bouquet;
  Blumenkohl m cauliflower;
  Blumenladen m flower shop;
  Blumenstrauß m bunch of flowers;
  Blumentopf m flowerpot; **Blumenvase** f
  vase
Bluse (-, -n) f blouse
Blut (-(e)s) nt blood; **Blutbild** nt blood
  count; **Blutdruck** m blood pressure
Blüte (-, -n) f (Pflanzenteil) flower, bloom;
  (Baumblüte) blossom; (fig) prime
bluten vi to bleed
Blütenstaub m pollen
Bluter (-s, -) m (Med) haemophiliac;
  Bluterguss m haematoma; (blauer Fleck)
  bruise; **Blutgruppe** f blood group; **blutig**
  adj bloody; **Blutkonserve** f unit of stored
  blood; **Blutprobe** f blood sample;
  Blutspende f blood donation;
  Bluttransfusion f blood transfusion;
  Blutung f bleeding; **Blutvergiftung** f
  blood poisoning; **Blutwurst** f black
  pudding (Brit), blood sausage (US)
BLZ abk = **Bankleitzahl**
Bob (-s, -s) m bob(sleigh)
Bock (-(e)s, Böcke) m (Reh) buck; (Schaf)
  ram; (Gestell) trestle; (Sport) vaulting
  horse; **ich hab keinen ~ (drauf)** (fam) I
  don't feel like it
Boden (-s, Böden) m ground; (Fußboden)
  floor; (von Meer, Fass) bottom; (Speicher)
  attic; **Bodennebel** m ground mist;
  Bodenpersonal nt ground staff;
  Bodenschätze pl mineral resources pl
Bodensee m **der ~** Lake Constance
Body (-s, -s) m body; **Bodybuilding** (-s) nt
  bodybuilding
bog imperf von **biegen**
Bogen (-s, -) m (Biegung) curve; (in der
  Architektur) arch; (Waffe, Instrument) bow;
  (Papier) sheet
Bohne (-, -n) f bean; **grüne ~n** pl green (o
  French (Brit)) beans pl; **weiße ~n** pl haricot
  beans pl; **Bohnenkaffee** m real coffee;
  Bohnensprosse f bean sprout
bohren vt to drill; **Bohrer** (-s, -) m drill
Boiler (-s, -) m water heater
Boje (-, -n) f buoy
Bolivien (-s) nt Bolivia
Bombe (-, -n) f bomb
Bon (-s, -s) m (Kassenzettel) receipt;
  (Gutschein) voucher, coupon

Bonbon (-s, -s) nt sweet (Brit), candy (US)
Bonus (- o -ses, -se o Boni) m bonus;
  (Punktvorteil) bonus points pl;
  (Schadenfreiheitsrabatt) no-claims bonus
Boot (-(e)s, -e) nt boat; **Bootsverleih** m
  boat hire (Brit) (o rental (US))
Bord (-(e)s, -e) m **an ~ (eines Schiffes)** on
  board (a ship); **an ~ gehen** (Schiff) to go on
  board; (Flugzeug) to board; **von ~ gehen** to
  disembark; **Bordcomputer** m dashboard
  computer
Bordell (-s, -e) nt brothel
Bordkarte f boarding card
Bordstein m kerb (Brit), curb (US)
borgen vt to borrow; **jdm etw ~** to lend
  sb sth; **sich** (dat) **etw ~** to borrow sth
Börse (-, -n) f stock exchange; (Geldbörse)
  purse
bös adj siehe **böse**; **bösartig** adj
  malicious; (Med) malignant
Böschung f slope; (Uferböschung)
  embankment
böse adj bad; (stärker) evil; (Wunde) nasty;
  (zornig) angry; **bist du mir ~?** are you
  angry with me?
boshaft adj malicious
Bosnien (-s) nt Bosnia;
  Bosnien-Herzegowina (-s) nt
  Bosnia-Herzegovina
böswillig adj malicious
bot imperf von **bieten**
botanisch adj **~er Garten** botanical
  gardens pl
Botschaft f message; (Pol) embassy;
  Botschafter(in) m(f) ambassador
Botsuana (-s) nt Botswana
Bouillon (-, -s) f stock
Boutique (-, -n) f boutique
Bowle (-, -n) f punch
Box (-, -en) f (Behälter, Pferdebox) box;
  (Lautsprecher) speaker; (bei Autorennen) pit
boxen vi to box; **Boxer** (-s, -) m (Hund,
  Sportler) boxer; **Boxershorts** pl boxer
  shorts pl; **Boxkampf** m boxing match
Boykott (-s, -e) m boycott
brach imperf von **brechen**
brachte imperf von **bringen**
Brainstorming (-s) nt brainstorming
Branchenverzeichnis nt yellow
  pages® pl
Brand (-(e)s, Brände) m fire; **einen
  ~ haben** (fam) to be parched
Brandenburg (-s) nt Brandenburg

Brandsalbe f ointment for burns
Brandung f surf
Brandwunde f burn
brannte imperf von **brennen**
Brasilien (-s) nt Brazil
braten (briet, gebraten) vt to roast; (auf dem Rost) to grill; (in der Pfanne) to fry; **Braten** (-s, -) m roast; (roher) joint; **Bratensoße** f gravy; **Brathähnchen** nt roast chicken; **Bratkartoffeln** pl fried potatoes pl; **Bratpfanne** f frying pan; **Bratspieß** m spit; **Bratwurst** f fried sausage; (gegrillte) grilled sausage
Brauch (-s, Bräuche) m custom
brauchen vt (nötig haben) to need (für, zu for); (erfordern) to require; (Zeit) to take; (gebrauchen) to use; **wie lange wird er ~?** how long will it take him?; **du brauchst es nur zu sagen** you only need to say; **das braucht (seine) Zeit** it takes time; **ihr braucht es nicht zu tun** you don't have (o need) to do it; **sie hätte nicht zu kommen ~** she needn't have come
brauen vt to brew; **Brauerei** f brewery
braun adj brown; (von Sonne) tanned; **Bräune** (-, -n) f brownness; (von Sonne) tan; **Bräunungsstudio** nt tanning studio
Brause (-, -n) f (Dusche) shower; (Getränk) fizzy drink (Brit), soda (US)
Braut (-, Bräute) f bride; **Bräutigam** (-s, -e) m bridegroom
brav adj (artig) good, well-behaved
bravo interj well done
BRD (-) f abk = **Bundesrepublik Deutschland** FRG

- **BRD**
-
- The **BRD** is the official name for the
- Federal Republic of Germany. It
- comprises 16 **Länder** (see **Land**). It was
- the name given to the former West
- Germany as opposed to East
- Germany (the **DDR**). The two
- Germanies were reunited on 3rd
- October 1990.

brechen (brach, gebrochen) vt to break; (erbrechen) to bring up; **sich** (dat) **den Arm ~** to break one's arm ▷ vi to break; (erbrechen) to vomit, to be sick; **Brechreiz** m nausea

Brei (-(e)s, -e) m (Breimasse) mush, pulp; (Haferbrei) porridge; (für Kinder) pap
breit adj wide; (Schultern) broad; **zwei Meter ~** two metres wide; **Breite** (-, -n) f breadth; (bei Maßangaben) width; (Geo) latitude; **der ~ nach** widthways; **Breitengrad** m (degree of) latitude
Bremen (-s) nt Bremen
Bremsbelag m brake lining; **Bremse** (-, -n) f brake; (Zool) horsefly; **bremsen** vi to brake ▷ vt (Auto) to brake; (fig) to slow down; **Bremsflüssigkeit** f brake fluid; **Bremslicht** nt brake light; **Bremspedal** nt brake pedal; **Bremsspur** f tyre marks pl; **Bremsweg** m braking distance
brennen (brannte, gebrannt) vi to burn; (in Flammen stehen) to be on fire; **es brennt!** fire!; **mir ~ die Augen** my eyes are smarting; **das Licht ~ lassen** to leave the light on; **Brennholz** nt firewood; **Brennnessel** f stinging nettle; **Brennspiritus** m methylated spirits pl; **Brennstab** m fuel rod; **Brennstoff** m fuel
Brett (-(e)s, -er) nt board; (länger) plank; (Regal) shelf; (Spielbrett) board; **schwarzes ~** notice board, bulletin board (US); **~er** pl (ski) skis pl; **Brettspiel** nt board game
Brezel (-, -n) f pretzel
Brief (-(e)s, -e) m letter; **Briefbombe** f letter bomb; **Brieffreund(in)** m(f) penfriend, pen pal; **Briefkasten** m letterbox (Brit), mailbox (US); **elektronischer ~** electronic mailbox; **Briefmarke** f stamp; **Briefpapier** nt writing paper; **Brieftasche** f wallet; **Briefträger(in)** m(f) postman/-woman; **Briefumschlag** m envelope; **Briefwaage** f letter scales pl
brief imperf von **braten**
Brille (-, -n) f glasses pl; (Schutzbrille) goggles pl; **Brillenetui** nt glasses case
bringen (brachte, gebracht) vt (herbringen) to bring; (mitnehmen, vom Sprecher weg) to take; (holen, herbringen) to get, to fetch; (Theat, Cine) to show; (Radio, Tv) to broadcast; **~ Sie mir bitte noch ein Bier** could you bring me another beer, please?; **jdn nach Hause ~** to take sb home; **jdn dazu ~, etw zu tun** to make sb do sth; **jdn auf eine Idee ~** to give sb an idea
Brise (-, -n) f breeze
Brite (-n, -n) m, **Britin** f British person,

Briton; **er ist ~** he is British; **die ~n** the British; **britisch** adj British

Brocken (-s, -) m bit; (größer) lump, chunk

Brokkoli m broccoli

Brombeere f blackberry

Bronchitis (-) f bronchitis

Bronze (-, -n) f bronze

Brosche (-, -n) f brooch

Brot (-(e)s, -e) nt bread; (Laib) loaf; **Brotaufstrich** m spread; **Brötchen** nt roll; **Brotzeit** f (Pause) break; (Essen) snack; **~ machen** to have a snack

Browser (-s, -) m (Inform) browser

Bruch (-(e)s, Brüche) m (Brechen) breaking; (Bruchstelle; mit Partei, Tradition etc) break; (Med: Eingeweidebruch) rupture, hernia; (Knochenbruch) fracture; (Math) fraction; **brüchig** adj brittle

Brücke (-, -n) f bridge

Bruder (-s, Brüder) m brother

Brühe (-, -n) f (Suppe) (clear) soup; (Grundlage) stock; (pej: Getränk) muck; **Brühwürfel** m stock cube

brüllen vi to roar; (Stier) to bellow; (vor Schmerzen) to scream (with pain)

brummen vi (Bär, Mensch) to growl; (brummeln) to mutter; (Insekt) to buzz; (Motor, Radio) to drone ▷ vt to growl

brünett adj brunette

Brunnen (-s, -) m fountain; (tief) well; (natürlich) spring

Brust (-, Brüste) f breast; (beim Mann) chest; **Brustschwimmen** (-s) nt breaststroke; **Brustwarze** f nipple

brutal adj brutal

brutto adv gross

BSE (-) nt abk = **bovine spongiforme Enzephalopathie** BSE

Bube (-n, -n) m boy, lad; (Karten) jack

Buch (-(e)s, Bücher) nt book

Buche (-, -n) f beech (tree)

buchen vt to book; (Betrag) to enter

Bücherei f library

Buchfink m chaffinch

Buchhalter(in) m(f) accountant

Buchhandlung f bookshop

Büchse (-, -n) f tin (Brit), can; **Büchsenfleisch** nt tinned meat (Brit), canned meat; **Büchsenmilch** f tinned milk (Brit), canned milk; **Büchsenöffner** m tin opener (Brit), can opener

Buchstabe (-ns, -n) m letter; **buchstabieren** vt to spell

Bucht (-, -en) f bay

Buchung f booking; (Comm) entry

Buckel (-s, -) m hump

bücken vr **sich ~** to bend down

Buddhismus (-) m Buddhism

Bude (-, -en) f (auf Markt) stall; (fam: Wohnung) pad, place

Büfett (-s, -s) nt sideboard; **kaltes ~** cold buffet

Büffel (-s, -) m buffalo

Bügel (-s, -) m (Kleidung) hanger; (Steigbügel) stirrup; (Brille) sidepiece; (von Skilift) T-bar; **Bügelbrett** nt ironing board; **Bügeleisen** nt iron; **Bügelfalte** f crease; **bügelfrei** adj non-iron; **bügeln** vt, vi to iron

buh interj boo

Bühne (-, -n) f stage; **Bühnenbild** nt set

Bulgare (-n, -n) m, **Bulgarin** f Bulgarian; **Bulgarien** (-s) nt Bulgaria; **bulgarisch** adj Bulgarian; **Bulgarisch** nt Bulgarian

Bulimie f bulimia

Bulle (-n, -n) m bull; (fam: Polizist) cop

Bummel (-s, -) m stroll; **bummeln** vi to stroll; (trödeln) to dawdle; (faulenzen) to loaf around; **Bummelzug** m slow train

bums interj bang

bumsen vi (vulg) to screw

Bund (-(e)s, Bünde) m (von Hose, Rock) waistband; (Freundschaftsbund) bond; (Organisation) association; (Pol) confederation; **der ~** (fam: Bundeswehr) the army ▷ (-(e)s, -e) nt bunch; (von Stroh etc) bundle

Bundes- in zW Federal; (auf Deutschland bezogen a.) German; **Bundesbahn** f German railway company; **Bundeskanzler(in)** m(f) Chancellor; **Bundesland** nt state, Land; **Bundesliga** f **erste/zweite ~** First/Second Division; **Bundespräsident(in)** m(f) President; **Bundesrat** m (in Deutschland) Upper House (of the German Parliament); (in der Schweiz) Council of Ministers; **Bundesregierung** f Federal Government; **Bundesrepublik** f Federal Republic; **~ Deutschland** Federal Republic of Germany; **Bundesstraße** f ≈ A road (Brit), ≈ state highway (US); **Bundestag** m Lower House (of the German Parliament); **Bundeswehr** f (German) armed forces pl

● **Bundeswehr**
●
● The **Bundeswehr** is the name for the
● German armed forces. It was
● established in 1955, first of all for
● volunteers, but since 1956 there has
● been compulsory military service for
● all able-bodied young men of 18. In
● peacetime the Defence Minister is
● the head of the 'Bundeswehr', but in
● wartime the **Bundeskanzler** takes over.
● The 'Bundeswehr' comes under the
● jurisdiction of NATO.

Bündnis *nt* alliance
Bungalow (-s, -s) *m* bungalow
Bungeejumping (-s) *nt* bungee jumping
bunt *adj* colourful; (*von Programm etc*)
varied; **~e Farben** bright colours ▷ *adv*
(*anstreichen*) in bright colours; **Buntstift** *m*
crayon, coloured pencil
Burg (-, -en) *f* castle
Bürger(in) (-s, -) *m(f)* citizen; **bürgerlich**
adj (*Rechte, Ehe etc*) civil; (*vom Mittelstand*)
middle-class; (*pej*) bourgeois; **Bürger-
meister(in)** *m(f)* mayor; **Bürgersteig**
(-(e)s, -e) *m* pavement (*Brit*), sidewalk (*US*)
Büro (-s, -s) *nt* office; **Büroklammer** *f*
paper clip
Bürokratie *f* bureaucracy
Bursche (-n, -n) *m* lad; (*Typ*) guy
Bürste (-, -n) *f* brush; **bürsten** *vt* to brush
Bus (-ses, -se) *m* bus; (*Reisebus*) coach (*Brit*),
bus; **Busbahnhof** *m* bus station
Busch (-(e)s, Büsche) *m* bush; (*Strauch*) shrub
Busen (-s, -) *m* breasts *pl*, bosom
Busfahrer(in) *m(f)* bus driver;
Bushaltestelle *f* bus stop
Businessclass (-) *f* business class
Busreise *f* coach tour (*Brit*), bus tour
Bußgeld *nt* fine
Büstenhalter (-s, -) *m* bra
Busverbindung *f* bus connection
Butter (-) *f* butter; **Butterbrot** *nt* slice of
bread and butter; **Butterkäse** *m type of
mild, full-fat cheese*; **Buttermilch** *f* butter-
milk; **Butterschmalz** *nt* clarified butter
Button (-s, -s) *m* badge (*Brit*), button (*US*)
b. w. *abk* = **bitte wenden** pto
Byte (-s, -s) *nt* byte
bzw. *adv abk* = **beziehungsweise**

ca. adv abk = **circa** approx
Cabrio (-s, -s) nt convertible
Café (-s, -s) nt café
Cafeteria (-, -s) f cafeteria
Call-Center (-s, -) nt call centre
campen vi to camp; **Camping** (-s) nt camping; **Campingbus** m camper; **Campingplatz** m campsite, camping ground (US)
Cappuccino (-s, -) m cappuccino
Carving (-s) nt (Ski) carving; **Carvingski** m carving ski
CD (-, -s) f abk = **Compact Disc** CD; **CD-Brenner** (-s, -) m CD burner, CD writer; **CD-Player** (-s, -) m CD player; **CD-ROM** (-, -s) f abk = **Compact Disc Read Only Memory** CD-ROM; **CD-ROM-Laufwerk** nt CD-ROM drive, **CD-Spieler** m CD player
Cello (-s, -s o Celli) nt cello
Celsius nt celsius; **20 Grad ~** 20 degrees Celsius, 68 degrees Fahrenheit
Cent (-, -s) m (von Dollar und Euro) cent
Chamäleon (-s, -s) nt chameleon
Champagner (-s, -) m champagne
Champignon (-s, -s) m mushroom

Champions League (-, -s) f Champions League
Chance (-, -n) f chance; **die ~n stehen gut** the prospects are good
Chaos (-) nt chaos; **Chaot(in)** (-en, -en) m(f) (fam) disorganized person, scatterbrain; **chaotisch** adj chaotic
Charakter (-s, -e) m character; **charakteristisch** adj characteristic (für of)
Charisma (-s, Charismen o Charismata) nt charisma
charmant adj charming
Charterflug m charter flight; **chartern** vt to charter
checken vt (überprüfen) to check; (fam: verstehen) to get
Check-in (-s, -s) m check-in; **Check-in-Schalter** m check-in desk
Chef(in) (-s, -s) m(f) boss; **Chefarzt** m, **Chefärztin** f senior consultant (Brit), medical director (US)
Chemie (-) f chemistry; **chemisch** adj chemical; **~e Reinigung** dry cleaning
Chemotherapie f chemotherapy
Chicoree (-s) m chicory
Chiffre (-, -n) f (Geheimzeichen) cipher; (in Zeitung) box number
Chile (-s) nt Chile
Chili (-s, -s) m chilli
China (-s) nt China; **Chinakohl** m Chinese leaves pl (Brit), bok choy (US); **Chinarestaurant** nt Chinese restaurant; **Chinese** (-n, -n) m Chinese; **Chinesin** (-, -nen) f Chinese (woman); **sie ist ~** she's Chinese; **chinesisch** adj Chinese; **Chinesisch** nt Chinese
Chip (-s, -s) m (Inform) chip; **Chipkarte** f smart card
Chips pl (Kartoffelchips) crisps pl (Brit), chips pl (US)
Chirurg(in) (-en, -en) m(f) surgeon
Chlor (-s) nt chlorine
Choke (-s, -s) m choke
Cholera (-) f cholera
Cholesterin (-s) nt cholesterol
Chor (-(e), Chöre) m choir; (Theat) chorus
Choreografie f choreography
Christ(in) (-en, -en) m(f) Christian; **Christbaum** m Christmas tree; **Christi Himmelfahrt** f the Ascension (of Christ); **Christkind** nt baby Jesus; (das Geschenke

bringt) ≈ Father Christmas, Santa Claus;
christlich *adj* Christian
Chrom *(-s) nt* chrome; *(Chem)* chromium
chronisch *adj* chronic
chronologisch *adj* chronological ▷ *adv*
in chronological order
Chrysantheme *(-, -n) f* chrysanthemum
circa *adv* about, approximately
City *(-) f* city centre, downtown *(US)*
Clementine *(-, -n) f* clementine
clever *adj* clever, smart
Clique *(-, -n) f* group; *(pej)* clique;
David und seine ~ David and his lot *o*
crowd
Clown *(-s, -s) m* clown
Club *(-s, -s) m* club; **Cluburlaub** *m* club
holiday *(Brit)*, club vacation *(US)*
Cocktail *(-s, -s) m* cocktail;
Cocktailtomate *f* cherry tomato
Cognac *(-s) m* cognac
Cola *(-, -s) f* Coke®, cola
Comic *(-s, -s) m* comic strip; *(Heft)* comic
Compact Disc *(-, -s) f* compact disc
Computer *(-s, -) m* computer;
Computerfreak *m* computer nerd;
computergesteuert *adj*
computer-controlled; **Computergrafik** *f*
computer graphics *pl*; **computerlesbar**
adj machine-readable; **Computerspiel** *nt*
computer game; **Computertomografie** *f*
computer tomography, scan;
Computervirus *m* computer virus
Container *(-s, -) m (zum Transport)*
container; *(für Bauschutt etc)* skip
Control-Taste *f* control key
Cookie *(-s, -s) nt (Inform)* cookie
cool *adj (fam)* cool
Cornflakes *pl* cornflakes *pl*
Couch *(-, -en) f* couch; **Couchtisch** *m*
coffee table
Coupé *(-s, -s) nt* coupé
Coupon *(-s, -s) m* coupon
Cousin *(-s, -s) m* cousin; **Cousine** *f*
cousin
Crack *(-s) nt (Droge)* crack
Creme *(-, -s) f* cream; *(Gastr)* mousse
Creutzfeld-Jakob-Krankheit *f*
Creutzfeld-Jakob disease, CJD
Croissant *(-s, -s) nt* croissant
Curry *(-s) m* curry powder ▷ *(-s) nt*
(indisches Gericht) curry; **Currywurst** *f fried*
sausage with ketchup and curry powder
Cursor *(-s, -) m (Inform)* cursor

Cybercafé *nt* cybercafé; **Cyberspace** *(-)*
m cyberspace

d

ich bleibe dabei I'm not changing my mind

dabei|haben *irr vt* **er hat seine Schwester dabei** he's brought his sister; **ich habe kein Geld dabei** I haven't got any money on me

Dach *(-(e)s, Dächer) nt* roof; **Dachboden** *m* attic, loft; **Dachgepäckträger** *m* roofrack; **Dachrinne** *f* gutter

Dachs *(-es, -e) m* badger

dachte *imperf von* **denken**

Dackel *(-s, -) m* dachshund

dadurch *adv (räumlich)* through it; *(durch diesen Umstand)* in that way; *(deshalb)* because of that, for that reason ▷ *conj* **~, dass** because; **~, dass er hart arbeitete** *(indem)* by working hard

dafür *adv* for it; *(anstatt)* instead; **~ habe ich 50 Euro bezahlt** I paid 50 euros for it; **ich bin ~ zu bleiben** I'm for (*o* in favour of) staying; **~ ist er ja da** that's what he's there for; **er kann nichts ~** he can't help it

dagegen *adv* against it; *(im Vergleich damit)* in comparison; *(bei Tausch)* for it; **ich habe nichts ~** I don't mind

daheim *adv* at home

daher *adv (räumlich)* from there; *(Ursache)* that's why ▷ *conj (deshalb)* that's why

dahin *adv (räumlich)* there; *(zeitlich)* then; *(vergangen)* gone; **bis ~** *(zeitlich)* till then; *(örtlich)* up to there; **bis ~ muss die Arbeit fertig sein** the work must be finished by then

dahinter *adv* behind it; **~ kommen** to find out

dahinterkommen *vi* to find out

Dahlie *f* dahlia

Dalmatiner *(-s, -) m* dalmatian

damals *adv* at that time, then

Dame *(-, -n) f* lady; *(Karten)* queen; *(Spiel)* draughts *sing (Brit)*, checkers *sing (US)*; **Damenbinde** *f* sanitary towel *(Brit)*, sanitary napkin *(US)*; **Damenfriseur** *m* ladies' hairdresser; **Damenkleidung** *f* ladies' wear; **Damentoilette** *f* ladies' toilet (*o* restroom *(US)*)

damit *adv* with it; *(begründend)* by that; **was meint er ~?** what does he mean by that?; **genug ~!** that's enough ▷ *conj* so that

Damm *(-(e)s, Dämme) m* dyke; *(Staudamm)* dam; *(am Hafen)* mole; *(Bahn-, Straßendamm)* embankment

---

da *adv* **1** *(örtlich)* there *(hier)* here; **da draußen** out there; **da sein** to be there; **da bin ich** here I am; **da, wo** where; **ist noch Milch da?** is there any milk left? **2** *(zeitlich)* then; *(folglich)* so **3**: **da haben wir Glück gehabt** we were lucky there; **da kann man nichts machen** nothing can be done about it ▷ *konj (weil)* as since

dabei *adv (räumlich)* close to it; *(zeitlich)* at the same time; *(obwohl, doch)* though; **sie hörte Radio und rauchte ~** she was listening to the radio and smoking (at the same time); **~ fällt mir ein ...** that reminds me ...; **~ kam es zu einem Unfall** this led to an accident; **... und ~ hat er gar keine Ahnung** ... even though he has no idea; **ich finde nichts ~** I don't see anything wrong with it; **es bleibt ~** that's settled; **~ sein** *(anwesend)* to be present; *(beteiligt)* to be involved; **ich bin ~!** count me in; **er war gerade ~ zu gehen** he was just (*o* on the point of) leaving

dabei|bleiben *irr vi* to stick with it;

Dämmerung *f* twilight; (*am Morgen*) dawn; (*am Abend*) dusk
Dampf (*-(e)s, Dämpfe*) *m* steam; (*Dunst*) vapour; **Dampfbad** *nt* Turkish bath; **Dampfbügeleisen** *nt* steam iron; **dampfen** *vi* to steam
dämpfen *vt* (*Gastr*) to steam; (*Geräusch*) to deaden; (*Begeisterung*) to dampen
Dampfer (*-s, -*) *m* steamer
Dampfkochtopf *m* pressure cooker
danach *adv* after that; (*zeitlich a.*) afterwards; (*demgemäß*) accordingly; **mir ist nicht ~** I don't feel like it; **~ sieht es aus** that's what it looks like
Däne (*-n, -n*) *m* Dane
daneben *adv* beside it; (*im Vergleich*) in comparison
Dänemark (*-s*) *nt* Denmark; **Dänin** *f* Dane, Danish woman/girl; **dänisch** *adj* Danish; **Dänisch** *nt* Danish
dank *prep* +*dat o gen* thanks to; **Dank** (*-(e)s*) *m* thanks *pl*; **vielen ~!** thank you very much; **jdm ~ sagen** to thank sb; **dankbar** *adj* grateful; (*Aufgabe*) rewarding; **danke** *interj* thank you, thanks; **nein ~!** no, thank you; **~, gerne!** yes, please; **~, gleichfalls!** thanks, and the same to you; **danken** *vi* **jdm für etw ~** to thank sb for sth; **nichts zu ~!** you're welcome
dann *adv* then; **bis ~!** see you (later); **~ eben nicht** okay, forget it, suit yourself
daran *adv* (*räumlich*) on it; (*befestigen*) to it; (*stoßen*) against it; **es liegt ~, dass ...** it's because ...
darauf *adv* (*räumlich*) on it; (*zielgerichtet*) towards it; (*danach*) afterwards; **es kommt ganz ~ an, ob ...** it all depends whether ...; **ich freue mich ~** I'm looking forward to it; **am Tag ~** the next day; **~ folgend** (*Tag, Jahr*) next, following
darauffolgend *adj* (*Tag, Jahr*) next, following
daraus *adv* from it; **was ist ~ geworden?** what became of it?
darin *adv* in it; **das Problem liegt ~, dass ...** the basic problem is that ...
Darlehen (*-s, -*) *nt* loan
Darm (*-(e)s, Därme*) *m* intestine; (*Wurstdarm*) skin; **Darmgrippe** *f* gastroenteritis
dar|stellen *vt* to represent; (*Theat*) to play; (*beschreiben*) to describe;

Darsteller(in) *m(f)* actor/actress;
Darstellung *f* representation; (*Beschreibung*) description
darüber *adv* (*räumlich*) above it, over it; (*fahren*) over it; (*mehr*) more; (*währenddessen*) meanwhile; (*sprechen, streiten, sich freuen*) about it
darum *adv* (*deshalb*) that's why; **es geht ~, dass ...** the point (*o* thing) is that ...
darunter *adv* (*räumlich*) under it; (*dazwischen*) among them; (*weniger*) less; **was verstehen Sie ~?** what do you understand by that?; **~ fallen** to be included
darunterfallen *vi* to be included
das *art* the; **~ Auto da** that car; **er hat sich ~ Bein gebrochen** he's broken his leg; **vier Euro ~ Kilo** four euros a kilo ▷ *pron* that (one), this (one); (*relativ, Sache*) that, which; (*relativ, Person*) who, that; (*demonstrativ*) this/that one; **~ Auto da** that car; **ich nehme ~ da** I'll take that one; **~ Auto, ~ er kaufte** the car (that (*o* which)) he bought; **~ Mädchen, ~ nebenan wohnt** the girl who (*o* that) lives next door; **~ heißt** that is; **~ sind Amerikaner** they're American
da sein *irr vi siehe* **da**
dass *conj* that; **so ~** so that; **es sei denn, ~** unless; **ohne ~ er grüßte** without saying hello
dasselbe *pron* the same
Datei *f* (*Inform*) file; **Dateimanager** *m* file manager
Daten *pl* data *pl*; **Datenbank** *f* database; **Datenmissbrauch** *m* misuse of data; **Datenschutz** *m* data protection; **Datenträger** *m* data carrier; **Datenverarbeitung** *f* data processing
datieren *vt* to date
Dativ *m* dative (case)
Dattel (*-, -n*) *f* date
Datum (*-s, Daten*) *nt* date
Dauer (*-, -n*) *f* duration; (*Länge*) length; **auf die ~** in the long run; **für die ~ von zwei Jahren** for (a period of) two years; **Dauerauftrag** *m* (*Fin*) standing order; **dauerhaft** *adj* lasting; (*Material*) durable; **Dauerkarte** *f* season ticket; **dauern** *vi* to last; (*Zeit benötigen*) to take; **es hat sehr lange gedauert, bis er ...** it took him a long time to ...; **wie lange dauert es denn noch?** how much longer will it be?; **das**

dauert mir zu lange I can't wait that long; **dauernd** adj lasting; (ständig) constant ▷ adv always, constantly; **er lachte ~** he kept laughing; **unterbrich mich nicht ~** stop interrupting me; **Dauerwelle** f perm (Brit), permanent (US)

Daumen (-s, -) m thumb

Daunendecke f eiderdown

davon adv of it; (räumlich) away; (weg von) from it; (Grund) because of it; **ich hätte gerne ein Kilo ~** I'd like one kilo of that; **~ habe ich gehört** I've heard of it; (Geschehen) I've heard about it; **das kommt ~, wenn ...** that's what happens when ...; **was hagte ich ~?** what's the point?; **auf und ~** up and away; **davon|laufen** irr vi to run away

davor adv (räumlich) in front of it; (zeitlich) before; **ich habe Angst ~** I'm afraid of it

dazu adv (zusätzlich) on top of that, as well; (zu diesem Zweck) for it, for that purpose; **ich möchte Reis ~** I'd like rice with it; **und ~ noch** and in addition; **~ fähig sein, etw zu tun** to be capable of doing sth; **wie kam es ~?** how did it happen?; **dazu|gehören** vi to belong to it; **dazu|kommen** irr vi (zu jdm ~) to join sb; **kommt noch etwas dazu?** anything else?

dazwischen adv in between; (Unterschied etc) between them; (in einer Gruppe) among them

dazwischen|kommen irr vi **wenn nichts dazwischenkommt** if all goes well; **mir ist etwas dazwischengekommen** something has cropped up

DDR (-) f abk = **Deutsche Demokratische Republik** (Hist) GDR

dealen vi (fam: mit Drogen) to deal in drugs; **Dealer(in)** (-s, -) m(f) (fam) dealer, pusher

Deck (-(e)s, -s o -e) nt deck; **an ~** on deck

Decke (-, -n) f cover; (für Bett) blanket; (für Tisch) tablecloth; (von Zimmer) ceiling

Deckel (-s, -) m lid

decken vt to cover; (Tisch) to lay, to set ▷ vr **sich ~** (Interessen) to coincide; (Aussagen) to correspond ▷ vi (den Tisch decken) to lay (o set) the table

Decoder (-s, -) m decoder

defekt adj faulty; **Defekt** (-(e)s, -e) m fault, defect

definieren vt to define; **Definition** (-, -en) f definition

deftig adj (Preise) steep; **ein ~es Essen** a good solid meal

dehnbar adj flexible, elastic; **dehnen** vt to stretch ▷ vr **sich ~** to stretch

Deich (-(e)s, -e) m dyke

dein pron (adjektivisch) your; **deine(r, s)** pron (substantivisch) yours, of you; **deiner** pron gen von **du**; of you; **deinetwegen** adv (wegen dir) because of you; (dir zuliebe) for your sake; (um dich) about you

deinstallieren vt (Programm) to uninstall

Dekolleté (-s, -s) nt low neckline

Dekoration f decoration; (in Laden) window dressing; **dekorativ** adj decorative; **dekorieren** vt to decorate; (Schaufenster) to dress

Delfin (-s, -e) m dolphin

delikat adj (lecker) delicious; (heikel) delicate

Delikatesse (-, -n) f delicacy

Delle (-, -en) f (fam) dent

Delphin (-s, -e) m dolphin

dem dat sing von **der/das**; **wie ~ auch sein mag** be that as it may

demnächst adv shortly, soon

Demo (-, -s) f (fam) demo

Demokratie (-, -n) f democracy; **demokratisch** adj democratic

demolieren vt to demolish

Demonstration f demonstration; **demonstrieren** vt, vi to demonstrate

den art akk sing, dat pl von **der**; **sie hat sich ~ Arm gebrochen** she's broken her arm ▷ pron him; (Sache) that one; (relativ: Person) who, that, whom; (relativ: Sache) which, that; **~ hab ich schon ewig nicht mehr gesehen** I haven't seen him in ages ▷ pron (Person) who, that, whom; (Sache) which, that; **der Typ, auf ~ sie steht** the guy (who) she fancies; **der Berg, auf ~ wir geklettert sind** the mountain (that) we climbed

denkbar adj **das ist ~** that's possible ▷ adv **~ einfach** extremely simple; **denken** (dachte, gedacht) vt, vi to think (über +akk about); **an jdn/etw ~** to think of sb/sth; (sich erinnern, berücksichtigen) to remember sb/sth; **woran denkst Du?** what are you thinking about?; **denk an den Kaffee!** don't forget the coffee ▷ vr

sich ~ (*sich vorstellen*) to imagine; **das kann ich mir ~** I can (well) imagine

Denkmal (*-s, Denkmäler*) *nt* monument; **Denkmalschutz** *m* monument preservation; **unter ~ stehen** to be listed

denn *conj* for, because ▷ *adv* then; (*nach Komparativ*) than; **was ist ~?** what's wrong?; **ist das ~ so schwierig?** is it really that difficult?

dennoch *conj* still, nevertheless

Deo (*-s, -s*) *nt*, **Deodorant** (*-s, -s*) *nt* deodorant; **Deoroller** *m* roll-on deodorant; **Deospray** *m o nt* deodorant spray

Deponie (*-, -n*) *f* waste disposal site, tip

Depressionen *pl* **an ~ leiden** to suffer from depression *sing*; **deprimieren** *vt* to depress

⬤ SCHLÜSSELWORT

der (*f* **die**, *nt* **das**, **gen des, der, des**, **dat dem, der, dem**, **akk den, die, das**, *pl* **die**) def art the; **der Rhein** the Rhine; **der Klaus** (*umg*) Klaus; **die Frau** (*im Allgemeinen*) women; **der Tod/das Leben** death/life; **der Fuß des Berges** the foot of the hill; **gib es der Frau** give it to the woman; **er hat sich die Hand verletzt** he has hurt his hand ▷ *relativ pron* (*bei Menschen*) who, that (*bei Tieren, Sachen*) which, that; **der Mann, den ich gesehen habe** the man who *od* whom *od* that I saw ▷ *demonstrativ pron* he/she/it (*jener, dieser*) that, (*pl*) those; **der/die war es** it was him/her; **der mit der Brille** the one with glasses; **ich will den (da)** I want that one

derart *adv* so; (*solcher Art*) such; **derartig** *adj* **ein ~er Fehler** such a mistake, a mistake like that

deren *gen von* **die** ▷ *pron* (*Person*) her; (*Sache*) its; (*Plural*) their ▷ *pron* (*Person*) whose; (*Sache*) of which; **meine Freundin und ~ Mutter** my friend and her mother; **das sind ~ Sachen** that's their stuff; **die Frau, ~ Tochter ...** the woman whose daughter ...; **ich bin mir ~ bewusst** I'm aware of that

dergleichen *pron* **und ~ mehr** and the like, and so on; **nichts ~** no such thing

derjenige *pron* the one; **~, der** (*relativ*) the one who (*o that*)

dermaßen *adv* so much; (*mit Adj*) so

derselbe *pron* the same (person/thing)

deshalb *adv* therefore; **~ frage ich ja** that's why I'm asking

Design (*-s, -s*) *nt* design; **Designer(in)** (*-s, -*) *m(f)* designer

Desinfektionsmittel *nt* disinfectant; **desinfizieren** *vt* to disinfect

dessen *gen von* **der, das** ▷ *pron* (*Person*) his; (*Sache*) its; **ich bin mir ~ bewusst** I'm aware of that ▷ *pron* (*Person*) whose; (*Sache*) of which; **mein Freund und ~ Mutter** my friend and his mother; **der Mann, ~ Tochter ...** the man whose daughter ...; **ich bin mir ~ bewusst** I'm aware of that

Dessert (*-s, -s*) *nt* dessert; **zum** (*o* **als**) **~** for dessert

destilliert *adj* distilled

desto *adv* **je eher, ~ besser** the sooner, the better

deswegen *conj* therefore

Detail (*-s, -s*) *nt* detail; **ins ~ gehen** to go into detail

Detektiv(in) (*-s, -e*) *m(f)* detective

deutlich *adj* clear; (*Unterschied*) distinct

deutsch *adj* German; **Deutsch** *nt* German; **auf ~** in German; **ins ~e übersetzen** to translate into German; **Deutsche(r)** *mf* German; **Deutschland** *nt* Germany

Devise (*-, -n*) *f* motto; **~n** *pl* (*Fin*) foreign currency *sing*; **Devisenkurs** *m* exchange rate

Dezember (*-(s), -*) *m* December; *siehe auch* **Juni**

dezent *adj* discreet

d.h. *abk von* **das heißt** i.e. (*gesprochen: i.e. oder that is*)

Dia (*-s, -s*) *nt* slide

Diabetes (*-, -*) *m* (*Med*) diabetes; **Diabetiker(in)** (*-s, -*) *m(f)* diabetic

Diagnose (*-, -n*) *f* diagnosis

diagonal *adj* diagonal

Dialekt (*-(e)s, -e*) *m* dialect

Dialog (*-(e)s, -e*) *m* dialogue; (*Inform*) dialog

Dialyse (*-, -n*) *f* (*Med*) dialysis

Diamant *m* diamond

Diaprojektor *m* slide projector

Diät (*-, -en*) *f* diet; **eine ~ machen** to be on a diet; (*anfangen*) to go on a diet

dich *pron akk von* **du** you; **~** (**selbst**)

(*reflexiv*) yourself; **pass auf ~ auf** look after yourself; **reg ~ nicht auf** don't get upset

dicht *adj* dense; (*Nebel*) thick; (*Gewebe*) close; (*wasserdicht*) watertight; (*Verkehr*) heavy ▷ *adv* **~ an/bei** close to; **~ bevölkert** densely populated

Dichter(in) (*-s, -*) *m(f)* poet; (*Autor*) writer

Dichtung *f* (*Auto*) gasket; (*Dichtungsring*) washer; (*Gedichte*) poetry

Dichtungsring *m* (*Tech*) washer

dick *adj* thick; (*Person*) fat; **jdn ~ haben** to be sick of sb; **Dickdarm** *m* colon; **Dickkopf** *m* stubborn (*o* pig-headed) person; **Dickmilch** *f* sour milk

die *art* the; **~ arme Sarah** poor Sarah ▷ *pron* (*sing, Person, als Subjekt*) she; (*Person, als Subjekt, Plural*) they; (*Person, als Objekt*) her; (*Person, als Objekt, Plural*) them; (*Sache*) that (one), this (one); (*Plural*) those (ones); (*Sache, Plural*) those (ones); (*relativ, auf Person*) who, that; (*relativ, auf Sache*) which, that; **~ mit den langen Haaren** the one (*o* her) with the long hair; **sie war ~ erste, ~ es erfuhr** she was the first to know; **ich nehme ~ da** I'll take that one/those ▷ *pl von* **der, die, das**

Dieb(in) (*-(e)s, -e*) *m(f)* thief; **Diebstahl** (*-(e)s, Diebstähle*) *m* theft; **Diebstahlsicherung** *f* burglar alarm

diejenige *pron* the one; **~, die** (*relativ*) the one who (*o* that); **~n** *pl* those *pl*, the ones

Diele (*-, -n*) *f* hall

Dienst (*-(e)s, -e*) *m* service; **außer ~** retired; **~ haben** to be on duty; **der ~ habende Arzt** the doctor on duty

Dienstag *m* Tuesday; *siehe auch* **Mittwoch**; **dienstags** *adv* on Tuesdays; *siehe auch* **mittwochs**

Dienstbereitschaft *f* **~ haben** (*Arzt*) to be on call; **Dienstleistung** *f* service; **dienstlich** *adj* official; **er ist ~ unterwegs** he's away on business; **Dienstreise** *f* business trip; **Dienststelle** *f* department; **Dienstwagen** *m* company car; **Dienstzeit** *f* office hours *pl*; (*Mil*) period of service

diesbezüglich *adj* (*formell*) on this matter

diese(r, s) *pron* this (one); *pl* these; **~ Frau** this woman; **~r Mann** this man; **~s Mädchen** this girl; **~ Leute** these people; **ich nehme ~/~n/~s** (*hier*) I'll take this one; (*dort*) I'll take that one; **ich nehme ~** *pl*

(*hier*) I'll take these (ones); (*dort*) I'll take those (ones)

Diesel (*-s, -*) *m* (*Auto*) diesel

dieselbe *pron* the same; **es sind immer ~n** it's always the same people

Dieselmotor *m* diesel engine; **Dieselöl** *nt* diesel (oil)

diesig *adj* hazy, misty

diesmal *adv* this time

Dietrich (*-s, -e*) *m* skeleton key

Differenz (*-, -en*) *f* difference

digital *adj* digital; **Digital-** *in zW* (*Kamera, Anzeige etc*) digital

Diktat (*-(e)s, -e*) *nt* dictation

Diktatur *f* dictatorship

Dill (*-s*) *m* dill

DIN *abk* = **Deutsche Industrienorm** DIN; **~ A4** A4

Ding (*-(e)s, -e*) *nt* thing; **vor allen ~en** above all; **der Stand der ~e** the state of affairs; **das ist nicht mein ~** (*fam*) it's not my sort of thing (*o* cup of tea); **Dingsbums** (*-*) *nt* (*fam*) thingy, thingummybob

Dinosaurier *m* dinosaur

Diphtherie *f* diphtheria

Diplom (*-(e)s, -e*) *nt* diploma

Diplomat(in) (*-en, -en*) *m(f)* diplomat

dir *pron dat von* **du** (to) you; **hat er ~ geholfen?** did he help you?; **ich werde es ~ erklären** I'll explain it to you; (*reflexiv*) **wasch ~ die Hände** go and wash your hands; **ein Freund von ~** a friend of yours

direkt *adj* direct; (*Frage*) straight; **~e Verbindung** through service ▷ *adv* directly; (*sofort*) immediately; **~ am Bahnhof** right next to the station; **Direktflug** *m* direct flight

Direktor(in) *m(f)* director; (*Schule*) headmaster/-mistress (*Brit*), principal (*US*)

Direktübertragung *f* live broadcast

Dirigent(in) *m(f)* conductor; **dirigieren** *vt* to direct; (*Mus*) to conduct

Discman® (*-s, -s*) *m* Discman®

Diskette *f* disk, diskette; **Diskettenlaufwerk** *nt* disk drive

Diskjockey (*-s, -s*) *m* disc jockey; **Disko** (*-, -s*) *f* (*fam*) disco, club; **Diskothek** (*-, -en*) *f* discotheque, club

diskret *adj* discreet

diskriminieren *vt* to discriminate against

Diskussion f discussion; **diskutieren** vt, vi to discuss

Display (-s, -s) nt display

disqualifizieren vt to disqualify

Distanz f distance

Distel (-, -n) f thistle

Disziplin (-, -en) f discipline

divers adj various

dividieren vt to divide (durch by); **8 dividiert durch 2 ist 4** 8 divided by 2 is 4

DJ (-s, -s) m abk = **Diskjockey** DJ

⬤ SCHLÜSSELWORT

doch adv **1** (dennoch) after all (sowieso) anyway; **er kam doch noch** he came after all; **du weißt es ja doch besser** you know better than I do anyway; **und doch ...** and yet ...

2 (als bejahende Antwort) yes I do/it does etc; **das ist nicht wahr — doch!** that's not true — yes it is!

3 (auffordernd): **komm doch** do come; **lass ihn doch** just leave him; **nicht doch!** oh no!

4: **sie ist doch noch so jung** but she's still so young; **Sie wissen doch, wie das ist** you know how it is(, don't you?); **wenn doch** if only

▷ konj (aber) but (trotzdem) all the same; **und doch hat er es getan** but still he did it

Doktor(in) m(f) doctor

Dokument nt document; **Dokumentarfilm** m documentary (film); **dokumentieren** vt to document; **Dokumentvorlage** f (Inform) document template

Dolch (-(e)s, -e) m dagger

Dollar (-(s), -s) m dollar

dolmetschen vt, vi to interpret; **Dolmetscher(in)** (-s, -) m(f) interpreter

Dolomiten pl Dolomites pl

Dom (-(e)s, -e) m cathedral

Domäne (-, -n) f domain, province; (Inform: Domain) domain

Dominikanische Republik f Dominican Republic

Domino (-s, -s) nt dominoes sing

Donau (-) f Danube

Döner (-s, -) m, **Döner Kebab** (-(s), -s) m doner kebab

Donner (-s, -) m thunder; **donnern** vi **es donnert** it's thundering

Donnerstag m Thursday; siehe auch **Mittwoch**; **donnerstags** adv on Thursdays; siehe auch **mittwochs**

doof adj (fam) stupid

dopen vt to dope; **Doping** (-s) nt doping; **Dopingkontrolle** f drugs test

Doppel (-s, -) nt duplicate; (Sport) doubles sing; **Doppelbett** nt double bed; **Doppeldecker** m double-decker; **Doppelhaushälfte** f semi-detached house (Brit), duplex (US); **doppelklicken** vi to double-click; **Doppelname** m double-barrelled name; **Doppelpunkt** m colon; **Doppelstecker** m two-way adaptor; **doppelt** adj double; **in -er Ausführung** in duplicate; **Doppelzimmer** nt double room

Dorf (-(e)s, Dörfer) nt village

Dorn (-(e)s, -en) m (Bot) thorn

Dörrobst nt dried fruit

Dorsch (-(e)s, -e) m cod

dort adv there; **~ drüben** over there; **dorther** adv from there

Dose (-, -n) f box; (Blechdose) tin (Brit), can; (Bierdose) can

dösen vi to doze

Dosenbier nt canned beer; **Dosenmilch** f canned milk, tinned milk (Brit); **Dosenöffner** m tin opener (Brit), can opener

Dotter (-s, -) m (egg) yolk

downloaden vt to download

Downsyndrom (-(e)s, -e) nt (Med) Down's syndrome

Dozent(in) m(f) lecturer

Dr. abk = **Doktor**

Drache (-n, -n) m dragon; **Drachen** (-s, -) m (Spielzeug) kite; (Sport) hang-glider; **Drachenfliegen** (-s) nt hang-gliding; **Drachenflieger(in)** (-s, -) m(f) hang-glider

Draht (-(e)s, Drähte) m wire; **Drahtseilbahn** f cable railway

Drama (-s, Dramen) nt drama; **dramatisch** adj dramatic

dran adv (fam) kontr von **daran**; **gut ~ sein** (reich) to be well-off; (glücklich) to be fortunate; (gesundheitlich) to be well; **schlecht ~ sein** to be in a bad way; **wer ist ~?** whose turn is it?; **ich bin ~** it's my turn; **bleib ~!** (Tel) hang on

drang imperf von **dringen**

Drang (-(e)s, Dränge) m (Trieb) urge (nach for); (Druck) pressure
drängeln vt, vi to push
drängen vt (schieben) to push; (antreiben) to urge ▷ vi (eilig sein) to be urgent; (Zeit) to press; **auf etw** (akk) **~** to press for sth
dran|kommen irr vi **wer kommt dran?** who's turn is it?, who's next?
drauf (fam) kontr von **darauf**; **gut/schlecht ~ sein** to be in a good/bad mood
Draufgänger(in) (-s, -) m(f) daredevil
drauf|kommen irr vi to remember; **ich komme nicht drauf** I can't think of it
drauf|machen vi (fam) **einen ~** to go on a binge
draußen adv outside
Dreck (-(e)s) m dirt, filth; **dreckig** adj dirty, filthy
drehen vt, vi to turn; (Zigaretten) to roll; (Film) to shoot ▷ vr **sich ~** to turn; (um Achse) to rotate; **sich ~ um** (handeln von) to be about
Drehstrom m three-phase current; **Drehtür** f revolving door; **Drehzahlmesser** m rev counter
drei num three; **~ viertel voll** three-quarters full; **es ist ~ viertel neun** it's a quarter to nine; **Drei** (-, -en) f three; (Schulnote) ≈ C; **Dreieck** nt triangle; **dreieckig** adj triangular; **dreifach** adj triple ▷ adv three times; **dreihundert** num three hundred; **Dreikönigstag** m Epiphany; **dreimal** adv three times; **Dreirad** nt tricycle; **dreispurig** adj three-lane
dreißig num thirty; **dreißigste(r, s)** adj thirtieth; siehe auch **dritte**
Dreiviertelstunde f **eine ~** three quarters of an hour
dreizehn num thirteen; **dreizehnte(r, s)** adj thirteenth; siehe auch **dritte**
dressieren vt to train
Dressing (-s, -s) nt (salad) dressing
Dressman (-s, Dressmen) m (male) model
Dressur (-, -en) f training
drin (fam) kontr von **darin** in it; **mehr war nicht ~** that was the best I could do
dringen (drang, gedrungen) vi (Wasser, Licht, Kälte) to penetrate (durch through, in +akk into); **auf etw** (akk) **~** to insist on sth; **dringend, dringlich** adj urgent

drinnen adv inside
dritt adv **wir sind zu ~** there are three of us; **dritte(r, s)** adj third; **die Dritte Welt** the Third World; **7. Juni** 7(th) June (gesprochen: the seventh of June); **am 7. Juni** on 7(th) June, on June 7(th) (gesprochen: on the seventh of June); **München, den 7. Juni** Munich, June 7(th); **Drittel** (-s, -) nt (Bruchteil) third; **drittens** adv thirdly
Droge (-, -n) f drug; **drogenabhängig, drogensüchtig** adj addicted to drugs
Drogerie f chemist's (Brit), drugstore (US); **Drogeriemarkt** m discount chemist's (Brit) (o drugstore (US))

⬡ **Drogerie**
⬡
⬡ The **Drogerie** as opposed to the
⬡ **Apotheke** sells medicines not
⬡ requiring a prescription. It tends to
⬡ be cheaper and also sells cosmetics,
⬡ perfume and toiletries.

drohen vi to threaten (jdm sb); **mit etw ~** to threaten to do sth
dröhnen vi (Motor) to roar; (Stimme, Musik) to boom; (Raum) to resound
Drohung f threat
Drossel (-, -n) f thrush
drüben adv over there; (auf der anderen Seite) on the other side
drüber (fam) kontr von **darüber**
Druck (-(e)s, Drücke) m (Phys) pressure; (fig: Belastung) stress; **jdn unter ~ setzen** to put sb under pressure ▷ (-(e)s, -e) m (Typo: Vorgang) printing; (Produkt, Schriftart) print; **Druckbuchstabe** m block letter; **in ~n schreiben** to print; **drucken** vt, vi to print
drücken vt, vi (Knopf, Hand) to press; (zu eng sein) to pinch; (fig: Preise) to keep down; **jdm etw in die Hand ~** to press sth into sb's hand ▷ vr **sich vor etw** (dat) **~** to get out of sth; **drückend** adj oppressive
Drucker (-s, -) m (Inform) printer; **Druckertreiber** m printer driver
Druckknopf m press stud (Brit), snap fastener (US); **Drucksache** f printed matter; **Druckschrift** f block letters pl
drunten adv down there
drunter (fam) kontr von **darunter**
Drüse (-, -n) f gland
Dschungel (-s, -) m jungle

du *pron* you; **bist ~ es?** is it you?; **wir sind per ~** we're on first-name terms

Dübel (*-s, -*) *m* Rawlplug®

ducken *vt* to duck ▷ *vr* **sich ~** to duck

Dudelsack *m* bagpipes *pl*

Duett (*-s, -e*) *nt* duet

Duft (*-(e)s, Düfte*) *m* scent; **duften** *vi* to smell nice; **es duftet nach ...** it smells of ...

dulden *vt* to tolerate

dumm *adj* stupid; **Dummheit** *f* stupidity; (*Tat*) stupid thing; **Dummkopf** *m* idiot

dumpf *adj* (*Ton*) muffled; (*Erinnerung*) vague; (*Schmerz*) dull

Düne (*-, -n*) *f* dune

Dünger (*-s, -*) *m* fertilizer

dunkel *adj* dark; (*Stimme*) deep; (*Ahnung*) vague; (*rätselhaft*) obscure; (*verdächtig*) dubious; **im Dunkeln tappen** (*fig*) to be in the dark; **dunkelblau** *adj* dark blue; **dunkelblond** *adj* light brown; **dunkelhaarig** *adj* dark-haired; **Dunkelheit** *f* darkness

dünn *adj* thin; (*Kaffee*) weak

Dunst (*-es, Dünste*) *m* haze; (*leichter Nebel*) mist; (*Chem*) vapour

dünsten *vt* (*Gastr*) to steam

Duo (*-s, -s*) *nt* duo

Dur (*-*) *nt* (*Mus*) major (key); **in G-~** in G major

⭕ **SCHLÜSSELWORT**

durch *präp* +akk **1** (*hindurch*) through; **durch den Urwald** through the jungle; **durch die ganze Welt reisen** to travel all over the world

2 (*mittels*) through, by (means of) (*aufgrund*) due to, owing to; **Tod durch Herzschlag/den Strang** death from a heart attack/by hanging; **durch die Post** by post; **durch seine Bemühungen** through his efforts

▷ *adv* **1** (*hindurch*) through; **die ganze Nacht durch** all through the night; **den Sommer durch** during the summer; **8 Uhr durch** past 8 o'clock; **durch und durch** completely

2 (*durchgebraten etc*): **(gut) durch** well-done

durchaus *adv* absolutely; **~ nicht** not at all

Durchblick *m* view; **den ~ haben** (*fig*) to know what's going on; **durch|blicken** *vi* to look through; (*fam: verstehen*) to understand (*bei etw* sth); **etw ~ lassen** (*fig*) to hint at sth

Durchblutung *f* circulation

durch|brennen *irr vi* (*Sicherung*) to blow; (*Draht*) to burn through; (*fam: davonlaufen*) to run away

durchdacht *adv* **gut ~** well thought-out

durch|drehen *vt* (*Fleisch*) to mince ▷ *vi* (*Räder*) to spin; (*fam: nervlich*) to crack up

durcheinander *adv* in a mess; (*fam: verwirrt*) confused; **~ bringen** to mess up; (*verwirren*) to confuse; **~ reden** to talk all at the same time; **~ trinken** to mix one's drinks; **Durcheinander** (*-s*) *nt* (*Verwirrung*) confusion; (*Unordnung*) mess

Durchfahrt *f* way through; **„~ verboten!"** 'no thoroughfare'

Durchfall *m* (*Med*) diarrhoea

durch|fallen *irr vi* to fall through; (*in Prüfung*) to fail

durch|fragen *vr* **sich ~** to ask one's way

durch|führen *vt* to carry out

Durchgang *m* passage; (*Sport*) round; (*bei Wahl*) ballot; **Durchgangsverkehr** *m* through traffic

durchgebraten *adj* well done

durchgefroren *adj* frozen to the bone

durch|gehen *irr vi* to go through (*durch etw* sth); (*ausreißen: Pferd*) to break loose; (*Mensch*) to run away; **durchgehend** *adj* (*Zug*) through; **~ geöffnet** open all day

durch|halten *irr vi* to hold out ▷ *vt* (*Tempo*) to keep up; **etw ~** (*bis zum Schluss*) to see sth through

durch|kommen *irr vi* to get through; (*Patient*) to pull through

durch|lassen *irr vt* (*jdn*) to let through; (*Wasser*) to let in

Durchlauf(wasser)erhitzer (*-s, -*) *m* instantaneous water heater

durch|lesen *irr vt* to read through

durchleuchten *vt* to X-ray

durch|machen *vt* to go through; (*Entwicklung*) to undergo; **die Nacht ~** to make a night of it, to have an all-nighter

Durchmesser (*-s, -*) *m* diameter

Durchreise *f* journey through; **auf der ~** passing through; (*Güter*) in

transit; **Durchreisevisum** *nt* transit
visa

durch|reißen *irr vt, vi* to tear (in two)

durchs *kontr von* **durch das**

Durchsage (-, -n) *f* announcement

durchschauen *vt* (*jdn, Lüge*) to see
through

durch|schlagen *irr vr* **sich ~** to struggle
through

durch|schneiden *irr vt* to cut (in two)

Durchschnitt *m* (*Mittelwert*) average; **im
~** on average; **durchschnittlich** *adj*
average ▷ *adv* (*im Durchschnitt*) on
average; **Durchschnittsgeschwindigkeit**
f average speed

durch|setzen *vt* to get through ▷ *vr* **sich
~** (*Erfolg haben*) to succeed; (*sich behaupten*)
to get one's way

durchsichtig *adj* transparent,
see-through

durch|stellen *vt* (*Tel*) to put through

durch|streichen *irr vt* to cross out

durchsuchen *vt* to search (*nach* for);
Durchsuchung *f* search

durchwachsen *adj* (*Speck*) streaky; (*fig:
mittelmäßig*) so-so

Durchwahl *f* direct dialling; (*Nummer*)
extension

durch|ziehen *irr vt* (*Plan*) to carry
through

Durchzug *m* draught

○ SCHLÜSSELWORT

dürfen *unreg vi* **1** (*Erlaubnis haben*) to be
allowed to; **ich darf das** I'm allowed to
(do that); **darf ich?** may I?; **darf ich ins
Kino?** can *od* may I go to the cinema?;
es darf geraucht werden you may
smoke

2 (*in Verneinungen*); **er darf das nicht** he's
not allowed to (do that); **das darf nicht
geschehen** that must not happen; **da
darf sie sich nicht wundern** that
shouldn't surprise her

3 (*in Höflichkeitsformeln*): **darf ich Sie
bitten, das zu tun?** may *od* could I ask you
to do that?; **was darf es sein?** what can I
do for you?

4 (*können*): **das dürfen Sie mir glauben**
you can believe me

5 (*Möglichkeit*): **das dürfte genug sein**
that should be enough; **es dürfte Ihnen**

bekannt sein, dass ... as you will
probably know ...

dürftig *adj* (*ärmlich*) poor; (*unzulänglich*)
inadequate

dürr *adj* dried-up; (*Land*) arid; (*mager*)
skinny

Durst (-(*e*)s) *m* thirst; **~ haben** to be
thirsty; **durstig** *adj* thirsty

Dusche (-, -n) *f* shower; **duschen** *vi* to
have a shower ▷ *vr* **sich ~** to have a
shower; **Duschgel** *nt* shower gel;
Duschvorhang *m* shower curtain

Düse (-, -n) *f* nozzle; (*Tech*) jet;
Düsenflugzeug *nt* jet (aircraft)

Dussel (-s, -) *m* (*fam*) dope; **duss(e)lig** *adj*
(*fam*) stupid

düster *adj* dark; (*Gedanken, Zukunft*)
gloomy

Dutyfreeshop (-s, -s) *m* duty-free shop

Dutzend (-s, -e) *nt* dozen

duzen *vt* to address as 'du' ▷ *vr* **sich ~** (**mit
jdm**) to address each other as 'du', to be on
first-name terms

DVD (-, -s) *f abk* = **Digital Versatile Disk**
DVD

dynamisch *adj* dynamic

Dynamo (-s, -s) *m* dynamo

D-Zug *m* fast train

Ebbe (-, -n) f low tide

eben adj level; (glatt) smooth ▷ adv just; (bestätigend) exactly

Ebene (-, -n) f plain; (fig) level

ebenfalls adv also, as well; (Antwort: gleichfalls!) you too; **ebenso** adv just as; **~ gut** just as well; **~ viel** just as much

Eber (-s, -) m boar

EC (-, -s) m abk = **Eurocityzug**

Echo (-s, -s) nt echo

echt adj (Leder, Gold) real, genuine; **ein ~er Verlust** a real loss

EC-Karte f ≈ debit card

Ecke (-, -n) f corner; (Math) angle; **an der ~** at the corner; **gleich um die ~** just round the corner; **eckig** adj rectangular; **Eckzahn** m canine

Economyclass (-) f coach (class), economy class

Ecstasy (-) f (Droge) ecstasy

edel adj noble; **Edelstein** m precious stone

EDV (-) f abk = **elektronische Datenverarbeitung** EDP

Efeu (-s) m ivy

Effekt (-s, -e) m effect

egal adj **das ist ~** it doesn't matter; **das ist** mir ~ I don't care, it's all the same to me; **~ wie teuer** no matter how expensive

egoistisch adj selfish

ehe conj before

Ehe (-, -n) f marriage; **Ehefrau** f wife; (verheiratete Frau) married woman; **Eheleute** pl married couple sing

ehemalig adj former; **ehemals** adv formerly

Ehemann m husband; (verheirateter Mann) married man; **Ehepaar** nt married couple

eher adv (früher) sooner; (lieber) rather, sooner; (mehr) more; **je ~, desto besser** the sooner the better

Ehering m wedding ring

eheste(r, s) adj (früheste) first ▷ adv **am ~n** (am wahrscheinlichsten) most likely

Ehre (-, -n) f honour; **ehren** vt to honour; **ehrenamtlich** adj voluntary; **Ehrengast** m guest of honour; **Ehrenwort** nt word of honour; **~!** I promise; **ich gebe dir mein ~** I give you my word

ehrgeizig adj ambitious

ehrlich adj honest

Ei (-(e)s, -er) nt egg; **hart gekochtes/weiches ~** hard-boiled/soft-boiled egg

Eiche (-, -n) f oak (tree); **Eichel** (-, -n) f acorn

Eichhörnchen nt squirrel

Eid (-(e)s, -e) m oath

Eidechse (-, -n) f lizard

Eierbecher m eggcup; **Eierstock** m ovary; **Eieruhr** f egg timer

Eifersucht f jealousy; **eifersüchtig** adj jealous (auf +akk of)

Eigelb (-(e)s, -) nt egg yolk

eigen adj own; (typisch) characteristic (jdm of sb); (eigenartig) peculiar; **eigenartig** adj peculiar; **Eigenschaft** f quality; (Chem, Phys) property; (Merkmal) characteristic

eigentlich adj actual, real ▷ adv actually, really; **was denken Sie sich ~ dabei?** what on earth do you think you're doing?

Eigentum nt property; **Eigentümer(in)** m(f) owner; **Eigentumswohnung** f owner-occupied flat (Brit), condominium (US)

eignen vr **sich ~ für** to be suited for; **er würde sich als Lehrer ~** he'd make a good teacher

Eilbrief m express letter, special-delivery

letter; **Eile** (-) f hurry; **eilen** vi (*dringend sein*) to be urgent; **es eilt nicht** there's no hurry; **eilig** adj hurried; (*dringlich*) urgent; **es ~ haben** to be in a hurry

Eimer (-s, -) m bucket

ein adv **nicht ~ noch aus wissen** not to know what to do; **~ - aus** (*Schalter*) on - off

ein(e) art a; (*vor gesprochenem Vokal*) an; **~ Mann** a man; **~ Apfel** an apple; **~e Stunde** an hour; **~ Haus** a house; **~ (gewisser) Herr Miller** a (certain) Mr Miller; **~es Tages** one day

einander pron one another, each other

ein|arbeiten vt to train ▷ vr **sich ~** to get used to the work

ein|atmen vt, vi to breathe in

Einbahnstraße f one-way street

ein|bauen vt to build in; (*Motor etc*) to install, to fit; **Einbauküche** f fitted kitchen

ein|biegen irr vi to turn (*in +akk* into)

ein|bilden vt **sich** (*dat*) **etw ~** to imagine sth

ein|brechen irr vi (*in Haus*) to break in; (*Dach etc*) to fall in, to collapse; **Einbrecher(in)** (-s, -) m(f) burglar

ein|bringen irr vt (*Ernte*) to bring in; (*Gewinn*) to yield; **jdm etw ~** to bring (*o* earn) sb sth ▷ vr **sich in** (*akk*) **etw ~** to make a contribution to sth

Einbruch m (*Haus*) break-in, burglary; **bei ~ der Nacht** at nightfall

Einbürgerung f naturalization

ein|checken vt to check in

ein|cremen vt to put some cream on ▷ vr **sich ~** to put some cream on

eindeutig adj clear, obvious ▷ adv clearly; **~ falsch** clearly wrong

ein|dringen irr vi (*gewaltsam*) to force one's way in (*in +akk* -to); (*in Haus*) to break in (*in +akk* -to); (*Gas, Wasser*) to get in (*in +akk* -to)

Eindruck m impression; **großen ~ auf jdn machen** to make a big impression on sb

eine(r, s) pron one; (*jemand*) someone; **~r meiner Freunde** one of my friends; **~r nach dem andern** one after the other

eineiig adj (*Zwillinge*) identical

eineinhalb num one and a half

einerseits adv on the one hand

einfach adj (*nicht kompliziert*) simple; (*Mensch*) ordinary; (*Essen*) plain; (*nicht mehrfach*) single; **~e Fahrkarte** single ticket (*Brit*), one-way ticket (*US*) ▷ adv simply; (*nicht mehrfach*) once

Einfahrt f (*Vorgang*) driving in; (*eines Zuges*) arrival; (*Ort*) entrance

Einfall m (*Idee*) idea; **ein|fallen** irr vi (*Licht etc*) to fall in; (*einstürzen*) to collapse; **ihm fiel ein, dass ...** it occurred to him that ...; **ich werde mir etwas ~ lassen** I'll think of something; **was fällt Ihnen ein!** what do you think you're doing?

Einfamilienhaus nt detached house

einfarbig adj all one colour; (*Stoff etc*) self-coloured

Einfluss m influence

ein|frieren irr vt, vi to freeze

ein|fügen vt to fit in; (*zusätzlich*) to add; (*Inform*) to insert; **Einfügetaste** f (*Inform*) insert key

Einfuhr (-, -en) f import; **Einfuhrbestimmungen** pl import regulations pl

ein|führen vt to introduce; (*Ware*) to import; **Einführung** f introduction

Eingabe f (*Dateneingabe*) input; **Eingabetaste** f (*Inform*) return (*o* enter) key

Eingang m entrance; **Eingangshalle** f entrance hall, lobby (*US*)

ein|geben irr vt (*Daten etc*) to enter, to key in

eingebildet adj imaginary; (*eitel*) arrogant

Eingeborene(r) mf native

ein|gehen irr vi (*Sendung, Geld*) to come in, to arrive; (*Tier, Pflanze*) to die; (*Stoff*) to shrink; **auf etw** (*akk*) **~** to agree to sth; **auf jdn ~** to respond to sb ▷ vt (*Vertrag*) to enter into; (*Wette*) to make; (*Risiko*) to take

eingelegt adj (*in Essig*) pickled

eingeschaltet adj (switched) on

eingeschlossen adj locked in; (*inklusive*) included

ein|gewöhnen vr **sich ~** to settle in

ein|gießen irr vt to pour

ein|greifen irr vi to intervene; **Eingriff** m intervention; (*Operation*) operation

ein|halten irr vt (*Versprechen etc*) to keep

ein|hängen vt (*Telefon*) (**den Hörer**) **~** to hang up

einheimisch adj (*Produkt, Mannschaft*) local; **Einheimische(r)** mf local

Einheit f (*Geschlossenheit*) unity; (*Maß*) unit; **einheitlich** adj uniform

ein|holen vt (*Vorsprung aufholen*) to catch

up with; (*Verspätung*) to make up for; (*Rat, Erlaubnis*) to ask for

Einhorn nt unicorn

einhundert num one (*o* a) hundred

einig adj (*vereint*) united; **sich** (*dat*) **~ sein** to agree

einige pron pl some; (*mehrere*) several ▷ adj some; **nach ~er Zeit** after some time; **~e hundert Euro** some hundred euros

einigen vr **sich ~** to agree (*auf +akk* on)

einigermaßen adv fairly, quite; (*leidlich*) reasonably

einiges pron something; (*ziemlich viel*) quite a bit; (*mehreres*) a few things; **es gibt noch ~ zu tun** there's still a fair bit to do

Einkauf m purchase; **Einkäufe (machen)** (to do one's) shopping; **ein|kaufen** vt to buy ▷ vi to go shopping; **Einkaufsbummel** m shopping trip; **Einkaufstasche** f, **Einkaufstüte** f shopping bag; **Einkaufswagen** m shopping trolley (*Brit*) (*o* cart (*US*)); **Einkaufszentrum** nt shopping centre (*Brit*) (*o* mall (*US*))

ein|klemmen vt to jam; **er hat sich** (*dat*) **den Finger eingeklemmt** he got his finger caught

Einkommen (*-s, -*) nt income

ein|laden irr vt (*jdn*) to invite; (*Gegenstände*) to load; **jdn zum Essen ~** to take sb out for a meal; **ich lade dich ein** (*bezahle*) it's my treat; **Einladung** f invitation

Einlass (*-es, Einlässe*) m admittance; **~ ab 18 Uhr** doors open at 6 pm; **ein|lassen** irr vr **sich mit jdm/auf etw** (*akk*) **~** to get involved with sb/sth

ein|leben vr **sich ~** to settle down

ein|legen vt (*Film etc*) to put in; (*marinieren*) to marinate; **eine Pause ~** to take a break

ein|leiten vt to start; (*Maßnahmen*) to introduce; (*Geburt*) to induce; **Einleitung** f introduction; (*von Geburt*) induction

ein|leuchten vi **jdm ~** to be (*o* become) clear to sb; **einleuchtend** adj clear

ein|loggen vi (*Inform*) to log on (*o* in)

ein|lösen vt (*Scheck*) to cash; (*Gutschein*) to redeem; (*Versprechen*) to keep

einmal adv once; (*früher*) before; (*in Zukunft*) some day; (*erstens*) first; **~ im Jahr** once a year; **noch ~** once more, again; **ich war schon ~ hier** I've been here before; **warst du schon ~ in London?** have you ever been to London?; **nicht ~** not even; **auf ~** suddenly; (*gleichzeitig*) at once; **einmalig** adj unique; (*einmal geschehend*) single; (*prima*) fantastic

ein|mischen vr **sich ~** to interfere (*in +akk* with)

Einnahme (*-, -n*) f (*Geld*) takings pl; (*von Medizin*) taking; **ein|nehmen** irr vt (*Medizin*) to take; (*Geld*) to take in; (*Standpunkt, Raum*) to take up; **jdn für sich ~** to win sb over

ein|ordnen vt to put in order; (*klassifizieren*) to classify; (*Akten*) to file ▷ vr **sich ~** (*Auto*) to get in lane; **sich rechts/links ~** to get into the right/left lane

ein|packen vt to pack (up)

ein|parken vt, vi to park

ein|planen vt to allow for

ein|prägen vt **sich** (*dat*) **etw ~** to remember (*o* memorize) sth

ein|räumen vt (*Bücher, Geschirr*) to put away; (*Schrank*) to put things in

ein|reden vt **jdm/sich etw ~** to talk sb/oneself into (believing) sth

ein|reiben irr vt **sich mit etw ~** to rub sth into one's skin

ein|reichen vt to hand in; (*Antrag*) to submit

Einreise f entry; **Einreisebestimmungen** pl entry regulations pl; **Einreiseerlaubnis** f, **Einreisegenehmigung** f entry permit; **ein|reisen** vi to enter (*in ein Land* a country); **Einreisevisum** nt entry visa

ein|renken vt (*Arm, Bein*) to set

ein|richten vt (*Wohnung*) to furnish; (*gründen*) to establish, to set up; (*arrangieren*) to arrange ▷ vr **sich ~** (*in Haus*) to furnish one's home; (*sich vorbereiten*) to prepare oneself (*auf +akk* for); (*sich anpassen*) to adapt (*auf +akk* to); **Einrichtung** f (*Wohnung*) furnishings pl; (*öffentliche Anstalt*) institution; (*Schwimmbad etc*) facility

eins num one; **Eins** (*-, -en*) f one; (*Schulnote*) ≈ A

einsam adj lonely

ein|sammeln vt to collect

Einsatz m (*Teil*) insert; (*Verwendung*) use;

(*Spieleinsatz*) stake; (*Risiko*) risk; (*Mus*) entry

ein|schalten *vt* (*Elek*) to switch on

ein|schätzen *vt* to estimate, to assess

ein|schenken *vt* to pour

ein|schiffen *vr* **sich ~** to embark (*nach* for)

ein|schlafen *irr vi* to fall asleep, to drop off; **mir ist der Arm eingeschlafen** my arm's gone to sleep

ein|schlagen *irr vt* (*Fenster*) to smash; (*Zähne, Schädel*) to smash in; (*Weg, Richtung*) to take ▷ *vi* to hit (*in etw akk* sth, *auf jdn* sb); (*Blitz*) to strike; (*Anklang finden*) to be a success

ein|schließen *irr vt* (*jdn*) to lock in; (*Gegenstand*) to lock away; (*umgeben*) to surround; (*fig: beinhalten*) to include; **einschließlich** *adv* inclusive ▷ *prep* +*gen* including; **von Montag bis ~ Freitag** from Monday up to and including Friday, Monday through Friday (*US*)

ein|schränken *vt* to limit, to restrict; (*verringern*) to cut down on ▷ *vr* **sich ~** to cut down (on expenditure)

ein|schreiben *irr vr* **sich ~** to register; (*Schule*) to enrol; **Einschreiben** (*-s, -*) *nt* registered letter; **etw per ~ schicken** to send sth by special delivery

ein|schüchtern *vt* to intimidate

ein|sehen *irr vt* (*verstehen*) to see; (*Fehler*) to recognize; (*Akten*) to have a look at

einseitig *adj* one-sided

ein|senden *irr vt* to send in

ein|setzen *vt* to put in; (*in Amt*) to appoint; (*Geld*) to stake; (*verwenden*) to use ▷ *vi* (*beginnen*) to set in; (*Mus*) to come in ▷ *vr* **sich ~** to work hard; **sich für jdn/etw ~** to support sb/sth

Einsicht *f* insight; **zu der ~ kommen, dass …** to come to realize that …

ein|sperren *vt* to lock up

ein|spielen *vt* (*Geld*) to bring in

ein|springen *irr vi* (*aushelfen*) to step in (*für* for)

Einspruch *m* objection (*gegen* to)

einspurig *adj* single-lane

Einstand *m* (*Tennis*) deuce

ein|stecken *vt* to pocket; (*Elek: Stecker*) to plug in; (*Brief*) to post, to mail (*US*); (*mitnehmen*) to take; (*hinnehmen*) to swallow

ein|steigen *irr vi* (*in Auto*) to get in; (*in Bus, Zug, Flugzeug*) to get on; (*sich beteiligen*) to get involved

ein|stellen *vt* (*beenden*) to stop; (*Geräte*) to adjust; (*Kamera*) to focus; (*Sender, Radio*) to tune in; (*unterstellen*) to put; (*in Firma*) to employ, to take on ▷ *vr* **sich auf jdn/etw ~** to adapt to sb/prepare oneself for sth; **Einstellung** *f* (*von Gerät*) adjustment; (*von Kamera*) focusing; (*von Arbeiter*) taking on; (*Meinung*) attitude

ein|stürzen *vi* to collapse

eintägig *adj* one-day

ein|tauschen *vt* to exchange (*gegen* for)

eintausend *num* one (*o* a) thousand

ein|teilen *vt* (*in Teile*) to divide (up) (*in* +*akk* into); (*Zeit*) to organize

eintönig *adj* monotonous

Eintopf *m* stew

ein|tragen *irr vt* (*in eine Liste*) to put down, to enter ▷ *vr* **sich ~** to put one's name down, to register

ein|treffen *irr vi* to happen; (*ankommen*) to arrive

ein|treten *irr vi* (*hineingehen*) to enter (*in etw akk* sth); (*in Klub, Partei*) to join (*in etw akk* sth); (*sich ereignen*) to occur; **~ für** to support; **Eintritt** *m* admission; **„~ frei"** 'admission free'; **Eintrittskarte** *f* (entrance) ticket; **Eintrittspreis** *m* admission charge

einverstanden *interj* okay, all right ▷ *adj* **mit etwas ~ sein** to agree to sth, to accept sth

Einwanderer *m*, **Einwanderin** *f* immigrant; **ein|wandern** *vi* to immigrate

einwandfrei *adj* perfect, flawless

Einwegflasche *f* non-returnable bottle; **Einwegwaschlappen** *m* disposable flannel (*Brit*) (*o* washcloth (*US*))

ein|weichen *vt* to soak

ein|weihen *vt* (*Gebäude*) to inaugurate, to open; **jdn in etw** (*akk*) **~** to let sb in on sth; **Einweihungsparty** *f* housewarming party

ein|werfen *irr vt* (*Ball, Bemerkung etc*) to throw in; (*Brief*) to post, to mail (*US*); (*Geld*) to put in, to insert; (*Fenster*) to smash

ein|wickeln *vt* to wrap up; (*fig*) **jdn ~** to take sb in

Einwohner(in) (*-s, -*) *m(f)* inhabitant; **Einwohnermeldeamt** *nt* registration office for residents

Einwurf *m* (*Öffnung*) slot; (*Sport*) throw-in

Einzahl *f* singular

ein|zahlen *vt* to pay in (*auf ein Konto* -to an account)

Einzel (*-s, -*) *nt* (*Tennis*) singles *sing*; **Einzelbett** *nt* single bed; **Einzelfahrschein** *m* single ticket (*Brit*), one-way ticket (*US*); **Einzelgänger(in)** *m(f)* loner; **Einzelhandel** *m* retail trade; **Einzelkind** *nt* only child

einzeln *adj* individual; (*getrennt*) separate; (*einzig*) single; **~e ...** several ..., some ...; **der/die Einzelne** the individual; **im Einzelnen** in detail ▷ *adv* separately; (*verpacken, aufführen*) individually; **~ angeben** to specify; **~ eintreten** to enter one by one

Einzelzimmer *nt* single room; **Einzelzimmerzuschlag** *m* single-room supplement

ein|ziehen *irr vt* **den Kopf ~** to duck ▷ *vi* (*in ein Haus*) to move in

einzig *adj* only; (*einzeln*) single; (*einzigartig*) unique; **kein ~er Fehler** not a single mistake; **das Einzige** the only thing; **der/die Einzige** the only person ▷ *adv* only; **die ~ richtige Lösung** the only correct solution; **einzigartig** *adj* unique

Eis (*-es, -*) *nt* ice; (*Speiseeis*) ice-cream; **~ laufen** to skate; **Eisbahn** *f* ice(skating) rink; **Eisbär** *m* polar bear; **Eisbecher** *m* (ice-cream) sundae; **Eisberg** *m* iceberg; **Eiscafé** *nt*, **Eisdiele** *f* ice-cream parlour

Eisen (*-s, -*) *nt* iron; **Eisenbahn** *f* railway (*Brit*), railroad (*US*); **eisern** *adj* iron

eisgekühlt *adj* chilled; **Eishockey** *nt* ice hockey; **Eiskaffee** *m* iced coffee; **eiskalt** *adj* ice-cold; (*Temperatur*) freezing; **Eiskunstlauf** *m* figure skating; **Eissalat** *m* iceberg lettuce; **Eisschokolade** *f* iced chocolate; **Eisschrank** *m* fridge, ice-box (*US*); **Eistee** *m* iced tea; **Eiswürfel** *m* ice cube; **Eiszapfen** *m* icicle

eitel *adj* vain

Eiter (*-s*) *m* pus

Eiweiß (*-es, -e*) *nt* egg white; (*Chem, Bio*) protein

ekelhaft, **ek(e)lig** *adj* disgusting, revolting; **ekeln** *vr* **sich ~** to be disgusted (*vor +dat* at)

EKG (*-s, -s*) *nt abk* = **Elektrokardiogramm** ECG

Ekzem (*-s, -e*) *nt* (*Med*) eczema

Elastikbinde *f* elastic bandage; **elastisch** *adj* elastic

Elch (*-(e)s, -e*) *m* elk; (*nordamerikanischer*) moose

Elefant *m* elephant

elegant *adj* elegant

Elektriker(in) (*-s, -*) *m(f)* electrician; **elektrisch** *adj* electric; **Elektrizität** *f* electricity; **Elektroauto** *nt* electric car; **Elektrogerät** *nt* electrical appliance; **Elektrogeschäft** *nt* electrical shop; **Elektroherd** *m* electric cooker; **Elektromotor** *m* electric motor; **Elektronik** *f* electronics *sing*; **elektronisch** *adj* electronic; **Elektrorasierer** (*-s, -*) *m* electric razor

Element (*-s, -e*) *nt* element

elend *adj* miserable; **Elend** (*-(e)s*) *nt* misery

elf *num* eleven; **Elf** (*-, -en*) *f* (*Sport*) eleven

Elfenbein *nt* ivory

Elfmeter *m* (*Sport*) penalty (kick)

elfte(r, s) *adj* eleventh; *siehe auch* **dritte**

Ell(en)bogen *m* elbow

Elster (*-, -n*) *f* magpie

Eltern *pl* parents *pl*

EM *f abk* = **Europameisterschaft** European Championship(s)

Email (*-s, -s*) *nt* enamel

E-Mail (*-, -s*) *f* (*Inform*) e-mail; **jdm eine ~ schicken** to e-mail sb, to send sb an e-mail; **jdm etwas per ~ schicken** to e-mail sth to sb; **E-Mail-Adresse** *f* e-mail address; **e-mailen** *vt* to e-mail

Emoticon (*-s, -s*) *nt* emoticon

emotional *adj* emotional

empfahl *imperf von* **empfehlen**

empfand *imperf von* **empfinden**

Empfang (*-(e)s, Empfänge*) *m* (*Rezeption; Veranstaltung*) reception; (*Erhalten*) receipt; **in ~ nehmen** to receive; **empfangen** (*empfing, empfangen*) *vt* to receive; **Empfänger(in)** (*-s, -*) *m(f)* recipient; (*Adressat*) addressee ▷ *m* (*Tech*) receiver; **Empfängnisverhütung** *f* contraception; **Empfangshalle** *f* reception area

empfehlen (*empfahl, empfohlen*) *vt* to recommend; **Empfehlung** *f* recommendation

empfinden (*empfand, empfunden*) *vt* to feel; **empfindlich** *adj* (*Mensch*) sensitive; (*Stelle*) sore; (*reizbar*) touchy; (*Material*) delicate

empfing *imperf von* **empfangen**

empfohlen *pp von* **empfehlen**

empfunden *pp von* **empfinden**

empört *adj* indignant (*über +akk* at)

Ende (*-s, -n*) *nt* end; (*Film, Roman*) ending; **am ~** at the end; (*schließlich*) in the end; **~ Mai** at the end of May; **~ der Achtzigerjahre** in the late eighties; **sie ist ~ zwanzig** she's in her late twenties; **zu ~** over, finished; **enden** *vi* to end; **der Zug endet hier** this service (*o* train) terminates here; **endgültig** *adj* final; (*Beweis*) conclusive

Endivie *f* endive

endlich *adv* at last, finally; (*am Ende*) eventually; **Endspiel** *nt* final; (*Endrunde*) finals *pl*; **Endstation** *f* terminus; **Endung** *f* ending

Energie *f* energy; **~ sparend** energy-saving; **Energiebedarf** *m* energy requirement; **Energieverbrauch** *m* energy consumption

energisch *adj* (*entschlossen*) forceful

eng *adj* narrow; (*Kleidung*) tight; (*fig: Freundschaft, Verhältnis*) close; **das wird ~** (*fam: zeitlich*) we're running out of time, it's getting tight ▷ *adv* **~ befreundet sein** to be close friends

engagieren *vt* to engage ▷ *vr* **sich ~** to commit oneself, to be committed (*für* to)

Engel (*-s, -*) *m* angel

England *nt* England; **Engländer(in)** (*-s, -*) *m(f)* Englishman/ -woman; **die ~** *pl* the English *pl*; **englisch** *adj* English; (*Gastr*) rare; **Englisch** *nt* English; **ins ~e übersetzen** to translate into English

Enkel (*-s, -*) *m* grandson; **Enkelin** *f* granddaughter

enorm *adj* enormous; (*fig*) tremendous

Entbindung *f* (*Med*) delivery

entdecken *vt* to discover; **Entdeckung** *f* discovery

Ente (*-, -n*) *f* duck

Enter-Taste *f* (*Inform*) enter (*o* return) key

entfernen *vt* to remove; (*Inform*) to delete ▷ *vr* **sich ~** to go away; **entfernt** *adj* distant; **15 km von X ~** 15 km away from X; **20 km voneinander ~** 20 km apart; **Entfernung** *f* distance; **aus der ~** from a distance

entführen *vt* to kidnap; **Entführer(in)** *m(f)* kidnapper; **Entführung** *f* kidnapping

entgegen *prep +dat* contrary to ▷ *adv* towards; **dem Wind ~** against the wind; **entgegengesetzt** *adj* (*Richtung*) opposite; (*Meinung*) opposing; **entgegen|kommen** *irr vi* **jdm ~** to come to meet sb; (*fig*) to accommodate sb; **entgegenkommend** *adj* (*Verkehr*) oncoming; (*fig*) obliging

entgegnen *vt* to reply (*auf +akk* to)

entgehen *irr vi* **jdm ~** to escape sb's notice; **sich** (*dat*) **etw ~ lassen** to miss sth

entgleisen *vi* (*Eisenb*) to be derailed; (*fig: Mensch*) to misbehave

Enthaarungscreme *f* hair remover

enthalten *irr vt* (*Behälter*) to contain; (*Preis*) to include ▷ *vr* **sich ~** to abstain (*gen* from)

entkoffeiniert *adj* decaffeinated

entkommen *irr vi* to escape

entkorken *vt* to uncork

entlang *prep +akk o dat* **~ dem Fluss, den Fluss ~** along the river; **entlang|gehen** *irr vi* to walk along

entlassen *irr vt* (*Patient*) to discharge; (*Arbeiter*) to dismiss

entlasten *vt* **jdn ~** (*Arbeit abnehmen*) to relieve sb of some of his/her work

entmutigen *vt* to discourage

entnehmen *vt* to take (*dat* from)

entrahmt *adj* (*Milch*) skimmed

entschädigen *vt* to compensate; **Entschädigung** *f* compensation

entscheiden *irr vt, vi* to decide ▷ *vr* **sich ~** to decide; **sich für/gegen etw ~** to decide on/against sth; **wir haben uns entschieden, nicht zu gehen** we decided not to go; **das entscheidet sich morgen** that'll be decided tomorrow; **entscheidend** *adj* decisive; (*Stimme*) casting; (*Frage, Problem*) crucial; **Entscheidung** *f* decision

entschließen *irr vr* **sich ~** to decide (*zu, für* on), to make up one's mind; **Entschluss** *m* decision

entschuldigen *vt* to excuse ▷ *vr* **sich ~** to apologize; **sich bei jdm für etw ~** to apologize to sb for sth ▷ *vi* **entschuldige!, ~ Sie!** (*vor einer Frage*) excuse me; (*Verzeihung!*) (I'm) sorry, excuse me (*US*); **Entschuldigung** *f* apology; (*Grund*) excuse; **jdn um ~ bitten** to apologize to sb; **~!** (*bei Zusammenstoß*) (I'm) sorry, excuse me (*US*); (*vor einer Frage*) excuse me; (*wenn man etw nicht verstanden hat*) (I beg your) pardon?

entsetzlich *adj* dreadful, appalling

entsorgen *vt* to dispose of

entspannen *vt* (*Körper*) to relax; (*Pol: Lage*) to ease ▷ *vr* **sich ~** to relax; (*fam*) to chill out; **Entspannung** *f* relaxation

entsprechen *irr vi* +*dat* to correspond to; (*Anforderungen, Wünschen etc*) to comply with; **entsprechend** *adj* appropriate ▷ *adv* accordingly ▷ *prep* +*dat* according to, in accordance with

entstehen *vi* (*Schwierigkeiten*) to arise; (*gebaut werden*) to be built; (*hergestellt werden*) to be created

enttäuschen *vt* to disappoint; **Enttäuschung** *f* disappointment

entweder *conj* **~ ... oder ...** either ... or ...; **~ oder!** take it or leave it

entwerfen *irr vt* (*Möbel, Kleider*) to design; (*Plan, Vertrag*) to draft

entwerten *vt* to devalue; (*Fahrschein*) to cancel; **Entwerter** (*-s, -*) *m* ticket-cancelling machine

entwickeln *vt* (*a. Foto*) to develop; (*Mut, Energie*) to show, to display ▷ *vr* **sich ~** to develop; **Entwicklung** *f* development; (*Foto*) developing; **Entwicklungshelfer(in)** (*-s, -*) *m(f)* development worker; **Entwicklungsland** *nt* developing country

Entwurf *m* outline; (*Design*) design; (*Vertragsentwurf, Konzept*) draft

entzückend *adj* delightful, charming

Entzug *m* withdrawal; (*Behandlung*) detox; **Entzugserscheinung** *f* withdrawal symptom

entzünden *vr* **sich ~** to catch fire; (*Med*) to become inflamed; **Entzündung** *f* (*Med*) inflammation

Epidemie *f* epidemic

Epilepsie *f* epilepsy

er *pron* (*Person*) he; (*Sache*) it; **er ists** it's him; **wo ist mein Mantel? - ~ ist ...** where's my coat? - it's ...

Erbe (*-n, -n*) *m* heir ▷ (*-s*) *nt* inheritance; (*fig*) heritage; **erben** *vt* to inherit; **Erbin** *f* heiress; **erblich** *adj* hereditary

erbrechen *irr vt* to vomit ▷ *vr* **sich ~** to vomit; **Erbrechen** *nt* vomiting

Erbschaft *f* inheritance

Erbse (*-, -n*) *f* pea

Erdapfel *m* potato; **Erdbeben** *nt* earthquake; **Erdbeere** *f* strawberry; **Erde** (*-, -n*) *f* (*Planet*) earth; (*Boden*) ground; **Erdgas** *nt* natural gas; **Erdgeschoss** *nt* ground floor (*Brit*), first floor (*US*); **Erdkunde** *f* geography; **Erdnuss** *f* peanut; **Erdöl** *nt* (mineral) oil; **Erdrutsch** *m* landslide; **Erdteil** *m* continent

ereignen *vr* **sich ~** to happen, to take place; **Ereignis** *nt* event

erfahren *irr vt* to learn, to find out; (*erleben*) to experience ▷ *adj* experienced; **Erfahrung** *f* experience

erfinden *irr vt* to invent; **erfinderisch** *adj* inventive, creative; **Erfindung** *f* invention

Erfolg (*-(e)s, -e*) *m* success; (*Folge*) result; **~ versprechend** promising; **viel ~!** good luck; **erfolglos** *adj* unsuccessful; **erfolgreich** *adj* successful

erforderlich *adj* necessary

erforschen *vt* to explore; (*untersuchen*) investigate

erfreulich *adj* pleasing, pleasant; (*Nachricht*) good; **erfreulicherweise** *adv* fortunately

erfrieren *irr vi* to freeze to death; (*Pflanzen*) to be killed by frost

Erfrischung *f* refreshment

erfüllen *vt* (*Raum*) to fill; (*Bitte, Wunsch etc*) to fulfil ▷ *vr* **sich ~** to come true

ergänzen *vt* (*hinzufügen*) to add; (*vervollständigen*) to complete ▷ *vr* **sich ~** to complement one another; **Ergänzung** *f* completion; (*Zusatz*) supplement

ergeben *irr vt* (*Betrag*) to come to; (*zum Ergebnis haben*) to result in ▷ *irr vr* **sich ~** to surrender; (*folgen*) to result (*aus* from) ▷ *adj* devoted; (*demütig*) humble

Ergebnis *nt* result

ergreifen *irr vt* to seize; (*Beruf*) to take up; (*Maßnahme, Gelegenheit*) to take; (*rühren*) to move

erhalten *irr vt* (*bekommen*) to receive; (*bewahren*) to preserve; **gut ~ sein** to be in good condition; **erhältlich** *adj* available

erheblich *adj* considerable

erhitzen *vt* to heat (up)

erhöhen *vt* to raise; (*verstärken*) to increase ▷ *vr* **sich ~** to increase

erholen *vr* **sich ~** to recover; (*sich ausruhen*) to have a rest; **erholsam** *adj* restful; **Erholung** f recovery; (*Entspannung*) relaxation, rest

erinnern vt to remind (*an +akk* of) ▷ vr **sich ~** to remember (*an etw akk* sth); **Erinnerung** f memory; (*Andenken*) souvenir; (*Mahnung*) reminder

erkälten vr **sich ~** to catch a cold; **erkältet** adj (**stark**) **~ sein** to have a (bad) cold; **Erkältung** f cold

erkennen irr vt to recognize; (*sehen, verstehen*) to see; **~, dass ...** to realize that ...; **erkenntlich** adj **sich ~ zeigen** to show one's appreciation

Erker (*-s, -*) m bay

erklären vt to explain; (*kundtun*) to declare; **Erklärung** f explanation; (*Aussage*) declaration

erkundigen vr **sich ~** to enquire (*nach* about)

erlauben vt to allow, to permit; **jdm ~, etw zu tun** to allow (*o* permit) sb to do sth; **sich** (*dat*) **etw ~** to permit oneself sth; **~ Sie(, dass ich rauche)?** do you mind (if I smoke)?; **was ~ Sie sich?** what do you think you're doing?; **Erlaubnis** f permission

Erläuterung f explanation; (*zu Text*) comment

erleben vt to experience; (*schöne Tage etc*) to have; (*Schlimmes*) to go through; (*miterleben*) to witness; (*noch miterleben*) to live to see; **Erlebnis** nt experience

erledigen vt (*Angelegenheit, Aufgabe*) to deal with; (*fam: ruinieren*) to finish; **erledigt** adj (*beendet*) finished; (*gelöst*) dealt with; (*fam: erschöpft*) whacked, knackered (*Brit*)

erleichtert adj relieved

Erlös (*-es, -e*) m proceeds pl

ermahnen vt (*warnend*) to warn

ermäßigt adj reduced; **Ermäßigung** f reduction

ermitteln vt to find out; (*Täter*) to trace ▷ vi (*Jur*) to investigate

ermöglichen vt to make possible (*dat* for)

ermorden vt to murder

ermüdend adj tiring

ermutigen vt to encourage

ernähren vt to feed; (*Familie*) to support ▷ vr **sich ~** to support oneself; **sich ~ von** to live on; **Ernährung** f (*Essen*) food; **Ernährungsberater(in)** m(f) nutritional (*o* dietary) adviser

erneuern vt to renew; (*restaurieren*) to restore; (*renovieren*) to renovate; (*auswechseln*) to replace

ernst adj serious ▷ adv **jdn/etw ~ nehmen** take sb/sth seriously; **Ernst** (*-es*) m seriousness; **das ist mein ~** I'm quite serious; **im ~?** seriously?; **ernsthaft** adj serious ▷ adv seriously

Ernte (*-, -n*) f harvest; **Erntedankfest** nt harvest festival (*Brit*), Thanksgiving (Day) (*US: 4. Donnerstag im November*); **ernten** vt to harvest; (*Lob etc*) to earn

erobern vt to conquer

eröffnen vt to open; **Eröffnung** f opening

erogen adj erogenous

erotisch adj erotic

erpressen vt (*jdn*) to blackmail; (*Geld etc*) to extort; **Erpressung** f blackmail; (*von Geld*) extortion

erraten irr vt to guess

erregen vt to excite; (*sexuell*) to arouse; (*ärgern*) to annoy; (*hervorrufen*) to arouse ▷ vr **sich ~** to get worked up; **Erreger** (*-s, -*) m (*Med*) germ; (*Virus*) virus

erreichbar adj **~ sein** to be within reach; (*Person*) to be available; **das Stadtzentrum ist zu Fuß/mit dem Wagen leicht ~** the city centre is within easy walking/driving distance; **erreichen** vt to reach; (*Zug etc*) to catch

Ersatz (*-es*) m replacement; (*auf Zeit*) substitute; (*Ausgleich*) compensation; **Ersatzreifen** m (*Auto*) spare tyre; **Ersatzteil** nt spare (part)

erscheinen irr vi to appear; (*wirken*) to seem

erschöpft adj exhausted; **Erschöpfung** f exhaustion

erschrecken vt to frighten ▷ (*erschrak, erschrocken*) vi to get a fright; **erschreckend** adj alarming; **erschrocken** adj frightened

erschwinglich adj affordable

ersetzen vt to replace; (*Auslagen*) to reimburse

SCHLÜSSELWORT

erst adv **1** first; **mach erst mal die Arbeit fertig** finish your work first; **wenn du das erst mal hinter dir hast** once you've got that behind you

2 (*nicht früher als, nur*) only; (*nicht bis*) not

till; **erst gestern** only yesterday; **erst morgen** not until tomorrow; **erst als** only when not until; **wir fahren erst später** we're not going until later; **er ist (gerade) erst angekommen** he's only just arrived

3: **wäre er doch erst zurück!** if only he were back!

erstatten vt (Kosten) to refund; **Bericht ~ to** report (über +akk on); **Anzeige gegen jdn ~ to** report sb to the police

erstaunlich adj astonishing; **erstaunt** adj surprised

erstbeste(r, s) adj **das ~ Hotel** any old hotel; **der Erstbeste** just anyone

erste(r, s) adj first; siehe auch **dritte zum ~n Mal** for the first time; **er wurde Erster** he came first; **auf den ~n Blick** at first sight

erstens adv first(ly), in the first place

ersticken vi (Mensch) to suffocate; **in Arbeit ~ to** be snowed under with work

erstklassig adj first-class; **erstmals** adv for the first time

erstrecken vr **sich ~ to** extend, to stretch (auf +akk to; über +akk over)

ertappen vt to catch

erteilen vt (Rat, Erlaubnis) to give

Ertrag (-(e)s, Erträge) m yield; (Gewinn) proceeds pl; **ertragen** irr vt (Schmerzen) to bear, to stand; (dulden) to put up with; **erträglich** adj bearable; (nicht zu schlecht) tolerable

ertrinken irr vi to drown

erwachsen adj grown-up; **~ werden to** grow up; **Erwachsene(r)** mf adult, grown-up

erwähnen vt to mention

erwarten vt to expect; (warten auf) to wait for; **ich kann den Sommer kaum ~ I** can hardly wait for the summer

erwerbstätig adj employed

erwidern vt to reply; (Gruß, Besuch) to return

erwischen vt (fam) to catch (bei etw doing sth)

erwünscht adj desired; (willkommen) welcome

Erz (-es, -e) nt ore

erzählen vt to tell (jdm etw sb sth); **Erzählung** f story, tale

erzeugen vt to produce; (Strom) to generate; **Erzeugnis** nt product

erziehen irr vt to bring up; (geistig) to educate; (Tier) to train; **Erzieher(in)** (-s, -) m(f) educator; (Kindergarten) (nursery school) teacher; **Erziehung** f upbringing; (Bildung) education

es pron (Sache, im Nom und Akk) it; (Baby, Tier) he/she; **ich bin ~** it's me; **~ ist kalt** it's cold; **~ gibt ...** there is .../there are ...; **ich hoffe ~ I** hope so; **ich kann ~ I** can do it

Escape-Taste f (Inform) escape key

Esel (-s, -) m donkey

Espresso (-s, -) m espresso

essbar adj edible; **essen** (aß, gegessen) vt, vi to eat; **zu Mittag/Abend ~ to** have lunch/dinner; **was gibt's zu ~?** what's for lunch/dinner?; **~ gehen** to eat out; **gegessen sein** (fig, fam) to be history; **Essen** (-s, -) nt (Mahlzeit) meal; (Nahrung) food

Essig (-s, -e) m vinegar; **Essiggurke** f gherkin

Esslöffel m dessert spoon; **Esszimmer** nt dining room

Estland nt Estonia

Etage (-, -n) f floor, storey; **in** (o **auf**) **der ersten ~** on the first (Brit) (o second (US)) floor; **Etagenbett** nt bunk bed

Etappe (-, -n) f stage

ethnisch adj ethnic

Etikett (-(e)s, -e) nt label

etliche pron pl several, quite a few; **etliches** pron quite a lot

etwa adv (ungefähr) about; (vielleicht) perhaps; (beispielsweise) for instance

etwas pron something; (verneinend, fragend) anything; (ein wenig) a little; **~ Neues** something/anything new; **~ zu essen** something to eat; **~ Salz** some salt; **wenn ich noch ~ tun kann ...** if I can do anything else ... ▷ adv a bit, a little; **~ mehr** a little more

EU (-) f abk = **Europäische Union** EU

euch pron akk, dat von **ihr**; you, (to) you; **~ (selbst)** (reflexiv) yourselves; **wo kann ich ~ treffen?** where can I meet you?; **sie schickt es ~** she'll send it to you; **ein Freund von ~** a friend of yours; **setzt ~ bitte** please sit down; **habt ihr ~ amüsiert?** did you enjoy yourselves?

euer pron (adjektivisch) your; **~ David** (am

Briefende) Yours, David ▷ *pron gen von* **ihr**; of you; **euere(r, s)** *pron siehe* **eure**

Eule *(-, -n) f* owl

eure(r, s) *pron (substantivisch)* yours; **das ist ~** that's yours; **euretwegen** *adv (wegen euch)* because of you; *(euch zuliebe)* for your sake; *(um euch)* about you

Euro *(-, -) m (Währung)* euro; **Eurocent** *m* eurocent; **Eurocity** *(-(s), -s) m,* **Eurocityzug** *m* European Intercity train; **Europa** *(-s) nt* Europe; **Europäer(in)** *(-s, -) m(f)* European; **europäisch** *adj* European; **Europäische Union** European Union; **Europameister(in)** *m(f)* European champion; *(Mannschaft)* European champions *pl;* **Europaparlament** *nt* European Parliament

Euter *(-s, -) nt* udder

evangelisch *adj* Protestant

eventuell *adj* possible ▷ *adv* possibly, perhaps

ewig *adj* eternal; **er hat ~ gebraucht** it took him ages; **Ewigkeit** *f* eternity

Ex- *in zW* ex-, former; **~frau** ex-wife; **~minister** former minister

exakt *adj* precise

Examen *(-s, -) nt* exam

Exemplar *(-s, -e) nt* specimen; *(Buch)* copy

Exil *(-s, -e) nt* exile

Existenz *f* existence; *(Unterhalt)* livelihood, living; **existieren** *vi* to exist

exklusiv *adj* exclusive; **exklusive** *adv, prep +gen* excluding

exotisch *adj* exotic

Experte *(-n, -n) m,* **Expertin** *f* expert

explodieren *vi* to explode; **Explosion** *f* explosion

Export *(-(e)s, -e) m* export; **exportieren** *vt* to export

Express *(-es) m,* **Expresszug** *m* express (train)

extra *adj inv (fam: gesondert)* separate; *(zusätzlich)* extra ▷ *adv (gesondert)* separately; *(speziell)* specially; *(absichtlich)* on purpose; **Extra** *(-s, -s) nt* extra

extrem *adj* extreme ▷ *adv* extremely; **~ kalt** extremely cold

exzellent *adj* excellent

Eyeliner *(-s, -) m* eyeliner

e

fabelhaft *adj* fabulous, marvellous

Fabrik *f* factory

Fach (*-(e)s, Fächer*) *nt* compartment; (*Schulfach, Sachgebiet*) subject; **Facharzt** *m*, **Fachärztin** *f* specialist; **Fachausdruck** (*-s, Fachausdrücke*) *m* technical term

Fächer (*-s, -*) *m* fan

Fachfrau *f* specialist, expert; **Fachmann** (*-leute*) *m* specialist, expert; **Fachwerkhaus** *nt* half-timbered house

Fackel (*-, -n*) *f* torch

fad(e) *adj* (*Essen*) bland; (*langweilig*) dull

Faden (*-s, Fäden*) *m* thread

fähig *adj* capable (*zu, gen* of); **Fähigkeit** *f* ability

Fahndung *f* search

Fahne (*-, -n*) *f* flag

Fahrausweis *m* ticket; **Fahrausweisautomat** *m* ticket machine; **Fahrausweiskontrolle** *f* ticket inspection

Fahrbahn *f* road; (*Spur*) lane

Fähre (*-, -n*) *f* ferry

fahren (*fuhr, gefahren*) *vt* to drive; (*Rad*) to ride; (*befördern*) to drive, to take; **50 km/h ~** to drive at (*o* do) 50 kph ▷ *vi* (*sich bewegen*) to go; (*Autofahrer*) to drive; (*Schiff*) to sail; (*abfahren*) to leave; **mit dem Auto/Zug ~** to go by car/train; **rechts ~!** keep to the right; **Fahrer(in)** (*-s, -*) *m(f)* driver; **Fahrerairbag** *m* driver airbag; **Fahrerflucht** *f* ~ **begehen** to fail to stop after an accident; **Fahrersitz** *m* driver's seat

Fahrgast *m* passenger; **Fahrgeld** *nt* fare; **Fahrgemeinschaft** *f* car pool; **Fahrkarte** *f* ticket; **Fahrkartenautomat** *m* ticket machine; **Fahrkartenschalter** *m* ticket office

fahrlässig *adj* negligent

Fahrlehrer(in) *m(f)* driving instructor; **Fahrplan** *m* timetable; **Fahrplanauszug** *m* individual timetable; **fahrplanmäßig** *adj* (*Eisenb*) scheduled; **Fahrpreis** *m* fare; **Fahrpreisermäßigung** *f* fare reduction; **Fahrrad** *nt* bicycle; **Fahrradschlauch** *m* bicycle tube; **Fahrradschloss** *nt* bicycle lock; **Fahrradverleih** *m* cycle hire (*Brit*) (*o* rental (*US*)); **Fahrradweg** *m* cycle path; **Fahrschein** *m* ticket; **Fahrscheinautomat** *m* ticket machine; **Fahrscheinentwerter** *m* ticket-cancelling machine; **Fahrschule** *f* driving school; **Fahrschüler(in)** *m(f)* learner (driver) (*Brit*), student driver (*US*); **Fahrspur** *f* lane; **Fahrstreifen** *m* lane; **Fahrstuhl** *m* lift (*Brit*), elevator (*US*)

Fahrt (*-, -en*) *f* journey; (*kurz*) trip; (*Auto*) drive; **auf der ~ nach London** on the way to London; **nach drei Stunden ~** after travelling for three hours; **gute ~!** have a good trip; **Fahrtkosten** *pl* travelling expenses *pl*; **Fahrtrichtung** *f* direction of travel

fahrtüchtig *f* (*Person*) fit to drive; (*Fahrzeug*) roadworthy

Fahrtunterbrechung *f* break in the journey, stop

Fahrverbot *nt* ~ **erhalten/haben** to be banned from driving; **Fahrzeug** *nt* vehicle; **Fahrzeugbrief** *m* (vehicle) registration document; **Fahrzeughalter(in)** *m(f)* registered owner; **Fahrzeugpapiere** *pl* vehicle documents *pl*

fair *adj* fair

Fakultät *f* faculty

Falke (*-n, -n*) *m* falcon

Fall (*-(e)s, Fälle*) *m* (*Sturz*) fall; (*Sachverhalt, juristisch*) case; **auf jeden ~, auf alle Fälle**

in any case; (*bestimmt*) definitely; **auf keinen ~** on no account; **für den ~, dass ...** in case ...

Falle (*-, -n*) *f* trap

fallen (*fiel, gefallen*) *vi* to fall; **etw ~ lassen** to drop sth

fällig *adj* due

falls *adv* if; (*für den Fall, dass*) in case

Fallschirm *m* parachute; **Fallschirmspringen** *nt* parachuting, parachute jumping; **Fallschirmspringer(in)** *m(f)* parachutist

falsch *adj* (*unrichtig*) wrong; (*unehrlich, unecht*) false; (*Schmuck*) fake; **~ verbunden** sorry, wrong number; **fälschen** *vt* to forge; **Falschfahrer(in)** *m(f) person driving the wrong way on the motorway*; **Falschgeld** *nt* counterfeit money; **Fälschung** *f* forgery, fake

Faltblatt *nt* leaflet

Falte (*-, -n*) *f* (*Knick*) fold; (*Haut*) wrinkle; (*Rock*) pleat; (*Bügel*) crease; **falten** *vt* to fold; **faltig** *adj* (*zerknittert*) creased; (*Haut, Gesicht*) wrinkled

Familie *f* family; **Familienangehörige(r)** *mf* family member; **Familienname** *m* surname; **Familienstand** *m* marital status

Fan (*-s, -s*) *m* fan

fand *imperf von* **finden**

fangen (*fing, gefangen*) *vt* to catch ▷ *vr* **sich ~** (*nicht fallen*) to steady oneself; (*fig*) to compose oneself

Fantasie *f* imagination

fantastisch *adj* fantastic

Farbbild *nt* colour photograph; **Farbdrucker** *m* colour printer; **Farbe** (*-, -n*) *f* colour; (*zum Malen etc*) paint; (*für Stoff*) dye; **farbecht** *adj* colourfast; **färben** *vt* to colour; (*Stoff, Haar*) to dye; **Farbfernsehen** *nt* colour television; **Farbfilm** *m* colour film; **Farbfoto** *nt* colour photo; **farbig** *adj* coloured; **Farbkopierer** *m* colour copier; **farblos** *adj* colourless; **Farbstoff** *m* dye; (*für Lebensmittel*) colouring

Farn (*-(e)s, -e*) *m* fern

Fasan (*-(e)s, -e(n)*) *m* pheasant

Fasching (*-s, -e*) *m* carnival, Mardi Gras (*US*); **Faschingsdienstag** (*-s, -e*) *m* Shrove Tuesday, Mardi Gras (*US*)

Faschismus *m* fascism

Faser (*-, -n*) *f* fibre

Fass (*-es, Fässer*) *nt* barrel; (*Öl*) drum

fassen *vt* (*ergreifen*) to grasp; (*enthalten*) to hold; (*Entschluss*) to take; (*verstehen*) to understand; **nicht zu ~!** unbelievable ▷ *vr* **sich ~** to compose oneself; **Fassung** *f* (*Umrahmung*) mount; (*Brille*) frame; (*Lampe*) socket; (*Wortlaut*) version; (*Beherrschung*) composure; **jdn aus der ~ bringen** to throw sb; **die ~ verlieren** to lose one's cool

fast *adv* almost, nearly

fasten *vi* to fast; **Fastenzeit** *f* **die ~** (*christlich*) Lent; (*muslimisch*) Ramadan

Fast Food (*-s*) *nt* fast food

Fastnacht *f* (*Fasching*) carnival

fatal *adj* (*verhängnisvoll*) disastrous; (*peinlich*) embarrassing

faul *adj* (*Obst, Gemüse*) rotten; (*Mensch*) lazy; (*Ausreden*) lame; **faulen** *vi* to rot

faulenzen *vi* to do nothing, to hang around; **Faulheit** *f* laziness

faulig *adj* rotten; (*Geruch, Geschmack*) foul

Faust (*-, Fäuste*) *f* fist; **Fausthandschuh** *m* mitten

Fax (*-, -(e)*) *nt* fax; **faxen** *vi, vt* to fax; **Faxgerät** *nt* fax machine; **Faxnummer** *f* fax number

FCKW (*-, -s*) *nt abk =* **Fluorchlorkohlenwasserstoff** CFC

Februar (*-(s), -e*) *m* February; *siehe auch* **Juni**

Fechten *nt* fencing

Feder (*-, -n*) *f* feather; (*Schreibfeder*) (pen-)nib; (*Tech*) spring; **Federball** *m* (*Ball*) shuttlecock; (*Spiel*) badminton; **Federung** *f* suspension

Fee (*-, -n*) *f* fairy

fegen *vi, vt* to sweep

fehl *adj* **~ am Platz** (*o* **Ort**) out of place

fehlen *vi* (*abwesend sein*) to be absent; **etw fehlt jdm** sb lacks sth; **was fehlt ihm?** what's wrong with him?; **du fehlst mir** I miss you; **es fehlt an ...** there's no...

Fehler (*-s, -*) *m* mistake, error; (*Mangel, Schwäche*) fault; **Fehlermeldung** *f* (*Inform*) error message

Fehlzündung *f* (*Auto*) misfire

Feier (*-, -n*) *f* celebration; (*Party*) party; **Feierabend** *m* *end of the working day*; **~ haben** to finish work; **nach ~** after work; **feierlich** *adj* solemn; **feiern** *vt, vi* to celebrate, to have a party; **Feiertag** *m*

holiday; **gesetzlicher ~** public (*o* bank (*Brit*) *o* legal (*US*)) holiday

feig(e) *adj* cowardly

Feige (-, -*n*) *f* fig

Feigling *m* coward

Feile (-, -*n*) *f* file

fein *adj* fine; (*vornehm*) refined; **~!** great!; **das schmeckt ~** that tastes delicious

Feind(in) (-(*e*)*s*, -*e*) *m(f)* enemy; **feindlich** *adj* hostile

Feinkost (-) *f* delicacies *pl*; **Feinkostladen** *m* delicatessen; **Feinschmecker(in)** (-*s*, -) *m(f)* gourmet

Feinwaschmittel *nt* washing powder for delicate fabrics

Feld (-(*e*)*s*, -*er*) *nt* field; (*Schach*) square; (*Sport*) pitch; **Feldsalat** *m* lamb's lettuce; **Feldweg** *m* path across the fields

Felge (-, -*n*) *f* (wheel) rim

Fell (-(*e*)*s*, -*e*) *nt* fur; (*von Schaf*) fleece

Fels (-*en*, -*en*) *m*, **Felsen** (-*s*, -) *m* rock; (*Klippe*) cliff; **felsig** *adj* rocky

feminin *adj* feminine; **Femininum** (-*s*, *Feminina*) *nt* (*Ling*) feminine noun

feministisch *adj* feminist

Fenchel (-*s*, -) *m* fennel

Fenster (-*s*, -) *nt* window; **Fensterbrett** *nt* windowsill; **Fensterladen** *m* shutter; **Fensterplatz** *m* windowseat; **Fensterscheibe** *f* windowpane

Ferien *pl* holidays *pl* (*Brit*), vacation *sing* (*US*); **~ haben/machen** to be/go on holiday (*Brit*) (*o* vacation (*US*)); **Ferienhaus** *nt* holiday (*Brit*) (*o* vacation (*US*)) home; **Ferienkurs** *m* holiday (*Brit*) (*o* vacation (*US*)) course; **Ferienlager** *nt* holiday camp (*Brit*), vacation camp (*US*); (*für Kinder im Sommer*) summer camp; **Ferienort** *m* holiday (*Brit*) (*o* vacation (*US*)) resort; **Ferienwohnung** *f* holiday flat (*Brit*), vacation apartment (*US*)

Ferkel (-*s*, -) *nt* piglet

fern *adj* distant, far-off; **von ~** from a distance; **Fernabfrage** *f* remote-control access; **Fernbedienung** *f* remote control; **Ferne** *f* distance; **aus der ~** from a distance

ferner *adj, adv* further; (*außerdem*) besides

Fernflug *m* long-distance flight; **Ferngespräch** *nt* long-distance call; **ferngesteuert** *adj* remote-controlled; **Fernglas** *nt* binoculars *pl*; **Fernlicht** *nt* full beam (*Brit*), high beam (*US*)

Fernsehapparat *m* TV (set); **fern|sehen** *irr vi* to watch television; **Fernsehen** *nt* television; **im ~** on television; **Fernseher** *m* TV (set); **Fernsehkanal** *m* TV channel; **Fernsehprogramm** *nt* (*Sendung*) TV programme; (*Zeitschrift*) TV guide; **Fernsehserie** *f* TV series *sing*; **Fernsehturm** *m* TV tower; **Fernsehzeitschrift** *f* TV guide

Fernstraße *f* major road; **Ferntourismus** *m* long-haul tourism; **Fernverkehr** *m* long-distance traffic

Ferse (-, -*n*) *f* heel

fertig *adj* (*bereit*) ready; (*beendet*) finished; (*gebrauchsfertig*) ready-made; **~ machen** (*beenden*) to finish; **jdn ~ machen** (*kritisieren*) to give sb hell; (*zur Verzweiflung bringen*) to drive sb mad; (*deprimieren*) to get sb down; **sich ~ machen** to get ready; **mit etw ~ werden** to be able to cope with sth; **auf die Plätze, ~, los!** on your marks, get set, go!; **Fertiggericht** *nt* ready meal

fest *adj* firm; (*Nahrung*) solid; (*Gehalt*) regular; (*Schuhe*) sturdy; (*Schlaf*) sound

Fest (-(*e*)*s*, -*e*) *nt* party; (*Rel*) festival

Festbetrag *m* fixed amount

fest|binden *irr vt* to tie (*an +dat* to); **fest|halten** *irr vt* to hold onto ▷ *vr* **sich ~** to hold on (*an +dat* to)

Festiger (-*s*, -) *m* setting lotion

Festival (-*s*, -*s*) *nt* festival

Festland *nt* mainland; **das europäische ~** the (European) continent

fest|legen *vt* to fix ▷ *vr* **sich ~** to commit oneself

festlich *adj* festive

fest|machen *vt* to fasten; (*Termin etc*) to fix; **fest|nehmen** *irr vt* to arrest; **Festnetz** *nt* (*Tel*) fixed-line network; **Festplatte** *f* (*Inform*) hard disk

fest|setzen *vt* to fix

Festspiele *pl* festival *sing*

fest|stehen *irr vi* to be fixed

fest|stellen *vt* to establish; (*sagen*) to remark

Feststelltaste *f* shift lock

Festung *f* fortress

Festzelt *nt* marquee

Fete (-, -*n*) *f* party

fett *adj* (*dick*) fat; (*Essen etc*) greasy; (*Schrift*) bold; **Fett** (-(*e*)*s*, -*e*) *nt* fat; (*Tech*) grease; **fettarm** *adj* low-fat; **fettig** *adj* fatty; (*schmierig*) greasy

fetzig adj (fam: Musik) funky
feucht adj damp; (Luft) humid;
  Feuchtigkeit f dampness;
  (Luftfeuchtigkeit) humidity;
  Feuchtigkeitscreme f moisturizing
  cream
Feuer (-s, -) nt fire; **haben Sie ~?** have you
  got a light?; **Feueralarm** m fire alarm;
  feuerfest adj fireproof; **feuergefährlich**
  adj inflammable; **Feuerlöscher** (-s, -) m
  fire extinguisher; **Feuermelder** (-s, -) m
  fire alarm; **Feuertreppe** f fire escape;
  Feuerwehr (-, -en) f fire brigade;
  Feuerwehrfrau f firewoman, fire
  fighter; **Feuerwehrmann** m fireman,
  fire fighter; **Feuerwerk** nt fireworks pl;
  Feuerzeug nt (cigarette) lighter
Fichte (-, -n) f spruce
ficken vt, vi (vulg) to fuck
Fieber (-s, -) nt temperature, fever;
  ~ haben to have a high temperature;
  Fieberthermometer nt thermometer
fiel imperf von **fallen**
fies adj (fam) nasty
Figur (-, -en) f figure; (im Schach) piece
Filet (-s, -s) nt fillet; **filetieren** vt to
  fillet; **Filetsteak** nt fillet steak
Filiale (-, -n) f (Comm) branch
Film (-(e)s, -e) m film, movie; **filmen** vt, vi
  to film
Filter (-s, -) m filter; **Filterkaffee** m filter
  coffee; **filtern** vt to filter; **Filterpapier**
  nt filter paper
Filz (-es, -e) m felt; **Filzschreiber** m,
  Filzstift m felt(-tip) pen, felt-tip
Finale (-s, -) nt (Sport) final
Finanzamt nt tax office; **finanziell** adj
  financial; **finanzieren** vt to finance
finden (fand, gefunden) vt to find; (meinen)
  to think; **ich finde nichts dabei, wenn ...**
  I don't see what's wrong if ...; **ich finde es
  gut/schlecht** I like/don't like it ▷ vr **es
  fanden sich nur wenige Helfer** there
  were only a few helpers
fing imperf von **fangen**
Finger (-s, -) m finger; **Fingerabdruck** m
  fingerprint; **Fingerhandschuh** m glove;
  Fingernagel m fingernail
Fink (-en, -en) m finch
Finne (-n, -n) m, **Finnin** f Finn, Finnish
  man/woman; **finnisch** adj Finnish;
  Finnisch nt Finnish; **Finnland** nt Finland
finster adj dark; (verdächtig) dubious;

(verdrossen) grim; (Gedanke) dark;
  Finsternis f darkness
Firewall (-, -s) f (Inform) firewall
Firma (-, Firmen) f firm
Fisch (-(e)s, -e) m fish; **~e** pl (Astr) Pisces
  sing; **fischen** vt, vi to fish; **Fischer(in)**
  (-s, -) m(f) fisherman/-woman;
  Fischerboot nt fishing boat; **Fischgericht**
  nt fish dish; **Fischhändler(in)** m(f)
  fishmonger; **Fischstäbchen** nt fish
  finger (Brit) (o stick (US))
Fisole (-, -n) f French bean
fit adj fit; **Fitness** (-) f fitness;
  Fitnesscenter (-s, -) nt fitness centre
fix adj (schnell) quick; **~ und fertig**
  exhausted
fixen vi (fam) to shoot up; **Fixer(in)** (-s, -)
  m(f) (fam) junkie
FKK f abk = **Freikörperkultur** nudism;
  FKK-Strand m nudist beach
flach adj flat; (Gewässer; Teller) shallow; **~er
  Absatz** low heel; **Flachbildschirm** m flat
  screen
Fläche (-, -n) f area; (Oberfläche) surface
Flagge (-, -n) f flag
flambiert adj flambé(ed)
Flamme (-, -n) f flame
Flanell (-s) m flannel
Flasche (-, -n) f bottle; **eine ~ sein** (fam)
  to be useless; **Flaschenbier** nt bottled
  beer; **Flaschenöffner** m bottle opener;
  Flaschenpfand nt deposit;
  Flaschentomate f plum tomato
flatterhaft adj fickle; **flattern** vi to
  flutter
flauschig adj fluffy
Flausen pl (fam) daft ideas pl
Flaute (-, -n) f calm; (Comm) recession
Flechte (-, -n) f plait; (Med) scab; (Bot)
  lichen; **flechten** (flocht, geflochten) vt to
  plait; (Kranz) to bind
Fleck (-(e)s, -e) m, **Flecken** (-s, -) m spot;
  (Schmutz) stain; (Stoff~) patch; (Makel)
  blemish; **Fleckentferner** (-s, -) m stain
  remover; **fleckig** adj spotted; (mit
  Schmutzflecken) stained
Fledermaus f bat
Fleisch (-(e)s) nt flesh; (Essen) meat;
  Fleischbrühe f meat stock; **Fleischer(in)**
  (-s, -) m(f) butcher; **Fleischerei** f
  butcher's (shop); **Fleischtomate** f beef
  tomato
fleißig adj diligent, hard-working

flexibel adj flexible
flicken vt to mend; **Flickzeug** nt repair kit
Flieder (-s, -) m lilac
Fliege (-, -n) f fly; (Krawatte) bow tie
fliegen (flog, geflogen) vt, vi to fly
Fliese (-, -n) f tile
Fließband nt conveyor belt; (als Einrichtung) production (o assembly) line; **fließen** (floss, geflossen) vi to flow; **fließend** adj (Rede, Deutsch) fluent; (Übergänge) smooth; **~(es) Wasser** running water
Flipper (-s, -) m pinball machine; **flippern** vi to play pinball
flippig adj (fam) eccentric
flirten vi to flirt
Flitterwochen pl honeymoon sing
flocht imperf von **flechten**
Flocke (-, -n) f flake
flog imperf von **fliegen**
Floh (-(e)s, Flöhe) m flea; **Flohmarkt** m flea market
Flop (-s, -s) m flop
Floskel (-, -n) f empty phrase
floss imperf von **fließen**
Floß (-es, Flöße) nt raft
Flosse (-, -n) f fin; (Schwimmflosse) flipper
Flöte (-, -n) f flute; (Blockflöte) recorder
flott adj lively; (elegant) smart; (Naut) afloat
Fluch (-(e)s, Flüche) m curse; **fluchen** vi to swear, to curse
Flucht (-, -en) f flight; **flüchten** vi to flee (vor +dat from); **flüchtig** adj **ich kenne ihn nur ~** I don't know him very well at all; **Flüchtling** m refugee
Flug (-(e)s, Flüge) m flight; **Flugbegleiter(in)** (-s, -) m(f) flight attendant; **Flugblatt** nt leaflet
Flügel (-s, -) m wing; (Mus) grand piano
Fluggast m passenger (on a plane); **Fluggesellschaft** f airline; **Flughafen** m airport; **Fluglotse** m air-traffic controller; **Flugnummer** f flight number; **Flugplan** m flight schedule; **Flugplatz** m airport; (klein) airfield; **Flugschein** m plane ticket; **Flugschreiber** m flight recorder, black box; **Flugsteig** (-s, -e) m gate; **Flugstrecke** f air route; **Flugticket** nt plane ticket; **Flugverbindung** f flight connection; **Flugverkehr** m air traffic; **Flugzeit** f flying time; **Flugzeug** nt plane; **Flugzeugentführung** f hijacking

Flunder (-, -n) f flounder
Fluor (-s) nt fluorine
Flur (-(e)s, -e) m hall
Fluss (-es, Flüsse) m river; (Fließen) flow
flüssig adj liquid; **Flüssigkeit** f liquid
flüstern vt, vi to whisper
Flut (-, -en) f (a. fig) flood; (Gezeiten) high tide; **Flutlicht** nt floodlight
Fohlen (-s, -) nt foal
Föhn (-(e)s, -e) m hairdryer; (Wind) foehn; **föhnen** vt to dry; (beim Friseur) to blow-dry
Folge (-, -n) f (Reihe, Serie) series sing; (Aufeinanderfolge) sequence; (Fortsetzung eines Romans) instalment; (Fortsetzung einer Fernsehserie) episode; (Auswirkung) result; **etw zur ~ haben** to result in sth; **~n haben** to have consequences; **folgen** vi to follow (jdm sb); (gehorchen) to obey (jdm sb); **jdm ~ können** (fig) to be able to follow sb; **folgend** adj following; **folgendermaßen** adv as follows; **folglich** adv consequently
Folie f foil; (für Projektor) transparency
Fön® m siehe **Föhn**
Fondue (-s, -s) nt fondue
fönen vt siehe **föhnen**
fordern vt to demand
fördern vt to promote; (unterstützen) to help
Forderung f demand
Forelle f trout
Form (-, -en) f form; (Gestalt) shape; (Gussform) mould; (Backform) baking tin (Brit) (o pan (US)); **in ~ sein** to be in good form; **Formalität** f formality; **Format** nt format; **von internationalem ~** of international standing; **formatieren** vt (Diskette) to format; (Text) to edit
Formblatt nt form; **formen** vt to form, to shape; **förmlich** adj formal; (buchstäblich) real; **formlos** adj informal; **Formular** (-s, -e) nt form; **formulieren** vt to formulate
forschen vi to search (nach for); (wissenschaftlich) to (do) research; **Forscher(in)** m(f) researcher; **Forschung** f research
Förster(in) (-s, -) m(f) forester; (für Wild) gamekeeper
fort adv away; (verschwunden) gone; **fort|bewegen** vt to move away ▷ vr **sich ~** to move; **Fortbildung** f further

education; (*im Beruf*) further training;
fort|fahren *irr vi* to go away;
(*weitermachen*) to continue; **fort|gehen** *irr*
vi to go away; **fortgeschritten** *adj*
advanced; **Fortpflanzung** *f* reproduction
Fortschritt *m* progress; **~e machen** to
make progress; **fortschrittlich** *adj*
progressive
fort|setzen *vt* to continue; **Fortsetzung**
f continuation; (*folgender Teil*) instalment;
~ folgt to be continued
Foto (*-s, -s*) *nt* photo ▷ (*-s, -s*) *m*
(*Fotoapparat*) camera; **Fotograf(in)** (*-en*,
-en) *m(f)* photographer; **Fotografie** *f*
photography; (*Bild*) photograph;
fotografieren *vt* to photograph ▷ *vi* to
take photographs; **Fotokopie** *f*
photocopy; **fotokopieren** *vt* to
photocopy
Foul (*-s, -s*) *nt* foul
Foyer (*-s, -s*) *nt* foyer
Fr. *f abk* = **Frau** Mrs; (*unverheiratet, neutral*) Ms
Fracht (*-, -en*) *f* freight; (*Naut*) cargo; (*Preis*)
carriage; **Frachter** (*-s, -*) *m* freighter
Frack (*-(e)s, Fräcke*) *m* tails *pl*
Frage (*-, -n*) *f* question; **das ist eine ~ der**
Zeit that's a matter (*o* question) of time;
das kommt nicht in ~ that's out of the
question; **Fragebogen** *m* questionnaire;
fragen *vt, vi* to ask; **Fragezeichen** *nt*
question mark; **fragwürdig** *adj* dubious
Franken (*-s, -*) *m* (*Schweizer Währung*)
Swiss franc ▷ (*-s*) *nt* (*Land*) Franconia
frankieren *vt* to stamp; (*maschinell*) to
frank
Frankreich (*-s*) *nt* France; **Franzose** (*-n*,
-n) *m*, **Französin** *f* Frenchman/-woman;
die ~n *pl* the French *pl*; **französisch** *adj*
French; **Französisch** *nt* French
fraß *imperf von* **fressen**
Frau (*-, -en*) *f* woman; (*Ehefrau*) wife;
(*Anrede*) Mrs; (*unverheiratet, neutral*) Ms;
Frauenarzt *m*, **Frauenärztin** *f*
gynaecologist; **Frauenbewegung** *f*
women's movement; **frauenfeindlich** *adj*
misogynous; **Frauenhaus** *nt* refuge (for
battered women)
Fräulein *nt* (*junge Dame*) young lady;
(*veraltet als Anrede*) Miss
Freak (*-s, -s*) *m* (*fam*) freak
frech *adj* cheeky; **Frechheit** *f* cheek; **so**
eine ~! what a cheek
Freeclimbing (*-s*) *nt* free climbing

frei *adj* free; (*Straße*) clear; (*Mitarbeiter*)
freelance; **ein ~er Tag** a day off; **~e**
Arbeitsstelle vacancy; **Zimmer ~** room(s)
to let (*Brit*), room(s) for rent (*US*); **im**
Freien in the open air; **Freibad** *nt*
open-air (swimming) pool; **freiberuflich**
adj freelance; **freig(i)ebig** *adj* generous;
Freiheit *f* freedom; **Freikarte** *f* free
ticket; **frei|lassen** *irr vt* to (set) free
freilich *adv* of course
Freilichtbühne *f* open-air theatre;
frei|machen *vr* **sich ~** to undress;
frei|nehmen *irr vt* **sich** (*dat*) **einen**
Tag ~ to take a day off; **Freisprechanlage**
f hands-free phone; **Freistoß** *m* free
kick
Freitag *m* Friday; *siehe auch* **Mittwoch**;
freitags *adv* on Fridays; *siehe auch*
mittwochs
freiwillig *adj* voluntary
Freizeichen *nt* (*Tel*) ringing tone
Freizeit *f* spare (*o* free) time;
Freizeithemd *nt* sports shirt;
Freizeitkleidung *f* leisure wear;
Freizeitpark *m* leisure park
fremd *adj* (*nicht vertraut*) strange;
(*ausländisch*) foreign; (*nicht eigen*) someone
else's; **Fremde(r)** *mf* (*Unbekannter*)
stranger; (*Ausländer*) foreigner;
fremdenfeindlich *adj* anti-foreigner,
xenophobic; **Fremdenführer(in)** *m(f)*
(*tourist*) guide; **Fremdenverkehr** *m*
tourism; **Fremdenverkehrsamt** *nt*
tourist information office;
Fremdenzimmer *nt* (*guest*) room;
Fremdsprache *f* foreign language;
Fremdsprachenkenntnisse *pl*
knowledge *sing* of foreign languages;
Fremdwort *nt* foreign word
Frequenz *f* (*Radio*) frequency
fressen (*fraß, gefressen*) *vt, vi* (*Tier*) to eat;
(*Mensch*) to guzzle
Freude (*-, -n*) *f* joy, delight; **freuen** *vt* to
please; **es freut mich, dass ...** I'm pleased
that ... ▷ *vr* **sich ~** to be pleased (*über +akk*
about); **sich auf etw** (*akk*) **~** to look
forward to sth
Freund (*-(e)s, -e*) *m* friend; (*in Beziehung*)
boyfriend; **Freundin** *f* friend; (*in*
Beziehung) girlfriend; **freundlich** *adj*
friendly; (*liebenswürdig*) kind;
freundlicherweise *adv* kindly;
Freundlichkeit *f* friendliness;

(*Liebenswürdigkeit*) kindness;
Freundschaft *f* friendship
Frieden (*-s, -*) *m* peace; **Friedhof** *m*
cemetery; **friedlich** *adj* peaceful
frieren (*fror, gefroren*) *vt, vi* to freeze; **ich
friere, es friert mich** I'm freezing
Frikadelle *f* rissole
Frisbeescheibe® *f* frisbee®
frisch *adj* fresh; (*lebhaft*) lively;
„**~ gestrichen"** 'wet paint'; **sich ~ machen**
to freshen up; **Frischhaltefolie** *f*
clingfilm® (*Brit*), plastic wrap (*US*);
Frischkäse *m* cream cheese
Friseur *m*, **Friseuse** *f* hairdresser;
frisieren *vt* **jdn ~** to do sb's hair ▷ *vr* **sich
~** to do one's hair; **Frisör** (*-s, -e*) *m*,
Frisöse (*-, -n*) *f* hairdresser
Frist (*-, -en*) *f* period; (*Zeitpunkt*) deadline;
**innerhalb einer ~ von zehn
Tagen** within a ten-day period; **eine
~ einhalten** to meet a deadline; **die ~ ist
abgelaufen** the deadline has expired;
fristgerecht *adj, adv* within the specified
time; **fristlos** *adj* **~e Entlassung**
dismissal without notice
Frisur *f* hairdo, hairstyle
frittieren *vt* to deep-fry
Frl. *f abk* = **Fräulein** Miss
froh *adj* happy; **~e Weihnachten!** Merry
Christmas
fröhlich *adj* happy, cheerful
Fronleichnam (*-(e)s*) *m* Corpus Christi
frontal *adj* frontal;
Frontalzusammenstoß *m* head-on
collision
fror *imperf von* **frieren**
Frosch (*-(e)s, Frösche*) *m* frog
Frost (*-(e)s, Fröste*) *m* frost; **bei ~** in frosty
weather; **Frostschutzmittel** *nt*
anti-freeze
Frottee *nt* terry(cloth); **frottieren** *vt*
to rub down; **Frottier(hand)tuch** *nt*
towel
Frucht (*-, Früchte*) *f* (*a. fig*) fruit; (*Getreide*)
corn; **Fruchteis** *nt* fruit-flavoured
ice-cream; **Früchtetee** *m* fruit tea;
fruchtig *adj* fruity; **Fruchtpresse** *f*
juicer; **Fruchtsaft** *m* fruit juice;
Fruchtsalat *m* fruit salad
früh *adj, adv* early; **heute ~** this morning;
um fünf Uhr ~ at five (o'clock) in the
morning; **~ genug** soon enough; **früher**
adj earlier; (*ehemalig*) former ▷ *adv*

formerly, in the past; **frühestens** *adv* at
the earliest
Frühjahr *nt*, **Frühling** *m* spring;
Frühlingsrolle *f* spring roll;
Frühlingszwiebel *f* spring onion (*Brit*),
scallion (*US*)
frühmorgens *adv* early in the morning
Frühschicht *f* **~ haben** to be on the early
shift
Frühstück *nt* breakfast; **frühstücken** *vi*
to have breakfast; **Frühstücksbüfett** *nt*
breakfast buffet; **Frühstücksfernsehen**
nt breakfast television; **Frühstücksspeck**
m bacon
frühzeitig *adj* early
Frust (*-s*) *m* (*fam*) frustration; **frustrieren**
vt to frustrate
Fuchs (*-es, Füchse*) *m* fox
fühlen *vt, vi* to feel ▷ *vr* **sich ~** to feel
fuhr *imperf von* **fahren**
führen *vt* to lead; (*Geschäft*) to run; (*Name*)
to bear; (*Buch*) to keep ▷ *vi* to lead, to be
in the lead ▷ *vr* **sich ~** to behave;
Führerschein *m* driving licence (*Brit*),
driver's license (*US*); **Führung** *f*
leadership; (*eines Unternehmens*)
management; (*Mil*) command; (*in Museum,
Stadt*) guided tour; **in ~ liegen** to be in the
lead
füllen *vt* to fill; (*Gastr*) to stuff ▷ *vr* **sich
~** to fill
Füller (*-s, -*) *m*, **Füllfederhalter** (*-s, -*) *m*
fountain pen
Füllung *f* filling
Fund (*-(e)s, -e*) *m* find; **Fundbüro** *nt* lost
property office (*Brit*), lost and found (*US*);
Fundsachen *pl* lost property *sing*
fünf *num* five; **Fünf** (*-, -en*) *f* five;
(*Schulnote*) ≈ E; **fünfhundert** *num* five
hundred; **fünfmal** *adv* five times;
fünfte(r, s) *adj* fifth; *siehe auch* **dritte**;
Fünftel (*-s, -*) *nt* (*Bruchteil*) fifth; **fünfzehn**
num fifteen; **fünfzehnte(r, s)** *adj*
fifteenth; *siehe auch* **dritte**; **fünfzig** *num*
fifty; **fünfzigste(r, s)** *adj* fiftieth
Funk (*-s*) *m* radio; **über ~** by radio
Funke (*-ns, -n*) *m* spark; **funkeln** *vi* to
sparkle
Funkgerät *nt* radio set; **Funktaxi** *nt*
radio taxi, radio cab
Funktion *f* function; **funktionieren** *vi* to
work, to function; **Funktionstaste** *f*
(*Inform*) function key

für *prep +akk* for; **was ~ (ein) ...?** what kind
(*o* sort) of ...?; **Tag ~ Tag** day after day

Furcht (-) *f* fear; **furchtbar** *adj* terrible;
fürchten *vt* to be afraid of, to fear ▷ *vr*
sich ~ to be afraid (*vor +dat* of);
fürchterlich *adj* awful

füreinander *adv* for each other

fürs *kontr von* **für das**

Fürst(in) (-en, -en) *m(f)* prince/princess;
Fürstentum *nt* principality; **fürstlich** *adj*
(*fig*) splendid

Furunkel (-s, -) *nt* boil

Furz (-es, -e) *m* (*vulg*) fart; **furzen** *vi* (*vulg*)
to fart

Fuß (-es, Füße) *m* foot; (*von Glas, Säule etc*)
base; (*von Möbel*) leg; **zu ~** on foot; **zu
~ gehen** to walk; **Fußball** *m* football (*Brit*),
soccer; **Fußballmannschaft** *f* football
(*Brit*) (*o* soccer) team; **Fußballplatz** *m*
football pitch (*Brit*), soccer field (*US*);
Fußballspiel *nt* football (*Brit*) (*o* soccer)
match; **Fußballspieler(in)** *m(f)*
footballer (*Brit*), soccer player; **Fußboden**
m floor; **Fußgänger(in)** (-s, -) *m(f)*
pedestrian; **Fußgängerüberweg** *m*
pedestrian crossing (*Brit*), crosswalk (*US*);
Fußgängerzone *f* pedestrian precinct
(*Brit*) (*o* zone (*US*)); **Fußgelenk** *nt* ankle;
Fußpilz *m* athlete's foot; **Fußtritt** *m*
kick; **jdm einen ~ geben** to give sb a kick,
to kick sb; **Fußweg** *m* footpath

Futon (-s, -s) *m* futon

futsch *adj* (*fam: kaputt*) broken;
(*zerschlagen*) smashed; (*weg, verloren*) gone

Futter (-s, -) *nt* feed; (*Heu etc*) fodder;
(*Stoff*) lining; **füttern** *vt* to feed; (*Kleidung*)
to line

Futur (-s, -e) *nt* (*Ling*) future (tense)

Fuzzi (-s, -s) *m* (*fam*) guy

f

nt daisy; **Gänsehaut** *f* goose pimples *pl* (*Brit*), goose bumps *pl* (*US*)

ganz *adj* whole; (*vollständig*) complete; **~ Europa** all of Europe; **sein ~es Geld** all his money; **den ~en Tag** all day; **die ~e Zeit** all the time ▷ *adv* quite; (*völlig*) completely; **es hat mir ~ gut gefallen** I quite liked it; **~ schön viel** quite a lot; **~ und gar nicht** not at all; **das ist etwas ~ anderes** that's a completely different matter; **ganztägig** *adj* all-day; (*Arbeit, Stelle*) full-time

gar *adj* done, cooked ▷ *adv* at all; **~ nicht/nichts/keiner** not/nothing/nobody at all; **~ nicht schlecht** not bad at all

Garage (-, -n) *f* garage

Garantie *f* guarantee; **garantieren** *vt* to guarantee

Garderobe (-, -n) *f* (*Kleidung*) wardrobe; (*Abgabe*) cloakroom

Gardine *f* curtain

Garn (-(e)s, -e) *nt* thread

Garnele (-, -n) *f* shrimp

garnieren *vt* to decorate; (*Speisen*) to garnish

Garten (-s, Gärten) *m* garden; **Gärtner(in)** (-s, -) *m(f)* gardener; **Gärtnerei** *f* nursery; (*Gemüsegärtnerei*) market garden (*Brit*), truck farm (*US*)

Garzeit *f* cooking time

Gas (-es, -e) *nt* gas; **~ geben** (*Auto*) to accelerate; (*fig*) to get a move on; **Gasanzünder** *m* gas lighter; **Gasbrenner** *m* gas burner; **Gasflasche** *f* gas bottle; **Gasheizung** *f* gas heating; **Gasherd** *m* gas stove, gas cooker (*Brit*); **Gaskocher** *m* camping stove; **Gaspedal** *nt* accelerator, gas pedal (*US*)

Gasse (-, -n) *f* alley

Gast (-es, Gäste) *m* guest; **Gäste haben** to have guests; **Gastarbeiter(in)** *m(f)* foreign worker; **Gästebett** *nt* spare bed; **Gästebuch** *nt* visitors' book; **Gästehaus** *nt* guest house; **Gästezimmer** *nt* guest room; **gastfreundlich** *adj* hospitable; **Gastgeber(in)** (-s, -) *m(f)* host/hostess; **Gasthaus** *nt*, **Gasthof** *m* inn; **Gastland** *nt* host country

Gastritis (-) *f* gastritis

Gastronomie *f* (*Gewerbe*) catering trade

Gastspiel *nt* (*Sport*) away game; **Gaststätte** *f* restaurant; (*Trinklokal*) pub

---

gab *imperf von* **geben**

Gabe (-, -n) *f* gift

Gabel (-, -n) *f* fork; **Gabelung** *f* fork

gaffen *vi* to gape

Gage (-, -n) *f* fee

gähnen *vi* to yawn

Galerie *f* gallery

Galle (-, -n) *f* gall; (*Organ*) gall bladder; **Gallenstein** *m* gallstone

Galopp (-s) *m* gallop; **galoppieren** *vi* to gallop

galt *imperf von* **gelten**

Gameboy® (-s, -s) *m* Gameboy®

gammeln *vi* to loaf (*o hang*) around; **Gammler(in)** (-s, -) *m(f)* layabout

gang *adj* **~ und gäbe sein** to be quite normal

Gang (-(e)s, Gänge) *m* walk; (*im Flugzeug*) aisle; (*Essen, Ablauf*) course; (*Flur etc*) corridor; (*Durchgang*) passage; (*Auto*) gear; **den zweiten ~ einlegen** to change into second (gear); **etw in ~ bringen** to get sth going; **Gangschaltung** *f* gears *pl*; **Gangway** (-, -s) *f* (*Aviat*) steps *pl*; (*Naut*) gangway

Gans (-, Gänse) *f* goose; **Gänseblümchen**

(*Brit*), bar; **Gastwirt(in)** *m(f)* landlord/
-lady

GAU (*-s, -s*) *m akr* = **größter
anzunehmender Unfall** MCA

Gaumen (*-s, -*) *m* palate

Gaze (*-, -n*) *f* gauze

geb. *adj abk* = **geboren** b. ▷ *adj abk* =
geborene née; *siehe* **geboren**

Gebäck (*-(e)s, -e*) *nt* pastries *pl*; (*Kekse*)
biscuits *pl* (*Brit*), cookies *pl* (*US*)

gebacken *pp von* **backen**

Gebärdensprache *f* sign language

Gebärmutter *f* womb

Gebäude (*-s, -*) *nt* building

geben (*gab, gegeben*) *vt, vi* to give (*jdm etw*
sb sth, sth to sb); (*Karten*) to deal; **lass dir
eine Quittung ~** ask for a receipt ▷ *vt
impers* **es gibt** there is/are; (*in Zukunft*)
there will be; **das gibt's nicht** I don't
believe it ▷ *vr* **sich ~** (*sich verhalten*) to
behave, to act; **das gibt sich wieder** it'll
sort itself out

Gebet (*-(e)s, -e*) *nt* prayer

gebeten *pp von* **bitten**

Gebiet (*-(e)s, -e*) *nt* area; (*Hoheitsgebiet*)
territory; (*fig*) field

gebildet *adj* educated; (*belesen*) well-read

Gebirge (*-s, -*) *nt* mountains *pl*; **gebirgig**
adj mountainous

Gebiss (*-es, -e*) *nt* teeth *pl*; (*künstlich*)
dentures *pl*; **gebissen** *pp von* **beißen**;
Gebissreiniger *m* denture tablets *pl*

Gebläse (*-s, -*) *nt* fan, blower

geblasen *pp von* **blasen**

geblieben *pp von* **bleiben**

gebogen *pp von* **biegen**

geboren *pp von* **gebären** ▷ *adj* born;
Andrea Jordan, ~e Christian Andrea
Jordan, née Christian

geborgen *pp von* **bergen** ▷ *adj* secure,
safe

geboten *pp von* **bieten**

gebracht *pp von* **bringen**

gebrannt *pp von* **brennen**

gebraten *pp von* **braten**

gebrauchen *vt* to use;
Gebrauchsanweisung *f* directions *pl* for
use; **gebrauchsfertig** *adj* ready to use;
gebraucht *adj* used; **etw ~ kaufen** to buy
sth secondhand; **Gebrauchtwagen** *m*
secondhand (*o* used) car

gebräunt *adj* tanned

gebrochen *pp von* **brechen**

Gebühr (*-, -en*) *f* charge; (*Maut*) toll;
(*Honorar*) fee; **Gebühreneinheit** *f* (*Tel*)
unit; **gebührenfrei** *adj* free of charge;
(*Telefonnummer*) freefone® (*Brit*), toll-free
(*US*); **gebührenpflichtig** *adj* subject to
charges; **~e Straße** toll road

gebunden *pp von* **binden**

Geburt (*-, -en*) *f* birth; **gebürtig** *adj* **er ist
~er Schweizer** he is Swiss by birth;
Geburtsdatum *nt* date of birth;
Geburtsjahr *nt* year of birth;
Geburtsname *m* birth name; (*einer Frau*)
maiden name; **Geburtsort** *m* birthplace;
Geburtstag *m* birthday; **herzlichen
Glückwunsch zum ~!** Happy Birthday;
Geburtsurkunde *f* birth certificate

Gebüsch (*-(e)s, -e*) *nt* bushes *pl*

gedacht *pp von* **denken**

Gedächtnis *nt* memory; **im ~ behalten**
to remember

Gedanke (*-ns, -n*) *m* thought; **sich** (*dat*)
über etw (*akk*) **~n machen** to think about
sth; (*besorgt*) to be worried about sth;
Gedankenstrich *m* dash

Gedeck (*-(e)s, -e*) *nt* place setting;
(*Speisenfolge*) set meal

Gedenkstätte *f* memorial; **Gedenktafel**
f commemorative plaque

Gedicht (*-(e)s, -e*) *nt* poem

Gedränge (*-s*) *nt* crush, crowd

gedrungen *pp von* **dringen**

Geduld (*-*) *f* patience; **geduldig** *adj*
patient

gedurft *pp von* **dürfen**

geehrt *adj* **Sehr ~er Herr Young** Dear Mr
Young

geeignet *adj* suitable

Gefahr (*-, -en*) *f* danger; **auf eigene ~** at
one's own risk; **außer ~** out of danger;
gefährden *vt* to endanger

gefahren *pp von* **fahren**

gefährlich *adj* dangerous

Gefälle (*-s, -*) *nt* gradient, slope

gefallen *pp von* **fallen** ▷ *irr vi* **jdm ~** to
please sb; **er/es gefällt mir** I like him/it;
sich (*dat*) **etw ~ lassen** to put up with
sth

Gefallen (*-s, -*) *m* favour; **jdm einen ~ tun**
to do sb a favour

gefälligst *adv* ..., will you!; **sei ~ still!** be
quiet, will you!

gefangen *pp von* **fangen**

Gefängnis *nt* prison

Gefäß (-es, -e) nt (Behälter) container, receptacle; (Anat, Bot) vessel

gefasst adj composed, calm; **auf etw** (akk) **~ sein** to be prepared (o ready) for sth

geflochten pp von **flechten**

geflogen pp von **fliegen**

geflossen pp von **fließen**

Geflügel (-s) nt poultry

gefragt adj in demand

gefressen pp von **fressen**

Gefrierbeutel m freezer bag; **gefrieren** irr vi to freeze; **Gefrierfach** nt freezer compartment; **Gefrierschrank** m (upright) freezer; **Gefriertruhe** f (chest) freezer

gefroren pp von **frieren**

Gefühl (-(e)s, -e) nt feeling

gefunden pp von **finden**

gegangen pp von **gehen**

gegeben pp von **geben**; **gegebenenfalls** adv if need be

⭕ SCHLÜSSELWORT

gegen präp +akk **1** against; **nichts gegen jdn haben** to have nothing against sb; **X gegen Y** (Sport, Jur) X versus Y; **ein Mittel gegen Schnupfen** something for colds

2 (in Richtung auf) towards; **gegen Osten** to(wards) the east; **gegen Abend** towards evening; **gegen einen Baum fahren** to drive into a tree

3 (ungefähr) round about; **gegen 3 Uhr** around 3 o'clock

4 (gegenüber) towards (ungefähr) around; **gerecht gegen alle** fair to all

5 (im Austausch für) for; **gegen bar** for cash; **gegen Quittung** against a receipt

6 (verglichen mit) compared with

Gegend (-, -en) f area; **hier in der ~** around here

gegeneinander adv against one another

Gegenfahrbahn f opposite lane; **Gegenmittel** nt remedy (gegen for); **Gegenrichtung** f opposite direction; **Gegensatz** m contrast; **im ~ zu** in contrast to; **gegensätzlich** adj conflicting; **gegenseitig** adj mutual; **sich ~ helfen** to help each other

Gegenstand m object; (Thema) subject

Gegenteil nt opposite; **im ~** on the contrary; **gegenteilig** adj opposite, contrary

gegenüber prep +dat opposite; (zu jdm) to(wards); (angesichts) in the face of ▷ adv opposite; **gegenüber|stehen** vt to face; (Problemen) to be faced with; **gegenüber|stellen** vt to confront (dat with); (fig) compare (dat with)

Gegenverkehr m oncoming traffic; **Gegenwart** (-) f present (tense)

Gegenwind m headwind

gegessen pp von **essen**

geglichen pp von **gleichen**

geglitten pp von **gleiten**

Gegner(in) (-s, -) m(f) opponent

gegolten pp von **gelten**

gegossen pp von **gießen**

gegraben pp von **graben**

gegriffen pp von **greifen**

gehabt pp von **haben**

Gehackte(s) nt mince(d meat) (Brit), ground meat (US)

Gehalt (-(e)s, -e) m content ▷ (-(e)s, Gehälter) nt salary

gehalten pp von **halten**

gehangen pp von **hängen**

gehässig adj spiteful, nasty

gehauen pp von **hauen**

gehbehindert adj **sie ist ~** she can't walk properly

geheim adj secret; **etw ~ halten** to keep sth secret; **Geheimnis** nt secret; (rätselhaft) mystery; **geheimnisvoll** adj mysterious; **Geheimnummer** f, **Geheimzahl** f (von Kreditkarte) PIN number

geheißen pp von **heißen**

gehen (ging, gegangen) vt, vi to go; (zu Fuß) to walk; (funktionieren) to work; **über die Straße ~** to cross the street; **~ nach** (Fenster) to face

▷ vi impers **wie geht es (dir)?** how are you (o things)?; **mir/ihm geht es gut** I'm/he's (doing) fine; **geht das?** is that possible?; **geht's noch?** can you still manage?; **es geht** not too bad, OK; **das geht nicht** that's not on; **es geht um ...** it's about ...

Gehirn (-(e)s, -e) nt brain; **Gehirnerschütterung** f concussion

gehoben pp von **heben**

geholfen pp von **helfen**

Gehör (-(e)s) nt hearing

gehorchen vi to obey (jdm sb)

gehören vi to belong (jdm to sb); **wem gehört das Buch?** whose book is this?; **gehört es dir?** is it yours? ▷ vr impers **das gehört sich nicht** it's not done

gehörlos adj deaf

gehorsam adj obedient

Gehsteig m

Gehweg (-s, -e) m pavement (Brit), sidewalk (US)

Geier (-s, -) m vulture

Geige (-, -n) f violin

geil adj randy (Brit), horny (US); (fam: toll) fantastic

Geisel (-, -n) f hostage

Geist (-(e)s, -er) m spirit; (Gespenst) ghost; (Verstand) mind; **Geisterbahn** f ghost train, tunnel of horror (US); **Geisterfahrer(in)** m(f) person driving the wrong way on the motorway

geizig adj stingy

gekannt pp von **kennen**

geklungen pp von **klingen**

geknickt adj (fig) dejected

gekniffen pp von **kneifen**

gekommen pp von **kommen**

gekonnt pp von **können** ▷ adj skilful

gekrochen pp von **kriechen**

Gel (-s, -s) nt gel

Gelächter (-s, -) nt laughter

geladen pp von **laden** ▷ adj loaded; (Elek) live; (fig) furious

gelähmt adj paralysed

Gelände (-s, -) nt land, terrain; (Fabrik, Sportgelände) grounds pl; (Baugelände) site

Geländer (-s, -) nt railing; (Treppengeländer) banister

Geländewagen m off-road vehicle

gelang imperf von **gelingen**

gelassen pp von **lassen** ▷ adj calm, composed

Gelatine f gelatine

gelaufen pp von **laufen**

gelaunt adj **gut/schlecht ~** in a good/bad mood

gelb adj yellow; (Ampel) amber, yellow (US); **gelblich** adj yellowish; **Gelbsucht** f jaundice

Geld (-(e)s, -er) nt money; **Geldautomat** m cash machine (o dispenser (Brit)), ATM (US); **Geldbeutel** m, **Geldbörse** f purse;

Geldbuße f fine; **Geldschein** m (bank)note (Brit), bill (US); **Geldstrafe** f fine; **Geldstück** nt coin; **Geldwechsel** m exchange of money; (Ort) bureau de change; **Geldwechselautomat** m, **Geldwechsler** (-s, -) m change machine

Gelee (-s, -s) nt jelly

gelegen pp von **liegen** ▷ adj situated; (passend) convenient; **etw kommt jdm ~** sth is convenient for sb

Gelegenheit f opportunity; (Anlass) occasion

gelegentlich adj occasional ▷ adv occasionally; (bei Gelegenheit) some time (or other)

Gelenk (-(e)s, -e) nt joint

gelernt adj skilled

gelesen pp von **lesen**

geliehen pp von **leihen**

gelingen (gelang, gelungen) vi to succeed; **es ist mir gelungen, ihn zu erreichen** I managed to get hold of him

gelitten pp von **leiden**

gelockt adj curly

gelogen pp von **lügen**

gelten (galt, gegolten) vt (wert sein) to be worth; **jdm viel/wenig ~** to mean a lot/not to mean much to sb ▷ vi (gültig sein) to be valid; (erlaubt sein) to be allowed; **jdm ~** (gemünzt sein auf) to be meant for (o aimed at) sb; **etw ~ lassen** to accept sth; **als etw ~** to be considered to be sth; **Geltungsdauer** f **eine ~ von fünf Tagen haben** to be valid for five days

gelungen pp von **gelingen**

gemahlen pp von **mahlen**

Gemälde (-s, -) nt painting, picture

gemäß prep +dat in accordance with ▷ adj appropriate (dat to)

gemein adj (niederträchtig) mean, nasty; (gewöhnlich) common

Gemeinde (-, -n) f district, community; (Pfarrgemeinde) parish; (Kirchengemeinde) congregation

gemeinsam adj joint, common ▷ adv together, jointly; **das Haus gehört uns beiden ~** the house belongs to both of us

Gemeinschaft f community; **~ Unabhängiger Staaten** Commonwealth of Independent States

gemeint pp von **meinen**; **das war nicht so ~** I didn't mean it like that

gemessen pp von **messen**

gemieden pp von **meiden**

gemischt adj mixed

gemocht pp von **mögen**

Gemüse (-s, -) nt vegetables pl;
Gemüsehändler(in) m(f) greengrocer

gemusst pp von **müssen**

gemustert adj patterned

gemütlich adj comfortable, cosy;
(Mensch) good-natured, easy-going; **mach es dir ~** make yourself at home

genannt pp von **nennen**

genau adj exact, precise ▷ adv exactly,
precisely; **~ in der Mitte** right in the
middle; **es mit etw ~ nehmen** to be
particular about sth; **~ genommen**
strictly speaking; **ich weiß es ~** I know for
certain (o for sure); **genauso** adv exactly
the same (way); **~ gut/viel/viele Leute**
just as well/much/many people (wie as)

genehmigen vt to approve; **sich** (dat)
etw ~ to indulge in sth; **Genehmigung** f
approval

Generalkonsulat nt consulate general

Generation f generation

Genf (-s) nt Geneva; **~er See** Lake
Geneva

genial adj brilliant

Genick (-(e)s, -e) nt (back of the) neck

Genie (-s, -s) nt genius

genieren vr **sich ~** to feel awkward; **ich
geniere mich vor ihm** he makes me feel
embarrassed

genießen (genoss, genossen) vt to enjoy

Genitiv m genitive (case)

genommen pp von **nehmen**

genoss imperf von **genießen**

genossen pp von **genießen**

genug adv enough

genügen vi to be enough (jdm for sb);
danke, das genügt thanks, that's enough
(o that will do)

Genuss (-es, Genüsse) m pleasure;
(Zusichnehmen) consumption

geöffnet adj (Geschäft etc) open

Geografie f geography

Geologie f geology

Georgien (-s) nt Georgia

Gepäck (-(e)s) nt luggage (Brit), baggage;
Gepäckabfertigung f luggage (Brit) (o
baggage) check-in; **Gepäckablage** f
luggage (Brit) (o baggage) rack;
Gepäckannahme f (zur Beförderung)
luggage (Brit) (o baggage) office; (zur

Aufbewahrung) left-luggage office (Brit),
baggage checkroom (US);
Gepäckaufbewahrung f left-luggage
office (Brit), baggage checkroom (US);
Gepäckausgabe f luggage (Brit) (o
baggage) office; (am Flughafen) baggage
reclaim; **Gepäckband** nt luggage (Brit) (o
baggage) conveyor; **Gepäckkontrolle** f
luggage (Brit) (o baggage) check;
Gepäckstück nt item of luggage (Brit) (o
baggage (US)); **Gepäckträger** m porter;
(an Fahrrad) carrier; **Gepäckversicherung**
f luggage (Brit) (o baggage) insurance;
Gepäckwagen m luggage van (Brit),
baggage car (US)

gepfiffen pp von **pfeifen**

gepflegt adj well-groomed; (Park) well
looked after

gequollen pp von **quellen**

 SCHLÜSSELWORT

gerade adj straight (aufrecht) upright;
eine gerade Zahl an even number
▷ adv **1** (genau) just exactly; (speziell)
especially; **gerade deshalb** that's just od
exactly why; **das ist es ja gerade!** that's
just it!; **gerade du** you especially; **warum
gerade ich?** why me (of all people)?; **jetzt
gerade nicht!** not now!; **gerade neben**
right next to

2 (eben, soeben) just; **er wollte gerade
aufstehen** he was just about to get up;
gerade erst only just; **gerade noch** (only)
just

gerannt pp von **rennen**

geraspelt adj grated

Gerät (-(e)s, -e) nt device, gadget;
(Werkzeug) tool; (Radio, Fernseher) set;
(Zubehör) equipment

geraten pp von **raten** ▷ irr vi to turn out;
gut/schlecht ~ to turn out well/badly; **an
jdn ~** to come across sb; **in etw** (akk) **~** to
get into sth

geräuchert adj smoked

geräumig adj roomy

Geräusch (-(e)s, -e) nt sound;
(unangenehm) noise

gerecht adj fair; (Strafe, Belohnung) just;
jdm/einer Sache ~ werden to do justice
to sb/sth

gereizt adj irritable

Gericht (-(e)s, -e) nt (Jur) court; (Essen) dish
gerieben pp von **reiben**
gering adj small; (unbedeutend) slight;
(niedrig) low; (Zeit) short; **geringfügig** adj
slight, minor ▷ adv slightly
gerissen pp von **reißen**
geritten pp von **reiten**
gern(e) adv willingly, gladly; ~ **haben,**
~ **mögen** to like; **etw ~ tun** to like doing
sth; ~ **geschehen** you're welcome
gerochen pp von **riechen**
Gerste (-, -n) f barley; **Gerstenkorn** nt
(im Auge) stye
Geruch (-(e)s, Gerüche) m smell
Gerücht (-(e)s, -e) nt rumour
gerufen pp von **rufen**
Gerümpel (-s) nt junk
gerungen pp von **ringen**
Gerüst (-(e)s, -e) nt (auf Bau) scaffolding;
(Gestell) trestle; (fig) framework (zu
of)
gesalzen pp von **salzen**
gesamt adj whole, entire; (Kosten) total;
(Werke) complete; **Gesamtschule** f ≈
comprehensive school
gesandt pp von **senden**
Gesäß (-es, -e) nt bottom
geschaffen pp von **schaffen**
Geschäft (-(e)s, -e) nt business; (Laden)
shop; (Geschäftsabschluss) deal;
geschäftlich adj commercial ▷ adv on
business; **Geschäftsfrau** f
businesswoman; **Geschäftsführer(in)**
m(f) managing director; (von Laden)
manager; **Geschäftsmann** m
businessman; **Geschäftsreise** f business
trip; **Geschäftsstraße** f shopping street;
Geschäftszeiten pl business (o opening)
hours pl
geschehen (geschah, geschehen) vi to
happen
Geschenk (-(e)s, -e) nt present, gift;
Geschenkgutschein m gift voucher;
Geschenkpapier nt gift-wrapping paper,
giftwrap
Geschichte (-, -n) f story; (Sache) affair;
(Hist) history
geschickt adj skilful
geschieden pp von **scheiden** ▷ adj
divorced
geschienen pp von **scheinen**
Geschirr (-(e)s, -e) nt crockery; (zum
Kochen) pots and pans pl; (von Pferd)

harness; ~ **spülen** to do (o wash) the
dishes, to do the washing-up (Brit);
Geschirrspülmaschine f dishwasher;
Geschirrspülmittel nt washing-up liquid
(Brit), dishwashing liquid (US);
Geschirrtuch nt tea towel (Brit), dish
towel (US)
geschissen pp von **scheißen**
geschlafen pp von **schlafen**
geschlagen pp von **schlagen**
Geschlecht (-(e)s, -er) nt sex; (Ling)
gender; **Geschlechtskrankheit** f sexually
transmitted disease, STD;
Geschlechtsorgan nt sexual organ;
Geschlechtsverkehr m sexual
intercourse
geschlichen pp von **schleichen**
geschliffen pp von **schleifen**
geschlossen adj closed
Geschmack (-(e)s, Geschmäcke) m taste;
geschmacklos adj tasteless;
Geschmack(s)sache f **das ist ~** that's a
matter of taste; **geschmackvoll** adj
tasteful
geschmissen pp von **schmeißen**
geschmolzen pp von **schmelzen**
geschnitten pp von **schneiden**
geschoben pp von **schieben**
Geschoss (-es, -e) nt (Stockwerk) floor
geschossen pp von **schießen**
Geschrei (-s) nt cries pl; (fig) fuss
geschrieben pp von **schreiben**
geschrie(e)n pp von **schreien**
geschützt adj protected
Geschwätz (-es) nt chatter; (Klatsch)
gossip; **geschwätzig** adj talkative,
gossipy
geschweige adv ~ **(denn)** let alone
geschwiegen pp von **schweigen**
Geschwindigkeit f speed; (Phys)
velocity; **Geschwindigkeitsbegrenzung**
f speed limit
Geschwister pl brothers and sisters pl
geschwollen adj (angeschwollen) swollen;
(Rede) pompous
geschwommen pp von **schwimmen**
geschworen pp von **schwören**
Geschwulst (-, Geschwülste) f growth
Geschwür (-(e)s, -e) nt ulcer
gesehen pp von **sehen**
gesellig adj sociable; **Gesellschaft** f
society; (Begleitung) company; (Abend~)
party; ~ **mit beschränkter Haftung**

g

limited company (*Brit*), limited corporation (*US*)

gesessen *pp von* **sitzen**

Gesetz (*-es, -e*) *nt* law; **gesetzlich** *adj* legal; **~er Feiertag** public (*o* bank (*Brit*) *o* legal (*US*)) holiday; **gesetzwidrig** *adj* illegal

Gesicht (*-(e)s, -er*) *nt* face; (*Miene*) expression; **mach doch nicht so ein ~!** stop pulling such a face; **Gesichtscreme** *f* face cream; **Gesichtswasser** *nt* toner

gesoffen *pp von* **saufen**

gesogen *pp von* **saugen**

gespannt *adj* tense; (*begierig*) eager; **ich bin ~, ob ...** I wonder if ...; **auf etw/jdn ~ sein** to look forward to sth/to seeing sb

Gespenst (*-(e)s, -er*) *nt* ghost

gesperrt *adj* closed

gesponnen *pp von* **spinnen**

Gespräch (*-(e)s, -e*) *nt* talk, conversation; (*Diskussion*) discussion; (*Anruf*) call

gesprochen *pp von* **sprechen**

gesprungen *pp von* **springen**

Gestalt (*-, -en*) *f* form, shape; (*Mensch*) figure

gestanden *pp von* **stehen, gestehen**

Gestank (*-(e)s*) *m* stench

gestatten *vt* to permit, to allow; **~ Sie?** may I?

Geste (*-, -n*) *f* gesture

gestehen *irr vt* to confess

gestern *adv* yesterday; **~ Abend/Morgen** yesterday evening/morning

gestiegen *pp von* **steigen**

gestochen *pp von* **stechen**

gestohlen *pp von* **stehlen**

gestorben *pp von* **sterben**

gestört *adj* disturbed; (*Empfang*) poor

gestoßen *pp von* **stoßen**

gestreift *adj* striped

gestrichen *pp von* **streichen**

gestritten *pp von* **streiten**

gestunken *pp von* **stinken**

gesund *adj* healthy; **wieder ~ werden** to get better; **Gesundheit** *f* health; **~!** bless you!; **gesundheitsschädlich** *adj* unhealthy

gesungen *pp von* **singen**

gesunken *pp von* **sinken**

getan *pp von* **tun**

getragen *pp von* **tragen**

Getränk (*-(e)s, -e*) *nt* drink;

Getränkeautomat *m* drinks machine; **Getränkekarte** *f* list of drinks

Getreide (*-s, -*) *nt* cereals *pl*, grain

getrennt *adj* separate; **~ leben** to live apart; **~ zahlen** to pay separately

getreten *pp von* **treten**

Getriebe (*-s, -*) *nt* (*Auto*) gearbox

getrieben *pp von* **treiben**

Getriebeschaden *m* gearbox damage

getroffen *pp von* **treffen**

getrunken *pp von* **trinken**

Getue *nt* fuss

geübt *adj* experienced

gewachsen *pp von* **wachsen** ▷ *adj* **jdm/einer Sache ~ sein** to be a match for sb/up to sth

Gewähr (*-*) *f* guarantee; **keine ~ übernehmen für** to accept no responsibility for

Gewalt (*-, -en*) *f* (*Macht*) power; (*Kontrolle*) control; (*große Kraft*) force; (*~taten*) violence; **mit aller ~** with all one's might; **gewaltig** *adj* tremendous; (*Irrtum*) huge

gewandt *pp von* **wenden** ▷ *adj* (*flink*) nimble; (*geschickt*) skilful

gewann *imperf von* **gewinnen**

gewaschen *pp von* **waschen**

Gewebe (*-s, -*) *nt* (*Stoff*) fabric; (*Bio*) tissue

Gewehr (*-(e)s, -e*) *nt* rifle, gun

Geweih (*-(e)s, -e*) *nt* antlers *pl*

gewellt *adj* (*Haare*) wavy

gewendet *pp von* **wenden**

Gewerbe (*-s, -*) *nt* trade; **Gewerbegebiet** *nt* industrial estate (*Brit*) (*o* park (*US*)); **gewerblich** *adj* commercial

Gewerkschaft *f* trade union

gewesen *pp von* **sein**

Gewicht (*-(e)s, -e*) *nt* weight; (*fig*) importance

gewiesen *pp von* **weisen**

Gewinn (*-(e)s, -e*) *m* profit; (*bei Spiel*) winnings *pl*; **gewinnen** (*gewann, gewonnen*) *vt* to win; (*erwerben*) to gain; (*Kohle, Öl*) to extract ▷ *vi* to win; (*profitieren*) to gain; **Gewinner(in)** (*-s, -*) *m(f)* winner

gewiss *adj* certain ▷ *adv* certainly

Gewissen (*-s, -*) *nt* conscience; **ein gutes/schlechtes ~ haben** to have a clear/bad conscience

Gewitter (*-s, -*) *nt* thunderstorm; **gewittern** *vi impers* **es gewittert** it's thundering

gewogen *pp von* **wiegen**

gewöhnen vt **jdn an etw** (akk) **~ to** accustom sb to sth ▷ vr **sich an jdn/etw ~ to** get used (o accustomed) to sb/sth; **Gewohnheit** f habit; (Brauch) custom; **gewöhnlich** adj usual; (durchschnittlich) ordinary; (pej) common; **wie ~** as usual; **gewohnt** adj usual; **etw ~ sein** to be used to sth

Gewölbe (-s, -) nt (Deckengewölbe) vault

gewonnen pp von **gewinnen**

geworben pp von **werben**

geworden pp von **werden**

geworfen pp von **werfen**

Gewürz (-es, -e) nt spice; **Gewürznelke** f clove; **gewürzt** adj seasoned

gewusst pp von **wissen**

Gezeiten pl tides pl

gezogen pp von **ziehen**

gezwungen pp von **zwingen**

Gibraltar (-s) nt Gibraltar

Gicht (-) f gout

Giebel (-s, -) m gable

gierig adj greedy

gießen (goss, gegossen) vt to pour; (Blumen) to water; (Metall) to cast; **Gießkanne** f watering can

Gift (-(e)s, -e) nt poison; **giftig** adj poisonous

Gigabyte nt gigabyte

Gin (-s, -s) m gin

ging imperf von **gehen**; **Gin Tonic** (-(s), -s) m gin and tonic

Gipfel (-s, -) m summit, peak; (Pol) summit; (fig: Höhepunkt) height

Gips (-es, -e) m (a. Med) plaster; **Gipsbein** nt **sie hat ein ~** she's got her leg in plaster; **Gipsverband** m plaster cast

Giraffe (-, -n) f giraffe

Girokonto nt current account (Brit), checking account (US)

Gitarre (-, -n) f guitar

Gitter (-s, -) nt bars pl

glänzen vi (a. fig) to shine; **glänzend** adj shining; (fig) brilliant

Glas (-es, Gläser) nt glass; (Marmelade) jar; **zwei ~ Wein** two glasses of wine; **Glascontainer** m bottle bank; **Glaser(in)** m(f) glazier; **Glasscheibe** f pane (of glass); **Glassplitter** m splinter of glass

Glasur f glaze; (Gastr) icing

glatt adj smooth; (rutschig) slippery; (Lüge) downright; **Glatteis** nt (black) ice

Glatze (-, -n) f bald head; (fam: Skinhead) skinhead

glauben vt, vi to believe (an +akk in); (meinen) to think; **jdm ~** to believe sb

gleich adj equal; (identisch) same, identical; **alle Menschen sind ~** all people are the same; **es ist mir ~** it's all the same to me ▷ adv equally; (sofort) straight away; (bald) in a minute; **~ groß/alt** the same size/age; **~ nach/an** right after/at; **Gleichberechtigung** f equal rights pl; **gleichen** (glich, geglichen) vi **jdm/einer Sache ~** to be like sb/sth ▷ vr **sich ~** to be alike; **gleichfalls** adv likewise; **danke ~!** thanks, and the same to you; **gleichgültig** adj indifferent; **gleichmäßig** adj regular; (Verteilung) even, equal; **gleichzeitig** adj simultaneous ▷ adv at the same time

Gleis (-es, -e) nt track, rails pl; (Bahnsteig) platform

gleiten (glitt, geglitten) vi to glide; (rutschen) to slide; **Gleitschirmfliegen** (-s) nt paragliding

Gletscher (-s, -) m glacier; **Gletscherfahren** nt glacier skiing; **Gletscherspalte** f crevasse

glich imperf von **gleichen**

Glied (-(e)s, -er) nt (Arm, Bein) limb; (von Kette) link; (Penis) penis; **Gliedmaßen** pl limbs pl

glitschig adj slippery

glitt imperf von **gleiten**

glitzern vi to glitter; (Sterne) to twinkle

Glocke (-, -n) f bell; **Glockenspiel** nt chimes pl

Glotze (-, -n) f (fam: TV) box; **glotzen** vi (fam) to stare

Glück (-(e)s) nt luck; (Freude) happiness; **~ haben** to be lucky; **viel ~!** good luck; **zum ~** fortunately; **glücklich** adj lucky; (froh) happy; **glücklicherweise** adv fortunately; **Glückwunsch** m congratulations pl; **herzlichen ~ zur bestandenen Prüfung** congratulations on passing your exam; **herzlichen ~ zum Geburtstag!** Happy Birthday

Glühbirne f light bulb; **glühen** vi to glow; **Glühwein** m mulled wine

GmbH (-, -s) f abk = **Gesellschaft mit beschränkter Haftung** ≈ Ltd (Brit), ≈ Inc (US)

Gokart (-(s), -s) m go-kart

Gold (-(e)s) nt gold; **golden** adj gold; (fig) golden; **Goldfisch** m goldfish; **Goldmedaille** f gold medal; **Goldschmied(in)** m(f) goldsmith

Golf (-(e)s, -e) m gulf; **der ~ von Biskaya** the Bay of Biscay ▷ (-s) nt golf; **Golfplatz** m golf course; **Golfschläger** m golf club

Gondel (-, -n) f gondola; (Seilbahn) cable-car

gönnen vt **ich gönne es ihm** I'm really pleased for him; **sich** (dat) **etw ~** to allow oneself sth

goss imperf von **gießen**

gotisch adj Gothic

Gott (-es, Götter) m God; (Gottheit) god; **Gottesdienst** m service; **Göttin** f goddess

Grab (-(e)s, Gräber) nt grave

graben (grub, gegraben) vt to dig; **Graben** (-s, Gräben) m ditch

Grabstein m gravestone

Grad (-(e)s, -e) m degree; **wir haben 30 ~ Celsius** it's 30 degrees Celsius, it's 86 degrees Fahrenheit; **bis zu einem gewissen ~** up to a certain extent

Graf (-en, -en) m count; (in Großbritannien) earl

Graffiti pl graffiti sing

Grafik (-, -en) f graph; (Kunstwerk) graphic; (Illustration) diagram; **Grafikkarte** f (Inform) graphics card; **Grafikprogramm** nt (Inform) graphics software

Gräfin (-, -nen) f countess

Gramm (-s) nt gram(me)

Grammatik f grammar

Grapefruit (-, -s) f grapefruit

Graphik f siehe **Grafik**

Gras (-es, Gräser) nt grass

grässlich adj horrible

Gräte (-, -n) f (fish)bone

gratis adj, adv free (of charge)

gratulieren vi **jdm (zu etw)** ~ to congratulate sb (on sth); (**ich**) **gratuliere!** congratulations!

grau adj grey, gray (US); **grauhaarig** adj grey-haired

grausam adj cruel

gravierend adj (Fehler) serious

greifen (griff, gegriffen) vt to seize; **zu etw ~** (fig) to resort to sth ▷ vi (Regel etc) to have an effect (bei on)

grell adj harsh

Grenze (-, -n) f boundary; (Staat) border; (Schranke) limit; **grenzen** vi to border (an +akk on); **Grenzkontrolle** f border control; **Grenzübergang** m border crossing point; **Grenzverkehr** m border traffic

Grieche (-n, -n) m Greek; **Griechenland** nt Greece; **Griechin** f Greek; **griechisch** adj Greek; **Griechisch** nt Greek

griesgrämig adj grumpy

Grieß (-es, -e) m (Gastr) semolina

griff imperf von **greifen**

Griff (-(e)s, -e) m grip; (Tür etc) handle; **griffbereit** adj handy

Grill (-s, -s) m grill; (im Freien) barbecue

Grille (-, -n) f cricket

grillen vt to grill ▷ vi to have a barbecue; **Grillfest** nt, **Grillfete** f barbecue; **Grillkohle** f charcoal

grinsen vi to grin; (höhnisch) to sneer

Grippe (-, -n) f flu; **Grippeschutzimpfung** f flu vaccination

grob adj coarse; (Fehler, Verstoß) gross; (Einschätzung) rough

Grönland (-s) nt Greenland

groß adj big, large; (hoch) tall; (fig) great; (Buchstabe) capital; (erwachsen) grown-up; **im Großen und Ganzen** on the whole ▷ adv greatly; **großartig** adj wonderful

Großbritannien (-s) nt (Great) Britain

Großbuchstabe m capital letter

Größe (-, -n) f size; (Länge) height; (fig) greatness; **welche ~ haben Sie?** what size do you take?

Großeltern pl grandparents pl; **Großhandel** m wholesale trade; **Großmarkt** m hypermarket; **Großmutter** f grandmother; **Großraum** m **der ~ Manchester** Greater Manchester; **groß|schreiben** irr vt to write with a capital letter; **Großstadt** f city; **Großvater** m grandfather; **großzügig** adj generous; (Planung) on a large scale

Grotte (-, -n) f grotto

grub imperf von **graben**

Grübchen nt dimple

Grube (-, -n) f pit

grüezi interj (schweizerisch) hello

Gruft -, -en vault

grün adj green; **~er Salat** lettuce; **~e Bohnen** French beans; **die Bananen sind noch zu ~** the bananas aren't ripe yet; **der ~e Punkt** symbol for recyclable packaging; **im ~en Bereich** hunky-dory

grüner Punkt

The **grüner Punkt** is the green spot symbol which appears on packaging, indicating that the packaging should not be thrown into the normal household refuse but kept separate to be recycled through the **DSD** (Duales System Deutschland) system. The recycling is financed by licences bought by the manufacturer from the 'DSD' and the cost of this is often passed on to the consumer.

Grünanlage f park

Grund (-(e)s, Gründe) m (Ursache) reason; (Erdboden) ground; (See, Gefäß) bottom; (Grundbesitz) land, property; **aus gesundheitlichen Gründen** for health reasons; **im ~e** basically; **aus diesem ~** for this reason

gründen vt to found; **Gründer(in)** m(f) founder

Grundgebühr f basic charge; **Grundgesetz** nt (German) Constitution

gründlich adj thorough

Gründonnerstag m Maundy Thursday

grundsätzlich adj fundamental, basic; **sie kommt ~ zu spät** she's always late; **Grundschule** f primary school; **Grundstück** nt plot; (Anwesen) estate; (Baugrundstück) site; **Grundwasser** nt ground water

Grüne(r) mf (Pol) Green; **die ~n** the Green Party

Gruppe (-, -n) f group; **Gruppenermäßigung** f group discount; **Gruppenreise** f group tour

Gruß (-es, Grüße) m greeting; **viele Grüße** best wishes; **Grüße an** (+akk) regards to; **mit freundlichen Grüßen** Yours sincerely (Brit), Sincerely yours (US); **sag ihm einen schönen ~** give him my regards; **grüßen** vt to greet; **grüß deine Mutter von mir** give your mother my regards; **Julia lässt (euch) ~** Julia sends (you) her regards

gucken vi to look

Gulasch (-(e)s, -e) nt goulash

gültig adj valid

Gummi (-s, -s) m o nt rubber; **Gummiband** nt rubber (o elastic (Brit)) band; **Gummibärchen** pl gums pl (in the shape of a bear) (Brit), gumdrops pl (in the shape of a bear) (US); **Gummihandschuhe** pl rubber gloves pl; **Gummistiefel** m wellington (boot) (Brit), rubber boot (US)

günstig adj favourable; (Preis) good

gurgeln vi to gurgle; (im Mund) to gargle

Gurke (-, -n) f cucumber; **saure ~** gherkin

Gurt (-(e)s, -e) m belt

Gürtel (-s, -) m belt; (Geo) zone; **Gürtelrose** f shingles sing

GUS (-) f akr = **Gemeinschaft Unabhängiger Staaten** CIS

SCHLÜSSELWORT

gut adj good; **alles Gute** all the best; **also gut** all right then

▷ adv well; **gut gehen** to work, to come off; **es geht jdm gut** sb's doing fine; **gut gemeint** well meant; **gut schmecken** to taste good; **jdm gut tun** to do sb good; **gut, aber ...** OK, but ...; **(na) gut, ich komme** all right, I'll come; **gut drei Stunden** a good three hours; **das kann gut sein** that may well be; **lass es gut sein** that'll do

Gutachten (-s, -) nt report; **Gutachter(in)** (-s, -) m(f) expert

gutartig adj (Med) benign

Güter pl goods pl; **Güterbahnhof** m goods station; **Güterzug** m goods train

gutgläubig adj trusting; **Guthaben** (-s) nt (credit) balance

gutmütig adj good-natured

Gutschein m voucher; **Gutschrift** f credit

Gymnasium nt ≈ grammar school (Brit), ≈ high school (US)

Gymnastik f exercises pl, keep-fit

Gynäkologe m, **Gynäkologin** f gynaecologist

Gyros (-, -) nt doner kebab

g

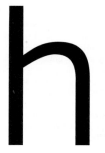

Haar (-(e)s, -e) nt hair; **um ein ~** nearly; **sich** (dat) **die ~e schneiden lassen** to have one's hair cut; **Haarbürste** f hairbrush; **Haarfestiger** m setting lotion; **Haargel** nt hair gel; **haarig** adj hairy; (fig) nasty; **Haarschnitt** m haircut; **Haarspange** f hair slide (Brit), barrette (US); **Haarspliss** m split ends pl; **Haarspray** nt hair spray; **Haartrockner** (-s, -) m hairdryer; **Haarwaschmittel** nt shampoo; **Haarwasser** nt hair tonic

haben (hatte, gehabt) vt, vaux to have; **Hunger/Angst ~** to be hungry/afraid; **Ferien ~** to be on holiday (Brit) (o vacation (US)); **welches Datum ~ wir heute?** what's the date today?; **ich hätte gerne ...** I'd like ...; **hätten Sie etwas dagegen, wenn ...?** would you mind if ...?; **was hast du denn?** what's the matter (with you)?

Haben nt (Comm) credit

Habicht (-(e)s, -e) m hawk

Hacke (-, -n) f (im Garten) hoe; (Ferse) heel; **hacken** vt to chop; (Loch) to hack; (Erde) to hoe; **Hacker(in)** (-s, -) m(f) (Inform) hacker; **Hackfleisch** nt mince(d meat) (Brit), ground meat (US)

Hafen (-s, Häfen) m harbour; (großer) port; **Hafenstadt** f port

Hafer (-s, -) m oats pl; **Haferflocken** pl rolled oats pl

Haft (-) f custody; **haftbar** adj liable, responsible; **haften** vi to stick; **~ für** to be liable (o responsible) for; **Haftnotiz** f Post-it®; **Haftpflichtversicherung** f third party insurance; **Haftung** f liability

Hagebutte (-, -n) f rose hip

Hagel (-s) m hail; **hageln** vi impers to hail

Hahn (-(e)s, Hähne) m cock; (Wasserhahn) tap (Brit), faucet (US); **Hähnchen** nt cockerel; (Gastr) chicken

Hai(fisch) (-(e)s, -e) m shark

häkeln vi, vt to crochet; **Häkelnadel** f crochet hook

Haken (-s, -) m hook; (Zeichen) tick

halb adj half; **~ eins** half past twelve; (fam) half twelve; **eine ~e Stunde** half an hour; **~ offen** half-open; **Halbfinale** nt semifinal; **halbieren** vt to halve; **Halbinsel** f peninsula; **Halbjahr** nt half-year; **halbjährlich** adj half-yearly; **Halbmond** m (Astr) half-moon; (Symbol) crescent; **Halbpension** f half board; **halbseitig** adj **~ gelähmt** paralyzed on one side; **halbtags** adv (arbeiten) part-time; **halbwegs** adv (leidlich) reasonably; **Halbzeit** f half; (Pause) half-time

half imperf von **helfen**; **Hälfte** (-, -n) f half

Halle (-, -n) f hall; **Hallenbad** nt indoor (swimming) pool

hallo interj hello, hi

Halogenlampe f halogen lamp; **Halogenscheinwerfer** m halogen headlight

Hals (-es, Hälse) m neck; (Kehle) throat; **Halsband** nt (für Tiere) collar; **Halsentzündung** f sore throat; **Halskette** f necklace; **Hals-Nasen-Ohren-Arzt** m, **Hals-Nasen-Ohren-Ärztin** f ear, nose and throat specialist; **Halsschmerzen** pl sore throat sing; **Halstuch** nt scarf

halt interj stop ▷ adv **das ist ~ so** that's just the way it is; **Halt** (-(e)s, -e) m stop; (fester) hold; (innerer) stability

haltbar adj durable; (Lebensmittel) non-perishable; **Haltbarkeitsdatum** nt best-before date

halten (*hielt, gehalten*) *vt* to keep; (*festhalten*) to hold; **~ für** to regard as; **~ von** to think of; **den Elfmeter ~** to save the penalty; **eine Rede ~** to give (*o* make) a speech ⊳ *vi* to hold; (*frisch bleiben*) to keep; (*stoppen*) to stop; **zu jdm ~** to stand by sb ⊳ *vr* **sich ~** (*frisch bleiben*) to keep; (*sich behaupten*) to hold out

Haltestelle *f* stop; **Halteverbot** *nt* **hier ist ~** you can't stop here

Haltung *f* (*Körper*) posture; (*fig*) attitude; (*Selbstbeherrschung*) composure; **~ bewahren** to keep one's composure

Hamburg (*-s*) *nt* Hamburg; **Hamburger** (*-s, -*) *m* (*Gastr*) hamburger

Hammelfleisch *nt* mutton

Hammer (*-s, Hämmer*) *m* hammer; (*fig, fam: Fehler*) howler; **das ist der ~** (*unerhört*) that's a bit much

Hämorr(ho)iden *pl* haemorrhoids *pl*, piles *pl*

Hamster (*-s, -*) *m* hamster

Hand (*-, Hände*) *f* hand; **jdm die ~ geben** to shake hands with sb; **jdn bei der ~ nehmen** to take sb by the hand; **eine ~ voll Reis/Leute** a handful of rice/people; **zu Händen von** attention; **Handarbeit** *f* (*Schulfach*) handicraft; **~ sein** to be handmade; **Handball** *m* handball; **Handbremse** *f* handbrake; **Handbuch** *nt* handbook, manual; **Handcreme** *f* hand cream; **Händedruck** *m* handshake

Handel (*-s*) *m* trade; (*Geschäft*) transaction; **handeln** *vi* to act; (*Comm*) to trade; **~ von** to be about ⊳ *vr impers* **sich ~ um** to be about; **es handelt sich um ...** it's about ...; **Handelskammer** *f* chamber of commerce; **Handelsschule** *f* business school

Handfeger (*-s, -*) *m* brush; **Handfläche** *f* palm; **Handgelenk** *nt* wrist; **handgemacht** *adj* handmade; **Handgepäck** *nt* hand luggage (*Brit*) (*o* baggage)

Händler(in) (*-s, -*) *m(f)* dealer

handlich *adj* handy

Handlung *f* act, action; (*von Roman, Film*) plot

Handschellen *pl* handcuffs *pl*; **Handschrift** *f* handwriting; **Handschuh** *m* glove; **Handschuhfach** *nt* glove compartment; **Handtasche** *f* handbag, purse (*US*); **Handtuch** *nt* towel;

Handwerk *nt* trade; (*Kunst~*) craft; **Handwerker** (*-s, -*) *m* workman

Handy (*-s, -s*) *nt* mobile (phone), cell phone (*US*)

Hanf (*-(e)s*) *m* hemp

Hang (*-(e)s, Hänge*) *m* (*Abhang*) slope; (*fig*) tendency

Hängebrücke *f* suspension bridge; **Hängematte** *f* hammock

hängen (*hing, gehangen*) *vi* to hang; **an der Wand/an der Decke ~** to hang on the wall/from the ceiling; **an jdm ~** (*fig*) to be attached to sb; **~ bleiben** to get caught (*an +dat* on); (*fig*) to get stuck ⊳ *vt* to hang (*an +akk* on)

Hantel (*-, -n*) *f* dumbbell

Hardware (*-, -s*) *f* (*Inform*) hardware

Harfe (*-, -n*) *f* harp

harmlos *adj* harmless

harmonisch *adj* harmonious

Harn (*-(e)s, -e*) *m* urine; **Harnblase** *f* bladder

Harpune (*-, -n*) *f* harpoon

hart *adj* hard; (*fig*) harsh; **zu jdm ~ sein** to be hard on sb; **~ gekocht** (*Ei*) hard-boiled; **hartnäckig** *adj* stubborn

Haschee (*-s, -s*) *nt* hash

Haschisch (*-*) *nt* hashish

Hase (*-n, -n*) *m* hare

Haselnuss *f* hazelnut

Hasenscharte *f* (*Med*) harelip

Hass (*-es*) *m* hatred (*auf, gegen +akk* of), hate; **einen ~ kriegen** (*fam*) to see red; **hassen** *vt* to hate

hässlich *adj* ugly; (*gemein*) nasty

Hast (*-*) *f* haste, hurry; **hastig** *adj* hasty

hatte *imperf von* **haben**

Haube (*-, -n*) *f* hood; (*Mütze*) cap; (*Auto*) bonnet (*Brit*), hood (*US*)

Hauch (*-(e)s, -e*) *m* breath; (*Luft~*) breeze; (*fig*) trace; **hauchdünn** *adj* (*Schicht, Scheibe*) wafer-thin

hauen (*haute, gehauen*) *vt* to hit

Haufen (*-s, -*) *m* pile; **ein ~ Geld** (*viel Geld*) a lot of money

häufig *adj* frequent ⊳ *adv* frequently, often

Haupt- *in zW* main; **Hauptbahnhof** *m* central (*o* main) station; **Hauptdarsteller(in)** *m(f)* leading actor/lady; **Haupteingang** *m* main entrance; **Hauptgericht** *nt* main course;

h

Hauptgeschäftszeiten *pl* peak shopping hours *pl*; **Hauptgewinn** *m* first prize
Häuptling *m* chief
Hauptquartier *nt* headquarters *pl*; **Hauptreisezeit** *f* peak tourist season; **Hauptrolle** *f* leading role; **Hauptsache** *f* main thing; **hauptsächlich** *adv* mainly, chiefly; **Hauptsaison** *f* high (*o* peak) season; **Hauptsatz** *m* main clause; **Hauptschule** *f* ≈ secondary school (*Brit*), ≈ junior high school (*US*); **Hauptspeicher** *m* (*Inform*) main storage (*o* memory); **Hauptstadt** *f* capital; **Hauptstraße** *f* main road; (*im Stadtzentrum*) main street; **Hauptverkehrszeit** *f* rush hour
Haus (*-es, Häuser*) *nt* house; **nach ~e** home; **zu ~e** at home; **jdn nach ~e bringen** to take sb home; **bei uns zu ~e** (*Heimat*) where we come from; (*Familie*) in my family; (*Haus*) at our place; **Hausarbeit** *f* housework; **Hausaufgabe** *f* (*Schule*) homework; **~n** *pl* homework *sing*; **Hausbesitzer(in)** (*-s, -*) *m(f)* house owner; (*Vermieter*) landlord/-lady; **Hausbesuch** *m* home visit; **Hausbewohner(in)** (*-s, -*) *m(f)* occupant; **Hausflur** *m* hall; **Hausfrau** *f* housewife; **hausgemacht** *adj* homemade; **Haushalt** *m* household; (*Pol*) budget; **Hausherr(in)** *m(f)* host/hostess; (*Vermieter*) landlord/-lady
häuslich *adj* domestic
Hausmann *m* house-husband; **Hausmannskost** *f good plain cooking*; **Hausmeister(in)** *m(f)* caretaker (*Brit*), janitor (*US*); **Hausnummer** *f* house number; **Hausordnung** *f* (house) rules *pl*; **Hausschlüssel** *m* front-door key; **Hausschuh** *m* slipper; **Haustier** *nt* pet; **Haustür** *f* front door
Haut (*-, Häute*) *f* skin; (*Tier*) hide; **Hautarzt** *m*, **Hautärztin** *f* dermatologist; **Hautausschlag** *m* skin rash; **Hautcreme** *f* skin cream; **Hautfarbe** *f* skin colour; **Hautkrankheit** *f* skin disease
Hawaii (*-s*) *nt* Hawaii
Hbf. *abk* = **Hauptbahnhof** central station
Hebamme (*-, -n*) *f* midwife
Hebel (*-s, -*) *m* lever
heben (*hob, gehoben*) *vt* to raise, to lift
Hebräisch (*-*) *nt* Hebrew
Hecht (*-(e)s, -e*) *m* pike
Heck (*-(e)s, -e*) *nt* (*von Boot*) stern; (*von Auto*) rear; **Heckantrieb** *m* rear-wheel drive

Hecke (*-, -n*) *f* hedge
Heckklappe *f* tailgate; **Hecklicht** *nt* tail-light; **Heckscheibe** *f* rear window; **Heckscheibenheizung** *f* rear-window defroster
Hefe (*-, -n*) *f* yeast
Heft (*-(e)s, -e*) *nt* notebook, exercise book; (*Ausgabe*) issue
heftig *adj* violent; (*Kritik, Streit*) fierce
Heftklammer *f* paper clip; **Heftpflaster** *nt* plaster (*Brit*), Band-Aid® (*US*)
Heide (*-, -n*) *f* heath, moor; **Heidekraut** *nt* heather
Heidelbeere *f* bilberry, blueberry
heidnisch *adj* (*Brauch*) pagan
heikel *adj* (*Angelegenheit*) awkward; (*wählerisch*) fussy
heil *adj* (*Sache*) in one piece, intact; (*Person*) unhurt; **heilbar** *adj* curable
Heilbutt (*-(e)s, -e*) *m* halibut
heilen *vt* to cure ▷ *vi* to heal
heilig *adj* holy; **Heiligabend** *m* Christmas Eve; **Heilige(r)** *mf* saint
Heilmittel *n* remedy, cure (*gegen* for); **Heilpraktiker(in)** (*-s, -*) *m(f)* non-medical practitioner
heim *adv* home; **Heim** (*-(e), -e*) *nt* home
Heimat (*-, -en*) *f* home (town/country); **Heimatland** *nt* home country
heim|fahren *irr vi* to drive home; **Heimfahrt** *f* journey home; **heimisch** *adj* (*Bevölkerung, Brauchtum*) local; (*Tiere, Pflanzen*) native; **heim|kommen** *irr vi* to come (*o* return) home
heimlich *adj* secret
Heimreise *f* journey home; **Heimspiel** *nt* (*Sport*) home game; **Heimvorteil** *m* (*Sport*) home advantage; **Heimweg** *m* way home; **Heimweh** (*-s*) *nt* homesickness; **~ haben** to be homesick; **Heimwerker(in)** *m(f)* DIY enthusiast
Heirat (*-, -en*) *f* marriage; **heiraten** *vi* to get married ▷ *vt* to marry; **Heiratsantrag** *m* proposal; **er hat ihr einen ~ gemacht** he proposed to her
heiser *adj* hoarse
heiß *adj* hot; (*Diskussion*) heated; **mir ist ~** I'm hot
heißen (*hieß, geheißen*) *vi* to be called; (*bedeuten*) to mean; **ich heiße Tom** my name is Tom; **wie ~ Sie?** what's your name?; **wie heißt sie mit Nachnamen?** what's her surname?; **wie heißt das auf**

Englisch? what's that in English? ▷ *vi impers* **es heißt** (*man sagt*) it is said; **es heißt in dem Brief ...** it says in the letter ...; **das heißt** that is
Heißluftherd *m* fan-assisted oven
heiter *adj* cheerful; (*Wetter*) bright
heizen *vt* to heat; **Heizkissen** *m* (*Med*) heated pad; **Heizkörper** *m* radiator; **Heizöl** *nt* fuel oil; **Heizung** *f* heating
Hektar (*-s, -*) *nt* hectare
Hektik (*-, -en*) *f* **nur keine ~!** take it easy; **hektisch** *adj* hectic
Held (*-en, -en*) *m* hero; **Heldin** *f* heroine
helfen (*half, geholfen*) *vi* to help (*jdm bei etw* sb with sth); (*nützen*) to be of use; **sie weiß sich** (*dat*) **zu ~** she can manage ▷ *vi impers* **es hilft nichts, du musst ...** it's no use, you have to ...; **Helfer(in)** *m(f)* helper; (*Mitarbeiter*) assistant
Helikopter-Skiing (*-s*) *nt* heliskiing, helicopter skiing
hell *adj* bright; (*Farbe*) light; (*Hautfarbe*) fair; **hellblau** *adj* light blue; **hellblond** *adj* ash-blond; **hellgelb** *adj* pale yellow; **hellgrün** *adj* light green; **Hellseher(in)** *m(f)* clairvoyant
Helm (*-(e)s, -e*) *m* helmet; **Helmpflicht** *f* compulsory wearing of helmets
Hemd (*-(e)s, -en*) *nt* shirt; (*Unter~*) vest
hemmen *vt* to check; (*behindern*) to hamper; **gehemmt sein** to be inhibited; **Hemmung** *f* (*psychisch*) inhibition; **sie hatte keine ~, ihn zu betrügen** she had no scruples about deceiving him; (*moralisch*) scruple
Henkel (*-s, -*) *m* handle
Henna (*-s*) *nt* henna
Henne (*-, -n*) *f* hen
Hepatitis (*-, Hepatitiden*) *f* hepatitis

⊘ SCHLÜSSELWORT

her *adv* **1** (*Richtung*): **komm her zu mir** come here (to me); **von England her** from England; **von weit her** from a long way away; **her damit!** hand it over!; **wo hat er das her?** where did he get that from?; **wo bist du her?** where do you come from?
2 (*Blickpunkt*): **von der Form her** as far as the form is concerned
3 (*zeitlich*): **das ist 5 Jahre her** that was 5

years ago; **ich kenne ihn von früher her** I know him from before

herab *adv* down; **herablassend** *adj* (*Bemerkung*) condescending; **herab|sehen** *irr vt* **auf jdn ~** to look down on sb; **herab|setzen** *vt* to reduce; (*fig*) to disparage
heran *adv* **näher ~!** come closer; **heran|kommen** *irr vi* to approach; **~ an** (*+akk*) to be able to get at; (*fig*) to be able to get hold of; **heran|wachsen** *irr vi* to grow up
herauf *adv* up; **herauf|beschwören** *irr vt* to evoke; (*verursachen*) to cause; **herauf|ziehen** *irr vt* to pull up ▷ *vi* to approach; (*Sturm*) to gather
heraus *adv* out; **heraus|bekommen** *irr vt* (*Geheimnis*) to find out; (*Rätsel*) to solve; **ich bekomme noch zwei Euro heraus** I've got two euros change to come; **heraus|bringen** *irr vt* to bring out; **heraus|finden** *irr vt* to find out; **heraus|fordern** *vt* to challenge; **Herausforderung** *f* challenge; **heraus|geben** *irr vt* (*Buch*) to edit; (*veröffentlichen*) to publish; **jdm zwei Euro ~** to give sb two euros change; **geben Sie mir bitte auf 20 Euro heraus** could you give me change for 20 euros, please?; **heraus|holen** *vt* to get out (*aus of*); **heraus|kommen** *irr vi* to come out; **dabei kommt nichts heraus** nothing will come of it; **heraus|stellen** *vr* **sich ~** to turn out (*als* to be); **heraus|ziehen** *irr vt* to pull out
Herbst (*-(e)s, -e*) *m* autumn, fall (*US*)
Herd (*-(e)s, -e*) *m* cooker, stove
Herde (*-, -n*) *f* herd; (*Schafe*) flock
herein *adv* in; **~!** come in; **herein|fallen** *irr vi* **wir sind auf einen Betrüger hereingefallen** we were taken in by a swindler; **herein|legen** *vt* **jdn ~** (*fig*) to take sb for a ride
Herfahrt *f* journey here; **auf der ~** on the way here
Hergang *m* course (of events); **schildern Sie mir den ~** tell me what happened
Hering (*-s, -e*) *m* herring
her|kommen *irr vi* to come; **wo kommt sie her?** where does she come from?
Heroin (*-s*) *nt* heroin
Herpes (*-*) *m* (*Med*) herpes

Herr (-(e)n, -en) m (vor Namen) Mr; (Mann) gentleman; (Adliger, Gott) Lord; **mein ~!** sir; **meine ~en!** gentlemen; **Sehr geehrte Damen und ~en** Dear Sir or Madam; **herrenlos** adj (Gepäckstück) abandoned; (Tier) stray; **Herrentoilette** f men's toilet, gents

her|richten vt to prepare

herrlich adj marvellous, splendid

Herrschaft f rule; (Macht) power; **meine ~en!** ladies and gentlemen!

herrschen vi to rule; (bestehen) to be

her|stellen vt to make; (industriell) to manufacture; **Hersteller(in)** m(f) manufacturer; **Herstellung** f production

herüber adv over

herum adv around; (im Kreis) round; **um etw ~** around sth; **du hast den Pulli falsch ~ an** you're wearing your sweater inside out; **anders ~** the other way round; **herum|fahren** irr vi to drive around; **herum|führen** vt **jdn in der Stadt ~** to show sb around the town ▷ vi **die Straße führt um das Zentrum herum** the road goes around the city centre; **herum|kommen** irr vi **sie ist viel in der Welt herumgekommen** she's been around the world; **um etw ~** (vermeiden) to get out of sth; **herum|kriegen** vt to talk round; **herum|treiben** irr vr **sich ~** to hang around

herunter adv down; **heruntergekommen** adj (Gebäude, Gegend) run-down; (Person) down-at-heel; **herunter|handeln** vt to get down; **herunter|holen** vt to bring down; **herunter|kommen** irr vi to come down; **herunter|laden** irr vt (Inform) to download

hervor adv out; **hervor|bringen** irr vt to produce; (Wort) to utter; **hervor|heben** irr vt to emphasize, to stress; **hervorragend** adj excellent; **hervor|rufen** irr vt to cause, to give rise to

Herz (-ens, -en) nt heart; (Karten) hearts pl; **von ganzem ~en** wholeheartedly; **sich** (dat) **etw zu ~en nehmen** to take sth to heart; **Herzanfall** m heart attack; **Herzbeschwerden** pl heart trouble sing; **Herzfehler** m heart defect; **herzhaft** adj (Essen) substantial; **~ lachen** to have a good laugh; **Herzinfarkt** m heart attack; **Herzklopfen** (-s) nt (Med) palpitations pl;

ich hatte ~ (vor Aufregung) my heart was pounding (with excitement); **herzkrank** adj **sie ist ~** she's got a heart condition; **herzlich** adj (Empfang, Mensch) warm; **~en Glückwunsch** congratulations

Herzog(in) (-s, Herzöge) m(f) duke/duchess

Herzschlag m heartbeat; (Herzversagen) heart failure; **Herzschrittmacher** m pacemaker; **Herzstillstand** m cardiac arrest

Hessen (-s) nt Hessen

heterosexuell adj heterosexual; **Heterosexuelle(r)** mf heterosexual

Hetze (-, -n) f (Eile) rush; **hetzen** vt to rush ▷ vr **sich ~** to rush

Heu (-(e)s) nt hay

heuer adv this year

heulen vi to howl; (weinen) to cry

Heuschnupfen m hay fever; **Heuschrecke** (-, -n) f grasshopper; (größer) locust

heute adv today; **~ Abend/früh** this evening/morning; **~ Nacht** tonight; (letzte Nacht) last night; **~ in acht Tagen** a week (from) today; **sie hat bis ~ nicht bezahlt** she hasn't paid to this day; **heutig** adj **die ~e Zeitung/Generation** today's paper/generation; **heutzutage** adv nowadays

Hexe (-, -n) f witch; **Hexenschuss** m lumbago

hielt imperf von **halten**

hier adv here; **~ entlang** this way; **~ bleiben** to stay here; **~ lassen** to leave here; **ich bin auch nicht von ~** I'm a stranger here myself; **hierher** adv here; **das gehört nicht ~** that doesn't belong here; **hiermit** adv with this; **hierzulande, hier zu Lande** adv in this country

hiesig adj local

hieß imperf von **heißen**

Hi-Fi-Anlage f hi-fi (system)

high adj (fam) high; **Highlife** (-s) nt high life; **~ machen** to live it up; **Hightech** (-s) nt high tech

Hilfe (-, -n) f help; (für Notleidende, finanziell) aid; **~!** help!; **erste ~ leisten** to give first aid; **um ~ bitten** to ask for help; **hilflos** adj helpless; **hilfsbereit** adj helpful; **Hilfsmittel** nt aid

Himbeere f raspberry

Himmel (-s, -) m sky; (Rel) heaven;
Himmelfahrt f Ascension;
Himmelsrichtung f direction;
himmlisch adj heavenly

⬤ SCHLÜSSELWORT

hin adv **1** Richtung): **hin und zurück** there
and back; **hin und her** to and fro; **bis zur
Mauer hin** up to the wall; **wo ist er hin?**
where has he gone?; **Geld hin, Geld her**
money or no money

2 (auf ... hin): **auf meine Bitte hin** at my
request; **auf seinen Rat hin** on the basis
of his advice

3: **mein Glück ist hin** my happiness has
gone

hinab adv down; **hinab|gehen** irr vi to go
down
hinauf adv up; **hinauf|gehen** irr vi, vt
to go up; **hinauf|steigen** irr vi to climb
(up)
hinaus adv out; **hinaus|gehen** irr vi to go
out; **das Zimmer geht auf den See
hinaus** the room looks out onto the lake;
~ über (+akk) to exceed; **hinaus|laufen** irr
vi to run out; **~ auf** (+akk) to come to, to
amount to; **hinaus|schieben** irr vi to put
off, to postpone; **hinaus|werfen** irr vt to
throw out; (aus Firma) to fire, to sack
(Brit); **hinaus|zögern** vr **sich ~** to take
longer than expected
Hinblick m **in** (o **im**) **~ auf** (+akk) with
regard to; (wegen) in view of
hin|bringen irr vt **ich bringe Sie hin** I'll
take you there
hindern vt to prevent; **jdn daran ~, etw
zu tun** to stop (o prevent) sb from doing
sth; **Hindernis** nt obstacle
Hinduismus m Hinduism
hindurch adv through; **das ganze Jahr
~** throughout the year, all year round; **die
ganze Nacht ~** all night (long)
hinein adv in; **hinein|gehen** irr vi to go
in; **~ in** (+akk) to go into, to enter;
hinein|passen vi to fit in; **~ in** (+akk) to
fit into
hin|fahren irr vi to go there ▷ vt to take
there; **Hinfahrt** f outward journey
hin|fallen irr vi to fall (down)
Hinflug m outward flight
hing imperf von **hängen**

hin|gehen irr vi to go there; (Zeit) to pass;
hin|halten irr vt to hold out; (warten
lassen) to put off
hinken vi to limp; **der Vergleich hinkt**
the comparison doesn't work
hin|knien vr **sich ~** to kneel down;
hin|legen vt to put down ▷ vr **sich ~** to
lie down; **hin|nehmen** irr vt (fig) to put
up with, to take; **Hinreise** f outward
journey; **hin|setzen** vr **sich ~** to sit down;
hinsichtlich prep +gen with regard to;
hin|stellen vt to put (down) ▷ vr **sich
~** to stand
hinten adv at the back; (im Auto) in the
back; (dahinter) behind
hinter prep +dat o akk behind; (nach) after;
~ jdm her sein to be after sb; **etw ~ sich**
(akk) **bringen** to get sth over (and done)
with; **Hinterachse** f rear axle;
Hinterausgang m rear exit; **Hinterbein** nt
hind leg; **Hinterbliebene(r)** mf
dependant; **hintere(r, s)** adj rear, back;
hintereinander adv (in einer Reihe) one
behind the other; (hintereinander her) one
after the other; **drei Tage ~** three days
running (o in a row); **Hintereingang** m
rear entrance; **Hintergedanke** m ulterior
motive; **hintergehen** irr vt to deceive;
Hintergrund m background; **hinterher**
adv (zeitlich) afterwards; **los, ~!** come on,
after him/her/them; **Hinterkopf** m back
of the head; **hinterlassen** vt to leave;
jdm eine Nachricht ~ to leave a
message for sb; **hinterlegen** vt to leave
(bei with)
Hintern (-, -) m (fam) backside, bum
Hinterradantrieb m (Auto) rear-wheel
drive; **Hinterteil** nt back (part); (Hintern)
behind; **Hintertür** f back door
hinüber adv over; **~ sein** (fam: kaputt) to
be ruined; (verdorben) to have gone bad;
hinüber|gehen irr vi to go over
hinunter adv down; **hinunter|gehen** irr
vi, vt to go down; **hinunter|schlucken** vt
(a. fig) to swallow
Hinweg m outward journey
hinweg|setzen vr **sich über etw** (akk)
~ to ignore sth
Hinweis (-es, -e) m (Andeutung) hint;
(Anweisung) instruction; (Verweis)
reference; **hin|weisen** irr vi **jdn auf etw**
(acc) **~** to point sth out to sb; **jdn nochmal
auf etw ~** to remind sb of sth

hinzu *adv* in addition; **hinzu|fügen** *vt* to add; **hinzu|kommen** *irr vi* **zu jdm ~** to join sb; **es war kalt, hinzu kam, dass es auch noch regnete** it was cold, and on top of that it was raining

Hirn *(-(e)s, -e) nt* brain; *(Verstand)* brains *pl*; **Hirnhautentzündung** *f* meningitis; **hirnverbrannt** *adj* crazy

Hirsch *(-(e)s, -e) m* deer; *(als Speise)* venison

Hirse *(-, -n) f* millet

Hirte *(-n, -n) m* shepherd

historisch *adj* historical

Hit *(-s, -s) m (fig, Mus, Inform)* hit; **Hitliste** *f*, **Hitparade** *f* charts *pl*

Hitze *(-) f* heat; **hitzebeständig** *adj* heat-resistant; **Hitzewelle** *f* heatwave; **hitzig** *adj* hot-tempered; *(Debatte)* heated; **Hitzschlag** *m* heatstroke

HIV *(-(s), -(s)) nt abk* = **Human Immunodeficiency Virus** HIV; **HIV-negativ** *adj* HIV-negative; **HIV-positiv** *adj* HIV-positive

H-Milch *f* long-life milk

hob *imperf von* **heben**

Hobby *(-s, -s) nt* hobby

Hobel *(-s, -) m* plane

hoch *adj* high; *(Baum, Haus)* tall; *(Schnee)* deep; **der Zaun ist drei Meter ~** the fence is three metres high; **~ auflösend** high-resolution; **~ begabt** extremely gifted; **das ist mir zu ~** that's above my head; **~ soll sie leben!, sie lebe ~!** three cheers for her; **4 ~ 2 ist 16** 4 squared is 16; **4 ~ 5** 4 to the power of 5

Hoch *(-s, -s) nt (Ruf)* cheer; *(Meteo)* high; **hochachtungsvoll** *adv (in Briefen)* Yours faithfully; **Hochbetrieb** *m* **es herrscht ~** they/we are extremely busy; **Hochdeutsch** *nt* High German; **Hochgebirge** *nt* high mountains *pl*; **Hochgeschwindigkeitszug** *m* high-speed train; **Hochhaus** *nt* high rise; **hoch|heben** *irr vt* to lift (up); **hochprozentig** *adj (Alkohol)* high-proof; **Hochsaison** *f* high season; **Hochschule** *f* college; *(Universität)* university; **hochschwanger** *adj* heavily pregnant; **Hochsommer** *m* midsummer; **Hochspannung** *f* great tension; *(Elek)* high voltage; **Hochsprung** *m* high jump

höchst *adv* highly, extremely; **höchste(r, s)** *adj* highest; *(äußerste)* extreme; **höchstens** *adv* at the most; **Höchstgeschwindigkeit** *f* maximum speed; **Höchstparkdauer** *f* maximum stay

Hochstuhl *m* high chair

höchstwahrscheinlich *adv* very probably

Hochwasser *nt* high water; *(Überschwemmung)* floods *pl*; **hochwertig** *adj* high-quality

Hochzeit *(-, -en) f* wedding; **Hochzeitsnacht** *f* wedding night; **Hochzeitsreise** *f* honeymoon; **Hochzeitstag** *m* wedding day; *(Jahrestag)* wedding anniversary

hocken *vi* to squat, to crouch

Hocker *(-s, -) m* stool

Hockey *(-s) nt* hockey

Hoden *(-s, -) m* testicle

Hof *(-(e)s, Höfe) m (Hinterhof)* yard; *(Innenhof)* courtyard; *(Bauernhof)* farm; *(Königshof)* court

hoffen *vi* to hope *(auf +akk* for); **ich hoffe es** I hope so; **hoffentlich** *adv* hopefully; **~ nicht** I hope not; **Hoffnung** *f* hope; **hoffnungslos** *adj* hopeless

höflich *adj* polite; **Höflichkeit** *f* politeness

hohe(r, s) *adj siehe* **hoch**

Höhe *(-, -n) f* height; *(Anhöhe)* hill; *(einer Summe)* amount; **in einer ~ von 5000 Metern** at an altitude of 5,000 metres; *(Flughöhe)* altitude; **Höhenangst** *f* vertigo; **Höhensonne** *f* sun lamp

Höhepunkt *m (einer Reise)* high point; *(einer Veranstaltung)* highlight; *(eines Films; sexuell)* climax

höher *adj, adv* higher

hohl *adj* hollow

Höhle *(-, -n) f* cave

holen *vt* to get, to fetch; *(abholen)* to pick up; *(Atem)* to catch; **die Polizei ~** to call the police; **jdn/etw ~ lassen** to send for sb/sth

Holland *nt* Holland; **Holländer(in)** *(-s, -) m(f)* Dutchman/-woman; **holländisch** *adj* Dutch

Hölle *(-, -n) f* hell

Hologramm *nt* hologram

holperig *adj* bumpy

Holunder *(-s, -) m* elder

Holz *(-es, Hölzer) nt* wood; **Holzboden** *m* wooden floor; **hölzern** *adj* wooden; **holzig** *adj (Stängel)* woody; **Holzkohle** *f* charcoal

Homebanking (-s) nt home banking, online banking; **Homepage** (-, -s) f home page; **Hometrainer** m exercise machine

homöopathisch adj homeopathic

homosexuell adj homosexual; **Homosexuelle(r)** mf homosexual

Honig (-s, -e) m honey; **Honigmelone** f honeydew melon

Honorar (-s, -e) nt fee

Hopfen (-s, -) m (Bot) hop; (beim Brauen) hops pl

hoppla interj whoops, oops

horchen vi to listen (auf +akk to); (an der Tür) to eavesdrop

hören vt, vi (passiv, mitbekommen) to hear; (zufällig) to overhear; (aufmerksam zuhören; Radio, Musik) to listen to; **ich habe schon viel von Ihnen gehört** I've heard a lot about you; **Hörer** m (Tel) receiver; **Hörer(in)** m(f) listener; **Hörgerät** nt hearing aid

Horizont (-(e)s, -e) m horizon; **das geht über meinen ~** that's beyond me

Hormon (-s, -e) nt hormone

Hornhaut f hard skin; (des Auges) cornea

Hornisse (-, -n) f hornet

Horoskop (-s, -e) nt horoscope

Hörsaal m lecture hall; **Hörsturz** m acute hearing loss; **Hörweite** f **in/außer ~** within/out of earshot

Höschenwindel (-, -n) f nappy (Brit), diaper (US)

Hose (-, -n) f trousers pl (Brit), pants pl (US); (Unterhose) (under)pants pl; **eine ~** a pair of trousers/pants; **kurze ~** (pair of) shorts pl; **Hosenanzug** m trouser suit (Brit), pantsuit (US); **Hosenschlitz** m fly, flies (Brit); **Hosentasche** f trouser pocket (Brit), pant pocket (US); **Hosenträger** m braces pl (Brit), suspenders pl (US)

Hospital (-s, Hospitäler) nt hospital

Hotdog (-s, -s) nt o m hot dog

Hotel (-s, -s) nt hotel; **in welchem ~ seid ihr?** which hotel are you staying at?; **Hoteldirektor(in)** m(f) hotel manager; **Hotelkette** f hotel chain; **Hotelzimmer** nt hotel room

Hotline (-, -s) f hot line

Hubraum m cubic capacity

hübsch adj (Mädchen, Kind, Kleid) pretty; (gutaussehend; Mann, Frau) good-looking, cute

Hubschrauber (-s, -) m helicopter

Huf (-(e)s, -e) m hoof; **Hufeisen** nt horseshoe

Hüfte (-, -n) f hip

Hügel (-s, -) m hill; **hügelig** adj hilly

Huhn (-(e)s, Hühner) nt hen; (Gastr) chicken; **Hühnchen** nt chicken; **Hühnerauge** nt corn; **Hühnerbrühe** f chicken broth

Hülle (-, -n) f cover; (für Ausweis) case; (Zellophan) wrapping

Hummel (-, -n) f bumblebee

Hummer (-s, -) m lobster; **Hummerkrabbe** f king prawn

Humor (-s) m humour; **~ haben** to have a sense of humour; **humorvoll** adj humorous

humpeln vi hobble

Hund (-(e)s, -e) m dog; **Hundeleine** f dog lead (Brit), dog leash (US)

hundert num hundred; **Hundertjahrfeier** f centenary; **hundertprozentig** adj, adv one hundred per cent; **hundertste(r, s)** adj hundredth

Hündin f bitch

Hunger (-s) m hunger; **~ haben/bekommen** to be/get hungry; **hungern** vi to go hungry; (ernsthaft, dauernd) to starve

Hupe (-, -n) f horn; **hupen** vi to sound one's horn

Hüpfburg f bouncy castle®; **hüpfen** vi to hop; (springen) to jump

Hürde (-, -n) f hurdle

Hure (-, -n) f whore

hurra interj hooray

husten vi to cough; **Husten** (-s) m cough; **Hustenbonbon** nt cough sweet; **Hustensaft** m cough mixture

Hut (-(e)s, Hüte) m hat

hüten vt to look after ▷ vr **sich ~** to watch out; **sich ~, etw zu tun** to take care not to do sth; **sich ~ vor** (+dat) to beware of

Hütte (-, -n) f hut, cottage; **Hüttenkäse** m cottage cheese

Hyäne (-, -n) f hyena

Hydrant m hydrant

hygienisch adj hygienic

Hyperlink (-s, -s) m hyperlink

Hypnose (-, -n) f hypnosis; **Hypnotiseur(in)** m(f) hypnotist; **hypnotisieren** vt to hypnotize

Hypothek (-, -en) f mortgage

hysterisch adj hysterical

ihnen *pron dat pl von* **sie**; (to) them; **wie geht es ~?** how are they?; **ein Freund von ~** a friend of theirs

Ihnen *pron dat sing u pl von* **Sie**; (to) you; **wie geht es ~?** how are you?; **ein Freund von ~** a friend of yours

○ SCHLÜSSELWORT

ihr *pron* **1** (*nom pl*) you; **ihr seid es** it's you

2 (*dat von sie*) to her; **gib es ihr** give it to her; **er steht neben ihr** he is standing beside her

▷ *possessiv pron* **1** (*sg*) her; (*bei Tieren, Dingen*) its; **ihr Mann** her husband

2 (*pl*) their; **die Bäume und ihre Blätter** the trees and their leaves

Ihr *pron von* **Sie**; (*adjektivisch*) your; **~(e) XY** (*am Briefende*) Yours, XY

ihre(r, s) *pron* (*substantivisch, sing*) hers; (*pl*) theirs; **das ist ~/~r/ihr(e)s** that's hers; (*pl*) that's theirs

Ihre(r, s) *pron* (*substantivisch*) yours; **das ist ~/~r/ihr(e)s** that's yours

ihretwegen *adv* (*wegen ihr*) because of her; (*ihr zuliebe*) for her sake; (*um sie*) about her; (*von ihr aus*) as far as she is concerned ▷ *adv* (*wegen ihnen*) because of them; (*ihnen zuliebe*) for their sake; (*um sie*) about them; (*von ihnen aus*) as far as they are concerned; **Ihretwegen** *adv* (*wegen Ihnen*) because of you; (*Ihnen zuliebe*) for your sake; (*um Sie*) about you; (*von Ihnen aus*) as far as you are concerned

Ikone (*-, -n*) *f* icon

illegal *adj* illegal

Illusion *f* illusion; **sich** (*dat*) **~en machen** to delude oneself; **illusorisch** *adj* illusory

Illustration *f* illustration

Illustrierte (*-n, -n*) *f* (*glossy*) magazine

im *kontr von* **in dem**; **~ Bett** in bed; **~ Fernsehen** on TV; **~ Radio** on the radio; **~ Bus/Zug** on the bus/train; **~ Januar** in January; **~ Stehen** (while) standing up

Imbiss (*-es, -e*) *m* snack; **Imbissbude** *f*, **Imbissstube** *f* snack bar

Imbussschlüssel *m* hex key

immer *adv* always; **~ mehr** more and more; **~ wieder** again and again; **~ noch** still; **~ noch nicht** still not; **für ~** forever; **~ wenn ich ...** every time I ...;

---

i. A. *abk* = **im Auftrag** pp

IC (*-, -s*) *m abk* = **Intercityzug** Intercity (train)

ICE (*-, -s*) *m abk* = **Intercityexpresszug** German high-speed train

ich *pron* I; **~ bin's** it's me; **~ nicht** not me; **du und ~** you and me; **hier bin ~!** here I am; **~ Idiot!** stupid me

Icon (*-s, -s*) *nt* (*Inform*) icon

IC-Zuschlag *m* Intercity supplement

ideal *adj* ideal; **Ideal** (*-s, -e*) *nt* ideal

Idee (*-, -n*) *f* idea

identifizieren *vt* to identify ▷ *vr* **sich mit jdm/etw ~** to identify with sb/sth

identisch *adj* identical

Idiot(in) (*-en, -en*) *m(f)* idiot; **idiotisch** *adj* idiotic

Idol (*-s, -e*) *nt* idol

Idylle *f* idyll; **idyllisch** *adj* idyllic

Igel (*-s, -*) *m* hedgehog

ignorieren *vt* to ignore

ihm *pron dat sing von* **er/es**; (to) him, (to) it; **wie geht es ~?** how is he?; **ein Freund von ~** a friend of his ▷ *pron dat von* **es**; (to) it

ihn *pron akk sing von* **er**; (*Person*) him; (*Sache*) it

~ **schöner/trauriger** more and more beautiful/sadder and sadder; **was/wer/ wo/wann (auch)**
~ whatever/whoever/wherever/whenever; **immerhin** *adv* after all; **immerzu** *adv* all the time
Immigrant(in) *m(f)* immigrant
Immobilien *pl* property *sing*, real estate *sing*; **Immobilienmakler(in)** *m(f)* estate agent (*Brit*), realtor (*US*)
immun *adj* immune (*gegen* to); **Immunschwäche** *f* immunodeficiency; **Immunschwächekrankheit** *f* immune deficiency syndrome; **Immunsystem** *nt* immune system
impfen *vt* to vaccinate; **ich muss mich gegen Pocken ~ lassen** I've got to get myself vaccinated against smallpox; **Impfpass** *m* vaccination card; **Impfstoff** *m* vaccine; **Impfung** *f* vaccination
imponieren *vi* to impress (*jdm* sb)
Import (*-(e)s, -e*) *m* import; **importieren** *vt* to import
impotent *adj* impotent
imstande *adj* ~ **sein** to be in a position; (*fähig*) to be able

🔵 SCHLÜSSELWORT

in *präp* +akk **1** (*räumlich: wohin?*) in, into; **in die Stadt** into town; **in die Schule gehen** to go to school
2 (*zeitlich*): **bis ins 20. Jahrhundert** into *od* up to the 20th century
▷ *präp* +dat ~ **1** (*räumlich: wo*) in; **in der Stadt** in town; **in der Schule sein** to be at school
2 (*zeitlich: wann*); **in diesem Jahr** this year (*in jenem Jahr*) in that year; **heute in zwei Wochen** two weeks today

inbegriffen *adj* included
indem *conj* **sie gewann, ~ sie mogelte** she won by cheating
Inder(in) (*-s, -*) *m(f)* Indian
Indianer(in) (*-s, -*) *m(f)* American Indian, Native American; **indianisch** *adj* American Indian, Native American
Indien (*-s*) *nt* India
indirekt *adj* indirect
indisch *adj* Indian
indiskret *adj* indiscreet

individuell *adj* individual
Indonesien (*-s*) *nt* Indonesia
Industrie *f* industry; **Industrie-** *in zW* industrial; **Industriegebiet** *nt* industrial area; **industriell** *adj* industrial
ineinander *adv* in(to) one another (*o* each other)
Infarkt (*-(e)s, -e*) *m* (*Herzinfarkt*) heart attack
Infektion *f* infection; **Infektionskrankheit** *f* infectious disease; **infizieren** *vt* to infect ▷ *vr* **sich ~** to be infected
Info (*-, -s*) *f* (*fam*) info
infolge *prep* +gen as a result of, owing to; **infolgedessen** *adv* consequently
Informatik *f* computer science; **Informatiker(in)** (*-s, -*) *m(f)* computer scientist
Information *f* information; **Informationsschalter** *m* information desk; **informieren** *vt* to inform; **falsch ~** to misinform ▷ *vr* **sich ~** to find out (*über* +akk about)
infrage *adv* **das kommt nicht ~** that's out of the question; **etw ~ stellen** to question sth
Infrastruktur *f* infrastructure
Infusion *f* infusion
Ingenieur(in) *m(f)* engineer
Ingwer (*-s*) *m* ginger
Inhaber(in) (*-s, -*) *m(f)* owner; (*Haus~*) occupier; (*von Lizenz*) holder; (*Fin*) bearer
Inhalt (*-(e)s, -e*) *m* contents *pl*; (*eines Buchs etc*) content; (*Math*) volume; (*Flächeninhalt*) area; **Inhaltsangabe** *f* summary; **Inhaltsverzeichnis** *nt* table of contents
Initiative *f* initiative; **die ~ ergreifen** to take the initiative
Injektion *f* injection
inklusive *adv, prep* inclusive (*gen* of)
inkonsequent *adj* inconsistent
Inland *nt* (*Pol, Comm*) home; **im ~** at home; (*Geo*) inland; **inländisch** *adj* domestic; **Inlandsflug** *m* domestic flight; **Inlandsgespräch** *nt* national call
Inlineskates *pl* Rollerblades® *pl*, inline skates *pl*
innen *adv* inside; **Innenarchitekt(in)** *m(f)* interior designer; **Innenhof** *m* (inner) courtyard; **Innenminister(in)** *m(f)* minister of the interior, Home Secretary (*Brit*); **Innenseite** *f* inside; **Innenspiegel**

m rearview mirror; **Innenstadt** *f* town centre; (*von Großstadt*) city centre

innere(r, s) *adj* inner; (*im Körper, inländisch*) internal; **Innere(s)** *nt* inside; (*Mitte*) centre; (*fig*) heart

Innereien *pl* innards *pl*

innerhalb *adv, prep +gen* within; (*räumlich*) inside

innerlich *adj* internal; (*geistig*) inner

innerste(r, s) *adj* innermost

Innovation *f* innovation; **innovativ** *adj* innovative

inoffiziell *adj* unofficial; (*zwanglos*) informal

ins *kontr von* **in das**

Insasse (*-n, -n*) *m*, **Insassin** *f* (*Auto*) passenger; (*Anstalt*) inmate

insbesondere *adv* particularly, in particular

Inschrift *f* inscription

Insekt (*-(e)s, -en*) *nt* insect, bug (*US*); **Insektenschutzmittel** *nt* insect repellent; **Insektenstich** *m* insect bite

Insel (*-, -n*) *f* island

Inserat *nt* advertisement

insgesamt *adv* altogether, all in all

Insider(in) (*-s, -*) *m(f)* insider

insofern *adv* in that respect; (*deshalb*) (and) so ▷ *conj* if; **~ als** in so far as

Installateur(in) *m(f)* (*Klempner*) plumber; (*Elektroinstallateur*) electrician; **installieren** *vt* (*Inform*) to install

Instinkt (*-(e)s, -e*) *m* instinct

Institut (*-(e)s, -e*) *nt* institute

Institution *f* institution

Instrument *nt* instrument

Insulin (*-s*) *nt* insulin

Inszenierung *f* production

intakt *adj* intact

intellektuell *adj* intellectual

intelligent *adj* intelligent; **Intelligenz** *f* intelligence

intensiv *adj* (*gründlich*) intensive; (*Gefühl, Schmerz*) intense; **Intensivkurs** *m* crash course; **Intensivstation** *f* intensive care unit

interaktiv *adj* interactive

Intercityexpress(zug) *m* German high-speed train; **Intercityzug** *m* Intercity (train); **Intercityzuschlag** *m* Intercity supplement

interessant *adj* interesting; **Interesse** (*-s, -n*) *nt* interest; **~ haben an** (*+dat*) to be interested in; **interessieren** *vt* to interest ▷ *vr* **sich ~** to be interested (*für* in)

Interface (*-, -s*) *nt* (*Inform*) interface

Internat *nt* boarding school

international *adj* international

Internet (*-s*) *nt* Internet, Net; **im ~** on the Internet; **im ~ surfen** to surf the Net; **Internetcafé** *nt* Internetcafé, cybercafé; **Internetfirma** *f* dotcom company; **Internethandel** *m* e-commerce; **Internetseite** *f* web page

interpretieren *vt* to interpret (*als* as)

Interpunktion *f* punctuation

Interregio (*-s, -s*) *m* regional train

Interview (*-s, -s*) *nt* interview; **interviewen** *vt* to interview

intim *adj* intimate

intolerant *adj* intolerant

investieren *vt* to invest

inwiefern *adv* in what way; (*in welchem Ausmaß*) to what extent; **inwieweit** *adv* to what extent

inzwischen *adv* meanwhile

Irak (*-(s)*) *m* (**der**) **~** Iraq

Iran (*-(s)*) *m* (**der**) **~** Iran

Ire (*-n, -n*) *m* Irishman

irgend *adv* **~ so ein Idiot** some idiot; **wenn ~ möglich** if at all possible; **irgendein** *pron*, **irgendeine(r, s)** *adj* some; (*fragend, im Bedingungssatz; beliebig*) any; **irgendetwas** *pron* something; (*fragend, im Bedingungssatz*) anything; **irgendjemand** *pron* somebody; (*fragend, im Bedingungssatz*) anybody; **irgendwann** *adv* sometime; (*zu beliebiger Zeit*) any time; **irgendwie** *adv* somehow; **irgendwo** *adv* somewhere; (*fragend, im Bedingungssatz*) anywhere

Irin *f* Irishwoman; **irisch** *adj* Irish; **Irland** *nt* Ireland

ironisch *adj* ironic

irre *adj* crazy, mad; (*toll*) terrific; **Irre(r)** *mf* lunatic; **irreführen** *irr vt* to mislead; **irremachen** *vt* to confuse; **irren** *vi* to be mistaken; (*umherirren*) to wander ▷ *vr* **sich ~** to be mistaken; **wenn ich mich nicht irre** if I'm not mistaken; **sich in der Nummer ~** (*Telefon*) to get the wrong number; **irrsinnig** *adj* mad, crazy; **Irrtum** (*-s, -tümer*) *m* mistake, error; **irrtümlich** *adj* mistaken ▷ *adv* by mistake

ISBN (*-*) *nt* *abk* = **industrial standard business network** ISBN ▷ (*-*) *f* *abk* =

Internationale Standard Buchnummer
ISBN
Ischias (-) *m* sciatica
ISDN (-) *nt* *abk* = **integrated services
digital network** ISDN
Islam (-*s*) *m* Islam; **islamisch** *adj* Islamic
Island *nt* Iceland; **Isländer(in)** (-*s*, -) *m(f)*
Icelander; **isländisch** *adj* Icelandic;
Isländisch *nt* Icelandic
Isolierband *nt* insulating tape; **isolieren**
vt to isolate; (*Elek*) to insulate
Isomatte *f* thermomat, karrymat®
Israel (-*s*) *nt* Israel; **Israeli** (-*(s)*, -*(s)*) *m*
(-, -*(s)*) *f* Israeli; **israelisch** *adj* Israeli
IT (-) *f* *abk* = **Informationstechnologie**
IT
Italien (-*s*) *nt* Italy; **Italiener(in)** (-*s*, -)
m(f) Italian; **italienisch** *adj* Italian;
Italienisch *nt* Italian

j

Jahreszeit *f* season; **Jahrgang** *m* (*Wein*) year, vintage; **der ~ 1989** (*Personen*) those born in 1989; **Jahrhundert** (*-s, -e*) *nt* century; **jährlich** *adj* yearly, annual; **Jahrmarkt** *m* fair; **Jahrtausend** *nt* millennium; **Jahrzehnt** *nt* decade
jähzornig *adj* hot-tempered
Jakobsmuschel *f* scallop
Jalousie *f* (venetian) blind
Jamaika (*-s*) *nt* Jamaica
jämmerlich *adj* pathetic
jammern *vi* to moan
Januar (*-(s), -e*) *m* January; *siehe auch* **Juni**
Japan (*-s*) *nt* Japan; **Japaner(in)** (*-s, -*) *m(f)* Japanese; **japanisch** *adj* Japanese; **Japanisch** *nt* Japanese
jaulen *vi* to howl
jawohl *adv* yes (of course)
Jazz (*-*) *m* jazz

 SCHLÜSSELWORT

je *adv* **1** (*jemals*) ever; **hast du so was je gesehen?** did you ever see anything like it?
2 (*jeweils*) every each; **sie zahlten je 3 Euro** they paid 3 euros each
▷ *konj* **1**: **je nach** depending on; **je nachdem** it depends; **je nachdem, ob ...** depending on whether ...
2: **je eher, desto** *od* **umso besser** the sooner the better

Jeans (*-, -*) *f* jeans *pl*
jede(r, s) *unbest Zahlwort* (*insgesamt gesehen*) every; (*einzeln gesehen*) each; (*jede(r, s) beliebige*) any; **~s Mal** every time, each time; **~n zweiten Tag** every other day; **sie hat an ~m Finger einen Ring** she's got a ring on each finger; **~r Computer reicht aus** any computer will do; **bei ~m Wetter** in any weather ▷ *pron* everybody; (*jeder Einzelne*) each; **~r von euch/uns** each of you/us; **jedenfalls** *adv* in any case; **jederzeit** *adv* at any time; **jedesmal** *adv* every time
jedoch *adv* however
jemals *adv* ever
jemand *pron* somebody; (*in Frage und Verneinung*) anybody
Jemen (*-(s)*) *m* Yemen
jene(r, s) *adj* that, those *pl* ▷ *pron* that (one), those *pl*

 SCHLÜSSELWORT

ja *adv* **1** yes; **haben Sie das gesehen?** — **ja** did you see it? — yes(, I did); **ich glaube ja** (yes,) I think so
2 (*fragend*) really?; **ich habe gekündigt — ja?** I've quit — have you?; **du kommst, ja?** you're coming, aren't you?
3: **sei ja vorsichtig** do be careful; **Sie wissen ja, dass ...** as you know, ...; **tu das ja nicht!** don't do that!; **ich habe es ja gewusst** I just knew it; **ja, also ...** well you see ...

Jacht (*-, -en*) *f* yacht; **Jachthafen** *m* marina
Jacke (*-, -n*) *f* jacket; (*Wolljacke*) cardigan
Jackett (*-s, -s o -e*) *nt* jacket
Jagd (*-, -en*) *f* hunt; (*Jagen*) hunting; **jagen** *vi* to hunt ▷ *vt* to hunt; (*verfolgen*) to chase; **Jäger(in)** *m(f)* hunter
Jaguar (*-s, -e*) *m* jaguar
Jahr (*-(e)s, -e*) *nt* year; **ein halbes ~** six months *pl*; **Anfang der neunziger ~e** in the early nineties; **mit sechzehn ~en** at (the age of) sixteen; **Jahrestag** *m* anniversary; **Jahreszahl** *f* date, year;

jenseits *adv* on the other side ▷ *prep* +*gen*
on the other side of; *(fig)* beyond

Jetlag (*-s*) *m* jet lag

jetzig *adj* present

jetzt *adv* now; **erst ~** only now; **~ gleich**
right now; **bis ~** so far, up to now; **von
~ an** from now on

jeweils *adv* **~ zwei zusammen** two at a
time; **zu ~ 5 Euro** at 5 euros each

Job (*-s, -s*) *m* job; **jobben** *vi* *(fam)* to work,
to have a job

Jod (*-(e)s*) *nt* iodine

Joga (*-s*) *nt* yoga

joggen *vi* to jog; **Jogging** (*-s*) *nt* jogging;
Jogginganzug *m* jogging suit, tracksuit;
Jogginghose *f* jogging pants *pl*

Jog(h)urt (*-s, -s*) *m o nt* yoghurt

Johannisbeere *f* **Schwarze
~** blackcurrant; **Rote ~** redcurrant

Joint (*-s, -s*) *m* *(fam)* joint

jonglieren *vi* to juggle

Jordanien (*-s*) *nt* Jordan

Joule (*-(s), -*) *nt* joule

Journalist(in) *m(f)* journalist

Joystick (*-s, -s*) *m* *(Inform)* joystick

jubeln *vi* to cheer

Jubiläum (*-s, Jubiläen*) *nt* jubilee;
(Jahrestag) anniversary

jucken *vi* to itch ▷ *vt* **es juckt mich am Arm**
my arm is itching; **das juckt mich nicht**
(fam) I couldn't care less; **Juckreiz** *m* itch

Jude (*-n, -n*) *m*, **Jüdin** *f* Jew; **sie ist Jüdin**
she's Jewish; **jüdisch** *adj* Jewish

Judo (*-(s)*) *nt* judo

Jugend (*-*) *f* youth; **jugendfrei** *adj* **ein ~er
Film** a U-rated film *(Brit)*, a G-rated film
(US); **ein nicht ~er Film** an X-rated film;
Jugendherberge (*-, -n*) *f* youth hostel;
jugendlich *adj* youthful; **Jugendliche(r)**
mf young person; **Jugendstil** *m* art
nouveau; **Jugendzentrum** *nt* youth
centre

Jugoslawien (*-s*) *nt* *(Hist)* Yugoslavia; **das
ehemalige ~** the former Yugoslavia

Juli (*-(s), -s*) *m* July; *siehe auch* **Juni**

jung *adj* young

Junge (*-n, -n*) *m* boy

Junge(s) (*-n, -n*) *nt* young animal; **die ~n**
pl the young *pl*

Jungfrau *f* virgin; *(Astr)* Virgo

Junggeselle (*-n, -n*) *m* bachelor;
Junggesellin *f* single woman

Juni (*-(s), -s*) *m* June; **im ~** in June; **am 4.**
~ on 4(th) June, on June 4(th) *(gesprochen:
on the fourth of June)*; **Anfang/Mitte/Ende
~** at the beginning/in the middle/at the
end of June; **letzten/nächsten
~** last/next June

Jupiter (*-s*) *m* Jupiter

Jura *ohne Artikel* *(Studienfach)* law;
~ studieren to study law; **Jurist(in)** *m(f)*
lawyer; **juristisch** *adj* legal

Justiz (*-*) *f* justice; **Justizminister(in)** *m(f)*
minister of justice

Juwel (*-s, -en*) *nt* jewel; **Juwelier(in)** (*-s, -e*)
m(f) jeweller

Jux (*-es, -e*) *m* joke, lark

j

k

Kabel (-s, -) nt (Elek) wire; (stark) cable; **Kabelfernsehen** nt cable television

Kabeljau (-s, -e o -s) m cod

Kabine f cabin; (im Schwimmbad) cubicle

Kabrio (-s, -s) nt convertible

Kachel (-, -n) f tile; **Kachelofen** m tiled stove

Käfer (-s, -) m beetle, bug (US)

Kaff (-s, -s) nt dump, hole

Kaffee (-s, -s) m coffee; ~ **kochen** to make some coffee; **Kaffeefilter** m coffee filter; **Kaffeekanne** f coffeepot; **Kaffeeklatsch** (-(e)s, -e) m chat over coffee and cakes, coffee klatch (US); **Kaffeelöffel** m coffee spoon; **Kaffeemaschine** f coffee maker (o machine); **Kaffeetasse** f coffee cup

Käfig (-s, -e) m cage

kahl adj (Mensch, Kopf) bald; (Baum, Wand) bare

Kahn (-(e)s, Kähne) m boat; (Lastkahn) barge

Kai (-s, -e o -s) m quay

Kaiser (-s, -) m emperor; **Kaiserin** f empress; **Kaiserschnitt** m (Med) caesarean (section)

Kajak (-s, -s) nt kayak

Kajal (-s) m kohl

Kajüte (-, -n) f cabin

Kakao (-s, -s) m cocoa; (Getränk) (hot) chocolate

Kakerlake (-, -n) f cockroach

Kaki (-, -s) f kaki

Kaktee (-, -n) f, **Kaktus** (-, -se) m cactus

Kalb (-(e)s, Kälber) nt calf; **Kalbfleisch** nt veal; **Kalbsbraten** m roast veal; **Kalbsschnitzel** nt veal cutlet; (paniert) escalope of veal

Kalender (-s, -) m calendar; (Taschenkalender) diary

Kalk (-(e)s, -e) m lime; (in Knochen) calcium

Kalorie f calorie; **kalorienarm** adj low-calorie

kalt adj cold; **mir ist (es) ~** I'm cold; **kaltblütig** adj cold-blooded; **Kälte** (-) f cold; (fig) coldness

kam imperf von **kommen**

Kambodscha (-s) nt Cambodia

Kamel (-(e)s, -e) nt camel

Kamera (-, -s) f camera

Kamerad(in) (-en, -en) m(f) friend; (als Begleiter) companion

Kamerafrau f, **Kameramann** m camerawoman/-man

Kamille (-, -n) f camomile; **Kamillentee** m camomile tea

Kamin (-s, -e) m (außen) chimney; (innen) fireplace

Kamm (-(e)s, Kämme) m comb; (Berg) ridge; (Hahn) crest; **kämmen** vr **sich ~, sich** (dat) **die Haare ~** to comb one's hair; **Kammermusik** f chamber music

Kampf (-(e)s, Kämpfe) m fight; (Schlacht) battle; (Wettbewerb) contest; (fig: Anstrengung) struggle; **kämpfen** vi to fight (für, um for); **Kampfsport** m martial art

Kanada (-s) nt Canada; **Kanadier(in)** (-s, -) m(f) Canadian; **kanadisch** adj Canadian

Kanal (-s, Kanäle) m (Fluss) canal; (Rinne, TV) channel; (für Abfluss) drain; **der ~** (Ärmelkanal) the (English) Channel; **Kanalinseln** pl Channel Islands pl; **Kanalisation** f sewerage system; **Kanaltunnel** m Channel Tunnel

Kanarienvogel m canary

Kandidat(in) (-en, -en) m(f) candidate

Kandis(zucker) (-) m rock candy

Känguru (-s, -s) nt kangaroo

Kaninchen nt rabbit

Kanister (-s, -) m can

Kännchen nt pot; **ein ~ Kaffee/Tee** a pot

of coffee/tea; **Kanne** (-, -n) f (Krug) jug; (Kaffeekanne) pot; (Milchkanne) churn; (Gießkanne) can

kannte imperf von **kennen**

Kante (-, -n) f edge

Kantine f canteen

Kanton (-s, -e) m canton

Kanu (-s, -s) nt canoe

Kanzler(in) (-s, -) m(f) chancellor

Kap (-s, -s) nt cape

Kapazität f capacity; (Fachmann) authority

Kapelle f (Gebäude) chapel; (Mus) band

Kaper (-, -n) f caper

kapieren vt, vi (fam) to understand; **kapiert?** got it?

Kapital (-s, -e o -ien) nt capital

Kapitän (-s, -e) m captain

Kapitel (-s, -) nt chapter

Kappe (-, -n) f cap

Kapsel (-, -n) f capsule

kaputt adj (fam) broken; (Mensch) exhausted; **kaputt|gehen** irr vi to break; (Schuhe) to fall apart; (Firma) to go bust; (Stoff) to wear out; **kaputt|machen** vt to break; (jdn) to wear out

Kapuze (-, -n) f hood

Kap Verde (-s) nt Cape Verde

Karaffe (-, -n) f carafe; (mit Stöpsel) decanter

Karambole (-, -n) f star fruit, carambola

Karamell (-s) m caramel, toffee

Karaoke (-(s)) nt karaoke

Karat (-s, -e) nt carat

Karate (-s) nt karate

Kardinal (-s, Kardinäle) m cardinal

Karfreitag m Good Friday

kariert adj checked; (Papier) squared

Karies (-) f (tooth) decay

Karikatur f caricature

Karneval (-s, -e o -s) m carnival

● **Karneval**
●
● **Karneval** is the name given to the days
● immediately before Lent when
● people gather to sing, dance, eat,
● drink and generally make merry
● before the fasting begins.
● **Rosenmontag**, the day before Shrove
● Tuesday, is the most important day
● of 'Karneval' on the Rhine. Most
● firms take a day's holiday on that day
● to enjoy the parades and revelry. In
● South Germany 'Karneval' is called
● **Fasching**.

Kärnten (-s) nt Carinthia

Karo (-s, -s) nt square; (Karten) diamonds pl

Karosserie f (Auto) body(work)

Karotte (-, -n) f carrot

Karpfen (-s, -) m carp

Karriere (-, -n) f career

Karte (-, -n) f card; (Landkarte) map; (Speisekarte) menu; (Eintrittskarte, Fahrkarte) ticket; **mit ~ bezahlen** to pay by credit card; **~n spielen** to play cards; **die ~n mischen/geben** to shuffle/deal the cards

Kartei f card index; **Karteikarte** f index card

Kartenspiel nt card game; **Kartentelefon** nt cardphone; **Kartenvorverkauf** m advance booking

Kartoffel (-, -n) f potato; **Kartoffelbrei** m mashed potatoes pl; **Kartoffelchips** pl crisps pl (Brit), chips pl (US); **Kartoffelpuffer** m potato cake (made from grated potatoes); **Kartoffelpüree** nt mashed potatoes pl; **Kartoffelsalat** m potato salad

Karton (-s, -s) m cardboard; (Schachtel) (cardboard) box

Kartusche (-, -n) f cartridge

Karussell (-s, -s) nt roundabout (Brit), merry-go-round

Kaschmir (-s, e) m (Stoff) cashmere

Käse (-s, -) m cheese; **Käsekuchen** m cheesecake; **Käseplatte** f cheeseboard

Kasino (-s, -s) nt (Spielkasino) casino

Kaskoversicherung f comprehensive insurance

Kasper(l) (-s, -) m Punch; (fig) clown; **Kasperl(e)theater** nt (Vorstellung) Punch and Judy show; (Gebäude) Punch and Judy theatre

Kasse (-, -n) f (in Geschäft) till, cash register; (im Supermarkt) checkout; (Geldkasten) cashbox; (Theater) box office; (Kino) ticket office; (Krankenkasse) health insurance; (Spar~) savings bank; **Kassenbon** (-s, -s) m, **Kassenzettel** m receipt; **Kassenzettel** m receipt

Kassette f (small) box; (Tonband)

cassette; **Kassettenrekorder** m cassette recorder

kassieren vt to take ▷ vi **darf ich ~?** would you like to pay now?; **Kassierer(in)** m(f) cashier

Kastanie f chestnut

Kasten (-s, Kästen) m (Behälter) box; (Getränkekasten) crate

Kat m abk = **Katalysator**

Katalog (-(e)s, -e) m catalogue

Katalysator m (Auto) catalytic converter; (Phys) catalyst

Katar (-s) nt Qatar

Katarr(h) (-s, -e) m catarrh

Katastrophe (-, -n) f catastrophe, disaster

Kategorie (-, -n) f category

Kater (-s, -) m tomcat; (fam: nach zu viel Alkohol) hangover

Kathedrale (-, -n) f cathedral

Katholik(in) m(f) Catholic; **katholisch** adj Catholic

Katze (-, -n) f cat

Kauderwelsch (-(s)) nt (unverständlich) gibberish; (Fachjargon) jargon

kauen vt, vi to chew

Kauf (-(e)s, Käufe) m purchase; (Kaufen) buying; **ein guter ~** a bargain; **etw in ~ nehmen** to put up with sth; **kaufen** vt to buy; **Käufer(in)** m(f) buyer; **Kauffrau** f businesswoman; **Kaufhaus** nt department store; **Kaufmann** m businessman; (im Einzelhandel) shopkeeper (Brit), storekeeper (US); **Kaufpreis** m purchase price; **Kaufvertrag** m purchase agreement

Kaugummi m chewing gum

Kaulquappe (-, -n) f tadpole

kaum adv hardly, scarcely

Kaution f deposit; (Jur) bail

Kaviar m caviar

KB (-, -) nt, **Kbyte** (-, -) nt abk = **Kilobyte** KB

Kebab (-(s), -s) m kebab

Kegel (-s, -) m skittle; (beim Bowling) pin; (Math) cone; **Kegelbahn** f bowling alley; **kegeln** vi to play skittles; (bowlen) to bowl

Kehle (-, -n) f throat; **Kehlkopf** m larynx

Kehre (-, -n) f sharp bend

kehren vt (fegen) to sweep

Keilriemen m (Auto) fan belt

kein pron no, not ... any; **ich habe ~ Geld** I have no money, I don't have money; **~ Mensch** no one; **du bist ~ Kind mehr**

you're not a child any more; **keine(r, s)** pron (Person) no one, nobody; (Sache) not ... any, none; **~r von ihnen** none of them; (bei zwei Personen/Sachen) neither of them; **ich will keins von beiden** I don't want either (of them); **keinesfalls** adv on no account, under no circumstances

Keks (-es, -e) m biscuit (Brit), cookie (US); **jdm auf den ~ gehen** (fam) to get on sb's nerves

Keller (-s, -) m cellar; (Geschoss) basement

Kellner (-s, -) m waiter; **Kellnerin** f waitress

Kenia (-s) nt Kenya

kennen (kannte, gekannt) vt to know; **wir ~ uns seit 1990** we've known each other since 1990; **wir ~ uns schon** we've already met; **kennst du mich noch?** do you remember me?; **~ lernen** to get to know; **sich ~ lernen** to get to know each other; (zum ersten Mal) to meet

Kenntnis f knowledge; **seine ~se** his knowledge

Kennwort nt (a. Inform) password; **Kennzeichen** nt mark, sign; (Auto) number plate (Brit), license plate (US); **besondere ~** distinguishing marks

Kerl (-s, -e) m guy, bloke (Brit)

Kern (-(e)s, -e) m (Obst) pip; (Pfirsich, Kirsche etc) stone; (Nuss) kernel; (Atomkern) nucleus; (fig) heart, core

Kernenergie f nuclear energy; **Kernkraft** f nuclear power; **Kernkraftwerk** nt nuclear power station

Kerze (-, -n) f candle; (Zündkerze) plug

Ket(s)chup (-(s), -s) m o nt ketchup

Kette (-, -n) f chain; (Halskette) necklace

keuchen vi to pant; **Keuchhusten** m whooping cough

Keule (-, -n) f club; (Gastr) leg; (von Hähnchen a.) drumstick

Keyboard (-s, -s) nt (Mus) keyboard

Kfz nt abk = **Kraftfahrzeug**

Kfz-Brief m ≈ logbook

Kfz-Steuer f ≈ road tax (Brit), vehicle tax (US)

KG (-, -s) f abk = **Kommanditgesellschaft** limited partnership

Kichererbse f chick pea

kichern vi to giggle

Kickboard® (-s, -s) nt micro scooter

Kicker (-s, -) m (Spiel) table football (Brit), foosball (US)

kidnappen vt to kidnap
Kidney-Bohne f kidney bean
Kiefer (-s, -) m jaw ▷ (-, -n) f pine
Kieme (-, -n) f gill
Kies (-es, -e) m gravel; **Kiesel** (-s, -) m,
  Kieselstein m pebble
kiffen vi (fam) to smoke pot
Kilo (-s, -(s)) nt kilo; **Kilobyte** nt kilobyte;
  Kilogramm nt kilogram; **Kilojoule** nt
  kilojoule; **Kilometer** m kilometre;
  Kilometerstand m ≈ mileage;
  Kilometerzähler m ≈ mileometer;
  Kilowatt nt kilowatt
Kind (-(e)s, -er) nt child; **sie bekommt ein
  ~** she's having a baby; **Kinderarzt** m,
  Kinderärztin f paediatrician;
  Kinderbetreuung f childcare;
  Kinderbett nt cot (Brit), crib (US);
  Kinderfahrkarte f child's ticket;
  Kindergarten m nursery school,
  kindergarten; **Kindergärtnerin** f
  nursery-school teacher; **Kindergeld** nt
  child benefit; **Kinderkrankheit** f
  children's illness; **Kinderkrippe** f crèche
  (Brit), daycare center (US);
  Kinderlähmung f polio;
  Kindermädchen nt nanny (Brit),
  nurse(maid); **kindersicher** adj childproof;
  Kindersicherung f childproof safety
  catch; (an Flasche) childproof cap;
  Kindersitz m child seat;
  Kindertagesstätte nt day nursery;
  Kinderteller m (im Restaurant) children's
  portion; **Kinderwagen** m pram (Brit),
  baby carriage (US); **Kinderzimmer** nt
  children's (bed)room; **Kindheit** f
  childhood; **kindisch** adj childish; **kindlich**
  adj childlike
Kinn (-(e)s, -e) nt chin
Kino (-s, -s) nt cinema (Brit), movie
  theater (US); **ins ~ gehen** to go to the
  cinema (Brit) (o to the movies (US))
Kiosk (-(e)s, -e) m kiosk
Kippe f (fam: Zigarettenstummel) cigarette
  end, fag end (Brit)
kippen vi to tip over ▷ vt to tilt;
  (Regierung, Minister) to topple
Kirche (-, -n) f church; **Kirchturm** m
  church tower; (mit Spitze) steeple
Kirmes (-, -sen) f fair
Kirsche (-, -n) f cherry; **Kirschtomate** f
  cherry tomato
Kissen (-s, -) nt cushion; (Kopfkissen)

pillow; **Kissenbezug** m cushion cover;
  (für Kopfkissen) pillowcase
Kiste (-, -n) f box; (Truhe) chest
kitschig adj kitschy, cheesy
kitzelig adj (a. fig) ticklish; **kitzeln** vt, vi
  to tickle
Kiwi (-, -s) f (Frucht) kiwi (fruit)
Klage (-, -n) f complaint; (Jur) lawsuit;
  klagen vi to complain (über +akk about,
  bei to); **kläglich** adj wretched
Klammer (-, -n) f (in Text) bracket;
  (Büroklammer) clip; (Wäscheklammer) peg
  (Brit), clothespin (US); (Zahnklammer)
  brace; **Klammeraffe** m (fam) at-sign, @;
  klammern vr **sich ~** to cling (an +akk to)
klang imperf von **klingen**
Klang (-(e)s, Klänge) m sound
Klappbett nt folding bed
klappen vi impers (gelingen) to work; **es
  hat gut geklappt** it went well
klappern vi to rattle; (Geschirr) to clatter;
  Klapperschlange f rattlesnake
Klappfahrad nt folding bicycle;
  Klappstuhl m folding chair
klar adj clear; (dat) **im Klaren sein** to
  be clear (über +akk about); **alles ~?**
  everything okay?
klären vt (Flüssigkeit) to purify; (Probleme,
  Frage) to clarify ▷ vr **sich ~** to clear itself up
Klarinette (-, -n) f clarinet
klar|kommen irr vi **mit etw ~** to cope
  with something; **kommst du klar?** are
  you managing all right?; **mit jdm ~** to get
  along with sb; **klar|machen** vt **jdm etw
  ~** to make sth clear to sb; **Klarsichtfolie** f
  clingfilm (Brit), plastic wrap (US);
  klar|stellen vt to clarify
Klärung f (von Frage, Problem) clarification
klasse adj inv (fam) great, brilliant
Klasse (-, -n) f class; (Schuljahr) form (Brit),
  grade (US); **erster ~ reisen** to travel first
  class; **in welche ~ gehst du?** which form
  (Brit) (o grade (US)) are you in?;
  Klassenarbeit f test; **Klassenlehrer(in)**
  m(f) class teacher; **Klassenzimmer** nt
  classroom
Klassik f (Zeit) classical period; (Musik)
  classical music
Klatsch (-(e)s, -e) m (Gerede) gossip;
  klatschen vi (schlagen) to smack; (Beifall)
  to applaud, to clap; (reden) to gossip;
  Klatschmohn m (corn) poppy;
  klatschnass adj soaking (wet)

k

Klaue (-, -n) f claw; (fam: Schrift) scrawl; **klauen** vt (fam) to pinch

Klavier (-s, -e) nt piano

Klebeband nt adhesive tape; **kleben** vt to stick (an +akk to) ▷ vi (klebrig sein) to be sticky; **klebrig** adj sticky; **Klebstoff** m glue; **Klebstreifen** m adhesive tape

Klecks (-es, -e) m blob; (Tinte) blot

Klee (-s) m clover

Kleid (-(e)s, -er) nt (Frauen~) dress; **~er** pl (Kleidung) clothes pl; **Kleiderbügel** m coat hanger; **Kleiderschrank** m wardrobe (Brit), closet (US); **Kleidung** f clothing

klein adj small, little; (Finger) little; **mein ~er Bruder** my little (o younger) brother; **als ich noch ~ war** when I was a little boy/girl; **etw ~ schneiden** to chop sth up; **etw ~ schreiben** to write sth with a small letter; **Kleinanzeige** f classified ad; **Kleinbuchstabe** m small letter; **Kleinbus** m minibus; **Kleingeld** nt change; **Kleinigkeit** f trifle; (Zwischenmahlzeit) snack; **Kleinkind** nt toddler; **klein|schreiben** vt to write with a small letter; **Kleinstadt** f small town

Kleister (-s, -) m paste

Klempner(in) m(f) plumber

klettern vi to climb

Klettverschluss m Velcro® fastening

klicken vi (a. Inform) to click

Klient(in) (-en, -en) m(f) client

Klima (-s, -s) nt climate; **Klimaanlage** f air conditioning; **klimatisiert** adj air-conditioned

Klinge (-, -n) f blade

Klingel (-, -n) f bell; **klingeln** vi to ring

klingen (klang, geklungen) vi to sound

Klinik f clinic; (Krankenhaus) hospital

Klinke (-, -n) f handle

Klippe (-, -n) f cliff; (im Meer) reef; (fig) hurdle

Klischee (-s, -s) nt (fig) cliché

Klo (-s, -s) nt (fam) loo (Brit), john (US); **Klobrille** f toilet seat; **Klopapier** nt toilet paper

klopfen vt, vi to knock; (Herz) to thump

Kloß (-es, Klöße) m (im Hals) lump; (Gastr) dumpling

Kloster (-s, Klöster) nt (für Männer) monastery; (für Frauen) convent

Klub (-s, -s) m club

klug adj clever

knabbern vt, vi to nibble

Knäckebrot nt crispbread

knacken vt, vi to crack

Knall (-(e)s, -e) m bang; **Knallbonbon** nt cracker; **knallen** vi to bang

knapp adj (kaum ausreichend) scarce; (Sieg) narrow; **~ bei Kasse sein** to be short of money; **~ zwei Stunden** just under two hours

Knauf (-s, Knäufe) m knob

Knautschzone f (Auto) crumple zone

kneifen (kniff, gekniffen) vt, vi to pinch; (sich drücken) to back out (vor +dat of); **Kneifzange** f pincers pl

Kneipe (-, -n) f (fam) pub (Brit), bar

Knete (-) f (fam: Geld) dough; **kneten** vt to knead; (formen) to mould

knicken vt, vi (brechen) to break; (Papier) to fold; **geknickt sein** (fig) to be downcast

Knie (-s, -) nt knee; **in die ~ gehen** to bend one's knees; **Kniebeuge** f knee bend; **Kniegelenk** nt knee joint; **Kniekehle** f back of the knee; **knien** vi to kneel; **Kniescheibe** f kneecap; **Knieschoner** (-s, -) m, **Knieschützer** (-s, -) m knee pad; **Kniestrumpf** m knee-length sock

kniff imperf von **kneifen**

knipsen vt to punch; (Foto) to snap ▷ vi (Foto) to take snaps

knirschen vi to crunch; **mit den Zähnen ~** to grind one's teeth

knitterfrei adj non-crease; **knittern** vi to crease

Knoblauch m garlic; **Knoblauchbrot** nt garlic bread; **Knoblauchzehe** f clove of garlic

Knöchel (-s, -) m (Finger) knuckle; (Fuß) ankle

Knochen (-s, -) m bone; **Knochenbruch** m fracture; **Knochenmark** nt marrow

Knödel (-s, -) m dumpling

Knollensellerie m celeriac

Knopf (-(e)s, Knöpfe) m button; **Knopfdruck** m **auf ~** at the touch of a botton; **Knopfloch** nt buttonhole

Knospe (-, -n) f bud

knoten vt to knot; **Knoten** (-s, -) m knot; (Med) lump

Know-how (-(s)) nt know-how, expertise

knurren vi (Hund) to growl; (Magen) to rumble; (Mensch) to grumble

knusprig adj crisp; (Keks) crunchy

knutschen vi (fam) to smooch

k. o. *adj inv* (*Sport*) knocked out; (*fig*) knackered

Koalition *f* coalition

Koch (-(e)s, Köche) *m* cook; **Kochbuch** *nt* cookery book, cookbook; **kochen** *vt, vi* to cook; (*Wasser*) to boil; (*Kaffee, Tee*) to make; **Köchin** *f* cook; **Kochlöffel** *m* wooden spoon; **Kochnische** *f* kitchenette; **Kochplatte** *f* hotplate; **Kochrezept** *nt* recipe; **Kochtopf** *m* saucepan

Kode (-s, -s) *m* code

Köder (-s, -) *m* bait

Koffein (-s) *nt* caffeine; **koffeinfrei** *adj* decaffeinated

Koffer (-s, -) *m* (suit)case; **Kofferraum** *m* (*Auto*) boot (*Brit*), trunk (*US*)

Kognak (-s, -s) *m* brandy

Kohl (-(e)s, -e) *m* cabbage

Kohle (-, -n) *f* coal; (*Holzkohle*) charcoal; (*Chem*) carbon; (*fam: Geld*) cash, dough; **Kohlehydrat** *nt* carbohydrate; **Kohlendioxid** *nt* carbon dioxide; **Kohlensäure** *f* (*in Getränken*) fizz; **ohne ~** still, non-carbonated (*US*); **mit ~** sparkling, carbonated (*US*); **Kohletablette** *f* charcoal tablet

Kohlrabi (-(s), -(s)) *m* kohlrabi

Kohlrübe *f* swede (*Brit*), rutabaga (*US*)

Koje (-, -n) *f* cabin; (*Bett*) bunk

Kokain (-s) *nt* cocaine

Kokosnuss *f* coconut

Kolben (-s, -) *m* (*Tech*) piston; (*Mais~*) cob

Kolik (-, -en) *f* colic

Kollaps (-es, -e) *m* collapse

Kollege (-n, -n) *m*, **Kollegin** *f* colleague

Köln (-s) *nt* Cologne

Kolonne (-, -n) *f* convoy; **in ~ fahren** to drive in convoy

Kölsch (-, -) *nt* (*Bier*) (strong) lager (*from the Cologne region*)

Kolumbien (-s) *nt* Columbia

Koma (-s, -s) *nt* coma

Kombi (-(s), -s) *m* estate (car) (*Brit*), station wagon (*US*); **Kombination** *f* combination; (*Folgerung*) deduction; (*Hemdhose*) combinations *pl*; (*Aviat*) flying suit; **kombinieren** *vt* to combine ▷ *vi* to reason; (*vermuten*) to guess; **Kombizange** *f* (pair of) pliers *pl*

Komfort (-s) *m* conveniences *pl*; (*Bequemlichkeit*) comfort

Komiker(in) *m(f)* comedian, comic; **komisch** *adj* funny

Komma (-s, -s) *nt* comma

Kommanditgesellschaft *f* limited partnership

kommen (kam, gekommen) *vi* to come; (*näher kommen*) to approach; (*passieren*) to happen; (*gelangen, geraten*) to get; (*erscheinen*) to appear; (*in die Schule, das Gefängnis etc*) to go; **~ lassen** to send for; **zu sich ~** to come round (*o* to); **zu etw ~** (*bekommen*) to acquire sth; (*Zeit dazu finden*) to get round to sth; **wer kommt zuerst?** who's first?; **kommend** *adj* coming; **~e Woche** next week; **in den ~en Jahren** in the years to come

Kommentar *m* commentary; **kein ~** no comment

Kommilitone (-n, -n) *m*, **Kommilitonin** *f* fellow student

Kommissar(in) *m(f)* inspector

Kommode (-, -n) *f* chest of drawers

Kommunikation *f* communication

Kommunion *f* (*Rel*) communion

Kommunismus *m* communism

Komödie *f* comedy

kompakt *adj* compact

Kompass (-es, -e) *m* compass

kompatibel *adj* compatible

kompetent *adj* competent

komplett *adj* complete

Kompliment *nt* compliment; **jdm ein ~ machen** to pay sb a compliment; **~!** congratulations

Komplize (-n, -n) *m* accomplice

kompliziert *adj* complicated

Komponist(in) *m(f)* composer

Kompost (-(e)s, -e) *m* compost; **Komposthaufen** *m* compost heap; **kompostierbar** *adj* biodegradable

Kompott (-(e)s, -e) *nt* stewed fruit

Kompresse (-, -n) *f* compress

Kompromiss (-es, -e) *m* compromise

Kondensmilch *f* condensed milk, evaporated milk

Kondition *f* (*Leistungsfähigkeit*) condition; **sie hat eine gute ~** she's in good shape

Konditorei *f* cake shop; (*mit Café*) café

Kondom (-s, -e) *nt* condom

Konfektionsgröße *f* size

Konferenz *f* conference

Konfession *f* religion; (*christlich*) denomination

Konfetti (-(s)) *nt* confetti

k

Konfirmation f (Rel) confirmation
Konfitüre (-, -n) f jam
Konflikt (-(e)s, -e) m conflict
konfrontieren vt to confront
Kongo (-s) m Congo
Kongress (-es, -e) m conference; **der
~** (Parlament der USA) Congress
König (-(e)s, -e) m king; **Königin** f
queen; **Königinpastete** f vol-au-vent;
königlich adj royal; **Königreich** nt
kingdom
Konkurrenz f competition

🔘 SCHLÜSSELWORT

können (pt **konnte**, pp **gekonnt** od (als
Hilfsverb) **können**) vt, vi **1** to be able to;
ich kann es machen I can do it, I am able
to do it,; **ich kann es nicht machen** I can't
do it, I'm not able to do it; **ich kann nicht
...** I can't ..., I cannot ...; **ich kann nicht
mehr** I can't go on
2 (wissen, beherrschen) to know; **können
Sie Deutsch?** can you speak German?; **er
kann gut Englisch** he speaks English well;
sie kann keine Mathematik she can't do
mathematics
3 (dürfen) to be allowed to; **kann ich
gehen?** can I go?; **könnte ich ...?** could I
...?; **kann ich mit?** (umg) can I come with
you?
4 (möglich sein): **Sie könnten Recht
haben** you may be right; **das kann sein**
that's possible; **kann sein** maybe

konsequent adj consistent;
Konsequenz f consequence
konservativ adj conservative
Konserven pl tinned food sing (Brit),
canned food sing; **Konservendose** f tin
(Brit), can
konservieren vt to preserve;
Konservierungsmittel nt preservative
Konsonant m consonant
Konsul(in) (-s, -n) m(f) consul; **Konsulat**
nt consulate
Kontakt (-(e)s, -e) m contact;
kontaktarm adj **er ist ~** he lacks contact
with other people; **kontaktfreudig** adj
sociable; **Kontaktlinsen** pl contact
lenses pl
Kontinent m continent
Konto (-s, Konten) nt account;

Kontoauszug m (bank) statement;
Kontoauszugsdrucker m bank-statement
machine; **Kontoinhaber(in)** m(f) account
holder; **Kontonummer** f account
number; **Kontostand** m balance
Kontrabass m double bass
Kontrast (-(e)s, -e) m contrast
Kontrolle (-, -n) f control; (Aufsicht)
supervision; (Passkontrolle) passport
control; **kontrollieren** vt to control;
(nachprüfen) to check
Konzentration f concentration;
Konzentrationslager nt (Hist)
concentration camp; **konzentrieren** vt
to concentrate ▷ vr **sich ~** to concentrate
Konzept (-(e)s, -e) nt rough draft; **jdn aus
dem ~ bringen** to put sb off
Konzert (-(e)s, -e) nt concert; (Stück)
concerto; **Konzertsaal** m concert hall
koordinieren vt to coordinate
Kopf (-(e)s, Köpfe) m head; **pro ~** per
person; **sich den ~ zerbrechen** to rack
one's brains; **Kopfhörer** m headphones
pl; **Kopfkissen** nt pillow; **Kopfsalat** m
lettuce; **Kopfschmerzen** pl headache
sing; **Kopfstütze** f headrest; **Kopftuch** nt
headscarf; **kopfüber** adv headfirst
Kopie f copy; **kopieren** vt (a. Inform) to
copy; **Kopierer** (-s, -) m, **Kopiergerät** nt
copier
Kopilot(in) m(f) co-pilot
Koralle (-, -n) f coral
Koran (-s) m (Rel) Koran
Korb (-(e)s, Körbe) m basket; **jdm einen
~ geben** (fig) to turn sb down
Kord (-(e)s, -e) m corduroy
Kordel (-, -n) f cord
Korinthe (-e, -n) f currant
Kork (-(e)s, -e) m cork; **Korken** (-s, -) m
cork; **Korkenzieher** (-s, -) m corkscrew
Korn (-(e)s, Körner) nt grain; **Kornblume** f
cornflower
Körper (-s, -) m body; **Körperbau** m
build; **körperbehindert** adj disabled;
Körpergeruch m body odour;
Körpergröße f height; **körperlich** adj
physical; **Körperteil** m part of the body;
Körperverletzung f physical injury
korrekt adj correct
Korrespondent(in) m(f) correspondent;
Korrespondenz f correspondence
korrigieren vt to correct
Kosmetik f cosmetics pl;

Kosmetikkoffer m vanity case;
Kosmetiksalon m beauty parlour;
Kosmetiktuch nt paper tissue
Kost (-) f (Nahrung) food; (Verpflegung) board
kostbar adj precious; (teuer) costly, expensive
kosten vt to cost ▷ vt, vi (versuchen) to taste; **Kosten** pl costs pl, cost; (Ausgaben) expenses pl; **auf ~ von** at the expense of; **kostenlos** adj free (of charge);
Kostenvoranschlag m estimate
köstlich adj (Essen) delicious; (Einfall) delightful; **sich ~ amüsieren** to have a marvellous time
Kostprobe f taster; (fig) sample;
kostspielig adj expensive
Kostüm (-s, -e) nt costume;
(Damenkostüm) suit
Kot (-(e)s) m excrement
Kotelett (-(e)s, -e o -s) nt chop, cutlet
Koteletten pl sideboards pl (Brit), sideburns pl (US)
Kotflügel m (Auto) wing
Krabbe (-, -n) f shrimp; (größer) prawn; (Krebs) crab
krabbeln vi to crawl
Krach (-(e)s, -s o -e) m crash; (andauernd) noise; (fam: Streit) row
Kraft (-, Kräfte) f strength; (Pol, Phys) force; (Fähigkeit) power; (Arbeits~) worker; **in ~ treten** to come into effect;
Kraftausdruck m swearword;
Kraftfahrzeug nt motor vehicle;
Kraftfahrzeugbrief m ≈ logbook;
Kraftfahrzeugschein m vehicle registration document;
Kraftfahrzeugsteuer f ≈ road tax (Brit), vehicle tax (US);
Kraftfahrzeugversicherung f car insurance; **kräftig** adj strong; (gesund) healthy; (Farben) intense, strong;
Kraftstoff m fuel; **Kraftwerk** nt power station
Kragen (-s, -) m collar
Krähe (-, -n) f crow
Kralle (-, -n) f claw; (Parkkralle) wheel clamp
Kram (-(e)s) m stuff
Krampf (-(e)s, Krämpfe) m cramp;
(zuckend) spasm; **Krampfader** f varicose vein
Kran (-(e)s, Kräne) m crane

Kranich (-s, -e) m (Zool) crane
krank adj ill, sick
kränken vt to hurt
Krankengymnastik f physiotherapy;
Krankenhaus nt hospital;
Krankenkasse f health insurance;
Krankenpfleger (-s, -) m (male) nurse;
Krankenschein m health insurance certificate; **Krankenschwester** f nurse;
Krankenversicherung f health insurance; **Krankenwagen** m ambulance; **Krankheit** f illness; (durch Infektion hervorgerufen) disease
Kränkung f insult
Kranz (-es, Kränze) m wreath
krass adj crass; (fam: toll) wicked
kratzen vt, vi to scratch; **Kratzer** (-s, -) m scratch
kraulen vi (schwimmen) to do the crawl ▷ vt (streicheln) to pet
Kraut (-(e)s, Kräuter) nt plant; (Gewürz) herb; (Gemüse) cabbage; **Kräuter** pl herbs pl; **Kräuterbutter** f herb butter;
Kräutertee m herbal tea; **Krautsalat** m coleslaw
Krawatte f tie
kreativ adj creative
Krebs (-es, -e) m (Zool) crab; (Med) cancer; (Astr) Cancer
Kredit (-(e)s, -e) m credit; **auf ~** on credit; **einen ~ aufnehmen** to take out a loan;
Kreditkarte f credit card
Kreide (-, -n) f chalk
Kreis (-es, -e) m circle; (Bezirk) district
kreischen vi to shriek; (Bremsen, Säge) to screech
Kreisel (-s, -) m (Spielzeug) top;
(Verkehrskreisel) roundabout (Brit), traffic circle (US)
Kreislauf m (Med) circulation; (fig: der Natur etc) cycle; **Kreislaufstörungen** pl (Med) **ich habe ~** I've got problems with my circulation; **Kreisverkehr** m roundabout (Brit), traffic circle (US), rotary (US)
Kren (-s) m horseradish
Kresse (-, -n) f cress
Kreuz (-es, -e) nt cross; (Anat) small of the back; (Karten) clubs pl; **mir tut das ~ weh** I've got backache; **Kreuzband** m cruciate ligament; **kreuzen** vt to cross ▷ vr **sich ~** to cross ▷ vi (Naut) to cruise;
Kreuzfahrt f cruise; **Kreuzgang** m

k

cloisters pl; **Kreuzotter** (-, -n) f adder;
Kreuzschlitzschraubenzieher m
Phillips® screwdriver; **Kreuzschlüssel** m
(Auto) wheel brace; **Kreuzschmerzen** pl
backache sing; **Kreuzung** f
(Verkehrskreuzung) crossroads sing,
intersection; (Züchtung) cross;
Kreuzworträtsel nt crossword (puzzle)
kriechen (kroch, gekrochen) vi to crawl;
(unauffällig) to creep; (fig, pej) (**vor jdm**) ~ to
crawl (to sb); **Kriechspur** f crawler lane
Krieg (-(e)s, -e) m war
kriegen vt (fam) to get; (erwischen) to
catch; **sie kriegt ein Kind** she's having a
baby; **ich kriege noch Geld von dir** you
still owe me some money
Krimi (-s, -s) m (fam) thriller; **Kriminalität**
f criminality; **Kriminalpolizei** f detective
force, ≈ CID (Brit), ≈ FBI (US);
Kriminalroman m detective novel;
kriminell adj criminal
Krippe (-, -n) f (Futterkrippe) manger;
(Weihnachtskrippe) crib (Brit), crèche (US);
(Kinderkrippe) crèche (Brit), daycare center
(US)
Krise (-, -n) f crisis
Kristall (-s, -e) m crystal ▷ (-s) nt (Glas)
crystal
Kritik f criticism; (Rezension) review;
Kritiker(in) m(f) critic; **kritisch** adj
critical
kritzeln vt, vi to scribble, to scrawl
Kroate (-n, -n) m Croat; **Kroatien** (-s) nt
Croatia; **Kroatin** f Croat; **kroatisch** adj
Croatian; **Kroatisch** nt Croatian
kroch imperf von **kriechen**
Krokodil (-s, -e) nt crocodile
Krokus (-, - o -se) m crocus
Krone (-, -n) f crown; **Kronleuchter** m
chandelier
Kropf (-(e)s, Kröpfe) m (Med) goitre; (von
Vogel) crop
Kröte (-, -n) f toad
Krücke (-, -n) f crutch
Krug (-(e)s, Krüge) m jug; (Bierkrug) mug
Krümel (-s, -) m crumb
krumm adj crooked
Krüppel (-s, -) m cripple
Kruste (-, -n) f crust
Kruzifix (-es, -e) nt crucifix
Kuba (-s) nt Cuba
Kübel (-s, -) m tub; (Eimer) bucket
Kubikmeter m cubic metre

Küche (-, -n) f kitchen; (Kochen) cooking
Kuchen (-s, -) m cake; (mit Teigdeckel) pie;
Kuchengabel f cake fork
Küchenmaschine f food processor;
Küchenpapier nt kitchen roll;
Küchenschrank m (kitchen) cupboard
Kuckuck (-s, -e) m cuckoo
Kugel (-, -n) f ball; (Math) sphere; (Mil)
bullet; (Weihnachtskugel) bauble;
Kugellager nt ball bearing;
Kugelschreiber m (ball-point) pen,
biro® (Brit); **Kugelstoßen** (-s) nt shot
put
Kuh (-, Kühe) f cow
kühl adj cool; **Kühlakku** (-s, -s) m ice
pack; **Kühlbox** f cool box; **kühlen** vt to
cool; **Kühler** (-s, -) m (Auto) radiator;
Kühlerhaube f (Auto) bonnet (Brit), hood
(US); **Kühlschrank** m fridge, refrigerator;
Kühltasche f cool bag; **Kühltruhe** f
freezer; **Kühlwasser** nt (Auto) radiator
water
Kuhstall m cowshed
Küken (-s, -) nt chick
Kuli (-s, -s) m (fam: Kugelschreiber) pen,
biro® (Brit)
Kulisse (-, -n) f scenery
Kult (-s, -e) m cult; **Kultfigur** f cult
figure
Kultur f culture; (Lebensform) civilization;
Kulturbeutel m toilet bag (Brit),
washbag; **kulturell** adj cultural
Kümmel (-s, -) m caraway seeds pl
Kummer (-s) m grief, sorrow
kümmern vr **sich um jdn** ~ to look after
sb; **sich um etw** ~ to see to sth ▷ vt to
concern; **das kümmert mich nicht** that
doesn't worry me
Kumpel (-s, -) m (fam) mate, pal
Kunde (-n, -n) m customer;
Kundendienst m after-sales (o customer)
service; **Kunden(kredit)karte** f
storecard, chargecard; **Kundennummer** f
customer number
kündigen vi to hand in one's notice;
(Mieter) to give notice that one is moving
out; **jdm** ~ to give sb his/her notice;
(Vermieter) to give sb notice to quit ▷ vt to
cancel; (Vertrag) to terminate; **jdm die
Stellung** ~ to give sb his/her notice; **jdm
die Wohnung** ~ to give sb notice to quit;
Kündigung f (Arbeitsverhältnis) dismissal;
(Vertrag) termination; (Abonnement)

cancellation; (*Frist*) notice;
Kündigungsfrist *f* period of notice
Kundin *f* customer; **Kundschaft** *f*
customers *pl*
künftig *adj* future
Kunst (*-, Künste*) *f* art; (*Können*) skill;
Kunstausstellung *f* art exhibition;
Kunstgewerbe *nt* arts and crafts *pl*;
Künstler(in) (*-s, -*) *m(f)* artist;
künstlerisch *adj* artistic
künstlich *adj* artificial
Kunststoff *m* synthetic material;
Kunststück *nt* trick; **Kunstwerk** *nt*
work of art
Kupfer (*-s, -*) *nt* copper
Kuppel (*-, -n*) *f* dome
kuppeln *vi* (*Auto*) to operate the clutch;
Kupplung *f* coupling; (*Auto*) clutch
Kur (*-, -en*) *f* course of treatment; (*am
Kurort*) cure
Kür (*-, -en*) *f* (*Sport*) free programme
Kurbel (*-, -n*) *f* crank; (*von Rollo, Fenster*)
winder
Kürbis (*-ses, -se*) *m* pumpkin
Kurierdienst *m* courier service
kurieren *vt* to cure
Kurort *m* health resort
Kurs (*-es, -e*) *m* course; (*Fin*) rate;
(*Wechselkurs*) exchange rate
kursiv *adj* italic ▷ *adv* in italics
Kursleiter(in) *m(f)* course tutor;
Kursteilnehmer(in) *m(f)* (course)
participant; **Kurswagen** *m* (*Eisenb*)
through carriage
Kurve (*-, -n*) *f* curve; (*Straßenkurve*) bend;
kurvenreich *adj* (*Straße*) winding
kurz *adj* short; (*zeitlich a.*) brief;
~ vorher/darauf shortly before/after;
kannst du ~ kommen? could you come
here for a minute?; **~ gesagt** in short;
kurzärmelig *adj* short-sleeved; **kürzen**
vt to cut short; (*in der Länge*) to shorten;
(*Gehalt*) to reduce; **kurzerhand** *adv* on the
spot; **kurzfristig** *adj* short-term; **das
Konzert wurde ~ abgesagt** the concert
was called off at short notice;
Kurzgeschichte *f* short story;
kurzhaarig *adj* short-haired; **kürzlich**
adv recently; **Kurznachrichten** *pl* news
summary *sing*; **Kurzparkzone** *f*
short-stay (*Brit*) (*o* short-term (*US*))
parking zone; **Kurzschluss** *m* (*Elek*) short
circuit; **kurzsichtig** *adj* short-sighted;

Kurzurlaub *m* short holiday (*Brit*), short
vacation (*US*); **Kurzwelle** *f* short wave
Kusine *f* cousin
Kuss (*-es, Küsse*) *m* kiss; **küssen** *vt* to kiss
▷ *vr* **sich ~** to kiss
Küste (*-, -n*) *f* coast; (*Ufer*) shore;
Küstenwache *f* coastguard
Kutsche (*-, -n*) *f* carriage; (*geschlossene*)
coach
Kuvert (*-s, -s*) *nt* envelope
Kuvertüre (*-, -n*) *f* coating
Kuwait (*-s*) *nt* Kuwait
KZ (*-s, -s*) *nt abk =* **Konzentrationslager**
(*Hist*) concentration camp

Labor (-s, -e o -s) nt lab

Labyrinth (-s, -e) nt maze

Lache (-, -n) f (Pfütze) puddle; (Blut~, Öl~) pool

lächeln vi to smile; **Lächeln** (-s) nt smile; **lachen** vi to laugh; **lächerlich** adj ridiculous

Lachs (-es, -e) m salmon

Lack (-s, -e) m varnish; (Farblack) lacquer; (an Auto) paint; **lackieren** vt to varnish; (Auto) to spray; **Lackschaden** m scratch (on the paintwork)

Ladegerät nt (battery) charger; **laden** (lud, geladen) vt (a. Inform) to load; (einladen) to invite; (Handy etc) to charge

Laden (-s, Läden) m shop; (Fensterladen) shutter; **Ladendieb(in)** m(f) shoplifter; **Ladendiebstahl** m shoplifting; **Ladenschluss** m closing time

Ladung f load; (Naut, Aviat) cargo; (Jur) summons sing

lag imperf von **liegen**

Lage (-, -n) f position, situation; (Schicht) layer; **in der ~ sein zu** to be in a position to

Lager (-s, -) nt camp; (Comm) warehouse; (Tech) bearing; **Lagerfeuer** nt campfire; **lagern** vi (Dinge) to be stored; (Menschen) to camp ▷ vt to store

Lagune f lagoon

lahm adj lame; (langweilig) dull; **lähmen** vt to paralyse; **Lähmung** f paralysis

Laib (-s, -e) m loaf

Laie (-n, -n) m layman

Laken (-s, -) nt sheet

Lakritze (-, -n) f liquorice

Lamm (-(e)s, Lämmer) nt (a. Lammfleisch) lamb

Lampe (-, -n) f lamp; (Glühbirne) bulb; **Lampenfieber** nt stage fright; **Lampenschirm** m lampshade

Lampion (-s, -s) m Chinese lantern

Land (-(e)s, Länder) nt (Gelände) land; (Nation) country; (Bundesland) state, Land; **auf dem ~(e)** in the country

● **Land**
●
● A **Land** (plural **Länder**) is a member
● state of the **BRD**. There are 16 **Länder**,
● namely Baden-Württemberg, Bayern,
● Berlin, Brandenburg, Bremen,
● Hamburg, Hessen,
● Mecklenburg-Vorpommern,
● Niedersachsen,
● Nordrhein-Westfalen,
● Rheinland-Pfalz, Saarland, Sachsen,
● Sachsen-Anhalt, Schleswig-Holstein
● and Thüringen. Each 'Land' has its
● own parliament and constitution.

Landebahn f runway; **landen** vt, vi to land; (Schiff) to dock

Länderspiel nt international (match)

Landesgrenze f national border, frontier; **Landesinnere** nt interior; **landesüblich** adj customary; **Landeswährung** f national currency; **landesweit** adj nationwide

Landhaus nt country house; **Landkarte** f map; **Landkreis** m administrative region, ≈ district

ländlich adj rural

Landschaft f countryside; (schöne) scenery; (Kunst) landscape; **Landstraße** f country road, B road (Brit)

Landung f landing; **Landungsbrücke** f, **Landungssteg** m gangway

Landwirt(in) m(f) farmer;

Landwirtschaft f agriculture, farming;
landwirtschaftlich adj agricultural
lang adj long; (Mensch) tall; **ein zwei
Meter ~er Tisch** a table two metres long;
den ganzen Tag ~ all day long; **die Straße
~** along the street; **langärmelig** adj
long-sleeved; **lange** adv (for) a long time;
ich musste ~ warten I had to wait (for) a
long time; **ich bleibe nicht ~** I won't stay
long; **es ist ~ her, dass wir uns gesehen
haben** it's a long time since we saw each
other; **Länge** (-, -n) f length; (Geo)
longitude
langen vi (fam: ausreichen) to be enough;
(fam: fassen) to reach (nach for); **mir
langt's** I've had enough
Langeweile f boredom
langfristig adj long-term ▷ adv in the
long term
Langlauf m cross-country skiing
längs prep +gen **die Bäume ~ der Straße**
the trees along(side) the road ▷ adv **die
Streifen laufen ~ über das Hemd** the
stripes run lengthways down the shirt
langsam adj slow ▷ adv slowly
Langschläfer(in) (-s, -) m(f) late riser
längst adv **das ist ~ fertig** that was
finished a long time ago; **sie sollte ~ da
sein** she should have been here long ago;
als sie kam, waren wir ~ weg when she
arrived we had long since left
Langstreckenflug m long-haul flight
Languste (-, -n) f crayfish, crawfish
(US)
langweilen vt to bore; **ich langweile
mich** I'm bored; **langweilig** adj boring;
Langwelle f long wave
Laos (-) nt Laos
Lappen (-s, -) m cloth, rag; (Staublappen)
duster
läppisch adj silly; (Summe) ridiculous
Laptop (-s, -s) m laptop
Lärche (-, -n) f larch
Lärm (-(e)s) m noise
las imperf von **lesen**
Lasche (-, -n) f flap
Laser (-s, -) m laser; **Laserdrucker** m
laser printer

○ SCHLÜSSELWORT

lassen (pt **ließ**, pp **gelassen** od (als
Hilfsverb) **lassen** vt **1** (unterlassen) to stop

(momentan) to leave; **lass das (sein)!** don't
(do it)!; (hör auf!) stop it!; **lass mich!** leave
me alone; **lassen wir das!** let's leave it; **er
kann das Trinken nicht lassen** he can't
stop drinking
2 (zurücklassen) to leave; **etw lassen, wie
es ist** to leave sth (just) as it is
3 (überlassen): **jdn ins Haus lassen** to let
sb into the house
▷ vi: **lass mal, ich mache das schon**
leave it, I'll do it
▷ Hilfsverb **1** (veranlassen): **etw machen
lassen** to have od get sth done; **sich dat
etw schicken lassen** to have sth sent (to one)
2 (zulassen): **jdn etw wissen lassen** to let
sb know sth; **das Licht brennen lassen** to
leave the light on; **jdn warten lassen** to
keep sb waiting; **das lässt sich machen**
that can be done
3: **lass uns gehen** let's go

lässig adj casual
Last (-, -en) f load; (Bürde) burden; (Naut,
Aviat) cargo
Laster (-s, -) nt vice; (fam) truck, lorry
(Brit)
lästern vi **über jdn/etw ~** to make nasty
remarks about sb/sth
lästig adj annoying; (Person) tiresome
Last-Minute-Flug m last-minute flight;
Last-Minute-Ticket nt last-minute ticket
Lastwagen m truck, lorry (Brit)
Latein (-s) nt Latin
Laterne (-, -n) f lantern; (Straßenlaterne)
streetlight
Latte (-, -n) f slat; (Sport) bar
Latz (-es, Lätze) m bib; **Lätzchen** nt bib;
Latzhose f dungarees pl
lau adj (Wind, Luft) mild
Laub (-(e)s) nt foliage; **Laubfrosch** m tree
frog; **Laubsäge** f fretsaw
Lauch (-(e)s, -e) m leeks pl; **eine Stange
~** a leek; **Lauchzwiebel** f spring onions pl
(Brit), scallions pl (US)
Lauf (-(e)s, Läufe) m run; (Wettlauf) race;
(Entwicklung) course; (von Gewehr) barrel;
Laufbahn f career; **laufen** (lief, gelaufen) vi,
vt to run; (gehen) to walk; (funktionieren) to
work; **mir läuft die Nase** my nose is
running; **was läuft im Kino?** what's on at
the cinema?; **wie läuft's so?** how are
things?; **laufend** adj running; (Monat,
Ausgaben) current; **auf dem Laufenden**

sein/halten to be/to keep up-to-date;
Läufer (-s, -) m (*Teppich*) rug; (*Schach*)
bishop; **Läufer(in)** m(f) (*Sport*) runner;
Laufmasche f ladder (*Brit*), run (*US*);
Laufwerk nt (*Inform*) drive
Laune (-, -n) f mood; **gute/schlechte**
~ haben to be in a good/bad mood;
launisch adj moody
Laus (-, *Läuse*) f louse
lauschen vi to listen; (*heimlich*) to
eavesdrop
laut adj loud ▷ adv loudly; (*lesen*) aloud
▷ prep +gen o dat according to
läuten vt, vi to ring
lauter adv (*fam: nichts als*) nothing but
Lautsprecher m loudspeaker;
Lautstärke f loudness; (*Radio, Tv*) volume
lauwarm adj lukewarm
Lava (-, *Laven*) f lava
Lavendel (-s, -) m lavender
Lawine f avalanche
LCD-Anzeige f LCD-display
leasen vt to lease; **Leasing** (-s) nt leasing
leben vt, vi to live; (*am Leben sein*) to be
alive; **wie lange ~ Sie schon hier?** how
long have you been living here?; **von ...**
~ (*Nahrungsmittel etc*) to live on ...; (*Beruf,*
Beschäftigung) to make one's living from
...; **Leben** (-s, -) nt life; **lebend** adj living;
lebendig adj alive; (*lebhaft*) lively;
lebensgefährlich adj very dangerous;
(*Verletzung*) critical; **Lebensgefährte** m,
Lebensgefährtin f partner;
Lebenshaltungskosten pl cost sing of
living; **lebenslänglich** adj for life;
~ bekommen to get life; **Lebenslauf** m
curriculum vitae (*Brit*), CV (*Brit*), resumé
(*US*); **Lebensmittel** pl food sing;
Lebensmittelgeschäft nt grocer's (shop);
Lebensmittelvergiftung f food
poisoning; **lebensnotwendig** adj vital;
Lebensretter(in) m(f) rescuer;
Lebensstandard m standard of living;
Lebensunterhalt m livelihood;
Lebensversicherung f life insurance (*o*
assurance (*Brit*)); **Lebenszeichen** nt sign
of life
Leber (-, -n) f liver; **Leberfleck** m mole;
Leberpastete f liver pâté
Lebewesen nt living being
lebhaft adj lively; (*Erinnerung, Eindruck*)
vivid; **Lebkuchen** m gingerbread; **ein ~** a
piece of gingerbread; **leblos** adj lifeless

Leck nt leak
lecken vi (*Loch haben*) to leak ▷ vt, vi
(*schlecken*) to lick
lecker adj delicious, tasty
Leder (-s, -) nt leather
ledig adj single
leer adj empty; (*Seite*) blank; (*Batterie*)
dead; **leeren** vt to empty ▷ vr **sich ~** to
empty; **Leerlauf** m (*Gang*) neutral;
Leertaste f space bar; **Leerung** f
emptying; (*Briefkasten*) collection;
Leerzeichen nt blank, space
legal adj legal, lawful
legen vt to put, to place; (*Eier*) to lay ▷ vr
sich ~ to lie down; (*Sturm, Begeisterung*) to
die down; (*Schmerz, Gefühl*) to wear off
Legende (-, -n) f legend
leger adj casual
Lehm (-(e)s, -e) m loam; (*Ton*) clay
Lehne (-, -n) f arm(rest); (*Rückenlehne*)
back(rest); **lehnen** vt to lean ▷ vr **sich**
~ to lean (*an/gegen* +akk against);
Lehnstuhl m armchair
Lehrbuch nt textbook; **Lehre** (-, -n) f
teaching; (*beruflich*) apprenticeship;
(*moralisch*) lesson; **lehren** vt to teach;
Lehrer(in) (-s, -) m(f) teacher; **Lehrgang**
m course; **Lehrling** m apprentice;
lehrreich adj instructive
Leib (-(e)s, -er) m body; **Leibgericht** nt,
Leibspeise f favourite dish;
Leibwächter(in) m(f) bodyguard
Leiche (-, -n) f corpse; **Leichenhalle** f
mortuary; **Leichenwagen** m hearse
leicht adj light; (*einfach*) easy, simple;
(*Erkrankung*) slight; **jdm ~ fallen** to be easy
for sb; **es sich** (*dat*) **~ machen** to take the
easy way out ▷ adv (*mühelos, schnell*)
easily; (*geringfügig*) slightly;
Leichtathletik f athletics sing;
leichtsinnig adj careless; (*stärker*)
reckless
leid adj **jdn/etw ~ sein** to be tired of
sb/sth; **Leid** (-(e)s) nt grief, sorrow; **es tut**
mir/ihm ~ I'm/he's sorry; **er tut mir ~** I'm
sorry for him; **~ tun**; *siehe auch* **leidtun**;
leiden (*litt, gelitten*) vi, vt to suffer (*an,*
unter +dat from); **ich kann ihn/es nicht ~** I
can't stand him/it; **Leiden** (-s, -) nt
suffering; (*Krankheit*) illness
Leidenschaft f passion;
leidenschaftlich adj passionate
leider adv unfortunately; **wir müssen**

jetzt ~ gehen I'm afraid we have to go now; **~ ja/nein** I'm afraid so/not
leidtun vi **es tut mir/ihm ~** I'm/he's sorry; **er tut mir ~** I'm sorry for him
Leihbücherei f lending library
leihen (lieh, geliehen) vt **jdm etw ~** to lend sb sth; **sich** (dat) **etw von jdm ~** to borrow sth from sb; **Leihfrist** f lending period; **Leihgebühr** f hire charge; (für Buch) lending charge; **Leihwagen** m hire car (Brit), rental car (US)
Leim (-(e)s, -e) m glue
Leine (-, -n) f cord; (für Wäsche) line; (Hundeleine) lead (Brit), leash (US)
Leinen (-s, -) nt linen; **Leintuch** nt (für Bett) sheet; **Leinwand** f (Kunst) canvas; (Cine) screen
leise adj quiet; (sanft) soft ▷ adv quietly
Leiste (-, -n) f ledge; (Zierleiste) strip; (Anat) groin
leisten vt (Arbeit) to do; (vollbringen) to achieve; **jdm Gesellschaft ~** to keep sb company; **sich** (dat) **etw ~** (gönnen) to treat oneself to sth; **ich kann es mir nicht ~** I can't afford it
Leistenbruch m hernia
Leistung f performance; (gute) achievement
Leitartikel m leading article (Brit), editorial (US)
leiten vt to lead; (Firma) to run; (in eine Richtung) to direct; (Elek) to conduct
Leiter (-, -n) f ladder
Leiter(in) (-s, -) m(f) (von Geschäft) manager
Leitplanke (-, -n) f crash barrier
Leitung f (Führung) direction; (Tel) line; (von Firma) management; (Wasserleitung) pipe; (Kabel) cable; **eine lange ~ haben** to be slow on the uptake; **Leitungswasser** nt tap water
Lektion f lesson
Lektüre (-, -n) f (Lesen) reading; (Lesestoff) reading matter
Lende (-, -n) f (Speise) loin; (vom Rind) sirloin; **die ~n** pl (Med) the lumbar region sing
lenken vt to steer; (Blick) to direct (auf +akk towards); **jds Aufmerksamkeit auf etw** (akk) **~** to draw sb's attention to sth; **Lenker** m (von Fahrrad, Motorrad) handlebars pl; **Lenkrad** nt steering

wheel; **Lenkradschloss** nt steering lock; **Lenkstange** f handlebars pl
Leopard (-en, -en) m leopard
Lepra (-) f leprosy
Lerche (-, -n) f lark
lernen vt, vi to learn; (für eine Prüfung) to study, to revise
lesbisch adj lesbian
Lesebuch nt reader; **lesen** (las, gelesen) vi, vt to read; (ernten) to pick; **Leser(in)** m(f) reader; **Leserbrief** m letter to the editor; **leserlich** adj legible; **Lesezeichen** nt bookmark
Lettland nt Latvia
letzte(r, s) adj last; (neueste) latest; (endgültig) final; **zum ~n Mal** for the last time; **am ~n Montag** last Monday; **in ~r Zeit** lately, recently; **letztens** adv (vor kurzem) recently; **letztere(r, s)** adj the latter
Leuchtanzeige f illuminated display; **Leuchte** (-, -n) f lamp, light; **leuchten** vi to shine; (Feuer, Zifferblatt) to glow; **Leuchter** (-s, -) m candlestick; **Leuchtfarbe** f fluorescent colour; (Anstrichfarbe) luminous paint; **Leuchtreklame** f neon sign; **Leuchtstift** m highlighter; **Leuchtstoffröhre** f strip light; **Leuchtturm** m lighthouse
leugnen vt to deny ▷ vi to deny everything
Leukämie f leukaemia (Brit), leukemia (US)
Leukoplast® (-(e)s, -e) nt Elastoplast® (Brit), Band-Aid® (US)
Leute pl people pl
Lexikon (-s, Lexika) nt encyclopaedia (Brit), encyclopedia (US); (Wörterbuch) dictionary
Libanon (-s) m **der ~** Lebanon
Libelle f dragonfly
liberal adj liberal
Libyen (-s) nt Libya
Licht (-(e)s, -er) nt light; **Lichtblick** m ray of hope; **lichtempfindlich** adj sensitive to light; **Lichempfindlichkeit** f (Foto) speed; **Lichthupe** f **die ~ betätigen** to flash one's lights; **Lichtjahr** nt light year; **Lichtmaschine** f dynamo; **Lichtschalter** m light switch; **Lichtschranke** f light barrier; **Lichtschutzfaktor** m sun protection factor, SPF
Lichtung f clearing

Lid (-(e)s, -er) nt eyelid; **Lidschatten** m eyeshadow

lieb adj (nett) nice; (teuer, geliebt) dear; (liebenswert) sweet; **das ist ~ von dir** that's nice of you; **Lieber Herr X** Dear Mr X; **Liebe** (-, -n) f love; **lieben** vt to love; (sexuell) to make love to; **liebenswürdig** adj kind; **lieber** adv rather; **ich möchte ~ nicht** I'd rather not; **welches ist dir ~?** which one do you prefer?; siehe auch **gern**, **lieb**; **Liebesbrief** m love letter; **Liebeskummer** m **~ haben** to be lovesick; **Liebespaar** nt lovers pl; **liebevoll** adj loving; **Liebhaber(in)** (-s, -) m(f) lover; **lieblich** adj lovely; (Wein) sweet; **Liebling** m darling; (Günstling) favourite; **Lieblings-** in zW favourite; **liebste(r, s)** adj favourite; **liebsten** adv **am ~ esse ich ...** my favourite food is ...; **am ~ würde ich bleiben** I'd really like to stay

Liechtenstein (-s) nt Liechtenstein

Lied (-(e)s, -er) nt song; (Rel) hymn

lief imperf von **laufen**

Lieferant(in) m(f) supplier

lieferbar adj available

liefern vt to deliver; (beschaffen) to supply

Lieferschein m delivery note; **Lieferung** f delivery; **Lieferwagen** m delivery van

Liege (-, -n) f (beim Arzt) couch; (Notbett) campbed; (Gartenliege) lounger; **liegen** (lag, gelegen) vi to lie; (sich befinden) to be; **mir liegt nichts/viel daran** it doesn't matter to me/it matters a lot to me; **woran liegt es nur, dass ...?** why is it that ...?; **~ bleiben** (Mensch) to stay lying down; (im Bett) to stay in bed; (Ding) to be left (behind); **~ lassen** (vergessen) to leave behind; **Liegestuhl** m deck chair; **Liegestütz** m press-up (Brit), push-up (US); **Liegewagen** m (Eisenb) couchette car

lieh imperf von **leihen**

ließ imperf von **lassen**

Lift (-(e)s, -e o -s) m lift, elevator (US)

Liga (-, Ligen) f league, division

light adj (Cola) diet; (fettarm) low-fat; (kalorienarm) low-calorie; (Zigaretten) mild

Likör (-s, -e) m liqueur

lila adj inv purple

Lilie f lily

Limette (-, -n) f lime

Limo (-, -s) f (fam) fizzy drink (Brit), soda

(US); **Limonade** f fizzy drink (Brit), soda (US); (mit Zitronengeschmack) lemonade

Limone (-, -n) f lime

Limousine (-, -n) f saloon (car) (Brit), sedan (US); (fam) limo

Linde (-, -n) f lime tree

lindern vt to relieve, to soothe

Lineal (-s, -e) nt ruler

Linie f line; **Linienflug** m scheduled flight; **Linienrichter** m linesman; **liniert** adj ruled, lined

Linke (-n, -n) f left-hand side; (Hand) left hand; (Pol) left (wing); **linke(r, s)** adj left; **auf der ~n Seite** on the left, on the left-hand side; **links** adv on the left; **~ abbiegen** to turn left; **~ von** to the left of; **~ oben** at the top left; **Linksaußen** m left winger; **Linkshänder(in)** (-s, -) m(f) left-hander; **linksherum** adv to the left, anticlockwise; **Linksverkehr** m driving on the left

Linse (-, -n) f lentil; (optisch) lens; **Linsensuppe** f lentil soup

Lippe (-, -n) f lip; **Lipgloss** nt lip gloss; **Lippenstift** m lipstick

lispeln vi to lisp

List (-, -en) f cunning; (Trick) trick

Liste (-, -n) f list

Litauen (-s) nt Lithuania

Liter (-s, -) m o nt litre

literarisch adj literary; **Literatur** f literature

Litschi (-, -s) f lychee, litchi

litt imperf von **leiden**

live adv (Radio, TV) live

Lizenz f licence

Lkw (-(s), -(s)) m abk = **Lastkraftwagen** truck, lorry (Brit)

Lob (-(e)s) nt praise; **loben** vt to praise

Loch (-(e)s, Löcher) nt hole; **lochen** vt to punch; **Locher** (-s, -) m (hole) punch

Locke (-, -n) f curl; **locken** vt (anlocken) to lure; (Haare) to curl; **Lockenstab** m curling tongs pl (Brit), curling irons pl (US); **Lockenwickler** (-s, -) m curler

locker adj (Schraube, Zahn) loose; (Haltung) relaxed; (Person) easy-going; **das schaffe ich ~** (fam) I'll manage it, no problem; **lockern** vt to loosen ▷ vr **sich ~** to loosen

lockig adj curly

Löffel (-s, -) m spoon; **einen ~ Mehl zugeben** add a spoonful of flour; **Löffelbiskuit** (-s, -s) m sponge finger

log *imperf von* **lügen**
Loge (-, -n) *f* (*Theat*) box
logisch *adj* logical
Logo (-s, -s) *nt* logo
Lohn (-(e)s, Löhne) *m* reward; (*Arbeitslohn*) pay, wages *pl*
lohnen *vr* **sich ~** to be worth it; **es lohnt sich nicht zu warten** it's no use waiting
Lohnerhöhung *f* pay rise (*Brit*), pay raise (*US*); **Lohnsteuer** *f* income tax
Lokal (-(e)s, -e) *nt* (*Gaststätte*) restaurant; (*Kneipe*) pub (*Brit*), bar
Lokomotive *f* locomotive
London (-s) *nt* London
Lorbeer (-s, -en) *m* laurel; **Lorbeerblatt** *nt* (*Gastr*) bay leaf
los *adj* loose; **~!** go on!; **jdn/etw ~ sein** to be rid of sb/sth; **was ist ~?** what's the matter?, what's up?; **dort ist nichts/viel ~** there's nothing/a lot going on there
Los (-es, -e) *nt* (*Schicksal*) lot, fate; (*Lotterie etc*) ticket
los|binden *irr vt* to untie
löschen *vt* (*Feuer, Licht*) to put out, to extinguish; (*Durst*) to quench; (*Tonband*) to erase; (*Daten, Zeile*) to delete; **Löschtaste** *f* delete key
lose *adj* loose
Lösegeld *nt* ransom
losen *vi* to draw lots
lösen *vt* (*lockern*) to loosen; (*Rätsel*) to solve; (*Chem*) to dissolve; (*Fahrkarte*) to buy ▷ *vr* **sich ~** (*abgehen*) to come off; (*Zucker etc*) to dissolve; (*Problem, Schwierigkeit*) to (re)solve itself
los|fahren *irr vi* to leave; **los|gehen** *irr vi* to set out; (*anfangen*) to start; **los|lassen** *irr vt* to let go
löslich *adj* soluble
Lösung *f* (*eines Rätsels, Problems, Flüssigkeit*) solution
los|werden *irr vt* to get rid of
Lotterie *f* lottery; **Lotto** (-s) *nt* National Lottery; **~ spielen** to play the lottery
Löwe (-n, -n) *m* (*Zool*) lion; (*Astr*) Leo; **Löwenzahn** *m* dandelion
Luchs (-es, -e) *m* lynx
Lücke (-, -n) *f* gap; **Lückenbüßer(in)** (-s, -) *m(f)* stopgap
lud *imperf von* **laden**
Luft (-, Lüfte) *f* air; (*Atem*) breath; **Luftballon** *m* balloon; **Luftblase** *f* (air) bubble; **luftdicht** *adj* airtight; **Luftdruck**

m (*Meteo*) atmospheric pressure; (*in Reifen*) air pressure
lüften *vt* to air; (*Geheimnis*) to reveal
Luftfahrt *f* aviation; **Luftfeuchtigkeit** *f* humidity; **Luftfilter** *m* air filter; **Luftfracht** *f* air freight; **Luftkissenfahrzeug** *nt* hovercraft; **Luftlinie** *f* **10 km ~** 10 km as the crow flies; **Luftmatratze** *f* airbed; **Luftpirat(in)** *m(f)* hijacker; **Luftpost** *f* airmail; **Luftpumpe** *f* (bicycle) pump; **Luftröhre** *f* windpipe
Lüftung *f* ventilation
Luftveränderung *f* change of air; **Luftverschmutzung** *f* air pollution; **Luftwaffe** *f* air force; **Luftzug** *m* draught (*Brit*), draft (*US*)
Lüge (-, -n) *f* lie; **lügen** (log, gelogen) *vi* to lie; **Lügner(in)** (-s, -) *m(f)* liar
Luke (-, -n) *f* hatch
Lumpen (-s, -) *m* rag
Lunchpaket *nt* packed lunch
Lunge (-, -n) *f* lungs *pl*; **Lungenentzündung** *f* pneumonia
Lupe (-, -n) *f* magnifying glass; **etw unter die ~ nehmen** (*fig*) to have a close look at sth
Lust (-, Lüste) *f* joy, delight; (*Neigung*) desire; **~ auf etw** (*akk*) **haben** to feel like sth; **~ haben, etw zu tun** to feel like doing sth
lustig *adj* (*komisch*) amusing, funny; (*fröhlich*) cheerful
lutschen *vt* to suck ▷ *vi* **~ an** (+*dat*) to suck; **Lutscher** (-s, -) *m* lollipop
Luxemburg (-s) *nt* Luxembourg
luxuriös *adj* luxurious
Luxus (-) *m* luxury
Lymphdrüse *f* lymph gland; **Lymphknoten** *m* lymph node
Lyrik (-) *f* poetry

m

machbar *adj* feasible

machen *vt* **1** to do; (*herstellen, zubereiten*) to make; **was machst du da?** what are you doing (there)?; **das ist nicht zu machen** that can't be done; **das Radio leiser machen** to turn the radio down; **aus Holz gemacht** made of wood

2 (*verursachen, bewirken*) to make; **jdm Angst machen** to make sb afraid; **das macht die Kälte** it's the cold that does that

3 (*ausmachen*) to matter; **das macht nichts** that doesn't matter; **die Kälte macht mir nichts** I don't mind the cold

4 (*kosten, ergeben*) to be; **3 und 5 macht 8** 3 and 5 is *o* are 8; **was *o* wie viel macht das?** how much does that make?

5: **was macht die Arbeit?** how's the work going?; **was macht dein Bruder?** how is your brother doing?; **das Auto machen lassen** to have the car done; **machs gut!** take care!; (*viel Glück*) good luck!

▷ *vi*: **mach schnell!** hurry up!; **Schluss machen** to finish (off); **mach schon!** come on!; **das macht müde** it makes you tired; **in etw** *dat* **machen** to be *o* deal in sth

▷ *vr* to come along (nicely); **sich an etw** *akk* **machen** to set about sth; **sich verständlich machen** to make o.s. understood; **sich** *dat* **viel aus jdm/etw machen** to like sb/sth

Macho (-s, -s) *m* (*fam*) macho (type)
Macht (-s, *Mächte*) *f* power; **mächtig** *adj* powerful; (*fam: ungeheuer*) enormous; **machtlos** *adj* powerless; **da ist man ~** there's nothing you can do (about it)
Mädchen *nt* girl; **Mädchenname** *m* maiden name
Made (-, -n) *f* maggot
Magazin (-s, -e) *nt* magazine
Magen (-s, - *o Mägen*) *m* stomach; **Magenbeschwerden** *pl* stomach trouble *sing*; **Magen-Darm-Infektion** *f* gastroenteritis; **Magengeschwür** *nt* stomach ulcer; **Magenschmerzen** *pl* stomachache *sing*
mager *adj* (*Fleisch, Wurst*) lean; (*Person*) thin; (*Käse, Joghurt*) low-fat; **Magermilch** *f* skimmed milk; **Magersucht** *f* anorexia; **magersüchtig** *adj* anorexic
magisch *adj* magical
Magnet (-s *o* -en, -en) *m* magnet
mähen *vt, vi* to mow
mahlen (*mahlte, gemahlen*) *vt* to grind
Mahlzeit *f* meal; (*für Baby*) feed ▷ *interj* (*guten Appetit*) enjoy your meal
Mähne (-, -n) *f* mane
mahnen *vt* to urge; **jdn schriftlich ~** to send sb a reminder; **Mahngebühr** *f* fine; **Mahnung** *f* warning; (*schriftlich*) reminder
Mai (-(s), -e) *m* May; *siehe auch* **Juni**; **Maifeiertag** *m* May Day; **Maiglöckchen** *nt* lily of the valley; **Maikäfer** *m* cockchafer
Mail (-, -s) *f* e-mail; **Mailbox** *f* (*Inform*) mailbox; **mailen** *vi, vt* to e-mail
Mais (-es, -e) *m* maize, corn (US); **Maiskolben** *m* corn cob; (*Gastr*) corn on the cob
Majestät (-, -en) *f* Majesty
Majonäse (-, -n) *f* mayonnaise
Majoran (-s, -e) *m* marjoram
makaber *adj* macabre
Make-up (-s, -s) *nt* make-up

Makler(in) (-s, -) m(f) broker; (Immobilienmakler) estate agent (Brit), realtor (US)

Makrele (-, -n) f mackerel

Makro (-s, -s) nt (Inform) macro

Makrone (-, -n) f macaroon

mal adv (beim Rechnen) times, multiplied by; (beim Messen) by; (fam: einmal = früher) once; (einmal = zukünftig) some day; **4 ~ 3 ist 12** 4 times 3 is (o equals) twelve; **da habe ich ~ gewohnt** I used to live there; **irgendwann ~ werde ich dort hinfahren** I'll go there one day; **das ist nun ~ so** well, that's just the way it is (o goes); **Mal** (-(e)s, -e) nt (Zeitpunkt) time; (Markierung) mark; **jedes ~** every time; **ein paar ~** a few times; **ein einziges ~** just once

Malaria (-) f malaria

Malaysia (-s) nt Malaysia

Malbuch nt colouring book

Malediven pl Maldives pl

malen vt, vi to paint; **Maler(in)** (-s, -) m(f) painter; **Malerei** f painting; **malerisch** adj picturesque

Mallorca (-s) nt Majorca, Mallorca

mal|nehmen irr vt to multiply (mit by)

Malta (-s) nt Malta

Malventee m mallow tea

Malz (-es) nt malt; **Malzbier** nt malt beer

Mama (-, -s) f mum(my) (Brit), mom(my) (US)

man pron you; (förmlich) one; (jemand) someone, somebody; (die Leute) they, people pl; **wie schreibt ~ das?** how do you spell that?; **~ hat ihr das Fahrrad gestohlen** someone stole her bike; **~ sagt, dass ...** they (o people) say that ...

managen vt (fam) to manage; **Manager(in)** (-s, -) m(f) manager

manche(r, s) adj many a; (mit pl) a number of, some ▷ pron (einige) some; (viele) many; **~ Politiker** many politicians pl, many a politician; **manchmal** adv sometimes

Mandant(in) m(f) client

Mandarine f mandarin, tangerine

Mandel (-, -n) f almond; **~n** (Anat) tonsils pl; **Mandelentzündung** f tonsillitis

Manege (-, -n) f ring

Mangel (-s, Mängel) m (Fehlen) lack; (Knappheit) shortage (an +dat of); (Fehler) defect, fault; **mangelhaft** adj (Ware) faulty; (Schulnote) ≈ E

Mango (-, -s) f mango

Mangold (-s) m mangel(wurzel)

Manieren pl manners pl

Maniküre (-, -n) f manicure

manipulieren vt to manipulate

Manko (-s, -s) nt deficiency

Mann (-(e)s, Männer) m man; (Ehemann) husband; **Männchen** nt **es ist ein ~** (Tier) it's a he; **männlich** adj masculine; (Bio) male

Mannschaft f (Sport, fig) team; (Naut, Aviat) crew

Mansarde (-, -n) f attic

Manschettenknopf m cufflink

Mantel (-s, Mäntel) m coat; (Tech) casing, jacket

Mappe (-, -n) f briefcase; (Aktenmappe) folder

Maracuja (-, -s) f passion fruit

Marathon (-s, -s) m marathon

Märchen nt fairy tale

Marder (-s, -) m marten

Margarine f margarine

Marienkäfer m ladybird (Brit), ladybug (US)

Marihuana (-s) nt marijuana

Marille (-, -n) f apricot

Marinade f marinade

Marine f navy

marinieren vt to marinate

Marionette f puppet

Mark (-(e)s) nt (Knochenmark) marrow; (Fruchtmark) pulp

Marke (-, -n) f (Warensorte) brand; (Fabrikat) make; (Briefmarke) stamp; (Essenmarke) voucher, ticket; (aus Metall etc) disc; (Messpunkt) mark; **Markenartikel** m branded item, brand name product; **Markenzeichen** nt trademark

markieren vt to mark; **Markierung** f marking; (Zeichen) mark

Markise (-, -n) f awning

Markt (-(e)s, Märkte) m market; **auf den ~ bringen** to launch; **Markthalle** f covered market; **Marktlücke** f gap in the market; **Marktplatz** m market place; **Marktwirtschaft** f market economy

Marmelade f jam; (Orangenmarmelade) marmalade

Marmor (-s, -e) m marble; **Marmorkuchen** m marble cake

m

Marokko (-s) nt Morocco
Marone (-, -n) f chestnut
Mars (-) m Mars
Marsch (-(e)s, Märsche) m march
Märtyrer(in) (-s, -) m(f) martyr
März (-es), -e) m March; siehe auch **Juni**
Marzipan (-s, -e) nt marzipan
Maschine f machine; (Motor) engine;
maschinell adj mechanical, machine-;
Maschinenbau m mechanical
engineering
Masern pl (Med) measles sing
Maske (-, -n) f mask; **Maskenball** m
fancy-dress ball; **maskieren** vr **sich**
~ (Maske aufsetzen) to put on a mask;
(verkleiden) to dress up
Maskottchen nt mascot
maß imperf von **messen**
Maß (-es, -e) nt measure; (Mäßigung)
moderation; (Grad) degree, extent; **~e**
(Person) measurements; (Raum)
dimensions; **in gewissem/hohem ~e** to a
certain/high degree; **in zunehmendem**
~e increasingly
Mass (-, -(en)) f (Bier) litre of beer
Massage (-, -n) f massage
Masse (-, -n) f mass; (von Menschen)
crowd; (Großteil) majority; **massenhaft**
adv masses (o loads) of; **am See sind**
~ Mücken there are masses of
mosquitoes at the lake;
Massenkarambolage f pile-up;
Massenmedien pl mass media pl;
Massenproduktion f mass production;
Massentourismus m mass tourism
Masseur(in) m(f) masseur/masseuse
maßgeschneidert adj (Kleidung)
made-to-measure
massieren vt to massage
mäßig adj moderate
massiv adj solid; (fig) massive
maßlos adj extreme
Maßnahme (-, -n) f measure, step
Maßstab m rule, measure; (fig) standard;
im ~ von 1:5 on a scale of 1:5
Mast (-(e)s, -e(n)) m mast; (Elek) pylon
Material (-s, -ien) nt material;
(Arbeitsmaterial) materials pl;
materialistisch adj materialistic
Materie f matter; **materiell** adj material
Mathematik f mathematics sing;
Mathematiker(in) m(f) mathematician
Matinee (-, -n) f ≈ matinee

Matratze (-, -n) f mattress
Matrose (-n, -n) m sailor
Matsch (-(e)s) m mud; (Schnee) slush;
matschig adj (Boden) muddy; (Schnee)
slushy; (Obst) mushy
matt adj weak; (glanzlos) dull; (Foto) matt;
(Schach) mate
Matte (-, -n) f mat
Matura (-) f Austrian school-leaving
examination; ≈ A-levels (Brit), ≈ High School
Diploma (US)
Mauer (-, -n) f wall
Maul (-(e)s, Mäuler) nt mouth; (fam) gob;
halt's ~! shut your face (o gob);
Maulbeere f mulberry; **Maulesel** m
mule; **Maulkorb** m muzzle; **Maul- und**
Klauenseuche f foot-and-mouth
disease; **Maulwurf** m mole
Maurer(in) (-s, -) m(f) bricklayer
Mauritius (-) nt Mauritius
Maus (-, Mäuse) f mouse; **Mausefalle** f
mousetrap; **Mausklick** (-s, -s) m mouse
click; **Mauspad** (-s, -s) nt mouse mat (o
pad); **Maustaste** f mouse key (o button)
Maut (-, -en) f toll; **Mautgebühr** f toll;
mautpflichtig adj **~e Straße** toll road,
turnpike (US); **Mautstelle** f tollbooth,
tollgate; **Mautstraße** f toll road,
turnpike (US)
maximal adv **ihr habt ~ zwei Stunden**
Zeit you've got two hours at (the) most;
~ vier Leute a maximum of four people
Mayonnaise f siehe **Majonäse**
Mazedonien (-s) nt Macedonia
MB (-, -) nt, **Mbyte** (-, -) nt abk =
Megabyte MB
Mechanik f mechanics sing; (Getriebe)
mechanics pl; **Mechaniker(in)** (-s, -) m(f)
mechanic; **mechanisch** adj mechanical;
Mechanismus m mechanism
meckern vi (Ziege) to bleat; (fam:
schimpfen) to moan
Mecklenburg-Vorpommern (-s) nt
Mecklenburg-Western Pomerania
Medaille (-, -n) f medal
Medien pl media pl
Medikament nt medicine
Meditation f meditation; **meditieren** vi
to meditate
medium adj (Steak) medium
Medizin (-, -en) f medicine (gegen for);
medizinisch adj medical
Meer (-(e)s, -e) nt sea; **am ~** by the sea;

Meerenge f straits pl; **Meeresfrüchte** pl seafood sing; **Meeresspiegel** m sea level; **Meerrettich** m horseradish; **Meerschweinchen** nt guinea pig; **Meerwasser** nt seawater

Megabyte nt megabyte; **Megahertz** nt megahertz

Mehl (-(e)s, -e) nt flour; **Mehlspeise** f sweet dish made from flour, eggs and milk

mehr pron, adv more; **~ will ich nicht ausgeben** I don't want to spend any more, that's as much as I want to spend; **was willst du ~?** what more do you want? ▷ adv **immer ~ (Leute)** more and more (people); **~ als fünf Minuten** more than five minutes; **je ~ ..., desto besser** the more ..., the better; **ich kann nicht ~ stehen** I can't stand any more (o longer); **es ist kein Brot ~ da** there's no bread left; **nie ~** never again; **mehrdeutig** adj ambiguous; **mehrere** pron several; **mehreres** pron several things; **mehrfach** adj multiple; (wiederholt) repeated; **Mehrfachstecker** m multiple plug; **Mehrheit** f majority; **mehrmals** adv repeatedly; **mehrsprachig** adj multilingual; **Mehrwegflasche** f returnable bottle, deposit bottle; **Mehrwertsteuer** f value added tax, VAT; **Mehrzahl** f majority; (Plural) plural

meiden (mied, gemieden) vt to avoid

Meile (-, -n) f mile

mein pron (adjektivisch) my; **meine(r, s)** pron (substantivisch) mine

meinen vt, vi (glauben, der Ansicht sein) to think; (sagen) to say; (sagen wollen, beabsichtigen) to mean; **das war nicht so gemeint** I didn't mean it like that

meinetwegen adv (wegen mir) because of me; (mir zuliebe) for my sake; (von mir aus) as far as I'm concerned

Meinung f opinion; **meiner ~ nach** in my opinion; **Meinungsumfrage** f opinion poll; **Meinungsverschiedenheit** f disagreement (über +akk about)

Meise (-, -n) f tit; **eine ~ haben** (fam) to be crazy

Meißel (-s, -) m chisel

meist adv mostly; **meiste(r, s)** pron (adjektivisch) most; **die ~n (Leute)** most people; **die ~ Zeit** most of the time; **das ~ (davon)** most of it; **die ~n von ihnen** most of them; (substantivisch) most of them; **am ~n** (the) most; **meistens** adv mostly; (zum größten Teil) for the most part

Meister(in) (-s, -) m(f) master; (Sport) champion; **Meisterschaft** f championship; **Meisterwerk** nt masterpiece

melden vt to report ▷ vr **sich ~** to report (bei to); (Schule) to put one's hand up; (freiwillig) to volunteer; (auf etw, am Telefon) to answer; **Meldung** f announcement; (Bericht) report; (Inform) message

Melodie f tune, melody

Melone (-, -n) f melon

Memoiren pl memoirs pl

Menge (-, -n) f quantity; (Menschen) crowd; **eine ~** (große Anzahl) a lot (gen of); **Mengenrabatt** m bulk discount

Meniskus (-, Menisken) m meniscus

Mensa (-, Mensen) f canteen, cafeteria (US)

Mensch (-en, -en) m human being, man; (Person) person; **kein ~** nobody; **~!** (bewundernd) wow!; (verärgert) bloody hell!; **Menschenmenge** f crowd; **Menschenrechte** pl human rights pl; **Menschenverstand** m **gesunder ~** common sense; **Menschheit** f humanity, mankind; **menschlich** adj human; (human) humane

Menstruation f menstruation

Mentalität f mentality, mindset

Menthol (-s) nt menthol

Menü (-s, -s) nt set meal; (Inform) menu; **Menüleiste** f (Inform) menu bar

Merkblatt nt leaflet; **merken** vt (bemerken) to notice; **sich** (dat) **etw ~** to remember sth; **Merkmal** nt feature

Merkur (-s) m Mercury

merkwürdig adj odd

Messbecher m measuring jug

Messe (-, -n) f fair; (Rel) mass; **Messebesucher(in)** m(f) visitor to a/the fair; **Messegelände** nt exhibition site

messen (maß, gemessen) vt to measure; (Temperatur, Puls) to take ▷ vr **sich ~** to compete; **sie kann sich mit ihm nicht ~** she's no match for him

Messer (-s, -) nt knife

Messgerät nt measuring device, gauge

Messing (-s) nt brass

Metall (-s, -e) nt metal

Meteorologe m, **Meteorologin** f meteorologist

m

Meter (-s, -) m o nt metre; **Metermaß** nt
tape measure
Methode (-, -n) f method
Metzger(in) (-s, -) m(f) butcher;
Metzgerei f butcher's (shop)
Mexiko (-s) nt Mexico
MEZ f abk = **mitteleuropäische Zeit** CET
miau interj miaow
mich pron akk von **ich** me; **~ (selbst)**
(reflexiv) myself; **stell dich hinter ~** stand
behind me; **ich fühle ~ wohl** I feel fine
mied imperf von **meiden**
Miene (-, -n) f look, expression
mies adj (fam) lousy
Miesmuschel f mussel
Mietauto nt siehe **Mietwagen**; **Miete**
(-, -n) f rent; **mieten** vt to rent; (Auto) to
hire (Brit), to rent (US); **Mieter(in)** (-s, -)
m(f) tenant; **Mietshaus** nt block of flats
(Brit), apartment house (US); **Mietvertrag**
m rental agreement; **Mietwagen** m hire
car (Brit), rental car (US); **sich** (dat) **einen
~ nehmen** to hire (Brit) (o rent (US)) a car
Migräne (-, -n) f migraine
Mikrofon (-s, -e) nt microphone
Mikrowelle (-, -n) f, **Mikrowellenherd** m
microwave (oven)
Milch (-) f milk; **Milcheis** nt ice-cream
(made with milk); **Milchglas** nt (dickes,
trübes Glas) frosted glass; **Milchkaffee** m
milky coffee; **Milchprodukte** pl dairy
products pl; **Milchpulver** nt powdered
milk; **Milchreis** m rice pudding;
Milchshake m milk shake; **Milchstraße** f
Milky Way
mild adj mild; (Richter) lenient; (freundlich)
kind
Militär (-s) nt military, army
Milliarde (-, -n) f billion; **Milligramm** nt
milligram; **Milliliter** m millilitre;
Millimeter m millimetre; **Million** f million;
Millionär(in) m(f) millionaire
Milz (-, -en) f spleen
Mimik f facial expression(s)
Minderheit f minority
minderjährig adj underage
minderwertig adj inferior;
Minderwertigkeitskomplex m
inferiority complex
Mindest- in zW minimum; **mindeste(r, s)**
adj least; **mindestens** adv at least;
Mindesthaltbarkeitsdatum nt
best-before date, sell-by date (Brit)

Mine (-, -n) f mine; (Bleistift) lead;
(Kugelschreiber) refill
Mineralwasser nt mineral water
Minibar f minibar; **Minigolf** nt miniature
golf, crazy golf (Brit)
minimal adj minimal
Minimum (-s, Minima) nt minimum
Minirock m miniskirt
Minister(in) (-s, -) m(f) minister;
Ministerium nt ministry;
Ministerpräsident(in) m(f) (von
Bundesland) Minister President (Prime
Minister of a Bundesland)
minus adv minus; **Minus** (-, -) nt deficit;
im ~ sein to be in the red; (Konto) to be
overdrawn
Minute (-, -n) f minute
Minze (-, -n) f mint
Mio. nt abk von **Million(en)** m
mir pron dat von **ich** (to) me; **kannst du
~ helfen?** can you help me?; **kannst du
es ~ erklären?** can you explain it to me?;
**ich habe ~ einen neuen Rechner
gekauft** I bought (myself) a new
computer; **ein Freund von ~** a friend of
mine
Mirabelle (-, -n) f mirabelle (small yellow
plum)
mischen vt to mix; (Karten) to shuffle;
Mischmasch m (fam) hotchpotch;
Mischung f mixture (aus of)
missachten vt to ignore; **Missbrauch** m
abuse; (falscher Gebrauch) misuse;
missbrauchen vt to misuse (zu for);
(sexuell) to abuse; **Misserfolg** m failure;
Missgeschick nt (Panne) mishap;
misshandeln vt to ill-treat
Mission f mission
misslingen (misslang, misslungen) vi to
fail; **der Versuch ist mir misslungen** my
attempt failed; **misstrauen** vt +dat to
distrust; **Misstrauen** (-s) nt mistrust,
suspicion (gegenüber of); **misstrauisch**
adj distrustful; (argwöhnisch) suspicious;
Missverständnis nt misunderstanding;
missverstehen irr vt to misunderstand
Mist (-(e)s) m (fam) rubbish; (von Kühen)
dung; (als Dünger) manure
Mistel (-, -n) f mistletoe
mit prep +dat with; (mittels) by; **~ der Bahn**
by train; **~ der Kreditkarte bezahlen** to
pay by credit card; **~ 10 Jahren** at the age
of 10; **wie wärs ~ ...?** how about ...? ▷ adv

along, too; **wollen Sie ~?** do you want to come along?

Mitarbeiter(in) *m(f)* *(Angestellter)* employee; *(an Projekt)* collaborator; *(freier)* freelancer

mit|bekommen *irr vt* *(fam: aufschnappen)* to catch; *(hören)* to hear; *(verstehen)* to get

mit|benutzen *vt* to share

Mitbewohner(in) *m(f)* *(in Wohnung)* flatmate *(Brit)*, roommate *(US)*

mit|bringen *irr vt* to bring along; **Mitbringsel** *(-s, -)* *nt* small present

miteinander *adv* with one another; *(gemeinsam)* together

mit|erleben *vt* to see (with one's own eyes)

Mitesser *(-s, -)* *m* blackhead

Mitfahrgelegenheit *f* ≈ lift, ride *(US)*; **Mitfahrzentrale** *f* agency for arranging lifts

mit|geben *irr vt* jdm etw ~ to give sb sth (to take along)

Mitgefühl *nt* sympathy

mit|gehen *irr vi* to go/come along

mitgenommen *adj* worn out, exhausted

Mitglied *nt* member

mithilfe *prep* +gen ~ **von** with the help of

mit|kommen *irr vi* to come along; *(verstehen)* to follow

Mitleid *nt* pity; ~ **haben mit** to feel sorry for

mit|machen *vt* to take part in ▷ *vi* to take part

mit|nehmen *irr vt* to take along; *(anstrengen)* to wear out, to exhaust

mit|schreiben *irr vi* to take notes ▷ *vt* to take down

Mitschüler(in) *m(f)* schoolmate

mit|spielen *vi* *(in Mannschaft)* to play; *(bei Spiel)* to join in; **in einem Film/Stück ~** to act in a film/play

Mittag *m* midday; **gestern ~** at midday yesterday, yesterday lunchtime; **über ~ geschlossen** closed at lunchtime; **zu ~ essen** to have lunch; **Mittagessen** *nt* lunch; **mittags** *adv* at lunchtime, at midday; **Mittagspause** *f* lunch break

Mitte *(-, -n)* *f* middle; **~ Juni** in the middle of June; **sie ist ~ zwanzig** she's in her mid-twenties

mit|teilen *vt* jdm etw ~ to inform sb of sth; **Mitteilung** *f* notification

Mittel *(-s -)* *nt* means *sing*; *(Maßnahme, Methode)* method; *(Med)* remedy *(gegen*

for); **das ist ein gutes ~, (um) junge Leute zu erreichen** that's a good way of engaging with young people

Mittelalter *nt* Middle Ages *pl*; **mittelalterlich** *adj* medieval; **Mittelamerika** *nt* Central America; **Mitteleuropa** *nt* Central Europe; **Mittelfeld** *nt* midfield; **Mittelfinger** *m* middle finger; **mittelmäßig** *adj* mediocre; **Mittelmeer** *nt* Mediterranean (Sea); **Mittelohrentzündung** *f* inflammation of the middle ear; **Mittelpunkt** *m* centre; **im ~ stehen** to be the centre of attention

mittels *prep* +gen by means of

Mittelstreifen *m* central reservation *(Brit)*, median *(US)*; **Mittelstürmer(in)** *m(f)* striker, centre-forward; **Mittelwelle** *f* medium wave

mitten *adv* in the middle; **~ auf der Straße/in der Nacht** in the middle of the street/night

Mitternacht *f* midnight

mittlere(r, s) *adj* middle; *(durchschnittlich)* average

mittlerweile *adv* meanwhile

Mittwoch *(-s, -e)* *m* Wednesday; **(am)** ~ on Wednesday; **(am)** ~ **Morgen/Nachmittag/Abend** (on) Wednesday morning/afternoon/evening; **diesen/letzten/nächsten** ~ this/last/next Wednesday; **jeden** ~ every Wednesday; **~ in einer Woche** a week on Wednesday, Wednesday week; **mittwochs** *adv* on Wednesdays; **~ abends** *(jeden Mittwochabend)* on Wednesday evenings

mixen *vt* to mix; **Mixer** *(-s, -)* *m* *(Küchengerät)* blender

MKS *f* abk = **Maul- und Klauenseuche** FMD

mobben *vt* to harass (o to bully) (at work)

Mobbing *(-s)* *nt* workplace bullying (o harassment)

Möbel *(-s, -)* *nt* piece of furniture; **die ~** *pl* the furniture *sing*; **Möbelwagen** *m* removal van

mobil *adj* mobile

Mobilfunknetz *nt* cellular network; **Mobiltelefon** *nt* mobile phone

möblieren *vt* to furnish

mochte *imperf von* **mögen**

m

Mode (-, -n) f fashion
Model (-s, -s) nt model
Modell (-s, -e) nt model
Modem (-s, -s) nt (Inform) modem
Mode(n)schau f fashion show
Moderator(in) m(f) presenter
modern adj modern; (modisch)
fashionable
Modeschmuck m costume jewellery;
modisch adj fashionable
Modus (-, Modi) m (Inform) mode; (fig) way
Mofa (-s, -s) nt moped
mogeln vi to cheat

⭘ SCHLÜSSELWORT

mögen (pt mochte, pp gemocht od (als
Hilfsverb) **mögen**) vt, vi to like; **magst
du/mögen Sie ihn?** do you like him?; **ich
möchte ...** I would like ... I'd like ...; **er
möchte in die Stadt** he'd like to go into
town; **ich möchte nicht, dass du ...** I
wouldn't like you to ...; **ich mag nicht
mehr** I've had enough
▷ Hilfsverb to like to (wollen) to want;
möchtest du etwas essen? would you
like something to eat?; **sie mag nicht
bleiben** she doesn't want to stay; **das
mag wohl sein** that may well be; **was
mag das heißen?** what might that
mean?; **Sie möchten zu Hause anrufen**
could you please call home?

möglich adj possible; **so bald wie ~** as
soon as possible; **möglicherweise** adv
possibly; **Möglichkeit** f possibility;
möglichst adv as ... as possible
Mohn (-(e)s, -e) m (Blume) poppy; (Samen)
poppy seed
Möhre (-, -n) f, **Mohrrübe** f carrot
Mokka (-s, -s) m mocha
Moldawien (-s) nt Moldova
Molkerei (-, -en) f dairy
Moll (-) nt minor (key); **a-~** A minor
mollig adj cosy; (dicklich) plump
Moment (-(e)s, -e) m moment; **im ~** at the
moment; **einen ~ bitte!** just a minute;
momentan adj momentary ▷ adv at the
moment
Monaco (-s) nt Monaco
Monarchie f monarchy
Monat (-(e)s, -e) m month; **sie ist im
dritten ~** (schwanger) she's three months

pregnant; **monatlich** adj, adv monthly;
~ 100 Euro zahlen to pay 100 euros a
month (o every month); **Monatskarte** f
monthly season ticket
Mönch (-s, -e) m monk
Mond (-(e)s, -e) m moon; **Mondfinsternis**
f lunar eclipse
Mongolei (-) f **die ~** Mongolia
Monitor m (Inform) monitor
monoton adj monotonous
Monsun (-s, -e) m monsoon
Montag m Monday; siehe auch **Mittwoch**;
montags adv on Mondays; siehe auch
mittwochs
Montenegro (-s) nt Montenegro
Monteur(in) (-s, -e) m(f) fitter;
montieren vt to assemble, to set up
Monument nt monument
Moor (-(e)s, -e) nt moor
Moos (-es, -e) nt moss
Moped (-s, -s) nt moped
Moral (-) f (Werte) morals pl; (einer
Geschichte) moral; **moralisch** adj moral
Mord (-(e)s, -e) m murder; **Mörder(in)**
(-s, -) m(f) murderer/murderess
morgen adv tomorrow; **~ früh** tomorrow
morning
Morgen (-s, -) m morning; **am ~** in the
morning; **Morgenmantel** m,
Morgenrock m dressing gown;
Morgenmuffel m **er ist ein ~** he's not a
morning person; **morgens** adv in the
morning; **um 3 Uhr ~** at 3 (o'clock) in the
morning, at 3 am
Morphium (-s) nt morphine
morsch adj rotten
Mosaik (-s, -e(n)) nt mosaic
Mosambik (-s) nt Mozambique
Moschee (-, -n) f mosque
Moskau (-s) nt Moscow
Moskito (-s, -s) m mosquito;
Moskitonetz nt mosquito net
Moslem (-s, -s) m, **Moslime** (-, -n) f
Muslim
Most (-(e)s, -e) m (unfermented) fruit
juice; (Apfelwein) cider
Motel (-s, -s) nt motel
motivieren vt to motivate
Motor m engine; (Elek) motor;
Motorboot nt motorboat; **Motorenöl** nt
engine oil; **Motorhaube** f bonnet (Brit),
hood (US); **Motorrad** nt motorbike,
motorcycle; **Motorradfahrer(in)** m(f)

motorcyclist; **Motorroller** m (motor) scooter; **Motorschaden** m engine trouble
Motte (-, -n) f moth
Motto (-s, -s) nt motto
Mountainbike (-s, -s) nt mountain bike
Möwe (-, -n) f (sea)gull
Mrd. f abk = **Milliarde(n)**
MS (-) f abk = **multiple Sklerose** MS
Mücke (-, -n) f midge; (tropische) mosquito; **Mückenstich** m mosquito bite
müde adj tired
muffig adj (Geruch) musty; (Gesicht, Mensch) grumpy
Mühe (-, -n) f trouble, pains pl; **sich** (dat) **große ~ geben** to go to a lot of trouble
muhen vi to moo
Mühle (-, -n) f mill; (Kaffeemühle) grinder
Mull (-(e)s, -e) m muslin; (Med) gauze
Müll (-(e)s) m rubbish (Brit), garbage (US); **Müllabfuhr** f rubbish (Brit) (o garbage (US)) disposal
Mullbinde f gauze bandage
Müllcontainer m waste container; **Mülldeponie** f rubbish (Brit) (o garbage (US)) dump; **Mülleimer** m rubbish bin (Brit), garbage can (US); **Mülltonne** f dustbin (Brit), garbage can (US); **Mülltrennung** f sorting and collecting household waste according to type of material; **Müllverbrennungsanlage** f incineration plant; **Müllwagen** m dustcart (Brit), garbage truck (US)
multikulturell adj multicultural
Multimedia- in zW multimedia
Multiple-Choice-Verfahren nt multiple choice
multiple Sklerose (-n, -n) f multiple sclerosis
Multiplexkino nt multiplex (cinema)
multiplizieren vt to multiply (mit by)
Mumie f mummy
Mumps (-) m mumps sing
München (-s) nt Munich
Mund (-(e)s, Münder) m mouth; **halt den ~!** shut up; **Mundart** f dialect; **Munddusche** f dental water jet
münden vi to flow (in +akk into)
Mundgeruch m bad breath; **Mundharmonika** (-, -s) f mouth organ
mündlich adj oral
Mundschutz m mask; **Mundwasser** nt mouthwash

Munition f ammunition
Münster (-s, -) nt minster, cathedral
munter adj lively
Münzautomat m vending machine; **Münze** (-, -n) f coin; **Münzeinwurf** m slot; **Münzrückgabe** f coin return; **Münztelefon** nt pay phone; **Münzwechsler** m change machine
murmeln vt, vi to murmur, to mutter
Murmeltier nt marmot
mürrisch adj sullen, grumpy
Mus (-es, -e) nt puree
Muschel (-, -n) f mussel; (~schale) shell
Museum (-s, Museen) nt museum
Musical (-s, -s) nt musical
Musik f music; **musikalisch** adj musical; **Musiker(in)** (-s, -) m(f) musician; **Musikinstrument** nt musical instrument; **musizieren** vi to play music
Muskat (-(e)s) m nutmeg
Muskel (-s, -n) m muscle; **Muskelkater** m **~ haben** to be stiff; **Muskelriss** m torn muscle; **Muskelzerrung** f pulled muscle; **muskulös** adj muscular
Müsli (-s, -) nt muesli
Muslim(in) (-s, -s) m(f) Muslim
Muss (-) nt must

🔵 SCHLÜSSELWORT

müssen (pt **musste**, pp **gemusst** od (als Hilfsverb) **müssen**) vi 1 (Zwang) must; (nur im Präsens) to have to; **ich muss es tun** I must do it, I have to do it; **ich musste es tun** I had to do it; **er muss es nicht tun** he doesn't have to do it; **muss ich?** must I?, do I have to?; **wann müsst ihr zur Schule?** when do you have to go to school?; **er hat gehen müssen** he (has) had to go; **muss das sein?** is that really necessary?; **ich muss mal** (umg) I need the toilet
2 (sollen): **das musst du nicht tun!** you oughtn't to od shouldn't do that; **Sie hätten ihn fragen müssen** you should have asked him
3: **es muss geregnet haben** it must have rained; **es muss nicht wahr sein** it needn't be true

Muster (-s, -) nt (Dessin) pattern, design; (Probe) sample; (Vorbild) model; **mustern** vt to have a close look at; **jdn ~** to look sb up and down

Mut *(-(e)s)* *m* courage; **jdm ~ machen** to encourage sb; **mutig** *adj* brave, courageous

Mutter *(-, Mütter)* *f* mother ▷ *(-, -n)* *f* *(Schraubenmutter)* nut; **Muttersprache** *f* mother tongue; **Muttertag** *m* Mother's Day; **Mutti** *f* mum(my) *(Brit)*, mom(my) *(US)*

mutwillig *adj* deliberate

Mütze *(-, -n)* *f* cap

MwSt. *abk* = **Mehrwertsteuer** VAT

Myanmar *(-s)* *nt* Myanmar

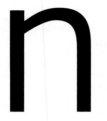

n

N *abk* = **Nord** N

na *interj* ~ **also!**, ~ **bitte!** see?, what did I tell you?; ~ **ja** well; ~ **und?** so what?

Nabel (-s, -) *m* navel

 SCHLÜSSELWORT

nach *präp* +dat **1** (*örtlich*) to; **nach Berlin** to Berlin; **nach links/rechts** (to the) left/right; **nach oben/hinten** up/back

2 (*zeitlich*) after; **einer nach dem anderen** one after the other; **nach Ihnen!** after you!; **zehn (Minuten) nach drei** ten (minutes) past three

3 (*gemäß*) according to; **nach dem Gesetz** according to the law; **dem Namen nach** judging by his/her name; **nach allem, was ich weiß** as far as I know

▷ *adv*: **ihm nach!** after him!; **nach und nach** gradually little by little; **nach wie vor** still

Nachbar(in) (-n, -n) *m(f)* neighbour; **Nachbarschaft** *f* neighbourhood
nach|bestellen *vt* to order some more
nachdem *conj* after; (*weil*) since; **je**

~ (**ob/wie**) depending on (whether/how)
nach|denken *irr vi* to think (*über +akk* about); **nachdenklich** *adj* thoughtful
nacheinander *adv* one after another (*o* the other)
Nachfolger(in) (-s, -) *m(f)* successor
nach|forschen *vt* to investigate
Nachfrage *f* inquiry; (*Comm*) demand; **nach|fragen** *vi* to inquire
Nachfüllpack *m* refill pack
nach|geben *irr vi* to give in (*jdm* to sb)
Nachgebühr *f* surcharge; (*für Briefe etc*) excess postage
nach|gehen *irr vi* to follow (*jdm* sb); (*erforschen*) to inquire (*einer Sache dat* into sth); **die Uhr geht (zehn Minuten) nach** this watch is (ten minutes) slow
nachher *adv* afterwards; **bis ~!** see you later
Nachhilfe *f* extra tuition
nach|holen *vt* to catch up with; (*Versäumtes*) to make up for
nach|kommen *irr vi* to follow; **einer Verpflichtung** (*dat*) ~ to fulfil an obligation
nach|lassen *irr vt* (*Summe*) to take off ▷ *vi* to decrease, to ease off; (*schlechter werden*) to deteriorate; **nachlässig** *adj* negligent, careless
nach|laufen *irr vi* to run after, to chase (*jdm* sb)
nach|lösen *vt* **eine Fahrkarte ~** to buy a ticket on the bus/train
nach|machen *vt* to imitate, to copy (*jdm etw* sth from sb); (*fälschen*) to counterfeit
Nachmittag *m* afternoon; **heute ~** this afternoon; **am ~** in the afternoon; **nachmittags** *adv* in the afternoon; **um 3 Uhr ~** at 3 (o'clock) in the afternoon, at 3 pm
Nachnahme (-, -n) *f* cash on delivery; **per ~** COD
Nachname *m* surname
Nachporto *nt* excess postage
nach|prüfen *vt* to check
nach|rechnen *vt* to check
Nachricht (-, -en) *f* (piece of) news *sing*; (*Mitteilung*) message; **Nachrichten** *pl* news *sing*
Nachsaison *f* off-season

nach|schauen vi jdm ~ to gaze after sb
▷ vt (prüfen) to check
nach|schicken vt to forward
nach|schlagen irr vt to look up
nach|sehen irr vt (prüfen) to check
nach|senden irr vt to forward
Nachspeise f dessert
nächstbeste(r, s) adj der ~ Zug/Job the
first train/job that comes along;
nächste(r, s) adj next; (nächstgelegen)
nearest
Nacht (-, Nächte) f night; **in der ~** during
the night; (bei Nacht) at night; **Nachtclub**
m nightclub; **Nachtdienst** m night duty;
~ haben (Apotheke) to be open all night
Nachteil m disadvantage
Nachtflug m night flight; **Nachtfrost** m
overnight frost; **Nachthemd** nt (für
Damen) nightdress; (für Herren)
nightshirt
Nachtigall (-, -en) f nightingale
Nachtisch m dessert, sweet (Brit),
pudding (Brit); **Nachtleben** nt nightlife
nach|tragen irr vt jdm etw ~ (übel
nehmen) to hold sth against sb
nachträglich adv ~ alles Gute zum
Geburtstag! Happy belated birthday
nachts adv at night; **um 11 Uhr ~** at 11
(o'clock) at night, at 11 pm; **um 2 Uhr ~** at 2
(o'clock) in the morning, at 2 am;
Nachtschicht f night shift; **Nachttarif** m
off-peak rate; **Nachttisch** m bedside
table; **Nachtzug** m night train
Nachweis (-es, -e) m proof
Nachwirkung f after-effect
nach|zahlen vi to pay extra ▷ vt **20 Euro**
~ to pay 20 euros extra
nach|zählen vt to check
Nacken (-s, -) m (nape of the) neck
nackt adj naked; (Tatsachen) plain, bare;
Nacktbadestrand m nudist beach
Nadel (-, -n) f needle; (Stecknadel) pin;
Nadelstreifen pl pinstripes pl
Nagel (-s, Nägel) m nail; **Nagelfeile** f
nail-file; **Nagellack** m nail varnish (o
polish); **Nagellackentferner** (-s, -) m
nail-varnish (o nail-polish) remover;
Nagelschere f nail scissors pl
nah(e) adj, adv (räumlich) near(by);
(zeitlich) near; (Verwandte, Freunde) close;
jdm ~e gehen to upset sb; **jdm etw ~e**
legen to suggest sth to sb; **~e liegen** to be
obvious ▷ prep +dat near (to), close to;

Nähe (-) f (Umgebung) vicinity; **in der**
~ nearby; **in der ~ von** near to
nähen vt, vi to sew
nähere(r, s) adj (Erklärung, Erkundigung)
more detailed; **die ~ Umgebung** the
immediate area; **Nähere(s)** nt details pl;
nähern vr **sich ~** to approach
nahezu adv virtually, almost
nahm imperf von **nehmen**
Nähmaschine f sewing machine;
Nähnadel f (sewing) needle
nahrhaft adj nourishing, nutritious;
Nahrung f food; **Nahrungsmittel** nt
food
Naht (-, Nähte) f seam; (Med) stitches pl,
suture; (Tech) join
Nahverkehr m local traffic;
Nahverkehrszug m local train
Nähzeug nt sewing kit
naiv adj naive
Name (-ns, -n) m name
nämlich adv that is to say, namely; (denn)
since
nannte imperf von **nennen**
Napf (-(e)s, Näpfe) m bowl, dish
Narbe (-, -n) f scar
Narkose (-, -n) f anaesthetic
Narzisse (-, -n) f narcissus
naschen vt, vi to nibble; **Naschkatze** f
(fam) nibbler; **eine ~ sein** to have a sweet
tooth
Nase (-, -n) f nose; **Nasenbluten** (-s) nt
nosebleed; **~ haben** to have a nosebleed;
Nasenloch nt nostril; **Nasentropfen** pl
nose drops pl
Nashorn nt rhinoceros
nass adj wet; **Nässe** (-) f wetness;
nässen vi (Wunde) to weep
Nation (-, -en) f nation; **national** adj
national; **Nationalfeiertag** m national
holiday; **Nationalhymne** (-, -n) f national
anthem; **Nationalität** f nationality;
Nationalmannschaft f national team;
Nationalspieler(in) m(f) international
(player)
NATO (-) f abk = **North Atlantic Treaty**
Organization NATO, Nato
Natur f nature; **Naturkost** f health food;
natürlich adj natural ▷ adv naturally;
(selbstverständlich) of course; **Naturpark** m
nature reserve; **naturrein** adj natural,
pure; **Naturschutz** m conservation;
Naturschutzgebiet nt nature reserve;

Naturwissenschaft f (natural) science; **Naturwissenschaftler(in)** m(f) scientist
Navigationssystem nt (Auto) navigation system
n. Chr. abk = **nach Christus** AD
Nebel (-s, -) m fog, mist; **nebelig** adj foggy, misty; **Nebelscheinwerfer** m foglamp; **Nebelschlussleuchte** f (Auto) rear foglight
neben prep +akk o dat next to; (außer) apart from, besides; **nebenan** adv next door; **Nebenausgang** m side exit; **nebenbei** adv at the same time; (außerdem) additionally; (beiläufig) incidentally; **nebeneinander** adv side by side; **Nebeneingang** m side entrance; **Nebenfach** nt subsidiary subject
nebenher adv (zusätzlich) besides; (gleichzeitig) at the same time; (daneben) alongside
Nebenkosten pl extra charges pl, extras pl; **Nebensache** f minor matter; **nebensächlich** adj minor; **Nebensaison** f low season; **Nebenstelle** f (Geschäft) branch; (Telefon) extension; **Nebenstraße** f side street; **Nebenwirkung** f side effect
neblig adj foggy, misty
necken vt to tease
Neffe (-n, -n) m nephew
negativ adj negative; **Negativ** nt (Foto) negative
nehmen (nahm, genommen) vt to take; **jdm etw ~** to take sth (away) from sb; **wie man's nimmt** it depends on how you look at it; **den Bus/Zug ~** to take the bus/train; **jdn/etw ernst ~** to take sb/sth seriously; **etw zu sich ~** to eat sth; **jdn zu sich ~** to have sb come and live with one; **jdn an die Hand ~** to take sb by the hand
neidisch adj envious
neigen vi **zu etw ~** to tend towards sth; **Neigung** f (des Geländes) slope; (Tendenz) inclination; (Vorliebe) liking
nein adv no
Nektarine f nectarine
Nelke (-, -n) f carnation; (Gewürz) clove
nennen (nannte, genannt) vt to name; (mit Namen) to call
Neonazi (-s, -s) m neo-Nazi
Neonlicht nt neon light; **Neonröhre** f neon tube
Nepal (-s) nt Nepal

Neptun (-s) m Neptune
Nerv (-s, -en) m nerve; **jdm auf die ~en gehen** to get on sb's nerves; **nerven** vt **jdn ~** (fam) to get on sb's nerves; **Nervenzusammenbruch** m nervous breakdown; **nervös** adj nervous
Nest (-(e)s, -er) nt nest; (pej: Ort) dump
nett adj nice; (freundlich) kind; **sei so ~ und ...** do me a favour and ...
netto adv net
Netz (-es, -e) nt net; (für Einkauf) string bag; (System) network; (Stromnetz) mains, power (US); **Netzanschluss** m mains connection; **Netzbetreiber(in)** m(f) network operator; (Inform) Internet (o Net) operator; **Netzgerät** nt power pack; **Netzkarte** f season ticket; **Netzwerk** nt (Inform) network; **Netzwerkkarte** f network card
neu adj new; (Sprache, Geschichte) modern; **die ~esten Nachrichten** the latest news; **Neubau** m new building; **neuerdings** adv recently; **Neueröffnung** f (Geschäft) new business; **Neuerung** f innovation; (Reform) reform
Neugier f curiosity; **neugierig** adj curious (auf +akk about); **ich bin ~, ob ...** I wonder whether (o if) ...; **ich bin ~ , was du dazu sagst** I'll be interested to hear what you have to say about it
Neuheit f novelty; **Neuigkeit** f news sing; **eine ~** a piece of news; **Neujahr** nt New Year; **prosit ~!** Happy New Year; **neulich** adv recently, the other day; **Neumond** m new moon
neun num nine; **neunhundert** num nine hundred; **neunmal** adv nine times; **neunte(r, s)** adj ninth; siehe auch **dritte**; **Neuntel** (-s, -) nt ninth; **neunzehn** num nineteen; **neunzehnte(r, s)** adj nineteenth; siehe auch **dritte**; **neunzig** num ninety; **in den ~er Jahren** in the nineties; **Neunzigerjahre** pl nineties pl; **neunzigste(r, s)** adj ninetieth
neureich adj nouveau riche
Neurologe m, **Neurologin** f neurologist; **Neurose** (-, -n) f neurosis; **neurotisch** adj neurotic
Neuseeland nt New Zealand
Neustart m (Inform) restart, reboot
neutral adj neutral
neuwertig adj nearly new
Nicaragua (-s) nt Nicaragua

🔵 SCHLÜSSELWORT

nicht adv **1** (Verneinung) not; **er ist es nicht** it's not him it isn't him; **er raucht nicht** (gerade) he isn't smoking (gewöhnlich) he doesn't smoke; **ich kann das nicht — ich auch nicht** I can't do it — neither od nor can I; **es regnet nicht mehr** it's not raining any more; **nicht rostend** stainless

2 (Bitte, Verbot): **nicht!** don't!, no!; **nicht berühren!** do not touch!; **nicht doch!** don't!

3 (rhetorisch): **du bist müde, nicht (wahr)?** you're tired, aren't you?; **das ist schön, nicht (wahr)?** it's nice, isn't it?

4: **was du nicht sagst!** the things you say!

Nichte (-, -n) f niece
Nichtraucher(in) m(f) non-smoker; **Nichtraucherabteil** nt non-smoking compartment; **Nichtraucherzone** f non-smoking area
nichts pron nothing; **für ~ und wieder ~** for nothing at all; **ich habe ~ gesagt** I didn't say anything; **~ sagend** meaningless; **macht ~** never mind
Nichtschwimmer(in) m(f) non-swimmer
nicken vi to nod
Nickerchen nt nap
nie adv never; **~ wieder** (o **mehr**) never again; **fast ~** hardly ever
nieder adj (niedrig) low; (gering) inferior ▷ adv down; **niedergeschlagen** adj depressed; **Niederlage** f defeat
Niederlande pl Netherlands pl; **Niederländer(in)** m(f) Dutchman/Dutchwoman; **niederländisch** adj Dutch; **Niederländisch** nt Dutch
Niederlassung f branch
Niederösterreich nt Lower Austria; **Niedersachsen** nt Lower Saxony
Niederschlag m (Meteo) precipitation; (Regen) rainfall
niedlich adj sweet, cute
niedrig adj low; (Qualität) inferior
niemals adv never
niemand pron nobody, no one; **ich habe**

~en gesehen I haven't seen anyone; **~ von ihnen** none of them
Niere (-, -n) f kidney; **Nierenentzündung** f kidney infection; **Nierensteine** pl kidney stones pl
nieseln vi impers to drizzle; **Nieselregen** m drizzle
niesen vi to sneeze
Niete (-, -n) f (Los) blank; (Reinfall) flop; (pej: Mensch) failure; (Tech) rivet
Nigeria (-s) nt Nigeria
Nikotin (-s) nt nicotine; **nikotinarm** adj low in nicotine
Nilpferd nt hippopotamus
nippen vi to sip; **an etw** (dat) **~** to sip sth
nirgends adv nowhere
Nische (-, -n) f niche
Nitrat nt nitrate
Niveau (-s, -s) nt level; **sie hat ~** she's got class
nobel adj (großzügig) generous; (fam: luxuriös) classy, posh; **Nobelpreis** m Nobel Prize

🔵 SCHLÜSSELWORT

noch adv **1** (weiterhin) still; **noch nicht** not yet; **noch nie** never (yet); **noch immer** od **immer noch** still; **bleiben Sie doch noch** stay a bit longer

2 (in Zukunft) still, yet; **das kann noch passieren** that might still happen; **er wird noch kommen** he'll come (yet)

3 (nicht später als): **noch vor einer Woche** only a week ago; **noch am selben Tag** the very same day; **noch im 19. Jahrhundert** as late as the 19th century; **noch heute** today

4 (zusätzlich): **wer war noch da?** who else was there?; **noch einmal** once more again; **noch dreimal** three more times; **noch einer** another one

5 (bei Vergleichen): **noch größer** even bigger; **das ist noch besser** that's better still; **und wenn es noch so schwer ist** however hard it is

6: **Geld noch und noch** heaps (and heaps) of money; **sie hat noch und noch versucht, ...** she tried again and again to ...

▷ konj: **weder A noch B** neither A nor B

Nominativ *m* nominative (case)
Nonne (-, -*n*) *f* nun
Non-Stop-Flug *m* nonstop flight
Nord north; **Nordamerika** *nt* North
America; **Norddeutschland** *nt* Northern
Germany; **Norden** (-*s*) *m* north; **im**
~ Deutschlands in the north of Germany;
Nordeuropa *nt* Northern Europe;
Nordirland *nt* Northern Ireland;
nordisch *adj* (*Völker, Sprache*) Nordic;
Nordkorea (-*s*) *nt* North Korea; **nördlich**
adj northern; (*Kurs, Richtung*) northerly;
Nordost(en) *m* northeast; **Nordpol** *m*
North Pole; **Nordrhein-Westfalen** (-*s*) *nt*
North Rhine-Westphalia; **Nordsee** *f*
North Sea; **nordwärts** *adv* north,
northwards; **Nordwest(en)** *m*
northwest; **Nordwind** *m* north wind
nörgeln *vi* to grumble
Norm (-, -*en*) *f* norm; (*Größenvorschrift*)
standard
normal *adj* normal; **Normalbenzin** *nt*
regular (petrol (*Brit*) *o* gas (*US*));
normalerweise *adv* normally
normen *vt* to standardize
Norwegen (-*s*) *nt* Norway; **Norweger(in)**
m(f) Norwegian; **norwegisch** *adj*
Norwegian; **Norwegisch** *nt* Norwegian
Not (-, *Nöte*) *f* need; (*Armut*) poverty;
(*Elend*) hardship; (*Bedrängnis*) trouble;
(*Mangel*) want; (*Mühe*) trouble; (*Zwang*)
necessity; **zur ~** if necessary; (*gerade noch*)
just about
Notar(in) *m(f)* public notary; **notariell**
adj **~ beglaubigt** attested by a notary
Notarzt *m*, **Notärztin** *f* emergency
doctor; **Notarztwagen** *m* emergency
ambulance; **Notausgang** *m* emergency
exit; **Notbremse** *f* emergency brake;
Notdienst *m* emergency service,
after-hours service; **notdürftig** *adj*
scanty; (*behelfsmäßig*) makeshift
Note (-, -*n*) *f* note; (*in Schule*) mark, grade
(*US*); (*Mus*) note
Notebook (-(*s*), -*s*) *nt* (*Inform*) notebook
Notfall *m* emergency; **notfalls** *adv* if
necessary
notieren *vt* to note down
nötig *adj* necessary; **etw ~ haben** to need
sth
Notiz (-, -*en*) *f* note; (*Zeitungs~*) item;
Notizblock *m* notepad; **Notizbuch** *nt*
notebook

Notlage *f* crisis; (*Elend*) plight;
notlanden *vi* to make a forced
(*o* emergency) landing; **Notruf**
m emergency call; **Notrufnummer**
f emergency number;
Notrufsäule *f* emergency telephone
notwendig *adj* necessary
Nougat (-*s*, -*s*) *m od nt* nougat
November (-(*s*), -) *m* November; *siehe*
auch **Juni**
Nr. *abk* = **Nummer** No., no.
Nu *m* **im ~** in no time
nüchtern *adj* sober; (*Magen*) empty
Nudel (-, -*n*) *f* noodle; **~n** *pl* (*italienische*)
pasta *sing*; **Nudelsuppe** *f* noodle
soup
null *num* zero; (*Tel*) O (*Brit*), zero (*US*);
~ Fehler no mistakes; **~ Uhr** midnight;
Null (-, -*en*) *f* nought, zero; (*pej: Mensch*)
dead loss; **Nulltarif** *m* **zum ~** free of
charge
Numerus clausus (-) *m* *restriction on the*
number of students allowed to study a
particular subject
Nummer (-, -*n*) *f* number; **nummerieren**
vt to number; **Nummernschild** *nt* (*Auto*)
number plate (*Brit*), license plate (*US*)
nun *adv* now; **von ~ an** from now on
▷ *interj* well; **~ gut!** all right, then; **es ist**
~ mal so that's the way it is
nur *adv* only; **nicht ~ ..., sondern auch ...**
not only ..., but also ...; **~ Anna nicht**
except Anna
Nürnberg (-*s*) *nt* Nuremberg
Nuss (-, *Nüsse*) *f* nut; **Nussknacker** (-*s*, -)
m nutcracker; **Nuss-Nougat-Creme** *f*
chocolate nut cream
Nutte (-, -*n*) *f* (*fam*) tart
nutz, nütze *adj* **zu nichts ~ sein** to be
useless; **nutzen, nützen** *vt* to use (*zu etw*
for sth); **was nützt es?** what use is it? ▷ *vi*
to be of use; **das nützt nicht viel** that
doesn't help much; **es nützt nichts(, es**
zu tun) it's no use (doing it); **Nutzen** (-*s*, -)
m usefulness; (*Gewinn*) profit; **nützlich**
adj useful
Nylon (-*s*) *nt* nylon

n

o *interj* oh

O *abk* = **Ost** E

Oase (-, -n) *f* oasis

ob *conj* if, whether; **so als ~** as if; **er tut so, als ~ er krank wäre** he's pretending to be sick; **und ~!** you bet

obdachlos *adj* homeless

oben *adv* (*am oberen Ende*) at the top; (*obenauf*) on (the) top; (*im Haus*) upstairs; (*in einem Text*) above; **~ erwähnt** (*o* **genannt**) above-mentioned; **mit dem Gesicht nach ~** face up; **da ~** up there; **von ~ bis unten** from top to bottom; **siehe ~** see above

Ober (-s, -) *m* waiter

obere(r, s) *adj* upper, top

Oberfläche *f* surface; **oberflächlich** *adj* superficial; **Obergeschoss** *nt* upper floor

oberhalb *adv, prep* +*gen* above

Oberhemd *nt* shirt; **Oberkörper** *m* upper body; **Oberlippe** *f* upper lip; **Oberösterreich** *nt* Upper Austria; **Oberschenkel** *m* thigh

oberste(r, s) *adj* very top, topmost

Oberteil *nt* top; **Oberweite** *f* bust/chest measurement

obig *adj* above(-mentioned)

Objekt (-(e)s, -e) *nt* object

objektiv *adj* objective; **Objektiv** *nt* lens

obligatorisch *adj* compulsory, obligatory

Oboe (-, -n) *f* oboe

Observatorium *nt* observatory

Obst (-(e)s) *nt* fruit; **Obstkuchen** *m* fruit tart; **Obstsalat** *m* fruit salad

obszön *adj* obscene

obwohl *conj* although

Ochse (-n, -n) *m* ox; **Ochsenschwanzsuppe** *f* oxtail soup

ocker *adj* ochre

öd(e) *adj* waste; (*unbebaut*) barren; (*fig*) dull

oder *conj* or; **~ aber** or else; **er kommt doch, ~?** he's coming, isn't he?

Ofen (-s, Öfen) *m* oven; (*Heizofen*) heater; (*Kohleofen*) stove; (*Herd*) cooker, stove; **Ofenkartoffel** *f* baked (*o* jacket) potato

offen *adj* open; (*aufrichtig*) frank; (*Stelle*) vacant ▷ *adv* frankly; **~ gesagt** to be honest

offenbar *adj* obvious; **offensichtlich** *adj* evident, obvious

öffentlich *adj* public; **Öffentlichkeit** *f* (*Leute*) public; (*einer Versammlung etc*) public nature

offiziell *adj* official

offline *adv* (*Inform*) offline

öffnen *vt* to open ▷ *vr* **sich ~** to open; **Öffner** (-s, -) *m* opener; **Öffnung** *f* opening; **Öffnungszeiten** *pl* opening times *pl*

oft *adv* often; **schon ~** many times; **öfter** *adv* more often (*o* frequently); **öfters** *adv* often, frequently

ohne *conj, prep* +*akk* without; **~ weiteres** without a second thought; (*sofort*) immediately; **~ ein Wort zu sagen** without saying a word; **~ mich** count me out

Ohnmacht (-machten) *f* unconsciousness; (*Hilflosigkeit*) helplessness; **in ~ fallen** to faint; **ohnmächtig** *adj* unconscious; **sie ist ~** she has fainted

Ohr (-(e)s, -en) *nt* ear; (*Gehör*) hearing

Öhr (-(e)s, -e) *nt* eye

Ohrenarzt *m*, **Ohrenärztin** *f* ear specialist; **Ohrenschmerzen** *pl* earache; **Ohrentropfen** *pl* ear drops *pl*; **Ohrfeige** *f*

slap (in the face); **Ohrläppchen** nt earlobe; **Ohrringe** pl earrings pl

oje interj oh dear

okay interj OK, okay

Ökoladen m health food store; **ökologisch** adj ecological; **~e Landwirtschaft** organic farming

ökonomisch adj economic; (sparsam) economical

Ökosystem nt ecosystem

Oktanzahl f (bei Benzin) octane rating

Oktober (-(s), -) m October; siehe auch **Juni**

- **Oktoberfest**
-
- The annual October beer festival, the
- **Oktoberfest**, takes place in Munich on
- a huge field where beer tents, roller
- coasters and many other
- amusements are set up. People sit at
- long wooden tables, drink beer from
- enormous litre beer mugs, eat
- pretzels and listen to brass bands. It
- is a great attraction for tourists and
- locals alike.

Öl (-(e)s, -e) nt oil; **Ölbaum** m olive tree; **ölen** vt to oil; (Tech) to lubricate; **Ölfarbe** f oil paint; **Ölfilter** m oil filter; **Ölgemälde** nt oil painting; **Ölheizung** f oil-fired central heating; **ölig** adj oily

oliv adj inv olive-green; **Olive** (-, -n) f olive; **Olivenöl** nt olive oil

Ölmessstab m dipstick; **Ölofen** m oil stove; **Ölpest** f oil pollution; **Ölsardine** f sardine in oil; **Ölstandanzeiger** m (Auto) oil gauge; **Ölteppich** m oil slick; **Ölwechsel** m oil change

Olympiade f Olympic Games pl; **olympisch** adj Olympic

Oma f, **Omi** (-s, -s) f grandma, gran(ny)

Omelett (-(e)s, -s) nt, **Omelette** f omelette

Omnibus m bus

onanieren vi to masturbate

Onkel (-s, -) m uncle

online adv (Inform) online; **Onlinedienst** m (Inform) online service

OP (-s, -s) m abk = **Operationssaal** operating theatre (Brit) (o room (US))

Opa m, **Opi** (-s, -s) m grandpa, grandad

Openairkonzert nt open-air concert

Oper (-, -n) f opera; (Gebäude) opera house

Operation f operation

Operette f operetta

operieren vi to operate ▷ vt to operate on

Opernsänger(in) m(f) opera singer

Opfer (-s, -) nt sacrifice; (Mensch) victim; **ein ~ bringen** to make a sacrifice

Opium (-s) nt opium

Opposition f opposition

Optiker(in) (-s, -) m(f) optician

optimal adj optimal, optimum

optimistisch adj optimistic

oral adj oral; **Oralverkehr** m oral sex

orange adj inv orange; **Orange** (-, -n) f orange; **Orangenmarmelade** f marmalade; **Orangensaft** m orange juice

Orchester (-s, -) nt orchestra

Orchidee (-, -n) f orchid

Orden (-s, -) m (Rel) order; (Mil) decoration

ordentlich adj (anständig) respectable; (geordnet) tidy, neat; (fam: annehmbar) not bad; (fam: tüchtig) proper ▷ adv properly

ordinär adj common, vulgar; (Witz) dirty

ordnen vt to sort out; **Ordner** (-s, -) m (bei Veranstaltung) steward; (Aktenordner) file; **Ordnung** f order; (Geordnetsein) tidiness; (**geht**) **in ~!** (that's) all right; **mit dem Drucker ist etwas nicht in ~** there's something wrong with the printer

Oregano (-s) m oregano

Organ (-s, -e) nt organ; (Stimme) voice

Organisation f organization; **organisieren** vt to organize; (fam: beschaffen) to get hold of ▷ vr **sich ~** to organize

Organismus m organism

Orgasmus m orgasm

Orgel (-, -n) f organ

Orgie f orgy

orientalisch adj oriental

orientieren vr **sich ~** to get one's bearings; **Orientierung** f orientation; **Orientierungssinn** m sense of direction

original adj original; (echt) genuine; **Original** (-s, -e) nt original; **Originalfassung** f original version

originell adj original; (komisch) witty

Orkan (-(e)s, -e) m hurricane

Ort (-(e)s, -e) m place; (Dorf) village; **an ~ und Stelle, vor ~** on the spot

Orthopäde (-n, -n) m, **Orthopädin** f orthopaedist

örtlich adj local; **Ortschaft** f village,

o

small town; **Ortsgespräch** *nt* local call;
Ortstarif *m* local rate; **Ortszeit** *f* local
time

● **Ossi**
●
● **Ossi** is a colloquial and rather
● derogatory word used to describe a
● German from the former **DDR**.

Ost east; **Ostdeutschland** *nt* (*als
Landesteil*) Eastern Germany; (*Hist*) East
Germany; **Osten** (*-s*) *m* east
Osterei *nt* Easter egg; **Osterglocke** *f*
daffodil; **Osterhase** *m* Easter bunny;
Ostermontag *m* Easter Monday; **Ostern**
(*-, -*) *nt* Easter; **an** (*o* **zu**) **~** at Easter; **frohe
~** Happy Easter
Österreich (*-s*) *nt* Austria;
Österreicher(in) (*-s, -*) *m(f)* Austrian;
österreichisch *adj* Austrian
Ostersonntag *m* Easter Sunday
Osteuropa *nt* Eastern Europe; **Ostküste**
f east coast; **östlich** *adj* eastern; (*Kurs,
Richtung*) easterly; **Ostsee** *f* **die ~** the
Baltic (Sea); **Ostwind** *m* east(erly) wind
OSZE (*-*) *f abk* = **Organisation für
Sicherheit und Zusammenarbeit in
Europa** OSCE
Otter (*-s, -*) *m* otter
out *adj* (*fam*) out; **outen** *vt* to out
oval *adj* oval
Overheadprojektor *m* overhead
projector
Ozean (*-s, -e*) *m* ocean; **der Stille ~** the
Pacific (Ocean)
Ozon (*-s*) *nt* ozone; **Ozonbelastung** *f*
ozone level; **Ozonloch** *nt* hole in the
ozone layer; **Ozonschicht** *f* ozone layer;
Ozonwerte *pl* ozone levels *pl*

paar *adj inv* **ein ~** a few; **ein ~ Mal** a few times; **ein ~ Äpfel** some apples

Paar (-(e)s, -e) *nt* pair; (*Ehepaar*) couple; **ein ~ Socken** a pair of socks

pachten *vt* to lease

Päckchen *nt* package; (*Zigaretten*) packet; (*zum Verschicken*) small parcel; **packen** *vt* to pack; (*fassen*) to grasp, to seize; (*fam: schaffen*) to manage; (*fig: fesseln*) to grip; **Packpapier** *nt* brown paper; **Packung** *f* packet, pack (*US*); **Packungsbeilage** *f* package insert, patient information leaflet

Pädagoge (-n, -n) *m*, **Pädagogin** *f* teacher; **pädagogisch** *adj* educational; **~e Hochschule** college of education

Paddel (-s, -) *nt* paddle; **Paddelboot** *nt* canoe; **paddeln** *vi* to paddle

Paket (-(e)s, -e) *nt* packet; (*Postpaket*) parcel; (*Inform*) package; **Paketbombe** *f* parcel bomb; **Paketkarte** *f* dispatch form (*to be filled in with details of the sender and the addressee when handing in a parcel at the post office*)

Pakistan (-s) *nt* Pakistan

Palast (-es, Paläste) *m* palace

Palästina (-s) *nt* Palestine; **Palästinenser(in)** (-s, -) *m(f)* Palestinian

Palatschinken *pl* filled pancakes *pl*

Palette *f* (*von Maler*) palette; (*Ladepalette*) pallet; (*Vielfalt*) range

Palme (-, -n) *f* palm (tree); **Palmsonntag** *m* Palm Sunday

Pampelmuse (-, -n) *f* grapefruit

pampig *adj* (*fam: frech*) cheeky; (*breiig*) gooey

Panda(bär) (-s, -s) *m* panda

panieren *vt* (*Gastr*) to coat with breadcrumbs; **paniert** *adj* breaded

Panik *f* panic

Panne (-, -n) *f* (*Auto*) breakdown; (*Missgeschick*) slip; **Pannendienst** *m*, **Pannenhilfe** *f* breakdown (*o* rescue) service

Pant(h)er (-s, -) *m* panther

Pantoffel (-s, -n) *m* slipper

Pantomime (-, -n) *f* mime

Panzer (-s, -) *m* (*Panzerung*) armour (plating); (*Mil*) tank

Papa (-s, -s) *m* dad(dy), pa (*US*)

Papagei (-s, -en) *m* parrot

Papaya (-, -s) *f* papaya

Papier (-s, -e) *nt* paper; **~e** *pl* (*Ausweispapiere*) papers *pl*; (*Dokumente, Urkunden*) papers *pl*, documents *pl*; **Papiercontainer** *m* paper bank; **Papierformat** *nt* paper size; **Papiergeld** *nt* paper money; **Papierkorb** *m* wastepaper basket; (*Inform*) recycle bin; **Papiertaschentuch** *nt* (paper) tissue; **Papiertonne** *f* paper bank

Pappbecher *m* paper cup; **Pappe** (-, -n) *f* cardboard; **Pappkarton** *m* cardboard box; **Pappteller** *m* paper plate

Paprika (-s, -s) *m* (*Gewürz*) paprika; (*Schote*) pepper

Papst (-(e)s, Päpste) *m* pope

Paradeiser (-s, -) *m* tomato

Paradies (-es, -e) *nt* paradise

Paragliding (-s) *nt* paragliding

Paragraph (-en, -en) *m* paragraph; (*Jur*) section

parallel *adj* parallel

Paranuss *f* Brazil nut

Parasit (-en, -en) *m* parasite

parat *adj* ready; **etw ~ haben** to have sth ready

Pärchen *nt* couple

Parfüm (-s, -s *o* -e) *nt* perfume; **Parfümerie** *f* perfumery; **parfümieren** *vt* to scent, to perfume

Pariser (-s, -) m (fam: Kondom) rubber
Park (-s, -s) m park
Park-and-ride-System nt
park-and-ride system; **Parkanlage** f
park; (um Gebäude) grounds pl; **Parkbank** f
park bench; **Parkdeck** nt parking level;
parken vt, vi to park
Parkett (-s, -e) nt parquet flooring; (Theat)
stalls pl (Brit), parquet (US)
Parkhaus nt multi-storey car park (Brit),
parking garage (US)
parkinsonsche Krankheit f
Parkinson's disease
Parkkralle f (Auto) wheel clamp;
Parklicht nt parking light; **Parklücke** f
parking space; **Parkplatz** m (für ein Auto)
parking space; (für mehrere Autos) car park
(Brit), parking lot (US); **Parkscheibe** f
parking disc; **Parkscheinautomat** m pay
point; (Parkscheinausgabegerät) ticket
machine; **Parkuhr** f parking meter;
Parkverbot nt (Stelle) no-parking zone;
hier ist ~ you can't park here
Parlament nt parliament
Parmesan (-s) m Parmesan (cheese)
Partei f party
Parterre (-s, -s) nt ground floor (Brit), first
floor (US)
Partie f part; (Spiel) game; (Mann, Frau)
catch; **mit von der ~ sein** to be in on it
Partitur f (Mus) score
Partizip (-s, -ien) nt participle
Partner(in) (-s, -) m(f) partner;
Partnerschaft f partnership;
eingetragene ~ civil partnership;
Partnerstadt f twin town
Party (-, -s) f party; **Partymuffel** (-s, -) m
party pooper; **Partyservice** m catering
service
Pass (-es, Pässe) m pass; (Ausweis) passport
passabel adj reasonable
Passagier (-s, -e) m passenger
Passamt nt passport office
Passant(in) m(f) passer-by; **Passbild** nt
passport photo
passen vi (Größe) to fit; (Farbe, Stil) to go
(zu with); (auf Frage) to pass; **passt (es) dir
morgen?** does tomorrow suit you?; **das
passt mir gut** that suits me fine;
passend adj suitable; (zusammenpassend)
matching; (angebracht) fitting; (Zeit)
convenient; **haben Sie es nicht ~?**
(Kleingeld) have you got the right change?

passieren vi to happen
passiv adj passive
Passkontrolle f passport control
Passwort nt password
Paste (-, -n) f paste
Pastellfarbe f pastel colour
Pastete (-, -n) f (warmes Gericht) pie;
(Pastetchen) vol-au-vent; (ohne Teig) pâté
Pastor(in) (-s, -en) m(f) minister, vicar
Pate (-n, -n) m godfather; **Patenkind** nt
godchild
Patient(in) m(f) patient
Patin f godmother
Patrone (-, -n) f cartridge
patsch interj splat; **Patsche** (-, -n) f
(Fliegen~) swat; (Bedrängnis) mess;
patschnass adj soaking wet
pauschal adj (Kosten) inclusive; (Urteil)
sweeping; **Pauschale** (-, -n) f,
Pauschalgebühr f flat rate (charge);
Pauschalpreis m flat rate; (für Hotel,
Reise) all-inclusive price; **Pauschalreise** f
package tour
Pause (-, -n) f break; (Theat) interval; (Kino
etc) intermission; (Innehalten) pause
Pavian (-s, -e) m baboon
Pavillon (-s, -s) m pavilion
Pay-TV (-s) nt pay-per-view television,
pay TV
Pazifik (-s) m Pacific (Ocean)
PC (-s, -s) m abk = **Personalcomputer** PC
Pech (-s, -e) nt (fig) bad luck; **~ haben** to
be unlucky; **~ gehabt!** tough (luck)
Pedal (-s, -e) nt pedal
Pediküre (-, -en) f pedicure
Peeling (-s, -s) nt (facial/body) scrub
peinlich adj (unangenehm) embarrassing,
awkward; (genau) painstaking; **es war mir
sehr ~** I was totally embarrassed
Peitsche (-, -n) f whip
Pelikan (-s, -e) m pelican
Pellkartoffeln pl potatoes pl boiled in
their skins
Pelz (-es, -e) m fur; **pelzig** adj (Zunge)
furred
pendeln vi (Zug, Bus) to shuttle; (Mensch)
to commute; **Pendelverkehr** m shuttle
traffic; (für Pendler) commuter traffic;
Pendler(in) (-s, -) m(f) commuter
penetrant adj sharp; (Mensch) pushy
Penis (-, -se) m penis
Pension f (Geld) pension; (Ruhestand)
retirement; (für Gäste) guesthouse, B&B;

pensioniert *adj* retired; **Pensionsgast** *m* guest (*in a guesthouse*)
Peperoni (-, -) *f* chilli
per *prep* +*akk* by, per; (*pro*) per; (*bis*) by
perfekt *adj* perfect
Pergamentpapier *nt* greaseproof paper
Periode (-, -*n*) *f* period
Perle (-, -*n*) *f* (*a. fig*) pearl
perplex *adj* dumbfounded
Person (-, -*en*) *f* person; **ein Tisch für drei ~en** a table for three; **Personal** (-*s*) *nt* staff, personnel; (*Bedienung*) servants *pl*; **Personalausweis** *m* identity card; **Personalien** *pl* particulars *pl*; **Personenschaden** *m* injury to persons; **Personenwaage** *f* (bathroom) scales *pl*; **Personenzug** *m* passenger train; **persönlich** *adj* personal; (*auf Briefen*) private ▷ *adv* personally; (*selbst*) in person; **Persönlichkeit** *f* personality
Peru (-*s*) *nt* Peru
Perücke (-, -*n*) *f* wig
pervers *adj* perverted
pessimistisch *adj* pessimistic
Pest (-) *f* plague
Petersilie *f* parsley
Petroleum (-*s*) *nt* paraffin (*Brit*), kerosene (*US*)
Pfad (-(*e*)*s*, -*e*) *m* path; **Pfadfinder** (-*s*, -) *m* boy scout; **Pfadfinderin** *f* girl guide
Pfahl (-(*e*)*s*, *Pfähle*) *m* post, stake
Pfand (-(*e*)*s*, *Pfänder*) *nt* security; (*Flaschenpfand*) deposit; (*im Spiel*) forfeit; **Pfandflasche** *f* returnable bottle
Pfanne (-, -*n*) *f* (frying) pan
Pfannkuchen *m* pancake
Pfarrei *f* parish; **Pfarrer(in)** (-*s*, -) *m(f)* priest
Pfau (-(*e*)*s*, -*en*) *m* peacock
Pfeffer (-*s*, -) *m* pepper; **Pfefferkuchen** *m* gingerbread; **Pfefferminze** (-*e*) *f* peppermint; **Pfefferminztee** *m* peppermint tea; **Pfeffermühle** *f* pepper mill; **pfeffern** *vt* to put pepper on/in; **Pfefferstreuer** (-*s*, -) *m* pepper pot
Pfeife (-, -*n*) *f* whistle; (*für Tabak, von Orgel*) pipe; **pfeifen** (*pfiff, gepfiffen*) *vt, vi* to whistle
Pfeil (-(*e*)*s*, -*e*) *m* arrow
Pfeiltaste *f* (*Inform*) arrow key
Pferd (-(*e*)*s*, -*e*) *nt* horse; **Pferdeschwanz** *m* (*Frisur*) ponytail; **Pferdestall** *m* stable; **Pferdestärke** *f* horsepower

pfiff *imperf von* **pfeifen**
Pfifferling *m* chanterelle
Pfingsten (-, -) *nt* Whitsun, Pentecost (*US*); **Pfingstmontag** *m* Whit Monday; **Pfingstsonntag** *m* Whit Sunday, Pentecost (*US*); **Pfingstrose** *f* peony
Pfirsich (-*s*, -*e*) *m* peach
Pflanze (-, -*n*) *f* plant; **pflanzen** *vt* to plant; **Pflanzenfett** *nt* vegetable fat
Pflaster (-*s*, -) *nt* (*für Wunde*) plaster, Band Aid® (*US*); (*Straßenpflaster*) road surface, pavement (*US*)
Pflaume (-, -*n*) *f* plum
Pflege (-, -*n*) *f* care; (*Krankenpflege*) nursing; (*von Autos, Maschinen*) maintenance; **pflegebedürftig** *adj* in need of care; **pflegeleicht** *adj* easy-care; (*fig*) easy to handle; **pflegen** *vt* to look after; (*Kranke*) to nurse; (*Beziehungen*) to foster; (*Fingernägel, Gesicht*) to take care of; (*Daten*) to maintain; **Pflegepersonal** *nt* nursing staff; **Pflegeversicherung** *f* long-term care insurance
Pflicht (-, -*en*) *f* duty; (*Sport*) compulsory section; **pflichtbewusst** *adj* conscientious; **Pflichtfach** *nt* (*Schule*) compulsory subject; **Pflichtversicherung** *f* compulsory insurance
pflücken *vt* to pick
Pforte (-, -*n*) *f* gate; **Pförtner(in)** (-*s*, -) *m(f)* porter
Pfosten (-*s*, -) *m* post
Pfote (-, -*n*) *f* paw
pfui *interj* ugh
Pfund (-(*e*)*s*, -*e*) *nt* pound
pfuschen *vi* (*fam*) to be sloppy
Pfütze (-, -*n*) *f* puddle
Phantasie *f siehe* **Fantasie**; **phantastisch** *adj siehe* **fantastisch**
Phase (-, -*n*) *f* phase
Philippinen *pl* Philippines *pl*
Philosophie *f* philosophy
Photo *nt siehe* **Foto**
pH-neutral *adj* pH-balanced; **pH-Wert** *m* pH-value
Physalis (-, *Physalen*) *f* physalis
Physik *f* physics *sing*
physisch *adj* physical
Pianist(in) (-*en*, -*en*) *m(f)* pianist
Pickel (-*s*, -) *m* pimple; (*Werkzeug*) pickaxe; (*Berg~*) ice-axe
Picknick (-*s*, -*e o* -*s*) *nt* picnic; **ein ~ machen** to have a picnic

piepsen *vi* to chirp

piercen *vt* **sich die Nase ~ lassen** to have one's nose pierced; **Piercing** (-s) *nt* (body) piercing

pieseln *vi* (*fam*) to pee

Pik (-, -) *nt* (*Karten*) spades *pl*

pikant *adj* spicy

Pilger(in) *m(f)* pilgrim; **Pilgerfahrt** *f* pilgrimage

Pille (-, -n) *f* pill; **sie nimmt die ~** she's on the pill

Pilot(in) (-en, -en) *m(f)* pilot

Pilz (-es, -e) *m* (*essbar*) mushroom; (*giftig*) toadstool; (*Med*) fungus

PIN (-, -s) *f* PIN (number)

pingelig *adj* (*fam*) fussy

Pinguin (-s, -e) *m* penguin

Pinie *f* pine; **Pinienkern** *m* pine nut

pink *adj* shocking pink

pinkeln *vi* (*fam*) to pee

Pinsel (-s, -) *m* (paint)brush

Pinzette *f* tweezers *pl*

Pistazie *f* pistachio

Piste (-, -n) *f* (*Ski*) piste; (*Aviat*) runway

Pistole (-, -n) *f* pistol

Pixel (-s) *nt* (*Inform*) pixel

Pizza (-, -s) *f* pizza; **Pizzaservice** *m* pizza delivery service; **Pizzeria** (-, Pizzerien) *f* pizzeria

Pkw (-(s), -(s)) *m* *abk* = **Personenkraftwagen** car

Plakat *nt* poster

Plakette *f* (*Schildchen*) badge; (*Aufkleber*) sticker

Plan (-(e)s, Pläne) *m* plan; (*Karte*) map; **planen** *vt* to plan

Planet (-en, -en) *m* planet; **Planetarium** *nt* planetarium

planmäßig *adj* scheduled

Plan(t)schbecken *nt* paddling pool; **plan(t)schen** *vi* to splash around

Planung *f* planning

Plastik *f* sculpture ▷ (-s) *nt* (*Kunststoff*) plastic; **Plastikfolie** *f* plastic film; **Plastiktüte** *f* plastic bag

Platin (-s) *nt* platinum

platsch *interj* splash

platt *adj* flat; (*fam: überrascht*) flabbergasted; (*fig: geistlos*) flat, boring

Platte (-, -n) *f* (*Foto, Tech, Gastr*) plate; (*Steinplatte*) flag; (*Schallplatte*) record; **Plattenspieler** *m* record player

Plattform *f* platform; **Plattfuß** *m* flat foot; (*Reifen*) flat (tyre)

Platz (-es, Plätze) *m* place; (*Sitzplatz*) seat; (*freier Raum*) space, room; (*in Stadt*) square; (*Sportplatz*) playing field; **nehmen Sie ~** please sit down, take a seat; **ist dieser ~ frei?** is this seat taken?; **Platzanweiser(in)** *m(f)* usher/usherette

Plätzchen *nt* spot; (*Gebäck*) biscuit

platzen *vi* to burst; (*Bombe*) to explode

Platzkarte *f* seat reservation; **Platzreservierung** *f* seat reservation; **Platzverweis** *m* **er erhielt einen ~** he was sent off; **Platzwunde** *f* laceration, cut

plaudern *vi* to chat, to talk

pleite *adj* (*fam*) broke; **Pleite** (-, -n) *f* (*Bankrott*) bankruptcy; (*fam: Reinfall*) flop

Plombe (-, -n) *f* lead seal; (*Zahnplombe*) filling; **plombieren** *vt* (*Zahn*) to fill

plötzlich *adj* sudden ▷ *adv* suddenly, all at once

plump *adj* clumsy; (*Hände*) ungainly; (*Körper*) shapeless

plumps *interj* thud; (*in Flüssigkeit*) plop

Plural (-s, -e) *m* plural

plus *adv* plus; **fünf ~ sieben ist zwölf** five plus seven is (*o* are) twelve; **zehn Grad ~** ten degrees above zero; **Plus** (-, -) *nt* plus; (*Fin*) profit; (*Vorteil*) advantage

Plüsch (-(e)s, -e) *m* plush

Pluto (-) *m* Pluto

PLZ *abk* = **Postleitzahl** postcode (*Brit*), zip code (*US*)

Po (-s, -s) *m* (*fam*) bottom, bum

Pocken *pl* smallpox *sing*

poetisch *adj* poetic

Pointe (-, -n) *f* punch line

Pokal (-s, -e) *m* goblet; (*Sport*) cup

pökeln *vt* to pickle

Pol (-s, -e) *m* pole

Pole (-n, -n) *m* Pole; **Polen** (-s) *nt* Poland

Police (-, -n) *f* (insurance) policy

polieren *vt* to polish

Polin *f* Pole, Polish woman

Politik *f* politics *sing*; (*eine bestimmte*) policy; **Politiker(in)** *m(f)* politician; **politisch** *adj* political

Politur *f* polish

Polizei *f* police *pl*; **Polizeibeamte(r)** *m*, **Polizeibeamtin** *f* police officer; **polizeilich** *adj* police; **sie wird ~ gesucht** the police are looking for her;

Polizeirevier *nt*, **Polizeiwache** *f* police station; **Polizeistunde** *f* closing time; **Polizeiwache** *f* police station; **Polizist(in)** *m(f)* policeman/-woman

Pollen (*-s, -*) *m* pollen; **Pollenflug** (*-s*) *m* pollen count

polnisch *adj* Polish; **Polnisch** *nt* Polish

Polo (*-s*) *nt* polo; **Polohemd** *nt* polo shirt

Polster (*-s, -*) *nt* cushion; (*Polsterung*) upholstery; (*in Kleidung*) padding; (*fig: Geld*) reserves *pl*; **Polstergarnitur** *f* living-room suite; **Polstermöbel** *pl* upholstered furniture *sing*; **polstern** *vt* to upholster; (*Kleidung*) to pad

Polterabend *m* party prior to a wedding, at which old crockery is smashed to bring good luck

poltern *vi* (*Krach machen*) to crash; (*schimpfen*) to rant

Polyester (*-s, -*) *m* polyester

Polypen *pl* (*Med*) adenoids *pl*

Pommes frites *pl* chips *pl* (*Brit*), French fries *pl* (*US*)

Pony (*-s, -s*) *m* (*Frisur*) fringe (*Brit*), bangs *pl* (*US*) ▷ (*-s, -s*) *nt* (*Pferd*) pony

Popcorn (*-s*) *nt* popcorn

Popmusik *f* pop (music)

populär *adj* popular

Pore (*-, -n*) *f* pore

Pornografie *f* pornography

Porree (*-s, -s*) *m* leeks *pl*; **eine Stange ~** a leek

Portemonnaie, **Portmonee** (*-s, -s*) *nt* purse

Portier (*-s, -s*) *m* porter; *siehe auch* **Pförtner**

Portion *f* portion, helping

Porto (*-s, -s*) *nt* postage

Portrait, **Porträt** (*-s, -s*) *nt* portrait

Portugal (*-s*) *nt* Portugal; **Portugiese** (*-n, -n*) *m* Portuguese; **Portugiesin** (*-, -nen*) *f* Portuguese; **portugiesisch** *adj* Portuguese; **Portugiesisch** *nt* Portuguese

Portwein (*-s, -e*) *m* port

Porzellan (*-s, -e*) *nt* china

Posaune (*-, -n*) *f* trombone

Position *f* position

positiv *adj* positive

Post® (*-, -en*) *f* post office; (*Briefe*) post (*Brit*), mail; **Postamt** *nt* post office; **Postanweisung** *f* postal order (*Brit*), money order (*US*); **Postbank** *f* German

post office bank; **Postbote** *m*, **-botin** *f* postman/-woman

Posten (*-s, -*) *m* post, position; (*Comm*) item; (*auf Liste*) entry

Poster (*-s, -*) *nt* poster

Postfach *nt* post-office box, PO box; **Postkarte** *f* postcard; **postlagernd** *adv* poste restante; **Postleitzahl** *f* postcode (*Brit*), zip code (*US*)

postmodern *adj* postmodern

Postsparkasse *f* post office savings bank; **Poststempel** *m* postmark; **Postweg** *m* **auf dem ~** by mail

Potenz *f* (*Math*) power; (*eines Mannes*) potency

PR (*-, -s*) *f abk* = **Public Relations** PR

prächtig *adj* splendid

prahlen *vi* to boast, to brag

Praktikant(in) *m(f)* trainee; **Praktikum** (*-s, Praktika*) *nt* practical training; **praktisch** *adj* practical; **~er Arzt** general practitioner

Praline *f* chocolate

Prämie *f* (*bei Versicherung*) premium; (*Belohnung*) reward; (*von Arbeitgeber*) bonus

Präparat *nt* (*Med*) medicine; (*Bio*) preparation

Präservativ *nt* condom

Präsident(in) *m(f)* president

Praxis (*-, Praxen*) *f* practice; (*Behandlungsraum*) surgery; (*von Anwalt*) office

präzise *adj* precise, exact

predigen *vt, vi* to preach; **Predigt** (*-, -en*) *f* sermon

Preis (*-es, -e*) *m* (*zu zahlen*) price; (*bei Sieg*) prize; **den ersten ~ gewinnen** to win first prize; **Preisausschreiben** *nt* competition

Preiselbeere *f* cranberry

preisgünstig *adj* inexpensive; **Preislage** *f* price range; **Preisliste** *f* price list; **Preisschild** *nt* price tag; **Preisträger(in)** *m(f)* prizewinner; **preiswert** *adj* inexpensive

Prellung *f* bruise

Premiere (*-, -n*) *f* premiere, first night

Premierminister(in) *m(f)* prime minister, premier

Presse (*-, -n*) *f* press

pressen *vt* to press

prickeln *vi* to tingle

Priester(in) (*-s, -*) *m(f)* priest/(woman) priest

P

Primel (-, -n) f primrose
primitiv adj primitive
Prinz (-en, -en) m prince; **Prinzessin** f princess
Prinzip (-s, -ien) nt principle; **im ~ basically; aus ~** on principle
Priorität f priority
privat adj private; **Privatfernsehen** nt commercial television; **Privatgrundstück** nt private property; **privatisieren** vt to privatize; **Privatquartier** nt private accommodation
pro prep +akk per; **5 Euro ~ Stück/Person** 5 euros each/per person; **Pro** (-s) nt pro
Probe (-, -n) f test; (Teststück) sample; (Theat) rehearsal; **Probefahrt** f test drive; **eine ~ machen** to go for a test drive; **Probezeit** f trial period; **probieren** vt, vi to try; (Wein, Speise) to taste, to sample
Problem (-s, -e) nt problem
Produkt (-(e)s, -e) nt product; **Produktion** f production; (produzierte Menge) output; **produzieren** vt to produce
Professor(in) (-s, -en) m(f) professor
Profi (-s, -s) m pro
Profil (-s, -e) nt profile; (von Reifen, Schuhsohle) tread
Profit (-(e)s, -e) m profit; **profitieren** vi to profit (von from)
Prognose (-, -n) f prediction; (Wetter) forecast
Programm (-s, -e) nt programme; (Inform) program; (TV) channel; **Programmheft** nt programme; **programmieren** vt to program; **Programmierer(in)** (-s, -) m(f) programmer; **Programmkino** nt arts (o repertory (US)) cinema
Projekt (-(e)s, -e) nt project
Projektor m projector
Promenade (-, -n) f promenade
Promille (-(s), -) nt (blood) alcohol level; **0,8 ~** 0,08 per cent; **Promillegrenze** f legal alcohol limit
prominent adj prominent; **Prominenz** f VIPs pl, prominent figures pl; (fam: Stars) the glitterati pl
Propeller (-s, -) m propeller
prosit interj cheers
Prospekt (-(e)s, -e) m leaflet, brochure
prost interj cheers
Prostituierte(r) mf prostitute
Protest (-(e)s, -e) m protest

Protestant(in) m(f) Protestant; **protestantisch** adj Protestant
protestieren vi to protest (gegen against)
Prothese (-, -n) f artificial arm/leg; (Gebiss) dentures pl
Protokoll (-s, -e) nt (bei Sitzung) minutes pl; (diplomatisch) (Inform) protocol; (bei Polizei) statement
protzen vi to show off; **protzig** adj flashy
Proviant (-s, -e) m provisions pl
Provider (-s, -) m (Inform) (service) provider
Provinz (-, -en) f province
Provision f (Comm) commission
provisorisch adj provisional
provozieren vt to provoke
Prozent (-(e)s, -e) nt per cent
Prozess (-es, -e) m (Vorgang) process; (Jur) trial; (Rechtsfall) (court) case; **prozessieren** vi to go to law (mit against)
Prozession f procession
Prozessor (-s, -en) m (Inform) processor
prüde adj prudish
prüfen vt to test; (nachprüfen) to check; **Prüfung** f (Schule) exam; (Überprüfung) check; **eine ~ machen** (Schule) to take an exam
Prügelei f fight; **prügeln** vt to beat ▷ vr **sich ~** to fight
PS abk = **Pferdestärke** hp ▷ abk = **Postskript(um)** PS
pseudo- präf pseudo; **Pseudokrupp** (-s) m (Med) pseudocroup; **Pseudonym** (-s, -e) nt pseudonym
pst interj ssh
Psychiater(in) (-s, -) m(f) psychiatrist; **psychisch** adj psychological; (Krankheit) mental; **Psychoanalyse** f psychoanalysis; **Psychologe** (-n, -n) m, **Psychologin** f psychologist; **Psychologie** f psychology
Psychopharmaka pl mind-affecting drugs pl, psychotropic drugs pl; **psychosomatisch** adj psychosomatic; **Psychoterror** m psychological intimidation; **Psychotherapie** f psychotherapy
Pubertät f puberty
Publikum (-s) nt audience; (Sport) crowd
Pudding (-s, -e o -s) m blancmange
Pudel (-s, -) m poodle

Puder (-s, -) m powder; **Puderzucker** m icing sugar

Puerto Rico (-s) nt Puerto Rico

Pulli (-s, -s) m, **Pullover** (-s, -) m sweater, pullover, jumper (Brit)

Puls (-es, -e) m pulse

Pulver (-s, -) nt powder; **Pulverkaffee** m instant coffee; **Pulverschnee** m powder snow

pummelig adj chubby

Pumpe (-, -n) f pump; **pumpen** vt to pump; (fam: verleihen) to lend; (fam: sich ausleihen) to borrow

Pumps pl court shoes pl (Brit), pumps pl (US)

Punk (-s, -s) m (Musik, Mensch) punk

Punkt (-(e)s, -e) m point; (bei Muster) dot; (Satzzeichen) full stop (Brit), period (US); ~ **zwei Uhr** at two o'clock sharp

pünktlich adj punctual, on time; **Pünktlichkeit** f punctuality

Punsch (-(e)s, -e) m punch

Pupille (-, -n) f pupil

Puppe (-, -n) f doll

pur adj pure; (völlig) sheer; (Whisky) neat

Püree (-s, -s) nt puree; (Kartoffelpüree) mashed potatoes pl

Puste (-) f (fam) puff; **außer ~ sein** to be puffed

Pustel (-, -n) f pustule; (Pickel) pimple; **pusten** vi to blow; (keuchen) to puff

Pute (-, -n) f turkey; **Putenschnitzel** nt turkey escalope

Putsch (-es, -e) m putsch

Putz (-es) m (Mörtel) plaster

putzen vt to clean; **sich** (dat) **die Nase** ~ to blow one's nose; **sich** (dat) **die Zähne** ~ to brush one's teeth; **Putzfrau** f cleaner; **Putzlappen** m cloth, **Putzmann** m cleaner; **Putzmittel** nt cleaning agent, cleaner

Puzzle (-s, -s) nt jigsaw (puzzle)

Pyjama (-s, -s) m pyjamas pl

Pyramide (-, -n) f pyramid

Python (-s, -s) m python

P

(*rechtwinklig*) at right angles; ~ **über die Straße** straight across the street; **querfeldein** *adv* across country; **Querflöte** *f* flute; **Querschnitt** *m* cross section; **querschnittsgelähmt** *adj* paraplegic; **Querstraße** *f* side street

quetschen *vt* to squash, to crush; (*Med*) to bruise; **Quetschung** *f* bruise

Queue (-s, -s) *m* (billiard) cue

quietschen *vi* to squeal; (*Tür, Bett*) to squeak; (*Bremsen*) to screech

Quirl (-s, -e) *m* whisk

quitt *adj* quits, even

Quitte (-, -n) *f* quince

Quittung *f* receipt

Quiz (-, -) *nt* quiz

Quote (-, -n) *f* rate; (*Comm*) quota

Quadrat *nt* square; **quadratisch** *adj* square; **Quadratmeter** *m* square metre

quaken *vi* (*Frosch*) to croak; (*Ente*) to quack

Qual (-, -en) *f* pain, agony; (*seelisch*) anguish; **quälen** *vt* to torment ▷ *vr* **sich ~** to struggle; (*geistig*) to torment oneself; **Quälerei** *f* torture, torment

qualifizieren *vt* to qualify; (*einstufen*) to label ▷ *vr* **sich ~** to qualify

Qualität *f* quality

Qualle (-, -n) *f* jellyfish

Qualm (-(e)s) *m* thick smoke; **qualmen** *vt, vi* to smoke

Quantität *f* quantity

Quarantäne (-, -n) *f* quarantine

Quark (-s) *m* quark; (*fam: Unsinn*) rubbish

Quartett (-s, -e) *nt* quartet; (*Kartenspiel*) happy families *sing*

Quartier (-s, -e) *nt* accommodation

quasi *adv* more or less

Quatsch (-es) *m* (*fam*) rubbish; **quatschen** *vi* (*fam*) to chat

Quecksilber *nt* mercury

Quelle (-, -n) *f* spring; (*eines Flusses*) source

quellen *vi* to pour

quer *adv* crossways, diagonally;

r

Rabatt (-(e)s, -e) m discount
Rabbi (-(s), -s) m rabbi; **Rabbiner** (-s, -) m rabbi
Rabe (-n, -n) m raven
Rache (-) f revenge, vengeance
Rachen (-s, -) m throat
rächen vt to avenge ▷ vr **sich ~** to take (one's) revenge (an +dat on)
Rad (-(e)s, Räder) nt wheel; (Fahrrad) bike; **~ fahren** to cycle; **mit dem ~ fahren** to go by bike
Radar (-s) m o nt radar; **Radarfalle** f speed trap; **Radarkontrolle** f radar speed check
radeln vi (fam) to cycle; **Radfahrer(in)** m(f) cyclist; **Radfahrweg** m cycle track (o path)
Radicchio (-s) m (Salatsorte) radicchio
radieren vt to rub out, to erase; **Radiergummi** m rubber (Brit), eraser; **Radierung** f (Kunst) etching
Radieschen nt radish
radikal adj radical
Radio (-s, -s) nt radio; **im ~** on the radio
radioaktiv adj radioactive
Radiologe (-n, -n) m, **Radiologin** f radiologist

Radiorekorder m radio cassette recorder; **Radiosender** m radio station; **Radiowecker** m radio alarm (clock)
Radkappe f (Auto) hub cap
Radler(in) (-s, -) m(f) cyclist
Radler (-s, -) nt ≈ shandy
Radlerhose f cycling shorts pl; **Radrennen** nt cycle racing; (einzelnes Rennen) cycle race; **Radtour** f cycling tour; **Radweg** m cycle track (o path)
raffiniert adj crafty, cunning; (Zucker) refined
Rafting (-s) nt white water rafting
Ragout (-s, -s) nt ragout
Rahm (-s) m cream
rahmen vt to frame; **Rahmen** (-s, -) m frame
Rakete (-, -n) f rocket
rammen vt to ram
Rampe (-, -n) f ramp
ramponieren vt (fam) to damage, to batter
Ramsch (-(e)s, -e) m junk
ran (fam) kontr von **heran**
Rand (-(e)s, Ränder) m edge; (von Brille, Tasse etc) rim; (auf Papier) margin; (Schmutzrand, unter Augen) ring; (fig) verge, brink
randalieren vi to (go on the) rampage; **Randalierer(in)** (-s, -) m(f) hooligan
Randstein m kerb (Brit), curb (US); **Randstreifen** m shoulder
rang imperf von **ringen**
Rang (-(e)s, Ränge) m rank; (in Wettbewerb) place; (Theat) circle
rannte imperf von **rennen**
ranzig adj rancid
Rap (-(s), -s) m (Mus) rap; **rappen** vi (Mus) to rap; **Rapper(in)** (-s, -) m(f) (Mus) rapper
rar adj rare, scarce
rasant adj quick, rapid
rasch adj quick
rascheln vi to rustle
rasen vi (sich schnell bewegen) to race; (toben) to rave; **gegen einen Baum ~ to** crash into a tree
Rasen (-s, -) m lawn
rasend adj (vor Wut) furious
Rasenmäher (-s, -) m lawnmower
Rasierapparat m razor; (elektrischer) shaver; **Rasiercreme** f shaving cream;

rasieren vt to shave ▷ vr **sich ~** to shave; **Rasierer** m shaver; **Rasiergel** nt shaving gel; **Rasierklinge** f razor blade; **Rasiermesser** nt (cutthroat) razor; **Rasierpinsel** m shaving brush; **Rasierschaum** m shaving foam

Rasse (-, -n) f race; (Tiere) breed

Rassismus m racism; **Rassist(in)** m(f) racist; **rassistisch** adj racist

Rast (-, -en) f rest, break; **~ machen** to have a rest (o break); **rasten** vi to rest; **Rastplatz** m (Auto) rest area; **Raststätte** f (Auto) service area; (Gaststätte) motorway (Brit) (o highway (US)) restaurant

Rasur f shave

Rat (-(e)s, Ratschläge) m (piece of) advice; **sie hat mir einen ~ gegeben** she gave me some advice; **um ~ fragen** to ask for advice

Rate (-, -n) f instalment; **etw auf ~n kaufen** to buy sth in instalments (Brit), to buy sth on the instalment plan (US)

raten (riet, geraten) vt, vi to guess; (empfehlen) to advise (jdm sb)

Rathaus nt town hall

Ration f ration

ratlos adj at a loss, helpless; **ratsam** adj advisable

Rätsel (-s, -) nt puzzle; (Worträtsel) riddle; **das ist mir ein ~** it's a mystery to me; **rätselhaft** adj mysterious

Ratte (-, -n) f rat

rau adj rough, coarse; (Wetter) harsh

Raub (-(e)s) m robbery; (Beute) loot, booty; **rauben** vt to steal; **jdm etw ~** to rob sb of sth; **Räuber(in)** (-s, -) m(f) robber; **Raubfisch** m predatory fish; **Raubkopie** f pirate copy; **Raubmord** m robbery with murder; **Raubtier** nt predator; **Raubüberfall** m mugging; **Raubvogel** m bird of prey

Rauch (-(e)s) m smoke; (Abgase) fumes pl; **rauchen** vt, vi to smoke; **Raucher(in)** (-s, -) m(f) smoker; **Raucherabteil** nt smoking compartment

Räucherlachs m smoked salmon; **räuchern** vt to smoke

rauchig adj smoky; **Rauchmelder** m smoke detector; **Rauchverbot** nt smoking ban; **hier ist ~** there's no smoking here

rauf (fam) kontr von **herauf**

rauh adj siehe **rau**; **Rauhreif** m siehe **Raureif**

Raum (-(e)s, Räume) m space; (Zimmer, Platz) room; (Gebiet) area

räumen vt to clear; (Wohnung, Platz) to vacate; (wegbringen) to shift, to move; (in Schrank etc) to put away

Raumfähre f space shuttle; **Raumfahrt** f space travel; **Raumschiff** nt spacecraft, spaceship; **Raumsonde** f space probe; **Raumstation** f space station

Raumtemperatur f room temperature

Räumungsverkauf m clearance sale, closing-down sale

Raupe (-, -n) f caterpillar

Raureif m hoarfrost

raus (fam) kontr von **heraus, hinaus**; **~!** (get) out!

Rausch (-(e)s, Räusche) m intoxication; **einen ~ haben/kriegen** to be/get drunk

rauschen vi (Wasser) to rush; (Baum) to rustle; (Radio etc) to hiss; **Rauschgift** nt drug; **Rauschgiftsüchtige(r)** mf drug addict

raus|fliegen irr vi (fam) to be kicked out

raus|halten irr vr (fam) **halt du dich da raus!** you (just) keep out of it

räuspern vr **sich ~** to clear one's throat

raus|schmeißen irr vt (fam) to throw out

Razzia (-, Razzien) f raid

reagieren vi to react (auf +akk to); **Reaktion** f reaction

real adj real; **realisieren** vt (merken) to realize; (verwirklichen) to implement; **realistisch** adj realistic; **Realität** (-, -en) f reality; **Reality-TV** (-s) nt reality TV

Realschule f ≈ secondary school, junior high (school) (US)

Rebe (-, -n) f vine

rebellieren vi to rebel

Rebhuhn nt partridge

rechnen vt, vi to calculate; **~ mit** to expect; (bauen auf) to count on ▷ vr **sich ~** to pay off, to turn out to be profitable; **Rechner** (-s, -) m calculator; (Computer) computer; **Rechnung** f calculation(s); (Comm) bill (Brit), check (US); **die ~, bitte!** can I have the bill, please?; **das geht auf meine ~** this is on me

recht adj (richtig, passend) right; **mir soll's ~ sein** it's alright by me; **mir ist es ~** I don't mind ▷ adv really, quite; (richtig) right(ly); **ich weiß nicht ~** I don't really know; **es geschieht ihm ~** it serves him right

Recht (-(e)s, -e) nt right; (Jur) law; **~ haben** to be right; **jdm ~ geben** to agree with sb

Rechte (-n, -n) f right-hand side; (Hand) right hand; (Pol) right (wing); **rechte(r, s)** adj right; **auf der ~n Seite** on the right, on the right-hand side; **Rechte(s)** nt right thing; **etwas/nichts ~s** something/nothing proper

Rechteck (-s, -e) nt rectangle; **rechteckig** adj rectangular

rechtfertigen vt to justify ▷ vr **sich ~** to justify oneself

rechtlich adj legal; **rechtmäßig** adj legal, lawful

rechts adv on the right; **~ abbiegen** to turn right; **~ von** to the right of; **~ oben** at the top right

Rechtsanwalt m, **-anwältin** f lawyer

Rechtschreibung f spelling

Rechtshänder(in) (-s, -) m(f) right-hander; **rechtsherum** adv to the right, clockwise; **rechtsradikal** adj (Pol) extreme right-wing

Rechtsschutzversicherung f legal costs insurance

Rechtsverkehr m driving on the right

rechtswidrig adj illegal

rechtwinklig adj right-angled; **rechtzeitig** adj timely ▷ adv in time

recycelbar adj recyclable; **recyceln** vt to recycle; **Recycling** (-s) nt recycling; **Recyclingpapier** nt recycled paper

Redakteur(in) m(f) editor; **Redaktion** f editing; (Leute) editorial staff; (Büro) editorial office(s)

Rede (-, -n) f speech; (Gespräch) talk; **eine ~ halten** to make a speech; **reden** vi to talk, to speak ▷ vt to say; (Unsinn etc) to talk; **Redewendung** f idiom; **Redner(in)** m(f) speaker

reduzieren vt to reduce

Referat (-s, -e) nt paper; **ein ~ halten** to give a paper (über +akk on)

reflektieren vt to reflect

Reform (-, -en) f reform; **Reformhaus** nt health food shop; **reformieren** vt to reform

Regal (-s, -e) nt shelf; (Möbelstück) shelves pl

Regel (-, -n) f rule; (Med) period;

regelmäßig adj regular; **regeln** vt to regulate, to control; (Angelegenheit) to settle ▷ vr **sich von selbst ~** to sort itself out; **Regelung** f regulation

Regen (-s, -) m rain; **Regenbogen** m rainbow; **Regenmantel** m raincoat; **Regenrinne** f gutter; **Regenschauer** m shower; **Regenschirm** m umbrella; **Regenwald** m rainforest; **Regenwurm** m earthworm

Regie f direction

regieren vt, vi to govern, to rule; **Regierung** f government; (von Monarch) reign

Region f region; **regional** adj regional

Regisseur(in) m(f) director

registrieren vt to register; (bemerken) to notice

regnen vi impers to rain; **regnerisch** adj rainy

regulär adj regular; **regulieren** vt to regulate, to adjust

Reh (-(e)s, -e) nt deer; (Fleisch) venison

Rehabilitationszentrum nt (Med) rehabilitation centre

Reibe (-, -n) f, **Reibeisen** nt grater; **reiben** (rieb, gerieben) vt to rub; (Gastr) to grate; **reibungslos** adj smooth

reich adj rich

Reich (-(e)s, -e) nt empire; (eines Königs) kingdom

reichen vi to reach; (genügen) to be enough, to be sufficient (jdm for sb) ▷ vt to hold out; (geben) to pass, to hand; (anbieten) to offer

reichhaltig adj ample, rich; **reichlich** adj (Trinkgeld) generous; (Essen) ample; **~ Zeit** plenty of time; **Reichtum** (-s, -tümer) m wealth

reif adj ripe; (Mensch, Urteil) mature

Reif (-(e)s) m (Raureif) hoarfrost ▷ (-(e)s, -e) m (Ring) ring, hoop

reifen vi to mature; (Obst) to ripen

Reifen (-s, -) m ring, hoop; (von Auto) tyre; **Reifendruck** m tyre pressure; **Reifenpanne** m puncture; **Reifenwechsel** m tyre change

Reihe (-, -n) f row; (von Tagen etc, fam: Anzahl) series sing; **der ~ nach** one after the other; **er ist an der ~** it's his turn; **Reihenfolge** f order, sequence; **Reihenhaus** nt terraced house (Brit), row house (US)

r

Reiher (-s, -) m heron

rein (fam) kontr von **herein, hinein** ▷ adj pure; (sauber) clean

Reinfall m (fam) letdown; **rein|fallen** irr vi (fam) **auf etw** (akk) ~ to fall for sth

reinigen vt to clean; **Reinigung** f cleaning; (Geschäft) (dry) cleaner's; **Reinigungsmittel** nt cleaning agent, cleaner

rein|legen vt jdn ~ to take sb for a ride

Reis (-es, -e) m rice

Reise (-, -n) f journey; (auf Schiff) voyage; **Reiseapotheke** f first-aid kit; **Reisebüro** nt travel agent's; **Reisebus** m coach; **Reiseführer(in)** m(f) (Mensch) courier; (Buch) guide(book); **Reisegepäck** nt luggage (Brit), baggage; **Reisegesellschaft** f (Veranstalter) tour operator; **Reiseleiter(in)** m(f) courier; **reisen** vi to travel; ~ **nach** to go to; **Reisende(r)** mf traveller; **Reisepass** m passport; **Reiseroute** f route, itinerary; **Reiserücktrittversicherung** f holiday cancellation insurance; **Reisescheck** m traveller's cheque; **Reisetasche** f holdall (Brit), carryall (US); **Reiseveranstalter** m tour operator; **Reiseverkehr** m holiday traffic; **Reiseversicherung** f travel insurance; **Reiseziel** nt destination

reißen (riss, gerissen) vt, vi to tear; (ziehen) to pull, to drag; (Witz) to crack

Reißnagel m drawing pin (Brit), thumbtack (US); **Reißverschluss** m zip (Brit), zipper (US); **Reißzwecke** f drawing pin (Brit), thumbtack (US)

reiten (ritt, geritten) vt, vi to ride; **Reiter(in)** m(f) rider; **Reithose** f riding breeches pl; **Reitsport** m riding; **Reitstiefel** m riding boot

Reiz (-es, -e) m stimulus; (angenehm) charm; (Verlockung) attraction; **reizen** vt to stimulate; (unangenehm) to annoy; (verlocken) to appeal to, to attract; **reizend** adj charming; **Reizgas** nt irritant gas; **Reizung** f irritation

Reklamation f complaint

Reklame (-, -n) f advertising; (Einzelwerbung) advertisement; (im Fernsehen) commercial

reklamieren vi to complain (wegen about)

Rekord (-(e)s, -e) m record

relativ adj relative ▷ adv relatively

relaxen vi to relax, to chill out

Religion f religion; **religiös** adj religious

Remoulade (-, -n) f tartar sauce

Renaissance f renaissance, revival; (Hist) Renaissance

Rennbahn f racecourse; (Auto) racetrack; **rennen** (rannte, gerannt) vt, vi to run; **Rennen** (-s, -) nt running; (Wettbewerb) race; **Rennfahrer(in)** m(f) racing driver; **Rennrad** nt racing bike; **Rennwagen** m racing car

renommiert adj famous, noted (wegen, für for)

renovieren vt to renovate; **Renovierung** f renovation

rentabel adj profitable

Rente (-, -n) f pension; **Rentenversicherung** f pension scheme

Rentier nt reindeer

rentieren vr **sich** ~ to pay, to be profitable

Rentner(in) (-s, -) m(f) pensioner, senior citizen

Reparatur f repair; **Reparaturwerkstatt** f repair shop; (Auto) garage; **reparieren** vt to repair

Reportage f report; **Reporter(in)** (-s, -) m(f) reporter

Reptil (-s, -ien) nt reptile

Republik f republic

Reservat (-s, -e) nt nature reserve; (für Ureinwohner) reservation; **Reserve** (-, -n) f reserve; **Reservekanister** m spare can; **Reserverad** nt (Auto) spare wheel; **Reservespieler(in)** m(f) reserve; **reservieren** vt to reserve; **Reservierung** f reservation

resignieren vi to give up; **resigniert** adj resigned

Respekt (-(e)s) m respect; **respektieren** vt to respect

Rest (-(e)s, -e) m rest, remainder; (Überreste) remains pl; **der** ~ **ist für Sie** (zur Bedienung) keep the change

Restaurant (-s, -s) nt restaurant

restaurieren vt to restore

Restbetrag m balance; **restlich** adj remaining; **restlos** adj complete

Resultat nt result

retten vt to save, to rescue

Rettich (-s, -e) m radish (large white or red variety)

Rettung f rescue; (Hilfe) help;

(*Rettungsdienst*) ambulance service; **Rettungsboot** *nt* lifeboat; **Rettungshubschrauber** *m* rescue helicopter; **Rettungsring** *m* lifebelt, life preserver (*US*); **Rettungswagen** *m* ambulance

Reue (-) *f* remorse; (*Bedauern*) regret; **reuen** *vt* **es reut ihn** he regrets it

revanchieren *vr* **sich ~** (*sich rächen*) to get one's own back, to get one's revenge; (*für Hilfe etc*) to return the favour

Revolution *f* revolution

Rezept (-(*e*)*s*, -*e*) *nt* (*Gastr*) recipe; (*Med*) prescription; **rezeptfrei** *adj* over-the-counter, non-prescription

Rezeption *f* (*im Hotel*) reception

rezeptpflichtig *adj* available only on prescription

R-Gespräch *nt* reverse-charge (*Brit*) (*o* collect (*US*)) call

Rhabarber (-*s*) *m* rhubarb

Rhein (-*s*) *m* Rhine; **Rheinland-Pfalz** (-) *nt* Rhineland-Palatinate

Rheuma (-*s*) *nt* rheumatism

Rhythmus *m* rhythm

richten *vt* (*lenken*) to direct (*auf +akk* to); (*Waffe, Kamera*) to point (*auf +akk* at); (*Brief, Anfrage*) to address (*an +akk* to); (*einstellen*) to adjust; (*instand setzen*) to repair; (*zurechtmachen*) to prepare ⊳ *vr* **sich ~ nach** (*Regel etc*) to keep to; (*Mode, Beispiel*) to follow; (*abhängen von*) to depend on

Richter(in) (-*s*, -) *m(f)* judge

Richtgeschwindigkeit *f* recommended speed

richtig *adj* right, correct; (*echt*) proper; **etw ~ stellen** to correct sth ⊳ *adv* (*fam: sehr*) really

Richtlinie *f* guideline

Richtung *f* direction; (*Tendenz*) tendency

rieb *imperf von* **reiben**

riechen (*roch, gerochen*) *vt, vi* to smell; **nach etw ~** to smell of sth; **an etw** (*dat*) **~** to smell sth

rief *imperf von* **rufen**

Riegel (-*s*, -) *m* bolt; (*Gastr*) bar

Riemen (-*s*, -) *m* strap; (*Gürtel*) belt

Riese (-*n*, -*n*) *m* giant; **Riesengarnele** *f* king prawn; **riesengroß** *adj* gigantic, huge; **Riesenrad** *nt* big wheel; **riesig** *adj* enormous, huge

riet *imperf von* **raten**

Riff (-(*e*)*s*, -*e*) *nt* reef

Rind (-(*e*)*s*, -*er*) *nt* cow; (*Bulle*) bull; (*Gastr*) beef; **~er** *pl* cattle *pl*

Rinde (-, -*n*) *f* (*Baum*) bark; (*Käse*) rind; (*Brot*) crust

Rinderbraten *m* roast beef; **Rinderwahn(sinn)** *m* mad cow disease; **Rindfleisch** *nt* beef

Ring (-(*e*)*s*, -*e*) *m* ring; (*Straße*) ring road; **Ringbuch** *nt* ring binder

ringen (*rang, gerungen*) *vi* to wrestle; **Ringer(in)** *m(f)* wrestler; **Ringfinger** *m* ring finger; **Ringkampf** *m* wrestling match; **ringsherum** *adv* round about

Rippe (-, -*n*) *f* rib; **Rippenfellentzündung** *f* pleurisy

Risiko (-*s*, -*s o* Risiken) *nt* risk; **auf eigenes ~** at one's own risk; **riskant** *adj* risky; **riskieren** *vt* to risk

riss *imperf von* **reißen**

Riss (-*es*, -*e*) *m* tear; (*in Mauer, Tasse etc*) crack; **rissig** *adj* cracked; (*Haut*) chapped

ritt *imperf von* **reiten**

Ritter (-*s*, -) *m* knight

Rivale (-*n*, -*n*) *m*, **Rivalin** *f* rival

Rizinusöl *nt* castor oil

Robbe (-, -*n*) *f* seal

Roboter (-*s*, -) *m* robot

robust *adj* robust

roch *imperf von* **riechen**

Rock (-(*e*)*s*, Röcke) *m* skirt

Rockband *f* (*Musikgruppe*) rock band; **Rockmusik** *f* rock (music)

Rodelbahn *f* toboggan run; **rodeln** *vi* to toboggan

Roggen (-*s*, -) *m* rye; **Roggenbrot** *nt* rye bread

roh *adj* raw; (*Mensch*) coarse, crude; **Rohkost** *f* raw vegetables and fruit *pl*

Rohr (-(*e*)*s*, -*e*) *nt* pipe; (*Bot*) cane; (*Schilf*) reed; **Röhre** (-, -*n*) *f* tube; (*Leitung*) pipe; (*Elek*) valve; (*Backröhre*) oven; **Rohrzucker** *m* cane sugar

Rohstoff *m* raw material

Rokoko (-*s*) *nt* rococo

Rolle (-, -*n*) *f* (*etw Zusammengerolltes*) roll; (*Theat*) role

rollen *vt, vi* to roll

Roller (-*s*, -) *m* scooter

Rollerblades® *pl* Rollerblades® *pl*; **Rollerskates** *pl* roller skates *pl*

r

Rollkragenpullover m polo-neck (Brit) (o turtleneck (US)) sweater; **Rollladen** m, **Rollo** (-s, -s) m (roller) shutters pl; **Rollschuh** m roller skate; **Rollstuhl** m wheelchair; **rollstuhlgerecht** adj suitable for wheelchairs; **Rolltreppe** f escalator

Roman (-s, -e) m novel

Romantik f romance; **romantisch** adj romantic

römisch-katholisch adj Roman Catholic

röntgen vt to X-ray; **Röntgenaufnahme** f, **Röntgenbild** nt X-ray; **Röntgenstrahlen** pl X-rays pl

rosa adj inv pink

Rose (-, -n) f rose

Rosenkohl m (Brussels) sprouts pl

Rosé(wein) m rosé (wine)

rosig adj rosy

Rosine f raisin

Rosmarin (-s) m rosemary

Rosskastanie f horse chestnut

Rost (-(e)s, -e) m rust; (zum Braten) grill, gridiron; **Rostbratwurst** f grilled sausage; **rosten** vi to rust; **rösten** vt to roast, to grill; (Brot) to toast; **rostfrei** adj rustproof; (Stahl) stainless; **rostig** adj rusty; **Rostschutz** m rustproofing

rot adj red; **~ werden** to blush; **~e Karte** red card; **~e Be(e)te** beetroot; **bei Rot über die Ampel fahren** to jump the lights; **das Rote Kreuz** the Red Cross

Röteln pl German measles sing

röten vt to redden ▷ vr **sich ~** to redden

rothaarig adj red-haired

rotieren vi to rotate; **am Rotieren sein** (fam) to be rushing around like a mad thing

Rotkehlchen nt robin; **Rotkohl** m, **Rotkraut** nt red cabbage; **Rotlichtviertel** nt red-light district; **Rotwein** m red wine

Rouge (-s, -s) nt rouge

Route (-, -n) f route

Routine f experience; (Trott) routine

Rubbellos nt scratchcard; **rubbeln** vt to rub

Rübe (-, -n) f turnip; **Gelbe ~** carrot; **Rote ~** beetroot

rüber (fam) kontr von **herüber, hinüber**

Rubin (-s, -e) m ruby

rücken vt, vi to move; **könntest du ein bisschen ~?** could you move over a bit?

Rücken (-s, -) m back; **Rückenlehne** f back(rest); **Rückenmark** nt spinal cord; **Rückenschmerzen** pl backache sing; **Rückenschwimmen** (-s) nt backstroke; **Rückenwind** m tailwind

Rückerstattung f refund; **Rückfahrkarte** f return ticket (Brit), round-trip ticket (US); **Rückfahrt** f return journey; **Rückfall** m relapse; **Rückflug** m return flight; **Rückgabe** f return; **rückgängig** adj **etw ~ machen** to cancel sth; **Rückgrat** (-(e)s, -e) nt spine, backbone; **Rückkehr** (-, -en) f return; **Rücklicht** nt rear light; **Rückreise** f return journey; **auf der ~** on the way back

Rucksack m rucksack, backpack; **Rucksacktourist(in)** m(f) backpacker

Rückschritt m step back; **Rückseite** f back; (hinterer Teil) rear; **siehe ~** see overleaf; **Rücksicht** f consideration; **~ nehmen auf** (+akk) to show consideration for; **rücksichtslos** adj inconsiderate; (Fahren) reckless; (unbarmherzig) ruthless; **rücksichtsvoll** adj considerate; **Rücksitz** m back seat; **Rückspiegel** m (Auto) rear-view mirror; **Rückstand** m **sie sind zwei Tore im ~** they're two goals down; **im ~ sein mit** (Arbeit, Miete) to be behind with; **Rücktaste** f backspace key; **Rückvergütung** f refund; **rückwärts** adv backwards, back; **Rückwärtsgang** m (Auto) reverse (gear); **Rückweg** m return journey, way back; **Rückzahlung** f repayment; **Rückzieher** m **einen ~ machen** to back out

Ruder (-s, -) nt oar; (Steuer) rudder; **Ruderboot** nt rowing boat (Brit), rowboat (US); **rudern** vt, vi to row

Ruf (-(e)s, -e) m call, cry; (Ansehen) reputation; **rufen** (rief, gerufen) vt, vi to call; (schreien) to cry; **Rufnummer** f telephone number

Ruhe (-) f rest; (Ungestörtheit) peace, quiet; (Gelassenheit, Stille) calm; (Schweigen) silence; **lass mich in ~!** leave me alone; **ruhen** vi to rest; **Ruhestand** m retirement; **im ~ sein** to be retired; **Ruhestörung** f disturbance of the peace; **Ruhetag** m closing day; **montags ~ haben** to be closed on Mondays

ruhig adj quiet; (bewegungslos) still; (Hand) steady; (gelassen) calm

Ruhm (-(e)s) m fame, glory

Rührei nt scrambled egg(s); **rühren** vt to move; (umrühren) to stir ▷ vr **sich ~** to move; (sich bemerkbar machen) to say something; **rührend** adj touching, moving; **Rührung** f emotion

Ruine (-, -n) f ruin; **ruinieren** vt to ruin

rülpsen vi to burp, to belch

rum (fam) kontr von **herum**

Rum (-s, -s) m rum

Rumänien (-s) nt Romania

Rummel (-s) m (Trubel) hustle and bustle; (Jahrmarkt) fair; (Medienrummel) hype; **Rummelplatz** m fairground

rumoren vi **es rumort in meinem Bauch/Kopf** my stomach is rumbling/my head is spinning

Rumpf (-(e)s, Rümpfe) m (Anat) trunk; (Aviat) fuselage; (Naut) hull

rümpfen vt **die Nase ~** to turn one's nose up (über at)

Rumpsteak nt rump steak

rund adj round ▷ adv (etwa) around; **~ um etw** (a)round sth; **Runde** (-, -n) f round; (in Rennen) lap; **Rundfahrt** f tour (durch of); **Rundfunk** m broadcasting; (Rundfunkanstalt) broadcasting service; **im ~** on the radio; **Rundgang** m tour (durch of); (von Wächter) round

rundlich adj plump; **Rundreise** f tour (durch of)

runter (fam) kontr von **herunter, hinunter**; **runterscrollen** vt (Inform) to scroll down

runzeln vt **die Stirn ~** to frown; **runzelig** adj wrinkled

ruppig adj gruff

Rüsche (-, -n) f frill

Ruß (-es) m soot

Russe (-n, -n) m Russian

Rüssel (-s, -) m (Elefant) trunk; (Schwein) snout

Russin f Russian; **russisch** adj Russian; **Russisch** nt Russian; **Russland** nt Russia

Rüstung f (mit Waffen) arming; (Ritterrüstung) armour; (Waffen) armaments pl

Rutsch (-(e)s, -e) m **guten ~ (ins neue Jahr)!** Happy New Year; **Rutschbahn** f, **Rutsche** f slide; **rutschen** vi to slide; (ausrutschen) to slip; **rutschig** adj slippery

rütteln vt, vi to shake

r

S *abk* = **Süd** S

s. *abk* = **siehe** see; **S.** *abk* = **Seite** p.

Saal (-(e)s, *Säle*) *m* hall; (*für Sitzungen*) room

Saarland *nt* Saarland

sabotieren *vt* to sabotage

Sache (-, -n) *f* thing; (*Angelegenheit*) affair, business; (*Frage*) matter; **bei der ~ bleiben** to keep to the point; **sachkundig** *adj* competent; **Sachlage** *f* situation; **sachlich** *adj* (*objektiv*) objective; (*nüchtern*) matter-of-fact; (*inhaltlich*) factual; **sächlich** *adj* (*Ling*) neuter; **Sachschaden** *m* material damage

Sachsen (-s) *nt* Saxony; **Sachsen-Anhalt** (-s) *nt* Saxony-Anhalt

sacht(e) *adv* softly, gently

Sachverständige(r) *mf* expert

Sack (-(e)s, *Säcke*) *m* sack; (*pej: Mensch*) bastard, bugger; **Sackgasse** *f* dead end, cul-de-sac

Safe (-s, -s) *m* safe

Safer Sex *m* safe sex

Safran (-s, -e) *m* saffron

Saft (-(e)s, *Säfte*) *m* juice; **saftig** *adj* juicy

Sage (-, -n) *f* legend

Säge (-, -n) *f* saw; **Sägemehl** *nt* sawdust

sagen *vt, vi* to say (*jdm* to sb), to tell (*jdm* sb); **wie sagt man ... auf Englisch?** what's ... in English?; **ich will dir mal was ~** let me tell you something

sägen *vt, vi* to saw

sagenhaft *adj* legendary; (*fam: großartig*) fantastic

sah *imperf von* **sehen**

Sahne (-) *f* cream; **Sahnetorte** *f* gateau

Saison (-, -s) *f* season; **außerhalb der ~** out of season

Saite (-, -n) *f* string

Sakko (-s, -s) *nt* jacket

Salami (-, -s) *f* salami

Salat (-(e)s, -e) *m* salad; (*Kopfsalat*) lettuce; **Salatbar** *f* salad bar; **Salatschüssel** *f* salad bowl; **Salatsoße** *f* salad dressing

Salbe (-, -n) *f* ointment

Salbei (-s) *m* sage

Salmonellenvergiftung *f* salmonella (poisoning)

salopp *adj* (*Kleidung*) casual; (*Sprache*) slangy

Salsamusik *f* salsa (music)

Salto (-s, -s) *m* somersault

Salz (-es, -e) *nt* salt; **salzarm** *adj* low-salt; **salzen** (*salzte, gesalzen*) *vt* to salt; **Salzgurke** *f* pickled gherkin; **Salzhering** *m* pickled herring; **salzig** *adj* salty; **Salzkartoffeln** *pl* boiled potatoes *pl*; **Salzstange** *f* pretzel stick; **Salzstreuer** *m* salt cellar (*Brit*) (o shaker (*US*)); **Salzwasser** *nt* salt water

Samba (-, -s) *f* samba

Samen (-s, -) *m* seed; (*Sperma*) sperm

sammeln *vt* to collect; **Sammler(in)** *m(f)* collector; **Sammlung** *f* collection; (*Ansammlung, Konzentration*) concentration

Samstag *m* Saturday; *siehe auch* **Mittwoch**; **samstags** *adv* on Saturdays; *siehe auch* **mittwochs**

samt *prep* +*dat* (along) with, together with

Samt (-(e)s, -e) *m* velvet

sämtliche(r, s) *adj* all (the)

Sanatorium (-s, *Sanatorien*) *nt* sanatorium (*Brit*), sanitarium (*US*)

Sand (-(e)s, -e) *m* sand

Sandale (-, -n) *f* sandal

sandig *adj* sandy; **Sandkasten** *m* sandpit (*Brit*), sandbox (*US*); **Sandpapier** *nt* sandpaper; **Sandstrand** *m* sandy beach

sandte *imperf von* **senden**

sanft *adj* soft, gentle

sang *imperf von* **singen**; **Sänger(in)** (-s, -) *m(f)* singer

Sangria (-, -s) *f* sangria

sanieren *vt* to redevelop; (*Gebäude*) to renovate; (*Betrieb*) to restore to profitability

sanitär *adj* sanitary; **~e Anlagen** *pl* sanitation

Sanitäter(in) (-s, -) *m(f)* ambulance man/woman, paramedic

sank *imperf von* **sinken**

Sankt Gallen (-s) *nt* St Gallen

Saphir (-s, -e) *m* sapphire

Sardelle *f* anchovy

Sardine *f* sardine

Sarg (-(e)s, *Särge*) *m* coffin

saß *imperf von* **sitzen**

Satellit (-en, -en) *m* satellite; **Satellitenfernsehen** *nt* satellite TV; **Satellitenschüssel** *f* (*fam*) satellite dish

Satire (-, -n) *f* satire (*auf +akk* on)

satt *adj* full; (*Farbe*) rich, deep; **~ sein** (*gesättigt*) to be full; **~ machen** to be filling; **jdn/etw ~ sein** (*o* **haben**) to be fed up with sb/sth

Sattel (-s, *Sättel*) *m* saddle

Saturn (-s) *m* Saturn

Satz (-es, *Sätze*) *m* (*Ling*) sentence; (*Mus*) movement; (*Tennis*) set; (*Kaffee*) grounds *pl*; (*Comm*) rate; (*Sprung*) jump; (*Comm*) rate

Satzzeichen *nt* punctuation mark

Sau (-, *Säue*) *f* sow; (*pej: Mensch*) dirty bugger

sauber *adj* clean; (*ironisch*) fine; **~ machen** to clean; **Sauberkeit** *f* cleanness; (*von Person*) cleanliness; **säubern** *vt* to clean

saublöd *adj* (*fam*) really stupid, dumb

Sauce (-, -n) *f* sauce; (*zu Braten*) gravy

Saudi-Arabien (-s) *nt* Saudi Arabia

sauer *adj* sour; (*Chem*) acid; (*fam: verärgert*) cross; **saurer Regen** acid rain; **Sauerkirsche** *f* sour cherry; **Sauerkraut** *nt* sauerkraut; **säuerlich** *adj* slighthly sour; **Sauermilch** *f* sour milk; **Sauerrahm** *m* sour cream; **Sauerstoff** *m* oxygen

saufen (*soff, gesoffen*) *vt* to drink; (*fam: Mensch*) to knock back ▷ *vi* to drink; (*fam: Mensch*) to booze

saugen (*sog o saugte, gesogen o gesaugt*) *vt, vi* to suck; (*mit Staubsauger*) to vacuum, to hoover (*Brit*); **Sauger** (-s, -) *m* (*auf Flasche*) teat; **Säugetier** *nt* mammal; **Säugling** *m* infant, baby

Säule (-, -n) *f* column, pillar

Saum (-s, *Säume*) *m* hem; (*Naht*) seam

Sauna (-, -s) *f* sauna

Säure (-, -n) *f* acid

sausen *vi* (*Ohren*) to buzz; (*Wind*) to howl; (*Mensch*) to rush

Saustall *m* pigsty; **Sauwetter** *nt* **was für ein ~** (*fam*) what lousy weather

Saxophon (-s, -e) *nt* saxophone

S-Bahn *f* suburban railway; **S-Bahn-Haltestelle** *f*, **S-Bahnhof** *m* suburban (train) station

scannen *vt* to scan; **Scanner** (-s, -) *m* scanner

schäbig *adj* shabby

Schach (-s, -s) *nt* chess; (*Stellung*) check; **Schachbrett** *nt* chessboard; **Schachfigur** *f* chess piece; **schachmatt** *adj* checkmate

Schacht (-(e)s, *Schächte*) *m* shaft

Schachtel (-, -n) *f* box

schade *interj* what a pity

Schädel (-s, -) *m* skull; **Schädelbruch** *m* fractured skull

schaden *vi* to damage, to harm (*jdm* sb); **das schadet nichts** it won't do any harm; **Schaden** (-s, *Schäden*) *m* damage; (*Verletzung*) injury; (*Nachteil*) disadvantage; **einen ~ verursachen** to cause damage; **Schadenersatz** *m* compensation, damages *pl*; **schadhaft** *adj* faulty; (*beschädigt*) damaged; **schädigen** *vt* to damage; (*jdn*) to do harm to, to harm; **schädlich** *adj* harmful (*für* to); **Schadstoff** *m* harmful substance; **schadstoffarm** *adj* low-emission

Schaf (-(e)s, -e) *nt* sheep; **Schafbock** *m* ram; **Schäfer** (-s, -) *m* shepherd; **Schäferhund** *m* Alsatian (*Brit*), German shepherd; **Schäferin** *f* shepherdess

schaffen (*schuf, geschaffen*) *vt* to create; (*Platz*) to make ▷ *vt* (*erreichen*) to manage, to do; (*erledigen*) to finish; (*Prüfung*) to pass; (*transportieren*) to take; **jdm zu ~ machen** to cause sb trouble

Schaffner(in) (-s, -) *m(f)* (*in Bus*) conductor/conductress; (*Eisenb*) guard

Schafskäse *m* sheep's (milk) cheese

schal *adj* (*Getränk*) flat

Schal (-s, -e *o* -s) *m* scarf

S

Schälchen nt (small) bowl

Schale (-, -n) f skin; (abgeschält) peel; (Nuss, Muschel, Ei) shell; (Geschirr) bowl, dish

schälen vt to peel; (Tomate, Mandel) to skin; (Erbsen, Eier, Nüsse) to shell; (Getreide) to husk ▷ vr **sich ~** to peel

Schall (-(e)s, -e) m sound; **Schalldämpfer** (-s, -) m (Auto) silencer (Brit), muffler (US); **Schallplatte** f record

Schalotte (-, -n) f shallot

schalten vt to switch ▷ vi (Auto) to change gear; (fam: begreifen) to catch on; **Schalter** (-s, -) m (auf Post, Bank) counter; (an Gerät) switch; **Schalterhalle** f main hall; **Schalteröffnungszeiten** pl business hours pl

Schaltfläche f (Inform) button; **Schalthebel** m gear lever (Brit) (o shift (US)); **Schaltjahr** nt leap year; **Schaltknüppel** m gear lever (Brit) (o shift (US)); **Schaltung** f gear change (Brit), gearshift (US)

Scham (-) f shame; (Schamgefühl) modesty; **schämen** vr **sich ~** to be ashamed

Schande (-) f disgrace

Schanze (-, -n) f ski jump

Schar (-, -en) f (von Vögeln) flock; (Menge) crowd; **in ~en** in droves

scharf adj (Messer, Kritik) sharp; (Essen) hot; **auf etw** (akk) **~ sein** (fam) to be keen on sth

Schärfe (-, -n) f sharpness; (Strenge) rigour; (Foto) focus

Scharlach (-s) m (Med) scarlet fever

Scharnier (-s, -e) nt hinge

Schaschlik (-s, -s) m o nt (shish) kebab

Schatten (-s, -) m shadow; **30 Grad im ~** 30 degrees in the shade; **schattig** adj shady

Schatz (-es, Schätze) m treasure; (Mensch) love

schätzen vt (abschätzen) to estimate; (Gegenstand) to value; (würdigen) to value, to esteem; (vermuten) to reckon; **Schätzung** f estimate; (das Schätzen) estimation; (von Wertgegenstand) valuation; **schätzungsweise** adv roughly, approximately

Schau (-, -en) f show; (Ausstellung) exhibition

schauen vi to look; **ich schau mal, ob ...**

I'll go and have a look whether ...; **schau, dass ...** see (to it) that ...

Schauer (-s, -) m (Regen) shower; (Schreck) shudder

Schaufel (-, -n) f shovel; **~ und Besen** dustpan and brush; **schaufeln** vt to shovel; **Schnee ~** to clear the snow away

Schaufenster nt shop window; **Schaufensterbummel** m window-shopping expedition

Schaukel (-, -n) f swing; **schaukeln** vi to rock; (mit Schaukel) to swing; **Schaukelstuhl** m rocking chair

Schaulustige(r) mf gawper (Brit), rubbernecker (US)

Schaum (-(e)s, Schäume) m foam; (Seifenschaum) lather; (Bierschaum) froth; **Schaumbad** nt bubble bath; **schäumen** vi to foam; **Schaumfestiger** (-s, -) m styling mousse; **Schaumgummi** m foam (rubber); **Schaumwein** m sparkling wine

Schauplatz m scene; **Schauspiel** nt spectacle; (Theat) play; **Schauspieler(in)** m(f) actor/actress

Scheck (-s, -s) m cheque; **Scheckheft** nt chequebook; **Scheckkarte** f cheque card

Scheibe (-, -n) f disc; (von Brot, Käse etc) slice; (Glasscheibe) pane; **Scheibenbremse** f (Auto) disc brake; **Scheibenwaschanlage** f (Auto) windscreen (Brit) (o windshield (US)) washer unit; **Scheibenwischer** (-s, -) m (Auto) windscreen (Brit) (o windshield (US)) wiper

Scheich (-s, -s) m sheik(h)

Scheide (-, -n) f (Anat) vagina

scheiden (schied, geschieden) vt (trennen) to separate; (Ehe) to dissolve; **sich ~ lassen** to get a divorce; **sie hat sich von ihm ~ lassen** she divorced him; **Scheidung** f divorce

Schein (-(e)s, -e) m light; (Anschein) appearance; (Geld) (bank)note; **scheinbar** adj apparent; **scheinen** (schien, geschienen) vi (Sonne) to shine; (den Anschein haben) to seem; **Scheinwerfer** (-s, -) m floodlight; (Theat) spotlight; (Auto) headlight

Scheiß- in zW (vulg) damned, bloody (Brit); **Scheiße** (-) f (vulg) shit, crap; **scheißegal** adj (vulg) **das ist mir ~** I don't give a damn (o toss); **scheißen** (schiss, geschissen) vi (vulg) to shit

Scheitel (-s, -) m parting (Brit), part (US)
scheitern vi to fail (an +dat because of)
Schellfisch m haddock
Schema (-s, -s o Schemata) nt scheme,
plan; (Darstellung) diagram
Schenkel (-s, -) m thigh
schenken vt to give; **er hat es mir
geschenkt** he gave it to me (as a present);
sich (dat) **etw ~** (fam: weglassen) to skip
sth
Scherbe (-, -n) f broken piece, fragment
Schere (-, -n) f scissors pl; (groß) shears pl;
eine ~ a pair of scissors/shears
Scherz (-es, -e) m joke
scheu adj shy
scheuen vr **sich ~ vor** (+dat) to be afraid
of, to shrink from ▷ vt to shun ▷ vi (Pferd)
to shy
scheuern vt to scrub; **jdm eine ~** (fam) to
slap sb in the face
Scheune (-, -n) f barn
scheußlich adj dreadful
Schi (-s, -er) m siehe **Ski**
Schicht (-, -en) f layer; (in Gesellschaft)
class; (in Fabrik etc) shift
schick adj stylish, chic
schicken vt to send ▷ vr **sich ~** (sich
beeilen) to hurry up
Schickimicki (-(s), -s) m (fam) trendy
Schicksal (-s, -e) nt fate
Schiebedach nt (Auto) sunroof; **schieben**
(schob, geschoben) vt, vi to push; **die Schuld
auf jdn ~** to put the blame on sb;
Schiebetür f sliding door
schied imperf von **scheiden**
Schiedsrichter(in) m(f); (Tennis) referee;
umpire; (Schlichter) arbitrator
schief adj crooked; (Blick) funny ▷ adv
crooked(ly); **~ gehen** (fam) to go wrong
schielen vi to squint
schien imperf von **scheinen**
Schienbein nt shin
Schiene (-, -n) f rail; (Med) splint
schier adj pure; (fig) sheer ▷ adv nearly,
almost
schießen (schoss, geschossen) vt to shoot;
(Ball) to kick; (Tor) to score; (Foto) to take
▷ vi to shoot (auf +akk at)
Schiff (-(e)s, -e) nt ship; (in Kirche) nave;
Schifffahrt f shipping; **Schiffsreise** f
voyage
schikanieren vt to harass; (Schule) to
bully

Schild (-(e)s, -e) m (Schutz) shield ▷ (-(e)s,
-er) nt sign; **was steht auf dem ~?** what
does the sign say?
Schilddrüse f thyroid gland
schildern vt to describe
Schildkröte f tortoise; (Wasserschildkröte)
turtle
Schimmel (-s, -) m mould; (Pferd) white
horse; **schimmeln** vi to go mouldy
schimpfen vt to tell off ▷ vi (sich
beklagen) to complain; **mit jdm ~** to tell sb
off; **Schimpfwort** nt swearword
Schinken (-s, -) m ham
Schirm (-(e)s, -e) m (Regenschirm)
umbrella; (Sonnenschirm) parasol,
sunshade
schiss imperf von **scheißen**
Schlacht (-, -en) f battle; **schlachten** vt to
slaughter; **Schlachter(in)** (-s, -) m(f)
butcher; **Schlachtfeld** nt battlefield
Schlaf (-(e)s) m sleep; **Schlafanzug** m
pyjamas pl; **Schlafcouch** f bed settee
Schläfe (-, -n) f temple
schlafen (schlief, geschlafen) vi to sleep;
schlaf gut! sleep well; **hast du gut
geschlafen?** did you sleep all right?; **er
schläft noch** he's still asleep; **~ gehen** to
go to bed
schlaff adj slack; (kraftlos) limp; (erschöpft)
exhausted
Schlafgelegenheit f place to sleep;
Schlaflosigkeit f sleeplessness;
Schlafmittel nt sleeping pill; **schläfrig**
adj sleepy
Schlafsaal m dormitory; **Schlafsack** m
sleeping bag; **Schlaftablette** f sleeping
pill; **er ist eine richtige ~** (fam: langweilig)
he's such a bore; **Schlafwagen** m
sleeping car, sleeper; **Schlafzimmer** nt
bedroom
Schlag (-(e)s, Schläge) m blow; (Puls) beat;
(Elek) shock; (fam: Portion) helping; (Art)
kind, type; **Schlagader** f artery;
Schlaganfall m (Med) stroke; **schlagartig**
adj sudden; **Schlagbohrmaschine** f
hammer drill
schlagen (schlug, geschlagen) vt to hit;
(besiegen) to beat; (Sahne) to whip; **jdn zu
Boden ~** to knock sb down ▷ vi (Herz) to
beat; (Uhr) to strike; **mit dem Kopf gegen
etw ~** to bang one's head against sth ▷ vr
sich ~ to fight
Schläger (-s, -) m (Sport) bat; (Tennis)

S

racket; (*Golf*) (golf) club; (*Hockey*) hockey stick; (*Mensch*) brawler; **Schlägerei** *f* fight, brawl

schlagfertig *adj* quick-witted; **Schlagloch** *nt* pothole; **Schlagsahne** *f* whipping cream; (*geschlagen*) whipped cream; **Schlagzeile** *f* headline; **Schlagzeug** *nt* drums *pl*; (*in Orchester*) percussion

Schlamm (-(*e*)*s*, -*e*) *m* mud

schlampig *adj* (*fam*) sloppy

schlang *imperf von* **schlingen**

Schlange (-, -*n*) *f* snake; (*von Menschen*) queue (*Brit*), line (*US*); **~ stehen** to queue (*Brit*), to stand in line (*US*); **Schlangenlinie** *f* wavy line; **in ~n fahren** to swerve about

schlank *adj* slim

schlapp *adj* limp; (*locker*) slack

Schlappe (-, -*n*) *f* (*fam*) setback

schlau *adj* clever, smart; (*raffiniert*) crafty, cunning

Schlauch (-(*e*)*s*, *Schläuche*) *m* hose; (*in Reifen*) inner tube; **Schlauchboot** *nt* rubber dinghy

schlecht *adj* bad; **mir ist ~** I feel sick; **jdn ~ machen** to run sb down; **die Milch ist ~** the milk has gone off ▷ *adv* badly; **es geht ihm ~** he's having a hard time; (*gesundheitlich*) he's not feeling well; (*finanziell*) he's pretty hard up

schleichen (*schlich, geschlichen*) *vi* to creep

Schleier (-*s*, -) *m* veil

Schleife (-, -*n*) *f* (*Inform, Aviat, Elek*) loop; (*Band*) bow

schleifen *vt* (*ziehen, schleppen*) to drag ▷ (*schliff, geschliffen*) *vt* (*schärfen*) to grind; (*Edelstein*) to cut

Schleim (-(*e*)*s*, -*e*) *m* slime; (*Med*) mucus; **Schleimer** (-*s*, -) *m* (*fam*) creep; **Schleimhaut** *f* mucous membrane

schlendern *vi* to stroll

schleppen *vt* to drag; (*Auto, Schiff*) to tow; (*tragen*) to lug; **Schlepplift** *m* ski tow

Schleswig-Holstein (-*s*) *nt* Schleswig-Holstein

Schleuder (-, -*n*) *f* catapult; (*für Wäsche*) spin-dryer; **schleudern** *vt* to hurl; (*Wäsche*) to spin-dry ▷ *vi* (*Auto*) to skid; **Schleudersitz** *m* ejector seat

schleunigst *adv* straight away

schlich *imperf von* **schleichen**

schlicht *adj* simple, plain

schlichten *vt* (*Streit*) to settle

schlief *imperf von* **schlafen**

schließen (*schloss, geschlossen*) *vt, vi* to close, to shut; (*beenden*) to close; (*Freundschaft, Ehe*) to enter into; (*folgern*) to infer (*aus* from) ▷ *vr* **sich ~** to close, to shut; **Schließfach** *nt* locker

schließlich *adv* finally; (*schließlich doch*) after all

schliff *imperf von* **schleifen**

schlimm *adj* bad; **schlimmer** *adj* worse; **schlimmste(r, s)** *adj* worst; **schlimmstenfalls** *adv* at (the) worst

Schlinge (-, -*n*) *f* loop; (*Med*) sling

Schlips (-*es*, -*e*) *m* tie

Schlitten (-*s*, -) *m* sledge, toboggan; (*mit Pferden*) sleigh; **Schlittenfahren** (-*s*) *nt* tobogganing

Schlittschuh *m* ice skate; **~ laufen** to ice-skate

Schlitz (-*es*, -*e*) *m* slit; (*für Münze*) slot; (*an Hose*) flies *pl*

schloss *imperf von* **schließen**

Schloss (-*es*, *Schlösser*) *nt* lock; (*Burg*) castle

Schlosser(in) *m(f)* mechanic

Schlucht (-, -*en*) *f* gorge, ravine

schluchzen *vi* to sob

Schluck (-(*e*)*s*, -*e*) *m* swallow; **Schluckauf** (-*s*) *m* hiccups *pl*; **schlucken** *vt, vi* to swallow

schludern *vi* (*fam*) to do sloppy work

schlug *imperf von* **schlagen**

Schlüpfer (-*s*, -) *m* panties *pl*

schlüpfrig *adj* slippery; (*fig*) lewd; (*Witz*) risqué

schlürfen *vt, vi* to slurp

Schluss (-*es*, *Schlüsse*) *m* end; (*Schlussfolgerung*) conclusion; **am ~** at the end; **mit jdm ~ machen** to finish (*o split up*) with sb

Schlüssel (-*s*, -) *m* (*a. fig*) key; **Schlüsselbein** *nt* collarbone; **Schlüsselblume** *f* cowslip; **Schlüsselbund** *m* bunch of keys; **Schlüsseldienst** *m* key-cutting service; **Schlüsselloch** *nt* keyhole

Schlussfolgerung *f* conclusion; **Schlusslicht** *nt* tail-light; (*fig*) tail-ender; **Schlusspfiff** *m* final whistle; **Schlussverkauf** *m* clearance sale

schmächtig *adj* frail

schmal *adj* narrow; (*Mensch, Buch etc*) slim; (*karg*) meagre

Schmalz (*-es, -e*) *nt* dripping, lard; (*fig: Sentimentalitäten*) schmaltz

schmatzen *vi* to eat noisily

schmecken *vt, vi* to taste (*nach* of); **es schmeckt ihm** he likes it; **lass es dir ~!** bon appétit

Schmeichelei *f* flattery; **schmeichelhaft** *adj* flattering; **schmeicheln** *vi* **jdm ~** to flatter sb

schmeißen (*schmiss, geschmissen*) *vt* (*fam*) to chuck, to throw

schmelzen (*schmolz, geschmolzen*) *vt, vi* to melt; (*Metall, Erz*) to smelt; **Schmelzkäse** *m* cheese spread

Schmerz (*-es, -en*) *m* pain; (*Trauer*) grief; **~en haben** to be in pain; **~en im Rücken haben** to have a pain in one's back; **schmerzen** *vt, vi* to hurt; **Schmerzensgeld** *nt* compensation; **schmerzhaft, schmerzlich** *adj* painful; **schmerzlos** *adj* painless; **Schmerzmittel** *nt* painkiller; **schmerzstillend** *adj* painkilling; **Schmerztablette** *f* painkiller

Schmetterling *m* butterfly

Schmied(in) (*-(e)s, -e*) *m(f)* blacksmith; **schmieden** *vt* to forge; (*Pläne*) to make

schmieren *vt* to smear; (*ölen*) to lubricate, to grease; (*bestechen*) to bribe ▷ *vt, vi* (*unsauber schreiben*) to scrawl; **Schmiergeld** *nt* (*fam*) bribe; **schmierig** *adj* greasy; **Schmiermittel** *nt* lubricant; **Schmierpapier** *nt* scrap paper; **Schmierseife** *f* soft soap

Schminke (*-, -n*) *f* make-up; **schminken** *vr* **sich ~** to put one's make-up on

schmiss *imperf von* **schmeißen**

schmollen *vi* to sulk; **schmollend** *adj* sulky

schmolz *imperf von* **schmelzen**

Schmuck (*-(e)s, -e*) *m* jewellery (*Brit*), jewelry (*US*); (*Verzierung*) decoration; **schmücken** *vt* to decorate

schmuggeln *vt, vi* to smuggle

schmunzeln *vi* to smile

schmusen *vi* to (kiss and) cuddle

Schmutz (*-es*) *m* dirt, filth; **schmutzig** *adj* dirty

Schnabel (*-s, Schnäbel*) *m* beak, bill; (*Ausguss*) spout

Schnake (*-, -n*) *f* mosquito

Schnalle (*-, -n*) *f* buckle

Schnäppchen *nt* (*fam*) bargain; **schnappen** *vt* (*fangen*) to catch ▷ *vi* **nach**

Luft ~ to gasp for breath; **Schnappschuss** *m* (*Foto*) snap(shot)

Schnaps (*-es, Schnäpse*) *m* schnapps

schnarchen *vi* to snore

schnaufen *vi* to puff, to pant

Schnauzbart *m* moustache; **Schnauze** (*-, -n*) *f* snout, muzzle; (*Ausguss*) spout; (*fam: Mund*) trap; **die ~ voll haben** to have had enough

schnäuzen *vr* **sich ~** to blow one's nose

Schnecke (*-, -n*) *f* snail; **Schneckenhaus** *nt* snail's shell

Schnee (*-s*) *m* snow; **Schneeball** *m* snowball; **Schneebob** *m* snowmobile; **Schneebrille** *f* snow goggles *pl*; **Schneeflocke** *f* snowflake; **Schneegestöber** (*-s, -*) *nt* snow flurry; **Schneeglöckchen** *nt* snowdrop; **Schneegrenze** *f* snowline; **Schneekanone** *f* snow thrower; **Schneekette** *f* (*Auto*) snow chain; **Schneemann** *m* snowman; **Schneematsch** *m* slush; **Schneepflug** *m* snowplough; **Schneeregen** *m* sleet; **Schneeschmelze** *f* thaw; **Schneesturm** *m* snowstorm, blizzard; **Schneetreiben** *nt* light blizzards *pl*; **Schneewehe** *f* snowdrift

Schneide (*-, -n*) *f* edge; (*Klinge*) blade; **schneiden** (*schnitt, geschnitten*) *vt* to cut; **sich** (*dat*) **die Haare ~ lassen** to have one's hair cut ▷ *vr* **sich ~** to cut oneself; **Schneider(in)** (*-s, -*) *m(f)* tailor; (*für Damenmode*) dressmaker; **Schneiderin** *f* dressmaker; **Schneidezahn** *m* incisor

schneien *vi impers* to snow

schnell *adj* quick, fast ▷ *adv* quickly, fast; **mach ~!** hurry up; **Schnelldienst** *m* express service; **Schnellhefter** *m* loose-leaf binder; **Schnellimbiss** *m* snack bar; **Schnellkochtopf** *m* pressure cooker; **Schnellreinigung** *f* express dry cleaning; (*Geschäft*) express (dry) cleaner's; **Schnellstraße** *f* expressway; **Schnellzug** *m* fast train

schneuzen *vr siehe* **schnäuzen**

schnitt *imperf von* **schneiden**

Schnitt (*-(e)s, -e*) *m* cut; (*Schnittpunkt*) intersection; (*Querschnitt*) (cross) section; (*Durchschnitt*) average; (*eines Kleides*) style; **Schnittblume** *f* cut flower; **Schnitte**

(-, -n) f slice; (belegt) sandwich;
Schnittkäse m cheese slices pl;
Schnittlauch m chives pl; **Schnittmuster**
nt pattern; **Schnittstelle** f (Inform, fig)
interface; **Schnittwunde** f cut, gash
Schnitzel (-s, -) nt (Papier) scrap; (Gastr)
escalope
schnitzen vt to carve
Schnorchel (-s, -) m snorkel;
schnorcheln vi to go snorkelling, to
snorkel; **Schnorcheln** (-s) nt snorkelling
schnüffeln vi to sniff
Schnuller (-s, -) m dummy (Brit), pacifier
(US)
Schnulze (-, -n) f (Film, Roman) weepie
Schnupfen (-s, -) m cold
schnuppern vi to sniff
Schnur (-, Schnüre) f string, cord; (Elek)
lead; **schnurlos** adj (Telefon) cordless
Schnurrbart m moustache
schnurren vi to purr
Schnürschuh m lace-up (shoe);
Schnürsenkel (-s, -) m shoelace
schob imperf von **schieben**
Schock (-(e)s, -e) m shock; **unter ~ stehen**
to be in a state of shock; **schockieren** vt
to shock
Schokolade f chocolate; **Schokoriegel**
m chocolate bar
Scholle (-, -n) f (Fisch) plaice; (Eis) ice floe

⊙ **SCHLÜSSELWORT**

schon adv **1** (bereits) already; **er ist schon
da** he's there already, he's already there;
ist er schon da? is he there yet?; **warst du
schon einmal da?** have you ever been
there?; **ich war schon einmal da** I've been
there before; **das war schon immer so**
that has always been the case; **schon oft**
often; **hast du schon gehört?** have you
heard?

2 (bestimmt) all right; **du wirst schon
sehen** you'll see (all right); **das wird
schon noch gut** that'll be OK
3 (bloß) just; **allein schon das Gefühl ...**
just the very feeling ...; **schon der
Gedanke** the very thought; **wenn ich
das schon höre** I only have to hear
that
4 (einschränkend): **ja schon, aber ...** yes
(well), but ...
5: **schon möglich** possible; **schon gut!**

OK!; **du weißt schon** you know; **komm
schon!** come on!

schön adj beautiful; (nett) nice; (Frau)
beautiful, pretty; (Mann) beautiful,
handsome; (Wetter) fine; **~e Grüße** best
wishes; **~es Wochenende** have a nice
weekend
schonen vt (pfleglich behandeln) to look
after ▷ vr **sich ~** to take it easy
Schönheit f beauty
Schonkost f light diet
schöpfen vt to scoop; (mit Kelle) to ladle;
Schöpfkelle f, **Schöpflöffel** m ladle
Schöpfung f creation
Schoppen (-s, -) m glass (of wine)
Schorf (-(e)s, -e) m scab
Schorle (-, -n) f spritzer
Schornstein m chimney;
Schornsteinfeger(in) (-s, -) m(f) chimney
sweep
schoss imperf von **schießen**
Schoß (-es, Schöße) m lap
Schotte (-n, -n) m Scot, Scotsman;
Schottin f Scot, Scotswoman;
schottisch adj Scottish, Scots;
Schottland nt Scotland
schräg adj slanting; (Dach) sloping; (Linie)
diagonal; (fam: unkonventionell) wacky
Schrank (-(e)s, Schränke) m cupboard;
(Kleiderschrank) wardrobe (Brit), closet
(US)
Schranke (-, -n) f barrier
Schrankwand f wall unit
Schraube (-, -n) f screw; **schrauben** vt to
screw; **Schraubendreher** (-s, -) m
screwdriver; **Schraubenschlüssel** m
spanner; **Schraubenzieher** (-s, -) m
screwdriver; **Schraubverschluss** m
screw top, screw cap
Schreck (-(e)s, -e) m, **Schrecken** (-s, -) m
terror; (Angst) fright; **jdm einen
~ einjagen** to give sb a fright;
schreckhaft adj jumpy; **schrecklich** adj
terrible, dreadful
Schrei (-(e)s, -e) m scream; (Ruf) shout
Schreibblock m writing pad; **schreiben**
(schrieb, geschrieben) vt, vi to write;
(buchstabieren) to spell; **wie schreibt man
...?** how do you spell ...?; **Schreiben** (-s, -)
nt writing; (Brief) letter; **Schreibfehler** m
spelling mistake; **schreibgeschützt** adj
(Diskette) write-protected; **Schreibtisch**

m desk; **Schreibwaren** *pl* stationery *sing*; **Schreibwarenladen** *m* stationer's

schreien (*schrie, geschrie(e)n*) *vt, vi* to scream; (*rufen*) to shout

Schreiner(in) *m(f)* joiner; **Schreinerei** *f* joiner's workshop

schrie *imperf von* **schreien**

schrieb *imperf von* **schreiben**

Schrift (-, *-en*) *f* writing; (*Handschrift*) handwriting; (*Schriftart*) typeface; (*Schrifttyp*) font; **schriftlich** *adj* written ▷ *adv* in writing; **würden Sie uns das bitte ~ geben?** could we have that in writing, please?; **Schriftsteller(in)** (-s, -) *m(f)* writer

Schritt (-(*e*)s, *-e*) *m* step; **~ für ~** step by step; **~e gegen etw unternehmen** to take steps against sth; **Schrittgeschwindigkeit** *f* walking speed; **Schrittmacher** *m* (*Med*) pacemaker

Schrott (-(*e*)s, *-e*) *m* scrap metal; (*fig*) rubbish

schrubben *vi, vt* to scrub; **Schrubber** (-s, -) *m* scrubbing brush

schrumpfen *vi* to shrink

Schubkarren (-s, -) *m* wheelbarrow; **Schublade** *f* drawer

schubsen *vt* to shove, to push

schüchtern *adj* shy

schuf *imperf von* **schaffen**

Schuh (-(*e*)s, *-e*) *m* shoe; **Schuhcreme** *f* shoe polish; **Schuhgeschäft** *nt* shoe shop; **Schuhgröße** *f* shoe size; **Schuhlöffel** *m* shoehorn; **Schuhsohle** *f* sole

Schulabschluss *m* school-leaving qualification

schuld *adj* **wer ist ~ daran?** whose fault is it?; **er ist ~** it's his fault, he's to blame; **Schuld** (-) *f* guilt; (*Verschulden*) fault; **~ haben** to be to blame (*an +dat* for); **er hat ~** it's his fault; **sie gibt mir die ~ an dem Unfall** she blames me for the accident; **schulden** *vt* to owe (*jdm etw* sb sth); **Schulden** *pl* debts *pl*; **~ haben** to be in debt; **~ machen** to run up debts; **seine ~ bezahlen** to pay off one's debts; **schuldig** *adj* guilty (*an +dat* of); (*gebührend*) due; **jdm etw ~ sein** to owe sb sth

Schule (-, *-n*) *f* school; **in der ~** at school; **in die ~ gehen** to go to school;

Schüler(in) (-s, -) *m(f)* (*jüngerer*) pupil; (*älterer*) student; **Schüleraustausch** *m* school exchange; **Schulfach** *nt* subject; **Schulferien** *pl* school holidays *pl* (*Brit*) (*o* vacation (*US*)); **schulfrei** *adj* **morgen ist ~** there's no school tomorrow; **Schulfreund(in)** *m(f)* schoolmate; **Schuljahr** *nt* school year; **Schulkenntnisse** *pl* **~ in Französisch** school(-level) French; **Schulklasse** *f* class; **Schulleiter(in)** *m(f)* headmaster/headmistress (*Brit*), principal (*US*)

Schulter (-, *-n*) *f* shoulder; **Schulterblatt** *nt* shoulder blade

Schulung *f* training; (*Veranstaltung*) training course

Schund (-(*e*)s) *m* trash

Schuppe (-, *-n*) *f* (*von Fisch*) scale; **schuppen** *vt* to scale ▷ *vr* **sich ~** to peel; **Schuppen** *pl* (*im Haar*) dandruff *sing*

Schürfwunde *f* graze

Schürze (-, *-n*) *f* apron

Schuss (-es, *Schüsse*) *m* shot; **mit einem ~ Wodka** with a dash of vodka

Schüssel (-, *-n*) *f* bowl

Schuster(in) (-s, -) *m(f)* shoemaker

Schutt (-(*e*)s) *m* rubble

Schüttelfrost *m* shivering fit; **schütteln** *vt* to shake ▷ *vr* **sich ~** to shake

schütten *vt* to pour; (*Zucker, Kies etc*) to tip ▷ *vi impers* to pour (down)

Schutz (-es) *m* protection (*gegen, vor* against, from); (*Unterschlupf*) shelter; **jdn in ~ nehmen** to stand up for sb; **Schutzblech** *nt* mudguard; **Schutzbrief** *m* travel insurance document for drivers; **Schutzbrille** *f* (safety) goggles *pl*

Schütze (-*n*, *-n*) *m* (*beim Fußball*) scorer; (*Astr*) Sagittarius

schützen *vt* **jdn gegen/vor etw ~** to protect sb against/from sth; **Schutzimpfung** *f* inoculation, vaccination

schwach *adj* weak; **~e Augen** poor eyesight *sing*; **Schwäche** (-, *-n*) *f* weakness; (*schwacher Punkt*) weak point; **Schwachstrom** *m* low-voltage current

Schwager (-s, *Schwäger*) *m* brother-in-law; **Schwägerin** *f* sister-in-law

Schwalbe (-, *-n*) *f* swallow; (*beim Fußball*) dive

S

schwamm *imperf von* **schwimmen**

Schwamm (-(e)s, Schwämme) *m* sponge; **~ drüber!** (fam) let's forget it!

Schwan (-(e)s, Schwäne) *m* swan

schwanger *adj* pregnant; **im vierten Monat ~ sein** to be four months pregnant; **Schwangerschaft** *f* pregnancy; **Schwangerschaftsabbruch** *m* abortion; **Schwangerschaftstest** *m* pregnancy test

schwanken *vi* to sway; (Preise, Zahlen) to fluctuate; (zögern) to hesitate; (taumeln) to stagger; **ich schwanke zwischen A und B** I can't decide between A and B

Schwanz (-es, Schwänze) *m* tail; (vulg: Penis) cock

Schwarm (-(e)s, Schwärme) *m* swarm; (fam: angehimmelte Person) heartthrob; **schwärmen** *vi* to swarm; **~ für** to be mad about

schwarz *adj* black; **~ sehen** (fam) to be pessimistic (für about); **mir wurde ~ vor Augen** everything went black; **Schwarzarbeit** *f* illicit work; **Schwarzbrot** *nt* black bread; **schwarz|fahren** *irr vi* to travel without a ticket; (ohne Führerschein) to drive without a licence; **Schwarzfahrer(in)** *m(f)* fare-dodger; **Schwarzmarkt** *m* black market; **Schwarzwald** *m* Black Forest; **schwarzweiß** *adj* black and white; **Schwarzwurzel** *f* black salsify

schwatzen *vi* to chatter; **Schwätzer(in)** (-s, -) *m(f)* chatterbox; (Schwafler) gasbag; (Klatschmaul) gossip

Schwebebahn *f* suspension railway; **schweben** *vi* to float; (hoch) to soar

Schwede (-n, -n) *m* Swede; **Schweden** (-s) *nt* Sweden; **Schwedin** *f* Swede; **schwedisch** *adj* Swedish; **Schwedisch** *nt* Swedish

Schwefel (-s) *m* sulphur

schweigen (schwieg, geschwiegen) *vi* to be silent; (nicht mehr reden) to stop talking; **Schweigen** (-s) *nt* silence; **Schweigepflicht** *f* duty of confidentiality; **die ärztliche ~** medical confidentiality

Schwein (-(e)s, -e) *nt* pig; (fam: Glück) luck; (fam: gemeiner Mensch) swine; **Schweinebraten** *m* roast pork; **Schweinefleisch** *nt* pork; **Schweinerei** *f* mess; (Gemeinheit) dirty trick

Schweiß (-es) *m* sweat

schweißen *vt, vi* to weld

Schweißfüße *pl* sweaty feet *pl*

Schweiz (-) *f* **die ~** Switzerland; **Schweizer(in)** (-s, -) *m(f)* Swiss; **Schweizerdeutsch** *nt* Swiss German; **schweizerisch** *adj* Swiss

Schwelle (-, -n) *f* doorstep; (a. fig) threshold

schwellen *vi* to swell (up); **Schwellung** *f* swelling

schwer *adj* heavy; (schwierig) difficult, hard; (schlimm) serious, bad; **er ist ~ zu verstehen** it's difficult to understand what he's saying ▷ *adv* (sehr) really; (verletzt etc) seriously, badly; **jdm ~ fallen** to be difficult for sb; **etw ~ nehmen** to take sth hard; **Schwerbehinderte(r)** *mf* severely disabled person; **schwerhörig** *adj* hard of hearing

Schwert (-(e)s, -er) *nt* sword; **Schwertlilie** *f* iris

Schwester (-, -n) *f* sister; (Med) nurse

schwieg *imperf von* **schweigen**

Schwiegereltern *pl* parents-in-law *pl*; **Schwiegermutter** *f* mother-in-law; **Schwiegersohn** *m* son-in-law; **Schwiegertochter** *f* daughter-in-law; **Schwiegervater** *m* father-in-law

schwierig *adj* difficult, hard; **Schwierigkeit** *f* difficulty; **in ~en kommen** to get into trouble; **jdm ~en machen** to make things difficult for sb

Schwimmbad *nt* swimming pool; **Schwimmbecken** *nt* swimming pool; **schwimmen** (schwamm, geschwommen) *vi* to swim; (treiben) to float; (fig: unsicher sein) to be all at sea; **Schwimmer(in)** *m(f)* swimmer; **Schwimmflosse** *f* flipper; **Schwimmflügel** *m* water wing; **Schwimmreifen** *m* rubber ring; **Schwimmweste** *f* life jacket

Schwindel (-s) *m* dizziness; (Anfall) dizzy spell; (Betrug) swindle; **schwindelfrei** *adj* **nicht ~ sein** to suffer from vertigo; **~ sein** to have a head for heights; **schwindlig** *adj* dizzy; **mir ist ~** I feel dizzy

Schwips *m* **einen ~ haben** to be tipsy

schwitzen *vi* to sweat

schwoll *imperf von* **schwellen**

schwor *imperf von* **schwören**

schwören (schwor, geschworen) *vt, vi* to swear; **einen Eid ~** to take an oath

schwul *adj* gay
schwül *adj* close
Schwung (-(e)s, Schwünge) *m* swing; (Triebkraft) momentum; (fig: Energie) energy; (fam: Menge) batch; **in ~ kommen** to get going
Schwur (-s, Schwüre) *m* oath
scrollen *vi* (Inform) to scroll
sechs *num* six; **Sechs** (-, -en) *f* six; (Schulnote) ≈ F; **Sechserpack** *m* sixpack; **sechshundert** *num* six hundred; **sechsmal** *adv* six times; **sechste(r, s)** *adj* sixth; siehe auch **dritte**; **Sechstel** (-s, -) *nt* sixth; **sechzehn** *num* sixteen; **sechzehnte(r, s)** *adj* sixteenth; siehe auch **dritte**; **sechzig** *num* sixty; **in den ~er Jahren** in the sixties; **sechzigste(r, s)** *adj* sixtieth
Secondhandladen *m* secondhand shop
See (-, -n) *f* sea; **an der ~** by the sea ▷ (-s, -n) *m* lake; **am ~** by the lake; **Seegang** *m* waves; **hoher/schwerer/leichter ~** rough/heavy/calm seas *pl*; **Seehund** *m* seal; **Seeigel** *m* sea urchin; **seekrank** *adj* seasick
Seele (-, -n) *f* soul
Seeleute *pl* seamen *pl*, sailors *pl*
seelisch *adj* mental, psychological
Seelöwe *m* sea lion; **Seemann** *m* sailor, seaman; **Seemeile** *f* nautical mile; **Seemöwe** *f* seagull; **Seenot** *f* distress (at sea); **Seepferdchen** *nt* sea horse; **Seerose** *f* water lily; **Seestern** *m* starfish; **Seezunge** *f* sole
Segel (-s, -) *nt* sail; **Segelboot** *nt* yacht; **Segelfliegen** (-s) *nt* gliding; **Segelflugzeug** *nt* glider; **segeln** *vt, vi* to sail; **Segelschiff** *nt* sailing ship
sehbehindert *adj* partially sighted
sehen (sah, gesehen) *vt, vi* to see; (in bestimmte Richtung) to look; **gut/schlecht ~** to have good/bad eyesight; **auf die Uhr ~** to look at one's watch; **kann ich das mal ~?** can I have a look at it?; **wir ~ uns morgen!** see you tomorrow!; **ich kenne sie nur vom Sehen** I only know her by sight; **Sehenswürdigkeiten** *pl* sights *pl*
Sehne (-, -n) *f* tendon; (an Bogen) string
sehnen *vr* **sich ~** to long (nach for)
Sehnenscheidenentzündung *f* (Med) tendovaginitis; **Sehnenzerrung** *f* (Med) pulled tendon

Sehnsucht *f* longing; **sehnsüchtig** *adj* longing
sehr *adv* (vor Adjektiv, Adverb) very; (mit Verben) a lot, very much; **zu ~** too much
seicht *adj* shallow
Seide (-, -n) *f* silk
Seife (-, -n) *f* soap; **Seifenoper** *f* soap (opera); **Seifenschale** *f* soap dish
Seil (-(e)s, -e) *nt* rope; (Kabel) cable; **Seilbahn** *f* cable railway

SCHLÜSSELWORT

sein (pt war, pp gewesen) *vi* **1** to be; **ich bin** I am; **du bist** you are; **er/sie/es ist** he/she/it is; **wir sind/ihr seid/sie sind** we/you/they are; **wir waren** we were; **wir sind gewesen** we have been
2: **seien Sie nicht böse** don't be angry; **sei so gut und ...** be so kind as to ...; **das wäre gut** that would od that'd be a good thing; **wenn ich Sie wäre** if I were od was you; **das wärs** that's all, that's it; **morgen bin ich in Rom** tomorrow I'll od I will od I shall be in Rome; **waren Sie mal in Rom?** have you ever been to Rome?
3: **wie ist das zu verstehen?** how is that to be understood?; **er ist nicht zu ersetzen** he cannot be replaced; **mit ihr ist nicht zu reden** you can't talk to her
4: **mir ist kalt** I'm cold; **was ist?** what's the matter?, what is it?; **ist was?** is something the matter?; **es sei denn, dass ...** unless ...; **wie dem auch sei** be that as it may; **wie wäre es mit ...?** how od what about ...?; **lass das sein!** stop that!

seit *conj* (bei Zeitpunkt) since; (bei Zeitraum) for; **er ist ~ Montag hier** he's been here since Monday; **er ist ~ einer Woche hier** he's been here for a week; **~ langem** for a long time; **seitdem** *adv, conj* since
Seite (-, -n) *f* side; (in Buch) page; **zur ~ gehen** to step aside; **Seitenairbag** *m* side-impact airbag; **Seitenaufprallschutz** *m* (Auto) side-impact protection; **Seitensprung** *m* affair; **Seitenstechen** (-s) *nt* **~ haben/bekommen** to have/get a stitch; **Seitenstraße** *f* side street; **Seitenstreifen** *m* hard shoulder (Brit), shoulder (US); **seitenverkehrt** *adj* the

wrong way round; **Seitenwind** *m* crosswind

seither *adv* since (then)

seitlich *adj* side

Sekretär(in) *m(f)* secretary

Sekt *(-(e)s, -e)* *m* sparkling wine *(similar to champagne)*

Sekte *(-, -n)* *f* sect

Sekunde *(-, -n)* *f* second; **Sekundenkleber** *(-s, -)* *m* superglue; **Sekundenschnelle** *f* **es geschah alles in ~** it was all over in a matter of seconds

⊙ SCHLÜSSELWORT

selbst *pron* **1**: **ich/er/wir selbst** I myself/he himself/we ourselves; **sie ist die Tugend selbst** she's virtue itself; **er braut sein Bier selbst** he brews his own beer; **wie gehts? — gut, und selbst?** how are things? — fine, and yourself? **2** *(ohne Hilfe)* alone on my/his/one's *etc* own; **von selbst** by itself; **er kam von selbst** he came of his own accord; **selbst gemacht** home-made ▷ *adv* even; **selbst wenn** even if; **selbst Gott** even God (himself)

selbständig *adj siehe* **selbstständig**

Selbstauslöser *(-s, -)* *m* *(Foto)* self-timer; **Selbstbedienung** *f* self-service; **Selbstbefriedigung** *f* masturbation; **Selbstbeherrschung** *f* self-control; **Selbstbeteiligung** *f* *(einer Versicherung)* excess; **selbstbewusst** *adj* (self-)confident; **Selbstbräuner** *(-s, -)* *m* self-tanning lotion; **selbstgemacht** *adj* self-made; **Selbstgespräch** *nt* **~e führen** to talk to oneself; **selbstklebend** *adj* self-adhesive; **Selbstkostenpreis** *m* cost price; **Selbstlaut** *m* vowel; **Selbstmord** *m* suicide; **selbstsicher** *adj* self-assured; **selbstständig** *adj* independent; *(arbeitend)* self-employed; **Selbstverpflegung** *f* self-catering; **selbstverständlich** *adj* obvious; **ich halte das für ~** I take that for granted ▷ *adv* naturally; **Selbstvertrauen** *nt* self-confidence

Sellerie *(-s, -(s))* *m* *(-, -n)* *f* *(Knollensellerie)* celeriac; *(Stangensellerie)* celery

selten *adj* rare ▷ *adv* seldom, rarely

seltsam *adj* strange;

~ schmecken/riechen to taste/smell strange

Semester *(-s, -)* *nt* semester; **Semesterferien** *pl* vacation *sing*

Semikolon *(-s, Semikola)* *nt* semicolon

Seminar *(-s, -e)* *nt* seminar

Semmel *(-, -n)* *f* roll; **Semmelbrösel** *pl* breadcrumbs

Senat *(-(e)s, -e)* *m* senate

senden *(sandte, gesandt)* *vt* to send ▷ *vt*, *vi* *(Radio, Tv)* to broadcast; **Sender** *(-s, -)* *m* *(TV)* channel; *(Radio)* station; *(Anlage)* transmitter; **Sendung** *f* *(Radio, Tv)* broadcasting; *(Programm)* programme

Senf *(-(e)s, -e)* *m* mustard

Senior(in) *m(f)* senior citizen; **Seniorenpass** *m* senior citizen's travel pass

senken *vt* to lower ▷ *vr* **sich ~** to sink

senkrecht *adj* vertical

Sensation *(-, -en)* *f* sensation

sensibel *adj* sensitive

sentimental *adj* sentimental

separat *adj* separate

September *(-(s), -)* *m* September; *siehe auch* **Juni**

Serbien *(-s)* *nt* Serbia

Serie *f* series *sing*

seriös *adj* *(ernsthaft)* serious; *(anständig)* respectable

Serpentine *f* hairpin (bend)

Serum *(-s, Seren)* *nt* serum

Server *(-s, -)* *m* *(Inform)* server

Service *(-(s), -)* *nt* *(Geschirr)* service ▷ *(-, -s)* *m* service

servieren *vt*, *vi* to serve

Serviette *f* napkin, serviette

Servolenkung *f* *(Auto)* power steering

Sesam *(-s, -s)* *m* sesame seeds *pl*

Sessel *(-s, -)* *m* armchair; **Sessellift** *m* chairlift

Set *(-s, -s)* *m o nt* set; *(Tischset)* tablemat

setzen *vt* to put; *(Baum etc)* to plant; *(Segel)* to set ▷ *vr* **sich ~** to settle; *(hinsetzen)* to sit down; **~ Sie sich doch** please sit down

Seuche *(-, -n)* *f* epidemic

seufzen *vt*, *vi* to sigh

Sex *(-(es))* *m* sex; **Sexismus** *m* sexism; **sexistisch** *adj* sexist; **Sextourismus** *m* sex tourism; **Sexualität** *f* sexuality; **sexuell** *adj* sexual

Seychellen *pl* Seychelles *pl*
sfr *abk* = **Schweizer Franken** Swiss
franc(s)
Shampoo (-*s*, -*s*) *nt* shampoo
Shareware (-, -*s*) *f* (*Inform*) shareware
Shorts *pl* shorts *pl*
Shuttlebus *m* shuttle bus

 SCHLÜSSELWORT

sich *pron* **1** (*akk*); **er/sie/es ... sich**
he/she/it ... himself/herself/itself; **sie**
pl/**man ... sich** they/one ...
themselves/oneself; **Sie ... sich** you ...
yourself/yourselves *pl*; **sich wiederholen**
to repeat oneself/itself
2 (*dat*): **er/sie/es ... sich** he/she/it ... to
himself/herself/itself; **sie** *pl*/**man ... sich**
they/one ... to themselves/oneself; **Sie ...
sich** you ... to yourself/yourselves *pl*; **sie
hat sich einen Pullover gekauft** she
bought herself a jumper; **sich die Haare
waschen** to wash one's hair
3 (*mit Präposition*): **haben Sie Ihren
Ausweis bei sich?** do you have your
pass on you?; **er hat nichts bei sich** he's
got nothing on him; **sie bleiben gern
unter sich** they keep themselves to
themselves
4 (*einander*) each other one another; **sie
bekämpfen sich** they fight each other *od*
one another
5: **dieses Auto fährt sich gut** this car
drives well; **hier sitzt es sich gut** it's good
to sit here

sicher *adj* safe (*vor +dat* from); (*gewiss*)
certain (*gen* of); (*zuverlässig*) reliable;
(*selbstsicher*) confident; **aber ~!** of course,
sure; **Sicherheit** *f* safety; (*Aufgabe von
Sicherheitsbeamten*) (*Fin*) security;
(*Gewissheit*) certainty; (*Selbstsicherheit*)
confidence; **mit ~** definitely;
Sicherheitsabstand *m* safe distance;
Sicherheitsgurt *m* seat belt;
sicherheitshalber *adv* just to be on the
safe side; **Sicherheitsnadel** *f* safety pin;
Sicherheitsvorkehrung *f* safety
precaution; **sicherlich** *adv* certainly;
(*wahrscheinlich*) probably
sichern *vt* to secure (*gegen* against);
(*schützen*) to protect; (*Daten*) to back up;
Sicherung *f* (*Sichern*) securing;

(*Vorrichtung*) safety device; (*an Waffen*)
safety catch; (*Elek*) fuse; (*Inform*) backup;
die ~ ist durchgebrannt the fuse has
blown
Sicht (-) *f* sight; (*Aussicht*) view; **sichtbar**
adj visible; **sichtlich** *adj* evident, obvious;
Sichtverhältnisse *pl* visibility *sing*;
Sichtweite *f* **in/außer ~** within/out of
sight
sie *pron* (*3. Person sing*) she; (*3. Person pl*)
they; (*akk von sing*) her; (*akk von pl*) them;
(*für eine Sache*) it; **da ist ~ ja** there she is; **da
sind ~ ja** there they are; **ich kenne ~** (*Frau*)
I know her; (*mehrere Personen*) I know
them; **~ lag gerade noch hier** (*meine Jacke,
Uhr*) it was here just a minute ago; **ich hab
~ gefunden** (*meine Jacke, Uhr*) I've found it;
**hast du meine Brille/Hose gesehen? -
ich kann ~ nirgends finden** have you
seen my glasses/trousers? - I can't find
them anywhere
Sie *pron* (*Höflichkeitsform, Nom und Akk*) you
Sieb (-(*e*)*s*, -*e*) *nt* sieve; (*Teesieb*) strainer
sieben *num* seven; **siebenhundert** *num*
seven hundred; **siebenmal** *adv* seven
times; **siebte(r, s)** *adj* seventh; *siehe auch*
dritte; **Siebtel** (-*s*, -) *nt* seventh; **siebzehn**
num seventeen; **siebzehnte(r, s)** *adj*
seventeenth; *siehe auch* **dritte**; **siebzig**
num seventy; **in den ~er Jahren** in the
seventies; **siebzigste(r, s)** *adj* seventieth
Siedlung (-, -*en*) *f* (*Wohngebiet*) housing
estate (*Brit*) (*o* development (*US*))
Sieg (-(*e*)*s*, -*e*) *m* victory; **siegen** *vi* to win;
Sieger(in) (-*s*, -) *m(f)* winner;
Siegerehrung *f* presentation ceremony
siehe *imper* see
siezen *vt* to address as 'Sie'
Signal (-*s*, -*e*) *nt* signal
Silbe (-, -*n*) *f* syllable
Silber (-*s*) *nt* silver; **Silberhochzeit** *f*
silver wedding; **Silbermedaille** *f* silver
medal
Silikon (-*s*, -*e*) *nt* silicone
Silvester (-*s*, -) *nt*, **Silvesterabend** *m*
New Year's Eve, Hogmanay (SCOT)

● **Silvester**
●
● **Silvester** is the German name for New
● Year's Eve. Although not an official
● holiday, most businesses close early
● and shops shut at midday. Most

● Germans celebrate in the evening
● and at midnight they let off
● fireworks and rockets; the revelry
● usually lasts until the early hours of
● the morning.

Simbabwe (-s) nt Zimbabwe
simpel adj simple
simultan adj simultaneous
simsen vt, vi (fam) to text
Sinfonie (-, -n) f symphony;
  Sinfonieorchester nt symphony
  orchestra
Singapur (-s) nt Singapore
singen (sang, gesungen) vt, vi to sing;
  richtig/falsch ~ to sing in tune/out of
  tune
Single (-, -s) f (CD) single ▷ (-s, -s) m
  (Mensch) single
Singular m singular
sinken (sank, gesunken) vi to sink; (Preise
  etc) to fall, to go down
Sinn (-(e)s, -e) m (Denken) mind;
  (Wahrnehmung) sense; (Bedeutung) sense,
  meaning; **~ machen** to make sense; **das
  hat keinen ~** it's no use; **sinnlich** adj
  sensuous; (erotisch) sensual;
  (Wahrnehmung) sensory; **sinnlos** adj
  (unsinnig) stupid; (Verhalten) senseless;
  (zwecklos) pointless; (bedeutungslos)
  meaningless; **sinnvoll** adj meaningful;
  (vernünftig) sensible
Sirup (-s, -e) m syrup
Sitte (-, -n) f custom
Situation f situation
Sitz (-es, -e) m seat; **sitzen** (saß, gesessen)
  vi to sit; (Bemerkung, Schlag) to strike
  home; (Gelerntes) to have sunk in; **der
  Rock sitzt gut** the skirt is a good fit;
  Sitzgelegenheit f place to sit down;
  Sitzplatz m seat; **Sitzung** f meeting
Sizilien (-s) nt Sicily
Skandal (-s, -e) m scandal
Skandinavien (-s) nt Scandinavia
Skateboard (-s, -s) nt skateboard;
  Skateboardfahrer(in) m(f) skateboarder
Skelett (-s, -e) nt skeleton
skeptisch adj sceptical
Ski (-s, -er) m ski; **~ laufen** (o **fahren**) to
  ski; **Skianzug** m ski suit; **Skibrille** f ski
  goggles pl; **Skifahren** (-s) nt skiing;
  Skigebiet (-s, -e) nt skiing area; **Skihose** f
  skiing trousers pl; **Skikurs** m skiing course;

Skilanglauf m cross-country skiing;
  Skiläufer(in) m(f) skier; **Skilehrer(in)**
  m(f) ski instructor; **Skilift** m ski-lift
Skinhead (-s, -s) m skinhead
Skipiste f ski run; **Skischanze** (-, -n) f ski
  jump; **Skischuh** m ski boot; **Skischule** f
  ski school; **Skispringen** (-s, -n) nt ski
  jumping; **Skistiefel** (-s, -) m ski boot;
  Skistock m ski pole; **Skiträger** m ski
  rack; **Skiurlaub** m skiing holiday (Brit) (o
  vacation (US))
Skizze (-, -n) f sketch
Skonto (-s, -s) m o nt discount
Skorpion (-s, -e) m (Zool) scorpion; (Astr)
  Scorpio
Skulptur (-, -en) f sculpture
S-Kurve f double bend
Slalom (-s, -s) m slalom
Slip (-s, -s) m (pair of) briefs pl; **Slipeinlage**
  f panty liner
Slowakei (-) f Slovakia; **slowakisch** adj
  Slovakian; **Slowakische Republik** Slovak
  Republic; **Slowakisch** nt Slovakian
Slowenien (-s) nt Slovenia; **slowenisch**
  adj Slovenian; **Slowenisch** nt
  Slovenian
Smiley (-s, -s) m smiley
Smog (-s) m smog; **Smogalarm** m smog
  alert
Smoking (-s, -s) m dinner jacket (Brit),
  tuxedo (US)
SMS nt abk = Short Message Service ▷ f
  (Nachricht) text message; **ich schicke dir
  eine ~** I'll text you, I'll send you a text
  (message)
Snowboard (-s, -s) nt snowboard;
  Snowboardfahren (-s) nt snowboarding;
  Snowboardfahrer(in) m(f) snowboarder

🔵 SCHLÜSSELWORT

so adv **1** (so sehr) so; **so groß/schön** etc so
  big/nice etc; **so groß/schön wie ...** as
  big/nice as ...; **so viel (wie)** as much as;
  rede nicht so viel don't talk so much; **so
  weit sein** to be ready; **so weit wie** od **als
  möglich** as far as possible; **ich bin so weit
  zufrieden** by and large I'm quite satisfied;
  so wenig (wie) as little (as); **das hat ihn
  so geärgert, dass ...** that annoyed him so
  much that ...; **so einer wie ich** somebody
  like me; **na so was!** well, well!
  2 (auf diese Weise) like this; **mach es nicht**

so don't do it like that; **so oder so** in one way or the other; **und so weiter** and so on; **... oder so was** ... or something like that; **das ist gut so** that's fine; **so gennant** so-called **3** (umg: umsonst); **ich habe es so bekommen** I got it for nothing ▷ konj: **so dass; sodass** so that; **so wie es jetzt ist** as things are at the moment ▷ excl: **so?** really?; **so, das wärs** so, that's it then

s. o. abk = **siehe oben** see above

sobald conj as soon as

Socke (-, -n) f sock

Sodbrennen (-s) nt heartburn

Sofa (-s, -s) nt sofa

sofern conj if, provided (that)

soff imperf von **saufen**

sofort adv immediately, at once; **Sofortbildkamera** f instant camera

Softeis nt soft ice-cream

Software (-, -s) f software

sog imperf von **saugen**

sogar adv even; **kalt, ~ sehr kalt** cold, in fact very cold

Sohle (-, -n) f sole

Sohn (-(e)s, Söhne) m son

Soja (-, Sojen) f soya; **Sojasprossen** pl bean sprouts pl

solang(e) conj as long as

Solarium nt solarium

Solarzelle f solar cell

solche(r, s) pron such; **eine ~ Frau, solch eine Frau** such a woman, a woman like that; **~ Sachen** things like that, such things; **ich habe ~ Kopfschmerzen** I've got such a headache; **ich habe ~n Hunger** I'm so hungry

Soldat(in) (-en, -en) m(f) soldier

solidarisch adj showing solidarity; **sich ~ erklären mit** to declare one's solidarity with

solid(e) adj solid; (Leben, Mensch) respectable

Soll (-(s), -(s)) nt (Fin) debit; (Arbeitsmenge) quota, target

○ SCHLÜSSELWORT

sollen (pt **sollte**, pp **gesollt** od (als Hilfsverb) **sollen**) Hilfsverb **1** (Pflicht, Befehl) to be

supposed to; **du hättest nicht gehen sollen** you shouldn't have gone, you oughtn't to have gone, **soll ich?** shall I?; **soll ich dir helfen?** shall I help you?; **sag ihm, er soll warten** tell him he's to wait; **was soll ich machen?** what should I do?

2 (Vermutung): **sie soll verheiratet sein** she's said to be married; **was soll das heißen?** what's that supposed to mean?; **man sollte glauben, dass ...** you would think that ...; **sollte das passieren, ...** if that should happen ...

▷ vt, vi: **was soll das?** what's all this?; **das sollst du nicht** you shouldn't do that; **was solls?** what the hell!

Solo (-s, -) nt solo

Sommer (-s, -) m summer; **Sommerfahrplan** m summer timetable; **Sommerferien** pl summer holidays pl (Brit) (o vacation sing (US)); **sommerlich** adj summery; (Sommer-) summer; **Sommerreifen** m normal tyre; **Sommersprossen** pl freckles pl; **Sommerzeit** f summertime; (Uhrzeit) daylight saving time

Sonderangebot nt special offer; **sonderbar** adj strange, odd; **Sondermarke** f special stamp; **Sondermaschine** f special plane; **Sondermüll** m hazardous waste

sondern conj but; **nicht nur ..., ~ auch** not only ..., but also

Sonderpreis m special price; **Sonderschule** f special school; **Sonderzeichen** nt (Inform) special character; **Sonderzug** m special train

Song (-s, -s) m song

Sonnabend m Saturday; siehe auch **Mittwoch**; **sonnabends** adv on Saturdays; **~ morgens** on Saturday mornings; siehe auch **mittwochs**

Sonne (-, -n) f sun; **sonnen** vr **sich ~** to sunbathe; **Sonnenallergie** f sun allergy; **Sonnenaufgang** m sunrise; **Sonnenblume** f sunflower; **Sonnenblumenkern** m sunflower seed; **Sonnenbrand** m sunburn; **Sonnenbrille** f sunglasses pl, shades pl; **Sonnencreme** f sun cream; **Sonnendach** nt (an Haus) awning; (Auto) sunroof; **Sonnendeck** nt sun deck; **Sonnenmilch** f suntan lotion;

S

Sonnenöl *nt* suntan oil; **Sonnenschein** *m* sunshine; **Sonnenschirm** *m* parasol, sunshade; **Sonnenschutzcreme** *f* sunscreen; **Sonnenstich** *m* sunstroke; **Sonnenstudio** *nt* solarium; **Sonnenuhr** *f* sundial; **Sonnenuntergang** *m* sunset; **sonnig** *adj* sunny

Sonntag *m* Sunday; *siehe auch* **Mittwoch**; **sonntags** *adv* on Sundays; *siehe auch* **mittwochs**

sonst *adv, conj* (*außerdem*) else; (*andernfalls*) otherwise, (or) else; (*mit Pron, in Fragen*) else; (*normalerweise*) normally, usually; **~ noch etwas?** anything else?; **~ nichts** nothing else

sooft *conj* whenever

Sopran (*-s, -e*) *m* soprano

Sorge (*-, -n*) *f* worry; (*Fürsorge*) care; **sich** (*dat*) **um jdn ~n machen** to be worried about sb; **sorgen** *vi* **für jdn ~** to look after sb; **für etw ~** to take care of sth, to see to sth ▷ *vr* **sich ~** to worry (*um* about); **sorgfältig** *adj* careful

sortieren *vt* to sort (out)

Sortiment *nt* assortment

sosehr *conj* however much

Soße (*-, -n*) *f* sauce; (*zu Braten*) gravy

Soundkarte *f* (*Inform*) sound card

Souvenir (*-s, -s*) *nt* souvenir

soviel *conj* as far as

soweit *conj* as far as

sowie *conj* (*wie auch*) as well as; (*sobald*) as soon as

sowohl *conj* **~ ... als** (*o* **wie**) **auch** both ... and

sozial *adj* social; **Sozialhilfe** *f* income support (*Brit*), welfare (aid) (*US*); **Sozialismus** *m* socialism; **Sozialversicherung** *f* social security; **Sozialwohnung** *f* council flat (*Brit*), state-subsidized apartment (*US*)

Soziologie *f* sociology

sozusagen *adv* so to speak

Spachtel (*-s, -*) *m* spatula

Spag(h)etti *pl* spaghetti *sing*

Spalte (*-, -n*) *f* crack; (*Gletscher*) crevasse; (*in Text*) column

spalten *vt* to split ▷ *vr* **sich ~** to split

Spange (*-, -n*) *f* clasp; (*Haarspange*) hair slide (*Brit*), barrette (*US*)

Spanien (*-s*) *nt* Spain; **Spanier(in)** (*-s, -*) *m(f)* Spaniard; **spanisch** *adj* Spanish; **Spanisch** *nt* Spanish

spann *imperf von* **spinnen**

spannen *vt* (*straffen*) to tighten; (*befestigen*) to brace ▷ *vi* to be tight

spannend *adj* exciting, gripping; **Spannung** *f* tension; (*Elek*) voltage; (*fig*) suspense

Sparbuch *nt* savings book; (*Konto*) savings account; **sparen** *vt, vi* to save

Spargel (*-s, -*) *m* asparagus; **Spargelsuppe** *f* asparagus soup

Sparkasse *f* savings bank; **Sparkonto** *f* savings account

spärlich *adj* meagre; (*Bekleidung*) scanty

sparsam *adj* economical; **Sparschwein** *nt* piggy bank

Spaß (*-es, Späße*) *m* joke; (*Freude*) fun; **es macht mir ~** I enjoy it, it's (great) fun; **viel ~!** have fun

spät *adj, adv* late; **zu ~ kommen** to be late

Spaten (*-s, -*) *m* spade

später *adj, adv* later; **spätestens** *adv* at the latest; **Spätlese** *f* late vintage (wine); **Spätvorstellung** *f* late-night performance

Spatz (*-en, -en*) *m* sparrow

spazieren *vi* to stroll, to walk; **~ gehen** to go for a walk; **Spaziergang** *m* walk

Specht (*-(e)s, -e*) *m* woodpecker

Speck (*-(e)s, -e*) *m* bacon fat; (*durchwachsen*) bacon

Spedition *f* (*für Umzug*) removal firm

Speiche (*-, -n*) *f* spoke

Speichel (*-s*) *m* saliva

Speicher (*-s, -*) *m* storehouse; (*Dachboden*) attic; (*Inform*) memory; **speichern** *vt* (*Inform*) to store; (*sichern*) to save

Speise (*-, -n*) *f* food; (*Gericht*) dish; **Speisekarte** *f* menu; **Speiseröhre** *f* gullet, oesophagus; **Speisesaal** *m* dining hall; **Speisewagen** *m* dining car

Spende (*-, -n*) *f* donation; **spenden** *vt* to donate, to give

spendieren *vt* **jdm etw ~** to treat sb to sth

Sperre (*-, -n*) *f* barrier; (*Verbot*) ban; **sperren** *vt* to block; (*Sport*) to suspend; (*verbieten*) to ban

Sperrgepäck *m* bulky luggage; **Sperrmüll** *m* bulky refuse; **Sperrstunde** *f* closing time; **Sperrung** *f* closing

Spesen *pl* expenses *pl*

spezialisieren *vr* **sich ~** to specialize (*auf*

+*akk* in); **Spezialist(in)** *m(f)* specialist; **Spezialität** *f* speciality (*Brit*), specialty (*US*); **speziell** *adj* special ▷ *adv* especially

Spiegel (*-s, -*) *m* mirror; **Spiegelei** *nt* fried egg (sunny-side up (*US*)); **spiegelglatt** *adj* very slippery; **Spiegelreflexkamera** *f* reflex camera

Spiel (*-(e)s, -e*) *nt* game; (*Tätigkeit*) play(ing); (*Karten*) pack, deck; (*Tech*) (free) play; **Spielautomat** *m* (*ohne Geldgewinn*) gaming machine; (*mit Geldgewinn*) slot machine; **spielen** *vt, vi* to play; (*um Geld*) to gamble; (*Theat*) to perform, to act; **Klavier ~** to play the piano; **spielend** *adv* easily; **Spieler(in)** (*-s, -*) *m(f)* player; (*um Geld*) gambler; **Spielfeld** *nt* (*für Fußball, Hockey*) field; (*für Basketball*) court; **Spielfilm** *m* feature film; **Spielkasino** *nt* casino; **Spielplatz** *m* playground; **Spielraum** *m* room to manoeuvre; **Spielregel** *f* rule; **sich an die ~n halten** to stick to the rules; **Spielsachen** *pl* toys *pl*; **Spielverderber(in)** (*-s, -*) *m(f)* spoilsport; **Spielzeug** *nt* toys *pl*; (*einzelnes*) toy

Spieß (*-es, -e*) *m* spear; (*Bratspieß*) spit; **Spießer(in)** (*-s, -*) *m(f)* square, stuffy type; **spießig** *adj* square, uncool

Spikes *pl* (*Sport*) spikes *pl*; (*Auto*) studs *pl*

Spinat (*-(e)s, -e*) *m* spinach

Spinne (*-, -n*) *f* spider; **spinnen** (*spann, gesponnen*) *vt, vi* to spin; (*fam: Unsinn reden*) to talk rubbish; (*verrückt sein*) to be crazy; **du spinnst!** you must be mad; **Spinnwebe** (*-, -n*) *f* cobweb

Spion(in) (*-s, -e*) *m(f)* spy; **spionieren** *vi* to spy; (*fig*) to snoop around

Spirale (*-, -n*) *f* spiral; (*Med*) coil

Spirituosen *pl* spirits *pl*, liquor *sing* (*US*)

Spiritus (*-, -se*) *m* spirit

spitz *adj* (*Nase, Kinn*) pointed; (*Bleistift, Messer*) sharp; (*Winkel*) acute; **Spitze** (*-, -n*) *f* point; (*von Finger, Nase*) tip; (*Bemerkung*) taunt, dig; (*erster Platz*) lead; (*Gewebe*) lace; **Spitzengeschwindigkeit** *f* top speed; **Spitzer** (*-s, -*) *m* pencil sharpener; **Spitzname** *m* nickname

Spliss (*-*) *m* split ends *pl*

sponsern *vt* to sponsor; **Sponsor(in)** (*-s, -en*) *m(f)* sponsor

spontan *adj* spontaneous

Sport (*-(e)s, -e*) *m* sport; **~ treiben** to do sport; **Sportanlage** *f* sports grounds *pl*; **Sportart** *f* sport; **Sportbekleidung** *f* sportswear; **Sportgeschäft** *nt* sports shop; **Sporthalle** *f* gymnasium, gym; **Sportlehrer(in)** (*-s, -*) *m(f)* sports instructor; (*Schule*) PE teacher; **Sportler(in)** (*-s, -*) *m(f)* sportsman/ -woman; **sportlich** *adj* sporting; (*Mensch*) sporty; **Sportplatz** *m* playing field; **Sporttauchen** *nt* (skin-)diving; (*mit Gerät*) scuba-diving; **Sportverein** *m* sports club; **Sportwagen** *m* sports car

sprach *imperf von* **sprechen**

Sprache (*-, -n*) *f* language; (*Sprechen*) speech; **Sprachenschule** *f* language school; **Sprachführer** *m* phrasebook; **Sprachkenntnisse** *pl* knowledge *sing* of languages; **gute englische ~ haben** to have a good knowledge of English; **Sprachkurs** *m* language course; **Sprachunterricht** *m* language teaching

sprang *imperf von* **springen**

Spray (*-s, -s*) *m o nt* spray

Sprechanlage *f* intercom; **sprechen** (*sprach, gesprochen*) *vt, vi* to speak (*jdn, mit jdm* to sb); (*sich unterhalten*) to talk (*mit* to, *über, von* about); **~ Sie Deutsch?** do you speak German?; **kann ich bitte mit David ~?** (*am Telefon*) can I speak to David, please?; **Sprecher(in)** *m(f)* speaker; (*Ansager*) announcer; **Sprechstunde** *f* consultation; (*Arzt*) surgery hours *pl*; (*Anwalt etc*) office hours *pl*; **Sprechzimmer** *nt* consulting room

Sprengstoff *m* explosive

Sprichwort *nt* proverb

Springbrunnen *m* fountain

springen (*sprang, gesprungen*) *vi* to jump; (*Glas*) to crack; (*mit Kopfsprung*) to dive

Sprit (*-(e)s, -e*) *m* (*fam: Benzin*) petrol (*Brit*), gas (*US*)

Spritze (*-, -n*) *f* (*Gegenstand*) syringe; (*Injektion*) injection; (*an Schlauch*) nozzle; **spritzen** *vt* to spray; (*Med*) to inject ▷ *vi* to splash; (*Med*) to give injections

Spruch (*-(e)s, Sprüche*) *m* saying

Sprudel (*-s, -*) *m* sparkling mineral water; (*süßer*) fizzy drink (*Brit*), soda (*US*); **sprudeln** *vi* to bubble

Sprühdose *f* aerosol (can); **sprühen** *vt, vi* to spray; (*fig*) to sparkle; **Sprühregen** *m* drizzle

Sprung (*-(e)s, Sprünge*) *m* jump; (*Riss*) crack; **Sprungbrett** *nt* springboard;

S

Sprungschanze f ski jump; **Sprungturm** m diving platforms pl

Spucke (-) f spit; **spucken** vt, vi to spit; (fam: sich erbrechen) to vomit; **Spucktüte** f sick bag

spuken vi (Geist) to walk; **hier spukt es** this place is haunted

Spülbecken nt sink

Spule (-, -n) f spool; (Elek) coil

Spüle (-, -n) f sink; **spülen** vt, vi to rinse; (Geschirr) to wash up; (Toilette) to flush; **Spülmaschine** f dishwasher; **Spülmittel** nt washing-up liquid (Brit), dishwashing liquid (US); **Spültuch** nt dishcloth; **Spülung** f (von WC) flush

Spur (-, -en) f trace; (Fußspur, Radspur) track; (Fährte) trail; (Fahrspur) lane; **die ~ wechseln** to change lanes pl

spüren vt to feel; (merken) to notice; **Spürhund** m sniffer dog

Squash (-) nt squash; **Squashschläger** m squash racket

Sri Lanka (-s) nt Sri Lanka

Staat (-(e)s, -en) m state; **staatlich** adj state(-); (vom Staat betrieben) state-run; **Staatsangehörigkeit** f nationality; **Staatsanwalt** m, **-anwältin** f prosecuting counsel (Brit), district attorney (US); **Staatsbürger(in)** m(f) citizen; **Staatsbürgerschaft** f nationality; **doppelte ~** dual nationality; **Staatsexamen** nt final exam taken by trainee teachers, medical and law students

Stab (-(e)s, Stäbe) m rod; (Gitter) bar; **Stäbchen** nt (Essstäbchen) chopstick; **Stabhochsprung** m pole vault

stabil adj stable; (Möbel) sturdy

stach imperf von stechen

Stachel (-s, -n) m spike; (von Tier) spine; (von Insekten) sting; **Stachelbeere** f gooseberry; **Stacheldraht** m barbed wire; **stachelig** adj prickly

Stadion (-s, Stadien) nt stadium

Stadt (-, Städte) f town; (groß) city; **in der ~** in town; **Stadtautobahn** f urban motorway (Brit) (o expressway (US)); **Stadtbummel** (-s, -) m **einen ~ machen** to go round town; **Städtepartnerschaft** f twinning; **Stadtführer** m (Heft) city guide; **Stadtführung** f city sightseeing tour; **Stadthalle** f municipal hall; **städtisch** adj municipal; **Stadtmauer** f city wall(s); **Stadtmitte** f town/city

centre, downtown (US); **Stadtplan** m (street) map; **Stadtrand** m outskirts pl; **Stadtrundfahrt** f city tour; **Stadtteil** m, **Stadtviertel** nt district, part of town; **Stadtzentrum** nt town/city centre, downtown (US)

stahl imperf von stehlen

Stahl (-(e)s, Stähle) m steel

Stall (-(e)s, Ställe) m stable; (Kaninchen) hutch; (Schweine) pigsty; (Hühner) henhouse

Stamm (-(e)s, Stämme) m (Baum) trunk; (von Menschen) tribe; **stammen** vi **~ aus** to come from; **Stammgast** m regular (guest); **Stammkunde** m, **Stammkundin** f regular (customer); **Stammtisch** m table reserved for regulars

stampfen vt, vi to stamp; (mit Werkzeug) to pound; (stapfen) to tramp

stand imperf von stehen

Stand (-(e)s, Stände) m (Wasser, Benzin) level; (Stehen) standing position; (Zustand) state; (Spielstand) score; (auf Messe etc) stand; (Klasse) class; **im ~e sein** to be in a position; (fähig) to be able

Standby-Betrieb m stand-by; **Standby-Ticket** nt stand-by ticket

Ständer (-s, -) m (Gestell) stand; (fam: Erektion) hard-on

Standesamt nt registry office

ständig adj permanent; (ununterbrochen) constant, continual

Standlicht nt sidelights pl (Brit), parking lights pl (US); **Standort** m position; **Standpunkt** m standpoint; **Standspur** f (Auto) hard shoulder (Brit), shoulder (US)

Stange (-, -n) f stick; (Stab) pole; (Metall) bar; (Zigaretten) carton; **Stangenbohne** f runner (Brit) (o string (US)) bean; **Stangenbrot** nt French stick; **Stangensellerie** m celery

stank imperf von stinken

Stapel (-s, -) m pile

Star (-(e)s, -e) m (Vogel) starling; (Med) cataract ▷ (-s, -s) m (in Film etc) star

starb imperf von sterben

stark adj strong; (heftig, groß) heavy; (Maßangabe) thick; **Stärke** (-, -n) f strength; (Dicke) thickness; (Wäschestärke, Speisestärke) starch; **stärken** vt to strengthen; (Wäsche) to starch; **Starkstrom** m high-voltage current;

Stärkung f strengthening; (*Essen*) refreshment

starr adj stiff; (*unnachgiebig*) rigid; (*Blick*) staring

starren vi to stare

Start (-(e)s, -e) m start; (*Aviat*) takeoff; **Startautomatik** f automatic choke; **Startbahn** f runway; **starten** vt, vi to start; (*Aviat*) to take off; **Starthilfekabel** nt jump leads pl (*Brit*), jumper cables pl (*US*); **Startmenü** nt (*Inform*) start menu

Station f (*Haltestelle*) stop; (*Bahnhof*) station; (*im Krankenhaus*) ward; **stationär** adj stationary; **~e Behandlung** in-patient treatment; **jdn ~ behandeln** to treat sb as an in-patient

Statistik f statistics pl

Stativ nt tripod

statt conj, prep +gen o dat instead of; **~ zu arbeiten** instead of working

statt|finden irr vi to take place

Statue (-, -n) f statue

Statusleiste f, **Statuszeile** f (*Inform*) status bar

Stau (-(e)s, -e) m (*im Verkehr*) (traffic) jam; **im ~ stehen** to be stuck in a traffic jam

Staub (-(e)s) m dust; **~ wischen** to dust; **staubig** adj dusty; **staubsaugen** vt, vi to vacuum, to hoover (*Brit*); **Staubsauger** m vacuum cleaner, hoover® (*Brit*); **Staubtuch** nt duster

Staudamm m dam

staunen vi to be astonished (*über +akk* at)

Stausee m reservoir; **Stauung** f (*von Wasser*) damming-up; (*von Blut, Verkehr*) congestion; **Stauwarnung** f traffic report

Std. abk = **Stunde** h

Steak (-s, -s) nt steak

stechen (stach, gestochen) vt, vi (*mit Nadel etc*) to prick; (*mit Messer*) to stab; (*mit Finger*) to poke; (*Biene*) to sting; (*Mücke*) to bite; (*Sonne*) to burn; (*Kartenspiel*) to trump; **Stechen** (-s, -) nt sharp pain, stabbing pain; **Stechmücke** f mosquito

Steckdose f socket; **stecken** vt to put; (*Nadel*) to stick; (*beim Nähen*) to pin ▷ vi (*festsitzen*) to be stuck; (*Nadeln*) (sticking); **der Schlüssel steckt** the key is in the door; **Stecker** (-s, -) m plug; **Stecknadel** f pin; **Steckrübe** f swede (*Brit*), rutabaga (*US*)

Steg (-s, -e) m bridge

stehen (stand, gestanden) vi to stand (*zu by*); (*sich befinden*) to be; (*stillstehen*) to have stopped; **was steht im Brief?** what does it say in the letter?; **jdm** (**gut**) **~** to suit sb; **~ bleiben** (*Uhr*) to stop; **~ lassen** to leave ▷ vi impers **wie steht's?** (*Sport*) what's the score?; **Stehlampe** f standard lamp (*Brit*), floor lamp (*US*)

stehlen (stahl, gestohlen) vt to steal

Stehplatz m (*im Konzert etc*) standing ticket

Steiermark (-) f Styria

steif adj stiff

steigen (stieg, gestiegen) vi (*Preise, Temperatur*) to rise; (*klettern*) to climb; **~ in/auf** (*+akk*) to get in/on

steigern vt to increase ▷ vr **sich ~** to increase

Steigung f incline, gradient

steil adj steep; **Steilhang** m steep slope; **Steilküste** f steep coast

Stein (-(e)s, -e) m stone; **Steinbock** m (*Zool*) ibex; (*Astr*) Capricorn; **Steinbutt** (-s, -e) m turbot; **steinig** adj stony; **Steinschlag** m falling rocks pl

Stelle (-, -n) f place, spot; (*Arbeit*) post, job; (*Amt*) office; **ich an deiner ~** if I were you; **auf der ~** straightaway; **stellen** vt to put; (*Uhr etc*) to set (*auf +akk* to); (*zur Verfügung stellen*) to provide ▷ vr **sich ~** (*bei Polizei*) to give oneself up; **sich schlafend ~** to pretend to be asleep; **Stellenangebot** nt job offer, vacancy; **stellenweise** adv in places; **Stellenwert** m (*fig*) status; **einen hohen ~ haben** to play an important role; **Stellplatz** m parking space; **Stellung** f position; **zu etw ~ nehmen** to comment on sth; **Stellvertreter(in)** m(f) representative; (*amtlich*) deputy; (*von Arzt*) locum (*Brit*), locum tenens (*US*)

Stempel (-s, -) m stamp; **stempeln** vt to stamp; (*Briefmarke*) to cancel

sterben (starb, gestorben) vi to die

Stereoanlage f stereo (system)

steril adj sterile; **sterilisieren** vt to sterilize

Stern (-(e)s, -e) m star; **ein Hotel mit vier ~en** a four-star hotel; **Sternbild** nt constellation; (*Sternzeichen*) star sign, sign of the zodiac; **Sternfrucht** f star fruit; **Sternschnuppe** (-, -n) f shooting star; **Sternwarte** (-e, -n) f observatory; **Sternzeichen** nt star sign, sign of the zodiac; **welches ~ bist du?** what's your star sign?

stets adv always

Steuer (-s, -) nt (Auto) steering wheel ▷ (-, -n) f tax; **Steuerberater(in)** m(f) tax adviser; **Steuerbord** nt starboard; **Steuererklärung** f tax declaration; **steuerfrei** adj tax-free; (Waren) duty-free; **Steuerknüppel** m control column; (Aviat, Inform) joystick; **steuern** vt, vi to steer; (Flugzeug) to pilot; (Entwicklung, Tonstärke) (Inform) to control; **steuerpflichtig** adj taxable; **Steuerung** f (Auto) steering; (Vorrichtung) controls pl; (Aviat) piloting; (fig) control; **Steuerungstaste** f (Inform) control key

Stich (-(e)s, -e) m (von Insekt) sting; (von Mücke) bite; (durch Messer) stab; (beim Nähen) stitch; (Färbung) tinge; (Kartenspiel) trick; (Kunst) engraving; **Stichprobe** f spot check

sticken vt, vi to embroider

Sticker (-s, -) m sticker

Stickerei f embroidery

stickig adj stuffy, close

Stiefbruder m stepbrother

Stiefel (-s, -) m boot

Stiefmutter f stepmother

Stiefmütterchen nt pansy

Stiefschwester f stepsister; **Stiefsohn** m stepson; **Stieftochter** f stepdaughter; **Stiefvater** m stepfather

stieg imperf von **steigen**

Stiege (-, -n) f steps pl

Stiel (-(e)s, -e) m handle; (Bot) stalk; **ein Eis am ~** an ice lolly (Brit), a Popsicle® (US)

Stier (-(e)s, -e) m (Zool) bull; (Astr) Taurus; **Stierkampf** m bullfight; **Stierkämpfer(in)** m(f) bullfighter

stieß imperf von **stoßen**

Stift (-(e)s, -e) m (aus Holz) peg; (Nagel) tack; (zum Schreiben) pen; (Farbstift) crayon; (Bleistift) pencil

Stil (-s, -e) m style

still adj quiet; (unbewegt) still

stillen vt (Säugling) to breast-feed

still|halten irr vi to keep still; **Stillleben** nt still life; **still|stehen** irr vi to stand still

Stimme (-, -n) f voice; (bei Wahl) vote

stimmen vi to be right; **stimmt!** that's right; **hier stimmt was nicht** there's something wrong here; **stimmt so!** (beim Bezahlen) keep the change

Stimmung f mood; (Atmosphäre) atmosphere

Stinkefinger m (fam) **jdm den ~ zeigen** to give sb the finger (o bird (US))

stinken (stank, gestunken) vi to stink (nach of)

Stipendium nt scholarship; (als Unterstützung) grant

Stirn (-, -en) f forehead; **Stirnhöhle** f sinus

Stock (-(e)s, Stöcke) m stick; (Bot) stock ▷ m (Stockwerke) floor, storey; **Stockbett** nt bunk bed; **Stöckelschuhe** pl high-heels; **Stockwerk** nt floor; **im ersten ~** on the first floor (Brit), on the second floor (US)

Stoff (-(e)s, -e) m (Gewebe) material; (Materie) matter; (von Buch etc) subject (matter); (fam: Rauschgift) stuff

stöhnen vi to groan (vor with)

stolpern vi to stumble, to trip

stolz adj proud

stopp interj hold it; (Moment mal!) hang on a minute; **stoppen** vt, vi to stop; (mit Uhr) to time; **Stoppschild** nt stop sign; **Stoppuhr** f stopwatch

Stöpsel (-s, -) m plug; (für Flaschen) stopper

Storch (-(e)s, Störche) m stork

stören vt to disturb; (behindern) to interfere with; **darf ich dich kurz ~?** can I trouble you for a minute?; **stört es dich, wenn ...?** do you mind if ...?

stornieren vt to cancel; **Stornogebühr** f cancellation fee

Störung f disturbance; (in der Leitung) fault

Stoß (-es, Stöße) m (Schub) push; (Schlag) blow; (mit Fuß) kick; (Haufen) pile; **Stoßdämpfer** (-s, -) m shock absorber

stoßen (stieß, gestoßen) vt (mit Druck) to shove, to push; (mit Schlag) to knock; (mit Fuß) to kick; (anstoßen) to bump; (zerkleinern) to pulverize ▷ vr **sich ~** to bang oneself; **sich ~ an** (+dat) (fig) to take exception to

Stoßstange f (Auto) bumper

stottern vt, vi to stutter

Str. abk von **Straße** St, Rd

Strafe (-, -n) f punishment; (Sport) penalty; (Gefängnisstrafe) sentence; (Geldstrafe) fine; **strafen** vt to punish; **Strafraum** m penalty area; **Strafstoß** m penalty kick; **Straftat** f (criminal) offence; **Strafzettel** m ticket

Strahl (-s, -en) m ray, beam; (*Wasser*) jet;
strahlen vi to radiate; (*fig*) to beam
Strähne (-, -n) f strand; (*weiß, gefärbt*)
streak
Strand (-(e)s, Strände) m beach; **am**
~ on the beach; **Strandcafé** nt beach
café; **Strandkorb** m *wicker beach chair*
with a hood; **Strandpromenade** f
promenade
strapazieren vt (*Material*) to be hard on;
(*Mensch, Kräfte*) to be a strain on
Straße (-, -n) f road; (*in der Stadt*) street;
Straßenarbeiten pl roadworks pl (*Brit*),
road repairs pl (*US*); **Straßenbahn** f tram
(*Brit*), streetcar (*US*); **Straßencafé** nt
pavement café (*Brit*), sidewalk café (*US*);
Straßenfest nt street party;
Straßenglätte f slippery roads pl;
Straßenkarte f road map; **Straßenrand**
m **am** ~ at the roadside; **Straßenschild** nt
street sign; **Straßensperre** f roadblock;
Straßenverhältnisse pl road conditions
pl
Strategie (-, -n) f strategy
Strauch (-(e)s, Sträucher) m bush, shrub;
Strauchtomate f vine-ripened tomato
Strauß (-es, Sträuße) m bunch; (*als
Geschenk*) bouquet ▷ m (*Strauße*) (*Vogel*)
ostrich
Strecke (-, -n) f route; (*Entfernung*)
distance; (*Eisenb*) line
strecken vt to stretch ▷ vr **sich** ~ to
stretch
streckenweise adv (*teilweise*) in parts;
(*zeitweise*) at times
Streich (-(e)s, -e) m trick, prank
streicheln vt to stroke
streichen (strich, gestrichen) vt (*anmalen*)
to paint; (*berühren*) to stroke; (*auftragen*) to
spread; (*durchstreichen*) to delete; (*nicht
genehmigen*) to cancel
Streichholz nt match;
Streichholzschachtel f matchbox;
Streichkäse m cheese spread
Streifen (-s, -) m (*Linie*) stripe; (*Stück*)
strip; (*Film*) film
Streifenwagen m patrol car
Streik (-(e)s, -s) m strike; **streiken** vi to be
on strike
Streit (-(e)s, -e) m argument (*um, wegen*
about, over); **streiten** (stritt, gestritten) vi
to argue (*um, wegen* about, over) ▷ vr **sich**
~ to argue (*um, wegen* about, over)

streng adj (*Blick*) severe; (*Lehrer*) strict;
(*Geruch*) sharp
Stress (-es) m stress; **stressen** vt to
stress (out); **stressig** adj (*fam*) stressful
Stretching (-s) nt (*Sport*) stretching
exercises pl
streuen vt to scatter; **die Straßen** ~ to
grit the roads; (*mit Salz*) to put salt down
on the roads; **Streufahrzeug** nt gritter
lorry (*Brit*), salt truck (*US*)
strich imperf von **streichen**
Strich (-(e)s, -e) m (*Linie*) line; **Stricher** m
(*fam: Strichjunge*) rent boy (*Brit*), boy
prostitute; **Strichkode** (-s, -s) m bar code;
Stricherin f (*fam: Strichmädchen*) hooker;
Strichpunkt m semicolon
Strick (-(e)s, -e) m rope
stricken vt, vi to knit; **Strickjacke** f
cardigan; **Stricknadel** f knitting needle
Stripper(in) m(f) stripper; **Striptease** (-)
m striptease
stritt imperf von **streiten**
Stroh (-(e)s) nt straw; **Strohdach** nt
thatched roof; **Strohhalm** m (*drinking*)
straw; **Strohhut** m straw hat
Strom (-(e)s, Ströme) m river; (*fig*) stream;
(*Elek*) current; **Stromanschluss** m
connection; **Stromausfall** m power
failure
strömen vi to stream, to pour; **Strömung**
f current
Stromverbrauch m power
consumption; **Stromzähler** m electricity
meter
Strophe (-, -n) f verse
Strudel (-s, -) m (*in Fluss*) whirlpool;
(*Gebäck*) strudel
Struktur f structure; (*von Material*)
texture
Strumpf (-(e)s, Strümpfe) m (*Damenstrumpf*)
stocking; (*Socke*) sock; **Strumpfhose** f
(pair of) tights pl (*Brit*), pantyhose (*US*)
Stück (-(e)s, -e) nt piece; (*von Zucker*) lump;
(*etwas*) bit; (*Zucker*) lump; (*Theat*) play; **ein**
~ **Käse** a piece of cheese
Student(in) m(f) student;
Studentenausweis m student card;
Studentenwohnheim nt hall of
residence (*Brit*), dormitory (*US*);
Studienabschluss m qualification (*at the
end of a course of higher education*);
Studienfahrt f study trip; **Studienplatz**
m university/college place; **studieren** vt,

S

vi to study; **Studium** *nt* studies *pl*;
während seines ~s while he is/was
studying

Stufe (-, -n) *f* step; (*Entwicklungsstufe*)
stage

Stuhl (-(e)s, Stühle) *m* chair

stumm *adj* silent; (*Med*) dumb

stumpf *adj* blunt; (*teilnahmslos, glanzlos*)
dull; **stumpfsinnig** *adj* dull

Stunde (-, -n) *f* hour; (*Unterricht*) lesson;
eine halbe ~ half an hour;
Stundenkilometer *m* **80 ~** 80 kilometres
an hour; **stundenlang** *adv* for hours;
Stundenlohn *m* hourly wage;
Stundenplan *m* timetable; **stündlich** *adj*
hourly

Stuntman (-s, Stuntmen) *m* stuntman;
Stuntwoman (-, Stuntwomen) *f*
stuntwoman

stur *adj* stubborn; (*stärker*) pigheaded

Sturm (-(e)s, Stürme) *m* storm; **stürmen** *vi*
(*Wind*) to blow hard; (*rennen*) to storm;
Stürmer(in) *m(f)* striker, forward;
Sturmflut *f* storm tide; **stürmisch** *adj*
stormy; (*fig*) tempestuous; (*Zeit*)
turbulent; (*Liebhaber*) passionate; (*Beifall*,
Begrüßung) tumultuous; **Sturmwarnung** *f*
gale warning

Sturz (-es, Stürze) *m* fall; (*Pol*) overthrow;
stürzen *vt* (*werfen*) to hurl; (*Pol*) to
overthrow; (*umkehren*) to overturn ▷ *vi* to
fall; (*rennen*) to dash; **Sturzhelm** *m* crash
helmet

Stute (-, -n) *f* mare

Stütze (-, -n) *f* support; (*Hilfe*) help; (*fam*:
Arbeitslosenunterstützung) dole (*Brit*),
welfare (*US*)

stützen *vt* to support; (*Ellbogen*) to prop

stutzig *adj* perplexed, puzzled;
(*misstrauisch*) suspicious

Styropor® (-s) *nt* polystyrene (*Brit*),
styrofoam (*US*)

subjektiv *adj* subjective

Substanz (-, -en) *f* substance

subtrahieren *vt* to subtract

Subvention *f* subsidy; **subventionieren**
vt to subsidize

Suche *f* search (*nach* for); **auf der ~ nach
etw sein** to be looking for sth; **suchen** *vt*
to look for; (*Inform*) to search ▷ *vi* to look,
to search (*nach* for); **Suchmaschine** *f*
(*Inform*) search engine

Sucht (-, Süchte) *f* mania; (*Med*) addiction;

süchtig *adj* addicted; **Süchtige(r)** *mf*
addict

Süd south; **Südafrika** *nt* South Africa;
Südamerika *nt* South America;
Süddeutschland *nt* Southern Germany;
Süden (-s) *m* south; **im ~ Deutschlands**
in the south of Germany; **Südeuropa** *nt*
Southern Europe; **Südkorea** (-s) *nt* South
Korea; **südlich** *adj* southern; (*Kurs,
Richtung*) southerly; **Verkehr in ~er
Richtung** southbound traffic;
Südost(en) *m* southeast; **Südpol** *m*
South Pole; **Südstaaten** *pl* (*der USA*) the
Southern States *pl*, the South *sing*;
südwärts *adv* south, southwards;
Südwest(en) *m* southwest; **Südwind** *m*
south wind

Sultanine *f* sultana

Sülze (-, -n) *f* jellied meat

Summe (-, -n) *f* sum; (*Gesamtsumme*) total

summen *vi, vt* to hum; (*Insekt*) to buzz

Sumpf (-(e)s, Sümpfe) *m* marsh;
(*subtropischer*) swamp; **sumpfig** *adj*
marshy

Sünde (-, -n) *f* sin

super *adj* (*fam*) super, great; **Super** (-s) *nt*
(*Benzin*) four star (petrol) (*Brit*), premium
(*US*); **Supermarkt** *m* supermarket

Suppe (-, -n) *f* soup; **Suppengrün** *nt*
*bunch of herbs and vegetables for flavouring
soup*; **Suppenlöffel** *m* soup spoon;
Suppenschüssel *f* soup tureen;
Suppentasse *f* soup cup; **Suppenteller**
m soup plate; **Suppenwürfel** *m* stock
cube

Surfbrett *nt* surfboard; **surfen** *vi* to surf;
im Internet ~ to surf the Internet;
Surfer(in) (-s, -) *m(f)* surfer

Surrealismus *m* surrealism

süß *adj* sweet; **süßen** *vt* to sweeten;
Süßigkeit *f* (*Bonbon etc*) sweet (*Brit*),
candy (*US*); **Süßkartoffel** *f* sweet potato,
yam (*US*); **süßsauer** *adj* sweet-and-sour;
Süßspeise *f* dessert; **Süßstoff** *m*
sweetener; **Süßwasser** *nt* fresh water

Sweatshirt (-s, -s) *nt* sweatshirt

Swimmingpool (-s, -s) *m* (swimming)
pool

Sylvester *nt* siehe **Silvester**

Symbol (-s, -e) *nt* symbol; **Symbolleiste** *f*
(*Inform*) toolbar

Symmetrie (-, -n) *f* symmetry;
symmetrisch *adj* symmetrical

sympathisch *adj* nice; **jdn ~ finden** to like sb
Symphonie (-, -n) *f* symphony
Symptom (-s, -e) *nt* symptom (*für* of)
Synagoge (-, -n) *f* synagogue
synchronisiert *adj* (*Film*) dubbed; **Synchronstimme** *f* dubbing voice
Synthesizer (-s, -) *m* (*Mus*) synthesizer
Synthetik (-, -en) *f* synthetic (fibre); **synthetisch** *adj* synthetic
Syrien (-s) *nt* Syria
System (-s, -e) *nt* system; **systematisch** *adj* systematic; **Systemsteuerung** *f* (*Inform*) control panel
Szene (-, -n) *f* scene

S

Tabak *(-s, -e) m* tobacco; **Tabakladen** *m* tobacconist's

Tabelle *f* table

Tablett *(-s, -s) nt* tray

Tablette *f* tablet, pill

Tabulator *m* tabulator, tab

Tacho(meter) *(-s, -) m (Auto)* speedometer

Tafel *(-, -n) f (a. Math)* table; *(Anschlagtafel)* board; *(Wandtafel)* blackboard; *(Schiefer~)* slate; *(Gedenktafel)* plaque; **eine ~ Schokolade** a bar of chocolate; **Tafelwasser** *nt* table water; **Tafelwein** *m* table wine

Tag *(-(e)s, -e) m* day; *(Tageslicht)* daylight; **guten ~!** good morning/afternoon; **am ~** during the day; **sie hat ihre ~e** she's got her period; **eines ~es** one day; **~ der Arbeit** Labour Day; **Tagebuch** *nt* diary; **tagelang** *adj* for days (on end); **Tagesanbruch** *m* daybreak; **Tagesausflug** *m* day trip; **Tagescreme** *f* day cream; **Tagesdecke** *f* bedspread; **Tagesgericht** *nt* dish of the day; **Tageskarte** *f (Fahrkarte)* day ticket; **die ~** *(Speisekarte)* today's menu; **Tageslicht** *nt* daylight; **Tagesmutter** *f* child minder;

Tagesordnung *f* agenda; **Tagestour** *f* day trip; **Tageszeitung** *f* daily newspaper; **täglich** *adj, adv* daily; **tags(über)** *adv* during the day; **Tagung** *f* conference

Tai Chi *(-) nt* tai chi

Taille *(-, -n) f* waist; **tailliert** *adj* fitted

Taiwan *(-s) nt* Taiwan

Takt *(-(e)s, -e) m (Taktgefühl)* tact; *(Mus)* time

Taktik *(-, -en) f* tactics *pl*

taktlos *adj* tactless; **taktvoll** *adj* tactful

Tal *(-(e)s, Täler) nt* valley

Talent *(-(e)s, -e) nt* talent; **talentiert** *adj* talented

Talkmaster(in) *(-s, -) m(f)* talk-show host; **Talkshow** *(-, -s) f* talkshow

Tampon *(-s, -s) m* tampon

Tandem *(-s, -s) nt* tandem

Tang *(-s, -e) m* seaweed

Tank *(-s, -s) m* tank; **Tankanzeige** *f* fuel gauge; **Tankdeckel** *m* fuel cap; **tanken** *vi* to get some petrol (*Brit*) (*o* gas (*US*)); *(Aviat)* to refuel; **Tanker** *(-s, -) m* (oil) tanker; **Tankstelle** *f* petrol station (*Brit*), gas station (*US*); **Tankwart(in)** *(-s, -e) m(f)* petrol pump attendant (*Brit*), gas station attendant (*US*)

Tanne *(-, -n) f* fir; **Tannenzapfen** *m* fir cone

Tansania *(-s) nt* Tanzania

Tante *(-, -n) f* aunt; **Tante-Emma-Laden** *m* corner shop (*Brit*), grocery store (*US*)

Tanz *(-es, Tänze) m* dance; **tanzen** *vt, vi* to dance; **Tänzer(in)** *m(f)* dancer; **Tanzfläche** *f* dance floor; **Tanzkurs** *m* dancing course; **Tanzlehrer(in)** *m(f)* dancing instructor; **Tanzstunde** *f* dancing lesson

Tapete *(-, -n) f* wallpaper; **tapezieren** *vt, vi* to wallpaper

Tarantel *(-, -n) f* tarantula

Tarif *(-s, -e) m* tariff, (scale of) fares/charges *pl*

Tasche *(-, -n) f* bag; *(Hosentasche)* pocket; *(Handtasche)* bag (*Brit*), purse (*US*); **Taschen-** *in zW* pocket; **Taschenbuch** *nt* paperback; **Taschendieb(in)** *m(f)* pickpocket; **Taschengeld** *nt* pocket money; **Taschenlampe** *f* torch (*Brit*), flashlight (*US*); **Taschenmesser** *nt* penknife; **Taschenrechner** *m* pocket calculator; **Taschentuch** *nt* handkerchief

Tasse (-, -n) f cup; **eine ~ Kaffee** a cup of coffee

Tastatur f keyboard; **Taste** (-, -n) f button; (von Klavier, Computer) key; **Tastenkombination** f (Inform) shortcut; **Tastentelefon** nt push-button telephone

tat imperf von **tun**

Tat (-, -en) f action

Tatar (-s, -s) nt raw minced beef

Täter(in) (-s, -) m(f) culprit

tätig adj active; **in einer Firma ~ sein** to work for a firm; **Tätigkeit** f activity; (Beruf) occupation

tätowieren vt to tattoo; **Tätowierung** f tattoo (an +dat on)

Tatsache f fact; **tatsächlich** adj actual ▷ adv really

Tau (-(e)s, -e) nt (Seil) rope ▷ (-(e)s) m dew

taub adj deaf; (Füße etc) numb (vor Kälte with cold)

Taube (-, -n) f pigeon; (Turtel~, fig: Friedenssymbol) dove

taubstumm adj deaf-and-dumb; **Taubstumme(r)** mf deaf-mute

tauchen vt to dip ▷ vi to dive; (Naut) to submerge; **Tauchen** (-s) nt diving; **Taucher(in)** (-s, -) m(f) diver; **Taucheranzug** m diving (o wet) suit; **Taucherbrille** f diving goggles pl; **Tauchermaske** f diving mask; **Tauchkurs** m diving course; **Tauchsieder** (-s, -) m portable immersion coil for heating water

tauen vi impers to thaw

Taufe (-, -n) f baptism; **taufen** vt to baptize; (nennen) to christen

taugen vi to be suitable (für for); **nichts ~** to be no good

Tausch (-(e)s, -e) m exchange; **tauschen** vt to exchange, to swap

täuschen vt to deceive ▷ vi to be deceptive ▷ vr **sich ~** to be wrong; **täuschend** adj deceptive; **Täuschung** f deception; (optisch) illusion

tausend num a thousand; **vier~** four thousand; **~ Dank!** thanks a lot; **tausendmal** adv a thousand times; **tausendste(r, s)** adj thousandth; **Tausendstel** (-s, -) nt (Bruchteil) thousandth

Tauwetter nt thaw

Taxi nt taxi; **Taxifahrer(in)** m(f) taxi driver; **Taxistand** m taxi rank (Brit), taxi stand (US)

Team (-s, -s) nt team; **Teamarbeit** f team work; **teamfähig** adj able to work in a team

Technik f technology; (angewandte) engineering; (Methode) technique; **Techniker(in)** (-s, -) m(f) engineer; (Sport, Mus) technician; **technisch** adj technical

Techno (-s) m (Mus) techno

Teddybär m teddy bear

Tee (-s, -s) m tea; **Teebeutel** m teabag; **Teekanne** f teapot; **Teelöffel** m teaspoon

Teer (-(e)s, -e) m tar

Teesieb nt tea strainer; **Teetasse** f teacup

Teich (-(e)s, -e) m pond

Teig (-(e)s, -e) m dough; **Teigwaren** pl pasta sing

Teil (-(e)s, -e) m part; (Anteil) share; **zum ~** partly ▷ (-(e)s, -e) nt part; (Bestandteil) component; **teilen** vt to divide; (mit jdm) to share (mit with); **20 durch 4 ~** to divide 20 by 4 ▷ vr **sich ~** to divide

Teilkaskoversicherung f third party, fire and theft insurance

teilmöbliert adj partly furnished

Teilnahme (-, -n) f participation (an +dat in); **teil|nehmen** irr vi to take part (an +dat in); **Teilnehmer(in)** (-s, -) m(f) participant

teils adv partly; **teilweise** adv partially, in part; **Teilzeit** f **~ arbeiten** to work part-time

Teint (-s, -s) m complexion

Tel. abk von **Telefon** tel.

Telefon (-s, -e) nt telephone; **Telefonanruf** m, **Telefonat** nt (tele)phone call; **Telefonanschluss** m telephone connection; **Telefonauskunft** f directory enquiries pl (Brit), directory assistance (US); **Telefonbuch** nt telephone directory; **Telefongebühren** pl telephone charges pl; **Telefongespräch** nt telephone conversation; **telefonieren** vi **ich telefoniere gerade (mit ...)** I'm on the phone (to ...); **telefonisch** adj telephone; (Benachrichtigung) by telephone; **Telefonkarte** f phonecard; **Telefonnummer** f (tele)phone number; **Telefonrechnung** f phone bill; **Telefonverbindung** f telephone connection; **Telefonzelle** f phone box (Brit), phone booth; **Telefonzentrale** f switchboard; **über die ~** through the switchboard

Telegramm nt telegram; **Teleobjektiv** nt telephoto lens; **Teleshopping** (-s) nt teleshopping; **Teleskop** (-s, -e) nt telescope

Teller (-s, -) m plate

Tempel (-s, -) m temple

Temperament nt temperament; (Schwung) liveliness; **temperamentvoll** adj lively

Temperatur f temperature; **bei ~en von 30 Grad** at temperatures of 30 degrees; **~ haben** to have a temperature; **~ bei jdm messen** to take sb's temperature

Tempo (-s, -s) nt (Geschwindigkeit) speed; **Tempolimit** (-s, -s) nt speed limit

Tempotaschentuch® nt (Papiertaschentuch) (paper) tissue, ≈ Kleenex®

Tendenz f tendency; (Absicht) intention

Tennis (-) nt tennis; **Tennisball** m tennis ball; **Tennisplatz** m tennis court; **Tennisschläger** m tennis racket; **Tennisspieler(in)** m(f) tennis player; **Tennisturnier** nt tennis tournament

Tenor (-s, Tenöre) m tenor

Teppich (-s, -e) m carpet; **Teppichboden** m (wall-to-wall) carpet

Termin (-s, -e) m (Zeitpunkt) date; (Frist) deadline; (Arzttermin etc) appointment

Terminal (-s, -s) nt (Inform, Aviat) terminal

Terminkalender m diary; **Terminplaner** m (in Buchform) personal organizer, Filofax®; (Taschencomputer) personal digital assistant, PDA

Terpentin (-s, -e) nt turpentine, turps sing

Terrasse (-, -n) f terrace; (hinter einem Haus) patio

Terror (-s) m terror; **Terroranschlag** m terrorist attack; **terrorisieren** vt to terrorize; **Terrorismus** m terrorism; **Terrorist(in)** m(f) terrorist

Tesafilm® m ≈ sellotape® (Brit), ≈ Scotch tape® (US)

Test (-s, -s) m test

Testament nt will; **das Alte/Neue ~** the Old/New Testament

testen vt to test; **Testergebnis** nt test results pl

Tetanus (-) m tetanus; **Tetanusimpfung** f (anti-)tetanus injection

teuer adj expensive, dear (Brit)

Teufel (-s, -) m devil; **was/wo zum ~** what/where the devil; **Teufelskreis** m vicious circle

Text (-(e)s, -e) m text; (Liedertext) words pl, lyrics pl; **Textmarker** (-s, -) m highlighter; **Textverarbeitung** f word processing; **Textverarbeitungsprogramm** nt word processing program

Thailand nt Thailand

Theater (-s, -) nt theatre; (fam) fuss; **ins ~ gehen** to go to the theatre; **Theaterkasse** f box office; **Theaterstück** nt (stage) play; **Theatervorstellung** f (stage) performance

Theke (-, -n) f (Schanktisch) bar; (Ladentisch) counter

Thema (-s, Themen) nt subject, topic; **kein ~!** no problem

Themse (-) f Thames

Theologie f theology

theoretisch adj theoretical; **~ stimmt das** that's right in theory; **Theorie** f theory

Therapeut(in) m(f) therapist; **Therapie** f therapy; **eine ~ machen** to undergo therapy

Thermalbad nt thermal bath; (Ort) thermal spa; **Thermometer** (-s, -) nt thermometer

Thermosflasche® f, **Thermoskanne®** f Thermos® (flask); **Thermostat** (-(e)s, -e) m thermostat

These (-, -n) f theory

Thron (-(e)s, -e) m throne

Thunfisch m tuna

Thüringen (-s) nt Thuringia

Thymian (-s, -e) m thyme

Tick (-(e)s, -s) m tic; (Eigenart) quirk; (Fimmel) craze; **ticken** vi to tick; **er tickt nicht ganz richtig** he's off his rocker

Ticket (-s, -s) nt (plane) ticket

Tiebreak (-s, -s) m (Sport: Tennis) tie break(er)

tief adj deep; (Ausschnitt, Ton, Sonne) low; **2 Meter ~** 2 metres deep; **Tief** (-s, -s) nt (Meteo) low; (seelisch) depression; **Tiefdruck** m (Meteo) low pressure; **Tiefe** (-, -n) f depth; **Tiefgarage** f underground car park (Brit) (o garage (US)); **tiefgekühlt** adj frozen; **Tiefkühlfach** nt freezer compartment; **Tiefkühlkost** f frozen food; **Tiefkühltruhe** *f* freezer; **Tiefpunkt** *m* low

Tier (*-(e)s, -e*) *nt* animal; **Tierarzt** *m*, **Tierärztin** *f* vet; **Tiergarten** *m* zoo; **Tierhandlung** *f* pet shop; **Tierheim** *nt* animal shelter; **tierisch** *adj* animal ▷ *adv* (*fam*) really; **~ ernst** deadly serious; **ich hatte ~ Angst** I was dead scared; **Tierkreiszeichen** *nt* sign of the zodiac; **Tierpark** *m* zoo; **Tierquälerei** *f* cruelty to animals; **Tierschützer(in)** (*-s, -*) *m(f)* animal rights campaigner; **Tierversuch** *m* animal experiment

Tiger (*-s, -*) *m* tiger

timen *vt* to time; **Timing** (*-s*) *nt* timing

Tinte (*-, -n*) *f* ink; **Tintenfisch** *m* cuttlefish; (*klein*) squid; (*achtarmig*) octopus; **Tintenfischringe** *pl* calamari *pl*; **Tintenstrahldrucker** *m* ink-jet printer

Tipp (*-s, -s*) *m* tip; **tippen** *vt, vi* to tap; (*fam: schreiben*) to type; (*fam: raten*) to guess

Tirol (*-s*) *nt* Tyrol

Tisch (*-(e)s, -e*) *m* table; **Tischdecke** *f* tablecloth; **Tischlerei** *f* joiner's workshop; (*Arbeit*) joinery; **Tischtennis** *nt* table tennis; **Tischtennisschläger** *m* table-tennis bat

Titel (*-s, -*) *m* title; **Titelbild** *nt* cover picture; **Titelmusik** *f* theme music; **Titelverteidiger(in)** *m(f)* defending champion

Toast (*-(e)s, -s*) *m* toast; **toasten** *vt* to toast; **Toaster** (*-s, -*) *m* toaster

Tochter (*-, Töchter*) *f* daughter

Tod (*-(e)s, -e*) *m* death; **Todesopfer** *nt* casualty; **Todesstrafe** *f* death penalty; **todkrank** *adj* terminally ill; (*sehr krank*) seriously ill; **tödlich** *adj* deadly, fatal; **er ist ~ verunglückt** he was killed in an accident; **todmüde** *adj* (*fam*) dead tired; **todsicher** *adj* (*fam*) dead certain

Tofu (*-(s)*) *m* tofu, bean curd

Toilette *f* toilet, restroom (*US*); **Toilettenpapier** *nt* toilet paper

toi, toi, toi *interj* good luck

tolerant *adj* tolerant (*gegen* of)

toll *adj* mad; (*Treiben*) wild; (*fam: großartig*) great; **Tollkirsche** *f* deadly nightshade; **Tollwut** *f* rabies *sing*

Tomate (*-, -n*) *f* tomato; **Tomatenmark** *nt* tomato purée (*Brit*) (o paste (*US*)); **Tomatensaft** *m* tomato juice

Tombola (*-, -s*) *f* raffle, tombola (*Brit*)

Ton (*-(e)s, -e*) *m* (*Erde*) clay ▷ *m* (*Töne*) (*Laut*) sound; (*Mus*) note; (*Redeweise*) tone; (*Farbton, Nuance*) shade; **Tonband** *nt* tape; **Tonbandgerät** *nt* tape recorder

tönen *vi* to sound ▷ *vt* to shade; (*Haare*) to tint

Toner (*-s, -*) *m* toner; **Tonerkassette** *f* toner cartridge

Tonne (*-, -n*) *f* (*Fass*) barrel; (*Gewicht*) tonne, metric ton

Tontechniker(in) *m(f)* sound engineer

Tönung *f* hue; (*für Haar*) rinse

Top (*-s, -s*) *nt* top

Topf (*-(e)s, Töpfe*) *m* pot

Töpfer(in) (*-s, -*) *m(f)* potter; **Töpferei** *f* pottery; (*Gegenstand*) piece of pottery

Tor (*-(e)s, -e*) *nt* gate; (*Sport*) goal; **ein ~ schießen** to score a goal; **Torhüter(in)** *m(f)* goalkeeper

torkeln *vi* to stagger

Torlinie *f* goal line

Tornado (*-s, -s*) *m* tornado

Torpfosten *m* goalpost; **Torschütze** *m*, **Torschützin** *f* (goal)scorer

Torte (*-, -n*) *f* cake; (*Obsttorte*) flan; (*Sahnetorte*) gateau

Torwart(in) (*-s, -e*) *m(f)* goalkeeper

tot *adj* dead; **~er Winkel** blind spot

total *adj* total, complete; **Totalschaden** *m* complete write-off

Tote(r) *mf* dead man/woman; (*Leiche*) corpse; **töten** *vt, vi* to kill; **Totenkopf** *m* skull

tot|lachen *vr* **sich ~** to kill oneself laughing

Toto (*-s, -s*) *m* o *nt* pools *pl*

tot|schlagen *irr vt* to beat to death; **die Zeit ~** to kill time

Touchscreen (*-s, -s*) *m* touch screen

Toupet (*-s, -s*) *nt* toupee

Tour (*-, -en*) *f* trip; (*Rundfahrt*) tour; **eine ~ nach York machen** to go on a trip to York; **Tourenski** *m* touring ski

Tourismus *m* tourism; **Tourist(in)** *m(f)* tourist; **Touristenklasse** *f* tourist class; **touristisch** *adj* tourist; (*pej*) touristy

traben *vi* to trot

Tournee (*-, -n*) *f* tour

Tracht (*-, -en*) *f* (*Kleidung*) traditional costume

Trackball (-s, -s) m (Inform) trackball
Tradition f tradition; **traditionell** adj
traditional
traf imperf von **treffen**
Trafik (-, -en) f tobacconist's
Tragbahre (-, -n) f stretcher
tragbar adj portable
träge adj sluggish, slow
tragen (trug, getragen) vt to carry;
(Kleidung, Brille, Haare) to wear; (Namen,
Früchte) to bear; **Träger** (-s, -) m (an
Kleidung) strap; (Hosen~) braces pl (Brit),
suspenders pl (US); (in der Architektur)
beam; (Stahl~, Eisen~) girder
Tragfläche f wing; **Tragflügelboot** nt
hydrofoil
tragisch adj tragic; **Tragödie** f tragedy
Trainer(in) (-s, -) m(f) trainer, coach;
trainieren vt, vi to train; (jdn a.) to
coach; (Übung) to practise; **Training**
(-s, -s) nt training; **Trainingsanzug** m
tracksuit
Traktor m tractor
Trambahn f tram (Brit), streetcar (US)
trampen vi to hitchhike; **Tramper(in)**
m(f) hitchhiker
Träne (-, -n) f tear; **tränen** vi to water;
Tränengas nt teargas
trank imperf von **trinken**
Transfusion f transfusion
Transitverkehr m transit traffic;
Transitvisum nt transit visa
Transplantation f transplant;
(Hauttransplantation) graft
Transport (-(e)s, -e) m transport;
transportieren vt to transport;
Transportmittel nt means sing of
transport; **Transportunternehmen** nt
haulage firm
Transvestit (-en, -en) m transvestite
trat imperf von **treten**
Traube (-, -n) f (einzelne Beere) grape;
(ganze Frucht) bunch of grapes;
Traubensaft m grape juice;
Traubenzucker m glucose
trauen vi jdm/einer Sache ~ to trust
sb/sth; **ich traute meinen Ohren nicht** I
couldn't believe my ears ▷ vr **sich ~** to
dare ▷ vt to marry; **sich ~ lassen** to get
married
Trauer (-) f sorrow; (für Verstorbenen)
mourning
Traum (-(e)s, Träume) m dream; **träumen**

vt, vi to dream (von of, about); **traumhaft**
adj dreamlike; (fig) wonderful
traurig adj sad (über +akk about)
Trauschein m marriage certificate;
Trauung f wedding ceremony;
Trauzeuge m, **Trauzeugin** f witness (at
wedding ceremony), ≈ best man/maid of
honour
Travellerscheck m traveller's cheque
treffen (traf, getroffen) vr **sich ~** to meet
▷ vt, vi to hit; (Bemerkung) to hurt;
(begegnen) to meet; (Entscheidung) to
make; (Maßnahmen) to take; **Treffen** (-s, -)
nt meeting; **Treffer** (-s, -) m (Tor) goal;
Treffpunkt m meeting place
treiben (trieb, getrieben) vt to drive; (Sport)
to do ▷ vi (im Wasser) to drift; (Pflanzen) to
sprout; (Tee, Kaffee) to be diuretic; **Treiber**
(-s, -) m (Inform) driver
Treibgas nt propellant; **Treibhaus** nt
greenhouse; **Treibstoff** m fuel
trennen vt to separate; (teilen) to divide
▷ vr **sich ~** to separate; **sich von jdm ~** to
leave sb; **sich von etw ~** to part with sth;
Trennung f separation
Treppe (-, -n) f stairs pl; (im Freien) steps pl;
Treppengeländer nt banister;
Treppenhaus nt staircase
Tresen (-s, -) m (in Kneipe) bar; (in Laden)
counter
Tresor (-s, -e) m safe
Tretboot nt pedal boat; **treten** (trat,
getreten) vi to step; **~ nach** to kick at; **mit
jdm in Verbindung ~** to get in contact
with sb ▷ vt to kick; (nieder~) to tread
treu adj (gegenüber Partner) faithful; (Kunde,
Fan) loyal; **Treue** (-) f (eheliche)
faithfulness; (von Kunde, Fan) loyalty
Triathlon (-s, -s) m triathlon
Tribüne (-, -n) f stand; (Rednertribüne)
platform
Trick (-s, -e o -s) m trick; **Trickfilm** m
cartoon
trieb imperf von **treiben**
Trieb (-(e)s, -e) m urge; (Instinkt) drive;
(Neigung) inclination; (an Baum etc) shoot;
Triebwerk nt engine
Trikot (-s, -s) nt shirt, jersey
Trimm-Dich-Pfad m fitness trail
trinkbar adj drinkable; **trinken** (trank,
getrunken) vt, vi to drink; **einen ~ gehen** to
go out for a drink; **Trinkgeld** nt tip;
Trinkhalm m (drinking) straw;

Trinkschokolade f drinking chocolate; **Trinkwasser** nt drinking water

Trio (-s, -s) nt trio

Tripper (-s, -) m gonorrhoea

Tritt (-(e)s, -e) m (Schritt) step; (Fußtritt) kick; **Trittbrett** nt running board

Triumph (-(e)s, -e) m triumph; **triumphieren** vi to triumph (über +akk over)

trivial adj trivial

trocken adj dry; **Trockenhaube** f hair-dryer; **Trockenheit** f dryness; **trocken|legen** vt (Baby) to change; **trocknen** vt, vi to dry; **Trockner** (-s, -) m dryer

Trödel (-s) m (fam) junk; **Trödelmarkt** m flea market

trödeln vi (fam) to dawdle

Trommel (-, -n) f drum; **Trommelfell** nt eardrum; **trommeln** vt, vi to drum

Trompete (-, -n) f trumpet

Tropen pl tropics pl

Tropf (-(e)s, -e) m (Med) drip; **am ~ hängen** to be on a drip; **tröpfeln** vi to drip; **es tröpfelt** it's drizzling; **tropfen** vt, vi to drip; **Tropfen** (-s, -) m drop; **tropfenweise** adv drop by drop; **tropfnass** adj dripping wet; **Tropfsteinhöhle** f stalactite cave

tropisch adj tropical

Trost (-es) m consolation, comfort; **trösten** vt to console, to comfort; **trostlos** adj bleak; (Verhältnisse) wretched; **Trostpreis** m consolation prize

Trottoir (-s, -s) nt pavement (Brit), sidewalk (US)

trotz prep +gen o dat in spite of; **Trotz** (-es) m defiance; **trotzdem** adv nevertheless ▷ conj although; **trotzig** adj defiant

trüb adj dull; (Flüssigkeit, Glas) cloudy; (fig) gloomy

Trüffel (-, -n) f truffle

trug imperf von tragen

trügerisch adj deceptive

Truhe (-, -n) f chest

Trümmer pl wreckage sing; (Bau~) ruins pl

Trumpf (-(e)s, Trümpfe) m trump

Trunkenheit f intoxication; **~ am Steuer** drink driving (Brit), drunk driving (US)

Truthahn m turkey

Tscheche (-n, -n) m, **Tschechin** f Czech; **Tschechien** (-s) nt Czech Republic; **tschechisch** adj Czech; **Tschechische**

Republik Czech Republic; **Tschechisch** nt Czech

Tschetschenien (-s) nt Chechnya

tschüs(s) interj bye

T-Shirt (-s, -s) nt T-shirt

Tube (-, -n) f tube

Tuberkulose (-, -n) f tuberculosis, TB

Tuch (-(e)s, Tücher) nt cloth; (Halstuch) scarf; (Kopftuch) headscarf

tüchtig adj competent; (fleißig) efficient; (fam: kräftig) good

Tugend (-, -en) f virtue; **tugendhaft** adj virtuous

Tulpe (-, -n) f tulip

Tumor (-s, -en) m tumour

Tümpel (-s, -) m pond

tun (tat, getan) vt (machen) to do; (legen) to put; **was tust du da?** what are you doing?; **das tut man nicht** you shouldn't do that; **jdm etw ~** (antun) to do sth to sb; **das tut es auch** that'll do ▷ vi to act; **so ~, als ob** to act as if ▷ vr impers **es tut sich etwas/viel** something/a lot is happening

Tuner (-s, -) m tuner

Tunesien (-s) nt Tunisia

Tunfisch m siehe **Thunfisch** tuna

Tunnel (-s, -s o -) m tunnel

Tunte (-, -n) f (pej, fam) fairy

tupfen vt, vi to dab; (mit Farbe) to dot; **Tupfen** (-s, -) m dot

Tür (-, -en) f door; **vor/an der ~** at the door; **an die ~ gehen** to answer the door

Türke (-n, -n) m Turk; **Türkei** (-) f **die ~** Turkey; **Türkin** f Turk

Türkis (-es, -e) m turquoise

türkisch adj Turkish; **Türkisch** nt Turkish

Turm (-(e)s, Türme) m tower; (spitzer Kirchturm) steeple; (Sprung~) diving platform; (Schach) rook, castle

turnen vi to do gymnastics; **Turnen** (-s) nt gymnastics sing; (Schule) physical education, PE; **Turner(in)** m(f) gymnast; **Turnhalle** f gym(nasium); **Turnhose** f gym shorts pl

Turnier (-s, -e) nt tournament

Turnschuh m gym shoe, sneaker (US)

Türschild nt doorplate; **Türschloss** nt lock

tuscheln vt, vi to whisper

Tussi (-, -s) f (pej, fam) chick

Tüte (-, -n) f bag

TÜV (-s, -s) m akr = **Technischer Überwachungsverein**

● **TÜV**
●
● The **TÜV** is the organization
● responsible for checking the safety of
● machinery, particularly vehicles. Cars
● over three years old have to be
● examined every two years for their
● safety and for their exhaust
● emissions. **TÜV** is also the name
● given to the test itself.

TÜV-Plakette *f badge attached to a vehicle's numberplate, indicating that it has passed the 'TÜV'*

Tweed *(-s, -s) m* tweed

Typ *(-s, -en) m* type; *(Auto)* model; *(Mann)* guy, bloke

Typhus *(-) m* typhoid

typisch *adj* typical *(für of)*; **ein ~er Fehler** a common mistake; **~ Marcus!** that's just like Marcus; **~ amerikanisch!** that's so American

u

u. *abk* = **und**

u. a. *abk* = **und andere(s)** and others; = **unter anderem, unter anderen** among other things

u. A. w. g. *abk* = **um Antwort wird gebeten** RSVP

U-Bahn *f* underground (*Brit*), subway (*US*)

übel *adj* bad; (*moralisch*) wicked; **mir ist ~** I feel sick; **diese Bemerkung hat er mir ~ genommen** he took offence at my remark; **Übelkeit** *f* nausea

üben *vt, vi* to practise

⊙ **SCHLÜSSELWORT**

über *präp* +dat **1** (*räumlich*) over above; **zwei Grad über null** two degrees above zero

2 (*zeitlich*) over; **über der Arbeit einschlafen** to fall asleep over one's work

▷ *präp* +akk

1 (*räumlich*) over; (*hoch über auch*) above; (*quer über auch*) across

2 (*zeitlich*) over; **über Weihnachten** over Christmas; **über kurz oder lang** sooner or later

3 (*mit Zahlen*): **Kinder über 12 Jahren** children over *od* above 12 years of age; **ein Scheck über 200 Euro** a cheque for 200 euros

4 (*auf dem Wege*) via; **nach Köln über Aachen** to Cologne via Aachen; **ich habe es über die Auskunft erfahren** I found out from information

5 (*betreffend*) about; **ein Buch über ...** a book about *od* on ...; **über jdn/etw lachen** to laugh about *od* at sb/sth

6: **Macht über jdn haben** to have power over sb; **sie liebt ihn über alles** she loves him more than everything

▷ *adv* over; **über und über** over and over; **den ganzen Tag über** all day long; **jdm in etw** *dat* **über sein** to be superior to sb in sth

überall *adv* everywhere

überanstrengen *vr* **sich ~** to overexert oneself

überbacken *adj* (**mit Käse**) **~** au gratin; **überbelichten** *vt* (*Foto*) to overexpose; **überbieten** *irr vt* to outbid; (*übertreffen*) to surpass; (*Rekord*) to break

Überbleibsel (-s, -) *nt* remnant

Überblick *m* overview; (*fig: in Darstellung*) survey; (*Fähigkeit zu verstehen*) grasp (*über* +akk of)

überbuchen *vt* to overbook; **Überbuchung** *f* overbooking

überdurchschnittlich *adj* above average

übereinander *adv* on top of each other; (*sprechen etc*) about each other

überein|stimmen *vi* to agree (*mit* with)

überempfindlich *adj* hypersensitive

überfahren *irr vt* (*Auto*) to run over; **Überfahrt** *f* crossing

Überfall *m* (*Banküberfall*) robbery; (*Mil*) raid; (*auf jdn*) assault; **überfallen** *irr vt* to attack; (*Bank*) to raid

überfällig *adj* overdue

überfliegen *irr vt* to fly over; (*Buch*) to skim through

Überfluss *m* overabundance, excess (*an* +dat of); **überflüssig** *adj* superfluous

überfordern *vt* to demand too much of; (*Kräfte*) to overtax; **da bin ich überfordert** (*bei Antwort*) you've got me there

Überführung *f* (*Brücke*) flyover (*Brit*), overpass (*US*)

überfüllt *adj* overcrowded

u

Übergabe f handover
Übergang m crossing; (Wandel, Überleitung) transition; **Übergangslösung** f temporary solution, stopgap
übergeben irr vt to hand over ▷ vr **sich ~** to be sick, to vomit
Übergepäck nt excess baggage
Übergewicht nt excess weight; (**10 Kilo**) **~ haben** to be (10 kilos) overweight
überglücklich adj overjoyed; (fam) over the moon
Übergröße f outsize
überhaupt adv at all; (im Allgemeinen) in general; (besonders) especially; **was willst du ~?** what is it you want?
überheblich adj arrogant
überholen vt to overtake; (Tech) to overhaul; **Überholspur** f overtaking (Brit) (o passing (US)) lane; **überholt** adj outdated
Überholverbot nt **hier herrscht ~** you can't overtake here
überhören vt to miss, not to catch; (absichtlich) to ignore; **überladen** irr vt to overload ▷ adj (fig) cluttered; **überlassen** irr vt **jdm etw ~** to leave sth to sb; **über|laufen** irr vi (Flüssigkeit) to overflow
überleben vt, vi to survive; **Überlebende(r)** mf survivor
überlegen vt to consider; **sich** (dat) **etw ~** to think about sth; **er hat es sich** (dat) **anders überlegt** he's changed his mind ▷ adj superior (dat to); **Überlegung** f consideration
überm kontr von **über dem**
übermäßig adj excessive
übermorgen adv the day after tomorrow
übernächste(r, s) adj **~ Woche** the week after next
übernachten vi to spend the night (bei jdm at sb's place); **übernächtigt** adj bleary-eyed, very tired; **Übernachtung** f overnight stay; **~ mit Frühstück** bed and breakfast
übernehmen irr vt to take on; (Amt, Geschäft) to take over ▷ vr **sich ~** to take on too much
überprüfen vt to check; **Überprüfung** f check; (Überprüfen) checking
überqueren vt to cross
überraschen vt to surprise; **Überraschung** f surprise

überreden vt to persuade; **er hat mich überredet** he talked me into it
überreichen vt to hand over
übers kontr von **über das**
überschätzen vt to overestimate; **überschlagen** irr vt (berechnen) to estimate; (auslassen: Seite) to skip ▷ vr **sich ~** to somersault; (Auto) to overturn; (Stimme) to crack; **überschneiden** irr vr **sich ~** (Linien etc) to intersect; (Termine) to clash
Überschrift f heading
Überschwemmung f flood
Übersee f **nach/in ~** overseas
übersehen irr vt (Gelände) to look (out) over; (nicht beachten) to overlook
übersetzen vt to translate (aus from, in +akk into); **Übersetzer(in)** (-s, -) m(f) translator; **Übersetzung** f translation
Übersicht f overall view; (Darstellung) survey; **übersichtlich** adj clear
überstehen irr vt (durchstehen) to get over; (Winter etc) to get through
Überstunden pl overtime sing
überstürzt adj hasty
überteuert adj overpriced
übertragbar adj transferable; (Med) infectious; **übertragen** irr vt to transfer (auf +akk to); (Radio) to broadcast; (Krankheit) to transmit ▷ vr to spread (auf +akk to) ▷ adj figurative; **Übertragung** f (Radio) broadcast; (von Daten) transmission
übertreffen irr vt to surpass
übertreiben irr vt, vi to exaggerate, to overdo; **Übertreibung** f exaggeration; **übertrieben** adj exaggerated, overdone
überwachen vt to supervise; (Verdächtigen) to keep under surveillance
überwand imperf von **überwinden**
überweisen irr vt to transfer; (Patienten) to refer (an +akk to); **Überweisung** f transfer; (von Patienten) referral
überwiegend adv mainly
überwinden (überwand, überwunden) vt to overcome ▷ vr **sich ~** to make an effort, to force oneself; **überwunden** pp von **überwinden**
Überzelt nt flysheet
überzeugen vt to convince; **Überzeugung** f conviction
überziehen irr vt (bedecken) to cover; (Jacke etc) to put on; (Konto) to overdraw;

die Betten frisch ~ to change the sheets; **Überziehungskredit** *m* overdraft facility

üblich *adj* usual

übrig *adj* remaining; **ist noch Saft ~?** is there any juice left?; **für jdn etwas ~ haben** (*fam*) to have a soft spot for sb; **die Übrigen** *pl* the rest *pl*; **im Übrigen** besides; **~ bleiben** to be left (over); **mir blieb nichts anderes ~(, als zu gehen)** I had no other choice (but to go); **übrigens** *adv* besides; (*nebenbei bemerkt*) by the way

Übung *f* practice; (*im Sport, Aufgabe etc*) exercise

Ufer (*-s, -*) *nt* (*Fluss*) bank; (*Meer, See*) shore; **am ~** on the bank/shore

Ufo (*-(s), -s*) *nt* *akr* = **unbekanntes Flugobjekt** UFO

Uhr (*-, -en*) *f* clock; (*am Arm*) watch; **wie viel ~ ist es?** what time is it?; **1 ~** 1 o'clock; **20 ~** 8 o'clock, 8 pm; **Uhrzeigersinn** *m* **im ~** clockwise; **gegen den ~** anticlockwise (*Brit*), counterclockwise (*US*); **Uhrzeit** *f* time (of day)

Ukraine (*-*) *f* **die ~** the Ukraine

UKW *abk* = **Ultrakurzwelle** VHF

Ulme (*-, -n*) *f* elm

Ultrakurzwelle *f* very high frequency; **Ultraschallaufnahme** *f* (*Med*) scan

○ SCHLÜSSELWORT

um *präp* +akk **1** (*um herum*) (a)round; **um Weihnachten** around Christmas; **er schlug um sich** he hit about him
2 (*mit Zeitangabe*) at; **um acht (Uhr)** at eight (o'clock)
3 (*mit Größenangabe*) by; **etw um 4 cm kürzen** to shorten sth by 4 cm; **um 10% teurer** 10% more expensive; **um vieles besser** better by far; **um so besser** so much the better
4: **der Kampf um den Titel** the battle for the title; **um Geld spielen** to play for money; **Stunde um Stunde** hour after hour; **Auge um Auge** an eye for an eye
▷ *präp* +gen: **um ... willen** for the sake of ...; **um Gottes willen** for goodness' *od* (*stärker*) God's sake
▷ *konj*: **um ... zu** (in order) to ...; **zu klug, um zu ...** too clever to ...; *siehe* **umso**
▷ *adv* **1** (*ungefähr*) about; **um (die) 30**

Leute about *od* around 30 people
2 (*vorbei*): **die 2 Stunden sind um** the two hours are up

umarmen *vt* to embrace

Umbau *m* rebuilding; (*zu etwas*) conversion (*zu* into); **um|bauen** *vt* to rebuild; (*zu etwas*) to convert (*zu* into)

um|blättern *vt, vi* to turn over

um|bringen *irr vt* to kill

um|buchen *vi* to change one's reservation/flight

um|drehen *vt* to turn (round); (*obere Seite nach unten*) to turn over ▷ *vr* **sich ~** to turn (round); **Umdrehung** *f* turn; (*Phys, Auto*) revolution

um|fahren *irr vt* to knock down

um|fallen *irr vi* to fall over

Umfang *m* (*Ausmaß*) extent; (*von Buch*) size; (*Reichweite*) range; (*Math*) circumference; **umfangreich** *adj* extensive

Umfeld *nt* environment

Umfrage *f* survey

Umgang *m* company; (*mit jdm*) dealings *pl*; **umgänglich** *adj* sociable; **Umgangssprache** *f* colloquial language, slang

Umgebung *f* surroundings *pl*; (*Milieu*) environment; (*Personen*) people around one

umgehen *irr vi* (*Gerücht*) to go round; **~ (können) mit** (know how to) handle ▷ *irr vt* (*Schwierigkeit, Verbot*) to get round

um|gehen *irr vi* **mit etw ~** to handle sth; **Umgehungsstraße** *f* bypass

umgekehrt *adj* reverse; (*gegenteilig*) opposite ▷ *adv* the other way round; **und ~** and vice versa

um|hören *vr* **sich ~** to ask around; **um|kehren** *vi* to turn back ▷ *vt* to reverse; (*Kleidungsstück*) to turn inside out; **um|kippen** *vt* to tip over ▷ *vi* to overturn; (*fig*) to change one's mind; (*fam: ohnmächtig werden*) to pass out

Umkleidekabine *f* changing cubicle (*Brit*), dressing room (*US*); **Umkleideraum** *m* changing room

Umkreis *m* neighbourhood; **im ~ von** within a radius of

um|leiten *vt* to divert; **Umleitung** *f* diversion

um|rechnen *vt* to convert (*in* +akk into);

Umrechnung f conversion;
Umrechnungskurs m rate of exchange
Umriss m outline
um|rühren vi, vt to stir
ums kontr von **um das**
Umsatz m turnover
um|schalten vi to turn over
Umschlag m cover; (Buch) jacket; (Med)
compress; (Brief) envelope
Umschulung f retraining
um|sehen irr vr **sich ~** to look around;
(suchen) to look out (nach for)
umso adv all the; **~ mehr** all the more;
~ besser so much the better
umsonst adv (vergeblich) in vain; (gratis)
for nothing
Umstand m circumstance; **Umstände**
(pl) (fig) fuss; **in anderen Umständen
sein** to be pregnant; **jdm Umstände
machen** to cause sb a lot of trouble;
machen Sie bitte keine Umstände
please, don't put yourself out; **unter
diesen/keinen Umständen** under
these/no circumstances; **unter
Umständen** possibly; **umständlich**
adj (Methode) complicated;
(Ausdrucksweise) long-winded;
(Mensch) ponderous; **Umstandsmode**
f maternity wear
um|steigen irr vi to change
(trains/buses)
um|stellen vt (an anderen Ort) to change
round; (Tech) to convert ▷ vr **sich ~** to
adapt (auf +akk to); **Umstellung** f
change; (Umgewöhnung) adjustment;
(Tech) conversion
Umtausch m exchange; **um|tauschen** vt
to exchange; (Währung) to change
Umweg m detour
Umwelt f environment;
Umweltbelastung f ecological damage;
umweltbewusst adj environmentally
aware; **umweltfreundlich** adj
environment-friendly; **Umweltpapier** nt
recycled paper; **umweltschädlich** adj
harmful to the environment;
Umweltschutz m environmental
protection; **Umweltschützer(in)** (-s, -)
m(f) environmentalist;
Umweltverschmutzung f pollution;
umweltverträglich adj
environment-friendly
um|werfen irr vt to knock over; (fig:

ändern) to upset; (fig, fam: jdn) to
flabbergast
um|ziehen irr vt to change ▷ vr **sich ~** to
change ▷ vi to move (house); **Umzug** m
(Straßenumzug) procession;
(Wohnungsumzug) move
unabhängig adj independent;
Unabhängigkeitstag m Independence
Day, Fourth of July (US)
unabsichtlich adv unintentionally
unangenehm adj unpleasant;
Unannehmlichkeit f inconvenience; **~en**
pl trouble sing
unanständig adj indecent;
unappetitlich adj (Essen) unappetizing;
(abstoßend) off-putting; **unbeabsichtigt**
adj unintentional; **unbedeutend** adj
insignificant, unimportant; (Fehler) slight
unbedingt adj unconditional ▷ adv
absolutely
unbefriedigend adj unsatisfactory;
unbegrenzt adj unlimited; **unbekannt**
adj unknown; **unbeliebt** adj unpopular;
unbemerkt adj unnoticed; **unbequem**
adj (Stuhl, Mensch) uncomfortable;
(Regelung) inconvenient; **unbeständig** adj
(Wetter) unsettled; (Lage) unstable;
(Mensch) unreliable; **unbestimmt** adj
indefinite; **unbeteiligt** adj (nicht
dazugehörig) uninvolved; (innerlich nicht
berührt) indifferent, unconcerned;
unbewacht adj unguarded; **unbewusst**
adj unconscious; **unbezahlt** adj unpaid;
unbrauchbar adj useless
und conj and; **~ so weiter** and so on; **na ~?**
so what?
undankbar adj (Person) ungrateful;
(Aufgabe) thankless; **undenkbar** adj
inconceivable; **undeutlich** adj indistinct;
undicht adj leaky; **uneben** adj uneven;
unecht adj (Schmuck etc) fake; **unehelich**
adj (Kind) illegitimate; **unendlich** adj
endless; (Math) infinite; **unentbehrlich**
adj indispensable; **unentgeltlich** adj free
(of charge)
unentschieden adj undecided; **~ enden**
(Sport) to end in a draw
unerfreulich adj unpleasant
unerhört adj unheard-of; (Bitte)
outrageous; **unerlässlich** adj
indispensable; **unerträglich** adj
unbearable; **unerwartet** adj
unexpected

unerwünscht *adj* unwelcome; (*Eigenschaften*) undesirable; **unfähig** *adj* incompetent; **~ sein, etw zu tun** to be incapable of doing sth; **unfair** *adj* unfair

Unfall *m* accident; **Unfallbericht** *m* accident report; **Unfallflucht** *f* failure to stop after an accident; **Unfallhergang** *m* **den ~ schildern** to give details of the accident; **Unfallstation** *f* casualty ward; **Unfallstelle** *f* scene of the accident; **Unfallversicherung** *f* accident insurance

unfreundlich *adj* unfriendly

Ungarn (*-s*) *nt* Hungary

Ungeduld *f* impatience; **ungeduldig** *adj* impatient

ungeeignet *adj* unsuitable

ungefähr *adj* approximate ▷ *adv* approximately; **~ 10 Kilometer** about 10 kilometres; **wann ~?** about what time?; **wo ~?** whereabouts?

ungefährlich *adj* harmless; (*sicher*) safe

ungeheuer *adj* huge ▷ *adv* (*fam*) enormously; **Ungeheuer** (*-s, -*) *nt* monster

ungehorsam *adj* disobedient (*gegenüber* to)

ungelegen *adj* inconvenient; **ungemütlich** *adj* unpleasant; (*Mensch*) disagreeable; **ungenießbar** *adj* inedible; (*Getränk*) undrinkable; **ungenügend** *adj* unsatisfactory; (*Schulnote*) ≈ F; **ungepflegt** *adj* (*Garten*) untended; (*Aussehen*) unkempt; (*Hände*) neglected; **ungerade** *adj* odd

ungerecht *adj* unjust; **ungerechtfertigt** *adj* unjustified; **Ungerechtigkeit** *f* injustice, unfairness

ungern *adv* reluctantly; **ungeschickt** *adj* clumsy; **ungeschminkt** *adj* without make-up; **ungesund** *adj* unhealthy; **ungewiss** *adj* uncertain; **ungewöhnlich** *adj* unusual

Ungeziefer (*-s*) *nt* vermin *pl*

ungezogen *adj* ill-mannered

ungezwungen *adj* relaxed

ungiftig *adj* non-toxic

unglaublich *adj* incredible

Unglück (*-(e)s, -e*) *nt* (*Unheil*) misfortune; (*Pech*) bad luck; (*Unglücksfall*) disaster; (*Verkehrs~*) accident; **das bringt ~** that's unlucky; **unglücklich** *adj* unhappy; (*erfolglos*) unlucky; (*unerfreulich*)

unfortunate; **unglücklicherweise** *adv* unfortunately

ungültig *adj* invalid

ungünstig *adj* inconvenient

unheilbar *adj* incurable; **~ krank sein** to be terminally ill

unheimlich *adj* eerie ▷ *adv* (*fam*) incredibly

unhöflich *adj* impolite

uni *adj* plain

Uni (*-, -s*) *f* uni

Uniform (*-, -en*) *f* uniform

Universität *f* university

Unkenntnis *f* ignorance

unklar *adj* unclear

Unkosten *pl* expenses *pl*; **Unkostenbeitrag** *m* contribution (towards expenses)

Unkraut *nt* weeds *pl*, ~art, weed

unlogisch *adj* illogical

unmissverständlich *adj* unambiguous

unmittelbar *adj* immediate; **~ darauf** immediately afterwards

unmöbliert *adj* unfurnished

unmöglich *adj* impossible

unnahbar *adj* unapproachable

unnötig *adj* unnecessary

UNO (*-*) *f akr* = **United Nations Organization** UN

unordentlich *adj* untidy; **Unordnung** *f* disorder

unpassend *adj* inappropriate; (*Zeit*) inconvenient; **unpersönlich** *adj* impersonal; **unpraktisch** *adj* impractical

Unrecht *nt* wrong; **zu ~** wrongly; **~ haben, im ~ sein** to be wrong

unregelmäßig *adj* irregular; **unreif** *adj* unripe; **unruhig** *adj* restless; **~ schlafen** to have a bad night

uns *pron akk, dat von* **wir**; us, (to) us; **~ (selbst)** (*reflexiv*) ourselves; **sehen Sie ~?** can you see us?; **er schickte es ~** he sent it to us; **lasst ~ in Ruhe** leave us alone; **ein Freund von ~** a friend of ours; **wir haben ~ hingesetzt** we sat down; **wir haben ~ amüsiert** we enjoyed ourselves; **wir mögen ~** we like each other

unscharf *adj* (*Foto*) blurred, out of focus

unscheinbar *adj* insignificant; (*Aussehen*) unprepossessing

unschlüssig *adj* undecided

unschuldig *adj* innocent

u

unser pron (adjektivisch) our ▷ pron gen von
wir; of us; **unsere(r, s)** pron
(substantivisch) ours; **unseretwegen** adv
(wegen uns) because of us; (uns zuliebe) for
our sake; (um uns) about us; (von uns aus)
as far as we are concerned
unseriös adj dubious; **unsicher** adj
(ungewiss) uncertain; (Person, Job) insecure
Unsinn m nonsense
unsterblich adj immortal; **~ verliebt**
madly in love
unsympathisch adj unpleasant; **er ist
mir ~** I don't like him
unten adv below; (im Haus) downstairs;
(an der Treppe etc) at the bottom; **nach
~** down; **unter** prep +akk o dat under,
below; (bei Menschen) among; (während)
during

O SCHLÜSSELWORT

unter präp +dat **1** (räumlich, mit Zahlen)
under; (drunter) underneath, below; **unter
18 Jahren** under 18 years
2 (zwischen) among(st); **sie waren unter
sich** they were by themselves; **einer
unter ihnen** one of them; **unter anderem**
among other things
▷ präp +akk under below

Unterarm m forearm
unterbelichtet adj (Foto) underexposed
Unterbewusstsein nt subconscious
unterbrechen irr vt to interrupt;
Unterbrechung f interruption; **ohne
~** nonstop
unterdrücken vt to suppress; (Leute) to
oppress
unterdurchschnittlich adj below
average
untere(r, s) adj lower
untereinander adv (räumlich) one below
the other; (gegenseitig) each other;
(miteinander) among
themselves/yourselves/ourselves
Unterführung f underpass
unter|gehen irr vi to go down; (Sonne) to
set; (Volk) to perish; (Welt) to come to an
end; (im Lärm) to be drowned out
Untergeschoss nt basement;
Untergewicht nt (**3 Kilo**) **~ haben** to be
(3 kilos) underweight; **Untergrund** m
foundation; (Pol) underground;

Untergrundbahn f underground (Brit),
subway (US)
unterhalb adv, prep +gen below; **~ von**
below
Unterhalt m maintenance; **unterhalten**
irr vt to maintain; (belustigen) to entertain
▷ vr **sich ~** to talk; (sich belustigen) to
enjoy oneself; **Unterhaltung** f
(Belustigung) entertainment; (Gespräch)
talk, conversation
Unterhemd nt vest (Brit), undershirt
(US); **Unterhose** f underpants pl; (für
Damen) briefs pl
unterirdisch adj underground
Unterkiefer m lower jaw
Unterkunft (-, -künfte) f accommodation
Unterlage f (Beleg) document;
(Schreibunterlage) pad
unterlassen irr vt **es ~, etw zu tun**
(versäumen) to fail to do sth; (bleiben lassen)
to refrain from doing sth
unterlegen adj inferior (dat to); (besiegt)
defeated
Unterleib m abdomen
Unterlippe f lower lip
Untermiete f **zur ~ wohnen** to be a
subtenant; **Untermieter(in)** m(f)
subtenant
unternehmen irr vt (Reise) to go on;
(Versuch) to make; **etwas ~** to do
something (gegen about); **Unternehmen**
(-s, -) nt undertaking; (Comm) company;
Unternehmensberater(in) (-s, -) m(f)
management consultant;
Unternehmer(in) (-s, -) m(f)
entrepreneur
Unterricht (-(e)s, -e) m lessons pl;
unterrichten vt to teach
unterschätzen vt to underestimate
unterscheiden irr vt to distinguish (von
from, zwischen +dat between) ▷ vr **sich
~** to differ (von from)
Unterschenkel m lower leg
Unterschied (-(e)s, -e) m difference; **im
~ zu dir** unlike you; **unterschiedlich** adj
different
unterschreiben irr vt to sign;
Unterschrift f signature
Untersetzer (-s, -) m tablemat; (für
Gläser) coaster
unterste(r, s) adj lowest, bottom
unter|stellen vr **sich ~** to take shelter
unterstellen vt (rangmäßig) to

subordinate (*dat* to); (*fig*) to impute (*jdm etw* sth to sb)

unterstreichen *irr vt* (*a. fig*) to underline

Unterstrich *m* (*Inform*) underscore

unterstützen *vt* to support; **Unterstützung** *f* support

untersuchen *vt* (*Med*) to examine; (*Polizei*) to investigate; **Untersuchung** *f* examination; (*polizeiliche*) investigation

untertags *adv* during the day

Untertasse *f* saucer

Unterteil *nt* lower part, bottom

Untertitel *m* subtitle

untervermieten *vt* to sublet

Unterwäsche *f* underwear

unterwegs *adv* on the way

unterzeichnen *vt* to sign

untreu *adj* unfaithful

untröstlich *adj* inconsolable; **unüberlegt** *adj* ill-considered ▷ *adv* without thinking; **unüblich** *adj* unusual; **unverantwortlich** *adj* irresponsible; (*unentschuldbar*) inexcusable

unverbindlich *adj* not binding; (*Antwort*) noncommittal ▷ *adv* (*Comm*) without obligation

unverbleit *adj* unleaded; **unverheiratet** *adj* unmarried, single; **unvermeidlich** *adj* unavoidable; **unvernünftig** *adj* silly; **unverschämt** *adj* impudent; **unverständlich** *adj* incomprehensible; **unverträglich** *adj* (*Person*) quarrelsome; (*Essen*) indigestible

unverwüstlich *adj* indestructible; (*Mensch*) irrepressible

unverzeihlich *adj* unpardonable; **unverzüglich** *adj* immediate; **unvollständig** *adj* incomplete; **unvorsichtig** *adj* careless

unwahrscheinlich *adj* improbable, unlikely ▷ *adv* (*fam*) incredibly

Unwetter *nt* thunderstorm

unwichtig *adj* unimportant

unwiderstehlich *adj* irresistible

unwillkürlich *adj* involuntary ▷ *adv* instinctively; **ich musste ~ lachen** I couldn't help laughing

unwohl *adj* unwell, ill

unzählig *adj* innumerable, countless

unzerbrechlich *adj* unbreakable; **unzertrennlich** *adj* inseparable; **unzufrieden** *adj* dissatisfied; **unzugänglich** *adj* inaccessible;

unzumutbar *adj* unacceptable

unzusammenhängend *adj* disconnected; (*Äußerung*) incoherent; **unzutreffend** *adj* inapplicable; (*unwahr*) incorrect; **unzuverlässig** *adj* unreliable

Update (*-s, -s*) *nt* (*Inform*) update

üppig *adj* (*Essen*) lavish; (*Vegetation*) lush

uralt *adj* ancient, very old

Uran (*-s*) *nt* uranium

Uranus (*-*) *m* Uranus

Uraufführung *f* premiere

Urenkel *m* great-grandson; **Urenkelin** *f* great-granddaughter; **Urgroßeltern** *pl* great-grandparents *pl*; **Urgroßmutter** *f* great-grandmother; **Urgroßvater** *m* great-grandfather

Urheber(in) (*-s, -*) *m(f)* originator; (*Autor*) author

Urin (*-s, -e*) *m* urine; **Urinprobe** *f* urine specimen

Urkunde (*-, -n*) *f* document

Urlaub (*-(e)s, -e*) *m* holiday (*Brit*), vacation (*US*); **im ~** on holiday (*Brit*), on vacation (*US*); **in ~ fahren** to go on holiday (*Brit*) (*o* vacation (*US*)); **Urlauber(in)** (*-s, -*) *m(f)* holiday-maker (*Brit*), vacationer (*US*); **Urlaubsort** *m* holiday resort; **urlaubsreif** *adj* ready for a holiday (*Brit*) (*o* vacation (*US*)); **Urlaubszeit** *f* holiday season (*Brit*), vacation period (*US*)

Urne (*-, -n*) *f* urn

Urologe *m*, **Urologin** *f* urologist

Ursache *f* cause (*für* of); **keine ~!** not at all; (*bei Entschuldigung*) that's all right

Ursprung *m* origin; (*von Fluss*) source; **ursprünglich** *adj* original ▷ *adv* originally; **Ursprungsland** *adj* country of origin

Urteil (*-s, -e*) *nt* (*Meinung*) opinion; (*Jur*) verdict; (*Strafmaß*) sentence; **urteilen** *vi* to judge

Uruguay (*-s*) *nt* Uruguay

Urwald *m* jungle

USA *pl* USA *sing*

User(in) (*-s, -*) *m(f)* (*Inform*) user

usw. *abk* = **und so weiter** etc

Utensilien *pl* utensils *pl*

u

vage *adj* vague

Vagina (-, *Vaginen*) *f* vagina

vakuumverpackt *adj* vacuum-packed

Valentinstag *m* St Valentine's Day

Vandalismus *m* vandalism

Vanille (-) *f* vanilla

variieren *vt, vi* to vary

Vase (-, *-n*) *f* vase

Vaseline (-) *f* Vaseline®

Vater (-s, *Väter*) *m* father; **väterlich** *adj*
paternal; **Vaterschaft** *f* fatherhood; (*Jur*)
paternity; **Vatertag** *m* Father's Day;
Vaterunser *nt* **das ~** (**beten**) (to say) the
Lord's Prayer

V-Ausschnitt *m* V-neck

v. Chr. *abk* = **vor Christus** BC

Veganer(in) (-s, -) *m(f)* vegan;
Vegetarier(in) (-s, -) *m(f)* vegetarian;
vegetarisch *adj* vegetarian

Veilchen *nt* violet

Velo (-s, -s) *nt* (*schweizerisch*) bicycle

Vene (-, *-n*) *f* vein

Venedig (-s) *nt* Venice

Venezuela (-s) *nt* Venezuela

Ventil (-s, *-e*) *nt* valve

Ventilator *m* ventilator

Venus (-) *f* Venus

Venusmuschel *f* clam

verabreden *vt* to arrange ▷ *vr* **sich ~** to
arrange to meet (*mit jdm* sb); **ich bin
schon verabredet** I'm already meeting
someone; **Verabredung** *f* arrangement;
(*Termin*) appointment; (*zum Ausgehen*) date

verabschieden *vt* (*Gäste*) to say goodbye
to; (*Gesetz*) to pass ▷ *vr* **sich ~** to say
goodbye

verachten *vt* to despise; **verächtlich** *adj*
contemptuous; (*verachtenswert*)
contemptible; **Verachtung** *f* contempt

verallgemeinern *vt* to generalize

Veranda (-, *Veranden*) *f* veranda, porch
(*US*)

veränderlich *adj* changeable; **verändern**
vt to change ▷ *vr* **sich ~** to change;
Veränderung *f* change

veranlassen *vt* to cause

veranstalten *vt* to organize;
Veranstalter(in) (-s, -) *m(f)* organizer;
Veranstaltung *f* event;
Veranstaltungsort *m* venue

verantworten *vt* to take responsibility
for ▷ *vr* **sich für etw ~** to answer for sth;
verantwortlich *adj* responsible (*für* for);
Verantwortung *f* responsibility (*für* for)

verärgern *vt* to annoy

verarschen *vt* (*fam*) to take the piss out
of (*Brit*), to make a sucker out of (*US*)

Verb (-s, *-en*) *nt* verb

Verband *m* (*Med*) bandage; (*Bund*)
association; **Verband(s)kasten** *m*
first-aid box; **Verband(s)zeug** *nt*
dressing material

verbergen *irr vt* to hide (*vor +dat* from)
▷ *vr* **sich ~** to hide (*vor +dat* from)

verbessern *vt* to improve; (*berichtigen*) to
correct ▷ *vr* **sich ~** to improve;
(*berichtigen*) to correct oneself;
Verbesserung *f* improvement;
(*Berichtigung*) correction

verbiegen *irr vi* to bend ▷ *vr* **sich ~** to
bend

verbieten *irr vt* to forbid; **jdm ~, etw zu
tun** to forbid sb to do sth

verbilligt *adj* reduced

verbinden *irr vt* to connect; (*kombinieren*)
to combine; (*Med*) to bandage; **können
Sie mich mit ... ~?** (*Tel*) can you put me
through to ...?; **ich verbinde** (*Tel*) I'm
putting you through ▷ *vr* (*Chem*) **sich ~** to
combine

verbindlich *adj* binding; (*freundlich*) friendly; **Verbindung** *f* connection

verbleit *adj* leaded

verblüffen *vt* to amaze

verblühen *vi* to fade

verborgen *adj* hidden

Verbot (*-(e)s, -e*) *nt* ban (*für, von* on); **verboten** *adj* forbidden; **es ist ~** it's not allowed; **es ist ~, hier zu parken** you're not allowed to park here; **Rauchen ~** no smoking

verbrannt *adj* burnt

Verbrauch (*-(e)s*) *m* consumption; **verbrauchen** *vt* to use up; **Verbraucher(in)** (*-s, -*) *m(f)* consumer

Verbrechen (*-s, -*) *nt* crime; **Verbrecher(in)** (*-s, -*) *m(f)* criminal

verbreiten *vt* to spread ▷ *vr* **sich ~** to spread

verbrennen *irr vt* to burn; **Verbrennung** *f* burning; (*in Motor*) combustion

verbringen *irr vt* to spend

verbunden *adj* **falsch ~** sorry, wrong number

Verdacht (*-(e)s*) *m* suspicion; **verdächtig** *adj* suspicious; **verdächtigen** *vt* to suspect

verdammt *interj* (*fam*) damn

verdanken *vt* **jdm etw ~** to owe sth to sb

verdarb *imperf von* **verderben**

verdauen *vt* (*a. fig*) to digest; **verdaulich** *adj* digestible; **das ist schwer ~** that is hard to digest; **Verdauung** *f* digestion

Verdeck (*-(e)s, -e*) *nt* top

verderben (*verdarb, verdorben*) *vt* to spoil; (*schädigen*) to ruin; (*moralisch*) to corrupt; **es sich** (*dat*) **mit jdm ~** to get into sb's bad books; **ich habe mir den Magen verdorben** I've got an upset stomach ▷ *vi* (*Lebensmittel*) to go off

verdienen *vt* to earn; (*moralisch*) to deserve; **Verdienst** (*-(e)s, -e*) *m* earnings *pl* ▷ (*-(e)s, -e*) *nt* merit; (*Leistung*) service (*um* to)

verdoppeln *vt* to double

verdorben *pp von* **verderben** ▷ *adj* spoilt; (*geschädigt*) ruined; (*moralisch*) corrupt

verdrehen *vt* to twist; (*Augen*) to roll; **jdm den Kopf ~** (*fig*) to turn sb's head

verdünnen *vt* to dilute

verdunsten *vi* to evaporate

verdursten *vi* to die of thirst

verehren *vt* to admire; (*Rel*) to worship; **Verehrer(in)** (*-s, -*) *m(f)* admirer

Verein (*-(e)s, -e*) *m* association; (*Klub*) club

vereinbar *adj* compatible

vereinbaren *vt* to arrange; **Vereinbarung** *f* agreement, arrangement

vereinigen *vt* to unite ▷ *vr* **sich ~** to unite; **Vereinigtes Königreich** *nt* United Kingdom; **Vereinigte Staaten (von Amerika)** *pl* United States *sing* (of America); **Vereinigung** *f* union; (*Verein*) association; **Vereinte Nationen** *pl* United Nations *pl*

vereisen *vi* (*Straße*) to freeze over; (*Fenster*) to ice up ▷ *vt* (*Med*) to freeze

vererben *vt* **jdm etw ~** to leave sth to sb; (*Bio*) to pass sth on to sb ▷ *vr* **sich ~** to be hereditary; **vererblich** *adj* hereditary

verfahren *irr vi* to proceed ▷ *vr* **sich ~** to get lost; **Verfahren** (*-s, -*) *nt* procedure; (*Tech*) method; (*Jur*) proceedings *pl*

verfallen *irr vi* to decline; (*Haus*) to be falling apart; (*Fin*) to lapse; (*Fahrkarte etc*) to expire; **~ in** (*+akk*) to lapse into; **Verfallsdatum** *nt* expiry (*Brit*) (*o* expiration (*US*)) date; (*von Lebensmitteln*) best-before date

verfärben *vr* **sich ~** to change colour; (*Wäsche*) to discolour

Verfasser(in) (*-s, -*) *m(f)* author, writer; **Verfassung** *f* (*gesundheitlich*) condition; (*Pol*) constitution

verfaulen *vi* to rot

verfehlen *vt* to miss

verfeinern *vt* to refine

Verfilmung *f* film (*o* screen) version

verfluchen *vt* to curse

verfolgen *vt* to pursue; (*Pol*) to persecute

verfügbar *adj* available; **verfügen** *vi* **über etw** (*akk*) **~** to have sth at one's disposal; **Verfügung** *f* order; **jdm zur ~ stehen** to be at sb's disposal; **jdm etw zur ~ stellen** to put sth at sb's disposal

verführen *vt* to tempt; (*sexuell*) to seduce; **verführerisch** *adj* seductive

vergangen *adj* past; **~e Woche** last week; **Vergangenheit** *f* past

Vergaser (*-s, -*) *m* (*Auto*) carburettor

vergaß *imperf von* **vergessen**

vergeben *irr vt* to forgive (*jdm etw* sb for sth); (*weggeben*) to award, to allocate;

V

vergebens *adv* in vain; **vergeblich** *adv* in vain ▷ *adj* vain, futile

vergehen *irr vi* to pass ▷ *vr* **sich an jdm ~** to indecently assault sb; **Vergehen** (-s, -) *nt* offence

Vergeltung *f* retaliation

vergessen (*vergaß, vergessen*) *vt* to forget; **vergesslich** *adj* forgetful

vergeuden *vt* to squander, to waste

vergewaltigen *vt* to rape; **Vergewaltigung** *f* rape

vergewissern *vr* **sich ~** to make sure

vergiften *vt* to poison; **Vergiftung** *f* poisoning

Vergissmeinnicht (-(e)s, -e) *nt* forget-me-not

Vergleich (-(e)s, -e) *m* comparison; (*Jur*) settlement; **im ~ zu** compared to (*o* with); **vergleichen** *irr vt* to compare (*mit* to, with)

Vergnügen (-s, -) *nt* pleasure; **viel ~!** enjoy yourself; **vergnügt** *adj* cheerful; **Vergnügungspark** *m* amusement park

vergoldet *adj* gold-plated

vergriffen *adj* (*Buch*) out of print; (*Ware*) out of stock

vergrößern *vt* to enlarge; (*Menge*) to increase; (*mit Lupe*) to magnify; **Vergrößerung** *f* enlargement; (*Menge*) increase; (*mit Lupe*) magnification; **Vergrößerungsglas** *nt* magnifying glass

verh. *adj abk* = **verheiratet** married

verhaften *vt* to arrest

verhalten *irr vr* **sich ~** (*sich benehmen*) to behave; (*Sache*) to be; **Verhalten** (-s) *nt* behaviour

Verhältnis *nt* relationship (*zu* with); (*Math*) ratio; **~se** *pl* circumstances *pl*, conditions *pl*; **im ~ von 1 zu 2** in a ratio of 1 to 2; **verhältnismäßig** *adj* relative ▷ *adv* relatively

verhandeln *vi* to negotiate (*über etw akk* sth); **Verhandlung** *f* negotiation

verheimlichen *vt* to keep secret (*jdm* from sb)

verheiratet *adj* married

verhindern *vt* to prevent; **sie ist verhindert** she can't make it

Verhör (-(e)s, -e) *nt* interrogation; (*gerichtlich*) examination; **verhören** *vt* to interrogate; (*bei Gericht*) to examine ▷ *vr* **sich ~** to mishear

verhungern *vi* to starve to death

verhüten *vt* to prevent; **Verhütung** *f* prevention; (*mit Pille, Kondom etc*) contraception; **Verhütungsmittel** *nt* contraceptive

verirren *vr* **sich ~** to get lost

Verkauf *m* sale; **verkaufen** *vt* to sell; **zu ~** for sale; **Verkäufer(in)** *m(f)* seller; (*beruflich*) salesperson; (*in Laden*) shop assistant (*Brit*), salesperson (*US*); **verkäuflich** *adj* for sale

Verkehr (-s, -e) *m* traffic; (*Sex*) intercourse; (*Umlauf*) circulation; **verkehren** *vi* (*Bus etc*) to run; **~ in** to frequent; **~ mit** to associate (*o* mix) with; **Verkehrsampel** *f* traffic lights *pl*; **Verkehrsamt** *nt* tourist information office; **verkehrsfrei** *adj* traffic-free; **Verkehrsfunk** *m* travel news *sing*; **Verkehrsinsel** *f* traffic island; **Verkehrsmeldung** *f* traffic report; **Verkehrsmittel** *nt* means *sing* of transport; **öffentliche ~** *pl* public transport *sing*; **Verkehrsschild** *nt* traffic sign; **Verkehrstote(r)** *mf* road casualty; **die Zahl der ~n** the number of deaths on the road; **Verkehrsunfall** *m* road accident; **Verkehrszeichen** *nt* traffic sign

verkehrt *adj* wrong; (*verkehrt herum*) the wrong way round; (*Pullover etc*) inside out; **du machst es ~** you're doing it wrong

verklagen *vt* to take to court

verkleiden *vt* to dress up (*als* as) ▷ *vr* **sich ~** to dress up (*als* as); (*um unerkannt zu bleiben*) to disguise oneself; **Verkleidung** *f* (*Karneval*) fancy dress; (*um nicht erkannt zu werden*) disguise

verkleinern *vt* to reduce; (*Zimmer, Gebiet etc*) to make smaller

verkneifen *irr vt* **sich** (*dat*) **etw ~** (*Lachen*) to stifle sth; (*Schmerz*) to hide sth; (*sich versagen*) to do without sth; **verkommen** *irr vi* to deteriorate; (*Mensch*) to go downhill ▷ *adj* (*Haus*) dilapidated; (*moralisch*) depraved; **verkraften** *vt* to cope with

verkratzt *adj* scratched

verkühlen *vr* **sich ~** to get a chill

verkürzen *vt* to shorten

Verlag (-(e)s, -e) *m* publishing company

verlangen *vt* (*fordern*) to demand; (*wollen*) to want; (*Preis*) to ask; (*Qualifikation*) to require; (*erwarten*) to ask (*von* of); (*fragen* *nach*) to ask for; (*Pass etc*) to ask to see; **~ Sie Herrn X** ask for Mr X ▷ *vi* **~ nach** to ask for

verlängern *vt* to extend; (*Pass, Erlaubnis*) renew; **Verlängerung** *f* extension; (*Sport*) extra time; (*von Pass, Erlaubnis*) renewal; **Verlängerungsschnur** *f* extension cable; **Verlängerungswoche** *f* extra week

verlassen *irr vt* to leave ▷ *irr vr* **sich ~** to rely (*auf +akk* on) ▷ *adj* desolate; (*Mensch*) abandoned; **verlässlich** *adj* reliable

Verlauf *m* course; **verlaufen** *irr vi* (*Weg, Grenze*) to run (*entlang* along); (*zeitlich*) to pass; (*Farben*) to run ▷ *vr* **sich ~** to get lost; (*Menschenmenge*) to disperse

verlegen *vt* to move; (*verlieren*) to mislay; (*Buch*) to publish ▷ *adj* embarrassed; **Verlegenheit** *f* embarrassment; (*Situation*) difficulty

Verleih (*-(e)s, -e*) *m* (*Firma*) hire company (*Brit*), rental company (*US*); **verleihen** *irr vt* to lend; (*vermieten*) to hire (out) (*Brit*), to rent (out) (*US*); (*Preis, Medaille*) to award

verleiten *vt* **jdn dazu ~, etw zu tun** to induce sb to do sth

verlernen *vt* to forget

verletzen *vt* to injure; (*fig*) to hurt; **Verletzte(r)** *mf* injured person; **Verletzung** *f* injury; (*Verstoß*) violation

verlieben *vr* **sich ~** to fall in love (*in jdn* with sb); **verliebt** *adj* in love

verlieren (*verlor, verloren*) *vt, vi* to lose

verloben *vr* **sich ~** to get engaged (*mit* to); **Verlobte(r)** *mf* fiancé/fiancée; **Verlobung** *f* engagement

verlor *imperf von* **verlieren**

verloren *pp von* **verlieren** ▷ *adj* lost; (*Eier*) poached; **~ gehen** to go missing

verlosen *vt* to raffle; **Verlosung** *f* raffle

Verlust (*-(e)s, -e*) *m* loss

vermehren *vt* to multiply; (*Menge*) to increase ▷ *vr* **sich ~** to multiply; (*Menge*) to increase

vermeiden *irr vt* to avoid

vermeintlich *adj* supposed

vermieten *vt* to rent (out), to let (out) (*Brit*); (*Auto*) to hire (out) (*Brit*), to rent (out) (*US*); **Vermieter(in)** *m(f)* landlord/ -lady

vermischen *vt* to mix ▷ *vr* **sich ~** to mix

vermissen *vt* to miss; **vermisst** *adj* missing; **jdn als ~ melden** to report sb missing

Vermittlung *f* (*bei Streit*) mediation; (*Herbeiführung*) arranging; (*Stelle*) agency

Vermögen (*-s, -*) *nt* fortune

vermuten *vt* to suppose; (*argwöhnen*) to suspect; **vermutlich** *adj* probable ▷ *adv* probably; **Vermutung** *f* supposition; (*Verdacht*) suspicion

vernachlässigen *vt* to neglect

vernichten *vt* to destroy; **vernichtend** *adj* (*fig*) crushing; (*Blick*) withering; (*Kritik*) scathing

Vernunft (*-*) *f* reason; **ich kann ihn nicht zur ~ bringen** I can't make him see reason; **vernünftig** *adj* sensible; (*Preis*) reasonable

veröffentlichen *vt* to publish

verordnen *vt* (*Med*) to prescribe; **Verordnung** *f* order; (*Med*) prescription

verpachten *vt* to lease (out) (*an +akk* to)

verpacken *vt* to pack; (*einwickeln*) to wrap up

Verpackung *f* packaging; **Verpackungskosten** *pl* packing charges *pl*

verpassen *vt* to miss

verpflegen *vt* to feed; **Verpflegung** *f* feeding; (*Kost*) food; (*in Hotel*) board

verpflichten *vt* to oblige; (*anstellen*) to engage ▷ *vr* **sich ~** to commit oneself (*etw zu tun* to doing sth)

verpfuschen *vt* (*fam*) to make a mess of; (*vulg*) to fuck up

verprügeln *vt* to beat up

verraten *irr vt* to betray; (*Geheimnis*) to divulge; **aber nicht ~!** but don't tell anyone ▷ *vr* **sich ~** to give oneself away

verrechnen *vt* **~ mit** to set off against ▷ *vr* **sich ~** to miscalculate; **Verrechnungsscheck** *m* crossed cheque (*Brit*), check for deposit only (*US*)

verregnet *adj* rainy

verreisen *vi* to go away (*nach* to); **sie ist (geschäftlich) verreist** she's away (on business); **verrenken** *vt* to contort; (*Med*) to dislocate; **sich** (*dat*) **den Knöchel ~** to sprain (*o* twist) one's ankle; **verringern** *vt* to reduce

verrostet *adj* rusty

verrückt *adj* mad, crazy; **es macht mich ~** it's driving me mad

versagen vi to fail; **Versagen** (-s) nt failure; **Versager(in)** (-s, -) m(f) failure

versalzen irr vt to put too much salt in/on

versammeln vt to assemble, to gather ▷ vr **sich ~** to assemble, to gather; **Versammlung** f meeting

Versand (-(e)s) m dispatch; (Abteilung) dispatch department; **Versandhaus** nt mail-order company

versäumen vt to miss; (unterlassen) to neglect; **~, etw zu tun** vt to fail to do sth

verschätzen vr **sich ~** to miscalculate

verschenken vt to give away; (Chance) to waste

verschicken vt to send off

verschieben vt irr (auf später) to postpone, to put off; (an anderen Ort) to move

verschieden adj (unterschiedlich) different; (mehrere) various; **sie sind ~ groß** they are of different sizes; **Verschiedene** pl various people/things pl; **Verschiedenes** various things pl

verschimmelt adj mouldy

verschlafen irr vt to sleep through; (fig) to miss ▷ vi to oversleep

verschlechtern vr **sich ~** to deteriorate, to get worse; **Verschlechterung** f deterioration

Verschleiß (-es) m wear and tear

verschließbar adj lockable; **verschließen** irr vt to close; (mit Schlüssel) to lock

verschlimmern vt to make worse ▷ vr **sich ~** to get worse

verschlossen adj locked; (fig) reserved

verschlucken vt to swallow ▷ vr **sich ~** to choke (an +dat on)

Verschluss m lock; (von Kleid) fastener; (Foto) shutter; (Stöpsel) stopper

verschmutzen vt to get dirty; (Umwelt) to pollute

verschnaufen vi **ich muss mal ~** I need to get my breath back

verschneit adj snow-covered

verschnupft adj **~ sein** to have a cold; (fam: beleidigt) to be peeved

verschonen vt to spare (jdn mit etw sb sth)

verschreiben irr vt (Med) to prescribe; **verschreibungspflichtig** adj available only on prescription

verschwand imperf von **verschwinden**

verschweigen irr vt to keep secret; **jdm etw ~** to keep sth from sb

verschwenden vt to waste; **Verschwendung** f waste

verschwiegen adj discreet; (Ort) secluded

verschwinden (verschwand, verschwunden) vi to disappear, to vanish; **verschwinde!** get lost!; **verschwunden** pp von **verschwinden**

Versehen (-s, -) nt **aus ~** by mistake; **versehentlich** adv by mistake

versenden irr vt to send off

versessen adj **~ auf** (+akk) mad about

versetzen vt to transfer; (verpfänden) to pawn; (fam: bei Verabredung) to stand up ▷ vr **sich in jdn** (o **jds Lage**) **~** to put oneself in sb's place

verseuchen vt to contaminate

versichern vt to insure; (bestätigen) to assure; **versichert sein** to be insured; **Versichertenkarte** f health-insurance card; **Versicherung** f insurance; **Versicherungskarte** f **grüne ~** green card (Brit), insurance document for driving abroad; **Versicherungspolice** f insurance policy

versilbert adj silver-plated

versinken irr vi to sink

Version f version

versöhnen vt to reconcile ▷ vr **sich ~** to become reconciled

versorgen vt to provide, to supply (mit with); (Familie) to look after ▷ vr **sich ~** to look after oneself; **Versorgung** f provision; (Unterhalt) maintenance; (für Alter etc) benefit

verspäten vr **sich ~** to be late; **verspätet** adj late; **Verspätung** f delay; (eine **Stunde**) **~ haben** to be (an hour) late

versprechen irr vt to promise ▷ vr **ich habe mich versprochen** I didn't mean to say that

Verstand m mind; (Vernunft) (common) sense; **den ~ verlieren** to lose one's mind; **verständigen** vt to inform ▷ vr **sich ~** to communicate; (sich einigen) to come to an understanding; **Verständigung** f communication; **verständlich** adj understandable; **Verständnis** nt understanding (für of); (Mitgefühl) sympathy; **verständnisvoll** adj understanding

Verstärker (-s, -) m amplifier

verstauchen vt to sprain

Versteck (-(e)s, -e) nt hiding place;

~ spielen to play hide-and-seek; **verstecken** vt to hide (vor +dat from) ▷ vr **sich ~** to hide (vor +dat from)

verstehen irr vt to understand; **falsch ~** to misunderstand ▷ vr **sich ~** to get on (mit with)

Versteigerung f auction

verstellbar adj adjustable; **verstellen** vt to move; (Uhr) to adjust; (versperren) to block; (Stimme, Handschrift) to disguise ▷ vr **sich ~** to pretend, to put on an act

verstopfen vt to block up; (Med) to constipate; **Verstopfung** f obstruction; (Med) constipation

Verstoß m infringement, violation (gegen of)

Versuch (-(e)s, -e) m attempt; (wissenschaftlich) experiment; **versuchen** vt to try

vertauschen vt to exchange; (versehentlich) to mix up

verteidigen vt to defend; **Verteidiger(in)** (-s, -) m(f) (Sport) defender; (Jur) defence counsel; **Verteidigung** f defence

verteilen vt to distribute

Vertrag (-(e)s, Verträge) m contract; (Pol) treaty

vertragen irr vt to stand, to bear ▷ vr **sich ~** to get along (with each other); (sich aussöhnen) to make it up

verträglich adj (Mensch) good-natured; (Speisen) digestible

vertrauen vi jdm/einer Sache **~** to trust sb/sth; **Vertrauen** (-s) nt trust (in +akk in, zu in); **ich habe kein ~ zu ihm** I don't trust him; **ich hab's ihm im ~ gesagt** I told him in confidence; **vertraulich** adj (geheim) confidential; **vertraut** adj **sich mit etw ~ machen** to familiarize oneself with sth

vertreten irr vt to represent; (Ansicht) to hold; **Vertreter(in)** (-s, -) m(f) representative

Vertrieb (-(e)s, -e) m (Abteilung) sales department

vertrocknen vi to dry up

vertun irr vr **sich ~** to make a mistake

vertuschen vt to cover up

verunglücken vi to have an accident; **tödlich ~** to be killed in an accident

verunsichern vt to make uneasy

verursachen vt to cause

verurteilen vt to condemn

vervielfältigen vt to make copies of

verwackeln vt (Foto) to blur

verwählen vr **sich ~** to dial the wrong number

verwalten vt to manage; (behördlich) to administer; **Verwalter(in)** (-s, -) m(f) manager; (Vermögens~) trustee; **Verwaltung** f management; (amtlich) administration

verwandt adj related (mit to); **Verwandte(r)** mf relative, relation; **Verwandtschaft** f relationship; (Menschen) relations pl

verwarnen vt to warn; (Sport) to caution

verwechseln vt to confuse (mit with); (halten für) to mistake (mit for)

verweigern vt to refuse

verwenden vt to use; (Zeit) to spend; **Mühe auf etw** (akk) **~** to take trouble over sth; **Verwendung** f use

verwirklichen vt to realize; **sich selbst ~** to fulfil oneself

verwirren vt to confuse; **Verwirrung** f confusion

verwitwet adj widowed

verwöhnen vt to spoil

verwunderlich adj surprising; **Verwunderung** f astonishment

verwüsten vt to devastate

verzählen vr **sich ~** to miscount

verzehren vt to consume

Verzeichnis nt (Liste) list; (Katalog) catalogue; (in Buch) index; (Inform) directory

verzeihen (verzieh, verziehen) vt, vi to forgive (jdm etw sb for sth); **~ Sie bitte, ...** (vor Frage etc) excuse me, ...; **~ Sie die Störung** sorry to disturb you; **Verzeihung** f **~!** sorry; **~, ...** (vor Frage etc) excuse me, ...; **(jdn) um ~ bitten** to apologize (to sb)

verzichten vi **auf etw** (akk) **~** to do without sth; (aufgeben) to give sth up

verzieh imperf von **verzeihen**

verziehen pp von **verzeihen**

verziehen irr vt (Kind) to spoil; **das Gesicht ~** to pull a face ▷ vr **sich ~** to go out of shape; (Gesicht) to contort; (verschwinden) to disappear

verzieren vt to decorate

verzögern vt to delay ▷ vr **sich ~** to be delayed; **Verzögerung** f delay

verzweifeln vi to despair (an +dat of);

V

verzweifelt adj desperate; **Verzweiflung** f despair

Veterinär(in) (-s, -e) m(f) veterinary surgeon (Brit), veterinarian (US)

Vetter (-s, -n) m cousin

vgl. abk = **vergleiche** cf

Viagra® (-s) nt Viagra®

Vibrator (-s, -en) m vibrator; **vibrieren** vi to vibrate

Video (-s, -s) nt video; **auf ~ aufnehmen** to video; **Videoclip** (-s, -s) m video clip; **Videofilm** m video; **Videogerät** nt video (recorder); **Videokamera** f video camera; **Videokassette** f video (cassette); **Videorekorder** m video recorder; **Videospiel** nt video game; **Videothek** (-, -en) f video library

Vieh (-(e)s) nt cattle

viel pron a lot (of), lots of; **~ Arbeit** a lot of work, lots of work; **~e Leute** a lot of people, lots of people, many people; **zu ~** too much; **zu ~e** too many; **sehr ~** a great deal of; **sehr ~e** a great many; **ziemlich ~/~e** quite a lot of; **nicht ~** not much, not a lot of; **nicht ~e** not many, not a lot of; **sie sagt nicht ~** she doesn't say a lot; **nicht ~** not much, not a lot of; **nicht ~e** not many, not a lot of; **gibt es ~?** is there much?, is there a lot?; **gibt es ~e?** are there many?, are there a lot? ▷ adv a lot; **er geht ~ ins Kino** he goes a lot to the cinema; **sehr ~** a great deal; **ziemlich ~** quite a lot; **~ besser** much better; **~ teurer** much more expensive; **~ zu ~** far too much

vielleicht adv perhaps; **~ ist sie krank** perhaps she's ill, she might be ill; **weißt du ~, wo er ist?** do you know where he is (by any chance)?

vielmal(s) adv many times; **danke ~s** many thanks; **vielmehr** adv rather; **vielseitig** adj very varied; (Mensch, Gerät) versatile

vier num four; **auf allen ~en** on all fours; **unter ~ Augen** in private, privately; **Vier** (-, -en) f four; (Schulnote) ≈ D; **Vierbettzimmer** nt four-bed room; **Viereck** (-(e)s, -e) nt four-sided figure; (Quadrat) square; **viereckig** adj four-sided; (quadratisch) square; **vierfach** adj **die ~e Menge** four times the amount; **vierhundert** num four hundred; **viermal** adv four times; **vierspurig** adj four-lane

viert adv **wir sind zu ~** there are four of us; **vierte(r, s)** adj fourth; siehe auch **dritte**

Viertel (-s, -) nt (Stadtviertel) quarter, district; (Bruchteil) quarter; (Viertelliter) quarter-litre; (Uhrzeit) quarter; **~ vor/nach drei** a quarter to/past three; **viertel drei** a quarter past two; **drei viertel drei** a quarter to three; **Viertelfinale** nt quarter-final; **vierteljährlich** adj quarterly; **Viertelstunde** f quarter of an hour

vierzehn num fourteen; **in ~ Tagen** in two weeks, in a fortnight (Brit); **vierzehntägig** adj two-week, fortnightly (Brit); **vierzehnte(r, s)** adj fourteenth; siehe auch **dritte**; **vierzig** num forty; **vierzigste(r, s)** adj fortieth

Vietnam (-s) nt Vietnam

Vignette f (Autobahn~) motorway (Brit) (o freeway (US)) permit

Villa (-, Villen) f villa

violett adj purple

Violine f violin

Virus (-, Viren) m o nt virus

Visitenkarte f card

Visum (-s, Visa o Visen) nt visa

Vitamin (-s, -e) nt vitamin

Vitrine (-, -n) f (glass) cabinet; (Schaukasten) display case

Vogel (-s, Vögel) m bird; **vögeln** vi, vt (vulg) to screw

Voicemail (-, -s) f voice mail

Vokal (-s, -e) m vowel

Volk (-(e)s, Völker) nt people pl; (Nation) nation; **Volksfest** nt festival; (Jahrmarkt) funfair; **Volkshochschule** f adult education centre; **Volkslied** nt folksong; **Volksmusik** f folk music; **volkstümlich** adj (einfach und beliebt) popular; (herkömmlich) traditional; (Kunst) folk

voll adj full (von of); **~ machen** to fill (up); **~ tanken** to fill up

Vollbart m beard; **Vollbremsung** f **eine ~ machen** to slam on the brakes; **vollends** adv completely

Volleyball m volleyball

Vollgas nt **mit ~** at full throttle; **~ geben** to step on it

völlig adj complete ▷ adv completely

volljährig adj of age; **Vollkaskoversicherung** f fully comprehensive insurance;

vollklimatisiert *adj* fully air-conditioned;
vollkommen *adj* perfect; **~er Unsinn**
complete rubbish ▷ *adv* completely
Vollkornbrot *nt* wholemeal (*Brit*) (*o*
whole wheat (*US*)) bread
Vollmacht (-, -en) *f* authority; (*Urkunde*)
power of attorney
Vollmilch *f* full-fat milk (*Brit*), whole milk
(*US*); **Vollmilchschokolade** *f* milk
chocolate; **Vollmond** *m* full moon;
Vollnarkose *f* general anaesthetic;
Vollpension *f* full board
vollständig *adj* complete
Volltreffer *m* direct hit; **Vollwaschmittel**
nt all-purpose washing powder;
Vollwertkost *f* wholefood; **vollzählig**
adj complete
Volt (-, -) *nt* volt
Volumen (-s, -) *nt* volume
vom *kontr von* **von dem** (*räumlich, zeitlich,
Ursache*) from; **ich kenne sie nur ~ Sehen** I
only know her by sight

○ SCHLÜSSELWORT

von *präp* +dat **1** (*Ausgangspunkt*) from; **von
... bis** from ... to; **von morgens bis
abends** from morning till night; **von ...
nach ...** from ... to ...; **von ... an** from ...;
von ... aus from ...; **von dort aus** from
there; **etw von sich aus tun** to do sth of
one's own accord; **von mir aus** (*umg*) if
you like I don't mind; **von wo/wann ...?**
where/when ... from?
2 (*Ursache, im Passiv*) by; **ein Gedicht von
Schiller** a poem by Schiller; **von etw
müde** tired from sth
3 (*als Genitiv*) of; **ein Freund von mir** a
friend of mine; **nett von dir** nice of you;
jeweils zwei von zehn two out of every
ten
4 (*über*) about; **er erzählte vom Urlaub**
he talked about his holiday
5: **von wegen!** (*umg*) no way!

○ SCHLÜSSELWORT

vor *präp* +dat **1** (*räumlich*) in front of; **vor
der Kirche links abbiegen** turn left before
the church
2 (*zeitlich*) before; **ich war vor ihm da** I
was there before him; **vor 2 Tagen** 2 days
ago; **5 (Minuten) vor 4** 5 (minutes) to 4;
vor kurzem a little while ago
3 (*Ursache*) with; **vor Wut/Liebe** with
rage/love; **vor Hunger sterben** to die of
hunger; **vor lauter Arbeit** because of
work
4: **vor allem, vor allen Dingen** most of all
▷ *präp* +akk (*räumlich*) in front of
▷ *adv*: **vor und zurück** backwards and
forwards

voran|gehen *irr vi* to go ahead; **einer
Sache** (*dat*) **~** to precede sth;
voran|kommen *irr vi* to make
progress
Vorarlberg (-s) *nt* Vorarlberg
voraus *adv* **jdm ~ sein** to be ahead of sb;
im Voraus in advance; **voraus|fahren** *irr
vi* to drive on ahead; **vorausgesetzt** *conj*
provided (that); **Voraussage** *f*
prediction; (*Wetter*) forecast;
voraus|sagen *vt* to predict;
voraus|sehen *irr vt* to foresee;
voraus|setzen *vt* to assume;
Voraussetzung *f* requirement,
prerequisite; **voraussichtlich** *adj*
expected ▷ *adv* probably; **voraus|zahlen**
vt to pay in advance
Vorbehalt (-(e)s, -e) *m* reservation;
vor|behalten *irr vt* **sich/jdm etw ~** to
reserve sth (for oneself)/for sb
vorbei *adv* past, over, finished;
vorbei|bringen *irr vt* to drop by (*o* in);
vorbei|fahren *irr vi* to drive past;
vorbei|gehen *irr vi* to pass by, to go past;
(*verstreichen, aufhören*) to pass;
vorbei|kommen *irr vi* to drop by;
vorbei|lassen *irr vt* **kannst du die Leute
~?** would you let these people pass?; **lässt
du mich bitte mal vorbei?** can I get past,
please?; **vorbei|reden** *vi* **aneinander ~** to
talk at cross-purposes
vor|bereiten *vt* to prepare ▷ *vr* **sich ~** to
get ready (*auf* +akk, *für* for); **Vorbereitung**
f preparation
vor|bestellen *vt* to book in advance;
(*Essen*) to order in advance;
Vorbestellung *f* booking, reservation
vor|beugen *vi* to prevent (*dat* sth);
vorbeugend *adj* preventive;
Vorbeugung *f* prevention
Vorbild *nt* (role) model; **vorbildlich** *adj*
model, ideal

V

Vorderachse f front axle; **vordere(r, s)** adj front; **Vordergrund** m foreground; **Vorderradantrieb** m (Auto) front-wheel drive; **Vorderseite** f front; **Vordersitz** m front seat; **Vorderteil** m o nt front (part)

vor|drängen vr **sich ~** to push forward

Vordruck m form

voreilig adj hasty, rash; **~e Schlüsse ziehen** to jump to conclusions; **voreingenommen** adj biased

vor|enthalten irr vt **jdm etw ~** to withhold sth from sb

vorerst adv for the moment

vor|fahren irr vi (vorausfahren) to drive on ahead; **vor das Haus ~** to drive up to the house; **fahren Sie bis zur Ampel vor** drive as far as the traffic lights

Vorfahrt f (Auto) right of way; **~ achten** give way (Brit), yield (US); **Vorfahrtsschild** nt give way (Brit) (o yield (US)) sign; **Vorfahrtsstraße** f major road

Vorfall m incident

vor|führen vt to demonstrate; (Film) to show; (Theaterstück, Trick) to perform

Vorgänger(in) m(f) predecessor

vor|gehen irr vi (vorausgehen) to go on ahead; (nach vorn) to go forward; (handeln) to act, to proceed; (Uhr) to be fast; (Vorrang haben) to take precedence; (passieren) to go on; **Vorgehen** (-s) nt procedure

Vorgesetzte(r) mf superior

vorgestern adv the day before yesterday

vor|haben irr vt to plan; **hast du schon was vor?** have you got anything on?; **ich habe vor, nach Rom zu fahren** I'm planning to go to Rome

vor|halten irr vt **jdm etw ~** to accuse sb of sth

Vorhand f forehand

vorhanden adj existing; (erhältlich) available

Vorhang m curtain

Vorhängeschloss nt padlock

Vorhaut f foreskin

vorher adv before; **zwei Tage ~** two days before; **~ essen wir** we'll eat first; **Vorhersage** f forecast; **vorher|sehen** irr vt to foresee

vorhin adv just now, a moment ago

vorig adj previous; (Woche etc) last

Vorkenntnisse pl previous knowledge sing

vor|kommen irr vi (nach vorne kommen) to come forward; (geschehen) to happen; (sich finden) to occur; (scheinen) to seem (to be); **sich** (dat) **dumm ~** to feel stupid

Vorlage f model

vor|lassen irr vt **jdn ~** to let sb go first

vorläufig adj temporary

vor|lesen irr vt to read out

Vorlesung f lecture

vorletzte(r, s) adj last but one; **am ~n Samstag** (on) the Saturday before last

Vorliebe f preference

vor|machen vt **kannst du es mir ~?** can you show me how to do it?; **jdm etwas ~** (fig: täuschen) to fool sb

vor|merken vt to note down; (Plätze) to book

Vormittag m morning; **am ~** in the morning; **heute ~** this morning; **vormittags** adv in the morning; **um 9 Uhr ~** at 9 (o'clock) in the morning, at 9 am

vorn(e) adv in front; **von ~ anfangen** to start at the beginning; **nach ~** to the front; **weiter ~** further up; **von ~ bis hinten** from beginning to end

Vorname m first name; **wie heißt du mit ~** what's your first name?

vornehm adj (von Rang) distinguished; (Benehmen) refined; (fein, elegant) elegant

vor|nehmen irr vt **sich** (dat) **etw ~** to start on sth; **sich** (dat) **~, etw zu tun** (beschließen) to decide to do sth

vornherein adv **von ~** from the start

Vorort m suburb

vorrangig adj priority

Vorrat m stock, supply; **vorrätig** adj in stock; **Vorratskammer** f pantry

Vorrecht nt privilege

Vorruhestand m early retirement

Vorsaison f early season

Vorsatz m intention; (Jur) intent; **vorsätzlich** adj intentional; (Jur) premeditated

Vorschau f preview; (Film) trailer

Vorschlag m suggestion, proposal; **vorschlagen** irr vt to suggest, to propose; **ich schlage vor, dass wir gehen** I suggest we go

vor|schreiben irr vt (befehlen) to stipulate; **jdm etw ~** to dictate sth to sb

Vorschrift *f* regulation, rule; (*Anweisung*) instruction; **vorschriftsmäßig** *adj* correct

Vorschule *f* nursery school, pre-school (*US*)

Vorsicht *f* care; **~!** look out; (*Schild*) caution; **~ Stufe!** mind the step; **vorsichtig** *adj* careful; **vorsichtshalber** *adv* just in case

Vorsorge *f* precaution; (*Vorbeugung*) prevention; **Vorsorgeuntersuchung** *f* checkup; **vorsorglich** *adv* as a precaution

Vorspann (-(*e*)*s*, -*e*) *m* credits *pl*

Vorspeise *f* starter

Vorsprung *m* projection; (*Abstand*) lead

vor|stellen *vt* (*bekannt machen*) to introduce; (*Uhr*) to put forward; (*vor etw*) to put in front; **sich** (*dat*) **etw ~** to imagine sth; **Vorstellung** *f* (*Bekanntmachen*) introduction; (*Theat*) performance; (*Gedanke*) idea; **Vorstellungsgespräch** *nt* interview

vor|täuschen *vt* to feign

Vorteil *m* advantage (*gegenüber* over); **die Vor- und Nachteile** the pros and cons; **vorteilhaft** *adj* advantageous

Vortrag (-(*e*)*s*, *Vorträge*) *m* talk (*über* +*akk* on); (*akademisch*) lecture; **einen ~ halten** to give a talk

vorüber *adv* over; **vorüber|gehen** *irr vi* to pass; **vorübergehend** *adj* temporary ▷ *adv* temporarily, for the time being

Vorurteil *nt* prejudice

Vorverkauf *m* advance booking

vor|verlegen *vt* to bring forward

Vorwahl *f* (*Tel*) dialling code (*Brit*), area code (*US*)

Vorwand (-(*e*)*s*, *Vorwände*) *m* pretext, excuse; **unter dem ~, dass** with the excuse that

vorwärts *adv* forward; **~ gehen** (*fig*) to progress; **Vorwärtsgang** *m* (*Auto*) forward gear

vorweg *adv* in advance; **vorweg|nehmen** *irr vt* to anticipate

Vorweihnachtszeit *f* pre-Christmas period, run-up to Christmas (*Brit*)

vor|werfen *irr vt* **jdm etw ~** to accuse sb of sth

vorwiegend *adv* mainly

Vorwort *nt* preface

Vorwurf *m* reproach; **sich** (*dat*) **Vorwürfe machen** to reproach oneself; **jdm**

Vorwürfe machen to accuse sb; **vorwurfsvoll** *adj* reproachful

vor|zeigen *vt* to show

vorzeitig *adj* premature, early

vor|ziehen *irr vt* (*lieber haben*) to prefer

Vorzug *m* preference; (*gute Eigenschaft*) merit; (*Vorteil*) advantage

vorzüglich *adj* excellent

vulgär *adj* vulgar

Vulkan (-*s*, -*e*) *m* volcano; **Vulkanausbruch** *m* volcanic eruption

V

W

W *abk* = **West** W

Waage (-, -n) *f* scales *pl*; (*Astr*) Libra;
waagerecht *adj* horizontal

wach *adj* awake; **~ werden** to wake up;
Wache (-, -n) *f* guard

Wachs (-es, -e) *nt* wax

wachsen (*wuchs, gewachsen*) *vi* to grow

wachsen *vt* (*Skier*) to wax

Wachstum *nt* growth

Wachtel (-, -n) *f* quail

Wächter(in) (-s, -) *m(f)* guard; (*auf Parkplatz*) attendant

wackelig *adj* wobbly; (*fig*) shaky;
Wackelkontakt *m* loose connection;
wackeln *vi* (*Stuhl*) to be wobbly; (*Zahn, Schraube*) to be loose; **mit dem Kopf ~** to waggle one's head

Wade (-, -n) *f* (*Anat*) calf

Waffe (-, -n) *f* weapon

Waffel (-, -n) *f* waffle; (*Keks, Eiswaffel*) wafer

wagen *vt* to risk; **es ~, etw zu tun** to dare to do sth

Wagen (-s, -) *m* (*Auto*) car; (*Eisenb*) carriage; **Wagenheber** (-s, -) *m* jack;
Wagentyp *m* model, make

Wahl (-, -en) *f* choice; (*Pol*) election

wählen *vt* to choose; (*Tel*) to dial; (*Pol*) to vote for; (*durch Wahl ermitteln*) to elect ▷ *vi* to choose; (*Tel*) to dial; (*Pol*) to vote;
Wähler(in) (-s, -) *m(f)* voter; **wählerisch** *adj* choosy

Wahlkampf *m* election campaign;
wahllos *adv* at random;
Wahlwiederholung *f* redial

Wahnsinn *m* madness; **~!** amazing!;
wahnsinnig *adj* insane, mad ▷ *adv* (*fam*) incredibly

wahr *adj* true; **das darf doch nicht ~ sein!**
I don't believe it; **nicht ~?** that's right, isn't it?

während *prep* +*gen* during ▷ *conj* while;
währenddessen *adv* meanwhile, in the meantime

Wahrheit *f* truth

wahrnehmbar *adj* noticeable,
perceptible; **wahr|nehmen** *irr vt* to perceive

Wahrsager(in) (-s, -) *m(f)* fortune-teller

wahrscheinlich *adj* probable, likely
▷ *adv* probably; **ich komme ~ zu spät** I'll probably be late; **Wahrscheinlichkeit** *f* probability

Währung *f* currency

Wahrzeichen *nt* symbol

Waise (-, -n) *f* orphan

Wal (-(e)s, -e) *m* whale

Wald (-(e)s, Wälder) *m* wood; (*groß*) forest;
Waldbrand *m* forest fire; **Waldlauf** *m* cross-country run; **Waldsterben** (-s) *nt* forest dieback

Wales (-) *nt* Wales; **Waliser(in)** *m(f)* Welshman/Welshwoman; **walisisch** *adj* Welsh; **Walisisch** *nt* Welsh

Walkie-Talkie (-(s), -s) *nt* walkie-talkie

Walkman® (-s, -s) *m* walkman®, personal stereo

Wall (-(e)s, Wälle) *m* embankment

Wallfahrt *f* pilgrimage; **Wallfahrtsort** *m* place of pilgrimage

Walnuss *f* walnut

Walross (-es, -e) *nt* walrus

wälzen *vt* to roll; (*Bücher*) to pore over;
(*Probleme*) to deliberate on ▷ *vr* **sich ~** to wallow; (*vor Schmerzen*) to roll about; (*im Bett*) to toss and turn

Walzer (-s, -) *m* waltz

Wand (-, Wände) *f* wall; (*Trenn~*) partition;
(*Berg~*) (rock) face

Wandel (-s) *m* change; **wandeln** *vt* to change ▷ *vr* **sich ~** to change

Wanderer (-s, -) m, **Wanderin** f hiker;
Wanderkarte f hiking map; **wandern** vi
to hike; (Blick) to wander; (Gedanken) to
stray; **Wanderschuh** m walking shoe;
Wanderstiefel m hiking boot;
Wanderung f hike; **eine ~ machen** to go
on a hike; **Wanderweg** m walking (o
hiking) trail

Wandleuchte f wall lamp;
Wandmalerei f mural; **Wandschrank** m
built-in cupboard (Brit), closet (US)

wandte imperf von **wenden**

Wange (-, -n) f cheek

wann adv when; **seit ~ ist sie da?** how
long has she been here?; **bis ~ bleibt ihr?**
how long are you staying?

Wanne (-, -n) f (bath) tub

Wappen (-s, -) nt coat of arms

war imperf von **sein**

warb imperf von **werben**

Ware (-, -n) f product; **~n** goods pl;
Warenhaus nt department store;
Warenprobe f sample; **Warensendung** f
consignment; **Warenzeichen** nt
trademark

warf imperf von **werfen**

warm adj warm; (Essen) hot; **~ laufen** to
warm up; **mir ist es zu ~** I'm too warm;
Wärme (-, -n) f warmth; **wärmen** vt to
warm; (Essen) to warm (o to heat) up ▷ vi
(Kleidung, Sonne) to be warm ▷ vr **sich ~** to
warm up; (gegenseitig) to keep each other
warm; **Wärmflasche** f hot-water bottle;
Warmstart m (Inform) warm start

Warnblinkanlage f (Auto) warning
flasher; **Warndreieck** nt (Auto) warning
triangle; **warnen** vt to warn (vor +dat
about, of); **Warnung** f warning

Warteliste f waiting list; **warten** vi to
wait (auf +akk for); **warte mal!** wait (o
hang on) a minute ▷ vt (Tech) to service

Wärter(in) m(f) attendant

Wartesaal m, **Wartezimmer** nt waiting
room

Wartung f service; (das Warten) servicing

warum adv why

Warze (-, -n) f wart

was pron what; (fam: etwas) something;
~ kostet das? what does it cost? how
much is it?; **~ für ein Auto ist das?** what
kind of car is that?; **~ für eine
Farbe/Größe?** what colour/size?; **~?** (fam:
wie bitte?) what?; **~ ist/gibt's?** what is it?

what's up? **du weißt, ~ ich meine** you
know what I mean; **~ (auch) immer**
whatever; **soll ich dir ~ mitbringen?** do
you want me to bring you anything?;
alles, ~ er hat everything he's got

Waschanlage f (Auto) car wash;
waschbar adj washable; **Waschbär** m
raccoon; **Waschbecken** nt washbasin

Wäsche (-, -n) f washing; (schmutzig)
laundry; (Bettwäsche) linen; (Unterwäsche)
underwear; **in der ~** in the wash;
Wäscheklammer f clothes peg (Brit) (o
pin (US)); **Wäscheleine** f clothesline

waschen (wusch, gewaschen) vt, vi to
wash; **Waschen und Legen** shampoo and
set ▷ vr **sich ~** to (have a) wash; **sich** (dat)
die Haare ~ to wash one's hair

Wäscherei f laundry; **Wäscheschleuder**
f spin-drier; **Wäscheständer** m clothes
horse; **Wäschetrockner** m tumble-drier

Waschgelegenheit f washing facilities
pl; **Waschlappen** m flannel (Brit),
washcloth (US); (fam: Mensch) wet
blanket; **Waschmaschine** f washing
machine; **Waschmittel** nt, **Waschpulver**
nt washing powder; **Waschraum** m
washroom; **Waschsalon** (-s, -s) m
launderette (Brit), laundromat (US);
Waschstraße f car wash

Wasser (-s, -) nt water; **fließendes
~** running water; **Wasserball** m (Sport)
water polo; **Wasserbob** m jet ski;
wasserdicht adj watertight; (Uhr etc)
waterproof; **Wasserfall** m waterfall;
Wasserfarbe f watercolour; **wasserfest**
adj watertight, waterproof; **Wasserhahn**
m tap (Brit), faucet (US); **wässerig** adj
watery; **Wasserkessel** m kettle;
Wasserkocher m electric kettle;
Wasserleitung f water pipe;
wasserlöslich adj water-soluble;
Wassermann m (Astr) Aquarius;
Wassermelone f water melon;
Wasserrutschbahn f water chute;
Wasserschaden m water damage;
wasserscheu adj scared of water;
Wasserski nt water-skiing;
Wasserspiegel m surface of the water;
(Wasserstand) water level; **Wassersport** m
water sports pl; **Wasserspülung** f flush;
wasserundurchlässig adj watertight,
waterproof; **Wasserverbrauch** m water
consumption; **Wasserversorgung** f

w

water supply; **Wasserwaage** f spirit
level; **Wasserwerk** nt waterworks pl
waten vi to wade
Watt (-(e)s, -en) nt (Geo) mud flats pl
▷ (-s, -) nt (Elek) watt
Watte (-, -n) f cotton wool; **Wattepad**
(-s, -s) m cotton pad; **Wattestäbchen** nt
cotton bud, Q-tip® (US)
WC (-s, -s) nt toilet, restroom (US);
WC-Reiniger m toilet cleaner
Web (-s) nt (Inform) Web; **Webseite** f
(Inform) web page
Wechsel (-s, -) m change; (Spieler~) (Sport)
substitution; **Wechselgeld** nt change;
wechselhaft adj (Wetter) changeable;
Wechseljahre pl menopause sing;
Wechselkurs m exchange rate;
wechseln vt to change; (Blicke) to
exchange; **Geld ~** to change some money;
(in Kleingeld) to get some change; **Euro in
Pfund ~** to change euros into pounds ▷ vi
to change; **kannst du ~?** can you change
this?; **Wechselstrom** m alternating
current, AC; **Wechselstube** f bureau de
change
Weckdienst m wake-up call service;
wecken vt to wake (up); **Wecker** (-s, -) m
alarm clock; **Weckruf** m wake-up call
wedeln vi (Ski) to wedel; **mit etw ~** to
wave sth; **mit dem Schwanz ~** to wag its
tail; **der Hund wedelte mit dem
Schwanz** the dog wagged its tail
weder conj **~ ... noch ...** neither ... nor ...
weg adv (entfernt, verreist) away; (los, ab)
off; **er war schon ~** he had already left (o
gone); **Hände ~!** hands off; **weit ~** a long
way away (o off)
Weg (-(e)s, -e) m way; (Pfad) path; (Route)
route; **jdn nach dem ~ fragen** to ask sb
the way; **auf dem ~ sein** to be on the
way
weg|bleiben irr vi to stay away;
weg|bringen irr vt to take away
wegen prep +gen o dat because of
weg|fahren irr vi to drive away; (abfahren)
to leave; (in Urlaub) to go away;
Wegfahrsperre f (Auto) (engine)
immobilizer; **weg|gehen** irr vi to go
away; **weg|kommen** irr vi to get away;
(fig) **gut/schlecht ~** to come off
well/badly; **weg|lassen** irr vt to leave
out; **weg|laufen** irr vi to run away;
weg|legen vt to put aside; **weg|machen**

vt (fam) to get rid of; **weg|müssen** irr vi
ich muss weg I've got to go;
weg|nehmen irr vt to take away;
weg|räumen vt to clear away;
weg|rennen irr vi to run away;
weg|schicken vt to send away;
weg|schmeißen irr vt to throw away;
weg|sehen irr vi to look away; **weg|tun**
irr vt to put away
Wegweiser (-s, -) m signpost
weg|werfen irr vt to throw away;
Wegwerfflasche f non-returnable bottle;
weg|wischen vt to wipe off; **weg|ziehen**
irr vi to move (away)
weh adj sore; siehe auch **wehtun**
wehen vt, vi to blow; (Fahne) to flutter
Wehen pl labour pains pl
Wehrdienst m military service
wehren vr **sich ~** to defend oneself
weh|tun irr vi to hurt; **jdm/sich ~** to hurt
sb/oneself
Weibchen nt **es ist ein ~** (Tier) it's a she;
weiblich adj feminine; (Bio) female
weich adj soft; **~ gekocht** (Ei) soft-boiled
Weichkäse m soft cheese; (Streichkäse)
cheese spread; **weichlich** adj soft;
(körperlich) weak; **Weichspüler** (-s, -) m
(für Wäsche) (fabric) softener
Weide (-, -n) f (Baum) willow; (Grasfläche)
meadow
weigern vr **sich ~** to refuse; **Weigerung** f
refusal
Weiher (-s, -) m pond
Weihnachten (-, -) nt Christmas;
Weihnachtsabend m Christmas Eve;
Weihnachtsbaum m Christmas tree;
Weihnachtsfeier f Christmas party;
Weihnachtsferien pl Christmas holidays
pl (Brit), Christmas vacation sing (US);
Weihnachtsgeschenk nt Christmas
present; **Weihnachtslied** nt Christmas
carol; **Weihnachtsmann** m Father
Christmas, Santa (Claus)

- **Weihnachtsmarkt**
-
- The **Weihnachtsmarkt** is a market held
- in most large towns in Germany in
- the weeks prior to Christmas. People
- visit it to buy presents, toys and
- Christmas decorations, and to enjoy
- the festive atmosphere. Food and
- drink associated with the Christmas

festivities can also be eaten and
drunk there, for example,
gingerbread and mulled wine.

Weihnachtsstern m (Bot) poinsettia;
Weihnachtstag m **erster ~** Christmas
Day; **zweiter ~** Boxing Day;
Weihnachtszeit f Christmas season
weil conj because
Weile (-) f while, short time; **es kann
noch eine ~ dauern** it could take some
time
Wein (-(e)s, -e) m wine; (Pflanze) vine;
Weinbeere f grape; **Weinberg** m
vineyard; **Weinbergschnecke** f snail;
Weinbrand m brandy
weinen vt, vi to cry
Weinglas nt wine glass; **Weinkarte** f
wine list; **Weinkeller** m wine cellar;
Weinlese (-, -n) f vintage; **Weinprobe** f
wine tasting; **Weintraube** f grape
weise adj wise
Weise (-, -n) f manner, way; **auf diese
(Art und) ~** this way
weisen (wies, gewiesen) vt to show
Weisheit f wisdom; **Weisheitszahn** m
wisdom tooth
weiß adj white; **Weißbier** nt ≈ wheat
beer; **Weißbrot** nt white bread;
weißhaarig adj white-haired; **Weißkohl**
m, **Weißkraut** nt (white) cabbage;
Weißwein m white wine
weit adj wide; (Begriff) broad; (Reise, Wurf)
long; (Kleid) loose; **wie ~ ist es ...?** how
far is it ...?; **so ~ sein** to be ready ▷ adv
far; **~ verbreitet** widespread; **~ gereist**
widely travelled; **~ offen** wide open; **das
geht zu ~** that's going too far, that's
pushing it
weiter adj wider; (~ weg) farther (away);
(zusätzlich) further; **~e Informationen**
further information sing ▷ adv further; **~!**
go on; (weitergehen!) keep moving;
~ nichts/niemand nothing/nobody else;
und so ~ and so on; **weiter|arbeiten** vi to
carry on working; **Weiterbildung** f
further training (o education);
weiter|empfehlen irr vt to recommend;
weiter|erzählen vt **nicht ~!** don't tell
anyone; **weiter|fahren** irr vi to go on
(nach to, bis as far as); **weiter|geben** irr vt
to pass on; **weiter|gehen** irr vi to go on;
weiter|helfen irr vi jdm **~** to help sb;

weiterhin adv **etw ~ tun** to go on doing
sth; **weiter|machen** vt, vi to continue;
weiter|reisen vi to continue one's
journey
weitgehend adj considerable ▷ adv
largely; **weitsichtig** adj long-sighted; (fig)
far-sighted; **Weitspringer(in)** m(f) long
jumper; **Weitsprung** m long jump;
Weitwinkelobjektiv nt (Foto) wide-angle
lens
Weizen (-s, -) m wheat; **Weizenbier** nt ≈
wheat beer

SCHLÜSSELWORT

welche(r, s) interrogativ pron which;
welcher von beiden? which (one) of the
two?; **welchen hast du genommen?**
which (one) did you take?; **welche eine
...!** what a ...!; **welche Freude!** what joy!
▷ indef pron some; (in Fragen) any; **ich habe
welche** I have some, **haben Sie welche?**
do you have any?
▷ relativ pron (bei Menschen) who (bei Sachen)
which that; **welche(r, s) auch immer**
whoever/whichever/whatever

welk adj withered; **welken** vi to wither
Welle (-, -n) f wave; **Wellengang** m
waves pl; **starker ~** heavy seas pl;
Wellenlänge f (a. fig) wavelength;
Wellenreiten nt surfing; **Wellensittich**
(-s, -e) m budgerigar, budgie; **wellig** adj
wavy
Welpe (-n, -n) m puppy
Welt (-, -en) f world; **auf der ~** in the
world; **auf die ~ kommen** to be born;
Weltall nt universe; **weltbekannt,
weltberühmt** adj world-famous;
Weltkrieg m world war; **Weltmacht** f
world power; **Weltmeister(in)** m(f)
world champion; **Weltmeisterschaft** f
world championship; (im Fußball) World
Cup; **Weltraum** m space; **Weltreise** f
trip round the world; **Weltrekord** m
world record; **Weltstadt** f metropolis;
weltweit adj worldwide, global
wem pron dat von **wer** who ... to, (to)
whom; **~ hast du's gegeben?** who did you
give it to?; **~ gehört es?** who does it
belong to?, whose is it?; **~ auch immer es
gehört** whoever it belongs to
wen pron akk von **wer** who, whom; **~ hast**

du besucht? who did you visit?;
~ möchten Sie sprechen? who would you
like to speak to?; **~ auch immer du
gesprochen hast** whoever you talked
to
Wende (-, -n) f turning point;
(*Veränderung*) change; **die ~** (*Hist*) the fall
of the Berlin Wall; **Wendekreis** m (*Auto*)
turning circle
Wendeltreppe f spiral staircase
wenden (*wendete o wandte, gewendet o
gewandt*) vt, vi to turn (round); (*um 180°*)
to make a U-turn; **sich an jdn ~** to turn
to sb; **bitte ~!** please turn over, PTO
▷ vr **sich ~** to turn; **sich an jdn ~** to turn
to sb
wenig pron, adv little; **~(e)** pl few; (**nur**) **ein**
(**klein**) **~** (just) a little (bit); **ein ~ Zucker** a
little bit of sugar, a little sugar; **wir haben
~ Zeit** we haven't got much time; **zu ~** too
little; pl too few; **nur ~ wissen** only a few
know ▷ adv **er spricht ~** he doesn't talk
much; **~ bekannt** little known; **wenige**
pron pl few pl; **wenigste(r, s)** adj least;
wenigstens adv at least

⬤ SCHLÜSSELWORT

wenn konj **1** (*falls, bei Wünschen*) if; **wenn
auch ..., selbst wenn ...** even if ...; **wenn
ich doch ...** if only I ...
2 (*zeitlich*) when; **immer wenn** whenever

wer pron who; **~ war das?** who was that?;
~ von euch? which (one) of you? ▷ pron
anybody who, anyone who; **~ das glaubt,
ist dumm** anyone who believes that is
stupid; **~ auch immer** whoever ▷ pron
somebody, someone; (*in Fragen*)
anybody, anyone; **ist da ~?** is (there)
anybody there?
Werbefernsehen nt TV commercials pl;
Werbegeschenk nt promotional gift;
werben (*warb, geworben*) vt to win;
(*Mitglied*) to recruit ▷ vi to advertise;
Werbespot (-s, -s) m commercial;
Werbung f advertising

⬤ SCHLÜSSELWORT

werden (pt **wurde**, pp **geworden** od (*bei
Passiv*) **worden**) vi to become; **was ist aus
ihm/aus der Sache geworden?** what

became of him/it?; **es ist nichts/gut
geworden** it came to nothing/turned out
well; **es wird Nacht/Tag** it's getting
dark/light; **mir wird kalt** I'm getting cold;
mir wird schlecht I feel ill; **Erster werden**
to come od be first; **das muss anders
werden** that'll have to change; **rot/zu Eis
werden** to turn red/to ice; **was willst du
(mal) werden?** what do you want to be?;
die Fotos sind gut geworden the photos
have come out nicely
▷ als Hilfsverb **1** (*bei Futur*): **er wird es tun**
he will od he'll do it; **er wird das nicht tun**
he will not od he won't do it; **es wird
gleich regnen** it's going to rain
2 (*bei Konjunktiv*): **ich würde ...** I would ...;
er würde gern ... he would od he'd like to
...; **ich würde lieber ...** I would od I'd
rather ...
3 (*bei Vermutung*): **sie wird in der Küche
sein** she will be in the kitchen
4 (*bei Passiv*): **gebraucht werden** to be
used; **er ist erschossen worden** he has od
he's been shot; **mir wurde gesagt, dass
...** I was told that ...

werfen (*warf, geworfen*) vt to throw
Werft (-, -en) f shipyard, dockyard
Werk (-(e)s, -e) nt (*Kunstwerk, Buch etc*)
work; (*Fabrik*) factory; (*Mechanismus*)
works pl; **Werkstatt** (-, -stätten) f
workshop; (*Auto*) garage; **Werktag** m
working day; **werktags** adv on weekdays,
during the week; **Werkzeug** nt tool;
Werkzeugkasten m toolbox
wert adj worth; **es ist etwa 50 Euro ~** it's
worth about 50 euros; **das ist nichts ~** it's
worthless; **Wert** (-(e)s, -e) m worth;
(*Zahlen~*) (*Fin*) value; **~ legen auf** (+akk) to
attach importance to; **es hat doch
keinen ~** (*Sinn*) it's pointless; **Wertangabe**
f declaration of value; **Wertbrief** m
insured letter; **Wertgegenstand** m
valuable object; **wertlos** adj worthless;
Wertmarke f token; **Wertpapiere** pl
securities pl; **Wertsachen** pl valuables pl;
Wertstoff m recyclable waste; **wertvoll**
adj valuable
Wesen (-s, -) nt being; (*Natur, Charakter*)
nature
wesentlich adj significant; (*beträchtlich*)
considerable ▷ adv considerably
weshalb adv why

Wespe (-, -n) f wasp; **Wespenstich** m wasp sting

wessen pron gen von **wer**; whose

● **Wessi**
●
● A **Wessi** is a colloquial and often
● derogatory word used to describe a
● German from the former West
● Germany. The expression
● 'Besserwessi' is used by East
● Germans to describe a West German
● who is considered to be a know-all.

West west; **Westdeutschland** nt (als Landesteil) Western Germany; (Hist) West Germany

Weste (-, -n) f waistcoat (Brit), vest (US); (Wollweste) cardigan

Westen (-s) m west; **im ~ Englands** in the west of England; **der Wilde ~** the Wild West; **Westeuropa** nt Western Europe; **Westküste** f west coast; **westlich** adj western; (Kurs, Richtung) westerly; **Westwind** m west(erly) wind

weswegen adv why

Wettbewerb m competition; **Wettbüro** nt betting office; **Wette** (-, -n) f bet; **eine ~ abschließen** to make a bet; **die ~ gilt!** you're on; **wetten** vt, vi to bet (auf +akk on); **ich habe mit ihm gewettet, dass ...** I bet him that ...; **ich wette mit dir um 50 Euro** I'll bet you 50 euros; **~, dass?** wanna bet?

Wetter (-s, -) nt weather; **Wetterbericht** m, **Wettervorhersage** f weather forecast; **Wetterkarte** f weather map; **Wetterlage** f weather situation; **Wettervorhersage** f weather forecast

Wettkampf m contest; **Wettlauf** m race; **Wettrennen** nt race

WG (-, -s) f abk = **Wohngemeinschaft**

Whirlpool® (-s, -s) m jacuzzi®

Whisky (-s, -s) m (schottisch) whisky; (irisch, amerikanisch) whiskey

wichtig adj important

wickeln vt (Schnur) to wind (um round); (Schal, Decke) to wrap (um round); **ein Baby ~** to change a baby's nappy (Brit) (o diaper (US)); **Wickelraum** m baby-changing room; **Wickeltisch** m baby-changing table

Widder (-s, -) m (Zool) ram; (Astr) Aries sing

wider prep +akk against

widerlich adj disgusting

widerrufen irr vt to withdraw; (Auftrag, Befehl etc) to cancel

widersprechen irr vi to contradict (jdm sb); **Widerspruch** m contradiction

Widerstand m resistance; **widerstandsfähig** adj resistant (gegen to)

widerwärtig adj disgusting

widerwillig adj unwilling, reluctant

widmen vt to dedicate ▷ vr **sich jdm/etw ~** to devote oneself to sb/sth; **Widmung** f dedication

○ SCHLÜSSELWORT

wie adv how; **wie groß/schnell?** how big/fast?; **wie wärs?** how about it?; **wie ist er?** what's he like?; **wie gut du das kannst!** you're very good at it; **wie bitte?** pardon?; (entrüstet) I beg your pardon!; **und wie!** and how!; **wie viel** how much; **wie viel Menschen** how many people; **wie weit** to what extent

▷ konj **1** (bei Vergleichen); **so schön wie ...** as beautiful as ...; **wie ich schon sagte** as I said; **wie du** like you; **singen wie ein ...** to sing like a ...; **wie (zum Beispiel)** such as (for example)

2 (zeitlich): **wie er das hörte, ging er** when he heard that he left; **er hörte, wie der Regen fiel** he heard the rain falling

wieder adv again; **~ ein(e) ...** another ...; **~ erkennen** to recognize; **etw ~ gutmachen** to make up for sth; **~ verwerten** to recycle

wieder|bekommen irr vt to get back

wiederholen vt to repeat; **Wiederholung** f repetition

Wiederhören nt (Tel) **auf ~** goodbye

wieder|kommen irr vi to come back

wieder|sehen irr vt to see again; (wieder treffen) to meet again; **Wiedersehen** (-s) nt reunion; **auf ~!** goodbye

Wiedervereinigung f reunification

Wiege (-, -n) f cradle; **wiegen** (wog, gewogen) vt, vi (Gewicht) to weigh

Wien (-s) nt Vienna

wies imperf von **weisen**

Wiese (-, -n) f meadow

Wiesel (-s, -) nt weasel

wieso adv why

W

wievielmal adv how often; **wievielte(r, s)** adj **zum ~n Mal?** how many times?; **den Wievielten haben wir heute?** what's the date today?; **am Wievielten hast du Geburtstag?** which day is your birthday?

wieweit conj to what extent

wild adj wild

Wild (-(e)s) nt game

wildfremd adj (fam) **ein ~er Mensch** a complete (o total) stranger; **Wildleder** nt suede; **Wildpark** m game park; **Wildschwein** nt (wild) boar; **Wildwasserfahren** (-s) nt whitewater canoeing (o rafting)

Wille (-ns, -n) m will

willen prep +gen **um ... ~** for the sake of ...; **um Himmels ~!** (vorwurfsvoll) for heaven's sake; (betroffen) goodness me

willkommen adj welcome

Wimper (-, -n) f eyelash; **Wimperntusche** f mascara

Wind (-(e)s, -e) m wind

Windel (-, -n) f nappy (Brit), diaper (US)

windgeschützt adj sheltered from the wind; **windig** adj windy; (fig) dubious; **Windjacke** f windcheater; **Windmühle** f windmill; **Windpocken** pl chickenpox sing; **Windschutzscheibe** f (Auto) windscreen (Brit), windshield (US); **Windstärke** f wind force; **Windsurfen** (-s) nt windsurfing; **Windsurfer(in)** m(f) windsurfer

Winkel (-s, -) m (Math) angle; (Gerät) set square; (in Raum) corner; **im rechten ~ zu** at right angles to

winken vt, vi to wave

Winter (-s, -) m winter; **Winterausrüstung** f (Auto) winter equipment; **Winterfahrplan** m winter timetable; **winterlich** adj wintry; **Wintermantel** m winter coat; **Winterreifen** m winter tyre; **Winterschlussverkauf** m winter sales pl; **Wintersport** m winter sports pl

Winterzeit f (Uhrzeit) winter time (Brit), standard time (US)

winzig adj tiny

wir pron we; **~ selbst** we ourselves; **~ alle** all of us; **~ drei** the three of us; **~ sind's** it's us; **~ nicht** not us

Wirbel (-s, -) m whirl; (Trubel) hurly-burly; (Aufsehen) fuss; (Anat) vertebra; **Wirbelsäule** f spine

wirken vi to be effective; (erfolgreich sein) to work; (scheinen) to seem

wirklich adj real; **Wirklichkeit** f reality

wirksam adj effective; **Wirkung** f effect

wirr adj confused; **Wirrwarr** (-s) m confusion

Wirsing (-s) m savoy cabbage

Wirt (-(e)s, -e) m landlord; **Wirtin** f landlady

Wirtschaft f (Comm) economy; (Gaststätte) pub; **wirtschaftlich** adj (Pol, Comm) economic; (sparsam) economical

Wirtshaus nt pub

wischen vt, vi to wipe; **Wischer** (-s, -) m wiper; **Wischlappen** m cloth

wissen (wusste, gewusst) vt to know; **weißt du schon, ...?** did you know ...?; **woher weißt du das?** how do you know?; **das musst du selbst ~** that's up to you; **Wissen** (-s) nt knowledge

Wissenschaft f science; **Wissenschaftler(in)** (-s, -) m(f) scientist; (Geisteswissenschaftler) academic; **wissenschaftlich** adj scientific; (geisteswissenschaftlich) academic

Witwe (-, -n) f widow; **Witwer** (-s, -) m widower

Witz (-(e)s, -e) m joke; **mach keine ~!** you're kidding!; **das soll wohl ein ~ sein** you've got to be joking; **witzig** adj funny

wo adv where; **zu einer Zeit, ~ ...** at a time when ...; **überall, ~ ich hingehe** wherever I go ▷ conj **jetzt, ~ du da bist** now that you're here; **~ ich dich gerade spreche** while I'm talking to you; **woanders** adv somewhere else

wobei adv **~ mir einfällt ...** which reminds me ...

Woche (-, -n) f week; **während** (o **unter**) **der ~** during the week; **einmal die ~** once a week; **Wochenende** nt weekend; **am ~** at (Brit) (o on (US)) the weekend; **wir fahren übers ~ weg** we're going away for the weekend; **Wochenendhaus** nt weekend cottage; **Wochenkarte** f weekly (season) ticket; **wochenlang** adv for weeks (on end); **Wochenmarkt** m weekly market; **Wochentag** m weekday; **wöchentlich** adj, adv weekly

Wodka (-s, -s) m vodka

wodurch adv **~ unterscheiden sie sich?** what's the difference between them?;

~ hast du es gemerkt? how did you notice?; **wofür** adv (relativ) for which; (Frage) what ... for; **~ brauchst du das?** what do you need that for?

wog imperf von **wiegen**

woher adv where ... from; **wohin** adv where ... to

◯ SCHLÜSSELWORT

wohl adv **1**: **sich wohl fühlen** (zufrieden) to feel happy; (gesundheitlich) to feel well; **jdm wohl tun** to do sb good; **wohl oder übel** whether one likes it or not

2 (wahrscheinlich) probably; (gewiss) certainly; (vielleicht) perhaps; **sie ist wohl zu Hause** she's probably at home; **das ist doch wohl nicht dein Ernst!** surely you're not serious!; **das mag wohl sein** that may well be; **ob das wohl stimmt?** I wonder if that's true; **er weiß das sehr wohl** he knows that perfectly well

Wohlwollen (-s) nt goodwill

Wohnblock m block of flats (Brit), apartment house (US); **wohnen** vi to live; **Wohngemeinschaft** f shared flat (Brit) (o apartment (US)); **ich wohne in einer ~** I share a flat (o apartment); **wohnhaft** adj resident; **Wohnküche** f kitchen-cum-living-room; **Wohnmobil** (-s, -e) nt camper, RV (US); **Wohnort** m place of residence; **Wohnsitz** m place of residence; **Wohnung** f flat (Brit), apartment (US); **Wohnungstür** f front door; **Wohnwagen** m caravan; **Wohnzimmer** nt living room

Wolf (-(e)s, Wölfe) m wolf

Wolke (-, -n) f cloud; **Wolkenkratzer** m skyscraper; **wolkenlos** adj cloudless; **wolkig** adj cloudy

Wolldecke f (woollen) blanket; **Wolle** (-, -n) f wool

◯ SCHLÜSSELWORT

wollen (pt **wollte**, pp **gewollt** od (als Hilfsverb) **wollen**) vt, vi to want; **ich will nach Hause** I want to go home; **er will nicht** he doesn't want to; **er wollte das nicht** he didn't want it; **wenn du willst** if you like; **ich will, dass du mir zuhörst** I want you to listen to me

▷ Hilfsverb: **er will ein Haus kaufen** he wants to buy a house; **ich wollte, ich wäre ...** I wish I were ...; **etw gerade tun wollen** to be going to do sth

Wolljacke f cardigan

womit adv what ... with; **~ habe ich das verdient?** what have I done to deserve that?

womöglich adv possibly

woran adv **~ denkst du?** what are you thinking of?; **~ ist er gestorben?** what did he die of?; **~ sieht man das?** how can you tell?

worauf adv **~ wartest du?** what are you waiting for?

woraus adv **~ ist das gemacht?** what is it made of?

Workshop (-s, -s) m workshop

World Wide Web nt World Wide Web

Wort (-(e)s, Wörter) nt (Vokabel) word ▷ (-(e)s, -e) nt (Äußerung) word; **mit anderen ~en** in other words; **jdn beim ~ nehmen** to take sb at his/her word; **Wörterbuch** nt dictionary; **wörtlich** adj literal

worüber adv **~ redet sie?** what is she talking about?

worum adv **~ gehts?** what is it about?

worunter adv **~ leidet er?** what is he suffering from?

wovon adv (relativ) from which; **~ redest du?** what are you talking about?; **wozu** adv (relativ) to/for which; (interrogativ) what ... for/to; (warum) why; **~?** what for?; **~ brauchst du das?** what do you need it for?; **~ soll das gut sein?** what's it for?; **~ hast du Lust?** what do you feel like doing?

Wrack (-(e)s, -s) nt wreck

Wucher (-s) m profiteering; **das ist ~!** that's daylight robbery!

wuchs imperf von **wachsen**

wühlen vi to rummage; (Tier) to root; (Maulwurf) to burrow

Wühltisch m bargain counter

wund adj sore; **Wunde** (-, -n) f wound

Wunder (-s, -) nt miracle; **es ist kein ~** it's no wonder; **wunderbar** adj wonderful, marvellous; **Wunderkerze** f sparkler; **Wundermittel** nt wonder cure; **wundern** vr **sich ~** to be surprised (über +akk at) ▷ vt

w

to surprise; **wunderschön** *adj* beautiful;
wundervoll *adj* wonderful
Wundsalbe *f* antiseptic ointment;
Wundstarrkrampf *m* tetanus
Wunsch (*-(e)s, Wünsche*) *m* wish (*nach* for);
wünschen *vt* to wish; **sich** (*dat*) **etw ~** to
want sth; **ich wünsche dir alles Gute** I
wish you all the best; **wünschenswert**
adj desirable
wurde *imperf von* **werden**
Wurf (*-s, Würfe*) *m* throw; (*Zool*) litter
Würfel (*-s, -*) *m* dice; (*Math*) cube;
würfeln *vi* to throw (the dice); (*Würfel
spielen*) to play dice ▷ *vt* (*Zahl*) to throw;
(*Gastr*) to dice; **Würfelzucker** *m* lump
sugar
Wurm (*-(e)s, Würmer*) *m* worm
Wurst (*-, Würste*) *f* sausage; **das ist mir
~** (*fam*) I couldn't care less
Würstchen *nt* frankfurter
Würze (*-, -n*) *f* seasoning, spice
Wurzel (*-, -n*) *f* root
würzen *vt* to season, to spice; **würzig** *adj*
spicy
wusch *imperf von* **waschen**
wusste *imperf von* **wissen**
wüst *adj* (*unordentlich*) chaotic;
(*ausschweifend*) wild; (*öde*) desolate; (*fam:
heftig*) terrible
Wüste (*-, -n*) *f* desert
Wut (*-*) *f* rage, fury; **ich habe eine ~ auf
ihn** I'm really mad at him; **wütend** *adj*
furious
WWW (*-*) *nt abk* = **World Wide Web**
WWW

X-Beine *pl* knock-knees *pl*; **x-beinig** *adj* knock-kneed

x-beliebig *adj* **ein ~es Buch** any book (you like)

x-mal *adv* umpteen times

Xylophon (-s, -e) *nt* xylophone

Yacht (-, -en) f yacht
Yoga (-(s)) m o nt yoga
Yuppie (-s, -s) m (-, -s) f yuppie

Zacke (-, -n) f point; (*Säge, Kamm*) tooth; (*Gabel*) prong; **zackig** adj (*Linie etc*) jagged; (*fam: Tempo*) brisk
zaghaft adj timid
zäh adj tough; (*Flüssigkeit*) thick
Zahl (-, -en) f number; **zahlbar** adj payable; **zahlen** vt, vi to pay; **~ bitte!** could I have the bill (*Brit*) (*o* check (*US*)) please?; **bar ~** to pay cash; **zählen** vt, vi to count (*auf +akk* on); **~ zu** to be one of; **Zahlenschloss** nt combination lock; **Zähler** (-s, -) m (*Gerät*) counter; (*für Strom, Wasser*) meter; **zahlreich** adj numerous; **Zahlung** f payment; **Zahlungsanweisung** f money order; **Zahlungsbedingungen** pl terms pl of payment
zahm adj tame; **zähmen** vt to tame
Zahn (-(e)s, *Zähne*) m tooth; **Zahnarzt** m, **Zahnärztin** f dentist; **Zahnbürste** f toothbrush; **Zahncreme** f toothpaste; **Zahnersatz** m dentures pl; **Zahnfleisch** nt gums pl; **Zahnfleischbluten** nt bleeding gums pl; **Zahnfüllung** f filling; **Zahnklammer** f brace; **Zahnpasta** f, **Zahnpaste** f toothpaste; **Zahnradbahn** f rack railway (*Brit*) (*o* railroad (*US*));

Zahnschmerzen pl toothache sing; **Zahnseide** f dental floss; **Zahnspange** f brace; **Zahnstocher** (-s, -) m toothpick
Zange (-, -n) f pliers pl; (*Zuckerzange*) tongs pl; (*Beißzange, Zool*) pincers pl; (*Med*) forceps pl
zanken vi to quarrel ▷ vr **sich ~** to quarrel
Zäpfchen nt (*Anat*) uvula; (*Med*) suppository
zapfen vt (*Bier*) to pull; **Zapfsäule** f petrol (*Brit*) (*o* gas (*US*)) pump
zappeln vi to wriggle; (*unruhig sein*) to fidget
zappen vi to zap, to channel-hop
zart adj (*weich, leise*) soft; (*Braten etc*) tender; (*fein, schwächlich*) delicate; **zartbitter** adj (*Schokolade*) plain, dark
zärtlich adj tender, affectionate; **Zärtlichkeit** f tenderness; **~en** pl hugs and kisses pl
Zauber (-s, -) m magic; (*Bann*) spell; **Zauberei** f magic; **Zauberer** (-s, -) m magician; (*Künstler*) conjuror; **Zauberformel** f (magic) spell; **zauberhaft** adj enchanting; **Zauberin** f sorceress; **Zauberkünstler(in)** m(f) magician, conjuror; **Zaubermittel** nt magic cure; **zaubern** vi to do magic; (*Künstler*) to do conjuring tricks; **Zauberspruch** m (magic) spell
Zaun (-(e)s, *Zäune*) m fence
z. B. abk = **zum Beispiel** e.g., eg
Zebra (-s, -s) nt zebra; **Zebrastreifen** m zebra crossing (*Brit*), crosswalk (*US*)
Zechtour f pub crawl
Zecke (-, -n) f tick
Zehe (-, -n) f toe; (*Knoblauch*) clove; **Zehennagel** m toenail; **Zehenspitze** f tip of the toes
zehn num ten; **Zehnerkarte** f ticket valid for ten trips; **Zehnkampf** m decathlon; **Zehnkämpfer(in)** m(f) decathlete; **zehnmal** adv ten times; **zehntausend** num ten thousand; **zehnte(r, s)** adj tenth; siehe auch **dritte**; **Zehntel** (-s, -) nt (*Bruchteil*) tenth; **Zehntelsekunde** f tenth of a second
Zeichen (-s, -) nt sign; (*Schriftzeichen*) character; **Zeichenblock** m sketch pad; **Zeichenerklärung** f key; **Zeichensetzung** f punctuation; **Zeichensprache** f sign language; **Zeichentrickfilm** m cartoon

z

zeichnen *vt, vi* to draw; **Zeichnung** *f* drawing

Zeigefinger *m* index finger; **zeigen** *vt* to show; **sie zeigte uns die Stadt** she showed us around the town; **zeig mal!** let me see ▷ *vi* to point (*auf +akk* to, at) ▷ *vr* **sich ~** to show oneself; **es wird sich ~** time will tell; **Zeiger** (*-s, -*) *m* pointer; (*Uhr*) hand

Zeile (*-, -n*) *f* line

Zeit (*-, -en*) *f* time; **ich habe keine ~** I haven't got time; **lass dir ~** take your time; **das hat ~** there's no rush; **von ~ zu ~** from time to time; **Zeitansage** *f* (*Tel*) speaking clock (*Brit*), correct time (*US*); **Zeitarbeit** *f* temporary work; **zeitgenössisch** *adj* contemporary, modern; **zeitgleich** *adj* simultaneous ▷ *adv* at exactly the same time; **zeitig** *adj* early; **Zeitkarte** *f* season ticket; **zeitlich** *adj* (*Reihenfolge*) chronological; **es passt ~ nicht** it isn't a convenient time; **ich schaff es ~ nicht** I'm not going to make it; **Zeitlupe** *f* slow motion; **Zeitplan** *m* schedule; **Zeitpunkt** *m* point in time; **Zeitraum** *m* period (of time); **Zeitschrift** *f* magazine; (*wissenschaftliche*) periodical

Zeitung *f* newspaper; **es steht in der ~** it's in the paper(s); **Zeitungsanzeige** *f* newspaper advertisement; **Zeitungsartikel** *m* newspaper article; **Zeitungskiosk** *m*, **Zeitungsstand** *m* newsstand

Zeitunterschied *m* time difference; **Zeitverschiebung** *f* time lag; **Zeitvertreib** (*-(e)s, -e*) *m* **zum ~** to pass the time; **zeitweise** *adv* occasionally; **Zeitzone** *f* time zone

Zelle (*-, -n*) *f* cell

Zellophan® (*-s*) *nt* cellophane®

Zelt (*-(e)s, -e*) *nt* tent; **zelten** *vi* to camp, to go camping; **Zeltplatz** *m* campsite, camping site

Zement (*-(e)s, -e*) *m* cement

Zentimeter *m o nt* centimetre

Zentner (*-s, -*) *m* (metric) hundredweight; (*in Deutschland*) fifty kilos; (*in Österreich und der Schweiz*) one hundred kilos

zentral *adj* central; **Zentrale** (*-, -n*) *f* central office; (*Tel*) exchange; **Zentralheizung** *f* central heating;

Zentralverriegelung *f* (*Auto*) central locking; **Zentrum** (*-s, Zentren*) *nt* centre

zerbrechen *irr vt, vi* to break; **zerbrechlich** *adj* fragile

Zeremonie (*-, -n*) *f* ceremony

zergehen *irr vi* to dissolve; (*schmelzen*) to melt

zerkleinern *vt* to cut up; (*zerhacken*) to chop (up); **zerkratzen** *vt* to scratch; **zerlegen** *vt* to take to pieces; (*Fleisch*) to carve; (*Gerät, Maschine*) to dismantle; **zerquetschen** *vt* to squash; **zerreißen** *irr vt* to tear to pieces ▷ *vi* to tear

zerren *vt* to drag; **sich** (*dat*) **einen Muskel ~** to pull a muscle ▷ *vi* to tug (*an +dat* at); **Zerrung** *f* (*Med*) pulled muscle

zerschlagen *irr vt* to smash ▷ *vr* **sich ~** to come to nothing

zerschneiden *irr vt* to cut up

Zerstäuber (*-s, -*) *m* atomizer

zerstören *vt* to destroy; **Zerstörung** *f* destruction

zerstreuen *vt* to scatter; (*Menge*) to disperse; (*Zweifel etc*) to dispel ▷ *vr* **sich ~** (*Menge*) to disperse; **zerstreut** *adj* scattered; (*Mensch*) absent-minded; (*kurzfristig*) distracted

zerteilen *vt* to split up

Zertifikat (*-(e)s, -e*) *nt* certificate

Zettel (*-s, -*) *m* piece of paper; (*Notizzettel*) note

Zeug (*-(e)s, -e*) *nt* (*fam*) stuff; (*Ausrüstung*) gear; **dummes ~** nonsense

Zeuge (*-n, -n*) *m*, **Zeugin** *f* witness

Zeugnis *nt* certificate; (*Schule*) report; (*Referenz*) reference

z. H(d). *abk* = **zu Händen von** attn

zickig *adj* (*fam*) touchy, bitchy

Zickzack (*-(e)s, -e*) *m* **im ~ fahren** to zigzag (across the road)

Ziege (*-, -n*) *f* goat

Ziegel (*-s, -*) *m* brick; (*Dach*) tile

Ziegenkäse *m* goat's cheese; **Ziegenpeter** *m* mumps

ziehen (*zog, gezogen*) *vt* to draw; (*zerren*) to pull; (*Spielfigur*) to move; (*züchten*) to rear ▷ *vi* (*zerren*) to pull; (*sich bewegen*) to move; (*Rauch, Wolke etc*) to drift; **den Tee ~ lassen** to let the tea stand ▷ *vi impers* **es zieht** there's a draught ▷ *vr* **sich ~** (*Treffen, Rede*) to drag on

Ziel (*-(e)s, -e*) *nt* (*Reise*) destination; (*Sport*) finish; (*Absicht*) goal, aim; **zielen** *vi* to aim (auf +akk at); **Zielgruppe** f target group; **ziellos** adj aimless; **Zielscheibe** f target

ziemlich adj considerable; **ein ~es Durcheinander** quite a mess; **mit ~er Sicherheit** with some certainty ▷ adv rather, quite; **~ viel** quite a lot

zierlich adj dainty; (Frau) petite

Ziffer (-, -n) f figure; **arabische/römische ~n** pl Arabic/Roman numerals pl; **Zifferblatt** nt dial, face

zig adj (fam) umpteen

Zigarette f cigarette; **Zigarettenautomat** m cigarette machine; **Zigarettenpapier** nt cigarette paper; **Zigarettenschachtel** f cigarette packet; **Zigarettenstummel** m cigarette end; **Zigarillo** (-s, -s) m cigarillo; **Zigarre** (-, -n) f cigar

Zigeuner(in) (-s, -) m(f) gipsy

Zimmer (-s, -) nt room; **haben Sie ein ~ für zwei Personen?** do you have a room for two?; **Zimmerlautstärke** f reasonable volume; **Zimmermädchen** nt chambermaid; **Zimmermann** m carpenter; **Zimmerpflanze** f house plant; **Zimmerschlüssel** m room key; **Zimmerservice** m room service; **Zimmervermittlung** f accommodation agency

Zimt (-(e)s, -e) m cinnamon; **Zimtstange** f cinnamon stick

Zink (-(e)s) nt zinc

Zinn (-(e)s) nt (Element) tin; (legiertes) pewter

Zinsen pl interest sing

Zipfel (-s, -) m corner; (spitz) tip; (Hemd) tail; (Wurst) end; (fam: Penis) willy; **Zipfelmütze** f pointed hat

zirka adv about, approximately

Zirkel (-s, -) m (Math) (pair of) compasses pl

Zirkus (-, -se) m circus

zischen vi to hiss

Zitat (-(e)s, -e) nt quotation (aus from); **zitieren** vt to quote

Zitronat nt candied lemon peel; **Zitrone** (-, -n) f lemon; **Zitronenlimonade** f lemonade; **Zitronensaft** m lemon juice

zittern vi to tremble (vor +dat with)

zivil adj civilian; (Preis) reasonable; **Zivil** (-s) nt plain clothes pl; (Mil) civilian clothes pl; **Zivildienst** m community service (for conscientious objectors)

zocken vi (fam) to gamble

Zoff (-s) m (fam) trouble

zog imperf von **ziehen**

zögerlich adj hesitant; **zögern** vi to hesitate

Zoll (-(e)s, Zölle) m customs pl; (Abgabe) duty; **Zollabfertigung** f customs clearance; **Zollamt** nt customs office; **Zollbeamte(r)** m, **-beamtin** f customs official; **Zollerklärung** f customs declaration; **zollfrei** adj duty-free; **Zollgebühren** pl customs duties pl; **Zollkontrolle** f customs check; **Zöllner(in)** m(f) customs officer; **zollpflichtig** adj liable to duty

Zombie (-s, -s) m zombie

Zone (-, -n) f zone

Zoo (-s, -s) m zoo

Zoom (-s, -s) nt zoom (shot); (Objektiv) zoom (lens)

Zopf (-(e)s, Zöpfe) m plait (Brit), braid (US)

Zorn (-(e)s) m anger; **zornig** adj angry (über etw akk about sth, auf jdn with sb)

O SCHLÜSSELWORT

zu präp +dat **1** (örtlich) to; **zum Bahnhof/ Arzt gehen** to go to the station/doctor; **zur Schule/Kirche gehen** to go to school/church; **sollen wir zu euch gehen?** shall we go to your place?; **sie sah zu ihm hin** she looked towards him; **zum Fenster herein** through the window; **zu meiner Linken** to od on my left

2 (zeitlich) at; **zu Ostern** at Easter; **bis zum 1. Mai** until May 1st; (nicht später als) by May 1st; **zu meiner Zeit** in my time

3 (Zusatz) with; **Wein zum Essen trinken** to drink wine with one's meal; **sich zu jdm setzen** to sit down beside sb; **setz dich doch zu uns** (come and) sit with us; **Anmerkungen zu etw** notes on sth

4 (Zweck) for; **Wasser zum Waschen** water for washing; **Papier zum Schreiben** paper to write on; **etw zum Geburtstag bekommen** to get sth for one's birthday

5 (Veränderung) into; **zu etw werden** to turn into sth; **jdn zu etw machen** to make sb (into) sth; **zu Asche verbrennen** to burn to ashes

z

6 (*mit Zahlen*); **3 zu 2** (*Sport*) 3-2; **das Stück zu 5 Euro** at 5 euros each; **zum ersten Mal** for the first time **7**: **zu meiner Freude** *etc* to my joy *etc*; **zum Glück** luckily; **zu Fuß** on foot; **es ist zum Weinen** it's enough to make you cry ▷ *konj* to; **etw zu essen** sth to eat; **um besser sehen zu können** in order to see better; **ohne es zu wissen** without knowing it; **noch zu bezahlende Rechnungen** bills that are still to be paid ▷ *adv* **1** (*allzu*) too; **zu sehr** too much; **zu viel** too much; **zu wenig** too little **2** (*örtlich*) toward(s); **er kam auf mich zu** he came up to me **3** (*geschlossen*) shut, closed; **die Geschäfte haben zu** the shops are closed; **„auf/zu"** (*Wasserhahn etc*) "on/off" **4** (*umg: los*); **nur zu!** just keep on!; **mach zu!** hurry up!

zuallererst *adv* first of all; **zuallerletzt** *adv* last of all
Zubehör (*-(e)s, -e*) *nt* accessories *pl*
zu|bereiten *vt* to prepare; **Zubereitung** *f* preparation
zu|binden *irr vt* to do (*o* tie) up
Zucchini *pl* courgettes *pl* (*Brit*), zucchini *pl* (*US*)
züchten *vt* (*Tiere*) to breed; (*Pflanzen*) to grow
zucken *vi* to jerk; (*krampfhaft*) to twitch; (*Strahl etc*) to flicker; **mit den Schultern ~** to shrug (one's shoulders)
Zucker (*-s, -*) *m* sugar; (*Med*) diabetes *sing*; **Zuckerdose** *f* sugar bowl; **zuckerkrank** *adj* diabetic; **Zuckerrohr** *nt* sugar cane; **Zuckerrübe** *f* sugar beet; **Zuckerwatte** *f* candy-floss (*Brit*), cotton candy (*US*)
zu|decken *vt* to cover up
zu|drehen *vt* to turn off
zueinander *adv* to one other; (*mit Verb*) together; **~ halten** to stick together
zuerst *adv* first; (*zu Anfang*) at first; **~ einmal** first of all
Zufahrt *f* access; (*Einfahrt*) drive(way); **Zufahrtsstraße** *f* access road; (*Autobahn*) slip road (*Brit*), ramp (*US*)
Zufall *m* chance; (*Ereignis*) coincidence; **durch ~** by accident; **so ein ~!** what a coincidence; **zufällig** *adj* chance ▷ *adv* by chance; **weißt du ~, ob ...?** do you happen to know whether ...?

zufrieden *adj* content(ed); (*befriedigt*) satisfied; **sich mit etw ~ geben** to settle for sth; **lass sie ~** leave her alone (*o* in peace); **sie ist schwer ~ zu stellen** she is hard to please; **Zufriedenheit** *f* contentment; (*Befriedigtsein*) satisfaction
zu|fügen *vt* to add (*dat* to); **jdm Schaden/Schmerzen ~** to cause sb harm/pain
Zug (*-(e)s, Züge*) *m* (*Eisenb*) train; (*Luft*) draught; (*Ziehen*) pull; (*Gesichtszug*) feature; (*Schach*) move; (*Charakterzug*) trait; (*an Zigarette*) puff, drag; (*Schluck*) gulp
Zugabe *f* extra; (*in Konzert etc*) encore
Zugabteil *nt* train compartment
Zugang *m* access; **„kein ~!"** 'no entry!'
Zugauskunft *f* (*Stelle*) train information office/desk; **Zugbegleiter(in)** *m(f)* guard (*Brit*), conductor (*US*)
zu|geben *irr vt* (*zugestehen*) admit; **zugegeben** *adv* admittedly
zu|gehen *irr vi* (*schließen*) to shut; **auf jdn/etw ~** to walk towards sb/sth; **dem Ende ~** to be coming to a close ▷ *vi impers* (*sich ereignen*) to happen; **es ging lustig zu** we/they had a lot of fun; **dort geht es streng zu** it's strict there
Zügel (*-s, -*) *m* rein
Zugführer(in) *m(f)* guard (*Brit*), conductor (*US*)
zugig *adj* draughty
zügig *adj* speedy
Zugluft *f* draught
Zugpersonal *nt* train staff
zu|greifen *irr vi* (*fig*) to seize the opportunity; (*beim Essen*) to help oneself; **~ auf** (+*akk*) (*Inform*) to access
Zugrestaurant *nt* dining car, diner (*US*)
Zugriffsberechtigung *f* (*Inform*) access right
zugrunde *adv* **~ gehen** to perish; **~ gehen an** (+*dat*) (*sterben*) to die of
Zugschaffner(in) *m(f)* ticket inspector; **Zugunglück** *nt* train crash
zugunsten *prep* +*gen o dat* in favour of
Zugverbindung *f* train connection
zu|haben *irr vi* to be closed
zu|halten *irr vt* **sich** (*dat*) **die Nase ~** to hold one's nose; **sich** (*dat*) **die Ohren ~** to hold one's hands over one's ears; **die Tür ~** to hold the door shut
Zuhause (*-s*) *nt* home

zu|hören *vi* to listen (*dat* to); **Zuhörer(in)** *m(f)* listener
zu|kleben *vt* to seal
zu|kommen *irr vi* to come up (*auf +akk* to); **jdm etw ~ lassen** to give/send sb sth; **etw auf sich** (*akk*) **~ lassen** to take sth as it comes
zu|kriegen *vt* **ich krieg den Koffer nicht zu** I can't shut the case
Zukunft (-, *Zukünfte*) *f* future; **zukünftig** *adj* future ▷ *adv* in future
zu|lassen *irr vt* (*hereinlassen*) to admit; (*erlauben*) to permit; (*Auto*) to license; (*fam: nicht öffnen*) to keep shut; **zulässig** *adj* permissible, permitted
zuletzt *adv* finally, at last
zuliebe *adv* **jdm ~** for sb's sake
zum *kontr von* **zu dem; ~ dritten Mal** for the third time; **~ Scherz** as a joke; **~ Trinken** for drinking
zu|machen *vt* to shut; (*Kleidung*) to do up ▷ *vi* to shut
zumindest *adv* at least
zu|muten *vt* **jdm etw ~** to expect sth of sb ▷ *vr* **sich** (*dat*) **zu viel ~** to overdo things
zunächst *adv* first of all; **~ einmal** to start with
Zunahme (-, -n) *f* increase
Zuname *m* surname, last name
zünden *vt, vi* (*Auto*) to ignite, to fire; **Zündholz** *nt* match; **Zündkabel** *f* (*Auto*) ignition cable; **Zündkerze** *f* (*Auto*) spark plug; **Zündschloss** *nt* ignition lock; **Zündschlüssel** *m* ignition key; **Zündung** *f* ignition
zu|nehmen *irr vi* to increase; (*Mensch*) to put on weight ▷ *vt* **5 Kilo ~** to put on 5 kilos
Zunge (-, -n) *f* tongue
Zungenkuss *m* French kiss
zunichte *adv* **~ machen** to ruin
zunutze *adv* **sich** (*dat*) **etw ~ machen** to make use of sth
zu|parken *vt* to block
zur *kontr von* **zu der**
zurecht|finden *irr vr* **sich ~** to find one's way around; **zurecht|kommen** *irr vi* to cope (*mit etw* with sth); **zurecht|machen** *vt* to prepare ▷ *vr* **sich ~** to get ready
Zürich (-s) *nt* Zurich
zurück *adv* back
zurück|bekommen *irr vt* to get back;

zurück|blicken *vi* to look back (*auf +akk* at); **zurück|bringen** *irr vt* (*hierhin*) to bring back; (*woandershin*) to take back;
zurück|erstatten *vt* to refund;
zurück|fahren *irr vi* to go back;
zurück|geben *irr vt* to give back; (*antworten*) to answer; **zurück|gehen** *irr vi* to go back; (*zeitlich*) to date back (*auf +akk* to)
zurück|halten *irr vt* to hold back; (*hindern*) to prevent ▷ *vr* **sich ~** to hold back; **zurückhaltend** *adj* reserved
zurück|holen *vt* to fetch back;
zurück|kommen *irr vi* to come back; **auf etw** (*akk*) **~** to return (*o* get back) to sth; **zurück|lassen** *irr vt* to leave behind; **zurück|legen** *vt* to put back; (*Geld*) to put by; (*reservieren*) to keep back; (*Strecke*) to cover; **zurück|nehmen** *irr vt* to take back; **zurück|rufen** *irr vt* to call back; **zurück|schicken** *vt* to send back; **zurück|stellen** *vt* to put back; **zurück|treten** *irr vi* to step back; (*von Amt*) to retire; **zurück|verlangen** *vt* **etw ~** to ask for sth back; **zurück|zahlen** *vt* to pay back
zurzeit *adv* at present
Zusage *f* promise; (*Annahme*) acceptance; **zu|sagen** *vt* to promise ▷ *vi* to accept; **jdm ~** (*gefallen*) to appeal to sb
zusammen *adv* together
Zusammenarbeit *f* collaboration; **zusammen|arbeiten** *vi* to work together
zusammen|brechen *irr vi* to collapse; (*psychisch*) to break down; **Zusammenbruch** *m* collapse; (*psychischer*) breakdown
zusammen|fassen *vt* to summarize; (*vereinigen*) to unite; **zusammenfassend** *adj* summarizing ▷ *adv* to summarize; **Zusammenfassung** *f* summary
zusammen|gehören *vi* to belong together; **zusammen|halten** *irr vi* to stick together
Zusammenhang *m* connection; **im/aus dem ~** in/out of context; **zusammen|hängen** *irr vi* to be connected; **zusammenhängend** *adj* coherent; **zusammenhang(s)los** *adj* incoherent
zusammen|klappen *vi, vt* to fold up
zusammen|knüllen *vt* to screw up
zusammen|kommen *irr vi* to meet;

(*sich ereignen*) to happen together; **zusammen|legen** *vt* to fold up ▷ *vi* (*Geld sammeln*) to club together;

zusammen|nehmen *irr vt* to summon up; **alles zusammengenommen** all in all ▷ *vr* **sich ~** to pull oneself together; (*fam*) to get a grip, to get one's act together;

zusammen|passen *vi* to go together; (*Personen*) to be suited;

zusammen|rechnen *vt* to add up

Zusammensein (*-s*) *nt* get-together

zusammen|setzen *vt* to put together ▷ *vr* **sich ~ aus** to be composed of; **Zusammensetzung** *f* composition

Zusammenstoß *m* crash, collision; **zusammen|stoßen** *irr vi* to crash (*mit* into)

zusammen|zählen *vt* to add up

zusammen|ziehen *irr vi* (*in Wohnung etc*) to move in together

Zusatz *m* addition; **Zusatzgerät** *nt* attachment; (*Inform*) add-on; **zusätzlich** *adj* additional ▷ *adv* in addition

zu|schauen *vi* to watch; **Zuschauer(in)** (*-s, -*) *m(f)* spectator; **die ~** (*pl*) (*Theat*) the audience *sing*; **Zuschauertribüne** *f* stand

zu|schicken *vt* to send

Zuschlag *m* extra charge; (*Fahrkarte*) supplement

zuschlagpflichtig *adj* subject to an extra charge; (*Eisenb*) subject to a supplement

zu|schließen *irr vt* to lock up

zu|sehen *irr vi* to watch (*jdm* sb); **~, dass** (*dafür sorgen*) to make sure that

zu|sichern *vt* **jdm etw ~** to assure sb of sth

Zustand *m* state, condition; **sie bekommt Zustände, wenn sie das sieht** (*fam*) she'll have a fit if she sees that

zustande *adv* **~ bringen** to bring about; **~ kommen** to come about

zuständig *adj* (*Behörde*) relevant; **~ für** responsible for

Zustellung *f* delivery

zu|stimmen *vi* to agree (*einer Sache dat* to sth, *jdm* with sb); **Zustimmung** *f* approval

zu|stoßen *irr vi* (*fig*) to happen (*jdm* to sb)

Zutaten *pl* ingredients *pl*

zu|trauen *vt* **jdm etw ~** to think sb is capable of sth; **das hätte ich ihm nie zugetraut** I'd never have thought he was capable of it; **ich würde es ihr ~** (*etw Negatives*) I wouldn't put it past her; **Zutrauen** (*-s*) *nt* confidence (*zu* in); **zutraulich** *adj* trusting; (*Tier*) friendly

zu|treffen *irr vi* to be correct; **~ auf** (*+akk*) to apply to; **Zutreffendes bitte streichen** please delete as applicable

Zutritt *m* entry; (*Zugang*) access; **~ verboten!** no entry

zuverlässig *adj* reliable; **Zuverlässigkeit** *f* reliability

Zuversicht *f* confidence; **zuversichtlich** *adj* confident

zuvor *adv* before; (*zunächst*) first; **zuvor|kommen** *irr vi* **jdm ~** to beat sb to it; **zuvorkommend** *adj* obliging

Zuwachs (*-es, Zuwächse*) *m* increase, growth; (*fam: Baby*) addition to the family

zuwider *adv* **es ist mir ~** I hate (*o detest*) it

zuzüglich *prep* +*gen* plus

zwang *imperf von* **zwingen**

Zwang (*-(e)s, Zwänge*) *m* (*innerer*) compulsion; (*Gewalt*) force

zwängen *vt* to squeeze (*in* +*akk* into) ▷ *vr* **sich ~** to squeeze (*in* +*akk* into)

zwanglos *adj* informal

zwanzig *num* twenty; **zwanzigste(r, s)** *adj* twentieth; *siehe auch* **dritte**

zwar *adv* **und ~ ...** (*genauer*) ..., to be precise; **das ist ~ schön, aber ...** it is nice, but ...; **ich kenne ihn ~, aber ...** I know him all right, but ...

Zweck (*-(e)s, -e*) *m* purpose; **zwecklos** *adj* pointless

zwei *num* two; **Zwei** (*-, -en*) *f* two; (*Schulnote*) ≈ B; **Zweibettzimmer** *nt* twin room; **zweideutig** *adj* ambiguous; (*unanständig*) suggestive; **zweifach** *adj, adv* double

Zweifel (*-s, -*) *m* doubt; **zweifellos** *adv* undoubtedly; **zweifeln** *vi* to doubt (*an etw dat* sth); **Zweifelsfall** *m* **im ~** in case of doubt

Zweig (*-(e)s, -e*) *m* branch

Zweigstelle *f* branch

zweihundert *num* two hundred; **zweimal** *adv* twice; **zweisprachig** *adj* bilingual; **zweispurig** *adj* (*Auto*) two-lane; **zweit** *adv* **wir sind zu ~** there are two of us; **zweite(r, s)** *adj* second; *siehe auch* **dritte eine ~ Portion** a second helping; **zweitens** *adv* secondly; (*bei Aufzählungen*)

second; **zweitgrößte(r, s)** *adj* second
largest; **Zweitschlüssel** *m* spare key
Zwerchfell *nt* diaphragm
Zwerg(in) (-(e)s, -e) *m(f)* dwarf
Zwetschge (-, -n) *f* plum
zwicken *vt* to pinch
Zwieback (-(e)s, -e) *m* rusk
Zwiebel (-, -n) *f* onion; (*von Blume*) bulb;
 Zwiebelsuppe *f* onion soup
Zwilling (-s, -e) *m* twin; **~e** (*pl*) (*Astr*)
 Gemini *sing*
zwingen (*zwang, gezwungen*) *vt* to force
zwinkern *vi* to blink; (*absichtlich*) to wink
zwischen *prep* +akk o dat between
Zwischenablage *f* (*Inform*) clipboard
zwischendurch *adv* in between
Zwischenfall *m* incident
Zwischenlandung *f* stopover
zwischenmenschlich *adj* interpersonal
Zwischenraum *m* space
Zwischenstopp (-s, -s) *m* stopover
Zwischensumme *f* subtotal
Zwischenzeit *f* **in der ~** in the meantime
zwitschern *vt, vi* to twitter, to chirp
zwölf *num* twelve; **zwölfte(r, s)** *adj*
 twelfth; *siehe auch* **dritte**
Zylinder (-s, -) *m* cylinder; (*Hut*) top hat;
 Zylinderkopfdichtung *f* cylinder-head
 gasket
zynisch *adj* cynical
Zypern (-s) *nt* Cyprus
Zyste (-, -n) *f* cyst

Z

a [eɪ, ə] (*before vowel or silent h: an*) *indef art*
1 ein; eine; **a woman** eine Frau; **a book** ein Buch; **an eagle** ein Adler; **she's a doctor** sie ist Ärztin
2 (*instead of the number "one"*) ein, eine; **a year ago** vor einem Jahr; **a hundred/thousand** *etc* **pounds** (ein) hundert/(ein) tausend *etc* Pfund
3 (*in expressing ratios, prices etc*) pro; **3 a day/week** 3 pro Tag/Woche 3 am Tag/in der Woche; **10 km an hour** 10 km pro Stunde/in der Stunde

---

AA *abbr* = **Automobile Association** *britischer Automobilklub*, ≈ ADAC *m*
aback *adv* **taken ~** erstaunt
abandon [ə'bændən] *vt* (*desert*) verlassen; (*give up*) aufgeben
abbey ['æbɪ] *n* Abtei *f*
abbreviate [əbri:vɪ'eɪt] *vt* abkürzen; **abbreviation** [əbri:vɪ'eɪʃən] *n* Abkürzung *f*
ABC ['eɪbi:'si:] *n* (*a. fig*) Abc *nt*
abdicate ['æbdɪkeɪt] *vi* (*king*) abdanken; **abdication** [æbdɪ'keɪʃən] *n* Abdankung *f*

abdomen ['æbdəmən] *n* Unterleib *m*
ability [ə'bɪlɪtɪ] *n* Fähigkeit *f*; **able** ['eɪbl] *adj* fähig; **to be ~ to do sth** etw tun können
abnormal [æb'nɔ:ml] *adj* anormal
aboard [ə'bɔ:d] *adv, prep* an Bord +*gen*
abolish [ə'bɒlɪʃ] *vt* abschaffen
aborigine [æbə'rɪdʒɪni:] *n* Ureinwohner(in) *m(f)* (Australiens)
abort [ə'bɔ:t] *vt* (*Med: foetus*) abtreiben; (*Space: mission*) abbrechen; **abortion** [ə'bɔ:ʃən] *n* Abtreibung *f*

KEYWORD

about [ə'baʊt] *adv* **1** (*approximately*) etwa, ungefähr; **about a hundred/thousand** *etc* etwa hundert/tausend *etc*; **at about 2 o'clock** etwa um 2 Uhr; **I've just about finished** ich bin gerade fertig
2 (*referring to place*) herum, umher; **to leave things lying about** Sachen herumliegen lassen; **to run/walk** *etc* **about** herumrennen/gehen *etc*
3: **to be about to do sth** im Begriff sein, etw zu tun; **he was about to go to bed** er wollte gerade ins Bett gehen
▷ *prep* **1** (*relating to*) über +*acc*; **a book about London** ein Buch über London; **what is it about?** worum geht es?; (*book etc*) wovon handelt es?; **we talked about it** wir haben darüber geredet; **what** *or* **how about doing this?** wollen wir das machen?
2 (*referring to place*) um (... herum); **to walk about the town** in der Stadt herumgehen; **her clothes were scattered about the room** ihre Kleider waren über das ganze Zimmer verstreut

above [ə'bʌv] *adv* oben; **children aged 8 and ~** Kinder ab 8 Jahren; **on the floor ~** ein Stockwerk höher ▷ *prep* über; **~ 40 degrees** über 40 Grad; **~ all** vor allem ▷ *adj* obig
abroad [ə'brɔ:d] *adv* im Ausland; **to go ~** ins Ausland gehen
abrupt [ə'brʌpt] *adj* (*sudden*) plötzlich, abrupt
abscess ['æbsɪs] *n* Geschwür *nt*
absence ['æbsəns] *n* Abwesenheit *f*; **absent** ['æbsənt] *adj* abwesend; **to be ~ fehlen**; **absent-minded** *adj* zerstreut

absolute ['æbsəluːt] *adj* absolut; (*power*) unumschränkt; (*rubbish*) vollkommen, total; **absolutely** *adv* absolut; (*true, stupid*) vollkommen; **~!** genau!; **you're ~ right** du hast/Sie haben völlig Recht

absorb [əb'zɔːb] *vt* absorbieren; (*fig: information*) in sich aufnehmen; **absorbed** *adj* **~ in sth** in etw vertieft; **absorbent** *adj* absorbierend; **~ cotton** (*US*) Watte *f*; **absorbing** *adj* (*fig*) faszinierend, fesselnd

abstain [əb'steɪn] *vi* **to ~ (from voting)** sich (der Stimme) enthalten

abstract ['æbstrækt] *adj* abstrakt

absurd [əb'sɜːd] *adj* absurd

abundance [ə'bʌndəns] *n* Reichtum *m* (*of* an +*dat*)

abuse [ə'bjuːs] *n* (*rude language*) Beschimpfungen *pl*; (*mistreatment*) Missbrauch *m* ▷ [ə'bjuːz] *vt* (*misuse*) missbrauchen; **abusive** [ə'bjuːsɪv] *adj* beleidigend

AC *abbr* = **alternating current** Wechselstrom *m* ▷ *abbr* = **air conditioning** Klimaanlage

a/c *abbr* = **account** Kto.

academic [ækə'demɪk] *n* Wissenschaftler(in) *m(f)* ▷ *adj* akademisch, wissenschaftlich

accelerate [æk'seləreɪt] *vi* (*car etc*) beschleunigen; (*driver*) Gas geben; **acceleration** [əkselə'reɪʃən] *n* Beschleunigung *f*; **accelerator** [ək'seləreɪtə*] *n* Gas(pedal) *nt*

accent ['æksent] *n* Akzent *m*

accept [ək'sept] *vt* annehmen; (*agree to*) akzeptieren; (*responsibility*) übernehmen; **acceptable** [ək'septəbl] *adj* annehmbar

access ['ækses] *n* Zugang *m*; (*Inform*) Zugriff *m*; **accessible** [æk'sesəbl] *adj* (*leicht*) zugänglich/erreichbar; (*place*) (leicht) erreichbar

accessory [æk'sesərɪ] *n* Zubehörteil *nt*

access road *n* Zufahrtsstraße *f*

accident ['æksɪdənt] *n* Unfall *m*; **by ~** zufällig; **accidental** [æksɪ'dentl] *adj* unbeabsichtigt; (*meeting*) zufällig; (*death*) durch Unfall; **~ damage** Unfallschaden *m*; **accident-prone** *adj* vom Pech verfolgt

acclimatize [ə'klaɪmətaɪz] *vt* **to ~ oneself** sich gewöhnen (*to* an +*akk*)

accommodate [ə'kɒmədeɪt] *vt* unterbringen; **accommodation(s)** [əkɒmə'deɪʃən(z)] *n* Unterkunft *f*

accompany [ə'kʌmpənɪ] *vt* begleiten

accomplish [ə'kʌmplɪʃ] *vt* erreichen

accord [ə'kɔːd] *n* **of one's own ~** freiwillig; **according to** *prep* nach, laut +*dat*

account [ə'kaʊnt] *n* (*in bank etc*) Konto *nt*; (*narrative*) Bericht *m*; **on ~ of** wegen; **on no ~** auf keinen Fall; **to take into ~** berücksichtigen, in Betracht ziehen; **accountant** [ə'kaʊntənt] *n* Buchhalter(in) *m(f)*; **account for** *vt* (*explain*) erklären; (*expenditure*) Rechenschaft ablegen für; **account number** *n* Kontonummer *f*

accumulate [ə'kjuːmjʊleɪt] *vt* ansammeln ▷ *vi* sich ansammeln

accuracy ['ækjʊrəsɪ] *n* Genauigkeit *f*; **accurate** ['ækjʊrɪt] *adj* genau

accusation [ækjʊ'zeɪʃən] *n* Anklage *f*, Beschuldigung *f*

accusative [ə'kjuːzətɪv] *n* Akkusativ *m*

accuse [ə'kjuːz] *vt* beschuldigen; (*Jur*) anklagen (*of wegen* +*gen*); **~ sb of doing sth** jdn beschuldigen, etw getan zu haben; **accused** *n* (*Jur*) Angeklagte(r) *mf*

accustom [ə'kʌstəm] *vt* gewöhnen (*to* an +*akk*); **accustomed** *adj* gewohnt; **to get ~ to sth** sich an etw *akk* gewöhnen

ace [eɪs] *n* Ass *nt* ▷ *adj* Star-

ache [eɪk] *n* Schmerz *m* ▷ *vi* wehtun

achieve [ə'tʃiːv] *vt* erreichen; **achievement** *n* Leistung *f*

acid ['æsɪd] *n* Säure *f* ▷ *adj* sauer; **~ rain** saurer Regen

acknowledge [ək'nɒlɪdʒ] *vt* (*recognize*) anerkennen; (*admit*) zugeben; (*receipt of letter etc*) bestätigen; **acknowledgement** *n* Anerkennung *f*; (*of letter*) Empfangsbestätigung *f*

acne ['æknɪ] *n* Akne *f*

acorn ['eɪkɔːn] *n* Eichel *f*

acoustic [ə'kuːstɪk] *adj* akustisch; **acoustics** [ə'kuːstɪks] *npl* Akustik *f*

acquaintance [ə'kweɪntəns] *n* (*person*) Bekannte(r) *mf*

acquire [ə'kwaɪə*] *vt* erwerben, sich aneignen; **acquisition** [ækwɪ'zɪʃn] *n* (*of skills etc*) Erwerb *m*; (*object*) Anschaffung *f*

acrobat ['ækrəbæt] *n* Akrobat(in) *m(f)*

across [ə'krɒs] *prep* über +*akk*; **he lives ~ the street** er wohnt auf der anderen

Seite der Straße ▷ *adv* hinüber, herüber;
100m ~ 100m breit

act [ækt] *n* (*deed*) Tat *f*; (*Jur: law*) Gesetz *nt*; (*Theat*) Akt *m*; (*fig: pretence*) Schau *f*; **it's all an ~** es ist alles nur Theater; **to be in the ~ of doing sth** gerade dabei sein, etw zu tun ▷ *vi* (*take action*) handeln; (*behave*) sich verhalten; (*Theat*) spielen; **to ~ as** (*person*) fungieren als; (*thing*) dienen als ▷ *vt* (*a part*) spielen

action ['ækʃən] *n* (*of play, novel etc*) Handlung *f*; (*in film etc*) Action *f*; (*Mil*) Kampf *m*; **to take ~** etwas unternehmen; **out of ~** (*machine*) außer Betrieb; **to put a plan into ~** einen Plan in die Tat umsetzen; **action replay** *n* (*Sport, Tv*) Wiederholung *f*

active ['æktɪv] *adj* aktiv; (*child*) lebhaft; **activity** [æk'tɪvɪtɪ] *n* Aktivität *f*; (*occupation*) Beschäftigung *f*; (*organized event*) Veranstaltung *f*

actor ['æktə*] *n* Schauspieler(in) *m(f)*; **actress** ['æktrɪs] *n* Schauspielerin *f*

actual ['æktjʊəl] *adj* wirklich; **actually** *adv* eigentlich; (*said in surprise*) tatsächlich

acupuncture ['ækjʊpʌŋktʃə*] *n* Akupunktur *f*

acute [ə'kjuːt] *adj* (*pain*) akut; (*sense of smell*) fein; (*Math: angle*) spitz

ad [æd] *abbr* = **advertisement**

AD *abbr* = **Anno Domini** nach Christi, n. Chr.

adapt [ə'dæpt] *vi* sich anpassen (*to +dat*) ▷ *vt* anpassen (*to +dat*); (*rewrite*) bearbeiten (*for* für); **adaptable** *adj* anpassungsfähig; **adaptation** *n* (*of book etc*) Bearbeitung *f*; **adapter** *n* (*Elec*) Zwischenstecker *m*, Adapter *m*

add [æd] *vt* (*ingredient*) hinzufügen; (*numbers*) addieren; **add up** *vi* (*make sense*) stimmen ▷ *vt* (*numbers*) addieren

addict ['ædɪkt] *n* Süchtige(r) *mf*; **addicted** [ə'dɪktɪd] *adj* ~ **to alcohol/drugs** alkohol-/drogensüchtig

addition [ə'dɪʃən] *n* Zusatz *m*; (*to bill*) Aufschlag *m*; (*Math*) Addition *f*; **in ~** außerdem, zusätzlich (*to zu*); **additional** *adj* zusätzlich, weiter; **additive** ['ædɪtɪv] *n* Zusatz *m*; **add-on** ['ædɒn] *n* Zusatzgerät *nt*

address [ə'dres] *n* Adresse *f* ▷ *vt* (*letter*) adressieren; (*person*) anreden

adequate ['ædɪkwɪt] *adj* (*appropriate*)

angemessen; (*sufficient*) ausreichend; (*time*) genügend

adhesive [əd'hiːsɪv] *n* Klebstoff *m*; **adhesive tape** *n* Klebstreifen *m*

adjacent [ə'dʒeɪsənt] *adj* benachbart

adjective ['ædʒəktɪv] *n* Adjektiv *nt*

adjoining [ə'dʒɔɪnɪŋ] *adj* benachbart, Neben-

adjust [ə'dʒʌst] *vt* einstellen; (*put right also*) richtig stellen; (*speed, flow*) regulieren; (*in position*) verstellen ▷ *vi* sich anpassen (*to +dat*); **adjustable** *adj* verstellbar

admin [əd'mɪn] *n* (*fam*) Verwaltung *f*; **administration** [ədmɪnɪs'treɪʃən] *n* Verwaltung *f*; (*Pol*) Regierung *f*

admirable ['ædmərəbl] *adj* bewundernswert; **admiration** [ædmɪ'reɪʃən] *n* Bewunderung *f*; **admire** [əd'maɪə*] *vt* bewundern

admission [əd'mɪʃən] *n* (*entrance*) Zutritt *m*; (*to university etc*) Zulassung *f*; (*fee*) Eintritt *m*; (*confession*) Eingeständnis *nt*; **admission charge**, **admission fee** *n* Eintrittspreis *m*; **admit** [əd'mɪt] *vt* (*let in*) hereinlassen (*to +akk*); (*to university etc*) zulassen; (*confess*) zugeben, gestehen; **to be ~ted to hospital** ins Krankenhaus eingeliefert werden

adolescent [ædə'lesnt] *n* Jugendliche(r) *mf*

adopt [ə'dɒpt] *vt* (*child*) adoptieren; (*idea*) übernehmen; **adoption** [ə'dɒptʃn] *n* (*of child*) Adoption *f*; (*of idea*) Übernahme *f*

adorable [ə'dɔːrəbl] *adj* entzückend; **adore** [ə'dɔː*] *vt* anbeten; (*person*) über alles lieben, vergöttern

adult ['ædʌlt] *adj* (*person*) erwachsen; (*film etc*) für Erwachsene ▷ *n* Erwachsene(r) *mf*

adultery [ə'dʌltərɪ] *n* Ehebruch *m*

advance [əd'vɑːns] *n* (*money*) Vorschuss *m*; (*progress*) Fortschritt *m*; **in ~** im Voraus; **to book in ~** vorbestellen ▷ *vi* (*move forward*) vorrücken ▷ *vt* (*money*) vorschießen; **advance booking** *n* Reservierung *f*; (*Theat*) Vorverkauf *m*; **advanced** *adj* (*modern*) fortschrittlich; (*course, study*) für Fortgeschrittene; **advance payment** *n* Vorauszahlung *f*

advantage [əd'vɑːntɪdʒ] *n* Vorteil *m*; **to take ~ of** (*exploit*) ausnutzen; (*profit from*)

Nutzen ziehen aus; **it's to your ~** es ist in deinem/Ihrem Interesse

adventure [əd'ventʃə*] n Abenteuer nt; **adventure holiday** n Abenteuerurlaub m; **adventure playground** n Abenteuerspielplatz m; **adventurous** [əd'ventʃərəs] adj (person) abenteuerlustig

adverb ['ædvɜ:b] n Adverb nt

adverse ['ædvɜ:s] adj (conditions etc) ungünstig; (effect, comment etc) negativ

advert ['ædvɜ:t] n Anzeige f; **advertise** ['ædvətaɪz] vt werben für; (in newspaper) inserieren; (job) ausschreiben ▷ vi Reklame machen; (in newspaper) annoncieren (for für); **advertisement** [əd'vɜ:tɪsmənt] n Werbung f; (announcement) Anzeige f; **advertising** n Werbung f

advice [əd'vaɪs] n Rat(schlag) m; **word** o **piece of ~** Ratschlag m; **take my ~** hör auf mich; **advisable** [əd'vaɪzəbl] adj ratsam; **advise** [əd'vaɪz] vt raten (sb jdm); **to ~ sb to do sth/not to do sth** jdm zuraten/abraten, etw zu tun

Aegean [iː'dʒiːən] n **the ~ (Sea)** die Ägäis

aerial ['ɛərɪəl] n Antenne f ▷ adj Luft-

aerobatics [ɛərəʊ'bætɪks] npl Kunstfliegen nt

aerobics [ɛə'rəʊbɪks] nsing Aerobic nt

aeroplane ['ɛərəpleɪn] n Flugzeug nt

afaik abbr = **as far as I know**; (SMS) ≈ soweit ich weiß

affair [ə'fɛə*] n (matter, business) Sache f, Angelegenheit f; (scandal) Affäre f; (love affair) Verhältnis nt

affect [ə'fekt] vt (influence) (ein)wirken auf +akk; (health, organ) angreifen; (move deeply) berühren; (concern) betreffen; **affection** [ə'fekʃən] n Zuneigung f; **affectionate** [ə'fekʃnɪt] adj liebevoll

affluent ['æfluənt] adj wohlhabend

afford [ə'fɔːd] vt sich leisten; **I can't ~ it** ich kann es mir nicht leisten; **affordable** [ə'fɔːdəbl] adj erschwinglich

Afghanistan [æf'gænɪstæn] n Afghanistan nt

aforementioned [əfɔː'menʃənd] adj oben genannt

afraid [ə'freɪd] adj **to be ~** Angst haben (of vor +dat); **to be ~ that ...** fürchten, dass ...; **I'm ~ I don't know** das weiß ich leider nicht

Africa ['æfrɪkə] n Afrika nt; **African** adj afrikanisch ▷ n Afrikaner(in) m(f); **African American**, **Afro-American** n Afroamerikaner(in) m(f)

after ['ɑːftə*] prep nach; **ten ~ five** (US) zehn nach fünf; **to be ~ sb/sth** (following, seeking) hinter jdm/etw her sein; **~ all** schließlich; (in spite of everything) (schließlich) doch ▷ conj nachdem ▷ adv **soon ~** bald danach; **aftercare** n Nachbehandlung f; **after-effect** n Nachwirkung f

afternoon n Nachmittag m; **~, good ~** guten Tag!; **in the ~** nachmittags

afters npl Nachtisch m; **after-sales service** n Kundendienst m; **after-shave (lotion)** n Rasierwasser nt; **after-sun lotion** n After-Sun-Lotion f; **afterwards** adv nachher; (after that) danach

again [ə'gen] adv wieder; (one more time) noch einmal; **not ~!** (nicht) schon wieder; **~ and ~** immer wieder; **the same ~ please** das Gleiche noch mal bitte

against [ə'genst] prep gegen; **~ my will** wider Willen; **~ the law** unrechtmäßig, illegal

age [eɪdʒ] n Alter nt; (period of history) Zeitalter nt; **at the ~ of four** im Alter von vier (Jahren); **what ~ is she?, what is her ~?** wie alt ist sie?; **to come of ~** volljährig werden; **under ~** minderjährig ▷ vi altern, alt werden; **aged** adj **~ thirty** dreißig Jahre alt; **a son ~ twenty** ein zwanzigjähriger Sohn ▷ adj ['eɪdʒɪd] (elderly) betagt; **age group** n Altersgruppe f; **ageism** n Diskriminierung f aufgrund des Alters; **age limit** n Altersgrenze f

agency ['eɪdʒənsɪ] n Agentur f

agenda [ə'dʒendə] n Tagesordnung f

agent ['eɪdʒənt] n (Comm) Vertreter(in) m(f); (for writer, actor etc) Agent(in) m(f)

aggression [ə'greʃn] n Aggression f; **aggressive** [ə'gresɪv] adj aggressiv

agitated adj aufgeregt; **to get ~** sich aufregen

AGM abbr = **Annual General Meeting** JHV f

ago [ə'gəʊ] adv **two days ~** heute vor zwei Tagen; **not long ~** (erst) vor kurzem

agonize ['ægənaɪz] vi sich den Kopf zerbrechen (over über dat); **agonizing** adj qualvoll; **agony** ['ægənɪ] n Qual f

agree [ə'griː] vt (date, price etc)

vereinbaren; **to ~ to do sth** sich bereit erklären, etw zu tun; **to ~ that ...** sich *dat* einig sein, dass ...; (*decide*) beschließen, dass ...; (*admit*) zugeben, dass ... ▷ vi (*have same opinion, correspond*) übereinstimmen (*with* mit); (*consent*) zustimmen; (*come to an agreement*) sich einigen (*about, on* auf +*akk*); (*food*) **not to ~ with sb** jdm nicht bekommen; **agreement** *n* (*agreeing*) Übereinstimmung *f*; (*contract*) Abkommen *nt*, Vereinbarung *f*

agricultural [ægrɪˈkʌltʃərəl] *adj* landwirtschaftlich, Landwirtschafts-; **agriculture** [ˈægrɪkʌltʃə*] *n* Landwirtschaft *f*

ahead [əˈhed] *adv* **to be ~** führen, vorne liegen; **~ of** vor +*dat*; **to be ~ of sb** (*person*) jdm voraus sein; (*thing*) vor jdm liegen; **to be 3 metres ~** 3 Meter Vorsprung haben

aid [eɪd] *n* Hilfe *f*; **in ~ of** zugunsten +*gen*; **with the ~ of** mithilfe +*gen* ▷ *vt* helfen +*dat*; (*support*) unterstützen

Aids [eɪdz] *n acr* = **acquired immune deficiency syndrome** Aids *nt*

aim [eɪm] *vt* (*gun, camera*) richten (*at* auf +*akk*) ▷ *vi* **to ~ at** (*with gun etc*) zielen auf +*akk*; (*fig*) abzielen auf +*akk*; **to ~ to do sth** beabsichtigen, etw zu tun ▷ *n* Ziel *nt*

air [ɛə*] *n* Luft *f*; **in the open ~** im Freien; (*Radio, Tv*) **to be on the ~** (*programme*) auf Sendung sein; (*station*) senden ▷ *vt* lüften; **airbag** *n* (*Auto*) Airbag *m*; **air-conditioned** *adj* mit Klimaanlage; **air-conditioning** *n* Klimaanlage *f*; **aircraft** *n* Flugzeug *nt*; **airfield** *n* Flugplatz *m*; **air force** *n* Luftwaffe *f*; **airgun** *n* Luftgewehr *nt*; **airline** *n* Fluggesellschaft *f*; **airmail** *n* Luftpost *f*; **by ~** mit Luftpost; **airplane** *n* (*US*) Flugzeug *nt*; **air pollution** *n* Luftverschmutzung *f*; **airport** *n* Flughafen *m*; **airsick** *adj* luftkrank; **airtight** *adj* luftdicht; **air-traffic controller** *n* Fluglotse *m*, Fluglotsin *f*; **airy** *adj* luftig; (*manner*) lässig

aisle [aɪl] *n* Gang *m*; (*in church*) Seitenschiff *nt*; **~ seat** Sitz *m* am Gang

ajar [əˈdʒɑ:*] *adj* (*door*) angelehnt

alarm [əˈlɑ:m] *n* (*warning*) Alarm *m*; (*bell etc*) Alarmanlage *f* ▷ *vt* beunruhigen; **alarm clock** *n* Wecker *m*; **alarmed** *adj* (*protected*) alarmgesichert; **alarming** *adj* beunruhigend

Albania [ælˈbeɪnɪə] *n* Albanien *nt*; **Albanian** *adj* albanisch ▷ *n* (*person*) Albaner(in) *m(f)*; (*language*) Albanisch *nt*

album [ˈælbəm] *n* Album *nt*

alcohol [ˈælkəhɒl] *n* Alkohol *m*; **alcohol-free** *adj* alkoholfrei; **alcoholic** [ælkəˈhɒlɪk] *adj* (*drink*) alkoholisch ▷ *n* Alkoholiker(in) *m(f)*; **alcoholism** *n* Alkoholismus *m*

ale [eɪl] *n* Ale *nt* (*helles englisches Bier*)

alert [əˈlɜ:t] *adj* wachsam ▷ *n* Alarm *m* ▷ *vt* warnen (*to* vor +*dat*)

algebra [ˈældʒɪbrə] *n* Algebra *f*

Algeria [ælˈdʒɪərɪə] *n* Algerien *nt*

alibi [ˈælɪbaɪ] *n* Alibi *nt*

alien [ˈeɪlɪən] *n* (*foreigner*) Ausländer(in) *m(f)*; (*from space*) Außerirdische(r) *mf*

align [əˈlaɪn] *vt* ausrichten (*with* auf +*akk*)

alike [əˈlaɪk] *adj, adv* gleich; (*similar*) ähnlich

alive [əˈlaɪv] *adj* lebendig; **to keep sth ~** etw am Leben erhalten; **he's still ~** er lebt noch

🔵 **KEYWORD**

all [ɔ:l] *adj* alle (r, s); **all day/night** den ganzen Tag/die ganze Nacht; **all men are equal** alle Menschen sind gleich; **all five came** alle fünf kamen; **all the books/food** die ganzen Bücher/das ganze Essen; **all the time** die ganze Zeit (über); **all his life** sein ganzes Leben (lang)

▷ *pron* **1** alles; **I ate it all, I ate all of it** ich habe alles gegessen; **all of us/the boys went** wir gingen alle/alle Jungen gingen; **we all sat down** wir setzten uns alle

2 (*in phrases*): **above all** vor allem; **after all** schließlich; **at all: not at all** (*in answer to question*) überhaupt nicht; (*in answer to thanks*) gern geschehen; **I'm not at all tired** ich bin überhaupt nicht müde; **anything at all will do** es ist egal, welche(r, s); **all in all** alles in allem

▷ *adv* ganz; **all alone** ganz allein; **it's not as hard as all that** so schwer ist es nun auch wieder nicht; **all the more/the better** umso mehr/besser; **all but** fast; **the score is 2 all** es steht 2 zu 2

allegation [ælɪˈgeɪʃən] *n* Behauptung *f*; **alleged** *adj* angeblich

allergic [əˈlɜːdʒɪk] adj allergisch (to gegen); **allergy** [ˈælədʒɪ] n Allergie f
alleviate [əˈliːvɪeɪt] vt (pain) lindern
alley [ˈælɪ] n (enge) Gasse; (passage) Durchgang m; (bowling) Bahn f
alliance [əˈlaɪəns] n Bündnis nt
alligator [ˈælɪɡeɪtə*] n Alligator m
all-night adj (café, cinema) die ganze Nacht geöffnet
allocate [ˈæləkeɪt] vt zuweisen, zuteilen (to dat)
allotment n (plot) Schrebergarten m
allow [əˈlaʊ] vt (permit) erlauben (sb jdm); (grant) bewilligen; (time) einplanen; **allow for** vt berücksichtigen; (cost etc) einkalkulieren; **allowance** n (from state) Beihilfe f; (from parent) Unterhaltsgeld nt
all right [ˈɔːlˈraɪt] adj okay, in Ordnung; **I'm ~** mir geht's gut ▷ adv (satisfactorily) ganz gut ▷ interj okay
all-time adj (record, high) aller Zeiten
allusion [əˈluːʒn] n Anspielung f (to auf +akk)
all-wheel drive [ˈɔːlwiːlˈdraɪv] n (Auto) Allradantrieb m
ally [ˈælaɪ] n Verbündete(r) mf; (Hist) Alliierte(r) mf
almond [ˈɑːmənd] n Mandel f
almost [ˈɔːlməʊst] adv fast
alone [əˈləʊn] adj, adv allein
along [əˈlɒŋ] prep entlang +akk; **~ the river** den Fluss entlang; (position) am Fluss entlang ▷ adv (onward) weiter; **~ with** zusammen mit; **all ~** die ganze Zeit; **alongside** prep neben +dat ▷ adv (walk) nebenher
aloud [əˈlaʊd] adv laut
alphabet [ˈælfəbet] n Alphabet nt
alpine [ˈælpaɪn] adj alpin; **Alps** [ælps] npl **the ~** die Alpen
already [ɔːlˈredɪ] adv schon, bereits
Alsace [ˈælsæs] n Elsass nt; **Alsatian** [ælˈseɪʃən] adj elsässisch ▷ n Elsässer(in) m(f); (Brit: dog) Schäferhund m
also [ˈɔːlsəʊ] adv auch
altar [ˈɔːltə*] n Altar m
alter [ˈɔːltə*] vt ändern; **alteration** [ɔːltəˈreɪʃən] n Änderung f; **~s** (to building) Umbau m
alternate [ɔːlˈtɜːnət] adj abwechselnd ▷ [ˈɔːltɜneɪt] vi abwechseln (with mit); **alternating current** n Wechselstrom m

alternative [ɔːlˈtɜːnətɪv] adj Alternativ- ▷ n Alternative f
although [ɔːlˈðəʊ] conj obwohl
altitude [ˈæltɪtjuːd] n Höhe f
altogether [ɔːltəˈɡeðə*] adv (in total) insgesamt; (entirely) ganz und gar
aluminium, **aluminum** (US) [æljʊˈmɪnɪəm, əˈluːmɪnəm] n Aluminium nt
always [ˈɔːlweɪz] adv immer
am [æm] present of **be**; bin
am, **a.m.** abbr = **ante meridiem** vormittags, vorm.
amateur [ˈæmətə*] n Amateur(in) m(f) ▷ adj Amateur-; (theatre, choir) Laien-
amaze [əˈmeɪz] vt erstaunen; **amazed** adj erstaunt (at über +akk); **amazing** adj erstaunlich
Amazon [ˈæməzən] n ~ (river) Amazonas m
ambassador [æmˈbæsədə*] n Botschafter m
amber [ˈæmbə*] n Bernstein m
ambiguity [æmbɪˈɡjʊɪti] n Zweideutigkeit f; **ambiguous** [æmˈbɪɡjʊəs] adj zweideutig
ambition [æmˈbɪʃən] n Ambition f; (ambitious nature) Ehrgeiz m; **ambitious** [æmˈbɪʃəs] adj ehrgeizig
ambulance [ˈæmbjʊləns] n Krankenwagen m
amend [əˈmend] vt (law etc) ändern
America [əˈmerɪkə] n Amerika nt; **American** adj amerikanisch ▷ n Amerikaner(in) m(f); **native ~** Indianer(in) m(f)
amiable [ˈeɪmɪəbl] adj liebenswürdig
amicable [ˈæmɪkəbl] adj freundlich; (relations) freundschaftlich; (Jur: settlement) gütlich
amnesia [æmˈniːzɪə] n Gedächtnisverlust m
among(st) [əˈmʌŋ(st)] prep unter +dat
amount [əˈmaʊnt] n (quantity) Menge f; (of money) Betrag m; **a large/small ~ of ...** ziemlich viel/wenig ... ▷ vi **to ~ to** (total) sich belaufen auf +akk
amp, **ampere** [æmp, ˈæmpɛə*] n Ampere nt
amplifier [ˈæmplɪfaɪə*] n Verstärker m
amputate [ˈæmpjʊteɪt] vt amputieren
Amtrak® [ˈæmtræk] n amerikanische Eisenbahngesellschaft

amuse [əˈmjuːz] vt amüsieren; (entertain) unterhalten; **amused** adj **I'm not ~** das finde ich gar nicht lustig; **amusement** n (enjoyment) Vergnügen nt; (recreation) Unterhaltung f; **amusement arcade** n Spielhalle f; **amusement park** n Vergnügungspark m; **amusing** adj amüsant

an [æn, ən] art ein(e)

anaemic [əˈniːmɪk] adj blutarm

anaesthetic [ænɪsˈθetɪk] n Narkose f; (substance) Narkosemittel nt

analyse, **analyze** [ˈænəlaɪz] vt analysieren; **analysis** [əˈnælɪsɪs] n Analyse f

anatomy [əˈnætəmɪ] n Anatomie f; (structure) Körperbau m

ancestor [ˈænsestə*] n Vorfahr m

anchor [ˈæŋkə*] n Anker m ▷ vt verankern; **anchorage** n Ankerplatz m

anchovy [ˈæntʃəvɪ] n Sardelle f

ancient [ˈeɪnʃənt] adj alt; (fam: person, clothes etc) uralt

and [ænd, ənd] conj und

Andorra [ænˈdɔːrə] n Andorra nt

anemic adj (US) see **anaemic**

anesthetic n (US) see **anaesthetic**

angel [ˈeɪndʒəl] n Engel m

anger [ˈæŋgə*] n Zorn m ▷ vt ärgern

angina, **angina pectoris** [ænˈdʒaɪnə(ˈpektərɪs)] n Angina Pectoris f

angle [ˈæŋgl] n Winkel m; (fig) Standpunkt m

angler [ˈæŋglə*] n Angler(in) m(f); **angling** [ˈæŋglɪŋ] n Angeln nt

angry [ˈæŋgrɪ] adj verärgert; (stronger) zornig; **to be ~ with sb** auf jdn böse sein

angular [ˈæŋgjʊlə*] adj eckig; (face) kantig

animal [ˈænɪməl] n Tier nt; **animal rights** npl Tierrechte pl

animated [ˈænɪmeɪtɪd] adj lebhaft; **~ film** Zeichentrickfilm m

aniseed [ˈænɪsiːd] n Anis m

ankle [ˈæŋkl] n (Fuß)knöchel m

annex [ˈæneks] n Anbau m

anniversary [ænɪˈvɜːsərɪ] n Jahrestag m

announce [əˈnaʊns] vt bekannt geben; (officially) bekannt machen; (on radio, TV etc) (Radio, Tv) ansagen; **announcement** n Bekanntgabe f; (official) Bekanntmachung f; (Radio, Tv) Ansage f;

announcer n (Radio, Tv) Ansager(in) m(f)

annoy [əˈnɔɪ] vt ärgern; **annoyance** n Ärger m; **annoyed** adj ärgerlich; **to be ~ with sb (about sth)** sich über jdn (über etw) ärgern; **annoying** adj ärgerlich; (person) lästig, nervig

annual [ˈænjʊəl] adj jährlich ▷ n Jahrbuch nt

anonymous [əˈnɒnɪməs] adj anonym

anorak [ˈænəræk] n Anorak m; (Brit fam: pej) Freak m

anorexia [ænəˈreksɪə] n Magersucht f; **anorexic** adj magersüchtig

another [əˈnʌðə*] adj, pron (different) ein(e) andere(r, s); (additional) noch eine(r, s); **let me put it ~ way** lass es mich anders sagen

answer [ˈɑːnsə*] n Antwort f (to auf +akk); (solution) Lösung f +gen ▷ vi antworten; (on phone) sich melden ▷ vt (person) antworten +dat; (letter, question) beantworten; (telephone) gehen an +akk, abnehmen; (door) öffnen; **answer back** vi widersprechen; **answering machine**, **answerphone** n Anrufbeantworter m

ant [ænt] n Ameise f

Antarctic [æntˈɑːktɪk] n Antarktis f; **Antarctic Circle** n südlicher Polarkreis

antelope [ˈæntɪləʊp] n Antilope f

antenna [ænˈtenə] (pl **antennae**) n (Zool) Fühler m; (Radio) Antenne f

anti- [ˈæntɪ] pref Anti-, anti-; **antibiotic** [ˈæntɪbaɪˈɒtɪk] n Antibiotikum nt

anticipate [ænˈtɪsɪpeɪt] vt (expect: trouble, question) erwarten, rechnen mit; **anticipation** [æntɪsɪˈpeɪʃən] n Erwartung f

anticlimax [æntɪˈklaɪmæks] n Enttäuschung f; **anticlockwise** [æntɪˈklɒkwaɪz] adv entgegen dem Uhrzeigersinn

antidote [ˈæntɪdəʊt] n Gegenmittel nt; **antifreeze** n Frostschutzmittel nt

Antipodes [ænˈtɪpədiːz] npl Australien und Neuseeland

antiquarian [æntɪˈkwɛərɪən] adj **~ bookshop** Antiquariat nt

antique [ænˈtiːk] n Antiquität f ▷ adj antik; **antique shop** n Antiquitätengeschäft nt

anti-Semitism [ænti'semitizm] *n*
Antisemitismus *m*; **antiseptic**
[ænti'septik] *n* Antiseptikum *nt* ▷ *adj*
antiseptisch; **antisocial** *adj* (*person*)
ungesellig; (*behaviour*) unsozial,
asozial
antlers ['æntləz] *npl* Geweih *nt*
anxiety [æŋ'zaɪəti] *n* Sorge *f* (*about* um);
anxious ['æŋkʃəs] *adj* besorgt (*about* um);
(*apprehensive*) ängstlich

⊙ KEYWORD

any ['eni] *adj* **1** (*in questions etc*): **have you
any butter?** haben Sie (etwas) Butter?;
have you any children? haben Sie
Kinder?; **if there are any tickets left** falls
noch Karten da sind
2 (*with negative*): **I haven't any
money/books** ich habe kein Geld/keine
Bücher
3 (*no matter which*) jede(r, s) (beliebige); **any
colour (at all)** jede beliebige Farbe;
choose any book you like nehmen Sie ein
beliebiges Buch
4 (*in phrases*): **in any case** in jedem Fall;
any day now jeden Tag; **at any
moment** jeden Moment; **at any rate**
auf jeden Fall
▷ *pron* **1** (*in questions etc*): **have you got
any?** haben Sie welche?; **can any of you
sing?** kann (irgend)einer von euch singen?
2 (*with negative*): **I haven't any (of them)**
ich habe keinen/keines (davon)
3 (*no matter which one(s)*): **take any of
those books (you like)** nehmen Sie
irgendeines dieser Bücher
▷ *adv* **1** (*in questions etc*): **do you want any
more soup/sandwiches?** möchten Sie
noch Suppe/Brote?; **are you feeling any
better?** fühlen Sie sich etwas besser?
2 (*with negative*): **I can't hear him any
more** ich kann ihn nicht mehr hören

⊙ KEYWORD

anything ['eniθiŋ] *pron* **1** (*in questions etc*)
(irgend)etwas; **can you see anything?**
können Sie etwas sehen?
2 (*with negative*): **I can't see anything** ich
kann nichts sehen
3 (*no matter what*): **you can say anything**

you like Sie können sagen, was Sie
wollen; **anything will do**
irgendetwas(, wird genügen)
irgendeine(r, s) (wird genügen); **he'll eat
anything** er ißt alles

apart [ə'pɑːt] *adv* auseinander; **~ from**
außer; **live ~** getrennt leben
apartment [ə'pɑːtmənt] *n* (*esp US*)
Wohnung *f*; **apartment block** *n* (*esp US*)
Wohnblock *m*
ape [eɪp] *n* (Menschen)affe *m*
aperitif [ə'peritif] *n* Aperitif *m*
aperture ['æpətjuə*] *n* Öffnung *f*; (*Foto*)
Blende *f*
apologize [ə'pɒlədʒaɪz] *vi* sich
entschuldigen; **apology** *n*
Entschuldigung *f*
apostrophe [ə'pɒstrəfi] *n* Apostroph *m*
appalled [ə'pɔːld] *adj* entsetzt (*at* über
+*akk*); **appalling** *adj* entsetzlich
apparatus [æpə'reɪtəs] *n* Apparat *m*;
(*piece of apparatus*) Gerät *nt*
apparent [ə'pærənt] *adj* (*obvious*)
offensichtlich (*to* für); (*seeming*) scheinbar;
apparently *adv* anscheinend
appeal [ə'piːl] *vi* (dringend) bitten (*for*
um, *to* +*akk*); (*Jur*) Berufung einlegen; **to
~ to sb** (*be attractive*) jdm zusagen ▷ *n*
Aufruf *m* (*to* an +*akk*); (*Jur*) Berufung *f*;
(*attraction*) Reiz *m*; **appealing** *adj*
ansprechend, attraktiv
appear [ə'pɪə*] *vi* erscheinen; (*Theat*)
auftreten; (*seem*) scheinen; **appearance** *n*
Erscheinen *nt*; (*Theat*) Auftritt *m*; (*look*)
Aussehen *nt*
appendicitis [əpendɪ'saɪtɪs] *n*
Blinddarmentzündung *f*; **appendix**
[ə'pendɪks] *n* Blinddarm *m*; (*to book*)
Anhang *m*
appetite ['æpɪtaɪt] *n* Appetit *m*; (*fig:
desire*) Verlangen *nt*; (*sexual*) Lust *f*;
appetizing ['æpɪtaɪzɪŋ] *adj* appetitlich,
appetitanregend
applause [ə'plɔːz] *n* Beifall *m*, Applaus *m*
apple ['æpl] *n* Apfel *m*; **apple crumble** *n*
mit Streuseln bestreutes Apfeldessert; **apple
juice** *n* Apfelsaft *m*; **apple pie** *n*
gedeckter Apfelkuchen *m*; **apple puree**,
apple sauce *n* Apfelmus *nt*; **apple tart** *n*
Apfelkuchen *m*; **apple tree** *n* Apfelbaum *m*
appliance [ə'plaɪəns] *n* Gerät *nt*;
applicable [ə'plɪkəbl] *adj* anwendbar; (*on*

forms) zutreffend; **applicant** ['æplɪkənt] _n_
Bewerber(in) _m(f)_; **application**
[æplɪ'keɪʃən] _n_ (_request_) Antrag _m_ (_for_ auf
+_akk_); (_for job_) Bewerbung _f_ (_for_ um);
application form _n_ Anmeldeformular _nt_;
apply [ə'plaɪ] _vi_ (_be relevant_) zutreffen
(_to_ auf +_akk_); (_for job etc_) sich bewerben
(_for_ um) ▷ _vt_ (_cream, paint etc_) auftragen;
(_put into practice_) anwenden; (_brakes_)
betätigen
appoint [ə'pɔɪnt] _vt_ (_to post_) ernennen;
appointment _n_ Verabredung _f_; (_at doctor,
hairdresser etc, in business_) Termin _m_; **by**
~ nach Vereinbarung
appreciate [ə'priːʃɪeɪt] _vt_ (_value_) zu
schätzen wissen; (_understand_) einsehen; **to
be much ~d** richtig gewürdigt werden ▷ _vi_
(_increase in value_) im Wert steigen;
appreciation [əpriːʃɪ'eɪʃən] _n_ (_esteem_)
Anerkennung _f_, Würdigung _f_; (_of person
also_) Wertschätzung _f_
apprehensive [æprɪ'hensɪv] _adj_
ängstlich
apprentice [ə'prentɪs] _n_ Lehrling _m_
approach [ə'prəʊtʃ] _vi_ sich nähern ▷ _vt_
(_place_) sich nähern +_dat_; (_person_)
herantreten an +_akk_; (_problem_) angehen
appropriate [ə'prəʊprɪət] _adj_ passend;
(_to occasion_) angemessen; (_remark_)
treffend; **appropriately** _adv_ passend;
(_expressed_) treffend
approval [ə'pruːvəl] _n_ (_show of
satisfaction_) Anerkennung _f_; (_permission_)
Zustimmung _f_ (_of_ zu); **approve** [ə'pruːv]
_vt_ billigen ▷ _vi_ **to ~ of sth/sb** etw
billigen/von jdm etwas halten; **I don't
~** ich missbillige das
approx [ə'prɒks] _abbr_ = **approximately**
ca.; **approximate** [ə'prɒksɪmɪt] _adj_
ungefähr; **approximately** _adv_ ungefähr,
circa
apricot ['eɪprɪkɒt] _n_ Aprikose _f_
April ['eɪprəl] _n_ April _m_; _see also_
September
apron ['eɪprən] _n_ Schürze _f_
aptitude [æptɪtjuːd] _n_ Begabung _f_
aquaplaning ['ækwəpleɪnɪŋ] _n_ (_Auto_)
Aquaplaning _nt_
aquarium [ə'kwɛərɪəm] _n_ Aquarium _nt_
Aquarius [ə'kwɛərɪəs] _n_ (_Astr_)
Wassermann _m_
Arab ['ærəb] _n_ Araber(in) _m(f)_; (_horse_)
Araber _m_; **Arabian** [ə'reɪbɪən] _adj_

arabisch; **Arabic** ['ærəbɪk] _n_ (_language_)
Arabisch _nt_ ▷ _adj_ arabisch
arbitrary ['ɑːbɪtrərɪ] _adj_ willkürlich
arcade [ɑː'keɪd] _n_ Arkade _f_; (_shopping
arcade_) Einkaufspassage _f_
arch [ɑːtʃ] _n_ Bogen _m_
archaeologist, **archeologist** (US)
[ɑːkɪ'ɒlədʒɪst] _n_ Archäologe _m_,
Archäologin _f_; **archaeology**, **archeology**
(US) [ɑːkɪ'ɒlədʒɪ] _n_ Archäologie _f_
archaic [ɑː'keɪɪk] _adj_ veraltet
archbishop [ɑːtʃ'bɪʃəp] _n_ Erzbischof _m_
archery ['ɑːtʃərɪ] _n_ Bogenschießen _nt_
architect ['ɑːkɪtekt] _n_ Architekt(in)
_m(f)_; **architecture** [ɑːkɪ'tektʃə] _n_
Architektur _f_
archive(s) ['ɑːkaɪv(z)] _n(pl)_ Archiv _nt_
archway ['ɑːtʃweɪ] _n_ Torbogen _m_
Arctic ['ɑːktɪk] _n_ Arktis _f_; **Arctic Circle** _n_
nördlicher Polarkreis
are [ə], _unstressed_ [ɑː*] _present of_ **be**
area ['ɛərɪə] _n_ (_region, district_) Gebiet _nt_,
Gegend _f_; (_amount of space_) Fläche _f_;
(_part of building etc_) Bereich _m_, Zone _f_; (_fig:
field_) Bereich _m_; **the London ~** der
Londoner Raum; **area code** _n_ (US)
Vorwahl _f_
aren't [ɑːnt] _contr of_ **are not**
Argentina [ɑːdʒən'tiːnə] _n_ Argentinien
_nt_
argue ['ɑːgjuː] _vi_ streiten (_about, over_ über
+_akk_); **to ~ that ...** behaupten, dass ...; **to
~ for/against ...** sprechen für/gegen ...;
argument _n_ (_reasons_) Argument _nt_;
(_quarrel_) Streit _m_; **to have an ~** sich
streiten
Aries ['ɛəriːz] _nsing_ (_Astr_) Widder _m_
arise [ə'raɪz] (**arose, arisen**) _vi_ sich
ergeben, entstehen; (_problem, question,
wind_) aufkommen
aristocracy [ærɪs'tɒkrəsɪ] _n_ (_class_) Adel
_m_; **aristocrat** ['ærɪstəkræt] _n_ Adlige(r)
_mf_; **aristocratic** [ærɪstə'krætɪk] _adj_
aristokratisch, adlig
arm [ɑːm] _n_ Arm _m_; (_sleeve_) Ärmel _m_; (_of
armchair_) Armlehne _f_ ▷ _vt_ bewaffnen;
armchair ['ɑːmtʃɛə*] _n_ Lehnstuhl _m_
armed [ɑːmd] _adj_ bewaffnet
armpit ['ɑːmpɪt] _n_ Achselhöhle _f_
arms [ɑːmz] _npl_ Waffen _pl_
army ['ɑːmɪ] _n_ Armee _f_, Heer _nt_
A road ['eɪrəʊd] _n_ (_Brit_) ≈ Bundesstraße _f_
aroma [ə'rəʊmə] _n_ Duft _m_, Aroma _nt_;

aromatherapy [ərəʊməˈθerəpɪ] *n*
Aromatherapie *f*
arose [əˈrəʊz] *pt of* **arise**
around [əˈraʊnd] *adv* herum, umher;
(*present*) hier (irgendwo); (*approximately*)
ungefähr; (*with time*) gegen; **he's**
~ somewhere er ist hier irgendwo in der
Nähe ▷ *prep* (*surrounding*) um … (herum);
(*about in*) in … herum
arr. *abbr* = **arrival, arrives** Ank.

arrange [əˈreɪndʒ] *vt* (*put in order*)
(an)ordnen; (*alphabetically*) ordnen;
(*artistically*) arrangieren; (*agree to: meeting*
etc) vereinbaren, festsetzen; (*holidays*)
festlegen; (*organize*) planen; **to ~ that …**
es so einrichten, dass …; **we ~d to meet**
at eight o'clock wir haben uns für acht
Uhr verabredet; **it's all ~d** es ist alles
arrangiert; **arrangement** *n* (*layout*)
Anordnung *f*; (*agreement*) Vereinbarung
f, Plan *m*; **make ~s** Vorbereitungen
treffen
arrest [əˈrest] *vt* (*person*) verhaften ▷ *n*
Verhaftung *f*; **under ~** verhaftet
arrival [əˈraɪvəl] *n* Ankunft *f*; **new**
~ (*person*) Neuankömmling *m*; **arrivals** *n*
(*airport*) Ankunftshalle *f*; **arrive** [əˈraɪv] *vi*
ankommen (*at* bei, *in* +*dat*); **to ~ at a**
solution eine Lösung finden
arrogant [ˈærəgənt] *adj* arrogant
arrow [ˈærəʊ] *n* (=*weapon, sign*) Pfeil *m*
art [ɑːt] *n* Kunst *f*, **~s** (*pl*)
Geisteswissenschaften *pl*
artery [ˈɑːtərɪ] *n* (*Med*) Schlagader *f*,
Arterie *f*
art gallery *n* Kunstgalerie *f*,
Kunstmuseum *nt*
arthritis [ɑːˈθraɪtɪs] *n* Arthritis *f*
artichoke [ˈɑːtɪtʃəʊk] *n* Artischocke *f*
article [ˈɑːtɪkl] *n* Artikel *m*; (*object*)
Gegenstand *m*
artificial [ɑːtɪˈfɪʃəl] *adj* künstlich, Kunst-;
(*smile etc*) gekünstelt
artist [ˈɑːtɪst] *n* Künstler(in) *m(f)*; **artistic**
[ɑːˈtɪstɪk] *adj* künstlerisch

○ **KEYWORD**

as [æz] *conj* **1** (*referring to time*) als; **as**
the years went by mit den Jahren; **he**
came in as I was leaving als er
hereinkam, ging ich gerade; **as from**
tomorrow ab morgen

2 (*in comparisons*): **as big as** so groß wie;
twice as big as zweimal so groß wie; **as**
much/many as so viel/so viele wie; **as**
soon as sobald
3 (*since, because*) da; **he left early as he**
had to be home by 10 er ging früher, da er
um 10 zu Hause sein musste
4 (*referring to manner, way*) wie; **do as you**
wish mach was du willst; **as she said** wie
sie sagte
5 (*concerning*): **as for** *or* **to that** was das
betrifft *or* angeht
6: **as if** *or* **though** als ob
▷ *prep* als; *see also* **long**; **he works as a**
driver er arbeitet als Fahrer; *see also*
such; **he gave it to me as a present** er
hat es mir als Geschenk gegeben; *see also*
well

asap [eɪeseɪˈpiː, ˈeɪsæp] *acr* = **as soon as**
possible möglichst bald
ascertain [æsəˈteɪn] *vt* feststellen
ash [æʃ] *n* (*dust*) Asche *f*; (*tree*)
Esche *f*
ashamed [əˈʃeɪmd] *adj* beschämt; **to**
be ~ (*of sb/sth*) sich (für jdn/etw)
schämen
ashore [əˈʃɔː*] *adv* an Land
ashtray [ˈæʃtreɪ] *n* Aschenbecher *m*
Asia [ˈeɪʃə] *n* Asien *nt*; **Asian** *adj* asiatisch
▷ *n* Asiat(in) *m(f)*
aside [əˈsaɪd] *adv* beiseite, zur Seite;
~ from (*esp US*) außer
ask [ɑːsk] *vt, vi* fragen; (*question*) stellen;
(*request*) bitten um; (*invite*) einladen; **to**
~ sb the way jdn nach dem Weg fragen;
to ~ sb to do sth jdn darum bitten, etw zu
tun; **ask for** *vt* bitten um
asleep [əˈsliːp] *adj, adv* **to be ~** schlafen;
to fall ~ einschlafen
asparagus [əsˈpærəgəs] *n* Spargel *m*
aspect [ˈæspekt] *n* Aspekt *m*
aspirin [ˈæsprɪn] *n* Aspirin® *nt*
ass [æs] *n* (*a. fig*) Esel *m*
assassinate [əˈsæsɪneɪt] *vt* ermorden;
assassination [əˈsæsɪneɪʃn] *n*
Ermordung *f*; **~ attempt** Attentat *nt*
assault [əˈsɔːlt] *n* Angriff *m*; (*Jur*)
Körperverletzung *f* ▷ *vt* überfallen,
herfallen über +*akk*
assemble [əˈsembl] *vt* (*parts*)
zusammensetzen; (*people*)
zusammenrufen ▷ *vi* sich versammeln;

assembly [ə'semblɪ] n (of people)
Versammlung f; (putting together)
Zusammensetzen nt; **assembly hall** n
Aula f
assert [ə'sɜːt] vt behaupten; **assertion**
[ə'sɜːʃən] n Behauptung f
assess [ə'ses] vt einschätzen;
assessment n Einschätzung f
asset ['æset] n Vermögenswert m; (fig)
Vorteil m; **~s** pl Vermögen nt
assign [ə'saɪn] vt zuweisen; **assignment**
n Aufgabe f; (mission) Auftrag m
assist [ə'sɪst] vt helfen +dat; **assistance** n
Hilfe f; **assistant** n Assistent(in) m(f),
Mitarbeiter(in) m(f); (in shop) Verkäufer(in)
m(f)
associate [ə'səʊʃɪət] n (partner)
Partner(in) m(f), Teilhaber(in) m(f)
▷ [ə'səʊʃɪeɪt] vt verbinden (with mit);
association [əsəʊsɪ'eɪʃən] n (organization)
Verband m, Vereinigung f; **in ~ with ...** in
Zusammenarbeit mit ...
assorted [ə'sɔːtɪd] adj gemischt;
assortment n Auswahl f (of an +dat); (of
sweets) Mischung f
assume [ə'sjuːm] vt annehmen (that
... dass ...); (role, responsibility)
übernehmen; **assumption** [ə'sʌmpʃən] n
Annahme f
assurance [ə'ʃʊərəns] n Versicherung f;
(confidence) Zuversicht f; **assure** [ə'ʃʊə*] vt
(say confidently) versichern +dat; **to ~ sb of
sth** jdm etw zusichern; **to be ~d of sth**
einer Sache sicher sein
asterisk ['æstərɪsk] n Sternchen nt
asthma ['æsmə] n Asthma nt
astonish [əs'tɒnɪʃ] vt erstaunen;
astonished adj erstaunt (at über);
astonishing adj erstaunlich;
astonishment n Erstaunen nt
astound [ə'staʊnd] vt sehr erstaunen;
astounding adj erstaunlich
astray [ə'streɪ] adv **to go ~** (letter etc)
verloren gehen; (person) vom Weg
abkommen; **to lead ~** irreführen, verführen
astrology [əs'trɒlədʒɪ] n Astrologie f
astronaut ['æstrənɔːt] n Astronaut(in)
m(f)
astronomy [əs'trɒnəmɪ] n Astronomie
f
asylum [ə'saɪləm] n (home) Anstalt f;
(political asylum) Asyl nt; **asylum seeker** n
Asylbewerber(in) m(f)

○ **KEYWORD**

at [æt] prep **1** (referring to position, direction)
an +dat, bei +dat; (with place) in +dat; **at the
top** an der Spitze; **at home/school** zu
Hause, zuhause (österreichisch,
schweizerisch)/in der Schule; **at the
baker's** beim Bäcker; **to look at sth** auf
etw acc blicken; **to throw sth at sb** etw
nach jdm werfen
2 (referring to time): **at 4 o'clock** um 4 Uhr;
at night bei Nacht; **at Christmas** zu
Weihnachten; **at times** manchmal
3 (referring to rates, speed etc): **at £1 a kilo** zu £1
pro Kilo; **two at a time** zwei auf einmal;
at 50 km/h mit 50 km/h
4 (referring to manner): **at a stroke** mit
einem Schlag; **at peace** in Frieden
5 (referring to activity): **to be at work** bei
der Arbeit sein; **to play at cowboys**
Cowboy spielen; **to be good at sth** gut in
etw dat sein
6 (referring to cause): **shocked/surprised/
annoyed at sth** schockiert/überrascht/
verärgert über etw acc; **I went at his
suggestion** ich ging auf seinen Vorschlag
hin

ate [et, eɪt] pt of **eat**
athlete ['æθliːt] n Athlet(in) m(f); (track
and field) Leichtathlet(in) m(f); (sportsman)
Sportler(in) m(f); **~'s foot** Fußpilz m;
athletic [æθ'letɪk] adj sportlich; (build)
athletisch; **athletics** npl Leichtathletik f
Atlantic [ət'læntɪk] n **the ~** (**Ocean**) der
Atlantik
atlas ['ætləs] n Atlas m
ATM abbr = **automated teller machine**
Geldautomat m
atmosphere ['ætməsfɪə*] n Atmosphäre
f; (fig) Stimmung f
atom ['ætəm] n Atom nt; **atom(ic) bomb**
n Atombombe f; **atomic** [ə'tɒmɪk] adj
Atom-; **~ energy** Atomenergie f; **~ power**
Atomkraft f
A to Z® ['eɪtə'zed] n Stadtplan m (in
Buchform)
atrocious [ə'trəʊʃəs] adj grauenhaft;
atrocity [ə'trɒsɪtɪ] n Grausamkeit f;
(deed) Gräueltat f
attach [ə'tætʃ] vt befestigen, anheften (to
an +dat); **to ~ importance to sth** Wert auf

etw *akk* legen; **to be ~ed to sb/sth** an jdm/etw hängen; **attachment** [ə'tætʃmənt] *n* (*affection*) Zuneigung *f;* (*Inform*) Attachment *nt*, Anhang *m*, Anlage *f*

attack [ə'tæk] *vt, vi* angreifen ▷ *n* Angriff +*akk* (*on* auf *m*); (*Med*) Anfall *m*

attempt [ə'tempt] *n* Versuch *m;* **to make an ~ to do sth** versuchen, etw zu tun ▷ *vt* versuchen

attend [ə'tend] *vt* (*go to*) teilnehmen an +*dat;* (*lectures, school*) besuchen ▷ *vi* (*be present*) anwesend sein; **attend to** *vt* sich kümmern um; (*customer*) bedienen; **attendance** *n* (*presence*) Anwesenheit *f;* (*people present*) Teilnehmerzahl *f;* **attendant** *n* (*in car park etc*) Wächter(in) *m(f);* (*in museum*) Aufseher(in) *m(f)*

attention [ə'tenʃən] *n* Aufmerksamkeit *f;* (**your**) **~ please** Achtung!; **to pay ~ to sth** etw beachten; **to pay ~ to sb** jdm aufmerksam zuhören; (*listen*) jdm/etw aufmerksam zuhören; **for the ~ of ...** zu Händen von ...; **attentive** [ə'tentɪv] *adj* aufmerksam

attic ['ætɪk] *n* Dachboden *m;* (*lived in*) Mansarde *f*

attitude ['ætɪtjuːd] *n* (*mental*) Einstellung *f* (*to, towards* zu); (*more general, physical*) Haltung *f*

attorney [ə'tɜːnɪ] *n* (*US: lawyer*) Rechtsanwalt *m*, Rechtsanwältin *f*

attract [ə'trækt] *vt* anziehen; (*attention*) erregen; **to be ~ed to** *o* **by sb** sich zu jdm hingezogen fühlen; **attraction** [ə'trækʃən] *n* Anziehungskraft *f;* (*thing*) Attraktion *f;* **attractive** *adj* attraktiv; (*thing, idea*) reizvoll

aubergine ['əʊbəʒiːn] *n* Aubergine *f*

auction ['ɔːkʃən] *n* Versteigerung *f*, Auktion *f* ▷ *vt* versteigern

audible ['ɔːdɪbl] *adj* hörbar

audience ['ɔːdɪəns] *n* Publikum *nt;* (*Radio*) Zuhörer *pl;* (*Tv*) Zuschauer *pl*

audio ['ɔːdɪəʊ] *adj* Ton-

audition [ɔː'dɪʃən] *n* Probe *f* ▷ *vi* (*Theat*) vorspielen, vorsingen

auditorium [ɔːdɪ'tɔːrɪəm] *n* Zuschauerraum *m*

Aug *abbr* = **August**

August ['ɔːgəst] *n* August *m; see also* **September**

aunt [ɑːnt] *n* Tante *f*

au pair [əʊ'pɛə*] *n* Aupairmädchen *nt*, Aupairjunge *m*

Australia [ɒ'streɪlɪə] *n* Australien *nt;* **Australian** *adj* australisch ▷ *n* Australier(in) *m(f)*

Austria ['ɒstrɪə] *n* Österreich *nt;* **Austrian** *adj* österreichisch ▷ *n* Österreicher(in) *m(f)*

authentic [ɔː'θentɪk] *adj* echt; (*signature*) authentisch; **authenticity** [ɔːθen'tɪsɪtɪ] *n* Echtheit *f*

author ['ɔːθə*] *n* Autor(in) *m(f);* (*of report etc*) Verfasser(in) *m(f)*

authority [ɔː'θɒrɪtɪ] *n* (*power, expert*) Autorität *f;* **an ~ on sth** eine Autorität auf dem Gebiet einer Sache; **the authorities** (*pl*) die Behörden *pl;* **authorize** ['ɔːθəraɪz] *vt* (*permit*) genehmigen; **to be ~d to do sth** offiziell berechtigt sein, etw zu tun

auto ['ɔːtəʊ] (*pl* **-s**) *n* (*US*) Auto *nt*

autobiography [ɔːtəʊbaɪ'ɒgrəfɪ] *n* Autobiographie *f;* **autograph** ['ɔːtəgrɑːf] *n* Autogramm *nt*

automatic [ɔːtə'mætɪk] *adj* automatisch; **~ gear change** (*Brit*), **~ gear shift** (*US*) Automatikschaltung *f* ▷ *n* (*car*) Automatikwagen *m*

automobile ['ɔːtəməbiːl] *n* (*US*) Auto(mobil) *nt;* **autotrain** ['ɔːtəʊtreɪn] *n* (*US*) Autoreisezug *m*

autumn ['ɔːtəm] *n* (*Brit*) Herbst *m*

auxiliary [ɔːg'zɪlɪərɪ] *adj* Hilfs-; **~ verb** Hilfsverb *nt* ▷ *n* Hilfskraft *f*

availability [əveɪlə'bɪlɪtɪ] *n* (*of product*) Lieferbarkeit *f;* (*of resources*) Verfügbarkeit *f;* **available** *adj* erhältlich; (*existing*) vorhanden; (*product*) lieferbar; (*person*) erreichbar; **to be/make ~ to sb** jdm zur Verfügung stehen/stellen; **they're only ~ in black** es gibt sie nur in Schwarz, sie sind nur in Schwarz erhältlich

avalanche ['ævəlɑːnʃ] *n* Lawine *f*

Ave *abbr* = **avenue**

avenue ['ævənjuː] *n* Allee *f*

average ['ævrɪdʒ] *n* Durchschnitt *m;* **on ~** im Durchschnitt ▷ *adj* durchschnittlich; **~ speed** Durchschnittsgeschwindigkeit *f;* **of ~ height** von mittlerer Größe

aviation [eɪvɪ'eɪʃən] *n* Luftfahrt *f*

avocado [ævə'kɑːdəʊ] (*pl* **-s**) *n* Avocado *f*

avoid [ə'vɔɪd] *vt* vermeiden; **to ~ sb** jdm aus dem Weg gehen; **avoidable** *adj* vermeidbar

awake [ə'weɪk] (**awoke, awoken**) vi
aufwachen ▷ adj wach

award [ə'wɔ:d] n (prize) Preis m; (for
bravery etc) Auszeichnung f ▷ vt
zuerkennen (to sb jdm); (present) verleihen
(to sb jdm)

aware [ə'wɛə*] adj bewusst; **to be ~ of
sth** sich dat einer Sache gen bewusst sein; **I
was not ~ that ...** es war mir nicht klar,
dass ...

away [ə'weɪ] adv weg; **to look
~** wegsehen; **he's ~** er ist nicht da; (on a
trip) er ist verreist; (from school, work) er
fehlt; (Sport) **they are (playing) ~** sie
spielen auswärts; (with distance) **three
miles ~** drei Meilen (von hier) entfernt; **to
work ~** drauflos arbeiten

awful ['ɔ:fʊl] adj schrecklich, furchtbar;
awfully adv furchtbar

awkward ['ɔ:kwəd] adj (clumsy)
ungeschickt; (embarrassing) peinlich;
(difficult) schwierig

awning ['ɔ:nɪŋ] n Markise f

awoke [ə'wəʊk] pt of **awake**; **awoken**
[ə'wəʊkən] pp of **awake**

ax (US), **axe** [æks] n Axt f

axle ['æksl] n (Tech) Achse f

verkehrt herum ⊳ vt (support)
unterstützen; (car) rückwärts fahren
⊳ vi (go backwards) rückwärts gehen o
fahren ⊳ adj Hinter-; **~ wheel** Hinterrad
nt ⊳ adv zurück; **they're ~** sie sind
wieder da; **back away** vi sich
zurückziehen; **back down** vi nachgeben;
back up vi (car etc) zurücksetzen ⊳ vt
(support) unterstützen; (Inform) sichern;
(car) zurückfahren

backache n Rückenschmerzen pl;
  backbone n Rückgrat nt; **backdate** vt
  zurückdatieren; **backdoor** n Hintertür f;
  backfire vi (plan) fehlschlagen; (Auto)
  fehlzünden; **background** n Hintergrund
  m; **backhand** n (Sport) Rückhand f;
  backlog n (of work) Rückstand m;
  backpack n (US) Rucksack m;
  backpacker n Rucksacktourist(in) m(f);
  backpacking n Rucksacktourismus m;
  back seat n Rücksitz m; **backside** n (fam)
  Po m; **back street** n Seitensträßchen nt;
  backstroke n Rückenschwimmen nt;
  back-up n (support) Unterstützung f;
  ~ (copy) (Inform) Sicherungskopie f;
  backward adj (child) zurückgeblieben;
  (region) rückständig; **~ movement**
  Rückwärtsbewegung f; **backwards** adv
  rückwärts; **backyard** n Hinterhof m
bacon ['beɪkən] n Frühstücksspeck m
bacteria [bæk'tɪərɪə] npl Bakterien pl
bad [bæd] (**worse, worst**) adj schlecht,
  schlimm; (smell) übel; **I have a ~ back** mir
  tut der Rücken weh; **I'm ~ at maths/sport**
  ich bin schlecht in Mathe/Sport; **to go
  ~** schlecht werden, verderben
badge [bædʒ] n Abzeichen nt
badger ['bædʒə*] n Dachs m
badly ['bædlɪ] adv schlecht; **~ wounded**
  schwer verwundet; **to need sth ~** etw
  dringend brauchen; **bad-tempered**
  ['bæd'tempəd] adj schlecht gelaunt
bag [bæg] n (small) Tüte f; (larger) Beutel
  m; (handbag) Tasche f; **my ~s** (luggage)
  mein Gepäck; **it's not my ~** (fam) das ist
  nicht mein Ding
baggage ['bægɪdʒ] n Gepäck nt; **baggage
  allowance** n Freigepäck nt; **baggage
  (re)claim** n Gepäckrückgabe f
baggy ['bægɪ] adj (zu) weit; (trousers, suit)
  ausgebeult
bag lady ['bægleɪdɪ] n Stadtstreicherin f
bagpipes ['bægpaɪps] npl Dudelsack m

BA abbr = **Bachelor of Arts**
BSc abbr = **Bachelor of Science**
babe [beɪb] n (fam) Baby nt; (fam:
  affectionate) Schatz m, Kleine(r) mf
baby ['beɪbɪ] n Baby nt; (of animal)
  Junge(s) nt; (fam: affectionate) Schatz m,
  Kleine(r) mf; **to have a ~** ein Kind
  bekommen; **it's your ~** (fam: responsibility)
  das ist dein Bier; **baby carriage** n (US)
  Kinderwagen m; **baby food** n
  Babynahrung f; **babyish** adj kindisch;
  baby shower n (US) Party für die werdende
  Mutter; **baby-sit** irr vi babysitten;
  baby-sitter n Babysitter(in) m(f)
bachelor ['bætʃələ*] n Junggeselle m;
  Bachelor of Arts/Science erster
  akademischer Grad, ≈ Magister/Diplom;
  bachelorette n Junggesellin f;
  bachelorette party n (US)
  Junggesellinnenabschied; **bachelor party** n
  (US) Junggesellenabschied
back [bæk] n (of person, animal) Rücken m;
  (of house, coin etc) Rückseite f; (of chair)
  Rückenlehne f; (of car) Rücksitz m; (of train)
  Ende nt; (Sport: defender) Verteidiger(in)
  m(f); **at the ~ of ...**, (US) **in ~ of** (inside)
  hinten in ...; (outside) hinter ...; **~ to front**

Bahamas [bə'hɑːməz] *npl* **the ~** die Bahamas *pl*

bail [beɪl] *n* (*money*) Kaution *f*

bait [beɪt] *n* Köder *m*

bake [beɪk] *vt*, *vi* backen; **baked beans** *npl* weiße Bohnen in Tomatensoße; **baked potato** (*pl* **-es**) *n* in der Schale gebackene Kartoffel, Ofenkartoffel *f*; **baker** *n* Bäcker(in) *m(f)*; **bakery** ['beɪkərɪ] *n* Bäckerei *f*; **baking powder** *n* Backpulver *nt*

balance ['bæləns] *n* (*equilibrium*) Gleichgewicht *nt* ▷ *vt* (*make up for*) ausgleichen; **balanced** *adj* ausgeglichen; **balance sheet** *n* Bilanz *f*

balcony ['bælkənɪ] *n* Balkon *m*

bald [bɔːld] *adj* kahl; **to be ~** eine Glatze haben

Balkans ['bɔːlkənz] *npl* **the ~** der Balkan, die Balkanländer *pl*

ball [bɔːl] *n* Ball *m*; **to have a ~** (*fam*) sich prima amüsieren

ballet ['bæleɪ] *n* Ballett *nt*; **ballet dancer** *n* Balletttänzer(in) *m(f)*

balloon [bə'luːn] *n* (Luft)ballon *m*

ballot ['bælət] *n* (geheime) Abstimmung; **ballot box** *n* Wahlurne *f*; **ballot paper** *n* Stimmzettel *m*

ballpoint (pen) ['bɔːlpɔɪnt] *n* Kugelschreiber *m*

ballroom ['bɔːlruːm] *n* Tanzsaal *m*

Baltic ['bɔːltɪk] *adj* **~ Sea** Ostsee *f*; **the ~ States** die baltischen Staaten

bamboo [bæm'buː] *n* Bambus *m*; **bamboo shoots** *npl* Bambussprossen *pl*

ban [bæn] *n* Verbot *nt* ▷ *vt* verbieten

banana [bə'nɑːnə] *n* Banane *f*; **he's ~s** er ist völlig durchgeknallt; **banana split** *n* Bananensplit *nt*

band [bænd] *n* (*group*) Gruppe *f*; (*of criminals*) Bande *f*; (*Mus*) Kapelle *f*; (*pop, rock etc*) Band *f*; (*strip*) Band *nt*

bandage ['bændɪdʒ] *n* Verband *m*; (*elastic*) Bandage *f* ▷ *vt* verbinden

B & B *abbr* = **bed and breakfast**

bang [bæŋ] *n* (*noise*) Knall *m*; (*blow*) Schlag *m* ▷ *vt*, *vi* knallen; (*door*) zuschlagen, zuknallen; **banger** ['bæŋə*] *n* (*Brit fam: firework*) Knallkörper *m*; (*sausage*) Würstchen *nt*; (*fam: old car*) Klapperkiste *f*

bangs [bæŋz] *npl* (*US: of hair*) Pony *m*

banish ['bænɪʃ] *vt* verbannen

banister(s) ['bænɪstə*] *n* (Treppen)geländer *nt*

bank [bæŋk] *n* (*Fin*) Bank *f*; (*of river etc*) Ufer *nt*; **bank account** *n* Bankkonto *nt*; **bank balance** *n* Kontostand *m*; **bank card** *n* Bankkarte *f*; **bank code** *n* Bankleitzahl *f*; **bank holiday** *n* gesetzlicher Feiertag

● **bank holiday**
●
● Als **bank holiday** wird in
● Großbritannien ein gesetzlicher
● Feiertag bezeichnet, an dem die
● Banken geschlossen sind. Die
● meisten dieser Feiertage, abgesehen
● von Weihnachten und Ostern, fallen
● auf Montage im Mai und August. An
● diesen langen Wochenenden (bank
● holiday weekends) fahren viele
● Briten in Urlaub, so dass dann auf
● den Straßen, Flughäfen und bei der
● Bahn sehr viel Betrieb ist.

bank manager *n* Filialleiter(in) *m(f)*; **banknote** *n* Banknote *f*

bankrupt *vt* ruinieren; **to go ~** Pleite gehen

bank statement *n* Kontoauszug *m*

baptism ['bæptɪzəm] *n* Taufe *f*; **baptize** ['bæptaɪz] *vt* taufen

bar [bɑː*] *n* (*for drinks*) Bar *f*; (*less smart*) Lokal *nt*; (*rod*) Stange *f*; (*of chocolate etc*) Riegel *m*, Tafel *f*; (*of soap*) Stück *nt*; (*counter*) Theke *f* ▷ *prep* außer; **~ none** ohne Ausnahme

barbecue ['bɑːbɪkjuː] *n* (*device*) Grill *m*; (*party*) Barbecue *nt*, Grillfete *f*; **to have a ~** grillen

barbed wire ['bɑːbd'waɪə*] *n* Stacheldraht *m*

barber ['bɑːbə*] *n* (Herren)friseur *m*

bar code ['bɑːkəʊd] *n* Strichkode *m*

bare [bɛə*] *adj* nackt; **~ patch** kahle Stelle; **barefoot** *adj*, *adv* barfuß; **bareheaded** *adj*, *adv* ohne Kopfbedeckung; **barely** *adv* kaum; (*with age*) knapp

bargain ['bɑːgɪn] *n* (*cheap offer*) günstiges Angebot, Schnäppchen *nt*; (*transaction*) Geschäft *nt*; **what a ~** das ist aber günstig! ▷ *vi* (ver)handeln

barge [bɑːdʒ] n (for freight) Lastkahn m; (unpowered) Schleppkahn m

bark [bɑːk] n (of tree) Rinde f; (of dog) Bellen nt ▷ vi (dog) bellen

barley ['bɑːlɪ] n Gerste f

barmaid ['bɑːmeɪd] n Bardame f; **barman** ['bɑːmən] (pl **-men**) n Barkeeper m

barn [bɑːn] n Scheune f

barometer [bə'rɒmɪtə*] n Barometer nt

baroque [bə'rɒk] adj barock, Barock-

barracks ['bærəks] npl Kaserne f

barrel ['bærəl] n Fass nt; **barrel organ** n Drehorgel f

barricade [bærɪ'keɪd] n Barrikade f

barrier ['bærɪə*] n (obstruction) Absperrung f, Barriere f; (across road etc) Schranke f

barrow ['bærəʊ] n (cart) Schubkarren m

bartender ['bɑːtendə*] n (US) Barkeeper m

base [beɪs] n Basis f; (of lamp, pillar etc) Fuß m; (Mil) Stützpunkt m ▷ vt gründen (on auf +akk); **to be ~d on sth** auf etw dat basieren; **baseball** n Baseball m; **baseball cap** n Baseballmütze f; **basement** n Kellergeschoss nt

bash [bæʃ] (fam) n Schlag m; (fam) Party f ▷ vt hauen

basic ['beɪsɪk] adj einfach; (fundamental) Grund-; (importance, difference) grundlegend; (in principle) grundsätzlich; **the accomodation is very ~** die Unterkunft ist sehr bescheiden; **basically** adv im Grunde; **basics** npl **the ~** das Wesentliche

basil ['bæzl] n Basilikum nt

basin ['beɪsn] n (for washing, valley) (Wasch)becken nt

basis ['beɪsɪs] n Basis f; **on the ~ of** aufgrund +gen; **on a monthly ~** monatlich

basket ['bɑːskɪt] n Korb m; **basketball** n Basketball m

Basque [bæsk] n (person) Baske m, Baskin f; (language) Baskisch nt ▷ adj baskisch

bass [beɪs] n (Mus) Bass m; (Zool) Barsch m ▷ adj (Mus) Bass-

bastard ['bɑːstəd] n (vulg: awful person) Arschloch nt

bat [bæt] n (Zool) Fledermaus f; (Sport: cricket, baseball) Schlagholz nt; (table tennis) Schläger m

batch [bætʃ] n Schwung m; (fam: of letters, books etc) Stoß m

bath [bɑːθ] n Bad nt; (tub) Badewanne f; **to have a ~** baden ▷ vt (child etc) baden

bathe [beɪð] vt, vi (wound etc) baden; **bathing cap** n Badekappe f; **bathing costume**, **bathing suit** (US) n Badeanzug m

bathmat ['bɑːθmæt] n Badevorleger m; **bathrobe** n Bademantel m; **bathroom** n Bad(ezimmer) nt; **baths** [bɑːðz] npl (Schwimm)bad nt; **bath towel** n Badetuch nt; **bathtub** n Badewanne f

baton ['bætən] n (Mus) Taktstock m; (police) Schlagstock m

batter ['bætə*] n Teig m ▷ vt heftig schlagen; **battered** adj übel zugerichtet; (hat, car) verbeult; (wife, baby) misshandelt

battery ['bætərɪ] n (Elec) Batterie f; **battery charger** n Ladegerät nt

battle ['bætl] n Schlacht f; (fig) Kampf m (for um +akk); **battlefield** n Schlachtfeld nt; **battlements** npl Zinnen pl

Bavaria [bə'vɛərɪə] n Bayern nt; **Bavarian** adj bay(e)risch ▷ n Bayer(in) m(f)

bay [beɪ] n (of sea) Bucht f; (on house) Erker m; (tree) Lorbeerbaum m; **bay leaf** n Lorbeerblatt nt; **bay window** n Erkerfenster nt

BBC abbr = **British Broadcasting Corporation** BBC f

BC abbr = **before Christ** vor Christi Geburt, v. Chr.

○ KEYWORD

be [biː] (pt **was**, **were**, pp **been**) aux vb **1** (with present participle: forming continuous tenses); **what are you doing?** was machst du (gerade)?; **it is raining** es regnet; **I've been waiting for you for hours** ich warte schon seit Stunden auf dich

2 (with pp: forming passives): **to be killed** getötet werden; **the thief was nowhere to be seen** der Dieb war nirgendwo zu sehen

3 (in tag questions): **it was fun, wasn't it?** es hat Spaß gemacht, nicht wahr?

4 (+to +infin): **the house is to be sold** das Haus soll verkauft werden; **he's not to open it** er darf es nicht öffnen b

▷ vb +complement **1** (*usu*) sein; **I'm tired** ich bin müde; **I'm hot/cold** mir ist heiß/kalt; **he's a doctor** er ist Arzt; **2 and 2 are 4** 2 und 2 ist *or* sind 4; **she's tall/pretty** sie ist groß/hübsch; **be careful/quiet** sei vorsichtig/ruhig
2 (*of health*): **how are you?** wie geht es dir?; **he's very ill** er ist sehr krank; **I'm fine now** jetzt geht es mir gut
3 (*of age*): **how old are you?** wie alt bist du?; **I'm sixteen (years old)** ich bin sechzehn (Jahre alt)
4 (*cost*): **how much was the meal?** was *or* wie viel hat das Essen gekostet?; **that'll be £5.75, please** das macht £5.75, bitte
▷ vi **1** (*exist, occur etc*) sein; **is there a God?** gibt es einen Gott?; **be that as it may** wie dem auch sei; **so be it** also gut
2 (*referring to place*) sein; **I won't be here tomorrow** iche werde morgen nicht hier sein
3 (*referring to movement*); **where have you been?** wo bist du gewesen?; **I've been in the garden** ich war im Garten
▷ impers vb **1** (*referring to time, distance, weather*) sein; **it's 5 o'clock** es ist 5 Uhr; **it's 10 km to the village** es sind 10 km bis zum Dorf; **it's too hot/cold** es ist zu heiß/kalt
2 (*emphatic*): **it's me** ich bins; **it's the postman** es ist der Briefträger

beach [biːtʃ] *n* Strand *m*; **beachwear** *n* Strandkleidung *f*
bead [biːd] *n* (*of glass, wood etc*) Perle *f*; (*drop*) Tropfen *m*
beak [biːk] *n* Schnabel *m*
beam [biːm] *n* (*of wood etc*) Balken *m*; (*of light*) Strahl *m* ▷ *vi* (*smile etc*) strahlen
bean [biːn] *n* Bohne *f*; **bean curd** *n* Tofu *m*
bear [bɛə*] (**bore, borne**) *vt* (*carry*) tragen; (*tolerate*) ertragen ▷ *n* Bär *m*; **bearable** *adj* erträglich
beard [bɪəd] *n* Bart *m*
beast [biːst] *n* Tier *nt*; (*brutal person*) Bestie *f*; (*disliked person*) Biest *nt*
beat [biːt] (**beat, beaten**) *vt* schlagen; (*as punishment*) prügeln; **to ~ sb at tennis** jdn im Tennis schlagen ▷ *n* (*of heart, drum etc*) Schlag *m*; (*Mus*) Takt *m*; (*type of music*) Beat *m*; **beat up** *vt* zusammenschlagen
beaten ['biːtn] *pp of* **beat**; **of the ~ track** abgelegen
beautiful ['bjuːtɪfʊl] *adj* schön; (*splendid*)

herrlich; **beauty** ['bjuːtɪ] *n* Schönheit *f*; **beauty spot** *n* (*place*) lohnendes Ausflugsziel
beaver ['biːvə*] *n* Biber *m*
became [bɪˈkeɪm] *pt of* **become**
because [bɪˈkɒz] *adv, conj* weil ▷ *prep* **~ of** wegen +*gen o dat*
become [bɪˈkʌm] (**became, become**) *vt* werden; **what's ~ of him?** was ist aus ihm geworden?
bed [bɛd] *n* Bett *nt*; (*in garden*) Beet *nt*; **bed and breakfast** *n* Übernachtung *f* mit Frühstück; **bedclothes** *npl* Bettwäsche *f*; **bedding** *n* Bettzeug *nt*; **bed linen** *n* Bettwäsche *f*; **bedroom** *n* Schlafzimmer *nt*; **bed-sit(ter)** *n* (*fam*) möblierte Einzimmerwohnung; **bedspread** *n* Tagesdecke *f*; **bedtime** *n* Schlafenszeit *f*
bee [biː] *n* Biene *f*
beech [biːtʃ] *n* Buche *f*
beef [biːf] *n* Rindfleisch *nt*; **beefburger** *n* Hamburger *m*; **beef tomato** (*pl* **-es**) *n* Fleischtomate *f*
beehive ['biːhaɪv] *n* Bienenstock *m*
been [biːn] *pp of* **be**
beer [bɪə*] *n* Bier *nt*; **beer garden** *n* Biergarten *m*
beetle ['biːtl] *n* Käfer *m*
beetroot ['biːtruːt] *n* Rote Bete
before [bɪˈfɔː*] *prep vor*; **the year ~ last** vorletztes Jahr; **the day ~ yesterday** vorgestern ▷ *conj* bevor ▷ *adv* (*of time*) vorher; **have you been there ~?** waren Sie/warst du schon einmal dort?; **beforehand** *adv* vorher
beg [bɛg] *vt* **to ~ sb to do sth** jdn inständig bitten, etw zu tun ▷ *vi* (*beggar*) betteln (*for* um +*akk*)
began [bɪˈgæn] *pt of* **begin**
beggar ['bɛgə*] *n* Bettler(in) *m(f)*
begin [bɪˈgɪn] (**began, begun**) *vt, vi* anfangen, beginnen; **to ~ to do sth** anfangen, etw zu tun; **beginner** *n* Anfänger(in) *m(f)*; **beginning** *n* Anfang *m*
begun [bɪˈgʌn] *pp of* **begin**
behalf [bɪˈhɑːf] *n* **on ~ of, in ~ of** (*US*) im Namen/Auftrag von; **on my ~** für mich
behave [bɪˈheɪv] *vi* sich benehmen; **~ yourself!** benimm dich!; **behavior** (*US*), **behaviour** [bɪˈheɪvjə*] *n* Benehmen *nt*
behind [bɪˈhaɪnd] *prep* hinter; **to be ~ time** Verspätung haben ▷ *adv* hinten; **to be ~ with one's work** mit seiner Arbeit

im Rückstand sein ▷ *n* (*fam*) Hinterteil *nt*

beige [beɪʒ] *adj* beige

being ['biːɪŋ] *n* (*existence*) Dasein *nt*; (*person*) Wesen *nt*

Belarus [belə'rʊs] *n* Weißrussland *nt*

belch [beltʃ] *n* Rülpser *m* ▷ *vi* rülpsen

belfry ['belfrɪ] *n* Glockenturm *m*

Belgian ['beldʒən] *adj* belgisch ▷ *n* Belgier(in) *m(f)*; **Belgium** ['beldʒəm] *n* Belgien *nt*

belief [bɪ'liːf] *n* Glaube *m* (*in an* +*akk*); (*conviction*) Überzeugung *f*; **it's my ~ that ...** ich bin der Überzeugung, dass ...; **believe** [bɪ'liːv] *vt* glauben; **believe in** *vi* glauben an +*akk*; **believer** *n* (*Rel*) Gläubige(r) *mf*

bell [bel] *n* (*church*) Glocke *f*; (*bicycle, door*) Klingel *f*; **bellboy** ['belbɔɪ] *n* (*esp US*) Page *m*

bellows ['beləʊz] *npl* (*for fire*) Blasebalg *m*

belly ['belɪ] *n* Bauch *m*; **bellyache** *n* Bauchweh *nt* ▷ *vi* (*fam*) meckern; **belly button** *n* (*fam*) Bauchnabel *m*; **bellyflop** *n* (*fam*) Bauchklatscher *m*

belong [bɪ'lɒŋ] *vi* gehören (*to sb* jdm); (*to club*) angehören +*dat*; **belongings** *npl* Habe *f*

below [bɪ'ləʊ] *prep* unter ▷ *adv* unten

belt [belt] *n* (*round waist*) Gürtel *m*; (*safety belt*) Gurt *m*; **below the ~** unter der Gürtellinie ▷ *vi* (*fam: go fast*) rasen, düsen; **beltway** *n* (*US*) Umgehungsstraße *f*

bench [bentʃ] *n* Bank *f*

bend [bend] *n* Biegung *f*; (*in road*) Kurve *f* ▷ *vt* (**bent, bent**) (*curve*) biegen; (*head, arm*) beugen ▷ *vi* sich biegen; (*person*) sich beugen; **bend down** *vi* sich bücken

beneath [bɪ'niːθ] *prep* unter ▷ *adv* darunter

beneficial [benɪ'fɪʃl] *adj* gut, nützlich (*to* für); **benefit** ['benɪfɪt] *n* (*advantage*) Vorteil *m*; (*profit*) Nutzen *m*; **for your/his ~** deinetwegen/seinetwegen; **unemployment ~** Arbeitslosengeld *nt* ▷ *vt* gut tun +*dat* ▷ *vi* Nutzen ziehen (*from* aus)

Benelux ['benɪlʌks] *n* Beneluxländer *pl*

benign [bɪ'naɪn] *adj* (*person*) gütig; (*climate*) mild; (*Med*) gutartig

bent [bent] *pt, pp of* **bend** ▷ *adj* krumm; (*fam*) korrupt

beret ['bereɪ] *n* Baskenmütze *f*

Bermuda [bə'mjuːdə] *n* **the ~s** *pl* die Bermudas *pl* ▷ *adj* **~ shorts** *pl* Bermudashorts *pl*; **the ~ triangle** das Bermudadreieck

berry ['berɪ] *n* Beere *f*

berth [bɜːθ] *n* (*for ship*) Ankerplatz *m*; (*in ship*) Koje *f*; (*in train*) Bett *nt* ▷ *vt* am Kai festmachen ▷ *vi* anlegen

beside [bɪ'saɪd] *prep* neben; **~ the sea/lake** am Meer/See; **besides** [bɪ'saɪdz] *prep* außer ▷ *adv* außerdem

besiege [bɪ'siːdʒ] *vt* belagern

best [best] *adj* beste(r, s); **my ~ friend** mein bester *o* engster Freund; **the ~ thing (to do) would be to ...** das Beste wäre zu ...; (*on food packaging*) **~ before ...** mindestens haltbar bis ... ▷ *n* der/die/das Beste; **all the ~** alles Gute; **to make the ~ of it** das Beste daraus machen ▷ *adv* am besten; **I like this ~** das mag ich am liebsten; **best-before date** *n* Mindesthaltbarkeitsdatum *nt*; **best man** ['best'mæn] (*pl* **men**) *n* Trauzeuge *m*; **bestseller** ['bestselə*] *n* Bestseller *m*

bet [bet] (**bet, bet**) *vt, vi* wetten (*on auf* +*akk*); **I ~ him £5 that ...** ich habe mit ihm um 5 Pfund gewettet, dass ...; **you ~** (*fam*) und ob!; **I ~ he'll be late** er kommt mit Sicherheit zu spät ▷ *n* Wette *f*

betray [bɪ'treɪ] *vt* verraten; **betrayal** *n* Verrat *m*

better ['betə*] *adj, adv* besser; **to get ~** (*healthwise*) sich erholen, wieder gesund werden; (*improve*) sich verbessern; **I'm much ~ today** es geht mir heute viel besser; **you'd ~ go** du solltest lieber gehen; **a change for the ~** eine Wendung zum Guten

betting ['betɪŋ] *n* Wetten *nt*; **betting shop** *n* Wettbüro *nt*

between [bɪ'twiːn] *prep* zwischen; (*among*) unter; **~ you and me, ...** unter uns gesagt, ... ▷ *adv* (*in*) **~** dazwischen

beverage ['bevərɪdʒ] *n* (*formal*) Getränk *nt*

beware [bɪ'wɛə*] *vt* **to ~ of sth** sich vor etw +*dat* hüten; **'~ of the dog'** „Vorsicht, bissiger Hund!"

bewildered [bɪ'wɪldəd] *adj* verwirrt

beyond [bɪ'jɒnd] *prep* (*place*) jenseits +*gen*; (*time*) über ... hinaus; (*out of reach*) außerhalb +*gen*; **it's ~ me** da habe ich keine Ahnung, da bin ich überfragt ▷ *adv* darüber hinaus

bias ['baɪəs] n (prejudice) Vorurteil nt, Voreingenommenheit f

bias(s)ed adj voreingenommen

bib [bɪb] n Latz m

Bible ['baɪbl] n Bibel f

bicycle ['baɪsɪkl] n Fahrrad nt

bid [bɪd] (**bid, bid**) vt (offer) bieten ▷ n (attempt) Versuch m; (offer) Gebot nt

big [bɪg] adj groß; **it's no ~ deal** (fam) es ist nichts Besonderes; **big dipper** n (Brit) Achterbahn f; **bigheaded** [bɪg'hedɪd] adj eingebildet

bike [baɪk] n (fam) Rad nt

bikini [bɪ'kiːnɪ] n Bikini m

bilberry ['bɪlbərɪ] n Heidelbeere f

bilingual [baɪ'lɪŋgwəl] adj zweisprachig

bill [bɪl] n (account) Rechnung f; (US: banknote) Banknote f; (Pol) Gesetzentwurf m; (Zool) Schnabel m; **billfold** ['bɪlfəʊld] n (US) Brieftasche f

billiards ['bɪlɪədz] nsing Billard nt; **billiard table** Billardtisch m

billion ['bɪlɪən] n Milliarde f

bin [bɪn] n Behälter m; (rubbish bin) (Müll)eimer m; (for paper) Papierkorb m

bind [baɪnd] (**bound, bound**) vt binden; (bind together) zusammenbinden; (wound) verbinden; **binding** n (ski) Bindung f; (book) Einband m

binge [bɪndʒ] n (fam: drinking) Sauferei f; **to go on a ~** auf Sauftour gehen

bingo ['bɪŋgəʊ] n Bingo nt

binoculars [bɪ'nɒkjʊləz] npl Fernglas nt

biodegradable ['baɪəʊdɪ'greɪdəbl] adj biologisch abbaubar

biography [baɪ'ɒgrəfɪ] n Biografie f

biological [baɪə'lɒdʒɪkəl] adj biologisch; **biology** [baɪ'ɒlədʒɪ] n Biologie f

birch [bɜːtʃ] n Birke f

bird [bɜːd] n Vogel m; (Brit fam: girl, girlfriend) Tussi f; **bird watcher** n Vogelbeobachter(in) m(f)

birth [bɜːθ] n Geburt f; **birth certificate** n Geburtsurkunde f; **birth control** n Geburtenkontrolle f; **birthday** n Geburtstag m; **happy ~** herzlichen Glückwunsch zum Geburtstag; **birthday card** n Geburtstagskarte f; **birthday party** n Geburtstagsfeier f; **birthplace** n Geburtsort m

biscuit ['bɪskɪt] n (Brit) Keks m

bisexual [baɪ'seksjʊəl] adj bisexuell

bishop ['bɪʃəp] n Bischof m; (in chess) Läufer m

bit [bɪt] pt of **bite** ▷ n (piece) Stück(chen) nt; (Inform) Bit nt; **a ~ (of ...)** (small amount) ein bisschen ...; **a ~ tired** etwas müde; **~ by ~** allmählich; (time) **for a ~** ein Weilchen; **quite a ~** (a lot) ganz schön viel

bitch [bɪtʃ] n (dog) Hündin f; **bitchy** adj gemein, zickig

bite [baɪt] (**bit, bitten**) vt, vi beißen ▷ n Biss m; (mouthful) Bissen m; (insect) Stich m; **to have a ~** eine Kleinigkeit essen;

bitten pp of **bite**

bitter ['bɪtə*] adj bitter; (memory etc) schmerzlich ▷ n (Brit: beer) halbdunkles Bier; **bitter lemon** n Bitter Lemon nt

bizarre [bɪ'zɑː*] adj bizarr

black [blæk] adj schwarz; **blackberry** n Brombeere f; **blackbird** n Amsel f; **blackboard** n (Wand)tafel f; **black box** n (Aviat) Flugschreiber m; **blackcurrant** n Schwarze Johannisbeere; **black eye** n blaues Auge; **Black Forest** n Schwarzwald m; **Black Forest gateau** n Schwarzwälder Kirschtorte f; **blackmail** n Erpressung f ▷ vt erpressen; **black market** n Schwarzmarkt m; **blackout** n (Med) Ohnmacht f; **to have a ~** ohnmächtig werden; **black pudding** n ≈ Blutwurst f; **Black Sea** n **the ~** das Schwarze Meer; **blacksmith** n Schmied(in) m(f); **black tie** n Abendanzug m, Smoking m; **is it ~?** ist/besteht da Smokingzwang?

bladder ['blædə*] n Blase f

blade [bleɪd] n (of knife) Klinge f; (of propeller) Blatt nt; (of grass) Halm m

blame [bleɪm] n Schuld f ▷ vt **to ~ sth on sb** jdm die Schuld an etw dat geben; **he is to ~** er ist daran schuld

bland [blænd] adj (taste) fade; (comment) nichts sagend

blank [blæŋk] adj (page, space) leer, unbeschrieben; (look) ausdruckslos; **~ cheque** Blankoscheck m

blanket ['blæŋkɪt] n (Woll)decke f

blast [blɑːst] n (of wind) Windstoß m; (of explosion) Druckwelle f ▷ vt (blow up) sprengen; **~!** (fam) Mist!, verdammt!

blatant ['bleɪtənt] adj (undisguised) offen; (obvious) offensichtlich

blaze [bleɪz] vi lodern; (sun) brennen ▷ n

(building) Brand m; (other fire) Feuer nt; **a ~ of colour** eine Farbenpracht

blazer ['bleɪzə*] n Blazer m

bleach [bliːtʃ] n Bleichmittel nt ▷ vt bleichen

bleak [bliːk] adj öde, düster; (future) trostlos

bleary ['blɪərɪ] adj (eyes) trübe, verschlafen

bleed [bliːd] (**bled, bled**) vi bluten

bleep [bliːp] n Piepton m ▷ vi piepen; **bleeper** n (fam) Piepser m

blend [blend] n Mischung f ▷ vt mischen ▷ vi sich mischen; **blender** n Mixer m

bless [bles] vt segnen; **~ you!** Gesundheit!; **blessing** n Segen m

blew [bluː] pt of **blow**

blind [blaɪnd] adj blind; (corner) unübersichtlich; **to turn a ~ eye to sth** bei etw ein Auge zudrücken ▷ n (for window) Rollo nt ▷ vt blenden; **blind alley** n Sackgasse f; **blind spot** n (Auto) toter Winkel; (fig) schwacher Punkt

blink [blɪŋk] vi blinzeln; (light) blinken

bliss [blɪs] n (Glück)seligkeit f

blister ['blɪstə*] n Blase f

blizzard ['blɪzəd] n Schneesturm m

bloated ['bləʊtɪd] adj aufgedunsen

block [blɒk] n (of wood, stone, ice) Block m, Klotz m; (of buildings) Häuserblock m; **~ of flats** (Brit) Wohnblock m ▷ vt (road etc) blockieren; (pipe, nose) verstopfen; **blockage** ['blɒkɪdʒ] n Verstopfung f; **blockbuster** ['blɒkbʌstə*] n Knüller m; **block letters** npl Blockschrift f

bloke [bləʊk] n (Brit fam) Kerl m, Typ m

blonde [blɒnd] adj blond ▷ n (person) Blondine f, blonder Typ

blood [blʌd] n Blut nt; **blood count** n Blutbild nt; **blood donor** n Blutspender(in) m(f); **blood group** n Blutgruppe f; **blood poisoning** n Blutvergiftung f; **blood pressure** n Blutdruck m; **blood sample** n Blutprobe f; **bloodsports** npl Sportarten, bei denen Tiere getötet werden; **bloodthirsty** adj blutrünstig; **bloody** adj (Brit fam) verdammt, Scheiß-; (literal sense) blutig

bloom [bluːm] n Blüte f ▷ vi blühen

blossom ['blɒsəm] n Blüte f ▷ vi blühen

blot ['blɒt] n (of ink) Klecks m; (fig) Fleck m

blouse [blaʊz] n Bluse f; **big girl's ~** (fam) Schwächling m, femininer Typ

blow [bləʊ] n Schlag m ▷ vi, vt (**blew, blown**) (wind) wehen, blasen; (person: trumpet etc) blasen; **to ~ one's nose** sich dat die Nase putzen; **blow out** vt (candle etc) ausblasen; **blow up** vi explodieren ▷ vt sprengen; (balloon, tyre) aufblasen; (Foto: enlarge) vergrößern; **blow-dry** vt föhnen; **blowjob** n (fam) **to give sb a ~** jdm einen blasen; **blown** [bləʊn] pp of **blow**; **blow-out** n (Auto) geplatzter Reifen

BLT n abbr = **bacon, lettuce and tomato sandwich** mit Frühstücksspeck, Kopfsalat und Tomaten belegtes Sandwich

blue [bluː] adj blau; (fam: unhappy) trübsinnig, niedergeschlagen; (film) pornografisch; (joke) anzüglich; (language) derb; **bluebell** n Glockenblume f; **blueberry** n Blaubeere f; **blue cheese** n Blauschimmelkäse m; **blues** npl **the ~** (Mus) der Blues; **to have the ~** (fam) niedergeschlagen sein

blunder ['blʌndə*] n Schnitzer m

blunt [blʌnt] adj (knife) stumpf; (fig) unverblümt; **bluntly** adv geradeheraus

blurred [blɜːd] adj verschwommen, unklar

blush [blʌʃ] vi erröten

board [bɔːd] n (of wood) Brett nt; (committee) Ausschuss m; (of firm) Vorstand m; **~ and lodging** Unterkunft und Verpflegung; **on ~** an Bord ▷ vt (train, bus) einsteigen in +akk; (ship) an Bord +gen gehen; **boarder** n Pensionsgast m; (school) Internatsschüler(in) m(f); **board game** n Brettspiel nt; **boarding card**, **boarding pass** n Bordkarte f, Einsteigekarte f; **boarding school** n Internat nt; **board meeting** n Vorstandssitzung f; **boardroom** n Sitzungssaal m (des Vorstands)

boast [bəʊst] vi prahlen (about mit) ▷ n Prahlerei f

boat [bəʊt] n Boot nt; (ship) Schiff nt; **boatman** n (hirer) Bootsverleiher m; **boat race** n Regatta f; **boat train** n Zug m mit Schiffsanschluss

bob(sleigh) ['bɒbsleɪ] n Bob m

bodily ['bɒdɪlɪ] adj körperlich ▷ adv (forcibly) gewaltsam; **body** ['bɒdɪ] n Körper m; (dead) Leiche f; (of car) Karosserie

b

_f;_ **bodybuilding** _n_ Bodybuilding _nt;_
bodyguard _n_ Leibwächter _m;_ _(group)_
Leibwache _f;_ **body jewellery** _n_
Intimschmuck _m;_ **body odour** _n_
Körpergeruch _m;_ **body piercing** _n_
Piercing _nt;_ **bodywork** _n_ Karosserie _f_
boil [bɔɪl] _vt, vi_ kochen ▷ _n_ _(Med)_
Geschwür _nt;_ **boiler** _n_ Boiler _m;_ **boiling**
adj _(water etc)_ kochend (heiß); **I was ~** _(hot)_
mir war fürchterlich heiß; _(with rage)_ ich
kochte vor Wut; **boiling point** _n_
Siedepunkt _m_
bold [bəʊld] _adj_ kühn, mutig; _(colours)_
kräftig; _(type)_ fett
Bolivia [bəˈlɪvɪə] _n_ Bolivien _nt_
bolt [bəʊlt] _n_ _(lock)_ Riegel _m;_ _(screw)_
Bolzen _m_ ▷ _vt_ verriegeln
bomb [bɒm] _n_ Bombe _f_ ▷ _vt_
bombardieren
bond [bɒnd] _n_ _(link)_ Bindung _f;_ _(Fin)_
Obligation _f_
bone [bəʊn] _n_ Knochen _m;_ _(of fish)_ Gräte
_f;_ **boner** _n_ _(US fam)_ Schnitzer _m;_ _(erection)_
Ständer _m_
bonfire [ˈbɒnfaɪə*] _n_ Feuer _nt_ (im Freien)
bonnet [ˈbɒnɪt] _n_ _(Brit Auto)_ Haube _f;_ _(for baby)_ Häubchen _nt_
bonny [ˈbɒnɪ] _adj_ _(esp Scottish)_ hübsch
bonus [ˈbəʊnəs] _n_ Bonus _m,_ Prämie _f_
boo [buː] _vt_ auspfeifen, ausbuhen ▷ _vi_
buhen ▷ _n_ Buhruf _m_
book [bʊk] _n_ Buch _nt;_ _(of tickets, stamps)_
Heft _nt_ ▷ _vt_ _(ticket etc)_ bestellen; _(hotel, flight etc)_ buchen; _(Sport)_ verwarnen; **fully ~ed (up)** ausgebucht; _(performance)_
ausverkauft; **book in** _vt_ eintragen; **to be ~ed in at a hotel** ein Zimmer in einem
Hotel bestellt haben; **bookable** _adj_ im
Vorverkauf erhältlich; **bookcase** _n_
Bücherregal _nt;_ **booking** _n_ Buchung _f;_
booking office _n_ _(Rail)_
Fahrkartenschalter _m;_ _(Theat)_
Vorverkaufsstelle _f;_ **book-keeping** _n_
Buchhaltung _f;_ **booklet** _n_ Broschüre _f;_
bookmark _n_ _(a. Inform)_ Lesezeichen _nt;_
bookshelf _n_ Bücherbord _nt;_ **bookshelves**
Bücherregal _nt;_ **bookshop, bookstore** _n_
(esp US) Buchhandlung _f_
boom [buːm] _n_ _(of business)_ Boom _m;_
(noise) Dröhnen _nt_ ▷ _vi_ _(business)_ boomen;
(fam) florieren; _(voice etc)_ dröhnen
boomerang [ˈbuːməræŋ] _n_ Bumerang _m_
boost [buːst] _n_ Auftrieb _m_ ▷ _vt_

(production, sales) ankurbeln; _(power, profits etc)_ steigern; **booster (injection)** _n_
Wiederholungsimpfung _f_
boot [buːt] _n_ Stiefel _m;_ _(Brit Auto)_
Kofferraum _m_ ▷ _vt_ _(Inform)_ laden, booten
booth [buːð] _n_ _(at fair etc)_ Bude _f;_ _(at trade fair etc)_ Stand _m_
booze [buːz] _n_ _(fam)_ Alkohol _m_ ▷ _vi_ _(fam)_
saufen
border [ˈbɔːdə*] _n_ Grenze _f;_ _(edge)_ Rand _m;_
north/south of the Border in
Schottland/England; **borderline** _n_
Grenze _f_
bore [bɔː*] _pt of_ **bear** ▷ _vt_ _(hole etc)_
bohren; _(person)_ langweilen ▷ _n_ _(person)_
Langweiler(in) _m(f),_ langweiliger Mensch;
(thing) langweilige Sache; **bored** _adj_ **to be ~** sich langweilen; **boredom** _n_
Langeweile _f;_ **boring** _adj_ langweilig
born [bɔːn] _adj_ **he was ~ in London** er ist
in London geboren
borne [bɔːn] _pp of_ **bear**
borough [ˈbʌrə] _n_ Stadtbezirk _m_
borrow [ˈbɒrəʊ] _vt_ borgen
Bosnia-Herzegovina
[ˈbɒznɪəhɜːtsəgəʊˈviːnə] _n_
Bosnien-Herzegowina _nt;_ **Bosnian**
[ˈbɒznɪən] _adj_ bosnisch ▷ _n_ Bosnier(in)
_m(f)_
boss [bɒs] _n_ Chef(in) _m(f),_ Boss _m;_ **boss around** _vt_ herumkommandieren; **bossy**
adj herrisch
botanical [bəˈtænɪkəl] _adj_ botanisch;
~ garden(s) botanischer Garten
both [bəʊθ] _adj_ beide; **~ the books** beide
Bücher ▷ _pron_ _(people)_ beide; _(things)_
beides; **~ (of) the boys** beide Jungs; **I like ~ of them** ich mag sie (alle) beide ▷ _adv_
~ X and Y sowohl X als auch Y
bother [ˈbɒðə*] _vt_ ärgern, belästigen; **it doesn't ~ me** das stört mich nicht; **he can't be ~ed with details** mit Details gibt
er sich nicht ab; **I'm not ~ed** das ist mir
egal ▷ _vi_ sich kümmern _(about_ um); **don't ~** (das ist) nicht nötig, lass es! ▷ _n_ _(trouble)_
Mühe _f;_ _(annoyance)_ Ärger _m_
bottle [ˈbɒtl] _n_ Flasche _f_ ▷ _vt_ _(in_
Flaschen) abfüllen; **bottle out** _vi_ _(fam)_
den Mut verlieren, aufgeben; **bottle bank**
_n_ Altglascontainer _m;_ **bottled** _adj_ in
Flaschen; **~ beer** Flaschenbier _nt;_
bottleneck _n_ _(fig)_ Engpass _m;_ **bottle opener** _n_ Flaschenöffner _m_

bottom ['bɒtəm] n (of container) Boden m; (underside) Unterseite f; (fam: of person) Po m; **at the ~ of the sea/table/page** auf dem Meeresgrund/am Tabellenende/unten auf der Seite ▷ adj unterste(r, s); **to be ~ of the class/league** Klassenletzte(r)/Tabellenletzte(r) sein; **~ gear** (Auto) erster Gang

bought [bɔ:t] pt, pp of **buy**

bounce [baʊns] vi (ball) springen, aufprallen; (cheque) platzen; **~ up and down** (person) herumhüpfen; **bouncy** adj (ball) gut springend; (person) munter; **bouncy castle®** n Hüpfburg f

bound [baʊnd] pt, pp of **bind** ▷ adj (tied up) gebunden; (obliged) verpflichtet; **to be ~ to do sth** (sure to) etw bestimmt tun (werden); (have to) etw tun müssen; **it's ~ to happen** es muss so kommen; **to be ~ for ...** auf dem Weg nach ... sein; **boundary** ['baʊndərɪ] n Grenze f

bouquet [bʊ'keɪ] n (flowers) Strauß m; (of wine) Blume f

boutique [bu:'ti:k] n Boutique f

bow [bəʊ] n (ribbon) Schleife f; (instrument, weapon) Bogen m ▷ [baʊ] vi sich verbeugen ▷ [baʊ] n (with head) Verbeugung f; (of ship) Bug m

bowels ['baʊəlz] npl Darm m

bowl [bəʊl] n (basin) Schüssel f; (shallow) Schale f; (for animal) Napf m ▷ vt, vi (in cricket) werfen

bowler ['bəʊlə*] n (in cricket) Werfer(in) m(f); (hat) Melone f

bowling ['bəʊlɪŋ] n Kegeln nt; **bowling alley** n Kegelbahn f; **bowling green** n Rasen m zum Bowling-Spiel; **bowls** [bəʊlz] nsing (game) Bowling-Spiel nt

bow tie [bəʊ'taɪ] n Fliege f

box [bɒks] n Schachtel f; (cardboard) Karton m; (bigger) Kasten m; (space on form) Kästchen nt; (Theat) Loge f; **boxer** n Boxer(in) m(f); **boxers, boxer shorts** npl Boxershorts pl; **boxing** n (Sport) Boxen nt; **Boxing Day** n zweiter Weihnachtsfeiertag

Boxing Day

Boxing Day ist ein Feiertag in Großbritannien. Fällt Weihnachten auf ein Wochenende, wird der Feiertag am nächsten Wochentag nachgeholt. Der Name geht auf einen alten Brauch zurück: früher erhielten Händler und Lieferanten an diesem Tag ein Geschenk, die so genannte Christmas Box.

boxing gloves npl Boxhandschuhe pl; **boxing ring** n Boxring m

box number n Chiffre f

box office n Kasse f

boy [bɔɪ] n Junge m

boycott ['bɔɪkɒt] n Boykott m ▷ vt boykottieren

boyfriend ['bɔɪfrend] n (fester) Freund m; **boy scout** n Pfadfinder m

bra [brɑ:] n BH m

brace [breɪs] n (Tech) Strebe f; (on teeth) Spange f

bracelet ['breɪslɪt] n Armband nt

braces ['breɪsɪz] npl (Brit) Hosenträger pl

bracket ['brækɪt] n (in text) Klammer f; (Tech) Träger m ▷ vt einklammern

brag [bræg] vi angeben

Braille [breɪl] n Blindenschrift f

brain [breɪn] n (Anat) Gehirn nt; (mind) Verstand m; **~s** (pl) (intelligence) Grips m; **brainwave** n Geistesblitz m; **brainy** adj schlau, clever

braise [breɪz] vt schmoren

brake [breɪk] n Bremse f ▷ vi bremsen; **brake fluid** n Bremsflüssigkeit f; **brake light** n Bremslicht nt; **brake pedal** n Bremspedal nt

branch [brɑ:ntʃ] n (of tree) Ast m; (of family, subject) Zweig m; (of firm) Filiale f, Zweigstelle f; **branch off** vi (road) abzweigen

brand [brænd] n (Comm) Marke f

brand-new ['brænd'nju:] adj (funkel)nagelneu

brandy ['brændɪ] n Weinbrand m

brass [brɑ:s] n Messing nt; (Brit fam: money) Knete f; **brass band** n Blaskapelle f

brat [bræt] n (pej, fam) Gör nt

brave [breɪv] adj tapfer, mutig; **bravery** ['breɪvərɪ] n Mut m

brawl [brɔ:l] n Schlägerei f

brawn [brɔ:n] n (strength) Muskelkraft f; (Gastr) Sülze f; **brawny** adj muskulös

Brazil [brə'zɪl] n Brasilien nt; **Brazilian** adj brasilianisch ▷ n Brasilianer(in) m(f); **brazil nut** n Paranuss f

bread [bred] n Brot nt; **breadbin** (Brit),

breadbox (US) n Brotkasten m;
breadcrumbs npl Brotkrumen pl; (Gastr)
Paniermehl nt; **breaded** adj paniert;
breadknife n Brotmesser nt
breadth [bredθ] n Breite f
break [breɪk] n (fracture) Bruch m; (rest)
Pause f; (short holiday) Kurzurlaub m; **give
me a ~** gib mir eine Chance, hör auf
damit! ▷ vt (**broke, broken**) (fracture)
brechen; (in pieces) zerbrechen; (toy, device)
kaputtmachen; (promise) nicht halten;
(silence) brechen; (law) verletzen; (journey)
unterbrechen; (news) mitteilen (to sb jdm);
I broke my leg ich habe mir das Bein
gebrochen; **he broke it to her gently** er
hat es ihr schonend beigebracht ▷ vi
(come apart) (auseinander) brechen; (in
pieces) zerbrechen; (toy, device)
kaputtgehen; (person) zusammenbrechen;
(day, dawn) anbrechen; (news) bekannt
werden; **break down** vi (car) eine Panne
haben; (machine) versagen; (person)
zusammenbrechen; **break in** vi (burglar)
einbrechen; **break into** vt einbrechen in
+akk; **break off** vi, vt abbrechen; **break
out** vi ausbrechen; **to ~ in a rash** einen
Ausschlag bekommen; **break up** vi
aufbrechen; (meeting, organisation) sich
auflösen; (marriage) in die Brüche gehen;
(couple) sich trennen; **school breaks up on
Friday** am Freitag beginnen die Ferien
▷ vt aufbrechen; (marriage) zerstören;
(meeting) auflösen; **breakable** adj
zerbrechlich; **breakage** n Bruch m;
breakdown n (of car) Panne f; (of machine)
Störung f; (of person, relations, system)
Zusammenbruch m; **breakdown service**
n Pannendienst m; **breakdown truck** n
Abschleppwagen m
breakfast ['brekfəst] n Frühstück nt; **to
have ~** frühstücken; **breakfast cereal** n
Cornflakes, Muesli etc; **breakfast television**
n Frühstücksfernsehen nt
break-in ['breɪkɪn] n Einbruch m;
breakup ['breɪkʌp] n (of meeting,
organization) Auflösung f; (of marriage)
Zerrüttung f
breast [brest] n Brust f; **breastfeed** vt
stillen; **breaststroke** n Brustschwimmen
nt
breath [breθ] n Atem m; **out of ~** außer
Atem; **breathalyse, breathalyze**
['breθəlaɪz] vt (ins Röhrchen) blasen

lassen; **breathalyser, breathalyzer** n
Promillemesser m; **breathe** [briːð] vt, vi
atmen; **breathe in** vt, vi einatmen;
breathe out vt, vi ausatmen;
breathless ['breθlɪs] adj atemlos;
breath-taking ['breθteɪkɪŋ] adj
atemberaubend
bred [bred] pt, pp of **breed**
breed [briːd] n (race) Rasse f ▷ vi (**bred,
bred**) sich vermehren ▷ vt züchten;
breeder n Züchter(in) m(f); (fam) Hetero
m; **breeding** n (of animals) Züchtung f; (of
person) (gute) Erziehung
breeze [briːz] n Brise f
brevity ['brevɪtɪ] n Kürze f
brew [bruː] vt (beer) brauen; (tea) kochen;
brewery n Brauerei f
bribe ['braɪb] n Bestechungsgeld nt ▷ vt
bestechen; **bribery** ['braɪbərɪ] n
Bestechung f
brick [brɪk] n Backstein m; **bricklayer** n
Maurer(in) m(f)
bride [braɪd] n Braut f; **bridegroom** n
Bräutigam m; **bridesmaid** n Brautjungfer
f
bridge [brɪdʒ] n Brücke f; (cards) Bridge nt
brief [briːf] adj kurz ▷ vt instruieren (on
über +akk); **briefcase** n Aktentasche f;
briefs npl Slip m
bright [braɪt] adj hell; (colour) leuchtend;
(cheerful) heiter; (intelligent) intelligent;
(idea) glänzend; **brighten up** vt aufhellen;
(person) aufheitern ▷ vi sich aufheitern;
(person) fröhlicher werden
brilliant ['brɪljənt] adj (sunshine, colour)
strahlend; (person) brillant; (idea)
glänzend; (Brit fam) **it was ~** es war
fantastisch
brim [brɪm] n Rand m
bring [brɪŋ] (**brought, brought**) vt
bringen; (with one) mitbringen; **bring
about** vt herbeiführen, bewirken; **bring
back** vt zurückbringen; (memories)
wecken; **bring down** vt (reduce) senken;
(government etc) zu Fall bringen; **bring in** vt
hereinbringen; (introduce) einführen; **bring
out** vt herausbringen; **bring round,
bring to** vt wieder zu sich bringen; **bring
up** vt (child) aufziehen; (question) zur
Sprache bringen
brisk [brɪsk] adj (trade) lebhaft; (wind)
frisch
bristle ['brɪsl] n Borste f

Brit [brɪt] n (fam) Brite m, Britin f; **Britain** ['brɪtn] n Großbritannien nt; **British** ['brɪtɪʃ] adj britisch; **the ~ Isles** (pl) die Britischen Inseln pl ▷ n **the ~** (pl) die Briten pl

Brittany ['brɪtənɪ] n die Bretagne

brittle ['brɪtl] adj spröde

broad [brɔːd] adj breit; (accent) stark; **in ~ daylight** am helllichten Tag ▷ (US fam) Frau f

B road ['biːrəʊd] n (Brit) ≈ Landstraße f

broadcast ['brɔːdkɑːst] n Sendung f ▷ irr vt, vi senden; (event) übertragen

broaden ['brɔːdn] vt **to ~ the mind** den Horizont erweitern; **broad-minded** adj tolerant

broccoli ['brɒkəlɪ] n Brokkoli pl

brochure ['brəʊʃjʊə*] n Prospekt m, Broschüre f

broke [brəʊk] pt of **break** ▷ adj (Brit fam) pleite; **broken** ['brəʊkən] pp of **break**; **broken-hearted** adj untröstlich

broker ['brəʊkə*] n Makler(in) m(f)

brolly ['brɒlɪ] n (Brit fam) Schirm m

bronchitis [brɒŋ'kaɪtɪs] n Bronchitis f

bronze [brɒnz] n Bronze f

brooch [brəʊtʃ] n Brosche f

broom [bruːm] n Besen m

Bros [brɒs] abbr = **brothers** Gebr.

broth [brɒθ] n Fleischbrühe f

brothel ['brɒθl] n Bordell nt

brother ['brʌðə*] n Bruder m; **~s** (pl) (Comm) Gebrüder pl; **brother-in-law** (pl **brothers-in-law**) n Schwager m

brought [brɔːt] pt, pp of **bring**

brow [braʊ] n (eyebrow) (Augen)braue f; (forehead) Stirn f

brown [braʊn] adj braun; **brown bread** n Mischbrot nt; (wholemeal) Vollkornbrot nt; **brownie** ['braʊnɪ] n (Gastr) Brownie m; (Brit) junge Pfadfinderin; **brown paper** n Packpapier nt; **brown rice** n Naturreis m; **brown sugar** n brauner Zucker

browse [braʊz] vi (in book) blättern; (in shop) schmökern, herumschauen; **browser** n (Inform) Browser m

bruise [bruːz] n blauer Fleck ▷ vt **to ~ one's arm** sich dat einen blauen Fleck (am Arm) holen

brunette [bruː'net] n Brünette f

brush [brʌʃ] n Bürste f; (for sweeping) Handbesen m; (for painting) Pinsel m ▷ vt bürsten; (sweep) fegen; **to ~ one's teeth** sich dat die Zähne putzen; **brush up** vt (French etc) auffrischen

Brussels sprouts [brʌsl'spraʊts] npl Rosenkohl m, Kohlsprossen pl

brutal ['bruːtl] adj brutal; **brutality** [bruː'tælɪtɪ] n Brutalität f

BSE abbr = **bovine spongiform encephalopathy** BSE f

bubble ['bʌbl] n Blase f; **bubble bath** n Schaumbad nt; **bubbly** ['bʌblɪ] adj sprudelnd; (person) temperamentvoll ▷ n (fam) Schampus m

buck [bʌk] n (animal) Bock m; (US fam) Dollar m

bucket ['bʌkɪt] n Eimer m

⬤ **Buckingham Palace**
⬤
⬤ Der **Buckingham Palace** ist die offizielle
⬤ Londoner Residenz der britischen
⬤ Monarchen und liegt am St James's
⬤ Park. Der Palast wurde 1703 für den
⬤ Herzog von Buckingham erbaut, 1762
⬤ von George III gekauft, zwischen 1821
⬤ und 1836 von John Nash umgebaut,
⬤ und Anfang des 20. Jahrhunderts
⬤ teilweise neu gestaltet. Teile des
⬤ Buckingham Palace sind heute der
⬤ Öffentlichkeit zugänglich.

buckle ['bʌkl] n Schnalle f ▷ vi (Tech) sich verbiegen ▷ vt zuschnallen

bud [bʌd] n Knospe f

Buddhism ['bʊdɪzəm] n Buddhismus m; **Buddhist** adj buddhistisch ▷ n Buddhist(in) m(f)

buddy ['bʌdɪ] n (fam) Kumpel m

budget ['bʌdʒɪt] n Budget nt

budgie ['bʌdʒɪ] n (fam) Wellensittich m

buff [bʌf] adj (US) muskulös; **in the ~** nackt ▷ n (enthusiast) Fan m

buffalo ['bʌfələʊ] (pl **-es**) n Büffel m

buffer ['bʌfə*] n (a. Inform) Puffer m

buffet ['bʊfeɪ] n (food) (kaltes) Büfett nt

bug [bʌg] n (Inform) Bug m, Programmfehler m; (listening device) Wanze f; (US: insect) Insekt nt; (fam: illness) Infektion f ▷ vt (fam) nerven

bugger ['bʌgə*] n (vulg) Scheißkerl m ▷ interj (vulg) Scheiße f; **bugger off** vi (vulg) abhauen, Leine ziehen

buggy® ['bʌgɪ] n (for baby) Buggy® m; (US: pram) Kinderwagen m

build [bɪld] (**built, built**) vt bauen; **build up** vt aufbauen; **builder** n Bauunternehmer(in) m(f); **building** n Gebäude nt; **building site** n Baustelle f; **building society** n Bausparkasse f
built pt, pp of **build**; **built-in** adj (cupboard) Einbau-, eingebaut
bulb [bʌlb] n (Bot) (Blumen)zwiebel f; (Elec) Glühbirne f
Bulgaria [bʌlˈgɛərɪə] n Bulgarien nt; **Bulgarian** adj bulgarisch ▷ n (person) Bulgare m, Bulgarin f; (language) Bulgarisch nt
bulimia [bəˈlɪmɪə] n Bulimie f
bulk [bʌlk] n (size) Größe f; (greater part) Großteil m (of +gen); **in ~** en gros; **bulky** adj (goods) sperrig; (person) stämmig
bull [bʊl] n Stier m; **bulldog** n Bulldogge f; **bulldoze** [ˈbʊldəʊz] vt planieren; **bulldozer** n Planierraupe f
bullet [ˈbʊlɪt] n Kugel f
bulletin [ˈbʊlɪtɪn] n Bulletin nt; (announcement) Bekanntmachung f; (Med) Krankenbericht m; **bulletin board** n (US: Inform) schwarzes Brett
bullfight [ˈbʊlfaɪt] n Stierkampf m; **bullshit** n (fam) Scheiß m
bully [ˈbʊlɪ] n Tyrann m
bum [bʌm] n (Brit fam: backside) Po m; (US: vagrant) Penner m; (worthless person) Rumtreiber m; **bum around** vi herumgammeln
bumblebee [ˈbʌmblbiː] n Hummel f
bump [bʌmp] n (fam: swelling) Beule f; (road) Unebenheit f; (blow) Stoß m ▷ vt stoßen; **to ~ one's head** sich dat den Kopf anschlagen (on an +dat); **bump into** vt stoßen gegen; (fam: meet) (zufällig) begegnen +dat; **bumper** n (Auto) Stoßstange f ▷ adj (edition etc) Riesen-; (crop etc) Rekord-; **bumpy** [ˈbʌmpɪ] adj holp(e)rig
bun [bʌn] n süßes Brötchen
bunch [bʌntʃ] n (of flowers) Strauß m; (fam: of people) Haufen m; **~ of keys** Schlüsselbund m; **~ of grapes** Weintraube f
bundle [ˈbʌndl] n Bündel nt
bungalow [ˈbʌŋgələʊ] n Bungalow m
bungee jumping [ˈbʌndʒɪdʒʌmpɪŋ] n Bungeejumping nt
bunk [bʌŋk] n Koje f; **bunk bed(s)** n(pl) Etagenbett nt

bunker [ˈbʌŋkə*] n (Mil) Bunker m
bunny [ˈbʌnɪ] n Häschen nt
buoy [bɔɪ] n Boje f; **buoyant** [ˈbɔɪənt] adj (floating) schwimmend
BUPA [ˈbuːpə] abbr (Brit) private Krankenkasse
burden [ˈbɜːdn] n Last f
bureau [ˈbjuːrəʊ] n Büro nt; (government department) Amt nt; **bureaucracy** [bjʊˈrɒkrəsɪ] n Bürokratie f; **bureaucratic** [bjuːrəˈkrætɪk] adj bürokratisch; **bureau de change** [ˈbjuːrəʊ də ˈʃɒnʒ] n Wechselstube f
burger [ˈbɜːgə*] n Hamburger m
burglar [ˈbɜːglə*] n Einbrecher(in) m(f); **burglar alarm** n Alarmanlage f; **burglarize** vt (US) einbrechen in +akk; **burglary** n Einbruch m; **burgle** [ˈbɜːgl] vt einbrechen in +akk
burial [ˈberɪəl] n Beerdigung f
burn [bɜːn] (**burnt** o **burned, burnt** o **burned**) vt verbrennen; (food, slightly) anbrennen; **to ~ one's hand** sich dat die Hand verbrennen ▷ vi brennen ▷ n (injury) Brandwunde f; (on material) verbrannte Stelle; **burn down** vt, vi abbrennen
burp [bɜːp] vi rülpsen ▷ vt (baby) aufstoßen lassen
bursary [ˈbɜːsərɪ] n Stipendium nt
burst [bɜːst] (**burst, burst**) vt platzen lassen ▷ vi platzen; **to ~ into tears** in Tränen ausbrechen
bury [ˈberɪ] vt begraben; (in grave) beerdigen; (hide) vergraben
bus [bʌs] n Bus m; **bus driver** n Busfahrer(in) m(f)
bush [bʊʃ] n Busch m
business [ˈbɪznɪs] n Geschäft nt; (enterprise) Unternehmen nt; (concern, affair) Sache f; **I'm here on ~** ich bin geschäftlich hier; **it's none of your ~** das geht dich nichts an; **business card** n Visitenkarte f; **business class** n (Aviat) Businessclass f; **business hours** npl Geschäftsstunden pl; **businessman** (pl **-men**) n Geschäftsmann m; **business studies** npl Betriebswirtschaftslehre f; **businesswoman** (pl **-women**) n Geschäftsfrau f
bus service n Busverbindung f; **bus shelter** n Wartehäuschen nt; **bus station** n Busbahnhof m; **bus stop** n Bushaltestelle f

bust [bʌst] n Büste f ▷ adj (broken)
kaputt; **to go ~** Pleite gehen; **bust-up** n
(fam) Krach m
busy ['bɪzɪ] adj beschäftigt; (street, place)
belebt; (esp US: telephone) besetzt; **~ signal**
(US) Besetztzeichen nt

 KEYWORD

but [bʌt] conj **1** (yet) aber; **not X but Y**
nicht X sondern Y
2 (however): **I'd love to come, but I'm
busy** ich würde gern kommen, bin aber
beschäftigt
3 (showing disagreement, surprise etc): **but
that's fantastic!** (aber) das ist ja
fantastisch!
▷ prep (apart from, except); **nothing but
trouble** nichts als Ärger; **no-one but him
can do it** niemand außer ihn kann es
machen; **but for you/your help** ohne
dich/deine Hilfe; **anything but that** alles,
nur das nicht
▷ adv (just, only); **she's but a child** sie ist
noch ein Kind; **had I but known** wenn es
es nur gewusst hätte; **I can but try** ich
kann es immerhin versuchen; **all but
finished** so gut wie fertig

butcher ['bʊtʃə*] n Fleischer(in) m(f),
Metzger(in) m(f)
butler ['bʌtlə*] n Butler m
butter ['bʌtə*] n Butter f ▷ vt buttern;
buttercup n Butterblume f; **butterfly** n
Schmetterling m
buttocks ['bʌtəks] npl Gesäß nt
button ['bʌtn] n Knopf m; (badge) Button
m ▷ vt zuknöpfen; **buttonhole** n
Knopfloch nt
buy [baɪ] n Kauf m ▷ vt (bought, bought)
kaufen (from von); **he bought me a ring** er
hat mir einen Ring gekauft; **buyer** n
Käufer(in) m(f)
buzz [bʌz] n Summen nt; **to give sb a
~** (fam) jdn anrufen ▷ vi summen; **buzzer**
['bʌzə*] n Summer m; **buzz word** n (fam)
Modewort nt

 KEYWORD

by [baɪ] prep **1** (referring to cause, agent) von
durch; **killed by lightning** vom Blitz
getötet; **a painting by Picasso** ein

Gemälde von Picasso
2 (referring to method, manner): **by
bus/car/train** mit dem
Bus/Auto/Zug; **to pay by cheque** per
Scheck bezahlen; **by moonlight** bei
Mondschein; **by saving hard, he ...** indem
er eisern sparte, ... er ...
3 (via, through) über +acc; **he came in by
the back door** er kam durch die Hintertür
herein
4 (close to, past) bei an +dat; **a holiday by
the sea** ein Urlaub am Meer; **she rushed
by me** sie eilte an mir vorbei
5 (not later than): **by 4 o'clock** bis 4 Uhr: **by
this time tomorrow** morgen um diese
Zeit; **by the time I got here it was too
late** als ich hier ankam, war es zu spät
6 (during): **by day** bei Tag
7 (amount): **by the kilo/metre**
kiloweise/meterweise; **paid by the hour**
stundenweise bezahlt
8 (Math, measure): **to divide by 3** durch 3
teilen; **to multiply by 3** mit 3 malnehmen;
a room 3 metres by 4 ein Zimmer 3 mal 4
Meter; **it's broader by a metre** es ist (um)
einem Meter breiter
9 (according to) nach; **it's all right by me**
von mir aus gern
10: (all) by oneself etc ganz allein
11: by the way übrigens
▷ adv **1:** see **go, pass** etc
2: by and by irgendwann: (with past tenses)
nach einiger Zeit; **by and large** (on the
whole) im Großen und Ganzen

bye-bye ['baɪ'baɪ] interj (fam)
Wiedersehen, tschüss
by-election n Nachwahl f; **bypass** n
Umgehungsstraße f; (Med) Bypass m;
byproduct n Nebenprodukt nt; **byroad** n
Nebenstraße f; **bystander** n
Zuschauer(in) m(f)
byte [baɪt] n Byte nt

C [siː] *abbr* = **Celsius** C

c *abbr* = **circa** ca

cab [kæb] *n* Taxi *nt*

cabbage ['kæbɪdʒ] *n* Kohl *m*

cabin ['kæbɪn] *n* (*Naut*) Kajüte *f*; (*Aviat*) Passagierraum *m*; (*wooden house*) Hütte *f*; **cabin crew** *n* Flugbegleitpersonal *nt*; **cabin cruiser** *n* Kajütboot *nt*

cabinet ['kæbɪnɪt] *n* Schrank *m*; (*for display*) Vitrine *f*; (*Pol*) Kabinett *nt*

cable ['keɪbl] *n* (*Elec*) Kabel *nt*; **cable-car** *n* Seilbahn *f*; **cable railway** *n* Drahtseilbahn *f*; **cable television**, **cablevision** (*US*) *n* Kabelfernsehen *nt*

cactus ['kæktəs] *n* Kaktus *m*

CAD *abbr* = **computer-aided design** CAD *nt*

Caesarean [siːˈzɛərɪən] *adj* **~** (**section**) Kaiserschnitt *m*

café ['kæfeɪ] *n* Café *nt*; **cafeteria** [kæfɪˈtɪərɪə] *n* Cafeteria *f*; **cafetiere** [kæfəˈtjɛə*] *n* Kaffeebereiter *m*

caffein(e) ['kæfiːn] *n* Koffein *nt*

cage [keɪdʒ] *n* Käfig *m*

Cairo ['kaɪərəʊ] *n* Kairo *nt*

cake [keɪk] *n* Kuchen *m*; **cake shop** *n* Konditorei *f*

calamity [kəˈlæmɪtɪ] *n* Katastrophe *f*

calculate ['kælkjʊleɪt] *vt* berechnen; (*estimate*) kalkulieren; **calculating** *adj* berechnend; **calculation** [kælkjʊˈleɪʃən] *n* Berechnung *f*; (*estimate*) Kalkulation *f*; **calculator** ['kælkjʊleɪtə*] *n* Taschenrechner *m*

calendar ['kælɪndə*] *n* Kalender *m*

calf [kɑːf] (*pl* **calves**) *n* Kalb *nt*; (*Anat*) Wade *f*

California [kælɪˈfɔːnɪə] *n* Kalifornien *nt*

call [kɔːl] *vt* rufen; (*name, describe as*) nennen; (*Tel*) anrufen; (*Inform, Aviat*) aufrufen; **what's this ~ed?** wie heißt das?; **that's what I ~ service** das nenne ich guten Service ▷ *vi* (*shout*) rufen (*for help* um Hilfe); (*visit*) vorbeikommen; **to ~ at the doctor's** beim Arzt vorbeigehen; (*of train*) **to ~ at …** in … halten ▷ *n* (*shout*) Ruf *m*; (*Tel*) Anruf; (*Inform, Aviat*) Aufruf *m*; **to make a ~** telefonieren; **to give sb a ~** jdn anrufen; **to be on ~** Bereitschaftsdienst haben; **call back** *vt, vi* zurückrufen; **call for** *vt* (*come to pick up*) abholen; (*demand, require*) verlangen; **call off** *vt* absagen

call centre *n* Callcenter *nt*; **caller** *n* Besucher(in) *m(f)*; (*Tel*) Anrufer(in) *m(f)*

calm [kɑːm] *n* Stille *f*; (*also of person*) Ruhe *f*; (*of sea*) Flaute *f* ▷ *vt* beruhigen ▷ *adj* ruhig; **calm down** *vi* sich beruhigen

calorie ['kælərɪ] *n* Kalorie *f*

calves [kɑːvz] *pl of* **calf**

Cambodia [kæmˈbəʊdɪə] *n* Kambodscha *nt*

camcorder ['kæmkɔːdə*] *n* Camcorder *m*

came [keɪm] *pt of* **come**

camel ['kæməl] *n* Kamel *nt*

camera ['kæmərə] *n* Fotoapparat *m*, Kamera *f*

camomile ['kæməmaɪl] *n* Kamille *f*

camouflage ['kæməflɑːʒ] *n* Tarnung *f*

camp [kæmp] *n* Lager *nt*; (*camping place*) Zeltplatz *m* ▷ *vi* zelten, campen ▷ *adj* (*fam*) theatralisch, tuntig

campaign [kæmˈpeɪn] *n* Kampagne *f*; (*Pol*) Wahlkampf *m* ▷ *vi* sich einsetzen (*for/against* für/gegen)

campbed ['kæmpbed] *n* Campingliege *f*; **camper** ['kæmpə*] *n* (*person*) Camper(in) *m(f)*; (*van*) Wohnmobil *nt*; **camping** ['kæmpɪŋ] *n* Zelten *nt*, Camping *nt*; **campsite** ['kæmpsaɪt] *n* Zeltplatz *m*, Campingplatz *m*

campus ['kæmpəs] n (of university)
Universitätsgelände nt, Campus m
can¹ [kæn] (**could, been able**) vb aux (be
able) können; (permission) dürfen; **I ~not** o
~'t see ich kann nichts sehen; **~ I go now?**
darf ich jetzt gehen? ▷ n (for food, beer)
Dose f; (for water, milk) Kanne f

⊙ **KEYWORD**

can² [kæn] (negative **cannot, can't**,
conditional **could**) aux vb **1** (be able to, know
how to) können; **I can see you tomorrow,
if you like** ich könnte Sie morgen sehen,
wenn Sie wollen; **I can swim** ich kann
schwimmen; **can you speak German?**
sprechen Sie Deutsch?
2 (may) können dürfen; **could I have a
word with you?** könnte ich Sie kurz
sprechen?

Canada ['kænədə] n Kanada nt;
Canadian [kə'neɪdjən] adj kanadisch ▷ n
Kanadier(in) m(f)
canal [kə'næl] n Kanal m
canary [kə'nɛərɪ] n Kanarienvogel m
cancel ['kænsəl] vt (plans) aufgeben;
(meeting, event) absagen; (Comm: order etc)
stornieren; (contract) kündigen; (Inform)
löschen; (Aviat: flight) streichen; **to be ~led**
(event, train, bus) ausfallen; **cancellation**
[kænsə'leɪʃən] n Absage f; (Comm)
Stornierung f; (Aviat) gestrichener Flug
cancer ['kænsə*] n (Med) Krebs m; **Cancer**
n (Astr) Krebs m
candid ['kændɪd] adj (person, conversation)
offen
candidate ['kændɪdət] n (for post)
Bewerber(in) m(f); (Pol) Kandidat(in) m(f)
candle ['kændl] n Kerze f; **candlelight** n
Kerzenlicht nt; **candlestick** n
Kerzenhalter m
candy ['kændɪ] n (US) Bonbon nt;
(quantity) Süßigkeiten pl; **candy-floss** n
(Brit) Zuckerwatte f
cane [keɪn] n Rohr nt; (stick) Stock
m
cannabis ['kænəbɪs] n Cannabis m
canned [kænd] adj Dosen-
cannot ['kænɒt] contr of **can not**
canny ['kænɪ] adj (shrewd) schlau
canoe [kə'nu:] n Kanu nt; **canoeing** n
Kanufahren nt

can opener ['kænəʊpnə*] n Dosenöffner m
canopy ['kænəpɪ] n Baldachin m; (awning)
Markise f; (over entrance) Vordach nt
can't [kɑ:nt] contr of **can not**
canteen [kæn'ti:n] n (in factory) Kantine
f; (in university) Mensa f
canvas ['kænvəs] n (for sails, shoes)
Segeltuch nt; (for tent) Zeltstoff m; (for
painting) Leinwand f
canvass ['kænvəs] vi um Stimmen
werben (for für)
canyon ['kænjən] n Felsenschlucht f;
canyoning ['kænjənɪŋ] n Canyoning nt
cap [kæp] n Mütze f; (lid) Verschluss m,
Deckel m
capability [keɪpə'bɪlɪtɪ] n Fähigkeit f;
capable ['keɪpəbl] adj fähig; **to be ~ of
sth** zu etw fähig (o imstande) sein; **to be
~ of doing sth** etw tun können
capacity [kə'pæsɪtɪ] n (of building,
container) Fassungsvermögen nt; (ability)
Fähigkeit f; (function) **in his ~ as ...** in
seiner Eigenschaft als ...
cape [keɪp] n (garment) Cape nt, Umhang
m; (Geo) Kap nt
caper ['keɪpə*] n (for cooking) Kaper f
capital ['kæpɪtl] n (Fin) Kapital nt; (letter)
Großbuchstabe m; **~ (city)** Hauptstadt f;
capitalism n Kapitalismus m; **capital
punishment** n die Todesstrafe
Capricorn ['kæprɪkɔ:n] n (Astr) Steinbock
m
capsize [kæp'saɪz] vi kentern
capsule ['kæpsju:l] n Kapsel f
captain ['kæptɪn] n Kapitän m; (army)
Hauptmann m
caption ['kæpʃən] n Bildunterschrift f
captive ['kæptɪv] n Gefangene(r) mf;
capture ['kæptʃə*] vt (person) fassen,
gefangen nehmen; (town etc) einnehmen;
(Inform: data) erfassen ▷ n
Gefangennahme f; (Inform) Erfassung f
car [kɑ:*] n Auto nt; (US Rail) Wagen m
carafe [kə'ræf] n Karaffe f
carambola [kærəm'bəʊlə] n Sternfrucht f
caramel ['kærəmel] n Karamelle f
caravan ['kærəvæn] n Wohnwagen m;
caravan site n Campingplatz m für
Wohnwagen
caraway (seed) ['kærəweɪ] n Kümmel m
carbohydrate [kɑ:bəʊ'haɪdreɪt] n
Kohle(n)hydrat nt
car bomb n Autobombe f

carbon [ˈkɑːbən] n Kohlenstoff m
car boot sale n auf einem Parkplatz stattfindender Flohmarkt
carburettor, carburetor (US) [ˈkɑːbjʊretə*] n Vergaser m
card [kɑːd] n Karte f; (material) Pappe f; **cardboard** n Pappe f; ~ (**box**) Karton m; (smaller) Pappschachtel f; **card game** n Kartenspiel nt
cardiac [ˈkɑːdɪæk] adj Herz-
cardigan [ˈkɑːdɪgən] n Strickjacke f
card index n Kartei f; **cardphone** [ˈkɑːdfəʊn] n Kartentelefon nt
care [kɛə*] n (worry) Sorge f; (carefulness) Sorgfalt f; (looking after things, people) Pflege f; **with** ~ sorgfältig; (cautiously) vorsichtig; **to take** ~ (watch out) vorsichtig sein; (in address) ~ **of** bei; **to take** ~ **of** sorgen für, sich kümmern um ▷ vi **I don't** ~ es ist mir egal; **to** ~ **about sth** Wert auf etw akk legen; **he** ~**s about her** sie liegt ihm am Herzen; **care for** vt (look after) sorgen für, sich kümmern um; (like) mögen
career [kəˈrɪə*] n Karriere f, Laufbahn f; **career woman** (pl **women**) n Karrierefrau f; **careers adviser** n Berufsberater(in) m(f)
carefree [ˈkɛəfriː] adj sorgenfrei; **careful, carefully** adj, adv sorgfältig; (cautious, cautiously) vorsichtig; **careless, carelessly** adj, adv nachlässig; (driving etc) leichtsinnig; (remark) unvorsichtig; **carer** [ˈkɛərə*] n Betreuer(in) m(f), Pfleger(in) m(f); **caretaker** [ˈkɛəteɪkə*] n Hausmeister(in) m(f); **careworker** n Pfleger(in) m(f)
car-ferry [ˈkɑːferɪ] n Autofähre f
cargo [ˈkɑːgəʊ] (pl **-(e)s**) n Ladung f
car hire, car hire company n Autovermietung f
Caribbean [kærɪˈbiːən] n Karibik f ▷ adj karibisch
caring [ˈkɛərɪŋ] adj mitfühlend; (parent, partner) liebevoll; (looking after sb) fürsorglich
car insurance n Kraftfahrzeugversicherung f
carnation [kɑːˈneɪʃən] n Nelke f
carnival [ˈkɑːnɪvəl] n Volksfest nt; (before Lent) Karneval m
carol [ˈkærəl] n Weihnachtslied nt
carp [kɑːp] n (fish) Karpfen m

car park n (Brit) Parkplatz m; (multi-storey car park) Parkhaus nt
carpenter [ˈkɑːpəntə*] n Zimmermann m; **carpet** [ˈkɑːpɪt] n Teppich m
car phone n Autotelefon nt; **carpool** n Fahrgemeinschaft f; (vehicles) Fuhrpark m ▷ vi eine Fahrgemeinschaft bilden; **car rental** n Autovermietung f
carriage [ˈkærɪdʒ] n (Brit Rail: coach) Wagen m; (compartment) Abteil nt; (horse-drawn) Kutsche f; (transport) Beförderung f; **carriageway** n (Brit: on road) Fahrbahn f
carrier [ˈkærɪə*] n (Comm) Spediteur(in) m(f); **carrier bag** n Tragetasche f
carrot [ˈkærət] n Karotte f
carry [ˈkærɪ] vt tragen; (in vehicle) befördern; (have on one) bei sich haben; **carry on** vi (continue) weitermachen; (fam: make a scene) ein Theater machen ▷ vt (continue) fortführen; **to** ~ **on working** weiter arbeiten; **carry out** vt (orders, plan) ausführen, durchführen
carrycot n Babytragetasche f
carsick [ˈkɑːsɪk] adj **he gets** ~ ihm wird beim Autofahren übel
cart [kɑːt] n Wagen m, Karren m; (US: shopping trolley) Einkaufswagen m
carton [ˈkɑːtən] n (Papp)karton m; (of cigarettes) Stange f
cartoon [kɑːˈtuːn] n Cartoon m o nt; (one drawing) Karikatur f; (film) (Zeichen)trickfilm m
cartridge [ˈkɑːtrɪdʒ] n (for film) Kassette f; (for gun, pen, printer) Patrone f; (for copier) Kartusche f
carve [kɑːv] vt, vi (wood) schnitzen; (stone) meißeln; (meat) schneiden, tranchieren; **carving** n (in wood) Schnitzerei f; (in stone) Skulptur f; (Ski) Carving nt
car wash n Autowaschanlage f
case [keɪs] n (crate) Kiste f; (box) Schachtel f; (for jewels) Schatulle f; (for spectacles) Etui nt; (Jur, matter) Fall m; **in** ~ falls; **in that** ~ in dem Fall; **in** ~ **of fire** bei Brand; **it's a** ~ **of ...** es handelt sich hier um ...
cash [kæʃ] n Bargeld nt; **in** ~ bar; ~ **on delivery** per Nachnahme ▷ vt (cheque) einlösen; **cash desk** n Kasse f; **cash dispenser** n Geldautomat m; **cashier** [kæˈʃɪə*] n Kassierer(in) m(f); **cash machine** n (Brit) Geldautomat m

cashmere ['kæʃmɪə*] n Kaschmirwolle f
cash payment n Barzahlung f;
 cashpoint n (Brit) Geldautomat m
casing ['keɪsɪŋ] n Gehäuse nt
casino [kə'si:nəʊ] (pl -s) n Kasino nt
cask [kɑːsk] n Fass nt
casserole ['kæsərəʊl] n Kasserole f; (food)
 Schmortopf m
cassette [kæ'set] n Kassette f; **cassette
 recorder** n Kassettenrekorder m
cast [kɑːst] (**cast, cast**) vt (throw) werfen;
 (Theat, Cine) besetzen; (roles) verteilen ▷ n
 (Theat, Cine) Besetzung f; (Med)
 Gipsverband m; **cast off** vi (Naut)
 losmachen
caster ['kɑːstə*] n ~ **sugar** Streuzucker
 m
castle ['kɑːsl] n Burg f
castrate [kæs'treɪt] vt kastrieren
casual ['kæʒjʊəl] adj (arrangement, remark)
 beiläufig; (attitude, manner) (nach)lässig,
 zwanglos; (dress) leger; (work, earnings)
 Gelegenheits-; (look, glance) flüchtig;
 ~ **wear** Freizeitkleidung f; ~ **sex**
 Gelegenheitssex m; **casually** adv (remark,
 say) beiläufig; (meet) zwanglos; (dressed)
 leger
casualty ['kæʒjʊəltɪ] n Verletzte(r) mf;
 (dead) Tote(r) mf; (department in hospital)
 Notaufnahme f
cat [kæt] n Katze f; (male) Kater m
catalog (US), **catalogue** ['kætəlɒg] n
 Katalog m ▷ vt katalogisieren
cataract ['kætərækt] n Wasserfall m;
 (Med) grauer Star
catarrh [kə'tɑː*] n Katarr(h) m
catastrophe [kə'tæstrəfɪ] n Katastrophe
 f
catch [kætʃ] n (fish etc) Fang m ▷ vt
 (**caught, caught**) fangen; (thief) fassen;
 (train, bus etc) nehmen; (not miss)
 erreichen; **to ~ a cold** sich erkälten; **to
 ~ fire** Feuer fangen; **I didn't ~ that** das
 habe ich nicht mitgekriegt; **catch on** vi
 (become popular) Anklang finden; **catch up**
 vt, vi **to ~ with sb** jdn einholen; **to ~ on
 sth** etw nachholen; **catching** adj
 ansteckend
category ['kætɪgərɪ] n Kategorie f
cater ['keɪtə*] vi die Speisen und Getränke
 liefern (for für); **cater for** vt (have facilities
 for) eingestellt sein auf +akk; **catering** n
 Versorgung f mit Speisen und Getränken,

Gastronomie f; **catering service** n
 Partyservice m
caterpillar ['kætəpɪlə*] n Raupe f
cathedral [kə'θiːdrəl] n Kathedrale f,
 Dom m
Catholic ['kæθəlɪk] adj katholisch
 ▷ Katholik(in) m(f)
cat nap n (Brit) kurzer Schlaf; **cat's eyes**
 ['kætsaɪz] npl (in road) Katzenaugen pl,
 Reflektoren pl
catsup ['kætsəp] n (US) Ketschup nt o m
cattle ['kætl] npl Vieh nt
caught [kɔːt] pt, pp of **catch**
cauliflower ['kɒlɪflaʊə*] n Blumenkohl m;
 cauliflower cheese n Blumenkohl m in
 Käsesoße
cause [kɔːz] n (origin) Ursache f (of für);
 (reason) Grund m (for zu); (purpose) Sache f;
 for a good ~ für wohltätige Zwecke; **no
 ~ for alarm/complaint** kein Grund zur
 Aufregung/Klage ▷ vt verursachen
causeway ['kɔːzweɪ] n Damm m
caution ['kɔːʃən] n Vorsicht f; (Jur, Sport)
 Verwarnung f ▷ vt (ver)warnen; **cautious**
 ['kɔːʃəs] adj vorsichtig
cave [keɪv] n Höhle f; **cave in** vi
 einstürzen
cavity ['kævɪtɪ] n Hohlraum m; (in tooth)
 Loch nt
cayenne (pepper) [keɪ'en] n
 Cayennepfeffer m
CCTV abbr = **closed circuit television**
 Videoüberwachungsanlage f
CD abbr = **Compact Disc** CD f; **CD player** n
 CD-Spieler m; **CD-ROM** abbr = **Compact
 Disc Read Only Memory** CD-ROM f;
 CD-RW abbr = **Compact Disc Rewritable**
 CD-RW f
cease [siːs] vi aufhören ▷ vt beenden; **to
 ~ doing sth** aufhören, etw zu tun; **cease
 fire** n Waffenstillstand m
ceiling ['siːlɪŋ] n Decke f
celebrate ['selɪbreɪt] vt, vi feiern;
 celebrated adj gefeiert; **celebration**
 [selɪ'breɪʃən] n Feier f; **celebrity**
 [sɪ'lebrɪtɪ] n Berühmtheit f, Star m
celeriac [sə'lerɪæk] n (Knollen)sellerie m
 o f; **celery** ['selərɪ] n (Stangen)sellerie m
 o f
cell [sel] n Zelle f; (US) see **cellphone**
cellar ['selə*] n Keller m
cello ['tʃeləʊ] (pl -s) n Cello nt
cellphone ['selfəʊn], **cellular phone**

['seljʊlə*'fəʊn] n Mobiltelefon nt, Handy nt

Celt [kelt] n Kelte m, Keltin f; **Celtic** ['keltɪk] adj keltisch ▷ n (language) Keltisch nt

cement [sɪ'ment] n Zement m

cemetery ['semɪtrɪ] n Friedhof m

censorship ['sensəʃɪp] n Zensur f

cent [sent] n (of dollar, euro etc) Cent m

center n (US) see centre

centiliter (US), **centilitre** ['sentɪliːtə*] n Zentiliter m; **centimeter** (US), **centimetre** ['sentɪmiːtə*] n Zentimeter m

central ['sentrəl] adj zentral; **Central America** n Mittelamerika nt; **Central Europe** n Mitteleuropa nt; **central heating** n Zentralheizung f; **centralize** vt zentralisieren; **central locking** n (Auto) Zentralverriegelung f; **central reservation** n (Brit) Mittelstreifen m; **central station** n Hauptbahnhof m

centre ['sentə*] n Mitte f; (building, of city) Zentrum nt ▷ vt zentrieren; **centre forward** n (Sport) Mittelstürmer m

century ['sentjʊrɪ] n Jahrhundert nt

ceramic [sɪ'ræmɪk] adj keramisch

cereal ['sɪərɪəl] n (any grain) Getreide nt; (breakfast cereal) Frühstücksflocken pl

ceremony ['serɪmənɪ] n Feier f, Zeremonie f

certain ['sɜːtən] adj sicher (of +gen); (particular) bestimmt; **for ~** mit Sicherheit; **certainly** adv sicher; (without doubt) bestimmt; **~!** aber sicher!; **~ not** ganz bestimmt nicht!

certificate [sə'tɪfɪkɪt] n Bescheinigung f; (in school, of qualification) Zeugnis nt; **certify** ['sɜːtɪfaɪ] vt, vi bescheinigen

cervical smear ['sɜːvɪkəl smɪə*] n Abstrich m

CFC abbr = **chlorofluorocarbon** FCKW nt

chain [tʃeɪn] n Kette f ▷ vt **to ~ (up)** anketten; **chain reaction** n Kettenreaktion f; **chain store** n Kettenladen m

chair [tʃɛə*] n Stuhl m; (university) Lehrstuhl m; (armchair) Sessel m; (chairperson) Vorsitzende(r) mf; **chairlift** n Sessellift m; **chairman** (pl **-men**) n Vorsitzende(r) m; (of firm) Präsident m; **chairperson** n Vorsitzende(r) mf; (of firm) Präsident(in) m(f); **chairwoman** (pl

-women) n Vorsitzende f; (of firm) Präsidentin f

chalet ['ʃæleɪ] n (in mountains) Berghütte f; (holiday dwelling) Ferienhäuschen nt

chalk ['tʃɔːk] n Kreide f

challenge ['tʃælɪndʒ] n Herausforderung f ▷ vt (person) herausfordern; (statement) bestreiten

chambermaid ['tʃeɪmbə*meɪd] n Zimmermädchen nt

chamois leather ['ʃæmwɑː'leðə*] n (for windows) Fensterleder nt

champagne [ʃæm'peɪn] n Champagner m

champion ['tʃæmpɪən] n (Sport) Meister(in) m(f); **championship** n Meisterschaft f; **Champions League** n Champions League f

chance [tʃɑːns] n (fate) Zufall m; (possibility) Möglichkeit f; (opportunity) Gelegenheit f; (risk) Risiko nt; **by ~** zufällig; **he doesn't stand a ~ (of winning)** er hat keinerlei Chance(, zu gewinnen)

chancellor ['tʃɑːnsələ*] n Kanzler(in) m(f)

chandelier [ʃændɪ'lɪə*] n Kronleuchter m

change [tʃeɪndʒ] vt verändern; (alter) ändern; (money, wheel, nappy) wechseln; (exchange) (um)tauschen; **to ~ one's clothes** sich umziehen; **to ~ trains** umsteigen; **to ~ gear** (Auto) schalten ▷ vi sich ändern; (esp outwardly) sich verändern; (get changed) sich umziehen ▷ n Veränderung f; (alteration) Änderung f; (money) Wechselgeld nt; (coins) Kleingeld nt; **for a ~** zur Abwechslung; **can you give me ~ for £10?** können Sie mir auf 10 Pfund herausgeben?; **change down** vi (Brit Auto) herunterschalten; **change over** vi sich umstellen (to auf +akk); **change up** vi (Brit Auto) hochschalten

changeable adj (weather) veränderlich, wechselhaft; **change machine** n Geldwechsler m; **changing room** n Umkleideraum m

channel ['tʃænl] n Kanal m; (Radio, TV) Kanal m, Sender m; **the (English) Channel** der Ärmelkanal; **the Channel Islands** die Kanalinseln; **the Channel Tunnel** der Kanaltunnel; **channel-hopping** n Zappen nt

chaos ['keɪɒs] n Chaos nt; **chaotic** [keɪ'ɒtɪk] adj chaotisch

chap [tʃæp] n (Brit fam) Bursche m, Kerl m

chapel ['tʃæpəl] *n* Kapelle *f*
chapped ['tʃæpt] *adj* (*lips*) aufgesprungen
chapter ['tʃæptə*] *n* Kapitel *nt*
character ['kærəktə*] *n* Charakter *m*,
Wesen *nt*; (*in a play, novel etc*) Figur *f*; (*Typo*)
Zeichen *nt*; **he's a real ~** er ist ein echtes
Original; **characteristic** [kærəktə'rɪstɪk]
n typisches Merkmal
charcoal ['tʃɑ:kəʊl] *n* Holzkohle *f*
charge [tʃɑ:dʒ] *n* (*cost*) Gebühr *f*; (*Jur*)
Anklage *f*; **free of ~** gratis, kostenlos; **to be
in ~ of** verantwortlich sein für ▷ *vt*
(*money*) verlangen; (*Jur*) anklagen; (*battery*)
laden; **charge card** *n* Kundenkreditkarte *f*
charity ['tʃærɪtɪ] *n* (*institution*) wohltätige
Organisation *f*; **a collection for ~** eine
Sammlung für wohltätige Zwecke;
charity shop *n* *Geschäft einer 'charity', in
dem freiwillige Helfer gebrauchte Kleidung,
Bücher etc verkaufen*
charm [tʃɑ:m] *n* Charme *m* ▷ *vt*
bezaubern; **charming** *adj* reizend,
charmant
chart [tʃɑ:t] *n* Diagramm *nt*; (*map*) Karte
f; **the ~s** *pl* die Charts, die Hitliste
charter ['tʃɑ:tə*] *n* Urkunde *f* ▷ *vt* (*Naut,
Aviat*) chartern; **charter flight** *n*
Charterflug *m*
chase [tʃeɪs] *vt* jagen, verfolgen ▷ *n*
Verfolgungsjagd *f*; (*hunt*) Jagd *f*
chassis ['ʃæsɪ] *n* (*Auto*) Fahrgestell *nt*
chat [tʃæt] *vi* plaudern; (*Inform*) chatten
▷ *n* Plauderei *f*; **chat up** *vt* anmachen,
anbaggern; **chatroom** *n* (*Inform*)
Chatroom *m*; **chat show** *n* Talkshow *f*;
chatty *adj* geschwätzig
chauffeur ['ʃəʊfə*] *n* Chauffeur(in) *m(f)*,
Fahrer(in) *m(f)*
cheap [tʃi:p] *adj* billig; (*of poor quality*)
minderwertig
cheat [tʃi:t] *vt, vi* betrügen; (*in school,
game*) mogeln
Chechen ['tʃetʃen] *adj* tschetschenisch
▷ *n* Tschetschene *m*, Tschetschenin *f*;
Chechnya ['tʃetʃnɪə] *n* Tschetschenien *nt*
check [tʃek] *vt* (*examine*) überprüfen (*for*
auf +*akk*); (*Tech: adjustment etc*)
kontrollieren; (*US: tick*) abhaken; (*Aviat:
luggage*) einchecken; (*US: coat*) abgeben
▷ *n* (*examination, restraint*) Kontrolle *f*; (*US:
restaurant bill*) Rechnung *f*; (*pattern*)
Karo(muster) *nt*; (*US*) *see* **cheque**; **check in**
vt, vi (*Aviat*) einchecken; (*into hotel*) sich

anmelden; **check out** *vi* sich abmelden,
auschecken; **check up** *vi* nachprüfen; **to
~ on sb** Nachforschungen über jdn
anstellen
checkers ['tʃekəz] *nsing* (*US*) Damespiel *nt*
check-in ['tʃekɪn] *n* (*airport*) Check-in *m*;
(*hotel*) Anmeldung *f*; **check-in desk** *n*
Abfertigungsschalter *m*; **checking
account** *n* (*US*) Scheckkonto *nt*; **check
list** *n* Kontrollliste *f*; **checkout** *n*
(*supermarket*) Kasse *f*; **checkout time** *n*
(*hotel*) Abreise(zeit) *f*; **checkpoint** *n*
Kontrollpunkt *m*; **checkroom** *n* (*US*)
Gepäckaufbewahrung *f*; **checkup** *n* (*Med*)
(ärztliche) Untersuchung
cheddar ['tʃedə*] *n* Cheddarkäse *m*
cheek [tʃi:k] *n* Backe *f*, Wange *f*;
(*insolence*) Frechheit *f*; **what a ~** so eine
Frechheit!; **cheekbone** *n* Backenknochen
m; **cheeky** *adj* frech
cheer [tʃɪə*] *n* Beifallsruf *m*; **~s** (*when
drinking*) prost!; (*Brit fam: thanks*) danke;
(*Brit: goodbye*) tschüs ▷ *vt* zujubeln +*dat*
▷ *vi* jubeln; **cheer up** *vt* aufmuntern ▷ *vi*
fröhlicher werden; **~!** Kopf hoch!; **cheerful**
['tʃɪəfʊl] *adj* fröhlich
cheese [tʃi:z] *n* Käse *m*; **cheeseboard** *n*
Käsebrett *nt*; (*as course*) (gemischte)
Käseplatte; **cheesecake** *n* Käsekuchen *m*
chef [ʃef] *n* Koch *m*; (*in charge of kitchen*)
Küchenchef(in) *m(f)*
chemical ['kemɪkəl] *adj* chemisch
▷ Chemikalie *f*; **chemist** ['kemɪst] *n*
(*pharmacist*) Apotheker(in) *m(f)*; (*industrial
chemist*) Chemiker(in) *m(f)*; **~'s** (**shop**)
Apotheke *f*; **chemistry** *n* Chemie *f*
cheque [tʃek] *n* (*Brit*) Scheck *m*; **cheque
account** *n* (*Brit*) Girokonto *nt*; **cheque
book** *n* (*Brit*) Scheckheft *nt*; **cheque card**
n (*Brit*) Scheckkarte *f*
chequered ['tʃekəd] *adj* kariert
cherish ['tʃerɪʃ] *vt* (*look after*) liebevoll
sorgen für; (*hope*) hegen; (*memory*)
bewahren
cherry ['tʃerɪ] *n* Kirsche *f*; **cherry tomato**
(*pl* **-es**) *n* Kirschtomate *f*
chess [tʃes] *n* Schach *nt*; **chessboard** *n*
Schachbrett *nt*
chest [tʃest] *n* Brust *f*; (*box*) Kiste *f*; **~ of
drawers** Kommode *f*
chestnut ['tʃesnʌt] *n* Kastanie *f*
chew [tʃu:] *vt, vi* kauen; **chewing gum** *n*
Kaugummi *m*

chick [tʃɪk] n Küken nt; **chicken** n Huhn nt; (food: roast) Hähnchen nt; (coward) Feigling m; **chicken breast** n Hühnerbrust f; **chicken Kiev** n paniertes Hähnchen, mit Knoblauchbutter gefüllt; **chickenpox** n Windpocken pl; **chickpea** n Kichererbse f

chicory ['tʃɪkərɪ] n Chicorée f

chief [tʃiːf] n (of department etc) Leiter(in) m(f); (boss) Chef(in) m(f); (of tribe) Häuptling m ▷ adj Haupt-; **chiefly** adv hauptsächlich

child [tʃaɪld] (pl **children**) n Kind nt; **child abuse** n Kindesmisshandlung f; **child allowance**, **child benefit** (Brit) n Kindergeld nt; **childbirth** n Geburt f, Entbindung f; **childhood** n Kindheit f; **childish** adj kindisch; **child lock** n Kindersicherung f; **childproof** adj kindersicher; **children** ['tʃɪldrən] pl of **child**; **child seat** n Kindersitz m

Chile ['tʃɪlɪ] n Chile nt

chill [tʃɪl] n Kühle f; (Med) Erkältung f ▷ vt (wine) kühlen; **chill out** vi (fam) relaxen; **chilled** adj gekühlt

chilli ['tʃɪlɪ] n Pepperoni pl; (spice) Chili m; **chilli con carne** ['tʃɪlɪkɒn'kɑːnɪ] n Chili con carne nt

chilly ['tʃɪlɪ] adj kühl, frostig

chimney ['tʃɪmnɪ] n Schornstein m; **chimneysweep** n Schornsteinfeger(in) m(f)

chimpanzee [tʃɪmpæn'ziː] n Schimpanse m

chin [tʃɪn] n Kinn nt

china ['tʃaɪnə] n Porzellan nt

China ['tʃaɪnə] n China nt; **Chinese** [tʃaɪ'niːz] adj chinesisch ▷ n (person) Chinese m, Chinesin f; (language) Chinesisch nt; **Chinese leaves** npl Chinakohl m

chip [tʃɪp] n (of wood etc) Splitter m; (damage) angeschlagene Stelle; (Inform) Chip m; **~s** (Brit: potatoes) Pommes frites pl; (US: crisps) Kartoffelchips pl ▷ vt anschlagen, beschädigen; **chippie** (fam), **chip shop** n Frittenbude f

chiropodist [kɪ'rɒpədɪst] n Fußpfleger(in) m(f)

chirp [tʃɜːp] vi zwitschern

chisel ['tʃɪzl] n Meißel m

chitchat ['tʃɪttʃæt] n Gerede nt

chives [tʃaɪvz] npl Schnittlauch m

chlorine ['klɔːriːn] n Chlor nt

chocaholic, **chocoholic** [tʃɒkə'hɒlɪk] n Schokoladenfreak m; **choc-ice** ['tʃɒkaɪs] n Eis nt mit Schokoladenüberzug; **chocolate** ['tʃɒklɪt] n Schokolade f; (chocolate-coated sweet) Praline f; **a bar of ~** eine Tafel Schokolade; **a box of ~s** eine Schachtel Pralinen; **chocolate cake** n Schokoladenkuchen m; **chocolate sauce** n Schokoladensoße f

choice [tʃɔɪs] n Wahl f; (selection) Auswahl f ▷ adj auserlesen; (product) Qualitäts-

choir ['kwaɪə*] n Chor m

choke [tʃəʊk] vi sich verschlucken; (Sport) die Nerven verlieren ▷ vt erdrosseln ▷ n (Auto) Choke m

cholera ['kɒlərə] n Cholera f

cholesterol [kə'lestərəl] n Cholesterin nt

choose [tʃuːz] (**chose**, **chosen**) vt wählen; (pick out) sich aussuchen; **there are three to ~ from** es stehen drei zur Auswahl

chop [tʃɒp] vt (zer)hacken; (meat etc) klein schneiden ▷ n (meat) Kotelett nt; **to get the ~** gefeuert werden; **chopper** n Hackbeil nt; (fam: helicopter) Hubschrauber m; **chopsticks** npl Essstäbchen pl

chorus ['kɔːrəs] n Chor m; (in song) Refrain m

chose, **chosen** [tʃəʊz, 'tʃəʊzn] pt, pp of **choose**

chowder ['tʃaʊdə*] n (US) dicke Suppe mit Meeresfrüchten

christen ['krɪsn] vt taufen; **christening** n Taufe f; **Christian** ['krɪstɪən] adj christlich ▷ n Christ(in) m(f); **Christian name** n (Brit) Vorname m

Christmas ['krɪsməs] n Weihnachten pl; **Christmas card** n Weihnachtskarte f; **Christmas carol** n Weihnachtslied nt; **Christmas Day** n der erste Weihnachtstag; **Christmas Eve** n Heiligabend m; **Christmas pudding** n Plumpudding m; **Christmas tree** n Weihnachtsbaum m

chronic ['krɒnɪk] adj (Med, fig) chronisch; (fam: very bad) miserabel

chrysanthemum [krɪ'sænθɪməm] n Chrysantheme f

chubby ['tʃʌbɪ] adj (child) pummelig; (adult) rundlich

chuck [tʃʌk] vt (fam) schmeißen; **chuck in** vt (fam: job) hinschmeißen; **chuck out** vt (fam) rausschmeißen; **chuck up** vi (fam) kotzen

chunk [tʃʌŋk] n Klumpen m; (of bread) Brocken m; (of meat) Batzen m; **chunky** adj (person) stämmig

Chunnel ['tʃʌnəl] n (fam) Kanaltunnel m

church [tʃɜːtʃ] n Kirche f; **churchyard** n Kirchhof m

chute [ʃuːt] n Rutsche f

chutney ['ʃʌtnɪ] n Chutney m

CIA abbr = **Central Intelligence Agency** (US) CIA f

CID abbr = **Criminal Investigation Department** (Brit) ≈ Kripo f

cider ['saɪdə*] n ≈ Apfelmost m

cigar [sɪ'gɑː*] n Zigarre f; **cigarette** [sɪgə'ret] n Zigarette f

cinema ['sɪnəmə] n Kino nt

cinnamon ['sɪnəmən] n Zimt m

circa ['sɜːkə] prep zirka

circle ['sɜːkl] n Kreis m ⊳ vi kreisen; **circuit** ['sɜːkɪt] n Rundfahrt f; (on foot) Rundgang m; (for racing) Rennstrecke f; (Elec) Stromkreis m; **circular** ['sɜːkjʊlə*] adj (kreis)rund, kreisförmig ⊳ n Rundschreiben nt; **circulation** [sɜːkjʊ'leɪʃən] n (of blood) Kreislauf m; (of newspaper) Auflage f

circumstances ['sɜːkəmstənsəz] npl (facts) Umstände pl; (financial condition) Verhältnisse pl; **in/under the ~** unter den Umständen; **under no ~** auf keinen Fall

circus ['sɜːkəs] n Zirkus m

cissy ['sɪsɪ] n (fam) Weichling m

cistern ['sɪstən] n Zisterne f; (of WC) Spülkasten m

cite [saɪt] vt zitieren

citizen ['sɪtɪzn] n Bürger(in) m(f); (of nation) Staatsangehörige(r) mf; **citizenship** n Staatsangehörigkeit f

city ['sɪtɪ] n Stadt f; (large) Großstadt f; **the ~** (London's financial centre) die (Londoner) City; **city centre** n Innenstadt f, Zentrum nt

civil ['sɪvɪl] adj (of town) Bürger-; (of state) staatsbürgerlich; (not military) zivil; **civil ceremony** n standesamtliche Hochzeit; **civil engineering** n Hoch- und Tiefbau m, Bauingenieurwesen nt; **civilian** [sɪ'vɪljən] n Zivilist(in) m(f); **civilization** [sɪvɪlaɪ'zeɪʃən] n Zivilisation f, Kultur f;

civilized ['sɪvɪlaɪzd] adj zivilisiert, kultiviert; **civil partnership** n eingetragene Partnerschaft; **civil rights** npl Bürgerrechte pl; **civil servant** n (Staats)beamte(r) m, (Staats)beamtin f; **civil service** n Staatsdienst m; **civil war** n Bürgerkrieg m

CJD abbr = **Creutzfeld-Jakob disease** Creutzfeld-Jakob-Krankheit f

cl abbr = **centilitre(s)** cl

claim [kleɪm] vt beanspruchen; (apply for) beantragen; (demand) fordern; (assert) behaupten (that dass) ⊳ n (demand) Forderung f (for für); (right) Anspruch m (to auf +akk); **~ for damages** Schadenersatzforderung f; **to make** o **put in a ~** (insurance) Ansprüche geltend machen; **claimant** n Antragsteller(in) m(f)

clam [klæm] n Venusmuschel f; **clam chowder** n (US) dicke Muschelsuppe (mit Sellerie, Zwiebeln etc)

clap [klæp] vi (Beifall) klatschen

claret ['klærɪt] n roter Bordeaux(wein)

clarify ['klærɪfaɪ] vt klären

clarinet [klærɪ'net] n Klarinette f

clarity ['klærɪtɪ] n Klarheit f

clash [klæʃ] vi (physically) zusammenstoßen (with mit); (argue) sich auseinandersetzen (with mit); (fig: colours) sich beißen ⊳ n Zusammenstoß m; (argument) Auseinandersetzung f

clasp [klɑːsp] n (on belt) Schnalle f

class [klɑːs] n Klasse f ⊳ vt einordnen, einstufen

classic ['klæsɪk] adj (mistake, example etc) klassisch ⊳ n Klassiker m; **classical** ['klæsɪkəl] adj (music, ballet etc) klassisch

classification [klæsɪfɪ'keɪʃn] n Klassifizierung f; **classify** ['klæsɪfaɪ] vt klassifizieren; **classified advertisement** Kleinanzeige f

classroom ['klɑːsrʊm] n Klassenzimmer nt

classy ['klɑːsɪ] adj (fam) nobel, exklusiv

clatter ['klætə*] vi klappern

clause [klɔːz] n (Ling) Satz m; (Jur) Klausel f

claw [klɔː] n Kralle f

clay [kleɪ] n Lehm m; (for pottery) Ton m

clean [kliːn] adj sauber; **~ driving licence** Führerschein ohne Strafpunkte ⊳ adv (completely) glatt ⊳ vt sauber machen;

(carpet etc) reinigen; (window, shoes, vegetables) putzen; (wound) säubern; **clean up** vt sauber machen ▷ vi aufräumen; **cleaner** n (person) Putzmann m, Putzfrau f; (substance) Putzmittel nt; **~'s** (firm) Reinigung f

cleanse [klenz] vt reinigen; (wound) säubern; **cleanser** n Reinigungsmittel nt

clear ['klɪə*] adj klar; (distinct) deutlich; (conscience) rein; (free, road etc) frei; **to be ~ about sth** sich über etw im Klaren sein ▷ adv **to stand ~** zurücktreten ▷ vt (road, room etc) räumen; (table) abräumen; (Jur: find innocent) freisprechen (of von) ▷ vi (fog, mist) sich verziehen; (weather) aufklaren; **clear away** vt wegräumen; (dishes) abräumen; **clear off** vi (fam) abhauen; **clear up** vi (tidy up) aufräumen; (weather) sich aufklären ▷ vt (room) aufräumen; (litter) wegräumen; (matter) klären

clearance sale n Räumungsverkauf m; **clearing** n Lichtung f; **clearly** adv klar; (speak, remember) deutlich; (obviously) eindeutig; **clearout** n Entrümpelungsaktion f; **clearway** n (Brit) Straße f mit Halteverbot nt

clench [klentʃ] vt (fist) ballen; (teeth) zusammenbeißen

clergyman ['klɜ:dʒɪmæn] (pl **-men**) n Geistliche(r) m

clerk [klɑ:k], (US) [klɜ:k] n (in office) Büroangestellte(r) mf; (US: salesperson) Verkäufer(in) m(f)

clever ['klevə*] adj schlau, klug; (idea) clever

cliché ['kli:ʃeɪ] n Klischee nt

click [klɪk] n Klicken nt; (Inform) Mausklick m ▷ vi klicken; **to ~ on sth** (Inform) etw anklicken; **it ~ed** (fam) ich hab's/er hat's etc geschnallt, es hat gefunkt, es hat Klick gemacht; **they ~ed** sie haben sich gleich verstanden; **click on** vt (Inform) anklicken

client ['klaɪənt] n Kunde m, Kundin f; (Jur) Mandant(in) m(f)

cliff [klɪf] n Klippe f

climate ['klaɪmɪt] n Klima nt

climax ['klaɪmæks] n Höhepunkt m

climb [klaɪm] vi (person) klettern; (aircraft, sun) steigen; (road) ansteigen ▷ vt (mountain) besteigen; (tree etc) klettern auf +akk ▷ n Aufstieg m; **climber** n (mountaineer) Bergsteiger(in) m(f);

climbing n Klettern nt, Bergsteigen nt; **climbing frame** n Klettergerüst nt

cling [klɪŋ] (**clung, clung**) vi sich klammern (to an +akk); **cling film®** n Frischhaltefolie f

clinic ['klɪnɪk] n Klinik f; **clinical** adj klinisch

clip [klɪp] n Klammer f ▷ vt (fix) anklemmen (to an +akk); (fingernails) schneiden; **clipboard** n Klemmbrett nt; **clippers** npl Schere f; (for nails) Zwicker m

cloak [kləʊk] n Umhang m; **cloakroom** n (for coats) Garderobe f

clock [klɒk] n Uhr f; (Auto: fam) Tacho m; **round the ~** rund um die Uhr; **clockwise** adv im Uhrzeigersinn; **clockwork** n Uhrwerk nt

clog [klɒg] n Holzschuh m ▷ vt verstopfen

cloister ['klɔɪstə*] n Kreuzgang m

clone [kləʊn] n Klon m ▷ vt klonen

close [kləʊs] adj nahe (to +dat); (friend, contact) eng; (resemblance) groß; **~ to the beach** in der Nähe des Strandes; **~ win** knapper Sieg; **on ~r examination** bei näherer o genauerer Untersuchung ▷ adv [kləʊs] dicht; **he lives ~ by** er wohnt ganz in der Nähe ▷ vt [kləʊz] schließen; (road) sperren; (discussion, matter) abschließen ▷ vi [kləʊz] schließen ▷ n [kləʊz] Ende nt; **close down** vi schließen; (factory) stillgelegt werden ▷ vt (shop) schließen; (factory) stilllegen; **closed** adj (road) gesperrt; (shop etc) geschlossen; **closed circuit television** n Videoüberwachungsanlage f; **closely** adv (related) eng, nah; (packed, follow) dicht; (attentively) genau

closet ['klɒzɪt] n (esp US) Schrank m

close-up ['kləʊsʌp] n Nahaufnahme f

closing ['kləʊzɪŋ] adj **~ date** letzter Termin; (for competition) Einsendeschluss m; **~ time** (of shop) Ladenschluss m; (Brit: of pub) Polizeistunde f

clot [klɒt] n (blood) **~** Blutgerinnsel nt; (fam: idiot) Trottel m ▷ vi (blood) gerinnen

cloth [klɒθ] n (material) Tuch nt; (for cleaning) Lappen m

clothe [kləʊð] vt kleiden; **clothes** npl Kleider pl, Kleidung f; **clothes line** n Wäscheleine f; **clothes peg, clothespin** (US) n Wäscheklammer f; **clothing** ['kləʊðɪŋ] n Kleidung f

clotted ['klɒtɪd] *adj* ~ **cream** dicke Sahne
(*aus erhitzter Milch*)

cloud [klaʊd] *n* Wolke *f*; **cloudy** *adj* (*sky*)
bewölkt; (*liquid*) trüb

clove [kləʊv] *n* Gewürznelke *f*; ~ **of garlic**
Knoblauchzehe *f*

clover ['kləʊvə*] *n* Klee *m*; **cloverleaf** (*pl*
-leaves) *n* Kleeblatt *nt*

clown [klaʊn] *n* Clown *m*

club [klʌb] *n* (*weapon*) Knüppel *m*;
(*society*) Klub *m*, Verein *m*; (*nightclub*)
Disko *f*; (*golf club*) Golfschläger *m*; **~s**
(*Cards*) Kreuz *nt*; **clubbing** *n* **to go ~** in
die Disko gehen; **club class** *n* (*Aviat*)
Businessclass *f*

clue [kluː] *n* Anhaltspunkt *m*, Hinweis *m*;
he hasn't a ~ er hat keine Ahnung

clumsy ['klʌmzɪ] *adj* unbeholfen,
ungeschickt

clung [klʌŋ] *pt, pp of* **cling**

clutch [klʌtʃ] *n* (*Auto*) Kupplung *f* ▷ *vt*
umklammern; (*book etc*) an sich *akk*
klammern

cm *abbr* = **centimetre(s)** cm

c/o *abbr* = **care of** bei

Co *abbr* = **company** Co

coach [kəʊtʃ] *n* (*Brit: bus*) Reisebus *m*;
(*Rail*) (Personen)wagen *m*; (*Sport: trainer*)
Trainer(in) *m(f)* ▷ *vt* Nachhilfeunterricht
geben +*dat*; (*Sport*) trainieren; **coach
(class)** *n* (*Aviat*) Economyclass *f*; **coach
driver** *n* Busfahrer(in) *m(f)*; **coach
station** *n* Busbahnhof *m*; **coach trip** *n*
Busfahrt *f*; (*tour*) Busreise *f*

coal [kəʊl] *n* Kohle *f*

coalition [kəʊə'lɪʃən] *n* (*Pol*) Koalition *f*

coalmine ['kəʊlmaɪn] *n* Kohlenbergwerk
nt; **coalminer** *n* Bergarbeiter *m*

coast [kəʊst] *n* Küste *f*; **coastguard** *n*
Küstenwache *f*; **coastline** *n* Küste *f*

coat [kəʊt] *n* Mantel *m*; (*jacket*) Jacke *f*; (*on
animals*) Fell *nt*, Pelz *m*; (*of paint*) Schicht *f*;
~ **of arms** Wappen *nt*; **coathanger** *n*
Kleiderbügel *m*; **coating** *n* Überzug *m*;
(*layer*) Schicht *f*

cobble(stone)s ['kɒbl(stəʊn)z] *npl*
Kopfsteine *pl*; (*surface*) Kopfsteinpflaster *nt*

cobweb ['kɒbweb] *n* Spinnennetz *nt*

cocaine [kə'keɪn] *n* Kokain *nt*

cock [kɒk] *n* Hahn *m*; (*vulg: penis*)
Schwanz *m*; **cockerel** ['kɒkərəl] *n* junger
Hahn

cockle ['kɒkl] *n* Herzmuschel *f*

cockpit ['kɒkpɪt] *n* (*in plane, racing car*)
Cockpit *nt*; **cockroach** ['kɒkrəʊtʃ] *n*
Kakerlake *f*; **cocksure** *adj* todsicher;

cocktail ['kɒkteɪl] *n* Cocktail *m*; **cock-up**
n (*Brit fam*) **to make a ~ of sth** bei etw
Mist bauen; **cocky** ['kɒkɪ] *adj* großspurig,
von sich selbst überzeugt

cocoa ['kəʊkəʊ] *n* Kakao *m*

coconut ['kəʊkənʌt] *n* Kokosnuss *f*

cod [kɒd] *n* Kabeljau *m*

COD *abbr* = **cash on delivery** per
Nachnahme

code [kəʊd] *n* Kode *m*

coeducational [kəʊedjʊ'keɪʃənl] *adj*
(*school*) gemischt

coffee ['kɒfɪ] *n* Kaffee *m*; **coffee bar** *n*
Café *nt*; **coffee break** *n* Kaffeepause *f*;
coffee maker *n* Kaffeemaschine *f*; **coffee
pot** *n* Kaffeekanne *f*; **coffee shop** *n* Café
nt; **coffee table** *n* Couchtisch *m*

coffin ['kɒfɪn] *n* Sarg *m*

coil [kɔɪl] *n* Rolle *f*; (*Elec*) Spule *f*; (*Med*)
Spirale *f*

coin [kɔɪn] *n* Münze *f*

coincide [kəʊɪn'saɪd] *vi* (*happen together*)
zusammenfallen (*with* mit); **coincidence**
[kəʊ'ɪnsɪdəns] *n* Zufall *m*

coke [kəʊk] *n* Koks *m*; **Coke®** Cola *f*

cola ['kəʊlə] *n* Cola *f*

cold [kəʊld] *adj* kalt; **I'm ~** mir ist kalt, ich
friere ▷ *n* Kälte *f*; (*illness*) Erkältung *f*,
Schnupfen *m*; **to catch a ~** sich erkälten;
cold box *n* Kühlbox *f*; **coldness** *n* Kälte *f*;
cold sore *n* Herpes *m*; **cold turkey** *n*
(*fam*) Totalentzug *m*; (*symptoms*)
Entzugserscheinungen *pl*

coleslaw ['kəʊlslɔː] *n* Krautsalat *m*

collaborate [kə'læbəreɪt] *vi*
zusammenarbeiten (*with* mit);
collaboration [kəlæbə'reɪʃən] *n*
Zusammenarbeit *f*; (*of one party*) Mitarbeit
f

collapse [kə'læps] *vi* zusammenbrechen;
(*building etc*) einstürzen ▷ *n*
Zusammenbruch *m*; (*of building*) Einsturz
m; **collapsible** [kə'læpsəbl] *adj*
zusammenklappbar, Klapp-

collar ['kɒlə*] *n* Kragen *m*; (*for dog, cat*)
Halsband *nt*; **collarbone** *n* Schlüsselbein
nt

colleague ['kɒliːg] *n* Kollege *m*, Kollegin *f*

collect [kə'lekt] *vt* sammeln; (*fetch*)
abholen ▷ *vi* sich sammeln; **collect call** *n*

(US) R-Gespräch nt; **collected** adj (works) gesammelt; (person) gefasst; **collector** n Sammler(in) m(f); **collection** [kə'lekʃən] n Sammlung f; (Rel) Kollekte f; (from postbox) Leerung f

college ['kɒlɪdʒ] n (residential) College nt; (specialist) Fachhochschule f; (vocational) Berufsschule f; (US: university) Universität f; **to go to ~** (US) studieren

collide [kə'laɪd] vi zusammenstoßen; **collision** [kə'lɪʒən] n Zusammenstoß m

colloquial [kə'ləʊkwɪəl] adj umgangssprachlich

Cologne [kə'ləʊn] n Köln nt

colon ['kəʊlən] n (punctuation mark) Doppelpunkt m

colonial [kə'ləʊnɪəl] adj Kolonial-; **colonize** ['kɒlənaɪz] vt kolonisieren; **colony** ['kɒlənɪ] n Kolonie f

color n (US), **colour** ['kʌlə*] n Farbe f; (of skin) Hautfarbe f ▷ vt anmalen; (bias) färben; **colour-blind** adj farbenblind; **coloured** adj farbig; (biased) gefärbt; **colour film** n Farbfilm m; **colourful** adj (lit, fig) bunt; (life, past) bewegt; **colouring** n (in food etc) Farbstoff m; (complexion) Gesichtsfarbe f; **colourless** adj (lit, fig) farblos; **colour photo(graph)** n Farbfoto nt; **colour television** n Farbfernsehen nt

column ['kɒləm] n Säule f; (of print) Spalte f

comb [kəʊm] n Kamm m ▷ vt kämmen; **to ~ one's hair** sich kämmen

combination [kɒmbɪ'neɪʃən] n Kombination f; (mixture) Mischung f (of aus); **combine** [kəm'baɪn] vt verbinden (with mit); (two things) kombinieren

come [kʌm] (came, come) vi kommen; (arrive) ankommen; (on list, in order) stehen; (with adjective: become) werden; **~ and see us** besuchen Sie uns mal; **coming** ich komm ja schon!; **to ~ first/second** erster/zweiter werden; **to ~ true** wahr werden; **to ~ loose** sich lockern; **the years to ~** die kommenden Jahre; **there's one more to ~** es kommt noch eins/noch einer; **how ~ ...?** (fam) wie kommt es, dass ...?; **~ to think of it** (fam) wo es mir gerade einfällt; **come across** vt (find) stoßen auf +akk; **come back** vi zurückkommen; **I'll ~ to that** ich komme darauf zurück; **come down** vi herunterkommen; (rain, snow, price) fallen;

come from vt (result) kommen von; **where do you ~?** wo kommen Sie her?; **I ~ London** ich komme aus London; **come in** vi hereinkommen; (arrive) ankommen; (in race) **to ~ fourth** Vierter werden; **come off** vi (button, handle etc) abgehen; (succeed) gelingen; **to ~ well/badly** gut/schlecht wegkommen; **come on** vi (progress) vorankommen; **~!** komm!; (hurry) beeil dich!; (encouraging) los!; **come out** vi herauskommen; (photo) was werden; (homosexual) sich outen; **come round** vi (visit) vorbeikommen; (regain consciousness) wieder zu sich kommen; **come to** vi (regain consciousness) wieder zu sich kommen ▷ vt (sum) sich belaufen auf +akk; **when it comes to ...** wenn es um ... geht; **come up** vi hochkommen; (sun, moon) aufgehen; **to ~ (for discussion)** zur Sprache kommen; **come up to** vt (approach) zukommen auf +akk; (water) reichen bis zu; (expectations) entsprechen +dat; **come up with** vt (idea) haben; (solution, answer) kommen auf +akk; **to ~ a suggestion** einen Vorschlag machen

comedian [kə'miːdɪən] n Komiker(in) m(f)

comedown ['kʌmdaʊn] n Abstieg m

comedy ['kɒmədɪ] n Komödie f

come-on ['kʌmɒn] n **to give sb the ~** (fam) jdn anmachen

comfort ['kʌmfət] n Komfort m; (consolation) Trost m ▷ vt trösten; **comfortable** adj bequem; (income) ausreichend; (temperature, life) angenehm; **comfort station** n (US) Toilette f; **comforting** adj tröstlich

comic ['kɒmɪk] n (magazine) Comic(heft) nt; (comedian) Komiker(in) m(f) ▷ adj komisch

coming ['kʌmɪŋ] adj kommend; (event) bevorstehend

comma ['kɒmə] n Komma nt

command [kə'mɑːnd] n Befehl m; (control) Führung f; (Mil) Kommando nt ▷ vt befehlen +dat

commemorate [kə'meməreɪt] vt gedenken +gen; **commemoration** [kəmemə'reɪʃən] n **in ~ of** in Gedenken an +akk

comment ['kɒment] n (remark) Bemerkung f; (note) Anmerkung f; (official) Kommentar m (on zu); **no ~** kein

Kommentar ▷ vi sich äußern (on zu);
commentary [ˈkɒməntrɪ] n Kommentar
m (on zu); (Tv, Sport) Livereportage f;
commentator [ˈkɒmənteɪtə*] n
Kommentator(in) m(f); (Tv, Sport)
Reporter(in) m(f)
commerce [ˈkɒmɜːs] n Handel m;
commercial [kəˈmɜːʃəl] adj kommerziell;
(training) kaufmännisch; **~ break**
Werbepause f; **~ vehicle** Lieferwagen m
▷ n (Tv) Werbespot m
commission [kəˈmɪʃən] n Auftrag m; (fee)
Provision f; (reporting body) Kommission f
▷ vt beauftragen
commit [kəˈmɪt] vt (crime) begehen ▷ vr
to ~ oneself (undertake) sich verpflichten
(to zu); **commitment** n Verpflichtung f;
(Pol) Engagement nt
committee [kəˈmɪtɪ] n Ausschuss m,
Komitee nt
commodity [kəˈmɒdɪtɪ] n Ware f
common [ˈkɒmən] adj (experience)
allgemein, alltäglich; (shared) gemeinsam;
(widespread, frequent) häufig; (pej)
gewöhnlich, ordinär; **to have sth in ~** etw
gemein haben ▷ n (Brit: land)
Gemeindewiese f; **commonly** adv häufig,
allgemein; **commonplace** adj alltäglich;
(pej) banal; **commonroom** n
Gemeinschaftsraum m; **Commons** n (Brit
Pol) **the (House of) ~** das Unterhaus;
common sense n gesunder
Menschenverstand; **Commonwealth** n
Commonwealth nt; **~ of Independent
States** Gemeinschaft f Unabhängiger
Staaten
communal [ˈkɒmjʊnl] adj gemeinsam;
(of a community) Gemeinschafts-,
Gemeinde-
communicate [kəˈmjuːnɪkeɪt] vi
kommunizieren (with mit);
communication [kəmjuːnɪˈkeɪʃən] n
Kommunikation f, Verständigung f;
communications satellite n
Nachrichtensatellit m;
communications technology n
Nachrichtentechnik f; **communicative**
adj gesprächig
communion [kəˈmjuːnɪən] n (Holy)
Communion Heiliges Abendmahl;
(Catholic) Kommunion f
communism [ˈkɒmjʊnɪzəm] n
Kommunismus m; **communist**

[ˈkɒmjʊnɪst] adj kommunistisch ▷ n
Kommunist(in) m(f)
community [kəˈmjuːnɪtɪ] n
Gemeinschaft f; **community centre** n
Gemeindezentrum nt; **community
service** n (Jur) Sozialdienst m
commutation ticket [kɒmjuˈteɪʃəntɪkɪt]
n (US) Zeitkarte f; **commute** [kəˈmjuːt] vi
pendeln; **commuter** n Pendler(in) m(f)
compact [kəmˈpækt] adj kompakt
▷ [ˈkɒmpækt] n (for make-up) Puderdose f;
(US: car) ≈ Mittelklassewagen m; **compact
camera** n Kompaktkamera f; **compact
disc** n Compact Disc f, CD f
companion [kəmˈpænɪən] n
Begleiter(in) m(f)
company [ˈkʌmpənɪ] n Gesellschaft f;
(Comm) Firma f; **to keep sb ~** jdm
Gesellschaft leisten; **company car** n
Firmenauto nt
comparable [ˈkɒmpərəbl] adj
vergleichbar (with, to mit)
comparative [kəmˈpærətɪv] adj relativ
▷ n (Ling) Komparativ m; **comparatively**
adv verhältnismäßig
compare [kəmˈpɛə*] vt vergleichen (with,
to mit); **~d with** o to im Vergleich zu;
beyond ~ unvergleichlich; **comparison**
[kəmˈpærɪsn] n Vergleich m; **in ~ with** im
Vergleich mit (o zu)
compartment [kəmˈpɑːtmənt] n (Rail)
Abteil nt; (in desk etc) Fach nt
compass [ˈkʌmpəs] n Kompass m; **~es** pl
Zirkel m
compassion [kəmˈpæʃən] n Mitgefühl nt
compatible [kəmˈpætɪbl] adj vereinbar
(with mit); (Inform) kompatibel; **we're not
~** wir passen nicht zueinander
compensate [ˈkɒmpenseɪt] vt (person)
entschädigen (for für) ▷ vi **to ~ for sth**
Ersatz für etw leisten; (make up for) etw
ausgleichen; **compensation**
[kɒmpenˈseɪʃən] n Entschädigung f;
(money) Schadenersatz m; (Jur) Abfindung f
compete [kəmˈpiːt] vi konkurrieren (for
um); (Sport) kämpfen (for um); (take part)
teilnehmen (in an +dat)
competence [ˈkɒmpɪtəns] n Fähigkeit f;
(Jur) Zuständigkeit f; **competent** adj
fähig; (Jur) zuständig
competition [kɒmpɪˈtɪʃən] n (contest)
Wettbewerb m; (Comm) Konkurrenz f (for
um); **competitive** [kəmˈpetɪtɪv] adj (firm,

price, product) konkurrenzfähig;
competitor [kəm'petɪtə*] n (Comm)
Konkurrent(in) m(f); (Sport) Teilnehmer(in)
m(f)
complain [kəm'pleɪn] vi klagen; (formally)
sich beschweren (about über +akk);
complaint n Klage f; (formal) Beschwerde
f; (Med) Leiden nt
complement vt ergänzen
complete [kəm'pliːt] adj vollständig;
(finished) fertig; (failure, disaster) total;
(happiness) vollkommen; **are we ~?** sind
wir vollzählig? ▷ vt vervollständigen;
(finish) beenden; (form) ausfüllen;
completely adv völlig; **not ~ ...** nicht
ganz ...
complex ['kɒmpleks] adj komplex; (task,
theory etc) kompliziert ▷ n Komplex m
complexion [kəm'plekʃən] n
Gesichtsfarbe f, Teint m
complicated ['kɒmplɪkeɪtɪd] adj
kompliziert; **complication**
['kɒmplɪkeɪʃən] n Komplikation f
compliment ['kɒmplɪmənt] n
Kompliment nt; **complimentary**
[kɒmplɪ'mentərɪ] adj lobend; (free of
charge) Gratis-; **~ ticket** Freikarte f
comply [kəm'plaɪ] vi **to ~ with the
regulations** den Vorschriften
entsprechen
component [kəm'pəʊnənt] n
Bestandteil m
compose [kəm'pəʊz] vt (music)
komponieren; **to ~ oneself** sich
zusammennehmen; **composed** adj
gefasst; **to be ~ of** bestehen aus;
composer n Komponist(in) m(f);
composition [kɒmpə'zɪʃən] n (of a group)
Zusammensetzung f; (Mus) Komposition f
comprehend [kɒmprɪ'hend] vt
verstehen; **comprehension**
[kɒmprɪ'henʃən] n Verständnis nt
comprehensive [kɒmprɪ'hensɪv] adj
umfassend; **~ school** Gesamtschule f
compress [kəm'pres] vt komprimieren
comprise [kəm'praɪz] vt umfassen,
bestehen aus
compromise ['kɒmprəmaɪz] n
Kompromiss m ▷ vi einen Kompromiss
schließen
compulsory [kəm'pʌlsərɪ] adj
obligatorisch; **~ subject** Pflichtfach nt
computer [kəm'pjuːtə*] n Computer m;

computer aided adj computergestützt;
computer-controlled adj
rechnergesteuert; **computer game** n
Computerspiel nt; **computer-literate** adj
to be ~ mit dem Computer umgehen
können; **computer scientist** n
Informatiker(in) m(f); **computing** n
(subject) Informatik f
con [kɒn] (fam) n Schwindel m ▷ vt
betrügen (out of um)
conceal [kən'siːl] vt verbergen (from vor
+dat)
conceivable [kən'siːvəbl] adj denkbar,
vorstellbar; **conceive** [kən'siːv] vt
(imagine) sich vorstellen; (child)
empfangen
concentrate ['kɒnsəntreɪt] vi sich
konzentrieren (on auf +akk);
concentration [kɒnsən'treɪʃən] n
Konzentration f
concept ['kɒnsept] n Begriff m
concern [kən'sɜːn] n (affair)
Angelegenheit f; (worry) Sorge f;
(Comm: firm) Unternehmen nt; **it's not my
~** das geht mich nichts an; **there's
no cause for ~** kein Grund zur
Beunruhigung ▷ vt (affect) angehen;
(have connection with) betreffen; (be
about) handeln von; **those ~ed** die
Betroffenen; **as far as I'm ~ed** was
mich betrifft; **concerned** adj (anxious)
besorgt; **concerning** prep bezüglich,
hinsichtlich +gen
concert ['kɒnsət] n Konzert nt; **~ hall**
Konzertsaal m
concession [kən'seʃən] n Zugeständnis
nt; (reduction) Ermäßigung f
concise [kən'saɪs] adj knapp gefasst,
prägnant
conclude [kən'kluːd] vt (end) beenden,
(ab)schließen; (infer) folgern (from aus); **to
~ that ...** zu dem Schluss kommen, dass
...; **conclusion** [kən'kluːʒən] n Schluss m,
Schlussfolgerung f
concrete ['kɒŋkriːt] n Beton m ▷ adj
konkret
concussion [kɒn'kʌʃən] n
Gehirnerschütterung f
condemn [kən'dem] vt verdammen; (esp
Jur) verurteilen
condensed milk n Kondensmilch f,
Dosenmilch f
condition [kən'dɪʃən] n (state) Zustand m;

(requirement) Bedingung f; **on ~ that ...** unter der Bedingung, dass ...; **~s** pl *(circumstances, weather)* Verhältnisse pl; **conditional** adj bedingt; *(Ling)* Konditional-; **conditioner** n Weichspüler m; *(for hair)* Pflegespülung f

condo [ˈkɒndəʊ] *(pl* **-s)** n see **condominium**

condolences [kənˈdəʊlənsɪz] npl Beileid nt

condom [ˈkɒndəm] n Kondom nt

condominium [kɒndəˈmɪnɪəm] n *(US: apartment)* Eigentumswohnung f

conduct [ˈkɒndʌkt] n *(behaviour)* Verhalten nt ▷ [kənˈdʌkt] vt führen, leiten; *(orchestra)* dirigieren; **conductor** [kənˈdʌktə*] n *(of orchestra)* Dirigent(in) m(f); *(in bus)* Schaffner(in) m(f); *(US: on train)* Zugführer(in) m(f)

cone [kəʊn] n Kegel m; *(for ice cream)* Waffeltüte f; *(fir cone)* (Tannen)zapfen m

conference [ˈkɒnfərəns] n Konferenz f

confess [kənˈfes] vt, vi **to ~ that ...** gestehen, dass ...; **confession** [kənˈfeʃən] n Geständnis nt; *(Rel)* Beichte f

confetti [kənˈfetɪ] n Konfetti nt

confidence [ˈkɒnfɪdəns] n Vertrauen nt *(in* zu); *(assurance)* Selbstvertrauen nt; **confident** adj *(sure)* zuversichtlich *(that ... dass ...)*, überzeugt *(of* von); *(self-assured)* selbstsicher; **confidential** [kɒnfɪˈdenʃəl] adj vertraulich

confine [kənˈfaɪn] vt beschränken *(to auf +akk)*

confirm [kənˈfɜːm] vt bestätigen; **confirmation** [kɒnfəˈmeɪʃən] n Bestätigung f; *(Rel)* Konfirmation f; **confirmed** adj überzeugt; *(bachelor)* eingefleischt

confiscate [ˈkɒnfɪskeɪt] vt beschlagnahmen, konfiszieren

conflict [ˈkɒnflɪkt] n Konflikt m

confuse [kənˈfjuːz] vt verwirren; *(sth with sth)* verwechseln *(with* mit); *(several things)* durcheinanderbringen; **confused** adj *(person)* konfus, verwirrt; *(account)* verworren; **confusing** adj verwirrend; **confusion** [kənˈfjuːʒən] n Verwirrung f; *(of two things)* Verwechslung f; *(muddle)* Chaos nt

congested [kənˈdʒestɪd] adj verstopft; *(overcrowded)* überfüllt; **congestion** [kənˈdʒestʃən] n Stau m

congratulate [kənˈɡrætjʊleɪt] vt gratulieren *(on* zu); **congratulations** [kənɡrætjʊˈleɪʃənz] npl Glückwünsche pl; **~!** gratuliere!, herzlichen Glückwunsch!

congregation [kɒnɡrɪˈɡeɪʃən] n *(Rel)* Gemeinde f

congress [ˈkɒnɡres] n Kongress m; *(US)* **Congress** der Kongress; **congressman** *(pl* **-men)**, **congresswoman** *(pl* **-women)** n *(US)* Mitglied nt des Repräsentantenhauses

conifer [ˈkɒnɪfə*] n Nadelbaum m

conjunction [kənˈdʒʌŋkʃən] n *(Ling)* Konjunktion f; **in ~ with** in Verbindung mit

conk out [kɒŋk ˈaʊt] vi *(fam: appliance, car)* den Geist aufgeben, streiken; *(person: die)* ins Gras beißen

connect [kəˈnekt] vt verbinden *(with, to* mit); *(Elec, Tech: appliance etc)* anschließen *(to an +akk)* ▷ vi *(train, plane)* Anschluss haben *(with an +akk)*; **~ing flight** Anschlussflug m; **~ing train** Anschlusszug m; **connection** [kəˈnekʃən] n Verbindung f; *(link)* Zusammenhang m; *(for train, plane, electrical appliance)* Anschluss m *(with, to an +akk)*; *(business etc)* Beziehung f; **in ~ with** in Zusammenhang mit; **bad ~** *(Tel)* schlechte Verbindung; *(Elec)* Wackelkontakt m; **connector** n *(Inform: computer)* Stecker m

conscience [ˈkɒnʃəns] n Gewissen nt; **conscientious** [kɒnʃɪˈenʃəs] adj gewissenhaft

conscious [ˈkɒnʃəs] adj *(act)* bewusst; *(Med)* bei Bewusstsein; **to be ~** bei Bewusstsein sein; **consciousness** n Bewusstsein nt

consecutive [kənˈsekjʊtɪv] adj aufeinander folgend

consent [kənˈsent] n Zustimmung f ▷ vi zustimmen *(to* dat)

consequence [ˈkɒnsɪkwəns] n Folge f, Konsequenz f; **consequently** [ˈkɒnsɪkwəntlɪ] adv folglich

conservation [kɒnsəˈveɪʃən] n Erhaltung f; *(of buildings)* Denkmalschutz m; *(nature conservation)* Naturschutz m; **conservation area** n Naturschutzgebiet nt; *(in town)* unter Denkmalschutz stehendes Gebiet

Conservative [kənˈsɜːvətɪv] adj *(Pol)* konservativ

conservatory [kənˈsɜːvətrɪ] n (greenhouse) Gewächshaus nt; (room) Wintergarten m

consider [kənˈsɪdə*] vt (reflect on) nachdenken über, sich überlegen; (take into account) in Betracht ziehen; (regard) halten für; **he is ~ed (to be) ...** er gilt als ...; **considerable** [kənˈsɪdərəbl] adj beträchtlich; **considerate** [kənˈsɪdərɪt] adj aufmerksam, rücksichtsvoll; **consideration** [kənsɪdəˈreɪʃən] n (thoughtfulness) Rücksicht f; (thought) Überlegung f; **to take sth into ~** etw in Betracht ziehen; **considering** [kənˈsɪdərɪŋ] prep in Anbetracht +gen ▷ conj da

consist [kənˈsɪst] vi **to ~ of ...** bestehen aus ...

consistent [kənˈsɪstənt] adj (behaviour, process etc) konsequent; (statements) übereinstimmend; (argument) folgerichtig; (performance, results) beständig

consolation [kɒnsəˈleɪʃən] n Trost m; **console** [kənˈsəʊl] vt trösten

consolidate [kənˈsɒlɪdeɪt] vt festigen

consonant [ˈkɒnsənənt] n Konsonant m

conspicuous [kənˈspɪkjʊəs] adj auffällig, auffallend

conspiracy [kənˈspɪrəsɪ] n Komplott nt; **conspire** [kənˈspaɪə*] vi sich verschwören (against gegen)

constable [ˈkʌnstəbl] n (Brit) Polizist(in) m(f)

Constance [ˈkɒnstəns] n Konstanz nt; **Lake ~** der Bodensee

constant [ˈkɒnstənt] adj (continual) ständig, dauernd; (unchanging: temperature etc) gleich bleibend; **constantly** adv dauernd

consternation [kɒnstəˈneɪʃən] n (dismay) Bestürzung f

constituency [kənˈstɪtjʊənsɪ] n Wahlkreis m

constitution [kɒnstɪˈtjuːʃən] n Verfassung f; (of person) Konstitution f

construct [kənˈstrʌkt] vt bauen; **construction** [kənˈstrʌkʃən] n (process, result) Bau m; (method) Bauweise f; **under ~** im Bau befindlich; **construction site** n Baustelle f; **construction worker** n Bauarbeiter(in) m(f)

consulate [ˈkɒnsjʊlət] n Konsulat nt

consult [kənˈsʌlt] vt um Rat fragen; (doctor) konsultieren; (book) nachschlagen in +dat; **consultant** n (Med) Facharzt m, Fachärztin f; **consultation** [kɒnsəlˈteɪʃən] n Beratung f; (Med) Konsultation f

consume [kənˈsjuːm] vt verbrauchen; (food) konsumieren; **consumer** n Verbraucher(in) m(f); **consumer-friendly** adj verbraucherfreundlich

contact [ˈkɒntækt] n (touch) Berührung f; (communication) Kontakt m; (person) Kontaktperson f; **to be/keep in ~ (with sb)** (mit jdm) in Kontakt sein/bleiben ▷ vt sich in Verbindung setzen mit; **contact lenses** npl Kontaktlinsen pl

contagious [kənˈteɪdʒəs] adj ansteckend

contain [kənˈteɪn] vt enthalten; **container** n Behälter m; (for transport) Container m

contaminate [kənˈtæmɪneɪt] vt verunreinigen; (chemically) verseuchen; **~d by radiation** strahlenverseucht, verstrahlt; **contamination** [kəntæmɪˈneɪʃən] n Verunreinigung f; (by radiation) Verseuchung f

contemporary [kənˈtempərərɪ] adj zeitgenössisch

contempt [kənˈtempt] n Verachtung f; **contemptuous** adj verächtlich; **to be ~** voller Verachtung sein (of für)

content [kənˈtent] adj zufrieden

content(s) [ˈkɒntent(s)] n pl Inhalt m

contest [ˈkɒntest] n (Wett)kampf m (for um); (competition) Wettbewerb m ▷ [kənˈtest] vt kämpfen um +akk; (dispute) bestreiten; **contestant** [kənˈtestənt] n Teilnehmer(in) m(f)

context [ˈkɒntekst] n Zusammenhang m; **out of ~** aus dem Zusammenhang gerissen

continent [ˈkɒntɪnənt] n Kontinent m, Festland nt; **the Continent** (Brit) das europäische Festland, der Kontinent; **continental** [kɒntɪˈnentl] adj kontinental; **~ breakfast** kleines Frühstück mit Brötchen und Marmelade, Kaffee oder Tee

continual [kənˈtɪnjʊəl] adj (endless) ununterbrochen; (constant) dauernd, ständig; **continually** adv dauernd; (again and again) immer wieder; **continuation** [kəntɪnjʊˈeɪʃən] n Fortsetzung f; **continue** [kənˈtɪnjuː] vi weitermachen (with mit); (esp talking) fortfahren (with mit); (*travelling*) weiterfahren; (*state, conditions*) fortdauern, anhalten ▷ *vt* fortsetzen; **to be ~d** Fortsetzung folgt; **continuous** [kən'tɪnjʊəs] *adj* (*endless*) ununterbrochen; (*constant*) ständig

contraceptive [kɒntrə'septɪv] *n* Verhütungsmittel *nt*

contract ['kɒntrækt] *n* Vertrag *m*

contradict [kɒntrə'dɪkt] *vt* widersprechen +*dat*; **contradiction** [kɒntrə'dɪkʃən] *n* Widerspruch *m*

contrary ['kɒntrərɪ] *n* Gegenteil *nt*; **on the ~** im Gegenteil ▷ *adj* **~ to** entgegen +*dat*

contrast ['kɒntrɑːst] *n* Kontrast *m*, Gegensatz *m*; **in ~ to** im Gegensatz zu ▷ [kən'trɑːst] *vt* entgegensetzen

contribute [kən'trɪbjuːt] *vt, vi* beitragen (*to* zu); (*money*) spenden (*to* für); **contribution** [kɒntrɪ'bjuːʃən] *n* Beitrag *m*

control [kən'trəʊl] *vt* (*master*) beherrschen; (*temper etc*) im Griff haben; (*esp Tech*) steuern; **to ~ oneself** sich beherrschen ▷ *n* Kontrolle *f*; (*mastery*) Beherrschung *f*; (*of business*) Leitung *f*; (*esp Tech*) Steuerung *f*; **~s** *pl* (*knobs, switches etc*) Bedienungselemente *pl*; (*collectively*) Steuerung *f*; **to be out of ~** außer Kontrolle sein; **control knob** *n* Bedienungsknopf *m*; **control panel** *n* Schalttafel *f*

controversial [kɒntrə'vɜːʃəl] *adj* umstritten

convalesce [kɒnvə'les] *vi* gesund werden; **convalescence** *n* Genesung *f*

convenience [kən'viːnɪəns] *n* (*quality, thing*) Annehmlichkeit *f*; **at your ~** wann es Ihnen passt; **with all modern ~s** mit allem Komfort; **convenience food** *n* Fertiggericht *nt*; **convenient** *adj* günstig, passend

convent ['kɒnvənt] *n* Kloster *nt*

convention [kən'venʃən] *n* (*custom*) Konvention *f*; (*meeting*) Konferenz *f*; **the Geneva Convention** die Genfer Konvention; **conventional** *adj* herkömmlich, konventionell

conversation [kɒnvə'seɪʃən] *n* Gespräch *nt*, Unterhaltung *f*

conversion [kən'vɜːʃən] *n* Umwandlung *f* (*into* in +*akk*); (*of building*) Umbau *m* (*into* zu); (*calculation*) Umrechnung *f*;

conversion table *n* Umrechnungstabelle *f*; **convert** [kən'vɜːt] *vt* umwandeln; (*person*) bekehren; (*Inform*) konvertieren; **to ~ into Euros** in Euro umrechnen; **convertible** *n* (*Auto*) Kabrio *nt* ▷ *adj* umwandelbar

convey [kən'veɪ] *vt* (*carry*) befördern; (*feelings*) vermitteln; **conveyor belt** *n* Förderband *nt*, Fließband *nt*

convict [kən'vɪkt] *vt* verurteilen (*of wegen*) ▷ ['kɒnvɪkt] *n* Strafgefangene(r) *mf*; **conviction** *n* (*Jur*) Verurteilung *f*; (*strong belief*) Überzeugung *f*

convince [kən'vɪns] *vt* überzeugen (*of von*); **convincing** *adj* überzeugend

cook [kʊk] *vt, vi* kochen ▷ *n* Koch *m*, Köchin *f*; **cookbook** *n* Kochbuch *nt*; **cooker** *n* Herd *m*; **cookery** *n* Kochkunst *f*; **~ book** Kochbuch *nt*; **cookie** *n* (*US*) Keks *m*; **cooking** *n* Kochen *nt*; (*style of cooking*) Küche *f*

cool [kuːl] *adj* kühl, gelassen; (*fam: brilliant*) cool, stark ▷ *vt, vi* (ab)kühlen; **~ it** reg dich ab! ▷ *n* **to keep/lose one's ~** (*fam*) ruhig bleiben/durchdrehen; **cool down** *vi* abkühlen; (*calm down*) sich beruhigen

cooperate [kəʊ'ɒpəreɪt] *vi* zusammenarbeiten, kooperieren; **cooperation** [kəʊɒpə'reɪʃən] *n* Zusammenarbeit *f*, Kooperation *f*; **cooperative** [kəʊ'ɒpərətɪv] *adj* hilfsbereit ▷ *n* Genossenschaft *f*

coordinate [kəʊ'ɔːdɪneɪt] *vt* koordinieren

cop [kɒp] *n* (*fam: policeman*) Bulle *m*

cope [kəʊp] *vi* zurechtkommen, fertig werden (*with* mit)

Copenhagen [kəʊpən'heɪgən] *n* Kopenhagen *nt*

copier ['kɒpɪə*] *n* Kopierer *m*

copper ['kɒpə*] *n* Kupfer *nt*; (*Brit fam: policeman*) Bulle *m*; (*fam: coin*) Kupfermünze *f*; **~s** Kleingeld *nt*

copy ['kɒpɪ] *n* Kopie *f*; (*of book*) Exemplar *nt* ▷ *vt* kopieren; (*imitate*) nachahmen; **copyright** *n* Urheberrecht *nt*

coral ['kɒrəl] *n* Koralle *f*

cord [kɔːd] *n* Schnur *f*; (*material*) Kordsamt *m*

cordial ['kɔːdɪəl] *adj* freundlich

cordless ['kɔːdlɪs] *adj* (*phone*) schnurlos

core [kɔː*] *n* (*a. fig*) Kern *m*; (*of apple, pear*)

Kerngehäuse nt; **core business** n
Kerngeschäft nt

cork [kɔːk] n (material) Kork m; (stopper)
Korken m; **corkscrew** ['kɔːkskruː] n
Korkenzieher m

corn [kɔːn] n Getreide nt, Korn nt; (US:
maize) Mais m; (on foot) Hühnerauge nt;
~ on the cob (gekochter) Maiskolben;
corned beef n Cornedbeef nt

corner ['kɔːnə*] n Ecke f; (on road) Kurve f;
(Sport) Eckstoß m ▷ vt in die Enge treiben;
corner shop n Laden m an der Ecke

cornflakes ['kɔːfleɪks] npl Cornflakes pl;
cornflour ['kɔːnflaʊə*] (Brit), **cornstarch**
['kɔːnstɑːtʃ] (US) n Maismehl nt

Cornish ['kɔːnɪʃ] adj kornisch; **~ pasty** mit
Fleisch und Kartoffeln gefüllte Pastete;
Cornwall ['kɔːnwəl] n Cornwall nt

coronary ['kɒrənərɪ] n (Med) Herzinfarkt
m

coronation [kɒrə'neɪʃən] n Krönung f

corporation [kɔːpə'reɪʃən] n (US Comm)
Aktiengesellschaft f

corpse [kɔːps] n Leiche f

correct [kə'rekt] adj (accurate) richtig;
(proper) korrekt ▷ vt korrigieren,
verbessern; **correction** n (esp written)
Korrektur f

correspond [kɒrɪ'spɒnd] vi entsprechen
(to dat); (two things) übereinstimmen;
(exchange letters) korrespondieren;
corresponding adj entsprechend

corridor ['kɒrɪdɔː*] n (in building) Flur m;
(in train) Gang m

corrupt [kə'rʌpt] adj korrupt

cosmetic [kɒz'metɪk] adj kosmetisch;
cosmetics npl Kosmetika pl; **cosmetic
surgeon** n Schönheitschirurg(in) m(f);
cosmetic surgery n Schönheitschirurgie f

cosmopolitan [kɒzmə'pɒlɪtən] adj
international; (attitude) weltoffen

cost [kɒst] (cost, cost) vt kosten ▷ n
Kosten pl; **at all ~s, at any ~** um jeden
Preis; **~ of living** Lebenshaltungskosten
pl; **costly** adj kostspielig

costume ['kɒstjuːm] n (Theat) Kostüm nt

cosy ['kəʊzɪ] adj gemütlich

cot [kɒt] n (Brit) Kinderbett nt; (US)
Campingliege f

cottage ['kɒtɪdʒ] n kleines Haus; (country
cottage) Landhäuschen nt; **cottage cheese**
n Hüttenkäse m; **cottage pie** n
Hackfleisch mit Kartoffelbrei überbacken

cotton ['kɒtn] n Baumwolle f; **cotton
candy** n (US) Zuckerwatte f; **cotton wool**
n (Brit) Watte f

couch [kaʊtʃ] n Couch f; (sofa) Sofa nt;
couchette [kuː'ʃet] n Liegewagen(platz)
m

cough [kɒf] vi husten ▷ n Husten m;
cough mixture n Hustensaft m; **cough
sweet** n Hustenbonbon nt

could [kʊd] pt of **can** konnte; conditional
könnte; **~ you come earlier?** könntest du
früher kommen?

couldn't contr of **could not**

council ['kaʊnsl] n (Pol) Rat m; (local ~)
Gemeinderat m; (town ~) Stadtrat m;
council estate n Siedlung f des sozialen
Wohnungsbaus; **council house** n
Sozialwohnung f; **councillor** ['kaʊnsɪlə*]
n Gemeinderat m, Gemeinderätin f;
council tax n Gemeindesteuer f

count [kaʊnt] vt, vi zählen; (include)
mitrechnen ▷ n Zählung f; (noble) Graf m;
count on vt (rely on) sich verlassen auf
+akk; (expect) rechnen mit

counter ['kaʊntə*] n (in shop) Ladentisch m;
(in café) Theke f; (in bank, post office)
Schalter m; **counter attack** n
Gegenangriff m ▷ vi zurückschlagen;
counter-clockwise adv (US) entgegen
dem Uhrzeigersinn

counterfoil ['kaʊntəfɔɪl] n
(Kontroll)abschnitt m

counterpart ['kaʊntəpɒːt] n Gegenstück
nt (of zu)

countess n Gräfin f

countless ['kaʊntlɪs] adj zahllos,
unzählig

country ['kʌntrɪ] n Land nt; **in the ~** auf
dem Land(e); **in this ~** hierzulande;
country cousin n (fam) Landei nt;
country dancing n Volkstanz m;
country house n Landhaus nt;
countryman n (compatriot) Landsmann
m; **country music** n Countrymusic f;
country road n Landstraße f;
countryside n Landschaft f; (rural area)
Land nt

county ['kaʊntɪ] n (Brit) Grafschaft f; (US)
Verwaltungsbezirk m; **county town** n
(Brit) ≈ Kreisstadt f

couple ['kʌpl] n Paar nt; **a ~ of** ein paar

coupon ['kuːpɒn] n (voucher) Gutschein
m

courage ['kʌrɪdʒ] n Mut m; **courageous** [kə'reɪdʒəs] adj mutig

courgette [kʊə'ʒet] n (Brit) Zucchini f

courier ['kʊrɪə*] n (for tourists) Reiseleiter(in) m(f); (messenger) Kurier m

course [kɔ:s] n (of study) Kurs m; (for race) Strecke f; (Naut, Aviat) Kurs m; (at university) Studiengang m; (in meal) Gang m; **of ~** natürlich; **in the ~ of** während

court [kɔ:t] n (Sport) Platz m; (Jur) Gericht nt

courteous ['kɜ:tɪəs] adj höflich; **courtesy** ['kɜ:təsɪ] n Höflichkeit f; **~ bus/coach** (gebührenfreier) Zubringerbus

courthouse ['kɔ:thaʊs] n (US) Gerichtsgebäude nt; **court order** n Gerichtsbeschluss m; **courtroom** n Gerichtssaal m

courtyard ['kɔ:tjɑ:d] n Hof m

cousin ['kʌzn] n (male) Cousin m; (female) Cousine f

cover ['kʌvə*] vt bedecken (in, with mit); (distance) zurücklegen; (loan, costs) decken ▷ n (for bed etc) Decke f; (of cushion) Bezug m; (lid) Deckel m; (of book) Umschlag m; (**insurance**) **~** Versicherungsschutz m; **cover up** vt zudecken; (error etc) vertuschen; **coverage** n Berichterstattung f (of über +akk); **cover charge** n Kosten pl für ein Gedeck; **covering** n Decke f; **covering letter** n Begleitbrief m; **cover story** n (newspaper) Titelgeschichte f

cow [kaʊ] n Kuh f

coward ['kaʊəd] n Feigling m; **cowardly** adj feig(e)

cowboy ['kaʊbɔɪ] n Cowboy m

coy [kɔɪ] adj gespielt schüchtern, kokett

cozy ['kəʊzɪ] adj (US) gemütlich

CPU abbr = **central processing unit** Zentraleinheit f

crab [kræb] n Krabbe f

crabby ['kræbɪ] adj mürrisch, reizbar

crack [kræk] n Riss m; (in pottery, glass) Sprung m; (drug) Crack nt; **to have a ~ at sth** etw ausprobieren ▷ vi (pottery, glass) einen Sprung bekommen; (wood, ice etc) einen Riss bekommen; **to get ~ing** (fam) loslegen ▷ vt (bone) anbrechen; (nut, code) knacken

cracker ['krækə*] n (biscuit) Kräcker m;

(Christmas ~) Knallbonbon nt; **crackers** adj (fam) verrückt, bekloppt; **he's ~** er hat nicht alle Tassen im Schrank

crackle ['krækl] vi knistern; (telephone, radio) knacken; **crackling** n (Gastr) Kruste f (des Schweinebratens)

cradle ['kreɪdl] n Wiege f

craft [krɑ:ft] n Handwerk nt; (art) Kunsthandwerk nt; (Naut) Boot nt; **craftsman** (pl **-men**) n Handwerker m; **craftsmanship** n Handwerkskunst f; (ability) handwerkliches Können

crafty ['krɑ:ftɪ] adj schlau

cram [kræm] vt stopfen (into in +akk); **to be ~med with ...** mit ... voll gestopft sein ▷ vi (revise for exam) pauken (for für)

cramp [kræmp] n Krampf m

cranberry ['krænbərɪ] n Preiselbeere f

crane [kreɪn] n (machine) Kran m; (bird) Kranich m

crash [kræʃ] vi einen Unfall haben; (two vehicles) zusammenstoßen; (plane, computer) abstürzen; (economy) zusammenbrechen; **to ~ into sth** gegen etw knallen ▷ vt einen Unfall haben mit ▷ n (car) Unfall m; (train) Unglück nt; (collision) Zusammenstoß m; (Aviat, Inform) Absturz m; (noise) Krachen nt; **crash barrier** n Leitplanke f; **crash course** n Intensivkurs m; **crash helmet** n Sturzhelm m; **crash landing** n Bruchlandung f

crate [kreɪt] n Kiste f; (of beer) Kasten m

crater ['kreɪtə*] n Krater m

craving [kreɪvɪŋ] n starkes Verlangen, Bedürfnis nt

crawl [krɔ:l] vi kriechen; (baby) krabbeln ▷ n (swimming) Kraul nt; **crawler lane** n Kriechspur f

crayfish ['kreɪfɪʃ] n Languste f

crayon ['kreɪən] n Buntstift m

crazy ['kreɪzɪ] adj verrückt (about nach)

cream [kri:m] n (from milk) Sahne f, Rahm m; (polish, cosmetic) Creme f ▷ adj cremefarben; **cream cake** n (small) Sahnetörtchen nt; (big) Sahnetorte f; **cream cheese** n Frischkäse m; **creamer** n Kaffeeweißer m; **cream tea** n (Brit) Nachmittagstee mit Törtchen, Marmelade und Schlagsahne; **creamy** adj sahnig

crease [kri:s] n Falte f ▷ vt falten; (untidy) zerknittern

create [kriˈeɪt] vt schaffen; (cause)
verursachen; **creative** [kriːˈeɪtɪv] adj
schöpferisch; (person) kreativ; **creature**
[ˈkriːtʃə*] n Geschöpf nt
crèche [kreɪʃ] n Kinderkrippe f
credible [ˈkredɪbl] adj (person)
glaubwürdig; **credibility** n
Glaubwürdigkeit f
credit [ˈkredɪt] n (Fin: amount allowed)
Kredit m; (amount possessed) Guthaben
nt; (recognition) Anerkennung f; **~s** (of
film) Abspann m; **credit card** n
Kreditkarte f
creep [kriːp] (**crept, crept**) vi kriechen;
creeps n **he gives me the ~** er ist mir
nicht ganz geheuer; **creepy** [ˈkriːpɪ] adj
(frightening) gruselig, unheimlich
crept [krept] pt, pp of **creep**
cress [kres] n Kresse f
crest [krest] n Kamm m; (coat of arms)
Wappen nt
crew [kruː] n Besatzung f, Mannschaft f
crib [krɪb] n (US) Kinderbett nt
cricket [ˈkrɪkɪt] n (insect) Grille f; (game)
Kricket nt
crime [kraɪm] n Verbrechen nt; **criminal**
[ˈkrɪmɪnl] n Verbrecher(in) m(f) ▷ adj
kriminell, strafbar
cripple [ˈkrɪpl] n Krüppel m ▷ vt
verkrüppeln, lähmen
crisis [ˈkraɪsɪs] (pl **crises**) n Krise f
crisp [krɪsp] adj knusprig; **crisps** npl
(Brit) Chips pl; **crispbread** n Knäckebrot
nt
criterion [kraɪˈtɪərɪən] n Kriterium nt;
critic [ˈkrɪtɪk] n Kritiker(in) m(f); **critical**
adj kritisch; **critically** adv kritisch;
~ ill/injured schwer krank/verletzt;
criticism [ˈkrɪtɪsɪzəm] n Kritik f; **criticize**
[ˈkrɪtɪsaɪz] vt kritisieren
Croat [ˈkrəʊæt] n Kroate m, Kroatin f;
Croatia [krəʊˈeɪʃə] n Kroatien nt;
Croatian [krəʊˈeɪʃən] adj kroatisch
crockery [ˈkrɒkərɪ] n Geschirr nt
crocodile [ˈkrɒkədaɪl] n Krokodil nt
crocus [ˈkrəʊkəs] n Krokus m
crop [krɒp] n (harvest) Ernte f; **crops** npl
Getreide nt; **crop up** vi auftauchen
croquette [krəˈket] n Krokette f
cross [krɒs] n Kreuz nt; **to mark sth with
a ~** etw ankreuzen ▷ vt (road, river etc)
überqueren; (legs) übereinander schlagen;
it ~ed my mind es fiel mir ein; **to ~ one's**
fingers die Daumen drücken ▷ adj
ärgerlich, böse; **cross out** vt
durchstreichen
crossbar n (of bicycle) Stange f; (Sport)
Querlatte f; **cross-country** adj **~ running**
Geländelauf m; **~ skiing** Langlauf m;
cross-examination n Kreuzverhör nt;
cross-eyed adj **to be ~** schielen; **crossing**
n (crossroads) (Straßen)kreuzung f; (for
pedestrians) Fußgängerüberweg m; (on
ship) Überfahrt f; **crossroads** nsing o pl
Straßenkreuzung f; **cross section** n
Querschnitt m; **crosswalk** n (US)
Fußgängerüberweg m; **crossword
(puzzle)** n Kreuzworträtsel nt
crouch [kraʊtʃ] vi hocken
crouton [ˈkruːtɒn] n Croûton m
crow [krəʊ] n Krähe f
crowbar [ˈkrəʊbɑː*] n Brecheisen nt
crowd [kraʊd] n Menge f ▷ vi sich
drängen (into in +akk; round um); **crowded**
adj überfüllt
crown [kraʊn] n Krone f ▷ vt krönen;
(fam) **and to ~ it all ...** und als Krönung ...;
crown jewels npl Kronjuwelen pl
crucial [ˈkruːʃəl] adj entscheidend
crude [kruːd] adj primitiv; (humour,
behaviour) derb, ordinär ▷ n **~ (oil)** Rohöl
nt
cruel [ˈkrʊəl] adj grausam (to zu, gegen);
(unfeeling) gefühllos; **cruelty** n
Grausamkeit f; **~ to animals** Tierquälerei f
cruise [kruːz] n Kreuzfahrt f ▷ vi (ship)
kreuzen; (car) mit Reisegeschwindigkeit
fahren; **cruise liner** n Kreuzfahrtschiff nt;
cruise missile n Marschflugkörper m;
cruising speed n Reisegeschwindigkeit f
crumb [krʌm] n Krume f
crumble [ˈkrʌmbl] vt, vi zerbröckeln ▷ n
mit Streuseln überbackenes Kompott
crumpet [ˈkrʌmpɪt] n weiches Hefegebäck
zum Toasten; (fam: attractive woman)
Schnecke f
crumple [ˈkrʌmpl] vt zerknittern;
crumple zone n (Auto) Knautschzone f
crunchy [ˈkrʌntʃɪ] adj (Brit) knusprig
crusade [kruːˈseɪd] n Kreuzzug m
crush [krʌʃ] vt zerdrücken; (finger etc)
quetschen; (spices, stone) zerstoßen ▷ n **to
have a ~ on sb** in jdn verknallt sein;
crushing adj (defeat, remark) vernichtend
crust [krʌst] n Kruste f; **crusty** adj
knusprig

crutch [krʌtʃ] n Krücke f
cry [kraɪ] vi (call) rufen; (scream) schreien; (weep) weinen ▷ n (call) Ruf m; (louder) Schrei m
crypt [krɪpt] n Krypta f
crystal ['krɪstl] n Kristall m
cu abbr = **see you** (SMS, E-Mail) bis bald
cub [kʌb] n (animal) Junge(s) nt
Cuba ['kjuːbə] n Kuba nt
cube [kjuːb] n Würfel m
cubic ['kjuːbɪk] adj Kubik-
cubicle ['kjuːbɪkl] n Kabine f
cuckoo ['kʊkuː] n Kuckuck m
cucumber ['kjuːkʌmbə*] n Salatgurke f
cuddle ['kʌdl] vt in den Arm nehmen; (amorously) schmusen mit ▷ n Liebkosung f, Umarmung f; **to have a ~** schmusen; **cuddly** adj verschmust; **cuddly toy** n Plüschtier nt
cuff [kʌf] n Manschette f; (US: trouser ~) Aufschlag m; **off the ~** aus dem Stegreif; **cufflink** n Manschettenknopf m
cuisine [kwɪ'ziːn] n Kochkunst f, Küche f
cul-de-sac ['kʌldəsæk] n (Brit) Sackgasse f
culprit ['kʌlprɪt] n Schuldige(r) mf; (fig) Übeltäter(in) m(f)
cult [kʌlt] n Kult m
cultivate ['kʌltɪveɪt] vt (Agr: land) bebauen; (crop) anbauen; **cultivated** adj (person) kultiviert, gebildet
cultural ['kʌltʃərəl] adj kulturell, Kultur-; **culture** ['kʌltʃə*] n Kultur f; **cultured** adj gebildet, kultiviert; **culture vulture** (Brit fam) n Kulturfanatiker(in) m(f)
cumbersome ['kʌmbəsəm] adj (object) unhandlich
cumin ['kʌmɪn] n Kreuzkümmel m
cunning ['kʌnɪŋ] adj schlau; (person a.) gerissen
cup [kʌp] n Tasse f; (prize) Pokal m; **it's not his ~ of tea** das ist nicht sein Fall; **cupboard** ['kʌbəd] n Schrank m; **cup final** n Pokalendspiel nt; **cup tie** n Pokalspiel nt
cupola ['kjuːpələ] n Kuppel f
curable ['kjʊrəbəl] adj heilbar
curb [kɜːb] n (US) see **kerb**
curd [kɜːd] n **~ cheese**, **~s** ≈ Quark m
cure [kjʊə*] n Heilmittel nt (for gegen); (process) Heilung f ▷ vt heilen; (Gastr) pökeln; (smoke) räuchern
curious ['kjʊərɪəs] adj neugierig; (strange) seltsam

curl [kɜːl] n Locke f ▷ vi sich kräuseln; **curly** adj lockig
currant ['kʌrənt] n (dried) Korinthe f; (red, black) Johannisbeere f
currency ['kʌrənsɪ] n Währung f; **foreign ~** Devisen pl
current ['kʌrənt] n (in water) Strömung f; (electric ~) Strom m ▷ adj (issue, affairs) aktuell, gegenwärtig; (expression) gängig; **current account** n Girokonto nt; **currently** adv zur Zeit
curriculum [kə'rɪkjʊləm] n Lehrplan m; **curriculum vitae** [kə'rɪkjʊləm'viːtaɪ] n (Brit) Lebenslauf m
curry ['kʌrɪ] n Currygericht nt; **curry powder** n Curry(pulver) nt
curse [kɜːs] vi (swear) fluchen (at auf +akk) ▷ n Fluch m
cursor ['kɜːsə*] n (Inform) Cursor m
curt [kɜːt] adj schroff, kurz angebunden
curtain ['kɜːtn] n Vorhang m; **it was ~s for Benny** für Benny war alles vorbei
curve [kɜːv] n Kurve f ▷ vi einen Bogen machen; **curved** adj gebogen
cushion ['kʊʃən] n Kissen nt
custard ['kʌstəd] n dicke Vanillesoße, die warm oder kalt zu vielen englischen Nachspeisen gegessen wird
custom ['kʌstəm] n Brauch m; (habit) Gewohnheit f; **customary** ['kʌstəmrɪ] adj üblich; **custom-built** adj nach Kundenangaben gefertigt; **customer** ['kʌstəmə*] n Kunde m, Kundin f; **customer loyalty card** n Kundenkarte f; **customer service** n Kundendienst m
customs ['kʌstəmz] npl (organization, location) Zoll m; **to pass through ~** durch den Zoll gehen; **customs officer** n Zollbeamte(r) m, Zollbeamtin f
cut [kʌt] (**cut, cut**) vt schneiden; (cake) anschneiden; (wages, benefits) kürzen; (prices) heruntersetzen; **I ~ my finger** ich habe mir in den Finger geschnitten ▷ n Schnitt m; (wound) Schnittwunde f; (reduction) Kürzung f (in gen); **price/tax ~** Preissenkung/Steuersenkung f; **to be a ~ above the rest** eine Klasse besser als die anderen sein; **cut back** vt (workforce etc) reduzieren; **cut down** vt (tree) fällen; **to ~ on sth** etwas einschränken; **cut in** vi (Auto) scharf einscheren; **to ~ on sb** jdn schneiden; **cut off** vt abschneiden; (gas,

electricity) abdrehen, abstellen; (*Tel*) **I was ~** ich wurde unterbrochen

cutback *n* Kürzung *f*

cute [kju:t] *adj* putzig, niedlich; (*US: shrewd*) clever

cutlery ['kʌtlərı] *n* Besteck *nt*

cutlet ['kʌtlɪt] *n* (*pork*) Kotelett *nt*; (*veal*) Schnitzel *nt*

cut-price *adj* verbilligt

cutting ['kʌtɪŋ] *n* (*from paper*) Ausschnitt *m*; (*of plant*) Ableger *m* ▷ *adj* (*comment*) verletzend

CV *abbr* = **curriculum vitae**

cwt *abbr* = **hundredweight** ≈ Zentner, Ztr.

cybercafé [saɪbə'kæfeɪ] *n* Internetcafé *nt*; **cyberspace** *n* Cyberspace *m*

cyclamen ['sɪkləmən] *n* Alpenveilchen *nt*

cycle ['saɪkl] *n* Fahrrad *nt* ▷ *vi* Rad fahren; **cycle lane**, **cycle path** *n* Radweg *m*; **cycling** *n* Radfahren *nt*; **cyclist** ['saɪklɪst] *n* Radfahrer(in) *m(f)*

cylinder ['sɪlɪndə*] *n* Zylinder *m*

cynical ['sɪnɪkəl] *adj* zynisch

cypress ['saɪprɪs] *n* Zypresse *f*

Cypriot ['sɪprɪət] *adj* zypriotisch ▷ *n* Zypriote *m*, Zypriotin *f*; **Cyprus** ['saɪprəs] *n* Zypern *nt*

czar [zɑ:*] *n* Zar *m*; **czarina** [zɑ'ri:nə] *n* Zarin *f*

Czech [tʃek] *adj* tschechisch ▷ *n* (*person*) Tscheche *m*, Tschechin *f*; (*language*) Tschechisch *nt*; **Czech Republic** *n* Tschechische Republik, Tschechien *nt*

d

dab [dæb] *vt* (*wound, nose etc*) betupfen (*with* mit)

dachshund ['dækshʊnd] *n* Dackel *m*

dad(dy) ['dæd(ɪ)] *n* Papa *m*, Vati *m*; **daddy-longlegs** *nsing* (*Brit*) Schnake; (*US*) Weberknecht *m*

daffodil ['dæfədɪl] *n* Osterglocke *f*

daft [dɑːft] *adj* (*fam*) blöd, doof

dahlia ['deɪlɪə] *n* Dahlie *f*

daily ['deɪlɪ] *adj, adv* täglich ▷ *n* (*paper*) Tageszeitung *f*

dairy ['dɛərɪ] *n* (*on farm*) Molkerei *f*; **dairy products** *npl* Milchprodukte *pl*

daisy ['deɪzɪ] *n* Gänseblümchen *nt*

dam [dæm] *n* Staudamm *m* ▷ *vt* stauen

damage ['dæmɪdʒ] *n* Schaden *m*; **~s** *pl* (*Jur*) Schadenersatz *m* ▷ *vt* beschädigen; (*reputation, health*) schädigen, schaden +*dat*

damn [dæm] *adj* (*fam*) verdammt ▷ *vt* (*condemn*) verurteilen; **~ (it)!** verflucht! ▷ *n* **he doesn't give a ~** es ist ihm völlig egal

damp [dæmp] *adj* feucht ▷ *n* Feuchtigkeit *f*; **dampen** ['dæmpən] *vt* befeuchten

dance [dɑːns] *n* Tanz *m*; (*event*) Tanzveranstaltung *f* ▷ *vi* tanzen; **dance**

floor *n* Tanzfläche *f*; **dancer** *n* Tänzer(in) *m(f)*; **dancing** *n* Tanzen *nt*

dandelion ['dændɪlaɪən] *n* Löwenzahn *m*

dandruff ['dændrəf] *n* Schuppen *pl*

Dane [deɪn] *n* Däne *m*, Dänin *f*

danger ['deɪndʒə*] *n* Gefahr *f*; **~ (sign)** Achtung!; **to be in ~** in Gefahr sein; **dangerous** *adj* gefährlich

Danish ['deɪnɪʃ] *adj* dänisch ▷ *n* (*language*) Dänisch *nt*; **the ~** *pl* die Dänen; **Danish pastry** *n* Plundergebäck *nt*

Danube ['dænjuːb] *n* Donau *f*

dare [dɛə*] *vi* **to ~ (to) do sth** es wagen, etw zu tun; **I didn't ~ ask** ich traute mich nicht, zu fragen; **how ~ you** was fällt dir ein!; **daring** *adj* (*person*) mutig; (*film, clothes etc*) gewagt

dark [dɑːk] *adj* dunkel; (*gloomy*) düster, trübe; (*sinister*) finster; **~ chocolate** Bitterschokolade *f*; **~ green/blue** dunkelgrün/dunkelblau ▷ *n* Dunkelheit *f*; **in the ~** im Dunkeln; **dark glasses** *npl* Sonnenbrille *f*; **darkness** *n* Dunkelheit *nt*

darling ['dɑːlɪŋ] *n* Schatz *m*; (*also favourite*) Liebling *m*

dart [dɑːt] *n* Wurfpfeil *m*; **darts** *nsing* (*game*) Darts *nt*

dash [dæʃ] *vi* stürzen, rennen ▷ *vt* **to ~ hopes** Hoffnungen zerstören ▷ *n* (*in text*) Gedankenstrich *m*; (*of liquid*) Schuss *m*; **dashboard** *n* Armaturenbrett *nt*

data ['deɪtə] *npl* Daten *pl*; **data bank, data base** *n* Datenbank *f*; **data capture** *n* Datenerfassung *f*; **data processing** *n* Datenverarbeitung *f*; **data protection** *n* Datenschutz *m*

date [deɪt] *n* Datum *nt*; (*for meeting, delivery etc*) Termin *m*; (*with person*) Verabredung *f*; (*with girlfriend etc*) Date *nt*; (*fruit*) Dattel *f*; **what's the ~ (today)?** der Wievielte ist heute?; **out of ~** *adj* veraltet; **up to ~** *adj* (*news*) aktuell; (*fashion*) zeitgemäß ▷ *vt* (*letter etc*) datieren; (*person*) gehen mit; **dated** *adj* altmodisch; **date of birth** *n* Geburtsdatum *nt*; **dating agency** *n* Partnervermittlung *f*

dative ['deɪtɪv] *n* Dativ *m*

daughter ['dɔːtə*] *n* Tochter *f*; **daughter-in-law** (*pl* **daughters-in-law**) *n* Schwiegertochter *f*

dawn [dɔːn] *n* Morgendämmerung *f* ▷ *vi*

dämmern; **it ~ed on me** mir ging ein Licht auf

day [deɪ] n Tag m; **one ~** eines Tages; **by ~** bei Tage; **~ after ~, ~ by ~** Tag für Tag; **the ~ after/before** am Tag danach/zuvor; **the ~ before yesterday** vorgestern; **the ~ after tomorrow** übermorgen; **these ~s** heutzutage; **in those ~s** damals; **let's call it a ~** Schluss für heute!; **daybreak** n Tagesanbruch m; **daydream** n Tagtraum m ▷ vi (mit offenen Augen) träumen; **daylight** n Tageslicht nt; **in ~** bei Tage; **daylight saving time** n Sommerzeit f; **day nursery** n Kindertagesstätte f; **day return** n (Brit Rail) Tagesrückfahrkarte f; **daytime** n **in the ~** bei Tage, tagsüber; **daytrip** n Tagesausflug m

dazed [deɪzd] adj benommen

dazzle ['dæzl] vt blenden; **dazzling** adj blendend, glänzend

dead [ded] adj tot; (limb) abgestorben ▷ adv genau; (fam) total, völlig; **~ tired** adj todmüde; **~ slow** (sign) Schritt fahren; **dead end** n Sackgasse f; **deadline** n Termin m; (period) Frist f; **~ for applications** Anmeldeschluss m; **deadly** adj tödlich ▷ adv **~ dull** todlangweilig

deaf [def] adj taub; **deafen** vt taub machen; **deafening** adj ohrenbetäubend

deal [diːl] (**dealt, dealt**) vt, vi (cards) geben, austeilen ▷ n (business ~) Geschäft nt; (agreement) Abmachung f; **it's a ~** abgemacht!; **a good/great ~ of** ziemlich/sehr viel; **deal in** vt handeln mit; **deal with** vt (matter) sich beschäftigen mit; (book, film) behandeln; (successfully: person, problem) fertig werden mit; (matter) erledigen; **dealer** n (Comm) Händler(in) m(f); (drugs) Dealer(in) m(f); **dealings** npl (Comm) Geschäfte pl

dealt [delt] pt, pp of **deal**

dear [dɪə*] adj lieb, teuer; **Dear Sir or Madam** Sehr geehrte Damen und Herren; **Dear David** Lieber David ▷ n Schatz m; (as address) mein Schatz, Liebling; **dearly** adv (love) (heiß und) innig; (pay) teuer

death [deθ] n Tod m; (of project, hopes) Ende nt; **~s** pl Todesfälle; (in accident) Todesopfer; **death certificate** n Totenschein m; **death penalty** n Todesstrafe f; **death toll** n Zahl f der

---

Todesopfer; **death trap** n Todesfalle f

debatable [dɪ'beɪtəbl] adj fraglich; (question) strittig; **debate** [dɪ'beɪt] n Debatte f ▷ vt debattieren

debauched [dɪ'bɔːtʃt] adj ausschweifend

debit ['debɪt] n Soll nt ▷ vt (account) belasten; **debit card** n Geldkarte f

debris ['debriː] n Trümmer pl

debt [det] n Schuld f; **to be in ~** verschuldet sein

decade ['dekeɪd] n Jahrzehnt nt

decadent ['dekədənt] adj dekadent

decaff ['diːkæf] n (fam) koffeinfreier Kaffee; **decaffeinated** [diː'kæfɪneɪtɪd] adj koffeinfrei

decanter [dɪ'kæntə*] n Dekanter m, Karaffe f

decay [dɪ'keɪ] n Verfall m; (rotting) Verwesung f; (of tooth) Fäule f ▷ vi verfallen; (rot) verwesen; (wood) vermodern; (teeth) faulen; (leaves) verrotten

deceased [dɪ'siːst] n **the ~** der/die Verstorbene

deceit [dɪ'siːt] n Betrug m; **deceive** [dɪ'siːv] vt täuschen

December [dɪ'sembə*] n Dezember m; see also **September**

decent ['diːsənt] adj anständig

deception [dɪ'sepʃən] n Betrug m; **deceptive** [dɪ'septɪv] adj täuschend, irreführend

decide [dɪ'saɪd] vt (question) entscheiden; (body of people) beschließen; **I can't ~ what to do** ich kann mich nicht entscheiden, was ich tun soll ▷ vi sich entscheiden; **to ~ on sth** (in favour of sth) sich für etw entscheiden, sich zu etw entschließen; **decided** adj entschieden; (clear) deutlich; **decidedly** adv entschieden

decimal ['desɪməl] adj Dezimal-; **decimal system** n Dezimalsystem nt

decipher [dɪ'saɪfə*] vt entziffern

decision [dɪ'sɪʒən] n Entscheidung f (on über +akk); (of committee, jury etc) Beschluss m; **to make a ~** eine Entscheidung treffen; **decisive** [dɪ'saɪsɪv] adj entscheidend; (person) entscheidungsfreudig

deck [dek] n (Naut) Deck nt; (of cards) Blatt nt; **deckchair** n Liegestuhl m

declaration [deklə'reɪʃən] n Erklärung f; **declare** [dɪ'kleə*] vt erklären; (state) behaupten (that dass); (at customs) **have**

you anything to ~? haben Sie etwas zu verzollen?

decline [dɪ'klaɪn] n Rückgang m ▷ vt (invitation, offer) ablehnen ▷ vi (become less) sinken, abnehmen; (health) sich verschlechtern

decode [di:'kəʊd] vt entschlüsseln

decompose [di:kəm'pəʊz] vi sich zersetzen

decontaminate [di:kən'tæmɪneɪt] vt entgiften; (from radioactivity) entseuchen

decorate ['dekəreɪt] vt (aus)schmücken; (wallpaper) tapezieren; (paint) anstreichen; **decoration** [dekə'reɪʃən] n Schmuck m; (process) Schmücken nt; (wallpapering) Tapezieren nt; (painting) Anstreichen nt; **Christmas ~s** Weihnachtsschmuck m; **decorator** n Maler(in) m(f)

decrease ['di:kri:s] n Abnahme f ▷ [di:'kri:s] vi abnehmen

dedicate ['dedɪkeɪt] vt widmen (to sb jdm); **dedicated** adj (person) engagiert; **dedication** [dedɪ'keɪʃən] n Widmung f; (commitment) Hingabe f, Engagement nt

deduce [dɪ'dju:s] vt folgern, schließen (from aus, that dass)

deduct [dɪ'dʌkt] vt abziehen (from von); **deduction** [dɪ'dʌkʃən] n (of money) Abzug m; (conclusion) (Schluss)folgerung f

deed [di:d] n Tat f

deep [di:p] adj tief; **deepen** vt vertiefen; **deep-freeze** n Tiefkühltruhe f; (upright) Gefrierschrank m; **deep-fry** vt frittieren

deer [dɪə*] n Reh nt; (with stag) Hirsch m

defeat [dɪ'fi:t] n Niederlage f; **to admit ~** sich geschlagen geben ▷ vt besiegen

defect ['di:fekt] n Defekt m, Fehler m; **defective** [dɪ'fektɪv] adj fehlerhaft

defence [dɪ'fens] n Verteidigung f; **defend** [dɪ'fend] vt verteidigen; **defendant** [dɪ'fendənt] n (Jur) Angeklagte(r) mf; **defender** n (Sport) Verteidiger(in) m(f); **defensive** [dɪ'fensɪv] adj defensiv

deficiency [dɪ'fɪʃənsɪ] n Mangel m; **deficient** adj mangelhaft; **deficit** ['defɪsɪt] n Defizit nt

define [dɪ'faɪn] vt (word) definieren; (duties, powers) bestimmen; **definite** ['defɪnɪt] adj (clear) klar, eindeutig; (certain) sicher; **it's ~** es steht fest; **definitely** adv bestimmt; **definition** [defɪ'nɪʃən] n Definition f; (Foto) Schärfe f

deflate [di:'fleɪt] vt die Luft ablassen aus

defrost [di:'frɒst] vt (fridge) abtauen; (food) auftauen

degrading [dɪ'greɪdɪŋ] adj erniedrigend

degree [dɪ'gri:] n Grad m; (at university) akademischer Grad; **a certain/high ~ of** ein gewisses/hohes Maß an +dat; **to a certain ~** einigermaßen; **I have a ~ in chemistry** ≈ ich habe Chemie studiert

dehydrated [di:haɪ'dreɪtɪd] adj (food) getrocknet, Trocken-; (person) ausgetrocknet

de-ice [di:'aɪs] vt enteisen

delay [dɪ'leɪ] vt (postpone) verschieben, aufschieben; **to be ~ed** (event) sich verzögern; **the train/flight was ~ed** der Zug/die Maschine hatte Verspätung ▷ vi warten; (hesitate) zögern ▷ n Verzögerung f; (of train etc) Verspätung f; **without ~** unverzüglich; **delayed** adj (train etc) verspätet

delegate n ['delɪgət] Delegierte(r) mf ▷ ['delɪgeɪt] vt delegieren; **delegation** [delɪ'geɪʃən] n Abordnung f; (foreign) Delegation f

delete [dɪ'li:t] vt (aus)streichen; (Inform) löschen; **deletion** n Streichung f; (Inform) Löschung f

deli ['delɪ] n (fam) Feinkostgeschäft nt

deliberate [dɪ'lɪbərət] adj (intentional) absichtlich; **deliberately** adv mit Absicht, extra

delicate ['delɪkɪt] adj (fine) fein; (fragile) zart; (a. Med) empfindlich; (situation) heikel

delicatessen [delɪkə'tesn] nsing Feinkostgeschäft nt

delicious [dɪ'lɪʃəs] adj köstlich, lecker

delight [dɪ'laɪt] n Freude f ▷ vt entzücken; **delighted** adj sehr erfreut (with über +akk); **delightful** adj entzückend; (weather, meal etc) herrlich

deliver [dɪ'lɪvə*] vt (goods) liefern (to sb jdm); (letter, parcel) zustellen; (speech) halten; (baby) entbinden; **delivery** n Lieferung f; (of letter, parcel) Zustellung f; (of baby) Entbindung f; **delivery van** n Lieferwagen m

delude [dɪ'lu:d] vt täuschen; **don't ~ yourself** mach dir nichts vor; **delusion** n Irrglaube m

de luxe [dɪ'lʌks] adj Luxus-

demand [dɪ'mɑ:nd] vt verlangen (from

von); (*time, patience etc*) erfordern ▷ *n* (*request*) Forderung *f*, Verlangen *nt* (*for* nach); (*Comm: for goods*) Nachfrage *f*; **on ~** auf Wunsch; **very much in ~** sehr gefragt; **demanding** *adj* anspruchsvoll

demented [dɪ'mentɪd] *adj* wahnsinnig

demerara [demə'rɛərə] *n* **~ (sugar)** brauner Zucker

demister *n* Defroster *m*

demo ['deməʊ] (*pl* **-s**) *n* (*fam*) Demo *f*

democracy [dɪ'mɒkrəsɪ] *n* Demokratie *f*; **democrat, Democrat** (*US Pol*) ['deməkræt] Demokrat(in) *m(f)*; **democratic** *adj* demokratisch; **the Democratic Party** (*US Pol*) die Demokratische Partei

demolish [dɪ'mɒlɪʃ] *vt* abreißen; (*fig*) zerstören; **demolition** [demə'lɪʃən] *n* Abbruch *m*

demonstrate ['demənstreɪt] *vt, vi* demonstrieren, beweisen; **demonstration** *n* Demonstration *f*

demoralize [dɪ'mɒrəlaɪz] *vt* demoralisieren

denationalization ['diːnæʃnəlaɪ'zeɪʃən] *n* Privatisierung *f*

denial [dɪ'naɪəl] *n* Leugnung *f*; (*official ~*) Dementi *nt*

denim ['denɪm] *n* Jeansstoff *m*; **denim jacket** *n* Jeansjacke *f*; **denims** *npl* Bluejeans *pl*

Denmark ['denmɑːk] *n* Dänemark *nt*

denomination [dɪnɒmɪ'neɪʃən] *n* (*Rel*) Konfession *f*; (*Comm*) Nennwert *m*

dense [dens] *adj* dicht; (*fam: stupid*) schwer von Begriff; **density** ['densɪtɪ] *n* Dichte *f*

dent [dent] *n* Beule *f*, Delle *f* ▷ *vt* einbeulen

dental ['dentl] *adj* Zahn-; **~ care** Zahnpflege *f*; **~ floss** Zahnseide *f*; **dentist** ['dentɪst] *n* Zahnarzt *m*, Zahnärztin; **dentures** ['dentʃəz] *npl* Zahnprothese *f*; (*full*) Gebiss *nt*

deny [dɪ'naɪ] *vt* leugnen, bestreiten; (*refuse*) ablehnen

deodorant [diː'əʊdərənt] *n* Deo(dorant) *nt*; **~ spray** Deospray *nt o m*

depart [dɪ'pɑːt] *vi* abreisen; (*bus, train*) abfahren (*for* nach, *from* von); (*plane*) abfliegen (*for* nach, *from* von)

department [dɪ'pɑːtmənt] *n* Abteilung *f*; (*at university*) Institut *nt*; (*Pol: ministry*)

Ministerium *nt*; **department store** *n* Kaufhaus *nt*

departure [dɪ'pɑːtʃə*] *n* (*of person*) Weggang *m*; (*on journey*) Abreise *f* (*for* nach); (*of train etc*) Abfahrt *f* (*for* nach); (*of plane*) Abflug *m* (*for* nach); **departure lounge** *n* (*Aviat*) Abflughalle *f*; **departure time** *n* Abfahrtzeit *f*; (*Aviat*) Abflugzeit *f*

depend [dɪ'pend] *vi* **it ~s** es kommt darauf an (*whether, if* ob); **depend on** *vt* (*thing*) abhängen von; (*person: rely on*) sich verlassen auf +*akk*; (*person, area etc*) angewiesen sein auf +*akk*; **it ~s on the weather** es kommt auf das Wetter an; **dependable** *adj* zuverlässig; **dependence** *n* Abhängigkeit *f* (*on* von); **dependent** *adj* abhängig (*on* von)

deplorable [dɪ'plɔːrəbl] *adj* bedauerlich; **deplore** *vt* bedauern

deport [dɪ'pɔːt] *vt* ausweisen, abschieben; **deportation** [diːpɔː'teɪʃən] *n* Abschiebung *f*

deposit [dɪ'pɒzɪt] *n* (*down payment*) Anzahlung *f*; (*security*) Kaution *f*; (*for bottle*) Pfand *nt*; (*to bank account*) Einzahlung *f*; (*in river etc*) Ablagerung *f* ▷ *vt* (*put down*) abstellen, absetzen; (*to bank account*) einzahlen; (*sth valuable*) deponieren; **deposit account** *n* Sparkonto *nt*

depot ['depəʊ] *n* Depot *nt*

depreciate [dɪ'priːʃɪeɪt] *vi* an Wert verlieren

depress [dɪ'pres] *vt* (*in mood*) deprimieren; **depressed** *adj* (*person*) niedergeschlagen, deprimiert; **~ area** Notstandsgebiet *nt*; **depressing** *adj* deprimierend; **depression** [dɪ'preʃən] *n* (*mood*) Depression *f*; (*Meteo*) Tief *nt*

deprive [dɪ'praɪv] *vt* **to ~ sb of sth** jdn einer Sache berauben; **deprived** *adj* (*child*) (sozial) benachteiligt

dept *abbr* = **department** Abt.

depth [depθ] *n* Tiefe *f*

deputy ['depjʊtɪ] *adj* stellvertretend, Vize- ▷ *n* Stellvertreter(in) *m(f)*; (*US Pol*) Abgeordnete(r) *mf*

derail [dɪ'reɪl] *vt* entgleisen lassen; **to be ~ed** entgleisen

deranged [dɪ'reɪndʒd] *adj* geistesgestört

derivation [derɪ'veɪʃən] *n* Ableitung *f*; **derive** [dɪ'raɪv] *vt* ableiten (*from* von) ▷ abstammen (*from* von)

dermatitis [dɜːməˈtaɪtɪs] n
Hautentzündung f

derogatory [dɪˈrɒgətərɪ] adj abfällig

descend [dɪˈsend] vt, vi hinabsteigen,
hinuntergehen; (person) **to ~ o be ~ed
from** abstammen von; **descendant** n
Nachkomme m; **descent** [dɪˈsent] n
(coming down) Abstieg m; (origin)
Abstammung f

describe [dɪsˈkraɪb] vt beschreiben;
description [dɪsˈkrɪpʃən] n Beschreibung
f

desert [ˈdezət] n Wüste f ▷ [dɪˈzɜːt] vt
verlassen; (abandon) im Stich lassen;
deserted adj verlassen; (empty)
menschenleer

deserve [dɪˈzɜːv] vt verdienen

design [dɪˈzaɪn] n (plan) Entwurf m; (of
vehicle, machine) Konstruktion f; (of object)
Design nt; (planning) Gestaltung f ▷ vt
entwerfen; (machine etc) konstruieren; **~ed
for sb/sth** (intended) für jdn/etw
konzipiert

designate [ˈdezɪgneɪt] vt bestimmen

designer [dɪˈzaɪnə*] n Designer(in) m(f);
(Tech) Konstrukteur(in) m(f); **designer
drug** n Designerdroge f

desirable [dɪˈzaɪərəbl] n wünschenswert;
(person) begehrenswert; **desire** [dɪˈzaɪə*]
n Wunsch m (for nach); (esp sexual)
Begierde f (for nach) ▷ vt wünschen; (ask
for) verlangen; **if ~d** auf Wunsch

desk [desk] n Schreibtisch m; (reception ~)
Empfang m; (at airport etc) Schalter m;
desktop publishing n Desktoppublishing
nt

desolate [ˈdesəlɪt] adj trostlos

despair [dɪsˈpɛə*] n Verzweiflung f (at
über +akk) ▷ vi verzweifeln (of an +dat)

despatch [dɪsˈpætʃ] see dispatch

desperate [ˈdespərɪt] adj verzweifelt;
(situation) hoffnungslos; **to be ~ for sth**
etw dringend brauchen, unbedingt
wollen; **desperation** [despəˈreɪʃən] n
Verzweiflung f

despicable [dɪˈspɪkəbl] adj
verachtenswert; **despise** [dɪsˈpaɪz] vt
verachten

despite [dɪsˈpaɪt] prep trotz +gen

dessert [dɪˈzɜːt] n Nachtisch m;
dessertspoon n Dessertlöffel m

destination [destɪˈneɪʃən] n (of person)
(Reise)ziel nt; (of goods) Bestimmungsort

m; **destine** vt **we're ~d for Hull** wir sind
auf dem Weg nach Hull; **he was ~d to die
young** er sollte früh sterben; **destiny**
[ˈdestɪnɪ] n Schicksal nt

destroy [dɪsˈtrɔɪ] vt zerstören;
(completely) vernichten; **destruction**
[dɪsˈtrʌkʃən] n Zerstörung f; (complete)
Vernichtung f; **destructive** [dɪsˈtrʌktɪv]
adj zerstörerisch; (esp fig) destruktiv

detach [dɪˈtætʃ] vt abnehmen; (from form
etc) abtrennen; (free) lösen (from von);
detachable adj abnehmbar; (from form
etc) abtrennbar; **detached** adj (attitude)
distanziert, objektiv; **~ house** Einzelhaus
nt

detail [ˈdiːteɪl,] (US) [diːˈteɪl] n Einzelheit
f, Detail nt; (**further**) **~s from ...** Näheres
erfahren Sie bei ...; **to go into ~** ins Detail
gehen; **in ~** ausführlich; **detailed** adj
detailliert, ausführlich

detain [dɪˈteɪn] vt aufhalten; (police) in
Haft nehmen

detect [dɪˈtekt] vt entdecken; (notice)
wahrnehmen; **detective** [dɪˈtektɪv] n
Detektiv(in) m(f); **detective story** n
Detektivroman, Krimi m

detention [dɪˈtenʃən] n Haft f; (Sch)
Nachsitzen nt

deter [dɪˈtɜː*] vt abschrecken (from
von)

detergent [dɪˈtɜːdʒənt] n
Reinigungsmittel nt; (soap powder)
Waschmittel nt

deteriorate [dɪˈtɪərɪəreɪt] vi sich
verschlechtern

determination [dɪtɜːmɪˈneɪʃən] n
Entschlossenheit f; **determine** [dɪˈtɜːmɪn]
vt bestimmen; **determined** adj (fest)
entschlossen

deterrent [dɪˈterənt] n
Abschreckungsmittel nt

detest [dɪˈtest] vt verabscheuen;
detestable adj abscheulich

detour [ˈdiːtʊə*] n Umweg m; (of traffic)
Umleitung f

deuce [djuːs] n (Tennis) Einstand m

devalue [diːˈvæljuː] vt abwerten

devastate [ˈdevəsteɪt] vt verwüsten;
devastating [ˈdevəsteɪtɪŋ] adj
verheerend

develop [dɪˈveləp] vt entwickeln; (illness)
bekommen ▷ vi sich entwickeln;
developing country n Entwicklungsland

nt; **development** *n* Entwicklung *f*; (*of land*) Erschließung *f*

device [dɪ'vaɪs] *n* Vorrichtung *f*, Gerät *nt*

devil ['devl] *n* Teufel *m*; **devilish** *adj* teuflisch

devote [dɪ'vəʊt] *vt* widmen (*to dat*); **devoted** *adj* liebend; (*servant etc*) treu ergeben; **devotion** *n* Hingabe *f*

devour [dɪ'vaʊə*] *vt* verschlingen

dew [dju:] *n* Tau *m*

diabetes [daɪə'bi:ti:z] *n* Diabetes *m*, Zuckerkrankheit *f*; **diabetic** [daɪə'betɪk] *adj* zuckerkrank, für Diabetiker ▷ *n* Diabetiker(in) *m(f)*

diagnosis (*diagnoses*) [daɪəg'nəʊsɪs] (*pl* **diagnoses**) *n* Diagnose *f*

diagonal [daɪ'ægənl] *adj* diagonal

diagram ['daɪəgræm] *n* Diagramm *nt*

dial ['daɪəl] *n* Skala *f*; (*of clock*) Zifferblatt *nt* ▷ *vt* (*Tel*) wählen; **dial code** *n* (*US*) Vorwahl *f*

dialect ['daɪəlekt] *n* Dialekt *m*

dialling code *n* (*Brit*) Vorwahl *f*; **dialling tone** *n* (*Brit*) Amtszeichen *nt*

dialogue, dialog (*US*) ['daɪəlɒg] *n* Dialog *m*

dial tone *n* (*US*) Amtszeichen *nt*

dialysis [daɪ'ælɪsɪs] *n* (*Med*) Dialyse *f*

diameter [daɪ'æmɪtə*] *n* Durchmesser *m*

diamond ['daɪəmənd] *n* Diamant *m*; (*Cards*) Karo *nt*

diaper ['daɪpə*] *n* (*US*) Windel *f*

diarrhoea [daɪə'ri:ə] *n* Durchfall *m*

diary ['daɪərɪ] *n* (Taschen)kalender *m*; (*account*) Tagebuch *nt*

dice [daɪs] *npl* Würfel *pl*; **diced** *adj* in Würfel geschnitten

dictate [dɪk'teɪt] *vt* diktieren; **dictation** [dɪk'teɪʃən] *n* Diktat *nt*

dictator [dɪk'teɪtə*] *n* Diktator(in) *m(f)*; **dictatorship** [dɪk'teɪtəʃɪp] *n* Diktatur *f*

dictionary ['dɪkʃənrɪ] *n* Wörterbuch *nt*

did [dɪd] *pt of* **do**

didn't ['dɪdnt] *contr of* **did not**

die [daɪ] *vi* sterben (*of an +dat*); (*plant, animal*) eingehen; (*engine*) absterben; **to be dying to do sth** darauf brennen, etw zu tun; **I'm dying for a drink** ich brauche unbedingt was zu trinken; **die away** *vi* schwächer werden; (*wind*) sich legen; **die down** *vi* nachlassen; **die out** *vi* aussterben

diesel ['di:zəl] *n* (*fuel, car*) Diesel *m*; **~ engine** Dieselmotor *m*

diet ['daɪət] *n* Kost *f*; (*special food*) Diät *f* ▷ *vi* eine Diät machen

differ ['dɪfə*] *vi* (*be different*) sich unterscheiden; (*disagree*) anderer Meinung sein; **difference** ['dɪfrəns] *n* Unterschied *m*; **it makes no ~ (to me)** es ist (mir) egal; **it makes a big ~** es macht viel aus; **different** *adj* andere(r, s); (*with pl*) verschieden; **to be quite ~** ganz anders sein (*from als*); (*two people, things*) völlig verschieden sein; **a ~ person** ein anderer Mensch; **differentiate** [dɪfə'renʃɪeɪt] *vt, vi* unterscheiden; **differently** ['dɪfrəntlɪ] *adv* anders (*from als*); (*from one another*) unterschiedlich

difficult ['dɪfɪkəlt] *adj* schwierig; **I find it ~** es fällt mir schwer; **difficulty** *n* Schwierigkeit *f*; **with ~** nur schwer; **to have ~ in doing sth** etw nur mit Mühe machen können

dig [dɪg] (**dug, dug**) *vt, vi* (*hole*) graben; **dig in** *vi* (*fam: to food*) reinhauen; **~!** greif(t) zu!; **dig up** *vt* ausgraben

digest [daɪ'dʒest] *vt* (*a. fig*) verdauen; **digestible** [dɪ'dʒestəbl] *adj* verdaulich; **digestion** [dɪ'dʒestʃən] *n* Verdauung *f*; **digestive** [dɪ'dʒestɪv] *adj* **~ biscuit** (*Brit*) Vollkornkeks *m*

digit ['dɪdʒɪt] *n* Ziffer *f*; **digital** ['dɪdʒɪtəl] *adj* digital; **~ computer** Digitalrechner *m*; **~ watch/clock** Digitaluhr *f*; **digital camera** *n* Digitalkamera *f*

dignified ['dɪgnɪfaɪd] *adj* würdevoll; **dignity** ['dɪgnɪtɪ] *n* Würde *f*

dilapidated [dɪ'læpɪdeɪtɪd] *adj* baufällig

dilemma [daɪ'lemə] *n* Dilemma *nt*

dill [dɪl] *n* Dill *m*

dilute [daɪ'lu:t] *vt* verdünnen

dim [dɪm] *adj* (*light*) schwach; (*outline*) undeutlich; (*stupid*) schwer von Begriff ▷ *vt* verdunkeln; (*US Auto*) abblenden; **~med headlights** (*US*) Abblendlicht *nt*

dime [daɪm] *n* (*US*) Zehncentstück *nt*

dimension [daɪ'menʃən] *n* Dimension *f*; **~s** *pl* Maße *pl*

diminish [dɪ'mɪnɪʃ] *vt* verringern ▷ *vi* sich verringern

dimple ['dɪmpl] *n* Grübchen *nt*

dine [daɪn] *vi* speisen; **dine out** *vi* außer Haus essen; **diner** *n* Gast *m*; (*Rail*) Speisewagen *m*; (*US*) Speiselokal *nt*

dinghy ['dɪŋgɪ] n Ding(h)i nt; (inflatable) Schlauchboot nt

dingy ['dɪndʒɪ] adj düster; (dirty) schmuddelig

dining car ['daɪnɪŋkɑ:*] n Speisewagen m; **dining room** n Esszimmer nt; (in hotel) Speiseraum m; **dining table** n Esstisch m

dinner ['dɪnə*] n Abendessen nt; (lunch) Mittagessen nt; (public) Diner nt; **to be at ~** beim Essen sein; **to have ~** zu Abend/Mittag essen; **dinner jacket** n Smoking m; **dinner party** n Abendgesellschaft f (mit Essen); **dinnertime** n Essenszeit f

dinosaur ['daɪnəsɔ:*] n Dinosaurier m

dip [dɪp] vt tauchen (in in +akk); **to ~ (one's headlights)** (Brit Auto) abblenden; **~ped headlights** Abblendlicht nt ▷ n (in ground) Bodensenke f; (sauce) Dip m

diploma [dɪ'pləʊmə] n Diplom nt

diplomat ['dɪpləmæt] n Diplomat(in) m(f); **diplomatic** [dɪplə'mætɪk] adj diplomatisch

dipstick ['dɪpstɪk] n Ölmessstab m

direct [daɪ'rekt] adj direkt; (cause, consequence) unmittelbar; **~ debit** (mandate) Einzugsermächtigung f; (transaction) Abbuchung f im Lastschriftverfahren; **~ train** durchgehender Zug ▷ vt (aim, send) richten (at, to an +akk); (film) die Regie führen bei; (traffic) regeln; **direct current** n (Elec) Gleichstrom m

direction [dɪ'rekʃən] n (course) Richtung f; (Cine) Regie f; **in the ~ of ...** in Richtung ...; **~s** pl for use Gebrauchsanweisung f; **~s** pl (to a place) Wegbeschreibung f

directly [dɪ'rektlɪ] adv direkt; (at once) sofort

director [dɪ'rektə*] n Direktor(in) m(f), Leiter(in) m(f); (of film) Regisseur(in) m(f)

directory [dɪ'rektərɪ] n Adressbuch nt; (Tel) Telefonbuch nt; **~ enquiries** o (US) **assistance** (Tel) Auskunft f

dirt [dɜ:t] n Schmutz m, Dreck m; **dirt cheap** adj spottbillig; **dirt road** n unbefestigte Straße; **dirty** adj schmutzig

disability [dɪsə'bɪlɪtɪ] n Behinderung f; **disabled** [dɪs'eɪbld] adj behindert, Behinderten- ▷ npl **the ~** die Behinderten

disadvantage [dɪsəd'vɑ:ntɪdʒ] n Nachteil m; **at a ~** benachteiligt;

disadvantageous [dɪsædvɑ:n'teɪdʒəs] adj nachteilig, ungünstig

disagree [dɪsə'gri:] vi anderer Meinung sein; (two people) sich nicht einig sein; (two reports etc) nicht übereinstimmen; **to ~ with sb** mit jdm nicht übereinstimmen; (food) jdm nicht bekommen; **disagreeable** adj unangenehm; (person) unsympathisch; **disagreement** n Meinungsverschiedenheit f

disappear [dɪsə'pɪə*] vi verschwinden; **disappearance** n Verschwinden nt

disappoint [dɪsə'pɔɪnt] vt enttäuschen; **disappointing** adj enttäuschend; **disappointment** n Enttäuschung f

disapproval [dɪsə'pru:vl] n Missbilligung f; **disapprove** [dɪsə'pru:v] vi missbilligen (of akk)

disarm [dɪs'ɑ:m] vt entwaffnen ▷ vi (Pol) abrüsten; **disarmament** n Abrüstung f; **disarming** adj (smile, look) gewinnend

disaster [dɪ'zɑ:stə*] n Katastrophe f; **disastrous** [dɪ'zɑ:strəs] adj katastrophal

disbelief [dɪsbə'li:f] n Ungläubigkeit f

disc [dɪsk] n Scheibe f, CD f; see also **disk** (Anat) Bandscheibe f; **disc brake** n Scheibenbremse f

discharge ['dɪstʃɑ:dʒ] n (Med) Ausfluss m ▷ [dɪs'tʃɑ:dʒ] vt (person) entlassen; (emit) ausstoßen; (Med) ausscheiden

discipline ['dɪsɪplɪn] n Disziplin f

disc jockey ['dɪskdʒɒkɪ] n Diskjockey m

disclose [dɪs'kləʊz] vt bekannt geben; (secret) enthüllen

disco ['dɪskəʊ] (pl -s) n Disko f, Diskomusik f

discomfort [dɪs'kʌmfət] n (slight pain) leichte Schmerzen pl; (unease) Unbehagen nt

disconnect [dɪskə'nekt] vt (electricity, gas, phone) abstellen; (unplug) **to ~ the TV (from the mains)** den Stecker des Fernsehers herausziehen; (Tel) **I've been ~ed** das Gespräch ist unterbrochen worden

discontent [dɪskən'tent] n Unzufriedenheit f; **discontented** adj unzufrieden

discontinue [dɪskən'tɪnju:] vt einstellen; (product) auslaufen lassen

discotheque ['dɪskəʊtek] n Diskothek f

discount ['dɪskaʊnt] n Rabatt m

discover [dɪsˈkʌvə*] vt entdecken; **discovery** n Entdeckung f
discredit [dɪsˈkredɪt] vt in Verruf bringen ▷ n Misskredit m
discreet [dɪsˈkriːt] adj diskret
discrepancy [dɪsˈkrepənsɪ] n Unstimmigkeit f, Diskrepanz f
discriminate [dɪsˈkrɪmɪneɪt] vi unterscheiden; **to ~ against sb** jdn diskriminieren; **discrimination** [dɪskrɪmɪˈneɪʃən] n (different treatment) Diskriminierung f
discus [ˈdɪskəs] n Diskus m
discuss [dɪsˈkʌs] vt diskutieren, besprechen; **discussion** [dɪsˈkʌʃən] n Diskussion f
disease [dɪˈziːz] n Krankheit f
disembark [dɪsɪmˈbɑːk] vi von Bord gehen
disentangle [ˈdɪsɪnˈtæŋgl] vt entwirren
disgrace [dɪsˈgreɪs] n Schande f ▷ vt Schande machen +dat; (family etc) Schande bringen über +akk; (less strong) blamieren; **disgraceful** adj skandalös; **it's ~** es ist eine Schande
disguise [dɪsˈgaɪz] vt verkleiden; (voice) verstellen ▷ n Verkleidung f; **in ~** verkleidet
disgust [dɪsˈgʌst] n Abscheu m; (physical) Ekel m ▷ vt anekeln, anwidern; **disgusting** adj widerlich; (physically) ekelhaft
dish [dɪʃ] n Schüssel f; (food) Gericht nt; **~es** pl (crockery) Geschirr nt; **to do/wash the ~es** abwaschen; **dishcloth** n (for washing) Spültuch nt; (for drying) Geschirrtuch nt
dishearten [dɪsˈhɑːtən] vt entmutigen; **don't be ~ed** lass den Kopf nicht hängen!
dishonest [dɪsˈɒnɪst] adj unehrlich
dishonour [dɪsˈɒnə*] n Schande f
dish towel n (US) Geschirrtuch nt; **dish washer** n Geschirrspülmaschine f
dishy [ˈdɪʃɪ] adj (Brit fam) klasse, attraktiv
disillusioned [dɪsɪˈluːʒənd] adj desillusioniert
disinfect [dɪsɪnˈfekt] vt desinfizieren; **disinfectant** n Desinfektionsmittel nt
disintegrate [dɪsˈɪntɪgreɪt] vi zerfallen; (group) sich auflösen
disjointed [dɪsˈdʒɔɪntɪd] adj unzusammenhängend

disk [dɪsk] n (Inform: floppy) Diskette f; **disk drive** n Diskettenlaufwerk nt; **diskette** [dɪˈsket] n Diskette f
dislike [dɪsˈlaɪk] n Abneigung f ▷ vt nicht mögen; **to ~ doing sth** etw ungern tun
dislocate [ˈdɪsləʊkeɪt] vt (Med) verrenken, ausrenken
dismal [ˈdɪzməl] adj trostlos
dismantle [dɪsˈmæntl] vt auseinander nehmen; (machine) demontieren
dismay [dɪsˈmeɪ] n Bestürzung f; **dismayed** adj bestürzt
dismiss [dɪsˈmɪs] vt (employee) entlassen; **dismissal** n Entlassung f
disobedience [dɪsəˈbiːdɪəns] n Ungehorsam m; **disobedient** adj ungehorsam; **disobey** [dɪsəˈbeɪ] vt nicht gehorchen +dat
disorder [dɪsˈɔːdə*] n (mess) Unordnung f; (riot) Aufruhr m; (Med) Störung f, Leiden nt
disorganized [dɪsˈɔːgənaɪzd] adj chaotisch
disparaging adj geringschätzig
dispatch [dɪˈspætʃ] vt abschicken, abfertigen
dispensable [dɪˈspensəbl] adj entbehrlich; **dispense** vt verteilen; **dispense with** vt verzichten auf +akk; **dispenser** n Automat m
disperse [dɪˈspɜːs] vi sich zerstreuen
display [dɪˈspleɪ] n (exhibition) Ausstellung f, Show f; (of goods) Auslage f; (Tech) Anzeige f, Display nt ▷ vt zeigen; (goods) ausstellen
disposable [dɪˈspəʊzəbl] adj (container, razor etc) Wegwerf-; **~ nappy** Wegwerfwindel f; **disposal** [dɪˈspəʊzəl] n Loswerden nt; (of waste) Beseitigung f; **to be at sb's ~** jdm zur Verfügung stehen; **dispose of** vt loswerden; (waste etc) beseitigen
dispute [dɪˈspjuːt] n Streit m; (industrial) Auseinandersetzung f ▷ vt bestreiten
disqualification [dɪskwɒlɪfɪˈkeɪʃən] n Disqualifikation f; **disqualify** [dɪsˈkwɒlɪfaɪ] vt disqualifizieren
disregard [dɪsrɪˈgɑːd] vt nicht beachten
disreputable [dɪsˈrepjʊtəbl] adj verrufen
disrespect [dɪsrɪˈspekt] n Respektlosigkeit f
disrupt [dɪsˈrʌpt] vt stören; (interrupt) unterbrechen; **disruption** [dɪsˈrʌpʃən] n Störung f; (interruption) Unterbrechung f

d

dissatisfied [dɪs'sætɪsfaɪd] adj unzufrieden

dissent [dɪ'sent] n Widerspruch m

dissolve [dɪ'zɒlv] vt auflösen ▷ vi sich auflösen

dissuade [dɪ'sweɪd] vt (davon abbringen) **to ~ sb from doing sth** jdn davon abbringen, etw zu tun

distance ['dɪstəns] n Entfernung f; **in the/from a ~** in/aus der Ferne; **distant** adj (a. in time) fern; (relative etc) entfernt; (person) distanziert

distaste [dɪs'teɪst] n Abneigung f (for gegen)

distil [dɪ'stɪl] vt destillieren; **distillery** n Brennerei f

distinct [dɪ'stɪŋkt] adj verschieden; (clear) klar, deutlich; **distinction** [dɪ'stɪŋkʃən] n (difference) Unterschied m; (in exam etc) Auszeichnung f; **distinctive** adj unverkennbar; **distinctly** adv deutlich

distinguish [dɪ'stɪŋgwɪʃ] vt unterscheiden (sth from sth etw von etw)

distort [dɪ'stɔːt] vt verzerren; (truth) verdrehen

distract [dɪ'strækt] vt ablenken; **distraction** [dɪ'strækʃən] n Ablenkung f; (diversion) Zerstreuung f

distress [dɪ'stres] n (need, danger) Not f; (suffering) Leiden nt; (mental) Qual f; (worry) Kummer m ▷ vt mitnehmen, erschüttern; **distressed area** n Notstandsgebiet nt; **distress signal** n Notsignal nt

distribute [dɪ'strɪbjuːt] vt verteilen; (Comm: goods) vertreiben; **distribution** [dɪstrɪ'bjuːʃən] n Verteilung f; (Comm: of goods) Vertrieb m; **distributor** [dɪ'strɪbjʊtə*] n (Auto) Verteiler m; (Comm) Händler(in) m(f)

district ['dɪstrɪkt] n Gegend f; (administrative) Bezirk m; **district attorney** n (US) Staatsanwalt m, Staatsanwältin f

distrust [dɪs'trʌst] vt misstrauen +dat ▷ n Misstrauen nt

disturb [dɪ'stɜːb] vt stören; (worry) beunruhigen; **disturbance** n Störung f; **disturbing** adj beunruhigend

ditch [dɪtʃ] n Graben m ▷ vt (fam: person) den Laufpass geben +dat; (plan etc) verwerfen

ditto ['dɪtəʊ] n dito, ebenfalls

dive [daɪv] n (into water) Kopfsprung m;

(Aviat) Sturzflug m; (fam) zwielichtiges Lokal ▷ vi (under water) tauchen; **diver** n Taucher(in) m(f)

diverse [daɪ'vɜːs] adj verschieden; **diversion** [daɪ'vɜːʃən] n (of traffic) Umleitung f; (distraction) Ablenkung f; **divert** [daɪ'vɜːt] vt ablenken; (traffic) umleiten

divide [dɪ'vaɪd] vt teilen; (in several parts, between people) aufteilen ▷ vi sich teilen; **dividend** ['dɪvɪdend] n Dividende f

divine [dɪ'vaɪn] adj göttlich

diving ['daɪvɪŋ] n (Sport)tauchen nt; (jumping in) Springen nt; (Sport: from board) Kunstspringen nt; **diving board** n Sprungbrett nt; **diving goggles** npl Taucherbrille f; **diving mask** n Tauchmaske f

division [dɪ'vɪʒən] n Teilung f; (Math) Division f; (department) Abteilung f; (Sport) Liga f

divorce [dɪ'vɔːs] n Scheidung f ▷ vt sich scheiden lassen von; **divorced** adj geschieden; **to get ~** sich scheiden lassen; **divorcee** [dɪvɔː'siː] n Geschiedene(r) mf

DIY [diː'aɪwaɪ] abbr = **do-it-yourself**; **DIY centre** n Baumarkt m

dizzy ['dɪzɪ] adj schwindlig

DJ [diː'dʒeɪ] abbr = **dinner jacket** Smoking m ▷ abbr = **disc jockey** Diskjockey m, DJ m

DNA abbr = **desoxyribonucleic acid** DNS f

KEYWORD

do [duː] (pt **did**, pp **done**) n (inf: party etc) Fete f

▷ aux vb **1** (in negative constructions and questions): **I don't understand** ich verstehe nicht; **didn't you know?** wusstest du das nicht?; **what do you think?** was meinen Sie?

2 (for emphasis, in polite phrases): **she does seem rather tired** sie scheint wirklich sehr müde zu sein; **do sit down/help yourself** setzen Sie sich doch hin/greifen Sie doch zu

3 (used to avoid repeating vb): **she swims better than I do** sie schwimmt besser als ich; **she lives in Glasgow — so do I** sie wohnt in Glasgow — ich auch

4 (in tag questions): **you like him, don't you?** du magst ihn doch, oder?

▷ vt **1** (carry out, perform etc) tun machen;

what are you doing tonight? was machst du heute Abend?; **I've got nothing to do** ich habe nichts zu tun; **to do one's hair/nails** sich die Haare/Nägel machen

2 (Aut etc) fahren

▷ vi **1** (act, behave): **do as I do** mach es wie ich

2 (get on, fare): **he's doing well/badly at school** er ist gut/schlecht in der Schule; **how do you do?** guten Tag

3 (be suitable) gehen (be sufficient) reichen; **to make do (with)** auskommen mit;

  do away with vt (kill) umbringen (abolish) (law etc) abschaffen;

  do up vt (laces, dress, buttons) zumachen (renovate) (room, house) renovieren;

  do with vt (need) brauchen (be connected) zu tun haben mit;

  do without vt, vi auskommen ohne

dock [dɒk] n Dock nt; (Jur) Anklagebank f; **docker** n Hafenarbeiter m; **dockyard** n Werft f

doctor ['dɒktə*] n Arzt m, Ärztin; (in title, also academic) Doktor m

document ['dɒkjʊmənt] n Dokument nt; **documentary** [dɒkjʊ'mentərɪ] n Dokumentarfilm m; **documentation** [dɒkjʊmen'teɪʃən] n Dokumentation f

docusoap ['dɒkjʊsəʊp] n Reality-Serie f, Dokusoap f

doddery ['dɒdərɪ] adj tatterig

dodgem ['dɒdʒəm] n Autoscooter m

dodgy ['dɒdʒɪ] adj nicht ganz in Ordnung; (dishonest, unreliable) zwielichtig; **he has a ~ stomach** er hat sich den Magen verdorben

dog [dɒg] n Hund m; **dog food** n Hundefutter nt; **doggie bag** ['dɒgɪ'bæg] n Tüte oder Box, in der Essensreste aus dem Restaurant mit nach Hause genommen werden können

do-it-yourself ['duːɪtjə'self] n Heimwerken nt, Do-it-yourself nt ▷ adj Heimwerker-; **do-it-yourselfer** n Bastler(in) m(f), Heimwerker(in) m(f)

doll [dɒl] n Puppe f

dollar ['dɒlə*] n Dollar m

dolphin ['dɒlfɪn] n Delphin m

domain n Domäne f; (Inform) Domain f

dome [dəʊm] n Kuppel f

domestic [də'mestɪk] adj häuslich; (within country) Innen-, Binnen-; **domestic animal** n Haustier nt; **domesticated** [də'mestɪkeɪtɪd] adj (person) häuslich; (animal) zahm; **domestic flight** n Inlandsflug m

domicile ['dɒmɪsaɪl] n (ständiger) Wohnsitz

dominant ['dɒmɪnənt] adj dominierend, vorherrschend; **dominate** ['dɒmɪneɪt] vt beherrschen

dominoes ['dɒmɪnəʊz] npl Domino(spiel) nt

donate [dəʊ'neɪt] vt spenden; **donation** n Spende f

done [dʌn] pp of do ▷ adj (cooked) gar; **well ~** durchgebraten

doner (kebab) ['dɒnəkə'bæb] n Döner (Kebab) m

donkey ['dɒŋkɪ] n Esel m

donor ['dəʊnə] n Spender(in) m(f)

don't [dəʊnt] contr of do not

doom [duːm] n Schicksal nt; (downfall) Verderben nt

door [dɔː*] n Tür f; **doorbell** n Türklingel f; **door handle** n Türklinke f; **doorknob** n Türknauf m; **doormat** n Fußabtreter m; **doorstep** n Türstufe f; **right on our ~** direkt vor unserer Haustür

dope [dəʊp] (Sport) n (for athlete) Aufputschmittel nt ▷ vt dopen; **dopey** adj (fam) bekloppt; (from drugs) benebelt; (sleepy) benommen

dormitory ['dɔːmɪtrɪ] n Schlafsaal m; (US) Studentenwohnheim nt

dosage ['dəʊsɪdʒ] n Dosierung f; **dose** [dəʊs] n Dosis f ▷ vt dosieren

dot [dɒt] n Punkt m; **on the ~** auf die Minute genau, pünktlich

dotcom ['dɒtkɒm] n **~ (company)** Internetfirma f, Dotcom-Unternehmen nt

dote on [dəʊt ɒn] vt abgöttisch lieben

dotted line n punktierte Linie

double ['dʌbl] adj, adv doppelt; **~ the quantity** die zweifache Menge, doppelt so viel ▷ vt verdoppeln ▷ n (person) Doppelgänger(in) m(f); (Cine) Double nt; **double bass** n Kontrabass m; **double bed** n Doppelbett nt; **double-click** vt (Inform) doppelklicken; **double cream** n Sahne mit hohem Fettgehalt; **doubledecker** n Doppeldecker m; **double glazing** n Doppelverglasung f; **double-park** vi in zweiter Reihe parken; **double room** n

Doppelzimmer *nt*; **doubles** *npl* (*Sport: also match*) Doppel *nt*

doubt [daʊt] *n* Zweifel *m*; **no ~** ohne Zweifel, zweifellos, wahrscheinlich; **to have one's ~s** Bedenken haben ▷ *vt* bezweifeln; (*statement, word*) anzweifeln; **I ~ it** das bezweifle ich; **doubtful** *adj* zweifelhaft, zweifelnd; **it is ~ whether ...** es ist fraglich, ob ...; **doubtless** *adv* ohne Zweifel, sicherlich

dough [dəʊ] *n* Teig *m*; **doughnut** *n* Donut *m* (*rundes Hefegebäck*)

dove [dʌv] *n* Taube *f*

down [daʊn] *n* Daunen *pl*; (*fluff*) Flaum *m* ▷ *adv* unten; (*motion*) nach unten; (*towards speaker*) herunter; (*away from speaker*) hinunter; **~ here/there** hier/dort unten; (*downstairs*) **they came ~ for breakfast** sie kamen zum Frühstück herunter; (*southwards*) **he came ~ from Scotland** er kam von Schottland herunter ▷ *prep* (*towards speaker*) herunter; (*away from speaker*) hinunter; **to drive ~ the hill/road** den Berg/die Straße hinunter fahren; (*along*) **to walk ~ the street** die Straße entlang gehen; **he's ~ the pub** (*fam*) er ist in der Kneipe ▷ *vt* (*fam: drink*) runterkippen ▷ *adj* niedergeschlagen, deprimiert

down-and-out *adj* heruntergekommen ▷ *n* Obdachlose(r) *mf*, Penner(in) *m(f)*; **downcast** *adj* niedergeschlagen; **downfall** *n* Sturz *m*; **down-hearted** *adj* entmutigt; **downhill** *adv* bergab; **he's going ~** (*fig*) mit ihm geht es bergab

● **Downing Street**
●
● **Downing Street** ist die Straße in
● London, die von Whitehall zum St
● James's Park führt, und in der sich
● der offizielle Wohnsitz des
● Premierministers (Nr. 10) und des
● Finanzministers (Nr. 11) befindet. Im
● weiteren Sinne bezieht sich der
● Begriff „Downing Street" auf die
● britische Regierung.

download ['daʊnləʊd] *vt* downloaden, herunterladen; **downmarket** *adj* für den Massenmarkt; **down payment** *n* Anzahlung *f*; **downpour** *n* Platzregen *m*; **downs** *npl* Hügelland *nt*; **downsize** *vt*

(*business*) verkleinern ▷ *vi* sich verkleinern

Down's syndrome ['daʊnz'sɪndrəʊm] *n* (*Med*) Downsyndrom *nt*

downstairs [daʊn'stɛəz] *adv* unten; (*motion*) nach unten; **downstream** *adv* flussabwärts; **downtime** *n* Ausfallzeit *f*; **downtown** *adv* (*be, work etc*) in der Innenstadt; (*go*) in die Innenstadt ▷ *adj* (*US*) in der Innenstadt; **~ Chicago** die Innenstadt von Chicago; **down under** *adv* (*fam: in/to Australia*) in/nach Australien; (*in/to New Zealand*) in/nach Neuseeland; **downwards** *adv, adj* nach unten; (*movement, trend*) Abwärts-

doze [dəʊz] *vi* dösen ▷ *n* Nickerchen *nt*

dozen ['dʌzn] *n* Dutzend *nt*; **two ~ eggs** zwei Dutzend Eier; **~s of times** x-mal

DP *abbr* = **data processing** DV *f*

drab [dræb] *adj* trist; (*colour*) düster

draft [drɑːft] *n* (*outline*) Entwurf *m*; (*US Mil*) Einberufung *f*

drag [dræg] *vt* schleppen ▷ *n* (*fam*) **to be a ~** (*boring*) stinklangweilig sein; (*laborious*) ein ziemlicher Schlauch sein; **drag on** *vi* sich in die Länge ziehen

dragon ['drægən] *n* Drache *m*; **dragonfly** *n* Libelle *f*

drain [dreɪn] *n* Abfluss *m* ▷ *vt* (*water, oil*) ablassen; (*vegetables etc*) abgießen; (*land*) entwässern, trockenlegen ▷ *vi* (*of water*) abfließen; **drainpipe** *n* Abflussrohr *nt*

drama ['drɑːmə] *n* (*a. fig*) Drama *nt*; **dramatic** [drə'mætɪk] *adj* dramatisch

drank [dræŋk] *pt of* **drink**

drapes [dreɪps] *npl* (*US*) Vorhänge *pl*

drastic ['dræstɪk] *adj* drastisch

draught [drɑːft] *n* (Luft)zug *m*; **there's a ~** es zieht; **on ~** (*beer*) vom Fass; **draughts** *nsing* Damespiel *nt*; **draughty** *adj* zugig

draw [drɔː] *n* (**drew, drawn**) *vt* (*pull*) ziehen; (*crowd*) anlocken, anziehen; (*picture*) zeichnen ▷ *vi* (*Sport*) unentschieden spielen ▷ *n* (*Sport*) Unentschieden *nt*; (*attraction*) Attraktion *f*; (*for lottery*) Ziehung *f*; **draw out** *vt* herausziehen; (*money*) abheben; **draw up** *vt* (*formulate*) entwerfen; (*list*) erstellen ▷ *vi* (*car*) anhalten; **drawback** *n* Nachteil *m*; **drawbridge** *n* Zugbrücke *f*

drawer ['drɔː*] *n* Schublade *f*

drawing ['drɔːɪŋ] *n* Zeichnung *f*; **drawing pin** *n* Reißzwecke *f*

drawn [drɔːn] *pp of* **draw**

dread [dred] *n* Furcht *f* (*of* vor +*dat*) ▷ *vt* sich fürchten vor +*dat*; **dreadful** *adj* furchtbar; **dreadlocks** *npl* Rastalocken *pl*

dream [driːm] (**dreamed** *o* **dreamt, dreamed** *o* **dreamt**) *vt, vi* träumen (*about* von) ▷ *n* Traum *m*; **dreamt** [dremt] *pt, pp of* **dream**

dreary ['drɪərɪ] *adj* (*weather, place*) trostlos; (*book etc*) langweilig

drench [drentʃ] *vt* durchnässen

dress [dres] *n* Kleidung *f*; (*garment*) Kleid *nt* ▷ *vt* anziehen; (*Med: wound*) verbinden; **to get ~ed** sich anziehen; **dress up** *vi* sich fein machen; (*in costume*) sich verkleiden (*as* als); **dress circle** *n* (*Theat*) erster Rang; **dresser** *n* Anrichte *f*; (*US: dressing table*) (Frisier)kommode *f*; **dressing** *n* (*Gastr*) Dressing *nt*, Soße *f*; (*Med*) Verband *m*; **dressing gown** *n* Morgenmantel *m*; **dressing room** *n* (*Sport*) Umkleideraum *m*; (*Theat*) Künstlergarderobe *f*; **dressing table** *n* Frisierkommode *f*; **dress rehearsal** *n* (*Theat*) Generalprobe *f*

drew [druː] *pt of* **draw**

dried [draɪd] *adj* getrocknet; (*milk, flowers*) Trocken-; **~ fruit** Dörrobst *nt*; **drier** ['draɪə*] *n see* **dryer**

drift [drɪft] *vi* treiben ▷ *n* (*of snow*) Verwehung *f*; (*fig*) Tendenz *f*; **if you get my ~** wenn du mich richtig verstehst

drill [drɪl] *n* Bohrer *m* ▷ *vt, vi* bohren

drink [drɪŋk] (**drank, drunk**) *vt, vi* trinken ▷ *n* Getränk *nt*; (*alcoholic*) Drink *m*; **drink-driving** *n* (*Brit*) Trunkenheit *f* am Steuer; **drinking water** *n* Trinkwasser *nt*

drip [drɪp] *n* Tropfen *m* ▷ *vi* tropfen; **drip-dry** *adj* bügelfrei; **dripping** *n* Bratenfett *nt* ▷ *adj* **~ (wet)** tropfnass

drive [draɪv] (**drove, driven**) *vt* (*car, person in car*) fahren; (*force: person, animal*) treiben; (*Tech*) antreiben; **to ~ sb mad** jdn verrückt machen ▷ *vi* fahren ▷ *n* Fahrt *f*; (*entrance*) Einfahrt *f*, Auffahrt *f*; (*Inform*) Laufwerk *nt*; **to go for a ~** spazieren fahren; **drive away, drive off** *vi* wegfahren ▷ *vt* vertreiben

drive-in *adj* Drive-in-; **~ cinema** (*US*) Autokino *nt*

driven ['drɪvn] *pp of* **drive**

driver ['draɪvə*] *n* Fahrer(in) *m(f)*; (*Inform*) Treiber *m*; **~'s license** (*US*) Führerschein *m*;

~'s seat Fahrersitz *m*; **driving** ['draɪvɪŋ] *n* (Auto)fahren *nt*; **he likes ~** er fährt gern Auto; **driving lesson** *n* Fahrstunde *f*; **driving licence** *n* (*Brit*) Führerschein *m*; **driving school** *n* Fahrschule *f*; **driving seat** *n* (*Brit*) Fahrersitz *m*; **to be in the ~** alles im Griff haben; **driving test** *n* Fahrprüfung *f*

drizzle ['drɪzl] *n* Nieselregen *m* ▷ *vi* nieseln

drop [drɒp] *n* (*of liquid*) Tropfen *m*; (*fall in price etc*) Rückgang *m* ▷ *vt* (*a. fig: give up*) fallen lassen ▷ *vi* (*fall*) herunterfallen; (*figures, temperature*) sinken, zurückgehen; **drop by, drop in** *vi* vorbeikommen; **drop off** *vi* (*to sleep*) einnicken; **drop out** *vi* (*withdraw*) aussteigen; (*university*) das Studium abbrechen; **dropout** *n* Aussteiger(in) *m(f)*

drought [draʊt] *n* Dürre *f*

drove [drəʊv] *pt of* **drive**

drown [draʊn] *vi* ertrinken ▷ *vt* ertränken

drowsy ['draʊzɪ] *adj* schläfrig

drug [drʌg] *n* (*Med*) Medikament *nt*, Arznei *f*; (*addictive*) Droge *f*; (*narcotic*) Rauschgift *nt*; **to be on ~s** drogensüchtig sein ▷ *vt* (mit Medikamenten) betäuben; **drug addict** *n* Rauschgiftsüchtige(r) *mf*; **drug dealer** *n* Drogenhändler(in) *m(f)*; **druggist** *n* (*US*) Drogist(in) *m(f)*; **drugstore** *n* (*US*) Drogerie *f*

drum [drʌm] *n* Trommel *f*; **~s** *pl* Schlagzeug *nt*; **drummer** *n* Schlagzeuger(in) *m(f)*

drunk [drʌŋk] *pp of* **drink** ▷ *adj* betrunken; **to get ~** sich betrinken ▷ *n* Betrunkene(r) *mf*; (*alcoholic*) Trinker(in) *m(f)*; **drunk-driving** *n* (*US*) Trunkenheit *f* am Steuer; **drunken** *adj* betrunken, besoffen

dry [draɪ] *adj* trocken ▷ *vt* trocknen; (*dishes, oneself, one's hands etc*) abtrocknen ▷ *vi* trocknen, trocken werden; **dry out** *vi* trocknen; **dry up** *vi* austrocknen; **dry-clean** *vt* chemisch reinigen; **dry-cleaning** *n* chemische Reinigung; **dryer** *n* Trockner *m*; (*for hair*) Föhn *m*; (*over head*) Trockenhaube *f*

DTP *abbr* = **desktop publishing** DTP *nt*

dual ['djʊəl] *adj* doppelt; **~ carriageway** (*Brit*) zweispurige Schnellstraße *f*; **~ nationality** doppelte

Staatsangehörigkeit; **dual-purpose** *adj* Mehrzweck-

dubbed [dʌbd] *adj (film)* synchronisiert

dubious ['djuːbɪəs] *adj* zweifelhaft

duchess ['dʌtʃəs] *n* Herzogin *f*

duck [dʌk] *n* Ente *f*

dude [duːd] *n (US fam)* Typ *m*; **a cool ~** ein cooler Typ

due [djuː] *adj (time)* fällig; *(fitting)* angemessen; **in ~ course** zu gegebener Zeit; **~ to** infolge +*gen*, wegen +*gen* ▷ *adv* **~ south/north etc** direkt nach Norden/Süden etc

dug [dʌg] *pt, pp of* **dig**

duke [djuːk] *n* Herzog *m*

dull [dʌl] *adj (colour, light, weather)* trübe; *(boring)* langweilig

duly ['djuːlɪ] *adv* ordnungsgemäß; *(as expected)* wie erwartet

dumb [dʌm] *adj* stumm; *(fam: stupid)* doof, blöde

dumb-bell ['dʌmbel] *n* Hantel *f*

dummy ['dʌmɪ] *n (sham)* Attrappe *f*; *(in shop)* Schaufensterpuppe *f*; *(Brit: teat)* Schnuller *m*; *(fam: person)* Dummkopf *m* ▷ *adj* unecht, Schein-; **~ run** Testlauf *m*

dump [dʌmp] *n* Abfallhaufen *m*; *(fam: place)* Kaff *nt* ▷ *vt (lit, fig)* abladen; *(fam)* **he ~ed her** er hat mir ihr Schluss gemacht

dumpling ['dʌmplɪŋ] *n* Kloß *m*, Knödel *m*

dune [djuːn] *n* Düne *f*

dung [dʌŋ] *n* Dung *m*; *(manure)* Mist *m*

dungarees [dʌŋgə'riːz] *npl* Latzhose *f*

dungeon ['dʌndʒən] *n* Kerker *m*

duplex ['djuːpleks] *n* zweistöckige Wohnung; *(US)* Doppelhaushälfte *f*

duplicate ['djuːplɪkɪt] *n* Duplikat *nt* ▷ ['djuːplɪkeɪt] *vt (make copies of)* kopieren; *(repeat)* wiederholen

durable ['djʊərəbl] *adj* haltbar; **duration** [djʊə'reɪʃən] *n* Dauer *f*

during ['djʊərɪŋ] *prep (time)* während +*gen*

dusk [dʌsk] *n* Abenddämmerung *f*

dust [dʌst] *n* Staub *m* ▷ *vt* abstauben; **dustbin** *n (Brit)* Mülleimer *m*; **dustcart** *n (Brit)* Müllwagen *m*; **duster** *n* Staubtuch *nt*; **dust jacket** *n* Schutzumschlag *m*; **dustman** *n (Brit)* Müllmann *m*; **dustpan** *n* Kehrschaufel *f*; **dusty** *adj* staubig

Dutch [dʌtʃ] *adj* holländisch ▷ *n (language)* Holländisch *nt*; **to speak/talk double ~** *(fam)* Quatsch reden; **the ~** *pl* die Holländer; **Dutchman** *(pl* **-men)** *n*

Holländer *m*; **Dutchwoman** *(pl* **-women)** *n* Holländerin *f*

duty ['djuːtɪ] *n* Pflicht *f*; *(task)* Aufgabe *f*; *(tax)* Zoll *m*; **on/off ~** im Dienst/nicht im Dienst; **to be on ~** Dienst haben; **duty-free** *adj* zollfrei; **~ shop** Dutyfreeshop *m*

duvet ['duːveɪ] *n* Federbett *nt*

DVD *n abbr* = **digital versatile disk** DVD *f*

dwarf [dwɔːf] *(pl* **dwarves)** *n* Zwerg(in) *m(f)*

dwelling ['dwelɪŋ] *n* Wohnung *f*

dwindle ['dwɪndl] *vi* schwinden

dye [daɪ] *n* Farbstoff *m* ▷ *vt* färben

dynamic [daɪ'næmɪk] *adj* dynamisch

dynamo ['daɪnəməʊ] *n* Dynamo *m*

dyslexia [dɪs'leksɪə] *n* Legasthenie *f*; **dyslexic** *adj* legasthenisch; **to be ~** Legastheniker(in) sein

dyspepsia [dɪs'pepsɪə] *n* Verdauungsstörung *f*

e

E [iː] *abbr* = **east** O

E111 form *n* ≈ Auslandskrankenschein *m*

each [iːtʃ] *adj* jeder/jede/jedes ▷ *pron* jeder/jede/jedes; **I'll have one of ~** ich nehme von jedem eins; **they ~ have a car** jeder von ihnen hat ein Auto; **~ other** einander, sich; **for/against ~ other** füreinander/gegeneinander ▷ *adv* je; **they cost 10 euros ~** sie kosten je 10 Euro, sie kosten 10 Euro das Stück

eager [ˈiːgə*] *adj* eifrig; **to be ~ to do sth** darauf brennen, etw zu tun

eagle [ˈiːgl] *n* Adler *m*

ear [ɪə*] *n* Ohr *nt*; **earache** *n* Ohrenschmerzen *pl*; **eardrum** *n* Trommelfell *nt*

earl [ɜːl] *n* Graf *m*

early [ˈɜːlɪ] *adj, adv* früh; **to be 10 minutes ~** 10 Minuten zu früh kommen; **at the earliest** frühestens; **in ~ June/2008** Anfang Juni/2008; **~ retirement** vorzeitiger Ruhestand; **~ warning system** Frühwarnsystem *nt*

earn [ɜːn] *vt* verdienen

earnest [ˈɜːnɪst] *adj* ernst; **in ~** im Ernst

earnings [ˈɜːnɪŋz] *npl* Verdienst *m*, Einkommen *nt*

earphones [ˈɪəfəʊnz] *npl* Kopfhörer *m*; **earplug** *n* Ohrenstöpsel *m*, Ohropax® *nt*; **earring** *n* Ohrring *m*

earth [ɜːθ] *n* Erde *f*; **what on ~ ...?** was in aller Welt ...? ▷ *vt* erden; **earthenware** *n* Tonwaren *pl*; **earthquake** *n* Erdbeben *nt*

earwig [ˈɪəwɪg] *n* Ohrwurm *m*

ease [iːz] *vt* (*pain*) lindern; (*burden*) erleichtern ▷ *n* (*easiness*) Leichtigkeit *f*; **to feel at ~** sich wohl fühlen; **to feel ill at ~** sich nicht wohl fühlen; **easily** [ˈiːzɪlɪ] *adv* leicht; **he is ~ the best** er ist mit Abstand der Beste

east [iːst] *n* Osten *m*; **to the ~ of** östlich von ▷ *adv* (*go, face*) nach Osten ▷ *adj* Ost-; **~ wind** Ostwind *m*; **eastbound** *adj* (in) Richtung Osten

Easter [ˈiːstə*] *n* Ostern *nt*; **at ~** zu Ostern; **Easter egg** *n* Osterei *nt*; **Easter Sunday** *n* Ostersonntag *m*

eastern [ˈiːstən] *adj* Ost-, östlich; **Eastern Europe** Osteuropa *nt*; **East Germany** *n* Ostdeutschland *nt*; **former ~** die ehemalige DDR, die neuen Bundesländer; **eastwards** [ˈiːstwədz] *adv* nach Osten

easy [ˈiːzɪ] *adj* leicht; (*task, solution*) einfach; (*life*) bequem; (*manner*) ungezwungen; **easy-care** *adj* pflegeleicht; **easy-going** *adj* gelassen

eat [iːt] (**ate, eaten**) *vt* essen; (*animal*) fressen; **eat out** *vi* zum Essen ausgehen; **eat up** *vt* aufessen; (*animal*) auffressen

eaten [ˈiːtn] *pp of* **eat**

eavesdrop [ˈiːvzdrɒp] *vi* (heimlich) lauschen; **to ~ on sb** jdn belauschen

eccentric [ɪkˈsentrɪk] *adj* exzentrisch

echo [ˈekəʊ] (*pl* **-es**) *n* Echo *nt* ▷ *vi* widerhallen

ecological [iːkəˈlɒdʒɪkl] *adj* ökologisch; **~ disaster** Umweltkatastrophe *f*; **ecology** [ɪˈkɒlədʒɪ] *n* Ökologie *f*

economic [iːkəˈnɒmɪk] *adj* wirtschaftlich, Wirtschafts-; **~ aid** Wirtschaftshilfe *f*; **economical** *adj* wirtschaftlich; (*person*) sparsam; **economics** *nsing o pl* Wirtschaftswissenschaft *f*; **economist** [ɪˈkɒnəmɪst] *n* Wirtschaftswissenschaftler(in) *m(f)*; **economize** [ɪˈkɒnəmaɪz] *vi* sparen (**on** an +*dat*); **economy** [ɪˈkɒnəmɪ] *n* (*of state*)

Wirtschaft f; (thrift) Sparsamkeit f;
economy class n (Aviat) Economyclass f
ecstasy ['ekstəsɪ] n Ekstase f; (drug)
Ecstasy f
eczema ['eksɪmə] n Ekzem nt
edge [edʒ] n Rand m; (of knife) Schneide f;
on ~ nervös; **edgy** ['edʒɪ] adj nervös
edible ['edɪbl] adj essbar
Edinburgh ['edɪnbərə] n Edinburg nt
edit ['edɪt] vt (series, newspaper etc)
herausgeben; (text) redigieren; (film)
schneiden; (Inform) editieren; **edition**
[ɪ'dɪʃən] n Ausgabe f; **editor** n
Redakteur(in) m(f); (of series etc)
Herausgeber(in) m(f); **editorial**
[edɪ'tɔːrɪəl] adj Redaktions- ▷ n
Leitartikel m
educate ['edjʊkeɪt] vt (child) erziehen; (at
school, university) ausbilden; (public)
aufklären; **educated** adj gebildet;
education [edjʊ'keɪʃən] n Erziehung f;
(studies, training) Ausbildung f; (subject of
study) Pädagogik f; (system) Schulwesen nt;
(knowledge) Bildung f; **educational** adj
pädagogisch; (instructive) lehrreich;
~ television Schulfernsehen nt
eel [iːl] n Aal m
eerie ['ɪərɪ] adj unheimlich
effect [ɪ'fekt] n Wirkung f (on auf +akk); **to
come into ~** in Kraft treten; **effective** adj
wirksam, effektiv
effeminate [ɪ'femɪnət] adj (of man)
tuntig
efficiency [ɪ'fɪʃənsɪ] n Leistungsfähigkeit
f; (of method) Wirksamkeit f; **efficient** adj
(Tech) leistungsfähig; (method) wirksam,
effizient
effort ['efət] n Anstrengung f; (attempt)
Versuch m; **to make an ~** sich anstrengen;
effortless adj mühelos
eg abbr = **exempli gratia (for example)** z.
B.
egg [eg] n Ei nt; **eggcup** n Eierbecher m;
eggplant n (US) Aubergine f; **eggshell** n
Eierschale f
ego ['iːgəʊ] (pl **-s**) n Ich nt; (self-esteem)
Selbstbewusstsein nt; **ego(t)ist**
['egəʊ(t)ɪst] n Egozentriker(in) m(f)
Egypt ['iːdʒɪpt] n Ägypten nt; **Egyptian**
[ɪ'dʒɪpʃən] adj ägyptisch ▷ n Ägypter(in)
m(f)
eiderdown ['aɪdədaʊn] n Daunendecke f
eight [eɪt] num acht; **at the age of ~** im

Alter von acht Jahren; **it's ~** (o'clock) es ist
acht Uhr ▷ n (a. bus etc) Acht f; (boat)
Achter m; **eighteen** [eɪ'tiːn] num
achtzehn ▷ n Achtzehn f; see also **eight**;
eighteenth adj achtzehnte(r, s); see also
eighth; **eighth** [eɪtθ] adj achte(r, s); **the
~ of June** der achte Juni ▷ n (fraction)
Achtel nt; **an ~ of a litre** ein Achtelliter;
eightieth ['eɪtɪəθ] adj achtzigste(r, s); see
also **eighth**; **eighty** ['eɪtɪ] num achtzig
▷ n Achtzig f; see also **eight**
Eire ['ɛərə] n die Republik Irland
either ['aɪðə*] conj **~ ... or** entweder ...
oder ▷ pron **~ of the two** eine(r, s) von
beiden ▷ adj **on ~ side** auf beiden Seiten
▷ adv **I won't go ~** ich gehe auch nicht
eject [ɪ'dʒekt] vt ausstoßen; (person)
vertreiben
elaborate [ɪ'læbərət] adj (complex)
kompliziert; (plan) ausgeklügelt;
(decoration) kunstvoll ▷ vi [ɪ'læbəreɪt]
could you ~ on that? könntest du mehr
darüber sagen?
elastic [ɪ'læstɪk] adj elastisch; **~ band**
Gummiband nt
elbow ['elbəʊ] n Ellbogen m
elder ['eldə*] adj (of two) älter ▷ n
Ältere(r) mf; (Bot) Holunder m; **elderly** adj
ältere(r, s) ▷ n **the ~** die älteren Leute;
eldest ['eldɪst] adj älteste(r, s)
elect [ɪ'lekt] vt wählen; **he was ~ed
chairman** er wurde zum Vorsitzenden
gewählt; **election** [ɪ'lekʃən] n Wahl f;
election campaign n Wahlkampf m;
electioneering [ɪlekʃə'nɪərɪŋ] n
Wahlpropaganda f; **electorate** [ɪ'lektərɪt]
n Wähler pl
electric [ɪ'lektrɪk] adj elektrisch; (car,
motor, razor etc) Elektro-; **~ blanket**
Heizdecke f; **~ cooker** Elektroherd m;
~ current elektrischer Strom; **~ shock**
Stromschlag m; **electrical** adj elektrisch;
~ goods/appliances Elektrogeräte;
electrician [ɪlek'trɪʃən] n Elektriker(in)
m(f); **electricity** [ɪlek'trɪsɪtɪ] n
Elektrizität f; **electrocute** [ɪ'lektrəʊkjuːt]
vt durch einen Stromschlag töten;
electronic [ɪlek'trɒnɪk] adj elektronisch
elegance ['elɪgəns] n Eleganz f; **elegant**
adj elegant
element ['elɪmənt] n Element nt; **an ~ of
truth** ein Körnchen Wahrheit;
elementary [elɪ'mentərɪ] adj einfach;

(*basic*) grundlegend; **~ stage**
Anfangsstadium *nt*; **~ school** (*US*)
Grundschule *f*; **~ maths/French**
Grundkenntnisse in
Mathematik/Französisch

elephant ['elɪfənt] *n* Elefant *m*

elevator ['elɪveɪtə*] *n* (*US*) Fahrstuhl *m*

eleven [ɪ'levn] *num* elf ▷ *n* (*team, bus etc*)
Elf *f see* **eight**; **eleventh** [ɪ'levnθ] *adj*
elfte(r, s) ▷ *n* (*fraction*) Elftel *nt see* **eighth**

eligible ['elɪdʒəbl] *adj* in Frage kommend;
(*for grant etc*) berechtigt; **~ for a**
pension/competition
pensions-/teilnahmeberechtigt;
~ bachelor begehrter Junggeselle

eliminate [ɪ'lɪmɪneɪt] *vt* ausschließen
(*from* aus), ausschalten; (*problem etc*)
beseitigen; **elimination** *n* Ausschluss *m*
(*from* aus); (*of problem etc*) Beseitigung *f*

elm [elm] *n* Ulme *f*

elope [ɪ'ləʊp] *vi* durchbrennen (*with sb* mit
jdm)

eloquent ['eləkwənt] *adj* redegewandt

else [els] *adv* **anybody/anything ~** (*in*
addition) sonst (noch) jemand/etwas;
(*other*) ein anderer/etwas anderes;
somebody ~ jemand anders; **everyone**
~ alle anderen; **or ~** sonst; **elsewhere** *adv*
anderswo, woanders; (*direction*)
woandershin

ELT *abbr* = **English Language Teaching**

e-mail, E-mail ['i:meɪl] *vi, vt* mailen (*sth*
to sb jdm etw) ▷ *n* E-Mail *f*; **e-mail**
address *n* E-Mail-Adresse *f*

emancipated [ɪ'mænsɪpeɪtɪd] *adj*
emanzipiert

embankment [ɪm'bæŋkmənt] *n*
Böschung *f*; (*for railway*) Bahndamm *m*

embargo [ɪm'bɑ:gəʊ] (*pl* **-es**) *n* Embargo
nt

embark [ɪm'bɑ:k] *vi* an Bord gehen

embarrass [ɪm'bærəs] *vt* in Verlegenheit
bringen; **embarrassed** *adj* verlegen;
embarrassing *adj* peinlich

embassy ['embəsɪ] *n* Botschaft *f*

embrace [ɪm'breɪs] *vt* umarmen ▷ *n*
Umarmung *f*

embroider [ɪm'brɔɪdə*] *vt* besticken;
embroidery *n* Stickerei *f*

embryo ['embrɪəʊ] (*pl* **-s**) *n* Embryo *m*

emerald ['emərəld] *n* Smaragd *m*

emerge [ɪ'mɜ:dʒ] *vi* auftauchen; **it ~d**
that ... es stellte sich heraus, dass ...

emergency [ɪ'mɜ:dʒənsɪ] *n* Notfall *m*
▷ *adj* Not-; **~ exit** Notausgang *m*; **~ room**
(*US*) Unfallstation *f*; **~ service** Notdienst
m; **~ stop** Vollbremsung *f*

emigrate ['emɪgreɪt] *vi* auswandern

emit [ɪ'mɪt] *vt* ausstoßen; (*heat*) abgeben

emotion [ɪ'məʊʃən] *n* Emotion *f*, Gefühl
nt; **emotional** *adj* (*person*) emotional;
(*experience, moment, scene*) ergreifend

emperor ['empərə*] *n* Kaiser *m*

emphasis ['emfəsɪs] *n* Betonung *f*;
emphasize ['emfəsaɪz] *vt* betonen;
emphatic, emphatically [ɪm'fætɪk, -lɪ]
adj, adv nachdrücklich

empire ['empaɪə*] *n* Reich *nt*

employ [ɪm'plɔɪ] *vt* beschäftigen; (*hire*)
anstellen; (*use*) anwenden; **employee**
[emplɔɪ'i:] *n* Angestellte(r) *mf*; **employer**
n Arbeitgeber(in) *m(f)*; **employment** *n*
Beschäftigung *f*; (*position*) Stellung *f*;
employment agency *n*
Stellenvermittlung *f*

empress ['emprɪs] *n* Kaiserin *f*

empty ['emptɪ] *adj* leer ▷ *vt* (*contents*)
leeren; (*container*) ausleeren

enable [ɪ'neɪbl] *vt* **to ~ sb to do sth** es
jdm ermöglichen, etw zu tun

enamel [ɪ'næməl] *n* Email *nt*; (*of teeth*)
Zahnschmelz *m*

enchanting [ɪn'tʃɑ:ntɪŋ] *adj* bezaubernd

enclose [ɪn'kləʊz] *vt* einschließen; (*in*
letter) beilegen (*in, with* dat); **enclosure**
[ɪn'kləʊʒə*] *n* (*for animals*) Gehege *nt*; (*in*
letter) Anlage *f*

encore ['ɒŋkɔ:*] *n* Zugabe *f*

encounter [ɪn'kaʊntə*] *n* Begegnung *f*
▷ *vt* (*person*) begegnen +dat; (*difficulties*)
stoßen auf +akk

encourage [ɪn'kʌrɪdʒ] *vt* ermutigen;
encouragement *n* Ermutigung *f*

encyclopaedia [ensaɪkləʊ'pi:dɪə] *n*
Lexikon *nt*, Enzyklopädie *f*

end [end] *n* Ende *nt*; (*of film, play etc*)
Schluss *m*; (*purpose*) Zweck *m*; **at the ~ of**
May Ende Mai; **in the ~** schließlich; **to**
come to an ~ zu Ende gehen ▷ *vt*
beenden ▷ *vi* enden; **end up** *vi* enden

endanger [ɪn'deɪndʒə*] *vt* gefährden;
~ed species vom Aussterben bedrohte Art

endeavour [ɪn'devə*] *n* Bemühung *f* ▷ *vt*
sich bemühen (*to do sth* etw zu tun)

ending ['endɪŋ] *n* (*of book*) Ausgang *m*;
(*last part*) Schluss *m*; (*of word*) Endung *f*

endive ['endaɪv] *n* Endiviensalat *m*
endless ['endlɪs] *adj* endlos; (*possibilities*)
unendlich
endurance [ɪn'djʊərəns] *n* Ausdauer *f*;
endure [ɪn'djʊə*] *vt* ertragen
enemy ['enɪmɪ] *n* Feind(in) *m(f)* ▷ *adj*
feindlich
energetic [enə'dʒetɪk] *adj*
energiegeladen; (*active*) aktiv; **energy**
['enədʒɪ] *n* Energie *f*
enforce [ɪn'fɔːs] *vt* durchsetzen;
(*obedience*) erzwingen
engage [ɪn'geɪdʒ] *vt* (*employ*) einstellen;
(*singer, performer*) engagieren; **engaged**
adj verlobt; (*toilet, telephone line*) besetzt;
to get ~ sich verloben (*to* mit); **engaged**
tone *n* (*Brit Tel*) Belegtzeichen *nt*;
engagement *n* (*to marry*) Verlobung *f*;
~ ring Verlobungsring *m*; **engaging** *adj*
gewinnend
engine ['endʒɪn] *n* (*Auto*) Motor *m*; (*Rail*)
Lokomotive *f*; **~ failure** (*Auto*)
Motorschaden *m*; **~ trouble** (*Auto*) Defekt
m am Motor; **engineer** [endʒɪ'nɪə*] *n*
Ingenieur(in) *m(f)*; (*US Rail*)
Lokomotivführer(in) *m(f)*; **engineering**
[endʒɪ'nɪərɪŋ] *n* Technik *f*; (*mechanical ~*)
Maschinenbau *m*; (*subject*)
Ingenieurwesen *nt*; **engine immobilizer** *n*
(*Auto*) Wegfahrsperre *f*
England ['ɪŋglənd] *n* England *nt*; **English**
adj englisch; **he's ~** er ist Engländer; **the**
~ Channel der Ärmelkanal ▷ *n* (*language*)
Englisch *nt*; **in ~** auf Englisch; **to translate**
into ~ ins Englische übersetzen; (*people*)
the ~ *pl* die Engländer; **Englishman** (*pl*
-men) *n* Engländer *m*; **Englishwoman** (*pl*
-women) *n* Engländerin *f*
engrave [ɪn'greɪv] *vt* eingravieren;
engraving *n* Stich *m*
engrossed [ɪn'grəʊst] *adj* vertieft (*in sth*
in etw *akk*)
enigma [ɪ'nɪgmə] *n* Rätsel *nt*
enjoy [ɪn'dʒɔɪ] *vt* genießen; **I ~ reading**
ich lese gern; **he ~s teasing her** es macht
ihm Spaß, sie aufzuziehen; **did you ~ the**
film? hat dir der Film gefallen?; **enjoyable**
adj angenehm; (*entertaining*)
unterhaltsam; **enjoyment** *n* Vergnügen
nt; (*stronger*) Freude *f* (*of* an +*dat*)
enlarge [ɪn'lɑːdʒ] *vt* vergrößern; (*expand*)
erweitern; **enlargement** *n* Vergrößerung
f

enormous, enormously [ɪ'nɔːməs, -lɪ]
adj, adv riesig, ungeheuer
enough [ɪ'nʌf] *adj* genug; **that's ~** das
reicht!; (*stop it*) Schluss damit!; **I've had**
~ das hat mir gereicht; (*to eat*) ich bin satt
▷ *adv* genug, genügend
enquire [ɪn'kwaɪə*] *vi* sich erkundigen
(*about* nach); **enquiry** [ɪn'kwaɪərɪ] *n*
(*question*) Anfrage *f*; (*for information*)
Erkundigung *f* (*about* über +*akk*);
(*investigation*) Untersuchung *f*; **'Enquiries'**
„Auskunft"
enrol [ɪn'rəʊl] *vi* sich einschreiben; (*for*
course, school) sich anmelden; **enrolment**
n Einschreibung *f*, Anmeldung *f*
en suite [ɒn'swiːt] *adj, n* **room with**
~ (*bathroom*) Zimmer *nt* mit eigenem Bad
ensure [ɪn'ʃʊə*] *vt* sicherstellen
enter ['entə*] *vt* eintreten in +*akk*,
betreten; (*drive into*) einfahren in +*akk*;
(*country*) einreisen in +*akk*; (*in list*)
eintragen; (*Inform*) eingeben; (*race, contest*)
teilnehmen an +*dat* ▷ *vi* (*towards speaker*)
hereinkommen; (*away from speaker*)
hineingehen
enterprise ['entəpraɪz] *n* (*Comm*)
Unternehmen *nt*
entertain [entə'teɪn] *vt* (*guest*) bewirten;
(*amuse*) unterhalten; **entertaining** *adj*
unterhaltsam; **entertainment** *n*
(*amusement*) Unterhaltung *f*
enthusiasm [ɪn'θjuːzɪæzəm] *n*
Begeisterung *f*; **enthusiastic**
[ɪnθjuːzɪ'æstɪk] *adj* begeistert (*about* von)
entice [ɪn'taɪs] *vt* locken; (*lead astray*)
verleiten
entire, entirely [ɪn'taɪə*, -lɪ] *adj, adv* ganz
entitle [ɪn'taɪtl] *vt* (*qualify*) berechtigen
(*to* zu); (*name*) betiteln
entrance ['entrəns] *n* Eingang *m*; (*for*
vehicles) Einfahrt *f*; (*entering*) Eintritt *m*;
(*Theat*) Auftritt *m*; **entrance exam** *n*
Aufnahmeprüfung *f*; **entrance fee** *n*
Eintrittsgeld *nt*
entrust [ɪn'trʌst] *vt* **to ~ sb with sth** jdm
etw anvertrauen
entry ['entrɪ] *n* (*way in*) Eingang *m*;
(*entering*) Eintritt *m*; (*in vehicle*) Einfahrt *f*;
(*into country*) Einreise *f*; (*admission*) Zutritt
m; (*in diary, accounts*) Eintrag *m*; **'no ~'**
„Eintritt verboten"; (*for vehicles*) „Einfahrt
verboten"; **entry phone** *n*
Türsprechanlage *f*

E-number n (food additive) E-Nummer f
envelope ['envələʊp] n (Brief)umschlag m
enviable ['enviəbl] adj beneidenswert; **envious** ['enviəs] adj neidisch
environment [ɪn'vaɪərənmənt] n Umgebung f; (ecology) Umwelt f; **environmental** [ɪnvaɪərən'mentəl] adj Umwelt-; **~ pollution** Umweltverschmutzung f; **environmentalist** n Umweltschützer(in) m(f)
envy ['envɪ] n Neid m (of auf +akk) ▷ vt beneiden (sb sth jdn um etw)
epic ['epɪk] n Epos nt; (film) Monumentalfilm m
epidemic [epɪ'demɪk] n Epidemie f
epilepsy [epɪ'lepsɪ] n Epilepsie f; **epileptic** [epɪ'leptɪk] adj epileptisch
episode ['epɪsəʊd] n Episode f; (Tv) Fortsetzung f, Folge f
epoch ['iːpɒk] n Zeitalter nt, Epoche f
equal ['iːkwl] adj gleich (to +dat) ▷ n Gleichgestellte(r) mf ▷ vt gleichen; (match) gleichkommen +dat; **two times two ~s four** zwei mal zwei ist gleich vier; **equality** [ɪ'kwɒlɪtɪ] n Gleichheit f; (equal rights) Gleichberechtigung f; **equalize** vi (Sport) ausgleichen; **equalizer** n (Sport) Ausgleichstreffer m; **equally** adv gleich; (on the other hand) andererseits; **equation** [ɪ'kweɪʒən] n (Math) Gleichung f
equator [ɪ'kweɪtə*] n Äquator m
equilibrium [iːkwɪ'lɪbrɪəm] n Gleichgewicht nt
equip [ɪ'kwɪp] vt ausrüsten; (kitchen) ausstatten; **equipment** n Ausrüstung f; (for kitchen) Ausstattung f; **electrical ~** Elektrogeräte pl
equivalent [ɪ'kwɪvələnt] adj gleichwertig (to dat); (corresponding) entsprechend (to dat) ▷ n Äquivalent nt; (amount) gleiche Menge; (in money) Gegenwert m
era ['ɪərə] n Ära f, Zeitalter nt
erase [ɪ'reɪz] vt ausradieren; (tape, disk) löschen; **eraser** n Radiergummi m
erect [ɪ'rekt] adj aufrecht ▷ vt (building, monument) errichten; (tent) aufstellen; **erection** n Errichtung f; (Anat) Erektion f
erode [ɪ'rəʊd] vt zerfressen; (land) auswaschen; (rights, power) aushöhlen; **erosion** [ɪ'rəʊʒən] n Erosion f

erotic [ɪ'rɒtɪk] adj erotisch
err [ɜː*] vi sich irren
errand ['erənd] n Besorgung f
erratic [ɪ'rætɪk] adj (behaviour) unberechenbar; (bus link etc) unregelmäßig; (performance) unbeständig
error ['erə*] n Fehler m; **in ~** irrtümlicherweise; **error message** n (Inform) Fehlermeldung f
erupt [ɪ'rʌpt] vi ausbrechen
escalator ['eskəleɪtə*] n Rolltreppe f
escalope ['eskələp] n Schnitzel nt
escape [ɪ'skeɪp] n Flucht f; (from prison etc) Ausbruch m; **to have a narrow ~** gerade noch davonkommen; **there's no ~** (fig) es gibt keinen Ausweg ▷ vt (pursuers) entkommen +dat; (punishment etc) entgehen +dat ▷ vi (from pursuers) entkommen (from dat); (from prison etc) ausbrechen (from dat); (leak: gas) ausströmen; (water) auslaufen
escort ['eskɔːt] n (companion) Begleiter(in) m(f); (guard) Eskorte f ▷ vt [ɪ'skɔːt] (lady) begleiten
especially [ɪ'speʃəlɪ] adv besonders
espionage ['espiəna:ʒ] n Spionage f
Esquire [ɪ'skwaɪə*] n (Brit: in address) **J. Brown, Esq** Herrn J. Brown
essay ['eseɪ] n Aufsatz m; (literary) Essay m
essential [ɪ'senʃəl] adj (necessary) unentbehrlich, unverzichtbar; (basic) wesentlich ▷ n **the ~s** pl das Wesentliche; **essentially** adv im Wesentlichen
establish [ɪ'stæblɪʃ] vt (set up) gründen; (introduce) einführen; (relations) aufnehmen; (prove) nachweisen; **to ~ that ...** feststellen, dass ...; **establishment** n Institution f; (business) Unternehmen nt
estate [ɪ'steɪt] n Gut nt; (of deceased) Nachlass m; (housing ~) Siedlung f; (country house) Landsitz m; **estate agent** n (Brit) Grundstücksmakler(in) m(f), Immobilienmakler(in) m(f); **estate car** n (Brit) Kombiwagen m
estimate ['estɪmət] n Schätzung f; (Comm: of price) Kostenvoranschlag m ▷ ['estɪmeɪt] vt schätzen
estuary ['estjʊərɪ] n Mündung f
etching ['etʃɪŋ] n Radierung f
eternal, **eternally** [ɪ'tɜːnl, -nəlɪ] adj, adv ewig; **eternity** n Ewigkeit f

ethical ['eθɪkəl] *adj* ethisch; **ethics**
['eθɪks] *npl* Ethik *f*
Ethiopia [iːθɪ'əʊpɪə] *n* Äthiopien *nt*
ethnic ['eθnɪk] *adj* ethnisch; (*clothes etc*)
landesüblich; **~ minority** ethnische
Minderheit
EU *abbr* = **European Union** EU *f*
euphemism ['juːfɪmɪzəm] *n*
Euphemismus *m*
euro ['jʊərəʊ] (*pl* **-s**) *n* (*Fin*) Euro *m*;
~ symbol Eurozeichen *nt*; **Eurocheque**
['jʊərəʊtʃek] *n* Euroscheck *m*; **Europe**
['jʊərəp] *n* Europa *nt*; **European**
[jʊərə'piːən] *adj* europäisch;
~ Parliament Europäisches Parlament;
~ Union Europäische Union ⊳ *n*
Europäer(in) *m(f)*; **Eurosceptic**
['jʊərəʊskeptɪk] *n* Euroskeptiker(in) *m(f)*;
Eurotunnel *n* Eurotunnel *m*
evacuate [ɪ'vækjʊeɪt] *vt* (*place*) räumen;
(*people*) evakuieren
evade [ɪ'veɪd] *vt* ausweichen +*dat*;
(*pursuers*) sich entziehen +*dat*
evaluate [ɪ'væljʊeɪt] *vt* auswerten
evaporate [ɪ'væpəreɪt] *vi* verdampfen;
(*fig*) verschwinden; **~d milk**
Kondensmilch *f*
even ['iːvən] *adj* (*flat*) eben; (*regular*)
gleichmäßig; (*equal*) gleich; (*number*)
gerade; **the score is ~** es steht
unentschieden ⊳ *adv* sogar; **~ you** selbst
(*o* sogar) du; **~ if** selbst wenn, wenn auch;
~ though obwohl; **not ~** nicht einmal;
~ better noch besser; **even out** *vi* (*prices*)
sich einpendeln
evening ['iːvnɪŋ] *n* Abend *m*; **in the**
~ abends, am Abend; **this ~** heute Abend;
evening class *n* Abendkurs *m*; **evening**
dress *n* (*generally*) Abendkleidung *f*;
(*woman's*) Abendkleid *nt*
evenly ['iːvənlɪ] *adv* gleichmäßig
event [ɪ'vent] *n* Ereignis *nt*; (*organized*)
Veranstaltung *f*; (*Sport: discipline*) Disziplin
f; **in the ~ of** im Falle +*gen*; **eventful** *adj*
ereignisreich
eventual [ɪ'ventʃʊəl] *adj* (*final*)
letztendlich; **eventually** [ɪ'ventʃʊəlɪ] *adv*
(*at last*) am Ende; (*given time*) schließlich
ever ['evə*] *adv* (*at any time*) je(mals);
don't ~ do that again tu das ja nie
wieder; **he's the best ~** er ist der Beste,
den es je gegeben hat; **have you ~ been**
to the States? bist du schon einmal in den

Staaten gewesen?; **for ~** (für) immer; **for**
~ and ~ auf immer und ewig; **~ so ...** (*fam*)
äußerst ...; **~ so drunk** ganz schön
betrunken
every ['evrɪ] *adj* jeder/jede/jedes; **~ day**
jeden Tag; **~ other day** jeden zweiten Tag;
~ five days alle fünf Tage; **I have ~ reason**
to believe that ... ich habe allen Grund
anzunehmen, dass ...; **everybody** *pron*
jeder, alle *pl*; **everyday** *adj* (*commonplace*)
alltäglich; (*clothes, language etc*) Alltags-;
everyone *pron* jeder, alle *pl*; **everything**
pron alles; **everywhere** *adv* überall; (*with*
direction) überallhin
evidence ['evɪdəns] *n* Beweise *pl*; (*single*
piece) Beweis *m*; (*testimony*) Aussage *f*;
(*signs*) Spuren *pl*; **evident, evidently** *adj*,
adv offensichtlich
evil ['iːvl] *adj* böse ⊳ *n* Böse(s) *nt*; **an ~** ein
Übel
evolution [iːvə'luːʃən] *n* Entwicklung *f*;
(*of life*) Evolution *f*; **evolve** [ɪ'vɒlv] *vi* sich
entwickeln
ex- [eks] *pref* Ex-, ehemalig; **~wife** frühere
Frau, Exfrau *f*; **ex** *n* (*fam*) Verflossene(r)
mf, Ex *mf*
exact [ɪg'zækt] *adj* genau; **exactly** *adv*
genau; **not ~ fast** nicht gerade schnell
exaggerate [ɪg'zædʒəreɪt] *vt, vi*
übertreiben; **exaggerated** *adj*
übertreiben; **exaggeration** *n*
Übertreibung *f*
exam [ɪg'zæm] *n* Prüfung *f*; **examination**
[ɪgzæmɪ'neɪʃən] *n* (*Med etc*) Untersuchung
f, Prüfung *f*; (*at university*) Examen *nt*; (*at*
customs etc) Kontrolle *f*; **examine**
[ɪg'zæmɪn] *vt* untersuchen (*for* auf +*akk*);
(*check*) kontrollieren, prüfen; **examiner** *n*
Prüfer(in) *m(f)*
example [ɪg'zɑːmpl] *n* Beispiel *nt*; **for**
~ zum Beispiel
excavation [ekskə'veɪʃən] *n* Ausgrabung
f
exceed [ɪk'siːd] *vt* überschreiten,
übertreffen; **exceedingly** *adv* äußerst
excel [ɪk'sel] *vt* übertreffen; **he ~led**
himself er hat sich selbst übertroffen ⊳ *vi*
sich auszeichnen (*in* in +*dat*, *at* bei);
excellent, excellently ['eksələnt, -lɪ] *adj*,
adv ausgezeichnet
except [ɪk'sept] *prep* **~** außer +*dat*; **~ for**
abgesehen von ⊳ *vt* ausnehmen;
exception [ɪk'sepʃən] *n* Ausnahme *f*;

exceptional, exceptionally [ɪkˈsepʃənl, -nəlɪ] *adj, adv* außergewöhnlich

excess [ekˈses] *n* Übermaß *nt* (*of* an +*dat*); **excess baggage** *n* Übergepäck *nt*; **excesses** *npl* Exzesse *pl*; (*drink, sex*) Ausschweifungen *pl*; **excess fare** *n* Nachlösegebühr *f*; **excessive, excessively** *adj, adv* übermäßig; **excess weight** *n* Übergewicht *nt*

exchange [ɪksˈtʃeɪndʒ] *n* Austausch *m* (*for* gegen); (*of bought items*) Umtausch *m* (*for* gegen); (*Fin*) Wechsel *m*; (*Tel*) Vermittlung *f*, Zentrale *f* ▷ *vt* austauschen; (*goods*) tauschen; (*bought items*) umtauschen (*for* gegen); (*money, blows*) wechseln; **exchange rate** *n* Wechselkurs *m*

excite [ɪkˈsaɪt] *vt* erregen; **excited** *adj* aufgeregt; **to get ~** sich aufregen; **exciting** *adj* aufregend; (*book, film*) spannend

exclamation [ekskləˈmeɪʃən] *n* Ausruf *m*; **exclamation mark, exclamation point** (*US*) *n* Ausrufezeichen *nt*

exclude [ɪksˈkluːd] *vt* ausschließen; **exclusion** [ɪksˈkluːʒən] *n* Ausschluss *m*; **exclusive** [ɪksˈkluːsɪv] *adj* (*select*) exklusiv; (*sole*) ausschließlich; **exclusively** *adv* ausschließlich

excrement [ˈekskrɪmənt] *n* Kot *m*, Exkremente *pl*

excruciating [ɪksˈkruːʃɪeɪtɪŋ] *adj* fürchterlich, entsetzlich

excursion [ɪksˈkɜːʃən] *n* Ausflug *m*

excusable [ɪksˈkjuːzəbl] *adj* entschuldbar; **excuse** [ɪksˈkjuːz] *vt* entschuldigen; **~ me** Entschuldigung!; **to ~ sb for sth** jdm etw verzeihen; **to ~ sb from sth** jdn von etw befreien ▷ [ɪksˈkjuːs] *n* Entschuldigung *f*, Ausrede *f*

ex-directory [eksdaɪˈrektərɪ] *adj* **to be ~** (*Brit Tel*) nicht im Telefonbuch stehen

execute [ˈeksɪkjuːt] *vt* (*carry out*) ausführen; (*kill*) hinrichten; **execution** *n* (*killing*) Hinrichtung *f*; (*carrying out*) Ausführung *f*; **executive** [ɪgˈzekjʊtɪv] *n* (*Comm*) leitender Angestellter, leitende Angestellte

exemplary [ɪgˈzemplərɪ] *adj* beispielhaft

exempt [ɪgˈzempt] *adj* befreit (*from* von) ▷ *vt* befreien

exercise [ˈeksəsaɪz] *n* (*in school, sports*) Übung *f*; (*movement*) Bewegung *f*; **to get more ~** mehr Sport treiben; **exercise bike** *n* Heimtrainer *m*; **exercise book** *n* Heft *nt*

exert [ɪgˈzɜːt] *vt* (*influence*) ausüben

exhaust [ɪgˈzɔːst] *n* (*fumes*) Abgase *pl*; (*Auto*) Auspuff *m*; **exhausted** *adj* erschöpft; **exhausting** *adj* anstrengend

exhibit [ɪgˈzɪbɪt] *n* (*in exhibition*) Ausstellungsstück *nt*; **exhibition** [eksɪˈbɪʃən] *n* Ausstellung *f*; **exhibitor** *n* Aussteller(in) *m(f)*

exhilarating [ɪgˈzɪləreɪtɪŋ] *adj* belebend, erregend

exile [ˈeksaɪl] *n* Exil *nt*; (*person*) Verbannte(r) *mf* ▷ *vt* verbannen

exist [ɪgˈzɪst] *vi* existieren; (*live*) leben (*on* von); **existence** *n* Existenz *f*; **to come into ~** entstehen; **existing** *adj* bestehend

exit [ˈeksɪt] *n* Ausgang *m*; (*for vehicles*) Ausfahrt *f*; **exit poll** *n* Umfrage direkt nach dem Wahlgang

exorbitant [ɪgˈzɔːbɪtənt] *adj* astronomisch

exotic [ɪgˈzɒtɪk] *adj* exotisch

expand [ɪksˈpænd] *vt* ausdehnen, erweitern ▷ *vi* sich ausdehnen; **expansion** [ɪksˈpænʃən] *n* Expansion *f*, Erweiterung *f*

expect [ɪksˈpekt] *vt* erwarten; (*suppose*) annehmen; **he ~s me to do it** er erwartet, dass ich es mache; **I ~ it'll rain** es wird wohl regnen; **I ~ so** ich denke schon ▷ *vi* **to be ~ing** ein Kind erwarten

expedition [ekspɪˈdɪʃən] *n* Expedition *f*

expenditure [ɪkˈspendɪtʃə*] *n* Ausgaben *pl*

expense [ɪkˈspens] *n* Kosten *pl*; (*single cost*) Ausgabe *f*; (**business**) **~s** *pl* Spesen *pl*; **at sb's ~** auf jds Kosten; **expensive** [ɪkˈspensɪv] *adj* teuer

experience [ɪkˈspɪərɪəns] *n* Erfahrung *f*; (*particular incident*) Erlebnis *nt*; **by/from ~** aus Erfahrung ▷ *vt* erfahren, erleben; (*hardship*) durchmachen; **experienced** *adj* erfahren

experiment [ɪkˈsperɪmənt] *n* Versuch *m*, Experiment *nt* ▷ *vi* experimentieren

expert [ˈekspɜːt] *n* Experte *m*, Expertin *f*; (*professional*) Fachmann *m*, Fachfrau *f*; (*Jur*) Sachverständige(r) *mf* ▷ *adj* fachmännisch; **expertise** [ekspəˈtiːz] *n* Sachkenntnis *f*

expire [ɪkˈspaɪə*] *vi* (*end*) ablaufen; **expiry date** [ɪkˈspaɪərɪdeɪt] *n* Verfallsdatum *nt*

explain [ɪkˈspleɪn] vt erklären (*sth to sb*
jdm etw); **explanation** [ekspləˈneɪʃən] n
Erklärung f
explicit [ɪkˈsplɪsɪt] adj ausdrücklich,
deutlich
explode [ɪkˈspləʊd] vi explodieren
exploit [ɪkˈsplɔɪt] vt ausbeuten
explore [ɪkˈsplɔː*] vt erforschen
explosion [ɪkˈspləʊʒən] n Explosion f;
explosive [ɪkˈspləʊsɪv] adj explosiv ▷ n
Sprengstoff m
export [ekˈspɔːt] vt, vi exportieren
▷ [ˈekspɔːt] n Export m ▷ adj (*trade*)
Export-
expose [ɪkˈspəʊz] vt (*to danger etc*)
aussetzen (*to dat*); (*uncover*) freilegen;
(*imposter*) entlarven; **exposed** adj
(*position*) ungeschützt; **exposure**
[ɪkˈspəʊʒə*] n (*Med*) Unterkühlung f; (*Foto:
time*) Belichtung(szeit) f; **24 ~s** 24
Aufnahmen
express [ɪkˈspres] adj (*speedy*) Express-,
Schnell-; **~ delivery** Eilzustellung f ▷ n
(*Rail*) Schnellzug m ▷ vt ausdrücken ▷ vr
to ~ oneself sich ausdrücken; **expression**
[ɪkˈspreʃən] n (*phrase*) Ausdruck m; (*look*)
Gesichtsausdruck m; **expressive** adj
ausdrucksvoll; **expressway** n (*US*)
Schnellstraße f
extend [ɪkˈstend] vt (*arms*) ausstrecken;
(*lengthen*) verlängern; (*building*)
vergrößern, ausbauen; (*business, limits*)
erweitern; **extension** [ɪkˈstenʃən] n
(*lengthening*) Verlängerung f; (*of building*)
Anbau m; (*Tel*) Anschluss m; (*of
business, limits*) Erweiterung f;
extensive [ɪkˈstensɪv] adj (*knowledge*)
umfangreich; (*use*) häufig; **extent**
[ɪkˈstent] n (*length*) Länge f; (*size*)
Ausdehnung f; (*scope*) Umfang m, Ausmaß
nt; **to a certain/large ~** in
gewissem/hohem Maße
exterior [ekˈstɪərɪə*] n Äußere(s) nt
external [ekˈstɜːnl] adj äußere(r, s),
Außen-; **externally** adv äußerlich
extinct [ɪkˈstɪŋkt] adj (*species*)
ausgestorben
extinguish [ɪkˈstɪŋgwɪʃ] vt löschen;
extinguisher n Löschgerät nt
extra [ˈekstrə] adj zusätzlich; **~ charge**
Zuschlag m; **~ time** (*Sport*) Verlängerung f
▷ adv besonders; **~ large** (*clothing*)
übergroß ▷ npl **~s** zusätzliche Kosten pl;

(*food*) Beilagen pl; (*accessories*) Zubehör nt;
(*for car etc*) Extras pl
extract [ɪkˈstrækt] vt herausziehen (*from
aus*); (*tooth*) ziehen ▷ [ˈekstrækt] n (*from
book etc*) Auszug m
extraordinary [ɪkˈstrɔːdnrɪ] adj
außerordentlich; (*unusual*) ungewöhnlich;
(*amazing*) erstaunlich
extreme [ɪkˈstriːm] adj äußerste(r, s);
(*drastic*) extrem ▷ n Extrem nt; **extremely**
adv äußerst, höchst; **extreme sports** npl
Extremsportarten pl; **extremist**
[ɪkˈstriːmɪst] adj extremistisch ▷ n
Extremist m
extricate [ˈekstrɪkeɪt] vt befreien (*from
aus*)
extrovert [ˈekstrəʊvɜːt] adj extrovertiert
exuberance [ɪgˈzuːbərəns] n
Überschwang m; **exuberant** adj
überschwänglich
exultation [egzʌlˈteɪʃən] n Jubel m
eye [aɪ] n Auge nt; **to keep an ~ on sb/sth**
auf jdn/etw aufpassen ▷ vt mustern;
eyebrow n Augenbraue f; **eyelash** n
Wimper f; **eyelid** n Augenlid nt; **eyeliner**
n Eyeliner m; **eyeopener** n **that was an
~** das hat mir die Augen geöffnet;
eyeshadow n Lidschatten m; **eyesight** n
Sehkraft f; **eyesore** n Schandfleck m; **eye
witness** n Augenzeuge m, Augenzeugin f

f

fabric ['fæbrɪk] *n* Stoff *m*
fabulous ['fæbjʊləs] *adj* sagenhaft
façade [fə'sɑːd] *n* (*a. fig*) Fassade *f*
face [feɪs] *n* Gesicht *nt*; (*of clock*)
Zifferblatt *nt*; (*of mountain*) Wand *f*; **in the
~ of** trotz +*gen*; **to be ~ to ~** (*people*)
einander gegenüberstehen ▷ *vt, vi*
(*person*) gegenüberstehen +*dat*; (*at table*)
gegenübersitzen +*dat*; **to ~ north** (*room*)
nach Norden gehen; **to ~** (**up to**) **the
facts** den Tatsachen ins Auge sehen; **to
be ~d with sth** mit etw konfrontiert
sein; **face cream** *n* Gesichtscreme *f*;
face lift *n* Gesichtsstraffung *f*; (*fig*)
Verschönerung *f*; **face powder** *n*
Gesichtspuder *m*
facet ['fæsɪt] *n* (*fig*) Aspekt *m*
face value *n* Nennwert *m*
facial ['feɪʃəl] *adj* Gesichts- ▷ *n* (*fam*)
(kosmetische) Gesichtsbehandlung
facilitate [fə'sɪlɪteɪt] *vt* erleichtern
facility [fə'sɪlɪtɪ] *n* (*building etc to be used*)
Einrichtung *f*, Möglichkeit *f*; (*installation*)
Anlage *f*; (*skill*) Gewandtheit *f*
fact [fækt] *n* Tatsache *f*; **as a matter of ~,
in ~** eigentlich, tatsächlich
factor ['fæktə*] *n* Faktor *m*

factory ['fæktərɪ] *n* Fabrik *f*; **factory
outlet** *n* Fabrikverkauf *m*
factual ['fæktjʊəl] *adj* sachlich
faculty ['fækəltɪ] *n* Fähigkeit *f*; (*at
university*) Fakultät *f*; (*US: teaching staff*)
Lehrkörper *m*
fade [feɪd] *vi* (*a. fig*) verblassen; **faded** *adj*
verblasst, verblichen
faff about ['fæfəbaʊt] *vi* (*Brit fam*)
herumwursteln
fag [fæg] *n* (*Brit fam: cigarette*) Kippe *f*; (*US
fam pej*) Schwule(r) *m*
Fahrenheit ['færənhaɪt] *n* Fahrenheit
fail [feɪl] *vt* (*exam*) nicht bestehen ▷ *vi*
versagen; (*plan, marriage*) scheitern;
(*student*) durchfallen; (*eyesight*)
nachlassen; **words ~ me** ich bin sprachlos;
failing *n* Schwäche *f*; **failure** ['feɪljə*] *n*
(*person*) Versager(in) *m(f)*; (*act*) (*a. Tech*)
Versagen *nt*; (*of engine etc*) Ausfall *m*; (*of
plan, marriage*) Scheitern *nt*
faint [feɪnt] *adj* schwach; (*sound*) leise;
(*fam*) **I haven't the ~est** (**idea**) ich habe
keine Ahnung ▷ *vi* ohnmächtig werden
(*with* vor +*dat*); **faintness** *n* (*Med*)
Schwächegefühl *nt*
fair [fɛə*] *adj* (*hair*) blond; (*skin*) hell; (*just*)
gerecht, fair; (*reasonable*) ganz ordentlich;
(*in school*) befriedigend; (*weather*) schön;
(*wind*) günstig; **a ~ number/amount of**
ziemlich viele/viel ▷ *adv* **to play ~** fair
spielen; (*fig*) fair sein; **~ enough** in
Ordnung! ▷ *n* (*fun~*) Jahrmarkt *m*; (*Comm*)
Messe *f*; **fair-haired** *adj* blond; **fairly** *adv*
(*honestly*) fair; (*rather*) ziemlich
fairy ['fɛərɪ] *n* Fee *f*; **fairy tale** *n* Märchen
nt
faith [feɪθ] *n* (*trust*) Vertrauen *nt* (*in sb* zu
jdm); (*Rel*) Glaube *m*; **faithful, faithfully**
adj, adv treu; **Yours ~ly** Hochachtungsvoll
fake [feɪk] *n* (*thing*) Fälschung *f* ▷ *adj*
vorgetäuscht ▷ *vt* fälschen
falcon ['fɔːlkən] *n* Falke *m*
fall [fɔːl] (**fell, fallen**) *vi* fallen; (*from a
height, badly*) stürzen; **to ~ ill** krank
werden; **to ~ asleep** einschlafen; **to ~ in
love** sich verlieben ▷ *n* Fall *m*; (*accident,
fig: of regime*) Sturz *m*; (*decrease*) Sinken *nt*
(*in* +*gen*); (*US: autumn*) Herbst *m*; **fall apart**
vi auseinanderfallen; **fall behind** *vi*
zurückbleiben; (*with work, rent*) in
Rückstand geraten; **fall down** *vi* (*person*)
hinfallen; **fall off** *vi* herunterfallen;

(*decrease*) zurückgehen; **fall out** *vi*
herausfallen; (*quarrel*) sich streiten; **fall
over** *vi* hinfallen; **fall through** *vi* (*plan
etc*) ins Wasser fallen

fallen ['fɔ:lən] *pp of* **fall**

fallout ['fɔ:laʊt] *n* radioaktiver
Niederschlag, Fall-out *m*

false [fɔ:ls] *adj* falsch; (*artificial*)
künstlich; **false alarm** *n* blinder Alarm;
false start *n* (*Sport*) Fehlstart *m*; **false
teeth** *npl* (künstliches) Gebiss

fame [feɪm] *n* Ruhm *m*

familiar [fə'mɪlɪə*] *adj* vertraut, bekannt;
to be ~ with vertraut sein mit, gut
kennen; **familiarity** [fəmɪlɪ'ærɪtɪ] *n*
Vertrautheit *f*

family ['fæmɪlɪ] *n* Familie *f*; (*including
relations*) Verwandtschaft *f*; **family man** *n*
Familienvater *m*; **family name** *n*
Familienname *m*, Nachname *m*

famine ['fæmɪn] *n* Hungersnot *f*;
famished ['fæmɪʃt] *adj* (*fam*)
ausgehungert

famous ['feɪməs] *adj* berühmt

fan [fæn] *n* (*hand-held*) Fächer *m*; (*Elec*)
Ventilator *m*; (*admirer*) Fan *m*

fanatic [fə'nætɪk] *n* Fanatiker(in) *m(f)*

fancy ['fænsɪ] *adj* (*elaborate*) kunstvoll;
(*unusual*) ausgefallen ▷ *vt* (*like*) gern
haben; **he fancies her** er steht auf sie;
~ that stell dir vor!, so was!; **fancy dress**
n Kostüm *nt*, Verkleidung *f*

fan heater ['fænhi:tə*] *n* Heizlüfter *m*;
fanlight *n* Oberlicht *nt*

fan mail *n* Fanpost *f*

fantasise ['fæntəsaɪz] *vi* träumen (*about*
von); **fantastic** [fæn'tæstɪk] *adj* (*a. fam*)
fantastisch; **that's ~** (*fam*) das ist ja toll!;
fantasy ['fæntəzɪ] *n* Fantasie *f*

far [fɑ:*] (**further** *o* **farther, furthest** *o*
farthest) *adj* weit; **the ~ end of the room**
das andere Ende des Zimmers; **the Far
East** der Ferne Osten ▷ *adv* weit; **~ better**
viel besser; **by ~ the best** bei weitem
der/die/das Beste; **as ~ as ...** bis zum *o* zur
...; (*with place name*) bis nach ...; **as ~ as I'm
concerned** was mich betrifft, von mir aus;
so ~ soweit, bisher; **faraway** *adj* weit
entfernt; (*look*) verträumt

fare [fɛə*] *n* Fahrpreis *m*; (*money*) Fahrgeld
nt

farm [fɑ:m] *n* Bauernhof *m*, Farm *f*;
farmer *n* Bauer *m*, Bäuerin *f*,

Landwirt(in) *m(f)*; **farmhouse** *n*
Bauernhaus *nt*; **farming** *n*
Landwirtschaft *f*; **farmland** *n* Ackerland
nt; **farmyard** *n* Hof *m*

far-reaching ['fɑ:ri:tʃɪŋ] *adj* weit
reichend; **far-sighted** *adj* weitsichtig;
(*fig*) weitblickend

farther ['fɑ:ðə*] *adj, adv* comparative of
far; *see* **further**

farthest ['fɑ:ðɪst] *adj, adv* superlative of
far; *see* **furthest**

fascinating ['fæsɪneɪtɪŋ] *adj*
faszinierend; **fascination** *n* Faszination *f*

fascism ['fæʃɪzəm] *n* Faschismus *m*;
fascist ['fæʃɪst] *adj* faschistisch
▷ *n* Faschist(in) *m(f)*

fashion ['fæʃən] *n* (*clothes*) Mode *f*;
(*manner*) Art (und Weise) *f*; **to be in ~** (in)
Mode sein; **out of ~** unmodisch;
fashionable, fashionably *adj, adv*
(*clothes, person*) modisch; (*author, pub etc*) in
Mode

fast [fɑ:st] *adj* schnell; (*dye*) waschecht;
to be ~ (*clock*) vorgehen ▷ *adv* schnell;
(*firmly*) fest; **to be ~ asleep** fest schlafen
▷ *n* Fasten *nt* ▷ *vi* fasten; **fastback** *n*
(*Auto*) Fließheck *nt*

fasten ['fɑ:sn] *vt* (*attach*) befestigen (*to
an +dat*); (*do up*) zumachen; **~ your
seatbelts** bitte anschnallen; **fastener,
fastening** *n* Verschluss *m*

fast food *n* Fast Food *nt*; **fast forward** *n*
(*for tape*) Schnellvorlauf *m*; **fast lane** *n*
Überholspur *f*

fat [fæt] *adj* dick; (*meat*) fett ▷ *n* (*Anat,
Gastr, Chem*) Fett *nt*

fatal ['feɪtl] *adj* tödlich

fate [feɪt] *n* Schicksal *nt*

fat-free *adj* (*food*) fettfrei

father ['fɑ:ðə*] *n* Vater *m*; (*priest*) Pfarrer
m ▷ *vt* (*child*) zeugen; **Father Christmas**
n der Weihnachtsmann; **father-in-law** (*pl*
fathers-in-law) *n* Schwiegervater *m*

fatigue [fə'ti:g] *n* Ermüdung *f*

fattening ['fætnɪŋ] *adj* **to be ~** dick
machen; **fatty** ['fætɪ] *adj* (*food*) fettig

faucet ['fɔ:sɪt] *n* (*US*) Wasserhahn *m*

fault [fɔ:lt] *n* Fehler *m*; (*Tech*) Defekt *m*;
(*Elec*) Störung *f*; (*blame*) Schuld *f*; **it's your
~** du bist daran schuld; **faulty** *adj*
fehlerhaft; (*Tech*) defekt

favor (*US*), **favour** ['feɪvə*] *n* (*approval*)
Gunst *f*; (*kindness*) Gefallen *m*; **in ~ of** für;

I'm in ~ (of going) ich bin dafür(, dass wir gehen); **to do sb a ~** jdm einen Gefallen tun ▷ vt (prefer) vorziehen; **favourable** adj günstig (to, for für); **favourite** ['feɪvərɪt] n Liebling m, Favorit(in) m(f) ▷ adj Lieblings-

fax [fæks] vt faxen ▷ n Fax nt; **fax number** n Faxnummer f

faze [feɪz] vt (fam) aus der Fassung bringen

FBI abbr = **Federal Bureau of Investigation** FBI nt

fear [fɪə*] n Angst f (of vor +dat) ▷ vt befürchten; **I ~ that most** davor habe ich am meisten Angst; **fearful** adj (timid) ängstlich, furchtsam; (terrible) fürchterlich; **fearless** adj furchtlos

feasible ['fi:zəbl] adj machbar

feast [fi:st] n Festessen nt

feather ['feðə*] n Feder f

feature ['fi:tʃə*] n (facial) (Gesichts)zug m; (characteristic) Merkmal nt; (of car etc) Ausstattungsmerkmal nt; (in the press) (Cine) Feature nt ▷ vt bringen, (als Besonderheit) zeigen; **feature film** n Spielfilm m

February ['februərɪ] n Februar m; see also **September**

fed [fed] pt, pp of **feed**

federal ['fedərəl] adj Bundes-; **the Federal Republic of Germany** die Bundesrepublik Deutschland

fed-up [fed'ʌp] adj **to be ~ with sth** etw satt haben; **I'm ~** ich habe die Nase voll

fee [fi:] n Gebühr f; (of doctor, lawyer) Honorar nt

feeble ['fi:bl] adj schwach

feed [fi:d] (**fed, fed**) vt (baby, animal) füttern; (support) ernähren ▷ n (for baby) Mahlzeit f; (for animals) Futter nt; (Inform: paper ~) Zufuhr f; **feed in** vt (information) eingeben; **feedback** n (information) Feed-back nt

feel [fi:l] (**felt, felt**) vt (sense) fühlen; (pain) empfinden; (touch) anfassen; (think) meinen ▷ vi (person) sich fühlen; **I ~ cold** mir ist kalt; **do you ~ like a walk?** hast du Lust, spazieren zu gehen?; **feeling** n Gefühl nt

feet [fi:t] pl of **foot**

fell [fel] pt of **fall** ▷ vt (tree) fällen

fellow ['feləʊ] n Kerl m, Typ m; **~ citizen** Mitbürger(in) m(f); **~ countryman** Landsmann m; **~ worker** Mitarbeiter(in) m(f)

felt [felt] pt, pp of **feel** ▷ n Filz m; **felt tip, felt-tip pen** n Filzstift m

female ['fi:meɪl] n (of animals) Weibchen nt ▷ adj weiblich; **~ doctor** Ärztin f; **~ dog** Hündin f; **feminine** ['femɪnɪn] adj weiblich; **feminist** ['femɪnɪst] n Feminist(in) m(f) ▷ adj feministisch

fence [fens] n Zaun m

fencing n (Sport) Fechten nt

fender ['fendə*] n (US Auto) Kotflügel m

fennel ['fenl] n Fenchel m

fern [fɜ:n] n Farn m

ferocious [fə'rəʊʃəs] adj wild

ferry ['ferɪ] n Fähre f ▷ vt übersetzen

fertile ['fɜ:taɪl] adj fruchtbar; **fertility** [fə'tɪlɪtɪ] n Fruchtbarkeit f; **fertilize** ['fɜ:tɪlaɪz] vt (Bio) befruchten; (Agr: land) düngen; **fertilizer** n Dünger m

festival ['festɪvəl] n (Rel) Fest nt; (Art, Mus) Festspiele pl; (pop music) Festival nt; **festive** ['festɪv] adj festlich; **festivities** [fe'stɪvɪtɪz] n Feierlichkeiten pl

fetch [fetʃ] vt holen; (collect) abholen; (in sale, money) einbringen; **fetching** adj reizend

fetish ['fetɪʃ] n Fetisch m

fetus ['fi:təs] n (US) Fötus m

fever ['fi:və*] n Fieber nt; **feverish** adj (Med) fiebrig; (fig) fieberhaft

few [fju:] adj, pron pl wenige pl; **a ~** pl ein paar; **fewer** adj weniger; **fewest** adj wenigste(r, s)

fiancé [fɪ'ã:nseɪ] n Verlobte(r) m; **fiancée** n Verlobte f

fiasco [fɪ'æskəʊ] (pl -s o US -es) n Fiasko nt

fiber (US), **fibre** ['faɪbə*] n Faser f; (material) Faserstoff m

fickle ['fɪkl] adj unbeständig

fiction ['fɪkʃən] n (novels) Prosaliteratur f; **fictional, fictitious** [fɪk'tɪʃəs] adj erfunden

fiddle ['fɪdl] n Geige f; (trick) Betrug m ▷ vt (accounts, results) frisieren; **fiddle with** vt herumfummeln an +dat; **fiddly** adj knifflig

fidelity [fɪ'delɪtɪ] n Treue f

fidget ['fɪdʒɪt] vi zappeln; **fidgety** adj zappelig

field [fi:ld] n Feld nt; (grass-covered) Wiese f; (fig: of work) (Arbeits)gebiet nt

fierce [fɪəs] *adj* heftig; (*animal, appearance*) wild; (*criticism, competition*) scharf

fifteen [fɪfˈtiːn] *num* fünfzehn ▷ *n* Fünfzehn *f*; *see also* **eight**; **fifteenth** *adj* fünfzehnte(r, s); *see also* **eighth**; **fifth** [fɪfθ] *adj* fünfte(r, s) ▷ *n* (*fraction*) Fünftel *nt*; *see also* **eighth**; **fifty** [ˈfɪftɪ] *num* fünfzig ▷ *n* Fünfzig *f*; *see also* **eight**; **fiftieth** *adj* fünfzigste(r, s); *see also* **eighth**

fig [fɪg] *n* Feige *f*

fight [faɪt] (**fought, fought**) *vi* kämpfen (*with, against* gegen, *for, over* um) ▷ *vt* (*person*) kämpfen mit; (*fig: disease, fire etc*) bekämpfen ▷ *n* Kampf *m*; (*brawl*) Schlägerei *f*; (*argument*) Streit *m*; **fight back** *vi* zurückschlagen; **fight off** *vt* abwehren; **fighter** *n* Kämpfer(in) *m(f)*

figurative [ˈfɪgərətɪv] *adj* übertragen

figure [ˈfɪgə*] *n* (*person*) Gestalt *f*; (*of person*) Figur *f*; (*number*) Zahl *f*, Ziffer *f*; (*amount*) Betrag *m*; **a four-figure sum** eine vierstellige Summe ▷ *vt* (*US: think*) glauben ▷ *vi* (*appear*) erscheinen; **figure out** *vt* (*work out*) herausbekommen; **I can't figure him out** ich werde aus ihm nicht schlau; **figure skating** *n* Eiskunstlauf *m*

file [faɪl] *n* (*tool*) Feile *f*; (*dossier*) Akte *f*; (*Inform*) Datei *f*; (*folder*) Aktenordner *m*; **on ~** in den Akten ▷ *vt* (*metal, nails*) feilen; (*papers*) ablegen (*under* unter) ▷ *vi* **to ~ in/out** hintereinander hereinkommen/hinausgehen; **filing cabinet** *n* Aktenschrank *m*

fill [fɪl] *vt* füllen; (*tooth*) plombieren; (*post*) besetzen; **fill in** *vt* (*hole*) auffüllen; (*form*) ausfüllen; (*tell*) informieren (*on* über); **fill out** *vt* (*form*) ausfüllen; **fill up** *vi* (*Auto*) voll tanken

fillet [ˈfɪlɪt] *n* Filet *nt*

filling [ˈfɪlɪŋ] *n* (*Gastr*) Füllung *f*; (*for tooth*) Plombe *f*; **filling station** *n* Tankstelle *f*

film [fɪlm] *n* Film *m* ▷ *vt* (*scene*) filmen; **film star** *n* Filmstar *m*; **film studio** *n* Filmstudio *nt*

filter [ˈfɪltə*] *n* Filter *m*; (*traffic lane*) Abbiegespur *f* ▷ *vt* filtern

filth [fɪlθ] *n* Dreck *m*; **filthy** *adj* dreckig

fin [fɪn] *n* Flosse *f*

final [ˈfaɪnl] *adj* letzte(r, s); (*stage, round*) End-; (*decision, version*) endgültig; **~ score**

Schlussstand *m* ▷ *n* (*Sport*) Endspiel *nt*; (*competition*) Finale *nt*; **~s** *pl* Abschlussexamen *nt*; **finalize** *vt* die endgültige Form geben +*dat*; **finally** *adv* (*lastly*) zuletzt; (*eventually*) schließlich, endlich

finance [faɪˈnæns] *n* Finanzwesen *nt*; **~s** *pl* Finanzen *pl* ▷ *vt* finanzieren; **financial** [faɪˈnænʃəl] *adj* finanziell; (*adviser, crisis, policy etc*) Finanz-

find [faɪnd] (**found, found**) *vt* finden; **he was found dead** er wurde tot aufgefunden; **I ~ myself in difficulties** ich befinde mich in Schwierigkeiten; **she ~s it difficult/easy** es fällt ihr schwer/leicht; **find out** *vt* herausfinden; **findings** *npl* (*Jur*) Ermittlungsergebnis *nt*; (*of report, Med*) Befund *m*

fine [faɪn] *adj* (*thin*) dünn, fein; (*good*) gut; (*splendid*) herrlich; (*clothes*) elegant; (*weather*) schön; **I'm ~** es geht mir gut; **that's ~** das ist OK ▷ *adv* (*well*) gut ▷ *n* (*Jur*) Geldstrafe *f* ▷ *vt* (*Jur*) mit einer Geldstrafe belegen; **fine arts** *npl* **the ~** die schönen Künste *pl*; **finely** *adv* (*cut*) dünn; (*ground*) fein

finger [ˈfɪŋgə*] *n* Finger *m* ▷ *vt* herumfingern an +*dat*; **fingernail** *n* Fingernagel *m*; **fingerprint** *n* Fingerabdruck *m*; **fingertip** *n* Fingerspitze *f*

finicky [ˈfɪnɪkɪ] *adj* (*person*) pingelig; (*work*) knifflig

finish [ˈfɪnɪʃ] *n* Ende *nt*; (*Sport*) Finish *nt*; (*line*) Ziel *nt*; (*of product*) Verarbeitung *f* ▷ *vt* beenden; (*book etc*) zu Ende lesen; (*food*) aufessen; (*drink*) austrinken ▷ *vi* zu Ende gehen; (*song, story*) enden; (*person*) fertig sein; (*stop*) aufhören; **have you ~ed?** bist du fertig?; **to ~ first/second** (*Sport*) als erster/zweiter durchs Ziel gehen; **finishing line** *n* Ziellinie *f*

Finland [ˈfɪnlənd] *n* Finnland *nt*; **Finn** *n* Finne *m*, Finnin *f*; **Finnish** *adj* finnisch ▷ *n* (*language*) Finnisch *nt*

fir [fɜː*] *n* Tanne *f*

fire [faɪə*] *n* Feuer *nt*; (*house etc*) Brand *m*; **to set ~ to sth** etw in Brand stecken; **to be on ~** brennen ▷ *vt* (*bullets, rockets*) abfeuern; (*fam: dismiss*) feuern ▷ *vi* (*Auto: engine*) zünden; **to ~ at sb** auf jdn schießen; **fire alarm** *n* Feuermelder *m*; **fire brigade** *n* Feuerwehr *f*; **fire engine**

n Feuerwehrauto *nt*; **fire escape** *n* Feuerleiter *f*; **fire extinguisher** *n* Feuerlöscher *m*; **firefighter** *n* Feuerwehrmann *m*, Feuerwehrfrau *f*; **fireman** *n* Feuerwehrmann *m*; **fireplace** *n* (offener) Kamin; **fireproof** *adj* feuerfest; **fire station** *n* Feuerwache *f*; **firewood** *n* Brennholz *nt*; **fireworks** *npl* Feuerwerk *nt*

firm [fɜːm] *adj* fest; (*person*) **to be ~** entschlossen auftreten ▷ *n* Firma *f*

first [fɜːst] *adj* erste(r, s) ▷ *adv* (*at first*) zuerst; (*firstly*) erstens; (*arrive, finish*) als erste(r); (*happen*) zum ersten Mal; **~ of all** zuallererst ▷ *n* (*person*) Erste(r) *mf*; (*Auto: gear*) erster Gang; **at ~** zuerst, anfangs; **first aid** *n* erste Hilfe; **first-class** *adj* erstklassig; (*compartment, ticket*) erster Klasse; **~ mail** (*Brit*) bevorzugt beförderte Post ▷ *adv* (*travel*) erster Klasse; **first floor** *n* (*Brit*) erster Stock; (*US*) Erdgeschoss *nt*; **first lady** *n* (*US*) Frau *f* des Präsidenten; **firstly** *adv* erstens; **first name** *n* Vorname *m*; **first night** *n* (*Theat*) Premiere *f*; **first-rate** *adj* erstklassig

fir tree *n* Tannenbaum *m*

fish [fɪʃ] *n* Fisch *m*; **~ and chips** (*Brit*) frittierter Fisch mit Pommes frites ▷ *vi* fischen; (*with rod*) angeln; **to go ~ing** fischen/angeln gehen; **fishbone** *n* Gräte *f*; **fishcake** *n* Fischfrikadelle *f*; **fish farm** *n* Fischzucht *f*; **fish finger** *n* (*Brit*) Fischstäbchen *nt*; **fishing** [ˈfɪʃɪŋ] *n* Fischen *nt*; (*with rod*) Angeln *nt*; (*as industry*) Fischerei *f*; **fishing boat** *n* Fischerboot *nt*; **fishing line** *n* Angelschnur *f*; **fishing rod** *n* Angelrute *f*; **fishing village** *n* Fischerdorf *nt*; **fishmonger** [ˈfɪʃmʌŋɡə*] *n* Fischhändler(in) *m(f)*; **fish stick** *n* (*US*) Fischstäbchen *nt*; **fish tank** *n* Aquarium *nt*

fishy [ˈfɪʃɪ] *adj* (*fam: suspicious*) faul

fist [fɪst] *n* Faust *f*

fit [fɪt] *adj* (*Med*) gesund; (*Sport*) in Form, fit; (*suitable*) geeignet; **to keep ~** sich in Form halten ▷ *vt* passen +*dat*; (*attach*) anbringen (*to* an +*dat*); (*install*) einbauen (*in* in +*akk*) ▷ *vi* passen; (*in space, gap*) hineinpassen ▷ *n* (*of clothes*) Sitz *m*; (*Med*) Anfall *m*; **it's a good ~** es passt gut; **fit in** *vt* (*accommodate*) unterbringen; (*find time for*) einschieben ▷ *vi* (*in space*)

hineinpassen; (*plans, ideas*) passen; **he doesn't ~** (**here**) er passt nicht hierher; **to ~ with sb's plans** sich mit jds Plänen vereinbaren lassen; **fitness** *n* (*Med*) Gesundheit *f*; (*Sport*) Fitness *f*; **fitted carpet** *n* Teppichboden *m*; **fitted kitchen** *n* Einbauküche *f*; **fitting** *adj* passend ▷ *n* (*of dress*) Anprobe *f*; **~s** *pl* Ausstattung *f*

five [faɪv] *num* fünf ▷ *n* Fünf *f*; *see also* **eight**; **fiver** *n* (*Brit fam*) Fünfpfundschein *m*

fix [fɪks] *vt* befestigen (*to* an +*dat*); (*settle*) festsetzen; (*place, time*) ausmachen; (*repair*) reparieren; **fixer** *n* (*drug addict*) Fixer(in) *m(f)*; **fixture** [ˈfɪkstʃə*] *n* (*Sport*) Veranstaltung *f*; (*match*) Spiel *nt*; (*in building*) Installationsteil *nt*; **~s** (**and fittings**) *pl* Ausstattung *f*

fizzy [ˈfɪzɪ] *adj* sprudelnd; **~ drink** Limo *f*

flabbergasted [ˈflæbəɡɑːstɪd] *adj* (*fam*) platt

flabby [ˈflæbɪ] *adj* (*fat*) wabbelig

flag [flæɡ] *n* Fahne *f*; **flagstone** *n* Steinplatte *f*

flake [fleɪk] *n* Flocke *f* ▷ *vi* **to ~** (**off**) abblättern

flamboyant [flæmˈbɔɪənt] *adj* extravagant

flame [fleɪm] *n* Flamme *f*; (*person*) **an old ~** eine alte Liebe

flan [flæn] *n* (*fruit ~*) Obstkuchen *m*

flannel [ˈflænl] *n* Flanell *m*; (*Brit: face ~*) Waschlappen *m*; (*fam: waffle*) Geschwafel *nt* ▷ *vi* herumlabern

flap [flæp] *n* Klappe *f*; (*fam*) **to be in a ~** rotieren ▷ *vt* (*wings*) schlagen mit ▷ *vi* flattern

flared [fleəd] *adj* (*trousers*) mit Schlag; **flares** *npl* Schlaghose *f*

flash [flæʃ] *n* Blitz *m*; (*news ~*) Kurzmeldung *f*; (*Foto*) Blitzlicht *nt*; **in a ~** im Nu ▷ *vt* **to ~ one's** (**head**)**lights** die Lichthupe betätigen ▷ *vi* aufblinken; (*brightly*) aufblitzen; **flashback** *n* Rückblende *f*, Flashback *m*; **flashlight** [ˈflæʃlaɪt] *n* (*Photo*) Blitzlicht *nt*; (*US: torch*) Taschenlampe *f*; **flashy** *adj* grell, schrill; (*pej*) protzig

flat [flæt] *adj* flach; (*surface*) eben; (*drink*) abgestanden; (*tyre*) platt; (*battery*) leer; (*refusal*) glatt ▷ *n* (*Brit: rooms*) Wohnung *f*; (*Auto*) Reifenpanne *f*; **flat screen** *n*

(*Inform*) Flachbildschirm *m*; **flatten** *vt* platt machen, einebnen

flatter ['flætə*] *vt* schmeicheln +*dat*; **flattering** *adj* schmeichelhaft

flatware ['flætwɛə] *n* (*US*) Besteck *nt*

flavor (*US*), **flavour** ['fleɪvə*] *n* Geschmack *m* ▷ *vt* Geschmack geben +*dat*; (*with spices*) würzen; **flavouring** *n* Aroma *nt*

flaw [flɔ:] *n* Fehler *m*; **flawless** *adj* fehlerlos; (*complexion*) makellos

flea [fli:] *n* Floh *m*

fled [fled] *pt, pp of* **flee**

flee [fli:] (**fled, fled**) *vi* fliehen

fleece [fli:s] *n* (*of sheep*) Vlies *nt*; (*soft material*) Fleece *m*; (*jacket*) Fleecejacke *f*

fleet [fli:t] *n* Flotte *f*

Flemish ['flemɪʃ] *adj* flämisch ▷ *n* (*language*) Flämisch *nt*

flesh [fleʃ] *n* Fleisch *nt*

flew [flu:] *pt of* **fly**

flex [fleks] *n* (*Brit Elec*) Schnur *f*

flexibility [fleksɪ'bɪlɪtɪ] *n* Biegsamkeit *f*; (*fig*) Flexibilität *f*; **flexible** ['fleksɪbl] *adj* biegsam; (*plans, person*) flexibel; **flexitime** *n* gleitende Arbeitszeit, Gleitzeit *f*

flicker ['flɪkə*] *vi* flackern; (*Tv*) flimmern

flies [flaɪz] *pl of* **fly** ▷ *n*

flight [flaɪt] *n* Flug *m*; (*escape*) Flucht *f*; ~ **of stairs** Treppe *f*; **flight attendant** *n* Flugbegleiter(in) *m(f)*; **flight recorder** *n* Flugschreiber *m*

flimsy ['flɪmzɪ] *adj* leicht gebaut, nicht stabil; (*thin*) hauchdünn; (*excuse*) fadenscheinig

fling [flɪŋ] (**flung, flung**) *vt* schleudern ▷ *n* **to have a** ~ eine (kurze) Affäre haben

flint [flɪnt] *n* Feuerstein *m*

flip [flɪp] *vt* schnippen; **to** ~ **a coin** eine Münze werfen; **flip through** *vt* (*book*) durchblättern; **flipchart** *n* Flipchart *nt*

flipper ['flɪpə*] *n* Flosse *f*

flirt [flɜ:t] *vi* flirten

float [fləʊt] *n* (*for fishing*) Schwimmer *m*; (*in procession*) Festwagen *m*; (*money*) Wechselgeld *nt* ▷ *vi* schwimmen; (*in air*) schweben

flock [flɒk] *n* (*of sheep*) (*Rel*) Herde *f*; (*of birds*) Schwarm *m*; (*of people*) Schar *f*

flog [flɒg] *vt* auspeitschen; (*Brit fam*) verscheuern

flood [flʌd] *n* Hochwasser *nt*, Überschwemmung *f*; (*fig*) Flut *f* ▷ *vt* überschwemmen; **floodlight** *n* Flutlicht *nt*; **floodlit** *adj* (*building*) angestrahlt

floor [flɔ:*] *n* Fußboden *m*; (*storey*) Stock *m*; **ground** ~ (*Brit*), **first** ~ (*US*) Erdgeschoss *nt*; **first** ~ (*Brit*), **second** ~ (*US*) erster Stock; **floorboard** *n* Diele *f*

flop [flɒp] *n* (*fam: failure*) Reinfall *m*, Flop *m* ▷ *vi* misslingen, floppen

floppy disk ['flɒpɪ'dɪsk] *n* Diskette *f*

Florence ['flɒrəns] *n* Florenz *nt*

florist ['flɒrɪst] *n* Blumenhändler(in) *m(f)*

flounder ['flaʊndə*] *n* (*fish*) Flunder *f*

flour ['flaʊə*] *n* Mehl *nt*

flourish ['flʌrɪʃ] *vi* gedeihen; (*business*) gut laufen; (*boom*) florieren ▷ *vt* (*wave about*) schwenken; **flourishing** *adj* blühend

flow [fləʊ] *n* Fluss *m*; **to go with the** ~ mit dem Strom schwimmen ▷ *vi* fließen

flower ['flaʊə*] *n* Blume *f* ▷ *vi* blühen; **flower bed** *n* Blumenbeet *nt*; **flowerpot** *n* Blumentopf *m*

flown [fləʊn] *pp of* **fly**

flu [flu:] *n* (*fam*) Grippe *f*

fluent *adj* (*Italian etc*) fließend; **to be** ~ **in German** fließend Deutsch sprechen

fluid ['flu:ɪd] *n* Flüssigkeit *f* ▷ *adj* flüssig

flung [flʌŋ] *pt, pp of* **fling**

fluorescent [flʊə'resnt] *adj* fluoreszierend, Leucht-

flush [flʌʃ] *n* (*lavatory*) Wasserspülung *f*; (*blush*) Röte *f* ▷ *vi* (*lavatory*) spülen

flute [flu:t] *n* Flöte *f*

fly [flaɪ] (**flew, flown**) *vt, vi* fliegen; **how time flies** wie die Zeit vergeht! ▷ *n* (*insect*) Fliege *f*; ~**/flies** (*pl*) (*on trousers*) Hosenschlitz *m*; **fly-drive** *n* Urlaub *m* mit Flug und Mietwagen; **flyover** *n* (*Brit*) Straßenüberführung *f*, Eisenbahnüberführung *f*; **flysheet** *n* Überzelt *nt*

FM *abbr* = **frequency modulation** ≈ UKW

FO *abbr* = **Foreign Office** ≈ AA *nt*

foal [fəʊl] *n* Fohlen *nt*

foam [fəʊm] *n* Schaum *m* ▷ *vi* schäumen

fob off [fɒb ɒf] *vt* **to fob sb off with sth** jdm etw andrehen

focus ['fəʊkəs] *n* Brennpunkt *m*; **in/out of** ~ (*photo*) scharf/unscharf; (*camera*) scharf/unscharf eingestellt ▷ *vt* (*camera*) scharf stellen ▷ *vi* sich konzentrieren (*on* auf +*akk*)

foetus ['fi:təs] *n* Fötus *m*

fog [fɒg] *n* Nebel *m*; **foggy** *adj* neblig; **fog**

light n (Auto: at rear) Nebelschlussleuchte f

foil [fɔɪl] vt vereiteln ▷ n Folie f

fold [fəʊld] vt falten ▷ vi (fam: business) eingehen ▷ n Falte f; **fold up** vt (map etc) zusammenfalten; (chair etc) zusammenklappen ▷ vi (fam: business) eingehen; **folder** n (portfolio) Aktenmappe f; (pamphlet) Broschüre f; (Inform) Ordner m; **folding** adj zusammenklappbar; (bicycle, chair) Klapp-

folk [fəʊk] n Leute pl; (Mus) Folk m; **my ~s** pl (fam) meine Leute ▷ adj Volks-

follow ['fɒləʊ] vt folgen +dat; (pursue) verfolgen; (understand) folgen können +dat; (career, news etc) verfolgen; **as ~s** wie folgt ▷ vi folgen; (result) sich ergeben (from aus); **follow up** vt (request, rumour) nachgehen +dat, weiter verfolgen; **follower** n Anhänger(in) m(f); **following** adj folgend; **the ~ day** am (darauf)folgenden Tag ▷ prep nach; **follow up** n (event, book etc) Fortsetzung f

fond [fɒnd] adj **to be ~ of** gern haben; **fondly** adv (with love) liebevoll; **fondness** n Vorliebe f; (for people) Zuneigung f

fondue ['fɒndu:] n Fondue nt

font [fɒnt] n Taufbecken nt; (Typo) Schriftart f

food [fu:d] n Essen nt, Lebensmittel pl; (for animals) Futter nt; (groceries) Lebensmittel pl; **food poisoning** n Lebensmittelvergiftung f; **food processor** n Küchenmaschine f; **foodstuff** n Lebensmittel nt

fool [fu:l] n Idiot m, Narr m; **to make a ~ of oneself** sich blamieren ▷ vt (deceive) hereinlegen ▷ vi **to ~ around** herumalbern; (waste time) herumtrödeln; **foolish** adj dumm; **foolproof** adj idiotensicher

foot [fʊt] (pl **feet**) n [fi:t] Fuß m; (measure) Fuß m (30,48 cm); **on ~** zu Fuß ▷ vt (bill) bezahlen; **foot-and-mouth disease** n Maul- und Klauenseuche f; **football** n Fußball m; (US: American ~) Football m; **footballer** n Fußballspieler(in) m(f); **footbridge** n Fußgängerbrücke f; **footing** n (hold) Halt m; **footlights** npl Rampenlicht nt; **footnote** n Fußnote f; **footpath** n Fußweg m;

footprint n Fußabdruck m; **footwear** n Schuhwerk nt

 KEYWORD

for [fɔ:*] prep **1** für; **is this for me?** ist das für mich?; **the train for London** der Zug nach London; **he went for the paper** er ging die Zeitung holen; **give it to me — what for?** gib es mir — warum?

2 (because of) wegen: **for this reason** aus diesem Grunde

3 (referring to distance); **there are roadworks for 5 km** die Baustelle ist 5 km lang; **we walked for miles** wir sind meilenweit gegangen

4 (referring to time) seit; (: with future sense) für; **he was away for 2 years** er war zwei Jahre lang weg

5 (+infin clauses): **it is not for me to decide** das kann ich nicht entscheiden; **for this to be possible ...** damit dies möglich wird/wurde ...

6 (in spite of) trotz +gen or (inf) dat; **for all his complaints** obwohl er sich ständig beschwert
▷ conj denn

forbade [fə'bæd] pt of **forbid**

forbid [fə'bɪd] (**forbade, forbidden**) vt verbieten

force [fɔ:s] n Kraft f; (compulsion) Zwang m, Gewalt; **to come into ~** in Kraft treten; **the Forces** pl die Streitkräfte ▷ vt zwingen; **forced** adj (smile) gezwungen; **~ landing** Notlandung f; **forceful** adj kraftvoll

forceps ['fɔ:seps] npl Zange f

forearm ['fɔ:rɑ:m] n Unterarm m

forecast ['fɔ:kɑ:st] vt voraussagen; (weather) vorhersagen ▷ n Vorhersage f

forefinger ['fɔ:fɪŋgə*] n Zeigefinger m

foreground ['fɔ:graʊnd] n Vordergrund m

forehand ['fɔ:hænd] n (Sport) Vorhand f

forehead ['fɔ:hed, 'fɒrɪd] n Stirn f

foreign ['fɒrən] adj ausländisch; **foreigner** n Ausländer(in) m(f); **foreign exchange** n Devisen pl; **foreign language** n Fremdsprache f; **foreign minister, foreign secretary** n Außenminister(in) m(f); **foreign policy** n Außenpolitik f

f

foremost ['fɔːməʊst] *adj* erste(r, s); (*leading*) führend

forerunner ['fɔːrʌnə*] *n* Vorläufer(in) *m(f)*

foresee [fɔː'siː] *irr vt* vorhersehen; **foreseeable** *adj* absehbar

forest ['fɒrɪst] *n* Wald *m*; **forestry** ['fɒrɪstrɪ] *n* Forstwirtschaft *f*

forever [fə'revə*] *adv* für immer

forgave [fə'geɪv] *pt of* **forgive**

forge [fɔːdʒ] *n* Schmiede *f* ▷ *vt* schmieden; (*fake*) fälschen; **forger** *n* Fälscher(in) *m(f)*; **forgery** *n* Fälschung *f*

forget [fə'get] (**forgot, forgotten**) *vt, vi* vergessen; **to ~ about sth** etw vergessen; **forgetful** *adj* vergesslich; **forgetfulness** *n* Vergesslichkeit *f*; **forget-me-not** *n* Vergissmeinnicht *nt*

forgive [fə'gɪv] (**forgave, forgiven**) *irr vt* verzeihen; **to ~ sb for sth** jdm etw verzeihen

forgot [fə'gɒt] *pt of* **forget**

forgotten [fə'gɒtn] *pp of* **forget**

fork [fɔːk] *n* Gabel *f*; (*in road*) Gabelung *f* ▷ *vi* (*road*) sich gabeln

form [fɔːm] *n* (*shape*) Form *f*, Klasse *f*; (*document*) Formular *nt*; (*person*) **to be in** (**good**) **~ in** Form sein ▷ *vt* bilden

formal ['fɔːməl] *adj* förmlich, formell; **formality** [fɔː'mælɪtɪ] *n* Formalität *f*

format ['fɔːmæt] *n* Format *nt* ▷ *vt* (*Inform*) formatieren

former ['fɔːmə*] *adj* frühere(r, s); (*opposite of latter*) erstere(r, s); **formerly** *adv* früher

formidable ['fɔːmɪdəbl] *adj* gewaltig; (*opponent*) stark

formula ['fɔːmjʊlə] *n* Formel *f*

formulate ['fɔːmjʊleɪt] *vt* formulieren

forth [fɔːθ] *adv* **and so ~** und so weiter; **forthcoming** [fɔːθ'kʌmɪŋ] *adj* kommend, bevorstehend

fortify ['fɔːtɪfaɪ] *vt* verstärken; (*for protection*) befestigen

fortieth ['fɔːtɪəθ] *adj* vierzigste(r, s); *see also* **eighth**

fortnight ['fɔːtnaɪt] *n* vierzehn Tage *pl*

fortress ['fɔːtrɪs] *n* Festung *f*

fortunate ['fɔːtʃənɪt] *adj* glücklich; **I was ~** ich hatte Glück; **fortunately** *adv* zum Glück; **fortune** ['fɔːtʃən] *n* (*money*) Vermögen *nt*; **good ~** Glück *nt*; **fortune-teller** *n* Wahrsager(in) *m(f)*

forty ['fɔːtɪ] *num* vierzig ▷ *n* Vierzig *f*; *see also* **eight**

forward ['fɔːwəd] *adv* vorwärts ▷ *n* (*Sport*) Stürmer(in) *m(f)* ▷ *vt* (*send on*) nachsenden; (*Inform*) weiterleiten; **forwards** *adv* vorwärts

foster child ['fɒstətʃaɪld] *n* Pflegekind *nt*; **foster parents** *npl* Pflegeeltern *pl*

fought [fɔːt] *pt, pp of* **fight**

foul [faʊl] *adj* (*weather*) schlecht; (*smell*) übel ▷ *n* (*Sport*) Foul *nt*

found [faʊnd] *pt, pp of* **find** ▷ *vt* (*establish*) gründen; **foundations** [faʊn'deɪʃənz] *npl* Fundament *nt*

fountain ['faʊntɪn] *n* Springbrunnen *m*; **fountain pen** *n* Füller *m*

four [fɔː*] *num* vier ▷ *n* Vier *f*; *see also* **eight**; **fourteen** ['fɔː'tiːn] *num* vierzehn ▷ *n* Vierzehn *f*; *see also* **eight**; **fourteenth** *adj* vierzehnte(r, s); *see also* **eighth**; **fourth** [fɔːθ] *adj* vierte(r, s); *see also* **eighth**

four-wheel drive *n* Allradantrieb *m*; (*car*) Geländewagen *m*

fowl [faʊl] *n* Geflügel *nt*

fox [fɒks] *n* Fuchs *m*

fraction ['frækʃən] *n* (*Math*) Bruch *m*; (*part*) Bruchteil *m*; **fracture** ['fræktʃə*] *n* (*Med*) Bruch *m* ▷ *vt* brechen

fragile ['frædʒaɪl] *adj* zerbrechlich

fragment ['frægmənt] *n* Bruchstück *nt*

fragrance ['freɪgrəns] *n* Duft *m*; **fragrant** *adj* duftend

frail [freɪl] *adj* gebrechlich

frame [freɪm] *n* Rahmen *m*; (*of spectacles*) Gestell *nt*; **~ of mind** Verfassung *f* ▷ *vt* einrahmen; **to ~ sb** (*fam: incriminate*) jdm etwas anhängen; **framework** *n* Rahmen *m*, Struktur *f*

France [frɑːns] *n* Frankreich *nt*

frank [fræŋk] *adj* offen

frankfurter ['fræŋkfɜːtə*] *n* (Frankfurter) Würstchen *nt*

frankly ['fræŋklɪ] *adv* offen gesagt; **quite ~** ganz ehrlich; **frankness** *n* Offenheit *f*

frantic ['fræntɪk] *adj* (*activity*) hektisch; (*effort*) verzweifelt; **~ with worry** außer sich vor Sorge

fraud [frɔːd] *n* (*trickery*) Betrug *m*; (*person*) Schwindler(in) *m(f)*

freak [friːk] *n* Anomalie *f*; (*animal, person*) Missgeburt *f*; (*fam: fan*) Fan *m*, Freak *m* ▷ *adj* (*conditions*)

außergewöhnlich, seltsam; **freak out** *vi*
(*fam*) ausflippen

freckle ['frekl] *n* Sommersprosse *f*

free [fri:] *adj, adv* frei; (*without payment*)
gratis, kostenlos; **for ~** umsonst ▷ *vt*
befreien; **freebie** ['fri:bɪ] *n* (*fam*)
Werbegeschenk *nt*; **it was a ~** es war
gratis; **freedom** ['fri:dəm] *n* Freiheit *f*;
freefone ['fri:fəʊn] *adj* **a ~ number** eine
gebührenfreie Nummer; **free kick** *n*
(*Sport*) Freistoß *m*

freelance ['fri:lɑːns] *adj* freiberuflich
tätig; (*artist*) freischaffend ▷ *n*
Freiberufler(in) *m(f)*

free-range ['fri:reɪndʒ] *adj* (*hen*) frei
laufend; **~ eggs** *pl* Freilandeier *pl*

freeway ['fri:weɪ] *n* (*US*) (gebührenfreie)
Autobahn

freeze [fri:z] (**froze, frozen**) *vi* (*feel cold*)
frieren; (*of lake etc*) zufrieren; (*water etc*)
gefrieren ▷ *vt* einfrieren; **freezer** *n*
Tiefkühltruhe *f*; (*in fridge*) Gefrierfach
nt; **freezing** *adj* eiskalt; **I'm ~** mir ist
eiskalt; **freezing point** *n* Gefrierpunkt *m*

freight [freɪt] *n* (*goods*) Fracht *f*; (*money
charged*) Frachtgebühr *f*; **freight car** *n*
(*US*) Güterwagen *m*; **freight train** *n* (*US*)
Güterzug *m*

French [frentʃ] *adj* französisch ▷ *n*
(*language*) Französisch *nt*; **the ~** *pl* die
Franzosen; **French bean** *n* grüne Bohne;
French bread *n* Baguette *f*; **French
dressing** *n* Vinaigrette *f*; **French fries**
(*US*) *npl* Pommes frites *pl*; **French kiss** *n*
Zungenkuss *m*; **Frenchman** (*pl* **-men**) *n*
Franzose *m*; **French toast** *n* (*US*) in Ei und
Milch getunktes gebratenes Brot; **French
window(s)** *n(pl)* Balkontür *f*,
Terrassentür *f*; **Frenchwoman** (*pl*
-women) *n* Französin *f*

frequency ['fri:kwənsɪ] *n* Häufigkeit
f; (*Phys*) Frequenz *f*; **frequent**
['fri:kwənt] *adj* häufig; **frequently** *adv*
häufig

fresco ['freskəʊ] (*pl* **-es**) *n* Fresko *nt*

fresh [freʃ] *adj* frisch; (*new*) neu; **freshen**
vi **to ~ (up**) (*person*) sich frisch machen;
freshman (*pl* **-men**) *n* Erstsemester *nt*;
freshwater fish *n* Süßwasserfisch *m*

Fri *abbr* = **Friday** Fr

friction ['frɪkʃən] *n* (*a. fig*) Reibung *f*

Friday ['fraɪdeɪ] *n* Freitag *m*; *see also*
Tuesday

fridge [frɪdʒ] *n* Kühlschrank *m*

fried [fraɪd] *adj* gebraten; **~ potatoes**
Bratkartoffeln *pl*; **~ egg** Spiegelei *nt*; **~ rice**
gebratener Reis

friend [frend] *n* Freund(in) *m(f)*; (*less
close*) Bekannte(r) *mf*; **to make ~s with sb**
sich mit jdm anfreunden; **we're good ~s**
wir sind gut befreundet; **friendly** *adj*
freundlich; **to be ~ with sb** mit jdm
befreundet sein ▷ *n* (*Sport*)
Freundschaftsspiel *nt*; **friendship**
['frendʃɪp] *n* Freundschaft *f*

fright [fraɪt] *n* Schrecken *m*; **frighten** *vt*
erschrecken; **to be ~ed** Angst haben;
frightening *adj* beängstigend

frill [frɪl] *n* Rüsche *f*; **~s** (*fam*)
Schnickschnack

fringe [frɪndʒ] *n* (*edge*) Rand *m*; (*on shawl
etc*) Fransen *pl*; (*hair*) Pony *m*

frivolous ['frɪvələs] *adj* leichtsinnig;
(*remark*) frivol

frizzy ['frɪzɪ] *adj* kraus

frog [frɒg] *n* Frosch *m*

○ **KEYWORD**

from [frɒm] *prep* **1** (*indicating starting
place*) von; (*indicating origin etc*) aus +*dat*; **a
letter/telephone call from my sister** ein
Brief/Anruf von meiner Schwester; **where
do you come from?** woher kommen Sie?;
to drink from the bottle aus der Flasche
trinken

2 (*indicating time*) von ... an; (*:past*)
seit; **from one o'clock to** *or* **until** *or* **till
two** von ein Uhr bis zwei; **from January
(on**) ab Januar

3 (*indicating distance*) von ... (entfernt)

4 (*indicating price, number etc*) ab +*dat*; **from
£10** ab £10; **there were from 20 to 30
people there** es waren zwischen 20 und
30 Leute da

5 (*indicating difference*): **he can't tell red
from green** er kann nicht zwischen Rot
und Grün unterscheiden; **to be
different from sb/sth** anders sein als
jd/etw

6 (*because of, based on*): **from what he says**
aus dem, was er sagt; **weak from hunger**
schwach vor Hunger

front [frʌnt] *n* Vorderseite *f*; (*of house*)
Fassade *f*; (*in war, of weather*) Front *f*; (*at*

seaside) Promenade *f*; **in ~, at the ~** vorne; **in ~ of** vor; **up ~** *(in advance)* vorher, im Voraus ▷ *adj* vordere(r, s), Vorder-; *(first)* vorderste(r, s); **~ door** Haustür *f*; **~ page** Titelseite *f*; **~ seat** Vordersitz *m*; **~ wheel** Vorderrad *nt*

frontier ['frʌntɪə*] *n* Grenze *f*

front-wheel drive *n (Auto)* Frontantrieb *m*

frost [frɒst] *n* Frost *m*; *(white ~)* Reif *m*; **frosting** *n (US)* Zuckerguss *m*; **frosty** *adj* frostig

froth [frɒθ] *n* Schaum *m*; **frothy** *adj* schaumig

frown [fraʊn] *vi* die Stirn runzeln

froze [frəʊz] *pt of* **freeze**

frozen ['frəʊzn] *pp of* **freeze** ▷ *adj (food)* tiefgekühlt, Tiefkühl-

fruit [fruːt] *n (as collective, a. type)* Obst *nt*; *(single ~, a. fig)* Frucht *f*; **fruit machine** *n* Spielautomat *m*; **fruit salad** *n* Obstsalat *m*

frustrated [frʌ'streɪtɪd] *adj* frustriert; **frustratration** *n* Frustration *f*, Frust *m*

fry [fraɪ] *vt* braten; **frying pan** *n* Bratpfanne *f*

fuchsia ['fjuːʃə] *n* Fuchsie *f*

fuck [fʌk] *vt (vulg)* ficken; **~ off** verpiss dich!; **fucking** *adj (vulg)* Scheiß-

fudge [fʌdʒ] *n* weiche Karamellsüßigkeit

fuel [fjʊəl] *n* Kraftstoff *m*; *(for heating)* Brennstoff *m*; **fuel consumption** *n* Kraftstoffverbrauch *m*; **fuel gauge** *n* Benzinuhr *f*; **fuel oil** *n* Gasöl *nt*; **fuel rod** *n* Brennstab *m*; **fuel tank** *n* Tank *m*; *(for oil)* Öltank *m*

fugitive ['fjuːdʒɪtɪv] *n* Flüchtling *m*

fulfil [fʊl'fɪl] *vt* erfüllen

full [fʊl] *adj* voll; *(person: satisfied)* satt; *(member, employment)* Voll(zeit)-; *(complete)* vollständig; **~ of ...** voller ... *gen*; **full beam** *n (Auto)* Fernlicht *nt*; **full moon** *n* Vollmond *m*; **full stop** *n* Punkt *m*; **full-time** *adj* **~ job** Ganztagsarbeit *f*; **fully** *adv* völlig; *(recover)* voll und ganz; *(discuss)* ausführlich

fumble ['fʌmbl] *vi* herumfummeln *(with, at* an *+dat)*

fumes [fjuːmz] *npl* Dämpfe *pl*; *(of car)* Abgase *pl*

fun [fʌn] *n* Spaß *m*; **for ~** zum Spaß; **it's ~** es macht Spaß; **to make ~ of** sich lustig machen über *+akk*

function ['fʌŋkʃən] *n* Funktion *f*; *(event)* Feier *f*; *(reception)* Empfang *m* ▷ *vi* funktionieren; **function key** *n (Inform)* Funktionstaste *f*

fund [fʌnd] *n* Fonds *m*; **~s** *pl* Geldmittel *pl*

fundamental [fʌndə'mentl] *adj* grundlegend; **fundamentally** *adv* im Grunde

funding ['fʌndɪŋ] *n* finanzielle Unterstützung

funeral ['fjuːnərəl] *n* Beerdigung *f*

funfair ['fʌnfɛə*] *n* Jahrmarkt *m*

fungus ['fʌŋgəs] *(pl* fungi *o* funguses) *n* Pilz *m*

funicular [fjuː'nɪkjʊlə*] *n* Seilbahn *f*

funnel ['fʌnl] *n* Trichter *m*; *(of steamer)* Schornstein *m*

funny ['fʌnɪ] *adj (amusing)* komisch, lustig; *(strange)* seltsam

fur [fɜ:*] *n* Pelz *m*; *(of animal)* Fell *nt*

furious ['fjʊərɪəs] *adj* wütend *(with sb* auf jdn)

furnished ['fɜ:nɪʃd] *adj* möbliert; **furniture** ['fɜ:nɪtʃə*] *n* Möbel *pl*; **piece of ~** Möbelstück *nt*

further ['fɜ:ðə*] *comparative of* **far** ▷ *adj* weitere(r, s); **~ education** Weiterbildung *f*; **until ~ notice** bis auf weiteres ▷ *adv* weiter; **furthest** ['fɜ:ðɪst] *superlative of* **far** ▷ *adj* am weitesten entfernt ▷ *adv* am weitesten

fury ['fjʊərɪ] *n* Wut *f*

fuse [fjuːz] *n (Elec)* Sicherung *f* ▷ *vi (Elec)* durchbrennen; **fuse box** *n* Sicherungskasten *m*

fuss [fʌs] *n* Theater *nt*; **to make a ~** ein Theater machen; **fussy** *adj (difficult)* schwierig, kompliziert; *(attentive to detail)* pingelig

future ['fjuːtʃə*] *adj* künftig ▷ *n* Zukunft *f*

fuze *(US) see* **fuse**

fuzzy ['fʌzɪ] *adj (indistinct)* verschwommen; *(hair)* kraus

gable ['geɪbl] n Giebel m

gadget ['gædʒɪt] n Vorrichtung f, Gerät nt

Gaelic ['geɪlɪk] adj gälisch ▷ n (language) Gälisch nt

gain [geɪn] vt (obtain, win) gewinnen; (advantage, respect) sich verschaffen; (wealth) erwerben; (weight) zunehmen ▷ vi (improve) gewinnen (in an +dat); (clock) vorgehen ▷ n Gewinn m (in an +dat)

gale [geɪl] n Sturm m

gall bladder ['gɔːlblædə*] n Gallenblase f

gallery ['gælərɪ] n Galerie f, Museum nt

gallon ['gælən] n Gallone f; ((Brit) 4,546 l, (US) 3,79 l)

gallop ['gæləp] n Galopp m ▷ vi galoppieren

gallstone ['gɔːlstəʊn] n Gallenstein m

Gambia ['gæmbɪə] n Gambia nt

gamble ['gæmbl] vi um Geld spielen, wetten ▷ n **it's a ~** es ist riskant; **gambling** n Glücksspiel nt

game [geɪm] n Spiel nt; (animals) Wild nt; **a ~ of chess** eine Partie Schach; **~s** (in school) Sport m; **game show** n (Tv) Gameshow f

gammon ['gæmən] n geräucherter Schinken

gang [gæŋ] n (of criminals, youths) Bande f, Gang f, Clique f ▷ vt **to ~ up on** sich verschwören gegen

gangster ['gæŋstə*] n Gangster m

gangway ['gæŋweɪ] n (for ship) Gangway f; (Brit: aisle) Gang m, Gangway f

gap [gæp] n (hole) Lücke f; (in time) Pause f; (in age) Unterschied m

gape [geɪp] vi (mit offenem Mund) starren

gap year n Jahr zwischen Schulabschluss und Studium, das oft zu Auslandsaufenthalten genutzt wird

garage ['gærɑːʒ] n Garage f; (for repair) (Auto)werkstatt f; (for fuel) Tankstelle f

garbage ['gɑːbɪdʒ] n (US) Müll m; (fam: nonsense) Quatsch m; **garbage can** n (US) Mülleimer m; (outside) Mülltonne f; **garbage truck** n (US) Müllwagen m

garbled ['gɑːbld] adj (story) verdreht

garden ['gɑːdn] n Garten m; (public) **~s** Park m; **garden centre** n Gartencenter nt; **gardener** n Gärtner(in) m(f); **gardening** n Gartenarbeit f

gargle ['gɑːgl] vi gurgeln

gargoyle ['gɑːgɔɪl] n Wasserspeier m

garlic ['gɑːlɪk] n Knoblauch m; **garlic bread** n Knoblauchbrot nt; **garlic butter** n Knoblauchbutter f

gas [gæs] n Gas nt; (US: petrol) Benzin nt; **to step on the ~** Gas geben; **gas cooker** n Gasherd m; **gas cylinder** n Gasflasche f; **gas fire** n Gasofen m

gasket ['gæskɪt] n Dichtung f

gas lighter n (for cigarettes) Gasfeuerzeug nt; **gas mask** n Gasmaske f; **gas meter** n Gaszähler m

gasoline ['gæsəliːn] n (US) Benzin nt

gasp [gɑːsp] vi keuchen; (in surprise) nach Luft schnappen

gas pedal n (US) Gaspedal nt; **gas pump** n (US) Zapfsäule f; **gas station** n (US) Tankstelle f; **gas tank** n (US) Benzintank m

gastric ['gæstrɪk] adj Magen-; **~ flu** Magen-Darm-Grippe f; **~ ulcer** Magengeschwür nt

gasworks ['gæswɜːks] n Gaswerk nt

gate [geɪt] n Tor nt; (barrier) Schranke f; (Aviat) Gate nt, Flugsteig m

gateau ['gætəʊ] n Torte f

gateway n Tor nt

gather ['gæðə*] vt (collect) sammeln; **to ~ speed** beschleunigen ▷ vi (assemble) sich versammeln; (understand) schließen (from aus); **gathering** n Versammlung f

gauge [geɪdʒ] n Meßgerät nt

gauze [gɔ:z] n Gaze f; (for bandages) Mull m

gave [geɪv] pt of **give**

gay [geɪ] adj (homosexual) schwul

gaze [geɪz] n Blick m ▷ vi starren

GCSE abbr = **general certificate of secondary education** (school) Abschlussprüfung f der Sekundarstufe, ≈ mittlere Reife

gear [gɪə*] n (Auto) Gang m; (equipment) Ausrüstung f; (clothes) Klamotten pl; **to change ~** schalten; **gearbox** n Getriebe nt; **gear change**, **gear shift** (US) n Gangschaltung f; **gear lever**, **gear stick** (US) n Schalthebel m

geese [gi:s] pl of **goose**

gel [dʒel] n Gel nt ▷ vi gelieren; **they really ~led** sie verstanden sich auf Anhieb

gelatine ['dʒeləti:n] n Gelatine f

gem [dʒem] n Edelstein m; (fig) Juwel nt

Gemini ['dʒemɪni:] nsing (Astr) Zwillinge pl

gender ['dʒendə*] n Geschlecht nt

gene [dʒi:n] n Gen nt

general ['dʒenərəl] adj allgemein; **~ knowledge** Allgemeinbildung f; **~ election** Parlamentswahlen pl; **generalize** ['dʒenrəlaɪz] vi verallgemeinern; **generally** ['dʒenrəlɪ] adv im Allgemeinen

generation [dʒenə'reɪʃən] n Generation f; **generation gap** n Generationsunterschied m

generator ['dʒenəreɪtə*] n Generator m

generosity [dʒenə'rɔsɪtɪ] n Großzügigkeit f; **generous** ['dʒenərəs] adj großzügig; (portion) reichlich

genetic [dʒɪ'netɪk] adj genetisch; **genetically modified** adj gentechnisch verändert, genmanipuliert; see also **GM**

Geneva [dʒɪ'ni:və] n Genf nt; **Lake ~** der Genfer See

genitals ['dʒenɪtlz] npl Geschlechtsteile pl

genitive ['dʒenɪtɪv] n Genitiv m

genius ['dʒi:nɪəs] n Genie nt

gentle ['dʒentl] adj sanft; (touch) zart;

gentleman (pl **-men**) n Herr m; (polite man) Gentleman m

gents [dʒents] n **'~'** (lavatory) „Herren"; **the ~** pl die Herrentoilette

genuine ['dʒenjʊɪn] adj echt

geographical [dʒɪə'græfɪkəl] adj geografisch; **geography** [dʒɪ'ɒgrəfɪ] n Geografie f; (at school) Erdkunde f

geological [dʒɪəʊ'lɒdʒɪkəl] adj geologisch; **geology** [dʒɪ'ɒlədʒɪ] n Geologie f

geometry [dʒɪ'ɒmɪtrɪ] n Geometrie f

geranium [dʒɪ'reɪnɪəm] n Geranie f

germ [dʒ3:m] n Keim m; (Med) Bazillus m

German ['dʒ3:mən] adj deutsch; **she's ~** sie ist Deutsche; **~ shepherd** Deutscher Schäferhund ▷ n (person) Deutsche(r) mf; (language) Deutsch nt; **in ~** auf Deutsch; **German measles** n sing Röteln pl; **Germany** ['dʒ3:mənɪ] n Deutschland nt

gesture ['dʒestʃə*] n Geste f

○ KEYWORD

get [ɡet] (pt, pp **got**, pp **gotten** (US)) vi
1 (become, be) werden; **to get old/tired** alt/müde werden; **to get married** heiraten
2 (go) (an)kommen gehen
3 (begin): **to get to know sb** jdn kennen lernen; **let's get going or started!** fangen wir an!
4 (modal aux vb): **you've got to do it** du musst es tun
▷ vt 1: **to get sth done** (do) etw machen: (have done) etw machen lassen; **to get sth going or to go** etw in Gang bringen or bekommen; **to get sb to do sth** jdn dazu bringen, etw zu tun
2 (obtain: money, permission, results) erhalten; (find: job, flat) finden; (fetch; person, object) holen; **to get sth for sb** jdm etw besorgen; **get me Mr Jones, please** (Tel) verbinden Sie mich bitte mit Mr Jones
3 (receive: present, letter) bekommen kriegen (acquire: reputation etc) erwerben
4 (catch) bekommen kriegen; (hit: target etc) treffen erwischen; **get him!** (to dog) fass!
5 (take, move) bringen; **to get sth to sb** jdm etw bringen

6 (*understand*) verstehen; (*hear*)
mitbekommen; **I've got it!** ich habs!
7 (*have, possess*): **to have got sth** etw
haben

get about *vi* herumkommen; (*news*) sich
verbreiten

get along *vi* (*people*) (gut)
zurechtkommen; (*depart*) sich *acc* auf den
Weg machen

get at *vt* (*facts*) herausbekommen; **to
get at sb** (*nag*) an jdm herumnörgeln

get away *vi* (*leave*) sich *acc* davonmachen
(*escape*); **to get away from sth** von etw
dat entkommen; **to get away with sth**
mit etw davonkommen

get back *vi* (*return*) zurückkommen ▷ *vt*
zurückbekommen

get by *vi* (*pass*) vorbeikommen; (*manage*)
zurechtkommen

get down *vi* (her)untergehen ▷ *vt*
(*depress*) fertig machen; **to get down to**
in Angriff nehmen (*find time to do*)
kommen zu

get in *vi* (*train*) ankommen; (*arrive home*)
heimkommen

get into *vt* (*enter*) hinein-/hereinkommen
in +*acc*; (: *car, train etc*) einsteigen in +*acc*;
(*clothes*) anziehen

get off *vi* (*from train etc*) aussteigen; (*from
horse*) absteigen ▷ *vt* aussteigen aus;
absteigen von

get on *vi* (*progress*) vorankommen; (*be
friends*) auskommen; (*age*) alt werden;
(*onto train etc*) einsteigen; (*onto horse*)
aufsteigen ▷ *vt* einsteigen in +*acc*; auf
etw *acc* aufsteigen

get out *vi* (*of house*) herauskommen; (*of
vehicle*) aussteigen ▷ *vt* (*take out*)
herausholen

get out of *vt* (*duty etc*) herumkommen
um

get over *vt* (*illness*) sich *acc* erholen von
(*surprise*) verkraften; (*news*) fassen; (*loss*)
sich abfinden mit

get round *vt* herumkommen; (*fig:
person*) herumkriegen

get through to *vt* (*Tel*) durchkommen zu

get together *vi* zusammenkommen

get up *vi* aufstehen ▷ *vt* hinaufbringen;
(*go up*) hinaufgehen; (*organize*) auf die
Beine stellen

get up to *vt* (*reach*) erreichen; (*prank etc*)
anstellen

Ghana ['gɑːnə] *n* Ghana *nt*

gherkin ['gɜːkɪn] *n* Gewürzgurke *f*

ghetto ['getəʊ] (*pl* **-es**) *n* Ghetto *nt*

ghost [gəʊst] *n* Gespenst *nt*; (*of sb*) Geist
m

giant ['dʒaɪənt] *n* Riese *m* ▷ *adj* riesig

giblets ['dʒɪblɪts] *npl* Geflügelinnereien *pl*

Gibraltar [dʒɪ'brɔːltə*] *n* Gibraltar *nt*

giddy ['gɪdɪ] *adj* schwindlig

gift [gɪft] *n* Geschenk *nt*; (*talent*)
Begabung *f*; **gifted** *adj* begabt; **giftwrap**
vt als Geschenk verpacken

gigantic [dʒaɪ'gæntɪk] *adj* riesig

giggle ['gɪgl] *vi* kichern ▷ *n* Gekicher *nt*

gill [gɪl] *n* (*of fish*) Kieme *f*

gimmick ['gɪmɪk] *n* (*for sales, publicity*)
Gag *m*

gin [dʒɪn] *n* Gin *m*

ginger ['dʒɪndʒə*] *n* Ingwer *m* ▷ *adj*
(*colour*) kupferrot; (*cat*) rötlichgelb; **ginger
ale** *n* Gingerale *nt*; **ginger beer** *n*
Ingwerlimonade *f*; **gingerbread** *n*
Lebkuchen *m* (*mit Ingwergeschmack*);
ginger(-haired) *adj* rotblond; **gingerly**
adv (*move*) vorsichtig

gipsy ['dʒɪpsɪ] *n* Zigeuner(in) *m(f)*

giraffe [dʒɪ'rɑːf] *n* Giraffe *f*

girl [gɜːl] *n* Mädchen *nt*; **girlfriend** *n*
(*feste*) Freundin *f*; **girl guide** *n* (*Brit*), **girl
scout** (*US*) Pfadfinderin *f*

gist [dʒɪst] *n* **to get the ~ (of it)** das
Wesentliche verstehen

give [gɪv] (**gave, given**) *vt* geben; (*as
present*) schenken (*to sb* jdm); (*state: name
etc*) angeben; (*speech*) halten; (*blood*)
spenden; **to ~ sb sth** jdm etw
geben/schenken ▷ *vi* (*yield*) nachgeben;
give away *vt* (*give free*) verschenken;
(*secret*) verraten; **give back** *vt*
zurückgeben; **give in** *vi* aufgeben; **give
up** *vt, vi* aufgeben; **give way** *vi* (*collapse,
yield*) nachgeben; (*traffic*) die Vorfahrt
beachten

given ['gɪvn] *pp* of **give** ▷ *adj* (*fixed*)
festgesetzt; (*certain*) bestimmt; **~ name**
(*US*) Vorname *m* ▷ *conj* **~ that ...**
angesichts der Tatsache, dass ...

glacier ['glæsɪə*] *n* Gletscher *m*

glad [glæd] *adj* froh (*about* über); **I was
~ (to hear) that ...** es hat mich gefreut,
dass ...; **gladly** ['glædlɪ] *adv* gerne

glance [glɑːns] *n* Blick *m* ▷ *vi* einen Blick
werfen (*at* auf +*akk*)

gland [glænd] n Drüse f; **glandular fever** n Drüsenfieber nt

glare [glɛə*] n grelles Licht; (stare) stechender Blick ▷ vi (angrily) **to ~ at sb** jdn böse anstarren; **glaring** adj (mistake) krass

glass [glɑ:s] n Glas nt; **~es** pl Brille f

glen [glen] n (SCOT) (enges) Bergtal nt

glide [glaɪd] vi gleiten; (hover) schweben; **glider** n Segelflugzeug nt; **gliding** n Segelfliegen nt

glimmer ['glɪmə*] n (of hope) Schimmer m

glimpse [glɪmps] n flüchtiger Blick

glitter ['glɪtə*] vi glitzern; (eyes) funkeln

glitzy [glɪtsɪ] adj (fam) glanzvoll, Schickimicki-

global ['gləʊbəl] adj global, Welt-; **~ warming** die Erwärmung der Erdatmosphäre; **globe** [gləʊb] n (sphere) Kugel f; (world) Erdball m; (map) Globus m

gloomily ['glu:mɪlɪ], **gloomy** adv, adj düster

glorious ['glɔ:rɪəs] adj (victory, past) ruhmreich; (weather, day) herrlich; **glory** ['glɔ:rɪ] n Herrlichkeit f

gloss [glɒs] n (shine) Glanz m

glossary ['glɒsərɪ] n Glossar nt

glossy ['glɒsɪ] adj (surface) glänzend ▷ n (magazine) Hochglanzmagazin nt

glove [glʌv] n Handschuh m; **glove compartment** n Handschuhfach nt

glow [gləʊ] vi glühen

glucose ['glu:kəʊs] n Traubenzucker m

glue [glu:] n Klebstoff m ▷ vt kleben

glutton ['glʌtn] n Vielfraß m; **a ~ for punishment** (fam) Masochist m

GM abbr = **genetically modified** Gen-; **~ foods** gentechnisch veränderte Lebensmittel

GMT abbr = **Greenwich Mean Time** WEZ f

go [gəʊ] (**went, gone**) vi gehen; (in vehicle, travel) fahren; (plane) fliegen; (road) führen (to nach); (depart: train, bus) (ab)fahren; (person) (fort)gehen; (disappear) verschwinden; (time) vergehen; (function) gehen, funktionieren; (machine, engine) laufen; (fit, suit) passen (with zu); (fail) nachlassen; **I have to ~ to the doctor/to London** ich muss zum Arzt/nach London; **to ~ shopping** einkaufen gehen; **to ~ for a walk/swim** spazieren/schwimmen gehen; **has he gone yet?** ist er schon weg?; **the wine ~es in the cupboard** der

Wein kommt in den Schrank; **to get sth ~ing** etw in Gang setzen; **to keep ~ing** weitermachen; (machine etc) weiterlaufen; **how's the job ~ing?** was macht der Job?; **his memory/eyesight is going** sein Gedächtnis lässt nach/seine Augen werden schwach; **to ~ deaf/mad/grey** taub/verrückt/grau werden ▷ vb aux **to be ~ing to do sth** etw tun werden; **I was ~ing to do it** ich wollte es tun ▷ n (pl **-es**) (attempt) Versuch m; **can I have another ~?** darf ich noch mal (probieren)?; **it's my ~** ich bin dran; **in one ~** auf einen Schlag; (drink) in einem Zug; **go after** vt nachlaufen +dat; (in vehicle) nachfahren +dat; **go ahead** vi (in front) vorausgehen; (start) anfangen; **go away** vi weggehen; (on holiday, business) verreisen; **go back** vi (return) zurückgehen; **we ~ a long way** (fam) wir kennen uns schon ewig; **go by** vi vorbeigehen; (vehicle) vorbeifahren; (years, time) vergehen ▷ vt (judge by) gehen nach; **go down** vi (sun, ship) untergehen; (flood, temperature) zurückgehen; (price) sinken; **to ~ well/badly** gut/schlecht ankommen; **go in** vi hineingehen; **go into** vt (enter) hineingehen in +akk; (crash) fahren gegen, hineinfahren in +akk; **to ~ teaching/politics/the army** Lehrer werden/in die Politik gehen/zum Militär gehen; **go off** vi (depart) weggehen; (in vehicle) wegfahren; (lights) ausgehen; (milk etc) sauer werden; (gun, bomb, alarm) losgehen ▷ vt (dislike) nicht mehr mögen; **go on** vi (continue) weitergehen; (lights) angehen; **to ~ with o doing sth** etw weitermachen; **go out** vi (leave house) hinausgehen; (fire, light, person socially) ausgehen; **to ~ for a meal** essen gehen; **go up** vi (temperature, price) steigen; (lift) hochfahren; **go without** vt verzichten auf +akk; (food, sleep) auskommen ohne

go-ahead ['gəʊəhed] adj (progressive) fortschrittlich ▷ n grünes Licht

goal [gəʊl] n (aim) Ziel nt; (Sport) Tor nt; **goalie, goalkeeper** n Torwart m, Torfrau f; **goalpost** n Torpfosten m

goat [gəʊt] n Ziege f

gob [gɒb] n (Brit fam) Maul nt; **shut your ~** halt's Maul! ▷ vi spucken; **gobsmacked** (fam: surprised) platt

god [gɒd] n Gott m; **thank God** Gott sei Dank; **godchild** (pl **-children**) n

Patenkind *nt*; **goddaughter** *n*
Patentochter *f*; **goddess** ['gɒdes] *n*
Göttin *f*; **godfather** *n* Pate *m*;
godmother *n* Patin *f*; **godson** *n*
Patensohn *m*

goggles *npl* Schutzbrille *f*; (*for skiing*)
Skibrille *f*; (*for diving*) Taucherbrille *f*

going ['gəʊɪŋ] *adj* (*rate*) üblich; **goings-on**
npl Vorgänge *pl*

go-kart ['gəʊkɑːt] *n* Gokart *m*

gold [gəʊld] *n* Gold *nt* ▷ *adj* golden;
goldfish *n* Goldfisch *m*; **gold-plated** *adj*
vergoldet

golf [gɒlf] *n* Golf *nt*; **golf ball** *n* Golfball
m; **golf club** *n* Golfschläger *m*;
(*association*) Golfklub *m*; **golf course** *n*
Golfplatz *m*; **golfer** *n* Golfspieler(in) *m(f)*

gone [gɒn] *pp of* **go**; **he's ~** er ist weg
▷ *prep* **just ~** gerade drei Uhr vorbei

good [gʊd] *n* (*benefit*) Wohl *nt*; (*morally
good things*) Gute(s) *nt*; **for the ~ of** zum
Wohle +*gen*; **it's for your own ~** es ist zu
deinem Besten *o* Vorteil; **it's no ~** (*doing
sth*) es hat keinen Sinn *o* Zweck; (*thing*) es
taugt nichts; **for ~** für immer ▷ *adj*
(**better, best**) gut; (*suitable*) passend;
(*thorough*) gründlich; (*well-behaved*) brav;
(*kind*) nett, lieb; **to be ~ at sport/maths**
gut in Sport/Mathe sein; **to be no ~ at
sport/maths** schlecht in Sport/Mathe
sein; **it's ~ for you** es tut dir gut; **this is
~ for colds** das ist gut gegen Erkältungen;
too ~ to be true zu schön, um wahr zu
sein; **this is just not ~ enough** so geht das
nicht; **a ~ three hours** gute drei Stunden;
~ morning/evening guten
Morgen/Abend; **~ night** gute Nacht; **to
have a ~ time** sich gut amüsieren

goodbye [gʊd'baɪ] *interj* auf Wiedersehen

Good Friday *n* Karfreitag *m*

good-looking *adj* gut aussehend

goods [gʊdz] *npl* Waren *pl*, Güter *pl*;
goods train *n* (*Brit*) Güterzug *m*

goodwill [gʊd'wɪl] *n* Wohlwollen *nt*

goose [guːs] (*pl* **geese**) *n* Gans *f* ▷ *vt*
(*fam*) **to ~ s.o.** jdn in den Arsch kneifen;
gooseberry ['gʊzbəri] *n* Stachelbeere *f*;
goose bumps *n*, **goose pimples** *npl*
Gänsehaut *f*

gorge [gɔːdʒ] *n* Schlucht *f*

gorgeous ['gɔːdʒəs] *adj* wunderschön;
he's ~ er sieht toll aus

gorilla [gə'rɪlə] *n* Gorilla *m*

gossip ['gɒsɪp] *n* (*talk*) Klatsch *m*; (*person*)
Klatschtante *f* ▷ *vi* klatschen, tratschen

got [gɒt] *pt, pp of* **get**

gotten ['gɒtn] (*US*) *pp of* **get**

govern ['gʌvən] *vt* regieren; (*province etc*)
verwalten; **government** *n* Regierung *f*;
governor *n* Gouverneur(in) *m(f)*; **govt**
abbr = **government** Regierung *f*

gown [gaʊn] *n* Abendkleid *nt*; (*academic*)
Robe *f*

GP *abbr* = **General Practitioner**
praktischer Arzt

GPS *n abbr* = **global positioning system**
GPS *nt*

grab [græb] *vt* packen; (*person*)
schnappen

grace [greɪs] *n* Anmut *f*; (*prayer*)
Tischgebet *nt*; **5 days' ~** 5 Tage Aufschub;
graceful *adj* anmutig

grade [greɪd] *n* Niveau *nt*; (*of goods*)
Güteklasse *f*; (*mark*) Note *f*; (*US: year*)
Klasse *f*; **to make the ~** es schaffen; **grade
crossing** *n* (*US*) Bahnübergang *m*; **grade
school** *n* (*US*) Grundschule *f*

gradient ['greɪdɪənt] *n* (*upward*) Steigung
f; (*downward*) Gefälle *nt*

gradual, gradually ['grædjʊəl, -lɪ] *adj, adv*
allmählich

graduate ['grædjʊɪt] *n* Uniabsolvent(in)
m(f), Akademiker(in) *m(f)*,
Hochschulabsolvent(in) *m(f)*
▷ ['grædjʊeɪt] *vi* einen akademischen
Grad erwerben

grain [greɪn] *n* (*cereals*) Getreide *nt*;
(*of corn, sand*) Korn *nt*; (*in wood*) Maserung
f

gram [græm] *n* Gramm *nt*

grammar ['græmə*] *n* Grammatik *f*;
grammar school *n* (*Brit*) ≈ Gymnasium *nt*

gran [græn] *n* (*fam*) Oma *f*

grand [grænd] *adj* (*pej*) hochnäsig; (*posh*)
vornehm ▷ *n* (*fam*) 1000 Pfund *bzw.* 1000
Dollar

grand(d)ad *n* (*fam*) Opa *m*;
granddaughter *n* Enkelin *f*; **grandfather**
n Großvater *m*; **grandma** *n* (*fam*) Oma *f*;
grandmother *n* Großmutter *f*; **grandpa**
n (*fam*) Opa *m*; **grandparents** *npl*
Großeltern *pl*; **grandson** *n* Enkel *m*

grandstand *n* (*Sport*) Tribüne *f*

granny ['grænɪ] *n* (*fam*) Oma *f*

grant [grɑːnt] *vt* gewähren (*sb sth* jdm
etw); **to take sb/sth for ~ed** jdn/etw als

selbstverständlich hinnehmen ▷ *n* Subvention *f*, finanzielle Unterstützung *f*; *(for university)* Stipendium *nt*

grape [greɪp] *n* Weintraube *f*; **grapefruit** *n* Grapefruit *f*; **grape juice** *n* Traubensaft *m*

graph [grɑːf] *n* Diagramm *nt*; **graphic** ['græfɪk] *adj* grafisch; *(description)* anschaulich

grasp [grɑːsp] *vt* ergreifen; *(understand)* begreifen

grass [grɑːs] *n* Gras *nt*; *(lawn)* Rasen *m*; **grasshopper** *n* Heuschrecke *f*

grate [greɪt] *n* Feuerrost *m* ▷ *vi* kratzen ▷ *vt* *(cheese)* reiben

grateful, gratefully ['greɪtfʊl, -fəlɪ] *adj*, *adv* dankbar

grater ['greɪtə*] *n* Reibe *f*

gratifying ['grætɪfaɪɪŋ] *adj* erfreulich

gratitude ['grætɪtjuːd] *n* Dankbarkeit *f*

grave [greɪv] *n* Grab *nt* ▷ *adj* ernst; *(mistake)* schwer

gravel ['grævəl] *n* Kies *m*

graveyard ['greɪvjɑːd] *n* Friedhof *m*

gravity ['grævɪtɪ] *n* Schwerkraft *f*; *(seriousness)* Ernst *m*

gravy ['greɪvɪ] *n* Bratensoße *f*

gray [greɪ] *adj* *(US)* grau

graze [greɪz] *vi* *(of animals)* grasen ▷ *vt* *(touch)* streifen; *(Med)* abschürfen ▷ *n* *(Med)* Abschürfung *f*

grease [griːs] *n* *(fat)* Fett *nt*; *(lubricant)* Schmiere *f* ▷ *vt* einfetten; *(Tech)* schmieren; **greasy** ['griːsɪ] *adj* fettig; *(hands, tools)* schmierig; *(fam: person)* schleimig

great [greɪt] *adj* groß; *(fam: good)* großartig, super; **a ~ deal of** viel; **Great Britain** ['greɪt'brɪtn] *n* Großbritannien *nt*; **great-grandfather** *n* Urgroßvater *m*; **great-grandmother** *n* Urgroßmutter *f*; **greatly** *adv* sehr; **~ disappointed** zutiefst enttäuscht

Greece [griːs] *n* Griechenland *nt*

greed [griːd] *n* Gier *f* *(for* nach); *(for food)* Gefräßigkeit *f*; **greedy** *adj* gierig; *(for food)* gefräßig

Greek [griːk] *adj* griechisch ▷ *n* *(person)* Grieche *m*, Griechin *f*; *(language)* Griechisch *nt*

green [griːn] *adj* grün ▷ *n* *(colour, for golf)* Grün *nt*; *(village ~)* Dorfwiese *f*; **~s** *(vegetables)* grünes Gemüse; **the Greens,**

the Green Party *(Pol)* die Grünen; **green card** *n* *(US: work permit)* Arbeitserlaubnis *f*; *(Brit: for car)* grüne Versicherungskarte; **greengage** *n* Reneklode *f*; **greengrocer** *n* Obst- und Gemüsehändler(in) *m(f)*; **greenhouse** *n* Gewächshaus *nt*; **~ effect** Treibhauseffekt *m*; **Greenland** *n* Grönland *nt*; **green pepper** *n* grüner Paprika; **green salad** *n* grüner Salat

Greenwich Mean Time ['grenɪdʒ'miːntaɪm] *n* westeuropäische Zeit

greet [griːt] *vt* grüßen; **greeting** *n* Gruß *m*

grew [gruː] *pt of* **grow**

grey [greɪ] *adj* grau; **grey-haired** *adj* grauhaarig; **greyhound** *n* Windhund *m*

grid [grɪd] *n* Gitter *nt*; **gridlock** *n* Verkehrsinfarkt *m*; **gridlocked** *adj* *(roads)* völlig verstopft; *(talks)* festgefahren

grief [griːf] *n* Kummer *m*; *(over loss)* Trauer *f*

grievance ['griːvəns] *n* Beschwerde *f*

grieve [griːv] *vi* trauern *(for* um)

grill [grɪl] *n* *(on cooker)* Grill *m* ▷ *vt* grillen

grim [grɪm] *adj* *(face, humour)* grimmig; *(situation, prospects)* trostlos

grin [grɪn] *n* Grinsen *nt* ▷ *vi* grinsen

grind [graɪnd] *(ground, ground)* *vt* mahlen; *(sharpen)* schleifen; *(US: meat)* durchdrehen, hacken

grip [grɪp] *n* Griff *m*; **get a ~** nimm dich zusammen!; **to get to ~s with sth** etw in den Griff bekommen ▷ *vt* packen; **gripping** *adj* *(exciting)* spannend

gristle ['grɪsl] *n* Knorpel *m*

groan [grəʊn] *vi* stöhnen *(with* vor +*dat*)

grocer ['grəʊsə*] *n* Lebensmittelhändler(in) *m(f)*; **groceries** *npl* Lebensmittel *pl*

groin [grɔɪn] *n* *(Anat)* Leiste *f*; **groin strain** *n* *(Med)* Leistenbruch *m*

groom [gruːm] *n* Bräutigam *m* ▷ *vt* **well ~ed** gepflegt

groovy ['gruːvɪ] *adj* *(fam)* cool

grope [grəʊp] *vi* tasten ▷ *vt* *(sexually harrass)* befummeln

gross [grəʊs] *adj* *(coarse)* derb; *(extreme: negligence, error)* grob; *(disgusting)* ekelhaft; *(Comm)* brutto; **~ national product** Bruttosozialprodukt *nt*; **~ salary** Bruttogehalt *nt*

grotty ['grɒtɪ] *adj* *(fam)* mies, vergammelt

ground [graʊnd] *pt, pp of* **grind** ▷ *n*
Boden *m*, Erde *f*; (*Sport*) Platz *m*; **~s** *pl*
(*around house*) (Garten)anlagen *pl*; (*reasons*)
Gründe *pl*; (*of coffee*) Satz *m*; **on (the) ~s of**
aufgrund von; **ground floor** *n* (*Brit*)
Erdgeschoss *nt*; **ground meat** *n* (*US*)
Hackfleisch *nt*

group [gruːp] *n* Gruppe *f* ▷ *vt*
gruppieren

grouse [graʊs] (*pl* **-**) *n* (*bird*) Schottisches
Moorhuhn; (*complaint*) Nörgelei *f*

grow [grəʊ] (**grew, grown**) *vi* wachsen;
(*increase*) zunehmen (*in an*); (*become*)
werden; **to ~ old** alt werden; **to ~ into ...**
sich entwickeln zu ... ▷ *vt* (*crop, plant*)
ziehen; (*commercially*) anbauen; **I'm ~ing a
beard** ich lasse mir einen Bart wachsen;
grow up *vi* aufwachsen; (*mature*)
erwachsen werden; **growing** *adj*
wachsend; **a ~ number of people** immer
mehr Leute

growl [graʊl] *vi* knurren

grown [grəʊn] *pp of* **grow**

grown-up [grəʊnˈʌp] *adj* erwachsen ▷ *n*
Erwachsene(r) *mf*; **growth** [grəʊθ] *n*
Wachstum *nt*; (*increase*) Zunahme *f*; (*Med*)
Wucherung *f*

grubby [ˈgrʌbɪ] *adj* schmuddelig

grudge [grʌdʒ] *n* Abneigung *f* (*against*
gegen) ▷ *vt* **to ~ sb sth** jdm etw nicht
gönnen

gruelling [ˈgrʊəlɪŋ] *adj* aufreibend; (*pace*)
mörderisch

gruesome [ˈgruːsəm] *adj* grausig

grumble [ˈgrʌmbl] *vi* murren (*about* über
+akk)

grumpy [ˈgrʌmpɪ] *adj* (*fam*) mürrisch,
grantig

grunt [grʌnt] *vi* grunzen

G-string [ˈdʒiːstrɪŋ] *n* ≈ Tanga *m*

guarantee [gærənˈtiː] *n* Garantie *f* (*of*
für); **it's still under ~** es ist noch Garantie
darauf ▷ *vt* garantieren

guard [gɑːd] *n* (*sentry*) Wache *f*; (*in prison*)
Wärter(in) *m(f)*; (*Brit Rail*) Schaffner(in)
m(f) ▷ *vt* bewachen; **a closely ~ed secret**
ein streng gehütetes Geheimnis

guardian [ˈgɑːdɪən] *n* Vormund *m*;
~ angel Schutzengel *m*

guess [ges] *n* Vermutung *f*; (*estimate*)
Schätzung *f*; **have a ~** rate mal! ▷ *vt, vi*
raten; (*estimate*) schätzen; **I ~ you're right**
du hast wohl recht; **I ~ so** ich glaube

schon; **guesstimate** [ˈgestɪmɪt] *n* (*fam*)
grobe Schätzung

guest [gest] *n* Gast *m*; **be my ~** nur zu!;
guest-house *n* Pension *f*; **guest room** *n*
Gästezimmer *nt*

guidance [ˈgaɪdəns] *n* (*direction*) Leitung
f; (*advice*) Rat *m*; (*counselling*) Beratung *f*;
for your ~ zu Ihrer Orientierung; **guide**
[gaɪd] *n* (*person*) Führer(in) *m(f)*; (*tour*)
Reiseleiter(in) *m(f)*; (*book*) Führer *m*; (*girl ~*)
Pfadfinderin *f* ▷ *vt* führen; **guidebook** *n*
Reiseführer *m*; **guide dog** *n* Blindenhund
m; **guided tour** *n* Führung *f* (*of* durch);
guidelines *npl* Richtlinien *pl*

guilt [gɪlt] *n* Schuld *f*; **guilty** *adj* schuldig
(*of gen*); (*look*) schuldbewusst; **to have a
~ conscience** ein schlechtes Gewissen
haben

guinea pig [ˈgɪnɪ pɪg] *n*
Meerschweinchen *nt*; (*person*)
Versuchskaninchen *nt*

guitar [gɪˈtɑː*] *n* Gitarre *f*

gulf [gʌlf] *n* Golf *m*; (*gap*) Kluft *f*; **Gulf
States** *npl* Golfstaaten *pl*

gull [gʌl] *n* Möwe *f*

gullible [ˈgʌlɪbl] *adj* leichtgläubig

gulp [gʌlp] *n* (kräftiger) Schluck ▷ *vi*
schlucken

gum [gʌm] *n* (*around teeth, usu pl*)
Zahnfleisch *nt*; (*chewing ~*) Kaugummi *m*

gun [gʌn] *n* Schusswaffe *f*; (*rifle*) Gewehr
nt; (*pistol*) Pistole *f*; **gunfire** *n* Schüsse *pl*,
Geschützfeuer *nt*; **gunpowder** *n*
Schießpulver *nt*; **gunshot** *n* Schuss *m*

gush [gʌʃ] *vi* (heraus)strömen (*from* aus)

gut [gʌt] *n* Darm *m*; **~s** *pl* (*intestines*)
Eingeweide; (*courage*) Mumm *m*

gutter [ˈgʌtə*] *n* (*for roof*) Dachrinne *f*; (*in
street*) Rinnstein *m*, Gosse *f*; **gutter press**
n Skandalpresse *f*

guy [gaɪ] *n* (*man*) Typ *m*, Kerl *m*; **~s** *pl* (*US*)
Leute *pl*

gym [dʒɪm] *n* Turnhalle *f*; (*for working out*)
Fitnesscenter *nt*; **gymnasium**
[dʒɪmˈneɪzɪəm] *n* Turnhalle *f*; **gymnastics**
[dʒɪmˈnæstɪks] *nsing* Turnen *nt*;
gym-toned *adj* durchtrainiert

gynaecologist [gaɪnɪˈkɒlədʒɪst] *n*
Frauenarzt *m*, Frauenärztin *f*, Gynäkologe
m, Gynäkologin *f*; **gynaecology** *n*
Gynäkologie *f*, Frauenheilkunde *f*

gypsy [ˈdʒɪpsɪ] *n* Zigeuner(in) *m(f)*

habit ['hæbɪt] *n* Gewohnheit *f*; **habitual** [hə'bɪtjʊəl] *adj* gewohnt; *(drinker, liar)* gewohnheitsmäßig

hack [hæk] *vt* hacken; **hacker** *n* (Inform) Hacker(in) *m(f)*

had [hæd] *pt, pp of* **have**

haddock ['hædək] *n* Schellfisch *m*

hadn't ['hædnt] *contr of* **had not**

haemophiliac, **hemophiliac** (US) [hi:məʊ'fɪlɪæk] *n* Bluter(in) *m(f)*; **haemorrhage**, **hemorrhage** (US) ['hemərɪdʒ] *n* Blutung *f* ▷ *vi* bluten; **haemorrhoids**, **hemorrhoids** (US) ['hemərɔɪdz] *npl* Hämorrhoiden *pl*

haggis ['hægɪs] *n* (Scot) *mit gehackten Schafsinnereien und Haferschrot gefüllter Schafsmagen*

Hague [heɪg] *n* **the ~** Den Haag

hail [heɪl] *n* Hagel *m* ▷ *vi* hageln ▷ *vt* **to ~ sb as sth** jdn als etw feiern; **hailstone** *n* Hagelkorn *nt*; **hailstorm** *n* Hagelschauer *m*

hair [hɛə*] *n* Haar *nt*, Haare *pl*; **to do one's ~** sich frisieren; **to get one's ~ cut** sich *dat* die Haare schneiden lassen; **hairbrush** *n* Haarbürste *f*; **hair conditioner** *n* Haarspülung *f*; **haircut** *n*

Haarschnitt *m*; **to have a ~** sich *dat* die Haare schneiden lassen; **hairdo** (*pl* **-s**) *n* Frisur *f*; **hairdresser** *n* Friseur *m*, Friseuse *f*; **hairdryer** *n* Haartrockner *m*; *(hand-held)* Fön® *m*; *(over head)* Trockenhaube *f*; **hair gel** *n* Haargel *nt*; **hairpin** *n* Haarnadel *f*; **hair remover** *n* Enthaarungsmittel *nt*; **hair spray** *n* Haarspray *nt*; **hair style** *n* Frisur *f*; **hairy** *adj* haarig, behaart; *(fam: dangerous)* brenzlig

hake [heɪk] *n* Seehecht *m*

half [hɑːf] (*pl* **halves**) *n* Hälfte *f*; *(Sport: of game)* Halbzeit *f*; **to cut in ~** halbieren ▷ *adj* halb; **three and a ~ pounds** dreieinhalb Pfund; **~ an hour, a ~ hour** eine halbe Stunde; **one and a ~** eineinhalb, anderthalb ▷ *adv* halb, zur Hälfte; **~ past three, ~ three** halb vier; **at ~ past** um halb; **~ asleep** fast eingeschlafen; **she's ~ German** sie ist zur Hälfte Deutsche; **~ as big (as)** halb so groß (wie); **half board** *n* Halbpension *f*; **half fare** *n* halber Fahrpreis; **half-hearted** *adj* halbherzig; **half-hour** *n* halbe Stunde; **half moon** *n* Halbmond *m*; **half pint** *n* ≈ Viertelliter *m o nt*; **half price** *n* (**at**) **~** zum halben Preis; **half-term** *n* (at school) Ferien *pl* in der Mitte des Trimesters; **half-time** *n* Halbzeit *f*; **halfway** *adv* auf halbem Wege; **halfwit** *n* (fam) Trottel *m*

halibut ['hælɪbət] *n* Heilbutt *m*

hall [hɔːl] *n* (building) Halle *f*; (for audience) Saal *m*; (entrance ~) Flur *m*; (large) Diele *f*; **~ of residence** (Brit) Studentenwohnheim *nt*

hallmark ['hɔːlmɑːk] *n* Stempel *m*; (fig) Kennzeichen *nt*

hallo [hʌ'ləʊ] *interj* hallo

Hallowe'en [hæləʊ'iːn] *n* Halloween *nt* *(Tag vor Allerheiligen, an dem sich Kinder verkleiden und von Tür zu Tür gehen)*

Hallowe'en

Hallowe'en ist der 31. Oktober, der Vorabend von Allerheiligen und nach altem Glauben der Abend, an dem man Geister und Hexen sehen kann. In Großbritannien und vor allem in den USA feiern die Kinder Hallowe'en, indem sie sich verkleiden und mit selbst gemachten

Laternen aus Kürbissen von Tür zu
Tür ziehen.

halo ['heɪləʊ] (pl **-es**) n (of saint)
Heiligenschein m
halt [hɔːlt] n Pause f, Halt m; **to come to
a ~** zum Stillstand kommen ▷ vt, vi
anhalten
halve [hɑːv] vt halbieren
ham [hæm] n Schinken m; **~ and eggs**
Schinken mit Spiegelei
hamburger ['hæmbɜːgə*] n (Gastr)
Hamburger m
hammer ['hæmə*] n Hammer m ▷ vt, vi
hämmern
hammock ['hæmək] n Hängematte f
hamper ['hæmpə*] vt behindern ▷ n (as
gift) Geschenkkorb m; (for picnic)
Picknickkorb m
hamster ['hæmstə*] n Hamster m
hand [hænd] n Hand f; (of clock,
instrument) Zeiger m; (in card game) Blatt nt;
to be made by ~ Handarbeit sein; **~s up!**
Hände hoch!; (at school) meldet euch!; **~s
off!** Finger weg!; **on the one ~ ..., on the
other ~...** einerseits ..., andererseits ...; **to
give sb a ~** jdm helfen (with bei); **it's in his
~s** er hat es in der Hand; **to be in good ~s**
gut aufgehoben sein; **to get out of
~** außer Kontrolle geraten ▷ vt (pass)
reichen (to sb jdm); **hand down** vt
(tradition) überliefern; (heirloom) vererben;
hand in vt einreichen; (at school, university
etc) abgeben; **hand out** vt verteilen;
hand over vt übergeben;
handbag n Handtasche f; **handbook** n
Handbuch nt; **handbrake** n (Brit)
Handbremse f; **hand cream** n
Handcreme f; **handcuffs** npl
Handschellen pl; **handful** n Handvoll f;
handheld PC n Handheld m
handicap ['hændɪkæp] n Behinderung f,
Handikap nt ▷ vt benachteiligen;
handicapped adj behindert; **the ~** die
Behinderten
handicraft ['hændɪkrɑːft] n
Kunsthandwerk nt
handkerchief ['hæŋkətʃɪf] n
Taschentuch nt
handle ['hændl] n Griff m; (of door) Klinke
f; (of cup etc) Henkel m; (for winding) Kurbel f
▷ vt (touch) anfassen; (deal with: matter)
sich befassen mit; (people, machine etc)

umgehen mit; (situation, problem) fertig
werden mit; **handlebars** npl Lenkstange f
hand luggage ['hændlʌgɪdʒ] n
Handgepäck nt; **handmade** adj
handgefertigt; **to be ~** Handarbeit sein;
handout n (sheet) Handout nt,
Thesenpapier nt; **handset** n Hörer m;
please replace the ~ bitte legen Sie auf;
hands-free phone n Freisprechanlage f;
handshake n Händedruck m
handsome ['hænsəm] adj (man) gut
aussehend
hands-on [hændz'ɒn] adj
praxisorientiert; **~ experience** praktische
Erfahrung
handwriting ['hændraɪtɪŋ] n
Handschrift f
handy ['hændɪ] adj (useful) praktisch
hang [hæŋ] (hung, hung) vt
(auf)hängen; (execute: hanged, hanged)
hängen; **to ~ sth on sth** etw an etw akk
hängen ▷ vi hängen ▷ n **he's got the ~ of
it** er hat den Dreh raus; **hang about** vi
sich herumtreiben, rumhängen; **hang on**
vi sich festhalten (to an +dat); (fam: wait)
warten; **to ~ to sth** etw behalten; **hang
up** vi (Tel) auflegen ▷ vt aufhängen
hangar ['hæŋə*] n Flugzeughalle f
hanger ['hæŋə*] n Kleiderbügel m
hang glider ['hæŋglaɪdə*] n
(Flug)drachen m; (person)
Drachenflieger(in) m(f); **hang-gliding** n
Drachenfliegen nt
hangover ['hæŋəʊvə*] n (bad head) Kater
m; (relic) Überbleibsel m
hankie ['hæŋkɪ] n (fam) Taschentuch nt
happen ['hæpən] vi geschehen; (sth
strange, unpleasant) passieren; **if anything
should ~ to me** wenn mir etwas passieren
sollte; **it won't ~ again** es wird nicht
wieder vorkommen; **I ~ed to be passing**
ich kam zufällig vorbei; **happening** n
Ereignis nt, Happening nt
happily ['hæpɪlɪ] adv fröhlich, glücklich;
(luckily) glücklicherweise; **happiness**
['hæpɪnɪs] n Glück nt; **happy** ['hæpɪ] adj
glücklich; (satisfied) **~ with sth** mit etw
zufrieden; (willing) **to be ~ to do sth** etw
gerne tun; **Happy Christmas** fröhliche
Weihnachten!; **Happy New Year** ein
glückliches Neues Jahr!; **Happy Birthday**
herzlichen Glückwunsch zum
Geburtstag!; **happy hour** n Happy Hour f

(Zeit, in der man in Bars Getränke zu günstigeren Preisen bekommt)

harass ['hærəs] vt (ständig) belästigen; **harassment** n Belästigung f; (at work) Mobbing nt; **sexual ~** sexuelle Belästigung

harbor (US), **harbour** ['hɑːbə*] n Hafen m

hard [hɑːd] adj hart; (difficult) schwer, schwierig; (harsh) hart(herzig); **don't be ~ on him** sei nicht zu streng zu ihm; **it's ~ to believe** es ist kaum zu glauben ▷ adv (work) schwer; (run) schnell; (rain, snow) stark; **to try ~/~er** sich dat große/mehr Mühe geben; **hardback** n gebundene Ausgabe; **hard-boiled** adj (egg) hart gekocht; **hard copy** n (Inform) Ausdruck m; **hard disk** n (Inform) Festplatte f; **harden** vt härten ▷ vi hart werden; **hardened** adj (person) abgehärtet (to gegen); **hard-hearted** adj hartherzig; **hardliner** n Hardliner(in) m(f); **hardly** ['hɑːdlɪ] adv kaum; **~ ever** fast nie; **hardship** ['hɑːdʃɪp] n Not f; **hard shoulder** n (Brit) Standspur f; **hardware** n (Inform) Hardware f, Haushalts- und Eisenwaren pl; **hard-working** adj fleißig, tüchtig

hare [hɛə*] n Hase m

harm [hɑːm] n Schaden m; (bodily) Verletzung f; **it wouldn't do any ~** es würde nicht schaden ▷ vt schaden +dat; (person) verletzen; **harmful** adj schädlich; **harmless** adj harmlos

harp [hɑːp] n Harfe f

harsh [hɑːʃ] adj (climate, voice) rau; (light, sound) grell; (severe) hart, streng

harvest ['hɑːvɪst] n Ernte f; (time) Erntezeit f ▷ vt ernten

has [hæz] pres of **have**

hash [hæʃ] n (Gastr) Haschee nt; (fam: hashish) Haschisch nt; **to make a ~ of sth** etw vermasseln; **hash browns** npl (US) ≈ Kartoffelpuffer pl

hassle ['hæsl] n Ärger m; (fuss) Theater nt; **no ~** kein Problem ▷ vt bedrängen

hasn't ['hæznt] contr of **has not**

haste [heɪst] n Eile f; **hastily, hasty** adv, adj hastig; (rash) vorschnell

hat [hæt] n Hut m

hatch [hætʃ] n (Naut) Luke f; (in house) Durchreiche f; **hatchback** ['hætʃbæk] n (car) Wagen m mit Hecktür

hate [heɪt] vt hassen; **I ~ doing this** ich mache das sehr ungern ▷ n Hass m (of auf +akk)

haul [hɔːl] vt ziehen, schleppen ▷ n (booty) Beute f; **haulage** ['hɔːlɪdʒ] n Transport m; (trade) Spedition f; **haunted** adj **a ~ house** ein Haus, in dem es spukt

⊙ KEYWORD

have [hæv] (pt, pp **had**) aux vb **1** haben (esp with vbs of motion) sein; **to have arrived/slept** angekommen sein/geschlafen haben; **to have been** gewesen sein; **having eaten** or **when he had eaten, he left** nachdem er gegessen hatte, ging er

2 (in tag questions): **you've done it, haven't you?** du hast es doch gemacht, oder nicht?

3 (in short answers and questions): **you've made a mistake — so I have/no I haven't** du hast einen Fehler gemacht — ja, stimmt/nein; **we haven't paid — yes we have!** wir haben nicht bezahlt — doch; **I've been there before, have you?** ich war schon einmal da, du auch?

▷ modal aux vb (be obliged); **to have (got) to do sth** etw tun müssen; **you haven't to tell her** du darfst es ihr nicht erzählen

▷ vt **1** (possess) haben; **he has (got) blue eyes** er hat blaue Augen; **I have (got) an idea** ich habe eine Idee

2 (referring to meals etc): **to have breakfast/a cigarette** frühstücken/eine Zigarette rauchen

3 (receive, obtain etc) haben; **may I have your address?** kann ich Ihre Adresse haben?; **to have a baby** ein Kind bekommen

4 (maintain, allow): **he will have it that he is right** er besteht darauf, dass er Recht hat; **I won't have it** das lasse ich mir nicht bieten

5: **to have sth done** etw machen lassen; **to have sb do sth** jdn etw machen lassen; **he soon had them all laughing** er brachte sie alle zum Lachen

6 (experience, suffer): **she had her bag stolen** man hat ihr die Tasche gestohlen; **he had his arm broken** er hat sich den Arm gebrochen

7 (+noun: take, hold etc); **to have a walk/rest** spazieren gehen/sich ausruhen; **to have a meeting/party** eine Besprechung/Party haben **have out** vt: **to have it out with sb** (settle problem) etw mit jdm bereden

Hawaii [hə'waɪiː] n Hawaii nt
hawk [hɔːk] n Habicht m
hay [heɪ] n Heu nt; **hay fever** n Heuschnupfen m
hazard ['hæzəd] n Gefahr f; (risk) Risiko nt; **hazardous** adj gefährlich; **~ waste** Sondermüll m; **hazard warning lights** npl Warnblinkanlage f
haze [heɪz] n Dunst m
hazelnut ['heɪzlnʌt] n Haselnuss f
hazy ['heɪzɪ] adj (misty) dunstig; (vague) verschwommen
he [hiː] pron er
head [hed] n Kopf m; (leader) Leiter(in) m(f); (at school) Schulleiter(in) m(f); **~ of state** Staatsoberhaupt nt; **at the ~ of** an der Spitze von; (tossing coin) **~s or tails?** Kopf oder Zahl? ▷ adj (leading) Ober-; **~ boy** Schulsprecher m; **~ girl** Schulsprecherin f ▷ vt anführen; (organization) leiten; **head for** vt zusteuern auf +akk; **he's heading for trouble** er wird Ärger bekommen
headache ['hedeɪk] n Kopfschmerzen pl, Kopfweh nt; **header** n (football) Kopfball m; (dive) Kopfsprung m; **headfirst** adj kopfüber; **headhunt** vt (Comm) abwerben; **heading** n Überschrift f; **headlamp, headlight** n Scheinwerfer m; **headline** n Schlagzeile f; **headmaster** n Schulleiter m; **headmistress** n Schulleiterin f; **head-on collision** adj Frontalzusammenstoß m; **headphones** npl Kopfhörer m; **headquarters** npl (of firm) Zentrale f; **headrest, head restraint** n Kopfstütze f; **headscarf** (pl **-scarves**) n Kopftuch nt; **head teacher** n Schulleiter(in) m(f)
heal [hiːl] vt, vi heilen
health [helθ] n Gesundheit f; **good/bad for one's ~** gesund/ungesund; **your ~!** zum Wohl!; **health centre** n Ärztezentrum nt; **health club** n Fitnesscenter nt; **health food** n Reformkost f; **~ store** Bioladen m; **health insurance** n Krankenversicherung f;

health service n Gesundheitswesen nt; **healthy** adj gesund
heap [hiːp] n Haufen m; **~s of** (fam) jede Menge ▷ vt, vi häufen
hear [hɪə*] (**heard, heard**) vt, vi hören; **to ~ about sth** von etw erfahren; **I've ~d of it/him** ich habe schon davon/von ihm gehört; **hearing** n Gehör nt; (Jur) Verhandlung f; **hearing aid** n Hörgerät nt; **hearsay** n **from ~** vom Hörensagen
heart [hɑːt] n Herz nt; **to loose/take ~** den Mut verlieren/Mut fassen; **to learn by ~** auswendig lernen; (cards) **~s** Herz nt; **queen of ~s** Herzdame f; **heart attack** n Herzanfall m; **heartbeat** n Herzschlag m; **heartbreaking** adj herzzerreißend; **heartbroken** adj todunglücklich, untröstlich; **heartburn** n Sodbrennen nt; **heart failure** n Herzversagen nt; **heartfelt** adj tief empfunden; **heartless** adj herzlos; **heart-throb** n (fam) Schwarm m; **heart-to-heart** n offene Aussprache; **hearty** ['hɑːtɪ] adj (meal, appetite) herzhaft; (welcome) herzlich
heat [hiːt] n Hitze f; (pleasant) Wärme f; (temperature) Temperatur f; (Sport) Vorlauf m ▷ vt (house, room) heizen; **heat up** vi warm werden ▷ vt aufwärmen; **heated** adj beheizt; (fig) hitzig; **heater** n Heizofen m; (Auto) Heizung f
heath [hiːθ] n (Brit) Heide f; **heather** ['heðə*] n Heidekraut nt
heating ['hiːtɪŋ] n Heizung f; **heat resistant** adj hitzebeständig; **heatstroke** n Hitzschlag m; **heatwave** n Hitzewelle f
heaven ['hevn] n Himmel m; **heavenly** adj himmlisch
heavily ['hevɪlɪ] adv (rain, drink etc) stark; **heavy** ['hevɪ] adj schwer; (rain, traffic, smoker etc) stark; **heavy goods vehicle** n Lastkraftwagen m
Hebrew ['hiːbruː] adj hebräisch ▷ n (language) Hebräisch nt
hectic ['hektɪk] adj hektisch
he'd [hiːd] contr of **he had; he would**
hedge [hedʒ] n Hecke f
hedgehog ['hedʒhɒg] n Igel m
heel [hiːl] n (Anat) Ferse f; (of shoe) Absatz m
hefty ['heftɪ] adj schwer; (person) stämmig; (fine, amount) saftig
height [haɪt] n Höhe f; (of person) Größe f

heir [ɛə*] n Erbe m; **heiress** ['ɛərɪs] n Erbin f
held [held] pt, pp of **hold**
helicopter ['helɪkɒptə*] n Hubschrauber m; **heliport** ['helɪpɔːt] n Hubschrauberlandeplatz m
hell [hel] n Hölle f; **go to ~** scher dich zum Teufel ▷ interj verdammt; **that's a ~ of a lot of money** das ist verdammt viel Geld
he'll [hiːl] contr of **he will; he shall**
hello [hʌ'ləʊ] interj hallo
helmet ['helmɪt] n Helm m
help [help] n Hilfe f ▷ vt, vi helfen +dat (with bei); **to ~ sb (to) do sth** jdm helfen, etw zu tun; **can I ~?** kann ich (Ihnen) behilflich sein?; **I couldn't ~ laughing** ich musste einfach lachen; **I can't ~ it** ich kann nichts dafür; **~ yourself** bedienen Sie sich; **helpful** adj (person) hilfsbereit; (useful) nützlich; **helping** n Portion f; **helpless** adj hilflos
hem [hem] n Saum m
hemophiliac [hiːməʊ'fɪlɪæk] n (US) Bluter m; **hemorrhage** ['hemərɪdʒ] n (US) Blutung f; **hemorrhoids** ['hemərɔɪdz] npl (US) Hämorrhoiden pl
hen [hen] n Henne f
hen night n (Brit) Junggesellinnenabschied m
hence [hens] adv (reason) daher
henpecked ['henpekt] adj **to be ~** unter dem Pantoffel stehen
hepatitis [hepə'taɪtɪs] n Hepatitis f
her [hɜː*] adj ihr; **she's hurt ~ leg** sie hat sich dat das Bein verletzt ▷ pron (direct object); (indirect object) ihr; **do you know ~?** kennst du sie?; **can you help ~?** kannst du ihr helfen?; **it's ~** sie ist's
herb [hɜːb] n Kraut nt
herbal medicine ['hɜːbəl-] n Pflanzenheilkunde f; **herbal tea** n Kräutertee m
herd [hɜːd] n Herde f; **herd instinct** n Herdentrieb m
here [hɪə*] adv hier; (to this place) hierher; **come ~** komm her; **I won't be ~ for lunch** ich bin zum Mittagessen nicht da; **~ and there** hier und da, da und dort
hereditary [hɪ'redɪtərɪ] adj erblich; **hereditary disease** n Erbkrankheit f; **heritage** ['herɪtɪdʒ] n Erbe nt
hernia ['hɜːnɪə] n Leistenbruch m, Eingeweidebruch m

hero ['hɪərəʊ] (pl -es) n Held m
heroin ['herəʊɪn] n Heroin nt
heroine ['herəʊɪn] n Heldin f; **heroism** ['herəʊɪzəm] n Heldentum nt
herring ['herɪŋ] n Hering m
hers [hɜːz] pron ihre(r, s); **this is ~** das gehört ihr; **a friend of ~** ein Freund von ihr
herself [hɜː'self] pron (reflexive) sich; **she's bought ~ a flat** sie hat sich eine Wohnung gekauft; **she needs it for ~** sie braucht es für sich (selbst); (emphatic) **she did it ~** sie hat es selbst gemacht; **(all) by ~** allein
he's [hiːz] contr of **he is; he has**
hesitant ['hezɪtənt] adj zögernd; **hesitate** ['hezɪteɪt] vi zögern; **don't ~ to ask** fragen Sie ruhig; **hesitation** n Zögern nt; **without ~** ohne zu zögern
heterosexual [hetərəʊ'seksʊəl] adj heterosexuell ▷ n Heterosexuelle(r) mf
HGV abbr = **heavy goods vehicle** LKW m
hi [haɪ] interj hi, hallo
hiccup ['hɪkʌp] n Schluckauf m; (minor problem) Problemchen nt; **to have (the) ~s** Schluckauf haben
hid [hɪd] pt of **hide**
hidden ['hɪdn] pp of **hide**
hide [haɪd] (**hid, hidden**) vt verstecken (from vor +dat); (feelings, truth) verbergen; (cover) verdecken ▷ vi sich verstecken (from vor +dat)
hideous ['hɪdɪəs] adj scheußlich
hiding ['haɪdɪŋ] n (beating) Tracht f Prügel; (concealment) **to be in ~** sich versteckt halten; **hiding place** n Versteck nt
hi-fi ['haɪfaɪ] n Hi-Fi nt; (system) Hi-Fi-Anlage f
high [haɪ] adj hoch; (wind) stark; (living) im großen Stil; (on drugs) high ▷ adv hoch ▷ n (Meteo) Hoch nt; **highchair** n Hochstuhl m; **higher** adj höher; **higher education** n Hochschulbildung f; **high flier** n Hochbegabte(r) (m)f; **high heels** npl Stöckelschuhe pl; **high jump** n Hochsprung m; **Highlands** npl (schottisches) Hochland nt; **highlight** n (in hair) Strähnchen nt; (fig) Höhepunkt m ▷ vt (with pen) hervorheben; **highlighter** n Textmarker m; **highly** adv hoch, sehr; **~ paid** hoch bezahlt; **I think ~ of him** ich habe eine hohe Meinung von ihm; **high-performance** adj Hochleistungs-; **high pressure** n Hochdruck m; **high**

school n (US) Highschool f, ≈ Gymnasium nt; **high-speed** adj Schnell-; **~ train** Hochgeschwindigkeitszug m; **high street** n Hauptstraße f; **high tech** adj Hightech- ▷ n Hightech nt; **high tide** n Flut f; **highway** n (US) ≈ Autobahn f; (Brit) Landstraße f

hijack ['haɪdʒæk] vt entführen, hijacken; **hijacker** n Entführer(in) m(f), Hijacker m

hike [haɪk] vi wandern ▷ n Wanderung f; **hiker** n Wanderer m, Wanderin f; **hiking** n Wandern nt

hilarious [hɪ'lɛərɪəs] adj zum Schreien komisch

hill [hɪl] n Hügel m; (higher) Berg m; **hilly** adj hügelig

him [hɪm] pron (direct object) ihn; (indirect object) ihm; **do you know ~?** kennst du ihn?; **can you help ~?** kannst du ihm helfen?; **it's ~** er ist's; **~ too** er auch

himself [hɪm'self] pron (reflexive) sich; **he's bought ~ a flat** er hat sich eine Wohnung gekauft; **he needs it for ~** er braucht es für sich (selbst); (emphatic) **he did it ~** er hat es selbst gemacht; **(all) by ~** allein

hinder ['hɪndə*] vt behindern; **hindrance** ['hɪndrəns] n Behinderung f

Hindu ['hɪndu:] adj hinduistisch ▷ n Hindu m; **Hinduism** ['hɪndu:ɪzəm] n Hinduismus m

hinge [hɪndʒ] n Scharnier nt; (on door) Angel f

hint [hɪnt] n Wink m, Andeutung f; (trace) Spur f ▷ vi andeuten (at akk)

hip [hɪp] n Hüfte f ▷ adj (trend) hip, trendy

hippopotamus [hɪpə'pɒtəməs] n Nilpferd nt

hire ['haɪə*] vt (worker) anstellen; (car, bike etc) mieten ▷ n Miete f; **for ~** (taxi) frei; **hire(d) car** n Mietwagen m; **hire purchase** n Ratenkauf m

his [hɪz] adj sein; **he's hurt ~ leg** er hat sich dat das Bein verletzt ▷ pron seine(r, s); **it's ~** es gehört ihm; **a friend of ~** ein Freund von ihm

historic [hɪ'stɒrɪk] adj (significant) historisch; **historical** adj (monument etc) historisch; (studies etc) geschichtlich; **history** ['hɪstərɪ] n Geschichte f

hit [hɪt] n (blow) Schlag m; (on target) Treffer m; (success) Erfolg m; (Mus) Hit m ▷ vt (hit, hit) schlagen; (bullet, stone etc)

treffen; **the car ~ the tree** das Auto fuhr gegen einen Baum; **to ~ one's head on sth** sich dat den Kopf an etw dat stoßen; **hit (up)on** vt stoßen auf +akk; **hit-and-run** adj **~ accident** Unfall m mit Fahrerflucht

hitch [hɪtʃ] vt (pull up) hochziehen ▷ n Schwierigkeit f; **without a ~** reibungslos

hitch-hike ['hɪtʃhaɪk] vi trampen; **hitch-hiker** n Tramper(in) m(f); **hitchhiking** n Trampen nt

HIV abbr = **human immunodeficiency virus** HIV nt; **~ positive/negative** HIV-positiv/negativ

hive [haɪv] n Bienenstock m

HM abbr = **His/Her Majesty**

HMS abbr = **His/Her Majesty's Ship**

hoarse [hɔ:s] adj heiser

hoax [həʊks] n Streich m, Jux m; (false alarm) blinder Alarm

hob [hɒb] n (of cooker) Kochfeld nt

hobble ['hɒbl] vi humpeln

hobby ['hɒbɪ] n Hobby nt

hobo ['həʊbəʊ] (pl -es) n (US) Penner(in) m(f)

hockey ['hɒkɪ] n Hockey nt

hold [həʊld] (held, held) vt halten; (contain) enthalten; (be able to contain) fassen; (post, office) innehaben; (value) behalten; (meeting) abhalten; (person as prisoner) gefangen halten; **to ~ one's breath** den Atem anhalten; **to ~ hands** Händchen halten; **~ the line** (Tel) bleiben Sie am Apparat ▷ vi halten; (weather) sich halten ▷ n (grasp) Halt m; (of ship, aircraft) Laderaum m; **hold back** vt zurückhalten; (keep secret) verheimlichen; **hold on** vi sich festhalten; (wait) warten; (Tel) dranbleiben; **to ~ to sth** etw festhalten; **hold out** vt ausstrecken; (offer) hinhalten; (offer) bieten ▷ vi durchhalten; **hold up** vt hochhalten; (support) stützen; (delay) aufhalten; **holdall** n Reisetasche f; **holder** n (person) Inhaber(in) m(f); **holdup** n (in traffic) Stau m; (robbery) Überfall m

hole [həʊl] n Loch nt; (of fox, rabbit) Bau m; **~ in the wall** (cash dispenser) Geldautomat m

holiday ['hɒlɪdeɪ] n (day off) freier Tag; (public ~) Feiertag m; (vacation) Urlaub m; (at school) Ferien pl; **on ~** im Urlaub; **to go on ~** Urlaub machen; **holiday camp** n Ferienlager nt; **holiday home** n

h

Ferienhaus *nt*; (*flat*) Ferienwohnung *f*;
holidaymaker *n* Urlauber(in) *m(f)*;
holiday resort *n* Ferienort *m*
Holland ['hɒlənd] *n* Holland *nt*
hollow ['hɒləʊ] *adj* hohl; (*words*) leer ▷ *n*
Vertiefung *f*
holly ['hɒlɪ] *n* Stechpalme *f*
holy ['həʊlɪ] *adj* heilig; **Holy Week** *n*
Karwoche *f*
home [həʊm] *n* Zuhause *nt*; (*area, country*)
Heimat *f*; (*institution*) Heim *nt*; **at ~** zu
Hause; **to make oneself at ~** es sich *dat*
bequem machen; **away from ~** verreist
▷ *adv* **to go ~** nach Hause gehen/fahren;
home address *n* Heimatadresse *f*; **home
country** *n* Heimatland *nt*; **home game** *n*
(*Sport*) Heimspiel *nt*; **homeless** *adj*
obdachlos; **homely** *adj* häuslich; (*US:
ugly*) unscheinbar; **home-made** *adj* selbst
gemacht; **home movie** *n* Amateurfilm
m; **Home Office** *n* (*Brit*)
Innenministerium *nt*
homeopathic *adj* (*US*) *see*
homoeopathic
home page ['həʊmpeɪdʒ] *n* (*Inform*)
Homepage *f*; **Home Secretary** *n* (*Brit*)
Innenminister(in) *m(f)*; **homesick** *adj* **to
be ~** Heimweh haben; **home town** *n*
Heimatstadt *f*; **homework** *n*
Hausaufgaben *pl*
homicide ['hɒmɪsaɪd] *n* (*US*) Totschlag *m*
homoeopathic [həʊmɪəʊ'pæθɪk] *adj*
homöopathisch
homosexual [hɒməʊ'sekʃʊəl] *adj*
homosexuell ▷ *n* Homosexuelle(r) *mf*
Honduras [hɒn'djʊərəs] *n* Honduras *nt*
honest ['ɒnɪst] *adj* ehrlich; **honesty** *n*
Ehrlichkeit *f*
honey ['hʌnɪ] *n* Honig *m*; **honeycomb** *n*
Honigwabe *f*; **honeydew melon** *n*
Honigmelone *f*; **honeymoon** *n*
Flitterwochen *pl*
Hong Kong [hɒŋ 'kɒŋ] *n* Hongkong *nt*
honor (*US*) *see* **honour**; **honorary**
['ɒnərərɪ] *adj* (*member, title etc*) Ehren-,
ehrenamtlich; **honour** ['ɒnə*] *vt* ehren;
(*cheque*) einlösen; (*contract*) einhalten ▷ *n*
Ehre *f*; **in ~ of** zu Ehren von; **honourable**
adj ehrenhaft; **honours degree** *n*
*akademischer Grad mit Prüfung im
Spezialfach*
hood [hʊd] *n* Kapuze *f*; (*Auto*) Verdeck *nt*;
(*US Auto*) Kühlerhaube *f*

hoof [huːf] (*pl* **hooves**) *n* Huf *m*
hook [hʊk] *n* Haken *m*; **hooked** *adj* (*keen*)
besessen (*on* von); (*drugs*) abhängig sein
(*on* von)
hooligan ['huːlɪgən] *n* Hooligan *m*
hoot [huːt] *vi* (*Auto*) hupen
Hoover® ['huːvə] *n* Staubsauger *m*;
hoover *vi*, *vt* staubsaugen
hop [hɒp] *vi* hüpfen ▷ *n* (*Bot*) Hopfen *m*
hope [həʊp] *vi*, *vt* hoffen (*for* auf +*akk*); **I
~ so/~ not** hoffentlich/hoffentlich nicht; **I
~ (that) we'll meet** ich hoffe, dass wir uns
sehen werden ▷ *n* Hoffnung *f*; **there's no
~** es ist aussichtslos; **hopeful** *adj*
hoffnungsvoll; **hopefully** *adv* (*full of hope*)
hoffnungsvoll; (*I hope so*) hoffentlich;
hopeless *adj* hoffnungslos; (*incompetent*)
miserabel
horizon [hə'raɪzn] *n* Horizont *m*;
horizontal [hɒrɪ'zɒntl] *adj* horizontal
hormone ['hɔːməʊn] *n* Hormon *nt*
horn [hɔːn] *n* Horn *nt*; (*Auto*) Hupe *f*
hornet ['hɔːnɪt] *n* Hornisse *f*
horny ['hɔːnɪ] *adj* (*fam*) geil
horoscope ['hɒrəskəʊp] *n* Horoskop *nt*
horrible, horribly ['hɒrɪbl, -blɪ] *adj*, *adv*
schrecklich; **horrid, horridly** ['hɒrɪd, -lɪ]
adj, *adv* abscheulich; **horrify** ['hɒrɪfaɪ] *vt*
entsetzen; **horror** ['hɒrə*] *n* Entsetzen
nt; **~s** (*things*) Schrecken *pl*
hors d'œuvre [ɔː'dɜːvr] *n* Vorspeise *f*
horse [hɔːs] *n* Pferd *nt*; **horse chestnut** *n*
Rosskastanie *f*; **horsepower** *n*
Pferdestärke *f*, PS *nt*; **horse racing** *n*
Pferderennen *nt*; **horseradish** *n*
Meerrettich *m*; **horse riding** *n* Reiten *nt*;
horseshoe *n* Hufeisen *nt*
horticulture ['hɔːtɪkʌltʃə*] *n* Gartenbau
m
hose, hosepipe [həʊz, 'həʊzpaɪp] *n*
Schlauch *m*
hospitable [hɒ'spɪtəbl] *adj*
gastfreundlich
hospital ['hɒspɪtl] *n* Krankenhaus *nt*
hospitality [hɒspɪ'tælɪtɪ] *n*
Gastfreundschaft *f*
host [həʊst] *n* Gastgeber *m*; (*Tv: of show*)
Moderator(in) *m(f)*, Talkmaster(in) *m(f)*
▷ *vt* (*party*) geben; (*TV show*)
moderieren
hostage ['hɒstɪdʒ] *n* Geisel *f*
hostel ['hɒstəl] *n* Wohnheim *nt*; (*youth ~*)
Jugendherberge *f*

hostess ['həʊstɪs] n (of a party)
Gastgeberin f
hostile ['hɒstaɪl] adj feindlich; **hostility**
[hɒs'tɪlɪtɪ] n Feindseligkeit f
hot [hɒt] adj heiß; (drink, food, water)
warm; (spiced) scharf; **I'm (feeling)** ~ mir
ist heiß; **hot cross bun** n Rosinenbrötchen
mit einem Kreuz darauf, hauptsächlich zu
Ostern gegessen; **hot dog** n Hotdog nt
hotel [həʊ'tel] n Hotel nt; **hotel room** n
Hotelzimmer nt
hothouse n Treibhaus nt; **hotline** n
Hotline f; **hotplate** n Kochplatte f;
hotpot n Fleischeintopf mit Kartoffeleinlage;
hot-water bottle n Wärmflasche f
hour ['aʊə*] n Stunde f; **to wait for ~s**
stundenlang warten; **~s** pl (of shops etc)
Geschäftszeiten pl; **hourly** adj stündlich
house [haʊs] (pl **houses**) n Haus nt; **at
my** ~ bei mir (zu Hause); **to my** ~ zu mir
(nach Hause); **on the** ~ auf Kosten des
Hauses; **the House of Commons/Lords**
das britische Unterhaus/Oberhaus; **the
Houses of Parliament** das britische
Parlamentsgebäude ▷ [haʊz] vt
unterbringen; **houseboat** n Hausboot nt;
household n Haushalt m; ~ **appliance**
Haushaltsgerät nt; **house-husband** n
Hausmann m; **housekeeping** n
Haushaltung f; (money) Haushaltsgeld nt;
house-trained adj stubenrein;
house-warming (party) n Einzugsparty
f; **housewife** (pl **-wives**) n Hausfrau f;
house wine n Hauswein m; **housework**
n Hausarbeit f
housing ['haʊzɪŋ] n (houses) Wohnungen
pl; (house building) Wohnungsbau m;
housing benefit n Wohngeld nt;
housing development, housing estate
(Brit) n Wohnsiedlung f
hover ['hɒvə*] vi schweben; **hovercraft** n
Luftkissenboot nt
how [haʊ] adv wie; ~ **many** wie viele;
~ **much** wie viel; ~ **are you?** wie geht es
Ihnen?; ~ **are things?** wie geht's?; ~**'s
work?** was macht die Arbeit?; ~ **about …?**
wie wäre es mit …?; **however** [haʊ'evə*]
conj (but) jedoch, aber ▷ adv (no matter
how) wie … auch; ~ **much it costs** wie viel
es auch kostet; ~ **you do it** wie man es
auch macht
howl [haʊl] vi heulen; **howler** ['haʊlə*] n
(fam) grober Schnitzer

HP, **hp** n (Brit) abbr = **hire purchase**
Ratenkauf m ▷ abbr = **horsepower** PS
HQ abbr = **headquarters**
hubcap ['hʌbkæp] n Radkappe f
hug [hʌg] vt umarmen ▷ n Umarmung f
huge [hju:dʒ] adj riesig
hum [hʌm] vi, vt summen
human ['hju:mən] adj menschlich;
~ **rights** Menschenrechte pl ▷ n ~ **(being)**
Mensch m; **humanitarian**
[hju:mænɪ'teərɪən] adj humanitär;
humanity [hju:'mænɪtɪ] n Menschheit f;
(kindliness) Menschlichkeit f; **humanities**
Geisteswissenschaften pl
humble ['hʌmbl] adj demütig; (modest)
bescheiden
humid ['hju:mɪd] adj feucht; **humidity**
[hju:'mɪdɪtɪ] n (Luft)feuchtigkeit f
humiliate [hju:'mɪlɪeɪt] vt demütigen;
humiliation [hju:mɪlɪ'eɪʃn] n
Erniedrigung f, Demütigung f
humor (US) see **humour**; **humorous**
['hju:mərəs] adj humorvoll; (story) lustig,
witzig; **humour** ['hju:mə*] n Humor m;
sense of ~ Sinn m für Humor
hump [hʌmp] n Buckel m
hunch [hʌntʃ] n Gefühl nt, Ahnung f ▷ vt
(back) krümmen; **hunchback** n
Bucklige(r) mf
hundred ['hʌndrəd] num **one** ~, **a**
~ (ein)hundert; **a** ~ **and one**
hundert(und)eins; **two** ~ zweihundert;
hundredth adj hundertste(r, s) ▷ n
(fraction) Hundertstel nt; **hundredweight**
n Zentner m (50,8 kg)
hung [hʌŋ] pt, pp of **hang**
Hungarian [hʌŋ'geərɪən] adj ungarisch
▷ n (person) Ungar(in) m(f); (language)
Ungarisch nt; **Hungary** ['hʌŋgərɪ] n
Ungarn nt
hunger ['hʌŋgə*] n Hunger m; **hungry**
['hʌŋgrɪ] adj hungrig; **to be** ~ Hunger
haben
hunk [hʌŋk] n (fam) gut aussehender
Mann
hunt [hʌnt] n Jagd f; (search) Suche f (for
nach) ▷ vt, vi jagen; (search) suchen (for
nach); **hunting** n Jagen nt, Jagd f
hurdle ['hɜ:dl] n (a. fig) Hürde f; **the
400m ~s** der 400m-Hürdenlauf
hurl [hɜ:l] vt schleudern
hurray [hʊ'reɪ] interj hurra
hurricane ['hʌrɪkən] n Orkan m

h

hurried ['hʌrɪd] *adj* eilig; **hurry** ['hʌrɪ] *n*
Eile *f*; **to be in a ~** es eilig haben; **there's
no ~** es eilt nicht ▷ *vi* sich beeilen; **~ (up)**
mach schnell! ▷ *vt* antreiben

hurt [hɜːt] **(hurt, hurt)** *vt* wehtun +*dat*;
(*wound: person, feelings*) verletzen; **I've
~ my arm** ich habe mir am Arm wehgetan
▷ *vi* wehtun; **my arm ~s** mir tut der Arm
weh

husband ['hʌzbənd] *n* Ehemann *m*

husky ['hʌskɪ] *adj* rau ▷ *n* Schlittenhund
m

hut [hʌt] *n* Hütte *f*

hyacinth ['haɪəsɪnθ] *n* Hyazinthe *f*

hybrid ['haɪbrɪd] *n* Kreuzung *f*

hydroelectric ['haɪdrəʊɪ'lektrɪk] *adj*
~ power station Wasserkraftwerk *nt*

hydrofoil ['haɪdrəʊfɔɪl] *n*
Tragflächenboot *nt*

hydrogen ['haɪdrədʒən] *n* Wasserstoff *m*

hygiene ['haɪdʒiːn] *n* Hygiene *f*; **hygienic**
[haɪ'dʒiːnɪk] *adj* hygienisch

hymn [hɪm] *n* Kirchenlied *nt*

hypermarket ['haɪpəmɑːkɪt] *n*
Großmarkt *m*; **hypersensitive** *adj*
überempfindlich

hyphen ['haɪfən] *n* Bindestrich *m*

hypnosis [hɪp'nəʊsɪs] *n* Hypnose *f*;
hypnotize ['hɪpnətaɪz] *vt* hypnotisieren

hypochondriac [haɪpəʊ'kɒndrɪæk] *n*
eingebildete(r) Kranke(r), eingebildete
Kranke

hypocrisy [hɪ'pəkrəsɪ] *n* Heuchelei *f*;
hypocrite ['hɪpəkrɪt] *n* Heuchler(in) *m(f)*

hypodermic [haɪpə'dɜmɪk] *adj*, *n*
~ (needle) Spritze *f*

hypothetical [haɪpəʊ'θetɪkəl] *adj*
hypothetisch

hysteria [hɪ'stɪərɪə] *n* Hysterie *f*;
hysterical [hɪ'sterɪkəl] *adj* hysterisch;
(*amusing*) zum Totlachen

identical [aɪˈdentɪkəl] *adj* identisch;
~ twins eineiige Zwillinge
identify [aɪˈdentɪfaɪ] *vt* identifizieren;
identity [aɪˈdentɪtɪ] *n* Identität *f*;
identity card *n* Personalausweis *m*
idiom [ˈɪdɪəm] *n* Redewendung *f*;
idiomatic *adj* idiomatisch
idiot [ˈɪdɪət] *n* Idiot(in) *m(f)*
idle [ˈaɪdl] *adj* *(doing nothing)* untätig;
(worker) unbeschäftigt; *(machines)* außer
Betrieb; *(lazy)* faul; *(promise, threat)* leer
idol [ˈaɪdl] *n* Idol *nt*; **idolize** [ˈaɪdəlaɪz] *vt*
vergöttern
idyllic [ɪˈdɪlɪk] *adj* idyllisch
i.e. *abbr* = **id est** d.h.

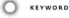 **KEYWORD**

if [ɪf] *conj* **1** wenn *(in case also)* falls; **if I
were you** wenn ich Sie wäre
2 *(although)*: **(even) if** (selbst *or* auch)
wenn
3 *(whether)* ob
4: **if so/not** wenn ja/nicht; **if only ...**
wenn ... doch nur ...; **if only I could** wenn
ich doch nur könnte; *see also* **as**

I [aɪ] *pron* ich
ice [aɪs] *n* Eis *nt* ▷ *vt* *(cake)* glasieren;
iceberg *n* Eisberg *m*; **iceberg lettuce** *n*
Eisbergsalat *m*; **icebox** *n* *(US)*
Kühlschrank *m*; **icecold** *adj* eiskalt;
ice cream *n* Eis *nt*; **ice cube** *n*
Eiswürfel *m*; **iced** *adj* eisgekühlt; *(coffee,
tea)* Eis-; *(cake)* glasiert; **ice hockey** *n*
Eishockey *nt*
Iceland [ˈaɪslənd] *n* Island *nt*; **Icelander** *n*
Isländer(in) *m(f)*; **Icelandic** [aɪsˈlændɪk]
adj isländisch ▷ *n* *(language)* Isländisch *nt*
ice lolly [ˈaɪslɒlɪ] *n* *(Brit)* Eis *nt* am Stiel;
ice rink *n* Kunsteisbahn *f*; **ice skating** *n*
Schlittschuhlaufen *nt*
icing [ˈaɪsɪŋ] *n* *(on cake)* Zuckerguss *m*
icon [ˈaɪkɒn] *n* Ikone *f*; *(Inform)* Icon *nt*,
Programmsymbol *nt*
icy [ˈaɪsɪ] *adj* *(slippery)* vereist; *(cold)* eisig
I'd [aɪd] *contr of* **I would; I had**
ID *abbr* = **identification** Ausweis *m*
idea [aɪˈdɪə] *n* Idee *f*; **(I've) no ~** (ich habe)
keine Ahnung; **that's my ~ of ...** so stelle
ich mir ... vor
ideal [aɪˈdɪəl] *n* Ideal *nt* ▷ *adj* ideal;
ideally *adv* ideal; *(before statement)*
idealerweise

ignition [ɪgˈnɪʃən] *n* Zündung *f*; **ignition
key** *n* *(Auto)* Zündschlüssel *m*
ignorance [ˈɪgnərəns] *n* Unwissenheit *f*;
ignorant *adj* unwissend; **ignore** [ɪgˈnɔ:*]
vt ignorieren, nicht beachten
I'll [aɪl] *contr of* **I will; I shall**
ill [ɪl] *adj* krank; **~ at ease** unbehaglich
illegal [ɪˈli:gəl] *adj* illegal
illegitimate [ɪlɪˈdʒɪtɪmət] *adj* unzulässig;
(child) unehelich
illiterate [ɪˈlɪtərət] *adj* **to be
~** Analphabet(in) sein
illness [ˈɪlnəs] *n* Krankheit *f*
illuminate [ɪˈlu:mɪneɪt] *vt* beleuchten;
illuminating *adj* *(remark)*
aufschlussreich
illusion [ɪˈlu:ʒən] *n* Illusion *f*; **to be under
the ~ that ...** sich einbilden, dass ...
illustrate [ˈɪləstreɪt] *vt* illustrieren;
illustration *n* Abbildung *f*, Bild *nt*
I'm [aɪm] *contr of* **I am**
image [ˈɪmɪdʒ] *n* Bild *nt*; *(public ~)* Image
nt; **imaginable** [ɪˈmædʒɪnəbl] *adj*
denkbar; **imaginary** [ɪˈmædʒɪnərɪ] *adj*
eingebildet; **~ world** Fantasiewelt *f*;
imagination [ɪmædʒɪˈneɪʃən] *n* Fantasie

f; (*mistaken*) Einbildung *f*; **imaginative**
[ɪ'mædʒɪnətɪv] *adj* fantasievoll; **imagine**
[ɪ'mædʒɪn] *vt* sich vorstellen; (*wrongly*)
sich einbilden; **~!** stell dir vor!
imbecile ['ɪmbəsiːl] *n* Trottel *m*
imitate ['ɪmɪteɪt] *vt* nachahmen,
nachmachen; **imitation** *n* Nachahmung *f*
▷ *adj* imitiert; **~ leather** Kunstleder *nt*
immaculate [ɪ'mækjʊlɪt] *adj* tadellos;
(*spotless*) makellos
immature [ɪmə'tjʊə*] *adj* unreif
immediate [ɪ'miːdɪət] *adj* unmittelbar;
(*instant*) sofortig; (*reply*) umgehend;
immediately *adv* sofort
immense, immensely [ɪ'mens, -lɪ] *adj*,
adv riesig, enorm
immersion heater [ɪ'mɜːʃn hiːtə] *n*
Boiler *m*
immigrant ['ɪmɪɡrənt] *n* Einwanderer *m*,
Einwanderin *f*; **immigration** [ɪmɪ'ɡreɪʃən]
n Einwanderung *f*; (*facility*)
Einwanderungskontrolle *f*
immobilize [ɪ'məʊbɪlaɪz] *vt* lähmen;
immobilizer *n* (*Auto*) Wegfahrsperre *f*
immoral [ɪ'mɒrəl] *adj* unmoralisch
immortal [ɪ'mɔːtl] *adj* unsterblich
immune [ɪ'mjuːn] *adj* (*Med*) immun (*from,
to* gegen); **immune system** *n*
Immunsystem *nt*
impact ['ɪmpækt] *n* Aufprall *m*; (*effect*)
Auswirkung *f* (*on auf +akk*)
impatience [ɪm'peɪʃəns] *n* Ungeduld *f*;
impatient, impatiently *adj, adv*
ungeduldig
impeccable [ɪm'pekəbl] *adj* tadellos
impede [ɪm'piːd] *vt* behindern
imperative [ɪm'perətɪv] *adj* unbedingt
erforderlich ▷ *n* (*Ling*) Imperativ *m*
imperfect [ɪm'pɜːfɪkt] *adj*
unvollkommen; (*goods*) fehlerhaft ▷ *n*
(*Ling*) Imperfekt *nt*; **imperfection**
[ɪmpə'fekʃən] *n* Unvollkommenheit *f*;
(*fault*) Fehler *m*
imperial [ɪm'pɪərɪəl] *adj* kaiserlich,
Reichs-; **imperialism** *n* Imperialismus *m*
impertinence [ɪm'pɜːtɪnəns] *n*
Unverschämtheit *f*, Zumutung *f*;
impertinent *adj* unverschämt
implant ['ɪmplɑːnt] *n* (*Med*) Implantat *nt*
implausible [ɪm'plɔːzəbl] *adj*
unglaubwürdig
implement ['ɪmplɪmənt] *n* Werkzeug *nt*,
Gerät *nt* ▷ [ɪmplɪ'ment] *vt* durchführen

implication [ɪmplɪ'keɪʃən] *n* Folge *f*,
Auswirkung *f*; (*logical*) Schlussfolgerung *f*;
implicit [ɪm'plɪsɪt] *adj* implizit,
unausgesprochen; **imply** [ɪm'plaɪ] *vt*
(*indicate*) andeuten; (*mean*) bedeuten; **are
you ~ing that ...** wollen Sie damit sagen,
dass ...
impolite [ɪmpə'laɪt] *adj* unhöflich
import [ɪm'pɔːt] *vt* einführen,
importieren ▷ *n* ['ɪmpɔːt] Einfuhr *f*,
Import *m*
importance [ɪm'pɔːtəns] *n* Bedeutung *f*;
of no ~ unwichtig; **important** *adj* wichtig
(*to sb* für jdn); (*significant*) bedeutend;
(*influential*) einflussreich
import duty ['ɪmpɔːtdjuːtɪ] *n*
Einfuhrzoll *m*; **import licence** *n*
Einfuhrgenehmigung *f*
impose [ɪm'pəʊz] *vt* (*conditions*)
auferlegen (*on dat*); (*penalty, sanctions*)
verhängen (*on gegen*); **imposing**
[ɪm'pəʊzɪŋ] *adj* eindrucksvoll, imposant
impossible [ɪm'pɒsəbl] *adj* unmöglich
impotence ['ɪmpətəns] *n* Machtlosigkeit
f; (*sexual*) Impotenz *f*; **impotent** *adj*
machtlos; (*sexually*) impotent
impractical [ɪm'præktɪkəl] *adj*
unpraktisch; (*plan*) undurchführbar
impress [ɪm'pres] *vt* beeindrucken;
impression [ɪm'preʃən] *n* Eindruck *m*;
impressive *adj* eindrucksvoll
imprison [ɪm'prɪzn] *vt* inhaftieren;
imprisonment *n* Inhaftierung *f*
improbability [ɪmprɒbə'bɪlɪtɪ] *n*
Unwahrscheinlichkeit *f*; **improbable**
[ɪm'prɒbəbl] *adj* unwahrscheinlich
improper [ɪm'prɒpə*] *adj* (*indecent*)
unanständig; (*use*) unsachgemäß
improve [ɪm'pruːv] *vt* verbessern ▷ *vi*
sich verbessern, besser werden; (*patient*)
Fortschritte machen; **improvement** *n*
Verbesserung *f* (*in +gen; on* gegenüber); (*in
appearance*) Verschönerung *f*
improvise ['ɪmprəvaɪz] *vt, vi*
improvisieren
impulse ['ɪmpʌls] *n* Impuls *m*; **impulsive**
[ɪm'pʌlsɪv] *adj* impulsiv

○ **KEYWORD**

in [ɪn] *prep* **1** (*indicating place, position*) in
+dat; (*with motion*) in *+acc*; **in here/there**
hier/dort; **in London** in London; **in the**

United States in den Vereinigten Staaten
2 (*indicating time: during*) in +*dat*; **in summer** im Sommer; **in 1988** (im Jahre) 1988; **in the afternoon** nachmittags, am Nachmittag
3 (*indicating time: in the space of*) innerhalb von; **I'll see you in 2 weeks** or **in 2 weeks' time** ich sehe Sie in zwei Wochen
4 (*indicating manner, circumstances, state etc*) in +*dat*; **in the sun/rain** in der Sonne/im Regen; **in English/French** auf Englisch/Französisch; **in a loud/soft voice** mit lauter/leiser Stimme
5 (*with ratios, numbers*): **1 in 10** jeder Zehnte; **20 pence in the pound** 20 Pence pro Pfund; **they lined up in twos** sie stellten sich in Zweierreihe auf
6 (*referring to people, works*): **the disease is common in children** die Krankheit ist bei Kindern häufig; **in Dickens** bei Dickens; **we have a loyal friend in him** er ist uns ein treuer Freund
7 (*indicating profession etc*): **to be in teaching/the army** Lehrer in/beim Militär sein; **to be in publishing** im Verlagswesen arbeiten
8 (*with present participle*): **in saying this, I ...** wenn ich das sage, ... ich; **in accepting this view, he ...** weil er diese Meinung akzeptierte, ... er
▷ *adv*; **to be in** (*person: at home, work*) da sein (*train, ship, plane*) angekommen sein (*in fashion*) in sein: **to ask sb in** jdn hereinbitten; **to run/limp etc in** hereingerannt/gehumpelt *etc* kommen
▷ *n*; **the ins and outs** (*of proposal, situation etc*) die Feinheiten

inability [ɪnə'bɪlɪtɪ] *n* Unfähigkeit *f*
inaccessible [ɪnæk'sesəbl] *adj* (*a. fig*) unzugänglich
inaccurate [ɪn'ækjʊrɪt] *adj* ungenau
inadequate [ɪn'ædɪkwət] *adj* unzulänglich
inapplicable [ɪnə'plɪkəbl] *adj* unzutreffend
inappropriate [ɪnə'prəʊprɪət] *adj* unpassend; (*clothing*) ungeeignet; (*remark*) unangebracht
inborn ['ɪn'bɔ:n] *adj* angeboren
incapable [ɪn'keɪpəbl] *adj* unfähig (*of* zu);

to be ~ of doing sth nicht imstande sein, etw zu tun
incense ['ɪnsens] *n* Weihrauch *m*
incentive [ɪn'sentɪv] *n* Anreiz *m*
incessant, incessantly [ɪn'sesnt, -lɪ] *adj, adv* unaufhörlich
incest ['ɪnsest] *n* Inzest *m*
inch [ɪntʃ] *n* Zoll *m* (2,54 *cm*)
incident ['ɪnsɪdənt] *n* Vorfall *m*; (*disturbance*) Zwischenfall *m*; **incidentally** [ɪnsɪ'dentlɪ] *adv* nebenbei bemerkt, übrigens
inclination [ɪnklɪ'neɪʃən] *n* Neigung *f*; **inclined** ['ɪnklaɪnd] *adj* **to be ~ to do sth** dazu neigen, etw zu tun
include [ɪn'klu:d] *vt* einschließen; (*on list, in group*) aufnehmen; **including** *prep* einschließlich (+*gen*); **not ~ service** Bedienung nicht inbegriffen; **inclusive** [ɪn'klu:sɪv] *adj* einschließlich (*of* +*gen*); (*price*) Pauschal-
incoherent [ɪnkəʊ'hɪərənt] *adj* zusammenhanglos
income ['ɪnkʌm] *n* Einkommen *nt*; (*from business*) Einkünfte *pl*; **income tax** *n* Einkommensteuer *f*; (*on wages, salary*) Lohnsteuer *f*; **incoming** ['ɪnkʌmɪŋ] *adj* ankommend; (*mail*) eingehend
incompatible [ɪnkəm'pætəbl] *adj* unvereinbar; (*people*) unverträglich; (*Inform*) nicht kompatibel
incompetent [ɪn'kɒmpɪtənt] *adj* unfähig
incomplete [ɪnkəm'pli:t] *adj* unvollständig
incomprehensible [ɪnkɒmprɪ'hensəbl] *adj* unverständlich
inconceivable [ɪnkən'si:vəbl] *adj* unvorstellbar
inconsiderate [ɪnkən'sɪdərət] *adj* rücksichtslos
inconsistency [ɪnkən'sɪstənsɪ] *n* Inkonsequenz *f*; (*contradictory*) Widersprüchlichkeit *f*; **inconsistent** *adj* inkonsequent; (*contradictory*) widersprüchlich; (*work*) unbeständig
inconvenience [ɪnkən'vi:nɪəns] *n* Unannehmlichkeit *f*; (*trouble*) Umstände *pl*; **inconvenient** *adj* ungünstig, unbequem; (*time*) **it's ~ for me** es kommt mir ungelegen; **if it's not too ~ for you** wenn es dir passt
incorporate [ɪn'kɔ:pəreɪt] *vt* aufnehmen (*into* in +*akk*); (*include*) enthalten

incorrect ['ɪnkərekt] *adj* falsch; (*improper*) inkorrekt

increase ['ɪnkriːs] *n* Zunahme *f* (*in* an +*dat*); (*in amount, speed*) Erhöhung *f* (*in* +*gen*); **~ in size** Vergrößerung *f* ▷ [ɪn'kriːs] *vt* (*price, taxes, salary, speed etc*) erhöhen; (*wealth*) vermehren; (*number*) vergrößern; (*business*) erweitern ▷ *vi* zunehmen (*in* an +*dat*); (*prices*) steigen; (*in size*) größer werden; (*in number*) sich vermehren; **increasingly** [ɪn'kriːsɪŋlɪ] *adv* zunehmend

incredible, incredibly [ɪn'kredəbl, -blɪ] *adj, adv* unglaublich; (*very good*) fantastisch

incredulous [ɪn'kredjʊləs] *adj* ungläubig, skeptisch

incriminate [ɪn'krɪmɪneɪt] *vt* belasten

incubator ['ɪnkjʊbeɪtə*] *n* Brutkasten *m*

incurable [ɪn'kjʊərəbl] *adj* unheilbar

indecent [ɪn'diːsnt] *adj* unanständig

indecisive [ɪndɪ'saɪsɪv] *adj* (*person*) unentschlossen; (*result*) nicht entscheidend

indeed [ɪn'diːd] *adv* tatsächlich; (*as answer*) allerdings; **very hot ~** wirklich sehr heiß

indefinite [ɪn'defɪnɪt] *adj* unbestimmt; **indefinitely** *adv* endlos; (*postpone*) auf unbestimmte Zeit

independence [ɪndɪ'pendəns] *n* Unabhängigkeit *f*

● **Independence Day**
●
● Der**Independence Day**,der4.Juli,istin
● den USA ein gesetzlicher Feiertag
● zum Gedenken an die
● Unabhängigkeitserklärung am 4. Juli
● 1776, mit der die 13 amerikanischen
● Kolonien ihre Freiheit und
● Unabhängigkeit von Großbritannien
● erklärten.

independent [ɪndɪ'pendənt] *adj* unabhängig (*of* von); (*person*) selbstständig

indescribable [ɪndɪ'skraɪbəbl] *adj* unbeschreiblich

index ['ɪndeks] *n* Index *m*, Verzeichnis *nt*; **index finger** *n* Zeigefinger *m*

India ['ɪndɪə] *n* Indien *nt*; **Indian** ['ɪndɪən] *adj* indisch; (*Native American*) indianisch

▷ *n* Inder(in) *m(f)*; (*Native American*) Indianer(in) *m(f)*; **Indian Ocean** *n* Indischer Ozean; **Indian summer** *n* Spätsommer *m*, Altweibersommer *m*

indicate ['ɪndɪkeɪt] *vt* (*show*) zeigen; (*instrument*) anzeigen; (*suggest*) hinweisen auf +*akk* ▷ *vi* (*Auto*) blinken; **indication** [ɪndɪ'keɪʃn] *n* (*sign*) Anzeichen *nt* (*of* für); **indicator** ['ɪndɪkeɪtə*] *n* (*Auto*) Blinker *m*

indifferent [ɪn'dɪfrənt] *adj* (*not caring*) gleichgültig (*to, towards* gegenüber); (*mediocre*) mittelmäßig

indigestible [ɪndɪ'dʒestəbl] *adj* unverdaulich; **indigestion** [ɪndɪ'dʒestʃən] *n* Verdauungsstörung *f*

indignity [ɪn'dɪgnɪtɪ] *n* Demütigung *f*

indirect, indirectly [ɪndɪ'rekt, -lɪ] *adj, adv* indirekt

indiscreet [ɪndɪ'skriːt] *adj* indiskret

indispensable [ɪndɪ'spensəbl] *adj* unentbehrlich

indisposed [ɪndɪ'spəʊzd] *adj* unwohl

indisputable [ɪndɪ'spjuːtəbl] *adj* unbestreitbar; (*evidence*) unanfechtbar

individual [ɪndɪ'vɪdjʊəl] *n* Einzelne(r) *mf* ▷ *adj* einzeln; (*distinctive*) eigen, individuell; **~ case** Einzelfall *m*; **individually** *adv* (*separately*) einzeln

Indonesia [ɪndəʊ'niːzjə] *n* Indonesien *nt*

indoor ['ɪndɔː*] *adj* (*shoes*) Haus-; (*plant, games*) Zimmer-; (*Sport: football, championship, record etc*) Hallen-; **indoors** *adv* drinnen, im Haus

indulge [ɪn'dʌldʒ] *vi* **to ~ in sth** sich *dat* etw gönnen; **indulgence** *n* Nachsicht *f*; (*enjoyment*) (übermäßiger) Genuss; (*luxury*) Luxus *m*; **indulgent** *adj* nachsichtig (*with* gegenüber)

industrial [ɪn'dʌstrɪəl] *adj* Industrie-, industriell; **~ estate** Industriegebiet *nt*; **industry** ['ɪndəstrɪ] *n* Industrie *f*

inedible [ɪn'edɪbl] *adj* nicht essbar, ungenießbar

ineffective [ɪnɪ'fektɪv] *adj* unwirksam, wirkungslos; **inefficient** *adj* unwirksam; (*use, machine*) unwirtschaftlich; (*method etc*) unrationell

ineligible [ɪn'elɪdʒəbl] *adj* nicht berechtigt (*for* zu)

inequality [ɪnɪ'kwɒlɪtɪ] *n* Ungleichheit *f*

inevitable [ɪn'evɪtəbl] *adj* unvermeidlich; **inevitably** *adv* zwangsläufig

inexcusable [ɪnɪks'kjuːzəbl] *adj*
unverzeihlich; **that's ~** das kann man
nicht verzeihen

inexpensive [ɪnɪks'pensɪv] *adj*
preisgünstig

inexperience [ɪnɪks'pɪərɪəns] *n*
Unerfahrenheit *f*; **inexperienced** *adj*
unerfahren

inexplicable [ɪnɪks'plɪkəbl] *adj*
unerklärlich

infallible [ɪn'fæləbl] *adj* unfehlbar

infamous ['ɪnfəməs] *adj* (*person*)
berüchtigt (*for* wegen); (*deed*)
niederträchtig

infancy ['ɪnfənsɪ] *n* frühe Kindheit;
infant ['ɪnfənt] *n* Säugling *m*; (*small child*)
Kleinkind *nt*; **infant school** *n* Vorschule *f*

infatuated [ɪn'fætjʊeɪtɪd] *adj* vernarrt
(*with* in +*akk*), verknallt (*with* in +*akk*)

infect [ɪn'fekt] *vt* (*person*) anstecken;
(*wound*) infizieren; **infection** [ɪn'fekʃən] *n*
Infektion *f*; **infectious** [ɪn'fekʃəs] *adj*
ansteckend

inferior [ɪn'fɪərɪə*] *adj* (*in quality*)
minderwertig; (*in rank*) untergeordnet;
inferiority [ɪnfɪərɪ'ɒrɪtɪ] *n*
Minderwertigkeit *f*; **~ complex**
Minderwertigkeitskomplex *m*

infertile [ɪn'fɜːtaɪl] *adj* unfruchtbar

infidelity [ɪnfɪ'delɪtɪ] *n* Untreue *f*

infinite ['ɪnfɪnɪt] *adj* unendlich

infinitive [ɪn'fɪnɪtɪv] *n* (*Ling*) Infinitiv *m*

infinity [ɪn'fɪnɪtɪ] *n* Unendlichkeit *f*

infirmary [ɪn'fɜːmərɪ] *n* Krankenhaus *nt*

inflame [ɪn'fleɪm] *vt* (*Med*) entzünden;
inflammation [ɪnflə'meɪʃən] *n* (*Med*)
Entzündung *f*

inflatable [ɪn'fleɪtəbl] *adj* aufblasbar;
~ dinghy Schlauchboot *nt*; **inflate** [ɪn'fleɪt]
vt aufpumpen; (*by blowing*) aufblasen;
(*prices*) hochtreiben

inflation [ɪn'fleɪʃən] *n* Inflation *f*

inflexible [ɪn'fleksəbl] *adj* unflexibel

inflict [ɪn'flɪkt] *vt* **to ~ sth on sb** jdm etw
zufügen; (*punishment*) jdm etw auferlegen;
(*wound*) jdm etw beibringen

in-flight [ɪn'flaɪt] *adj* (*catering, magazine*)
Bord-; **~ entertainment** Bordprogramm
nt

influence ['ɪnflʊəns] *n* Einfluss *m* (*on* auf
+*akk*) ▷ *vt* beeinflussen; **influential**
[ɪnflʊ'enʃəl] *adj* einflussreich

influenza [ɪnflʊ'enzə] *n* Grippe *f*

inform [ɪn'fɔːm] *vt* informieren (*of, about*
über +*akk*); **to keep sb ~ed** jdn auf dem
Laufenden halten

informal [ɪn'fɔːməl] *adj* zwanglos,
ungezwungen

information [ɪnfə'meɪʃən] *n* Auskunft *f*,
Informationen *pl*; **for your ~** zu Ihrer
Information; **further ~** weitere
Informationen, weiteres; **information
desk** *n* Auskunftsschalter *m*;
information technology *n*
Informationstechnik *f*; **informative**
[ɪn'fɔːmətɪv] *adj* aufschlussreich

infra-red ['ɪnfrə'red] *adj* infrarot

infrastructure *n* Infrastruktur *f*

infuriate [ɪn'fjʊərɪeɪt] *vt* wütend
machen; **infuriating** *adj* äußerst
ärgerlich

infusion [ɪn'fjuːʒən] *n* (*herbal tea*)
Aufguss *m*; (*Med*) Infusion *f*

ingenious [ɪn'dʒiːnɪəs] *adj* (*person*)
erfinderisch; (*device*) raffiniert; (*idea*)
genial

ingredient [ɪn'griːdɪənt] *n* (*Gastr*) Zutat *f*

inhabit [ɪn'hæbɪt] *vt* bewohnen;
inhabitant *n* Einwohner(in) *m(f)*

inhale [ɪn'heɪl] *vt* einatmen; (*cigarettes,
Med*) inhalieren; **inhaler** *n*
Inhalationsgerät *nt*

inherit [ɪn'herɪt] *vt* erben; **inheritance** *n*
Erbe *nt*

inhibited [ɪn'hɪbɪtɪd] *adj* gehemmt;
inhibition [ɪnhɪ'bɪʃən] *n* Hemmung *f*

in-house ['ɪnhaʊs] *adj* intern

inhuman [ɪn'hjuːmən] *adj* unmenschlich

initial [ɪ'nɪʃəl] *adj* anfänglich; **~ stage**
Anfangsstadium *nt* ▷ *vt* mit Initialen
unterschreiben; **initially** *adv* anfangs;
initials *npl* Initialen *pl*

initiative [ɪ'nɪʃətɪv] *n* Initiative *f*

inject [ɪn'dʒekt] *vt* (*drug etc*) einspritzen;
to ~ sb with sth jdm etw (ein)spritzen;
injection *n* Spritze *f*, Injektion *f*

in-joke ['ɪndʒəʊk] *n* Insiderwitz *m*

injure ['ɪndʒə*] *vt* verletzen; **to ~ one's
leg** sich *dat* das Bein verletzen; **injury**
['ɪndʒərɪ] *n* Verletzung *f*

injustice [ɪn'dʒʌstɪs] *n* Ungerechtigkeit *f*

ink [ɪŋk] *n* Tinte *f*; **ink-jet printer** *n*
Tintenstrahldrucker *m*

inland ['ɪnlənd] *adj* Binnen- ▷ *adv*
landeinwärts; **inland revenue** *n* (*Brit*)
Finanzamt *nt*

in-laws [ˈɪnlɔːz] npl (fam)
Schwiegereltern pl
inline skates [ˈɪnlaɪnskeɪts] npl
Inlineskates pl, Inliner pl
inmate [ˈɪnmeɪt] n Insasse m
inn [ɪn] n Gasthaus nt
innate [ɪˈneɪt] adj angeboren
inner [ˈɪnəʳ] adj innere(r, s); **~ city**
Innenstadt f
innocence [ˈɪnəsns] n Unschuld f;
innocent adj unschuldig
innovation [ɪnəʊˈveɪʃən] n Neuerung f
innumerable [ɪˈnjuːmərəbl] adj
unzählig
inoculate [ɪˈnɒkjʊleɪt] vt impfen (against
gegen); **inoculation** [ɪnɒkjʊˈleɪʃən] n
Impfung f
in-patient [ˈɪnpeɪʃənt] n stationärer
Patient, stationäre Patientin
input [ˈɪnpʊt] n (contribution) Beitrag m;
(Inform) Eingabe f
inquest [ˈɪnkwest] n gerichtliche
Untersuchung (einer Todesursache)
inquire [ɪnˈkwaɪəʳ] see **enquire**; **inquiry**
[ɪnˈkwaɪərɪ] see **enquiry**
insane [ɪnˈseɪn] adj wahnsinnig; (Med)
geisteskrank; **insanity** [ɪnˈsænɪtɪ] n
Wahnsinn m
insatiable [ɪnˈseɪʃəbl] adj unersättlich
inscription [ɪnˈskrɪpʃən] n (on stone etc)
Inschrift f
insect [ˈɪnsekt] n Insekt nt; **insecticide**
[ɪnˈsektɪsaɪd] n
Insektenbekämpfungsmittel nt; **insect
repellent** n Insektenschutzmittel nt
insecure [ɪnsɪˈkjʊəʳ] adj (person)
unsicher; (shelves) instabil
insensitive [ɪnˈsensɪtɪv] adj
unempfindlich (to gegen); (unfeeling)
gefühllos; **insensitivity** [ɪnsensɪˈtɪvɪtɪ] n
Unempfindlichkeit f (to gegen); (unfeeling
nature) Gefühllosigkeit f
inseparable [ɪnˈsepərəbl] adj
unzertrennlich
insert [ɪnˈsɜːt] vt einfügen; (coin)
einwerfen; (key etc) hineinstecken ▷ n (in
magazine) Beilage f; **insertion** n (in text)
Einfügen nt
inside [ˈɪnˈsaɪd] n the **~** das Innere;
(surface) die Innenseite; **from the ~** von
innen ▷ adj innere(r, s), Innen-; **~ lane**
(Auto) Innenspur f; (Sport) Innenbahn f
▷ adv (place) innen; (direction) hinein; **to**

go ~ hineingehen ▷ prep (place) in +dat;
(into) in +akk ... hinein; (time, within)
innerhalb +gen; **inside out** adv verkehrt
herum; (know) in- und auswendig; **insider**
n Eingeweihte(r) mf, Insider(in) m(f)
insight [ˈɪnsaɪt] n Einblick m (into in
+akk)
insignificant [ɪnsɪɡˈnɪfɪkənt] adj
unbedeutend
insincere [ɪnsɪnˈsɪəʳ] adj unaufrichtig,
falsch
insinuate [ɪnˈsɪnjʊeɪt] vt andeuten;
insinuation [ɪnsɪnjʊˈeɪʃən] n Andeutung
f
insist [ɪnˈsɪst] vi darauf bestehen; **to ~ on
sth** auf etw dat bestehen; **insistent** adj
hartnäckig
insoluble [ɪnˈsɒljʊbl] adj unlösbar
insomnia [ɪnˈsɒmnɪə] n Schlaflosigkeit f
inspect [ɪnˈspekt] vt prüfen,
kontrollieren; **inspection** n Prüfung f;
(check) Kontrolle f; **inspector** n (police ~)
Inspektor(in) m(f); (senior) Kommissar(in)
m(f); (on bus etc) Kontrolleur(in) m(f)
inspiration [ɪnspɪˈreɪʃən] n Inspiration f;
inspire [ɪnˈspaɪəʳ] vt (respect) einflößen
(in dat); (person) inspirieren
install [ɪnˈstɔːl] vt (software) installieren;
(furnishings) einbauen
installment, instalment [ɪnˈstɔːlmənt] n
Rate f; (of story) Folge f; **to pay in ~s** auf
Raten zahlen; **installment plan** n (US)
Ratenkauf m
instance [ˈɪnstəns] n (of discrimination)
Fall m; (example) Beispiel nt; **for ~** zum
Beispiel
instant [ˈɪnstənt] n Augenblick m ▷ adj
sofortig; **instant coffee** n Instantkaffee
m; **instantly** adv sofort
instead [ɪnˈsted] adv stattdessen;
instead of prep (an)statt +gen; **~ of me** an
meiner Stelle; **~ of going** (an)statt zu
gehen
instinct [ˈɪnstɪŋkt] n Instinkt m;
instinctive, instinctively [ɪnˈstɪŋktɪv, -lɪ]
adj, adv instinktiv
institute [ˈɪnstɪtjuːt] n Institut nt;
institution [ɪnstɪˈtjuːʃən] n (organisation)
Institution f, Einrichtung f; (home) Anstalt f
instruct [ɪnˈstrʌkt] vt anweisen;
instruction [ɪnˈstrʌkʃən] n (teaching)
Unterricht m; (command) Anweisung f; **~s
for use** Gebrauchsanweisung f;

instructor *n* Lehrer(in) *m(f)*; *(US)* Dozent(in) *m(f)*

instrument ['ɪnstrʊmənt] *n* Instrument *nt*; **instrument panel** *n* Armaturenbrett *nt*

insufficient [ɪnsə'fɪʃənt] *adj* ungenügend

insulate ['ɪnsjʊleɪt] *vt* *(Elec)* isolieren; **insulating tape** *n* Isolierband *nt*; **insulation** [ɪnsjʊ'leɪʃən] *n* Isolierung *f*

insulin ['ɪnsjʊlɪn] *n* Insulin *nt*

insult ['ɪnsʌlt] *n* Beleidigung *f* ▷ [ɪn'sʌlt] *vt* beleidigen; **insulting** [ɪn'sʌltɪŋ] *adj* beleidigend

insurance [ɪn'ʃʊərəns] *n* Versicherung *f*; **~ company** Versicherungsgesellschaft *f*; **~ policy** Versicherungspolice *f*; **insure** [ɪn'ʃʊə*] *vt* versichern *(against* gegen)

intact [ɪn'tækt] *adj* intakt

intake ['ɪnteɪk] *n* Aufnahme *f*

integrate ['ɪntɪgreɪt] *vt* integrieren *(into* in *+akk)*; **integration** *n* Integration *f*

integrity [ɪn'tegrətɪ] *n* Integrität *f*, Ehrlichkeit *f*

intellect ['ɪntɪlekt] *n* Intellekt *m*; **intellectual** [ɪntɪ'lektjʊəl] *adj* intellektuell; *(interests etc)* geistig

intelligence [ɪn'telɪdʒəns] *n* *(understanding)* Intelligenz *f*; **intelligent** *adj* intelligent

intend [ɪn'tend] *vt* beabsichtigen; **to ~ to do sth** vorhaben, etw zu tun

intense [ɪn'tens] *adj* intensiv; *(pressure)* enorm; *(competition)* heftig; **intensity** *n* Intensität *f*; **intensive** *adj* intensiv; **intensive care unit** *n* Intensivstation *f*; **intensive course** *n* Intensivkurs *m*

intent [ɪn'tent] *adj* **to be ~ on doing sth** fest entschlossen sein, etw zu tun; **intention** [ɪn'tenʃən] *n* Absicht *f*; **intentional, intentionally** *adj, adv* absichtlich

interact [ɪntər'ækt] *vi* aufeinander einwirken; **interaction** *n* Interaktion *f*, Wechselwirkung *f*; **interactive** *adj* interaktiv

interchange ['ɪntətʃeɪndʒ] *n* *(of motorways)* Autobahnkreuz *nt*; **interchangeable** [ɪntə'tʃeɪndʒəbl] *adj* austauschbar

intercity [ɪntə'sɪtɪ] *n* Intercityzug *m*, IC *m*

intercom ['ɪntəkɒm] *n* (Gegen)sprechanlage *f*

intercourse ['ɪntəkɔːs] *n* *(sexual)* Geschlechtsverkehr *m*

interest ['ɪntrest] *n* Interesse *nt*; *(Fin: on money)* Zinsen *pl*; *(Comm: share)* Anteil *m*; **to be of ~** von Interesse sein *(to* für) ▷ *vt* interessieren; **interested** *adj* interessiert *(in* an *+dat)*; **to be ~ed in** sich interessieren für; **are you ~ in coming?** hast du Lust, mitzukommen?; **interest-free** *adj* zinsfrei; **interesting** *adj* interessant; **interest rate** *n* Zinssatz *m*

interface ['ɪntəfeɪs] *n* *(Inform)* Schnittstelle *f*

interfere [ɪntə'fɪə*] *vi* *(meddle)* sich einmischen *(with, in* in *+akk)*; **interference** *n* Einmischung *f*; *(Tv, Radio)* Störung *f*

interior [ɪn'tɪərɪə*] *adj* Innen- ▷ *n* Innere(s) *nt*; *(of car)* Innenraum *m*; *(of house)* Innenausstattung *f*

intermediate [ɪntə'miːdɪət] *adj* Zwischen-; **~ stage** Zwischenstadium *nt*

intermission [ɪntə'mɪʃən] *n* Pause *f*

intern [ɪn'tɜːn] *n* Assistent(in) *m(f)*

internal [ɪn'tɜːnl] *adj* innere(r, s); *(flight)* Inlands-; **~ revenue** *(US)* Finanzamt *nt*; **internally** *adv* innen; *(in body)* innerlich

international [ɪntə'næʃnəl] *adj* international; **~ match** Länderspiel *nt*; **~ flight** Auslandsflug *m* ▷ *n* *(Sport: player)* Nationalspieler(in) *m(f)*

Internet ['ɪntənet] *n* *(Inform)* Internet *nt*; **Internet banking** *n* Onlinebanking *nt*; **Internet café** *n* Internetcafé *nt*; **Internet provider** *n* Internetprovider *m*

interpret [ɪn'tɜːprɪt] *vi, vt* *(translate)* dolmetschen; *(explain)* interpretieren; **interpretation** [ɪntɜːprɪ'teɪʃən] *n* Interpretation *f*; **interpreter** [ɪn'tɜːprɪtə*] *n* Dolmetscher(in) *m(f)*

interrogate [ɪn'terəgeɪt] *vt* verhören; **interrogation** *n* Verhör *nt*

interrupt [ɪntə'rʌpt] *vt* unterbrechen; **interruption** [ɪntə'rʌpʃən] *n* Unterbrechung *f*

intersection [ɪntə'sekʃən] *n* *(of roads)* Kreuzung *f*

interstate [ɪntə'steɪt] *n* *(US)* zwischenstaatlich; **~ highway** ≈ Bundesautobahn *f*

interval ['ɪntəvəl] *n* *(space, time)* Abstand *m*; *(theatre etc)* Pause *f*

intervene [ɪntə'viːn] *vi* eingreifen *(in* in);

intervention [ɪntə'venʃən] n Eingreifen
nt; (Pol) Intervention f
interview ['ɪntəvju:] n Interview nt; (for
job) Vorstellungsgespräch nt ▷ vt
interviewen; (job applicant) ein
Vorstellungsgespräch führen mit;
interviewer n Interviewer(in) m(f)
intestine [ɪn'testɪn] n Darm m; **~s** pl
Eingeweide pl
intimate ['ɪntɪmət] adj (friends) vertraut,
eng; (atmosphere) gemütlich; (sexually)
intim
intimidate [ɪn'tɪmɪdeɪt] vt
einschüchtern; **intimidation** n
Einschüchterung f
into ['ɪntʊ] prep in +akk; (crash) gegen;
to change ~ sth (turn ~) zu etw werden;
(put on) sich dat etw anziehen; **to
translate ~ French** ins Französische
übersetzen; **to be ~ sth** (fam) auf etw akk
stehen
intolerable [ɪn'tɒlərəbl] adj unerträglich
intolerant [ɪn'tɒlərənt] adj intolerant
intoxicated [ɪn'tɒksɪkeɪtɪd] adj
betrunken; (fig) berauscht
intricate ['ɪntrɪkət] adj kompliziert
intrigue [ɪn'tri:g] vt faszinieren;
intriguing adj faszinierend, fesselnd
introduce [ɪntrə'dju:s] vt (person)
vorstellen (to sb jdm); (sth new) einführen
(to in +akk); **introduction** [ɪntrə'dʌkʃən]
n Einführung f (to in +akk); (to book)
Einleitung f (to zu); (to person) Vorstellung f
introvert ['ɪntrəʊvɜ:t] n Introvertierte(r)
mf
intuition [ɪntju:'ɪʃn] n Intuition f
invade [ɪn'veɪd] vt einfallen in +akk
invalid ['ɪnvəlɪd] n Kranke(r) mf; (disabled)
Invalide m ▷ adj [ɪn'vælɪd] (not valid)
ungültig
invaluable [ɪn'væljʊəbl] adj äußerst
wertvoll, unschätzbar
invariably [ɪn'veərɪəblɪ] adv ständig;
(every time) jedes Mal, ohne Ausnahme
invasion [ɪn'veɪʒən] n Invasion f (of in
+akk), Einfall m (of in +akk)
invent [ɪn'vent] vt erfinden; **invention**
[ɪn'venʃən] n Erfindung f; **inventor** n
Erfinder(in) m(f)
inverted commas [ɪn'vɜ:tɪd 'kɒməz] npl
Anführungszeichen pl
invest [ɪn'vest] vt, vi investieren (in in
+akk)

investigate [ɪn'vestɪgeɪt] vt
untersuchen; **investigation**
[ɪnvestɪ'geɪʃən] n Untersuchung f (into
+gen)
investment [ɪn'vestmənt] n Investition
f; **it's a good ~** es ist eine gute Anlage; (it'll
be useful) es macht sich bezahlt
invigorating [ɪn'vɪgəreɪtɪŋ] adj
erfrischend, belebend; (tonic) stärkend
invisible [ɪn'vɪzəbl] adj unsichtbar
invitation [ɪnvɪ'teɪʃən] n Einladung f;
invite [ɪn'vaɪt] vt einladen
invoice ['ɪnvɔɪs] n (bill) Rechnung f
involuntary [ɪn'vɒləntərɪ] adj
unbeabsichtigt
involve [ɪn'vɒlv] vt verwickeln (in sth in
etw akk); (entail) zur Folge haben; **to be ~d
in sth** (participate in) an etw dat beteiligt
sein; **I'm not ~d** (affected) ich bin nicht
betroffen
inward ['ɪnwəd] adj innere(r, s);
inwardly adv innerlich; **inwards** adv
nach innen
iodine ['aɪədi:n] n Jod nt
IOU [aɪəʊ'ju:] abbr = **I owe you**
Schuldschein m
IQ abbr = **intelligence quotient** IQ m
Iran [ɪ'rɑ:n] n der Iran
Iraq [ɪ'rɑ:k] n der Irak
Ireland ['aɪələnd] n Irland nt
iris ['aɪrɪs] n (flower) Schwertlilie f; (of eye)
Iris f
Irish ['aɪrɪʃ] adj irisch; **~ coffee** Irishcoffee
m; **~ Sea** die Irische See ▷ n (language)
Irisch nt; **the ~** pl die Iren pl; **Irishman** (pl
-men) n Ire m; **Irishwoman** (pl **-women**)
n Irin f
iron ['aɪən] n Eisen nt; (for ironing)
Bügeleisen nt ▷ adj eisern ▷ vt bügeln
ironic(al) [aɪ'rɒnɪk(əl)] adj ironisch
ironing board n Bügelbrett nt
irony ['aɪrənɪ] n Ironie f
irrational [ɪ'ræʃənl] adj irrational
irregular [ɪ'regjʊlə*] adj unregelmäßig;
(shape) ungleichmäßig
irrelevant [ɪ'reləvənt] adj belanglos,
irrelevant
irreplaceable [ɪrɪ'pleɪsəbl] adj
unersetzlich
irresistible [ɪrɪ'zɪstəbl] adj
unwiderstehlich
irrespective of [ɪrɪ'spektɪv ɒv] prep
ungeachtet +gen

irresponsible [ɪrɪ'spɒnsəbl] *adj* verantwortungslos

irretrievable [ɪrɪ'triːvəbl] *adv* unwiederbringlich; (*loss*) unersetzlich

irritable ['ɪrɪtəbl] *adj* reizbar; **irritate** ['ɪrɪteɪt] *vt* (*annoy*) ärgern; (*deliberately*) reizen; **irritation** [ɪrɪ'teɪʃən] *n* (*anger*) Ärger *m*; (*Med*) Reizung *f*

IRS *abbr* = **Internal Revenue Service** (*US*) Finanzamt *nt*

is [ɪz] *present of* **be** ist

Islam ['ɪzlɑːm] *n* Islam *m*; **Islamic** [ɪz'læmɪk] *adj* islamisch

island ['aɪlənd] *n* Insel *f*; **Isle** [aɪl] *n* (*in names*) **the ~ of Man** die Insel Man; **the ~ of Wight** die Insel Wight; **the British ~s** die Britischen Inseln

isn't ['ɪznt] *contr of* **is not**

isolate ['aɪsəleɪt] *vt* isolieren; **isolated** *adj* (*remote*) abgelegen; (*cut off*) abgeschnitten (*from* von); **an ~ case** ein Einzelfall; **isolation** [aɪsə'leɪʃən] *n* Isolierung *f*

Israel ['ɪzreɪl] *n* Israel *nt*; **Israeli** [ɪz'reɪlɪ] *adj* israelisch ▷ *n* Israeli *m o f*

issue ['ɪʃuː] *n* (*matter*) Frage *f*; (*problem*) Problem *nt*; (*subject*) Thema *nt*; (*of newspaper etc*) Ausgabe *f*; **that's not the ~** darum geht es nicht ▷ *vt* ausgeben; (*document*) ausstellen; (*orders*) erteilen; (*book*) herausgeben

◯ **KEYWORD**

it [ɪt] *pron* **1** (*specific: subject*) er/sie/es; (*: direct object*) ihn/sie/es; (*: indirect object*) ihm/ihr/ihm; **about/from/in/of it** darüber/davon/darin/davon
2 (*impers*) es; **it's raining** es regnet; **it's Friday tomorrow** morgen ist Freitag; **who is it? — it's me** wer ist da? — ich (bins)

IT *abbr* = **information technology** IT *f*

Italian [ɪ'tæljən] *adj* italienisch ▷ *n* Italiener(in) *m(f)*; (*language*) Italienisch *nt*

italic [ɪ'tælɪk] *adj* kursiv ▷ *npl* **in ~s** kursiv

Italy ['ɪtəlɪ] *n* Italien *nt*

itch [ɪtʃ] *n* Juckreiz *m*; **I have an ~** mich juckt es ▷ *vi* jucken; **he is ~ing to ...** es juckt ihn, zu ...; **itchy** *adj* juckend

it'd ['ɪtd] *contr of* **it would; it had**

item ['aɪtəm] *n* (*article*) Gegenstand *m*; (*in catalogue*) Artikel *m*; (*on list, in accounts*) Posten *m*; (*on agenda*) Punkt *m*; (*in show programme*) Nummer *f*; (*in news*) Bericht *m*; (*Tv: radio*) Meldung *f*

itinerary [aɪ'tɪnərərɪ] *n* Reiseroute *f*

it'll ['ɪtl] *contr of* **it will; it shall**

its [ɪts] *pron* sein; (*feminine form*) ihr

it's [ɪts] *contr of* **it is; it has**

itself [ɪt'self] *pron* (*reflexive*) sich; (*emphatic*) **the house ~ is OK** das Haus selbst o an sich ist in Ordnung; **by ~** allein; **the door closes (by) ~** die Tür schließt sich von selbst

I've [aɪv] *contr of* **I have**

ivory ['aɪvərɪ] *n* Elfenbein *nt*

ivy ['aɪvɪ] *n* Efeu *m*

i

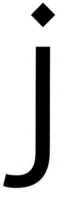

J

jab [dʒæb] vt (needle, knife) stechen (into in +akk) ▷ n (fam) Spritze f
jack [dʒæk] n (Auto) Wagenheber m; (Cards) Bube m; **jack in** vt (fam) aufgeben, hinschmeißen; **jack up** vt (car etc) aufbocken
jacket ['dʒækɪt] n Jacke f; (of man's suit) Jackett nt; (of book) Schutzumschlag m; **jacket potato** (pl **-es**) n (in der Schale) gebackene Kartoffel
jack-knife ['dʒæknaɪf] (pl **jack-knives**) n Klappmesser nt ▷ vi (truck) sich quer stellen
jackpot ['dʒækpɒt] n Jackpot m
jacuzzi® [dʒə'ku:zɪ] n (bath) Whirlpool® m
jail [dʒeɪl] n Gefängnis nt ▷ vt einsperren
jam [dʒæm] n Konfitüre f, Marmelade f; (traffic ~) Stau m ▷ vt (street) verstopfen; (machine) blockieren; **to be ~med** (stuck) klemmen; **to ~ on the brakes** eine Vollbremsung machen
Jamaica [dʒə'meɪkə] n Jamaika nt
jam-packed adj proppenvoll
janitor ['dʒænɪtə*] n (US) Hausmeister(in) m(f)
Jan abbr = **January** Jan

January ['dʒænjʊərɪ] n Januar m
Japan [dʒə'pæn] n Japan nt; **Japanese** [dʒæpə'ni:z] adj japanisch ▷ n (person) Japaner(in) m(f); (language) Japanisch nt
jar [dʒɑ:*] n Glas nt
jaundice ['dʒɔ:ndɪs] n Gelbsucht f
javelin ['dʒævlɪn] n Speer m; (Sport) Speerwerfen nt
jaw [dʒɔ:] n Kiefer m
jazz [dʒæz] n Jazz m
jealous ['dʒeləs] adj eifersüchtig (of auf +akk); **don't make me ~** mach mich nicht neidisch; **jealousy** n Eifersucht f
jeans [dʒi:nz] npl Jeans pl
jeep® [dʒi:p] n Jeep® m
jelly ['dʒelɪ] n Gelee nt; (on meat) Gallert nt; (dessert) Götterspeise f; (US: jam) Marmelade f; **jelly baby** n (sweet) Gummibärchen nt; **jellyfish** n Qualle f
jeopardize ['dʒepədaɪz] vt gefährden
jerk [dʒɜ:k] n Ruck m; (fam: idiot) Trottel m ▷ vt ruckartig bewegen ▷ vi (rope) rucken; (muscles) zucken
Jerusalem [dʒə'ru:sələm] n Jerusalem nt
jet [dʒet] n (of water etc) Strahl m; (nozzle) Düse f; (aircraft) Düsenflugzeug nt; **jet foil** n Tragflächenboot nt; **jetlag** n Jetlag m (Müdigkeit nach langem Flug)
jetty ['dʒetɪ] n Landesteg m; (larger) Landungsbrücke f
Jew [dʒu:] n Jude m, Jüdin f
jewel ['dʒu:əl] n Edelstein m; (esp fig) Juwel nt; **jeweller, jeweler** (US) n Juwelier(in) m(f); **jewellery, jewelery** (US) n Schmuck m
Jewish ['dʒu:ɪʃ] adj jüdisch; **she's ~** sie ist Jüdin
jigsaw (puzzle) ['dʒɪgsɔ:(pʌzl)] n Puzzle nt
jilt [dʒɪlt] vt den Laufpass geben +dat
jingle ['dʒɪŋgl] n (advert) Jingle m; (verse) Reim m
jitters ['dʒɪtərz] npl (fam) **to have the ~** Bammel haben; **jittery** adj (fam) ganz nervös
job [dʒɒb] n (piece of work) Arbeit f; (task) Aufgabe f; (occupation) Stellung f, Job m; **what's your ~?** was machen Sie beruflich?; **it's a good ~ you did that** gut, dass du das gemacht hast; **jobcentre** n Arbeitsvermittlungsstelle f, Arbeitsamt nt; **job-hunting** n **to go ~** auf Arbeitssuche gehen; **jobless** adj

arbeitslos; **job seeker** n
Arbeitsuchende(r) mf; **jobseeker's**
allowance n Arbeitslosengeld nt;
job-sharing n Arbeitsplatzteilung f
jockey ['dʒɒkɪ] n Jockey m
jog [dʒɒg] vt (person) anstoßen ▷ vi (run)
joggen; **jogging** n Jogging nt; **to go**
~ joggen gehen
john [dʒɒn] n (US fam) Klo nt
join [dʒɔɪn] vt (put together) verbinden (to
mit); (club etc) beitreten +dat; **to ~ sb** sich
jdm anschließen; (sit with) sich zu jdm
setzen ▷ vi (unite) sich vereinigen; (rivers)
zusammenfließen ▷ n Verbindungsstelle
f; (seam) Naht f; **join in** vi, vt mitmachen
(sth bei etw)
joinery ['dʒɔɪnərɪ] n Schreinerei f
joint [dʒɔɪnt] n (of bones) Gelenk nt; (in pipe
etc) Verbindungsstelle f; (of meat) Braten
m; (of marijuana) Joint m ▷ adj gemeinsam;
joint account n Gemeinschaftskonto nt;
jointly adv gemeinsam
joke [dʒəʊk] n Witz m; (prank) Streich m;
for a ~ zum Spaß; **it's no ~** das ist nicht
zum Lachen ▷ vi Witze machen; **you**
must be joking das ist ja wohl nicht dein
Ernst!
jolly ['dʒɒlɪ] adj lustig, vergnügt
Jordan ['dʒɔːdən] n (country) Jordanien nt;
(river) Jordan m
jot down [dʒɒt daʊn] vt sich notieren;
jotter n Notizbuch nt
journal ['dʒɜːnl] n (diary) Tagebuch nt;
(magazine) Zeitschrift f; **journalism** n
Journalismus m; **journalist** n
Journalist(in) m(f)
journey ['dʒɜːnɪ] n Reise f; (esp on stage,
by car, train) Fahrt f
joy [dʒɔɪ] n Freude f (at über +akk);
joystick n (Inform) Joystick m; (Aviat)
Steuerknüppel m
judge [dʒʌdʒ] n Richter(in) m(f); (Sport)
Punktrichter(in) m(f) ▷ vt beurteilen (by
nach); **as far as I can ~** meinem Urteil
nach ▷ vi urteilen (by nach); **judg(e)ment**
n (Jur) Urteil nt; (opinion) Ansicht f; **an**
error of ~ Fehleinschätzung f
judo ['dʒuːdəʊ] n Judo nt
jug [dʒʌg] n Krug m
juggle ['dʒʌgl] vi (lit, fig) jonglieren (with
mit)
juice [dʒuːs] n Saft m; **juicy** adj saftig;
(story, scandal) pikant

July [dʒuːˈlaɪ] n Juli m; see also **September**
jumble ['dʒʌmbl] n Durcheinander nt ▷ vt
to ~ (up) durcheinander werfen; (facts)
durcheinander bringen; **jumble sale** n
(for charity) Wohltätigkeitsbasar m
jumbo ['dʒʌmbəʊ] adj (sausage etc)
Riesen-; **jumbo jet** n Jumbojet m
jump [dʒʌmp] vi springen; (nervously)
zusammenzucken; **to ~ to conclusions**
voreilige Schlüsse ziehen; **to ~ from one**
thing to another dauernd das Thema
wechseln ▷ vt (a. fig: omit) überspringen;
to ~ the lights bei Rot über die Kreuzung
fahren; **to ~ the queue** sich vordrängen
▷ n Sprung m; (for horses) Hindernis nt;
jumper n Pullover m; (US: dress)
Trägerkleid nt; (person, horse) Springer(in)
m(f); **jumper cables** npl (US), **jump leads**
npl (Brit Auto) Starthilfekabel nt
junction ['dʒʌŋkʃən] n (of roads) Kreuzung
f; (Rail) Knotenpunkt m
June [dʒuːn] n Juni m; see also **September**
jungle ['dʒʌŋgl] n Dschungel m
junior ['dʒuːnɪə*] adj (younger) jünger;
(lower position) untergeordnet (to sb jdm)
▷ n **she's two years my ~** sie ist zwei
Jahre jünger als ich; **junior high (school)**
n (US) ≈ Mittelschule f; **junior school** n
(Brit) Grundschule f
junk [dʒʌŋk] n (trash) Plunder m;
junkfood n Nahrungsmittel pl mit
geringem Nährwert, Junkfood nt; **junkie**
n (fam) Junkie m, Fixer(in) m(f); (fig: fan)
Freak m; **junk mail** n Reklame f; (Inform)
Junkmail f; **junk shop** n Trödelladen m
jury ['dʒʊərɪ] n Geschworene pl; (in
competition) Jury f
just [dʒʌst] adj gerecht ▷ adv (recently)
gerade; (exactly) genau; **~ as expected**
genau wie erwartet; **~ as nice** genauso
nett; (barely) **~ in time** gerade noch
rechtzeitig; (immediately) **~ before/after**
... gleich vor/nach ...; (small distance)
~ round the corner gleich um die Ecke; (a
little) **~ over an hour** etwas mehr als eine
Stunde; (only) **~ the two of us** nur wir
beide; **~ a moment** Moment mal;
(absolutely, simply) **it was ~ fantastic** es
war einfach klasse; **~ about** so etwa;
(more or less) mehr oder weniger; **~ about**
ready fast fertig
justice ['dʒʌstɪs] n Gerechtigkeit f;
justifiable [dʒʌstɪˈfaɪəbl] adj

berechtigt; **justifiably** *adv* zu
Recht; **justify** ['dʒʌstɪfaɪ] *vt*
rechtfertigen
jut [dʒʌt] *vi* **to ~ (out)** herausragen
juvenile ['dʒuːvənaɪl] *n adj* Jugend-,
jugendlich ▷ *n* Jugendliche(r) *mf*

K

to **~ sth clean/secret** etw sauber/geheim halten; **'~ clear'** „(bitte) freihalten"; **~ this to yourself** behalten Sie das für sich ▷ vi (*food*) sich halten; (*remain, with adj*) bleiben; **~ quiet** sei ruhig!; **~ left** links fahren; **to ~ doing sth** (*repeatedly*) etw immer wieder tun; **~ at it** mach weiter so!; **it ~s happening** es passiert immer wieder ▷ n (*livelihood*) Unterhalt m; **keep back** vi zurückbleiben ▷ vt zurückhalten; (*information*) verschweigen (*from sb* jdm); **keep off** vt (*person, animal*) fernhalten; **'~ off the grass'** „Betreten des Rasens verboten"; **keep on** vi weitermachen; (*walking*) weitergehen; (*in car*) weiterfahren; **to ~ doing sth** (*persistently*) etw immer wieder tun ▷ vt (*coat etc*) anbehalten; **keep out** vt nicht hereinlassen ▷ vi draußen bleiben; **~** (*on sign*) Eintritt verboten; **keep to** vt (*road, path*) bleiben auf +dat; (*plan etc*) sich halten an +akk; **to ~ the point** bei der Sache bleiben; **keep up** vi Schritt halten (*with* mit) ▷ vt (*maintain*) aufrechterhalten; (*speed*) halten; **to ~ appearances** den Schein wahren; **keep it up!** (*fam*) weiter so!

keeper n (*museum etc*) Aufseher(in) m(f); (*goal~*) Torwart m; (*zoo ~*) Tierpfleger(in) m(f); **keep-fit** n Fitnesstraining nt; **~ exercises** Gymnastik f

kennel ['kenl] n Hundehütte f; **kennels** n Hundepension f

Kenya ['kenjə] n Kenia nt

kept [kept] pt, pp of **keep**

kerb ['kɜːb] n Randstein m

kerosene ['kerəsiːn] n (US) Petroleum m

ketchup ['ketʃʌp] n Ket(s)chup nt o m

kettle ['ketl] n Kessel m

key [kiː] n Schlüssel m; (*of piano, computer*) Taste f; (*Mus*) Tonart f; (*for map etc*) Zeichenerklärung f ▷ vt **to ~ (in)** (*Inform*) eingeben ▷ adj entscheidend; **keyboard** n (*piano, computer*) Tastatur f; **keyhole** n Schlüsselloch nt; **keypad** n (*Inform*) Nummernblock m; **keyring** n Schlüsselring m

kick [kɪk] n Tritt m; (*Sport*) Stoß m; **I get a ~ out of it** (*fam*) es turnt mich an ▷ vt, vi treten; **kick out** vt (*fam*) rausschmeißen (*of* aus); **kick-off** n (*Sport*) Anstoß m

kid [kɪd] n (*child*) Kind nt ▷ vt (*tease*) auf den Arm nehmen ▷ vi Witze machen;

---

k abbr = **thousand**; **15k** 15 000
K abbr = **kilobyte** KB
kangaroo [kæŋgə'ruː] n Känguru nt
karaoke [kærɪ'əʊkɪ] n Karaoke nt
karate [kə'rɑːtɪ] n Karate nt
kart [kɑːt] n Gokart m
kayak ['kaɪæk] n Kajak m o nt
Kazakhstan [kæzæk'stɑːn] n Kasachstan nt
kebab [kə'bæb] n (*shish ~*) Schaschlik nt o m; (*doner ~*) Kebab m
keel [kiːl] n (*Naut*) Kiel m; **keel over** vi (*boat*) kentern; (*person*) umkippen
keen [kiːn] adj begeistert (*on* von); (*hardworking*) eifrig; (*mind, wind*) scharf; (*interest, feeling*) stark; **to be ~ on sb** von jdm angetan sein; **she's ~ on riding** sie reitet gern; **to be ~ to do sth** darauf erpicht sein, etw zu tun
keep [kiːp] (**kept, kept**) vt (*retain*) behalten; (*secret*) für sich behalten; (*observe*) einhalten; (*promise*) halten; (*run: shop, diary, accounts*) führen; (*animals*) halten; (*support, family etc*) unterhalten, versorgen; (*store*) aufbewahren; **to ~ sb waiting** jdn warten lassen; **to ~ sb from doing sth** jdn davon abhalten, etw zu tun;

you're ~ding das ist doch nicht dein Ernst!; **no ~ding** aber echt!
kidnap ['kɪdnæp] vt entführen; **kidnapper** n Entführer(in) m(f); **kidnapping** n Entführung f
kidney ['kɪdnɪ] n Niere f; **kidney machine** n künstliche Niere
kill [kɪl] vt töten; (esp intentionally) umbringen; (weeds) vernichten; **killer** n Mörder(in) m(f)
kilo ['kiːləʊ] (pl -s) n Kilo nt; **kilobyte** n Kilobyte nt; **kilogramme** n Kilogramm nt; **kilometer** (US), **kilometre** n Kilometer m; **~s per hour** Stundenkilometer pl; **kilowatt** n Kilowatt nt
kilt [kɪlt] n Schottenrock m
kind [kaɪnd] adj nett, freundlich (to zu) ▷ n Art f; (of coffee, cheese etc) Sorte f; **what ~ of …?** was für ein(e) …?; **this ~ of … so ein(e) …**; **~ of** (+ adj) irgendwie
kindergarten ['kɪndəgɑːtn] n Kindergarten m
kindly ['kaɪndlɪ] adj nett, freundlich ▷ adv liebenswürdigerweise; **kindness** ['kaɪndnəs] n Freundlichkeit f
king [kɪŋ] n König m; **kingdom** n Königreich nt; **kingfisher** n Eisvogel m; **king-size** adj im Großformat; (bed) extra groß
kipper ['kɪpə*] n Räucherhering m
kiss [kɪs] n Kuss m; **~ of life** Mund-zu-Mund-Beatmung f ▷ vt küssen
kit [kɪt] n (equipment) Ausrüstung f; (fam) Sachen pl; (sports ~) Sportsachen pl; (belongings, clothes) Sachen pl; (for building sth) Bausatz m
kitchen ['kɪtʃɪn] n Küche f; **kitchen foil** n Alufolie f; **kitchen scales** n Küchenwaage f; **kitchen unit** n Küchenschrank m; **kitchenware** n Küchengeschirr nt
kite [kaɪt] n Drachen m
kitten ['kɪtn] n Kätzchen nt
kiwi ['kiːwiː] n (fruit) Kiwi f
km abbr = **kilometres** km
knack [næk] n Dreh m, Trick m; **to get/have got the ~** den Dreh herauskriegen/heraushaben; **knackered** ['nækəd] adj (Brit fam) fix und fertig, kaputt
knee [niː] n Knie nt; **kneecap** n Kniescheibe f; **knee-jerk** adj (reaction) reflexartig; **kneel** [niːl] (**knelt** o **kneeled,**

knelt o **kneeled**) vi knien; (action, ~ down) sich hinknien
knelt [nelt] pt, pp of **kneel**
knew [njuː] pt of **know**
knickers ['nɪkəz] npl (Brit) Schlüpfer m
knife [naɪf] (pl **knives**) n Messer nt
knight [naɪt] n Ritter m; (in chess) Pferd nt, Springer m
knit [nɪt] vt, vi stricken; **knitting** n (piece of work) Strickarbeit f; (activity) Stricken nt; **knitting needle** n Stricknadel f; **knitwear** n Strickwaren pl
knob [nɒb] n (on door) Knauf m; (on radio etc) Knopf m
knock [nɒk] vt schlagen; (accidentally) stoßen; **to ~ one's head** sich dat den Kopf anschlagen ▷ vi klopfen (on, at an +akk) ▷ n (blow) Schlag m; (on door) Klopfen nt; **there was a ~ (at the door)** es hat geklopft; **knock down** vt (object) umstoßen; (person) niederschlagen; (with car) anfahren; (building) abreißen; **knock out** vt (stun) bewusstlos schlagen; (boxer) k.o. schlagen; **knock over** vt umstoßen; (with car) anfahren; **knocker** n Türklopfer m; **knockout** n Knockout m, K.o. m
knot [nɒt] n Knoten m
know [nəʊ] (**knew, known**) vt, vi wissen; (be acquainted with: people, places) kennen; (recognize) erkennen; (language) können; **I'll let you ~** ich sage dir Bescheid; **I ~ some French** ich kann etwas Französisch; **to get to ~ sb** jdn kennen lernen; **to be ~n as** bekannt sein als; **know about** vt Bescheid wissen über +akk; (subject) sich auskennen in +dat; (cars, horses etc) sich auskennen mit; **know of** vt kennen; **not that I ~** nicht dass ich wüsste; **know-all** n (fam) Klugscheißer m; **know-how** n Kenntnis f, Know-how nt; **knowing** adj wissend; (look, smile) vielsagend; **knowledge** ['nɒlɪdʒ] n Wissen nt; (of a subject) Kenntnisse pl; **to (the best of) my ~** meines Wissens
known [nəʊn] pp of **know**
knuckle ['nʌkl] n (Finger)knöchel m; (Gastr) Hachse f; **knuckle down** vi sich an die Arbeit machen
Koran [kɒˈrɑːn] n Koran m
Korea [kəˈrɪə] n Korea nt
Kosovo ['kɒsəvəʊ] n der Kosovo
kph abbr = **kilometres per hour** km/h

Kremlin ['kremlın] *n* the ~ der
Kreml
Kurd [kɛːd] *n* Kurde *m*, Kurdin *f*; **Kurdish**
adj kurdisch
Kuwait [kʊ'wəɪt] *n* Kuwait *nt*

L *abbr* (Brit Auto) = **learner**

LA *abbr* = **Los Angeles**

lab [læb] *n* (*fam*) Labor *nt*

label ['leɪbl] *n* Etikett *nt*; (*tied*) Anhänger *m*; (*adhesive*) Aufkleber *m*; (*record* ~) Label *nt* ▷ *vt* etikettieren; (*pej*) abstempeln

laboratory [lə'bɒrətərɪ] *n* Labor *nt*

Labor Day

Der **Labor Day** ist in den USA und Kanada der Name für den Tag der Arbeit. Er wird dort als gesetzlicher Feiertag am ersten Montag im September begangen.

laborious [lə'bɔːrɪəs] *adj* mühsam; **labor** (*US*), **labour** ['leɪbə*] *n* Arbeit *f*; (*Med*) Wehen *pl*; **to be in** ~ Wehen haben ▷ *adj* (*Pol*) Labour-; ~ **Party** Labour Party *f*; **labor union** *n* (*US*) Gewerkschaft *f*; **labourer** *n* Arbeiter(in) *m(f)*

lace [leɪs] *n* (*fabric*) Spitze *f*; (*of shoe*) Schnürsenkel *m* ▷ *vt* **to ~ (up)** zuschnüren; **lace-up** *n* Schnürschuh *m*

lack [læk] *vt, vi* **to be ~ing** fehlen; **sb ~s** *o* **is ~ing in sth** es fehlt jdm an etw *dat*; **we**

~ **the time** uns fehlt die Zeit ▷ *n* Mangel *m*; **for ~ of** aus Mangel an +*dat*

lacquer ['lækə*] *n* Lack *m*; (*Brit: hair* ~) Haarspray *nt*

lad [læd] *n* Junge *m*

ladder ['lædə*] *n* Leiter *f*; (*in tight*) Laufmasche *f*

laddish ['lædɪʃ] *adj* (*Brit*) machohaft

laden ['leɪdn] *adj* beladen (*with* mit)

ladies ['leɪdɪz], **ladies' room** *n* Damentoilette *f*; **lady** ['leɪdɪ] *n* Dame *f*; (*as title*) Lady *f*; **ladybird**, **ladybug** (*US*) *n* Marienkäfer *m*

lag [læg] *vi* **to ~ (behind)** zurückliegen ▷ *vt* (*pipes*) isolieren

lager ['lɑːgə*] *n* helles Bier; ~ **lout** betrunkener Rowdy

lagging ['lægɪŋ] *n* Isolierung *f*

laid [leɪd] *pt, pp of* **lay**; **laid-back** *adj* (*fam*) cool, gelassen

lain [leɪn] *pp of* **lie**

lake [leɪk] *n* See *m*; **the Lake District** *Seengebiet im Nordwesten Englands*

lamb [læm] *n* Lamm *nt*; (*meat*) Lammfleisch *nt*; **lamb chop** *n* Lammkotelett *nt*

lame [leɪm] *adj* lahm; (*excuse*) faul; (*argument*) schwach

lament [lə'ment] *n* Klage *f* ▷ *vt* beklagen

laminated ['læmɪneɪtɪd] *adj* beschichtet

lamp [læmp] *n* Lampe *f*; (*in street*) Laterne *f*; (*in car*) Licht *nt*, Scheinwerfer *m*; **lamppost** *n* Laternenpfahl *m*; **lampshade** *n* Lampenschirm *m*

land [lænd] *n* Land *nt* ▷ *vi* (*from ship*) an Land gehen; (*Aviat*) landen ▷ *vt* (*passengers*) absetzen; (*goods*) abladen; (*plane*) landen; **landing** *n* Landung *f*; (*on stairs*) Treppenabsatz *m*; **landing stage** *n* Landesteg *m*; **landing strip** *n* Landebahn *f*

landlady *n* Hauswirtin *f*, Vermieterin *f*; **landlord** *n* (*of house*) Hauswirt *m*, Vermieter *m*; (*of pub*) Gastwirt *m*; **landmark** *n* Wahrzeichen *nt*; (*event*) Meilenstein *m*; **landowner** *n* Grundbesitzer(in) *m(f)*; **landscape** *n* Landschaft *f*; (*format*) Querformat *nt*; **landslide** *n* (*Geo*) Erdrutsch *m*

lane [leɪn] *n* (*in country*) enge Landstraße, Weg *m*; (*in town*) Gasse *f*; (*of motorway*) Spur *f*; (*Sport*) Bahn *f*; **to get in ~** (*in car*) sich einordnen

language ['læŋgwɪdʒ] *n* Sprache *f*; (*style*) Ausdrucksweise *f*

lantern ['læntən] *n* Laterne *f*

lap [læp] *n* Schoß *m*; (*in race*) Runde *f* ▷ *vt* (*in race*) überholen

lapse [læps] *n* (*mistake*) Irrtum *m*; (*moral*) Fehltritt *m* ▷ *vi* ablaufen

laptop ['læptɒp] *n* Laptop *m*

large [lɑːdʒ] *adj* groß; **by and ~** im Großen und Ganzen; **largely** *adv* zum größten Teil; **large-scale** *adj* groß angelegt, Groß-

lark [lɑːk] *n* (*bird*) Lerche *f*

laryngitis [lærɪnˈdʒaɪtɪs] *n* Kehlkopfentzündung *f*; **larynx** ['lærɪŋks] *n* Kehlkopf *m*

laser ['leɪzə*] *n* Laser *m*; **laser printer** *n* Laserdrucker *m*

lash [læʃ] *vt* peitschen; **lash out** *vi* (*with fists*) um sich schlagen; (*spend money*) sich in Unkosten stürzen (*on* mit)

lass [læs] *n* Mädchen *nt*

last [lɑːst] *adj* letzte(r, s); **the ~ but one** der/die/das vorletzte; **~ night** gestern Abend; **~ but not least** nicht zuletzt ▷ *adv* zuletzt; (*last time*) das letzte Mal; **at ~** endlich ▷ *n* (*person*) Letzte(r) *mf*; (*thing*) Letzte(s) *nt*; **he was the ~ to leave** er ging als Letzter ▷ *vi* (*continue*) dauern; (*remain in good condition*) durchhalten; (*remain good*) sich halten; (*money*) ausreichen; **lasting** *adj* dauerhaft; (*impression*) nachhaltig; **lastly** *adv* schließlich; **last-minute** *adj* in letzter Minute; **last name** *n* Nachname *m*

late [leɪt] *adj* spät; (*after proper time*) zu spät; (*train etc*) verspätet; (*dead*) verstorben; **to be ~** zu spät kommen; (*train etc*) Verspätung haben ▷ *adv* spät; (*after proper time*) zu spät; **late availibility flight** *n* Last-Minute-Flug *m*; **lately** *adv* in letzter Zeit; **late opening** *n* verlängerte Öffnungszeiten *pl*; **later** ['leɪtə*] *adj, adv* später; **see you ~** bis später; **latest** ['leɪtɪst] *adj* späteste(r, s); (*most recent*) neueste(r, s) ▷ *n* **the ~** (*news*) das Neueste; **at the ~** spätestens

Latin ['lætɪn] *n* Latein *nt* ▷ *adj* lateinisch; **Latin America** *n* Lateinamerika *nt*; **Latin-American** *adj* lateinamerikanisch ▷ *n* Lateinamerikaner(in) *m(f)*

latitude ['lætɪtjuːd] *n* (*Geo*) Breite *f*

latter ['lætə*] *adj* (*second of two*) letztere(r, s); (*last: part, years*) letzte(r, s), später

Latvia ['lætvɪə] *n* Lettland *nt*

laugh [lɑːf] *n* Lachen *nt*; **for a ~** aus Spaß ▷ *vi* lachen (*at, about* über +*akk*); **to ~ at sb** sich über jdn lustig machen; **it's no ~ing matter** es ist nicht zum Lachen; **laughter** ['lɑːftə*] *n* Gelächter *nt*

launch [lɔːntʃ] *n* (*launching, of ship*) Stapellauf *m*; (*of rocket*) Abschuss *m*; (*of product*) Markteinführung *f*; (*with hype*) Lancierung *f*; (*event*) Eröffnungsfeier *f* ▷ *vt* (*ship*) vom Stapel lassen; (*rocket*) abschießen; (*product*) einführen; (*with hype*) lancieren; (*project*) in Gang setzen

launder ['lɔːndə*] *vt* waschen und bügeln; (*fig: money*) waschen; **laundrette** [lɔːnˈdret] *n* (*Brit*), **laundromat** ['lɔːndrəmæt] *n* (*US*) Waschsalon *m*; **laundry** ['lɔːndrɪ] *n* (*place*) Wäscherei *f*; (*clothes*) Wäsche *f*

lavatory ['lævətrɪ] *n* Toilette *f*

lavender ['lævɪndə*] *n* Lavendel *m*

lavish ['lævɪʃ] *adj* verschwenderisch; (*furnishings etc*) üppig; (*gift*) großzügig

law [lɔː] *n* Gesetz *nt*; (*system*) Recht *nt*; (*for study*) Jura; (*of sport*) Regel *f*; **against the ~** gesetzwidrig; **law-abiding** *adj* gesetzestreu; **law court** *n* Gerichtshof *m*; **lawful** *adj* rechtmäßig

lawn [lɔːn] *n* Rasen *m*; **lawnmower** *n* Rasenmäher *m*

lawsuit ['lɔːsuːt] *n* Prozess *m*; **lawyer** ['lɔːjə*] *n* Rechtsanwalt *m*, Rechtsanwältin *f*

laxative ['læksətɪv] *n* Abführmittel *nt*

lay [leɪ] *pt of* **lie** ▷ *vt* (**laid, laid**) legen; (*table*) decken; (*vulg*) poppen, bumsen; (*egg*) legen ▷ *adj* Laien-; **lay down** *vt* hinlegen; **lay off** *vt* (*workers*) (vorübergehend) entlassen; (*stop attacking*) in Ruhe lassen; **lay on** *vt* (*provide*) anbieten; (*organize*) veranstalten, bereitstellen; **layabout** *n* Faulenzer(in) *m(f)*; **lay-by** *n* Parkbucht *f*; (*bigger*) Parkplatz *m*

layer ['leɪə*] *n* Schicht *f*

layman ['leɪmən] *n* Laie *m*

layout ['leɪaʊt] *n* Gestaltung *f*; (*of book etc*) Lay-out *nt*

laze [leɪz] *vi* faulenzen; **laziness** ['leɪzɪnɪs] *n* Faulheit *f*; **lazy** ['leɪzɪ] *adj* faul; (*day, time*) gemütlich

lb *abbr* = **pound** Pfd.
lead [led] *n* Blei *nt* ▷ *vt, vi* [li:d] (**led, led**)
führen; (*group etc*) leiten; **to ~ the way**
vorangehen; **this is ~ing us nowhere** das
bringt uns nicht weiter ▷ [li:d] *n* (*race*)
Führung *f*; (*distance, time ahead*) Vorsprung
m (*over* vor +*dat*); (*of police*) Spur *f*; (*Theat*)
Hauptrolle *f*; (*dog's*) Leine *f*; (*Elec: flex*)
Leitung *f*; **lead astray** *vt* irreführen; **lead
away** *vt* wegführen; **lead back** *vi*
zurückführen; **lead on** *vt* anführen; **lead
to** *vt* (*street*) hinführen nach; (*result in*)
führen zu; **lead up to** *vt* (*drive*) führen zu
leaded ['lɛdɪd] *adj* (*petrol*) verbleit
leader ['li:də*] *n* Führer(in) *m(f)*; (*of party*)
Vorsitzende(r) *mf*; (*of project, expedition*)
Leiter(in) *m(f)*; (*Sport: in race*) der/die Erste;
(*in league*) Tabellenführer *m*; **leadership**
['li:dəʃɪp] *n* Führung *f*
lead-free ['lɛd'fri:] *adj* (*petrol*) bleifrei
leading ['li:dɪŋ] *adj* führend, wichtig
leaf [li:f] (*pl* **leaves**) *n* Blatt *nt*; **leaflet**
['li:flɪt] *n* Prospekt *m*; (*pamphlet*) Flugblatt
nt; (*with instructions*) Merkblatt *nt*
league [li:g] *n* Bund *m*; (*Sport*) Liga *f*
leak [li:k] *n* (*gap*) undichte Stelle; (*escape*)
Leck *nt*; **to take a ~** (*fam*) pinkeln gehen
▷ *vi* (*pipe etc*) undicht sein; (*liquid etc*)
auslaufen; **leaky** *adj* undicht
lean [li:n] *adj* (*meat*) mager; (*face*) schmal;
(*person*) drahtig ▷ *vi* (**leant** *o* **leaned,
leant** *o* **leaned**) (*not vertical*) sich neigen;
(*rest*) **to ~ against sth** sich an etw *akk*
lehnen; (*support oneself*) **to ~ on sth** sich
auf etw *akk* stützen ▷ *vt* lehnen (*on,
against* an +*akk*); **lean back** *vi* sich
zurücklehnen; **lean forward** *vi* sich
vorbeugen; **lean over** *vi* sich
hinüberbeugen; **lean towards** *vt*
tendieren zu
leant [lɛnt] *pt, pp of* **lean**
leap [li:p] *n* Sprung *m* ▷ *vi* (**leapt** *o* **leaped,
lept** *o* **leaped**) springen; **leap year** *n*
Schaltjahr *nt*
learn [lɜ:n] (**learnt** *o* **learned, learnt** *o*
learned) *vt, vi* lernen; (*find out*) erfahren;
to ~ (how) to swim schwimmen lernen;
learned ['lɜ:nɪd] *adj* gelehrt; **learner** *n*
Anfänger(in) *m(f)*; (*Brit: driver*)
Fahrschüler(in) *m(f)*
learnt [lɜ:nt] *pt, pp of* **learn**
lease [li:s] *n* (*of land, premises etc*) Pacht *f*;
(*contract*) Pachtvertrag *m*; (*of house, car etc*)

Miete *f*; (*contract*) Mietvertrag *m* ▷ *vt*
pachten; (*house, car etc*) mieten; **lease out**
vt vermieten; **leasing** ['li:sɪŋ] *n* Leasing
nt
least [li:st] *adj* wenigste(r, s); (*slightest*)
geringste(r, s) ▷ *adv* am wenigsten;
~ expensive billigste(r, s) ▷ *n* **the ~** das
Mindeste; **not in the ~** nicht im
geringsten; **at ~** wenigstens; (*with number*)
mindestens
leather ['lɛðə*] *n* Leder *nt* ▷ *adj* ledern,
Leder-
leave [li:v] *n* (*time off*) Urlaub *m*; **on ~** auf
Urlaub; **to take one's ~** Abschied nehmen
(*of* von) ▷ *vt* (**left, left**) (*place, person*)
verlassen; (*not remove, not change*) lassen;
(*~ behind: message, scar etc*) hinterlassen;
(*forget*) hinter sich lassen; (*after death*)
hinterlassen (*to sb* jdm); (*entrust*)
überlassen (*to sb* jdm); **to be left** (*remain*)
übrig bleiben; **~ me alone** lass mich in
Ruhe!; **don't ~ it to the last minute**
warte nicht bis zur letzten Minute ▷ *vi*
(weg)gehen, (weg)fahren; (*on journey*)
abreisen; (*bus, train*) abfahren (*for* nach);
leave behind *vt* zurücklassen; (*scar etc*)
hinterlassen; (*forget*) hinter sich lassen;
leave out *vt* auslassen; (*person*)
ausschließen (*of* von)
leaves [li:vz] *pl of* **leaf**
leaving do [li:vɪŋdu:] *n* Abschiedsfeier *f*
Lebanon ['lɛbənən] *n* **the ~** der Libanon
lecture ['lɛktʃə*] *n* Vortrag *m*; (*at
university*) Vorlesung *f*; **to give a ~** einen
Vortrag/eine Vorlesung halten; **lecturer**
n Dozent(in) *m(f)*; **lecture theatre** *n*
Hörsaal *m*
led [lɛd] *pt, pp of* **lead**
LED *abbr* = **light-emitting diode**
Leuchtdiode *f*
ledge [lɛdʒ] *n* Leiste *f*; (*window* ~) Sims *m o*
nt
leek [li:k] *n* Lauch *m*
left [lɛft] *pt, pp of* **leave** ▷ *adj* linke(r, s)
▷ *adv* (*position*) links; (*movement*) nach
links ▷ *n* (*side*) linke Seite; **the Left** (*Pol*)
die Linke; **on/to the ~** links (*of* von);
move/fall to the ~ nach links
rücken/fallen; **left-hand** *adj* linke(r, s);
~ bend Linkskurve *f*; **~ drive**
Linkssteuerung *f*; **left-handed** *adj*
linkshändig; **left-hand side** *n* linke
Seite

left-luggage locker n
Gepäckschließfach nt; **left-luggage office** n Gepäckaufbewahrung f
left-overs npl Reste pl
left wing n linker Flügel; **left-wing** adj (Pol) linksgerichtet
leg [leg] n Bein nt; (of meat) Keule f
legacy ['legəsɪ] n Erbe nt, Erbschaft f
legal ['liːgəl] adj Rechts-, rechtlich; (allowed) legal; (limit, age) gesetzlich; **~ aid** Rechtshilfe f; **legalize** vt legalisieren; **legally** adv legal
legend ['ledʒənd] n Legende f
legible, legibly ['ledʒəbl, -blɪ] adj, adv leserlich
legislation [ledʒɪs'leɪʃn] n Gesetze pl
legitimate [lɪ'dʒɪtɪmət] adj rechtmäßig, legitim
legroom ['legrʊm] n Platz m für die Beine
leisure ['leʒə*] n (time) Freizeit f ▷ adj Freizeit-; **~ centre** Freizeitzentrum nt; **leisurely** ['leʒəlɪ] adj gemächlich
lemon ['lemən] n Zitrone f; **lemonade** [lemə'neɪd] n Limonade f; **lemon curd** n Brotaufstrich aus Zitronen, Butter, Eiern und Zucker; **lemon juice** n Zitronensaft m; **lemon sole** n Seezunge f
lend [lend] (**lent, lent**) vt leihen; **to ~ sb sth** jdm etw leihen; **to (sb) ~ a hand** (jdm) behilflich sein; **lending library** n Leihbücherei f
length [leŋθ] n Länge f; **4 metres in ~** 4 Meter lang; **what ~ is it?** wie lange ist es?; **for any ~ of time** für längere Zeit; **at ~** (lengthily) ausführlich; **lengthen** ['leŋθən] vt verlängern; **lengthy** adj sehr lange; (dragging) langwierig
lenient ['liːnɪənt] adj nachsichtig
lens [lenz] n Linse f; (Foto) Objektiv nt
lent [lent] pt, pp of **lend**
Lent [lent] n Fastenzeit f
lentil ['lentl] n (Bot) Linse f
Leo ['liːəʊ] (pl **-s**) n (Astr) Löwe m
leopard ['lepəd] n Leopard m
lept [lept] pt, pp of **leap**
lesbian ['lezbɪən] adj lesbisch ▷ n Lesbe f
less [les] adj, adv, n weniger; **~ and ~** immer weniger; (~ often) immer seltener; **lessen** ['lesn] vi abnehmen, nachlassen ▷ vt verringern; (pain) lindern; **lesser** ['lesə*] adj geringer; (amount) kleiner
lesson ['lesn] n (at school) Stunde f; (unit of study) Lektion f; (fig) Lehre f; (Rel) Lesung f; **~s start at 9** der Unterricht beginnt um 9
let [let] (**let, let**) vt lassen; (lease) vermieten; **to ~ sb have sth** jdm etw geben; **~'s go** gehen wir; **to ~ go (of sth)** (etw) loslassen; **let down** vt herunterlassen; (fail to help) im Stich lassen; (disappoint) enttäuschen; **let in** vt hereinlassen; **let off** vt (bomb) hochgehen lassen; (person) laufen lassen; **let out** vt hinauslassen; (secret) verraten; (scream etc) ausstoßen; **let up** vi nachlassen; (stop) aufhören
lethal ['liːθəl] adj tödlich
let's contr = **let us**
letter ['letə*] n (of alphabet) Buchstabe m; (message) Brief m; (official ~) Schreiben nt; **letter bomb** n Briefbombe f; **letterbox** n Briefkasten m
lettuce ['letɪs] n Kopfsalat m
leukaemia, leukemia (US) [luː'kiːmɪə] n Leukämie f
level ['levl] adj (horizontal) waagerecht; (ground) eben; (two things, two runners) auf selber Höhe; **to be ~ with sb/sth** mit jdm/etw auf gleicher Höhe sein; **~ on points** punktgleich ▷ adv (run etc) auf gleicher Höhe, gleich auf; **to draw ~** (in race) gleichziehen (with mit); (in game) ausgleichen ▷ n (altitude) Höhe f; (standard) Niveau nt; (amount, degree) Grad m; **to be on a ~ with** auf gleicher Höhe sein mit ▷ vt (ground) einebnen; **level crossing** n (Brit) (schienengleicher) Bahnübergang m; **level-headed** adj vernünftig
lever ['liːvə*], (US) ['levə*] n Hebel m; (fig) Druckmittel nt; **lever up** vt hochstemmen
liability [laɪə'bɪlɪtɪ] n Haftung f; (burden) Belastung f; (obligation) Verpflichtung f; **liable** ['laɪəbl] adj **to be ~ for sth** (responsible) für etw haften; **~ for tax** steuerpflichtig
liar ['laɪə*] n Lügner(in) m(f)
Lib Dem [lɪb'dem] abbr = **Liberal Democrat**
liberal ['lɪbərəl] adj (generous) großzügig; (broad-minded) liberal; **Liberal Democrat** n (Brit Pol) Liberaldemokrat(in) m(f) ▷ adj liberaldemokratisch; **the ~ Party** die Liberaldemokratische Partei

liberate ['lɪbəreɪt] vt befreien; **liberation** [lɪbə'reɪʃn] n Befreiung f

Liberia [laɪ'bɪərɪə] n Liberia nt

liberty ['lɪbətɪ] n Freiheit f

Libra ['liːbrə] n (Astr) Waage f

library ['laɪbrərɪ] n Bibliothek f; (lending ~) Bücherei f

Libya ['lɪbɪə] n Libyen nt

lice [laɪs] pl of **louse**

licence ['laɪsəns] n (permit) Genehmigung f; (Comm) Lizenz f; (driving ~) Führerschein m; **license** ['laɪsəns] n (US) see **licence** ▷ vt genehmigen; **licensed** adj (restaurant etc) mit Schankerlaubnis; **license plate** n (US Auto) Nummernschild nt; **licensing hours** npl Ausschankzeiten pl

lick [lɪk] vt lecken ▷ n Lecken nt

licorice ['lɪkərɪs] n Lakritze f

lid [lɪd] n Deckel m; (eye~) Lid nt

lie [laɪ] n Lüge f; **~ detector** Lügendetektor m ▷ vi lügen; **to ~ to sb** jdn belügen ▷ vi (**lay, lain**) (rest, be situated) liegen; (~ down) sich legen; (snow) liegen bleiben; **to be lying third** an dritter Stelle liegen; **lie about** vi herumliegen; **lie down** vi sich hinlegen

Liechtenstein ['lɪktənstaɪn] n Liechtenstein nt

lie in [laɪ'ɪn] n **to have a ~** ausschlafen

life [laɪf] (pl **lives**) n Leben nt; **to get ~** lebenslänglich bekommen; **there isn't much ~ here** hier ist nicht viel los; **how many lives were lost?** wie viele sind ums Leben gekommen?; **life assurance** n Lebensversicherung f; **lifebelt** n Rettungsring m; **lifeboat** n Rettungsboot nt; **lifeguard** n Bademeister(in) m(f), Rettungsschwimmer(in) m(f); **life insurance** n Lebensversicherung f; **life jacket** n Schwimmweste f; **lifeless** adj (dead) leblos; **lifelong** adj lebenslang; **life preserver** n (US) Rettungsring m; **life-saving** adj lebensrettend; **life-size(d)** adj in Lebensgröße; **life span** n Lebensspanne f; **life style** n Lebensstil m; **lifetime** n Lebenszeit f

lift [lɪft] vt (hoch)heben; (ban) aufheben ▷ n (Brit: elevator) Aufzug m, Lift m; **to give sb a ~** jdn im Auto mitnehmen; **lift up** vt hochheben; **lift-off** n Start m

ligament ['lɪgəmənt] n Band nt

light [laɪt] (**lit** o **lighted**, **lit** o **lighted**) vt beleuchten; (fire, cigarette) anzünden ▷ n Licht nt; (lamp) Lampe f; **~s** pl (Auto) Beleuchtung f; (traffic ~s) Ampel f; **in the ~ of** angesichts +gen ▷ adj (bright) hell; (not heavy, easy) leicht; (punishment) milde; (taxes) niedrig; **~ blue/green** hellblau/hellgrün; **light up** vt (illuminate) beleuchten ▷ vi (a. eyes) aufleuchten

light bulb n Glühbirne f

lighten ['laɪtn] vi hell werden ▷ vt (give light to) erhellen; (make less heavy) leichter machen; (fig) erleichtern

lighter ['laɪtə*] n (cigarette ~) Feuerzeug nt

light-hearted adj unbeschwert; **lighthouse** n Leuchtturm m; **lighting** n Beleuchtung f; **lightly** adv leicht; **light meter** n (Foto) Belichtungsmesser m

lightning ['laɪtnɪŋ] n Blitz m

lightweight adj leicht

like [laɪk] vt mögen, gern haben; **he ~s swimming** er schwimmt gern; **would you ~ ...?** hätten Sie gern ...?; **I'd ~ to go home** ich möchte nach Hause (gehen); **I don't ~ the film** der Film gefällt mir nicht ▷ prep wie; **what's it/he ~?** wie ist es/er?; **he looks ~ you** er sieht dir ähnlich; **~ that/this** so; **likeable** ['laɪkəbl] adj sympathisch

likelihood ['laɪklɪhʊd] n Wahrscheinlichkeit f; **likely** ['laɪklɪ] adj wahrscheinlich; **the bus is ~ to be late** der Bus wird wahrscheinlich Verspätung haben; **he's not (at all) ~ to come** (höchst)wahrscheinlich kommt er nicht

like-minded [laɪk'maɪndɪd] adj gleich gesinnt

likewise ['laɪkwaɪz] adv ebenfalls; **to do ~** das Gleiche tun

liking ['laɪkɪŋ] n (for person) Zuneigung f; (for type, things) Vorliebe f (for für)

lilac ['laɪlək] n Flieder m ▷ adj fliederfarben

lily ['lɪlɪ] n Lilie f; **~ of the valley** Maiglöckchen nt

limb [lɪm] n Glied nt

limbo ['lɪmbəʊ] n **in ~** (plans) auf Eis gelegt

lime [laɪm] n (tree) Linde f; (fruit) Limone f; (substance) Kalk m; **lime juice** n Limonensaft m; **limelight** n (fig) Rampenlicht nt

limerick ['lɪmərɪk] n Limerick m (fünfzeiliges komisches Gedicht)

limestone ['laɪmstəʊn] n Kalkstein m

limit ['lɪmɪt] n Grenze f; (for pollution etc) Grenzwert m; **there's a ~ to that** dem sind Grenzen gesetzt; **to drive over the ~** das Tempolimit überschreiten; **that's the ~** jetzt reicht's!, das ist die Höhe! ▷ vt beschränken (to auf +akk); (freedom, spending) einschränken; **limitation** [lɪmɪ'teɪʃən] n Beschränkung f; (of freedom, spending) Einschränkung f; **limited** adj begrenzt; **~ liability company** Gesellschaft f mit beschränkter Haftung, GmbH f; **public ~ company** Aktiengesellschaft f

limousine ['lɪməziːn] n Limousine f

limp [lɪmp] vi hinken ▷ adj schlaff

line [laɪn] n Linie f; (written) Zeile f; (rope) Leine f; (on face) Falte f; (row) Reihe f; (US: queue) Schlange f; (Rail) Bahnlinie f; (between A and B) Strecke f; (Tel) Leitung f; (range of items) Kollektion f; **hold the ~** bleiben Sie am Apparat; **to stand in ~** Schlange stehen; **in ~ with** in Übereinstimmung mit; **something along those ~s** etwas in dieser Art; **drop me a ~** schreib mir ein paar Zeilen; **~s** (Theat) Text m ▷ vt (clothes) füttern; (streets) säumen; **lined** adj (paper) liniert; (face) faltig; **line up** vi sich aufstellen; (US: form queue) sich anstellen

linen ['lɪnɪn] n Leinen nt; (sheets etc) Wäsche f

liner ['laɪnə*] n Überseedampfer m, Passagierschiff nt

linesman ['laɪnzmən] n (pl -men) n (Sport) Linienrichter m

linger ['lɪŋgə*] vi verweilen; (smell) nicht weggehen

lingerie ['lænʒəriː] n Damenunterwäsche f

lining ['laɪnɪŋ] n (of clothes) Futter nt; (brake ~) Bremsbelag m

link [lɪŋk] n (connection) Verbindung f; (of chain) Glied nt; (relationship) Beziehung f (with zu); (between events) Zusammenhang m; (Internet) Link m ▷ vt verbinden

lion ['laɪən] n Löwe m; **lioness** n Löwin f

lip [lɪp] n Lippe f; **lipstick** n Lippenstift m

liqueur [lɪ'kjʊə*] n Likör m

liquid ['lɪkwɪd] n Flüssigkeit f ▷ adj flüssig

liquidate ['lɪkwɪdeɪt] vt liquidieren

liquidizer ['lɪkwɪdaɪzə*] n Mixer m

liquor ['lɪkə*] n Spirituosen pl

liquorice ['lɪkərɪs] n Lakritze f

Lisbon ['lɪzbən] n Lissabon nt

lisp [lɪsp] vt, vi lispeln

list [lɪst] n Liste f ▷ vi (ship) Schlagseite haben ▷ vt auflisten, aufzählen; **~ed building** unter Denkmalschutz stehendes Gebäude

listen ['lɪsn] vi zuhören, horchen (for sth auf etw akk); **listen to** vt (person) zuhören +dat; (radio) hören; (advice) hören auf; **listener** n Zuhörer(in) m(f); (to radio) Hörer(in) m(f)

lit [lɪt] pt, pp of **light**

liter ['liːtə*] n (US) Liter m

literacy ['lɪtərəsɪ] n Fähigkeit f zu lesen und zu schreiben; **literal** ['lɪtərəl] adj (translation, meaning) wörtlich; (actual) buchstäblich; **literally** adv (translate, take sth) wörtlich; (really) buchstäblich, wirklich; **literary** ['lɪtərərɪ] adj literarisch; (critic, journal etc) Literatur-; (language) gehoben; **literature** ['lɪtrətʃə*] n Literatur f; (brochures etc) Informationsmaterial nt

Lithuania [lɪθjuː'eɪnjə] n Litauen nt

litre ['liːtə*] n Liter m

litter ['lɪtə*] n Abfälle pl; (of animals) Wurf m ▷ vt **to be ~ed with** übersät sein mit; **litter bin** n Abfalleimer m

little ['lɪtl] adj (smaller, smallest) klein; (in quantity) wenig; **a ~ while ago** vor kurzer Zeit ▷ adv, n (fewer, fewest) wenig; **a ~** ein bisschen, ein wenig; **as ~ as possible** so wenig wie möglich; **for as ~ as £5** ab nur 5 Pfund; **I see very ~ of them** ich sehe sie sehr selten; **~ by ~** nach und nach; **little finger** n kleiner Finger

live [laɪv] adj lebendig; (Elec) geladen, unter Strom; (TV, Radio: event) live; **~ broadcast** Direktübertragung f ▷ [lɪv] vi leben; (not die) überleben; (dwell) wohnen; **you ~ and learn** man lernt nie aus ▷ vt (life) führen; **to ~ a life of luxury** im Luxus leben; **live on** vi weiterleben ▷ vt **to ~ sth** von etw leben; (feed) sich von etw ernähren; **to earn enough to ~** genug verdienen, um davon zu leben; **live together** vi zusammenleben; **live up to** vt (reputation) gerecht werden +dat; (expectations) entsprechen +dat; **live with** vt (parents etc) wohnen bei; (partner) zusammenleben mit; (difficulty) **you'll just have to ~ it** du musst dich eben damit abfinden

liveliness ['laɪvlɪnɪs] n Lebhaftigkeit f; **lively** ['laɪvlɪ] adj lebhaft

liver ['lɪvə*] n Leber f

lives [laɪvz] pl of **life**

livestock ['laɪvstɒk] n Vieh nt

living ['lɪvɪŋ] n Lebensunterhalt m; **what do you do for a ~?** was machen Sie beruflich? ▷ adj lebend; **living room** n Wohnzimmer nt

lizard ['lɪzəd] n Eidechse f

load [ləʊd] n Last f; (cargo) Ladung f; (Tech, fig) Belastung f; **~s of** (fam) massenhaft; **it was a ~ of rubbish** (fam) es war grottenschlecht ▷ vt (vehicle) beladen; (Inform) laden; (film) einlegen

loaf [ləʊf] (pl **loaves**) n **~ (of bread)** Brot nt; **loaf about** vi faulenzen

loan [ləʊn] n (item leant) Leihgabe f; (Fin) Darlehen nt; **on ~** geliehen ▷ vt leihen (to sb jdm)

loathe [ləʊð] vt verabscheuen

loaves [ləʊvz] pl of **loaf**

lobby ['lɒbɪ] n Vorhalle f; (Pol) Lobby f

lobster ['lɒbstə*] n Hummer m

local ['ləʊkəl] adj (traffic, time etc) Orts-; (radio, news, paper) Lokal-; (government, authority) Kommunal-; (anaesthetic) örtlich; **~ call** (Tel) Ortsgespräch nt; **~ elections** Kommunalwahlen pl; **~ time** Ortszeit f; **~ train** Nahverkehrszug m; **the ~ shops** die Geschäfte am Ort ▷ n (pub) Stammlokal nt; **the ~s** pl die Ortsansässigen pl; **locally** adv örtlich, am Ort

locate [ləʊ'keɪt] vt (find) ausfindig machen; (position) legen; (establish) errichten; **to be ~d** sich befinden (in, at in +dat); **location** [ləʊ'keɪʃən] n (position) Lage f; (Cine) Drehort m

loch [lɒx] n (Scot) See m

lock [lɒk] n Schloss nt; (Naut) Schleuse f; (of hair) Locke f ▷ vt (door etc) abschließen ▷ vi (door etc) sich abschließen lassen; (wheels) blockieren; **lock in** vt einschließen, einsperren; **lock out** vt aussperren; **lock up** vt (house) abschließen; (person) einsperren

locker ['lɒkə*] n Schließfach nt; **locker room** n (US) Umkleideraum m

locksmith ['lɒksmɪθ] n Schlosser(in) m(f)

locust ['ləʊkəst] n Heuschrecke f

lodge [lɒdʒ] n (small house) Pförtnerhaus nt; (porter's ~) Pförtnerloge f ▷ vi in Untermiete wohnen (with bei); (get stuck) stecken bleiben; **lodger** n Untermieter(in) m(f); **lodging** n Unterkunft f

loft [lɒft] n Dachboden m

log [lɒg] n Klotz m; (Naut) Log nt; **to keep a ~ of sth** über etw Buch führen; **log in** vi (Inform) sich einloggen; **log off** vi (Inform) sich ausloggen; **log on** vi (Inform) sich einloggen; **log out** vi (Inform) sich ausloggen

logic ['lɒdʒɪk] n Logik f; **logical** adj logisch

logo ['lɒgəʊ] (pl **-s**) n Logo nt

loin [lɔɪn] n Lende f

loiter ['lɔɪtə*] vi sich herumtreiben

lollipop ['lɒlɪpɒp] n Lutscher m; **~ man/lady** (Brit) Schülerlotse m, Schülerlotsin f

lolly ['lɒlɪ] n Lutscher m; (fam: money) Knete f

London ['lʌndən] n London nt; **Londoner** n Londoner(in) m(f)

loneliness ['ləʊnlɪnɪs] n Einsamkeit f; **lonely** ['ləʊnlɪ], (esp US) **lonesome** ['ləʊnsəm] adj einsam

long [lɒŋ] adj lang; (distance) weit; **it's a ~ way** es ist weit (to nach); **for a ~ time** lange; **how ~ is the film?** wie lange dauert der Film?; **in the ~ run** auf die Dauer ▷ adv lange; **not for ~** nicht lange; **~ ago** vor langer Zeit; **before ~** bald; **all day ~** den ganzen Tag; **no ~er** nicht mehr; **as ~ as** solange ▷ vi sich sehnen (for nach); (be waiting) sehnsüchtig warten (for auf); **long-distance call** n Ferngespräch nt; **long drink** n Longdrink m; **long-haul flight** n Langstreckenflug m; **longing** n Sehnsucht f (for nach); **longingly** adv sehnsüchtig; **longitude** ['lɒŋgɪtjuːd] n Länge f; **long jump** n Weitsprung m; **long-life milk** n H-Milch f; **long-range** adj Langstrecken-, Fern-; **~ missile** Langstreckenrakete f; **long-sighted** adj weitsichtig; **long-standing** adj alt, langjährig; **long-term** adj langfristig; (car park, effect etc) Langzeit-; **~ unemployment** Langzeitarbeitslosigkeit f; **long wave** n Langwelle f

loo [lu:] n (Brit fam) Klo nt

look [lʊk] n Blick m; (appearance) **~(s)** pl Aussehen nt; **I'll have a ~** ich schau mal nach; **to have a ~ at sth** sich dat etw ansehen; **can I have a ~?** darf ich mal sehen? ▷ vi schauen, gucken; (with prep) sehen; (search) nachsehen; (appear) aussehen; **(I'm) just ~ing** ich schaue nur; **it ~s like rain** es sieht nach Regen aus ▷ vt **~ what you've done** sieh dir mal an, was du da angestellt hast; (appear) **he ~s his age** man sieht ihm sein Alter an; **to ~ one's best** sehr vorteilhaft aussehen; **look after** vt (care for) sorgen für; (keep an eye on) aufpassen auf +akk; **look at** vt ansehen, anschauen; **look back** vi sich umsehen; (fig) zurückblicken; **look down on** vt (fig) herabsehen auf +akk; **look for** vt suchen; **look forward to** vt sich freuen auf +akk; **look into** vt (investigate) untersuchen; **look out** vi hinaussehen (of the window zum Fenster); (watch out) Ausschau halten (for nach); (be careful) aufpassen, Acht geben (for auf +akk); **~!** Vorsicht!; **look up** vi aufsehen ▷ vt (word etc) nachschlagen; **look up to** vt aufsehen zu

loony ['lu:nɪ] adj (fam) bekloppt

loop [lu:p] n Schleife f

loose [lu:s] adj locker; (knot, button) lose; **loosen** vt lockern; (knot) lösen

loot [lu:t] n Beute f

lop-sided ['lɒp'saɪdɪd] adj schief

lord [lɔ:d] n (ruler) Herr m; (Brit: title) Lord m; **the Lord** (God) Gott der Herr; **the (House of) Lords** (Brit) das Oberhaus

lorry ['lɒrɪ] n (Brit) Lastwagen m

lose [lu:z] (lost, lost) vt verlieren; (chance) verpassen; **to ~ weight** abnehmen; **to ~ one's life** umkommen ▷ vi verlieren; (clock, watch) nachgehen; **loser** n Verlierer(in) m(f); **loss** [lɒs] n Verlust m; **lost** [lɒst] pt, pp of **lose**; **we're ~** wir haben uns verlaufen ▷ adj verloren; **lost-and-found** (US), **lost property (office)** n Fundbüro nt

lot [lɒt] n (fam: batch) Menge f, Haufen m, Stoß m; **this is the first ~** das ist die erste Ladung; **a ~** viel(e); **a ~ of money** viel Geld; **~s of people** viele Leute; **the (whole) ~** alles; (people) alle; (parking) **~** (US) Parkplatz m

lotion ['ləʊʃən] n Lotion f

lottery ['lɒtərɪ] n Lotterie f

loud [laʊd] adj laut; (colour) schreiend; **loudspeaker** n Lautsprecher m; (of stereo) Box f

lounge [laʊndʒ] n Wohnzimmer nt; (in hotel) Aufenthaltsraum m; (at airport) Warteraum m ▷ vi sich herumlümmeln

louse [laʊs] (pl lice) n Laus f; **lousy** ['laʊzɪ] adj (fam) lausig

lout [laʊt] n Rüpel m

lovable ['lʌvəbl] adj liebenswert

love [lʌv] n Liebe f (of zu); (person, address) Liebling m, Schatz m; (Sport) null; **to be in ~** verliebt sein (with sb in jdn); **to fall in ~** sich verlieben (with sb in jdn); **to make ~** (sexually) sich lieben; **to make ~ to (o with)** sb mit jdm schlafen; (in letter) **he sends his ~** er lässt grüßen; **give her my ~** grüße sie von mir; **~, Tom** liebe Grüße, Tom ▷ vt (person) lieben; (activity) sehr gerne mögen; **to ~ to do sth** etw für sein Leben gerne tun; **I'd ~ a cup of tea** ich hätte liebend gern eine Tasse Tee; **love affair** n (Liebes)verhältnis nt; **love letter** n Liebesbrief m; **love life** n Liebesleben nt; **lovely** ['lʌvlɪ] adj schön, wunderschön; (charming) reizend; **we had a ~ time** es war sehr schön; **lover** ['lʌvə] n Liebhaber(in) m(f); **loving** adj liebevoll

low [ləʊ] adj niedrig; (rank) niedere(r, s); (level, note, neckline) tief; (intelligence, density) gering; (quality, standard) schlecht; (not loud) leise; (depressed) niedergeschlagen; **we're ~ on petrol** wir haben kaum noch Benzin ▷ n (Meteo) Tief nt; **low-calorie** adj kalorienarm; **lowcut** adj (dress) tief ausgeschnitten; **low-emission** adj schadstoffarm; **lower** ['ləʊə*] adj niedriger; (storey, class etc) untere(r, s) ▷ vt herunterlassen; (eyes, price) senken; (pressure) verringern; **low-fat** adj fettarm; **low tide** [ləʊ'taɪd] n Ebbe f

loyal ['lɔɪəl] adj treu; **loyalty** n Treue f

lozenge ['lɒzɪndʒ] n Pastille f

● **L-Plates**

● Als **L-Plates** werden in
● Großbritannien die weißen Schilder
● mit einem roten „L" bezeichnet, die
● vorn und hinten an jedem von einem
● Fahrschüler gesteuerten Fahrzeug

- befestigt werden müssen.
- Fahrschüler müssen einen
- vorläufigen Führerschein
- beantragen und dürfen damit unter
- der Aufsicht eines erfahrenen
- Autofahrers auf allen Straßen außer
- Autobahnen fahren.

Ltd *abbr* = **limited** ≈ GmbH *f*

lubricant [ˈluːbrɪkənt] *n* Schmiermittel *nt*, Gleitmittel *nt*

luck [lʌk] *n* Glück *nt*; **bad ~** Pech *nt*; **luckily** *adv* glücklicherweise, zum Glück; **lucky** *adj* (*number, day etc*) Glücks-; **to be ~** Glück haben; **~ coincidence** glücklicher Zufall

ludicrous [ˈluːdɪkrəs] *adj* grotesk

luggage [ˈlʌɡɪdʒ] *n* Gepäck *nt*; **luggage compartment** *n* Gepäckraum *m*; **luggage rack** *n* Gepäcknetz *nt*

lukewarm [ˈluːkwɔːm] *adj* lauwarm

lullaby [ˈlʌləbaɪ] *n* Schlaflied *nt*

lumbago [lʌmˈbeɪɡəʊ] *n* Hexenschuss *m*

luminous [ˈluːmɪnəs] *adj* leuchtend

lump [lʌmp] *n* Klumpen *m*; (*Med*) Schwellung *f*; (*in breast*) Knoten *m*; (*of sugar*) Stück *nt*; **lump sum** *n* Pauschalsumme *f*; **lumpy** *adj* klumpig

lunacy [ˈluːnəsɪ] *n* Wahnsinn *m*; **lunatic** [ˈluːnətɪk] *adj* wahnsinnig ▷ *n* Wahnsinnige(r) *mf*

lunch, luncheon [lʌntʃ, -ən] *n* Mittagessen *nt*; **to have ~** zu Mittag essen; **lunch break, lunch hour** *n* Mittagspause *f*; **lunch packet** *n* Lunchpaket *nt*; **lunchtime** *n* Mittagszeit *f*

lung [lʌŋ] *n* Lunge *f*

lurid [ˈljʊərɪd] *adj* (*colour*) grell; (*details*) widerlich

lurk [lɜːk] *vi* lauern

lust [lʌst] *n* (sinnliche) Begierde (*for* nach)

luster (*US*), **lustre** [ˈlʌstə*] *n* Glanz *m*

Luxembourg [ˈlʌksəmbɜːɡ] *n* Luxemburg *nt*; **Luxembourger** [lʌksəmˈbɜːɡə*] *n* Luxemburger(in) *m(f)*

luxurious [lʌɡˈʒʊərɪəs] *adj* luxuriös, Luxus-; **luxury** [ˈlʌkʃərɪ] *n* (*a. luxuries pl*) Luxus *m*; **~ goods** Luxusgüter *pl*

lynx [lɪŋks] *n* Luchs *m*

lyrics *npl* (*words for song*) Liedtext *m*

m *abbr* = **metre** m

M *abbr* (*street*) = **Motorway** A; (*size*) = **medium** M

MA *abbr* = **Master of Arts** Magister Artium m

ma [ma:] *n* (*fam*) Mutti *f*

mac [mæk] *n* (*Brit fam*) Regenmantel *m*

Macedonia [mæʃə'dəʊnɪə] *n* Mazedonien *nt*

machine [mə'ʃi:n] *n* Maschine *f*; **machine gun** *n* Maschinengewehr *nt*; **machinery** [mə'ʃi:nərɪ] *n* Maschinen *pl*; (*fig*) Apparat *m*; **machine washable** *adj* waschmaschinenfest

mackerel ['mækrəl] *n* Makrele *f*

macro ['mækrəʊ] (*pl* **-s**) *n* (*Inform*) Makro *nt*

mad [mæd] *adj* wahnsinnig, verrückt; (*dog*) tollwütig; (*angry*) wütend, sauer (*at* auf +*akk*); (*fam*) **~ about** (*fond of*) verrückt nach; **to work like ~** wie verrückt arbeiten; **are you ~?** spinnst du?

madam ['mædəm] *n* gnädige Frau

mad cow disease [mæd'kaʊdɪ'zi:z] *n* Rinderwahnsinn *m*; **maddening** *adj* zum Verrücktwerden

made [meɪd] *pt, pp of* **make**

made-to-measure ['meɪdtə'meʒə*] *adj* nach Maß; **~ suit** Maßanzug *m*

madly ['mædlɪ] *adv* wie verrückt; (*with adj*) wahnsinnig; **madman** ['mædmən] (*pl* **-men**) *n* Verrückte(r) *m*; **madwoman** ['mædwʊmən] (*pl* **-women**) *n* Verrückte *f*; **madness** ['mædnɪs] *n* Wahnsinn *m*

magazine ['mægəzi:n] *n* Zeitschrift *f*

maggot ['mægət] *n* Made *f*

magic ['mædʒɪk] *n* Magie *f*; (*activity*) Zauberei *f*; (*fig: effect*) Zauber *m*; **as if by ~** wie durch Zauberei ▷ *adj* Zauber-; (*powers*) magisch; **magician** [mə'dʒɪʃən] *n* Zauberer *m*, Zaub(r)erin *f*

magnet ['mægnɪt] *n* Magnet *m*; **magnetic** [mæg'netɪk] *adj* magnetisch; **magnetism** ['mægnɪtɪzəm] *n* (*fig*) Anziehungskraft *f*

magnificent, magnificently [mæg'nɪfɪsənt, -lɪ] *adj, adv* herrlich, großartig

magnify ['mægnɪfaɪ] *vt* vergrößern; **magnifying glass** *n* Vergrößerungsglas *nt*, Lupe *f*

magpie ['mægpaɪ] *n* Elster *f*

maid [meɪd] *n* Dienstmädchen *nt*; **maiden name** *n* Mädchenname *m*; **maiden voyage** *n* Jungfernfahrt *f*

mail [meɪl] *n* Post *f*; (*e-mail*) Mail *f* ▷ *vt* (*post*) aufgeben; (*send*) mit der Post schicken (*to* an +*akk*); **mailbox** *n* (*US*) Briefkasten *m*; (*Inform*) Mailbox *f*; **mailing list** *n* Adressenliste *f*; **mailman** *n* (*pl* **-men**) (*US*) Briefträger *m*; **mail order** *n* Bestellung *f* per Post; **mail order firm** *n* Versandhaus *nt*; **mailshot** *n* Mailing *nt*

main [meɪn] *adj* Haupt-; **~ course** Hauptgericht *nt*; **the ~ thing** die Hauptsache ▷ *n* (*pipe*) Hauptleitung *f*; **mainframe** *n* Großrechner *m*; **mainland** *n* Festland *nt*; **mainly** *adv* hauptsächlich; **main road** *n* Hauptverkehrsstraße *f*; **main street** *n* (*US*) Hauptstraße *f*

maintain [meɪn'teɪn] *vt* (*keep up*) aufrechterhalten; (*machine, roads*) instand halten; (*service*) warten; (*claim*) behaupten; **maintenance** ['meɪntənəns] *n* Instandhaltung *f*; (*Tech*) Wartung *f*

maize [meɪz] *n* Mais *m*

majestic [mə'dʒestɪk] *adj* majestätisch; **majesty** ['mædʒɪstɪ] *n* Majestät *f*; **his/her Majesty** seine/ihre Majestät

major ['meɪdʒə*] adj (bigger) größer; (important) bedeutend; ~ **part** Großteil m; (role) wichtige Rolle; ~ **road** Hauptverkehrsstraße f; (Mus) **A** ~ A-Dur nt ▷ vi (US) **to ~ in sth** etw als Hauptfach studieren

Majorca [mə'jɔːkə] n Mallorca nt

majority [mə'dʒɒrɪtɪ] n Mehrheit f; **to be in the ~** in der Mehrzahl sein

make [meɪk] n Marke f ▷ vt (**made, made**) machen; (manufacture) herstellen; (clothes) anfertigen; (dress) nähen; (soup) zubereiten; (bread, cake) backen; (tea, coffee) kochen; (speech) halten; (earn) verdienen; (decision) treffen; **it's made of gold** es ist aus Gold; **to ~ sb do sth** jdn dazu bringen, etw zu tun; (force) jdn zwingen, etw zu tun; **she made us wait** sie ließ uns warten; **what ~s you think that?** wie kommen Sie darauf?; **it ~s the room look smaller** es lässt den Raum kleiner wirken; **to ~ (it to) the airport** (reach) den Flughafen erreichen; (in time) es zum Flughafen schaffen; **he never really made it** er hat es nie zu etwas gebracht; **she didn't ~ it through the night** sie hat die Nacht nicht überlebt; (calculate) **I ~ it £5/a quarter to six** nach meiner Rechnung kommt es auf 5 Pfund/nach meiner Uhr ist es dreiviertel sechs; **he's just made for this job** er ist für diese Arbeit wie geschaffen; **make for** vt zusteuern auf +akk; **make of** vt (think of) halten von; **I couldn't ~ anything of it** ich wurde daraus nicht schlau; **make off** vi sich davonmachen (with mit); **make out** vi zurechtkommen ▷ vt (cheque) ausstellen; (list) aufstellen; (understand) verstehen; (discern) ausmachen; **to ~ (that) ...** es so hinstellen, als ob ...; **make up** vt (team etc) bilden; (face) schminken; (invent: story etc) erfinden; **to ~ one's mind** sich entscheiden; **to make it up with sb** sich mit jdm aussöhnen ▷ vi sich versöhnen; **make up for** vt ausgleichen; (time) aufholen

make-believe adj Fantasie-; **makeover** n gründliche Veränderung, Verschönerung f; **maker** n (Comm) Hersteller(in) m(f); **makeshift** adj behelfsmäßig; **make-up** n Make-up nt, Schminke f; **making** ['meɪkɪŋ] n Herstellung f

maladjusted [mælə'dʒʌstɪd] adj verhaltensgestört

malaria [mə'lɛərɪə] n Malaria f

Malaysia [mə'leɪzɪə] n Malaysia nt

male [meɪl] n Mann m; (animal) Männchen nt ▷ adj männlich; ~ **chauvinist** Chauvi m, Macho m; ~ **nurse** Krankenpfleger m

malfunction [mæl'fʌŋkʃən] vi nicht richtig funktionieren ▷ n Defekt m

malice ['mælɪs] n Bosheit f; **malicious** [mə'lɪʃəs] adj boshaft; (behaviour, action) böswillig; (damage) mutwillig

malignant [mə'lɪgnənt] adj bösartig

mall [mɔːl] n (US) Einkaufszentrum nt

malnutrition [mælnjʊ'trɪʃən] n Unterernährung f

malt [mɔːlt] n Malz nt

Malta ['mɔːltə] n Malta nt; **Maltese** [mɔːl'tiːz] adj maltesisch ▷ n (person) Malteser(in) m(f); (language) Maltesisch nt

maltreat [mæl'triːt] vt schlecht behandeln; (violently) misshandeln

mammal ['mæməl] n Säugetier nt

mammoth ['mæməθ] adj Mammut-, Riesen-

man [mæn] (pl **men**) n (male) Mann m; (human race) der Mensch, die Menschen pl; (in chess) Figur f ▷ vt besetzen

manage ['mænɪdʒ] vi zurechtkommen; **can you ~?** schaffst du es?; **to ~ without sth** ohne etw auskommen, auf etw verzichten können ▷ vt (control) leiten; (musician, sportsman) managen; (cope with) fertig werden mit; (task, portion, climb etc) schaffen; **to ~ to do sth** es schaffen, etw zu tun; **manageable** adj (object) handlich; (task) zu bewältigen; **management** n Leitung f; (directors) Direktion f; (subject) Management nt, Betriebswirtschaft f; **management consultant** n Unternehmensberater(in) m(f); **manager** n Geschäftsführer(in) m(f); (departmental ~) Abteilungsleiter(in) m(f); (of branch, bank) Filialleiter(in) m(f); (of musician, sportsman) Manager(in) m(f); **managing director** n Geschäftsführer(in) m(f)

mane [meɪn] n Mähne f

maneuver (US) see **manoeuvre**

mango ['mæŋgəʊ] (pl **-es**) n Mango f

man-hour n Arbeitsstunde f

manhunt n Fahndung f

mania ['meɪnɪə] n Manie f; **maniac**

['meɪnɪæk] n Wahnsinnige(r) mf; (fan) Fanatiker(in) m(f)

manicure ['mænɪkjʊə*] n Maniküre f

manipulate [mə'nɪpjʊleɪt] vt manipulieren

mankind [mæn'kaɪnd] n Menschheit f

manly ['mænlɪ] adj männlich

man-made ['mænmeɪd] adj (product) künstlich

manner ['mænə*] n Art f; **in this ~** auf diese Art und Weise; **~s** pl Manieren pl

manoeuvre [mə'nu:və*] n Manöver nt ⊳ vt, vi manövrieren

manor ['mænə*] n **~ (house)** Herrenhaus nt

manpower ['mænpaʊə*] n Arbeitskräfte pl

mansion ['mænʃən] n Villa f; (of old family) Herrenhaus nt

manslaughter ['mænslɔ:tə*] n Totschlag m

mantelpiece ['mæntlpi:s] n Kaminsims m

manual ['mænjʊəl] adj manuell, Hand- ⊳ n Handbuch nt

manufacture [mænjʊ'fæktʃə*] vt herstellen ⊳ n Herstellung f; **manufacturer** n Hersteller m

manure [mə'njʊə*] n Dung m; (esp artificial) Dünger m

many ['menɪ] **(more, most)** adj, pron viele; **~ times** oft; **not ~ people** nicht viele Leute; **too ~ problems** zu viele Probleme

map [mæp] n Landkarte f; (of town) Stadtplan m

maple ['meɪpl] n Ahorn m

marathon ['mærəθən] n Marathon m

marble ['mɑ:bl] n Marmor m; (for playing) Murmel f

march [mɑ:tʃ] vi marschieren ⊳ n Marsch m; (protest) Demonstration f

March [mɑ:tʃ] n März m; see also **September**

mare [meə] n Stute f

margarine [mɑ:dʒə'ri:n] n Margarine f

margin ['mɑ:dʒɪn] n Rand m; (extra amount) Spielraum m; (Comm) Gewinnspanne f; **marginal** adj (difference etc) geringfügig

marijuana [mærjʊ'ɑ:nə] n Marihuana nt

marinade ['mærɪneɪd] n (Gastr)

Marinade f; **marinated** ['mærɪneɪtd] adj mariniert

marine [mə'ri:n] adj Meeres-

marital ['mærɪtl] adj ehelich; **~ status** Familienstand m

maritime ['mærɪtaɪm] adj See-

marjoram ['mɑ:dʒərəm] n Majoran m

mark [mɑ:k] n (spot) Fleck m; (at school) Note f; (sign) Zeichen nt ⊳ vt (make ~) Flecken machen auf +akk; (indicate) markieren; (schoolwork) benoten, korrigieren, Flecken machen auf +akk; **markedly** ['mɑ:kɪdlɪ] adv merklich; (with comp adj) wesentlich; **marker** n (in book) Lesezeichen nt; (pen) Marker m

market ['mɑ:kɪt] n Markt m; (stock ~) Börse f ⊳ vt (Comm: new product) auf den Markt bringen; (goods) vertreiben; **marketing** n Marketing nt; **market leader** n Marktführer m; **market place** n Marktplatz m; **market research** n Marktforschung f

marmalade ['mɑ:məleɪd] n Orangenmarmelade f

maroon [mə'ru:n] adj rötlich braun

marquee [mɑ:'ki:] n großes Zelt

marriage ['mærɪdʒ] n Ehe f; (wedding) Heirat f (to mit); **married** ['mærɪd] adj (person) verheiratet

marrow ['mærəʊ] n (bone ~) Knochenmark nt; (vegetable) Kürbis m

marry ['mærɪ] vt heiraten; (join) trauen; (take as husband, wife) heiraten ⊳ vi **to ~ / to get married** heiraten

marsh [mɑ:ʃ] n Marsch f, Sumpf m

marshal ['mɑ:ʃəl] n (at rally etc) Ordner m; (US: police) Bezirkspolizeichef m

martial arts ['mɑ:ʃəl'ɑ:ts] npl Kampfsportarten pl

martyr ['mɑ:tə*] n Märtyrer(in) m(f)

marvel ['mɑ:vəl] n Wunder nt ⊳ vi staunen (at über +akk); **marvellous**, **marvelous** (US) adj wunderbar

marzipan [mɑ:zɪ'pæn] n Marzipan nt o m

mascara [mæ'skɑ:rə] n Wimperntusche f

mascot ['mæskɒt] n Maskottchen nt

masculine ['mæskjʊlɪn] adj männlich

mashed [mæʃt] adj **~ potatoes** pl Kartoffelbrei m, Kartoffelpüree nt

mask [mɑ:sk] n (a. Inform) Maske f ⊳ vt (feelings) verbergen

masochist ['mæsəʊkɪst] n Masochist(in) m(f)

mason ['meɪsn] n (stone~) Steinmetz(in) m(f); **masonry** n Mauerwerk nt

mass [mæs] n Masse f; (of people) Menge f; (Rel) Messe f; **~es of** massenhaft

massacre ['mæsəkə*] n Blutbad nt

massage ['mæsɑ:ʒ] n Massage f ▷ vt massieren

massive ['mæsɪv] adj (powerful) gewaltig; (very large) riesig

mass media ['mæs'mi:dɪə] npl Massenmedien pl; **mass-produce** vt in Massenproduktion herstellen; **mass production** n Massenproduktion f

master ['mɑ:stə*] n Herr m; (of dog) Besitzer m, Herrchen nt; (teacher) Lehrer m; (artist) Meister m ▷ vt meistern; (language etc) beherrschen; **masterly** adj meisterhaft; **masterpiece** n Meisterwerk nt

masturbate ['mæstəbeɪt] vi masturbieren

mat [mæt] n Matte f; (for table) Untersetzer m

match [mætʃ] n Streichholz nt; (Sport) Wettkampf m; (ball games) Spiel nt; (tennis) Match nt ▷ vt (be like, suit) passen zu; (equal) gleichkommen +dat ▷ vi zusammenpassen; **matchbox** n Streichholzschachtel f; **matching** adj (one item) passend; (two items) zusammenpassend

mate [meɪt] n (companion) Kumpel m; (of animal) Weibchen nt/Männchen nt ▷ vi sich paaren

material [mə'tɪərɪəl] n Material nt; (for book etc, cloth) Stoff m; **materialistic** [mətɪərɪə'lɪstɪk] adj materialistisch; **materialize** [mə'tɪərɪəlaɪz] vi zustande kommen; (hope) wahr werden

maternal [mə'tɜ:nl] adj mütterlich; **maternity** [mə'tɜ:nɪtɪ] adj **~ dress** Umstandskleid nt; **~ leave** Elternzeit f (der Mutter); **~ ward** Entbindungsstation f

math [mæθ] n (US fam) Mathe f; **mathematical** [mæθə'mætɪkəl] adj mathematisch; **mathematics** [mæθə'mætɪks] nsing Mathematik f; **maths** [mæθs] nsing (Brit fam) Mathe f

matinée ['mætɪneɪ] n Nachmittagsvorstellung f

matter ['mætə*] n (substance) Materie f; (affair) Sache f; **a personal ~** eine persönliche Angelegenheit; **a ~ of taste** eine Frage des Geschmacks; **no ~ how/what** egal wie/was; **what is the ~?** was ist los?; **as a ~ of fact** eigentlich; **a ~ of time** eine Frage der Zeit ▷ vi darauf ankommen, wichtig sein; **it doesn't ~** es macht nichts; **matter-of-fact** adj sachlich, nüchtern

mattress ['mætrəs] n Matratze f

mature [mə'tjʊə*] adj reif ▷ vi reif werden; **maturity** [mə'tjʊərɪtɪ] n Reife f

maximum ['mæksɪməm] adj Höchst-, höchste(r, s); **~ speed** Höchstgeschwindigkeit f ▷ n Maximum nt

may [meɪ] (**might**) vb aux (be possible) können; (have permission) dürfen; **it ~ rain** es könnte regnen; **~ I smoke?** darf ich rauchen?; **it ~ not happen** es passiert vielleicht gar nicht; **we ~ as well go** wir können ruhig gehen

May [meɪ] n Mai m; see also **September**

maybe ['meɪbi:] adv vielleicht

May Day ['meɪdeɪ] n der erste Mai

mayo ['meɪəʊ] (US fam), **mayonnaise** [meɪə'neɪz] n Mayo f, Mayonnaise f, Majonäse f

mayor [mɛə*] n Bürgermeister m

maze [meɪz] n Irrgarten m; (fig) Wirrwarr nt

MB abbr = **megabyte** MB nt

⃝ KEYWORD

me [mi:] pron 1 (direct) mich; **it's me** ich bins

2 (indirect) mir; **give them to me** gib sie mir

3 (after prep: +acc) mich; (+dat) mir; **with/without me** mit mir/ohne mich

meadow ['medəʊ] n Wiese f

meal [mi:l] n Essen nt, Mahlzeit f; **to go out for a ~** essen gehen; **meal pack** n (US) tiefgekühltes Fertiggericht; **meal time** n Essenszeit f

mean [mi:n] (**meant, meant**) vt (signify) bedeuten; (have in mind) meinen; (intend) vorhaben; **I ~ it** ich meine das ernst; **what do you ~ (by that)?** was willst du damit sagen?; **to ~ to do sth** etw tun wollen; **it was ~t for you** es war für dich bestimmt (o gedacht); **it was ~t to be a joke** es sollte ein Witz sein ▷ *vi* **he ~s well** er meint es gut ▷ *adj* (*stingy*) geizig; (*spiteful*) gemein (*to zu*); **meaning** ['miːnɪŋ] *n* Bedeutung *f*; (*of life, poem*) Sinn *m*; **meaningful** *adj* sinnvoll; **meaningless** *adj* (*text*) ohne Sinn

means [miːnz] (*pl* **means**) *n* Mittel *nt*; (*pl: funds*) Mittel *pl*; **by ~ of** durch, mittels; **by all ~** selbstverständlich; **by no ~** keineswegs; **~ of transport** Beförderungsmittel

meant [ment] *pt, pp of* **mean**

meantime [miːnˈtaɪm] *adv* **in the ~** inzwischen; **meanwhile** [miːnˈwaɪl] *adv* inzwischen

measles ['miːzlz] *nsing* Masern *pl*; **German ~** Röteln *pl*

measure ['meʒə*] *vt, vi* messen ▷ *n* (*unit, device for measuring*) Maß *nt*; (*step*) Maßnahme *f*; **to take ~s** Maßnahmen ergreifen; **measurement** *n* (*amount measured*) Maß *nt*

meat [miːt] *n* Fleisch *nt*; **meatball** *n* Fleischbällchen *nt*

mechanic [mɪˈkænɪk] *n* Mechaniker(in) *m(f)*; **mechanical** *adj* mechanisch; **mechanics** *nsing* Mechanik *f*; **mechanism** ['mekənɪzəm] *n* Mechanismus *m*

medal ['medl] *n* Medaille *f*; (*decoration*) Orden *m*; **medalist** (*US*), **medallist** ['medəlɪst] *n* Medaillengewinner(in) *m(f)*

media ['miːdɪə] *npl* Medien *pl*

median strip ['miːdɪən strɪp] *n* (*US*) Mittelstreifen *m*

mediate ['miːdɪeɪt] *vi* vermitteln

medical ['medɪkəl] *adj* medizinisch; (*treatment etc*) ärztlich; **~ student** Medizinstudent(in) *m(f)* ▷ *n* Untersuchung *f*; **Medicare** ['medɪkɛə*] *n* (*US*) Krankenkasse *f* für ältere Leute; **medication** [medɪˈkeɪʃən] *n* Medikamente *pl*; **to be on ~** Medikamente nehmen; **medicinal** [meˈdɪsɪnl] *adj* Heil-; **~ herbs** Heilkräuter *pl*; **medicine** ['medsɪn] *n* Arznei *f*; (*science*) Medizin *f*

medieval [medɪˈiːvəl] *adj* mittelalterlich

mediocre [miːdɪˈəʊkə*] *adj* mittelmäßig

meditate ['medɪteɪt] *vi* meditieren; (*fig*) nachdenken (*on über +akk*)

Mediterranean [medɪtəˈreɪnɪən] *n* (*sea*) Mittelmeer *nt*; (*region*) Mittelmeerraum *m*

medium ['miːdɪəm] *adj* (*quality, size*) mittlere(r, s); (*steak*) halbdurch; **~** (**dry**) (*wine*) halbtrocken; **~ sized** mittelgroß; **~ wave** Mittelwelle *f* ▷ *n* (*pl* **media**) Medium *nt*; (*means*) Mittel *nt*

meet [miːt] (**met, met**) *vt* treffen; (*by arrangement*) sich treffen mit; (*difficulties*) stoßen auf +*akk*; (*get to know*) kennen lernen; (*requirement, demand*) gerecht werden +*dat*; (*deadline*) einhalten; **pleased to ~ you** sehr angenehm!; **to ~ sb at the station** jdn vom Bahnhof abholen ▷ *vi* sich treffen; (*become acquainted*) sich kennen lernen; **we've met** (**before**) wir kennen uns schon; **meet up** *vt* sich treffen (*with mit*); **meet with** *vt* (*group*) zusammenkommen mit; (*difficulties, resistance etc*) stoßen auf +*akk*; **meeting** *n* Treffen *nt*; (*business ~*) Besprechung *f*; (*of committee*) Sitzung *f*; (*assembly*) Versammlung *f*; **meeting place**, **meeting point** *n* Treffpunkt *m*

megabyte ['megəbaɪt] *n* Megabyte *nt*

melody ['melədɪ] *n* Melodie *f*

melon ['melən] *n* Melone *f*

melt [melt] *vt, vi* schmelzen

member ['membə*] *n* Mitglied *nt*; (*of tribe, species*) Angehörige(r) *mf*; **Member of Parliament** Parlamentsabgeordnete(r) *mf*; **membership** *n* Mitgliedschaft *f*; **membership card** *n* Mitgliedskarte *f*

memento [məˈmentəʊ] (*pl* **-es**) *n* Andenken *nt* (*of an +akk*)

memo ['meməʊ] (*pl* **-s**) *n* Mitteilung *f*, Memo *nt*; **memo pad** *n* Notizblock *m*

memorable ['memərəbl] *adj* unvergesslich; **memorial** [mɪˈmɔːrɪəl] *n* Denkmal *nt* (*to für*); **memorize** ['meməraɪz] *vt* sich einprägen, auswendig lernen; **memory** ['memərɪ] *n* Gedächtnis *nt*; (*Inform: of computer*) Speicher *m*; (*sth recalled*) Erinnerung *f*; **in ~ of** zur Erinnerung an +*akk*

men [men] *pl of* **man**

menace ['menɪs] *n* Bedrohung *f*; (*danger*) Gefahr *f*

mend [mend] *vt* reparieren; (*clothes*) flicken ▷ *n* **to be on the ~** auf dem Wege der Besserung sein

meningitis [menɪnˈdʒaɪtɪs] *n* Hirnhautentzündung *f*

menopause ['menəʊpɔːz] *n* Wechseljahre *pl*

m

mental ['mentl] *adj* geistig; **~ hospital** psychiatrische Klinik; **mentality** [men'tælıtı] *n* Mentalität *f*; **mentally** ['mentəlı] *adv* geistig; **~ handicapped** geistig behindert; **~ ill** geisteskrank

mention ['menʃən] *n* Erwähnung *f* ▷ *vt* erwähnen (*to sb* jdm gegenüber); **don't ~ it** bitte sehr, gern geschehen

menu ['menju:] *n* Speisekarte *f*; (*Inform*) Menü *nt*

merchandise ['mɜːtʃəndaɪz] *n* Handelsware *f*; **merchant** ['mɜːtʃənt] *adj* Handels-

merciful ['mɜːsɪfʊl] *adj* gnädig; **mercifully** *adv* glücklicherweise

mercury ['mɜːkjʊrı] *n* Quecksilber *nt*

mercy ['mɜːsɪ] *n* Gnade *f*

mere [mıə*] *adj* bloß; **merely** ['mıəlı] *adv* bloß, lediglich

merge [mɜːdʒ] *vi* verschmelzen; (*Auto*) sich einfädeln; (*Comm*) fusionieren; **merger** *n* (*Comm*) Fusion *f*

meringue [mə'ræŋ] *n* Baiser *nt*

merit ['merɪt] *n* Verdienst *nt*; (*advantage*) Vorzug *m*

merry ['merı] *adj* fröhlich; (*fam: tipsy*) angeheitert; **Merry Christmas** Fröhliche Weihnachten!; **merry-go-round** *n* Karussell *nt*

mess [mes] *n* Unordnung *f*; (*muddle*) Durcheinander *nt*; (*dirty*) Schweinerei *f*; (*trouble*) Schwierigkeiten *pl*; **in a ~** (*muddled*) durcheinander; (*untidy*) unordentlich; (*fig: person*) in der Klemme; **to make a ~ of sth** etw verpfuschen; **to look a ~** unmöglich aussehen; **mess about** *vi* (*tinker with*) herummurksen (*with an +dat*); (*play the fool*) herumalbern; (*do nothing in particular*) herumgammeln; **mess up** *vt* verpfuschen; (*make untidy*) in Unordnung bringen; (*dirty*) schmutzig machen

message ['mesıdʒ] *n* Mitteilung *f*, Nachricht *f*; (*meaning*) Botschaft *f*; **can I give him a ~?** kann ich ihm etwas ausrichten?; **please leave a ~** (*on answerphones*) bitte hinterlassen Sie eine Nachricht; **I get the ~** ich hab's verstanden

messenger ['mesındʒə*] *n* Bote *m*

messy ['mesı] *adj* (*untidy*) unordentlich; (*situation etc*) verfahren

met [met] *pt, pp of* **meet**

metal ['metl] *n* Metall *nt*; **metallic** [mı'tælık] *adj* metallisch

meteorology [mi:tıə'rɒlədʒı] *n* Meteorologie *f*

meter ['mi:tə*] *n* Zähler *m*; (*parking meter*) Parkuhr *f*; (*US*) *see* **metre**

method ['meθəd] *n* Methode *f*; **methodical** [mı'θɒdıkəl] *adj* methodisch

meticulous [mı'tıkjʊləs] *adj* (*peinlich*) genau

metre ['mi:tə*] *n* Meter *m o nt*; **metric** ['metrık] *adj* metrisch; **~ system** Dezimalsystem *nt*

Mexico ['meksıkəʊ] *n* Mexiko *nt*

mice [maıs] *pl of* **mouse**

mickey ['mıkı] *n* **to take the ~ (out of sb)** (*fam*) (jdn) auf den Arm nehmen

microchip ['maıkrəʊtʃıp] *n* (*Inform*) Mikrochip *m*; **microphone** *n* Mikrofon *nt*; **microscope** *n* Mikroskop *nt*; **microwave (oven)** *n* Mikrowelle(nherd) *f(m)*

mid [mıd] *adj* **in ~ January** Mitte Januar; **he's in his ~ forties** er ist Mitte vierzig; **midday** ['mıddeı] *n* Mittag *m*; **at ~** mittags

middle ['mıdl] *n* Mitte *f*; (*waist*) Taille *f*; **in the ~ of** mitten in +*dat*; **to be in the ~ of doing sth** gerade dabei sein, etw zu tun ▷ *adj* mittlere(r, s), Mittel-; **the ~ one** der/die/das Mittlere; **middle-aged** *adj* mittleren Alters; **Middle Ages** *npl* **the ~** das Mittelalter; **middle-class** *adj* mittelständisch; (*bourgeois*) bürgerlich; **middle classes** *npl* **the ~** der Mittelstand; **Middle East** *n* **the ~** der Nahe Osten; **middle name** *n* zweiter Vorname

Midlands ['mıdləndz] *npl* **the ~** Mittelengland *nt*

midnight ['mıdnaıt] *n* Mitternacht *f*

midst [mıdst] *n* **in the ~ of** mitten in +*dat*

midsummer ['mıdsʌmə*] *n* Hochsommer *m*; **Midsummer's Day** Sommersonnenwende *f*

midway [mıd'weı] *adv* auf halbem Wege; **~ through the film** nach der Hälfte des Films; **midweek** [mıd'wi:k] *adj, adv* in der Mitte der Woche

midwife ['mıdwaıf] (*pl* **-wives**) *n* Hebamme *f*

midwinter [mıd'wıntə*] *n* tiefster Winter

might [maıt] *pt of* **may**; (*possibility*) könnte; (*permission*) dürfte; (*would*) würde;

they ~ still come sie könnten noch kommen; **he ~ have let me know** er hätte mir doch Bescheid sagen können; **I thought she ~ change her mind** ich dachte schon, sie würde sich anders entscheiden ▷ *n* Macht *f*, Kraft *f*

mighty ['maɪtɪ] *adj* gewaltig; (*powerful*) mächtig

migraine ['miːgreɪn] *n* Migräne *f*

migrant ['maɪgrənt] *n* (*bird*) Zugvogel *m*; **~ worker** Gastarbeiter(in) *m(f)*; **migrate** [maɪ'greɪt] *vi* abwandern; (*birds*) nach Süden ziehen

mike [maɪk] *n* (*fam*) Mikro *nt*

Milan [mɪ'læn] *n* Mailand *nt*

mild [maɪld] *adj* mild; (*person*) sanft; **mildly** *adv* **to put it ~** gelinde gesagt; **mildness** *n* Milde *f*

mile [maɪl] *n* Meile *f* (= 1,609 *km*); **for ~s (and ~s)** ≈ kilometerweit; **~s per hour** Meilen pro Stunde; **~s better than** hundertmal besser als; **mileage** *n* Meilen *pl*, Meilenzahl *f*; **mileometer** [maɪ'lɒmɪtə*] *n* ≈ Kilometerzähler *m*; **milestone** *n* (*a. fig*) Meilenstein *m*

militant ['mɪlɪtənt] *adj* militant; **military** ['mɪlɪtərɪ] *adj* Militär-, militärisch

milk [mɪlk] *n* Milch *f* ▷ *vt* melken; **milk chocolate** *n* Vollmilchschokolade *f*; **milkman** (*pl* **-men**) *n* Milchmann *m*; **milk shake** *n* Milkshake *m*, Milchmixgetränk *nt*

mill [mɪl] *n* Mühle *f*; (*factory*) Fabrik *f*

millennium [mɪ'lenɪəm] *n* Jahrtausend *nt*

millet ['mɪlɪt] *n* Hirse *f*

milligramme ['mɪlɪgræm] *n* Milligramm *nt*; **milliliter** (*US*), **millilitre** *n* Milliliter *m*; **millimeter** (*US*), **millimetre** *n* Millimeter *m*

million ['mɪljən] *n* Million *f*; **five ~** fünf Millionen; **~s of people** Millionen von Menschen; **millionaire** [mɪljə'nɛə*] *n* Millionär(in) *m(f)*

mime [maɪm] *n* Pantomime *f* ▷ *vt*, *vi* mimen; **mimic** ['mɪmɪk] *n* Imitator(in) *m(f)* ▷ *vt*, *vi* nachahmen; **mimicry** ['mɪmɪkrɪ] *n* Nachahmung *f*

mince [mɪns] *vt* (*zer*)hacken ▷ *n* (*meat*) Hackfleisch *nt*; **mincemeat** *n* süße Gebäckfüllung aus Rosinen, Äpfeln, Zucker, Gewürzen und Talg; **mince pie** *n* mit 'mincemeat' gefülltes süßes Weihnachtsgebäck

mind [maɪnd] *n* (*intellect*) Verstand *m*;

(*also person*) Geist *m*; **out of sight, out of ~** aus den Augen, aus dem Sinn; **he is out of his ~** er ist nicht bei Verstand; **to keep sth in ~** etw im Auge behalten; **do you have sth in ~?** denken Sie an etwas Besonderes?; **I've a lot on my ~** mich beschäftigt so vieles im Moment; **to change one's ~** es sich *dat* anders überlegen ▷ *vt* (*look after*) aufpassen auf +*akk*; (*object to*) etwas haben gegen; **~ you, ...** allerdings ...; **I wouldn't ~ ...** ich hätte nichts gegen ...; **'~ the step'** „Vorsicht Stufe!" ▷ *vi* etwas dagegen haben; **do you ~ if I ...** macht es Ihnen etwas aus, wenn ich ...; **I don't ~** es ist mir egal, meinetwegen; **never ~** macht nichts

mine [maɪn] *pron* meine(r, s); **this is ~** das gehört mir; **a friend of ~** ein Freund von mir ▷ *n* (*coalmine*) Bergwerk *nt*; (*Mil*) Mine *f*; **miner** *n* Bergarbeiter *m*

mineral ['mɪnərəl] *n* Mineral *nt*; **mineral water** *n* Mineralwasser *nt*

mingle ['mɪŋgl] *vi* sich mischen (*with* unter +*akk*)

miniature ['mɪnɪtʃə*] *adj* Miniatur-

minibar ['mɪnɪbɑː] *n* Minibar *f*; **minibus** *n* Kleinbus *m*; **minicab** *n* Kleintaxi *nt*

minimal ['mɪnɪml] *adj* minimal; **minimize** ['mɪnɪmaɪz] *vt* auf ein Minimum reduzieren; **minimum** ['mɪnɪməm] *n* Minimum *nt* ▷ *adj* Mindest-

mining ['maɪnɪŋ] *n* Bergbau *m*

miniskirt *n* Minirock *m*

minister ['mɪnɪstə*] *n* (*Pol*) Minister(in) *m(f)*; (*Rel*) Pastor(in) *m(f)*, Pfarrer(in) *m(f)*; **ministry** ['mɪnɪstrɪ] *n* (*Pol*) Ministerium *nt*

minor ['maɪnə*] *adj* kleiner; (*insignificant*) unbedeutend; (*operation, offence*) harmlos; **~ road** Nebenstraße *f*; (*Mus*) **A -** a-Moll *nt* ▷ *n* (*Brit: under 18*) Minderjährige(r) *mf*; **minority** [maɪ'nɒrɪtɪ] *n* Minderheit *f*

mint [mɪnt] *n* Minze *f*; (*sweet*) Pfefferminz(bonbon) *nt*; **mint sauce** *n* Minzsoße *f*

minus ['maɪnəs] *prep* minus; (*without*) ohne

minute [maɪ'njuːt] *adj* winzig; **in ~ detail** genauestens ▷ ['mɪnɪt] *n* Minute *f*; **just a ~** Moment mal!; **any ~** jeden Augenblick; **~s** *pl* (*of meeting*) Protokoll *nt*

miracle ['mɪrəkl] *n* Wunder *nt*;

m

miraculous [mɪˈrækjʊləs] adj unglaublich

mirage [ˈmɪrɑːʒ] n Fata Morgana f, Luftspiegelung f

mirror [ˈmɪrə*] n Spiegel m

misbehave [mɪsbɪˈheɪv] vi sich schlecht benehmen

miscalculation [ˈmɪskælkjʊˈleɪʃən] n Fehlkalkulation f; (misjudgement) Fehleinschätzung f

miscarriage [mɪsˈkærɪdʒ] n (Med) Fehlgeburt f

miscellaneous [mɪsɪˈleɪnɪəs] adj verschieden

mischief [ˈmɪstʃɪf] n Unfug m; **mischievous** [ˈmɪstʃɪvəs] adj (person) durchtrieben; (glance) verschmitzt

misconception [mɪskənˈsepʃən] n falsche Vorstellung

misconduct [mɪsˈkɒndʌkt] n Vergehen nt

miser [ˈmaɪzə*] n Geizhals m

miserable [ˈmɪzərəbl] adj (person) todunglücklich; (conditions, life) elend; (pay, weather) miserabel

miserly [ˈmaɪzəlɪ] adj geizig

misery [ˈmɪzərɪ] n Elend nt; (suffering) Qualen pl

misfit [ˈmɪsfɪt] n Außenseiter(in) m(f)

misfortune [mɪsˈfɔːtʃən] n Pech nt

misguided [mɪsˈgaɪdɪd] adj irrig; (optimism) unangebracht

misinform [mɪsɪnˈfɔːm] vt falsch informieren

misinterpret [mɪsɪnˈtɜːprɪt] vt falsch auslegen

misjudge [mɪsˈdʒʌdʒ] vt falsch beurteilen

mislay [mɪsˈleɪ] irr vt verlegen

mislead [mɪsˈliːd] irr vt irreführen; **misleading** adj irreführend

misprint [ˈmɪsprɪnt] n Druckfehler m

mispronounce [mɪsprəˈnaʊns] vt falsch aussprechen

miss [mɪs] vt (fail to hit, catch) verfehlen; (not notice, hear) nicht mitbekommen; (be too late for) verpassen; (chance) versäumen; (regret the absence of) vermissen; **I ~ you** du fehlst mir ▷ vi nicht treffen; (shooting) danebenschießen; (ball, shot etc) danebengehen; **miss out** vt auslassen ▷ vi **to ~ on sth** etw verpassen

Miss [mɪs] n (unmarried woman) Fräulein nt

missile [ˈmɪsaɪl] n Geschoss nt; (rocket) Rakete f

missing [ˈmɪsɪŋ] adj (person) vermisst; (thing) fehlend; **to be/go ~** vermisst werden, fehlen

mission [ˈmɪʃən] n (Pol, Mil, Rel) Auftrag m, Mission f; **missionary** [ˈmɪʃənrɪ] n Missionar(in) m(f)

mist [mɪst] n (feiner) Nebel m; (haze) Dunst m; **mist over, mist up** vi sich beschlagen

mistake [mɪˈsteɪk] n Fehler m; **by ~** aus Versehen ▷ irr vt (**mistook, mistaken**) (misunderstand) falsch verstehen; (mix up) verwechseln (for mit); **there's no mistaking ...** ist unverkennbar; (meaning) ... ist unmissverständlich; **mistaken** adj (idea, identity) falsch; **to be ~** sich irren, falsch liegen

mistletoe [ˈmɪsltəʊ] n Mistel f

mistreat [mɪsˈtriːt] vt schlecht behandeln

mistress [ˈmɪstrɪs] n (lover) Geliebte f

mistrust [mɪsˈtrʌst] n Misstrauen nt (of gegen) ▷ vt misstrauen +dat

misty [ˈmɪstɪ] adj neblig; (hazy) dunstig

misunderstand [mɪsʌndəˈstænd] irr vt, vi falsch verstehen; **misunderstanding** n Missverständnis nt; (disagreement) Differenz f

mitten [ˈmɪtn] n Fausthandschuh m

mix [mɪks] n (mixture) Mischung f ▷ vt mischen; (blend) vermischen (with mit); (drinks, music) mixen; **to ~ business with pleasure** das Angenehme mit dem Nützlichen verbinden ▷ vi (liquids) sich vermischen lassen; **mix up** vt (mix) zusammenmischen; (confuse) verwechseln (with mit); **mixed** adj gemischt; **a ~ bunch** eine bunt gemischte Truppe; **~ grill** Mixedgrill m; **~ vegetables** Mischgemüse nt; **mixer** n (for food) Mixer m; **mixture** [ˈmɪkstʃə*] n Mischung f; (Med) Saft m; **mix-up** n Durcheinander nt

ml abbr = **millilitre** ml

mm abbr = **millimetre** mm

moan [məʊn] n Stöhnen nt; (complaint) Gejammer nt ▷ vi stöhnen; (complain) jammern, meckern (about über +akk)

mobile [ˈməʊbaɪl] adj beweglich; (on wheels) fahrbar ▷ n (phone) Handy nt; **mobile phone** n Mobiltelefon nt, Handy nt

mobility [məʊ'bɪlɪtɪ] n Beweglichkeit f
mock [mɒk] vt verspotten ▷ adj Schein-;
  mockery n Spott m
mod cons ['mɒd'kɒnz] abbr = **modern**
  conveniences (moderner) Komfort
mode [məʊd] n Art f; (*Inform*) Modus m
model ['mɒdl] n Modell nt; (*example*)
  Vorbild nt; (*fashion ~*) Model nt ▷ adj
  (*miniature*) Modell-; (*perfect*) Muster- ▷ vt
  (*make*) formen ▷ vi **she ~s for Versace** sie
  arbeitet als Model bei Versace
modem ['məʊdem] n Modem nt
moderate ['mɒdərət] adj mäßig; (*views,
  politics*) gemäßigt; (*income, success*)
  mittelmäßig ▷ n (*Pol*) Gemäßigte(r) mf
  ▷ ['mɒdəreɪt] vt mäßigen; **moderation**
  [mɒdə'reɪʃən] n Mäßigung f; **in ~** mit
  Maßen
modern ['mɒdən] adj modern; **~ history**
  neuere Geschichte; **~ Greek**
  Neugriechisch nt; **modernize** ['mɒdənaɪz]
  vt modernisieren
modest ['mɒdɪst] adj bescheiden;
  modesty n Bescheidenheit f
modification [mɒdɪfɪ'keɪʃən] n
  Abänderung f; **modify** ['mɒdɪfaɪ] vt
  abändern
moist [mɔɪst] adj feucht; **moisten**
  ['mɔɪsn] vt befeuchten; **moisture**
  ['mɔɪstʃə*] n Feuchtigkeit f; **moisturizer**
  n Feuchtigkeitscreme f
molar ['məʊlə*] n Backenzahn m
mold (*US*) see **mould**
mole [məʊl] n (*spot*) Leberfleck m; (*animal*)
  Maulwurf m
molecule ['mɒlɪkjuːl] n Molekül nt
molest [məʊ'lest] vt belästigen
molt (*US*) see **moult**
molten ['məʊltən] adj geschmolzen
mom [mɒm] n (*US*) Mutti f
moment ['məʊmənt] n Moment m,
  Augenblick m; **just a ~** Moment mal!; **at (o
  for) the ~** im Augenblick; **in a ~** gleich
momentous [məʊ'mentəs] adj
  bedeutsam
Monaco ['mɒnəkəʊ] n Monaco nt
monarchy ['mɒnəkɪ] n Monarchie f
monastery ['mɒnəstrɪ] n (*for monks*)
  Kloster nt
Monday ['mʌndeɪ] n Montag m; *see also*
  Tuesday
monetary ['mʌnɪtərɪ] adj (*reform, policy,
  union*) Währungs-; **~ unit** Geldeinheit f

money ['mʌnɪ] n Geld nt; **to get one's ~'s
  worth** auf seine Kosten kommen; **money
  order** n Postanweisung f
mongrel ['mʌŋgrəl] n
  Promenadenmischung f
monitor ['mɒnɪtə*] n (*screen*) Monitor m
  ▷ vt (*progress etc*) überwachen;
  (*broadcasts*) abhören
monk [mʌŋk] n Mönch m
monkey ['mʌŋkɪ] n Affe m; **~ business**
  Unfug m
monopolize [mə'nɒpəlaɪz] vt
  monopolisieren; (*fig: person, thing*) in
  Beschlag nehmen; **monopoly** [mə'nɒpəlɪ]
  n Monopol nt
monotonous [mə'nɒtənəs] adj eintönig,
  monoton
monsoon [mɒn'suːn] n Monsun m
monster ['mɒnstə*] n (*animal, thing*)
  Monstrum nt ▷ adj Riesen-; **monstrosity**
  [mɒn'strɒsɪtɪ] n Monstrosität f; (*thing*)
  Ungetüm nt
month [mʌnθ] n Monat m; **monthly** adj
  monatlich; (*ticket, salary*) Monats- ▷ adv
  monatlich ▷ n (*magazine*)
  Monats(zeit)schrift f
monty ['mɒntɪ] n **to go the full ~** (*fam:
  strip*) alle Hüllen fallen lassen; (*go the whole
  hog*) aufs Ganze gehen
monument ['mɒnjʊmənt] n Denkmal nt
  (*to für*); **monumental** [mɒnjʊ'mentl] adj
  (*huge*) gewaltig
mood [muːd] n (*of person*) Laune f; (*a.
  general*) Stimmung f; **to be in a good/bad
  ~** gute/schlechte Laune haben,
  gut/schlecht gelaunt sein; **to be in the ~ for
  sth** zu etw aufgelegt sein; **I'm not in the
  ~** ich fühle mich nicht danach; **moody** adj
  launisch
moon [muːn] n Mond m; **to be over the
  ~** (*fam*) überglücklich sein; **moonlight** n
  Mondlicht nt ▷ vi schwarzarbeiten;
  moonlit adj (*night, landscape*) mondhell
moor [mɔː*] n Moor nt ▷ vt, vi
  festmachen; **moorings** npl Liegeplatz m;
  moorland n Moorland nt, Heideland nt
moose [muːs] (*pl -*) n Elch m
mop [mɒp] n Mopp m; **mop up** vt
  aufwischen
mope [məʊp] vi Trübsal blasen
moped ['məʊped] n (*Brit*) Moped nt
moral ['mɒrəl] adj moralisch; (*values*)
  sittlich ▷ n Moral f; **~s** pl Moral f; **morale**

[mɒˈrɑːl] n Stimmung f, Moral f; **morality**
[məˈrælɪtɪ] n Moral f, Ethik f
morbid [ˈmɔːbɪd] adj krankhaft

  KEYWORD

more [mɔː*] adj (greater in number etc)
mehr; (additional) noch mehr; **do you
want (some) more tea?** möchten Sie
noch etwas Tee?; **I have no** or **I don't have
any more money** ich habe kein Geld mehr
▷ pron (greater amount) mehr; (further or
additional amount) noch mehr; **is there any
more?** gibt es noch mehr?; (left over) ist
noch etwas da?; **there's no more** es ist
nichts mehr da ▷ adv mehr; **more
dangerous/easily** etc **(than)**
gefährlicher/einfacher etc (als); **more and
more** immer mehr; **more and more
excited** immer aufgeregter; **more or less**
mehr oder weniger; **more than ever** mehr
denn je; **more beautiful than ever**
schöner denn je

morgue [mɔːg] n Leichenschauhaus nt
morning [ˈmɔːnɪŋ] n Morgen m; **in the
~** am Morgen, morgens; (tomorrow)
morgen früh; **this ~** heute morgen ▷ adj
Morgen-; (early) Früh-; (walk etc)
morgendlich; **morning after pill** n die
Pille danach; **morning sickness** n
Schwangerschaftsübelkeit f
Morocco [məˈrɒkəʊ] n Marokko nt
moron [ˈmɔːrɒn] n Idiot(in) m(f)
morphine [ˈmɔːfiːn] n Morphium nt
morsel [ˈmɔːsl] n Bissen m
mortal [ˈmɔːtl] adj sterblich; (wound)
tödlich ▷ n Sterbliche(r) mf; **mortality**
[mɔːˈtælɪtɪ] n (death rate)
Sterblichkeitsziffer f; **mortally** adv
tödlich
mortgage [ˈmɔːgɪdʒ] n Hypothek f ▷ vt
mit einer Hypothek belasten
mortified [ˈmɔːtɪfaɪd] adj **I was ~** es war
mir schrecklich peinlich
mortuary [ˈmɔːtjʊərɪ] n Leichenhalle f
mosaic [məʊˈzeɪɪk] n Mosaik nt
Moscow [ˈmɒskəʊ] n Moskau nt
Moslem [ˈmɒzləm] adj, n see **Muslim**
mosque [mɒsk] n Moschee f
mosquito [mɒˈskiːtəʊ] (pl **-es**) n
(Stech)mücke f; (tropical) Moskito m; **~ net**
Moskitonetz nt

moss [mɒs] n Moos nt
most [məʊst] adj meiste pl, die meisten;
in ~ cases in den meisten Fällen ▷ adv
(with verbs) am meisten; (with adj) ...ste;
(with adv) am ...sten; (very) äußerst,
höchst; **he ate (the) ~** er hat am meisten
gegessen; **the ~ beautiful/interesting**
der/die/das schönste/interessanteste;
~ interesting hochinteressant! ▷ n das
meiste, der größte Teil; (people) die
meisten; **~ of the money/players** das
meiste Geld/die meisten Spieler; **for the
~ part** zum größten Teil; **five at the
~** höchstens fünf; **to make the ~ of sth**
etw voll ausnützen; **mostly** adv (most of
the time) meistens; (mainly) hauptsächlich;
(for the most part) größtenteils
MOT abbr = **Ministry of Transport**;
~ (test) ≈ TÜV m
motel [məʊˈtel] n Motel nt
moth [mɒθ] n Nachtfalter m; (wool-eating)
Motte f; **mothball** n Mottenkugel f
mother [ˈmʌðə*] n Mutter f ▷ vt
bemuttern; **mother-in-law** (pl
mothers-in-law) n Schwiegermutter f;
mother-to-be (pl **mothers-to-be**) n
werdende Mutter
motif [məʊˈtiːf] n Motiv nt
motion [ˈməʊʃən] n Bewegung f; (in
meeting) Antrag m; **motionless** adj
bewegungslos
motivate [ˈməʊtɪveɪt] vt motivieren;
motive [ˈməʊtɪv] n Motiv nt
motor [ˈməʊtə*] n Motor m; (fam: car)
Auto nt ▷ adj Motor-; **Motorail train®** n
(Brit) Autoreisezug m; **motorbike** n
Motorrad nt; **motorboat** n Motorboot nt;
motorcycle n Motorrad nt; **motor
industry** n Automobilindustrie f;
motoring [ˈməʊtərɪŋ] n Autofahren nt;
~ organization Automobilklub m;
motorist [ˈməʊtərɪst] n Autofahrer(in)
m(f); **motor oil** n Motorenöl nt; **motor
racing** n Autorennsport m; **motor
scooter** n Motorroller m; **motor show** n
Automobilausstellung f; **motor vehicle** n
Kraftfahrzeug nt; **motorway** n (Brit)
Autobahn f
motto [ˈmɒtəʊ] n (pl **-es**) n Motto nt
mould [məʊld] n Form f; (mildew)
Schimmel m ▷ vt (a. fig) formen; **mouldy**
[ˈməʊldɪ] adj schimmelig
moult [məʊlt] vi sich mausern, haaren

mount [maʊnt] vt (horse) steigen auf +akk; (exhibition etc) organisieren; (painting) mit einem Passepartout versehen ▷ vi **to ~ (up)** (an)steigen ▷ n Passepartout nt

mountain ['maʊntɪn] n Berg m; **mountain bike** n Mountainbike nt; **mountaineer** [maʊntɪ'nɪə*] n Bergsteiger(in) m(f); **mountaineering** [maʊntɪ'nɪərɪŋ] n Bergsteigen nt; **mountainous** adj bergig; **mountainside** n Berghang m

mourn [mɔːn] vt betrauern ▷ vi trauern (for um); **mourner** n Trauernde(r) mf; **mournful** adj trauervoll; **mourning** n Trauer f; **to be in ~** trauern (for um)

mouse [maʊs] (pl **mice**) n (a. Inform) Maus f; **mouse mat**, **mouse pad** (US) n Mauspad nt; **mouse trap** n Mausefalle f

mousse [muːs] n (Gastr) Creme f; (styling ~) Schaumfestiger m

moustache [mə'stæʃ] n Schnurrbart m

mouth [maʊθ] n Mund m; (of animal) Maul nt; (of cave) Eingang m; (of bottle etc) Öffnung f; (of river) Mündung f; **to keep one's ~ shut** (fam) den Mund halten; **mouthful** n (of drink) Schluck m; (of food) Bissen m; **mouth organ** n Mundharmonika f; **mouthwash** n Mundwasser nt; **mouthwatering** adj appetitlich, lecker

move [muːv] n (movement) Bewegung f; (in game) Zug m; (step) Schritt m; (moving house) Umzug m; **to make a ~** (in game) ziehen; (leave) sich auf den Weg machen; **to get a ~ on (with sth)** sich (mit etw) beeilen ▷ vt bewegen; (object) rücken; (car) wegfahren; (transport: goods) befördern; (people) transportieren; (in job) versetzen; (emotionally) bewegen, rühren; **I can't ~ it** (stuck, too heavy) ich bringe es nicht von der Stelle; **to ~ house** umziehen ▷ vi sich bewegen; (change place) gehen; (vehicle, ship) fahren; (move house, town etc) umziehen; (in game) ziehen; **move about** vi sich bewegen; (travel) unterwegs sein; **move away** vi weggehen; (move town) wegziehen; **move in** vi (to house) einziehen; **move off** vi losfahren; **move on** vi weitergehen; (vehicle) weiterfahren; **move out** vi ausziehen; **move up** vi (in queue etc) aufrücken; **movement** n Bewegung f

movie ['muːvɪ] n Film m; **the ~s** (the cinema) das Kino

moving ['muːvɪŋ] adj (emotionally) ergreifend, berührend

mow [məʊ] (**mowed**, **mown** o **mowed**) vt mähen; **mower** n (lawn~) Rasenmäher m

mown [məʊn] pp of **mow**

Mozambique [məʊzæm'biːk] n Mosambik nt

MP abbr = **Member of Parliament** Parlamentsabgeordnete(r) mf

mph abbr = **miles per hour** Meilen pro Stunde

MPV abbr = **multi-purpose vehicle** Mehrzweckfahrzeug nt

MP3 n MP3 nt

Mr [mɪstə*] n (form of address) Herr

Mrs ['mɪsɪz] n (form of address) Frau

Ms [məz] n (form of address for any woman, married or unmarried) Frau

MS n abbr = **multiple sclerosis** MS f

Mt abbr = **Mount** Berg m

much [mʌtʃ] (**more**, **most**) adj viel; **we haven't got ~ time** wir haben nicht viel Zeit; **how ~ money?** wie viel Geld? ▷ adv viel; (with verb) sehr; **~ better** viel besser; **I like it very ~** es gefällt mir sehr gut; **I don't like it ~** ich mag es nicht besonders; **thank you very ~** danke sehr; **I thought as ~** das habe ich mir gedacht; **~ as I like him** so sehr ich ihn mag; **we don't see them ~** wir sehen sie nicht sehr oft; **~ the same** fast gleich ▷ n viel; **as ~ as you want** so viel du willst; **he's not ~ of a cook** er ist kein großer Koch

muck [mʌk] n (fam) Dreck m; **muck about** vi (fam) herumalbern; **muck up** vt (fam) dreckig machen; (spoil) vermasseln; **mucky** adj dreckig

mucus ['mjuːkəs] n Schleim m

mud [mʌd] n Schlamm m

muddle ['mʌdl] n Durcheinander nt; **to be in a ~** ganz durcheinander sein ▷ vt **to ~ (up)** durcheinander bringen; **muddled** adj konfus

muddy ['mʌdɪ] adj schlammig; (shoes) schmutzig; **mudguard** ['mʌdgɑːd] n Schutzblech nt

muesli ['muːzlɪ] n Müsli nt

muffin ['mʌfɪn] n Muffin m; (Brit) weiches, flaches Milchbrötchen aus Hefeteig, das meist getoastet und mit Butter gegessen wird

muffle ['mʌfl] vt (sound) dämpfen; **muffler** n (US) Schalldämpfer m

mug [mʌg] n (cup) Becher m; (fam: fool) Trottel m ▷ vt (attack and rob) überfallen; **mugging** n Raubüberfall m

muggy ['mʌgɪ] adj (weather) schwül

mule [mju:l] n Maulesel m

mull over [mʌl 'əʊvə*] vt nachdenken über +akk

mulled [mʌld] adj ~ **wine** Glühwein m

multicolored (US), **multicoloured** ['mʌltɪ'kʌləd] adj bunt; **multicultural** adj multikulturell; **multi-grade** adj ~ **oil** Mehrbereichsöl nt; **multilingual** adj mehrsprachig; **multinational** n (company) Multi m

multiple ['mʌltɪpl] n Vielfache(s) nt ▷ adj mehrfach; (several) mehrere; **multiple-choice (method)** n Multiple-Choice-Verfahren nt; **multiple sclerosis** ['mʌltɪplskle'rəʊsɪs] n Multiple Sklerose f

multiplex ['mʌltɪpleks] adj, n ~ (cinema) Multiplexkino nt

multiplication [mʌltɪplɪ'keɪʃən] n Multiplikation f; **multiply** ['mʌltɪplaɪ] vt multiplizieren (by mit) ▷ vi sich vermehren

multi-purpose ['mʌltɪ'pɜ:pəs] adj Mehrzweck-; **multistorey (car park)** n Parkhaus nt; **multitasking** n (Inform) Multitasking nt

mum [mʌm] n (fam: mother) Mutti f, Mami f

mumble ['mʌmbl] vt, vi murmeln

mummy ['mʌmɪ] n (dead body) Mumie f; (fam: mother) Mutti f, Mami f

mumps [mʌmps] nsing Mumps m

munch [mʌntʃ] vt, vi mampfen

Munich ['mju:nɪk] n München nt

municipal [mju:'nɪsɪpəl] adj städtisch

mural ['mjʊərəl] n Wandgemälde nt

murder ['mɜ:də*] n Mord m; **the traffic was ~** der Verkehr war die Hölle ▷ vt ermorden; **murderer** n Mörder(in) m(f)

murky ['mɜ:kɪ] adj düster; (water) trüb

murmur ['mɜ:mə*] vt, vi murmeln

muscle ['mʌsl] n Muskel m; **muscular** ['mʌskjʊlə*] adj (strong) muskulös; (cramp, pain etc) Muskel-

museum [mju:'zɪəm] n Museum nt

mushroom ['mʌʃru:m] n (essbarer) Pilz; (button ~) Champignon m ▷ vi (fig) emporschießen

mushy ['mʌʃɪ] adj breiig; ~ **peas** Erbsenmus nt

music ['mju:zɪk] n Musik f; (printed) Noten pl; **musical** adj (sound) melodisch; (person) musikalisch; ~ **instrument** Musikinstrument nt ▷ n (show) Musical nt; **musically** adv musikalisch; **musician** [mju:'zɪʃən] n Musiker(in) m(f)

Muslim ['mʊzlɪm] adj moslemisch ▷ n Moslem m, Muslime f

mussel ['mʌsl] n Miesmuschel f

must [mʌst] (had to, had to) vb aux (need to) müssen; (in negation) dürfen; **I ~n't forget that** ich darf das nicht vergessen; (certainty) **he ~ be there by now** er ist inzwischen bestimmt schon da; (assumption) **I ~ have lost it** ich habe es wohl verloren; ~ **you?** muss das sein? ▷ n Muss nt

mustache ['mʌstæʃ] n (US) Schnurrbart m

mustard ['mʌstəd] n Senf m; **to cut the ~** es bringen

mustn't ['mʌsnt] contr of **must not**

mute [mju:t] adj stumm

mutter ['mʌtə*] vt, vi murmeln

mutton ['mʌtn] n Hammelfleisch nt

mutual ['mju:tjʊəl] adj gegenseitig; **by ~ consent** in gegenseitigem Einvernehmen

my [maɪ] adj mein; **I've hurt ~ leg** ich habe mir das Bein verletzt

Myanmar ['maɪænma:] n Myanmar nt

myself [maɪ'self] pron (reflexive) mich akk, mir dat; **I've hurt ~** ich habe mich verletzt; **I've bought ~ a flat** ich habe mir eine Wohnung gekauft; **I need it for ~** ich brauche es für mich (selbst); (emphatic) **I did it ~** ich habe es selbst gemacht; (all) **by ~** allein

mysterious [mɪ'stɪərɪəs] adj geheimnisvoll, mysteriös; (inexplicable) rätselhaft; **mystery** ['mɪstərɪ] n Geheimnis nt; (puzzle) Rätsel nt; **it's a ~ to me** es ist mir schleierhaft; **mystify** ['mɪstɪfaɪ] vt verblüffen

myth [mɪθ] n Mythos m; (fig: untrue story) Märchen nt; **mythical** adj mythisch; (fig: untrue) erfunden; **mythology** [mɪ'θɒlədʒɪ] n Mythologie f

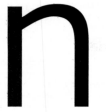

N *abbr* = **north** N

nag [næg] *vt, vi* herumnörgeln (*sb* an jdm); **nagging** *n* Nörgelei *f*

nail [neɪl] *n* Nagel *m* ▷ *vt* nageln (*to* an); **nail down** *vt* festnageln; **nailbrush** *n* Nagelbürste *f*; **nail clippers** *npl* Nagelknipser *m*; **nailfile** *n* Nagelfeile *f*; **nail polish** *n* Nagellack *m*; **nail polish remover** *n* Nagellackentferner *m*; **nail scissors** *npl* Nagelschere *f*; **nail varnish** *n* Nagellack *m*

naive [naɪˈiːv] *adj* naiv

naked [ˈneɪkɪd] *adj* nackt

name [neɪm] *n* Name *m*; **his ~ is ...** er heißt ...; **what's your ~?** wie heißen Sie?; (*reputation*) **to have a good/bad ~** einen guten/schlechten Ruf haben ▷ *vt* nennen (*after* nach); (*sth new*) benennen; (*nominate*) ernennen (*as* als/zu); **a boy ~d ...** ein Junge namens ...; **namely** *adv* nämlich; **name plate** *n* Namensschild *nt*

nan bread [ˈnɑːnˈbred] *n* (*warm serviertes*) *indisches Fladenbrot*

nanny [ˈnænɪ] *n* Kindermädchen *nt*

nap [næp] *n* **to have a ~** ein Nickerchen machen

napkin [ˈnæpkɪn] *n* (*at table*) Serviette *f*

Naples [ˈneɪplz] *n* Neapel *nt*

nappy [ˈnæpɪ] *n* (*Brit*) Windel *f*

narcotic [nɑːˈkɒtɪk] *n* Rauschgift *nt*

narrate [nəˈreɪt] *vt* erzählen; **narration** [nəˈreɪʃən], **narrative** [ˈnærətɪv] *n* Erzählung *f*; **narrator** [nəˈreɪtə*] *n* Erzähler(in) *m(f)*

narrow [ˈnærəʊ] *adj* eng, schmal; (*victory, majority*) knapp; **to have a ~ escape** mit knapper Not davonkommen ▷ *vi* sich verengen; **narrow down** *vt* einschränken (*to sth* auf etw *akk*); **narrow-minded** *adj* engstirnig

nasty [ˈnɑːstɪ] *adj* ekelhaft; (*person*) fies; (*remark*) gehässig; (*accident, wound etc*) schlimm

nation [ˈneɪʃən] *n* Nation *f*; **national** [ˈnæʃənl] *adj* national; **~ anthem** Nationalhymne *f*; **National Health Service** (*Brit*) staatlicher Gesundheitsdienst; **~ insurance** (*Brit*) Sozialversicherung *f*; **~ park** Nationalpark *m*; **~ service** Wehrdienst *m*; **~ socialism** (*Hist*) Nationalsozialismus *m* ▷ *n* Staatsbürger(in) *m(f)*

nationality [næʃˈnælɪtɪ] *n* Staatsangehörigkeit *f*, Nationalität *f*; **nationalize** [ˈnæʃnəlaɪz] *vt* verstaatlichen; **nationwide** *adj, adv* landesweit

- **National Trust**
-
- Der **National Trust** ist ein 1895
- gegründeter Natur- und
- Denkmalschutzverband in
- Großbritannien, der Gebäude und
- Gelände von besonderem
- historischem oder ästhetischem
- Interesse erhält und der
- Öffentlichkeit zugänglich macht.

native [ˈneɪtɪv] *adj* einheimisch; (*inborn*) angeboren, natürlich; **Native American** Indianer(in) *m(f)*; **~ country** Heimatland *nt*; **a ~ German** ein gebürtiger Deutscher, eine gebürtige Deutsche; **~ language** Muttersprache *f*; **~ speaker** Muttersprachler(in) *m(f)* ▷ *n* Einheimische(r) *mf*; (*in colonial context*) Eingeborene(r) *mf*

nativity play [nəˈtɪvətɪpleɪ] *n* Krippenspiel *nt*

NATO ['neɪtəʊ] *acr* = **North Atlantic Treaty Organization** Nato *f*

natural ['nætʃrəl] *adj* natürlich; (*law, science, forces etc*) Natur-; (*inborn*) angeboren; **~ gas** Erdgas *nt*; **~ resources** Bodenschätze *pl*; **naturally** *adv* natürlich; (*by nature*) von Natur aus; **it comes ~ to her** es fällt ihr leicht

nature ['neɪtʃə*] *n* Natur *f*; (*type*) Art *f*; **it is not in my ~** es entspricht nicht meiner Art; **by ~** von Natur aus; **nature reserve** *n* Naturschutzgebiet *nt*

naughty ['nɔːtɪ] *adj* (*child*) ungezogen; (*cheeky*) frech

nausea ['nɔːsɪə] *n* Übelkeit *f*

nautical ['nɔːtɪkəl] *adj* nautisch; **~ mile** Seemeile *f*

nave [neɪv] *n* Hauptschiff *nt*

navel ['neɪvəl] *n* Nabel *m*

navigate ['nævɪgeɪt] *vi* navigieren; (*in car*) lotsen, dirigieren; **navigation** [nævɪ'geɪʃən] *n* Navigation *f*; (*in car*) Lotsen *nt*

navy ['neɪvɪ] *n* Marine *f*; **~ blue** Marineblau *m*

Nazi ['nɑːtsɪ] *n* Nazi *m*

NB *abbr* = **nota bene** NB

NE *abbr* = **northeast** NO

near [nɪə*] *adj* nahe; **my ~est relations** meine nächsten Verwandten; **in the ~ future** in nächster Zukunft; **that was a ~ miss** (*o thing*) das war knapp; (*with price*) **... or ~est offer** Verhandlungsbasis ... ▷ *adv* in der Nähe; **so ~** so nahe; **come ~er** näher kommen; (*event*) näher rücken ▷ *prep* **~ (to)** (*space*) nahe an +*dat*; (*vicinity*) in der Nähe +*gen*; **~ the sea** nahe am Meer; **~ the station** in der Nähe des Bahnhofs, in Bahnhofsnähe; **nearby** *adj* nahe gelegen ▷ *adv* in der Nähe; **nearly** *adv* fast; **nearside** *n* (*Auto*) Beifahrerseite *f*; **near-sighted** *adj* kurzsichtig

neat ['niːt] *adj* ordentlich; (*work, writing*) sauber; (*undiluted*) pur

necessarily [nesə'serəlɪ] *adv* notwendigerweise; **not ~** nicht unbedingt; **necessary** ['nesəsərɪ] *adj* notwendig, nötig; **it's ~ to ...** man muss ...; **it's not ~ for him to come** er braucht nicht mitzukommen; **necessity** [nɪ'sesɪtɪ] *n* Notwendigkeit *f*; **the bare necessities** das absolut Notwendigste; **there is no**

~ to ... man braucht nicht (zu) ..., man muss nicht ...

neck [nek] *n* Hals *m*; (*size*) Halsweite *f*; **back of the ~** Nacken *m*; **necklace** ['neklɪs] *n* Halskette *f*; **necktie** *n* (*US*) Krawatte *f*

nectarine ['nektərɪn] *n* Nektarine *f*

née [neɪ] *adj* geborene

need [niːd] *n* (*requirement*) Bedürfnis *nt* (*for* für); (*necessity*) Notwendigkeit *f*; (*poverty*) Not *f*; **to be in ~ of sth** etw brauchen; **if ~(s) be** wenn nötig; **there is no ~ to ...** man braucht nicht (zu) ..., man muss nicht ... ▷ *vt* brauchen; **I ~ to speak to you** ich muss mit dir reden; **you ~n't go** du brauchst nicht (zu) gehen, du musst nicht gehen

needle ['niːdl] *n* Nadel *f*

needless, needlessly ['niːdlɪs, -lɪ] *adj, adv* unnötig; **~ to say** selbstverständlich

needy ['niːdɪ] *adj* bedürftig

negative ['negətɪv] *n* (*Ling*) Verneinung *f*; (*Foto*) Negativ *nt* ▷ *adj* negativ; (*answer*) verneinend

neglect [nɪ'glekt] *n* Vernachlässigung *f* ▷ *vt* vernachlässigen; **to ~ to do sth** es versäumen, etw zu tun; **negligence** ['neglɪdʒəns] *n* Nachlässigkeit *f*; **negligent** *adj* nachlässig

negligible ['neglɪdʒəbl] *adj* unbedeutend; (*amount*) geringfügig

negotiate [nɪ'gəʊʃɪeɪt] *vi* verhandeln; **negotiation** [nɪgəʊʃɪ'eɪʃən] *n* Verhandlung *f*

neigh [neɪ] *vi* (*horse*) wiehern

neighbor (*US*), **neighbour** ['neɪbə*] *n* Nachbar(in) *m(f)*; **neighbo(u)rhood** *n* Nachbarschaft *f*; **neighbo(u)ring** *adj* benachbart

neither ['naɪðə*] *adj, pron* keine(r, s) von beiden; **~ of you/us** keiner von euch/uns beiden ▷ *adv* **~ ... nor ...** weder ... noch ... ▷ *conj* **I'm not going - ~ am I** ich gehe nicht - ich auch nicht

neon ['niːɒn] *n* Neon *nt*; **~ sign** (*advertisement*) Leuchtreklame *f*

nephew ['nefjuː] *n* Neffe *m*

nerd [nɜːv] *n* (*fam*) Schwachkopf *m*; **he's a real computer ~** er ist ein totaler Computerfreak

nerve [nɜːv] *n* Nerv *m*; **he gets on my ~s** er geht mir auf die Nerven; (*courage*) **to keep/lose one's ~** die Nerven

behalten/verlieren; (*cheek*) **to have the
~ to do sth** die Frechheit besitzen, etw zu
tun; **nerve-racking** *adj*
nervenaufreibend; **nervous** ['nɜːvəs] *adj*
(*apprehensive*) ängstlich; (*on edge*) nervös;
nervous breakdown *n*
Nervenzusammenbruch *m*
nest [nest] *n* Nest *nt* ▷ *vi* nisten
net [net] *n* Netz *nt*; **the Net** (*Internet*) das
Internet; **on the ~** im Netz ▷ *adj* (*price,
weight*) Netto-; **~ profit** Reingewinn *m*;
netball *n* Netzball *m*
Netherlands ['neðələndz] *npl* **the ~** die
Niederlande *pl*
nettle ['netl] *n* Nessel *f*
network ['netwɜːk] *n* Netz *nt*; (*Tv, Radio*)
Sendenetz *nt*; (*Inform*) Netzwerk *nt*
neurosis [njʊə'rəʊsɪs] *n* Neurose *f*;
neurotic [njʊə'rɒtɪk] *adj* neurotisch
neuter ['njuːtə*] *adj* (*Bio*) geschlechtslos;
(*Ling*) sächlich
neutral ['njuːtrəl] *adj* neutral ▷ *n* (*gear in
car*) Leerlauf *m*
never ['nevə*] *adv* nie(mals); **~ before**
noch nie; **~ mind** macht nichts!;
never-ending *adj* endlos; **nevertheless**
[nevəðə'les] *adv* trotzdem
new [njuː] *adj* neu; **this is all ~ to me** das
ist für mich noch ungewohnt; **newcomer**
n Neuankömmling *m*; (*in job, subject*)
Neuling *m*
New England [njuː'ɪŋglənd] *n*
Neuengland *nt*
Newfoundland ['njuːfəndlənd] *n*
Neufundland *nt*
newly ['njuːlɪ] *adv* neu; **~ made** (*cake*)
frisch gebacken; **newly-weds** *npl*
Frischvermählte *pl*; **new moon** *n*
Neumond *m*
news [njuːz] *nsing* (*item of ~*) Nachricht *f*;
(*Radio, Tv*) Nachrichten *pl*; **good ~** eine
erfreuliche Nachricht; **what's the ~?** was
gibt's Neues?; **have you heard the ~?** hast
du das Neueste gehört?; **that's ~ to me**
das ist mir neu; **newsagent**, **news dealer**
(*US*) *n* Zeitungshändler(in) *m(f)*; **news
bulletin** *n* Nachrichtensendung *f*; **news
flash** *n* Kurzmeldung *f*; **newsgroup** *n*
(*Inform*) Diskussionsforum *nt*, Newsgroup
f; **newsletter** *n* Mitteilungsblatt *nt*;
newspaper ['njuːspeɪpə*] *n* Zeitung *f*
New Year ['njuː'jɪə*] *n* das neue Jahr;
Happy ~ (ein) frohes Neues Jahr!; (*toast*)

Prosit Neujahr!; **~'s Day** Neujahr *nt*,
Neujahrstag *m*; **~'s Eve** Silvesterabend *m*;
~'s resolution *guter Vorsatz fürs neue Jahr*
New York [njuː'jɔːk] *n* New York *nt*
New Zealand [njuː'ziːlənd] *n*
Neuseeland *nt* ▷ *adj* neuseeländisch; **New
Zealander** *n* Neuseeländer(in) *m(f)*
next [nekst] *adj* nächste(r, s); **the week
after ~** übernächste Woche; **~ time I see
him** wenn ich ihn das nächste Mal sehe;
you're ~ du bist jetzt dran ▷ *adv* als
Nächstes; (*then*) dann, darauf; **~ to** neben
+*dat*; **~ to last** vorletzte(r, s); **~ to
impossible** nahezu unmöglich; **the ~ best
thing** das Nächstbeste; **~ door** nebenan
NHS *abbr* = **National Health Service**
Niagara Falls [naɪ'ægrə'fɔːlz] *npl*
Niagarafälle *pl*
nibble ['nɪbl] *vt* knabbern an +*dat*;
nibbles *npl* Knabberzeug *nt*
Nicaragua [nɪkə'rægjʊə] *n* Nicaragua *nt*
nice [naɪs] *adj* nett, sympathisch; (*taste,
food, drink*) gut; (*weather*) schön; **~ and ...**
schön ...; **be ~ to him** sei nett zu ihm;
have a ~ day (*US*) schönen Tag noch!;
nicely *adv* nett; (*well*) gut; **that'll do
~** das genügt vollauf
nick [nɪk] *vt* (*fam: steal*) klauen; (*capture*)
schnappen
nickel ['nɪkl] *n* (*Chem*) Nickel *nt*; (*US: coin*)
Nickel *m*
nickname ['nɪkneɪm] *n* Spitzname *m*
nicotine ['nɪkətiːn] *n* Nikotin *nt*;
nicotine patch *n* Nikotinpflaster *nt*
niece [niːs] *n* Nichte *f*
Nigeria [naɪ'dʒɪərɪə] *n* Nigeria *nt*
night [naɪt] *n* Nacht *f*; (*before bed*) Abend
m; **good ~** gute Nacht!; **at** (*o by*) **~** nachts;
to have an early ~ früh schlafen gehen;
nightcap *n* Schlummertrunk *m*;
nightclub *n* Nachtklub *m*; **nightdress** *n*
Nachthemd *nt*; **nightie** ['naɪtɪ] *n* (*fam*)
Nachthemd *nt*
nightingale ['naɪtɪŋgeɪl] *n* Nachtigall *f*
night life ['naɪtlaɪf] *n* Nachtleben *nt*;
nightly *adv* (*every evening*) jeden Abend;
(*every night*) jede Nacht; **nightmare**
['naɪtmɛə*] *n* Albtraum *m*; **nighttime** *n*
Nacht *f*; **at ~** nachts
nil [nɪl] *n* (*Sport*) null
Nile [naɪl] *n* Nil *m*
nine [naɪn] *num* neun; **~ times out of ten**
so gut wie immer ▷ *n* (*a. bus etc*) Neun *f*;

see also **eight**; **nineteen** [naɪn'tiːn] *num*
neunzehn ▷ *n* (*a. bus etc*) Neunzehn *f*; *see
also* **eight**; **nineteenth** *adj* neunzehnte(r,
s); *see also* **eighth**; **ninetieth** ['naɪntɪəθ]
adj neunzigste(r, s); *see also* **eighth**;
ninety ['naɪntɪ] *num* neunzig ▷ *n*
Neunzig *f*; *see also* **eight**; **ninth** [naɪnθ]
adj neunte(r, s) ▷ *n* (*fraction*) Neuntel *nt*;
see also **eighth**

nipple ['nɪpl] *n* Brustwarze *f*

nitrogen ['naɪtrədʒən] *n* Stickstoff *m*

🔵 **KEYWORD**

no [nəʊ] (*pl* **noes** *adv* (*opposite of yes*) nein;
to answer no (*to question*) mit Nein
antworten; (*to request*) Nein *or* nein sagen;
no thank you nein, danke
▷ *adj* (*not any*) kein(e); **I have no
money/time** ich habe kein Geld/keine
Zeit; **"no smoking"** "Rauchen
verboten"
▷ *n* Nein *nt* (*no vote*) Neinstimme *f*

nobility [nəʊ'bɪlɪtɪ] *n* Adel *m*; **noble**
['nəʊbl] *adj* (*rank*) adlig; (*quality*) edel ▷ *n*
Adlige(r) *mf*

nobody ['nəʊbədɪ] *pron* niemand;
(*emphatic*) keiner; **~ knows** keiner weiß es;
~ else sonst niemand, kein anderer ▷ *n*
Niemand *m*

no-claims bonus [nəʊ'kleɪmzbəʊnəs] *n*
Schadenfreiheitsrabatt *m*

nod [nɒd] *vi, vt* nicken; **nod off** *vi*
einnicken

noise [nɔɪz] *n* (*loud*) Lärm *m*; (*sound*)
Geräusch *nt*; **noisy** *adj* laut; (*crowd*)
lärmend

nominate ['nɒmɪneɪt] *vt* (*in election*)
aufstellen; (*appoint*) ernennen

nominative ['nɒmɪnətɪv] *n* (*Ling*)
Nominativ *m*

nominee [nɒmɪ'niː] *n* Kandidat(in) *m(f)*

non- [nɒn] *pref* Nicht-; (*with adj*) nicht-,
un-; **non-alcoholic** *adj* alkoholfrei

none [nʌn] *pron* keine(r, s); **~ of them**
keiner von ihnen; **~ of it is any use** nichts
davon ist brauchbar; **there are ~ left** es
sind keine mehr da; (*with comparative*) **to
be ~ the wiser** auch nicht schlauer sein; **I
was ~ the worse for it** es hat mir nichts
geschadet

nonentity [nɒ'nentɪtɪ] *n* Null *f*

nonetheless [nʌnðə'les] *adv*
nichtsdestoweniger, dennoch

non-event *n* Reinfall *m*; **non-existent**
adj nicht vorhanden; **non-fiction** *n*
Sachbücher *pl*; **non-iron** *adj* bügelfrei;
non-polluting *adj* schadstofffrei;
non-resident *n* **'open to ~s'** „auch für
Nichthotelgäste"; **non-returnable** *adj*
~ bottle Einwegflasche *f*

nonsense ['nɒnsəns] *n* Unsinn *m*; **don't
talk ~** red keinen Unsinn

non-smoker [nɒn'sməʊkə*] *n*
Nichtraucher(in) *m(f)*; **non-smoking** *adj*
Nichtraucher-; **~ area**
Nichtraucherbereich *m*; **non-standard** *adj*
nicht serienmäßig; **nonstop** *adj* (*train*)
durchgehend; (*flight*) Nonstop- ▷ *adv*
(*talk*) ununterbrochen; (*travel*) ohne
Unterbrechung; (*fly*) ohne
Zwischenlandung; **non-violent** *adj*
gewaltfrei

noodles ['nuːdlz] *npl* Nudeln *pl*

noon [nuːn] *n* Mittag *m*; **at ~** um 12 Uhr
mittags

no one ['nəʊwʌn] *pron* niemand;
(*emphatic*) keiner; **~ else** sonst niemand,
kein anderer

nor [nɔː] *conj* **neither ... ~ ...** weder ...
noch ...; **I don't smoke, ~ does he** ich
rauche nicht, er auch nicht

norm [nɔːm] *n* Norm *f*

normal ['nɔːməl] *adj* normal; **to get back
to ~** sich wieder normalisieren; **normally**
adv (*usually*) normalerweise

north [nɔːθ] *n* Norden *m*; **to the ~ of**
nördlich von ▷ *adv* (*go, face*) nach Norden
▷ *adj* Nord-; **~ wind** Nordwind *m*; **North
America** *n* Nordamerika *nt*; **northbound**
adj (in) Richtung Norden; **northeast** *n*
Nordosten *m*; **to the ~ of** nordöstlich von
▷ *adv* (*go, face*) nach Nordosten ▷ *adj*
Nordost-; **northern** ['nɔːðən] *adj*
nördlich; **~ France** Nordfrankreich *nt*;
Northern Ireland *n* Nordirland *nt*; **North
Pole** *n* Nordpol *m*; **North Sea** *n* Nordsee
f; **northwards** *adv* nach Norden;
northwest *n* Nordwesten *m*; **to the ~ of**
nordwestlich von ▷ *adv* (*go, face*) nach
Nordwesten ▷ *adj* Nordwest-

Norway ['nɔːweɪ] *n* Norwegen *nt*;
Norwegian [nɔː'wiːdʒən] *adj*
norwegisch ▷ *n* (*person*) Norweger(in)
m(f); (*language*) Norwegisch *nt*

nos. *abbr* = **numbers** Nr.

nose [nəʊz] *n* Nase *f*; **nose around** *vi* herumschnüffeln; **nosebleed** *n* Nasenbluten *nt*; **nose-dive** *n* Sturzflug *m*; **to take a ~** abstürzen

nosey ['nəʊzɪ] *see* **nosy**

nostalgia [nɒ'stældʒɪə] *n* Nostalgie *f* (*for* nach); **nostalgic** *adj* nostálgisch

nostril ['nɒstrɪl] *n* Nasenloch *nt*

nosy ['nəʊzɪ] *adj* neugierig

not [nɒt] *adv* nicht; **~ a** kein; **~ one of them** kein einziger von ihnen; **he is ~ an expert** er ist kein Experte; **I told him ~ to (do it)** ich sagte ihm, er solle es nicht tun; **~ at all** überhaupt nicht, keineswegs; (*don't mention it*) gern geschehen; **~ yet** noch nicht

notable ['nəʊtəbl] *adj* bemerkenswert; **note** [nəʊt] *n* (*written*) Notiz *f*; (*short letter*) paar Zeilen *pl*; (*on scrap of paper*) Zettel *m*; (*comment in book etc*) Anmerkung *f*; (*bank~*) Schein *m*; (*Mus: sign*) Note *f*; (*sound*) Ton *m*; **to make a ~ of sth** sich *dat* etw notieren; **~s** (*of lecture etc*) Aufzeichnungen *pl*; **to take ~s** sich *dat* Notizen machen (*of* über +*akk*) ▷ *vt* (*notice*) bemerken (*that* dass); (*write down*) notieren; **notebook** *n* Notizbuch *nt*; (*Inform*) Notebook *nt*; **notepad** *n* Notizblock *m*; **notepaper** *n* Briefpapier *nt*

nothing ['nʌθɪŋ] *n* nichts; **~ but ...** lauter ...; **for ~** umsonst; **he thinks ~ of it** er macht sich nichts daraus

notice ['nəʊtɪs] *n* (*announcement*) Bekanntmachung *f*; (*on ~ board*) Anschlag *m*; (*attention*) Beachtung *f*; (*advance warning*) Ankündigung *f*; (*to leave job, flat etc*) Kündigung *f*; **at short ~** kurzfristig; **until further ~** bis auf weiteres; **to give sb ~** jdm kündigen; **to hand in one's ~** kündigen; **to take (no) ~ of (sth)** etw (nicht) beachten; **take no ~** kümmere dich nicht darum! ▷ *vt* bemerken; **noticeable** *adj* erkennbar; (*visible*) sichtbar; **to be ~** auffallen; **notice board** *n* Anschlagtafel *f*

notification [nəʊtɪfɪ'keɪʃən] *n* Benachrichtigung *f* (*of* von); **notify** ['nəʊtɪfaɪ] *vt* benachrichtigen (*of* von)

notion ['nəʊʃən] *n* Idee *f*

notorious [nəʊ'tɔːrɪəs] *adj* berüchtigt

nought [nɔːt] *n* Null *f*

noun [naʊn] *n* Substantiv *nt*

nourish ['nʌrɪʃ] *vt* nähren; **nourishing** *adj* nahrhaft; **nourishment** *n* Nahrung *f*

novel ['nɒvəl] *n* Roman *m* ▷ *adj* neuartig; **novelist** *n* Schriftsteller(in) *m(f)*; **novelty** *n* Neuheit *f*

November [nəʊ'vembə*] *n* November *m*; *see also* **September**

novice ['nɒvɪs] *n* Neuling *m*

now [naʊ] *adv* (*at the moment*) jetzt; (*introductory phrase*) also; **right ~** jetzt gleich; **just ~** gerade; **by ~** inzwischen; **from ~ on** ab jetzt; **~ and again** (*o then*) ab und zu; **nowadays** *adv* heutzutage

nowhere ['nəʊwɛə*] *adv* nirgends; **we're getting ~** wir kommen nicht weiter; **~ near** noch lange nicht

nozzle ['nɒzl] *n* Düse *f*

nuclear ['njuːklɪə*] *adj* (*energy etc*) Kern-; **~ power station** Kernkraftwerk *nt*; **nuclear waste** *n* Atommüll *m*

nude [njuːd] *adj* nackt ▷ *n* (*person*) Nackte(r) *mf*; (*painting etc*) Akt *m*

nudge [nʌdʒ] *vt* stupsen; **nudist** ['njuːdɪst] *n* Nudist(in) *m(f)*, FKK-Anhänger(in) *m(f)*; **nudist beach** *n* FKK-Strand *m*

nuisance ['njuːsns] *n* Ärgernis *nt*; (*person*) Plage *f*; **what a ~** wie ärgerlich!

nuke [njuːk] (*US fam*) *n* (*bomb*) Atombombe *f* ▷ *vt* eine Atombombe werfen auf +*akk*

numb [nʌm] *adj* taub, gefühllos ▷ *vt* betäuben

number ['nʌmbə*] *n* Nummer *f*; (*Math*) Zahl *f*; (*quantity*) (An)zahl *f*; **in small/large ~s** in kleinen/großen Mengen; **a ~ of times** mehrmals ▷ *vt* (*give a number to*) nummerieren; (*count*) zählen (*among* zu); **his days are ~ed** seine Tage sind gezählt; **number plate** *n* (*Brit Auto*) Nummernschild *nt*

numeral ['njuːmərəl] *n* Ziffer *f*; **numerical** [njuː'merɪkəl] *adj* numerisch; (*superiority*) zahlenmäßig; **numerous** ['njuːmərəs] *adj* zahlreich

nun [nʌn] *n* Nonne *f*

Nuremberg ['njʊərəmbɜːg] *n* Nürnberg *nt*

nurse [nɜːs] *n* Krankenschwester *f*; (*male ~*) Krankenpfleger *m* ▷ *vt* (*patient*) pflegen; (*baby*) stillen; **nursery** *n* Kinderzimmer *nt*; (*for plants*) Gärtnerei *f*; (*tree*) Baumschule *f*; **nursery rhyme** *n* Kinderreim *m*; **nursery school** *n* Kindergarten *m*; **~ teacher**

Kindergärtner(in) *m(f)*, Erzieher(in) *m(f)*;
nursing *n* (*profession*) Krankenpflege *f*;
~ home Privatklinik *f*
nut [nʌt] *n* Nuss *f*; (*Tech: for bolt*) Mutter *f*;
nutcase *n* (*fam*) Spinner(in) *m(f)*;
nutcracker *n*, **nutcrackers** *npl*
Nussknacker *m*
nutmeg ['nʌtmeg] *n* Muskat *m*,
Muskatnuss *f*
nutrient ['nju:trɪənt] *n* Nährstoff *m*
nutrition [nju:'trɪʃən] *n* Ernährung *f*;
nutritious [nju:'trɪʃəs] *adj* nahrhaft
nuts [nʌts] (*fam*) *adj* verrückt; **to be
~ about sth** nach etw verrückt sein ▷ *npl*
(*testicles*) Eier *pl*
nutshell ['nʌtʃel] *n* Nussschale *f*; **in a
~** kurz gesagt
nutter ['nʌtə*] *n* (*fam*) Spinner(in) *m(f)*;
nutty ['nʌtɪ] *adj* (*fam*) verrückt
NW *abbr* = **northwest** NW
nylon® ['naɪlɒn] *n* Nylon® *nt* ▷ *adj*
Nylon-

O [əʊ] *n* (*Tel*) Null *f*

oak [əʊk] *n* Eiche *f* ▷ *adj* Eichen-

OAP *abbr* = **old-age pensioner** Rentner(in) *m(f)*

oar [ɔ:*] *n* Ruder *nt*

oasis [əʊˈeɪsɪs] *n* (*pl* **oases**) *n* Oase *f*

oatcake [ˈəʊtkeɪk] *n* Haferkeks *m*

oath [əʊθ] *n* (*statement*) Eid *m*

oats [əʊts] *npl* Hafer *m*; (*Gastr*) Haferflocken *pl*

obedience [əˈbiːdɪəns] *n* Gehorsam *m*; **obedient** *adj* gehorsam; **obey** [əˈbeɪ] *vt, vi* gehorchen +*dat*

object [ˈɒbdʒekt] *n* Gegenstand *m*; (*abstract*) Objekt *nt*; (*purpose*) Ziel *nt* ▷ [əbˈdʒekt] *vi* dagegen sein; (*raise objection*) Einwände erheben (*to* gegen); (*morally*) Anstoß nehmen (*to* an +*dat*); **do you ~ to my smoking?** haben Sie etwas dagegen, wenn ich rauche?; **objection** [əbˈdʒekʃən] *n* Einwand *m*

objective [əbˈdʒektɪv] *n* Ziel *nt* ▷ *adj* objektiv; **objectivity** [ɒbdʒekˈtɪvɪtɪ] *n* Objektivität *f*

obligation [ɒblɪˈɡeɪʃən] *n* (*duty*) Pflicht *f*; (*commitment*) Verpflichtung *f*; **no ~** unverbindlich; **obligatory** [əˈblɪɡətərɪ]

adj obligatorisch; **oblige** [əˈblaɪdʒ] *vt* **to ~ sb to do sth** jdn (dazu) zwingen, etw zu tun; **he felt ~d to accept the offer** er fühlte sich verpflichtet, das Angebot anzunehmen

oblique [əˈbliːk] *adj* schräg; (*angle*) schief

oblong [ˈɒblɒŋ] *n* Rechteck *nt* ▷ *adj* rechteckig

oboe [ˈəʊbəʊ] *n* Oboe *f*

obscene [əbˈsiːn] *adj* obszön

obscure [əbˈskjʊə*] *adj* unklar; (*unknown*) unbekannt

observant [əbˈzɜːvənt] *adj* aufmerksam; **observation** [ɒbzəˈveɪʃən] *n* (*watching*) Beobachtung *f*; (*remark*) Bemerkung *f*; **observe** [əbˈzɜːv] *vt* (*notice*) bemerken; (*watch*) beobachten; (*customs*) einhalten

obsessed [əbˈsest] *adj* besessen (*with an idea etc* von einem Gedanken etc); **obsession** [əbˈseʃən] *n* Manie *f*

obsolete [ˈɒbsəliːt] *adj* veraltet

obstacle [ˈɒbstəkl] *n* Hindernis *nt* (*to* für); **to be an ~ to sth** einer Sache im Weg stehen

obstinate [ˈɒbstɪnət] *adj* hartnäckig

obstruct [əbˈstrʌkt] *vt* versperren; (*pipe*) verstopfen; (*hinder*) behindern, aufhalten; **obstruction** [əbˈstrʌkʃən] *n* Blockierung *f*; (*of pipe*) Verstopfung *f*; (*obstacle*) Hindernis *nt*

obtain [əbˈteɪn] *vt* erhalten; **obtainable** *adj* erhältlich

obvious [ˈɒbvɪəs] *adj* offensichtlich; **it was ~ to me that ...** es war mir klar, dass ...; **obviously** *adj* offensichtlich

occasion [əˈkeɪʒən] *n* Gelegenheit *f*; (*special event*) (großes) Ereignis; **on the ~ of** anlässlich +*gen*; **special ~** besonderer Anlass; **occasional**, **occasionally** *adj, adv* gelegentlich

occupant [ˈɒkjʊpənt] *n* (*of house*) Bewohner(in) *m(f)*; (*of vehicle*) Insasse *m*, Insassin *f*; **occupation** [ɒkjʊˈpeɪʃən] *n* Beruf *m*; (*pastime*) Beschäftigung *f*; (*of country etc*) Besetzung *f*; **occupied** *adj* (*country, seat, toilet*) besetzt; (*person*) beschäftigt; **to keep sb/oneself ~** jdn/sich beschäftigen; **occupy** [ˈɒkjʊpaɪ] *vt* (*country*) besetzen; (*time*) beanspruchen; (*mind, person*) beschäftigen

occur [əˈkɜː*] *vi* vorkommen; **~ to sb** jdm

einfallen; **occurrence** [əˈkʌrəns] n (event) Ereignis nt; (presence) Vorkommen nt

ocean [ˈəʊʃən] n Ozean m; (US: sea) das Meer nt

o'clock [əˈklɒk] adv **5 ~** 5 Uhr; **at 10 ~** um 10 Uhr

octagon [ˈɒktəgən] n Achteck nt

October [ɒkˈtəʊbə*] n Oktober m; see also **September**

octopus [ˈɒktəpəs] n Tintenfisch m

odd [ɒd] adj (strange) sonderbar; (not even) ungerade; (one missing) einzeln; **to be the ~ one out** nicht dazugehören; **~ jobs** Gelegenheitsarbeiten pl; **odds** npl Chancen pl; **against all ~** entgegen allen Erwartungen; **~ and ends** (fam) Kleinkram pl

odometer [əʊˈdɒmətə*] n (US Auto) Meilenzähler m

odor (US), **odour** [ˈəʊdə*] n Geruch m

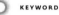 **KEYWORD**

of [ɒv, əv] prep **1** von +dat ≈ use of gen; **the history of Germany** die Geschichte Deutschlands; **a friend of ours** ein Freund von uns; **a boy of 10** ein 10-jähriger Junge; **that was kind of you** das war sehr freundlich von Ihnen

2 (expressing quantity, amount, dates etc): **a kilo of flour** ein Kilo Mehl; **how much of this do you need?** wie viel brauchen Sie (davon)?; **there were 3 of them** (people) sie waren zu dritt; (objects) es gab 3 (davon); **a cup of tea/vase of flowers** eine Tasse Tee/Vase mit Blumen; **the 5th of July** der 5 Juli

3 (from, out of) aus; **a bridge made of wood** eine Holzbrücke eine Brücke aus Holz

off [ɒf] adv (away) weg, fort; (free) frei; (switch) ausgeschaltet; (milk) sauer; **a mile ~** eine Meile entfernt; **I'll be ~ now** ich gehe jetzt; **to have the day/Monday ~** heute/Montag freihaben; **the lights are ~** die Lichter sind aus; **the concert is ~** das Konzert fällt aus; **I got 10% ~** ich habe 10% Nachlass bekommen ▷ prep (away from) von; **to jump/fall ~ the roof** vom Dach springen/fallen; **to get ~ the bus** aus dem Bus aussteigen; **he's ~ work/school** er hat frei/schulfrei; **to take £20 ~ the**

price den Preis um 20 Pfund herabsetzen

offence [əˈfens] n (crime) Straftat f; (minor) Vergehen nt; (to feelings) Kränkung f; **to cause/take ~** Anstoß erregen/nehmen; **offend** [əˈfend] vt kränken; (eye, ear) beleidigen; **offender** n Straffällige(r) mf; **offense** (US) see **offence; offensive** [əˈfensɪv] adj anstößig; (insulting) beleidigend; (smell) übel, abstoßend ▷ n (Mil) Offensive f

offer [ˈɒfə*] n Angebot nt; **on ~** (Comm) im Angebot ▷ vt anbieten (to sb jdm); (money, a chance etc) bieten

offhand [ɒfˈhænd] adj lässig ▷ adv (say) auf Anhieb

office [ˈɒfɪs] n Büro nt; (position) Amt nt; **doctor's ~** (US) Arztpraxis f; **office block** n Bürogebäude nt; **office hours** npl Dienstzeit f; (notice) Geschäftszeiten pl; **officer** [ˈɒfɪsə*] n (Mil) Offizier(in) m(f); (official) Polizeibeamte(r) m, Polizeibeamtin f; **office worker** [ˈɒfɪswɜːkə*] n Büroangestellte(r) mf; **official** [əˈfɪʃəl] adj offiziell; (report etc) amtlich; **~ language** Amtssprache f ▷ n Beamte(r) m, Beamtin f, Repräsentant(in) m(f)

off-licence [ˈɒflaɪsəns] n (Brit) Wein- und Spirituosenhandlung f; **off-line** adj (Inform) offline; **off-peak** adj außerhalb der Stoßzeiten; (rate, ticket) verbilligt; **off-putting** adj abstoßend, entmutigend, irritierend; **off-season** adj außerhalb der Saison

offshore [ˈɒfʃɔː*] adj küstennah, Küsten-; (oil rig) im Meer; **offside** [ˈɒfˈsaɪd] n (Auto) Fahrerseite f; (Sport) Abseits nt

often [ˈɒfən] adv oft; **every so ~** von Zeit zu Zeit

oil [ɔɪl] n Öl nt ▷ vt ölen; **oil level** n Ölstand m; **oil painting** n Ölgemälde nt; **oil-rig** n (Öl)bohrinsel f; **oil slick** n Ölteppich m; **oil tanker** n Öltanker m; (truck) Tankwagen m; **oily** adj ölig; (skin, hair) fettig

ointment [ˈɔɪntmənt] n Salbe f

OK, **okay** [əʊˈkeɪ] adj (fam) okay, in Ordnung; **that's ~ by** (o **with**) **me** das ist mir recht

old [əʊld] adj alt; **old age** n Alter nt; **~ pension** Rente f; **~ pensioner** Rentner(in) m(f); **old-fashioned** adj

altmodisch; **old people's home** *n*
Altersheim *nt*

olive ['ɒlɪv] *n* Olive *f*; **olive oil** *n* Olivenöl
nt

Olympic [əʊ'lɪmpɪk] *adj* olympisch; **the
~ Games, the ~s** *pl* die Olympischen Spiele
pl, die Olympiade

omelette ['ɒmlət] *n* Omelett *nt*

omission [əʊ'mɪʃən] *n* Auslassung *f*; **omit**
[əʊ'mɪt] *vt* auslassen

 KEYWORD

on [ɒn] *prep* **1** (*indicating position*) auf +*dat*;
(*with vb of motion*) auf +*acc*; (*on vertical
surface, part of body*) an +*dat/acc*; **it's on the
table** es ist auf dem Tisch; **she put the
book on the table** sie legte das Buch auf
den Tisch; **on the left** links
2 (*indicating means, method, condition etc*):
on foot (*go, be*) zu Fuß; **on the
train/plane** (*go*) mit dem Zug/Flugzeug;
(*be*) im Zug/Flugzeug; **on the
telephone/television** am Telefon/im
Fernsehen; **to be on drugs** Drogen
nehmen; **to be on holiday/business** im
Urlaub/auf Geschäftsreise sein
3 (*referring to time*): **on Friday** (am)
Freitag; **on Fridays** freitags; **on June 20th**
am 20. Juni; **a week on Friday** Freitag in
einer Woche; **on arrival he ...** als er
ankam, ... er ...
4 (*about, concerning*) über +*acc*
▷ *adv* **1** (*referring to dress*): **she put her
boots/hat on** sie zog ihre Stiefel
an/setzte ihren Hut auf
2 (*further, continuously*) weiter; **to walk on**
weitergehen
▷ *adj* **1** (*functioning, in operation: machine,
TV, light*) an; (: *tap*) aufgedreht; (: *brakes*)
angezogen; **is the meeting still on?**
findet die Versammlung noch statt?;
there's a good film on es läuft ein guter
Film
2: **that's not on!** (*inf: of behaviour*) das
liegt nicht drin!

once [wʌns] *adv* (*one time, in the past*)
einmal; **at ~** sofort; (*at the same time*)
gleichzeitig; **~ more** noch einmal; **for
~** ausnahmsweise (einmal); **~ in a while**
ab und zu mal ▷ *conj* wenn ... einmal;

~ you've got used to it sobald Sie sich
daran gewöhnt haben

oncoming ['ɒnkʌmɪŋ] *adj*
entgegenkommend; **~ traffic**
Gegenverkehr *m*

 KEYWORD

one [wʌn] *num* eins (*with noun, referring
back to noun*) ein/eine/ein); **it is one
(o'clock)** es ist eins es ist ein Uhr; **one
hundred and fifty** einhundertfünfzig
▷ *adj* **1** (*sole*) einzige(r, s); **the one book
which** das einzige Buch, welches
2 (*same*) derselbe/dieselbe/dasselbe;
they came in the one car sie kamen alle
in dem einen Auto
3 (*indef*): **one day I discovered ...** eines
Tages bemerkte ich ...
▷ *pron* **1** eine(r, s); **do you have a red
one?** haben Sie einen roten/eine rote/ein
rotes?; **this one** diese(r, s); **that one**
der/die/das; **which one?** welche(r, s)?;
one by one einzeln
2: **one another** einander; **do you two
ever see one another?** seht ihr beide
euch manchmal?
3 (*impers*) man; **one never knows** man
kann nie wissen; **to cut one's finger** sich
in den Finger schneiden

onion ['ʌnjən] *n* Zwiebel *f*

on-line ['ɒnlaɪn] *adj* (*Inform*) online;
~ banking Homebanking *nt*

only ['əʊnlɪ] *adv* nur; (*with time*) erst;
~ yesterday erst gestern; **he's ~ four** er
ist erst vier; **~ just arrived** gerade erst
angekommen ▷ *adj* einzige(r, s); **~ child**
Einzelkind *nt*

o.n.o. *abbr* = **or nearest offer** VB

onside [ɒn'saɪd] *adv* (*Sport*) nicht im
Abseits

onto ['ɒntʊ] *prep* auf +*akk*; (*vertical surface*)
an +*akk*; **to be ~ sb** jdm auf die Schliche
gekommen sein

onwards ['ɒnwədz] *adv* voran, vorwärts;
from today ~ von heute an, ab heute

opaque [əʊ'peɪk] *adj* undurchsichtig

open ['əʊpən] *adj* offen; **in the ~ air** im
Freien; **~ to the public** für die
Öffentlichkeit zugänglich; **the shop is
~ all day** das Geschäft hat den ganzen Tag

offen ▷ vt öffnen, aufmachen; (*meeting, account, new building*) eröffnen; (*road*) dem Verkehr übergeben ▷ vi (*door, window etc*) aufgehen, sich öffnen; (*shop, bank*) öffnen, aufmachen; (*begin*) anfangen (*with* mit); **open-air** *adj* Freiluft-; **open day** *n* Tag *m* der offenen Tür; **opening** *n* Öffnung *f*; (*beginning*) Anfang *m*; (*official, of exhibition etc*) Eröffnung *f*; (*opportunity*) Möglichkeit *f*; **~ hours** (*o* **times**) Öffnungszeiten *pl*; **openly** *adv* offen; **open-minded** *adj* aufgeschlossen; **open-plan** *adj* **~ office** Großraumbüro *nt*

opera ['ɒpərə] *n* Oper *f*; **opera glasses** *npl* Opernglas *nt*; **opera house** *n* Oper *f*, Opernhaus *nt*; **opera singer** *n* Opernsänger(in) *m(f)*

operate ['ɒpəreɪt] *vt* (*machine*) bedienen; (*brakes, lights*) betätigen ▷ vi (*machine*) laufen; (*bus etc*) verkehren (*between* zwischen); **to ~ (on sb)** (*Med*) (jdn) operieren; **operating theatre** *n* Operationssaal *m*; **operation** [ɒpə'reɪʃən] *n* (*of machine*) Bedienung *f*; (*functioning*) Funktionieren *nt*; (*Med*) Operation *f* (*on* an +*dat*); (*undertaking*) Unternehmen *nt*; **in ~** (*machine*) in Betrieb; **to have an ~** operiert werden (*for* wegen); **operator** ['ɒpəreɪtə*] *n* **to phone the ~** die Vermittlung anrufen

opinion [ə'pɪnjən] *n* Meinung *f* (*on* zu); **in my ~** meiner Meinung nach

opponent [ə'pəʊnənt] *n* Gegner(in) *m(f)*

opportunity [ɒpə'tju:nɪtɪ] *n* Gelegenheit *f*

oppose [ə'pəʊz] *vt* sich widersetzen +*dat*; (*idea*) ablehnen; **opposed** *adj* **to be ~ to sth** gegen etw sein; **as ~ to** im Gegensatz zu; **opposing** *adj* (*team*) gegnerisch; (*points of view*) entgegengesetzt

opposite ['ɒpəzɪt] *adj* (*house*) gegenüberliegend; (*direction*) entgegengesetzt; **the ~ sex** das andere Geschlecht ▷ adv gegenüber ▷ prep gegenüber; **~ me** mir gegenüber ▷ n Gegenteil *nt*

opposition [ɒpə'zɪʃən] *n* Widerstand *m* (*to* gegen); (*Pol*) Opposition *f*

oppress [ə'pres] *vt* unterdrücken; **oppressive** *adj* (*heat*) drückend

opt [ɒpt] *vi* **to ~ for sth** sich für etw

entscheiden; **to ~ to do sth** sich entscheiden, etw zu tun

optician [ɒp'tɪʃən] *n* Optiker(in) *m(f)*

optimist ['ɒptɪmɪst] *n* Optimist(in) *m(f)*; **optimistic** [ɒptɪ'mɪstɪk] *adj* optimistisch

optimum ['ɒptɪməm] *adj* optimal

option ['ɒpʃən] *n* Möglichkeit *f*; (*Comm*) Option *f*; **to have no ~** keine Wahl haben; **optional** *adj* freiwillig; **~ extras** (*Auto*) Extras *pl*

or [ɔ:*] *conj* oder; (*otherwise*) sonst; (*after neg*) noch; **hurry up, ~** (*else*) **we'll be late** beeil dich, sonst kommen wir zu spät

oral ['ɔ:rəl] *adj* mündlich; **~ sex** Oralverkehr *m* ▷ *n* (*exam*) Mündliche(s) *nt*

orange ['ɒrɪndʒ] *n* Orange *f* ▷ *adj* orangefarben; **orange juice** *n* Orangensaft *m*

orbit ['ɔ:bɪt] *n* Umlaufbahn *f*; **to be out of ~** (*fam*) nicht zu erreichen sein ▷ vt umkreisen

orchard ['ɔ:tʃəd] *n* Obstgarten *m*

orchestra ['ɔ:kɪstrə] *n* Orchester *nt*; (*US Theat*) Parkett *nt*

orchid ['ɔ:kɪd] *n* Orchidee *f*

ordeal [ɔ:'di:l] *n* Tortur *f*; (*emotional*) Qual *f*

order ['ɔ:də*] *n* (*sequence*) Reihenfolge *f*; (*good arrangement*) Ordnung *f*; (*command*) Befehl *m*; (*Jur*) Anordnung *f*; (*condition*) Zustand *m*; (*Comm*) Bestellung *f*; **out of ~** (*not functioning*) außer Betrieb; (*unsuitable*) nicht angebracht; **in ~** (*items*) richtig geordnet; (*all right*) in Ordnung; **in ~ to do sth** um etw zu tun ▷ vt (*arrange*) ordnen; (*command*) befehlen; **to ~ sb to do sth** jdm befehlen, etw zu tun; (*food, product*) bestellen; **order form** *n* Bestellschein *m*

ordinary ['ɔ:dnrɪ] *adj* gewöhnlich, normal; (*average*) durchschnittlich

ore [ɔ:*] *n* Erz *nt*

organ ['ɔ:gən] *n* (*Mus*) Orgel *f*; (*Anat*) Organ *nt*

organic [ɔ:'gænɪk] *adj* organisch; (*farming, vegetables*) Bio-, Öko-; **~ farmer** Biobauer *m*, Biobäuerin *f*; **~ food** Biokost *f*

organization [ɔ:gənaɪ'zeɪʃən] *n* Organisation *f*; (*arrangement*) Ordnung *f*; **organize** ['ɔ:gənaɪz] *vt* organisieren; **organizer** *n* (elektronisches) Notizbuch

orgasm ['ɔ:gæzəm] *n* Orgasmus *m*

orgy ['ɔ:dʒɪ] n Orgie f
oriental [ɔ:rɪ'entəl] adj orientalisch
orientation ['ɔ:rɪenteɪʃən] n
Orientierung f
origin ['ɒrɪdʒɪn] n Ursprung m; (of person)
Herkunft f; **original** [ə'rɪdʒɪnl] adj (first)
ursprünglich; (painting) original; (idea)
originell ▷ n Original nt; **originality**
[ərɪdʒɪ'nælɪtɪ] n Originalität f; **originally**
adv ursprünglich
Orkneys ['ɔ:knɪz] npl, **Orkney Islands**
npl Orkneyinseln pl
ornament ['ɔ:nəmənt] n
Schmuckgegenstand m; **ornamental**
[ɔ:nə'məntl] adj dekorativ
orphan ['ɔ:fən] n Waise f, Waisenkind nt;
orphanage ['ɔ:fənɪdʒ] n Waisenhaus nt
orthodox ['ɔ:θədɒks] adj orthodox
orthopedic, orthopaedic (US)
[ɔ:θəʊ'pi:dɪk] adj orthopädisch
ostentatious [ɒsten'teɪʃəs] adj protzig
ostrich ['ɒstrɪtʃ] n (Zool) Strauß m
other ['ʌðə*] adj, pron andere(r, s); **any
~ questions?** sonst noch Fragen?; **the
~ day** neulich; **every ~ day** jeden zweiten
Tag; **any person ~ than him** alle außer
ihm; **someone/something or ~** irgend
jemand/irgend etwas; **otherwise** adv
sonst; (differently) anders
OTT adj abbr = **over the top** übertrieben
otter ['ɒtə*] n Otter m
ought [ɔ:t] vb aux (obligation) sollte;
(probability) dürfte; (stronger) müsste; **you
~ to do that** Sie sollten das tun; **he ~ to
win** er müsste gewinnen; **that ~ to do** das
müsste (o dürfte) reichen
ounce [aʊns] n Unze f (28,35 g)
our [aʊə*] adj unser; **ours** pron unsere(r,
s); **this is ~** das gehört uns; **a friend of
~** ein Freund von uns; **ourselves** pron
(reflexive) uns; **we enjoyed ~** wir haben uns
amüsiert; **we've got the house to ~** wir
haben das Haus für uns; (emphatic) **we did
it ~** wir haben es selbst gemacht; (**all**) **by
~** allein
out [aʊt] adv hinaus/heraus; (not indoors)
draußen; (not at home) nicht zu Hause; (not
alight) aus; (unconscious) bewusstlos;
(published) herausgekommen; (results)
bekannt gegeben; **have you been ~ yet?**
waren Sie schon draußen?; **I was ~ when
they called** ich war nicht da, als sie
vorbeikamen; **to be ~ and about**

unterwegs sein; **the sun is ~** die Sonne
scheint; **the fire is ~** das Feuer ist
ausgegangen; (wrong) **the calculation is**
(**way**) **~** die Kalkulation stimmt (ganz und
gar) nicht; **they're ~ to get him** sie sind
hinter ihm her
outback ['aʊtbæk] n (in Australia) **the
~** das Hinterland
outboard ['aʊtbɔ:d] adj **~ motor**
Außenbordmotor m
outbreak ['aʊtbreɪk] n Ausbruch m
outburst ['aʊtbɜ:st] n Ausbruch m
outcome ['aʊtkʌm] n Ergebnis nt
outcry ['aʊtkraɪ] n (public protest)
Protestwelle f (against gegen)
outdo [aʊt'du:] irr vt übertreffen
outdoor ['aʊtdɔ:*] adj Außen-; (Sport) im
Freien; **~ swimming pool** Freibad nt;
outdoors [aʊt'dɔ:z] adv draußen, im
Freien
outer ['aʊtə*] adj äußere(r, s); **outer
space** n Weltraum m
outfit ['aʊtfɪt] n Ausrüstung f; (clothes)
Kleidung f
outgoing ['aʊtgəʊɪŋ] adj kontaktfreudig
outgrow [aʊt'grəʊ] irr vt (clothes)
herauswachsen aus
outing ['aʊtɪŋ] n Ausflug m
outlet ['aʊtlet] n Auslass m, Abfluss m;
(US) Steckdose f; (shop) Verkaufsstelle f
outline ['aʊtlaɪn] n Umriss m; (summary)
Abriss m
outlive [aʊt'lɪv] vt überleben
outlook ['aʊtlʊk] n Aussicht(en) f(pl);
(prospects) Aussichten pl; (attitude)
Einstellung f (on zu)
outnumber [aʊt'nʌmbə*] vt
zahlenmäßig überlegen sein +dat; **~ed**
zahlenmäßig unterlegen
out of ['aʊtɒv] prep (motion, motive, origin)
aus; (position, away from) außerhalb +gen;
~ danger/sight/breath außer
Gefahr/Sicht/Atem; **made ~ wood** aus
Holz gemacht; **we are ~ bread** wir haben
kein Brot mehr; **out-of-date** adj veraltet;
out-of-the-way adj abgelegen
outpatient ['aʊtpeɪʃənt] n ambulanter
Patient, ambulante Patientin
output ['aʊtpʊt] n Produktion f; (of
engine) Leistung f; (Inform) Ausgabe f
outrage ['aʊtreɪdʒ] n (great anger)
Empörung f (at über); (wicked deed)
Schandtat f; (crime) Verbrechen nt;

(*indecency*) Skandal *m*; **outrageous**
[aʊtˈreɪdʒəs] *adj* unerhört; (*clothes,
behaviour etc*) unmöglich, schrill
outright [ˈaʊtraɪt] *adv* (*killed*) sofort ▷ *adj*
total; (*denial*) völlig; (*winner*) unbestritten
outside [aʊtˈsaɪd] *n* Außenseite *f*; **on the
~** außen ▷ *adj* äußere(r, s), Außen-;
(*chance*) sehr gering ▷ *adv* außen; **to
go ~** nach draußen gehen ▷ *prep*
außerhalb +*gen*; **outsider** *n*
Außenseiter(in) *m(f)*
outsize [ˈaʊtsaɪz] *adj* übergroß; (*clothes*)
in Übergröße
outskirts [ˈaʊtskɜːts] *npl* (*of town*)
Stadtrand *m*
outstanding [aʊtˈstændɪŋ] *adj*
hervorragend; (*debts etc*) ausstehend
outward [ˈaʊtwəd] *adj* äußere(r, s);
~ journey Hinfahrt *f*; **outwardly** *adv*
nach außen hin; **outwards** *adv* nach
außen
oval [ˈəʊvəl] *adj* oval
ovary [ˈəʊvərɪ] *n* Eierstock *m*
ovation [əʊˈveɪʃən] *n* Ovation *f*, Applaus
m
oven [ˈʌvn] *n* Backofen *m*; **oven glove** *n*
Topfhandschuh *m*; **ovenproof** *adj*
feuerfest; **oven-ready** *adj* bratfertig
over [ˈəʊvə*] *prep* (*position*) über +*dat*;
(*motion*) über +*akk*; **they spent a long
time ~ it** sie haben lange dazu gebraucht;
from all ~ England aus ganz England;
~ £20 mehr als 20 Pfund; **~ the
phone/radio** am Telefon/im Radio; **to
talk ~ a glass of wine** sich bei einem Glas
Wein unterhalten; **~ and above this**
darüber hinaus; **~ the summer** während
des Sommers ▷ *adv* (*across*)
hinüber/herüber; (*finished*) vorbei; (*match,
play etc*) zu Ende; (*left*) übrig; (*more*) mehr;
~ there/in America da drüben/drüben in
Amerika; **~ to you** Sie sind dran; **it's (all)
~ between us** es ist aus zwischen uns;
~ and ~ again immer wieder; **to start (all)
~ again** noch einmal von vorn anfangen;
children of 8 and ~ Kinder von 8 Jahren
und darüber
over- [ˈəʊvə*] *pref* über-
overall [ˈəʊvərɔːl] *n* (*Brit*) Kittel *m* ▷ *adj*
(*situation*) allgemein; (*length*) Gesamt-;
~ majority absolute Mehrheit ▷ *adv*
insgesamt; **overalls** *npl* Overall *m*
overboard [ˈəʊvəbɔːd] *adv* über Bord

overbooked [əʊvəˈbʊkt] *adj* überbucht;
overbooking *n* Überbuchung *f*
overcharge [əʊvəˈtʃɑːdʒ] *vt* zu viel
verlangen von
overcoat [ˈəʊvəkəʊt] *n* Wintermantel *m*
overcome [əʊvəˈkʌm] *irr vt* überwinden;
~ by sleep/emotion von Schlaf/Rührung
übermannt; **we shall ~** wir werden siegen
overcooked [əʊvəˈkʊkt] *adj* zu lange
gekocht; (*meat*) zu lange gebraten
overcrowded [əʊvəˈkraʊdɪd] *adj*
überfüllt
overdo [əʊvəˈduː] *irr vt* übertreiben;
you're ~ing it du übertreibst es; (*doing too
much*) Sie übernehmen sich; **overdone** *adj*
übertrieben; (*food*) zu lange gekocht; (*meat*)
zu lange gebraten
overdose [ˈəʊvədəʊs] *n* Überdosis *f*
overdraft [ˈəʊvədrɑːft] *n*
Kontoüberziehung *f*; **overdrawn**
[əʊvəˈdrɔːn] *adj* überzogen
overdue [əʊvəˈdjuː] *adj* überfällig
overestimate [əʊvərˈestɪmeɪt] *vt*
überschätzen
overexpose [əʊvərɪksˈpəʊz] *vt* (*Foto*)
überbelichten
overflow [əʊvəˈfləʊ] *vi* überlaufen
overhead [ˈəʊvəhed] *adj* (*Aviat*) **~ locker**
Gepäckfach *nt*; **~ projector**
Overheadprojektor *m*; **~ railway**
Hochbahn *f* ▷ [əʊvəˈhed] *adv* oben
overhear [əʊvəˈhɪə*] *irr vt* zufällig mit
anhören
overheat [əʊvəˈhiːt] *vi* (*engine*) heiß
laufen
overjoyed [əʊvəˈdʒɔɪd] *adj* überglücklich
(*at* über)
overland [ˈəʊvəlænd] *adj* Überland-
▷ [əʊvəˈlænd] *adv* (*travel*) über Land
overlap [əʊvəˈlæp] *vi* (*dates etc*) sich
überschneiden; (*objects*) sich teilweise
decken
overload [əʊvəˈləʊd] *vt* überladen
overlook [əʊvəˈlʊk] *vt* (*view from above*)
überblicken; (*not notice*) übersehen;
(*pardon*) hinwegsehen über +*akk*
overnight [əʊvəˈnaɪt] *adj* (*journey, train*)
Nacht-; **~ bag** Reisetasche *f*; **~ stay**
Übernachtung *f* ▷ *adv* über Nacht
overpass [ˈəʊvəpɑːs] *n* Überführung *f*
overpay [əʊvəˈpeɪ] *vt* überbezahlen
overrule [əʊvəˈruːl] *vt* verwerfen;
(*decision*) aufheben

overseas [əʊvə'siːz] *adj* Übersee-; (*fam*)
Auslands-; **~ students** Studenten aus
Übersee ▷ *adv* (*go*) nach Übersee; (*live*,
work) in Übersee
oversee [əʊvə'siː] *irr vt* beaufsichtigen
overshadow [əʊvə'ʃædəʊ] *vt*
überschatten
overshoot [əʊvə'ʃuːt] *irr vt* (*runway*)
hinausschießen über +*akk*; (*turning*)
vorbeifahren +*dat*
oversight ['əʊvəsaɪt] *n* Versehen *nt*
oversimplify [əʊvə'sɪmplɪfaɪ] *vt* zu sehr
vereinfachen
oversleep [əʊvə'sliːp] *irr vi* verschlafen
overtake [əʊvə'teɪk] *irr vt, vi* überholen
overtime ['əʊvətaɪm] *n* Überstunden
pl
overturn [əʊvə'tɜːn] *vt, vi* umkippen
overweight [əʊvə'weɪt] *adj* **to be**
~ Übergewicht haben
overwhelm [əʊvə'welm] *vt*
überwältigen; **overwhelming** *adj*
überwältigend
overwork [əʊvə'wɜːk] *n* Überarbeitung *f*
▷ *vi* sich überarbeiten; **overworked** *adj*
überarbeitet
owe [əʊ] *vt* schulden; **to ~ sth to sb**
(*money*) jdm etw schulden; (*favour etc*) jdm
etw verdanken; **how much do I ~ you?**
was bin ich Ihnen schuldig?; **owing to**
prep wegen +*gen*
owl [aʊl] *n* Eule *f*
own [əʊn] *vt* besitzen ▷ *adj* eigen; **on**
one's ~ allein; **he has a flat of his ~** er hat
eine eigene Wohung; **own up** *vi* **to ~ to**
sth etw zugeben; **owner** *n* Besitzer(in)
m(f); (*of business*) Inhaber(in) *m(f)*;
ownership *n* Besitz *m*; **under new**
~ unter neuer Leitung
ox [ɒks] (*pl* **oxen**) *n* Ochse *m*; **oxtail**
['ɒksteɪl] *n* Ochsenschwanz *m*; **~ soup**
Ochsenschwanzsuppe *f*; **oxygen**
['ɒksɪdʒən] *n* Sauerstoff *m*
oyster ['ɔɪstə*] *n* Auster *f*
oz *abbr* = **ounces** Unzen *pl*
Oz ['ɒz] *n* (*fam*) Australien *nt*
ozone ['əʊzəʊn] *n* Ozon *nt*; **~ layer**
Ozonschicht *f*

o

p *abbr* = **page** S.; *abbr* = **penny, pence**

p.a. *abbr* = **per annum**

pace [peɪs] *n* (*speed*) Tempo *nt*; (*step*) Schritt *m*; **pacemaker** *n* (*Med*) Schrittmacher *m*

Pacific [pə'sɪfɪk] *n* **the ~** (*Ocean*) der Pazifik; **Pacific Standard Time** *n* pazifische Zeit

pacifier ['pæsɪfaɪə] *n* (*US: for baby*) Schnuller *m*

pack [pæk] *n* (*of cards*) Spiel *nt*; (*esp US: of cigarettes*) Schachtel *f*; (*gang*) Bande *f*; (*US: backpack*) Rucksack *m* ▷ *vt* (*case*) packen; (*clothes*) einpacken ▷ *vi* (*for holiday*) packen; **pack in** *vt* (*Brit fam: job*) hinschmeißen; **package** ['pækɪdʒ] *n* (*a. Inform, fig*) Paket *nt*; **package deal** *n* Pauschalangebot *nt*; **package holiday**, **package tour** *n* Pauschalreise *f*; **packaging** *n* (*material*) Verpackung *f*; **packed lunch** *n* (*Brit*) Lunchpaket *nt*; **packet** *n* Päckchen *nt*; (*of cigarettes*) Schachtel *f*

pad [pæd] *n* (*of paper*) Schreibblock *m*; (*padding*) Polster *nt*; **padded envelope** *n* wattierter Umschlag; **padding** *n* (*material*) Polsterung *f*

paddle ['pædl] *n* (*for boat*) Paddel *nt* ▷ *vi* (*in boat*) paddeln; **paddling pool** *n* (*Brit*) Planschbecken *nt*

padlock ['pædlɒk] *n* Vorhängeschloss *nt*

page [peɪdʒ] *n* (*of book etc*) Seite *f*

pager ['peɪdʒə*] *n* Piepser *m*

paid [peɪd] *pt, pp of* **pay** ▷ *adj* bezahlt

pain [peɪn] *n* Schmerz *m*; **to be in ~** Schmerzen haben; **she's a (real) ~** sie nervt; **painful** *adj* (*physically*) schmerzhaft; (*embarrassing*) peinlich; **painkiller** *n* schmerzstillendes Mittel

painstaking *adj* sorgfältig

paint [peɪnt] *n* Farbe *f* ▷ *vt* anstreichen; (*picture*) malen; **paintbrush** *n* Pinsel *m*; **painter** *n* Maler(in) *m(f)*; **painting** *n* (*picture*) Bild *nt*, Gemälde *nt*

pair [peə*] *n* Paar *nt*; **a ~ of shoes** ein Paar Schuhe; **a ~ of scissors** eine Schere; **a ~ of trousers** eine Hose

pajamas [pə'dʒɑːməz] *npl* (*US*) Schlafanzug *m*

Pakistan [pɑːkɪ'stɑːn] *n* Pakistan *nt*

pal [pæl] *n* (*fam*) Kumpel *m*

palace ['pæləs] *n* Palast *m*

pale [peɪl] *adj* (*face*) blass, bleich; (*colour*) hell

palm [pɑːm] *n* (*of hand*) Handfläche *f*; **~ (tree)** Palme *f*; **palmtop (computer)** *n* Palmtop(computer) *m*

pamper ['pæmpə*] *vt* verhätscheln

pan [pæn] *n* (*saucepan*) Topf *m*; (*frying pan*) Pfanne *f*; **pancake** ['pænkeɪk] *n* Pfannkuchen *m*; **Pancake Day** *n* (*Brit*) Fastnachtsdienstag *m*

panda ['pændə] *n* Panda *m*

pane [peɪn] *n* Scheibe *f*

panel ['pænl] *n* (*of wood*) Tafel *f*; (*in discussion*) Diskussionsteilnehmer *pl*

panic ['pænɪk] *n* Panik *f* ▷ *vi* in Panik geraten; **panicky** ['pænɪkɪ] *adj* panisch

pansy ['pænzɪ] *n* (*flower*) Stiefmütterchen *nt*

panties ['pæntɪz] *npl* (Damen)slip *m*

pantomime ['pæntəmaɪm] *n* (*Brit*) *um die Weihnachtszeit aufgeführte Märchenkomödie*

pants [pænts] *npl* Unterhose *f*; (*esp US: trousers*) Hose *f*

pantyhose ['pæntɪhəʊz] *npl* (*US*) Strumpfhose *f*; **panty-liner** *n* Slipeinlage *f*

paper ['peɪpə*] *n* Papier *nt*; (*newspaper*) Zeitung *f*; (*exam*) Klausur *f*; (*for reading at*

conference) Referat nt; **~s** pl *(identity papers)*
Papiere pl; **~ bag** Papiertüte f; **~ cup**
Pappbecher m ▷ vt *(wall)* tapezieren;
paperback n Taschenbuch nt; **paper clip**
n Büroklammer f; **paper feed** n *(of printer)*
Papiereinzug m; **paper round** n **to do a
~** Zeitungen austragen; **paperwork** n
Schreibarbeit f

parachute ['pærəʃuːt] n Fallschirm m
▷ vi abspringen

paracetamol [pærə'siːtəmɒl] n *(tablet)*
Paracetamoltablette f

parade [pə'reɪd] n *(procession)* Umzug m;
(Mil) Parade f ▷ vi vorbeimarschieren

paradise ['pærədaɪs] n Paradies nt

paragliding ['pærəglaɪdɪŋ] n
Gleitschirmfliegen nt

paragraph ['pærəgrɑːf] n Absatz m

parallel ['pærəlel] adj parallel ▷ n *(Math,
fig)* Parallele f

paralyze ['pærəlaɪz] vt lähmen; *(fig)*
lahm legen

paranoid ['pærənɔɪd] adj paranoid

paraphrase ['pærəfreɪz] vt umschreiben;
(sth spoken) anders ausdrücken

parasailing ['pærəseɪlɪŋ] n Parasailing nt

parasol ['pærəsɒl] n Sonnenschirm m

parcel ['pɑːsl] n Paket nt

pardon ['pɑːdn] n *(Jur)* Begnadigung f;
~ me/I beg your ~ verzeihen Sie bitte;
(objection) aber ich bitte Sie; **I beg your ~?/
~ me?** wie bitte?

parent ['pɛərənt] n Elternteil m; **~s** pl
Eltern pl; **~s-in-law** pl Schwiegereltern pl;
parental [pə'rentl] adj elterlich, Eltern-

parish ['pærɪʃ] n Gemeinde f

park [pɑːk] n Park m ▷ vt, vi parken;
parking n Parken nt; **'no ~'** „Parken
verboten"; **parking brake** n *(US)*
Handbremse f; **parking disc** n
Parkscheibe f; **parking fine** n Geldbuße f
für falsches Parken; **parking lights** npl
(US) Standlicht nt; **parking lot** n *(US)*
Parkplatz m; **parking meter** n Parkuhr f;
parking place, parking space n
Parkplatz m; **parking ticket** n
Strafzettel m

parliament ['pɑːləmənt] n Parlament nt

parrot ['pærət] n Papagei m

parsley ['pɑːslɪ] n Petersilie f

parsnip ['pɑːsnɪp] n Pastinake f
(längliches, weißes Wurzelgemüse)

part [pɑːt] n Teil m; *(of machine)* Teil nt;
(Theat) Rolle f; *(US: in hair)* Scheitel m; **to
take ~** teilnehmen *(in an +dat)*; **for the
most ~** zum größten Teil ▷ adj Teil- ▷ vt
(separate) trennen; *(hair)* scheiteln ▷ vi
(people) sich trennen

partial ['pɑːʃəl] adj *(incomplete)* teilweise,
Teil-; *(biased)* parteiisch

participant [pɑː'tɪsɪpənt] n
Teilnehmer(in) m(f); **participate**
[pɑː'tɪsɪpeɪt] vi teilnehmen *(in an +dat)*

particular [pə'tɪkjʊlə*] adj *(specific)*
bestimmt; *(exact)* genau; *(fussy)* eigen; **in
~** insbesondere ▷ n **~s** pl *(details)*
Einzelheiten pl; *(about person)* Personalien
pl; **particularly** adv besonders

parting ['pɑːtɪŋ] n *(farewell)* Abschied m;
(Brit: in hair) Scheitel m

partly ['pɑːtlɪ] adv teilweise

partner ['pɑːtnə*] n Partner(in) m(f);
partnership n Partnerschaft f

partridge ['pɑːtrɪdʒ] n Rebhuhn nt

part-time ['pɑːt'taɪm] adj Teilzeit- ▷ adv
to work ~ Teilzeit arbeiten

party ['pɑːtɪ] n *(celebration)* Party f;
(Pol, Jur) Partei f; *(group)* Gruppe f ▷ vi
feiern

pass [pɑːs] vt *(on foot)* vorbeigehen an
+dat; *(in car etc)* vorbeifahren an +dat;
(time) verbringen; *(exam)* bestehen; *(law)*
verabschieden; **to ~ sth to sb, to ~ sb sth**
jdm etw reichen; **to ~ the ball to sb** jdm
den Ball zuspielen ▷ vi *(on foot)*
vorbeigehen; *(in car etc)* vorbeifahren;
(years) vergehen; *(in exam)* bestehen ▷ n
(document) Ausweis m; *(Sport)* Pass m; **pass
away** vi *(die)* verscheiden; **pass by** vi *(on
foot)* vorbeigehen; *(in car etc)* vorbeifahren
▷ vt *(on foot)* vorbeigehen an +dat; *(in car
etc)* vorbeifahren an +dat; **pass on** vt
weitergeben *(to an +akk)*; *(disease)*
übertragen *(to auf +akk)*; **pass out** vi
(faint) ohnmächtig werden; **pass round** vt
herumreichen

passage ['pæsɪdʒ] n *(corridor)* Gang m; *(in
book, music)* Passage f; **passageway** n
Durchgang m

passenger ['pæsɪndʒə*] n Passagier(in)
m(f); *(on bus)* Fahrgast m; *(on train)*
Reisende(r) mf; *(in car)* Mitfahrer(in) m(f)

passer-by ['pɑːsə'baɪ] *(pl* **passers-by**) n
Passant(in) m(f)

passion ['pæʃən] n Leidenschaft f;
passionate ['pæʃənɪt] adj

p

leidenschaftlich; **passion fruit** *n*
Passionsfrucht

passive ['pæsɪv] *adj* passiv ▷ *n* ~ **(voice)**
(*Ling*) Passiv *nt*

passport ['pɑːspɔːt] *n* (Reise)pass *m*;
passport control *n* Passkontrolle *f*

password ['pɑːswɜːd] *n* (*Inform*)
Passwort *nt*

past [pɑːst] *n* Vergangenheit *f* ▷ *adv* (*by*)
vorbei; **it's five** ~ es ist fünf nach ▷ *adj*
(*years*) vergangen; (*president etc*) ehemalig;
in the ~ **two months** in den letzten zwei
Monaten ▷ *prep* (*telling time*) nach; **it's
half** ~ **10** es ist halb 11; **to go** ~ **sth** an etw
dat vorbeigehen/-fahren

pasta ['pæstə] *n* Nudeln *pl*

paste [peɪst] *vt* (*stick*) kleben; (*Inform*)
einfügen ▷ *n* (*glue*) Kleister *m*

pastime ['pɑːstaɪm] *n* Zeitvertreib *m*

pastry ['peɪstrɪ] *n* Teig *m*; (*cake*)
Stückchen

pasty ['pæstɪ] *n* (*Brit*) Pastete *f*

patch [pætʃ] *n* (*area*) Fleck *m*; (*for mending*)
Flicken ▷ *vt* flicken; **patchy** *adj* (*uneven*)
ungleichmäßig

pâté ['pæteɪ] *n* Pastete *f*

paternal [pə'tɜːnl] *adj* väterlich;
~ **grandmother** Großmutter *f*
väterlicherseits; **paternity leave**
[pə'tɜːnɪtɪliːv] *n* Elternzeit *f* (des Vaters)

path [pɑːθ] *n* (*a. Inform*) Pfad *m*; (*a. fig*)
Weg *m*

pathetic [pə'θetɪk] *adj* (*bad*) kläglich,
erbärmlich; **it's** ~ es ist zum Heulen

patience ['peɪʃəns] *n* Geduld *f*; (*Brit Cards*)
Patience *f*; **patient** *adj* geduldig ▷ *n*
Patient(in) *m(f)*

patio ['pætɪəʊ] *n* Terrasse *f*

patriotic [pætrɪ'ɒtɪk] *adj* patriotisch

patrol car [pə'trəʊlkɑː*] *n* Streifenwagen
m; **patrolman** (*pl* -**men**) *n* (*US*)
Streifenpolizist *m*

patron ['peɪtrən] *n* (*sponsor*) Förderer *m*,
Förderin *f*; (*in shop*) Kunde *m*, Kundin *f*

patronize ['pætrənaɪz] *vt* (*treat
condescendingly*) von oben herab
behandeln; **patronizing** *adj* (*attitude*)
herablassend

pattern ['pætən] *n* Muster *nt*

pause [pɔːz] *n* Pause *f* ▷ *vi* (*speaker*)
innehalten

pavement *n* (*Brit*) Bürgersteig *m*; (*US*)
Pflaster *nt*

pay [peɪ] (**paid, paid**) *vt* bezahlen; **he
paid** (**me**) **£20 for it** er hat (mir) 20 Pfund
dafür gezahlt; **to** ~ **attention** Acht geben
(*to* auf +*akk*); **to** ~ **sb a visit** jdn besuchen
▷ *vi* zahlen; (*be profitable*) sich bezahlt
machen; **to** ~ **for sth** etw bezahlen ▷ *n*
Bezahlung *f*, Lohn *m*; **pay back** *vt* (*money*)
zurückzahlen; **pay in** *vt* (*into account*)
einzahlen; **payable** *adj* zahlbar; (*due*)
fällig; **payday** *n* Zahltag *m*; **payee** [peɪ'iː]
n Zahlungsempfänger(in) *m(f)*; **payment**
n Bezahlung *f*; (*money*) Zahlung *f*;
pay-per-view *adj* Pay-per-View-; **pay
phone** *n* Münzfernsprecher *m*; **pay TV** *n*
Pay-TV *nt*

PC *abbr* = **personal computer** PC
m; *abbr* = **politically correct** politisch
korrekt

PDA *abbr* = **personal digital assistant**
PDA *m*

PE *abbr* = **physical education** (*school*)
Sport *m*

pea [piː] *n* Erbse *f*

peace [piːs] *n* Frieden *m*; **peaceful** *adj*
friedlich

peach [piːtʃ] *n* Pfirsich *m*

peacock ['piːkɒk] *n* Pfau *m*

peak [piːk] *n* (*of mountain*) Gipfel *m*; (*fig*)
Höhepunkt *m*; **peak period** *n* Stoßzeit *f*;
(*season*) Hochsaison

peanut ['piːnʌt] *n* Erdnuss *f*; **peanut
butter** *n* Erdnussbutter *f*

pear [pɛə*] *n* Birne *f* ·

pearl [pɜːl] *n* Perle *f*

pebble ['pebl] *n* Kiesel *m*

pecan [pɪ'kæn] *n* Pekannuss

peck [pek] *vt, vi* picken; **peckish** *adj* (*Brit
fam*) ein bisschen hungrig

peculiar [pɪ'kjuːlɪə*] *adj* (*odd*) seltsam;
~ **to** charakteristisch für; **peculiarity**
[pɪkjʊlɪ'ærɪtɪ] *n* (*singular quality*)
Besonderheit *f*; (*strangeness*)
Eigenartigkeit *f*

pedal ['pedl] *n* Pedal *nt*

pedestrian [pɪ'destrɪən] *n* Fußgänger(in)
m(f); **pedestrian crossing** *n*
Fußgängerüberweg *m*

pee [piː] *vi* (*fam*) pinkeln

peel [piːl] *n* Schale *f* ▷ *vt* schälen ▷ *vi*
(*paint etc*) abblättern; (*skin etc*) sich
schälen

peer [pɪə*] *n* Gleichaltrige(r) *mf* ▷ *vi*
starren

peg [peg] n (for coat etc) Haken m; (for tent) Hering m; (**clothes**) ~ (Wäsche)klammer f
pelvis ['pelvɪs] n Becken nt
pen [pen] n (ball-point) Kuli m, Kugelschreiber; (fountain ~) Füller m
penalize ['pi:nəlaɪz] vt (punish) bestrafen; **penalty** ['penltɪ] n (punishment) Strafe f; (in football) Elfmeter m
pence [pens] pl of **penny**
pencil ['pensl] n Bleistift m; **pencil sharpener** n (Bleistift)spitzer m
penetrate ['penɪtreɪt] vt durchdringen; (enter into) eindringen in +akk
penfriend ['penfrend] n Brieffreund(in) m(f)
penguin ['peŋgwɪn] n Pinguin m
penicillin [penɪ'sɪlɪn] n Penizillin nt
peninsula [pɪ'nɪnsjʊlə] n Halbinsel f
penis ['pi:nɪs] n Penis m
penknife ['pennaɪf] (pl **penknives**) n Taschenmesser nt
penny ['penɪ] (pl **pence** o **pennies**) n (Brit) Penny m; (US) Centstück nt
pension ['penʃən] n Rente f; (for civil servants, executives etc) Pension f; **pensioner** n Rentner(in) m(f); **pension plan, pension scheme** n Rentenversicherung f
penultimate [pɪ'nʌltɪmət] adj vorletzte(r, s)
people ['pi:pl] npl (persons) Leute pl; (von Staat) Volk nt; (inhabitants) Bevölkerung f; **people carrier** n Minivan m
pepper ['pepə*] n Pfeffer m; (vegetable) Paprika m; **peppermint** n (sweet) Pfefferminz nt
per [pɜ:*] prep pro; ~ **annum** pro Jahr; ~ **cent** Prozent nt
percentage [pə'sentɪdʒ] n Prozentsatz m
perceptible [pə'septəbl] adj wahrnehmbar
percolator ['pɜ:kəleɪtə*] n Kaffeemaschine f
percussion [pɜ:'kʌʃən] n (Mus) Schlagzeug nt
perfect ['pɜ:fɪkt] adj perfekt; (utter) völlig ▷ [pə'fekt] vt vervollkommnen; **perfectly** adv perfekt; (utterly) völlig
perform [pə'fɔ:m] vt (task) ausführen; (play) aufführen; (Med: operation) durchführen ▷ vi (Theat) auftreten;

performance n (show) Vorstellung f; (efficiency) Leistung f
perfume ['pɜ:fju:m] n Duft m; (substance) Parfüm nt
perhaps [pə'hæps] adv vielleicht
peril ['perɪl] n Gefahr f
period ['pɪərɪəd] n (length of time) Zeit f; (in history) Zeitalter nt; (school) Stunde f; (Med) Periode f; (US: full stop) Punkt m; **for a ~ of three years** für einen Zeitraum von drei Jahren; **periodical** [pɪərɪ'ɒdɪkəl] n Zeitschrift f
peripheral [pə'rɪfərəl] n (Inform) Peripheriegerät nt
perish ['perɪʃ] vi (die) umkommen; (material) verderben
perjury ['pɜ:dʒərɪ] n Meineid m
perm [pɜ:m] n Dauerwelle f
permanent, permanently ['pɜ:mənənt, -lɪ] adj, adv ständig
permission [pə'mɪʃən] n Erlaubnis f; **permit** ['pɜ:mɪt] n Genehmigung f ▷ [pə'mɪt] vt erlauben, zulassen; **to ~ sb to do sth** jdm erlauben, etw zu tun
persecute ['pɜ:sɪkju:t] vt verfolgen
perseverance [pɜ:sɪ'vɪərəns] n Ausdauer f
Persian ['pɜ:ʃən] adj persisch
persist [pə'sɪst] vi (in belief etc) bleiben (in bei); (rain, smell) andauern; **persistent** adj beharrlich
person ['pɜ:sn] n Mensch m; (in official context) Person f; **in ~** persönlich; **personal** adj persönlich; (private) privat; **personality** [pɜ:sə'nælɪtɪ] n Persönlichkeit f; **personal organizer** n Organizer m; **personal stereo** (pl **-s**) n Walkman® m; **personnel** [pɜ:sə'nel] n Personal nt
perspective [pə'spektɪv] n Perspektive f
perspire [pə'spaɪə*] vi schwitzen
persuade [pə'sweɪd] vt überreden; (convince) überzeugen; **persuasive** [pə'sweɪsɪv] adj überzeugend
perverse [pə'vɜ:s] adj pervers; (obstinate) eigensinnig; **pervert** ['pɜ:vɜ:t] n Perverse(r) mf ▷ [pə'vɜ:t] vt (morally) verderben
pessimist ['pesɪmɪst] n Pessimist(in) m(f); **pessimistic** [pesɪ'mɪstɪk] adj pessimistisch
pest [pest] n (insect) Schädling m; (fig: person) Nervensäge f; (thing) Plage f;

pester ['pestə*] vt plagen; **pesticide** ['pestɪsaɪd] n Schädlingsbekämpfungsmittel nt
pet [pet] n (animal) Haustier nt; (person) Liebling m
petal ['petl] n Blütenblatt nt
petition [pə'tɪʃən] n Petition f
petrol ['petrəl] n (Brit) Benzin nt; **petrol pump** n (at garage) Zapfsäule f; **petrol station** n Tankstelle f; **petrol tank** n Benzintank m
pharmacy ['fɑːməsɪ] n (shop) Apotheke f
phase [feɪz] n Phase f
PhD abbr = **Doctor of Philosophy** Dr. phil; (dissertation) Doktorarbeit f; **to do one's ~** promovieren
pheasant ['feznt] n Fasan m
phenomenon [fɪ'nɒmɪnən] (pl **phenomena**) n Phänomen nt
Philippines ['fɪlɪpiːnz] npl Philippinen pl
philosophical [fɪlə'sɒfɪkəl] adj philosophisch; (fig) gelassen; **philosophy** [fɪ'lɒsəfɪ] n Philosophie f
phone [fəʊn] n Telefon nt ▷ vt, vi anrufen; **phone book** n Telefonbuch nt; **phone bill** n Telefonrechnung f; **phone booth**, **phone box** (Brit) n Telefonzelle f; **phonecall** n Telefonanruf m; **phonecard** n Telefonkarte f; **phone-in** n Rundfunkprogramm, bei dem Hörer anrufen können; **phone number** n Telefonnummer f
photo ['fəʊtəʊ] (pl **-s**) n Foto nt; **photo booth** n Fotoautomat m; **photocopier** ['fəʊtəʊ'kɒpɪə*] n Kopiergerät nt; **photocopy** ['fəʊtəʊkɒpɪ] n Fotokopie f ▷ vt fotokopieren; **photograph** ['fəʊtəgrɑːf] n Fotografie f, Aufnahme f ▷ vt fotografieren; **photographer** [fə'tɒɡrəfə*] n Fotograf(in) m(f); **photography** [fə'tɒɡrəfɪ] n Fotografie f
phrase [freɪz] n (expression) Redewendung f, Ausdruck m; **phrase book** n Sprachführer m
physical ['fɪzɪkəl] adj (bodily) körperlich, physisch ▷ n ärztliche Untersuchung; **physically** adv (bodily) körperlich, physisch; **~ handicapped** körperbehindert
physician [fɪ'zɪʃən] n Arzt m, Ärztin f
physics ['fɪzɪks] nsing (=subject) Physik f

physiotherapy [fɪzɪə'θerəpɪ] n Physiotherapie f
physique [fɪ'ziːk] n Körperbau m
piano ['pjɑːnəʊ] (pl **-s**) n Klavier nt
pick [pɪk] vt (flowers, fruit) pflücken; (choose) auswählen; (team) aufstellen; **pick out** vt auswählen; **pick up** vt (lift up) aufheben; (collect) abholen; (learn) lernen
pickle ['pɪkl] n (food) (Mixed) Pickles pl ▷ vt einlegen
pickpocket ['pɪkpɒkɪt] n Taschendieb(in) m(f)
picnic ['pɪknɪk] n Picknick nt
picture ['pɪktʃə*] n Bild nt; **to go to the ~s** (Brit) ins Kino gehen ▷ vt (visualize) sich vorstellen; **picture book** n Bilderbuch nt; **picturesque** [pɪktʃə'resk] adj malerisch
pie [paɪ] n (meat) Pastete f; (fruit) Kuchen m
piece [piːs] n Stück nt; (part) Teil nt; (in chess) Figur f; (in draughts) Stein m; **a ~ of cake** ein Stück Kuchen; **to fall to ~s** auseinanderfallen
pier [pɪə*] n Pier m
pierce [pɪəs] vt durchstechen, durchbohren; (cold, sound) durchdringen; **pierced** adj (part of body) gepierct; **piercing** adj durchdringend
pig [pɪg] n Schwein nt
pigeon ['pɪdʒən] n Taube f; **pigeonhole** n (compartment) Ablegefach nt
piggy ['pɪgɪ] adj (fam) verfressen; **pigheaded** ['pɪg'hedɪd] adj dickköpfig; **piglet** ['pɪglət] n Ferkel nt; **pigsty** ['pɪgstaɪ] n Schweinestall m; **pigtail** ['pɪgteɪl] n Zopf m
pile [paɪl] n (heap) Haufen m; (one on top of another) Stapel m; **pile up** vi (accumulate) sich anhäufen
piles [paɪlz] npl Hämorr(ho)iden pl
pile-up ['paɪlʌp] n (Auto) Massenkarambolage f
pilgrim ['pɪlgrɪm] n Pilger(in) m(f)
pill [pɪl] n Tablette f; **the ~** die (Antibaby)pille; **to be on the ~** die Pille nehmen
pillar ['pɪlə*] n Pfeiler m
pillow ['pɪləʊ] n (Kopf)kissen nt; **pillowcase** n (Kopf)kissenbezug m
pilot ['paɪlət] n (Aviat) Pilot(in) m(f)
pimple ['pɪmpl] n Pickel m

pin [pɪn] n (for fixing) Nadel f; (in sewing) Stecknadel f; (Tech) Stift m; **I've got ~s and needles in my leg** mein Bein ist mir eingeschlafen ▷ vt (fix with ~) heften (to an +akk)

PIN [pɪn] acr = **personal identification number, PIN (number)** PIN f, Geheimzahl f

pincers ['pɪnsəz] npl (tool) Kneifzange f

pinch [pɪntʃ] n (of salt) Prise f ▷ vt zwicken; (fam: steal) klauen ▷ vi (shoe) drücken

pine [paɪn] n Kiefer f

pineapple ['paɪnæpl] n Ananas f

pink [pɪŋk] adj rosa

pinstripe(d) ['pɪnstraɪp(t)] adj Nadelstreifen-

pint [paɪnt] n Pint nt (Brit: 0,57 l, US: 0,473l); (Brit: glass of beer) Bier nt

pious ['paɪəs] adj fromm

pip [pɪp] n (of fruit) Kern m

pipe [paɪp] n (for smoking) Pfeife f; (for water, gas) Rohrleitung f

pirate ['paɪərɪt] n Pirat(in) m(f); **pirated copy** n Raubkopie f

Pisces ['paɪsiːz] nsing (Astr) Fische pl; **she's a ~** sie ist Fisch

pistachio [pɪˈstɑːʃɪəʊ] (pl -s) n Pistazie f

piste [piːst] n (Ski) Piste f

pistol ['pɪstl] n Pistole f

pit [pɪt] n (hole) Grube f; (coalmine) Zeche f; **the ~s** (in motor racing) die Box; **to be the ~s** (fam) grottenschlecht sein

pitch [pɪtʃ] n (Sport) Spielfeld nt; (Mus: of instrument) Tonlage f; (of voice) Stimmlage f ▷ vt (tent) aufschlagen; (throw) werfen; **pitch-black** adj pechschwarz

pitcher ['pɪtʃə*] n (US: jug) Krug m

pitiful ['pɪtɪfʊl] adj (contemptible) jämmerlich

pitta bread ['pɪtəbred] n Pittabrot nt

pity ['pɪtɪ] n Mitleid nt; **what a ~** wie schade; **it's a ~** es ist schade ▷ vt Mitleid haben mit

pizza ['piːtsə] n Pizza f

place [pleɪs] n m (spot, in text) Stelle f; (town etc) Ort; (house) Haus nt; (position, seat, on course) Platz m; **~ of birth** Geburtsort m; **at my ~** bei mir; **in third ~** auf dem dritten Platz; **to three decimal ~s** bis auf drei Stellen nach dem Komma; **out of ~** nicht an der richtigen Stelle; (fig: remark) unangebracht; **in ~ of** anstelle von; **in the first ~** (firstly) erstens; (immediately) gleich; (in any case) überhaupt ▷ vt (put) stellen, setzen; (lay flat) legen; (advertisement) setzen (in in +akk); (Comm: order) aufgeben; **place mat** n Set nt

plague [pleɪg] n Pest f

plaice [pleɪs] n Scholle f

plain [pleɪn] adj (clear) klar, deutlich; (simple) einfach; (not beautiful) unattraktiv; (yoghurt) Natur-; (Brit: chocolate) (Zart)bitter- ▷ n Ebene f; **plainly** adv (frankly) offen; (simply) einfach; (obviously) eindeutig

plait [plæt] n Zopf m ▷ vt flechten

plan [plæn] n Plan m; (for essay etc) Konzept nt ▷ vt planen; **to ~ to do sth, to ~ on doing sth** vorhaben, etw zu tun ▷ vi planen

plane [pleɪn] n (aircraft) Flugzeug nt; (tool) Hobel m; (Math) Ebene f

planet ['plænɪt] n Planet m

plank [plæŋk] n Brett nt

plant [plɑːnt] n Pflanze f; (equipment) Maschinen pl; (factory) Werk nt ▷ vt (tree etc) pflanzen; **plantation** [plænˈteɪʃən] n Plantage f

plaque [plæk] n Gedenktafel f; (on teeth) Zahnbelag m

plaster ['plɑːstə*] n (Brit Med: sticking plaster) Pflaster nt; (on wall) Verputz m; **to have one's arm in ~** den Arm in Gips haben

plastered ['plɑːstəd] adj (fam) besoffen; **to get (absolutely) ~** sich besaufen

plastic ['plæstɪk] n Kunststoff m; **to pay with ~** mit Kreditkarte bezahlen ▷ adj Plastik-; **plastic bag** n Plastiktüte f; **plastic surgery** n plastische Chirurgie f

plate [pleɪt] n (for food) Teller m; (flat sheet) Platte f; (plaque) Schild nt

platform ['plætfɔːm] n (Rail) Bahnsteig m; (at meeting) Podium nt

platinum ['plætɪnəm] n Platin nt

play [pleɪ] n Spiel nt; (Theat) (Theater)stück nt ▷ vt spielen; (another player or team) spielen gegen; **to ~ the piano** Klavier spielen; **to ~ a part in** (fig) eine Rolle spielen bei ▷ vi spielen; **play at** vt **what are you ~ing at?** was soll das?; **play back** vt abspielen; **play down** vt herunterspielen

P

playacting n Schauspielerei f; **playback** n Wiedergabe f; **player** n Spieler(in) m(f); **playful** adj (person) verspielt; (remark) scherzhaft; **playground** n Spielplatz m; (in school) Schulhof m; **playgroup** n Spielgruppe f; **playing card** n Spielkarte f; **playing field** n Sportplatz m; **playmate** n Spielkamerad(in) m(f); **playwright** n Dramatiker(in) m(f)

plc abbr = **public limited company** AG f

plea [pliː] n Bitte f (for um)

plead [pliːd] vi dringend bitten (with sb jdn); (Jur) **to ~ guilty** sich schuldig bekennen

pleasant, pleasantly ['pleznt, -lɪ] adj, adv angenehm

please [pliːz] adv bitte; **more tea? - yes, ~** noch Tee? - ja, bitte ▷ vt (be agreeable to) gefallen +dat; **~ yourself** wie du willst; **pleased** adj zufrieden; (glad) erfreut; **~ to meet you** freut mich, angenehm; **pleasing** adj erfreulich; **pleasure** ['pleʒə*] n Vergnügen nt, Freude f; **it's a ~** gern geschehen

pledge [pledʒ] n (promise) Versprechen nt ▷ vt (promise) versprechen

plenty ['plentɪ] n **~ of** eine Menge, viel(e); **to be ~** genug sein, reichen; **I've got ~** ich habe mehr als genug ▷ adv (US fam) ganz schön

pliable ['plaɪəbl] adj biegsam

pliers ['plaɪəz] npl (Kombi)zange f

plimsolls ['plɪmsəlz] npl (Brit) Turnschuhe pl

plonk [plɒŋk] n (Brit fam: wine) billiger Wein ▷ vt **to ~ sth (down)** etw hinknallen

plot [plɒt] n (of story) Handlung f; (conspiracy) Komplott nt; (of land) Stück nt Land, Grundstück nt ▷ vi ein Komplott schmieden

plough, plow (US) [plaʊ] n Pflug m ▷ vt, vi (Agr) pflügen; **ploughman's lunch** n (Brit) in einer Kneipe serviertes Gericht aus Käse, Brot, Mixed Pickles etc

pluck [plʌk] vt (eyebrows, guitar) zupfen; (chicken) rupfen; **pluck up** vt **to ~ (one's) courage** Mut aufbringen

plug [plʌg] n (for sink, bath) Stöpsel m; (Elec) Stecker m; (Auto) (Zünd)kerze f; (fam: publicity) Schleichwerbung f ▷ vt (fam: advertise) Reklame machen für; **plug in** vt anschließen

plum [plʌm] n Pflaume f ▷ adj (fam: job etc) Super-

plumber ['plʌmə*] n Klempner(in) m(f); **plumbing** ['plʌmɪŋ] n (fittings) Leitungen pl; (craft) Installieren nt

plump [plʌmp] adj rundlich

plunge [plʌndʒ] vt (knife) stoßen; (into water) tauchen ▷ vi stürzen; (into water) tauchen

plural ['plʊərəl] n Plural m

plus [plʌs] prep plus; (as well as) und ▷ adj Plus-; **20 ~** mehr als 20 ▷ n (fig) Plus nt

plywood ['plaɪwʊd] n Sperrholz nt

pm abbr = **post meridiem at 3 ~** um 3 Uhr nachmittags; **at 8 ~** um 8 Uhr abends

pneumonia [njuː'məʊnɪə] n Lungenentzündung f

poached [pəʊtʃt] adj (egg) pochiert, verloren

PO Box abbr = **post office box** Postfach nt

pocket ['pɒkɪt] n Tasche f ▷ vt (put in ~) einstecken; **pocketbook** n (US: wallet) Brieftasche f; **pocket calculator** n Taschenrechner m; **pocket money** n Taschengeld nt

poem ['pəʊəm] n Gedicht nt; **poet** ['pəʊɪt] n Dichter(in) m(f); **poetic** [pəʊ'etɪk] adj poetisch; **poetry** ['pəʊɪtrɪ] n (art) Dichtung f; (poems) Gedichte pl

point [pɔɪnt] n Punkt m; (spot) Stelle f; (sharp tip) Spitze f; (moment) Zeitpunkt m; (purpose) Zweck m; (idea) Argument nt; (decimal) Dezimalstelle f; **~s** pl (Rail) Weiche f; **~ of view** Standpunkt m; **three ~ two** drei Komma zwei; **at some ~** irgendwann (mal); **to get to the ~** zur Sache kommen; **there's no ~** es hat keinen Sinn; **I was on the ~ of leaving** ich wollte gerade gehen ▷ vt (gun etc) richten (at auf +akk); **to ~ one's finger at** mit dem Finger zeigen auf +akk ▷ vi (with finger etc) zeigen (at, to auf +akk); **point out** vt (indicate) aufzeigen; (mention) hinweisen auf +akk; **pointed** adj spitz; (question) gezielt; **pointer** n (on dial) Zeiger m; (tip) Hinweis m; **pointless** adj sinnlos

poison ['pɔɪzn] n Gift nt ▷ vt vergiften; **poisonous** adj giftig

poke [pəʊk] vt (with stick, finger) stoßen, stupsen; (put) stecken

Poland ['pəʊlənd] n Polen nt

polar ['pəʊlə*] adj Polar-, polar; **~ bear** Eisbär m

pole [pəʊl] *n* Stange *f*; (*Geo, Elec*) Pol *m*
Pole [pəʊl] *n* Pole *m*, Polin *f*
pole vault *n* Stabhochsprung *m*
police [pə'li:s] *n* Polizei *f*; **police car** *n* Polizeiwagen *m*; **policeman** (*pl* **-men**) *n* Polizist *m*; **police station** *n* (Polizei)wache *f*; **policewoman** (*pl* **-women**) *n* Polizistin *f*
policy ['pɒlɪsɪ] *n* (*plan*) Politik *f*; (*principle*) Grundsatz *m*; (*insurance ~*) (Versicherungs)police *f*
polio ['pəʊlɪəʊ] *n* Kinderlähmung *f*
polish ['pɒlɪʃ] *n* (*for furniture*) Politur *f*; (*floor*) Wachs *nt*; (*for shoes*) Creme *f*; (*shine*) Glanz *m*; (*fig*) Schliff *m* ▷ *vt* polieren; (*shoes*) putzen; (*fig*) den letzten Schliff geben +*dat*
Polish ['pəʊlɪʃ] *adj* polnisch ▷ *n* Polnisch *nt*
polite [pə'laɪt] *adj* höflich; **politeness** *n* Höflichkeit *f*
political, **politically** [pə'lɪtɪkəl, -ɪ] *adj, adv* politisch; **~ly correct** politisch korrekt; **politician** [pɒlɪ'tɪʃən] *n* Politiker(in) *m(f)*; **politics** ['pɒlɪtɪks] *nsing o pl* Politik *f*
poll [pəʊl] *n* (*election*) Wahl *f*; (*opinion ~*) Umfrage *f*
pollen ['pɒlən] *n* Pollen *m*, Blütenstaub *m*; **pollen count** *n* Pollenflug *m*
polling station ['pəʊlɪŋsteɪʃən] *n* Wahllokal *nt*
pollute [pə'lu:t] *vt* verschmutzen; **pollution** [pə'lu:ʃən] *n* Verschmutzung *f*
pompous ['pɒmpəs] *adj* aufgeblasen; (*language*) geschwollen
pond [pɒnd] *n* Teich *m*
ponder ['pɒndə*] *vt* nachdenken über +*akk*
pony ['pəʊnɪ] *n* Pony *nt*; **ponytail** *n* Pferdeschwanz *m*
poodle ['pu:dl] *n* Pudel *m*
pool [pu:l] *n* (*swimming ~*) Schwimmbad *nt*; (*private*) Swimmingpool *m*; (*of spilt liquid, blood*) Lache *f*; (*game*) Poolbillard *nt* ▷ *vt* (*money etc*) zusammenlegen
poor [pɔ:*] *adj* arm; (*not good*) schlecht ▷ *npl* **the ~** die Armen *pl*; **poorly** *adv* (*badly*) schlecht ▷ *adj* (*Brit*) krank
pop [pɒp] *n* (*music*) Pop *m*; (*noise*) Knall *m* ▷ *vt* (*put*) stecken; (*balloon*) platzen lassen ▷ *vi* (*balloon*) platzen; (*cork*) knallen; **to ~ in** (*person*) vorbeischauen; **pop concert** *n* Popkonzert *nt*; **popcorn** *n* Popcorn *nt*

Pope [pəʊp] *n* Papst *m*
pop group ['pɒpgru:p] *n* Popgruppe *f*; **pop music** *n* Popmusik *f*
poppy ['pɒpɪ] *n* Mohn *m*
Popsicle® ['pɒpsɪkl] *n* (*US*) Eis *nt* am Stiel
pop star ['pɒpstɑ:*] *n* Popstar *m*
popular ['pɒpjʊlə*] *adj* (*well-liked*) beliebt (*with* bei); (*widespread*) weit verbreitet
population [pɒpjʊ'leɪʃən] *n* Bevölkerung *f*; (*of town*) Einwohner *pl*
porcelain ['pɔ:slɪn] *n* Porzellan *nt*
porch [pɔ:tʃ] *n* Vorbau *m*; (*US: verandah*) Veranda *f*
porcupine ['pɔ:kjʊpaɪn] *n* Stachelschwein *nt*
pork [pɔ:k] *n* Schweinefleisch *nt*; **pork chop** *n* Schweinekotelett; **pork pie** *n* Schweinefleischpastete *f*
porn [pɔ:n] *n* Porno *m*; **pornographic** [pɔ:nə'græfɪk] *adj* pornografisch; **pornography** [pɔ:'nɒgrəfɪ] *n* Pornografie *f*
porridge ['pɒrɪdʒ] *n* Haferbrei *m*
port [pɔ:t] *n* (*harbour*) Hafen *m*; (*town*) Hafenstadt *f*; (*Naut: left side*) Backbord *nt*; (*wine*) Portwein *m*; (*Inform*) Anschluss *m*
portable ['pɔ:təbl] *adj* tragbar; (*radio*) Koffer-
portal ['pɔ:tl] *n* (*Inform*) Portal *nt*
porter ['pɔ:tə*] *n* Pförtner(in) *m(f)*; (*for luggage*) Gepäckträger *m*
porthole ['pɔ:thəʊl] *n* Bullauge *nt*
portion ['pɔ:ʃən] *n* Teil *m*; (*of food*) Portion *f*
portrait ['pɔ:trɪt] *n* Porträt *nt*
portray [pɔ:'treɪ] *vt* darstellen
Portugal ['pɔ:tʃʊgl] *n* Portugal *nt*; **Portuguese** [pɔ:tʃʊ'gi:z] *adj* portugiesisch ▷ *n* Portugiese *m*, Portugiesin *f*; (*language*) Portugiesisch *nt*
pose [pəʊz] *n* Haltung *f* ▷ *vi* posieren ▷ *vt* (*threat, problem*) darstellen
posh [pɒʃ] *adj* (*fam*) piekfein
position [pə'zɪʃən] *n* Stellung *f*; (*place*) Position *f*, Lage *f*; (*job*) Stelle *f*; (*opinion*) Standpunkt *m*; **to be in a ~ to do sth** in der Lage sein, etw zu tun; **in third ~** auf dem dritten Platz ▷ *vt* aufstellen; (*Inform: cursor*) positionieren
positive ['pɒzɪtɪv] *adj* positiv; (*convinced*) sicher; (*definite*) eindeutig
possess [pə'zes] *vt* besitzen; **possession**

p

[pəˈzeʃən] n ~(s pl) Besitz m; **possessive**
adj (person) Besitz ergreifend
possibility [pɒsəˈbɪlɪtɪ] n Möglichkeit f;
possible [ˈpɒsəbl] adj möglich; **if ~** wenn
möglich; **as big/soon as ~** so groß/bald
wie möglich; **possibly** adv (perhaps)
vielleicht; **I've done all I ~ can** ich habe
mein Möglichstes getan
post [pəʊst] n (mail) Post f; (pole) Pfosten
m; (job) Stelle f ▷ vt (letters) aufgeben; **to
keep sb ~ed** jdn auf dem Laufenden
halten; **postage** [ˈpəʊstɪdʒ] n Porto nt;
~ and packing Porto und Verpackung;
postal adj Post-; (Brit) **~ order**
Postanweisung f; **postbox** n Briefkasten
m; **postcard** n Postkarte f; **postcode** n
(Brit) Postleitzahl f
poster [ˈpəʊstə*] n Plakat nt, Poster nt
postgraduate [pəʊstˈɡrædjuɪt] n jmd, der
seine Studien nach dem ersten akademischen
Grad weiterführt
postman [ˈpəʊstmən] (pl **-men**) n
Briefträger m; **postmark** n Poststempel
m
postmortem [pəʊstˈmɔːtəm] n Autopsie
f
post office [ˈpəʊstɒfɪs] n Post® f; **post
office box** n Postfach nt
postpone [pəˈspəʊn] vt verschieben (till
auf +akk)
posture [ˈpɒstʃə*] n Haltung f
pot [pɒt] n Topf m; (tea~, coffee ~) Kanne f;
(fam: marijuana) Pot nt ▷ vt (plant)
eintopfen
potato [pəˈteɪtəʊ] (pl **-es**) n Kartoffel f;
potato chips (US) npl Kartoffelchips pl;
potato peeler n Kartoffelschäler m
potent [ˈpəʊtənt] adj stark
potential [pəʊˈtenʃəl] adj potenziell ▷ n
Potenzial nt; **potentially** adv potenziell
pothole [ˈpɒthəʊl] n Höhle f; (in road)
Schlagloch nt
potter about [ˈpɒtərəbaʊt] vi
herumhantieren
pottery [ˈpɒtərɪ] n (objects) Töpferwaren
pl
potty [ˈpɒtɪ] adj (Brit fam) verrückt ▷ n
Töpfchen nt
poultry [ˈpəʊltrɪ] n Geflügel nt
pounce [paʊns] vi **to ~ on** sich stürzen
auf +akk
pound [paʊnd] n (money) Pfund nt;
(weight) Pfund nt (0,454 kg); **a ~ of cherries**

ein Pfund Kirschen; **ten-~ note**
Zehnpfundschein m
pour [pɔː*] vt (liquid) gießen; (rice, sugar
etc) schütten; **to ~ sb sth** (drink) jdm etw
eingießen; **pouring** adj (rain) strömend
poverty [ˈpɒvətɪ] n Armut f
powder [ˈpaʊdə*] n Pulver nt; (cosmetic)
Puder m; **powdered milk** n Milchpulver
nt; **powder room** n Damentoilette f
power [ˈpaʊə*] n Macht f; (ability)
Fähigkeit f; (strength) Stärke f; (Elec) Strom
m; **to be in ~** an der Macht sein ▷ vt
betreiben, antreiben; **power-assisted
steering** n Servolenkung f; **power cut** n
Stromausfall m; **powerful** adj (politician
etc) mächtig; (engine, government) stark;
(argument) durchschlagend; **powerless**
adj machtlos; **power station** n
Kraftwerk nt
p&p abbr = postage and packing
PR abbr = public relations ▷ abbr =
proportional representation
practical, practically [ˈpræktɪkəl, -ɪ] adj,
adv praktisch; **practice** [ˈpræktɪs] n
(training) Übung f; (custom) Gewohnheit f;
(doctor's, lawyer's) Praxis f; **in ~** (in reality) in
der Praxis; **out of ~** außer Übung; **to put
sth into ~** etw in die Praxis umsetzen ▷ vt,
vi (US) see **practise**; **practise** [ˈpræktɪs] vt
(instrument, movement) üben; (profession)
ausüben ▷ vi üben; (doctor, lawyer)
praktizieren
Prague [prɑːɡ] n Prag nt
praise [preɪz] n Lob nt ▷ vt loben
pram [præm] n (Brit) Kinderwagen m
prawn [prɔːn] n Garnele f, Krabbe f;
prawn crackers npl Krabbenchips pl
pray [preɪ] vi beten; **to ~ for sth** (fig)
stark auf etw akk hoffen; **prayer** [ˈprɛə*] n
Gebet nt
pre- [priː] pref vor-, prä-
preach [priːtʃ] vi predigen
prearrange [priːəˈreɪndʒ] vt im Voraus
vereinbaren
precaution [prɪˈkɔːʃən] n
Vorsichtsmaßnahme f
precede [prɪˈsiːd] vt vorausgehen +dat;
preceding adj vorhergehend
precinct [ˈpriːsɪŋkt] n (Brit: pedestrian ~)
Fußgängerzone f; (Brit: shopping ~)
Einkaufsviertel nt; (US: district) Bezirk m
precious [ˈpreʃəs] adj kostbar; **~ stone**
Edelstein m

précis ['preɪsiː] n Zusammenfassung f
precise, **precisely** [prɪ'saɪs, -lɪ] adj, adv
genau
precondition [priːkən'dɪʃən] n
Vorbedingung f
predecessor ['priːdɪsesə*] n
Vorgänger(in) m(f)
predicament [prɪ'dɪkəmənt] n missliche
Lage
predict [prɪ'dɪkt] vt voraussagen;
predictable adj vorhersehbar; (person)
berechenbar
predominant [prɪ'dɒmɪnənt] adj
vorherrschend; **predominantly** adv
überwiegend
preface ['prefɪs] n Vorwort nt
prefer [prɪ'fɜː*] vt vorziehen (to dat),
lieber mögen (to als); **to ~ to do sth** etw
lieber tun; **preferably** ['prefrəblɪ] adv
vorzugsweise, am liebsten; **preference**
['prefərəns] n (liking) Vorliebe f;
preferential [prefə'renʃəl] adj **to get**
~ treatment bevorzugt behandelt
werden
prefix ['priːfɪks] n (US Tel) Vorwahl f
pregnancy ['pregnənsɪ] n
Schwangerschaft f; **pregnant** ['pregnənt]
adj schwanger; **two months ~** im zweiten
Monat schwanger
prejudice ['predʒʊdɪs] n Vorurteil nt;
prejudiced adj (person)
voreingenommen
preliminary [prɪ'lɪmɪnərɪ] adj (measures)
vorbereitend; (results) vorläufig; (remarks)
einleitend
premature ['premətʃʊə*] adj vorzeitig;
(hasty) voreilig
premiere ['premɪɛə*] n Premiere f
premises ['premɪsɪz] npl (offices)
Räumlichkeiten pl; (of factory, school)
Gelände nt
premium-rate ['priːmɪəmreɪt] adj (Tel)
zum Höchsttarif
preoccupied [priː'ɒkjʊpaɪd] adj **to be**
~ with sth mit etw sehr beschäftigt sein
prepaid [priː'peɪd] adj vorausbezahlt;
(envelope) frankiert
preparation [prepə'reɪʃən] n
Vorbereitung f; **prepare** [prɪ'pɛə*] vt
vorbereiten (for auf +akk); (food)
zubereiten; **to be ~d to do sth** bereit sein,
etw zu tun ▷ vi sich vorbereiten (for auf
+akk)

prerequisite [priː'rekwɪzɪt] n
Voraussetzung f
prescribe [prɪ'skraɪb] vt vorschreiben;
(Med) verschreiben; **prescription**
[prɪ'skrɪpʃən] n Rezept nt
presence ['prezns] n Gegenwart f;
present ['preznt] adj (in attendance)
anwesend (at bei); (current) gegenwärtig;
~ tense Gegenwart f, Präsens nt ▷ n
Gegenwart f; (gift) Geschenk nt; **at**
~ zurzeit ▷ [prɪ'zent] vt (Tv, Radio)
präsentieren; (problem) darstellen; (report
etc) vorlegen; **to ~ sb with sth** jdm etw
überreichen; **present-day** adj heutig;
presently adv bald; (at present) zurzeit
preservative [prɪ'zɜːvətɪv] n
Konservierungsmittel nt; **preserve**
[prɪ'zɜːv] vt erhalten; (food) einmachen,
konservieren
president ['prezɪdənt] n Präsident(in)
m(f); **presidential** [prezɪ'denʃəl] adj
Präsidenten-; (election) Präsidentschafts-
press [pres] n (newspapers, machine) Presse
f ▷ vt (push) drücken; **to ~ a button** auf
einen Knopf drücken ▷ vi (push) drücken;
pressing adj dringend; **press-stud** n
Druckknopf m; **press-up** n (Brit)
Liegestütz m; **pressure** ['preʃə*] n Druck
m; **to be under ~** unter Druck stehen; **to**
put ~ on sb jdn unter Druck setzen;
pressure cooker n Schnellkochtopf m;
pressurize ['preʃəraɪz] vt (person) unter
Druck setzen
presumably [prɪ'zjuːməblɪ] adv
vermutlich; **presume** [prɪ'zjuːm] vt, vi
annehmen
presumptuous [prɪ'zʌmptʃʊəs] adj
anmaßend
presuppose [priːsə'pəʊz] vt
voraussetzen
pretend [prɪ'tend] vt **to ~ that** so tun als
ob; **to ~ to do sth** vorgeben, etw zu tun
▷ vi **she's ~ing** sie tut nur so
pretentious [prɪ'tenʃəs] adj anmaßend;
(person) wichtigtuerisch
pretty ['prɪtɪ] adj hübsch ▷ adv ziemlich
prevent [prɪ'vent] vt verhindern; **to ~ sb**
from doing sth jdn daran hindern, etw zu
tun
preview ['priːvjuː] n (Cine)
Voraufführung f; (trailer) Vorschau f
previous, **previously** ['priːvɪəs, -lɪ] adj,
adv früher

p

prey [preɪ] *n* Beute *f*

price [praɪs] *n* Preis *m* ▷ *vt* **it's ~d at £10** es ist mit 10 Pfund ausgezeichnet; **priceless** *adj* unbezahlbar; **price list** *n* Preisliste *f*; **price tag** *n* Preisschild *nt*

prick [prɪk] *n* Stich *m*; (*vulg: penis*) Schwanz *m*; (*vulg: person*) Arsch *m* ▷ *vt* stechen in +*akk*; **to ~ one's finger** sich *dat* in den Finger stechen; **prickly** ['prɪklɪ] *adj* stachelig

pride [praɪd] *n* Stolz *m*; (*arrogance*) Hochmut *m* ▷ *vt* **to ~ oneself on sth** auf etw *akk* stolz sein

priest [priːst] *n* Priester *m*

primarily ['praɪmərɪlɪ] *adv* vorwiegend; **primary** ['praɪmərɪ] *adj* Haupt-; **~ education** Grundschulausbildung *f*; **~ school** Grundschule *f*

prime [praɪm] *adj* Haupt-; (*excellent*) erstklassig ▷ *n* **in one's ~** in den besten Jahren; **prime minister** *n* Premierminister(in) *m(f)*; **prime time** *n* (*TV*) Hauptsendezeit *f*

primitive ['prɪmɪtɪv] *adj* primitiv

primrose ['prɪmrəʊz] *n* Schlüsselblume *f*

prince [prɪns] *n* Prinz *m*; (*ruler*) Fürst *m*; **princess** [prɪn'ses] *n* Prinzessin *f*; (*wife of ruler*) Fürstin *f*

principal ['prɪnsɪpəl] *adj* Haupt-, wichtigste(r, s) ▷ *n* (*school*) Rektor(in) *m(f)*

principle ['prɪnsəpl] *n* Prinzip *nt*; **in ~** im Prinzip; **on ~** aus Prinzip

print [prɪnt] *n* (*picture*) Druck *m*; (*Foto*) Abzug *m*; (*made by feet, fingers*) Abdruck *m*; **out of ~** vergriffen ▷ *vt* drucken; (*photo*) abziehen; (*write in block letters*) in Druckschrift schreiben; **print out** *vt* (*Inform*) ausdrucken; **printed matter** *n* Drucksache *f*; **printer** *n* Drucker *m*; **printout** *n* (*Inform*) Ausdruck *m*

prior ['praɪə*] *adj* früher; **a ~ engagement** eine vorher getroffene Verabredung; **~ to sth** vor etw *dat*; **~ to going abroad, she had …** bevor sie ins Ausland ging, hatte sie …

priority [praɪ'ɒrɪtɪ] *n* (*thing having precedence*) Priorität *f*

prison ['prɪzn] *n* Gefängnis *nt*; **prisoner** *n* Gefangene(r) *mf*; **~ of war** Kriegsgefangene(r) *mf*

privacy ['prɪvəsɪ] *n* Privatleben *nt*; **private** ['praɪvɪt] *adj* privat; (*confidential*) vertraulich ▷ *n* einfacher Soldat; **in ~** privat; **privately** *adv* privat; (*confidentially*) vertraulich; **privatize** ['praɪvətaɪz] *vt* privatisieren

privilege ['prɪvɪlɪdʒ] *n* Privileg *nt*; **privileged** *adj* privilegiert

prize [praɪz] *n* Preis *m*; **prize money** *n* Preisgeld *nt*; **prizewinner** *n* Gewinner(in) *m(f)*; **prizewinning** *adj* preisgekrönt

pro [prəʊ] (*pl* **-s**) *n* (*professional*) Profi *m*; **the ~s and cons** *pl* das Für und Wider

pro- [prəʊ] *pref* pro-

probability [prɒbə'bɪlɪtɪ] *n* Wahrscheinlichkeit *f*; **probable, probably** ['prɒbəbl, -blɪ] *adj, adv* wahrscheinlich

probation [prə'beɪʃən] *n* Probezeit *f*; (*Jur*) Bewährung *f*

probe [prəʊb] *n* (*investigation*) Untersuchung *f* ▷ *vt* untersuchen

problem ['prɒbləm] *n* Problem *nt*; **no ~** kein Problem!

procedure [prə'siːdʒə*] *n* Verfahren *nt*

proceed [prə'siːd] *vi* (*continue*) fortfahren; (*set about sth*) vorgehen ▷ *vt* **to ~ to do sth** anfangen, etw zu tun; **proceedings** *npl* (*Jur*) Verfahren *nt*; **proceeds** ['prəʊsiːds] *npl* Erlös *m*

process ['prəʊses] *n* Prozess *m*, Vorgang *m*; (*method*) Verfahren *nt* ▷ *vt* (*application etc*) bearbeiten; (*food, data*) verarbeiten; (*film*) entwickeln

procession [prə'seʃən] *n* Umzug *m*

processor ['prəʊsesə*] *n* (*Inform*) Prozessor *m*; (*Gastr*) Küchenmaschine *f*

produce ['prɒdjuːs] *n* (*Agr*) Produkte *pl*, Erzeugnisse *pl* ▷ [prə'djuːs] *vt* (*manufacture*) herstellen, produzieren; (*on farm*) erzeugen; (*film, play, record*) produzieren; (*cause*) hervorrufen; (*evidence, results*) liefern; **producer** *n* (*manufacturer*) Hersteller(in) *m(f)*; (*of film, play, record*) Produzent(in) *m(f)*; **product** ['prɒdʌkt] *n* Produkt *nt*, Erzeugnis *nt*; **production** [prə'dʌkʃən] *n* Produktion *f*; (*Theat*) Inszenierung *f*; **productive** [prə'dʌktɪv] *adj* produktiv; (*land*) ertragreich

prof [prɒf] *n* (*fam*) Professor(in) *m(f)*

profession [prə'feʃən] *n* Beruf *m*; **professional** [prə'feʃnl] *n* Profi *m* ▷ *adj* beruflich; (*expert*) fachlich; (*sportsman, actor etc*) Berufs-

professor [prə'fesə*] *n* Professor(in) *m(f)*; (*US: lecturer*) Dozent(in) *m(f)*

proficient [prə'fɪʃənt] adj kompetent (in in +dat)

profile ['prəufaɪl] n Profil nt; **to keep a low ~** sich rar machen

profit ['prɒfɪt] n Gewinn m ▷ vi profitieren (by, from von); **profitable** adj rentabel

profound [prə'faund] adj tief; (idea, thinker) tiefgründig; (knowledge) profund

program ['prəugræm] n (Inform) Programm nt; (US) see **programme** ▷ vt (Inform) programmieren; (US) see **programme**

programme ['prəugræm] n Programm nt; (Tv, Radio) Sendung f ▷ vt programmieren; **programmer** n Programmierer(in) m(f); **programming** n (Inform) Programmieren nt; **~ language** Programmiersprache f

progress ['prəugres] n Fortschritt m; **to make ~** Fortschritte machen ▷ [prə'gres] vi (work, illness etc) fortschreiten; (improve) Fortschritte machen; **progressive** [prə'gresɪv] adj (person, policy) fortschrittlich; **progressively** [prə'gresɪvlɪ] adv zunehmend

prohibit [prə'hɪbɪt] vt verbieten

project ['prɒdʒekt] n Projekt nt

projector [prə'dʒektə*] n Projektor m

prolong [prə'lɒŋ] vt verlängern

prom [prɒm] n (at seaside) Promenade f; (Brit: concert) Konzert nt (bei dem ein Großteil des Publikums im Parkett Stehplätze hat); (US: dance) Ball für die Schüler und Studenten von Highschools oder Colleges

prominent ['prɒmɪnənt] adj (politician, actor etc) prominent; (easily seen) auffallend

promiscuous [prə'mɪskjuəs] adj promisk

promise ['prɒmɪs] n Versprechen nt ▷ vt versprechen; **to ~ sb sth** jdm etw versprechen; **to ~ to do sth** versprechen, etw zu tun ▷ vi versprechen; **promising** adj viel versprechend

promote [prə'məut] vt (in rank) befördern; (help on) fördern; (Comm) werben für; **promotion** [prə'məuʃən] n (in rank) Beförderung f; (Comm) Werbung f (of für)

prompt [prɒmpt] adj prompt; (punctual) pünktlich ▷ adv **at two o'clock ~** Punkt zwei Uhr ▷ vt (Theat: actor) soufflieren +dat

prone [prəun] adj **to be ~ to sth** zu etw neigen

pronounce [prə'nauns] vt (word) aussprechen; **pronounced** adj ausgeprägt; **pronunciation** [prənʌnsɪ'eɪʃən] n Aussprache f

proof [pru:f] n Beweis m; (of alcohol) Alkoholgehalt m

prop [prɒp] n Stütze f; (Theat) Requisit nt ▷ vt **to ~ sth against sth** etw gegen etw lehnen; **prop up** vt stützen; (fig) unterstützen

proper ['prɒpə*] adj richtig; (morally correct) anständig

property ['prɒpətɪ] n (possession) Eigentum nt; (house) Haus nt; (land) Grundbesitz m; (characteristic) Eigenschaft f

proportion [prə'pɔːʃən] n Verhältnis nt; (share) Teil m; **~s** pl (size) Proportionen pl; **in ~ to** im Verhältnis zu; **proportional** adj proportional; **~ representation** Verhältniswahlrecht nt

proposal [prə'pəuzl] n Vorschlag m; **~ (of marriage)** (Heirats)antrag m; **propose** [prə'pəuz] vt vorschlagen ▷ vi (offer marriage) einen Heiratsantrag machen (to sb jdm)

proprietor [prə'praɪətə*] n Besitzer(in) m(f); (of pub, hotel) Inhaber(in) m(f)

prose [prəuz] n Prosa f

prosecute ['prɒsɪkjuːt] vt verfolgen (for wegen)

prospect ['prɒspekt] n Aussicht f

prosperity [prɒ'sperɪtɪ] n Wohlstand m; **prosperous** adj wohlhabend; (business) gut gehend

prostitute ['prɒstɪtjuːt] n Prostituierte(r) mf

protect [prə'tekt] vt schützen (from, against vor +dat, gegen); **protection** [prə'tekʃən] n Schutz m (from, against vor +dat, gegen); **protective** adj beschützend; (clothing etc) Schutz-

protein ['prəutiːn] n Protein nt, Eiweiß nt

protest ['prəutest] n Protest m; (demonstration) Protestkundgebung f ▷ [prə'test] vi protestieren (against gegen); (demonstrate) demonstrieren

Protestant ['prɒtəstənt] adj protestantisch ▷ n Protestant(in) m(f)

proud, proudly [praud, -lɪ] adj, adv stolz (of auf +akk)

prove [pruːv] *vt* beweisen; (*turn out to be*) sich erweisen als

proverb ['prɒvɜːb] *n* Sprichwort *nt*

provide [prə'vaɪd] *vt* zur Verfügung stellen; (*drinks, music etc*) sorgen für; (*person*) versorgen (*with* mit); **provide for** *vt* (*family etc*) sorgen für; **provided** *conj* **~ (that)** vorausgesetzt, dass; **provider** *n* (*Inform*) Provider *m*

provision [prə'vɪʒən] *n* (*condition*) Bestimmung *f*; **~s** *pl* (*food*) Proviant *m*

provisional, provisionally [prə'vɪʒnl, -ɪ] *adj, adv* provisorisch

provoke [prə'vəuk] *vt* provozieren; (*cause*) hervorrufen

proximity [prɒk'sɪmɪtɪ] *n* Nähe *f*

prudent ['pruːdənt] *adj* klug; (*person*) umsichtig

prudish ['pruːdɪʃ] *adj* prüde

prune [pruːn] *n* Backpflaume *f* ▷ *vt* (*tree etc*) zurechtstutzen

PS *abbr* = **postscript** PS *nt*

psalm [sɑːm] *n* Psalm *m*

pseudo ['sjuːdəu] *adj* pseudo-, Pseudo-; **pseudonym** ['sjuːdənɪm] *n* Pseudonym *nt*

PST *abbr* = **Pacific Standard Time**

psychiatric [saɪkɪ'ætrɪk] *adj* psychiatrisch; (*illness*) psychisch; **psychiatrist** [saɪ'kaɪətrɪst] *n* Psychiater(in) *m(f)*; **psychiatry** [saɪ'kaɪətrɪ] *n* Psychiatrie *f*; **psychic** ['saɪkɪk] *adj* übersinnlich; **I'm not ~** ich kann keine Gedanken lesen; **psychoanalysis** [saɪkəuə'næləsɪs] *n* Psychoanalyse *f*; **psychoanalyst** [saɪkəu'ænəlɪst] *n* Psychoanalytiker(in) *m(f)*; **psychological** [saɪkə'lɒdʒɪkəl] *adj* psychologisch; **psychology** [saɪ'kɒlədʒɪ] *n* Psychologie *f*; **psychopath** ['saɪkəupæθ] *n* Psychopath(in) *m(f)*

pt *abbr* = **pint**

pto *abbr* = **please turn over** b.w.

pub [pʌb] *n* (*Brit*) Kneipe *f*

● **pub**
●
● Ein **pub** ist ein Gasthaus mit einer
● Lizenz zum Ausschank von
● alkoholischen Getränken. Ein „Pub"
● besteht meist aus verschiedenen
● gemütlichen (**lounge, snug**) oder
● einfacheren (**public bar**) Räumen, in
● denen oft auch Spiele wie Darts,
● Domino und Poolbillard zur
● Verfügung stehen. In „Pubs" werden
● vor allem mittags auch Mahlzeiten
● angeboten (**pub lunch**). „Pubs" sind
● normalerweise von 11 bis 23 Uhr
● geöffnet, aber manchmal
● nachmittags geschlossen.

puberty ['pjuːbətɪ] *n* Pubertät *f*

public ['pʌblɪk] *n* **the (general) ~** die (breite) Öffentlichkeit; **in ~** in der Öffentlichkeit ▷ *adj* öffentlich; (*relating to the State*) Staats-; **~ convenience** (*Brit*) öffentliche Toilette; **~ holiday** gesetzlicher Feiertag; **~ opinion** die öffentliche Meinung; **~ relations** *pl* Öffentlichkeitsarbeit *f*, Public Relations *pl*; **~ school** (*Brit*) Privatschule *f*; **publication** [pʌblɪ'keɪʃən] *n* Veröffentlichung *f*; **publicity** [pʌb'lɪsɪtɪ] *n* Publicity *f*; (*advertisements*) Werbung *f*; **publish** ['pʌblɪʃ] *vt* veröffentlichen; **publisher** *n* Verleger(in) *m(f)*; (*company*) Verlag *m*; **publishing** *n* Verlagswesen *nt*

pub lunch ['pʌb'lʌntʃ] *n* (*oft einfacheres*) Mittagessen in einer Kneipe

pudding ['pudɪŋ] *n* (*course*) Nachtisch *m*

puddle ['pʌdl] *n* Pfütze *f*

puff [pʌf] *vi* (*pant*) schnaufen

puffin ['pʌfɪn] *n* Papageientaucher *m*

puff paste (*US*), **puff pastry** ['pʌf'peɪstrɪ] *n* Blätterteig *m*

pull [pul] *n* Ziehen *nt*; **to give sth a ~** an etw *dat* ziehen ▷ *vt* (*cart, tooth*) ziehen; (*rope, handle*) ziehen an +*dat*; (*fam: drag*) abschleppen; **to ~ a muscle** sich *dat* einen Muskel zerren; **to ~ sb's leg** jdn auf den Arm nehmen ▷ *vi* ziehen; **pull apart** *vt* (*separate*) auseinander ziehen; **pull down** *vt* (*blind*) herunterziehen; (*house*) abreißen; **pull in** *vi* hineinfahren; (*stop*) anhalten; **pull off** *vt* (*clothes*) ausziehen; (*deal etc*) zuwege bringen; **pull on** *vt* (*clothes*) anziehen; **pull out** *vi* (*car from lane*) ausscheren; (*train*) abfahren; (*withdraw*) aussteigen (*of* aus) ▷ *vt* herausziehen; (*tooth*) ziehen; (*troops*) abziehen; **pull round, pull through** *vi* durchkommen; **pull up** *vt* (*raise*) hochziehen; (*chair*) heranziehen ▷ *vi* anhalten

pullover ['puləuvə*] *n* Pullover *m*

pulp [pʌlp] *n* Brei *m*; (*of fruit*) Fruchtfleisch *nt*

pulpit ['pʊlpɪt] *n* Kanzel *f*

pulse [pʌls] *n* Puls *m*

pump [pʌmp] *n* Pumpe *f*; (*in petrol station*) Zapfsäule *f*; **pump up** *vt* (*tyre etc*) aufpumpen

pumpkin ['pʌmpkɪn] *n* Kürbis *m*

pun [pʌn] *n* Wortspiel *nt*

punch [pʌntʃ] *n* (*blow*) (Faust)schlag *m*; (*tool*) Locher *m*; (*hot drink*) Punsch *m*; (*cold drink*) Bowle *f* ▷ *vt* (*strike*) schlagen; (*ticket, paper*) lochen

punctual, punctually ['pʌŋktjʊəl, -ɪ] *adj, adv* pünktlich

punctuation [pʌŋktjʊ'eɪʃən] *n* Interpunktion *f*; **punctuation mark** *n* Satzzeichen *nt*

puncture ['pʌŋktʃə*] *n* (*flat tyre*) Reifenpanne *f*

punish ['pʌnɪʃ] *vt* bestrafen; **punishment** *n* Strafe *f*; (*action*) Bestrafung *f*

pupil ['pjuːpl] *n* (*school*) Schüler(in) *m(f)*

puppet ['pʌpɪt] *n* Puppe *f*; (*string ~*) Marionette *f*

puppy ['pʌpɪ] *n* junger Hund

purchase ['pɜːtʃɪs] *n* Kauf *m* ▷ *vt* kaufen

pure [pjʊə*] *adj* rein; (*clean*) sauber; (*utter*) pur; **purely** ['pjʊəlɪ] *adv* rein; **purify** ['pjʊərɪfaɪ] *vt* reinigen; **purity** ['pjʊərɪtɪ] *n* Reinheit *f*

purple ['pɜːpl] *adj* violett

purpose ['pɜːpəs] *n* Zweck *m*; (*of person*) Absicht *f*; **on ~** absichtlich

purr [pɜː*] *vi* (*cat*) schnurren

purse [pɜːs] *n* Geldbeutel *m*; (*US: handbag*) Handtasche *f*

pursue [pə'sjuː] *vt* (*person, car*) verfolgen; (*hobby, studies*) nachgehen +*dat*; **pursuit** [pə'sjuːt] *n* (*chase*) Verfolgung *f*; (*occupation*) Beschäftigung *f*; (*hobby*) Hobby *nt*

pus [pʌs] *n* Eiter *m*

push [pʊʃ] *n* Stoß *m* ▷ *vt* (*person*) stoßen; (*car, chair etc*) schieben; (*button*) drücken; (*drugs*) dealen ▷ *vi* (*in crowd*) drängeln; **push in** *vi* (*in queue*) sich vordrängeln; **push off** *vi* (*fam: leave*) abhauen; **push on** *vi* (*with job*) weitermachen; **push up** *vt* (*prices*) hochtreiben; **pushchair** *n* (*Brit*) Sportwagen *m*; **pusher** *n* (*of drugs*) Dealer(in) *m(f)*; **push-up** *n* (*US*)

Liegestütz *m*; **pushy** *adj* (*fam*) aufdringlich, penetrant

put [pʊt] (**put, put**) *vt* tun; (*upright*) stellen; (*flat*) legen; (*express*) ausdrücken; (*write*) schreiben; **he ~ his hand in his pocket** er steckte die Hand in die Tasche; **he ~ his hand on her shoulder** er legte ihr die Hand auf die Schulter; **to ~ money into one's account** Geld auf sein Konto einzahlen; **put aside** *vt* (*money*) zurücklegen; **put away** *vt* (*tidy away*) wegräumen; **put back** *vt* zurücklegen; (*clock*) zurückstellen; **put down** *vt* (*in writing*) aufschreiben; (*Brit: animal*) einschläfern; (*rebellion*) niederschlagen; **to put the phone down** (den Hörer) auflegen; **to put one's name down for sth** sich für etw eintragen; **put forward** *vt* (*idea*) vorbringen; (*name*) vorschlagen; (*clock*) vorstellen; **put in** *vt* (*install*) einbauen; (*submit*) einreichen; **put off** *vt* (*switch off*) ausschalten; (*postpone*) verschieben; **to put sb off doing sth** jdn davon abbringen, etw zu tun; **put on** *vt* (*switch on*) anmachen; (*clothes*) anziehen; (*hat, glasses*) aufsetzen; (*make-up, CD*) auflegen; (*play*) aufführen; **to put the kettle on** Wasser aufsetzen; **to put weight on** zunehmen; **put out** *vt* (*hand, foot*) ausstrecken; (*light, cigarette*) ausmachen; **put up** *vt* (*hand*) hochheben; (*picture*) aufhängen; (*tent*) aufstellen; (*building*) errichten; (*price*) erhöhen; (*person*) unterbringen; **to ~ with** sich abfinden mit; **I won't ~ with it** das lasse ich mir nicht gefallen

putt [pʌt] *vt, vi* (*Sport*) putten

puzzle ['pʌzl] *n* Rätsel *nt*; (*toy*) Geduldsspiel *nt*; (**jigsaw**) **~** Puzzle *nt* ▷ *vt* vor ein Rätsel stellen; **it ~s me** es ist mir ein Rätsel; **puzzling** *adj* rätselhaft

pyjamas [pɪ'dʒɑːməz] *npl* Schlafanzug *m*

pylon ['paɪlən] *n* Mast *m*

pyramid ['pɪrəmɪd] *n* Pyramide *f*

quack [kwæk] *vi* quaken

quaint [kweɪnt] *adj* (*idea, tradition*) kurios; (*picturesque*) malerisch

qualification [kwɒlɪfɪˈkeɪʃən] *n* (*for job*) Qualifikation *f*; (*from school, university*) Abschluss *m*; **qualified** [ˈkwɒlɪfaɪd] *adj* (*for job*) qualifiziert; **qualify** *vt* (*limit*) einschränken; **to be qualified to do sth** berechtigt sein, etw zu tun ▷ *vi* (*finish training*) seine Ausbildung abschließen; (*Sport*) sich qualifizieren

quality [ˈkwɒlɪtɪ] *n* Qualität *f*; (*characteristic*) Eigenschaft *f*

quantity [ˈkwɒntɪtɪ] *n* Menge *f*, Quantität *f*

quarantine [ˈkwɒrənti:n] *n* Quarantäne *f*

quarrel [ˈkwɒrəl] *n* Streit *m* ▷ *vi* sich streiten; **quarrelsome** *adj* streitsüchtig

quarter [ˈkwɔ:tə*] *n* Viertel *nt*; (*of year*) Vierteljahr *nt*; (*US: coin*) Vierteldollar *m*; **a ~ of an hour** eine Viertelstunde; **~ to/past** (*Brit*) (*o* **~ of/after** (*US*)) **three** Viertel vor/nach drei ▷ *vt* vierteln; **quarter final** *n* Viertelfinale *nt*; **quarters** *npl* (*Mil*) Quartier *nt*

quartet [kwɔ:ˈtet] *n* Quartett *nt*

quay [ki:] *n* Kai *m*

queasy [ˈkwi:zɪ] *adj* **I feel ~** mir ist übel

queen [kwi:n] *n* Königin *f*; (*in cards, chess*) Dame *f*

queer [kwɪə*] *adj* (*strange*) seltsam, sonderbar; (*pej: homosexual*) schwul ▷ *n* (*pej*) Schwule(r) *m*

quench [kwentʃ] *vt* (*thirst*) löschen

query [ˈkwɪərɪ] *n* Frage *f* ▷ *vt* in Frage stellen; (*bill*) reklamieren

question [ˈkwestʃən] *n* Frage *f*; **that's out of the ~** das kommt nicht in Frage ▷ *vt* (*person*) befragen; (*suspect*) verhören; (*express doubt about*) bezweifeln; **questionable** *adj* zweifelhaft; (*improper*) fragwürdig; **question mark** *n* Fragezeichen *nt*; **questionnaire** [kwestʃəˈnɛə*] *n* Fragebogen *m*

queue [kju:] *n* (*Brit*) Schlange *f*; **to jump the ~** sich vordrängeln ▷ *vi* **to ~ (up)** Schlange stehen

quibble [ˈkwɪbl] *vi* kleinlich sein; (*argue*) streiten

quiche [ki:ʃ] *n* Quiche *f*

quick [kwɪk] *adj* schnell; (*short*) kurz; **be ~ mach schnell!**; **quickly** *adv* schnell

quid [kwɪd] *n* (*pl* **quid**) *n* (*Brit fam*) Pfund *nt*; **20 ~** 20 Pfund

quiet [ˈkwaɪət] *adj* (*not noisy*) leise; (*peaceful, calm*) still, ruhig; **be ~** sei still!; **to keep ~ about sth** über etw *akk* nichts sagen ▷ *n* Stille *f*, Ruhe *f*; **quiet down** (*US*), **quieten down** [ˈkwaɪətənˈdaʊn] *vi* sich beruhigen ▷ *vt* beruhigen; **quietly** *adv* leise; (*calmly*) ruhig

quilt [kwɪlt] *n* (Stepp)decke *f*

quit [kwɪt] (*pt, pp* **quitted, quit** *o* **quitted**) *vt* (*leave*) verlassen; (*job*) aufgeben; **to ~ doing sth** aufhören, etw zu tun ▷ *vi* aufhören; (*resign*) kündigen

quite [kwaɪt] *adv* (*fairly*) ziemlich; (*completely*) ganz, völlig; **I don't ~ understand** ich verstehe das nicht ganz; **~ a few** ziemlich viele; **~ so!** richtig!

quits [kwɪts] *adj* **to be ~ with sb** mit jdm quitt sein

quiver [ˈkwɪvə*] *vi* zittern

quiz [kwɪz] *n* (*competition*) Quiz *nt*

quota [ˈkwəʊtə] *n* Anteil *m*; (*Comm, Pol*) Quote *f*

quotation [kwəʊˈteɪʃən] *n* Zitat *nt*; (*price*) Kostenvoranschlag *m*; **quotation marks** *npl* Anführungszeichen *pl*; **quote** [kwəʊt] *vt* (*text, author*) zitieren; (*price*) nennen ▷ *n* Zitat *nt*; (*price*) Kostenvoranschlag *m*; **in ~s** in Anführungszeichen

q

r

rabbi ['ræbaɪ] n Rabbiner m
rabbit ['ræbɪt] n Kaninchen nt
rabies ['reɪbiːz] nsing Tollwut f
raccoon [rə'kuːn] n Waschbär m
race [reɪs] n (competition) Rennen nt; (people) Rasse f ▷ vt um die Wette laufen/fahren ▷ vi (rush) rennen; **racecourse** n Rennbahn f; **racehorse** n Rennpferd nt; **racetrack** n Rennbahn f
racial ['reɪʃəl] adj Rassen-; **~ discrimination** Rassendiskriminierung f
racing ['reɪsɪŋ] n (horse) **~** Pferderennen nt; (motor) **~** Autorennen nt; **racing car** n Rennwagen m
racism ['reɪsɪzəm] n Rassismus m; **racist** n Rassist(in) m(f) ▷ adj rassistisch
rack [ræk] n Ständer m, Gestell nt ▷ vt **to ~ one's brains** sich dat den Kopf zerbrechen
racket ['rækɪt] n (Sport) Schläger m; (noise) Krach m
radar ['reɪdɑ:*] n Radar nt o m; **radar trap** n Radarfalle f
radiation [reɪdɪ'eɪʃən] n (radioactive) Strahlung f
radiator ['reɪdɪeɪtə*] n Heizkörper m; (Auto) Kühler m

radical ['rædɪkəl] adj radikal
radio ['reɪdɪəʊ] (pl **-s**) n Rundfunk m, Radio nt
radioactivity [reɪdɪəʊæk'tɪvɪtɪ] n Radioaktivität f
radio alarm ['reɪdɪəʊə'lɑːm] n Radiowecker m; **radio station** n Rundfunkstation f
radiotherapy [reɪdɪəʊ'θerəpɪ] n Strahlenbehandlung f
radish ['rædɪʃ] n Radieschen nt
radius ['reɪdɪəs] n Radius m; **within a five-mile ~** im Umkreis von fünf Meilen (of um)
raffle ['ræfl] n Tombola f; **raffle ticket** n Los nt
raft [rɑːft] n Floß nt
rag [ræg] n Lumpen m; (for cleaning) Lappen m
rage [reɪdʒ] n Wut f; **to be all the ~** der letzte Schrei sein ▷ vi toben; (disease) wüten
raid [reɪd] n Überfall m (on auf +akk); (by police) Razzia f (on gegen) ▷ vt (bank etc) überfallen; (by police) eine Razzia machen in +dat
rail [reɪl] n (on stairs, balcony etc) Geländer nt; (of ship) Reling f; (Rail) Schiene f; **railcard** n (Brit) ≈ Bahncard® f; **railing** n Geländer nt; **~s** pl (fence) Zaun m; **railroad** n (US) Eisenbahn f; **railroad station** n (US) Bahnhof m; **railway** n (Brit) Eisenbahn f; **railway line** n Bahnlinie f; (track) Gleis m; **railway station** n Bahnhof m
rain [reɪn] n Regen m ▷ vi regnen; **it's ~ing** es regnet; **rainbow** n Regenbogen m; **raincoat** n Regenmantel m; **rainfall** n Niederschlag m; **rainforest** n Regenwald m; **rainy** adj regnerisch
raise [reɪz] n (US: of wages/salary) Gehalts-/Lohnerhöhung f ▷ vt (lift) hochheben; (increase) erhöhen; (family) großziehen; (livestock) züchten; (money) aufbringen; (objection) erheben; **to ~ one's voice** (in anger) laut werden
raisin ['reɪzən] n Rosine f
rally ['rælɪ] n (Pol) Kundgebung f; (Auto) Rallye f; (Tennis) Ballwechsel m
RAM [ræm] acr = **random access memory** RAM m
ramble ['ræmbl] n Wanderung f ▷ vi (walk) wandern; (talk) schwafeln

ramp [ræmp] n Rampe f
ran [ræn] pt of **run**
ranch [rɑːntʃ] n Ranch f
rancid ['rænsɪd] adj ranzig
random ['rændəm] adj willkürlich ▷ n **at ~ (choose)** willkürlich; (fire) ziellos
randy ['rændɪ] adj (Brit fam) geil, scharf
rang [ræŋ] pt of **ring**
range [reɪndʒ] n (selection) Auswahl f (of an +dat); (Comm) Sortiment nt (of an +dat); (of missile, telescope) Reichweite f; (of mountains) Kette f; **in this price ~** in dieser Preisklasse ▷ vi **to ~ from ... to ...** gehen von ... bis ...; (temperature, sizes, prices) liegen zwischen ... und ...
rank [ræŋk] n (Mil) Rang m; (social position) Stand m ▷ vt einstufen ▷ vi **to ~ among** zählen zu
ransom ['rænsəm] n Lösegeld nt
rap [ræp] n (Mus) Rap m
rape [reɪp] n Vergewaltigung f ▷ vt vergewaltigen
rapid, rapidly ['ræpɪd, -lɪ] adj, adv schnell
rapist ['reɪpɪst] n Vergewaltiger m
rare [rɛə*] adj selten, rar; (especially good) vortrefflich; (steak) blutig; **rarely** adv selten; **rarity** ['rɛərɪtɪ] n Seltenheit f
rash [ræʃ] adj unbesonnen ▷ n (Med) (Haut)ausschlag m
rasher ['ræʃə*] n **~ (of bacon)** (Speck)scheibe f
raspberry ['rɑːzbərɪ] n Himbeere f
rat [ræt] n Ratte f; (pej: person) Schwein nt
rate [reɪt] n (proportion, frequency) Rate f; (speed) Tempo nt; **~ (of exchange)** (Wechsel)kurs m; **~ of inflation** Inflationsrate f; **~ of interest** Zinssatz m; **at any ~** auf jeden Fall ▷ vt (evaluate) einschätzen (as als)
rather ['rɑːðə*] adv (in preference) lieber; (fairly) ziemlich; **I'd ~ stay here** ich würde lieber hier bleiben; **I'd ~ not** lieber nicht; **or ~** (more accurately) vielmehr
ratio ['reɪʃɪəʊ] (pl **-s**) n Verhältnis nt
rational ['ræʃənl] adj rational; **rationalize** ['ræʃnəlaɪz] vt rationalisieren
rattle ['rætl] n (toy) Rassel f ▷ vt (keys, coins) klimpern mit; (person) durcheinander bringen ▷ vi (window) klappern; (bottles) klirren; **rattle off** vt herunterrasseln; **rattlesnake** n Klapperschlange f

rave [reɪv] vi (talk wildly) fantasieren; (rage) toben; (enthuse) schwärmen (about von) ▷ n (Brit: event) Raveparty f
raven ['reɪvn] n Rabe m
raving ['reɪvɪŋ] adv **~ mad** total verrückt
ravishing ['rævɪʃɪŋ] adj hinreißend
raw [rɔː] adj (food) roh; (skin) wund; (climate) rau
ray [reɪ] n (of light) Strahl m; **~ of hope** Hoffnungsschimmer m
razor ['reɪzə*] n Rasierapparat m; **razor blade** n Rasierklinge f
Rd n abbr = **road** Str.
re [riː] prep (Comm) betreffs +gen
RE abbr = **religious education**
reach [riːtʃ] n **within/out of (sb's) ~ in/außer** (jds) Reichweite; **within easy ~ of the shops** nicht weit von den Geschäften ▷ vt (arrive at, contact) erreichen; (come down/up as far as) reichen bis zu; (contact) **can you ~ it?** kommen Sie dran?; **reach for** vt greifen nach; **reach out** vi die Hand ausstrecken; **to ~ for** greifen nach
react [riːˈækt] vi reagieren (to auf +akk); **reaction** [riːˈækʃən] n Reaktion f (to auf +akk); **reactor** [rɪˈæktə*] n Reaktor m
read [riːd] (read, read) vt lesen; (meter) ablesen; **to ~ sth to sb** jdm etw vorlesen ▷ vi lesen; **to ~ to sb** jdm vorlesen; **it ~s well** es liest sich gut; **it ~s as follows** es lautet folgendermaßen; **read out** vt vorlesen; **read through** vt durchlesen; **read up on** vt nachlesen über +akk; **readable** adj (book) lesenswert; (handwriting) lesbar; **reader** n Leser(in) m(f)
readily ['redɪlɪ] adv (willingly) bereitwillig; **~ available** leicht erhältlich
reading ['riːdɪŋ] n (action) Lesen nt; (from meter) Zählerstand m; **reading glasses** npl Lesebrille f; **reading lamp** n Leselampe f; **reading list** n Leseliste f; **reading matter** n Lektüre f
readjust [riːəˈdʒʌst] vt (mechanism etc) neu einstellen ▷ vi sich wieder anpassen (to an +akk)
ready ['redɪ] adj fertig, bereit; **to be ~ to do sth** (willing) bereit sein, etw zu tun; **are you ~ to go?** bist du so weit?; **to get sth ~** etw fertig machen; **to get (oneself) ~** sich fertig machen; **ready cash** n

r

Bargeld *nt*; **ready-made** *adj* (*product*)
Fertig-; (*clothes*) Konfektions-; **~ meal**
Fertiggericht *nt*

real [rɪəl] *adj* wirklich; (*actual*) eigentlich;
(*genuine*) echt; (*idiot etc*) richtig; **for ~** echt;
this time it's for ~ diesmal ist es ernst;
get ~ sei realistisch! ▷ *adv* (*fam*, *esp US*)
echt ▷ *n* **for ~** echt; **this time it's for
~** diesmal ist es ernst; **get ~** sei
realistisch!; **real ale** *n* Ale *nt*; **real estate**
n Immobilien *pl*

realistic, **realistically** [rɪəˈlɪstɪk, -əlɪ] *adj*,
adv realistisch; **reality** [riːˈælɪtɪ] *n*
Wirklichkeit *f*; **in ~** in Wirklichkeit; **reality
TV** *n* Reality-TV *nt*; **realization**
[rɪəlaɪˈzeɪʃən] *n* (*awareness*) Erkenntnis *f*;
realize [ˈrɪəlaɪz] *vt* (*understand*) begreifen;
(*plan*, *idea*) realisieren; **I ~d (that) …** mir
wurde klar, dass …

really [ˈriːəlɪ] *adv* wirklich

real time [rɪəlˈtaɪm] *n* (*Inform*) **in ~** in
Echtzeit

realtor [ˈrɪəltɔ*] *n* (*US*)
Grundstücksmakler(in) *m(f)*

reappear [riːəˈpɪə*] *vi* wieder erscheinen

rear [rɪə*] *adj* hintere(r, s), Hinter- ▷ *n* (*of
building*, *vehicle*) hinterer Teil; **at the ~ of**
hinter +*dat*; (*inside*) hinten in +*dat*; **rear
light** *n* (*Auto*) Rücklicht *nt*

rearm [riːˈɑːm] *vi* wieder aufrüsten

rearrange [riːəˈreɪndʒ] *vt* (*furniture*,
system) umstellen; (*meeting*) verlegen (*for
auf +akk*)

rear-view mirror [ˈrɪəvjuːˈmɪrə*] *n*
Rückspiegel *m*; **rear window** *n* (*Auto*)
Heckscheibe *f*

reason [ˈriːzn] *n* (*cause*) Grund *m* (*for für*);
(*ability to think*) Verstand *m*; (*common sense*)
Vernunft *f*; **for some ~** aus irgendeinem
Grund ▷ *vi* **to ~ with sb** mit jdm
vernünftig reden; **reasonable** *adj* (*person*,
price) vernünftig; (*offer*) akzeptabel;
(*chance*) reell; (*food*, *weather*) ganz gut;
reasonably *adv* vernünftig; (*fairly*)
ziemlich

reassure [riːəˈʃʊə*] *vt* beruhigen; **she ~d
me that …** sie versicherte mir, dass …

rebel [ˈrebl] *n* Rebell(in) *m(f)* ▷ [rɪˈbel] *vi*
rebellieren; **rebellion** [rɪˈbelɪən] *n*
Aufstand *m*

reboot [riːˈbuːt] *vt*, *vi* (*Inform*) rebooten

rebound [rɪˈbaʊnd] *vi* (*ball etc*)
zurückprallen

rebuild [riːˈbɪld] *irr vt* wieder aufbauen

recall [rɪˈkɔːl] *vt* (*remember*) sich erinnern
an +*akk*; (*call back*) zurückrufen

recap [ˈriːkæp] *vt*, *vi* rekapitulieren

receipt [rɪˈsiːt] *n* (*document*) Quittung *f*;
(*receiving*) Empfang *m*; **~s** *pl* (*money*)
Einnahmen *pl*

receive [rɪˈsiːv] *vt* (*news etc*) erhalten,
bekommen; (*visitor*) empfangen; **receiver**
n (*Tel*) Hörer *m*; (*Radio*) Empfänger *m*

recent [ˈriːsnt] *adj* (*event*) vor kurzem
stattgefunden; (*photo*) neueste(r,s);
(*invention*) neu; **in ~ years** in den letzten
Jahren; **recently** *adv* vor kurzem; (*in the
last few days or weeks*) in letzter Zeit

reception [rɪˈsepʃən] *n* Empfang *m*;
receptionist *n* (*in hotel*) Empfangschef *m*,
Empfangsdame *f*; (*woman in firm*)
Empfangsdame *f*; (*Med*)
Sprechstundenhilfe *f*

recess [rɪˈses] *n* (*in wall*) Nische *f*; (*US: in
school*) Pause *f*

recession [rɪˈseʃən] *n* Rezession *f*

recharge [riːˈtʃɑːdʒ] *vt* (*battery*) aufladen;
rechargeable [riːˈtʃɑːdʒəbl] *adj* wieder
aufladbar

recipe [ˈresɪpɪ] *n* Rezept *nt* (*for für*)

recipient [rɪˈsɪpɪənt] *n* Empfänger(in)
m(f)

reciprocal [rɪˈsɪprəkəl] *adj* gegenseitig

recite [rɪˈsaɪt] *vt* vortragen; (*details*)
aufzählen

reckless [ˈrekləs] *adj* leichtsinnig; (*driving*)
gefährlich

reckon [ˈrekən] *vt* (*calculate*) schätzen;
(*think*) glauben ▷ *vi* **to ~ with** rechnen mit

reclaim [rɪˈkleɪm] *vt* (*baggage*) abholen;
(*expenses*, *tax*) zurückverlangen

recline [rɪˈklaɪn] *vi* (*person*) sich
zurücklehnen; **reclining seat** *n* Liegesitz
m

recognition [rekəgˈnɪʃən] *n*
(*acknowledgement*) Anerkennung *f*; **in ~ of**
in Anerkennung +*gen*; **recognize**
[ˈrekəgnaɪz] *vt* erkennen; (*approve
officially*) anerkennen

recommend [rekəˈmend] *vt* empfehlen;
recommendation [rekəmenˈdeɪʃən] *n*
Empfehlung *f*

reconcile [ˈrekənsaɪl] *vt* (*people*)
versöhnen; (*facts*) (miteinander)
vereinbaren

reconsider [riːkənˈsɪdə*] *vt* noch einmal

überdenken ▷ vi es sich dat noch einmal überlegen

reconstruct [ri:kən'strʌkt] vt wieder aufbauen; (crime) rekonstruieren

record ['rekɔ:d] n (Mus) (Schall)platte f; (best performance) Rekord m; **~s** pl (files) Akten pl; **to keep a ~ of** Buch führen über +akk ▷ adj (time etc) Rekord- ▷ [rɪ'kɔ:d] vt (write down) aufzeichnen; (on tape etc) aufnehmen; **~ed message** Ansage f; **recorded delivery** n (Brit) **by ~** per Einschreiben

recorder [rɪ'kɔ:də*] n (Mus) Blockflöte f; (**cassette**) ~ (Kassetten)rekorder m; **recording** [rɪ'kɔ:dɪŋ] n (on tape etc) Aufnahme f; **record player** ['rekɔ:dpleɪə*] n Plattenspieler m

recover [rɪ'kʌvə*] vt (money, item) zurückbekommen; (appetite, strength) wiedergewinnen ▷ vi sich erholen

recreation [rekrɪ'eɪʃən] n Erholung f; **recreational** adj Freizeit-; **~ vehicle** (US) Wohnmobil nt

recruit [rɪ'kru:t] n (Mil) Rekrut(in) m(f); (in firm, organization) neues Mitglied ▷ vt (Mil) rekrutieren; (members) anwerben; (staff) einstellen; **recruitment agency** n Personalagentur f

rectangle ['rektæŋgl] n Rechteck nt; **rectangular** [rek'tæŋgʊlə*] adj rechteckig

rectify ['rektɪfaɪ] vt berichtigen

recuperate [rɪ'ku:pəreɪt] vi sich erholen

recyclable [ri:'saɪkləbl] adj recycelbar, wieder verwertbar; **recycle** [ri:'saɪkl] vt recyceln, wieder verwerten; **~d paper** Recyclingpapier nt; **recycling** n Recycling nt, Wiederverwertung f

red [red] adj rot ▷ n **in the ~** in den roten Zahlen; **Red Cross** n Rotes Kreuz; **red cabbage** n Rotkohl m; **redcurrant** n (rote) Johannisbeere

redeem [rɪ'di:m] vt (Comm) einlösen

red-handed [red'hændɪd] adj **to catch sb ~** jdn auf frischer Tat ertappen; **redhead** n Rothaarige(r) mf

redial [ri:'daɪəl] vt, vi nochmals wählen

redirect [ri:daɪ'rekt] vt (traffic) umleiten; (forward) nachsenden

red light [red'laɪt] n (traffic signal) rotes Licht; **to go through the ~** bei Rot über die Ampel fahren; **red meat** n Rind-, Lamm-, Rehfleisch

redo [ri:'du:] irr vt nochmals machen

reduce [rɪ'dju:s] vt reduzieren (to auf +akk, by um); **reduction** [rɪ'dʌkʃən] n Reduzierung f; (in price) Ermäßigung f

redundant [rɪ'dʌndənt] adj überflüssig; **to be made ~** entlassen werden

red wine [red'waɪn] n Rotwein m

reef [ri:f] n Riff nt

reel [ri:l] n Spule f; (on fishing rod) Rolle f; **reel off** vt herunterrasseln

ref [ref] n (fam: referee) Schiri m

refectory [rɪ'fektərɪ] n (at college) Mensa f

refer [rɪ'fɜ:*] vt **to ~ sb to sb/sth** jdn an jdn/etw verweisen; **to ~ sth to sb** (query, problem) etw an jdn weiterleiten ▷ vi **to ~ to** (mention, allude to) sich beziehen auf +akk; (book) nachschlagen in +dat

referee [refə'ri:] n Schiedsrichter(in) m(f); (in boxing) Ringrichter m; (Brit: for job) Referenz f

reference ['refrəns] n (allusion) Anspielung f (to auf +akk); (for job) Referenz f; (in book) Verweis m; **~ (number)** (in document) Aktenzeichen nt; **with ~ to** mit Bezug auf +akk; **reference book** n Nachschlagewerk nt

referendum [refə'rendəm] (pl **referenda**) n Referendum nt

refill ['ri:fɪl] vt [ri:'fɪl] nachfüllen ▷ n (for ballpoint pen) Ersatzmine f

refine [rɪ'faɪn] vt (purify) raffinieren; (improve) verfeinern; **refined** adj (genteel) fein

reflect [rɪ'flekt] vt reflektieren; (fig) widerspiegeln ▷ vi nachdenken (on über +akk); **reflection** [rɪ'flekʃən] n (image) Spiegelbild nt; (thought) Überlegung f

reflex ['ri:fleks] n Reflex m

reform [rɪ'fɔ:m] n Reform f ▷ vt reformieren; (person) bessern

refrain [rɪ'freɪn] vi **to ~ from doing sth** es unterlassen, etw zu tun

refresh [rɪ'freʃ] vt erfrischen; **refresher course** n Auffrischungskurs m; **refreshing** adj erfrischend; **refreshments** npl Erfrischungen pl

refrigerator [rɪ'frɪdʒəreɪtə*] n Kühlschrank m

refuel [ri:'fjʊəl] vt, vi auftanken

refuge ['refju:dʒ] n Zuflucht f (from vor +dat); **to take ~** sich flüchten (from vor +dat, in in +akk); **refugee** [refjʊ'dʒi:] n Flüchtling m

refund ['riːfʌnd] *n* (*of money*)
Rückerstattung *f*; **to get a ~ (on sth)** sein
Geld (für etw) zurückbekommen
▷ [rɪ'fʌnd] *vt* zurückerstatten

refusal [rɪ'fjuːzəl] *n* (*to do sth*) Weigerung
f; **refuse** ['refjuːs] *n* Müll *m*, Abfall *m*
▷ [rɪ'fjuːz] *vt* ablehnen; **to ~ sb sth** jdm
etw verweigern; **to ~ to do sth** sich
weigern, etw zu tun ▷ *vi* sich weigern

regain [rɪ'geɪn] *vt* wiedergewinnen,
wiedererlangen; **to ~ consciousness**
wieder zu Bewusstsein kommen

regard [rɪ'gɑːd] *n* **with ~ to** in Bezug auf
+*akk*; **in this ~** in dieser Hinsicht; **~s** (*at end
of letter*) mit freundlichen Grüßen; **give my
~s to ...** viele Grüße an ..., +*akk* ▷ *vt* **to
~ sb/sth as sth** jdn/etw als etw
betrachten; **as ~s ...** was ... betrifft;
regarding *prep* bezüglich +*gen*;
regardless *adj* **~ of** ohne Rücksicht auf
+*akk* ▷ *adv* trotzdem; **to carry on
~** einfach weitermachen

regime [reɪ'ʒiːm] *n* (*Pol*) Regime *nt*

region ['riːdʒən] *n* (*of country*) Region *f*,
Gebiet *nt*; **in the ~ of** (*about*) ungefähr;
regional *adj* regional

register ['redʒɪstə*] *n* Register *nt*; (*school*)
Namensliste *f* ▷ *vt* (*with an authority*)
registrieren lassen; (*birth, death, vehicle*)
anmelden ▷ *vi* (*at hotel, for course*) sich
anmelden; (*at university*) sich einschreiben;
registered *adj* eingetragen; (*letter*)
eingeschrieben; **by ~ post** per
Einschreiben; **registration** [redʒɪ'streɪʃən]
n (*for course*) Anmeldung *f*; (*at university*)
Einschreibung *f*; (*Auto: number*)
(polizeiliches) Kennzeichen; **registration
form** *n* Anmeldeformular *nt*;
registration number *n* (*Auto*)
(polizeiliches) Kennzeichen; **registry
office** ['redʒɪstrɪɒfɪs] *n* Standesamt *nt*

regret [rɪ'gret] *n* Bedauern *nt* ▷ *vt*
bedauern; **regrettable** *adj* bedauerlich

regular ['regjʊlə*] *adj* regelmäßig; (*size*)
normal ▷ *n* (*client*) Stammkunde *m*,
Stammkundin *f*; (*in bar*) Stammgast *m*;
(*petrol*) Normalbenzin *nt*; **regularly** *adv*
regelmäßig

regulate ['regjʊleɪt] *vt* regulieren; (*using
rules*) regeln; **regulation** [regjʊ'leɪʃən] *n*
(*rule*) Vorschrift *f*

rehabilitation [riːəbɪlɪ'teɪʃən] *n*
Rehabilitation *f*

rehearsal [rɪ'hɜːsəl] *n* Probe *f*; **rehearse**
vt, vi proben

reign [reɪn] *n* Herrschaft *f* ▷ *vi* herrschen
(*over* über +*akk*)

reimburse [riːɪm'bɜːs] *vt* (*person*)
entschädigen; (*expenses*) zurückerstatten

reindeer ['reɪndɪə*] *n* Rentier *nt*

reinforce [riːɪn'fɔːs] *vt* verstärken

reinstate [riːɪn'steɪt] *vt* (*employee*) wieder
einstellen; (*passage in text*) wieder
aufnehmen

reject ['riːdʒekt] *n* (*Comm*)
Ausschussartikel *m* ▷ [rɪ'dʒekt] *vt*
ablehnen; **rejection** [rɪ'dʒekʃən] *n*
Ablehnung *f*

relapse [rɪ'læps] *n* Rückfall *m*

relate [rɪ'leɪt] *vt* (*story*) erzählen; (*connect*)
in Verbindung bringen (*to* mit) ▷ *vi* **to ~ to**
(*refer*) sich beziehen auf +*akk*; **related** *adj*
verwandt (*to* mit); **relation** [rɪ'leɪʃən] *n*
(*relative*) Verwandte(r) *mf*; (*connection*)
Beziehung *f*; **~s** *pl* (*dealings*) Beziehungen
pl; **relationship** *n* (*connection*) Beziehung
f; (*between people*) Verhältnis *nt*

relative ['relətɪv] *n* Verwandte(r) *mf* ▷ *adj*
relativ; **relatively** *adv* relativ,
verhältnismäßig

relax [rɪ'læks] *vi* sich entspannen; **~!** reg
dich nicht auf! ▷ *vt* (*grip, conditions*)
lockern; **relaxation** [riːlæk'seɪʃən] *n*
(*rest*) Entspannung *f*; **relaxed** *adj*
entspannt; **relaxing** *adj* entspannend

release [rɪ'liːs] *n* (*from prison*) Entlassung
f; **new/recent ~** (*film, CD*)
Neuerscheinung *f* ▷ *vt* (*animal, hostage*)
freilassen; (*prisoner*) entlassen; (*handbrake*)
lösen; (*news*) veröffentlichen; (*film, CD*)
herausbringen

relent [rɪ'lent] *vi* nachgeben; **relentless**,
relentlessly *adj, adv* (*merciless*)
erbarmungslos; (*neverending*)
unaufhörlich

relevance ['reləvəns] *n* Relevanz *f* (*to*
für); **relevant** *adj* relevant (*to* für)

reliable, **reliably** [rɪ'laɪəbl, -blɪ] *adj, adv*
zuverlässig; **reliant** [rɪ'laɪənt] *adj* **~ on**
abhängig von

relic ['relɪk] *n* (*from past*) Relikt *nt*

relief [rɪ'liːf] *n* (*from anxiety, pain*)
Erleichterung *f*; (*assistance*) Hilfe *f*; **relieve**
[rɪ'liːv] *vt* (*pain*) lindern; (*boredom*)
überwinden; (*take over from*) ablösen; **I'm
~d** ich bin erleichtert

religion [rɪˈlɪdʒən] n Religion f; **religious** [rɪˈlɪdʒəs] adj religiös

relish [ˈrelɪʃ] n (for food) würzige Soße ▷ vt (enjoy) genießen; **I don't ~ the thought of getting up early** der Gedanke, früh aufzustehen, behagt mir gar nicht

reluctant [rɪˈlʌktənt] adj widerwillig; **to be ~ to do sth** etw nur ungern tun; **reluctantly** adv widerwillig

rely on [rɪˈlaɪ ɒn] vt sich verlassen auf +akk; (depend on) abhängig sein von

remain [rɪˈmeɪn] vi bleiben; (be left over) übrig bleiben; **remainder** n (a. Math) Rest m; **remaining** adj übrig; **remains** npl Überreste pl

remark [rɪˈmɑːk] n Bemerkung f ▷ vt **to ~ that** bemerken, dass ▷ vi **to ~ on sth** über etw akk eine Bemerkung machen; **remarkable**, **remarkably** adj, adv bemerkenswert

remarry [riːˈmærɪ] vi wieder heiraten

remedy [ˈremədɪ] n Mittel nt (for gegen) ▷ vt abhelfen +dat

remember [rɪˈmembə*] vt sich erinnern an +akk; **to ~ to do sth** daran denken, etw zu tun; **I ~ seeing her** ich erinnere mich daran, sie gesehen zu haben; **I must ~ that** das muss ich mir merken ▷ vi sich erinnern

Remembrance Day [rɪˈmembrəns'deɪ] n (Brit) ≈ Volkstrauertag m

● **Remembrance Day**
●
● **Remembrance Sunday/Day** ist der
● britische Gedenktag für die
● Gefallenen der beiden Weltkriege
● und anderer Kriege. Er fällt auf einen
● Sonntag vor oder nach dem 11.
● November (am 11.11.1918 endete der
● Erste Weltkrieg) und wird mit einer
● Schweigeminute,
● Kranzniederlegungen an
● Kriegerdenkmälern und dem Tragen
● von Anstecknadeln in Form einer
● Mohnblume begangen.

remind [rɪˈmaɪnd] vt **to ~ sb of/about sb/sth** jdn an jdn/etw erinnern; **to ~ sb to do sth** jdn daran erinnern, etw zu tun; **that ~s me** dabei fällt mir ein ...; **reminder** n (to pay) Mahnung f

reminisce [remɪˈnɪs] vi in Erinnerungen schwelgen (about an +akk); **reminiscent** [remɪˈnɪsənt] adj **to be ~ of** erinnern an +akk

remittance n Überweisung f (to an +akk)

remnant [ˈremnənt] n Rest m

remote [rɪˈməʊt] adj (place) abgelegen; (slight) gering ▷ n (Tv) Fernbedienung f; **remote control** n Fernsteuerung f; (device) Fernbedienung f

removal [rɪˈmuːvəl] n Entfernung f; (Brit: move from house) Umzug m; **removal firm** n (Brit) Spedition f; **remove** [rɪˈmuːv] vt entfernen; (lid) abnehmen; (clothes) ausziehen; (doubt, suspicion) zerstreuen

rename [riːˈneɪm] vt umbenennen

renew [rɪˈnjuː] vt erneuern; (licence, passport, library book) verlängern lassen

renounce [rɪˈnaʊns] vt verzichten auf +akk; (faith, opinion) abschwören +dat

renovate [ˈrenəveɪt] vt renovieren

renowned [rɪˈnaʊnd] adj berühmt (for für)

rent [rent] n Miete f; **for ~** (US) zu vermieten ▷ vt (as hirer, tenant) mieten; (as owner) vermieten; **~ed car** Mietwagen m; **rent out** vt vermieten; **rental** n Miete f; (for car, TV etc) Leihgebühr f ▷ adj Miet-

reorganize [riːˈɔːgənaɪz] vt umorganisieren

rep [rep] n (Comm) Vertreter(in) m(f)

repair [rɪˈpeə*] n Reparatur f ▷ vt reparieren; (damage) wieder gutmachen; **repair kit** n Flickzeug nt

repay [riːˈpeɪ] irr vt (money) zurückzahlen; **to ~ sb for sth** (fig) sich bei jdm für etw revanchieren

repeat [rɪˈpiːt] n (Radio, Tv) Wiederholung f ▷ vt wiederholen; **repetition** [repəˈtɪʃən] n Wiederholung f; **repetitive** [rɪˈpetɪtɪv] adj sich wiederholend

rephrase [riːˈfreɪz] vt anders formulieren

replace [rɪˈpleɪs] vt ersetzen (with durch); (put back) zurückstellen, zurücklegen; **replacement** n (thing, person) Ersatz m; (temporarily in job) Vertretung f; **replacement part** n Ersatzteil nt

replay [ˈriːpleɪ] n (action) ~ Wiederholung f ▷ [riːˈpleɪ] vt (game) wiederholen

replica [ˈreplɪkə] n Kopie f

reply [rɪˈplaɪ] n Antwort f ▷ vi antworten; **to ~ to sb/sth** jdm/auf etw *akk* antworten ▷ *vt* **to ~ that** antworten, dass

report [rɪ'pɔːt] *n* Bericht *m*; (*school*) Zeugnis *nt* ▷ *vt* (*tell*) berichten; (*give information against*) melden; (*to police*) anzeigen ▷ *vi* (*present oneself*) sich melden; **to ~ sick** sich krankmelden; **report card** *n* (*US: school*), Zeugnis *nt*; **reporter** *n* Reporter(in) *m(f)*

represent [reprɪ'zent] *vt* darstellen; (*speak for*) vertreten; **representation** [reprɪzen'teɪʃən] *n* (*picture etc*) Darstellung *f*; **representative** [reprɪ'zentətɪv] *n* Vertreter(in) *m(f)*; (*US Pol*) Abgeordnete(r) *mf* ▷ *adj* repräsentativ (*of* für)

reprimand ['reprɪmɑːnd] *n* Tadel *m* ▷ *vt* tadeln

reprint ['riːprɪnt] *n* Nachdruck *m*

reproduce [riːprə'djuːs] *vt* (*copy*) reproduzieren ▷ *vi* (*Bio*) sich fortpflanzen; **reproduction** [riːprə'dʌkʃən] *n* (*copy*) Reproduktion *f*; (*Bio*) Fortpflanzung *f*

reptile ['reptaɪl] *n* Reptil *nt*

republic [rɪ'pʌblɪk] *n* Republik *f*; **republican** *adj* republikanisch ▷ *n* Republikaner(in) *m(f)*

repulsive [rɪ'pʌlsɪv] *adj* abstoßend

reputable ['repjʊtəbl] *adj* seriös

reputation [repjʊ'teɪʃən] *n* Ruf *m*; **he has a ~ for being difficult** er hat den Ruf, schwierig zu sein

request [rɪ'kwest] *n* Bitte *f* (*for* um); **on ~** auf Wunsch ▷ *vt* bitten um; **to ~ sb to do sth** jdn bitten, etw zu tun

require [rɪ'kwaɪə*] *vt* (*need*) brauchen; (*desire*) verlangen; **what qualifications are ~d?** welche Qualifikationen sind erforderlich?; **required** *adj* erforderlich; **requirement** *n* (*condition*) Anforderung *f*; (*need*) Bedingung *f*

rerun ['riːrʌn] *n* Wiederholung *f*

rescue ['reskjuː] *n* Rettung *f*; **to come to sb's ~** jdm zu Hilfe kommen ▷ *vt* retten; **rescue party** *n* Rettungsmannschaft *f*

research [rɪ'sɜːtʃ] *n* Forschung *f* ▷ *vi* forschen (*into* über +*akk*) ▷ *vt* erforschen; **researcher** *n* Forscher(in) *m(f)*

resemblance [rɪ'zembləns] *n* Ähnlichkeit *f* (*to* mit); **resemble** [rɪ'zembl] *vt* ähneln +*dat*

resent [rɪ'zent] *vt* übel nehmen

reservation [rezə'veɪʃən] *n* (*booking*) Reservierung *f*; (*doubt*) Vorbehalt *m*; **I**

have a ~ (*in hotel, restaurant*) ich habe reserviert; **reserve** [rɪ'zɜːv] *n* (*store*) Vorrat *m* (*of* an +*dat*); (*manner*) Zurückhaltung *f*; (*Sport*) Reservespieler(in) *m(f)*; (*game ~*) Naturschutzgebiet *nt* ▷ *vt* (*book in advance*) reservieren; **reserved** *adj* reserviert

reservoir ['rezəvwɑː*] *n* (*for water*) Reservoir *nt*

reside [rɪ'zaɪd] *vi* wohnen; **residence** ['rezɪdəns] *n* Wohnsitz *m*; (*living*) Aufenthalt *m*; **~ permit** Aufenthaltsgenehmigung *f*; **~ hall** Studentenwohnheim *nt*; **resident** ['rezɪdənt] *n* (*in house*) Bewohner(in) *m(f)*; (*in town, area*) Einwohner(in) *m(f)*

resign [rɪ'zaɪn] *vt* (*post*) zurücktreten von; (*job*) kündigen ▷ *vi* (*from post*) zurücktreten; (*from job*) kündigen; **resignation** [rezɪg'neɪʃən] *n* (*from post*) Rücktritt *m*; (*from job*) Kündigung *f*; **resigned** *adj* resigniert; **he is ~ to it** er hat sich damit abgefunden

resist [rɪ'zɪst] *vt* widerstehen +*dat*; **resistance** *n* Widerstand *m* (*to* gegen)

resit [riː'sɪt] (*Brit*) *irr vt* wiederholen ▷ ['riːsɪt] *n* Wiederholungsprüfung *f*

resolution [rezə'luːʃən] *n* (*intention*) Vorsatz *m*; (*decision*) Beschluss *m*

resolve [rɪ'zɒlv] *vt* (*problem*) lösen

resort [rɪ'zɔːt] *n* (*holiday ~*) Urlaubsort *m*; (*health ~*) Kurort *m*; **as a last ~** als letzter Ausweg ▷ *vi* **to ~ to** greifen zu; (*violence*) anwenden

resources [rɪ'sɔːsɪz] *npl* (*money*) (Geld)mittel *pl*; (*mineral ~*) Bodenschätze *pl*

respect [rɪ'spekt] *n* Respekt *m* (*for* vor +*dat*); (*consideration*) Rücksicht *f* (*for* auf +*akk*); **with ~ to** in Bezug auf +*akk*; **in this ~** in dieser Hinsicht; **in all due ~** bei allem Respekt ▷ *vt* respektieren; **respectable** [rɪ'spektəbl] *adj* (*person, family*) angesehen; (*district*) anständig; (*achievement, result*) beachtlich; **respected** [rɪ'spektɪd] *adj* angesehen

respective [rɪ'spektɪv] *adj* jeweilig; **respectively** *adv* **5% and 10% ~** 5% beziehungsweise 10%

respiratory [rɪ'spɪrətərɪ] *adj* **~ problems** (*o* **trouble**) Atembeschwerden *pl*

respond [rɪ'spɒnd] *vi* antworten (*to* auf +*akk*); (*react*) reagieren (*to* auf +*akk*); (*to*

treatment) ansprechen (to auf +akk);
response [rɪ'spɒns] n Antwort f;
(reaction) Reaktion f; **in ~ to** als Antwort
auf +akk
responsibility [rɪspɒnsə'bɪlɪtɪ] n
Verantwortung f; **that's her ~** dafür ist sie
verantwortlich; **responsible** [rɪ'spɒnsəbl]
adj verantwortlich (for für); (trustworthy)
verantwortungsbewusst; (job)
verantwortungsvoll
rest [rest] n (relaxation) Ruhe f; (break)
Pause f; (remainder) Rest m; **to have** (o
take) **a ~** sich ausruhen; (break) Pause
machen; **the ~ of the wine/the people**
der Rest des Weins/der Leute ▷ vi (relax)
sich ausruhen; (lean) lehnen (on, against an
+dat, gegen)
restaurant ['restərɒnt] n Restaurant nt;
restaurant car n (Brit) Speisewagen m
restful ['restful] adj (holiday etc)
erholsam, ruhig; **restless** ['restləs] adj
unruhig
restore [rɪ'stɔ:*] vt (painting, building)
restaurieren; (order) wiederherstellen;
(give back) zurückgeben
restrain [rɪ'streɪn] vt (person, feelings)
zurückhalten; **to ~ oneself** sich
beherrschen
restrict [rɪ'strɪkt] vt beschränken (to auf
+akk); **restricted** adj beschränkt;
restriction [rɪ'strɪkʃən] n Einschränkung
f (on +gen)
rest room ['restru:m] n (US) Toilette f
result [rɪ'zʌlt] n Ergebnis nt; (consequence)
Folge f; **as a ~ of** infolge +gen ▷ vi **to ~ in**
führen zu; **to ~ from** sich ergeben aus
resume [rɪ'zju:m] vt (work, negotiations)
wieder aufnehmen; (journey) fortsetzen
résumé ['rezjumeɪ] n Zusammenfassung
f; (US: curriculum vitae) Lebenslauf m
resuscitate [rɪ'sʌsɪteɪt] vt wieder
beleben
retail ['ri:teɪl] adv im Einzelhandel;
retailer n Einzelhändler(in) m(f)
retain [rɪ'teɪn] vt behalten; (heat) halten
rethink [ri:'θɪŋk] irr vt noch einmal
überdenken
retire [rɪ'taɪə*] vi (from work) in den
Ruhestand treten; (withdraw) sich
zurückziehen; **retired** adj (person)
pensioniert; **retirement** n (time of life)
Ruhestand m; **retirement age** n
Rentenalter nt

retrace [rɪ'treɪs] vt zurückverfolgen
retrain [ri:'treɪn] vi sich umschulen
lassen
retreat [rɪ'tri:t] n (Mil) Rückzug m (from
aus); (refuge) Zufluchtsort m ▷ vi (Mil) sich
zurückziehen; (step back) zurückweichen
retrieve [rɪ'tri:v] vt (recover)
wiederbekommen; (rescue) retten; (data)
abrufen
retrospect ['retrəʊspekt] n **in
~** rückblickend; **retrospective**
[retrəʊ'spektɪv] adj rückblickend; (pay rise)
rückwirkend
return [rɪ'tɜ:n] n (going back) Rückkehr f;
(giving back) Rückgabe f; (profit) Gewinn m;
(Brit: ~ ticket) Rückfahrkarte f; (plane ticket)
Rückflugticket nt; (Tennis), Return m; **in
~** als Gegenleistung (for für); **many happy
~s (of the day)** herzlichen Glückwunsch
zum Geburtstag! ▷ vi (person)
zurückkehren; (doubts, symptoms) wieder
auftreten; **to ~ to school/work** wieder in
die Schule/die Arbeit gehen ▷ vt (give
back) zurückgeben; **I ~ed his call** ich habe
ihn zurückgerufen; **returnable** adj (bottle)
Pfand-; **return flight** n (Brit) Rückflug m;
(both ways) Hin- und Rückflug m; **return
key** n (Inform) Eingabetaste f; **return
ticket** n (Brit) Rückfahrkarte f; (for plane)
Rückflugticket nt
reunification [ri:ju:nɪfɪ'keɪʃən] n
Wiedervereinigung f
reunion [ri:'ju:njən] n (party) Treffen nt;
reunite [ri:ju:'naɪt] vt wieder vereinigen
reusable [ri:'ju:zəbl] adj wieder
verwendbar
reveal [rɪ'vi:l] vt (make known) enthüllen;
(secret) verraten; (show) zeigen; **revealing**
adj aufschlussreich; (dress) freizügig
revenge [rɪ'vendʒ] n Rache f; (in game)
Revanche f; **to take ~ on sb (for sth)** sich
an jdm (für etw) rächen
revenue ['revənju:] n Einnahmen pl
reverse [rɪ'vɜ:s] n (back) Rückseite f;
(opposite) Gegenteil nt; (Auto) **~ (gear)**
Rückwärtsgang m ▷ adj **in ~ order** in
umgekehrter Reihenfolge ▷ vt (order)
umkehren; (decision) umstoßen; (car)
zurücksetzen; **to ~ the charges** (Brit) ein
R-Gespräch führen ▷ vi (Auto) rückwärts
fahren
review [rɪ'vju:] n (of book, film etc)
Rezension f; **to be under ~** überprüft

werden ▷ vt (book, film etc) rezensieren; (re-examine) überprüfen

revise [rɪ'vaɪz] vt revidieren; (text) überarbeiten; (Brit: in school) wiederholen ▷ vi (Brit: in school) den Stoff wiederholen; **revision** [rɪ'vɪʒən] n (of text) Überarbeitung f; (Brit: in school) Wiederholung f

revitalize [ri:'vaɪtəlaɪz] vt neu beleben

revive [rɪ'vaɪv] vt wieder beleben; (tradition, interest) wieder aufleben lassen ▷ vi (regain consciousness) wieder zu sich kommen

revolt [rɪ'vəʊlt] n Aufstand m; **revolting** adj widerlich

revolution [revə'lu:ʃən] n (Pol, fig) Revolution f; (turn) Umdrehung f; **revolutionary** adj revolutionär ▷ n Revolutionär(in) m(f)

revolve [rɪ'vɒlv] vi sich drehen (around um); **revolver** n Revolver m; **revolving door** n Drehtür f

reward [rɪ'wɔ:d] n Belohnung f ▷ vt belohnen; **rewarding** adj lohnend

rewind [ri:'waɪnd] irr vt (tape) zurückspulen

rewrite [ri:'raɪt] irr vt (write again; recast) umschreiben

rheumatism ['ru:mətɪzəm] n Rheuma nt

Rhine [raɪn] n Rhein m

rhinoceros [raɪ'nɒsərəs] n Nashorn nt

Rhodes [rəʊdz] n Rhodos nt

rhubarb ['ru:bɑ:b] n Rhabarber m

rhyme [raɪm] n Reim m ▷ vi sich reimen (with auf +akk)

rhythm ['rɪðəm] n Rhythmus m

rib [rɪb] n Rippe f

ribbon ['rɪbən] n Band nt

rice [raɪs] n Reis m; **rice pudding** n Milchreis m

rich [rɪtʃ] adj reich; (food) schwer ▷ npl **the ~** die Reichen pl

rickety ['rɪkɪtɪ] adj wackelig

rid [rɪd] (**rid, rid**) vt **to get ~ of sb/sth** jdn/etw loswerden

ridden ['rɪdn] pp of **ride**

riddle ['rɪdl] n Rätsel nt

ride [raɪd] (**rode, ridden**) vt (horse) reiten; (bicycle) fahren ▷ vi (on horse) reiten; (on bike) fahren ▷ n (in vehicle, on bike) Fahrt f; (on horse) (Aus)ritt m; **to go for a ~** (in car, on bike) spazieren fahren; (on horse) reiten gehen; **to take sb for a ~** (fam) jdn

verarschen; **rider** n (on horse) Reiter(in) m(f); (on bike) Fahrer(in) m(f)

ridiculous [rɪ'dɪkjʊləs] adj lächerlich; **don't be ~** red keinen Unsinn!

riding ['raɪdɪŋ] n Reiten nt; **to go ~** reiten gehen ▷ adj Reit-

rifle ['raɪfl] n Gewehr nt

rig [rɪg] n **oil ~** Bohrinsel f ▷ vt (election etc) manipulieren

right [raɪt] adj (correct, just) richtig; (opposite of left) rechte(r, s); (clothes, job etc) passend; **to be ~** (person) Recht haben; (clock) richtig gehen; **that's ~** das stimmt! ▷ n Recht nt (to auf +akk); (side) rechte Seite; **the Right** (Pol) die Rechte; **to take a ~** (Auto) rechts abbiegen; **on the ~** rechts (of von); **to the ~** nach rechts; (on the ~) rechts (of von) ▷ adv (towards the ~) nach rechts; (directly) direkt; (exactly) genau; **to turn ~** (Auto) rechts abbiegen; **~ away** sofort; **~ now** im Moment; (immediately) sofort; **right angle** n rechter Winkel; **right-hand drive** n Rechtssteuerung f ▷ adj rechtsgesteuert; **right-handed** adj **he is ~** er ist Rechtshänder; **right-hand side** n rechte Seite; **on the ~** auf der rechten Seite; **rightly** adv zu Recht; **right of way** n **to have ~** (Auto) Vorfahrt haben; **right wing** n (Pol, Sport) rechter Flügel; **right-wing** adj Rechts-; **~ extremist** Rechtsradikale(r) mf

rigid ['rɪdʒɪd] adj (stiff) starr; (strict) streng

rigorous, rigorously ['rɪgərəs, -lɪ] adj, adv streng

rim [rɪm] n (of cup etc) Rand m; (of wheel) Felge f

rind [raɪnd] n (of cheese) Rinde f; (of bacon) Schwarte f; (of fruit) Schale f

ring [rɪŋ] (**rang, rung**) vt, vi (bell) läuten; (Tel) anrufen ▷ n (on finger, in boxing) Ring m; (circle) Kreis m; (at circus) Manege f; **to give sb a ~** (Tel) jdn anrufen; **ring back** vt, vi zurückrufen; **ring up** vt, vi anrufen

ring binder n Ringbuch nt

ringing tone n (Tel) Rufzeichen nt

ringleader n Anführer(in) m(f)

ring road n (Brit) Umgehungsstraße f

ringtone n Klingelton m

rink [rɪŋk] n (ice ~) Eisbahn f; (for roller-skating) Rollschuhbahn f

rinse [rɪns] vt spülen

riot ['raɪət] n Aufruhr m

rip [rɪp] n Riss m ▷ vt zerreißen; **to ~ sth**

open etw aufreißen ▷ vi reißen; **rip off** vt (fam: person) übers Ohr hauen; **rip up** vt zerreißen

ripe [raɪp] adj (fruit) reif; **ripen** vi reifen

rip-off ['rɪpɒf] n **that's a ~** (fam: too expensive) das ist Wucher

rise [raɪz] (**rose, risen**) vi (from sitting, lying) aufstehen; (sun) aufgehen; (prices, temperature) steigen; (ground) ansteigen; (in revolt) sich erheben ▷ n (increase) Anstieg m (in +gen); (pay ~) Gehaltserhöhung f; (to power, fame) Aufstieg m (to zu); (slope) Steigung f; **risen** ['rɪzn] pp of **rise**

risk [rɪsk] n Risiko nt ▷ vt riskieren; **to ~ doing sth** es riskieren, etw zu tun; **risky** adj riskant

risotto [rɪ'zɒtəʊ] (pl **-s**) n Risotto nt

ritual ['rɪtjʊəl] n Ritual nt ▷ adj rituell

rival ['raɪvəl] n Rivale m, Rivalin f (for um); (Comm) Konkurrent(in) m(f); **rivalry** n Rivalität f; (Comm, Sport) Konkurrenz f

river ['rɪvə*] n Fluss m; **the River Thames** (Brit), **the Thames River** (US) die Themse; **riverside** n Flussufer nt ▷ adj am Flussufer

road [rəʊd] n Straße f; (fig) Weg m; **on the ~** (travelling) unterwegs, mit dem Auto/Bus etc fahren; **roadblock** n Straßensperre f; **roadmap** n Straßenkarte f; **road rage** n aggressives Verhalten im Straßenverkehr; **roadside** n **at** (o **by**) **the ~** am Straßenrand; **roadsign** n Verkehrsschild nt; **road tax** n Kraftfahrzeugssteuer f; **roadworks** npl Straßenarbeiten pl; **roadworthy** adj fahrtüchtig

roar [rɔ:*] n (of person, lion) Brüllen nt; (von Verkehr) Donnern nt ▷ vi (person, lion) brüllen (with vor +dat)

roast [rəʊst] n Braten m ▷ adj **~ beef** Rinderbraten m; **~ chicken** Brathähnchen nt; **~ pork** Schweinebraten m; **~ potatoes** pl im Backofen gebratene Kartoffeln ▷ vt (meat) braten

rob [rɒb] vt bestehlen; (bank, shop) ausrauben; **robber** n Räuber(in) m(f); **robbery** n Raub m

robe [rəʊb] n (US: dressing gown) Morgenrock m; (of judge, priest etc) Robe f, Talar m

robin ['rɒbɪn] n Rotkehlchen nt

robot ['rəʊbɒt] n Roboter m

robust [rəʊ'bʌst] adj robust; (defence) stark

rock [rɒk] n (substance) Stein m; (boulder) Felsbrocken m; (Mus) Rock m; **stick of ~** (Brit) Zuckerstange f; **on the ~s** (drink) mit Eis; (marriage) gescheitert ▷ vt, vi (swing) schaukeln; (dance) rocken; **rock climbing** n Klettern nt; **to go ~** klettern gehen

rocket ['rɒkɪt] n Rakete f; (in salad) Rucola f

rocking chair ['rɒkɪŋtʃeə*] n Schaukelstuhl m

rocky ['rɒkɪ] adj (landscape) felsig; (path) steinig

rod [rɒd] n (bar) Stange f; (fishing ~) Rute f

rode [rəʊd] pt of **ride**

rogue [rəʊg] n Schurke m, Gauner m

role [rəʊl] n Rolle f; **role model** n Vorbild nt

roll [rəʊl] n (of film, paper etc) Rolle f; (bread ~) Brötchen nt ▷ vt (move by ~ing) rollen; (cigarette) drehen ▷ vi (move by ~ing) rollen; (ship) schlingern; (camera) laufen; **roll out** vt (pastry) ausrollen; **roll over** vi (person) sich umdrehen; **roll up** vi (fam: arrive) antanzen ▷ vt (carpet) aufrollen; **to roll one's sleeves up** die Ärmel hochkrempeln

roller n (hair ~) (Locken)wickler m; **Rollerblades®** npl Inlineskates pl; **rollerblading** n Inlineskaten nt; **roller coaster** n Achterbahn f; **roller skates** npl Rollschuhe pl; **roller-skating** n Rollschuhlaufen nt; **rolling pin** n Nudelholz nt; **roll-on (deodorant)** n Deoroller m

ROM [rɒm] acr = **read only memory** ROM m

Roman ['rəʊmən] adj römisch ▷ n Römer(in) m(f); **Roman Catholic** adj römisch-katholisch ▷ n Katholik(in) m(f)

romance [rəʊ'mæns] n Romantik f; (love affair) Romanze f

Romania [rəʊ'meɪnɪə] n Rumänien nt; **Romanian** adj rumänisch ▷ n Rumäne m, Rumänin f; (language) Rumänisch nt

romantic [rəʊ'mæntɪk] adj romantisch

roof [ru:f] n Dach nt; **roof rack** n Dachgepäckträger m

rook [rʊk] n (in chess) Turm m

room [ru:m] n Zimmer nt, Raum m; (large, for gatherings etc) Saal m; (space) Platz m; (fig) Spielraum m; **to make ~ for** Platz

machen für; **roommate** *n*
Zimmergenosse *m*, Zimmergenossin *f*; *(US:*
sharing apartment) Mitbewohner(in) *m(f)*;
room service *n* Zimmerservice *m*; **roomy**
adj geräumig; *(garment)* weit

root [ruːt] *n* Wurzel *f*; **root out** *vt*
(eradicate) ausrotten; **root vegetable** *n*
Wurzelgemüse *nt*

rope [rəʊp] *n* Seil *nt*; **to know the ~s** *(fam)*
sich auskennen

rose [rəʊz] *pt of* **rise** ▷ *n* Rose *f*

rosé ['rəʊzeɪ] *n* Rosé(wein) *m*

rot [rɒt] *vi* verfaulen

rota ['rəʊtə] *n (Brit)* Dienstplan *m*

rotate [rəʊ'teɪt] *vt (turn)* rotieren lassen
▷ *vi* rotieren; **rotation** [rəʊ'teɪʃən] *n*
(turning) Rotation *f*; **in ~** abwechselnd

rotten ['rɒtn] *adj (decayed)* faul; *(mean)*
gemein; *(unpleasant)* scheußlich; *(ill)* elend

rough [rʌf] *adj (not smooth)* rau; *(path)*
uneben; *(coarse, violent)* grob; *(crossing)*
stürmisch; *(without comforts)* hart;
(unfinished, makeshift) grob; *(approximate)*
ungefähr; **~ draft** Rohentwurf *m*; **I have a**
~ idea ich habe eine ungefähre
Vorstellung ▷ *adv* **to sleep ~** im Freien
schlafen ▷ *vt* **to ~ it** primitiv leben ▷ *n* **to**
write sth in ~ etw ins Unreine schreiben;
roughly *adv* grob; *(approximately)*
ungefähr

round [raʊnd] *adj* rund ▷ *adv* **all ~** *(on all*
sides) rundherum; **the long way ~** der
längere Weg; **I'll be ~ at 8** ich werde um
acht Uhr da sein; **the other way**
~ umgekehrt ▷ *prep (surrounding)* um (...
herum); **~ (about)** *(approximately)*
ungefähr; **~ the corner** um die Ecke; **to go**
~ the world um die Welt reisen; **she lives**
~ here sie wohnt hier in der Gegend ▷ *n*
Runde *f*; *(of bread, toast)* Scheibe *f*; **it's my**
~ *(of drinks)* die Runde geht auf mich ▷ *vt*
(corner) biegen um; **round off** *vt*
abrunden; **round up** *vt (number, price)*
aufrunden

roundabout *n (Brit Auto)* Kreisverkehr *m*;
(Brit: merry-go-round) Karussell *nt* ▷ *adj*
umständlich; **round-the-clock** *adj* rund
um die Uhr; **round trip** *n* Rundreise *f*;
round-trip ticket *n (US)* Rückfahrkarte *f*;
(for plane) Rückflugticket *nt*

rouse [raʊz] *vt (from sleep)* wecken

route [ruːt] *n* Route *f*; *(bus, plane etc*
service) Linie *f*; *(fig)* Weg *m*

routine [ruː'tiːn] *n* Routine *f* ▷ *adj*
Routine-

row [rəʊ] *n (line)* Reihe *f*; **three times in a**
~ dreimal hintereinander ▷ *vt, vi (boat)*
rudern ▷ [raʊ] *n (noise)* Krach *m*; *(dispute)*
Streit *m*

rowboat ['rəʊbəʊt] *n (US)* Ruderboot *nt*

row house ['rəʊhaʊs] *n (US)* Reihenhaus
nt

rowing ['rəʊɪŋ] *n* Rudern *nt*; **rowing boat**
n (Brit) Ruderboot *nt*; **rowing machine** *n*
Rudergerät *nt*

royal ['rɔɪəl] *adj* königlich; **royalty** *n*
(family) Mitglieder *pl* der königlichen
Familie; **royalties** *pl (from book, music)*
Tantiemen *pl*

RSPCA *abbr =* **Royal Society for the**
Prevention of Cruelty to Animals
britischer Tierschutzverein

RSPCC *abbr =* **Royal Society for the**
Prevention of Cruelty to Children
britischer Kinderschutzverein

RSVP *abbr =* **répondez s'il vous plaît** u. A.
w. g.

rub [rʌb] *vt* reiben; **rub in** *vt*
einmassieren; **rub out** *vt (with eraser)*
ausradieren

rubber ['rʌbə*] *n* Gummi *m*; *(Brit: eraser)*
Radiergummi *m*; *(US fam: contraceptive)*
Gummi *m*; **rubber band** *n* Gummiband
nt; **rubber stamp** *n* Stempel *m*

rubbish ['rʌbɪʃ] *n* Abfall *m*; *(nonsense)*
Quatsch *m*; *(poor-quality thing)* Mist *m*;
don't talk ~ red keinen Unsinn!; **rubbish**
bin *n* Mülleimer *m*; **rubbish dump** *n*
Müllabladeplatz *m*

rubble ['rʌbl] *n* Schutt *m*

ruby ['ruːbɪ] *n (stone)* Rubin *m*

rucksack ['rʌksæk] *n* Rucksack *m*

rude [ruːd] *adj (impolite)* unhöflich;
(indecent) unanständig

rug [rʌg] *n* Teppich *m*; *(next to bed)*
Bettvorleger *m*; *(for knees)* Wolldecke *f*

rugby ['rʌgbɪ] *n* Rugby *nt*

rugged ['rʌgɪd] *adj (coastline)* zerklüftet;
(features) markant

ruin ['ruːɪn] *n* Ruine *f*; *(financial, social)*
Ruin *m* ▷ *vt* ruinieren

rule [ruːl] *n* Regel *f*; *(governing)* Herrschaft
f; **as a ~** in der Regel ▷ *vt, vi (govern)*
regieren; *(decide)* entscheiden; **ruler** *n*
Lineal *nt*; *(person)* Herrscher(in) *m(f)*

rum [rʌm] *n* Rum *m*

rumble ['rʌmbl] *vi* (*stomach*) knurren; (*train, truck*) rumpeln

rummage ['rʌmɪdʒ] *vi* ~ (**around**) herumstöbern

rumor (*US*), **rumour** ['ruːmə*] *n* Gerücht *nt*

run [rʌn] (*ran, run*) *vt* (*race, distance*) laufen; (*machine, engine, computer program, water*) laufen lassen; (*manage*) leiten, führen; (*car*) unterhalten; **I ran her home** ich habe sie nach Hause gefahren ▷ *vi* laufen; (*move quickly*) rennen; (*bus, train*) fahren; (*path etc*) verlaufen; (*machine, engine, computer program*) laufen; (*flow*) fließen; (*colours, make-up*) verlaufen; **to ~ for President** für die Präsidentschaft kandidieren; **to be ~ning low** knapp werden; **my nose is ~ning** mir läuft die Nase; **it ~s in the family** es liegt in der Familie ▷ *n* (*on foot*) Lauf *m*; (*in car*) Spazierfahrt *f*; (*series*) Reihe *f*; (*sudden demand*) Ansturm *m* (*on auf +akk*); (*in tights*) Laufmasche *f*; (*in cricket, baseball*) Lauf *m*; **to go for a ~** laufen gehen; (*in car*) eine Spazierfahrt machen; **in the long ~** auf die Dauer; **on the ~** auf der Flucht (*from* vor *+dat*); **run about** *vi* herumlaufen; **run away** *vi* weglaufen; **run down** *vt* (*with car*) umfahren; (*criticize*) heruntermachen; **to be ~** (*tired*) abgespannt sein; **run into** *vt* (*meet*) zufällig treffen; (*problem*) stoßen auf *+akk*; **run off** *vi* weglaufen; **run out** *vi* (*person*) hinausrennen; (*liquid*) auslaufen; (*lease, time*) ablaufen; (*money, supplies*) ausgehen; **he ran ~ of money** ihm ging das Geld aus; **run over** *vt* (*with car*) überfahren; **run up** *vt* (*debt, bill*) machen

rung [rʌŋ] *pp of* **ring**

runner ['rʌnə*] *n* (*athlete*) Läufer(in) *m(f)*; **to do a ~** (*fam*) wegrennen; **runner beans** *npl* (*Brit*) Stangenbohnen *pl*

running ['rʌnɪŋ] *n* (*Sport*) Laufen *nt*; (*management*) Leitung *f*, Führung *f* ▷ *adj* (*water*) fließend; **~ costs** Betriebskosten *pl*; (*for car*) Unterhaltskosten *pl*; **3 days ~** 3 Tage hintereinander

runny ['rʌnɪ] *adj* (*food*) flüssig; (*nose*) laufend

runway ['rʌnweɪ] *n* Start- und Landebahn *f*

rural ['ruərəl] *adj* ländlich

rush [rʌʃ] *n* Eile *f*; (*for tickets etc*) Ansturm *m* (*for auf +akk*); **to be in a ~** es eilig haben; **there's no ~** es eilt nicht ▷ *vt* (*do too quickly*) hastig machen; (*meal*) hastig essen; **to ~ sb to hospital** jdn auf dem schnellsten Weg ins Krankenhaus bringen; **don't ~ me** dräng mich nicht ▷ *vi* (*hurry*) eilen; **don't ~** lass dir Zeit; **rush hour** *n* Hauptverkehrszeit *f*

rusk [rʌsk] *n* Zwieback *m*

Russia ['rʌʃə] *n* Russland *nt*; **Russian** *adj* russisch ▷ *n* Russe *m*, Russin *f*; (*language*) Russisch *nt*

rust [rʌst] *n* Rost *m* ▷ *vi* rosten; **rustproof** ['rʌstpruːf] *adj* rostfrei; **rusty** ['rʌstɪ] *adj* rostig

ruthless ['ruːθləs] *adj* rücksichtslos; (*treatment, criticism*) schonungslos

rye [raɪ] *n* Roggen *m*; **rye bread** *n* Roggenbrot *nt*

S

S *abbr* = **south** S

sabotage ['sæbətɑːʒ] *vt* sabotieren

sachet ['sæʃeɪ] *n* Päckchen *nt*

sack [sæk] *n* (*bag*) Sack *m*; **to get the ~** (*fam*) rausgeschmissen werden ▷ *vt* (*fam*) rausschmeißen

sacred ['seɪkrɪd] *adj* heilig

sacrifice ['sækrɪfaɪs] *n* Opfer *nt* ▷ *vt* opfern

sad [sæd] *adj* traurig

saddle ['sædl] *n* Sattel *m*

sadistic [sə'dɪstɪk] *adj* sadistisch

sadly ['sædlɪ] *adv* (*unfortunately*) leider

safari [sə'fɑːrɪ] *n* Safari

safe [seɪf] *adj* (*free from danger*) sicher; (*out of danger*) in Sicherheit; (*careful*) vorsichtig; **have a ~ journey** gute Fahrt! ▷ *n* Safe *m*; **safeguard** *n* Schutz *m* ▷ *vt* schützen (*against* vor +*dat*); **safely** *adv* sicher; (*arrive*) wohlbehalten; (*drive*) vorsichtig; **safety** *n* Sicherheit *f*; **safety belt** *n* Sicherheitsgurt *m*; **safety pin** *n* Sicherheitsnadel *f*

Sagittarius [sædʒɪ'teərɪəs] *n* (*Astr*) Schütze *m*

Sahara [sə'hɑːrə] *n* **the ~** (**Desert**) die (Wüste) Sahara

said [sed] *pt, pp of* **say**

sail [seɪl] *n* Segel *nt*; **to set ~** losfahren (*for* nach) ▷ *vi* (*in yacht*) segeln; (*on ship*) mit dem Schiff fahren; (*ship*) auslaufen (*for* nach) ▷ *vt* (*yacht*) segeln mit; (*ship*) steuern; **sailboat** *n* (*US*) Segelboot *nt*; **sailing** *n* **to go ~** segeln gehen; **sailing boat** *n* (*Brit*) Segelboot *nt*; **sailor** *n* Seemann *m*; (*in navy*) Matrose *m*

saint [seɪnt] *n* Heilige(r) *mf*

sake [seɪk] *n* **for the ~ of** um +*gen* ... willen; **for your ~** deinetwegen, dir zuliebe

salad ['sæləd] *n* Salat *m*; **salad cream** *n* (*Brit*) majonäseartige Salatsoße; **salad dressing** *n* Salatsoße *f*

salary ['sælərɪ] *n* Gehalt *nt*

sale [seɪl] *n* Verkauf *m*; (*at reduced prices*) Ausverkauf *m*; **the ~s** *pl* (*in summer, winter*) der Schlussverkauf; **for ~** zu verkaufen; **sales clerk** *n* (*US*) Verkäufer(in) *m(f)*; **salesman** (*pl* **-men**) *n* Verkäufer *m*; (*rep*) Vertreter *m*; **sales rep** *n* Vertreter(in) *m(f)*; **sales tax** *n* (*US*) Verkaufssteuer *f*; **saleswoman** (*pl* **-women**) *n* Verkäuferin *f*; (*rep*) Vertreterin *f*

saliva [sə'laɪvə] *n* Speichel *m*

salmon ['sæmən] *n* Lachs *m*

saloon [sə'luːn] *n* (*ship's lounge*) Salon *m*; (*US: bar*) Kneipe *f*

salt [sɔːlt] *n* Salz *nt* ▷ *vt* (*flavour*) salzen; (*roads*) mit Salz streuen; **salt cellar**, **salt shaker** (*US*) *n* Salzstreuer *m*; **salty** *adj* salzig

salvage ['sælvɪdʒ] *vt* bergen (*from* aus); (*fig*) retten

same [seɪm] *adj* **the ~** (*similar*) der/die/das gleiche, die gleichen *pl*; (*identical*) der-/die-/dasselbe, dieselben *pl*; **they live in the ~ house** sie wohnen im selben Haus ▷ *pron* **the ~** (*similar*) der/die/das Gleiche, die Gleichen *pl*; (*identical*) der-/die-/dasselbe, dieselben *pl*; **I'll have the ~ again** ich möchte noch mal das Gleiche; **all the ~** trotzdem; **the ~ to you** gleichfalls; **it's all the ~ to me** es ist mir egal ▷ *adv* **the ~** gleich; **they look the ~** sie sehen gleich aus

sample ['sɑːmpl] *n* Probe *f*; (*of fabric*) Muster *nt* ▷ *vt* probieren

sanctions ['sæŋkʃənz] *npl* (*Pol*) Sanktionen *pl*

sanctuary ['sæŋktjʊərɪ] *n* (*refuge*) Zuflucht *f*; (*for animals*) Schutzgebiet *nt*

sand [sænd] *n* Sand *m*

sandal ['sændl] *n* Sandale *f*

sandpaper *n* Sandpapier *nt* ▷ *vt* schmirgeln

sandwich ['sænwɪdʒ] *n* Sandwich *nt*

sandy ['sændɪ] *adj* (*full of sand*) sandig; **~ beach** Sandstrand *m*

sane [seɪn] *adj* geistig gesund, normal; (*sensible*) vernünftig

sang [sæŋ] *pt of* **sing**

sanitary ['sænɪtərɪ] *adj* hygienisch; **sanitary napkin** (*US*), **sanitary towel** *n* Damenbinde *f*

sank [sæŋk] *pt of* **sink**

Santa (Claus) ['sæntə('klɔːz)] *n* der Weihnachtsmann

sarcastic [sɑːˈkæstɪk] *adj* sarkastisch

sardine [sɑːˈdiːn] *n* Sardine *f*

Sardinia [sɑːˈdɪnɪə] *n* Sardinien *nt*

sari [sɑːrɪ] *n* Sari *m* (*von indischen Frauen getragenes Gewand*)

sat [sæt] *pt, pp of* **sit**

Sat *abbr* = **Saturday** Sa.

satellite ['sætəlaɪt] *n* Satellit *m*; **satellite dish** *n* Satellitenschüssel *f*; **satellite TV** *n* Satellitenfernsehen *nt*

satin ['sætɪn] *n* Satin *m*

satisfaction [sætɪsˈfækʃən] *n* (*contentment*) Zufriedenheit *f*; **is that to your ~?** sind Sie damit zufrieden?; **satisfactory** [sætɪsˈfæktərɪ] *adj* zufrieden stellend; **satisfied** ['sætɪsfaɪd] *adj* zufrieden (*with* mit); **satisfy** ['sætɪsfaɪ] *vt* zufrieden stellen; (*convince*) überzeugen; (*conditions*) erfüllen; (*need, demand*) befriedigen; **satisfying** *adj* befriedigend

Saturday ['sætədeɪ] *n* Samstag *m*, Sonnabend *m*; *see also* **Tuesday**

sauce [sɔːs] *n* Soße *f*; **saucepan** *n* Kochtopf *m*; **saucer** *n* Untertasse *f*

saucy ['sɔːsɪ] *adj* frech

Saudi Arabia ['saʊdɪə'reɪbɪə] *n* Saudi-Arabien *nt*

sauna ['sɔːnə] *n* Sauna *f*

sausage ['sɒsɪdʒ] *n* Wurst *f*; **sausage roll** *n* mit Wurst gefülltes Blätterteigröllchen

savage ['sævɪdʒ] *adj* (*person, attack*) brutal; (*animal*) wild

save [seɪv] *vt* (*rescue*) retten (*from* vor +*dat*); (*money, time, electricity etc*) sparen; (*strength*) schonen; (*Inform*) speichern; **to ~ sb's life** jdm das Leben retten ▷ *vi* sparen ▷ *n* (*in football*) Parade *f*; **save up** *vi* sparen (*for* auf +*akk*); **saving** *n* (*of money*) Sparen *nt*; **~s** *pl* Ersparnisse *pl*; **~s account** Sparkonto *nt*

savory (*US*), **savoury** ['seɪvərɪ] *adj* (*not sweet*) pikant

saw [sɔː] (**sawed, sawn**) *vt, vi* sägen ▷ *n* (*tool*) Säge *f* ▷ *pt of* **see**; **sawdust** *n* Sägemehl *nt*

saxophone ['sæksəfəʊn] *n* Saxophon *nt*

say [seɪ] (**said, said**) *vt* sagen (*to sb* jdm); (*prayer*) sprechen; **what does the letter ~?** was steht im Brief?; **the rules ~ that ...** in den Regeln heißt es, dass ...; **he's said to be rich** er soll reich sein ▷ *n* **to have a ~ in sth** bei etw ein Mitspracherecht haben ▷ *adv* zum Beispiel; **saying** *n* Sprichwort *nt*

scab [skæb] *n* (*on cut*) Schorf *m*

scaffolding ['skæfəʊldɪŋ] *n* (Bau)gerüst *nt*

scale [skeɪl] *n* (*of map etc*) Maßstab *m*; (*on thermometer etc*) Skala *f*; (*of pay*) Tarifsystem *nt*; (*Mus*) Tonleiter *f*; (*of fish, snake*) Schuppe *f*; **to ~** maßstabsgerecht; **on a large/small ~** in großem/kleinem Umfang; **scales** *npl* (*for weighing*) Waage *f*

scalp [skælp] *n* Kopfhaut *f*

scan [skæn] *vt* (*examine*) genau prüfen; (*read quickly*) überfliegen; (*Inform*) scannen ▷ *n* (*Med*) Ultraschall *m*; **scan in** *vt* (*Inform*) einscannen

scandal ['skændl] *n* Skandal *m*; **scandalous** *adj* skandalös

Scandinavia [skændɪˈneɪvɪə] *n* Skandinavien *nt*; **Scandinavian** *adj* skandinavisch ▷ *n* Skandinavier(in) *m(f)*

scanner ['skænə*] *n* Scanner *m*

scapegoat ['skeɪpgəʊt] *n* Sündenbock *m*

scar [skɑː*] *n* Narbe *f*

scarce ['skeəs] *adj* selten; (*in short supply*) knapp; **scarcely** *adv* kaum

scare ['skeə*] *n* (*general alarm*) Panik *f* ▷ *vt* erschrecken; **to be ~d** Angst haben (*of* vor +*dat*)

scarf [skɑːf] (*pl* **-scarves**) *n* Schal *m*; (*on head*) Kopftuch *nt*

scarlet ['skɑːlət] *adj* scharlachrot; **scarlet fever** *n* Scharlach *m*

scary ['skeərɪ] *adj* (*film, story*) gruselig

scatter ['skætə*] *vt* verstreuen; (*seed,*

gravel) streuen; *(disperse)* auseinander treiben

scene [si:n] *n (location)* Ort *m; (division of play) (Theat)* Szene *f; (view)* Anblick *m;* **to make a ~** eine Szene machen; **scenery** ['si:nərɪ] *n (landscape)* Landschaft *f; (Theat)* Kulissen *pl;* **scenic** ['si:nɪk] *adj (landscape)* malerisch; **~ route** landschaftlich schöne Strecke

scent [sent] *n (perfume)* Parfüm *nt; (smell)* Duft *m*

sceptical ['skeptɪkəl] *adj (Brit)* skeptisch

schedule ['ʃedju:l, 'skedʒʊəl] *n (plan)* Programm *nt; (of work)* Zeitplan *m; (list)* Liste *f; (US: of trains, buses, air traffic)* Fahr-, Flugplan *m;* **on ~** planmäßig; **to be behind ~ with sth** mit etw in Verzug sein ▷ *vt* **the meeting is ~d for next Monday** die Besprechung ist für nächsten Montag angesetzt; **scheduled** *adj (departure, arrival)* planmäßig; **~ flight** Linienflug *m*

scheme [ski:m] *n (plan)* Plan *m; (project)* Projekt *nt; (dishonest)* Intrige *f* ▷ *vi* intrigieren

schizophrenic [skɪtsə'frenɪk] *adj* schizophren

scholar ['skɒlə*] *n* Gelehrte(r) *mf;* **scholarship** *n (grant)* Stipendium *nt*

school [sku:l] *n* Schule *f; (university department)* Fachbereich *m; (US: university)* Universität *f;* **school bag** *n* Schultasche *f;* **schoolbook** *n* Schulbuch *nt;* **schoolboy** *n* Schüler *m;* **school bus** *n* Schulbus *m;* **schoolgirl** *n* Schülerin *f;* **schoolteacher** *n* Lehrer(in) *m(f);* **schoolwork** *n* Schularbeiten *pl*

sciatica [saɪ'ætɪkə] *n* Ischias *m*

science ['saɪəns] *n* Wissenschaft *f; (natural ~)* Naturwissenschaft *f;* **science fiction** *n* Sciencefiction *f;* **scientific** [saɪən'tɪfɪk] *adj* wissenschaftlich; **scientist** ['saɪəntɪst] *n* Wissenschaftler(in) *m(f); (in natural sciences)* Naturwissenschaftler(in) *m(f)*

scissors ['sɪzəz] *npl* Schere *f*

scone [skɒn] *n kleines süßes Hefebrötchen mit oder ohne Rosinen, das mit Butter oder Dickrahm und Marmelade gegessen wird*

scoop [sku:p] *n (exclusive story)* Exklusivbericht *m;* **a ~ of ice-cream** eine Kugel Eis ▷ *vt* **to ~ (up)** schaufeln

scooter ['sku:tə*] *n (Motor)roller *m; (toy)* (Tret)roller *m*

scope [skəʊp] *n* Umfang *m; (opportunity)* Möglichkeit *f*

score [skɔ:*] *n (Sport)* Spielstand *m; (final result)* Spielergebnis *nt; (in quiz etc)* Punktestand *m; (Mus)* Partitur *f;* **to keep (the) ~** mitzählen ▷ *vt (goal)* schießen; *(points)* machen ▷ *vi (keep ~)* mitzählen; **scoreboard** *n* Anzeigetafel *f*

scorn ['skɔ:n] *n* Verachtung *f;* **scornful** *adj* verächtlich

Scorpio ['skɔ:pɪəʊ] *(pl -s) n (Astr)* Skorpion *m*

scorpion ['skɔ:pɪən] *n* Skorpion *m*

Scot [skɒt] *n* Schotte *m,* Schottin *f;* **Scotch** [skɒtʃ] *adj* schottisch ▷ *n (whisky)* schottischer Whisky, Scotch *m*

Scotch tape® *n (US)* Tesafilm® *m*

Scotland ['skɒtlənd] *n* Schottland *nt;* **Scotsman** *(pl -men) n* Schotte *m;* **Scotswoman** *(pl -women) n* Schottin *f;* **Scottish** *adj* schottisch

scout [skaʊt] *n (boy ~)* Pfadfinder *m*

scowl [skaʊl] *vi* finster blicken

scrambled eggs *npl* Rührei *nt*

scrap [skræp] *n (bit)* Stückchen *nt,* Fetzen *m; (metal)* Schrott *m* ▷ *vt (car)* verschrotten; *(plan)* verwerfen; **scrapbook** *n* Sammelalbum *nt*

scrape [skreɪp] *n (scratch)* Kratzer *m* ▷ *vt (car)* schrammen; *(wall)* streifen; **to ~ one's knee** sich das Knie schürfen; **scrape through** *vi (exam)* mit knapper Not bestehen

scrap heap ['skræphi:p] *n* Schrotthaufen *m;* **scrap metal** *n* Schrott *m;* **scrap paper** *n* Schmierpapier *nt*

scratch ['skrætʃ] *n (mark)* Kratzer *m;* **to start from ~** von vorne anfangen ▷ *vt* kratzen; *(car)* zerkratzen; **to ~ one's arm** sich am Arm kratzen ▷ *vi* kratzen; *(~ oneself)* sich kratzen

scream [skri:m] *n* Schrei *m* ▷ *vi* schreien *(with vor +dat);* **to ~ at sb** jdn anschreien

screen [skri:n] *n (Tv, Inform)* Bildschirm *m; (Cine)* Leinwand *f* ▷ *vt (protect)* abschirmen; *(hide)* verdecken; *(film)* zeigen; *(applicants, luggage)* überprüfen; **screenplay** *n* Drehbuch *nt;* **screen saver** *n (Inform)* Bildschirmschoner *m*

screw [skru:] *n* Schraube *f* ▷ *vt (vulg: have sex with)* poppen; **to ~ sth to sth** etw an etw *akk* schrauben; **to ~ off/on** *(lid)* ab-/aufschrauben; **screw up** *vt (paper)*

zusammenknüllen; (make a mess of)
vermasseln; **screwdriver** n
Schraubenzieher m; **screw top** n
Schraubverschluss m

scribble ['skrɪbl] vt, vi kritzeln

script [skrɪpt] n (of play) Text m; (of film)
Drehbuch nt; (style of writing) Schrift f

scroll down ['skrəʊl'daʊn] vi (Inform)
runterscrollen; **scroll up** vi (Inform)
raufscrollen; **scroll bar** n (Inform)
Scrollbar f

scrub [skrʌb] vt schrubben; **scrubbing
brush**, **scrub brush** (US) n Scheuerbürste
f

scruffy ['skrʌfɪ] adj vergammelt

scrupulous, scrupulously ['skru:pjʊləs,
-lɪ] adj, adv gewissenhaft; (painstaking)
peinlich genau

scuba-diving ['sku:bədaɪvɪŋ] n
Sporttauchen nt

sculptor ['skʌlptə*] n Bildhauer(in) m(f);
sculpture ['skʌlptʃə*] n (Art) Bildhauerei
f; (statue) Skulptur f

sea [si:] n Meer nt, See f; **seafood** n
Meeresfrüchte pl; **sea front** n
Strandpromenade f; **seagull** n Möwe f

seal [si:l] n (animal) Robbe f; (stamp,
impression) Siegel nt; (Tech) Verschluss m;
(ring etc) Dichtung f ▷ vt versiegeln;
(envelope) zukleben

seam [si:m] n Naht f

seaport ['si:pɔ:t] n Seehafen m

search [sɜ:tʃ] n Suche f (for nach); **to do a
~ for** (Inform) suchen nach; **in ~ of** auf der
Suche nach ▷ vi suchen (for nach) ▷ vt
durchsuchen; **search engine** n (Inform)
Suchmaschine f

seashell ['si:ʃel] n Muschel f; **seashore** n
Strand m; **seasick** adj seekrank; **seaside**
n **at the ~** am Meer; **to go to the ~** ans
Meer fahren; **seaside resort** n Seebad nt

season ['si:zn] n Jahreszeit f; (Comm)
Saison f; **high/low ~** Hoch-/Nebensaison f
▷ vt (flavour) würzen

seasoning n Gewürz nt

season ticket n (Rail) Zeitkarte f; (Theat)
Abonnement nt; (Sport) Dauerkarte f

seat [si:t] n (place) Platz m; (chair) Sitz m;
take a ~ setzen Sie sich ▷ vt **the hall ~s
300** der Saal hat 300 Sitzplätze; **please be
~ed** bitte setzen Sie sich; **to remain ~ed**
sitzen bleiben; **seat belt** n
Sicherheitsgurt m

sea view ['si:vju:] n Seeblick m; **seaweed**
n Seetang m

secluded [sɪ'klu:dɪd] adj abgelegen

second ['sekənd] adj zweite(r, s); **the ~ of
June** der zweite Juni ▷ adv (in ~ position) an
zweiter Stelle; (secondly) zweitens; **he
came ~** er ist Zweiter geworden ▷ n (of
time) Sekunde f; (moment) Augenblick m;
~ (gear) der zweite Gang; (~ helping)
zweite Portion; **just a ~** (einen)
Augenblick!; **secondary** adj (less
important) zweitrangig; **~ education**
höhere Schulbildung f; **~ school**
weiterführende Schule; **second-class**
adj (ticket) zweiter Klasse; **~ stamp**
Briefmarke für nicht bevorzugt beförderte
Sendungen ▷ adv (travel) zweiter Klasse;
secondhand adj, adv gebraucht;
(information) aus zweiter Hand; **secondly**
adv zweitens; **second-rate** adj (pej)
zweitklassig

secret ['si:krət] n Geheimnis nt ▷ adj
geheim; (admirer) heimlich

secretary ['sekrətrɪ] n Sekretär(in) m(f);
(minister) Minister(in) m(f); **Secretary of
State** n (US) Außenminister(in) m(f)

secretive ['si:krətɪv] adj (person)
geheimnistuerisch; **secretly** ['si:krətlɪ]
adv heimlich

sect [sekt] n Sekte f

section ['sekʃən] n (part) Teil m; (of
document) Abschnitt m; (department)
Abteilung f

secure [sɪ'kjʊə*] adj (safe) sicher (from vor
+dat); (firmly fixed) fest ▷ vt (make firm)
befestigen; (window, door) fest
verschließen; (obtain) sich sichern;
securely adv fest; (safely) sicher; **security**
[sɪ'kjʊərɪtɪ] n Sicherheit f

sedative ['sedətɪv] n Beruhigungsmittel
nt

seduce [sɪ'dju:s] vt verführen; **seductive**
[sɪ'dʌktɪv] adj verführerisch; (offer)
verlockend

see [si:] (**saw, seen**) vt sehen; (understand)
verstehen; (check) nachsehen; (accompany)
bringen; (visit) besuchen; (talk to)
sprechen; **to ~ the doctor** zum Arzt
gehen; **to ~ sb home** jdn nach Hause
begleiten; **I saw him swimming** ich habe
ihn schwimmen sehen; **~ you** tschüs!;
~ you on Friday bis Freitag! ▷ vi sehen;
(understand) verstehen; (check) nachsehen;

S

(**you**) **~** siehst du!; **we'll ~** mal sehen; **see about** vt (attend to) sich kümmern um; **see off** vt (say goodbye to) verabschieden; **see out** vt (show out) zur Tür bringen; **see through** vt **to see sth through** etw zu Ende bringen; **to ~ sb/sth** jdn/etw durchschauen; **see to** vt sich kümmern um; **~ it that …** sieh zu, dass …

seed [siːd] n (of plant) Samen m; (in fruit) Kern m; **seedless** adj kernlos

seek [siːk] (**sought, sought**) vt suchen; (fame) streben nach; **to ~ sb's advice** jdn um Rat fragen

seem [siːm] vi scheinen; **he ~s (to be) honest** er scheint ehrlich zu sein; **it ~s to me that …** es scheint mir, dass …

seen [siːn] pp of **see**

seesaw ['siːsɔː] n Wippe f

segment ['segmənt] n Teil m

seize [siːz] vt packen; (confiscate) beschlagnahmen; (opportunity, power) ergreifen

seldom ['seldəm] adv selten

select [sɪ'lekt] adj (exclusive) exklusiv ▷ vt auswählen; **selection** [sɪ'lekʃən] n Auswahl f (of an +dat); **selective** adj (choosy) wählerisch

self [self] (pl **selves**) n Selbst nt, Ich nt; **he's his old ~ again** er ist wieder ganz der Alte; **self-adhesive** adj selbstklebend; **self-assured** n selbstsicher; **self-catering** adj für Selbstversorger; **self-centred** adj egozentrisch; **self-confidence** n Selbstbewusstsein nt; **self-confident** adj selbstbewusst; **self-conscious** adj befangen, verklemmt; **self-contained** adj (flat) separat; **self-control** n Selbstbeherrschung f; **self-defence** n Selbstverteidigung f; **self-employed** adj selbstständig; **self-evident** adj offensichtlich

selfish, selfishly ['selfɪʃ, -lɪ] adj, adv egoistisch, selbstsüchtig; **selfless, selflessly** adj, adv selbstlos

self-pity [self'pɪtɪ] n Selbstmitleid nt; **self-portrait** n Selbstporträt nt; **self-respect** n Selbstachtung f; **self-service** n Selbstbedienung f ▷ adj Selbstbedienungs-

sell [sel] (**sold, sold**) vt verkaufen; **to ~ sb sth, to ~ sth to sb** jdm etw verkaufen; **do you ~ postcards?** haben Sie Postkarten?

▷ vi (product) sich verkaufen; **sell out** vt **to be sold ~** ausverkauft sein; **sell-by date** n Haltbarkeitsdatum nt

Sellotape® ['seləteɪp] n (Brit) Tesafilm® m

semester [sɪ'mestə*] n Semester nt

semi ['semɪ] n (Brit: house) Doppelhaushälfte f; **semicircle** n Halbkreis m; **semicolon** n Semikolon nt; **semidetached (house)** n (Brit) Doppelhaushälfte f; **semifinal** n Halbfinale nt

seminar ['semɪnɑː*] n Seminar nt

semiskimmed milk ['semɪskɪmd'mɪlk] n Halbfettmilch f

senate ['senət] n Senat m; **senator** n Senator(in) m(f)

send [send] (**sent, sent**) vt schicken; **to ~ sb sth, to ~ sth to sb** jdm etw schicken; **~ her my best wishes** grüße sie von mir; **send away** vt wegschicken ▷ vi **to ~ for** anfordern; **send back** vt zurückschicken; **send for** vt (person) holen lassen; (by post) anfordern; **send off** vt (by post) abschicken; **send out** vt (invitations etc) verschicken ▷ vi **to ~ for sth** etw holen lassen

sender ['sendə*] n Absender(in) m(f)

senior ['siːnɪə*] adj (older) älter; (high-ranking) höher; (pupils) älter; **he is ~ to me** er ist mir übergeordnet ▷ n **he's eight years my ~** er ist acht Jahre älter als ich; **senior citizen** n Senior(in) m(f)

sensation [sen'seɪʃən] n Gefühl nt; (excitement, person, thing) Sensation f; **sensational** adj sensationell

sense [sens] n (faculty, meaning) Sinn m; (feeling) Gefühl nt; (understanding) Verstand m; **~ of smell/taste** Geruchs-/Geschmackssinn m; **to have a ~ of humour** Humor haben; **to make ~** (sentence etc) einen Sinn ergeben; (be sensible) Sinn machen; **in a ~** gewissermaßen ▷ vt spüren; **senseless** adj (stupid) sinnlos

sensible, sensibly ['sensəbl, -blɪ] adj, adv vernünftig

sensitive ['sensɪtɪv] adj empfindlich (to gegen); (easily hurt) sensibel; (subject) heikel

sensual ['sensjʊəl] adj sinnlich

sensuous ['sensjʊəs] adj sinnlich

sent [sent] pt, pp of **send**

sentence ['sentəns] n (Ling) Satz m; (Jur) Strafe f ▷ vt verurteilen (to zu)
sentiment ['sentimənt] n (sentimentality) Sentimentalität f; (opinion) Ansicht f; **sentimental** [senti'mentl] adj sentimental
separate ['seprət] adj getrennt, separat; (individual) einzeln ▷ ['sepəreit] vt trennen (from von); **they are ~d** (couple) sie leben getrennt ▷ vi sich trennen; **separately** adv getrennt; (singly) einzeln
September [sep'tembə*] n September m; **in ~** im September; **on the 2nd of ~** am 2. September; **at the beginning/in the middle/at the end of ~** Anfang/Mitte/Ende September; **last/next ~** letzten/nächsten September
septic ['septik] adj vereitert
sequel ['si:kwəl] n (to film, book) Fortsetzung f (to von)
sequence ['si:kwəns] n (order) Reihenfolge f
Serb ['sɜ:b] n Serbe m, Serbin f; **Serbia** ['sɜ:bjə] n Serbien nt
sergeant ['sɑ:dʒənt] n Polizeimeister(in) m(f); (Mil) Feldwebel(in) m(f)
serial ['siəriəl] n (TV) Serie f; (in newspaper etc) Fortsetzungsroman m ▷ adj (Inform) seriell; **~ number** Seriennummer f
series ['siəriz] nsing Reihe f; (TV, Radio) Serie f
serious ['siəriəs] adj ernst; (injury, illness, mistake) schwer; (discussion) ernsthaft; **are you ~?** ist das dein Ernst?; **seriously** adv ernsthaft; (hurt) schwer; **~?** im Ernst?; **to take sb ~** jdn ernst nehmen
sermon ['sɜ:mən] n (Rel) Predigt f
servant ['sɜ:vənt] n Diener(in) m(f); **serve** [sɜ:v] vt (customer) bedienen; (food) servieren; (one's country etc) dienen +dat; (sentence) verbüßen; **I'm being ~d** ich werde schon bedient; **it ~s him right** es geschieht ihm recht ▷ vi dienen (as als), aufschlagen ▷ n Aufschlag m
server n (Inform) Server m
service ['sɜ:vis] n (in shop, hotel) Bedienung f; (activity, amenity) Dienstleistung f; (set of dishes) Service nt; (Auto) Inspektion f; (Tech) Wartung f; (Rel) Gottesdienst m, Aufschlag m; **train/bus ~** Zug-/Busverbindung f; **'~ not included'** „Bedienung nicht inbegriffen" ▷ vt (Auto, Tech) warten;

service area n (on motorway) Raststätte f (mit Tankstelle); **service charge** n Bedienung f; **service provider** n (Inform) Provider m; **service station** n Tankstelle f
serving ['sɜ:viŋ] n (portion) Portion f
session ['seʃən] n (of court, assembly) Sitzung f
set [set] (set, set) vt (place) stellen; (lay flat) legen; (arrange) anordnen; (table) decken; (trap, record) aufstellen; (time, price) festsetzen; (watch, alarm) stellen (for auf +akk); **to ~ sb a task** jdm eine Aufgabe stellen; **to ~ free** freilassen; **to ~ a good example** ein gutes Beispiel geben; **the novel is ~ in London** der Roman spielt in London ▷ vi (sun) untergehen; (become hard) fest werden; (bone) zusammenwachsen ▷ n (collection of things) Satz m; (of cutlery, furniture) Garnitur f; (group of people) Kreis m; (Radio, TV) Apparat m, Satz m; (Theat) Bühnenbild nt; (Cine) (Film)kulisse f ▷ adj (agreed, prescribed) festgelegt; (ready) bereit; **~ meal** Menü nt; **set aside** vt (money) beiseite legen; (time) einplanen; **set off** vi aufbrechen (for nach) ▷ vt (alarm) auslösen; (enhance) hervorheben; **set out** vi aufbrechen (for nach) ▷ vt (chairs, chesspieces etc) aufstellen; (state) darlegen; **to ~ to do sth** (intend) beabsichtigen, etw zu tun; **set up** vt (firm, organization) gründen; (stall, tent, camera) aufbauen; (meeting) vereinbaren ▷ vi **to ~ as a doctor** sich als Arzt niederlassen
setback n Rückschlag m
settee [se'ti:] n Sofa nt, Couch f
setting ['setiŋ] n (of novel, film) Schauplatz m; (surroundings) Umgebung f
settle ['setl] vt (bill, debt) begleichen; (dispute) beilegen; (question) klären; (stomach) beruhigen ▷ vi **to ~ (down)** (feel at home) sich einleben; (calm down) sich beruhigen; **settle in** vi (in place) sich einleben; (in job) sich eingewöhnen; **settle up** vi (be)zahlen; **to ~ with sb** mit jdm abrechnen; **settlement** n (of bill, debt) Begleichung f; (colony) Siedlung f; **to reach a ~** sich einigen
setup ['setʌp] n (organization) Organisation f; (situation) Situation f
seven ['sevn] num sieben ▷ n Sieben f; see also **eight**; **seventeen** ['sevn'ti:n] num

S

siebzehn ▷ *n* Siebzehn *f*; *see also* **eight**;
seventeenth *adj* siebzehnte(r, s); *see also*
eighth; **seventh** ['sevnθ] *adj* siebte(r, s)
▷ *n* (*fraction*) Siebtel *nt*; *see also* **eighth**;
seventieth ['sevntɪɪθ] *adj* siebzigste(r, s);
see also **eighth**; **seventy** ['sevntɪ] *num*
siebzig; **~-one** einundsiebzig ▷ *n* Siebzig *f*;
to be in one's seventies in den Siebzigern
sein; *see also* **eight**

several ['sevrəl] *adj, pron* mehrere

severe [sɪ'vɪə*] *adj* (*strict*) streng; (*serious*)
schwer; (*pain*) stark; (*winter*) hart;
severely *adv* (*harshly*) hart; (*seriously*)
schwer

sew [səʊ] (**sewed, sewn**) *vt, vi* nähen

sewage ['su:ɪdʒ] *n* Abwasser *nt*; **sewer**
['sʊə*] *n* Abwasserkanal *m*

sewing ['səʊɪŋ] *n* Nähen *nt*; **sewing
machine** *n* Nähmaschine *f*

sewn [səʊn] *pp of* **sew**

sex [seks] *n* Sex *m*; (*gender*) Geschlecht *nt*;
to have ~ Sex haben (*with* mit); **sexism**
['seksɪzəm] *n* Sexismus *m*; **sexist**
['seksɪst] *adj* sexistisch ▷ *n* Sexist(in)
m(f); **sex life** *n* Sex(ual)leben *nt*

sexual ['seksjʊəl] *adj* sexuell;
~ discrimination/harassment sexuelle
Diskriminierung/Belästigung;
~ intercourse Geschlechtsverkehr *m*;
sexuality [seksjʊ'ælɪtɪ] *n* Sexualität *f*;
sexually *adv* sexuell

sexy ['seksɪ] *adj* sexy

Seychelles ['seɪʃelz] *npl* Seychellen *pl*

shabby ['ʃæbɪ] *adj* schäbig

shack [ʃæk] *n* Hütte *f*

shade [ʃeɪd] *n* (*shadow*) Schatten *m*; (*for
lamp*) (Lampen)schirm *m*; (*colour*) Farbton
m; (*US: sunglasses*) Sonnenbrille *f* ▷ *vt*
(*from sun*) abschirmen; (*in drawing*)
schattieren

shadow ['ʃædəʊ] *n* Schatten *m*

shady ['ʃeɪdɪ] *adj* schattig; (*fig*)
zwielichtig

shake [ʃeɪk] (**shook, shaken**) *vt*
schütteln; (*shock*) erschüttern; **to ~ hands
with sb** jdm die Hand geben; **to ~ one's
head** den Kopf schütteln ▷ *vi* (*tremble*)
zittern; (*building, ground*) schwanken;
shake off *vt* abschütteln; **shaken** ['ʃeɪkn]
pp of **shake**; **shaky** ['ʃeɪkɪ] *adj* (*trembling*)
zittrig; (*table, chair, position*) wackelig;
(*weak*) unsicher

shall [ʃæl] (**should**) *vb aux* werden; (*in

questions*) sollen; **I ~ do my best** ich werde
mein Bestes tun; **~ I come too?** soll ich
mitkommen?; **where ~ we go?** wo gehen
wir hin?

shallow ['ʃæləʊ] *adj* (*a. fig*) seicht; (*person*)
oberflächlich

shame [ʃeɪm] *n* (*feeling of* ~) Scham *f*;
(*disgrace*) Schande *f*; **what a ~** wie schade!;
~ on you schäm dich!; **it's a ~ that ...**
schade, dass ...

shampoo [ʃæm'pu:] *n* Shampoo *nt*; **to
have a ~ and set** sich die Haare waschen
und legen lassen ▷ *vt* (*hair*) waschen;
(*carpet*) schamponieren

shandy ['ʃændɪ] *n* Radler *m*, Alsterwasser
nt

shan't [ʃɑ:nt] *contr of* **shall not**

shape [ʃeɪp] *n* Form *f*; (*unidentified figure*)
Gestalt *f*; **in the ~ of** in Form +*gen*; **to be in
good ~** (*healthwise*) in guter Verfassung
sein; **to take ~** (*plan, idea*) Gestalt
annehmen ▷ *vt* (*clay, person*) formen;
-shaped [ʃeɪpt] *suf* -förmig;
heart~ herzförmig; **shapeless** *adj*
formlos

share [ʃeə*] *n* Anteil +*dat* (*in, of* an *m*); (*Fin*)
Aktie *f* ▷ *vt, vi* teilen; **shareholder** *n*
Aktionär(in) *m(f)*

shark [ʃɑ:k] *n* (*Zool*) Haifisch *m*

sharp [ʃɑ:p] *adj* scharf; (*pin*) spitz; (*person*)
scharfsinnig; (*pain*) heftig; (*increase, fall*)
abrupt; **C/F ~** (*Mus*) Cis/Dis *nt* ▷ *adv* **at 2
o'clock ~** Punkt 2 Uhr; **sharpen** *vt* (*knife*)
schärfen; (*pencil*) spitzen; **sharpener** *n*
(*pencil ~*) Spitzer *m*

shatter ['ʃætə*] *vt* zerschmettern; (*fig*)
zerstören ▷ *vi* zerspringen; **shattered** *adj*
(*exhausted*) kaputt

shave [ʃeɪv] (**shaved, shaved** *o* **shaven**) *vt*
rasieren ▷ *vi* sich rasieren ▷ *n* Rasur *f*;
that was a close ~ (*fig*) das war knapp;
shave off *vt* **to shave one's beard off**
sich den Bart abrasieren; **shaven** ['ʃeɪvn]
pp of **shave** ▷ *adj* (*head*) kahl geschoren;
shaver *n* (*Elec*) Rasierapparat *m*; **shaving
brush** *n* Rasierpinsel *m*; **shaving foam** *n*
Rasierschaum *m*

shawl [ʃɔ:l] *n* Tuch *nt*

she [ʃi:] *pron* sie

shed [ʃed] (**shed, shed**) *n* Schuppen *m*
▷ *vt* (*tears, blood*) vergießen; (*hair, leaves*)
verlieren

she'd [ʃi:d] *contr of* **she had; she would**

sheep [ʃiːp] (pl -) n Schaf nt; **sheepdog** n Schäferhund m; **sheepskin** n Schaffell nt

sheer [ʃɪə*] adj (madness) rein; (steep) steil; (transparent) hauchdünn; **by ~ chance** rein zufällig

sheet [ʃiːt] n (on bed) Betttuch nt; (of paper) Blatt nt; (of metal) Platte f; (of glass) Scheibe f; **a ~ of paper** ein Blatt Papier

shelf [ʃelf] (pl **shelves**) n Bücherbord nt, Regal nt; **shelves** pl (item of furniture) Regal nt

she'll [ʃiːl] contr of **she will; she shall**

shell [ʃel] n (of egg, nut) Schale f; (sea~) Muschel f ▷ vt (peas, nuts) schälen; **shellfish** n (as food) Meeresfrüchte pl

shelter ['ʃeltə*] n (protection) Schutz m; (accommodation) Unterkunft f; (bus ~) Wartehäuschen nt ▷ vt schützen (from vor +dat) ▷ vi sich unterstellen; **sheltered** adj (spot) geschützt; (life) behütet

shelve [ʃelv] vt (fig) aufschieben; **shelves** pl of **shelf**

shepherd ['ʃepəd] n Schäfer m; **shepherd's pie** n Hackfleischauflauf mit Decke aus Kartoffelpüree

sherry ['ʃerɪ] n Sherry m

she's [ʃiːz] contr of **she is; she has**

shield [ʃiːld] n Schild m; (fig) Schutz m ▷ vt schützen (from vor +dat)

shift [ʃɪft] n (change) Veränderung f; (period at work, workers) Schicht f; (on keyboard) Umschalttaste f ▷ vt (furniture etc) verrücken; (stain) entfernen; **to ~ gear(s)** (US Auto) schalten ▷ vi (move) sich bewegen; (move up) rutschen; **shift key** n Umschalttaste f

shin [ʃɪn] n Schienbein nt

shine [ʃaɪn] (**shone, shone**) vi (be shiny) glänzen; (sun) scheinen; (lamp) leuchten ▷ vt (polish) polieren ▷ n Glanz m

shingles ['ʃɪŋglz] nsing (Med) Gürtelrose f

shiny ['ʃaɪnɪ] adj glänzend

ship [ʃɪp] n Schiff nt ▷ vt (send) versenden; (by ship) verschiffen; **shipment** n (goods) Sendung f; (sent by ship) Ladung f; **shipwreck** n Schiffbruch m; **shipyard** n Werft f

shirt [ʃɜːt] n Hemd nt

shiver ['ʃɪvə*] vi zittern (with vor +dat)

shock [ʃɒk] n (mental, emotional) Schock m;

to be in ~ unter Schock stehen; **to get a ~** (Elec) einen Schlag bekommen ▷ vt schockieren; **shock absorber** n Stoßdämpfer m; **shocked** adj schockiert (by über +akk); **shocking** adj schockierend; (awful) furchtbar

shoe [ʃuː] n Schuh m; **shoehorn** n Schuhlöffel m; **shoelace** n Schnürsenkel m; **shoe polish** n Schuhcreme f

shone [ʃɒn] pt, pp of **shine**

shook [ʃʊk] pt of **shake**

shoot [ʃuːt] (**shot, shot**) vt (wound) anschießen; (kill) erschießen; (Cine) drehen; (fam: heroin) drücken ▷ vi (with gun, move quickly) schießen; **to ~ at sb** auf jdn schießen ▷ n (of plant) Trieb m; **shooting** n (exchange of gunfire) Schießerei f; (killing) Erschießung f

shop [ʃɒp] n Geschäft nt, Laden m ▷ vi einkaufen; **shop assistant** n Verkäufer(in) m(f); **shopkeeper** n Geschäftsinhaber(in) m(f); **shoplifting** n Ladendiebstahl m; **shopper** n Käufer(in) m(f); **shopping** n (activity) Einkaufen nt; (goods) Einkäufe pl; **to do the ~** einkaufen; **to go ~** einkaufen gehen; **shopping bag** n Einkaufstasche f; **shopping cart** n (US) Einkaufswagen m; **shopping center** (US), **shopping centre** n Einkaufszentrum nt; **shopping list** n Einkaufszettel m; **shopping trolley** n (Brit) Einkaufswagen m; **shop window** n Schaufenster nt

shore [ʃɔː*] n Ufer nt; **on ~** an Land

short [ʃɔːt] adj kurz; (person) klein; **to be ~ of money** knapp bei Kasse sein; **to be ~ of time** wenig Zeit haben; **~ of breath** kurzatmig; **to cut ~** (holiday) abbrechen; **we are two ~** wir haben zwei zu wenig; **it's ~ for ...** das ist die Kurzform von ... ▷ n (drink, Elec) Kurze(r) m; **shortage** n Knappheit f (of an +dat); **shortbread** n Buttergebäck nt; **short circuit** n Kurzschluss m; **shortcoming** n Unzulänglichkeit f; (of person) Fehler m; **shortcut** n (quicker route) Abkürzung f; (Inform) Shortcut m; **shorten** vt kürzen; (in time) verkürzen; **shorthand** n Stenografie f; **shortlist** n **to be on the ~** in der engeren Wahl sein; **short-lived** adj kurzlebig; **shortly** adv bald; **shorts** npl Shorts pl; **short-sighted** adj (a. fig) kurzsichtig; **short-sleeved** adj kurzärmelig; **short-stay car park** n

Kurzzeitparkplatz m; **short story** n Kurzgeschichte f; **short-term** adj kurzfristig; **short wave** n Kurzwelle f

shot [ʃɒt] pt, pp of **shoot** ▷ n (from gun, in football) Schuss m; (Foto, Cine) Aufnahme f; (injection) Spritze f; (of alcohol) Schuss m

should [ʃʊd] pt of **shall** ▷ vb aux **I ~ go now** ich sollte jetzt gehen; **what ~ I do?** was soll ich tun?; **you ~n't have said that** das hättest du nicht sagen sollen; **that ~ be enough** das müsste reichen

shoulder [ˈʃəʊldə*] n Schulter f

shouldn't [ˈʃʊdnt] contr of **should not**

should've [ˈʃʊdəv] contr of **should have**

shout [ʃaʊt] n Schrei m; (call) Ruf m ▷ vt rufen; (order) brüllen ▷ vi schreien; **to ~ at** anschreien; **to ~ for help** um Hilfe rufen

shove [ʃʌv] vt (person) schubsen; (car, table etc) schieben ▷ vi (in crowd) drängeln

shovel [ˈʃʌvl] n Schaufel f ▷ vt schaufeln

show [ʃəʊ] (**showed, shown**) vt zeigen; **to ~ sb sth, to ~ sth to sb** jdm etw zeigen; **to ~ sb in** jdn hereinführen; **to ~ sb out** jdn zur Tür bringen ▷ n (Cine, Theat) Vorstellung f; (Tv) Show f; (exhibition) Ausstellung f; **show off** vi (pej) angeben; **show round** vt herumführen; **to show sb round the house/the town** jdm das Haus/die Stadt zeigen; **show up** vi (arrive) auftauchen

shower [ˈʃaʊə*] n Dusche f; (rain) Schauer m; **to have** (o **take**) **a ~** duschen ▷ vi (wash) duschen

showing [ˈʃəʊɪŋ] n (Cine) Vorstellung f

shown [ʃəʊn] pp of **show**

showroom [ˈʃəʊruːm] n Ausstellungsraum m

shrank [ʃræŋk] pt of **shrink**

shred [ʃred] n (of paper, fabric) Fetzen m ▷ vt (in shredder) (im Reißwolf) zerkleinern; **shredder** n (for paper) Reißwolf m

shrimp [ʃrɪmp] n Garnele f

shrink [ʃrɪŋk] (**shrank, shrunk**) vi schrumpfen; (clothes) eingehen

shrivel [ˈʃrɪvl] vi **to ~ (up)** schrumpfen; (skin) runzlig werden; (plant) welken

Shrove Tuesday [ˈʃrəʊvˈtjuːzdeɪ] n Fastnachtsdienstag m

shrub [ʃrʌb] n Busch m, Strauch m

shrug [ʃrʌg] vt, vi **to ~ (one's shoulders)** mit den Achseln zucken

shrunk [ʃrʌŋk] pp of **shrink**

shudder [ˈʃʌdə*] vi schaudern; (ground, building) beben

shuffle [ˈʃʌfl] vt, vi mischen

shut [ʃʌt] (**shut, shut**) vt zumachen, schließen; **~ your mouth** (fam) halt den Mund! ▷ vi schließen ▷ adj geschlossen; **we're ~** wir haben geschlossen; **shut down** vt schließen; (computer) ausschalten ▷ vi schließen; (computer) sich ausschalten; **shut in** vt einschließen; **shut out** vt (lock out) aussperren; **to shut oneself out** sich aussperren; **shut up** vt (lock up) abschließen; (silence) zum Schweigen bringen ▷ vi (keep quiet) den Mund halten; **~!** halt den Mund!; **shutter** n (on window) (Fenster)laden m; **shutter release** n Auslöser m; **shutter speed** n Belichtungszeit f

shuttle bus [ˈʃʌtlbʌs] n Shuttlebus m

shuttlecock [ˈʃʌtlkɒk] n Federball m

shuttle service [ˈʃʌtlsɜːvɪs] n Pendelverkehr m

shy [ʃaɪ] adj schüchtern; (animal) scheu

Siberia [saɪˈbɪərɪə] n Sibirien nt

Sicily [ˈsɪsɪlɪ] n Sizilien nt

sick [sɪk] adj krank; (joke) makaber; **to be ~** (Brit: vomit) sich übergeben; **to be off ~** wegen Krankheit fehlen; **I feel ~** mir ist schlecht; **to be ~ of sb/sth** jdn/etw satt haben; **it makes me ~** (fig) es ekelt mich an; **sickbag** n Spucktüte f; **sick leave** n **to be on ~** krankgeschrieben sein; **sickness** n Krankheit f; (Brit: nausea) Übelkeit f; **sickness benefit** n (Brit) Krankengeld nt

side [saɪd] n Seite f; (of road) Rand m; (of mountain) Hang m; (Sport) Mannschaft f; **by my ~** neben mir; **~ by ~** nebeneinander ▷ adj (door, entrance) Seiten-; **sideboard** n Anrichte f; **sideboards, sideburns** (US) npl Koteletten pl; **side dish** n Beilage f; **side effect** n Nebenwirkung f; **sidelight** n (Brit Auto) Parklicht nt; **side order** n Beilage f; **side road** n Nebenstraße f; **side street** n Seitenstraße f; **sidewalk** n (US) Bürgersteig m; **sideways** adv seitwärts

sieve [sɪv] n Sieb nt

sift [sɪft] vt (flour etc) sieben

sigh [saɪ] vi seufzen

sight [saɪt] n (power of seeing) Sehvermögen nt; (view, thing seen) Anblick m; **~s** pl (of city etc) Sehenswürdigkeiten pl;

to have bad ~ schlecht sehen; **to lose ~ of** aus den Augen verlieren; **out of ~** außer Sicht; **sightseeing** n **to go ~** Sehenswürdigkeiten besichtigen; **~ tour** Rundfahrt f

sign [saɪn] n Zeichen nt; (notice, road ~) Schild nt ▷ vt unterschreiben ▷ vi unterschreiben; **to ~ for sth** den Empfang einer Sache gen bestätigen; **to ~ in/out** sich ein-/austragen; **sign on** vi (Brit: register as unemployed) sich arbeitslos melden; **sign up** vi (for course) sich einschreiben; (Mil) sich verpflichten

signal ['sɪgnl] n Signal nt ▷ vi (car driver) blinken

signature ['sɪgnətʃə*] n Unterschrift f

significant [sɪg'nɪfɪkənt] adj (important) bedeutend, wichtig; (meaning sth) bedeutsam; **significantly** adv (considerably) bedeutend

sign language ['saɪnlæŋgwɪdʒ] n Zeichensprache f; **signpost** n Wegweiser m

silence ['saɪləns] n Stille f; (of person) Schweigen nt; **~!** Ruhe! ▷ vt zum Schweigen bringen; **silent** adj still; (taciturn) schweigsam; **she remained ~** sie schwieg

silk [sɪlk] n Seide f ▷ adj Seiden-

silly ['sɪlɪ] adj dumm, albern; **don't do anything ~** mach keine Dummheiten

silver ['sɪlvə*] n Silber nt; (coins) Silbermünzen pl ▷ adj Silber-, silbern; **silver-plated** adj versilbert; **silver wedding** n silberne Hochzeit

similar ['sɪmɪlə*] adj ähnlich (to dat); **similarity** [sɪmɪ'lærɪtɪ] n Ähnlichkeit f (to mit); **similarly** adv (equally) ebenso

simple ['sɪmpl] adj einfach; (unsophisticated) schlicht; **simplify** ['sɪmplɪfaɪ] vt vereinfachen; **simply** adv einfach; (merely) bloß; (dress) schlicht

simulate ['sɪmjʊleɪt] vt simulieren

simultaneous, simultaneously [sɪməl'teɪnɪəs, -lɪ] adj, adv gleichzeitig

sin [sɪn] n Sünde f ▷ vi sündigen

since [sɪns] adv seitdem; (in the meantime) inzwischen ▷ prep seit +dat; **ever ~ 1995** schon seit 1995 ▷ conj (time) seit, seitdem; (because) da, weil; **ever ~ I've known her** seit ich sie kenne; **it's ages ~ I've seen him** ich habe ihn seit langem nicht mehr gesehen

sincere [sɪn'sɪə*] adj aufrichtig; **sincerely** adv aufrichtig; **Yours ~** mit freundlichen Grüßen

sing [sɪŋ] (sang, sung) vt, vi singen

Singapore [sɪŋgə'pɔː*] n Singapur nt

singer ['sɪŋə*] n Sänger(in) m(f)

single ['sɪŋgl] adj (one only) einzig; (not double) einfach; (bed, room) Einzel-; (unmarried) ledig; (Brit: ticket) einfach ▷ n (Brit: ticket) einfache Fahrkarte; (Mus) Single f; **a ~ to London, please** (Brit Rail) einfach nach London, bitte; **single out** vt (choose) auswählen; **single-handed, single-handedly** adv im Alleingang; **single parent** n Alleinerziehende(r) mf; **single supplement** n (for hotel room) Einzelzimmerzuschlag m

singular ['sɪŋgjʊlə*] n Singular m

sinister ['sɪnɪstə*] adj unheimlich

sink [sɪŋk] (sank, sunk) vt (ship) versenken ▷ vi sinken ▷ n Spülbecken nt; (in bathroom) Waschbecken nt

sip [sɪp] vt nippen an +dat

sir [sɜː*] n **yes, ~** ja(, mein Herr); **can I help you, ~?** kann ich Ihnen helfen?; **Sir James** (title) Sir James

sister ['sɪstə*] n Schwester f; (Brit: nurse) Oberschwester f; **sister-in-law** (pl **sisters-in-law**) n Schwägerin f

sit [sɪt] (sat, sat) vi (be sitting) sitzen; (~ down) sich setzen; (committee, court) tagen ▷ vt (Brit: exam) machen; **sit down** vi sich hinsetzen; **sit up** vi (from lying position) sich aufsetzen

sitcom ['sɪtkɒm] n Situationskomödie f

site [saɪt] n Platz m; (building ~) Baustelle f; (web~) Site f

sitting ['sɪtɪŋ] n (meeting, for portrait) Sitzung f; **sitting room** n Wohnzimmer nt

situated ['sɪtjʊeɪtɪd] adj **to be ~** liegen

situation [sɪtjʊ'eɪʃən] n (circumstances) Situation f, Lage f; (job) Stelle f; **'~s vacant/wanted'** (Brit) „Stellenangebote/Stellengesuche"

six [sɪks] num sechs ▷ n Sechs f; see also **eight**; **sixpack** n (of beer etc) Sechserpack nt; **sixteen** ['sɪks'tiːn] num sechzehn ▷ n Sechzehn f; see also **eight**; **sixteenth** adj sechzehnte(r, s); see also **eighth**; **sixth** [sɪksθ] adj sechste(r, s); **~ form** (Brit) ≈ Oberstufe f ▷ n (fraction) Sechstel nt; see also **eighth**; **sixtieth** ['sɪkstɪɪθ] adj sechzigste(r, s); *see also* **eighth**; **sixty** ['sɪkstɪ] *num* sechzig; **~-one** einundsechzig ▷ *n* Sechzig *f*; **to be in one's sixties** in den Sechzigern sein; *see also* **eight**

size [saɪz] *n* Größe *f*; **what ~ are you?** welche Größe haben Sie?; **a ~ too big** eine Nummer zu groß

sizzle ['sɪzl] *vi* (*Gastr*) brutzeln

skate [skeɪt] *n* Schlittschuh *m*; (*roller ~*) Rollschuh *m* ▷ *vi* Schlittschuh laufen; (*roller-~*) Rollschuh laufen; **skateboard** *n* Skateboard *nt*; **skating** *n* Eislauf *m*; (*roller-~*) Rollschuhlauf *m*; **skating rink** *n* Eisbahn *f*; (*for roller-skating*) Rollschuhbahn *f*

skeleton ['skelɪtn] *n* (*a. fig*) Skelett *nt*

skeptical *n* (*US*) *see* **sceptical**

sketch [sketʃ] *n* Skizze *f*; (*Theat*) Sketch *m* ▷ *vt* skizzieren; **sketchbook** *n* Skizzenbuch *nt*

ski [skiː] *n* Ski *m* ▷ *vi* Ski laufen; **ski boot** *n* Skistiefel *m*

skid [skɪd] *vi* (*Auto*) schleudern

skier ['skiːə*] *n* Skiläufer(in) *m(f)*; **skiing** *n* Skilaufen *nt*; **to go ~** Ski laufen gehen; **~ holiday** Skiurlaub *m*; **skiing instructor** *n* Skilehrer(in) *m(f)*

skilful, skilfully ['skɪlfʊl, -fəlɪ] *adj, adv* geschickt

ski-lift ['skiːlɪft] *n* Skilift *m*

skill [skɪl] *n* Geschick *nt*; (*acquired technique*) Fertigkeit *f*; **skilled** *adj* geschickt (*at, in* +*dat*); (*worker*) Fach-; (*work*) fachmännisch

skim [skɪm] *vt* **to ~ (off)** (*fat etc*) abschöpfen; **to ~ (through)** (*read*) überfliegen; **skimmed milk** *n* Magermilch *f*

skin [skɪn] *n* Haut *f*; (*fur*) Fell *nt*; (*peel*) Schale *f*; **skin diving** *n* Sporttauchen *nt*; **skinny** *adj* dünn

skip [skɪp] *vi* hüpfen; (*with rope*) Seil springen ▷ *vt* (*miss out*) überspringen; (*meal*) ausfallen lassen; (*school, lesson*) schwänzen

ski pants ['skiːpænts] *npl* Skihose *f*; **ski pass** *n* Skipass *m*; **ski pole** *n* Skistock *m*; **ski resort** *n* Skiort *m*

skirt [skɜːt] *n* Rock *m*

ski run ['skiːrʌn] *n* (Ski)abfahrt *f*; **ski stick** *n* Skistock *m*; **ski tow** *n* Schlepplift *m*

skittle ['skɪtl] *n* Kegel *m*; **~s** (*game*) Kegeln *nt*

skive [skaɪv] *vi* **to ~ (off)** (*Brit fam*) sich drücken; (*from school*) schwänzen; (*from work*) blaumachen

skull [skʌl] *n* Schädel *m*

sky [skaɪ] *n* Himmel *m*; **skydiving** *n* Fallschirmspringen *nt*; **skylight** *n* Dachfenster *nt*; **skyscraper** *n* Wolkenkratzer *m*

slam [slæm] *vt* (*door*) zuschlagen; **slam on** *vt* **to slam the brakes on** voll auf die Bremse treten

slander ['slɑːndə*] *n* Verleumdung *f* ▷ *vt* verleumden

slang [slæŋ] *n* Slang *m*

slap [slæp] *n* Klaps *m*; (*across face*) Ohrfeige *f* ▷ *vt* schlagen; **to ~ sb's face** jdn ohrfeigen

slash [slæʃ] *n* (*punctuation mark*) Schrägstrich *m* ▷ *vt* (*face, tyre*) aufschlitzen; (*prices*) stark herabsetzen

slate [sleɪt] *n* (*rock*) Schiefer *m*; (*roof ~*) Schieferplatte *f*

slaughter ['slɔːtə*] *vt* (*animals*) schlachten; (*people*) abschlachten

Slav [slɑːv] *adj* slawisch ▷ *n* Slawe *m*, Slawin *f*

slave [sleɪv] *n* Sklave *m*, Sklavin *f*; **slave away** *vi* schuften; **slave-driver** *n* (*fam*) Sklaventreiber(in) *m(f)*; **slavery** ['sleɪvərɪ] *n* Sklaverei *f*

sleaze [sliːz] *n* (*corruption*) Korruption *f*; **sleazy** *adj* (*bar, district*) zwielichtig

sledge ['sledʒ] *n* Schlitten *m*

sleep [sliːp] (**slept, slept**) *vi* schlafen; **to ~ with sb** mit jdm schlafen ▷ *n* Schlaf *m*; **to put to ~** (*animal*) einschläfern; **sleep in** *vi* (*lie in*) ausschlafen; **sleeper** *n* (*Rail: train*) Schlafwagenzug *m*; (*carriage*) Schlafwagen *m*; **sleeping bag** *n* Schlafsack *m*; **sleeping car** *n* Schlafwagen *m*; **sleeping pill** *n* Schlaftablette *f*; **sleepless** *adj* schlaflos; **sleepy** *adj* schläfrig; (*place*) verschlafen

sleet [sliːt] *n* Schneeregen *m*

sleeve [sliːv] *n* Ärmel *m*; **sleeveless** *adj* ärmellos

sleigh [sleɪ] *n* (Pferde)schlitten *m*

slender ['slendə*] *adj* schlank; (*fig*) gering

slept [slept] *pt, pp of* **sleep**

slice [slaɪs] *n* Scheibe *f*; (*of cake, tart, pizza*)

Stück nt ▷ vt **to ~ (up)** in Scheiben schneiden; **sliced bread** n geschnittenes Brot

slid [slɪd] pt, pp of **slide**

slide [slaɪd] **(slid, slid)** vt gleiten lassen; (push) schieben ▷ vi gleiten; (slip) rutschen ▷ n (Foto) Dia nt; (in playground) Rutschbahn f; (Brit: for hair) Spange f

slight [slaɪt] adj leicht; (problem, difference) klein; **not in the ~est** nicht im Geringsten; **slightly** adv etwas; (injured) leicht

slim [slɪm] adj (person) schlank; (book) dünn; (chance, hope) gering ▷ vi abnehmen

slime [slaɪm] n Schleim m; **slimy** adj schleimig

sling [slɪŋ] **(slung, slung)** vt werfen ▷ n (for arm) Schlinge f

slip [slɪp] n (mistake) Flüchtigkeitsfehler m; **~ of paper** Zettel m ▷ vt (put) stecken; **to ~ on/off** (garment) an-/ausziehen; **it ~ped my mind** ich habe es vergessen ▷ vi (lose balance) (aus)rutschen; **slip away** vi (leave) sich wegstehlen; **slipper** n Hausschuh m; **slippery** adj (path, road) glatt; (soap, fish) glitschig; **slip-road** n (Brit: onto motorway) Auffahrt f; (off motorway) Ausfahrt f

slit [slɪt] **(slit, slit)** vt aufschlitzen ▷ n Schlitz m

slope [sləʊp] n Neigung f; (side of hill) Hang m ▷ vi (be sloping) schräg sein; **slope down** vi (land, road) abfallen; **sloping** adj (floor, roof) schräg

sloppy ['slɒpɪ] adj (careless) schlampig; (sentimental) rührselig

slot [slɒt] n (opening) Schlitz m; (Inform) Steckplatz m; **we have a ~ free at 2** (free time) um 2 ist noch ein Termin frei; **slot machine** n Automat m; (for gambling) Spielautomat m

Slovak ['sləʊvæk] adj slowakisch ▷ n (person) Slowake m, Slowakin f; (language) Slowakisch nt; **Slovakia** [sləʊ'vækɪə] n Slowakei f

Slovene ['sləʊviːn], **Slovenian** [sləʊ'viːnɪən] adj slowenisch ▷ n (person) Slowene m, Slowenin f; (language) Slowenisch nt; **Slovenia** [sləʊ'viːnɪə] n Slowenien nt

slow [sləʊ] adj langsam; (business) flau; **to be ~** (clock) nachgehen; (stupid)

begriffsstutzig sein; **slow down** vi langsamer werden; (when driving/walking) langsamer fahren/gehen; **slowly** adv langsam; **slow motion** n **in ~** in Zeitlupe

slug [slʌg] n (Zool) Nacktschnecke f

slum [slʌm] n Slum m

slump [slʌmp] n Rückgang m (in an +dat) ▷ vi (onto chair etc) sich fallen lassen; (prices) stürzen

slung [slʌŋ] pt, pp of **sling**

slur [slɜː*] n (insult) Verleumdung f; **slurred** [slɜːd] adj undeutlich

slush [slʌʃ] n (snow) Schneematsch m; **slushy** adj matschig; (fig) schmalzig

slut [slʌt] n (pej) Schlampe f

smack [smæk] n Klaps m ▷ vt **to ~ sb** jdm einen Klaps geben ▷ vi **to ~ of** riechen nach

small [smɔːl] adj klein; **small ads** npl (Brit) Kleinanzeigen pl; **small change** n Kleingeld nt; **small letters** npl **in ~** in Kleinbuchstaben; **smallpox** n Pocken pl; **small print** n **the ~** das Kleingedruckte; **small-scale** adj (map) in kleinem Maßstab; **small talk** n Konversation f, Smalltalk m

smart [smɑːt] adj (elegant) schick; (clever) clever; **smart card** n Chipkarte f; **smartly** adv (dressed) schick

smash [smæʃ] n (car crash) Zusammenstoß m, Schmetterball m ▷ vt (break) zerschlagen; (fig: record) deutlich übertreffen ▷ vi (break) zerbrechen; **to ~ into** (car) krachen gegen; **smashing** adj (fam) toll

smear [smɪə*] n (mark) Fleck m; (Med) Abstrich m; (fig) Verleumdung f ▷ vt (spread) schmieren; (make dirty) beschmieren; (fig) verleumden

smell [smel] **(smelt** o **smelled, smelt** o **smelled)** vt riechen ▷ vi riechen (of nach); (unpleasantly) stinken ▷ n Geruch m; (unpleasant) Gestank m; **smelly** adj übel riechend; **smelt** [smelt] pt, pp of **smell**

smile [smaɪl] n Lächeln nt ▷ vi lächeln; **to ~ at sb** jdn anlächeln

smock [smɒk] n Kittel m

smog [smɒg] n Smog m

smoke [sməʊk] n Rauch m ▷ vt rauchen; (food) räuchern ▷ vi rauchen; **smoke alarm** n Rauchmelder m; **smoked** adj (food) geräuchert; **smoke-free** adj (zone, building) rauchfrei; **smoker** n Raucher(in)

S

m(f); **smoking** n Rauchen nt; **'no ~'** „Rauchen verboten"

smooth [smu:ð] adj glatt; (flight, crossing) ruhig; (movement) geschmeidig; (without problems) reibungslos; (pej: person) aalglatt ▷ vt (hair, dress) glatt streichen; (surface) glätten; **smoothly** adv reibungslos; **to run ~** (engine) ruhig laufen

smudge [smʌdʒ] vt (writing, lipstick) verschmieren

smug [smʌg] adj selbstgefällig

smuggle ['smʌgl] vt schmuggeln; **to ~ in/out** herein-/herausschmuggeln

smutty ['smʌtɪ] adj (obscene) schmutzig

snack [snæk] n Imbiss m; **to have a ~** eine Kleinigkeit essen; **snack bar** n Imbissstube f

snail [sneɪl] n Schnecke f; **snail mail** n (fam) Schneckenpost f

snake [sneɪk] n Schlange f

snap [snæp] n (photo) Schnappschuss m ▷ adj (decision) spontan ▷ vt (break) zerbrechen; (rope) zerreißen ▷ vi (break) brechen; (rope) reißen; (bite) schnappen (at nach); **snap off** vt (break) abbrechen; **snap fastener** n (US) Druckknopf m; **snapshot** n Schnappschuss m

snatch [snætʃ] vt (grab) schnappen

sneak [sni:k] vi (move) schleichen; **sneakers** npl (US) Turnschuhe pl

sneeze [sni:z] vi niesen

sniff [snɪf] vi schniefen; (smell) schnüffeln (at an +dat) ▷ vt schnuppern an +dat; (glue) schnüffeln

snob [snɒb] n Snob m; **snobbish** adj versnobt

snog [snɒg] vi, vt knutschen

snooker ['snu:kə*] n Snooker nt

snoop [snu:p] vi **to ~ (around)** (herum)schnüffeln

snooze [snu:z] n, vi **to (have a) ~** ein Nickerchen machen

snore [snɔ:*] vi schnarchen

snorkel ['snɔ:kl] n Schnorchel m; **snorkelling** n Schnorcheln nt; **to go ~** schnorcheln gehen

snout [snaʊt] n Schnauze f

snow [snəʊ] n Schnee m ▷ vi schneien; **snowball** n Schneeball m; **snowboard** n Snowboard nt; **snowboarding** n Snowboarding nt; **snowdrift** n Schneewehe f; **snowdrop** n

Schneeglöckchen nt; **snowflake** n Schneeflocke f; **snowman** (pl **-men**) n Schneemann m; **snowplough, snowplow** (US) n Schneepflug m; **snowstorm** n Schneesturm m; **snowy** adj (region) schneereich; (landscape) verschneit

snug [snʌg] adj (person, place) gemütlich

snuggle up ['snʌglʌp] vi **to ~ to sb** sich an jdn ankuscheln

KEYWORD

so [səʊ] adv **1** (thus) so; (likewise) auch; **so saying he walked away** indem er das sagte, ging er; **if so** wenn ja; **I didn't do it — you did so!** ich hab das nicht gemacht — hast du wohl!; **so do I, so am I** etc ich auch; **so it is!** tatsächlich!; **I hope/think so** hoffentlich/ich glaube schon; **so far** bis jetzt

2 (in comparisons etc: to such a degree) so; **so quickly/big (that)** so schnell/groß, dass; **I'm so glad to see you** ich freue mich so, dich zu sehen

3: **so many** so viele; **so much work** so viel Arbeit; **I love you so much** ich liebe dich so sehr

4 (phrases): **10 or so** etwa 10; **so long!** (inf: goodbye) tschüss!

▷ conj **1** (expressing purpose); **so as to** um ... zu; **so (that)** damit

2 (expressing result) also; **so I was right after all** ich hatte also doch Recht; **so you see ...** wie du siehst ...

soak [səʊk] vt durchnässen; (leave in liquid) einweichen; **I'm ~ed** ich bin durchnässt; **soaking** adj **~ (wet)** durchnässt

soap [səʊp] n Seife f; **soap (opera)** n Seifenoper f; **soap powder** n Waschpulver nt

sob [sɒb] vi schluchzen

sober ['səʊbə*] adj nüchtern; **sober up** vi nüchtern werden

so-called ['səʊ'kɔ:ld] adj so genannt

soccer ['sɒkə*] n Fußball m

sociable ['səʊʃəbl] adj gesellig

social ['səʊʃəl] adj sozial; (sociable) gesellig; **socialist** adj sozialistisch ▷ n Sozialist(in) m(f); **socialize** vi unter die Leute gehen; **social security** n (Brit) Sozialhilfe f; (US) Sozialversicherung f

society [sə'saɪətɪ] n Gesellschaft f; (club) Verein m

sock [sɒk] n Socke f

socket ['sɒkɪt] n (Elec) Steckdose f

soda ['səʊdə] n (~ water) Soda f; (US: pop) Limo f; **soda water** n Sodawasser nt

sofa ['səʊfə] n Sofa nt; **sofa bed** n Schlafcouch f

soft [sɒft] adj weich; (quiet) leise; (lighting) gedämpft; (kind) gutmütig; (weak) nachgiebig; **~ drink** alkoholfreies Getränk; **softly** adv sanft; (quietly) leise; **software** n (Inform) Software f

soil [sɔɪl] n Erde f; (ground) Boden m

solar ['səʊlə*] adj Sonnen-, Solar-

solarium [sə'lɛərɪəm] n Solarium nt

sold [səʊld] pt, pp of **sell**

soldier ['səʊldʒə*] n Soldat(in) m(f)

sole [səʊl] n Sohle f; (fish) Seezunge f ▷ vt besohlen ▷ adj einzig; (owner, responsibility) alleinig; **solely** adv nur

solemn ['sɒləm] adj feierlich; (person) ernst

solicitor [sə'lɪsɪtə*] n (Brit) Rechtsanwalt m, Rechtsanwältin f

solid ['sɒlɪd] adj (hard) fest; (gold, oak etc) massiv; (~ly built) solide; (meal) kräftig; **three hours ~** drei volle Stunden

solitary ['sɒlɪtərɪ] adj einsam; (single) einzeln; **solitude** ['sɒlɪtjuːd] n Einsamkeit f

solo ['səʊləʊ] n (Mus) Solo nt

soluble ['sɒljʊbl] adj löslich; (problem) lösbar; **solution** [sə'luːʃən] n Lösung f (to +gen); **solve** [sɒlv] vt lösen

somber (US), **sombre** ['sɒmbə*] adj düster

 KEYWORD

some [sʌm] adj **1** (a certain amount or number of) einige; (a few) ein paar; (with singular nouns) etwas; **some tea/biscuits** etwas Tee/ein paar Plätzchen; **I've got some money, but not much** ich habe ein bisschen Geld, aber nicht viel

2 (certain: in contrasts) manche(r, s); **some people say that ...** manche Leute sagen, dass ...

3 (unspecified) irgendein(e); **some woman was asking for you** da hat eine Frau nach Ihnen gefragt; **some day** eines Tages;

some day next week irgendwann nächste Woche

▷ pron **1** (a certain number) einige; **have you got some?** haben Sie welche?

2 (a certain amount) etwas; **I've read some of the book** ich habe das Buch teilweise gelesen

▷ adv : **some 10 people** etwa 10 Leute

somebody pron jemand; **~ (or other)** irgendjemand; **~ else** jemand anders; **someday** adv irgendwann; **somehow** adv irgendwie; **someone** pron see **somebody**; **someplace** adv (US) see **somewhere**; **something** ['sʌmθɪŋ] pron etwas; **~ (or other)** irgendetwas; **~ else** etwas anderes; **~ nice** etwas Nettes; **would you like ~ to drink?** möchten Sie etwas trinken? ▷ adv **~ like 20** ungefähr 20; **sometime** adv irgendwann; **sometimes** adv manchmal; **somewhat** adv ein wenig; **somewhere** adv irgendwo; (to a place) irgendwohin; **~ else** irgendwo anders; (to another place) irgendwo anders hin; **~ around 6** ungefähr 6

son [sʌn] n Sohn m

song [sɒŋ] n Lied nt

son-in-law ['sʌnɪnlɔː] (pl **sons-in-law**) n Schwiegersohn m

soon [suːn] adv bald; (early) früh; **too ~** zu früh; **as ~ as I ...** sobald ich ...; **as ~ as possible** so bald wie möglich; **sooner** adv (time) früher; (for preference) lieber

soot [sʊt] n Ruß m

soothe [suːð] vt beruhigen; (pain) lindern

sophisticated [sə'fɪstɪkeɪtɪd] adj (person) kultiviert; (machine) hoch entwickelt; (plan) ausgeklügelt

sophomore ['sɒfəmɔː*] n (US) College-Student(in) m(f) im zweiten Jahr

soppy ['sɒpɪ] adj (fam) rührselig

soprano [sə'prɑːnəʊ] n Sopran m

sore [sɔː*] adj **to be ~** weh tun; **to have a ~ throat** Halsschmerzen haben ▷ n wunde Stelle

sorrow ['sɒrəʊ] n Kummer m

sorry ['sɒrɪ] adj (sight, figure) traurig; **(I'm) ~** (excusing) Entschuldigung!; **I'm ~** (regretful) es tut mir leid; **~?** wie bitte?; **I feel ~ for him** er tut mir leid

sort [sɔːt] *n* Art *f*; **what ~ of film is it?**
was für ein Film ist das?; **a ~ of** eine Art
+*gen*; **all ~s of things** alles Mögliche ▷ *adv*
~ of *(fam)* irgendwie ▷ *vt* sortieren;
everything's ~ed *(dealt with)* alles ist
geregelt; **sort out** *vt* *(classify etc)*
sortieren; *(problems)* lösen
sought [sɔːt] *pt, pp of* **seek**
soul [səʊl] *n* Seele *f*; *(music)* Soul *m*
sound [saʊnd] *adj* *(healthy)* gesund; *(safe)*
sicher; *(sensible)* vernünftig; *(theory)*
stichhaltig; *(thrashing)* tüchtig ▷ *adv* **to be
~ asleep** fest schlafen ▷ *n* *(noise)*
Geräusch *nt*; *(Mus)* Klang *m*; *(TV)* Ton *m* ▷ *vt*
to ~ the alarm Alarm schlagen; **to ~ one's
horn** hupen ▷ *vi* *(seem)* klingen *(like* wie);
soundcard *n* *(Inform)* Soundkarte *f*;
sound effects *npl* Klangeffekte *pl*;
soundproof *adj* schalldicht; **soundtrack**
n *(of film)* Filmmusik *f*, Soundtrack *m*
soup [suːp] *n* Suppe *f*
sour ['saʊə*] *adj* sauer; *(fig)* mürrisch
source [sɔːs] *n* Quelle *f*; *(fig)* Ursprung
m
sour cream [saʊə'kriːm] *n* saure Sahne
south [saʊθ] *n* Süden *m*; **to the ~ of**
südlich von ▷ *adv* *(go, face)* nach Süden
▷ *adj* Süd-; **South Africa** *n* Südafrika *nt*;
South African *adj* südafrikanisch ▷ *n*
Südafrikaner(in) *m(f)*; **South America** *n*
Südamerika *nt*; **South American** *adj*
südamerikanisch ▷ *n* Südamerikaner(in)
m(f); **southbound** *adj* (in) Richtung
Süden; **southern** ['sʌðən] *adj*
Süd-, südlich; **~ Europe** Südeuropa *nt*;
southwards ['saʊθwədz] *adv* nach Süden
souvenir [suːvə'nɪə*] *n* Andenken *nt* *(of*
an +*akk)*
sow [saʊ] **(sowed, sown** *o* **sowed)** *vt* *(a.
fig)* säen; *(field)* besäen ▷ [saʊ] *n* *(pig)*
Sau *f*
soya bean ['sɔɪə'biːn] *n* Sojabohne *f*
soy sauce ['sɔɪ'sɔːs] *n* Sojasoße *f*
spa [spɑː] *n* *(place)* Kurort *m*
space [speɪs] *n* *(room)* Platz *m*, Raum *m*;
(outer ~) Weltraum *m*; *(gap)* Zwischenraum
m; *(for parking)* Lücke *f*; **space bar** *n*
Leertaste *f*; **spacecraft** *(pl -)* *n*
Raumschiff *nt*; **space ship** *n* Raumschiff
nt; **space shuttle** *n* Raumfähre *f*
spacing ['speɪsɪŋ] *n* *(in text)*
Zeilenabstand *m*; **double ~** zweizeiliger
Abstand

spacious ['speɪʃəs] *adj* geräumig
spade [speɪd] *n* Spaten *m*; **~s** Pik *nt*
spaghetti [spə'getɪ] *nsing* Spaghetti *pl*
Spain [speɪn] *n* Spanien *nt*
spam [spæm] *n* *(Inform)* Spam *m*
Spaniard ['spænɪəd] *n* Spanier(in) *m(f)*;
Spanish ['spænɪʃ] *adj* spanisch ▷ *n*
(language) Spanisch *nt*
spanner ['spænə*] *n* *(Brit)*
Schraubenschlüssel *m*
spare [speə*] *adj* *(as replacement)* Ersatz-;
~ part Ersatzteil *nt*; **~ room** Gästezimmer
nt; **~ time** Freizeit *f*; **~ tyre** Ersatzreifen *m*
▷ *n* *(~ part)* Ersatzteil *nt* ▷ *vt* *(lives,
feelings)* verschonen; **can you ~ (me) a
moment?** hätten Sie einen Moment Zeit?
spark [spɑːk] *n* Funke *m*; **sparkle**
['spɑːkl] *vi* funkeln; **sparkling wine** *n*
Schaumwein *m*, Sekt *m*; **spark plug**
['spɑːkplʌg] *n* Zündkerze *f*
sparrow ['spærəʊ] *n* Spatz *m*
sparse [spɑːs] *adj* spärlich; **sparsely** *adv*
~ populated dünn besiedelt
spasm ['spæzəm] *n* *(Med)* Krampf *m*
spat [spæt] *pt, pp of* **spit**
speak [spiːk] **(spoke, spoken)** *vt*
sprechen; **can you ~ French?** sprechen Sie
Französisch?; **to ~ one's mind** seine
Meinung sagen ▷ *vi* sprechen *(to* mit, zu);
(make speech) reden; **~ing** *(Tel)* am Apparat;
so to ~ sozusagen; **~ for yourself** das
meinst auch nur du!; **speak up** *vi* *(louder)*
lauter sprechen; **speaker** *n* Sprecher(in)
m(f); *(public ~)* Redner(in) *m(f)*; *(loud~)*
Lautsprecher *m*
spear [spɪə*] *n* Speer *m*
special ['speʃəl] *adj* besondere(r, s),
speziell ▷ *n* *(on menu)* Tagesgericht *nt*; *(TV,
Radio)* Sondersendung *f*; **special delivery**
n Eilzustellung *f*; **special effects** *npl*
Spezialeffekte *pl*; **specialist** *n*
Spezialist(in) *m(f)*; *(Tech)* Fachmann *m*,
Fachfrau *f*; *(Med)* Facharzt *m*, Fachärztin *f*;
speciality [speʃɪ'ælɪtɪ] *n* Spezialität *f*;
specialize *vi* sich spezialisieren *(in* auf
+*akk)*; **specially** *adv* besonders;
(specifically) extra; **special offer** *n*
Sonderangebot *nt*; **specialty** *n* *(US)* see
speciality
species ['spiːʃiːz] *nsing* Art *f*
specific [spə'sɪfɪk] *adj* spezifisch; *(precise)*
genau; **specify** ['spesɪfaɪ] *vt* genau
angeben

specimen ['spesɪmən] n (sample) Probe f;
(example) Exemplar nt

specs [speks] npl (fam) Brille f

spectacle ['spektəkl] n Schauspiel nt

spectacles npl Brille f

spectacular [spek'tækjʊlə*] adj
spektakulär

spectator [spek'teɪtə*] n Zuschauer(in)
m(f)

sped [sped] pt, pp of **speed**

speech [spi:tʃ] n (address) Rede f; (faculty)
Sprache f; **to make a ~** eine Rede halten;
speechless adj sprachlos (with vor +dat)

speed [spi:d] (**sped** o **speeded, sped** o
speeded) vi rasen; (exceed ~ limit) zu
schnell fahren ▷ n Geschwindigkeit f; (of
film) Lichtempfindlichkeit f; **speed up** vt
beschleunigen ▷ vi schneller
werden/fahren; (drive faster) schneller
fahren; **speedboat** n Rennboot nt; **speed
bump** n Bodenschwelle f; **speed camera**
n Blitzgerät nt; **speed limit** n
Geschwindigkeitsbegrenzung f;
speedometer [spɪ'dɒmɪtə*] n
Tachometer m; **speed trap** n Radarfalle f;
speedy adj schnell

spell [spel] (**spelt** o **spelled, spelt** o
spelled) vt buchstabieren; **how do you
~ ...?** wie schreibt man ...? ▷ n (period)
Weile f; (enchantment) Zauber m; **a
cold/hot ~** (weather) ein
Kälteeinbruch/eine Hitzewelle;
spellchecker n (Inform)
Rechtschreibprüfung f; **spelling** n
Rechtschreibung f; (of a word)
Schreibweise f; **~ mistake** Schreibfehler m

spelt [spelt] pt, pp of **spell**

spend [spend] (**spent, spent**) vt (money)
ausgeben (on für); (time) verbringen;
spending money n Taschengeld nt

spent [spent] pt, pp of **spend**

sperm [spɜ:m] n Sperma nt

sphere [sfɪə*] n (globe) Kugel f; (fig)
Sphäre f

spice [spaɪs] n Gewürz nt; (fig) Würze f
▷ vt würzen; **spicy** ['spaɪsɪ] adj würzig;
(fig) pikant

spider ['spaɪdə*] n Spinne f

spike [spaɪk] n (on railing etc) Spitze f; (on
shoe, tyre) Spike m

spill [spɪl] (**spilt** o **spilled, spilt** o **spilled**)
vt verschütten

spin [spɪn] (**spun, spun**) vi (turn) sich

drehen; (washing) schleudern; **my head is
~ning** mir dreht sich alles ▷ vt (turn)
drehen; (coin) hochwerfen ▷ n (turn)
Drehung f

spinach ['spɪnɪtʃ] n Spinat m

spin-drier ['spɪndraɪə*] n
Wäscheschleuder f; **spin-dry** vt
schleudern

spine [spaɪn] n Rückgrat nt; (of animal,
plant) Stachel m; (of book) Rücken m

spiral ['spaɪrəl] n Spirale f ▷ adj
spiralförmig; **spiral staircase** n
Wendeltreppe f

spire ['spaɪə*] n Turmspitze f

spirit ['spɪrɪt] n (essence, soul) Geist m;
(humour, mood) Stimmung f; (courage) Mut
m; (verve) Elan m; **~s** pl (drinks) Spirituosen
pl

spiritual ['spɪrɪtjʊəl] adj geistig; (Rel)
geistlich

spit [spɪt] (**spat, spat**) vi spucken ▷ n (for
roasting) (Brat)spieß m; (saliva) Spucke f;
spit out vt ausspucken

spite [spaɪt] n Boshaftigkeit f; **in ~ of**
trotz +gen; **spiteful** adj boshaft

spitting image ['spɪtɪŋ'ɪmɪdʒ] n **he's the
~ of you** er ist dir wie aus dem Gesicht
geschnitten

splash [splæʃ] vt (person, object)
bespritzen ▷ vi (liquid) spritzen; (play in
water) planschen

splendid ['splendɪd] adj herrlich

splinter ['splɪntə*] n Splitter m

split [splɪt] (**split, split**) vt (stone, wood)
spalten; (share) teilen ▷ vi (stone, wood)
sich spalten; (seam) platzen ▷ n (in stone,
wood) Spalt m; (in clothing) Riss m; (fig)
Spaltung f; **split up** vi (couple) sich
trennen ▷ vt (divide up) aufteilen; **split
ends** npl (Haar)spliss m; **splitting** adj
(headache) rasend

spoil [spɔɪl] (**spoiled** o **spoilt, spoiled** o
spoilt) vt verderben; (child) verwöhnen
▷ vi (food) verderben

spoilt [spɔɪlt] pt, pp of **spoil**

spoke [spəʊk] pt of **speak** ▷ n Speiche f

spoken ['spəʊkən] pp of **speak**

spokesperson ['spəʊkspɜ:sən] (pl
-people) n Sprecher(in) m(f)

sponge [spʌndʒ] n (for washing)
Schwamm m; **sponge bag** n Kulturbeutel
m; **sponge cake** n Biskuitkuchen m

sponsor ['spɒnsə*] n (of event, programme)

S

Sponsor(in) *m(f)* ▷ *vt* unterstützen; (*event, programme*) sponsern

spontaneous, spontaneously [spɒn'teɪnɪəs, -lɪ] *adj, adv* spontan

spool [spuːl] *n* Spule *f*

spoon [spuːn] *n* Löffel *m*

sport [spɔːt] *n* Sport *m*; **sports car** *n* Sportwagen *m*; **sports centre** *n* Sportzentrum *nt*; **sports club** *n* Sportverein *m*; **sportsman** (*pl* **-men**) *n* Sportler *m*; **sportswear** *n* Sportkleidung *f*; **sportswoman** (*pl* **-women**) *n* Sportlerin *f*; **sporty** *adj* sportlich

spot [spɒt] *n* (*dot*) Punkt *m*; (*of paint, blood etc*) Fleck *m*; (*place*) Stelle *f*; (*pimple*) Pickel *m*; **on the ~** vor Ort; (*at once*) auf der Stelle ▷ *vt* (*notice*) entdecken; (*difference*) erkennen; **spotless** *adj* (*clean*) blitzsauber; **spotlight** *n* (*lamp*) Scheinwerfer *m*; **spotty** *adj* (*pimply*) pickelig

spouse [spaʊs] *n* Gatte *m*, Gattin *f*

spout [spaʊt] *n* Schnabel *m*

sprain [spreɪn] *n* Verstauchung *f* ▷ *vt* **to ~ one's ankle** sich den Knöchel verstauchen

sprang [spræŋ] *pt of* **spring**

spray [spreɪ] *n* (*liquid in can*) Spray *nt o m*; (~ (*can*)) Spraydose *f* ▷ *vt* (*plant, insects*) besprühen; (*car*) spritzen

spread [spred] (**spread, spread**) *vt* (*open out*) ausbreiten; (*news, disease*) verbreiten; (*butter, jam*) streichen; (*bread, surface*) bestreichen ▷ *vi* (*news, disease, fire*) sich verbreiten ▷ *n* (*of disease, religion etc*) Verbreitung *f*; (*for bread*) Aufstrich *m*; **spreadsheet** *n* (*Inform*) Tabellenkalkulation *f*

spring [sprɪŋ] (**sprang, sprung**) *vi* (*leap*) springen ▷ *n* (*season*) Frühling *m*; (*coil*) Feder *f*; (*water*) Quelle *f*; **springboard** *n* Sprungbrett *nt*; **spring onion** *n* (*Brit*) Frühlingszwiebel *f*; **spring roll** *n* (*Brit*) Frühlingsrolle *f*; **springy** *adj* (*mattress*) federnd

sprinkle ['sprɪŋkl] *vt* streuen; (*liquid*) (be)träufeln; **to ~ sth with sth** etw mit etw bestreuen; (*with liquid*) etw mit etw besprengen; **sprinkler** *n* (*for lawn*) Rasensprenger *m*; (*for fire*) Sprinkler *m*

sprint [sprɪnt] *vi* rennen; (*Sport*) sprinten

sprout [spraʊt] *n* (*of plant*) Trieb *m*; (*from seed*) Keim *m*; (**Brussels**) **~s** *pl* Rosenkohl *m* ▷ *vi* sprießen

sprung [sprʌŋ] *pp of* **spring**

spun [spʌn] *pt, pp of* **spin**

spy [spaɪ] *n* Spion(in) *m(f)* ▷ *vi* spionieren; **to ~ on sb** jdm nachspionieren ▷ *vt* erspähen

squad [skwɒd] *n* (*Sport*) Mannschaft *f*; (*police ~*) Kommando *nt*

square [skweə*] *n* (*shape*) Quadrat *nt*; (*open space*) Platz *m*; (*on chessboard etc*) Feld *nt* ▷ *adj* (*in shape*) quadratisch; **2 ~ metres** 2 Quadratmeter; **2 metres ~** 2 Meter im Quadrat ▷ *vt* **3 ~d** 3 hoch 2; **square root** *n* Quadratwurzel *f*

squash [skwɒʃ] *n* (*drink*) Fruchtsaftgetränk *nt*; (*Sport*) Squash *nt*; (*US: vegetable*) Kürbis *m* ▷ *vt* zerquetschen

squat [skwɒt] *vi* (*be crouching*) hocken; **to ~ (down)** sich (hin)hocken

squeak [skwiːk] *vi* (*door, shoes etc*) quietschen; (*animal*) quieken

squeal [skwiːl] *vi* (*person*) kreischen (*with* vor +*dat*)

squeeze [skwiːz] *vt* drücken; (*orange*) auspressen ▷ *vi* **to ~ into the car** sich in den Wagen hineinzwängen; **squeeze up** *vi* (*on bench etc*) zusammenrücken

squid [skwɪd] *n* Tintenfisch *m*

squint [skwɪnt] *vi* schielen; (*in bright light*) blinzeln

squirrel ['skwɪrəl] *n* Eichhörnchen *nt*

squirt [skwɜːt] *vt, vi* (*liquid*) spritzen

Sri Lanka [sriː'læŋkə] *n* Sri Lanka *nt*

st *abbr* = **stone** Gewichtseinheit (*6,35 kg*)

St *abbr* = **saint** St.; *abbr* = **street** Str.

stab [stæb] *vt* (*person*) einstechen auf +*akk*; (*to death*) erstechen; **stabbing** *adj* (*pain*) stechend

stabilize ['steɪbəlaɪz] *vt* stabilisieren ▷ *vi* sich stabilisieren

stable ['steɪbl] *n* Stall *m* ▷ *adj* stabil

stack [stæk] *n* (*pile*) Stapel *m* ▷ *vt* **to ~ (up)** (auf)stapeln

stadium ['steɪdɪəm] *n* Stadion *nt*

staff [stɑːf] *n* (*personnel*) Personal *nt*, Lehrkräfte *pl*

stag [stæg] *n* Hirsch *m*

stag night *n* (*Brit*) Junggesellenabschied *m*

stage [steɪdʒ] *n* (*Theat*) Bühne *f*; (*of project, life etc*) Stadium *nt*; (*of journey*) Etappe *f*; **at this ~** zu diesem Zeitpunkt ▷ *vt* (*Theat*) aufführen, inszenieren; (*demonstration*) veranstalten

stagger ['stægə*] *vi* wanken ▷ *vt* (*amaze*) verblüffen; **staggering** *adj* (*amazing*) umwerfend; (*amount, price*) Schwindel erregend

stagnant ['stægnənt] *adj* (*water*) stehend; **stagnate** [stæg'neɪt] *vi* (*fig*) stagnieren

stain [steɪn] *n* Fleck *m*; **stained-glass window** *n* Buntglasfenster *nt*; **stainless steel** *n* rostfreier Stahl; **stain remover** *n* Fleck(en)entferner *m*

stair [stɛə*] *n* (Treppen)stufe *f*; **~s** *pl* Treppe *f*; **staircase** *n* Treppe *f*

stake [steɪk] *n* (*post*) Pfahl *m*; (*in betting*) Einsatz *m*; (*Fin*) Anteil *m* (*in an* +*dat*); **to be at ~** auf dem Spiel stehen

stale [steɪl] *adj* (*bread*) alt; (*beer*) schal

stalk [stɔ:k] *n* Stiel *m* ▷ *vt* (*wild animal*) sich anpirschen an +*akk*; (*person*) nachstellen +*dat*

stall [stɔ:l] *n* (*in market*) (Verkaufs)stand *m*; (*in stable*) Box *f*; **~s** *pl* (*Theat*) Parkett *nt* ▷ *vt* (*engine*) abwürgen ▷ *vi* (*driver*) den Motor abwürgen; (*car*) stehen bleiben; (*delay*) Zeit schinden

stamina ['stæmɪnə] *n* Durchhaltevermögen *nt*

stammer ['stæmə*] *vi, vt* stottern

stamp [stæmp] *n* (*postage ~*) Briefmarke *f*; (*for document*) Stempel *m* ▷ *vt* (*passport etc*) stempeln; (*mail*) frankieren; **stamped addressed envelope** *n* frankierter Rückumschlag

stand [stænd] (**stood, stood**) *vi* stehen; (*as candidate*) kandidieren ▷ *vt* (*place*) stellen; (*endure*) aushalten; **I can't ~ her** ich kann sie nicht ausstehen ▷ *n* (*stall*) Stand *m*; (*seats in stadium*) Tribüne *f*; (*for coats, bicycles*) Ständer *m*; (*for small objects*) Gestell *nt*; **stand around** *vi* herumstehen; **stand by** *vi* (*be ready*) sich bereithalten; (*be inactive*) danebenstehen ▷ *vt* (*fig: person*) halten zu; (*decision, promise*) stehen zu; **stand for** *vt* (*represent*) stehen für; (*tolerate*) hinnehmen; **stand in for** *vt* einspringen für; **stand out** *vi* (*be noticeable*) auffallen; **stand up** *vi* (*get up*) aufstehen ▷ *vt* (*girlfriend, boyfriend*) versetzen; **stand up for** *vt* sich einsetzen für; **stand up to** *vt* **to ~ sb** jdm die Stirn bieten

standard ['stændəd] *n* (*norm*) Norm *f*; **~ of living** Lebensstandard *m* ▷ *adj* Standard-

standardize ['stændədaɪz] *vt* vereinheitlichen

stand-by ['stændbaɪ] *n* (*thing in reserve*) Reserve *f*; **on ~** in Bereitschaft ▷ *adj* (*flight, ticket*) Standby-; **standing order** *n* (*at bank*) Dauerauftrag *m*; **standpoint** ['stændpɔɪnt] *n* Standpunkt *m*; **standstill** ['stændstɪl] *n* Stillstand *m*; **to come to a ~** stehen bleiben; (*fig*) zum Erliegen kommen

stank [stæŋk] *pt of* **stink**

staple ['steɪpl] *n* (*for paper*) Heftklammer *f* ▷ *vt* heften (*to an* +*akk*); **stapler** *n* Hefter *m*

star [stɑ:*] *n* Stern *m*; (*person*) Star *m* ▷ *vt* **the film ~s Hugh Grant** der Film zeigt Hugh Grant in der Hauptrolle ▷ *vi* die Hauptrolle spielen

starch [stɑ:tʃ] *n* Stärke *f*

stare [stɛə*] *vi* starren; **to ~ at** anstarren

starfish ['stɑ:fɪʃ] *n* Seestern *m*

star sign ['stɑ:saɪn] *n* Sternzeichen *nt*

start [stɑ:t] *n* (*beginning*) Anfang *m*, Beginn *m*; (*Sport*) Start *m*; (*lead*) Vorsprung *m*; **from the ~** von Anfang an ▷ *vt* anfangen; (*car, engine*) starten; (*business, family*) gründen; **to ~ to do sth, to ~ doing sth** anfangen, etw zu tun ▷ *vi* (*begin*) anfangen; (*car*) anspringen; (*on journey*) aufbrechen; (*Sport*) starten; (*jump*) zusammenfahren; **~ing from Monday** ab Montag; **start off** *vt* (*discussion, process etc*) anfangen, beginnen ▷ *vi* (*begin*) anfangen, beginnen; (*on journey*) aufbrechen; **start over** *vi* (*US*) wieder anfangen; **start up** *vi* (*in business*) anfangen ▷ *vt* (*car, engine*) starten; (*business*) gründen; **starter** *n* (*Brit: first course*) Vorspeise *f*; (*Auto*) Anlasser *m*; **starting point** *n* (*a. fig*) Ausgangspunkt *m*

startle ['stɑ:tl] *vt* erschrecken; **startling** *adj* überraschend

starve [stɑ:v] *vi* hungern; (*to death*) verhungern; **I'm ~ing** ich habe einen Riesenhunger

state [steɪt] *n* (*condition*) Zustand *m*; (*Pol*) Staat *m*; **~ of health/mind** Gesundheits-/Geisteszustand *m*; **the (United) States** die (Vereinigten) Staaten

▷ adj Staats-; (control, education) staatlich
▷ vt erklären; (facts, name etc) angeben;
stated adj (fixed) festgesetzt

statement ['steɪtmənt] n (official
declaration) Erklärung f; (to police) Aussage
f; (from bank) Kontoauszug m

state-of-the-art [steɪtəvðiː'ɑːt] adj
hochmodern, auf dem neuesten Stand der
Technik

static ['stætɪk] adj (unchanging)
konstant

station ['steɪʃən] n (for trains, buses)
Bahnhof m; (underground ~) Station f; (police
~, fire ~) Wache f; (Tv, Radio) Sender m ▷ vt
(Mil) stationieren

stationer's ['steɪʃənəz] n ~ (shop)
Schreibwarengeschäft nt; **stationery** n
Schreibwaren pl

station wagon ['steɪʃənwægən] n (US)
Kombiwagen m

statistics [stə'tɪstɪks] nsing (science)
Statistik f; (figures) Statistiken pl

statue ['stætjuː] n Statue f

status ['steɪtəs] n Status m; (prestige)
Ansehen nt; **status bar** n (Inform)
Statuszeile f

stay [steɪ] n Aufenthalt m ▷ vi bleiben;
(with friends, in hotel) wohnen (with bei); **to
~ the night** übernachten; **stay away** vi
wegbleiben; **to ~ from sb** sich von jdm
fern halten; **stay behind** vi
zurückbleiben; (at work) länger bleiben;
stay in vi (at home) zu Hause bleiben;
stay out vi (not come home) wegbleiben;
stay up vi (at night) aufbleiben

steady ['stedɪ] adj (speed) gleichmäßig;
(progress, increase) stetig; (job, income,
girlfriend) fest; (worker) zuverlässig; (hand)
ruhig; **they've been going ~ for two
years** sie sind seit zwei Jahren fest
zusammen ▷ vt (nerves) beruhigen; **to
~ oneself** Halt finden

steak [steɪk] n Steak nt; (of fish) Filet nt

steal [stiːl] (**stole, stolen**) vt stehlen; **to
~ sth from sb** jdm etw stehlen

steam [stiːm] n Dampf m ▷ vt (Gastr)
dämpfen; **steam up** vi (window)
beschlagen; **steamer** n (Gastr)
Dampfkochtopf m; (ship) Dampfer m;
steam iron n Dampfbügeleisen nt

steel [stiːl] n Stahl m ▷ adj Stahl-

steep [stiːp] adj steil

steeple ['stiːpl] n Kirchturm m

steer [stɪə*] vt, vi steuern; (car, bike etc)
lenken; **steering** n (Auto) Lenkung f;
steering wheel n Steuer nt, Lenkrad nt

stem [stem] n (of plant, glass) Stiel m

step [step] n Schritt m; (stair) Stufe f;
(measure) Maßnahme f; **~ by ~** Schritt für
Schritt ▷ vi treten; **~ this way, please**
hier entlang, bitte; **step down** vi (resign)
zurücktreten

stepbrother n Stiefbruder m; **stepchild** n
(pl **-children**) n Stiefkind nt; **stepfather** n
Stiefvater m

stepladder n Trittleiter f

stepmother n Stiefmutter f; **stepsister**
n Stiefschwester f

stereo ['sterɪəʊ] (pl **-s**) n ~ (system)
Stereoanlage f

sterile ['steraɪl] adj steril; **sterilize**
['sterɪlaɪz] vt sterilisieren

sterling ['stɜːlɪŋ] n (Fin) das Pfund
Sterling

stern [stɜːn] adj streng ▷ n Heck nt

stew [stjuː] n Eintopf m

steward ['stjuːəd] n (on plane, ship)
Steward m; **stewardess** n Stewardess f

stick [stɪk] (**stuck, stuck**) vt (with glue etc)
kleben; (pin etc) stecken; (fam: put) tun ▷ vi
(get jammed) klemmen; (hold fast) haften
▷ n Stock m; (hockey ~) Schläger m; (of
chalk) Stück nt; (of celery, rhubarb) Stange f;
stick out vt **to stick one's tongue out**
(**at sb**) (jdm) die Zunge herausstrecken
▷ vi (protrude) vorstehen; (ears) abstehen;
(be noticeable) auffallen; **stick to** vt (rules,
plan etc) sich halten an +akk; **sticker**
['stɪkə*] n Aufkleber m; **sticky** ['stɪkɪ] adj
klebrig; (weather) schwül; **~ label**
Aufkleber m; **~ tape** Klebeband nt

stiff [stɪf] adj steif

stifle ['staɪfl] vt (yawn etc, opposition)
unterdrücken; **stifling** adj drückend

still [stɪl] adj still; (drink) ohne
Kohlensäure ▷ adv (yet, even now) (immer)
noch; (all the same) immerhin; (sit, stand)
still; **he ~ doesn't believe me** er glaubt
mir immer noch nicht; **keep ~** halt still!;
bigger/better ~ noch größer/besser

still life (pl **still lives**) n Stillleben nt

stimulate ['stɪmjʊleɪt] vt anregen,
stimulieren; **stimulating** adj anregend;
stimulus ['stɪmjʊləs] n (incentive) Anreiz
m

sting [stɪŋ] [stɪŋ] (**stung, stung**) vt (wound with

~) stechen ▷ vi (eyes, ointment etc) brennen
▷ n (insect wound) Stich m
stingy ['stɪndʒɪ] adj (fam) geizig
stink [stɪŋk] (stank, stunk) vi stinken (of
nach) ▷ n Gestank m
stir [stɜ:*] vt (mix) (um)rühren; **stir up** vt
(mob) aufhetzen; (memories) wachrufen; **to
~ trouble** Unruhe stiften; **stir-fry** vt
(unter Rühren) kurz anbraten
stitch [stɪtʃ] n (in sewing) Stich m; (in
knitting) Masche f; **to have a ~** (pain)
Seitenstechen haben; **he had to have ~es**
er musste genäht werden; **she had her
~es out** ihr wurden die Fäden gezogen; **to
be in ~es** (fam) sich kaputtlachen ▷ vt
nähen; **stitch up** vt (hole, wound) nähen
stock [stɒk] n (supply) Vorrat m (of an
+dat); (of shop) Bestand m; (for soup etc)
Brühe f; **~s and shares** pl Aktien und
Wertpapiere pl; **to be in/out of
~** vorrätig/nicht vorrätig sein; **to take
~** Inventur machen; (fig) Bilanz ziehen
▷ vt (keep in shop) führen; **stock up** vi sich
eindecken (on, with mit)
stockbroker n Börsenmakler(in) m(f)
stock cube n Brühwurfel m
stock exchange n Börse f
stocking ['stɒkɪŋ] n Strumpf m
stock market ['stɒkmɑ:kɪt] n Börse f
stole [stəʊl] pt of **steal**; **stolen** ['stəʊlən]
pp of **steal**
stomach ['stʌmək] n Magen m; (belly)
Bauch m; **on an empty ~** auf leeren
Magen; **stomach-ache** n
Magenschmerzen pl; **stomach upset** n
Magenverstimmung f
stone [stəʊn] n Stein m; (seed) Kern m,
Stein m; (weight) britische Gewichtseinheit
(6,35 kg) ▷ adj Stein-, aus Stein; **stony** adj
(ground) steinig
stood [stʊd] pt, pp of **stand**
stool [stu:l] n Hocker m
stop [stɒp] n Halt m; (for bus, tram, train)
Haltestelle f; **to come to a ~** anhalten ▷ vt
(vehicle, passer-by) anhalten; (put an end to)
ein Ende machen +dat; (cease) aufhören
mit; (prevent from happening) verhindern;
(bleeding) stillen; (engine, machine)
abstellen; (payments) einstellen; (cheque)
sperren; **to ~ doing sth** aufhören, etw zu
tun; **to ~ sb (from) doing sth** jdn daran
hindern, etw zu tun; **~ it** hör auf (damit)!
▷ vi (vehicle) anhalten; (during journey) Halt

machen; (pedestrian, clock, heart) stehen
bleiben; (rain, noise) aufhören; (stay)
bleiben; **stop by** vi vorbeischauen; **stop
over** vi Halt machen; (overnight)
übernachten; **stopover** n (on journey)
Zwischenstation f; **stopper** n Stöpsel m;
stop sign n Stoppschild nt; **stopwatch** n
Stoppuhr f
storage ['stɔ:rɪdʒ] n Lagerung f; **store**
[stɔ:*] n (supply) Vorrat m (of an +dat);
(place for storage) Lager nt; (large shop)
Kaufhaus nt; (US: shop) Geschäft nt ▷ vt
lagern; (Inform) speichern; **storecard** n
Kundenkreditkarte f; **storeroom** n
Lagerraum m
storey ['stɔ:rɪ] n (Brit) Stock m,
Stockwerk nt
storm [stɔ:m] n Sturm m; (thunder~)
Gewitter nt ▷ vt, vi (with movement)
stürmen; **stormy** adj stürmisch
story ['stɔ:rɪ] n Geschichte f; (plot)
Handlung f; (US: of building) Stock m,
Stockwerk nt
stout [staʊt] adj (fat) korpulent; (shoes)
fest
stove [stəʊv] n Herd m; (for heating) Ofen
m
stow [stəʊ] vt verstauen; **stowaway** n
blinder Passagier
straight [streɪt] adj (not curved) gerade;
(hair) glatt; (honest) ehrlich (with zu); (fam:
heterosexual) hetero ▷ adv (directly) direkt;
(immediately) sofort; (drink) pur; (think)
klar; **~ ahead** geradeaus; **to go ~ on**
geradeaus weitergehen/weiterfahren;
straightaway adv sofort;
straightforward adj einfach; (person)
aufrichtig
strain [streɪn] n Belastung f ▷ vt (eyes)
überanstrengen; (rope, relationship)
belasten; (vegetables) abgießen; **to ~ a
muscle** sich einen Muskel zerren;
strained adj (laugh, smile) gezwungen;
(relations) gespannt; **~ muscle**
Muskelzerrung f; **strainer** n Sieb nt
strand [strænd] n (of wool) Faden m; (of
hair) Strähne f ▷ vt **to be (left) ~ed**
(person) festsitzen
strange [streɪndʒ] adj seltsam;
(unfamiliar) fremd; **strangely** adv seltsam;
~ enough seltsamerweise; **stranger** n
Fremde(r) mf; **I'm a ~ here** ich bin hier
fremd

S

strangle ['stræŋgl] vt (kill) erdrosseln
strap [stræp] n Riemen m; (on dress etc) Träger m; (on watch) Band nt ▷ vt (fasten) festschnallen (to an +dat); **strapless** adj trägerlos
strategy ['strætɪdʒɪ] n Strategie f
straw [strɔː] n Stroh nt; (drinking ~) Strohhalm m
strawberry n Erdbeere f
stray [streɪ] n streunendes Tier ▷ adj (cat, dog) streunend ▷ vi streunen
streak ['striːk] n (of colour, dirt) Streifen m; (in hair) Strähne f; (in character) Zug m
stream [striːm] n (flow of liquid) Strom m; (brook) Bach m ▷ vi strömen; **streamer** n (of paper) Luftschlange f
street [striːt] n Straße f; **streetcar** n (US) Straßenbahn f; **street lamp**, **street light** n Straßenlaterne f; **street map** n Stadtplan m
strength [strɛŋθ] n Kraft f, Stärke f; **strengthen** vt verstärken; (fig) stärken
strenuous ['strɛnjʊəs] adj anstrengend
stress [strɛs] n Stress m; (on word) Betonung f; **to be under ~** im Stress sein ▷ vt betonen; (put under ~) stressen; **stressed** adj ~ **(out)** gestresst
stretch [strɛtʃ] n (of land) Stück nt; (of road) Strecke f ▷ vt (material, shoes) dehnen; (rope, canvas) spannen; (person in job etc) fordern; **to ~ one's legs** (walk) sich die Beine vertreten ▷ vi (person) sich strecken; (area) sich erstrecken (to bis zu); **stretch out** vt **to stretch one's hand/legs out** die Hand/die Beine ausstrecken, ausstrecken ▷ vi (reach) sich strecken; (lie down) sich ausstrecken; **stretcher** n Tragbahre f
strict, **strictly** [strɪkt, -lɪ] adj, adv (severe(ly)) streng; (exact(ly)) genau
strike [straɪk] (**struck, struck**) vt (match) anzünden; (hit) schlagen; (find) finden; **it struck me as strange** es kam mir seltsam vor ▷ vi (stop work) streiken; (attack) zuschlagen; (clock) schlagen ▷ n (by workers) Streik m; **to be on ~** streiken; **strike up** vt (conversation) anfangen; (friendship) schließen; **striking** adj auffallend; (resemblance) verblüffend
string [strɪŋ] n (for tying) Schnur f; (Mus, Tennis) Saite f; **the ~s** pl (section of orchestra) die Streicher pl
strip [strɪp] n Streifen m; (Brit: of footballer

etc) Trikot nt ▷ vt (undress) ausziehen ▷ vi (undress) sich ausziehen, strippen
stripe [straɪp] n Streifen m; **striped** adj gestreift
stripper ['strɪpə*] n Stripper(in) m(f); (paint ~) Farbentferner m
strip-search ['strɪpsɜːtʃ] n Leibesvisitation f (bei der man sich ausziehen muss)
striptease ['strɪptiːz] n Striptease m
strive [straɪv] (**strove, striven**) vi **to ~ to do sth** bemüht sein, etw zu tun; **to ~ for sth** nach etw streben
stroke [strəʊk] n (Med, Tennis etc) Schlag m; (of pen, brush) Strich m ▷ vt streicheln
stroll [strəʊl] n Spaziergang m ▷ vi spazieren; **stroller** n (US: for baby) Buggy m
strong [strɒŋ] adj stark; (healthy) robust; (wall, table) stabil; (shoes) fest; (influence, chance) groß; **strongly** adv stark; (believe) fest; (constructed) stabil
strove [strəʊv] pt of **strive**
struck [strʌk] pt, pp of **strike**
structural, **structurally** ['strʌktʃərəl, -lɪ] adj strukturell; **structure** ['strʌktʃə*] n Struktur f; (building, bridge) Konstruktion f, Bau m
struggle ['strʌgl] n Kampf m (for um) ▷ vi (fight) kämpfen (for um); (do sth with difficulty) sich abmühen; **to ~ to do sth** sich abmühen, etw zu tun
stub [stʌb] n (of cigarette) Kippe f; (of ticket, cheque) Abschnitt m ▷ vt **to ~ one's toe** sich dat den Zeh stoßen (on an +dat)
stubble ['stʌbl] n Stoppeln pl
stubborn ['stʌbən] adj (person) stur
stuck [stʌk] pt, pp of **stick** ▷ adj **to be ~** (jammed) klemmen; (at a loss) nicht mehr weiterwissen; **to get ~** (car in snow etc) stecken bleiben
student ['stjuːdənt] n Student(in) m(f), Schüler(in) m(f)
studio ['stjuːdɪəʊ] n (pl **-s**) n Studio nt
studious ['stjuːdɪəs] adj fleißig
study ['stʌdɪ] n (investigation) Untersuchung f; (studying) Studium nt; (room) Arbeitszimmer nt ▷ vt, vi studieren; **to ~ for an exam** sich auf eine Prüfung vorbereiten
stuff [stʌf] n Zeug nt, Sachen pl ▷ vt (push) stopfen; (Gastr) füllen; **to ~ oneself**

(*fam*) sich voll stopfen; **stuffing** *n* (*Gastr*)
Füllung *f*

stuffy ['stʌfɪ] *adj* (*room*) stickig; (*person*)
spießig

stumble ['stʌmbl] *vi* stolpern; (*when
speaking*) stocken

stun [stʌn] *vt* (*shock*) fassungslos
machen; **I was ~ned** ich war fassungslos
(*o* völlig überrascht)

stung [stʌŋ] *pt, pp of* **sting**

stunk [stʌŋk] *pp of* **stink**

stunning ['stʌnɪŋ] *adj* (*marvellous*)
fantastisch; (*beautiful*) atemberaubend;
(*very surprising, shocking*) überwältigend;
unfassbar

stunt [stʌnt] *n* (*Cine*) Stunt *m*

stupid ['stjuːpɪd] *adj* dumm; **stupidity**
[stjuːˈpɪdɪtɪ] *n* Dummheit *f*

sturdy ['stɜːdɪ] *adj* robust; (*building, car*)
stabil

stutter ['stʌtə*] *vi, vt* stottern

stye [staɪ] *n* (*Med*) Gerstenkorn *nt*

style [staɪl] *n* Stil *m* ▷ *vt* (*hair*) stylen;
styling mousse *n* Schaumfestiger *m*;
stylish ['staɪlɪʃ] *adj* elegant

subconscious [sʌbˈkɒnʃəs] *adj*
unterbewusst ▷ *n* **the ~** das
Unterbewusstsein

subdivide [sʌbdɪˈvaɪd] *vt* unterteilen

subject ['sʌbdʒɪkt] *n* (*topic*) Thema *nt*; (*in
school*) Fach *nt*; (*citizen*)
Staatsangehörige(r) *mf*; (*of kingdom*)
Untertan(in) *m(f)*; (*Ling*) Subjekt *nt*; **to
change the ~** das Thema wechseln ▷ *adj*
[səbˈdʒekt] **to be ~ to** (*dependent on*)
abhängen von; (*under control of*)
unterworfen sein +*dat*

subjective [səbˈdʒektɪv] *adj* subjektiv

sublet [sʌbˈlet] *irr vt* untervermieten (*to
an* +*akk*)

submarine [sʌbməˈriːn] *n* U-Boot *nt*

submerge [səbˈmɜːdʒ] *vt* (*put in water*)
eintauchen ▷ *vi* tauchen

submit [səbˈmɪt] *vt* (*application, claim*)
einreichen ▷ *vi* (*surrender*) sich ergeben

subordinate [səˈbɔːdɪnət] *adj*
untergeordnet (*to* +*dat*) ▷ *n*
Untergebene(r) *mf*

subscribe [səbˈskraɪb] *vi* **to ~ to** (*magazine
etc*) abonnieren; **subscription**
[səbˈskrɪpʃən] *n* (*to magazine etc*)
Abonnement *nt*; (*to club etc*)
(Mitglieds)beitrag *m*

subsequent ['sʌbsɪkwənt] *adj*
nach(folgend); **subsequently** *adv* später,
anschließend

subside [səbˈsaɪd] *vi* (*floods*) zurückgehen;
(*storm*) sich legen; (*building*) sich senken

substance ['sʌbstəns] *n* Substanz *f*

substantial [səbˈstænʃəl] *adj*
beträchtlich; (*improvement*) wesentlich;
(*meal*) reichhaltig; (*furniture*) solide

substitute ['sʌbstɪtjuːt] *n* Ersatz *m*;
(*Sport*) Ersatzspieler(in) *m(f)* ▷ *vt* **to ~ A
for B** B durch A ersetzen

subtitle ['sʌbtaɪtl] *n* Untertitel *m*

subtle ['sʌtl] *adj* (*difference, taste*) fein;
(*plan*) raffiniert

subtotal ['sʌbtəʊtl] *n* Zwischensumme
f

subtract [səbˈtrækt] *vt* abziehen (*from
von*)

suburb ['sʌbɜːb] *n* Vorort *m*; **in the ~s** am
Stadtrand; **suburban** [səˈbɜːbən] *adj*
vorstädtisch, Vorstadt-

subway ['sʌbweɪ] *n* (*Brit*) Unterführung *f*;
(*US Rail*) U-Bahn *f*

succeed [səkˈsiːd] *vi* erfolgreich sein; **he
~ed** (**in doing it**) es gelang ihm(, es zu tun)
▷ *vt* nachfolgen +*dat*; **succeeding** *adj*
nachfolgend; **success** [səkˈses] *n* Erfolg
m; **successful, successfully** *adj, adv*
erfolgreich

successive [səkˈsesɪv] *adj* aufeinander
folgend; **successor** *n* Nachfolger(in) *m(f)*

succulent ['sʌkjʊlənt] *adj* saftig

succumb [səˈkʌm] *vi* erliegen (*to* +*dat*)

such [sʌtʃ] *adj* solche(r, s); **~ a book** so
ein Buch, ein solches Buch; **it was ~ a
success that ...** es war solch ein Erfolg,
dass ...; **~ as** wie ▷ *adv* so; **~ a hot day**
so ein heißer Tag ▷ *pron* **as ~** als solche(r,
s); **suchlike** *adj* derartig ▷ *pron*
dergleichen

suck [sʌk] *vt* (*toffee etc*) lutschen; (*liquid*)
saugen; **it ~s** (*fam*) das ist beschissen

Sudan [sʊˈdaːn] *n* (**the**) **~** der Sudan

sudden ['sʌdn] *adj* plötzlich; **all of a
~** ganz plötzlich; **suddenly** *adv* plötzlich

sue [suː] *vt* verklagen

suede [sweɪd] *n* Wildleder *nt*

suffer ['sʌfə*] *vt* erleiden ▷ *vi* leiden; **to
~ from** (*Med*) leiden an +*dat*

sufficient, sufficiently [səˈfɪʃənt, -lɪ] *adj,
adv* ausreichend

suffocate ['sʌfəkeɪt] *vt, vi* ersticken

S

sugar ['ʃʊgə*] *n* Zucker *m* ▷ *vt* zuckern;
sugar bowl *n* Zuckerdose *f*; **sugary** *adj*
(*sweet*) süß

suggest [sə'dʒest] *vt* vorschlagen; (*imply*)
andeuten; **I ~ saying nothing** ich schlage
vor, nichts zu sagen; **suggestion**
[sə'dʒestʃən] *n* (*proposal*) Vorschlag *m*;
suggestive *adj* vielsagend; (*sexually*)
anzüglich

suicide ['sʊɪsaɪd] *n* (*act*) Selbstmord *m*

suit [suːt] *n* (*man's clothes*) Anzug *m*; (*lady's
clothes*) Kostüm *nt*; (*Cards*) Farbe *f* ▷ *vt* (*be
convenient for*) passen +*dat*; (*clothes, colour*)
stehen +*dat*; (*climate, food*) bekommen
+*dat*; **suitable** *adj* geeignet (*for* für);
suitcase *n* Koffer *m*

suite [swiːt] *n* (*of rooms*) Suite *f*; (*sofa and
chairs*) Sitzgarnitur *f*

sulk [sʌlk] *vi* schmollen; **sulky** *adj*
eingeschnappt

sultana [sʌl'tɑːnə] *n* (*raisin*) Sultanine *f*

sum [sʌm] *n* Summe *f*; (*money a.*) Betrag
m; (*calculation*) Rechenaufgabe *f*; **sum up**
vt, vi (*summarize*) zusammenfassen

summarize ['sʌməraɪz] *vt, vi*
zusammenfassen; **summary** *n*
Zusammenfassung *f*

summer ['sʌmə*] *n* Sommer *m*; **summer
camp** *n* (US) Ferienlager *nt*; **summer
holidays** *n* Sommerferien *pl*;
summertime *n* **in** (**the**) **~** im Sommer

summit ['sʌmɪt] *n* (*a. Pol*) Gipfel *m*

summon ['sʌmən] *vt* (*doctor, fire brigade
etc*) rufen; (*to one's office*) zitieren;
summon up *vt* (*courage, strength*)
zusammennehmen

summons ['sʌmənz] *nsing* (*Jur*)
Vorladung *f*

sumptuous ['sʌmptjʊəs] *adj* luxuriös;
(*meal*) üppig

sun [sʌn] *n* Sonne *f* ▷ *vt* **to ~ oneself** sich
sonnen

Sun *abbr* = **Sunday** So.

sunbathe *vi* sich sonnen; **sunbathing**
n Sonnenbaden *nt*; **sunbed** *n*
Sonnenbank *f*; **sunblock** *n* Sunblocker *m*;
sunburn *n* Sonnenbrand *m*; **sunburnt** *adj*
to be/get ~ einen Sonnenbrand
haben/bekommen

sundae ['sʌndeɪ] *n* Eisbecher *m*

Sunday ['sʌndɪ] *n* Sonntag *m*; *see also*
Tuesday

sung [sʌŋ] *pp of* **sing**

sunglasses ['sʌnglɑːsɪz] *npl* Sonnenbrille
f; **sunhat** *n* Sonnenhut *m*

sunk [sʌŋk] *pp of* **sink**

sunlamp ['sʌnlæmp] *n* Höhensonne *f*;
sunlight *n* Sonnenlicht *nt*; **sunny** ['sʌnɪ]
adj sonnig; **sun protection factor** *n*
Lichtschutzfaktor *m*; **sunrise** *n*
Sonnenaufgang *m*; **sunroof** *n* (*Auto*)
Schiebedach *nt*; **sunscreen** *n*
Sonnenschutzmittel *nt*; **sunset** *n*
Sonnenuntergang *m*; **sunshade** *n*
Sonnenschirm *m*; **sunshine** *n*
Sonnenschein *m*; **sunstroke** *n*
Sonnenstich *m*; **suntan** *n*
(Sonnen)bräune *f*; **to get/have a
~** braun werden/sein; **~ lotion** (*o* **oil**)
Sonnenöl *nt*

super ['suːpə*] *adj* (*fam*) toll

superb, superbly [suː'pɜːb, -lɪ] *adj, adv*
ausgezeichnet

superficial, superficially [suːpə'fɪʃəl, -ɪ]
adj, adv oberflächlich

superfluous [sʊ'pɜːflʊəs] *adj* überflüssig

superglue ['suːpəgluː] *n* Sekundenkleber
m

superior [sʊ'pɪərɪə*] *adj* (*better*) besser (*to*
als); (*higher in rank*) höher gestellt (*to* als),
höher ▷ *n* (*in rank*) Vorgesetzte(r) *mf*

supermarket ['suːpəmɑːkɪt] *n*
Supermarkt *m*

supersede [suːpə'siːd] *vt* ablösen

supersonic [suːpə'sɒnɪk] *adj* Überschall-

superstitious [suːpə'stɪʃəs] *adj*
abergläubisch

superstore ['suːpəstɔː*] *n*
Verbrauchermarkt *m*

supervise ['suːpəvaɪz] *vt* beaufsichtigen;
supervisor ['suːpəvaɪzə] *n* Aufsicht *f*; (*at
university*) Doktorvater *m*

supper ['sʌpə*] *n* Abendessen *nt*;
(*late-night snack*) Imbiss

supplement ['sʌplɪmənt] *n* (*extra
payment*) Zuschlag *m*; (*of newspaper*)
Beilage *f* ▷ *vt* ergänzen; **supplementary**
[sʌplɪ'mentərɪ] *adj* zusätzlich

supplier [sə'plaɪə*] *n* Lieferant(in) *m(f)*;
supply [sə'plaɪ] *vt* (*deliver*) liefern; (*drinks,
music etc*) sorgen für; **to ~ sb with sth**
(*provide*) jdn mit etw versorgen ▷ *n* (*stock*)
Vorrat *m* (*of* an +*dat*)

support [sə'pɔːt] *n* Unterstützung *f*;
(*Tech*) Stütze *f* ▷ *vt* (*hold up*) tragen,
stützen; (*provide for*) ernähren,

unterhalten; (speak in favour of)
unterstützen; **he ~s Manchester United**
er ist Manchester-United-Fan
suppose [sə'pəʊz] vt (assume) annehmen;
I ~ so ich denke schon; **I ~ not**
wahrscheinlich nicht; **you're not ~d to
smoke here** du darfst hier nicht rauchen;
supposedly [sə'pəʊzɪdlɪ] adv angeblich;
supposing conj angenommen
suppress [sə'pres] vt unterdrücken
surcharge ['sɜːtʃɑːdʒ] n Zuschlag m
sure [ʃʊə*] adj sicher; **I'm (not) ~** ich bin
mir (nicht) sicher; **make ~ you lock up**
vergiss nicht abzuschließen ⊳ adv **~!** klar!;
~ enough tatsächlich; **surely** adv **~ you
don't mean it?** das ist nicht dein Ernst,
oder?
surf [sɜːf] n Brandung f ⊳ vi (Sport) surfen
⊳ vt **to ~ the net** im Internet surfen
surface ['sɜːfɪs] n Oberfläche f ⊳ vi
auftauchen; **surface mail** n **by ~** auf dem
Land-/Seeweg
surfboard ['sɜːfbɔːd] n Surfbrett nt;
surfer n Surfer(in) m(f); **surfing** n Surfen
nt; **to go ~** surfen gehen
surgeon ['sɜːdʒən] n Chirurg(in) m(f);
surgery ['sɜːdʒərɪ] n (operation)
Operation f; (room) Praxis f, Sprechzimmer
nt; (consulting time) Sprechstunde f; **to
have ~** operiert werden
surname ['sɜːneɪm] n Nachname m
surpass [sɜː'pɑːs] vt übertreffen
surplus ['sɜːpləs] n Überschuss m (of an
+dat)
surprise [sə'praɪz] n Überraschung f ⊳ vt
überraschen; **surprising** adj
überraschend; **surprisingly** adv
überraschenderweise, erstaunlicherweise
surrender [sə'rendə*] vi sich ergeben (to
+dat) ⊳ vt (weapon, passport) abgeben
surround [sə'raʊnd] vt umgeben; (stand
all round) umringen; **surrounding** adj
(countryside) umliegend ⊳ n **~s** pl
Umgebung f
survey ['sɜːveɪ] n (opinion poll) Umfrage
f; (of literature etc) Überblick m (of über
+akk); (of land) Vermessung f ⊳ [sɜː'veɪ] vt
(look out over) überblicken; (land)
vermessen
survive [sə'vaɪv] vt, vi überleben
susceptible [sə'septəbl] adj empfänglich
(to für); (Med) anfällig (to für)
suspect ['sʌspekt] n Verdächtige(r) mf

⊳ adj verdächtig ⊳ [sə'spekt] vt
verdächtigen (of +gen); (think likely)
vermuten
suspend [sə'spend] vt (from work)
suspendieren; (payment) vorübergehend
einstellen; (player) sperren; (hang up)
aufhängen; **suspender** n (Brit)
Strumpfhalter m; **~s** pl (US: for trousers)
Hosenträger pl
suspense [sə'spens] n Spannung f
suspicious [sə'spɪʃəs] adj misstrauisch (of
sb/sth jdm/etw gegenüber); (causing
suspicion) verdächtig
swallow ['swɒləʊ] n (bird) Schwalbe f
⊳ vt, vi schlucken
swam [swæm] pt of swim
swamp [swɒmp] n Sumpf m
swan [swɒn] n Schwan m
swap [swɒp] vt, vi tauschen; **to ~ sth for
sth** etw gegen etw eintauschen
sway [sweɪ] vi schwanken
swear [swɛə*] (**swore, sworn**) vi (promise)
schwören; (curse) fluchen; **to ~ at sb** jdn
beschimpfen; **swear by** vt (have faith in)
schwören auf +akk; **swearword** n Fluch m
sweat [swet] n Schweiß m ⊳ vi
schwitzen; **sweatband** n Schweißband
nt; **sweater** n Pullover m; **sweatshirt** n
Sweatshirt nt; **sweaty** adj verschwitzt
swede [swiːd] n Steckrübe f
Swede [swiːd] n Schwede m, Schwedin f;
Sweden n Schweden nt; **Swedish** adj
schwedisch ⊳ n (language) Schwedisch nt
sweep [swiːp] (**swept, swept**) vt, vi (with
brush) kehren, fegen; **sweep up** vt (dirt
etc) zusammenkehren, zusammenfegen
sweet [swiːt] n (Brit: candy) Bonbon nt;
(dessert) Nachtisch m ⊳ adj süß; (kind) lieb;
sweet-and-sour adj süßsauer;
sweetcorn n Mais m; **sweeten** vt (tea
etc) süßen; **sweetener** n (substance)
Süßstoff m
swell [swel] (**swelled, swollen** o **swelled**)
vi **to ~ (up)** (an)schwellen ⊳ adj (US fam)
toll; **swelling** n (Med) Schwellung f
sweltering ['sweltərɪŋ] adj (heat)
drückend
swept [swept] pt, pp of sweep
swift, **swiftly** [swɪft] adj, adv schnell
swig [swɪg] n (fam) Schluck m
swim [swɪm] (**swam, swum**) vi
schwimmen ⊳ n **to go for a
~** schwimmen gehen; **swimmer** n

S

Schwimmer(in) *m(f)*; **swimming** *n*
Schwimmen *nt*; **to go ~** schwimmen
gehen; **swimming cap** *n* (*Brit*)
Badekappe *f*; **swimming costume** *n* (*Brit*)
Badeanzug *m*; **swimming pool** *n*
Schwimmbad *nt*; (*private, in hotel*)
Swimmingpool *m*; **swimming trunks** *npl*
(*Brit*) Badehose *f*; **swimsuit** *n* Badeanzug
m
swindle ['swɪndl] *vt* betrügen (*out of* um)
swine [swaɪn] *n* (*person*) Schwein *nt*
swing [swɪŋ] (**swung, swung**) *vt, vi*
(*object*) schwingen ▷ *n* (*for child*) Schaukel *f*
swipe [swaɪp] *vt* (*credit card etc*)
durchziehen; (*fam: steal*) klauen; **swipe
card** *n* Magnetkarte *f*
Swiss [swɪs] *adj* schweizerisch ▷ *n*
Schweizer(in) *m(f)*
switch [swɪtʃ] *n* (*Elec*) Schalter *m* ▷ *vt*
(*change*) wechseln; **to ~ sth for sth** etw
gegen etw eintauschen ▷ *vi* (*change*)
wechseln (*to* zu); **switch off** *vt*
abschalten, ausschalten; **switch on** *vt*
anschalten, einschalten; **switchboard** *n*
(*Tel*) Vermittlung *f*
Switzerland ['swɪtsələnd] *n* die Schweiz
swivel ['swɪvl] *vi* sich drehen ▷ *vt*
drehen; **swivel chair** *n* Drehstuhl *m*
swollen ['swəʊlən] *pp of* **swell** ▷ *adj* (*Med*)
geschwollen; (*stomach*) aufgebläht
swop [swɒp] *see* **swap**
sword [sɔːd] *n* Schwert *nt*
swore [swɔː*] *pt of* **swear**
sworn [swɔːn] *pp of* **swear**
swot [swɒt] *vi* (*Brit fam*) büffeln (*for* für)
swum [swʌm] *pp of* **swim**
swung [swʌŋ] *pt, pp of* **swing**
syllable ['sɪləbl] *n* Silbe *f*
syllabus ['sɪləbəs] *n* Lehrplan *m*
symbol ['sɪmbəl] *n* Symbol *nt*; **symbolic**
[sɪm'bɒlɪk] *adj* symbolisch; **symbolize** *vt*
symbolisieren
symmetrical [sɪ'metrɪkəl] *adj*
symmetrisch
sympathetic [sɪmpə'θetɪk] *adj*
mitfühlend; (*understanding*)
verständnisvoll; **sympathize** ['sɪmpəθaɪz]
vi mitfühlen (*with sb* mit jdm); **sympathy**
['sɪmpəθɪ] *n* Mitleid *nt*; (*after death*) Beileid
nt; (*understanding*) Verständnis *nt*
symphony ['sɪmfənɪ] *n* Sinfonie *f*
symptom ['sɪmptəm] *n* (*a. fig*) Symptom
nt

synagogue ['sɪnəgɒg] *n* Synagoge *f*
synonym ['sɪnənɪm] *n* Synonym *nt*;
synonymous [sɪ'nɒnɪməs] *adj* synonym
(*with* mit)
synthetic [sɪn'θetɪk] *adj* (*material*)
synthetisch
syphilis ['sɪfɪlɪs] *n* Syphilis *f*
Syria ['sɪrɪə] *n* Syrien *nt*
syringe [sɪ'rɪndʒ] *n* Spritze *f*
system ['sɪstəm] *n* System *nt*;
systematic [sɪstə'mætɪk] *adj*
systematisch; **system disk** *n* (*Inform*)
Systemdiskette *f*; **system(s) software** *n*
(*Inform*) Systemsoftware *f*

t

tab [tæb] *n* (*for hanging up coat etc*) Aufhänger *m*; (*Inform*) Tabulator *m*; **to pick up the ~** (*fam*) die Rechnung übernehmen

table ['teɪbl] *n* Tisch *m*; (*list*) Tabelle *f*; **~ of contents** Inhaltsverzeichnis *nt*; **tablecloth** *n* Tischdecke *f*; **tablelamp** *n* Tischlampe *f*; **tablemat** *n* Set *nt*; **tablespoon** *n* Servierlöffel *m*; (*in recipes*) Esslöffel *m*

tablet ['tæblət] *n* (*Med*) Tablette *f*

table tennis ['teɪbltənɪs] *n* Tischtennis *nt*; **table wine** *n* Tafelwein *m*

tabloid ['tæblɔɪd] *n* Boulevardzeitung *f*

taboo [tə'bu:] *n* Tabu *nt* ▷ *adj* tabu

tacit, tacitly ['tæsɪt, -lɪ] *adj, adv* stillschweigend

tack [tæk] *n* (*small nail*) Stift *m*; (*US: thumb~*) Reißzwecke *f*

tackle ['tækl] *n* (*Sport*) Angriff *m*; (*equipment*) Ausrüstung *f* ▷ *vt* (*deal with*) in Angriff nehmen; (*Sport*) angreifen; (*verbally*) zur Rede stellen (*about* wegen)

tact [tækt] *n* Takt *m*; **tactful, tactfully** *adj, adv* taktvoll; **tactic(s)** ['tæktɪk(s)] *n(pl)* Taktik *f*; **tactless, tactlessly** ['tæktləs, -lɪ] *adj, adv* taktlos

tag [tæg] *n* (*label*) Schild *nt*; (*with maker's name*) Etikett *nt*

Tahiti [tɑː'hiːtɪ] *n* Tahiti *nt*

tail [teɪl] *n* Schwanz *m*; **heads or ~s?** Kopf oder Zahl?; **tailback** *n* (*Brit*) Rückstau *m*; **taillight** *n* (*Auto*) Rücklicht *nt*

tailor ['teɪlə*] *n* Schneider(in) *m(f)*

tailpipe ['teɪlpaɪp] *n* (*US Auto*) Auspuffrohr *nt*

tainted ['teɪntɪd] *adj* (*US: food*) verdorben

Taiwan [taɪ'wæn] *n* Taiwan *nt*

take [teɪk] (**took, taken**) *vt* nehmen; (*~ along with one*) mitnehmen; (*~ to a place*) bringen; (*subtract*) abziehen (*from* von); (*capture: person*) fassen; (*gain, obtain*) bekommen; (*Fin, Comm*) einnehmen; (*train, taxi*) nehmen, fahren mit; (*trip, walk, holiday, exam, course, photo*) machen; (*bath*) nehmen; (*phone call*) entgegennehmen; (*decision, precautions*) treffen; (*risk*) eingehen; (*advice, job*) annehmen; (*consume*) zu sich nehmen; (*tablets*) nehmen; (*heat, pain*) ertragen; (*react to*) aufnehmen; (*have room for*) Platz haben für; **I'll ~ it** (*item in shop*) ich nehme es; **how long does it ~?** wie lange dauert es?; **it ~s 4 hours** man braucht 4 Stunden; **do you ~ sugar?** nehmen Sie Zucker?; **I ~ it that ...** ich nehme an, dass ...; **to ~ place** stattfinden; **take after** *vt* nachschlagen +*dat*; **take along** *vt* mitnehmen; **take apart** *vt* auseinander nehmen; **take away** *vt* (*remove*) wegnehmen (*from sb* jdm); (*subtract*) abziehen (*from* von); **take back** *vt* (*return*) zurückbringen; (*retract*) zurücknehmen; (*remind*) zurückversetzen (*to* in +*akk*); **take down** *vt* (*picture, curtains*) abnehmen; (*write down*) aufschreiben; **take in** *vt* (*understand*) begreifen; (*give accommodation to*) aufnehmen; (*deceive*) hereinlegen; (*include*) einschließen; (*show, film etc*) mitnehmen; **take off** *vi* (*plane*) starten ▷ *vt* (*clothing*) ausziehen; (*hat, lid*) abnehmen; (*deduct*) abziehen; (*Brit: imitate*) nachmachen; **to take a day off** sich einen Tag freinehmen; **take on** *vt* (*undertake*) übernehmen; (*employ*) einstellen; (*Sport*) antreten gegen; **take out** *vt* (*wallet etc*) herausnehmen; (*person, dog*) ausführen; (*insurance*) abschließen; (*money from bank*) abheben; (*book from library*) ausleihen; **take over** *vt* übernehmen ▷ *vi* **he took over** (**from me**) er hat mich abgelöst; **take to** vt **I've taken to her/it** ich mag sie/es; **to ~ doing sth** (begin) anfangen, etw zu tun; **take up** vt (carpet) hochnehmen; (space) einnehmen; (time) in Anspruch nehmen; (hobby) anfangen mit; (new job) antreten; (offer) annehmen

takeaway n (Brit: meal) Essen nt zum Mitnehmen

taken ['teɪkn] pp of **take** ▷ adj (seat) besetzt; **to be ~ with** angetan sein von

takeoff ['teɪkɒf] n (Aviat) Start m; (imitation) Nachahmung f; **takeout** (US) see **takeaway**; **takeover** n (Comm) Übernahme f

takings ['teɪkɪŋz] npl Einnahmen pl

tale [teɪl] n Geschichte f

talent ['tælənt] n Talent nt; **talented** adj begabt

talk [tɔːk] n (conversation) Gespräch nt; (rumour) Gerede nt; (to audience) Vortrag m ▷ vi sprechen, reden; (have conversation) sich unterhalten; **to ~ to** (o **with**) **sb** (**about sth**) mit jdm (über etw akk) sprechen ▷ vt (language) sprechen; (nonsense) reden; (politics, business) reden über +akk; **to ~ sb into doing/out of doing sth** jdn überreden/jdm ausreden, etw zu tun; **talk over** vt besprechen

talkative adj gesprächig; **talk show** n Talkshow f

tall [tɔːl] adj groß; (building, tree) hoch; **he is 6ft ~** er ist 1,80m groß

tame [teɪm] adj zahm; (joke, story) fade ▷ vt (animal) zähmen

tampon ['tæmpɒn] n Tampon m

tan [tæn] n (on skin) (Sonnen)bräune f; **to get/have a ~** braun werden/sein ▷ vi braun werden

tangerine [tændʒə'riːn] n Mandarine f

tango ['tæŋgəʊ] n Tango m

tank [tæŋk] n Tank m; (for fish) Aquarium nt; (Mil) Panzer m

tanker ['tæŋkə*] n (ship) Tanker m; (vehicle) Tankwagen m

tanned [tænd] adj (by sun) braun

tantalizing ['tæntəlaɪzɪŋ] adj verlockend

Tanzania [tænzə'nɪə] n Tansania nt

tap [tæp] n (for water) Hahn m ▷ vt, vi (strike) klopfen; **to ~ sb on the shoulder** jdm auf die Schulter klopfen; **tap-dance** vi steppen

tape [teɪp] n (adhesive ~) Klebeband nt; (for tape recorder) Tonband nt; (cassette) Kassette f; (video) Video nt ▷ vt (record) aufnehmen; **tape up** vt (parcel) zukleben; **tape measure** n Maßband nt; **tape recorder** n Tonbandgerät nt

tapestry ['tæpɪstrɪ] n Wandteppich m

tap water ['tæpwɔː'tə*] n Leitungswasser nt

tar [tɑː*] n Teer m

target ['tɑːgɪt] n Ziel nt; (board) Zielscheibe f

tariff ['tærɪf] n (price list) Preisliste f; (tax) Zoll m

tarmac ['tɑːmæk] n (Aviat) Rollfeld nt

tart [tɑːt] n (fruit ~) (Obst)kuchen m; (small) (Obst)törtchen nt; (fam, pej: prostitute) Nutte f; (fam: promiscuous person) Schlampe f

tartan ['tɑːtən] n Schottenkaro nt; (material) Schottenstoff m

tartar(e) sauce ['tɑː'tə'sɔːs] n Remouladensoße f

task [tɑːsk] n Aufgabe f; (duty) Pflicht f; **taskbar** n (Inform) Taskbar f

Tasmania [tæz'meɪnɪə] n Tasmanien nt

taste [teɪst] n Geschmack m; (sense of ~) Geschmacksinn m; (small quantity) Kostprobe f; **it has a strange ~** es schmeckt komisch ▷ vt schmecken; (try) probieren ▷ vi (food) schmecken (of nach); **to ~ good/strange** gut/komisch schmecken; **tasteful, tastefully** adj, adv geschmackvoll; **tasteless, tastelessly** adj, adv geschmacklos; **tasty** adj schmackhaft

tattered ['tætəd] adj (clothes) zerlumpt; (fam: person) angespannt; **I'm absolutely ~** ich bin mit den Nerven am Ende

tattoo [tə'tuː] n (on skin) Tätowierung f

taught [tɔːt] pt, pp of **teach**

Taurus ['tɔːrəs] n (Astr) Stier m

tax [tæks] n Steuer f (on auf +akk) ▷ vt besteuern; **taxable** adj steuerpflichtig; **taxation** [tæk'seɪʃən] n Besteuerung f; **tax bracket** n Steuerklasse f; **tax disc** n (Brit Auto) Steuermarke f; **tax-free** adj steuerfrei

taxi ['tæksɪ] n Taxi nt ▷ vi (plane) rollen; **taxi driver** n Taxifahrer(in) m(f); **taxi rank** (Brit), **taxi stand** n Taxistand m

tax return ['tæksrɪ'tɜːn] n Steuererklärung f

tea [ti:] n Tee m; (afternoon ~) ≈ Kaffee und Kuchen; (meal) frühes Abendessen; **teabag** n Teebeutel m; **tea break** n (Tee)pause f

teach [ti:tʃ] (**taught, taught**) vt (person, subject) unterrichten; **to ~ sb (how) to dance** jdm das Tanzen beibringen ▷ vi unterrichten; **teacher** n Lehrer(in) m(f); **teaching** n (activity) Unterrichten nt; (profession) Lehrberuf m

teacup ['ti:kʌp] n Teetasse f

team [ti:m] n (Sport) Mannschaft f, Team nt; **teamwork** n Teamarbeit f

teapot ['ti:pɒt] n Teekanne f

tear [tɪə*] n (in eye) Träne f

tear [teə*] (**tore, torn**) vt zerreißen; **to ~ a muscle** sich einen Muskel zerren ▷ n (in material etc) Riss m; **tear down** vt (building) abreißen; **tear up** vt (paper) zerreißen

tearoom ['ti:rʊm] n Teestube f, Café, in dem in erster Linie Tee serviert wird

tease [ti:z] vt (person) necken (about wegen)

tea set ['ti:set] n Teeservice nt; **teashop** n Teestube f; **teaspoon** n Teelöffel m; **tea towel** n Geschirrtuch nt

technical ['teknɪkəl] adj technisch; (knowledge, term, dictionary) Fach-; **technically** adv technisch; **technique** [tek'ni:k] n Technik f

techno ['teknəʊ] n Techno f

technological [teknə'lɒdʒɪkəl] adj technologisch; **technology** [tek'nɒlədʒɪ] n Technologie f

tedious ['ti:dɪəs] adj langweilig

teen(age) ['ti:n(eɪdʒ)] adj (fashions etc) Teenager-; **teenager** n Teenager m; **teens** [ti:nz] npl **in one's ~** im Teenageralter

teeth [ti:θ] pl of **tooth**

teetotal ['ti:'təʊtl] adj abstinent

telegraph pole ['telɪgrɑ:fpəʊl] n (Brit) Telegrafenmast m

telephone ['telɪfəʊn] n Telefon nt ▷ vi telefonieren ▷ vt anrufen; **telephone banking** n Telefonbanking nt; **telephone book** n Telefonbuch nt; **telephone booth**, **telephone box** (Brit) n Telefonzelle f; **telephone call** n Telefonanruf m; **telephone directory** n Telefonbuch nt; **telephone number** n Telefonnummer f

telephoto lens ['telɪfəʊtəʊ'lenz] n Teleobjektiv nt

telescope ['telɪskəʊp] n Teleskop nt

televise ['telɪvaɪz] vt im Fernsehen übertragen; **television** ['telɪvɪʒən] n Fernsehen nt; **television programme** n Fernsehsendung f; **television set** n Fernsehapparat m

teleworking ['telɪwɜ:kɪŋ] n Telearbeit f

tell [tel] (**told, told**) vt (say, inform) sagen (sb sth jdm etw); (story) erzählen; (truth) sagen; (difference) erkennen; (reveal secret) verraten; **to ~ sb about sth** jdm von etw erzählen; **to ~ sth from sth** etw von etw unterscheiden ▷ vi (be sure) wissen; **tell apart** vt unterscheiden; **tell off** vt schimpfen

telling adj aufschlussreich

telly ['telɪ] n (Brit fam) Glotze f; **on (the) ~** in der Glotze

temp [temp] n Aushilfskraft f ▷ vi als Aushilfskraft arbeiten

temper ['tempə*] n (anger) Wut f; (mood) Laune f; **to lose one's ~** die Beherrschung verlieren; **to have a bad ~** jähzornig sein; **temperamental** [tempərə'mentl] adj (moody) launisch

temperature ['temprɪtʃə*] n Temperatur f; (Med: high ~) Fieber nt; **to have a ~** Fieber haben

temple ['templ] n Tempel m; (Anat) Schläfe f

tempo ['tempəʊ] (pl **-s**) n Tempo nt

temporarily ['tempərərɪlɪ] adv vorübergehend; **temporary** ['tempərərɪ] adj vorübergehend; (road, building) provisorisch

tempt [tempt] vt in Versuchung führen; **I'm ~ed to accept** ich bin versucht anzunehmen; **temptation** [temp'teɪʃən] n Versuchung f; **tempting** adj verlockend

ten [ten] num zehn ▷ n Zehn f; see also **eight**

tenant ['tenənt] n Mieter(in) m(f); (of land) Pächter(in) m(f)

tend [tend] vi **to ~ to do sth** (person) dazu neigen, etw zu tun; **to ~ towards** neigen zu; **tendency** ['tendənsɪ] n Tendenz f; **to have a ~ to do sth** (person) dazu neigen, etw zu tun

tender ['tendə*] adj (loving) zärtlich; (sore) empfindlich; (meat) zart

tendon ['tendən] *n* Sehne *f*
Tenerife [tenə'ri:f] *n* Teneriffa *nt*
tenner ['tenə*] *n* (*Brit fam: note*)
Zehnpfundschein *m*; (*amount*) zehn Pfund
tennis ['tenɪs] *n* Tennis *nt*; **tennis ball** *n*
Tennisball *m*; **tennis court** *n* Tennisplatz
m; **tennis racket** *n* Tennisschläger *m*
tenor ['tenə*] *n* Tenor *m*
tenpin bowling, tenpins (*US*)
['tenpɪn'bəʊlɪŋ, 'tenpɪnz] *n* Bowling *nt*
tense [tens] *adj* angespannt; (*stretched
tight*) gespannt; **tension** ['tenʃən] *n*
Spannung *f*; (*strain*) Anspannung *f*
tent [tent] *n* Zelt *nt*
tenth [tenθ] *adj* zehnte(r, s) ▷ *n* (*fraction*)
Zehntel *nt*; *see also* **eighth**
tent peg ['tentpeg] *n* Hering *m*; **tent pole**
n Zeltstange *f*
term [tɜ:m] *n* (*in school, at university*)
Trimester *nt*; (*expression*) Ausdruck *m*; **~s** *pl*
(*conditions*) Bedingungen *pl*; **to be on good
~s with sb** mit jdm gut auskommen; **to
come to ~s with sth** sich mit etw
abfinden; **in the long/short
~** langfristig/kurzfristig; **in ~s of ...** was ...
betrifft
terminal ['tɜ:mɪnl] *n* (*bus ~ etc*)
Endstation *f*; (*Aviat*) Terminal *m*; (*Inform*)
Terminal *nt*; (*Elec*) Pol *m* ▷ *adj* (*Med*)
unheilbar; **terminally** *adv* (*ill*) unheilbar
terminate ['tɜ:mɪneɪt] *vt* (*contract*)
lösen; (*pregnancy*) abbrechen ▷ *vi* (*train,
bus*) enden
terminology [tɜ:mɪ'nɒlədʒɪ] *n*
Terminologie *f*
terrace ['terəs] *n* (*of houses*) Häuserreihe *f*;
(*in garden etc*) Terrasse *f*; **terraced** *adj*
(*garden*) terrassenförmig angelegt;
terraced house *n* (*Brit*) Reihenhaus *nt*
terrible ['terəbl] *adj* schrecklich
terrific [tə'rɪfɪk] *adj* (*very good*)
fantastisch
terrify ['terɪfaɪ] *vt* erschrecken; **to be
terrified** schreckliche Angst haben (*of* vor
+dat)
territory ['terɪtərɪ] *n* Gebiet *nt*
terror ['terə*] *n* Schrecken *m*; (*Pol*) Terror
m; **terrorism** *n* Terrorismus *m*; **terrorist**
n Terrorist(in) *m(f)*
test [test] *n* Test *m*, Klassenarbeit *f*;
(*driving ~*) Prüfung *f*; **to put to the ~** auf die
Probe stellen ▷ *vt* testen, prüfen;
(*patience, courage etc*) auf die Probe stellen

Testament ['testəmənt] *n* **the Old/New
~** das Alte/Neue Testament
test-drive ['testdraɪv] *vt* Probe fahren
testicle ['testɪkl] *n* Hoden *m*
testify ['testɪfaɪ] *vi* (*Jur*) aussagen
test tube ['testtju:b] *n* Reagenzglas *nt*
tetanus ['tetənəs] *n* Tetanus *m*
text [tekst] *n* Text *m*; (*of document*)
Wortlaut *m*; (*sent by mobile phone*) SMS *f*
▷ *vt* (*message*) simsen, SMSen; **to ~ sb** jdm
simsen, jdm eine SMS schicken; **I'll ~ it to
you** ich schicke es dir per SMS
textbook *n* Lehrbuch *nt*
texting ['tekstɪŋ] *n* SMS-Messaging *nt*;
text message *n* SMS *f*; **text messaging**
n SMS-Messaging *nt*
texture ['tekstʃə*] *n* Beschaffenheit *f*
Thailand ['taɪlənd] *n* Thailand *nt*
Thames [temz] *n* Themse *f*
than [ðæn] *prep, conj* als; **bigger/faster
~ me** größer/schneller als ich; **I'd rather
walk ~ drive** ich gehe lieber zu Fuß als mit
dem Auto
thank [θæŋk] *vt* danken *+dat*; **~ you**
danke; **~ you very much** vielen Dank;
thankful *adj* dankbar; **thankfully** *adv*
(*luckily*) zum Glück; **thankless** *adj*
undankbar; **thanks** *npl* Dank *m*; **~** danke!;
~ to dank *+gen*

● **Thanksgiving Day**
●
● **Thanksgiving (Day)** ist ein Feiertag in
● den USA, der auf den vierten
● Donnerstag im November fällt. Er
● soll daran erinnern, wie die
● Pilgerväter die gute Ernte im Jahre
● 1621 feierten. In Kanada gibt es einen
● ähnlichen Erntedanktag (, der aber
● nichts mit den Pilgervätern zu tun
● hat) am zweiten Montag im Oktober.

⬤ **KEYWORD**

that [ðæt, ðət] *adj* (*demonstrative*) (*pl
those*) der/die/das; jene(r, s); **that one** das
da ▷ *pron*
1 (*demonstrative*) (*pl those*) das;
who's/what's that? wer ist da/was ist
das?; **is that you?** bist du das?; **that's
what he said** genau das hat er gesagt;
what happened after that? was
passierte danach?; **that is** das heißt

2 (*relative: subj*) der/die/das die; (*: direct obj*) den/die/das die; (*: indirect obj*) dem/der/dem denen; **all (that) I have** alles, was ich habe
3 (*relative: of time*); **the day (that)** an dem Tag, als; **the winter (that) he came** in dem Winter, in dem er kam
▷ *conj* dass; **he thought that I was ill** er dachte, dass ich krank sei er dachte, ich sei krank
▷ *adv* (*demonstrative*) so; **I can't work that much** ich kann nicht so viel arbeiten

that's [ðæts] *contr of* **that is; that has**
thaw [θɔ:] *vi* tauen; (*frozen food*) auftauen
▷ *vt* auftauen lassen

🔵 **KEYWORD**

the [ði:, ðə] *def art* **1** der/die/das; **to play the piano/violin** Klavier/Geige spielen; **I'm going to the butcher's/ the cinema** ich gehe zum Fleischer/ins Kino; **Elizabeth the First** Elisabeth die Erste
2 (+*adj to form noun*) das die; **the rich and the poor** die Reichen und die Armen
3 (*in comparisons*): **the more he works the more he earns** je mehr er arbeitet, desto mehr verdient er

theater (*US*), **theatre** ['θɪətə*] *n* Theater *nt*; (*for lectures etc*) Saal *m*
theft [θeft] *n* Diebstahl *m*
their [ðɛə*] *adj* ihr; (*unidentified person*) sein; **they cleaned ~ teeth** sie putzten sich die Zähne; **someone has left ~ umbrella here** jemand hat seinen Schirm hier vergessen; **theirs** *pron* ihre(r, s); (*unidentified person*) seine(r, s); **it's ~** es gehört ihnen; **a friend of ~** ein Freund von ihnen; **someone has left ~ here** jemand hat seins hier liegen lassen
them [ðem, ðəm] *pron* (*direct object*) sie; (*indirect object*) ihnen; (*unidentified person*) ihn/ihm, sie/ihr; **do you know ~?** kennst du sie?; **can you help ~?** kannst du ihnen helfen?; **it's ~** sie sind's; **if anyone has a problem you should help ~** wenn jemand ein Problem hat, solltest du ihm helfen
theme [θi:m] *n* Thema *nt*; (*Mus*) Motiv *nt*; **~ park** Themenpark *m*; **~ song** Titelmusik *f*

themselves [ðəm'selvz] *pron* sich; **they hurt ~** sie haben sich verletzt; **they ~ were not there** sie selbst waren nicht da; **they did it ~** sie haben es selbst gemacht; **they are not dangerous in ~** an sich sind sie nicht gefährlich; **(all) by ~ allein**
then [ðen] *adv* (*at that time*) damals; (*next*) dann; (*therefore*) also; (*furthermore*) ferner; **from ~ on** von da an; **by ~** bis dahin ▷ *adj* damalig; **our ~ boss** unser damaliger Chef
theoretical, **theoretically** [θɪə'retɪkəl, -ɪ] *adj*, *adv* theoretisch
theory ['θɪərɪ] *n* Theorie *f*; **in ~** theoretisch
therapy ['θerəpɪ] *n* Therapie *f*

🔵 **KEYWORD**

there [ðɛə*] *adv* **1**: **there is, there are** es *or* da ist/sind; (*there exists/exist also*) es gibt; **there are 3 of them** (*people, things*) es gibt 3 davon; **there has been an accident** da war ein Unfall
2 (*place*) da dort; (*direction*) dahin, dorthin; **put it in/on there** leg es dahinein/dorthinauf
3: **there, there** (*esp to child*) na, na

thermometer [θə'mɒmɪtə*] *n* Thermometer *nt*
Thermos® ['θɜ:məs] *n* **~ (flask)** Thermosflasche® *f*
these [ði:z] *pron*, *adj* diese; **I don't like ~ apples** ich mag diese Äpfel nicht; **~ are not my books** das sind nicht meine Bücher
thesis ['θi:sɪs] (*pl* **theses**) *n* (*for PhD*) Doktorarbeit *f*
they [ðeɪ] *pron pl* sie; (*people in general*) man; (*unidentified person*) er/sie; **~ are rich** sie sind reich; **~ say that ...** man sagt, dass ...; **if anyone looks at this, ~ will see that ...** wenn sich jemand dies ansieht, wird er erkennen, dass ...
they'd [ðeɪd] *contr of* **they had; they would**
they'll [ðeɪl] *contr of* **they will; they shall**
they've [ðeɪv] *contr of* **they have**
thick [θɪk] *adj* dick; (*fog*) dicht; (*liquid*) dickflüssig; (*fam: stupid*) dumm; **thicken** *vi* (*fog*) dichter werden; (*sauce*) dick werden
▷ *vt* (*sauce*) eindicken

t

thief [θiːf] (*pl* **thieves**) *n* Dieb(in) *m(f)*

thigh [θaɪ] *n* Oberschenkel *m*

thimble ['θɪmbl] *n* Fingerhut *m*

thin [θɪn] *adj* dünn

thing [θɪŋ] *n* Ding *nt*; (*affair*) Sache *f*; **my ~s** *pl* meine Sachen *pl*; **how are ~s?** wie geht's?; **I can't see a ~** ich kann nichts sehen; **he knows a ~ or two about cars** er kennt sich mit Autos aus

think [θɪŋk] (**thought, thought**) *vt, vi* denken; (*believe*) meinen; **I ~ so** ich denke schon; **I don't ~ so** ich glaube nicht; **think about** *vt* denken an +*akk*; (*reflect on*) nachdenken über +*akk*; (*have opinion of*) halten von; **think of** *vt* denken an +*akk*; (*devise*) sich ausdenken; (*have opinion of*) halten von; (*remember*) sich erinnern an +*akk*; **think over** *vt* überdenken; **think up** *vt* sich ausdenken

third [θɜːd] *adj* dritte(r, s); **the Third World** die Dritte Welt ▷ *n* (*fraction*) Drittel *nt*; **in ~** (**gear**) im dritten Gang; *see also* **eighth**; **thirdly** *adv* drittens; **third-party insurance** *n* Haftpflichtversicherung *f*

thirst [θɜːst] *n* Durst *m* (*for* nach); **thirsty** *adj* **to be ~** Durst haben

thirteen ['θɜː'tiːn] *num* dreizehn ▷ *n* Dreizehn *f*; *see also* **eight**; **thirteenth** *adj* dreizehnte(r, s); *see also* **eighth**; **thirtieth** ['θɜːtɪɪθ] *adj* dreißigste(r, s); *see also* **eighth**; **thirty** ['θɜːtɪ] *num* dreißig; **~-one** einunddreißig ▷ *n* Dreißig *f*; **to be in one's thirties** in den Dreißigern sein; *see also* **eight**

⊙ KEYWORD

this [ðɪs] *adj* (*demonstrative: pl these*) diese(r, s); **this evening** heute Abend; **this one** diese(r, s) (da)
▷ *pron* (*demonstrative: pl these*) dies das; **who/what is this?** wer/was ist das?; **this is where I live** hier wohne ich; **this is what he said** das hat er gesagt; **this is Mr Brown** dies ist Mr Brown; (*on telephone*) hier ist Mr Brown
▷ *adv* (*demonstrative*); **this high/long** *etc* so groß/lang *etc*

thistle ['θɪsl] *n* Distel *f*

thorn [θɔːn] *n* Dorn *m*, Stachel *m*

thorough ['θʌrə] *adj* gründlich;

thoroughly *adv* gründlich; (*agree etc*) völlig

those [ðəʊz] *pron* die da, jene; **~ who** diejenigen, die ▷ *adj* die, jene

though [ðəʊ] *conj* obwohl; **as ~** als ob ▷ *adv* aber

thought [θɔːt] *pt, pp of* **think** ▷ *n* Gedanke *m*; (*thinking*) Überlegung *f*; **thoughtful** *adj* (*kind*) rücksichtsvoll; (*attentive*) aufmerksam; (*in Gedanken versunken*) nachdenklich; **thoughtless** *adj* (*unkind*) rücksichtslos, gedankenlos

thousand ['θaʊzənd] *num* (**one**) **~, a ~** tausend; **five ~** fünftausend; **~s of** Tausende von

thrash [θræʃ] *vt* (*hit*) verprügeln; (*defeat*) vernichtend schlagen

thread [θred] *n* Faden *m* ▷ *vt* (*needle*) einfädeln; (*beads*) auffädeln

threat [θret] *n* Drohung *f*; (*danger*) Bedrohung *f* (*to* für); **threaten** *vt* bedrohen; **threatening** *adj* bedrohlich

three [θriː] *num* drei ▷ *n* Drei *f*; *see also* **eight**; **three-dimensional** *adj* dreidimensional; **three-piece suit** *n* Anzug *m* mit Weste; **three-quarters** *npl* drei Viertel *pl*

threshold ['θreʃhəʊld] *n* Schwelle *f*

threw [θruː] *pt of* **throw**

thrifty ['θrɪftɪ] *adj* sparsam

thrilled [θrɪld] *adj* **to be ~** (**with sth**) sich (über etw *akk*) riesig freuen; **thriller** *n* Thriller *m*; **thrilling** *adj* aufregend

thrive [θraɪv] *vi* gedeihen (*on* bei); (*fig, business*) florieren

throat [θrəʊt] *n* Hals *m*, Kehle *f*

throbbing ['θrɒbɪn] *adj* (*pain, headache*) pochend

thrombosis [θrɒm'bəʊsɪs] *n* Thrombose *f*; **deep vein ~** tiefe Venenthrombose *f*

throne [θrəʊn] *n* Thron *m*

through [θruː] *prep* durch; (*time*) während +*gen*; (*because of*) aus, durch; (*US: up to and including*) bis; **arranged ~ him** durch ihn arrangiert ▷ *adv* durch; **to put sb ~** (*Tel*) jdn verbinden (*to* mit) ▷ *adj* (*ticket, train*) durchgehend; **~ flight** Direktflug *m*; **to be ~ with sb/sth** mit jdm/etw fertig sein; **throughout** [θruː'aʊt] *prep* (*place*) überall in +*dat*; (*time*) während +*gen*; **~ the night** die ganze Nacht hindurch ▷ *adv* überall; (*time*) die ganze Zeit

throw [θrəʊ] (**threw, thrown**) vt werfen; (rider) abwerfen; (party) geben; **to ~ sth to sb, to ~ sb sth** jdm etw zuwerfen; **I was ~n by his question** seine Frage hat mich aus dem Konzept gebracht ▷ n Wurf m; **throw away** vt wegwerfen; **throw in** vt (include) dazugeben; **throw out** vt (unwanted object) wegwerfen; (person) hinauswerfen (of aus); **throw up** vt, vi (fam: vomit) sich übergeben; **throw-in** n Einwurf m

thrown [θrəʊn] pp of **throw**

thru (US) see **through**

thrush [θrʌʃ] n Drossel f

thrust [θrʌst] (**thrust, thrust**) vt, vi (push) stoßen

thruway ['θruːweɪ] n (US) Schnellstraße f

thumb [θʌm] n Daumen m ▷ vt **to ~ a lift** per Anhalter fahren; **thumbtack** n (US) Reißzwecke f

thunder ['θʌndə*] n Donner m ▷ vi donnern; **thunderstorm** n Gewitter nt

Thur(s) abbr = **Thursday** Do.

Thursday ['θɜːzdɪ] n Donnerstag m; see also **Tuesday**

thus [ðʌs] adv (in this way) so; (therefore) somit, also

thyme [taɪm] n Thymian m

Tibet [tɪ'bet] n Tibet nt

tick [tɪk] n (Brit: mark) Häkchen nt ▷ vt (name) abhaken; (box, answer) ankreuzen ▷ vi (clock) ticken

ticket ['tɪkɪt] n (for train, bus) (Fahr)karte f; (plane ~) Flugschein m, Ticket nt; (for theatre, match, museum etc) (Eintritts)karte f; (price ~) (Preis)schild nt; (raffle ~) Los nt; (for car park) Parkschein m; (for traffic offence) Strafzettel m; **ticket collector, ticket inspector** (Brit) n Fahrkartenkontrolleur(in) m(f); **ticket machine** n (for public transport) Fahrscheinautomat m; (in car park) Parkscheinautomat m; **ticket office** n (Rail) Fahrkartenschalter m; (Theat) Kasse f

tickle ['tɪkl] vt kitzeln; **ticklish** ['tɪklɪʃ] adj kitzlig

tide [taɪd] n Gezeiten pl; **the ~ is in/out** es ist Flut/Ebbe

tidy ['taɪdɪ] adj ordentlich ▷ vt aufräumen; **tidy up** vt, vi aufräumen

tie [taɪ] n (neck~) Krawatte f; (Sport) Unentschieden nt; (bond) Bindung f ▷ vt (attach, do up) binden (to an +akk); (~ together) zusammenbinden; (knot) machen ▷ vi (Sport) unentschieden spielen; **tie down** vt festbinden (to an +dat); (fig) binden; (knot) anbinden; (parcel) verschnüren; (shoelace) binden; (boat) festmachen; **I'm tied up** (fig) ich bin beschäftigt

tiger ['taɪgə*] n Tiger m

tight [taɪt] adj (clothes) eng; (knot) fest; (screw, lid) fest sitzend; (control, security measures) streng; (timewise) knapp; (schedule) eng ▷ adv (shut) fest; (pull) stramm; **hold ~** festhalten!; **sleep ~** schlaf gut!; **tighten** vt (knot, rope, screw) anziehen; (belt) enger machen; (restrictions, control) verschärfen; **tights** npl (Brit) Strumpfhose f

tile [taɪl] n (on roof) Dachziegel m; (on wall, floor) Fliese f; **tiled** adj (roof) Ziegel-; (floor, wall) gefliest

till [tɪl] n Kasse f ▷ prep, conj see **until**

tilt [tɪlt] vt kippen; (head) neigen ▷ vi sich neigen

time [taɪm] n Zeit f; (occasion) Mal nt; (Mus) Takt m; **local ~** Ortszeit; **what ~ is it?, what's the ~?** wie spät ist es?, wie viel Uhr ist es?; **to take one's ~** (over sth) sich (bei etw) Zeit lassen; **to have a good ~** Spaß haben; **in two weeks' ~** in zwei Wochen; **at ~s** manchmal; **at the same ~** gleichzeitig; **all the ~** die ganze Zeit; **by the ~ he ...** bis er ...; (in past) als er ...; **for the ~ being** vorläufig; **in ~** (not late) rechtzeitig; **on ~** pünktlich; **the first ~** das erste Mal; **this ~** diesmal; **five ~s** fünfmal; **five ~s six** fünf mal sechs; **four ~s a year** viermal im Jahr; **three at a ~** drei auf einmal ▷ vt (with stopwatch) stoppen; **you ~d that well** das hast du gut getimt; **time difference** n Zeitunterschied m; **time limit** n Frist f; **timer** n Timer m; (switch) Schaltuhr f; **time-saving** adj Zeit sparend; **time switch** n Schaltuhr f; **timetable** n (for public transport) Fahrplan m; (school) Stundenplan m; **time zone** n Zeitzone f

timid ['tɪmɪd] adj ängstlich

timing ['taɪmɪŋ] n (coordination) Timing nt, zeitliche Abstimmung

tin [tɪn] n (metal) Blech nt; (Brit: can) Dose f; **tinfoil** n Alufolie f; **tinned** [tɪnd] adj (Brit) aus der Dose; **tin opener** n (Brit) Dosenöffner m

tinsel ['tɪnsəl] *n* ≈ Lametta *nt*

tint [tɪnt] *n* (Farb)ton *m*; (*in hair*) Tönung *f*; **tinted** *adj* getönt

tiny ['taɪnɪ] *adj* winzig

tip [tɪp] *n* (*money*) Trinkgeld *nt*; (*hint*) Tipp *m*; (*end*) Spitze *f*; (*of cigarette*) Filter *m*; (*Brit: rubbish ~*) Müllkippe *f* ▷ *vt* (*waiter*) Trinkgeld geben +*dat*; **tip over** *vt, vi* (*overturn*) umkippen

tipsy ['tɪpsɪ] *adj* beschwipst

tiptoe ['tɪptəʊ] *n* **on ~** auf Zehenspitzen

tire ['taɪə*] *n* (*US*) *see* **tyre** ▷ *vt* müde machen ▷ *vi* müde werden; **tired** *adj* müde; **to be ~ of sb/sth** jdn/etw satt haben; **to be ~ of doing sth** es satt haben, etw zu tun; **tireless, tirelessly** *adv* unermüdlich; **tiresome** *adj* lästig; **tiring** *adj* ermüdend

Tirol [tɪ'rəʊl] *see* **Tyrol**

tissue ['tɪʃuː] *n* (*Anat*) Gewebe *nt*; (*paper handkerchief*) Tempotaschentuch® *nt*, Papier(taschen)tuch *nt*; **tissue paper** *n* Seidenpapier *nt*

tit [tɪt] *n* (*bird*) Meise *f*; (*fam: breast*) Titte *f*

title ['taɪtl] *n* Titel *m*

KEYWORD

to [tuː, tə] *prep* **1** (*direction*) zu nach; **I go to France/school** ich gehe nach Frankreich/ zur Schule; **to the left** nach links
2 (*as far as*) bis
3 (*with expressions of time*) vor; **a quarter to 5** Viertel vor 5
4 (*for, of*) für; **secretary to the director** Sekretärin des Direcktors
5 (*expressing indirect object*): **to give sth to sb** jdm etw geben; **to talk to sb** mit jdm sprechen; **I sold it to a friend** ich habe es einem Freund verkauft
6 (*in relation to*) zu; **30 miles to the gallon** 30 Meilen pro Gallone
7 (*purpose, result*) zu; **to my surprise** zu meiner Überraschung
▷ *with vb* **1** (*infin*): **to go/eat** gehen/essen; **to want to do sth** etw tun wollen; **to try/start to do sth** versuchen/anfangen, etw zu tun; **he has a lot to lose** er hat viel zu verlieren
2 (*with vb omitted*): **I don't want to** ich will (es) nicht

3 (*purpose, result*) um; **I did it to help you** ich tat es, um dir zu helfen
4 (*after adj etc*): **ready to use** gebrauchsfertig; **too old/young to ... zu** alt/jung, um ... zu ...
▷ *adv* ; **push/pull the door to** die Tür zuschieben/zuziehen

toad [təʊd] *n* Kröte *f*; **toadstool** *n* Giftpilz *m*

toast [təʊst] *n* (*bread, drink*) Toast *m*; **a piece** (*o* **slice**) **of ~** eine Scheibe Toast; **to propose a ~ to sb** einen Toast auf jdn ausbringen ▷ *vt* (*bread*) toasten; (*person*) trinken auf +*akk*; **toaster** *n* Toaster *m*

tobacco [tə'bækəʊ] (*pl* **-es**) *n* Tabak *m*; **tobacconist's** [tə'bækənɪsts] *n* ~ (**shop**) Tabakladen *m*

toboggan [tə'bɒgən] *n* Schlitten *m*

today [tə'deɪ] *adv* heute; **a week ~** heute in einer Woche; **~'s newspaper** die Zeitung von heute

toddler ['tɒdlə*] *n* Kleinkind *nt*

toe [təʊ] *n* Zehe *f*, Zeh *m*; **toenail** *n* Zehennagel *m*

toffee ['tɒfɪ] *n* (*sweet*) Karamellbonbon *nt*; **toffee apple** *n* kandierter Apfel

tofu ['təʊfuː] *n* Tofu *m*

together [tə'geðə*] *adv* zusammen; **I tied them ~** ich habe sie zusammengebunden

toilet ['tɔɪlət] *n* Toilette *f*; **to go to the ~** auf die Toilette gehen; **toilet bag** *n* Kulturbeutel *m*; **toilet paper** *n* Toilettenpapier *m*; **toiletries** ['tɔɪlətrɪz] *npl* Toilettenartikel *pl*; **toilet roll** *n* Rolle *f* Toilettenpapier

token ['təʊkən] *n* Marke *f*; (*in casino*) Spielmarke *f*; (*voucher, gift ~*) Gutschein *m*; (*sign*) Zeichen *nt*

Tokyo ['təʊkɪəʊ] *n* Tokio *nt*

told [təʊld] *pt, pp of* **tell**

tolerant ['tɒlərənt] *adj* tolerant (*of* gegenüber); **tolerate** ['tɒləreɪt] *vt* tolerieren; (*noise, pain, heat*) ertragen

toll [təʊl] *n* (*charge*) Gebühr *f*; **the death ~** die Zahl der Toten; **toll-free** *adj, adv* (*US Tel*) gebührenfrei; **toll road** *n* gebührenpflichtige Straße

tomato [tə'mɑːtəʊ] (*pl* **-es**) *n* Tomate *f*; **tomato juice** *n* Tomatensaft *m*; **tomato ketchup** *n* Tomatenket(s)chup *m o nt*;

tomato sauce n Tomatensoße f; (Brit: ketchup) Tomatenket(s)chup m o nt

tomb [tu:m] n Grabmal nt; **tombstone** n Grabstein m

tomorrow [tə'mɒrəʊ] adv morgen; ~ **morning** morgen früh; ~ **evening** morgen Abend; **the day after** ~ übermorgen; **a week (from) ~/~ week** morgen in einer Woche

ton [tʌn] n (Brit) Tonne f (1016 kg); (US) Tonne f (907 kg); ~**s of books** (fam) eine Menge Bücher

tone [təʊn] n Ton m; **tone down** vt mäßigen; **toner** ['təʊnə*] n (for printer) Toner m; **toner cartridge** n Tonerpatrone f

tongs [tɒŋz] npl Zange f; (curling ~) Lockenstab m

tongue [tʌŋ] n Zunge f

tonic ['tɒnɪk] n (Med) Stärkungsmittel nt; ~ **(water)** Tonic nt; **gin and** ~ Gin m Tonic

tonight [tə'naɪt] adv heute Abend; (during night) heute Nacht

tonsils ['tɒnslz] n Mandeln pl; **tonsillitis** [tɒnsɪ'laɪtɪs] n Mandelentzündung f

too [tu:] adv zu; (also) auch; ~ **fast** zu schnell; ~ **much/many** zu viel/viele; **me** ~ ich auch; **she liked it** ~ ihr gefiel es auch

took [tʊk] pt of **take**

tool [tu:l] n Werkzeug nt; **toolbar** n (Inform) Symbolleiste f; **toolbox** n Werkzeugkasten m

tooth [tu:θ] (pl **teeth**) n Zahn m; **toothache** n Zahnschmerzen pl; **toothbrush** n Zahnbürste f; **toothpaste** n Zahnpasta f; **toothpick** n Zahnstocher m

top [tɒp] n (of tower, class, company etc) Spitze f; (of mountain) Gipfel m; (of tree) Krone f; (of street) oberes Ende; (of tube, pen) Kappe f; (of box) Deckel m; (of bikini) Oberteil nt; (sleeveless) Top nt; **at the** ~ **of the page** oben auf der Seite; **at the** ~ **of the league** an der Spitze der Liga; **on** ~ oben; **on** ~ **of** auf +dat; (in addition to) zusätzlich zu; **in** ~ **(gear)** im höchsten Gang; **over the** ~ übertrieben ▷ adj (floor, shelf) oberste(r, s); (price, note) höchste(r, s); (best) Spitzen-; (pupil, school) beste(r, s) ▷ vt (exceed) übersteigen; (be better than) übertreffen; (league) an erster Stelle liegen in +dat; ~**ped with cream** mit Sahne obendrauf; **top up** vt auffüllen; **can I top you up?** darf ich dir nachschenken?

topic ['tɒpɪk] n Thema nt; **topical** adj aktuell

topless ['tɒpləs] adj, adv oben ohne

topping ['tɒpɪŋ] n (on top of pizza, ice-cream etc) Belag m, Garnierung f

top-secret ['tɒp'si:krət] adj streng geheim

torch [tɔ:tʃ] n (Brit) Taschenlampe f

tore [tɔ:*] pt of **tear**

torment [tɔ:'ment] vt quälen

torn [tɔ:n] pp of **tear**

tornado [tɔ:'neɪdəʊ] (pl -es) n Tornado m

torrential [tə'renʃəl] adj (rain) sintflutartig

tortoise ['tɔ:təs] n Schildkröte f

torture ['tɔ:tʃə*] n Folter f; (fig) Qual f ▷ vt foltern

Tory ['tɔ:rɪ] (Brit) n Tory m, Konservative(r) mf ▷ adj Tory-

toss [tɒs] vt (throw) werfen; (salad) anmachen; **to** ~ **a coin** eine Münze werfen ▷ n **I don't give a** ~ (fam) es ist mir scheißegal

total ['təʊtl] n (of figures, money) Gesamtsumme f; **a** ~ **of 30** insgesamt 30; **in** ~ insgesamt ▷ adj total; (sum etc) Gesamt- ▷ vt (amount to) sich belaufen auf +akk; **totally** adv total

touch [tʌtʃ] n (act of ~ing) Berührung f; (sense of ~) Tastsinn m; (trace) Spur f; **to be/keep in** ~ **with sb** mit jdm in Verbindung stehen/bleiben; **to get in** ~ **with sb** sich mit jdm in Verbindung setzen; **to lose** ~ **with sb** den Kontakt zu jdm verlieren ▷ vt (feel) berühren; (emotionally) bewegen; **touch on** vt (topic) berühren; **touchdown** n (Aviat) Landung f; (Sport) Touchdown m; **touching** adj (moving) rührend; **touch screen** n Touchscreen m, Berührungsbildschirm m; **touchy** adj empfindlich, zickig

tough [tʌf] adj hart; (meat) zäh; (material) robust; (meat) zäh

tour ['tʊə*] n Tour f (of durch); (of town, building) Rundgang m (of durch); (of pop group etc) Tournee f ▷ vt eine Tour/einen Rundgang/eine Tournee machen durch ▷ vi (on holiday) umherreisen; **tour guide** n Reiseleiter(in) m(f)

tourism ['tʊərɪzəm] n Tourismus m, Fremdenverkehr m; **tourist** n Tourist(in) m(f); **tourist class** n Touristenklasse f; **tourist guide** n (book) Reiseführer m;

(*person*) Fremdenführer(in) *m(f)*; **tourist office** *n* Fremdenverkehrsamt *nt*

tournament ['tʊənəmənt] *n* Tournier *nt*

tour operator ['tʊərɒpəreɪtə*] *n* Reiseveranstalter *m*

tow [təʊ] *vt* abschleppen; (*caravan, trailer*) ziehen; **tow away** *vt* abschleppen

towards [tə'wɔːdz] *prep* ~ **me** mir entgegen, auf mich zu; **we walked ~ the station** wir gingen in Richtung Bahnhof; **my feelings ~ him** meine Gefühle ihm gegenüber; **she was kind ~ me** sie war nett zu mir

towel ['taʊəl] *n* Handtuch *nt*

tower ['taʊə*] *n* Turm *m*; **tower block** *n* (*Brit*) Hochhaus *nt*

town [taʊn] *n* Stadt *f*; **town center** (*US*), **town centre** *n* Stadtmitte *f*, Stadtzentrum *nt*; **town hall** *n* Rathaus *nt*

towrope ['təʊrəʊp] *n* Abschleppseil *nt*; **tow truck** *n* (*US*) Abschleppwagen *m*

toxic ['tɒksɪk] *adj* giftig, Gift-

toy [tɔɪ] *n* Spielzeug *nt*; **toy with** *vt* spielen mit; **toyshop** *n* Spielwarengeschäft *nt*

trace [treɪs] *n* Spur *f*; **without ~** spurlos ▷ *vt* (*find*) ausfindig machen; **tracing paper** *n* Pauspapier *nt*

track [træk] *n* (*mark*) Spur *f*; (*path*) Weg *m*; (*Rail*) Gleis *nt*; (*on CD, record*) Stück *nt*; **to keep/lose ~ of sb/sth** jdn/etw im Auge behalten/aus den Augen verlieren; **track down** *vt* ausfindig machen; **trackball** *n* (*Inform*) Trackball *m*; **tracksuit** *n* Trainingsanzug *m*

tractor ['træktə*] *n* Traktor *m*

trade [treɪd] *n* (*commerce*) Handel *m*; (*business*) Geschäft *nt*; (*skilled job*) Handwerk *nt* ▷ *vi* handeln (*in* mit) ▷ *vt* (*exchange*) tauschen (*for* gegen); **trademark** *n* Warenzeichen *nt*; **tradesman** (*pl* **-men**) *n* (*shopkeeper*) Geschäftsmann *m*; (*workman*) Handwerker *m*; **trade(s) union** *n* (*Brit*) Gewerkschaft *f*

tradition [trə'dɪʃən] *n* Tradition *f*; **traditional, traditionally** *adj, adv* traditionell

traffic ['træfɪk] *n* Verkehr *m*; (*pej: trading*) Handel *m* (*in* mit); **traffic circle** *n* (*US*) Kreisverkehr *m*; **traffic island** *n* Verkehrsinsel *f*; **traffic jam** *n* Stau *m*;

traffic lights *npl* Verkehrsampel *f*; **traffic warden** *n* (*Brit*) ≈ Politesse *f*

tragedy ['trædʒədɪ] *n* Tragödie *f*; **tragic** ['trædʒɪk] *adj* tragisch

trail [treɪl] *n* Spur *f*; (*path*) Weg *m* ▷ *vt* (*follow*) verfolgen; (*drag*) schleppen; (*drag behind*) hinter sich herziehen; (*Sport*) zurückliegen hinter +*dat* ▷ *vi* (*hang loosely*) schleifen; (*Sport*) weit zurückliegen; **trailer** *n* Anhänger *m*; (*US: caravan*) Wohnwagen *m*; (*Cine*) Trailer *m*

train [treɪn] *n* (*Rail*) Zug *m* ▷ *vt* (*teach*) ausbilden; (*Sport*) trainieren ▷ *vi* (*Sport*) trainieren; **to ~ as** (*o to be*) **a teacher** eine Ausbildung als Lehrer machen; **trained** *adj* (*person, voice*) ausgebildet; **trainee** *n* Auszubildende(r) *mf*; (*academic, practical*) Praktikant(in) *m(f)*; **trainer** *n* (*Sport*) Trainer(ih) *m(f)*; **~s** (*Brit: shoes*) Turnschuhe *pl*; **training** *n* Ausbildung *f*; (*Sport*) Training *nt*; **train station** *n* Bahnhof *m*

tram ['træm] *n* (*Brit*) Straßenbahn *f*

tramp [træmp] *n* Landstreicher(in) *m(f)* ▷ *vi* trotten

tranquillizer ['træŋkwɪlaɪzə*] *n* Beruhigungsmittel *nt*

transaction *n* (*piece of business*) Geschäft *nt*

transatlantic ['trænzət'læntɪk] *adj* transatlantisch; **~ flight** Transatlantikflug *m*

transfer ['trænsfə*] *n* (*of money*) Überweisung *f*; (*US: ticket*) Umsteigekarte *f* ▷ [træns'fɜː*] *vt* (*money*) überweisen (*to sb* an jdn); (*patient*) verlegen; (*employee*) versetzen; (*Sport*) transferieren ▷ *vi* (*on journey*) umsteigen; **transferable** [træns'fɜːrəbl] *adj* übertragbar

transform [træns'fɔːm] *vt* umwandeln; **transformation** [trænsfə'meɪʃən] *n* Umwandlung *f*

transfusion [træns'fjuːʒən] *n* Transfusion *f*

transistor [træn'zɪstə*] *n* Transistor *m*; **~ (radio)** Transistorradio *nt*

transition [træn'zɪʃən] *n* Übergang *m* (*from ... to* von ... zu)

transit lounge ['trænzɪtlaʊndʒ] *n* Transitraum *m*; **transit passenger** *n* Transitreisende(r) *mf*

translate [trænz'leɪt] *vt, vi* übersetzen; **translation** [trænz'leɪʃən] *n* Übersetzung

f; **translator** [trænz'leɪtə*] *n*
Übersetzer(in) *m(f)*

transmission [trænz'mɪʃən] *n* (*Tv, Radio*)
Übertragung *f*; (*Auto*) Getriebe *nt*

transparent [træns'pærənt] *adj*
durchsichtig; (*fig*) offenkundig

transplant [træns'plɑ:nt] (*Med*) *vt*
transplantieren ▷ ['trænsplɑ:nt] *n*
(*operation*) Transplantation *f*

transport ['trænspɔ:t] *n* (*of goods, people*)
Beförderung *f*; **public ~** öffentliche
Verkehrsmittel *pl* ▷ [træns'pɔ:t] *vt*
befördern, transportieren;
transportation [trænspɔ:'teɪʃən] *n see*
transport

trap [træp] *n* Falle *f* ▷ *vt* **to be ~ped** (*in
snow, job etc*) festsitzen

trash [træʃ] *n* (*book, film etc*) Schund *m*;
(*US: refuse*) Abfall *m*; **trash can** *n* (*US*)
Abfalleimer *m*; **trashy** *adj* niveaulos;
(*novel*) Schund-

traumatic [trɔ:'mætɪk] *adj*
traumatisch

travel ['trævl] *n* Reisen *nt* ▷ *vi* (*journey*)
reisen ▷ *vt* (*distance*) zurücklegen;
(*country*) bereisen; **travel agency, travel
agent** *n* (*company*) Reisebüro *nt*; **traveler**
(*US*) *see* **traveller**; **traveler's check** (*US*)
see **traveller's cheque**; **travel insurance**
n Reiseversicherung *f*; **traveller** *n*
Reisende(r) *mf*; **traveller's cheque** *n*
(*Brit*) Reisescheck *m*; **travelsick** *n*
reisekrank

tray [treɪ] *n* Tablett *nt*; (*for mail etc*) Ablage
f; (*of printer, photocopier*) Fach *nt*

tread [tred] *n* (*on tyre*) Profil *nt*; **tread on**
[tred] (**trod, trodden**) *vt* treten auf +*akk*

treasure ['treʒə*] *n* Schatz *m* ▷ *vt*
schätzen

treat [tri:t] *n* besondere Freude; **it's my
~** das geht auf meine Kosten ▷ *vt*
behandeln; **to ~ sb** (**to sth**) jdn (zu etw)
einladen; **to ~ oneself to sth** sich etw
leisten; **treatment** ['tri:tmənt] *n*
Behandlung *f*

treaty ['tri:tɪ] *n* Vertrag *m*

tree [tri:] *n* Baum *m*

tremble ['trembl] *vi* zittern

tremendous [trə'mendəs] *adj* gewaltig;
(*fam: very good*) toll

trench [trentʃ] *n* Graben *m*

trend [trend] *n* Tendenz *f*; (*fashion*) Mode
f, Trend *m*; **trendy** *adj* trendy

trespass ['trespəs] *vi* **'no ~ing'** „Betreten
verboten"

trial ['traɪəl] *n* (*Jur*) Prozess *m*; (*test*)
Versuch *m*; **by ~ and error** durch
Ausprobieren; **trial period** *n* (*for employee*)
Probezeit *f*

triangle ['traɪæŋgl] *n* Dreieck *nt*; (*Mus*)
Triangel *m*; **triangular** [traɪ'æŋgjʊlə*] *adj*
dreieckig

tribe [traɪb] *n* Stamm *m*

trick [trɪk] *n* Trick *m*; (*mischief*) Streich *m*
▷ *vt* hereinlegen

tricky ['trɪkɪ] *adj* (*difficult*) schwierig;
(*situation*) verzwickt

trifle ['traɪfl] *n* Kleinigkeit *f*; (*Brit Gastr*)
Trifle *nt* (*Nachspeise aus Biskuit,
Wackelpudding, Obst, Vanillesoße und Sahne*)

trigger ['trɪgə*] *n* (*of gun*) Abzug *m* ▷ *vt* **to
~** (**off**) auslösen

trim [trɪm] *vt* (*hair, beard*) nachschneiden;
(*nails*) schneiden; (*hedge*) stutzen ▷ *n* **just
a ~, please** nur etwas nachschneiden,
bitte; **trimmings** *npl* (*decorations*)
Verzierungen *pl*; (*extras*) Zubehör *nt*;
(*Gastr*) Beilagen *pl*

trip [trɪp] *n* Reise *f*; (*outing*) Ausflug *m* ▷ *vi*
stolpern (*over* über +*akk*)

triple ['trɪpl] *adj* dreifach ▷ *adv* **~ the
price** dreimal so teuer ▷ *vi* sich
verdreifachen; **triplets** ['trɪplɪts] *npl*
Drillinge *pl*

tripod ['traɪpɒd] *n* (*Foto*) Stativ *nt*

trite [traɪt] *adj* banal

triumph ['traɪʌmf] *n* Triumph *m*

trivial ['trɪvɪəl] *adj* trivial

trod [trɒd] *pt of* **tread**

trodden *pp of* **tread**

trolley ['trɒlɪ] *n* (*Brit: in shop*)
Einkaufswagen *m*; (*for luggage*) Kofferkuli
m; (*serving ~*) Teewagen *m*

trombone [trɒm'bəʊn] *n* Posaune *f*

troops [tru:ps] *npl* (*Mil*) Truppen *pl*

trophy ['trəʊfɪ] *n* Trophäe *f*

tropical ['trɒpɪkl] *adj* tropisch

trouble ['trʌbl] *n* (*problems*)
Schwierigkeiten *pl*; (*worry*) Sorgen *pl*;
(*effort*) Mühe *f*; (*unrest*) Unruhen *pl*;
(*Med*) Beschwerden *pl*; **to be in ~** in
Schwierigkeiten sein; **to get into
~** (*with authority*) Ärger bekommen; **to
make ~** Schwierigkeiten machen ▷ *vt*
(*worry*) beunruhigen; (*disturb*) stören; **my
back's troubling me** mein Rücken macht

t

mir zu schaffen; **sorry to ~ you** ich muss dich leider kurz stören; **troubled** adj (worried) beunruhigt; **trouble-free** adj problemlos; **troublemaker** n Unruhestifter(in) m(f); **troublesome** adj lästig

trousers ['traʊzəz] npl Hose f; **trouser suit** n (Brit) Hosenanzug m

trout [traʊt] n Forelle f

truck [trʌk] n Lastwagen m; (Brit Rail) Güterwagen m; **trucker** n (US: driver) Lastwagenfahrer(in) m(f)

true [truː] adj (factually correct) wahr; (genuine) echt; **to come ~** wahr werden

truly ['truːlɪ] adv wirklich; **Yours ~** (in letter) mit freundlichen Grüßen

trump [trʌmp] n (Cards) Trumpf m

trumpet ['trʌmpɪt] n Trompete f

trunk [trʌŋk] n (of tree) Stamm m; (Anat) Rumpf m; (of elephant) Rüssel m; (piece of luggage) Überseekoffer m; (US Auto) Kofferraum m; **trunks** npl (**swimming**) ~ Badehose f

trust [trʌst] n (confidence) Vertrauen nt (in zu) ▷ vt vertrauen +dat; **trusting** adj vertrauensvoll; **trustworthy** adj vertrauenswürdig

truth [truːθ] n Wahrheit f; **truthful** adj ehrlich; (statement) wahrheitsgemäß

try [traɪ] n Versuch m ▷ vt (attempt) versuchen; (~ out) ausprobieren; (sample) probieren; (Jur: person) vor Gericht stellen; (courage, patience) auf die Probe stellen ▷ vi versuchen; (make effort) sich bemühen; **~ and come** versuch zu kommen; **try on** vt (clothes) anprobieren; **try out** vt ausprobieren

T-shirt ['tiːʃɜːt] n T-Shirt nt

tub [tʌb] n (for ice-cream, margarine) Becher m

tube [tjuːb] n (pipe) Rohr nt; (of rubber, plastic) Schlauch m; (for toothpaste, glue etc) Tube f; **the Tube** (in London) die U-Bahn

tube station ['tjuːbsteɪʃən] n U-Bahn-Station f

tuck [tʌk] vt (put) stecken; **tuck in** vt (shirt) in die Hose stecken; (blanket) feststecken; (person) zudecken ▷ vi (eat) zulangen

Tue(s) abbr = **Tuesday** Di.

Tuesday ['tjuːzdɪ] n Dienstag m; **on ~** (am) Dienstag; **on ~s** dienstags;

this/last/next ~ diesen/letzten/nächsten Dienstag; (**on**) ~ **morning/afternoon/evening** (am) Dienstag Morgen/Nachmittag/Abend; **every ~** jeden Dienstag; **a week on ~/ ~ week** Dienstag in einer Woche

tug [tʌɡ] vt ziehen; **she ~ged his sleeve** sie zog an seinem Ärmel ▷ vi ziehen (at an +dat)

tuition [tjuːˈɪʃən] n Unterricht m; (US: fees) Studiengebühren pl; **~ fees** pl Studiengebühren pl

tulip ['tjuːlɪp] n Tulpe f

tumble ['tʌmbl] vi (person, prices) fallen; **tumble dryer** n Wäschetrockner m; **tumbler** n (glass) (Becher)glas nt

tummy ['tʌmɪ] n (fam) Bauch m; **tummyache** n (fam) Bauchweh nt

tumor (US), **tumour** ['tjuːmə*] n Tumor m

tuna ['tjuːnə] n Thunfisch m

tune [tjuːn] n Melodie f; **to be in/out of ~** (instrument) gestimmt/verstimmt sein; (singer) richtig/falsch singen ▷ vt (instrument) stimmen; (radio) einstellen (to auf +akk); **tuner** n (in stereo system) Tuner m

Tunisia [tjuːˈnɪzɪə] n Tunesien nt

tunnel ['tʌnl] n Tunnel m; (under road, railway) Unterführung f

turban ['tɜːbən] n Turban m

turbulence ['tɜːbjʊləns] n (Aviat) Turbulenzen pl; **turbulent** adj stürmisch

Turk [tɜːk] n Türke m, Türkin f

turkey ['tɜːkɪ] n Truthahn m

Turkey ['tɜːkɪ] n die Türkei; **Turkish** adj türkisch ▷ n (language) Türkisch nt

turmoil ['tɜːmɔɪl] n Aufruhr m

turn [tɜːn] n (rotation) Drehung f; (performance) Nummer f; **to make a left ~** nach links abbiegen; **at the ~ of the century** um die Jahrhundertwende; **it's your ~** du bist dran; **in ~, by ~s** abwechselnd; **to take ~s** sich abwechseln ▷ vt (wheel, key, screw) drehen; (to face other way) umdrehen; (corner) biegen um; (page) umblättern; (transform) verwandeln (into in +akk) ▷ vi (rotate) sich drehen; (to face other way) sich umdrehen; (change direction: driver, car) abbiegen; (become) werden; (weather) umschlagen; **to ~ into sth** (become) sich in etw akk verwandeln; **to ~ cold/green** kalt/grün werden; **to ~ left/right** links/rechts abbiegen; **turn**

away vt (person) abweisen; **turn back** vt (person) zurückweisen ▷ vi (go back) umkehren; **turn down** vt (refuse) ablehnen; (radio, TV) leiser stellen; (heating) kleiner stellen; **turn off** vi abbiegen ▷ vt (switch off) ausschalten; (tap) zudrehen; (engine, electricity) abstellen; **turn on** vt (switch on) einschalten; (tap) aufdrehen; (engine, electricity) anstellen; (fam: person) anmachen, antörnen; **turn out** vt (light) ausmachen; (pockets) leeren ▷ vi (develop) sich entwickeln; **as it turned out** wie sich herausstellte; **turn over** vt onto other side, umdrehen; (page) umblättern ▷ vi (person) sich umdrehen; (car) sich überschlagen; (TV) umschalten (to auf +akk); **turn round** vt (to face other way) umdrehen ▷ vi (person) sich umdrehen; (go back) umkehren; **turn to** vt sich zuwenden +dat; **turn up** vi (person, lost object) auftauchen ▷ vt (radio, TV) lauter stellen; (heating) höher stellen; **turning** n (in road) Abzweigung f; **turning point** n Wendepunkt m

turnip ['tɜːnɪp] n Rübe f
turnover ['tɜːnəʊvə*] n (Fin) Umsatz m
turnpike ['tɜːnpaɪk] n (US) gebührenpflichtige Autobahn
turntable ['tɜːnteɪbl] n (on record player) Plattenteller m
turn-up ['tɜːnʌp] n (Brit: on trousers) Aufschlag m
turquoise ['tɜːkwɔɪz] adj türkis
turtle ['tɜːtl] n (Brit) Wasserschildkröte f; (US) Schildkröte f
tutor ['tjuːtə*] n (private) Privatlehrer(in) m(f); (Brit: at university) Tutor(in) m(f)
tuxedo [tʌk'siːdəʊ] (pl -s) n (US) Smoking m
TV [tiː'viː] n Fernsehen nt; (~ set) Fernseher m; **to watch ~** fernsehen; **on ~** im Fernsehen ▷ adj Fernseh-; **~ programme** Fernsehsendung f
tweed [twiːd] n Tweed m
tweezers ['twiːzəz] npl Pinzette f
twelfth [twelfθ] adj zwölfte(r, s); see also **eighth**; **twelve** [twelv] num zwölf ▷ n Zwölf f; see also **eight**
twentieth ['twentɪɪθ] adj zwanzigste(r, s); see also **eighth**; **twenty** ['twentɪ] num zwanzig; **~-one** einundzwanzig ▷ n

Zwanzig f; **to be in one's twenties** in den Zwanzigern sein; see also **eight**
twice [twaɪs] adv zweimal; **~ as much/many** doppelt so viel/viele
twig [twɪg] n Zweig m
twilight ['twaɪlaɪt] n (in evening) Dämmerung f
twin [twɪn] n Zwilling m ▷ adj (brother etc) Zwillings-; **~ beds** zwei Einzelbetten
twinge [twɪndʒ] n (pain) stechender Schmerz
twinkle ['twɪŋkl] vi funkeln
twin room ['twɪn'ruːm] n Zweibettzimmer nt; **twin town** n Partnerstadt f
twist [twɪst] vt (turn) drehen, winden; (distort) verdrehen; **I've ~ed my ankle** ich bin mit dem Fuß umgeknickt
two [tuː] num zwei; **to break sth in ~** etw in zwei Teile brechen ▷ n Zwei f; **the ~ of them** die beiden; see also **eight**; **two-dimensional** adj zweidimensional; (fig) oberflächlich; **two-faced** adj falsch, heuchlerisch; **two-piece** adj zweiteilig; **two-way** adj **~ traffic** Gegenverkehr
type [taɪp] n (sort) Art f; (typeface) Schrift(art) f; **what ~ of car is it?** was für ein Auto ist das?; **he's not my ~** er ist nicht mein Typ; **typeface** n Schrift(art) f; **typewriter** n Schreibmaschine f
typhoid ['taɪfɔɪd] n Typhus m
typhoon [taɪ'fuːn] n Taifun m
typical ['tɪpɪkəl] adj typisch (of für)
typing error ['taɪpɪŋerə*] n Tippfehler m
tyre [taɪə*] n (Brit) Reifen m; **tyre pressure** n Reifendruck m
Tyrol [tɪ'rəʊl] n **the ~** Tirol nt

t

UFO ['juːfəʊ] *acr* = **unidentified flying object** Ufo *nt*

Uganda [juːˈgændə] *n* Uganda *nt*

ugly ['ʌglɪ] *adj* hässlich; (*bad*) schlimm

UHT *adj abbr* = **ultra-heat treated ~ milk** H-Milch *f*

UK *abbr* = **United Kingdom**

Ukraine [juːˈkreɪn] *n* **the ~** die Ukraine

ulcer ['ʌlsə*] *n* Geschwür *nt*

ulterior [ʌlˈtɪərɪə*] *adj* **~ motive** Hintergedanke *m*

ultimate ['ʌltɪmət] *adj* (*final*) letzte(r, s); (*authority*) höchste(r, s); **ultimately** *adv* letzten Endes; (*eventually*) schließlich; **ultimatum** [ʌltɪˈmeɪtəm] *n* Ultimatum *nt*

ultra- ['ʌltrə] *pref* ultra-

ultrasound ['ʌltrəsaʊnd] *n* (*Med*) Ultraschall *m*

umbrella [ʌmˈbrelə] *n* Schirm *m*

umpire ['ʌmpaɪə*] *n* Schiedsrichter(in) *m(f)*

umpteen ['ʌmptiːn] *num* (*fam*) zig; **~ times** zigmal

un- [ʌn] *pref* un-

UN *nsing abbr* = **United Nations** UNO *f*

unable [ʌnˈeɪbl] *adj* **to be ~ to do sth** etw nicht tun können

unacceptable [ʌnəˈkseptəbl] *adj* unannehmbar

unaccountably [ʌnəˈkaʊntəblɪ] *adv* unerklärlicherweise

unaccustomed [ʌnəˈkʌstəmd] *adj* **to be ~ to sth** etw nicht gewohnt sein

unanimous, unanimously [juːˈnænɪməs, -lɪ] *adj, adv* einmütig

unattached [ʌnəˈtætʃt] *adj* (*without partner*) ungebunden

unattended [ʌnəˈtendɪd] *adj* (*luggage, car*) unbeaufsichtigt

unauthorized [ʌnˈɔːθəraɪzd] *adj* unbefugt

unavailable [ʌnəˈveɪləbl] *adj* nicht erhältlich; (*person*) nicht erreichbar

unavoidable [ʌnəˈvɔɪdəbl] *adj* unvermeidlich

unaware [ʌnəˈwɛə*] *adj* **to be ~ of sth** sich einer Sache *dat* nicht bewusst sein; **I was ~ that ...** ich wusste nicht, dass ...

unbalanced [ʌnˈbælənst] *adj* unausgewogen; (*mentally*) gestört

unbearable [ʌnˈbɛərəbl] *adj* unerträglich

unbeatable [ʌnˈbiːtəbl] *adj* unschlagbar

unbelievable [ʌnbɪˈliːvəbl] *adj* unglaublich

unblock [ʌnˈblɒk] *vt* (*pipe*) frei machen

unbutton [ʌnˈbʌtn] *vt* aufknöpfen

uncertain [ʌnˈsɜːtən] *adj* unsicher

uncle ['ʌŋkl] *n* Onkel *m*

uncomfortable [ʌnˈkʌmfətəbl] *adj* unbequem

unconditional [ʌnkənˈdɪʃənl] *adj* bedingungslos

unconscious [ʌnˈkɒnʃəs] *adj* (*Med*) bewusstlos; **to be ~ of sth** sich einer Sache *dat* nicht bewusst sein; **unconsciously** *adv* unbewusst

uncork [ʌnˈkɔːk] *vt* entkorken

uncover [ʌnˈkʌvə*] *vt* aufdecken

undecided [ʌndɪˈsaɪdɪd] *adj* unschlüssig

undeniable [ʌndɪˈnaɪəbl] *adj* unbestreitbar

under ['ʌndə*] *prep* (*beneath*) unter +*dat*; (*with motion*) unter +*akk*; **children ~ eight** Kinder unter acht; **~ an hour** weniger als eine Stunde ▷ *adv* (*beneath*) unten; (*with motion*) darunter; **children aged eight and ~** Kinder bis zu acht Jahren; **under-age** *adj* minderjährig

undercarriage ['ʌndəkærɪdʒ] *n* Fahrgestell *nt*

underdog ['ʌndədɒg] n Unterlegene(r) mf; (outsider) Außenseiter(in) m(f)

underdone [ʌndə'dʌn] adj (Gastr) nicht gar, durch; (deliberately) nicht durchgebraten

underestimate [ʌndər'estɪmeɪt] vt unterschätzen

underexposed [ʌndərɪks'pəʊzd] adj (Foto) unterbelichtet

undergo [ʌndə'gəʊ] irr vt (experience) durchmachen; (operation, test) sich unterziehen +dat

undergraduate [ʌndə'grædjʊət] n Student(in) m(f)

underground ['ʌndəgraʊnd] adj unterirdisch ▷ n (Brit Rail) U-Bahn f; **underground station** n U-Bahn-Station f

underlie [ʌndə'laɪ] irr vt zugrunde liegen +dat

underline [ʌndə'laɪn] vt unterstreichen

underlying [ʌndə'laɪɪŋ] adj zugrunde liegend

underneath [ʌndə'niːθ] prep unter; (with motion) unter +akk ▷ adv darunter

underpants ['ʌndəpænts] npl Unterhose f; **undershirt** ['ʌndəʃɜːt] n (US) Unterhemd nt; **undershorts** ['ʌndəʃɔːts] npl (US) Unterhose f

understand [ʌndə'stænd] irr vt, vi verstehen; **I ~ that ...** (been told) ich habe gehört, dass ...; (sympathize) ich habe Verständnis dafür, dass ...; **to make oneself understood** sich verständlich machen; **understandable** adj verständlich; **understanding** adj verständnisvoll

undertake [ʌndə'teɪk] irr vt (task) übernehmen; **to ~ to do sth** sich verpflichten, etw zu tun; **undertaker** n Leichenbestatter(in) m(f); **~'s** (firm) Bestattungsinstitut nt

underwater [ʌndə'wɔːtə*] adv unter Wasser ▷ adj Unterwasser-

underwear ['ʌndəweə*] n Unterwäsche f

undesirable [ʌndɪ'zaɪərəbl] adj unerwünscht

undo [ʌn'duː] irr vt (unfasten) aufmachen; (work) zunichte machen; (Inform) rückgängig machen

undoubtedly [ʌn'daʊtɪdlɪ] adv zweifellos

undress [ʌn'dres] vt ausziehen; **to get ~ed** sich ausziehen ▷ vi sich ausziehen

undue [ʌn'djuː] adj übermäßig

unduly [ʌn'djuːlɪ] adv übermäßig

unearth [ʌn'ɜːθ] vt (dig up) ausgraben; (find) aufstöbern

unease [ʌn'iːz] n Unbehagen nt; **uneasy** adj (person) unbehaglich; **I'm ~ about it** mir ist nicht wohl dabei

unemployed [ʌnɪm'plɔɪd] adj arbeitslos ▷ ▷ npl **the ~** die Arbeitslosen pl; **unemployment** [ʌnɪm'plɔɪmənt] n Arbeitslosigkeit f; **unemployment benefit** n Arbeitslosengeld nt

unequal [ʌn'iːkwəl] adj ungleich

uneven [ʌn'iːvən] adj (surface, road) uneben; (contest) ungleich

unexpected [ʌnɪk'spektɪd] adj unerwartet

unfair [ʌn'feə*] adj unfair

unfamiliar [ʌnfə'mɪljə*] adj **to be ~ with sb/sth** jdn/etw nicht kennen

unfasten [ʌn'fɑːsn] vt aufmachen

unfit [ʌn'fɪt] adj ungeeignet (for für); (in bad health) nicht fit

unforeseen [ʌnfɔː'siːn] adj unvorhergesehen

unforgettable [ʌnfə'getəbl] adj unvergesslich

unforgivable [ʌnfə'gɪvəbl] adj unverzeihlich

unfortunate [ʌn'fɔːtʃnət] adj (unlucky) unglücklich; **it is ~ that ...** es ist bedauerlich, dass ...; **unfortunately** adv leider

unfounded [ʌn'faʊndɪd] adj unbegründet

unhappy [ʌn'hæpɪ] adj (sad) unglücklich, unzufrieden; **to be ~ with sth** mit etw unzufrieden sein

unhealthy [ʌn'helθɪ] adj ungesund

unheard-of [ʌn'hɜːdɒv] adj (unknown) gänzlich unbekannt; (outrageous) unerhört

unhelpful [ʌn'helpfʊl] adj nicht hilfreich

unhitch [ʌn'hɪtʃ] vt (caravan, trailer) abkoppeln

unhurt [ʌn'hɜːt] adj unverletzt

uniform ['juːnɪfɔːm] n Uniform f ▷ adj einheitlich

unify ['juːnɪfaɪ] vt vereinigen

unimportant [ʌnɪm'pɔːtənt] adj unwichtig

uninhabited [ʌnɪn'hæbɪtɪd] adj unbewohnt

u

uninstall [ʌnɪn'stɔːl] *vt* (*Inform*) deinstallieren

unintentional [ʌnɪn'tenʃənl] *adj* unabsichtlich

union ['juːnjən] *n* (*uniting*) Vereinigung *f*; (*alliance*) Union *f*; **Union Jack** *n* Union Jack *m* (*britische Nationalflagge*)

unique [juː'niːk] *adj* einzigartig

unit ['juːnɪt] *n* Einheit *f*; (*of system, machine*) Teil *nt*; (*in school*) Lektion *f*

unite [juː'naɪt] *vt* vereinigen; **the United Kingdom** das Vereinigte Königreich; **the United Nations** *pl* die Vereinten Nationen *pl*; **the United States** (**of America**) *pl* die Vereinigten Staaten (von Amerika) *pl* ▷ *vi* sich vereinigen

universe ['juːnɪvɜːs] *n* Universum *nt*

university [juːnɪ'vɜːsɪtɪ] *n* Universität *f*

unkind [ʌn'kaɪnd] *adj* unfreundlich (*to* zu)

unknown [ʌn'nəʊn] *adj* unbekannt (*to* +*dat*)

unleaded [ʌn'ledɪd] *adj* bleifrei

unless [ən'les] *conj* es sei denn, wenn ... nicht; **don't do it ~ I tell you to** mach das nicht, es sei denn, ich sage es dir; **~ I'm mistaken ...** wenn ich mich nicht irre ...

unlicensed [ʌn'laɪsənst] *adj* (*to sell alcohol*) ohne Lizenz

unlike [ʌn'laɪk] *prep* (*in contrast to*) im Gegensatz zu; **it's ~ her to be late** es sieht ihr gar nicht ähnlich, zu spät zu kommen; **unlikely** [ʌn'laɪklɪ] *adj* unwahrscheinlich

unload [ʌn'ləʊd] *vt* ausladen

unlock [ʌn'lɒk] *vt* aufschließen

unlucky [ʌn'lʌkɪ] *adj* unglücklich; **to be ~** Pech haben

unmistakable [ʌnmɪ'steɪkəbl] *adj* unverkennbar

unnecessary [ʌn'nesəsərɪ] *adj* unnötig

unobtainable [ʌnəb'teɪnəbl] *adj* nicht erhältlich

unoccupied [ʌn'ɒkjʊpaɪd] *adj* (*seat*) frei; (*building, room*) leer stehend

unpack [ʌn'pæk] *vt, vi* auspacken

unpleasant [ʌn'pleznt] *adj* unangenehm

unplug [ʌn'plʌg] *vt* **to ~ sth** den Stecker von etw herausziehen

unprecedented [ʌn'presɪdəntɪd] *adj* beispiellos

unpredictable [ʌnprɪ'dɪktəbl] *adj* (*person, weather*) unberechenbar

unreasonable [ʌn'riːznəbl] *adj* unvernünftig; (*demand*) übertrieben

unreliable [ʌnrɪ'laɪəbl] *adj* unzuverlässig

unsafe [ʌn'seɪf] *adj* nicht sicher; (*dangerous*) gefährlich

unscrew [ʌn'skruː] *vt* abschrauben

unsightly [ʌn'saɪtlɪ] *adj* unansehnlich

unskilled [ʌn'skɪld] *adj* (*worker*) ungelernt

unsuccessful [ʌnsək'sesfʊl] *adj* erfolglos

unsuitable [ʌn'suːtəbl] *adj* ungeeignet (*for* für)

until [ən'tɪl] *prep* bis; **not ~** erst; **from Monday ~ Friday** von Montag bis Freitag; **he didn't come home ~ midnight** er kam erst um Mitternacht nach Hause; **~ then** bis dahin ▷ *conj* bis; **she won't come ~ you invite her** sie kommt erst, wenn du sie einlädst

unusual, unusually [ʌn'juːʒʊəl, -ɪ] *adj, adv* ungewöhnlich

unwanted [ʌn'wɒntɪd] *adj* unerwünscht, ungewollt

unwell [ʌn'wel] *adj* krank; **to feel ~** sich nicht wohl fühlen

unwilling [ʌn'wɪlɪŋ] *adj* **to be ~ to do sth** nicht bereit sein, etw zu tun

unwind [ʌn'waɪnd] *irr vt* abwickeln ▷ *vi* (*relax*) sich entspannen

unwrap [ʌn'ræp] *vt* auspacken

unzip [ʌn'zɪp] *vt* den Reißverschluss aufmachen an +*dat*; (*Inform*) entzippen

KEYWORD

up [ʌp] *prep*: **to be up sth** oben auf etw *dat* sein; **to go up sth** (auf) etw *acc* hinaufgehen; **go up that road** gehen Sie die Straße hinauf

▷ *adv* **1** (*upwards, higher*) oben; **put it up a bit higher** stell es etwas weiter nach oben; **up there** da oben dort oben; **up above** hoch oben

2: **to be up** (*out of bed*) auf sein (*prices, level*) gestiegen sein (*building, tent*) stehen

3: **up to** (*as far as*) bis; **up to now** bis jetzt

4: **to be up to** (*depending on*); **it's up to you** das hängt von dir ab; (*equal to*); **he's not up to it** (*job, task etc*) er ist dem nicht gewachsen (*inf: be doing: showing disapproval, suspicion*); **what is he up to?** was führt er im Schilde?; **it's not up to me to decide** die Entscheidung liegt nicht bei mir; **his work is not up to the required standard** seine Arbeit entspricht nicht dem geforderten Niveau

▷ n ; **ups and downs** (in life, career) Höhen und Tiefen pl

upbringing [ˈʌpbrɪŋɪŋ] n Erziehung f
update [ʌpˈdeɪt] n (list etc) Aktualisierung f; (software) Update nt ▷ vt (list etc, person) auf den neuesten Stand bringen, aktualisieren
upgrade [ʌpˈgreɪd] vt (computer) aufrüsten; **we were ~d** das Hotel hat uns ein besseres Zimmer gegeben
upheaval [ʌpˈhiːvəl] n Aufruhr m; (Pol) Umbruch m
uphill [ʌpˈhɪl] adv bergauf
upon [əˈpɒn] prep see **on**
upper [ˈʌpə*] adj obere(r, s); (arm, deck) Ober-
upright [ˈʌpraɪt] adj, adv aufrecht
uprising [ˈʌpraɪzɪŋ] n Aufstand m
uproar [ˈʌprɔː*] n Aufruhr m
upset [ʌpˈset] irr vt (overturn) umkippen; (disturb) aufregen; (sadden) bestürzen; (offend) kränken; (plans) durcheinander bringen ▷ adj (disturbed) aufgeregt; (sad) bestürzt; (offended) gekränkt; **~ stomach** [ˈʌpset] Magenverstimmung f
upside down [ʌpsaɪdˈdaʊn] adv verkehrt herum; (fig) drunter und drüber; **to turn sth ~** (box etc) etw umdrehen/durchwühlen
upstairs [ʌpˈstɛəz] adv oben; (go, take) nach oben
up-to-date [ˈʌptəˈdeɪt] adj modern; (fashion, information) aktuell; **to keep sb ~** jdn auf dem Laufenden halten
upwards [ˈʌpwədz] adv nach oben
urban [ˈɜːbən] adj städtisch, Stadt-
urge [ɜːdʒ] n Drang m ▷ vt **to ~ sb to do sth** jdn drängen, etw zu tun; **urgent, urgently** [ˈɜːdʒənt, -lɪ] adj, adv dringend
urine [ˈjʊərɪn] n Urin m
us [ʌs] pron uns; **do they know ~?** kennen sie uns?; **can he help ~?** kann er uns helfen?; **it's ~** wir sind's; **both of ~** wir beide
US, USA nsing abbr = **United States (of America)** USA pl
use [juːs] n (using) Gebrauch m; (for specific purpose) Verwendung f; **to make ~ of** Gebrauch machen von; **in/out of ~** in/außer Gebrauch; **it's no ~ (doing that)** es hat keinen Zweck(, das zu tun); **it's (of) no ~ to me** das kann ich nicht

brauchen ▷ [juːz] vt benutzen, gebrauchen; (for specific purpose) verwenden; (method) anwenden; **use up** vt aufbrauchen
used [juːzd] adj (secondhand) gebraucht ▷ vb aux **to be ~d to sb/sth** an jdn/etw gewöhnt sein; **to get ~d to sb/sth** sich an jdn/etw gewöhnen; **she ~d to live here** sie hat früher mal hier gewohnt; **useful** adj nützlich; **useless** adj nutzlos; (unusable) unbrauchbar; (pointless) zwecklos; **user** [ˈjuːzə*] n Benutzer(in) m(f); **user-friendly** adj benutzerfreundlich
usual [ˈjuːʒəl] adj üblich, gewöhnlich; **as ~** wie üblich; **usually** adv normalerweise
utensil [juːˈtensl] n Gerät nt
uterus [ˈjuːtərəs] n Gebärmutter f
utilize [ˈjuːtɪlaɪz] vt verwenden
utmost [ˈʌtməʊst] adj äußerst; **to do one's ~** sein Möglichstes tun
utter [ˈʌtə*] adj völlig ▷ vt von sich geben; **utterly** adv völlig
U-turn [ˈjuːtɜːn] n (Auto) Wende f; **to do a ~** wenden; (fig) eine Kehrtwendung machen

u

gültig; (*argument*) stichhaltig; (*claim*) berechtigt

valley ['vælɪ] *n* Tal *nt*

valuable ['væljʊəbl] *adj* wertvoll; (*time*) kostbar; **valuables** *npl* Wertsachen *pl*

value ['vælju:] *n* Wert *m* ▷ *vt* (*appreciate*) schätzen; **value added tax** *n* Mehrwertsteuer *f*

valve [vælv] *n* Ventil *nt*

van [væn] *n* (*Auto*) Lieferwagen *m*

vanilla [və'nɪlə] *n* Vanille *f*

vanish ['vænɪʃ] *vi* verschwinden

vanity ['vænɪtɪ] *n* Eitelkeit *f*; **vanity case** *n* Schminkkoffer *m*

vapor (*US*), **vapour** ['veɪpə*] *n* (*mist*) Dunst *m*; (*steam*) Dampf *m*

variable ['vɛərɪəbl] *adj* (*weather, mood*) unbeständig; (*quality*) unterschiedlich; (*speed, height*) regulierbar; **varied** ['vɛərɪd] *adj* (*interests, selection*) vielseitig; (*career*) bewegt; (*work, diet*) abwechslungsreich; **variety** [və'raɪətɪ] *n* (*diversity*) Abwechslung *f*; (*assortment*) Vielfalt *f* (*of an* +*dat*); (*type*) Art *f*; **various** ['vɛərɪəs] *adj* verschieden

varnish ['vɑ:nɪʃ] *n* Lack *m* ▷ *vt* lackieren

vary ['vɛərɪ] *vt* (*alter*) verändern ▷ *vi* (*be different*) unterschiedlich sein; (*fluctuate*) sich verändern; (*prices*) schwanken

vase [vɑ:z, ç veɪz] (*US*) *n* Vase *f*

vast [vɑ:st] *adj* riesig; (*area*) weit

VAT *abbr* = **value added tax** Mehrwertsteuer *f*, MwSt.

Vatican ['vætɪkən] *n* **the ~** der Vatikan

VCR *abbr* = **video cassette recorder** Videorekorder *m*

VD *abbr* = **venereal disease**

VDU *abbr* = **visual display unit**

veal [vi:l] *n* Kalbfleisch *nt*

vegan ['vi:gən] *n* Veganer(in) *m(f)*

vegetable ['vedʒətəbl] *n* Gemüse *nt*

vegetarian [vedʒɪ'tɛərɪən] *n* Vegetarier(in) *m(f)* ▷ *adj* vegetarisch

vehicle ['vi:ɪkl] *n* Fahrzeug *nt*

veil [veɪl] *n* Schleier *m*

vein [veɪn] *n* Ader *f*

Velcro® ['velkrəʊ] *n* Klettband *nt*

velvet ['velvɪt] *n* Samt *m*

vending machine ['vendɪŋməʃi:n] *n* Automat *m*

venereal disease [vɪ'nɪərɪəldɪzi:z] *n* Geschlechtskrankheit *f*

vacancy ['veɪkənsɪ] *n* (*job*) offene Stelle; (*room*) freies Zimmer; **vacant** ['veɪkənt] *adj* (*room, seat*) frei; (*post*) offen; (*building*) leer stehend; **vacate** [və'keɪt] *vt* (*room, building*) räumen; (*seat*) frei machen

vacation [və'keɪʃən] *n* (*US*) Ferien *pl*, Urlaub *m*; (*at university*) (Semester)ferien *pl*; **to go on ~** in Urlaub fahren; **~ course** Ferienkurs *m*

vaccinate ['væksɪneɪt] *vt* impfen; **vaccination** [væksɪ'neɪʃən] *n* Impfung *f*; **~ card** Impfpass *m*

vacuum ['vækjʊm] *n* Vakuum *nt* ▷ *vt, vi* (staub)saugen; **vacuum cleaner** *n* Staubsauger *m*

vagina [və'dʒaɪnə] *n* Scheide *f*

vague [veɪg] *adj* (*imprecise*) vage; (*resemblance*) entfernt; **vaguely** *adv* in etwa, irgendwie

vain [veɪn] *adj* (*attempt*) vergeblich; (*conceited*) eitel; **vainly** *adv* (*in vain*) vergeblich

valentine (card) ['væləntaɪn(kɑ:d)] *n* Valentinskarte *f*; **Valentine's Day** *n* Valentinstag *m*

valid ['vælɪd] *adj* (*ticket, passport etc*)

venetian blind [vɪˈniːʃənˈblaɪnd] n
Jalousie f
Venezuela [veneˈzweɪlə] n Venezuela nt
vengeance [ˈvendʒəns] n Rache f
Venice [ˈvenɪs] n Venedig nt
venison [ˈvenɪsn] n Rehfleisch nt
vent [vent] n Öffnung f
ventilate [ˈventɪleɪt] vt lüften;
  ventilation [ventɪˈleɪʃən] n Belüftung f;
  ventilator [ˈventɪleɪtə*] n (in room)
  Ventilator m; **to be on a ~** (Med) künstlich
  beatmet werden
venture [ˈventʃə*] n (project)
  Unternehmung f; (Comm) Unternehmen nt
  ▷ vi (go) (sich) wagen
venue [ˈvenjuː] n (for concert etc)
  Veranstaltungsort m; (Sport)
  Austragungsort m
verb [vɜːb] n Verb nt; **verbal** adj
  (agreement) mündlich; (skills) sprachlich;
  verbally adv mündlich
verdict [ˈvɜːdɪkt] n Urteil nt
verge [vɜːdʒ] n (of road) (Straßen)rand m;
  to be on the ~ of doing sth im Begriff
  sein, etw zu tun ▷ vi **to ~ on** grenzen an
  +akk
verification [verɪfɪˈkeɪʃən] n
  (confirmation) Bestätigung f; (check)
  Überprüfung f; **verify** [ˈverɪfaɪ] vt
  (confirm) bestätigen; (check) überprüfen
vermin [ˈvɜːmɪn] npl Schädlinge pl;
  (insects) Ungeziefer nt
verruca [veˈruːkə] n Warze f
versatile [ˈvɜːsətaɪl] adj vielseitig
verse [vɜːs] n (poetry) Poesie f; (stanza)
  Strophe f
version [ˈvɜːʃən] n Version f
versus [ˈvɜːsəs] prep gegen; (in contrast
  to) im Gegensatz zu
vertical [ˈvɜːtɪkəl] adj senkrecht,
  vertikal
very [ˈverɪ] adv sehr; **~ much** sehr ▷ adj
  the ~ book I need genau das Buch, das ich
  brauche; **at that ~ moment** gerade in
  dem Augenblick; **at the ~ top** ganz oben;
  the ~ best der/die/das Allerbeste
vest [vest] n (Brit) Unterhemd nt; (US:
  waistcoat) Weste f
vet [vet] n Tierarzt m, Tierärztin f
veto [ˈviːtəʊ] n (pl **-es**) n Veto nt ▷ vt sein
  Veto einlegen gegen
VHF abbr = **very high frequency** UKW
via [ˈvaɪə] prep über +akk

viable [ˈvaɪəbl] adj (plan) realisierbar;
  (company) rentabel
vibrate [vaɪˈbreɪt] vi vibrieren; **vibration**
  [vaɪˈbreɪʃən] n Vibration f
vicar [ˈvɪkə*] n Pfarrer(in) m(f)
vice [vaɪs] n (evil) Laster nt; (Tech)
  Schraubstock m ▷ pref Vize-;
  ~~chairman stellvertretender
  Vorsitzender; **~~president**
  Vizepräsident(in) m(f)
vice versa [ˈvaɪsˈvɜːsə] adv umgekehrt
vicinity [vɪˈsɪnɪtɪ] n **in the ~** in der Nähe
  (of +gen)
vicious [ˈvɪʃəs] adj (violent) brutal;
  (malicious) gemein; **vicious circle** n
  Teufelskreis m
victim [ˈvɪktɪm] n Opfer nt
Victorian [vɪkˈtɔːrɪən] adj viktorianisch
victory [ˈvɪktərɪ] n Sieg m
video [ˈvɪdɪəʊ] (pl **-s**) adj Video- ▷ n Video
  nt; (recorder) Videorekorder m ▷ vt (auf
  Video) aufnehmen; **video camera** n
  Videokamera f; **video cassette** n
  Videokassette f; **video clip** n Videoclip m;
  video game n Videospiel nt; **video
  recorder** n Videorekorder m; **video shop**
  n Videothek f; **videotape** n Videoband nt
  ▷ vt (auf Video) aufnehmen
Vienna [vɪˈenə] n Wien nt
Vietnam [vjetˈnæm] n Vietnam nt
view [vjuː] n (sight) Blick m (of auf +akk);
  (vista) Aussicht f; (opinion) Ansicht f,
  Meinung f; **in ~ of** angesichts +gen ▷ vt
  (situation, event) betrachten; (house)
  besichtigen; **viewer** n (for slides)
  Diabetrachter m; (TV) Zuschauer(in) m(f);
  viewpoint n (fig) Standpunkt m
vigilant [ˈvɪdʒɪlənt] adj wachsam
vile [vaɪl] adj abscheulich; (weather, food)
  scheußlich
village [ˈvɪlɪdʒ] n Dorf nt; **villager** n
  Dorfbewohner(in) m(f)
villain [ˈvɪlən] n Schurke m; (in film, story)
  Bösewicht m
vine [vaɪn] n (Wein)rebe f
vinegar [ˈvɪnɪgə*] n Essig m
vineyard [ˈvɪnjəd] n Weinberg m
vintage [ˈvɪntɪdʒ] n (of wine) Jahrgang m;
  vintage wine n edler Wein
vinyl [ˈvaɪnɪl] n Vinyl nt
viola [vɪˈəʊlə] n Bratsche f
violate [ˈvaɪəleɪt] vt (treaty) brechen;
  (rights, rule) verletzen

violence ['vaɪələns] *n* (*brutality*) Gewalt *f*; (*of person*) Gewalttätigkeit *f*; **violent** *adj* (*brutal*) brutal; (*death*) gewaltsam

violet ['vaɪələt] *n* Veilchen *nt*

violin [vaɪə'lɪn] *n* Geige *f*, Violine *f*

VIP *abbr* = **very important person** VIP *mf*

virgin ['vɜːdʒɪn] *n* Jungfrau *f*

Virgo ['vɜːgəʊ] *n* (*Astr*) Jungfrau *f*

virile ['vɪraɪl] *adj* (*man*) männlich

virtual ['vɜːtjʊəl] *adj* (*Inform*) virtuell; **virtually** *adv* praktisch; **virtual reality** *n* virtuelle Realität

virtue ['vɜːtjuː] *n* Tugend *f*; **by ~ of** aufgrund +*gen*; **virtuous** ['vɜːtjʊəs] *adj* tugendhaft

virus ['vaɪrəs] *n* (*Med, Inform*) Virus *nt*

visa ['viːzə] *n* Visum *nt*

visibility [vɪzɪ'bɪlɪtɪ] *n* (*Meteo*) Sichtweite *f*; **good/poor ~** gute/schlechte Sicht; **visible** ['vɪzəbl] *adj* sichtbar; (*evident*) sichtlich; **visibly** *adv* sichtlich

vision ['vɪʒən] *n* (*power of sight*) Sehvermögen *nt*; (*foresight*) Weitblick *m*; (*dream, image*) Vision *f*

visit ['vɪzɪt] *n* Besuch *m*; (*stay*) Aufenthalt *m* ▷ *vt* besuchen; **visiting hours** *npl* Besuchszeiten *pl*; **visitor** *n* Besucher(in) *m(f)*; **~s' book** Gästebuch *nt*; **visitor centre** *n* Informationszentrum *nt*

visor ['vaɪzə*] *n* (*on helmet*) Visier *nt*; (*Auto*) Blende *f*

visual ['vɪzjʊəl] *adj* Seh-; (*image, joke*) visuell; **~ aid** Anschauungsmaterial *nt*; **~ display unit** Monitor *m*; **visualize** *vt* sich vorstelle; **visually** *adv* visuell; **~ impaired** sehbehindert

vital ['vaɪtl] *adj* (*essential*) unerlässlich, wesentlich; (*argument, moment*) entscheidend; **vitality** [vaɪ'tælɪtɪ] *n* Vitalität *f*; **vitally** *adv* äußerst

vitamin ['vɪtəmɪn] *n* Vitamin *nt*

vivacious [vɪ'veɪʃəs] *adj* lebhaft

vivid ['vɪvɪd] *adj* (*description*) anschaulich; (*memory*) lebhaft; (*colour*) leuchtend

V-neck ['viːnek] *n* V-Ausschnitt *m*

vocabulary [vəʊ'kæbjʊlərɪ] *n* Wortschatz *m*, Vokabular *nt*

vocal ['vəʊkəl] *adj* (*of the voice*) Stimm-; (*group*) Gesangs-; (*protest, person*) lautstark

vocation [vəʊ'keɪʃən] *n* Berufung *f*; **vocational** *adj* Berufs-

vodka ['vɒdkə] *n* Wodka *m*

voice [vɔɪs] *n* Stimme *f* ▷ *vt* äußern; **voice mail** *n* Voicemail *f*

void [vɔɪd] *n* Leere *f* ▷ *adj* (*Jur*) ungültig; **~ of** (*ganz*) ohne

volcano [vɒl'keɪnəʊ] (*pl* **-es**) *n* Vulkan *m*

volley ['vɒlɪ] *n* (*Tennis*) Volley *m*; **volleyball** *n* Volleyball *m*

volt [vəʊlt] *n* Volt *nt*; **voltage** *n* Spannung *f*

volume ['vɒljuːm] *n* (*of sound*) Lautstärke *f*; (*space occupied by sth*) Volumen *nt*; (*size, amount*) Umfang *m*; (*book*) Band *m*; **volume control** *n* Lautstärkeregler *m*

voluntary, voluntarily ['vɒləntərɪ, -lɪ] *adj, adv* freiwillig; (*unpaid*) ehrenamtlich; **volunteer** [vɒlən'tɪə*] *n* Freiwillige(r) *mf* ▷ *vi* sich freiwillig melden ▷ *vt* **to ~ to do sth** sich anbieten, etw zu tun

voluptuous [və'lʌptjʊəs] *adj* sinnlich

vomit ['vɒmɪt] *vi* sich übergeben

vote [vəʊt] *n* Stimme *f*; (*ballot*) Wahl *f*; (*result*) Abstimmungsergebnis *nt*; (*right to vote*) Wahlrecht *nt* ▷ *vt* (*elect*) wählen; **they ~d him chairman** sie wählten ihn zum Vorsitzenden ▷ *vi* wählen; **to ~ for/against sth** für/gegen etw stimmen; **voter** *n* Wähler(in) *m(f)*

voucher ['vaʊtʃə*] *n* Gutschein *m*

vow [vaʊ] *n* Gelöbnis *nt* ▷ *vt* **to ~ to do sth** geloben, etw zu tun

vowel ['vaʊəl] *n* Vokal *m*

voyage ['vɔɪɪdʒ] *n* Reise *f*

vulgar ['vʌlgə*] *adj* vulgär, ordinär

vulnerable ['vʌlnərəbl] *adj* verwundbar; (*sensitive*) verletzlich

vulture ['vʌltʃə*] *n* Geier *m*

W

W *abbr* = **west** W

wade [weɪd] *vi (in water)* waten

wafer ['weɪfə*] *n* Waffel *f*; *(Rel)* Hostie *f*; **wafer-thin** *adj* hauchdünn

waffle ['wɒfl] *n* Waffel *f*; *(Brit fam: empty talk)* Geschwafel *nt* ▷ *vi (Brit fam)* schwafeln

wag [wæg] *vt (tail)* wedeln mit

wage [weɪdʒ] *n* Lohn *m*

waggon *(Brit)*, **wagon** ['wægən] *n (horse-drawn)* Fuhrwerk *nt*; *(Brit Rail)* Waggon *m*; *(US Auto)* Wagen *m*

waist [weɪst] *n* Taille *f*; **waistcoat** *n (Brit)* Weste *f*; **waistline** *n* Taille *f*

wait [weɪt] *n* Wartezeit *f* ▷ *vi* warten *(for* auf +*akk)*; **to ~ and see** abwarten; **~ a minute** Moment mal!; **wait up** *vi* aufbleiben

waiter *n* Kellner *m*; **~!** Herr Ober!

waiting *n* **'no ~'** „Halteverbot"; **waiting list** *n* Warteliste *f*; **waiting room** *n (Med)* Wartezimmer *nt*; *(Rail)* Wartesaal *m*

waitress *n* Kellnerin *f*

wake [weɪk] *(woke o waked, woken o waked) vt* wecken ▷ *vi* aufwachen; **wake up** *vt* aufwecken ▷ *vi* aufwachen; **wake-up call** *n (Tel)* Weckruf *m*

Wales ['weɪlz] *n* Wales *nt*

walk [wɔːk] *n* Spaziergang *m*; *(ramble)* Wanderung *f*; *(route)* Weg *m*; **to go for a ~** spazieren gehen; **it's only a five-minute ~** es sind nur fünf Minuten zu Fuß ▷ *vi* gehen; *(stroll)* spazieren gehen; *(ramble)* wandern ▷ *vt (dog)* ausführen; **walking** *n* **to go ~** wandern; **walking shoes** *npl* Wanderschuhe *pl*; **walking stick** *n* Spazierstock *m*

Walkman®*(pl* **-s)** *n* Walkman® *m*

wall [wɔːl] *n (inside)* Wand *f*; *(outside)* Mauer *f*

wallet ['wɒlɪt] *n* Brieftasche *f*

wallpaper ['wɔːlpeɪpə*] *n* Tapete *f*; *(Inform)* Bildschirmhintergrund *m* ▷ *vt* tapezieren

walnut ['wɔːlnʌt] *n (nut)* Walnuss *f*

waltz [wɔːlts] *n* Walzer *m*

wander ['wɒndə*] *vi (person)* herumwandern

want [wɒnt] *n (lack)* Mangel *m (of* an +*dat)*; *(need)* Bedürfnis *nt*; **for ~ of** aus Mangel an +*dat* ▷ *vt (desire)* wollen; *(need)* brauchen; **I ~ to stay here** ich will hier bleiben; **he doesn't ~ to** er will nicht

WAP phone ['wæpfəʊn] *n* WAP-Handy *nt*

war [wɔː*] *n* Krieg *m*

ward [wɔːd] *n (in hospital)* Station *f*; *(child)* Mündel *nt*

warden ['wɔːdən] *n* Aufseher(in) *m(f)*; *(in youth hostel)* Herbergsvater *m*, Herbergsmutter *f*

wardrobe ['wɔːdrəʊb] *n* Kleiderschrank *m*

warehouse ['wɛəhaʊs] *n* Lagerhaus *nt*

warfare ['wɔːfɛə*] *n* Krieg *m*; *(techniques)* Kriegsführung *f*

warm [wɔːm] *adj* warm; *(welcome)* herzlich; **I'm ~** mir ist warm ▷ *vt* wärmen; *(food)* aufwärmen; **warm over** *vt (US: food)* aufwärmen; **warm up** *vt (food)* aufwärmen; *(room)* erwärmen ▷ *vi (food, room)* warm werden; *(Sport)* sich aufwärmen; **warmly** *adv* warm; *(welcome)* herzlich; **warmth** *n* Wärme *f*; *(of welcome)* Herzlichkeit *f*

warn [wɔːn] *vt* warnen *(of, against* vor +*dat)*; **to ~ sb not to do sth** jdn davor warnen, etw zu tun; **warning** *n* Warnung *f*; **warning light** *n* Warnlicht *nt*; **warning triangle** *n (Auto)* Warndreieck *nt*

warranty ['wɒrəntɪ] *n* Garantie *f*

wart [wɔːt] *n* Warze *f*

wary ['wεərɪ] *adj* vorsichtig; (*suspicious*) misstrauisch

was [wɒz, wəz] *pt of* **be**

wash [wɒʃ] *n* **to have a ~** sich waschen; **it's in the ~** es ist in der Wäsche ▷ *vt* waschen; (*plates, glasses etc*) abwaschen; **to ~ one's hands** sich *dat* die Hände waschen; **to ~ the dishes** (das Geschirr) abwaschen ▷ *vi* (*clean oneself*) sich waschen; **wash off** *vt* abwaschen; **wash up** *vi* (*Brit: wash dishes*) abwaschen; (*US: clean oneself*) sich waschen; **washable** *adj* waschbar; **washbag** *n* (US) Kulturbeutel *m*; **washbasin** *n* Waschbecken *nt*; **washcloth** *n* (*US*) Waschlappen *m*; **washer** *n* (*Tech*) Dichtungsring *m*; (*washing machine*) Waschmaschine *f*; **washing** *n* (*laundry*) Wäsche *f*; **washing machine** *n* Waschmaschine *f*; **washing powder** *n* Waschpulver *nt*; **washing-up** *n* (*Brit*) Abwasch *m*; **to do the ~** abwaschen; **washing-up liquid** *n* (*Brit*) Spülmittel *nt*; **washroom** *n* (US) Toilette *f*

wasn't ['wɒznt] *contr of* **was not**

wasp [wɒsp] *n* Wespe *f*

waste [weɪst] *n* (*materials*) Abfall *m*; (*wasting*) Verschwendung *f*; **it's a ~ of time** das ist Zeitverschwendung ▷ *adj* (*superfluous*) überschüssig ▷ *vt* verschwenden (*on an +akk*); (*opportunity*) vertun; **waste bin** *n* Abfalleimer *m*; **wastepaper basket** *n* Papierkorb *m*

watch [wɒtʃ] *n* (*timepiece*) (Armband)uhr *f* ▷ *vt* (*observe*) beobachten; (*guard*) aufpassen auf +akk; (*film, play, programme*) sich *dat* ansehen; **to ~ TV** fernsehen ▷ *vi* zusehen; (*guard*) Wache halten; **to ~ for sb/sth** nach jdm/etw Ausschau halten; **~ out** pass auf!; **watchdog** *n* Wachhund *m*; (*fig*) Aufsichtsbehörde *f*; **watchful** *adj* wachsam

water ['wɔ:tə*] *n* Wasser *nt*; **~s** *pl* (*territory*) Gewässer *pl* ▷ *vt* (*plant*) gießen ▷ *vi* (*eye*) tränen; **my mouth is ~ing** mir läuft das Wasser im Mund zusammen; **water down** *vt* verdünnen; **watercolor** (*US*), **watercolour** *n* (*painting*) Aquarell *nt*; (*paint*) Wasserfarbe *f*; **watercress** *n* (Brunnen)kresse *f*; **waterfall** *n* Wasserfall *m*; **watering can** *n* Gießkanne *f*; **water level** *n* Wasserstand *m*; **watermelon** *n* Wassermelone *f*; **waterproof** *adj* wasserdicht; **water-skiing** *n* Wasserskilaufen *nt*; **water sports** *npl* Wassersport *m*; **watertight** *adj* wasserdicht; **water wings** *npl* Schwimmflügel *pl*; **watery** *adj* wässerig

wave [weɪv] *n* Welle *f* ▷ *vt* (*move to and fro*) schwenken; (*hand, flag*) winken mit ▷ *vi* (*person*) winken; (*flag*) wehen; **wavelength** *n* Wellenlänge *f*; **to be on the same ~** (*fig*) die gleiche Wellenlänge haben; **wavy** ['weɪvɪ] *adj* wellig

wax [wæks] *n* Wachs *nt*; (*in ear*) Ohrenschmalz *nt*

way [weɪ] *n* Weg *m*; (*direction*) Richtung *f*; (*manner*) Art *f*; **can you tell me the ~ to ... ?** wie komme ich (am besten) zu ... ?; **we went the wrong ~** wir sind in die falsche Richtung gefahren/gegangen; **to lose one's ~** sich verirren; **to make ~ for sb/sth** jdm/etw Platz machen; **to get one's own ~** seinen Willen durchsetzen; **'give ~'** (*Auto*) „Vorfahrt achten"; **the other ~ round** andersherum; **one ~ or another** irgendwie; **in a ~** in gewisser Weise; **in the ~** im Weg; **by the ~** übrigens; **'~ in'** „Eingang"; **'~ out'** „Ausgang"; **no ~** (*fam*) kommt nicht infrage!

we [wi:] *pron* wir

weak [wi:k] *adj* schwach; **weaken** *vt* schwächen ▷ *vi* schwächer werden

wealth [welθ] *n* Reichtum *m*; **wealthy** *adj* reich

weapon ['wepən] *n* Waffe *f*

wear [wεə*] (**wore, worn**) *vt* (*have on*) tragen; **what shall I ~?** was soll ich anziehen? ▷ *vi* (*become worn*) sich abnutzen ▷ *n* **~ (and tear)** Abnutzung *f*; **wear off** *vi* (*diminish*) nachlassen; **wear out** *vt* abnutzen; (*person*) erschöpfen ▷ *vi* sich abnutzen

weary ['wɪərɪ] *adj* müde

weather ['weðə*] *n* Wetter *nt*; **I'm feeling under the ~** ich fühle mich nicht ganz wohl; **weather forecast** *n* Wettervorhersage *f*

weave [wi:v] (**wove** *o* **weaved, woven** *o* **weaved**) *vt* (*cloth*) weben; (*basket etc*) flechten

web [web] *n* (*a. fig*) Netz *nt*; **the Web** das Web, das Internet; **webcam** ['webkæm] *n* Webcam *f*; **web page** *n* Webseite *f*; **website** *n* Website *f*

we'd [wi:d] *contr of* we had; we would
Wed *abbr* = **Wednesday** Mi.
wedding ['wedɪŋ] *n* Hochzeit *f*; **wedding anniversary** *n* Hochzeitstag *m*; **wedding dress** *n* Hochzeitskleid *nt*; **wedding ring** *n* Ehering *m*
wedding shower *n* (US) Party für die zukünftige Braut
wedge [wedʒ] *n* (under door etc) Keil *m*; (of cheese etc) Stück *nt*, Ecke *f*
Wednesday ['wenzdeɪ] *n* Mittwoch *m*; *see also* **Tuesday**
wee [wi:] *adj* klein ▷ *vi* (fam) Pipi machen
weed [wi:d] *n* Unkraut *nt* ▷ *vt* jäten
week [wi:k] *n* Woche *f*; **twice a ~** zweimal in der Woche; **a ~ on Friday/Friday ~** Freitag in einer Woche; **a ~ last Friday** letzten Freitag vor einer Woche; **in two ~s' time, in two ~s** in zwei Wochen; **for ~s** wochenlang; **weekday** *n* Wochentag *m*; **weekend** *n* Wochenende *nt*; **weekly** *adj, adv* wöchentlich; (magazine) Wochen-
weep [wi:p] (**wept, wept**) *vi* weinen
weigh [weɪ] *vt, vi* wiegen; **it ~s 20 kilos** es wiegt 20 Kilo; **weigh up** *vt* abwägen; (person) einschätzen; **weight** [weɪt] *n* Gewicht *nt*; **to lose/put on ~** abnehmen/zunehmen; **weightlifting** *n* Gewichtheben *nt*; **weight training** *n* Krafttraining *nt*; **weighty** *adj* (important) schwer wiegend
weird [wɪəd] *adj* seltsam; **weirdo** ['wɪədəʊ] *n* Spinner(in) *m(f)*
welcome ['welkəm] *n* Empfang *m* ▷ *adj* willkommen; (news) angenehm; **~ to London** willkommen in London! ▷ *vt* begrüßen; **welcoming** *adj* freundlich
welfare ['welfeə*] *n* Wohl *nt*; (US: social security) Sozialhilfe *f*; **welfare state** *n* Wohlfahrtsstaat *m*
well [wel] *n* Brunnen *m* ▷ *adj* (in good health) gesund; **are you ~?** geht es dir gut?; **to feel ~** sich wohl fühlen; **get ~ soon** gute Besserung! ▷ *interj* nun; **~, I don't know** nun, ich weiß nicht ▷ *adv* gut; **~ done** gut gemacht!; **it may ~ be** das kann wohl sein; **as ~** (in addition) auch; **~ over 60** weit über 60
we'll [wi:l] *contr of* we will; we shall
well-behaved [welbɪ'heɪvd] *adj* brav; **well-being** *n* Wohl *nt*; **well-built** *adj*

(person) gut gebaut; **well-done** *adj* (steak) durchgebraten; **well-earned** *adj* wohlverdient
wellingtons ['welɪŋtənz] *npl* Gummistiefel *pl*
well-known [wel'nəʊn] *adj* bekannt; **well-off** *adj* (wealthy) wohlhabend; **well-paid** *adj* gut bezahlt
Welsh [welʃ] *adj* walisisch ▷ *n* (language) Walisisch *nt*; **the ~** *pl* die Waliser *pl*; **Welshman** (*pl* **-men**) *n* Waliser *m*; **Welshwoman** (*pl* **-women**) *n* Waliserin *f*
went [went] *pt of* **go**
wept [wept] *pt, pp of* **weep**
were [wɜ:] *pt of* **be**
we're [wɪə*] *contr of* we are
weren't [wɜ:nt] *contr of* were not
west [west] *n* Westen *m*; **the West** (Pol) der Westen ▷ *adv* (go, face) nach Westen ▷ *adj* West-; **westbound** *adj* (in) Richtung Westen; **western** *adj* West-, westlich; **Western Europe** Westeuropa *nt* ▷ *n* (Cine) Western *m*; **West Germany** *n* (**the former**) **~** (das ehemalige) Westdeutschland, Westdeutschland *nt*; **westwards** ['westwədz] *adv* nach Westen
wet [wet] (**wet, wet**) *vt* **to ~ oneself** in die Hose machen ▷ *adj* nass, feucht; **'~ paint'** „frisch gestrichen"; **wet suit** *n* Taucheranzug *m*
we've [wi:v] *contr of* we have
whale [weɪl] *n* Wal *m*
wharf [wɔ:f] (*pl* **-s** *o* **wharves**) *n* Kai *m*

◯ **KEYWORD**

what [wɒt] *adj* **1** (in questions) welche(r, s) was für ein(e); **what size is it?** welche Größe ist das?
2 (in exclamations) was für ein(e); **what a mess!** was für ein Durcheinander!
▷ *pron* (interrogative/relative) was; **what are you doing?** was machst du gerade?; **what are you talking about?** wovon reden Sie?; **what is it called?** wie heißt das?; **what about ...?** wie wärs mit ...?; **I saw what you did** ich habe gesehen, was du gemacht hast
▷ *excl* (disbelieving) wie was; **what, no coffee!** wie, kein Kaffee?; **I've crashed the car — what!** ich hatte einen Autounfall — was!

w

what's [wɒts] *contr of* **what is; what has**

wheat [wi:t] *n* Weizen *m*

wheel [wi:l] *n* Rad *nt*; *(steering wheel)* Lenkrad *nt* ▷ *vt (bicycle, trolley)* schieben; **wheelbarrow** *n* Schubkarren *m*; **wheelchair** *n* Rollstuhl *m*; **wheel clamp** *n* Parkkralle *f*

KEYWORD

when [wɛn] *adv* wann ▷ *conj* **1** *(at, during, after the time that)* wenn; *(in past)* als; **she was reading when I came in** sie las, als ich hereinkam; **be careful when you cross the road** seien Sie vorsichtig, wenn Sie über die Straße gehen

2 *(on, at which)* als; **on the day when I met him** an dem Tag, an dem ich ihn traf

3 *(whereas)* wo ... doch

where [wɛə*] *adv* wo; **~ are you going?** wohin gehst du?; **~ are you from?** woher kommst du? ▷ *conj* wo; **that's ~ I used to live** da habe ich früher gewohnt; **whereabouts** [wɛərə'baʊts] *adv* wo ▷ *npl* ['wɛərəbaʊts] Aufenthaltsort *m*; **whereas** [wɛər'æz] *conj* während, wohingegen; **whereby** *adv* wodurch; **wherever** [wɛər'evə*] *conj* wo immer; **~ that may be** wo immer das sein mag; **~ I go** überall, wohin ich gehe

whether ['wɛðə*] *conj* ob

KEYWORD

which [wɪtʃ] *adj* **1** *(interrogative: direct, indirect)* welche(r, s); **which one?** welche(r, s)?

2: **in which case** in diesem Fall; **by which time** zu dieser Zeit

▷ *pron* **1** *(interrogative)* welche(r, s); *(of people also)* wer

2 *(relative)* der/die/das *(referring to people)* was; **the apple which you ate/which is on the table** der Apfel, den du gegessen hast/der auf dem Tisch liegt; **he said he saw her, which is true** er sagte, er habe sie gesehen, was auch stimmt

while [waɪl] *n* **a ~** eine Weile; **for a ~** eine Zeit lang; **a short ~ ago** vor kurzem ▷ *conj* während; *(although)* obwohl

whine [waɪn] *vi (person)* jammern

whip [wɪp] *n* Peitsche *f* ▷ *vt (beat)* peitschen; **~ped cream** Schlagsahne *f*

whirl [wɜ:l] *vt, vi* herumwirbeln; **whirlpool** *n (in river, sea)* Strudel *m*; *(pool)* Whirlpool *m*

whisk [wɪsk] *n* Schneebesen *m* ▷ *vt (cream etc)* schlagen

whisker ['wɪskə*] *n (of animal)* Schnurrhaar *nt*; **~s** *pl (of man)* Backenbart *m*

whisk(e)y ['wɪskɪ] *n* Whisky *m*

whisper ['wɪspə*] *vi, vt* flüstern; **to ~ sth to sb** jdm etw zuflüstern

whistle ['wɪsl] *n* Pfiff *m*; *(instrument)* Pfeife *f* ▷ *vt, vi* pfeifen

white [waɪt] *n (of egg)* Eiweiß *nt*; *(of eye)* Weiße *nt* ▷ *adj* weiß; *(with fear)* blass; *(coffee)* mit Milch; **White House** *n* **the ~** das Weiße Haus; **white lie** *n* Notlüge *f*; **white meat** *n* helles Fleisch; **white sauce** *n* weiße Soße; **white water rafting** *n* Rafting *nt*; **white wine** *n* Weißwein *m*

Whitsun ['wɪtsn] *n* Pfingsten *nt*

KEYWORD

who [hu:] *pron* **1** *(interrogative)* wer; *(acc)* wen; *(dat)* wem; **who is it?, who's there?** wer ist da?

2 *(relative)* der/die/das; **the woman/man who spoke to me** die Frau/der Mann, die/der mit mir sprach

KEYWORD

whole [həʊl] *adj* ganz ▷ *n* Ganze(s) *nt*; **the ~ of my family** meine ganze Familie; **on the ~** im Großen und Ganzen; **wholefood** *n (Brit)* Vollwertkost *f*; **wholeheartedly** *adv* voll und ganz; **wholemeal** *adj (Brit)* Vollkorn-; **wholesale** *adv (buy, sell)* im Großhandel; **wholesome** *adj* gesund; **wholewheat** *adj* Vollkorn-; **wholly** ['həʊlɪ] *adv* völlig

KEYWORD

whom [hu:m] *pron* **1** *(interrogative: acc)* wen; (: *dat*) wem; **whom did you see?** wen haben Sie gesehen?; **to whom did you give it?** wem haben Sie es gegeben?

2 *(relative: acc)* den/die/das; (: *dat*) dem/der/dem; **the man whom I saw/to**

whom I spoke der Mann, den ich sah/mit dem ich sprach

whooping cough [ˈhuːpɪŋkɒf] *n* Keuchhusten *m*

whose [huːz] *adj* (*in questions*) wessen; (*in relative clauses*) dessen/deren/dessen, deren *pl*; **~ bike is that?** wessen Fahrrad ist das? ▷ *pron* (*in questions*) wessen; **~ is this?** wem gehört das?

 KEYWORD

why [waɪ] *adv* warum weshalb ▷ *conj* warum weshalb; **that's not why I'm here** ich bin nicht deswegen hier; **that's the reason why** deshalb ▷ *excl* (*expressing surprise, shock*) na so was (*explaining*) also dann; **why, it's you!** na so was, du bist es!

wicked [ˈwɪkɪd] *adj* böse; (*fam: great*) geil

wide [waɪd] *adj* breit; (*skirt, trousers*) weit; (*selection*) groß ▷ *adv* weit; **wide-angle lens** *n* Weitwinkelobjektiv *nt*; **wide-awake** *adj* hellwach; **widely** *adv* weit; **~ known** allgemein bekannt; **widen** *vt* verbreitern; (*fig*) erweitern; **wide-open** *adj* weit offen; **widescreen TV** *n* Breitbildfernseher *m*; **widespread** *adj* weit verbreitet

widow [ˈwɪdəʊ] *n* Witwe *f*; **widowed** *adj* verwitwet; **widower** *n* Witwer *m*

width [wɪdθ] *n* Breite *f*

wife [waɪf] (*pl* **wives**) *n* (Ehe)frau *f*

wig [wɪg] *n* Perücke *f*

wiggle [ˈwɪgl] *vt* wackeln mit

wild [waɪld] *adj* wild; (*violent*) heftig; (*plan, idea*) verrückt ▷ *n* **in the ~** in freier Wildbahn; **wildlife** *n* Tier- und Pflanzenwelt *f*; **wildly** *adv* wild; (*enthusiastic, exaggerated*) maßlos

 KEYWORD

will [wɪl] *aux vb* **1** (*forms future tense*) werden; **I will finish it tomorrow** ich mache es morgen zu Ende

2 (*in conjectures, predictions*): **he will or he'll be there by now** er dürfte jetzt da sein; **that will be the postman** das wird der Postbote sein

3 (*in commands, requests, offers*): **will you be**

quiet! sei endlich still!; **will you help me?** hilfst du mir?; **will you have a cup of tea?** trinken Sie eine Tasse Tee?; **I won't put up with it!** das lasse ich mir nicht gefallen! ▷ *vt* wollen ▷ *n* Wille *m* (*Jur*) Testament *nt*

willow [ˈwɪləʊ] *n* Weide *f*

willpower [ˈwɪlpaʊə*] *n* Willenskraft *f*

wimp [wɪmp] *n* Weichei *nt*

win [wɪn] (**won, won**) *vt, vi* gewinnen ▷ *n* Sieg *m*; **win over, win round** *vt* für sich gewinnen

wind [waɪnd] (**wound, wound**) *vt* (*rope, bandage*) wickeln; **wind down** *vt* (*car window*) herunterkurbeln; **wind up** *vt* (*clock*) aufziehen; (*car window*) hochkurbeln; (*meeting, speech*) abschließen; (*person*) aufziehen, ärgern

wind [wɪnd] *n* Wind *m*; (*Med*) Blähungen *pl*

wind instrument [ˈwɪndɪnstrʊmənt] *n* Blasinstrument *nt*; **windmill** *n* Windmühle *f*

window [ˈwɪndəʊ] *n* Fenster *nt*; (*counter*) Schalter *m*; **window box** *n* Blumenkasten *m*; **windowpane** *n* Fensterscheibe *f*; **window-shopping** *n* **to go ~** einen Schaufensterbummel machen; **windowsill** *n* Fensterbrett *nt*

windpipe [ˈwɪndpaɪp] *n* Luftröhre *f*; **windscreen** *n* (*Brit*) Windschutzscheibe *f*; **windscreen wiper** *n* (*Brit*) Scheibenwischer *m*; **windshield** *n* (*US*) Windschutzscheibe *f*; **windshield wiper** *n* (*US*) Scheibenwischer *m*; **windsurfer** *n* Windsurfer(in) *m(f)*; (*board*) Surfbrett *nt*; **windsurfing** *n* Windsurfen *nt*

windy [ˈwɪndɪ] *adj* windig

wine [waɪn] *n* Wein *m*; **wine bar** *n* Weinlokal *nt*; **wineglass** *n* Weinglas *nt*; **wine list** *n* Weinkarte *f*; **wine tasting** *n* (*event*) Weinprobe *f*

wing [wɪŋ] *n* Flügel *m*; (*Brit Auto*) Kotflügel *m*; **~s** *pl* (*Theat*) Kulissen *pl*

wink [wɪŋk] *vi* zwinkern; **to ~ at sb** jdm zuzwinkern

winner [ˈwɪnə*] *n* Gewinner(in) *m(f)*; (*Sport*) Sieger(in) *m(f)*; **winning** *adj* (*team, horse etc*) siegreich; **~ number** Gewinnzahl *f* ▷ *n* **~s** *pl* Gewinn *m*

winter [ˈwɪntə*] *n* Winter *m*; **winter sports** *npl* Wintersport *m*; **wint(e)ry** [ˈwɪntrɪ] *adj* winterlich

w

wipe [waɪp] vt abwischen; **to ~ one's nose** sich dat die Nase putzen; **to ~ one's feet** (on mat) sich dat die Schuhe abtreten; **wipe off** vt abwischen; **wipe out** vt (destroy) vernichten; (data, debt) löschen; (epidemic etc) ausrotten

wire ['waɪə*] n Draht m; (Elec) Leitung f; (US: telegram) Telegramm nt ▷ vt (plug in) anschließen; (US Tel) telegrafieren (sb sth jdm etw); **wireless** ['waɪələs] adj drahtlos

wisdom ['wɪzdəm] n Weisheit f; **wisdom tooth** n Weisheitszahn m

wise, wisely [waɪz, -lɪ] adj, adv weise

wish [wɪʃ] n Wunsch m (for nach); **with best ~es** (in letter) herzliche Grüße ▷ vt wünschen, wollen; **to ~ sb good luck/Merry Christmas** jdm viel Glück/frohe Weihnachten wünschen; **I ~ I'd never seen him** ich wünschte, ich hätte ihn nie gesehen

witch [wɪtʃ] n Hexe f

🔵 KEYWORD

with [wɪð, wɪθ] prep **1** (accompanying, in the company of) mit; **we stayed with friends** wir übernachteten bei Freunden; **I'll be with you in a minute** einen Augenblick ich bin sofort da; **I'm not with you** (I don't understand) das verstehe ich nicht; **to be with it** (inf) (up-to-date) auf dem Laufenden sein (ooo) (alert) (voll) da sein inf

2 (descriptive, indicating manner etc) mit; **the man with the grey hat** der Mann mit dem grauen Hut; **red with anger** rot vor Wut

withdraw [wɪð'drɔ:] irr vt zurückziehen; (money) abheben; (comment) zurücknehmen ▷ vi sich zurückziehen

wither ['wɪðə*] vi (plant) verwelken

withhold [wɪð'həʊld] irr vt vorenthalten (from sb jdm)

within [wɪð'ɪn] prep innerhalb +gen; **~ walking distance** zu Fuß erreichbar

without [wɪð'aʊt] prep ohne; **~ asking** ohne zu fragen

withstand [wɪð'stænd] irr vt standhalten +dat

witness ['wɪtnəs] n Zeuge m, Zeugin f ▷ vt Zeuge sein; **witness box, witness stand** (US) n Zeugenstand m

witty ['wɪtɪ] adj geistreich

wives [waɪvz] pl of **wife**

wobble ['wɒbl] vi wackeln; **wobbly** adj wackelig

wok [wɒk] n Wok m

woke [wəʊk] pt of **wake**

woken ['wəʊkn] pp of **wake**

wolf [wʊlf] (pl **wolves**) n Wolf m

woman ['wʊmən] (pl **women**) n Frau f

womb [wu:m] n Gebärmutter f

women ['wɪmɪn] pl of **woman**

won [wʌn] pt, pp of **win**

wonder ['wʌndə*] n (marvel) Wunder nt; (surprise) Staunen nt ▷ vt, vi (speculate) sich fragen; **I ~ what/if ...** ich frage mich, was/ob ...; **wonderful, wonderfully** adj, adv wunderbar

won't [wəʊnt] contr of **will not**

wood [wʊd] n Holz nt; **~s** Wald m; **wooden** adj Holz-; (fig) hölzern; **woodpecker** n Specht m; **woodwork** n (wooden parts) Holzteile pl; (in school) Werken nt

wool [wʊl] n Wolle f; **woollen, woolen** (US) adj Woll-

word [wɜ:d] n Wort nt; (promise) Ehrenwort nt; **~s** pl (of song) Text m; **to have a ~ with sb** mit jdm sprechen; **in other ~s** mit anderen Worten ▷ vt formulieren; **wording** n Wortlaut m, Formulierung f; **word processing** n Textverarbeitung f; **word processor** n (program) Textverarbeitungsprogramm nt

wore [wɔ:*] pt of **wear**

work [wɜ:k] n Arbeit f; (of art, literature) Werk nt; **~ of art** Kunstwerk nt; **he's at ~** er ist in/auf der Arbeit; **out of ~** arbeitslos ▷ vi arbeiten (at, on an +dat); (machine, plan) funktionieren; (medicine) wirken; (succeed) klappen ▷ vt (machine) bedienen; **work out** vi (plan) klappen; (sum) aufgehen; (person) trainieren ▷ vt (price, speed etc) ausrechnen; (plan) ausarbeiten; **work up** vt **to get worked up** sich aufregen; **workaholic** [wɜ:kə'hɒlɪk] n Arbeitstier nt; **worker** n Arbeiter(in) m(f); **working class** n Arbeiterklasse f; **workman** (pl **-men**) n Handwerker m; **workout** n (Sport) Fitnesstraining nt, Konditionstraining nt; **work permit** n Arbeitserlaubnis f; **workplace** n Arbeitsplatz m; **workshop** n Werkstatt f; (meeting) Workshop m;

work station n (Inform) Workstation f
world [wɜːld] n Welt f; **world championship** n Weltmeisterschaft f; **World War** n ~ I/II, **the First/Second** ~ der Erste/Zweite Weltkrieg; **world-wide** adj, adv weltweit; **World Wide Web** n World Wide Web nt
worm [wɜːm] n Wurm m
worn [wɔːn] pp of **wear** ▷ adj (clothes) abgetragen; (tyre) abgefahren; **worn-out** adj abgenutzt; (person) erschöpft
worried ['wʌrɪd] adj besorgt; **be ~ about** sich dat Sorgen machen um; **worry** ['wʌrɪ] n Sorge f ▷ vt Sorgen machen +dat ▷ vi sich Sorgen machen (about um); **don't ~** keine Sorge!; **worrying** adj beunruhigend
worse [wɜːs] adj comparative of **bad**; schlechter; (pain, mistake etc) schlimmer ▷ adv comparative of **badly**; schlechter; **worsen** vt verschlechtern ▷ vi sich verschlechtern
worship ['wɜːʃɪp] vt anbeten, anhimmeln
worst [wɜːst] adj superlative of **bad**; schlechteste(r, s); (pain, mistake etc) schlimmste(r, s) ▷ adv superlative of **badly**; am schlechtesten ▷ n **the ~ is over** das Schlimmste ist vorbei; **at (the) ~** schlimmstenfalls
worth [wɜːθ] n Wert m; **£10 ~ of food** Essen für 10 Pfund ▷ adj **it is ~ £50** es ist 50 Pfund wert; **~ seeing** sehenswert; **it's ~ it** (rewarding) es lohnt sich; **worthless** adj wertlos; **worthwhile** adj lohnend, lohnenswert; **worthy** ['wɜːðɪ] adj (deserving respect) würdig; **to be ~ of sth** etw verdienen

○ **KEYWORD**

would [wʊd] aux vb **1** (conditional tense): **if you asked him he would do it** wenn du ihn fragtest, würde er es tun; **if you had asked him he would have done it** wenn du ihn gefragt hättest, hätte er es getan
2 (in offers, invitations, requests): **would you like a biscuit?** möchten Sie ein Plätzchen?; **would you ask him to come in?** würden Sie ihn bitte hineinbitten?
3 (in indirect speech): **I said I would do it** ich sagte, ich würde es tun
4 (emphatic): **it WOULD have to snow**

today! es musste ja ausgerechnet heute schneien!
5 (insistence): **she wouldn't behave** sie wollte sich partout nicht anständig benehmen
6 (conjecture): **it would have been midnight** es mag ungefähr Mitternacht gewesen sein; **it would seem so** es sieht wohl so aus
7 (indicating habit): **he would go there on Mondays** er ging jeden Montag dorthin

wouldn't ['wʊdnt] contr of **would not**
would've ['wʊdəv] contr of **would have**
wound [wuːnd] n Wunde f ▷ vt verwunden; (fig) verletzen ▷ [waʊnd] pt, pp of **wind**
wove [wəʊv] pt of **weave**
woven ['wəʊvn] pp of **weave**
wrap [ræp] vt (parcel, present) einwickeln; **to ~ sth round sth** etw um etw wickeln; **wrap up** vt (parcel, present) einwickeln ▷ vi (dress warmly) sich warm anziehen; **wrapper** n (of sweet) Papier nt; **wrapping paper** n Packpapier nt; (giftwrap) Geschenkpapier nt
wreath [riːθ] n Kranz m
wreck [rek] n (ship, plane, car) Wrack nt; **a nervous ~** ein Nervenbündel m ▷ vt (car) zu Schrott fahren; (fig) zerstören; **wreckage** ['rekɪdʒ] n Trümmer pl
wrench [rentʃ] n (tool) Schraubenschlüssel m
wrestling ['reslɪŋ] n Ringen nt
wring out ['rɪŋ'aʊt] (wrung, wrung) vt auswringen
wrinkle ['rɪŋkl] n Falte f
wrist [rɪst] n Handgelenk nt; **wristwatch** n Armbanduhr f
write [raɪt] (wrote, written) vt schreiben; (cheque) ausstellen ▷ vi schreiben; **to ~ to sb** jdm schreiben; **write down** vt aufschreiben; **write off** vt (debt, person) abschreiben; (car) zu Schrott fahren ▷ vi **to ~ off for sth** etw anfordern; **write out** vt (name etc) ausschreiben; (cheque) ausstellen; **write-protected** adj (Inform) schreibgeschützt; **writer** n Verfasser(in) m(f); (author) Schriftsteller(in) m(f); **writing** n Schrift f; (profession) Schreiben nt; **writing paper** n Schreibpapier nt
written ['rɪtən] pp of **write**

w

wrong [rɒŋ] *adj* (*incorrect*) falsch; (*morally*)
unrecht; **you're ~** du hast Unrecht;
what's ~ with your leg? was ist mit
deinem Bein los?; **you've got the
~ number** Sie sind falsch verbunden; **I
dialled the ~ number** ich habe mich
verwählt; **don't get me ~** versteh mich
nicht falsch; **to go ~** (*plan*) schief gehen;
wrongly *adv* falsch; (*unjustly*) zu Unrecht
wrote [rəʊt] *pt of* **write**
WWW *abbr* = **World Wide Web** WWW

xenophobia [zenəˈfəʊbɪə] *n*
Ausländerfeindlichkeit *f*
XL *abbr* = **extra large** XL, übergroß
Xmas [ˈeksməs] *n* Weihnachten *nt*
X-ray [ˈeksreɪ] *n* (*picture*)
Röntgenaufnahme *f* ▷ *vt* röntgen
xylophone [ˈzaɪləfəʊn] *n* Xylophon *nt*

yacht [jɒt] *n* Jacht *f*; **yachting** *n* Segeln *nt*; **to go ~** segeln gehen

yard [jɑːd] *n* Hof *m*; (*US: garden*) Garten *m*; (*measure*) Yard *nt* (*0,91 m*)

yawn [jɔːn] *vi* gähnen

yd *abbr* = **yard(s)**

year ['jɪə*] *n* Jahr *nt*; **this/last/next ~** dieses/letztes/nächstes Jahr; **he is 28 ~s old** er ist 28 Jahre alt; **~s ago** vor Jahren; **a five-year-old** ein(e) Fünfjährige(r); **yearly** *adj, adv* jährlich

yearn [jɜːn] *vi* sich sehnen (*for* nach +*dat*); **to ~ to do sth** sich danach sehnen, etw zu tun

yeast [jiːst] *n* Hefe *f*

yell [jel] *vi, vt* schreien; **to ~ at sb** jdn anschreien

yellow ['jeləʊ] *adj* gelb; **~ card** (*Sport*) gelbe Karte; **~ fever** Gelbfieber *nt*; **~ line** (*Brit*) ≈ Halteverbot *nt*; **double ~ line** (*Brit*) ≈ absolutes Halteverbot; **the Yellow Pages®** *pl* die Gelben Seiten *pl*

yes [jes] *adv* ja; (*answering negative question*) doch; **to say ~ to sth** ja zu etw sagen ▷ *n* Ja *nt*

yesterday ['jestədeɪ] *adv* gestern; **~ morning/evening** gestern Morgen/ Abend; **the day before ~** vorgestern; **~'s newspaper** die Zeitung von gestern

yet [jet] *adv* (*still*) noch; (*up to now*) bis jetzt; (*in a question: already*) schon; **he hasn't arrived ~** er ist noch nicht gekommen; **have you finished ~?** bist du schon fertig?; **~ again** schon wieder; **as ~** bis jetzt ▷ *conj* doch

yield [jiːld] *n* Ertrag *m* ▷ *vt* (*result, crop*) hervorbringen; (*profit, interest*) bringen ▷ *vi* nachgeben (*to* +*dat*); (*Mil*) sich ergeben (*to* +*dat*); **'~'** (*US Auto*) „Vorfahrt beachten"

yoga ['jəʊɡə] *n* Joga *nt*

yog(h)urt [jɒɡət] *n* Jog(h)urt *m*

yolk [jəʊk] *n* Eigelb *nt*

Yorkshire pudding ['jɔːkʃə'pʊdɪŋ] *n* gebackener Eierteig, der meist zum Roastbeef gegessen wird

🔘 **KEYWORD**

you [juː] *pron* **1** (*subj, in comparisons: familiar form: sg*) du; (: *pl*) ihr; (*in letters also*) du ihr; (: *polite form*) Sie; **you Germans** ihr Deutschen; **she's younger than you** sie ist jünger als du/Sie
2 (*direct object, after prep* +*acc: familiar form: sg*) dich; (: *pl*) euch; (*in letters also*) dich euch; (: *polite form*) Sie; **I know you** ich kenne dich/euch/Sie
3 (*indirect object, after prep* +*dat: familiar form*) (*sg*) dir; (*pl*) euch; (*in letters also*) dir euch; (: *polite form*) Ihnen; **I gave it to you** ich gab es dir/euch/Ihnen
4 (*impers: one: subj*) man; (: *direct object*) einen; (*indirect object*) einem; **fresh air does you good** frische Luft tut gut

you'd [juːd] *contr of* **you had; you would**; **~ better leave** du solltest gehen

you'll [juːl] *contr of* **you will; you shall**

young [jʌŋ] *adj* jung ▷ *n* **the ~** *pl* (*~ people*) die jungen Leute *pl*; (*animals*) die Jungen *pl*; **youngster** ['jʌŋstə*] *n* Jugendliche(r) *mf*

your ['jɔː*] *adj sing* dein; *polite form* Ihr; *pl* euer; *polite form* Ihr; **have you hurt ~ leg?** hast du dir das Bein verletzt?

you're ['jʊə*] *contr of* **you are**

yours ['jɔːz] *pron sing* deine(r, s); *polite form* Ihre(r, s); *pl* eure(r, s); *polite form* Ihre(r, s); **is this ~?** gehört das dir/Ihnen?; **a**

friend of ~ ein Freund von dir/Ihnen; **~ ...**, dein/deine ..., Ihr/Ihre ...

yourself [jɔːˈself] *pron sing* dich; *polite form* sich; **have you hurt ~?** hast du dich/haben Sie sich verletzt?; **did you do it ~?** hast du es selbst gemacht?; **(all) by ~** allein; **yourselves** *pron pl* euch; *polite form* sich; **have you hurt ~?** habt ihr euch/haben Sie sich verletzt?; **did you do it ~?** habt ihr es selbst gemacht?; **(all) by ~** allein

youth [juːθ] *n* (*period*) Jugend *f*; (*young man*) junger Mann; (*young people*) Jugend *f*; **youth hostel** *n* Jugendherberge *f*

you've [juːv] *contr of* **you have**

yucky [ˈjʌkɪ] *adj* (*fam*) eklig

Yugoslav [juːgəˈslɑːv] *adj* jugoslawisch ▷ *n* Jugoslawe *m*, Jugoslawin *f*; **Yugoslavia** *n* (*hist*) Jugoslawien *nt*; **the former ~** das ehemalige Jugoslawien; **Yugoslavian** *see* **Yugoslav**

yummy [ˈjʌmɪ] *adj* (*fam*) lecker

yuppie, **yuppy** [ˈjʌpɪ] *n* Yuppie *m*

y

zoo [zu:] *n* Zoo *m*
zoom [zu:m] *vi* (*move fast*) brausen, sausen ▷ *n* ~ (**lens**) Zoomobjektiv *nt*; **zoom in** *vi* (*Foto*) heranzoomen (*on* an +*akk*)
zucchini [zu:'ki:nɪ] (*pl* -(**s**)) *n* (*US*) Zucchini *f*

zap [zæp] *vt* (*Inform*) löschen; (*in computer game*) abknallen ▷ *vi* (*Tv*) zappen; **zapper** *n* (*Tv*) Fernbedienung *f*; **zapping** *n* (*Tv*) ständiges Umschalten, Zapping *nt*
zebra ['zebrə, ç'zi:brə] (*US*) *n* Zebra *nt*; **zebra crossing** *n* (*Brit*) Zebrastreifen *m*
zero [zɪərəʊ] (*pl* -**es**) *n* Null *f*; **10 degrees below** ~ 10 Grad unter null
zest [zest] *n* (*enthusiasm*) Begeisterung *f*
zigzag ['zɪgzæg] *n* Zickzack *m* ▷ *vi* (*person, vehicle*) im Zickzack gehen/fahren; (*path*) im Zickzack verlaufen
zinc [zɪŋk] *n* Zink *nt*
zip [zɪp] *n* (*Brit*) Reißverschluss *m* ▷ *vt* **to** ~ (**up**) den Reißverschluss zumachen; (*Inform*) zippen; **zip code** *n* (*US*) Postleitzahl *f*; **Zip disk®** *n* (*Inform*) ZIP-Diskette® *f*; **Zip drive®** *n* (*Inform*) ZIP-Laufwerk® *nt*; **Zip file®** *n* (*Inform*) ZIP-Datei® *f*; **zipper** *n* (*US*) Reißverschluss *m*
zit [zɪt] *n* (*fam*) Pickel *m*
zodiac ['zəʊdɪæk] *n* Tierkreis *m*; **sign of the** ~ Tierkreiszeichen *nt*
zone [zəʊn] *n* Zone *f*; (*area*) Gebiet *nt*; (*in town*) Bezirk *m*